ISBN 978-1-5276-4640-7
PIBN 10878028

FB &c Ltd, Dalton House, 60 Windsor Avenue, London, SW19 2RR.
Company number 08720141. Registered in England and Wales.

For support please visit www.forgottenbooks.com

NUEVO
DICCIONARIO PORTATIL,
ESPAÑOL É INGLES,

PUESTO SEGUN LOS MEJORES DICCIONARIOS QUE HASTA AHORA HAN SALIDO A LUZ EN AMBAS NACIONES.

POR C. M. GATTEL,

PROFESOR DE GRAMATICA GENERAL.

ESPAÑOL É INGLES.

VALENCIA.
POR P. J. MALLEN Y C.
MDCCCIII.

ADVERTENCIA.

GENERALMENTE hablando, ningun Diccionario de Lenguas, aun el mas bien hecho, puede esperar el aprecio y la estimacion del publico por otro titulo que el de la utilidad que le proporciona.

Rara vez se considera en su autor otra especie de merito; no obstante que esta clase de obras exige mucho cuidado y trabajo, conocimientos muy extensos, un gusto mas delicado de lo que comunmente se imagina, y que reuna dos qualidades que pocas veces se hallan juntas: á saber la claridad y la precision. Todo esto es aun mas necesario en un Diccionario manual, que por su mismo destino no admite las explicaciones que los demas Vocabularios; y que, debiendose ceñir á los mas estrechos limites, es preciso que exprese el significado de cada palabra con otra: y si esto no puede ser, que lo haga por una definicion la mas breve, lo que no es siempre facil de componer con la claridad.

Esta dificultad, que solo conocen bien los que trabajan en superarla, da derecho á la indulgencia de los lectores. Y en quanto á mi, aunque no me lisongeo de haberla vencido totalmente, puedo asegurar que no he omitido diligencia ni eficacia para conseguirlo. Con esta mira me he valido de todos los auxilios que podian serme utiles. He consultado las fuentes mas acreditadas, y me he fundado sobre las autoridades mas bien establecidas para asegurarme de la exacti y merecer la confianza.

Mi guia, en quanto al Ingles, ha sido el Diccionario manual *Nugent*, que es la primera obra que se ha publicado de esta espec sirviendo de modelo á todos los posteriores, y que al mismo tiempc uno de los mas justamente estimados. Tambien me he servido d ultima edicion del grande Diccionario Ingles y Frances de *Roy* del Diccionario Ingles de *Sheridan*, del de *Ash*, y aun del de *Jonh* quando las circunstancias lo han exigido.

En quanto al Español, me he servido con preferencia del Dicc nario Español y Frances que yo publiqué en 1790: el qual, por lo c hace á la primera de dichas lenguas, fue fielmente extractado del la Real Academia Española; á quien sin embargo he recurrido sie pre que se ha presentado alguna duda que aclarar, o alguna omis que suplir.

Por lo demas, este Vocabulario Ingles y Español casi puede deci el primero que se ha publicado; pues á pesar de la eficacia de algu lexicographos en seguir el util exemplo que les dió *Nugent*, aun se ha publicado un Diccionario de estas dos lenguas, pudiendose de sin separarse mucho de la verdad, que no le habia. El de *Steve* compuesto mucho antes del establecimiento de la Academia Es ñola, puede servir de poco; pues sobre ser muy incompleto, opone, como tan viejo, á la Ortografia, y á los principios de la Sy taxis y de la pronunciacion establecidos por la citada Acaden *Pineda*, que siguió á *Stevens*, no ha hecho sino mutilarle, y añ á sus yerros, que ya eran muchos, la falta grave, inexcusable y temeraria, de apartarse de intento del systema gramatical de la Academia, pretendiendo subrogar su autoridad propia en lugar de la de un cuerpo de literatos especialmente ocupado por instituto en estudiar su lengua, y en perfeccionarla, como felizmente lo ha conseguido.

A estos dos lexicographos se siguio *Delpino*, cuyo Diccionario Ingles y Español, mas conforme á los verdaderos principios que los de sus predecesores, fue despues corregido y aumentado por *Baretti*. La obra de este ultimo en un tomo en fol. pareció en Londres en 1778, y fue reimpresa en Leon en dos tomos in-4º. en 1786, baxo el titulo supuesto de Londres. Pero a pesar de las numerosas adiciones y correcciones, que dice el autor habia hecho al Diccionario de *Delpino*, el suyo es tan incompleto é inexacto, que se debe mirar como guia poco segura, y casi siempre insuficiente (1).

Aunque el Diccionario que ofrezco al publico està reducido á un volumen mucho menor, me parece poder asegurar, que es muy superior á todos los mencionados, tanto por su mayor fidelidad y correccion, como porque comprehende una nomenclatura infinita-

(1) Ademas de los Diccionarios Ingles y Español, y Español é Ingles que acabo de mencionar, he sabido que habia uno recientemente impreso en Madrid, en 4 tomos en 4to. compuesto, por *Thomas Connelly* y *Thomas Higging* confesores de la Familia Real. No habiendolo tenido en mi poder, me ha sido imposible de juzgarlo, y siento infinito que la dificultad de comunicacion entre las dos naciones, respeto al comercio de libros, me haya imposibilitado de sacar de esta importante obra los auxilios que segun todas apariencias, me hubiera ofrecido.

mente mas cómpleta. Yo me creeré dichoso, si, como me lo h(puesto, puedo con esta obra contribuir á facilitar y extender l municacion entre dos pueblos estimables, poco separados p(situacion geografica, pero aun mas reunidos en varias parte glovo por sus relaciones politicas y de comercio.

Lista alfabética de los nombres propios de hombres y mugeres en Español é Ingles con sus acentos.

An alphabetical list of the proper names of men and women in Spanish and English with their accents.

A

Aarón, *Adron.*
Abél, *A'bel.*
Abrahán, *A'braham.*
Adán, *A'dam.*
Adólfo, *Adólphus.*
Adrián, *A'drian.*
Aláno, *A'lan*, or *A'llen.*
Alarico, *A'larick*, or *Alric.*
Albérto, *A'lbert.*
Alexándro, *Alexánder.*
Alfrédo, *A'lfred.*
Alfónso, ó Alónso, *Alphónsus.*
Alnino, *A'lwin.*
Ambrósio, *Ambrósius.*
Amedéo, *Amadéus.*
Andrés, *A'ndrew.*
A'na, *A'nne.*
Anselmo, *A'nselm.*
Antón, nio, *A'nthony.*
Antonino, *A'nthonine.*
Aníbal, *Hánibal.*
Aquiles, ó Achíles, *Achiles.*
Archibáldo, *A'rchibald.*
Arnáldo, *A'rnald.*
Artúro, *A'rthur.*
Augústo, *Augústus.*
Agustin, *A'ustin*, or *A'ugustin.*

B

Baltasár, *Bálthasar.*
Baptista, ó Bautista, *Báptist.*
Bartolomé, *Barthólomew*
Basílio, *Básil.*
Balduino, *Baldwin.*
Benjamin, *Bénjamin.*
Benito, *Bénedict.*
Bernabé, *Bárnaby.*
Bertrán, *Bértram.*
Bernárdo, *Bérnard.*
Blas, *Bláse.*
Bonifácio, *Bóniface.*
Buenaventúra, *Bonavénture.*

C

Cárlos, *Chárles.*
César, *Cæsar.*
Ciprián, *Cyprian.*
Cirilo, *Cyril.*
Cláudio, *Cláudius.*
Cleménte, *Clément.*
Conrádo, *Cónrad.*
Constantino, *Cónstantine.*
Cornélio, *Cornélius.*
Crisóstomo, *Chrysóstom.*
Cristóbal, *Christopher.*

D

Daniél, *Dániel.*
David, *Dávid.*
Dionísio, *Dénys*, or *Dénnis.*
Donstáno, *Dúnstan.*

E

Edmóndo, *E'dmund.*
Eleázaro, *Eléazar.*
Elías, *Elías.*
Eliséo, *Elísha*, *Ellis.*
Erásmo, *Erásmus.*
Estéban, *Stéphen*, or *Steéven.*
Eugénio, *Eugéne*, *owen*
Eusébio, *Eusebius.*
Eustáquio, *Eustace.*
Ezequías, *Ezechías.*
Ezequiél, *Ezechiel.*

F

Fabian, *Fábrian.*
Félix, *Félix.*
Fernándo, *Férdinand.*
Francisco, *Fráncis.*
Federico, *Fréderick.*
Fúlquio, *Fulk*, or *Fowk.*

G

Gabriél, *Gábriel.*
Gaspár, *Gáspar.*
Gedónio, *Gideon.*
Gedevino, *Góodwin.*
Geofrédo, *Géffery.*
Gerónimo, *Hiérome*, or *Jérome.*
Gérvasio, *Gérvas.*
Gil, *Giles.*
Gilbérto, *Gilbert.*
Godefrédo, *Gódfrey*
Gregório, *Grégory.*
Gualtério, *Wálter.*
Guillélmo, *William.*
Guido, *Gúy.*

H

Hectór, *Héctor.*
Henríque, *Hénry.*
Herbérto, *Hérbert.*
Hércules, *Hércules.*
Hilário, *Hílary.*
Horácio, *Hórace.*

Hubérto, *Húbert*, or *Hóbart.*
Húgo, *Hugh.*
Humfrédo, *Húmfrey*

I

Ignácio, *Ignátius.*
Irenéo, *Iréneus.*
Isaác, *Isáac.*

J

Jacób, *Jácob.*
Jacóbo, *Jámes.*
Jáymo, *Jámes.*
Jeremías, *Jéremy.*
Job, *Job.*
Jonatas, *Jónathan.*
Jórge, *George.*
Joséf, ó Joséph, *Jóseph.*
Josías, *Jósiah.*
Joselíno, *Jósselin.*
Josué, *Jóshua.*
Júdas, *Júdas.*
Julián, *Júlian.*
Júlio, *Július.*

L

Lázaro, *Lázarus.*
Leopóldo, *Léopold.*
Lorénzo, *Láarence.*
Lúcas, *Lúke.*
Luís, *Léwis.*

M

Malaquías, *Málachy.*
Márco, *Mark.*
Martín, *Mártin.*
Matéo, *Máthew.*
Matías, *Máthias.*
Mauricio, *Márris*, *Máurice*, or *Mórice*
Maxîmiliáno, *Maximílian.*
Miguél, *Míchael.*
Moysés, *Móses.*

N

Natán, *Náthan.*
Natanaél, *Nathánael.*
Nehemías, *Nehémiah.*
Nicolás, *Nícholas.*

O

Olivério, *O'liver.*
Otónio, *O'tho.*

P

Patrício, *Pátrick.*
Páblo, *Pául.*
Pédro, *Péter.*
Phinées, *Phíneus.*

R

Randólfo, *Róndel.*
Rafaél, *Ráphael.*
Raymúndo, *Ráymund.*
Reynáldo, *Réynold.*
Ricárdo, *Ríchard.*
Robérto, *Róbert*, *Rápert.*
Rodólfo, *Rulph*, *Rolph.*
Rogério, *Róger.*
Rolándo, *Rówland.*

S

Salómon, *Sálomon.*
Samuél, *Sámuel.*
Sansón, *Sámpson.*
Sebastián, *Sebástian.*
Sigismúndo, *Sígismun*
Silváno, *Sílvan.*
Silvéstre, *Silvéster.*
Simeón, *Símeon.*
Simón, *Símon.*

T

Tadéo, *Thady.*
Teodóro, *Théodore.*
Teodoríco, *Dórick.*
Teodósio, *Theodósius*
Teófilo, *Theóphilus.*
Teobáldo, *Theóbald*, *Tíbald.*
Timotéo, *Tímothy.*
Tobías, *Tóby.*
Tomás, *Thómas.*

U V

Urbáno, *U'rban.*
Valentín, *Válentine.*
Vicénte, *Víncent.*

Z

Zacarías, *Zácharу.*

A

ix, *Abigáil.*
i. *A'lice.*
A'gath.
Alíthea.
Amélia.
nn.
i, *Antónia.*

B

, *Bárbara.*
Beátriz.
Benedícta.
óna.
Brídget.

C

Chárlot.
, *Caroline.*
a, *Cássandra.*
, *Cátharine.*
Cécily.
láre.
a, *Cláudina.*
, *Clotílda.*
za, *Cónstance.*
, *Christína.*

D

Diána.
Dionísia, *Dénnis.*
Dorotéa, *Dórothy.*

E

Eléna, *Héllen.*
Engrácia, *Grace.*
Estér, *Ester*, or *Héster.*
Éva, *Eve.*

F

Felípa, *Philíppa.*
Flóra, *Flóra.*
Floréncia, *Florénce.*
Francísca, *Fráncis*

G

Gertrúdis, *Gértrude.*

I

Isabél, *I'sabel.*

J

Juána, *Jáne.*
Judít, *Júdith.*
Juliána, *Júlian.*

L

Leonór, *Eleonor.*
Luísa, *Lóuisa.*
Lucía, *Lúcy.*
Lucrécia, *Lucrétia.*

M

Magdaléna, *Mágdalen.*
Margaríta, *Márgaret*, or *Márgery*
María, *Máry.*
Matílde, *Mawl.*

P

Penélope, *Pénelope.*
Prudéncia, *Prúdence.*

R

Raquél, *Ráchel.*
Rebéca, *Rébecca.*
Rósa, *Rósamund.*

S

Sabína, *Sábina.*
Sára, *Sárah.*
Sofía, *Sóphia.*
Susána, *Súsan.*

T

Terésa, *Thérese.*

U

U'rsula, *U'rsula.*

Diminutivos de algunos nombres Ingleses.

por Adelaida.
Bautista.
Bárbara.
Bartolome.
Benjamin.
Betty *por* Isabel.
or *Brígida.*
Billy *por* Guillermo.
Bob *por* Roberto.
Cis *por* Cecilia.
Clem *por* Clemente.
Dan *por* Daniel.
Dick *por* Ricardo.
Doll por Dorotea.
Dy por Diana.
Frank, Fanny *por* Francisca.
Harry *por* Henrique.
Jack *por* Juan.
Jemmy *por* Jayme.
Jenny *por* Juana.
Jo por Joseph.
Jonny por Juan.

Kit *por* Christobal.
Kitty *por* Catalina.
Madgy *por* Magdalena.
Mat *por* Mateo.
Mich *por* Miguel.
Molly *por* María.
Mun *por* Edmundo.
Nam *por* Ambrosio.
Nancy *por* Ana.
Nick *por* Nicolas.
Polly *por* María.

Peggy *por* Margaríta.
Phil *por* Felipe.
Pru *por* Prudencia.
Robin *por* Roberto
Sally *por* Sara.
Sam *por* Samuel.
Sib. *por* Sebastiana.
Sil *por* Silvestre.
Sim *por* Simon.
Susy *por* Susana.
Tid *por* Teodoro.

Tim *por* Timoteo.
Tom *por* Tomas.
Tony *por* Antonio.
Tracy *por* Teresa.
Vin *por* Vicente.
Val *por* Valentin.
Wat *por* Gualtero *ó* Baltazar.
Will *por* Guillermo.
Zack *por* Zacarias

ALOGO ALFABÉTICO DE LOS VERBOS

nsonante final se duplica o repite en el prétérito activo y s participios, y de los verbos irregulares cuyo consonante se repite en el participio activo.

. . abetted.
. . abhorred.
. . abuttet.
. . acquitted.
. . admitted.
. . allotted.
. . amitted.
. . annulled.
. . appalled.
. . apparelled.
. . avelled.
. . averred.
. . bagged.
. . barred.
. . barrelled.
. . bedded.
. . bedimmed.
. . bedropped.
. . befalling.
. . befitted.
. . begged.
. . begetting.
. . beginning.
. . besetting.
. . besmutted.
. . besotted.
. . bespotted.
. . bestirred.
. . bestudded.
. . betted.
. . bethralled.
. . betrimmed.
. . baissed.
. . bidding.
. . blabbed.
. . blotted.
. . blurred.
. . bowelled.
. . bragged.
. . *brimmed.*
. . *budded.*

Cabal . . . . caballed.
Cancel . . . cancelled.
Cap. . . . . capped.
Capot. . . . capotted.
Carol. . . . carolled.
Cavil. . . . cavilled.
Channel . . channelled.
Chap . . . . chapped.
Char . . . . charred.
Chat . . . . chatted.
Chip . . . . chipped.
Chisel. . . . chiselled.
Chit. . . . . chitted.
Chop . . . . chopped.
Clap . . . . clapped.
Clip. . . . . clipped.
Clod . . . . clodded.
Clog . . . . clogged.
Clot. . . . . clotted.
Club . . . . clubbed.
Cod. . . . . codded.
Cog. . . . . cogged.
Commit. . . committed.
Compel. . . compelled.
Complot . . complotted.
Con. . . . . conned.
Concur . . . concurred.
Confer . . . conferred.
Control. . . controlled.
Coquet . . . coquetted.
Counsel. . . counselled.
Cram . . . . crammed.
Crib. . . . . cribbed.
Crop. . . . . cropped.
Crum. . . . crummed.
Cub. . . . . cubbed.
Cudgel . . . cudgelled.
Cup. . . . . cupped.
Cut . . . . . cutting.
Dab. . . . . dabbed.
Dag. . . . . *dagged.*
Dam. . . . . dammed.

Dap. . . . . dapped.
Debar. . . . debarred.
Debel. . . . debelled.
Defer. . . . deferred.
Demit. . . . demitted.
Demur . . . demurred.
Deter . . . . deterred.
Dig . . . . . digging.
Dim. . . . . dimmed.
Din. . . . . dinned.
Dip. . . . . dipped.
Disannul . . disannulled.
Discounsel. disconnselled
Disenthral. disenthralled.
Dishevel. . . dishevelled.
Disinter. . . disinterred.
Dispel. . . . dispelled.
Distil. . . . distilled.
Dog. . . . . dogged.
Dod. . . . . donned.
Dot. . . . . dotted.
Drag . . . . dragged.
Dram. . . . drammed.
Drib. . . . . dribbed.
Drip. . . . . dripped.
Drivel. . . . drivelled.
Drop . . . . dropped.
Drup . . . . drubbed.
Drum. . . . drummed.
Dub. . . . . dubbed.
Duel . . . . duelled.
Dun. . . . . dunned.
Embar . . . embarred.
Embowel. . embowelled.
Emit . . . . emitted.
Empannel . empannelled
Enamel. . . enamelled.
Englut . . . englutted.
Enrol. . . . enrolled.
Entrap . . . entrapped.
Equal. . . . equalled.
Equip. . . . equipped.

Excel. . . . excelled.
Expel. . . . expelled.
Extil . . . . extilled.
Extol. . . . extolled.
Fag. . . . . fagged.
Fan. . . . . fanned.
Fat. . . . . fatted.
Fib . . . . . fibbed.
Fig . . . . . figged.
Fin . . . . . finned.
Fit. . . . . . fitted.
Flag. . . . . flagged.
Flam . . . . flammed.
Flap. . . . . flapped.
Flat . . . . . flatted.
Flit . . . . . flitted.
Flog. . . . . flogged.
Plop. . . . . floopped.
Fob. . . . . Fobbeb.
Forbid. . . . forbidding.
Forerun. . . forerunning
Forestal. . . forestalled.
Foretel . . . foretelling.
Forget . . . forgetting.
Fret. . . . . fretted.
Fub. . . . . fubbed.
Fulfil. . . . . fulfilled.
Fur. . . . . furred.
Gab. . . . . gabbed.
Gad. . . . . gadded.
Gag. . . . . gagged.
Gambol. . . gambolled.
Gem . . . . gemmed.
Get. . . . . getting.
Gip. . . . . gipped.
Glad. . . . . gladded.
Glib. . . . . glibbed.
Glut. . . . . glutted.
Gnar . . . . gnarret.
God. . . . . godded.
Gospel. . . . gospelled.
Gravel . . . gravelled.
Grin. . . . . grinned.
Grovel . . . grovelled.
Grub . . . . grubbed.
Gum . . . . gummed.
Gut. . . . . gutted
Hag. . . . . hagged.
Handsel. . . handselled.

Hap . . . . . happed.
Hatchel. . . hatchelled.
Hem. . . . . hemmed.
Hip. . . . . hipped.
Hit . . . . . hitting.
Hitchel. . . hitchelled.
Hop. . . . . hopped.
Hovel. . . . hovelled.
Housel . . . houselled.
Hug. . . . . hugged.
Hum . . . . Hummed.
Hyp. . . . . hypped.
Jam. . . . . jammed.
Japan. . . . japanned.
Jar. . . . . . jarret.
Jet. . . . . . jetted.
Jig . . . . . jigged.
Immit. . . . immitted.
Impel. . . . impelled.
Inclip. . . . inclipped.
Incur . . . . incurred.
Infer. . . . . inferred.
Inship. . . . inshipped.
Instal. . . . installed.
Instil . . . . instilled.
Instop. . . . instopped.
Inter. . . . . interred.
Intermit. . . intermitted.
Inthral . . . inthralled.
Intromit. . . intromitted.
Inwrap . . . inwrapped.
Job . . . . . jobbed.
Jog . . . . . jogged.
Jug. . . . . jugged.
Jut . . . . . jutted.
Ken. . . . . kenned.
Kennel. . . kennelled.
Kernel . . . kernelled.
Kid . . . . . kidded.
Kidnap . . . kidnapped.
Knit. . . . . knitting.
Knot . . . . knotted.
Knub . . . . knubbed.
Lag . . . . . lagged.
Landdam. . landdammed.
Lap . . . . . lapped.
Let . . . . . letting.
Level. . . . levelled.
Libel . . . . libelled.

Lig . . . . .
Lip. . . . .
Lob. . . . .
Lop. . . . .
Lug. . . . .
Mad. . . . .
Man. . . . .
Manumit . .
Map. . . . .
Mar. . . . .
Marshal. . .
Marvel . . .
Mat. . . . .
Miscal. . . .
Misinfer . .
Mistel . . .
Mob. . . . .
Model. . . .
Mop. . . . .
Mud. . . . .
Nab. . . . .
Nap. . . . .
Net. . . . .
Newmodel
Nib. . . . .
Nim. . . . .
Nip . . . . .
Nod. . . . .
Nousel . . .
Nut. . . . .
Occur. . . .
Omit . . . .
Onset. . . .
Overbid. . .
Overget . .
Overred. . .
Overrun . .
Overset. . .
Overskip . .
Overslip . .
Overtop . .
Overtrip . .
Outbid . . .
Outrun . . .
Outsit. . . .
Outstrip . .
Outwit . . .
Pad. . . . .
Pan. . . . .

. . parcelled.
. . patted.
. . patrolled.
. . pegged.
. . penning.
. . permitted.
. . pigged.
. . pinned.
. . pipped.
. . pistolled.
. . pitted.
. . planned.
. . platted.
. . plodded.
. . plotted.
. . plugged.
. . podded.
. . pommelled.
. . popped.
. . postilled.
. . potted.
. . preferred.
. pretermitted.
. . prigged.
. . primmed.
. . progged.
. . propped.
. . propelled.
. . pulvilled.
. . punned.
. . pupped.
. . putting.
. . quarrelled.
. . quipped.
. . quitting.
. . quobbed.
. . rammed.
. . rapped.
. . ravelled.
. . readmitted.
. . rebelled.
. . recalled.
.t. recommitted.
. . recurred.
. . refelled.
. . referred.
. . refitted.
. . regretted.
. . reinstalled.

Remit. . . . remitted.
Repel. . . . repelled.
Restem. . . restemmed.
Revel. . . . revelled.
Revictual. . revictualled.
Rid. . . . . ridding.
Rig. . . . . rigged.
Rip. . . . . ripped.
Rival. . . . rivalled.
Rivel. . . . rivelled.
Rivet. . . . rivetted.
Rob. . . . . robbed.
Rot. . . . . rotting.
Rowel . . . rowelled.
Rub. . . . . rubbed.
Run . . . . running.
Rut. . . . . rutted.
Sag. . . . . sagged.
Sap. . . . . sapped.
Scab. . . . . scabbed.
Scan. . . . . scanned.
Scar. . . . . scarred.
Scrub. . . . scrubbed.
Scud. . . . . scudded.
Scum. . . . scummed.
Set . . . . . setting.
Sham . . . . shammed.
Shed . . . . shedding.
Ship. . . . . shipped.
Shog. . . . . shogged.
Shovel. . . . shovelled.
Shred . . . . shredding.
Shrivel . . . shrivelled.
Shrub. . . . shrubbed.
Shrug. . . . shrugged.
Shun . . . . shunned.
Shut. . . . . shutting.
Sin . . . . . sinned.
Sip . . . . . sipped.
Sit. . . . . . sitting.
Skim . . . . skimmed.
Skin . . . . skinned.
Skip . . . . skipped.
Slam . . . . slammed.
Slap. . . . . slapped.
Slip. . . . . slipped.
Slit . . . . . slitting.
Slop. . . . . slopped.
Slot. . . . . slotted.

Slur. . . . . slurred.
Smut. . . . smutted.
Snap . . . . snapped.
Snip . . . . snipped.
Snivel . . . snivelled.
Snub . . . . snubbed.
Snug . . . . snugged.
Sob. . . . . sobbed.
Sop. . . . . sopped.
Sot . . . . . sotted.
Span . . . . spanned.
Spar . . . . sparred.
Spet. . . . . spetted.
Spin . . . . spinning.
Spit. . . . . spitting.
Split . . . . splitting.
Spot. . . . . spotted.
Sprig . . . . sprigged.
Sprit. . . . . spritted.
Spur. . . . . spurred.
Squab. . . . squabbed.
Squat. . . . squatted.
Stab. . . . . stabbet.
Star. . . . . starret.
Stem. . . . . stemmed.
Step. . . . . stepped.
Stir. . . . . stirred.
Stop. . . . . stopped.
Strap . . . . strapped.
Strip. . . . . stripped.
Strut. . . . strutted.
Stub . . . . stubbed.
Stud . . . . studded.
Stum. . . . stummed.
Stun. . . . stunned.
Stut . . . . stutted.
Submit. . . submitted.
Sum . . . . summet.
Sup. . . . . supped.
Swab. . . . swabbed.
Swag. . . . swagged.
Swap. . . . swapped.
Swin. . . . swigged.
Swim. . . . swimming.
Swop. . . . swopped.
Tag. . . . . tagged.
Tan. . . . . tanned.
Tap. . . . . tapped.
Tar. . . . . tarred.

Ted. . . . . tedded.
Thin . . . . thinned.
Thrid. . . . thridded.
Throb. . . . throbbed.
Thrum. . . thrummed.
Tin. . . . . tinned.
Tinsel . . . tinselled.
Tip . . . . . tipped,
Top . . . . . topped.
Trammel. . trammelled.
Transcur. . transcurred.
Transfer. . transferred.
Transmit. . transmitted.
Trap. . . . . trapped.
Travel . . . travelled.
Trepan. . . trepanned.
Trig. . . . . trigged.
Trim . . . . trimmed.
Trip. . . . . tripped.
Trot. . . . . trotted.
Tug. . . . . tugged.
Tunnel. . . tunnelled.

Tup. . . . . tupped.
Twin. . . . twinned.
Twit. . . . twitted.
Van. . . . . vanned.
Victual . . victualled.
Unbar . . . unbarred.
Unbed . . . unbedded.
Unbias . . . unbiassed.
Unbowel . unbowelled.
Unclog. . . unclogged.
Undam. . . undamned.
Underbid . underbidding.
Underpin . underpinned.
Underprop. underpropped.
Underset . undersetting.
Unfit. . . . unfitted.
Ungod . . . ungodded.
Unkennel. unkennelled.
Unknit. . . unknitting.
Unknot . . unknotted.
Unman. . . unmanned.
Unpeg . . . unpegged.

Unpin . . . unpinned.
Unravel . . unravelled.
Unrig. . . . unrigged.
Unrip. . . . unripped.
Unrivet . . unriveted.
Unrol. . . . unrolled.
Unship. . . unshipped.
Unstop . . . unstopped.
Unwit . . . unwitted.
Wad . . . . wadded.
Wag . . . . wagged.
War. . . . . warred.
Wed . . . . wedded.
Wet. . . . . wetting.
Whet. . . . whetted.
Whip. . . . whipped.
Whiz. . . . whizzed.
Win. . . . . winning.
Wit . . . . . witting,
Worship. . worshipped.
Wot. . . . . wotted.
Wrap. . . . wrapped.

NUEVO
DICCIONARIO
ESPAÑOL E INGLES.
PART I.
Conteniente el ESPAÑOL ántes del INGLES.

ABREVIACIONES.

a. ó *adj.* significa Adjectivo : *adv.* Adverbio : *art.* Articulo : *aum.* Aumentativo : *dim.* Diminutivo : *c.* ó *conj.* Conjuncion : *int.* Interjeccion : *p.* Participio : p. a. *Participio Activo* : p. p. *Participio Pasivo* : *pl.* Plural : *pr.* ó *prep.* Preposicion : *pro.* Pronombre : *s.* Substantivo : *m.* Masculino : *f.* femenino : *v.* Verbo : *v. a.* Verbo activo : *v. n.* Verbo neutro : *v. r.* Verbo reflexo, ó réciproco : *v. imp.* Verbo impersonal : *v. defect.* Verbo defectivo : 2. los dos géneros. *V.* Véase.

ABA, *s. f. a litle span of ground of about two yards*
Ababa, *s. f. Poppy*
Abaca, *s. f. a kind of flax*
Abacería, *sub. f. an oil-shop*
Abacero, ra, *s. the master or mistress of an oil-shop, etc.*
Abacial, *a. belonging to an abbot*
Abaco, *s. m. abacus*
Abad, *s. m. an abbot*
Abada, *s. f. the female of a rhinoceros*
Abadejo, *s. m. stock-fish || spanish-fly || a wren*
Abadengo, ga, *a. belonging to an abbot*
Abades, *s. m. pl. spanish-flies*
Abadeza, *s. f. an abbess*
Abadía, *s. f. abby*
Abalanzado, da, *a. audacious*
Abalanzar, *v. a. to make the balance even || to balance*
Abalanzarse, *v. r. to rush on suddenly || to dare*
Abaldonar, *v. a. to taunt, to debase*
Abalear, *v. a. to winow*
Aballar, *v. a. to pull or beat down || to carry*

away ; to lead || *to move* [*to ale*
Aballestar, *v. a. to tow ;*
Abalorio, *sub. m. bugles* (*beads of glass*)
Abanderado, *s. m. ensign-bearer*
Abanderados, *plur. those that carry the colours at the procession*
Abanderizador, *s. masc a factious, a ring-leader* [*a rebellion*
Abanderizar, *v. a. to raise*
Abandonamiento, *sub. m. V.* Abandono
Abandonar, *v. a. to abandon*
Abandono, *s. m. abandoning* || *prostitution*
Abanicar, *v. a. to fan*
Abanicazo, *s. m. a stroke with a fan*
Abanico, *s. m. a fan*
Abanillo, *s. m. a litle fan* || *a puff* or *ruffle*
Abaniquero, *s. m. a fan-maker*, or *fan-seller*
Abano, *s. m. a fan to drive away the flies*
Abanto, *s. m. a bird like the vulture*
Abaratar, *v. a. to diminish the price; to cheapen, etc.*
Abarca, *s. f. shoes made of raw skins*
Abarcador, *s. m. one who embraces*
Abarcadura, *s. f.* } *an embrace*
Abarcamiento, *s. m.* } *an embrace*
Abarcar, *v. a. to embrace*
Abarcon, *sub. m. an iron circle to fasten the pole of a coach*
Abarquillar, *v. a. to bend in the shape of a litle boat*
Abarracarse, *v. r. to shelter one's self by entering into barracks*
Abarrancadero, *sub m. a deep way* || *a precipice*
Abarrancar, *v. a. to make the ways deep* || *to put into troublesome business, etc.*
Abarrotar, *v. a. to bind* or *press hard*
Abarrote, *subs. m. small parcel of goods to fill up the cavities of a ship ; dennage*
Abastecedor, *s. m. provider*
Abastecer, *v. a. to furnish* or *provide*
Abastecimiento, *s. m. the care and action of providing* || *provisions*
Abastionar, *v. a. to fortify with bastions*
Abasto, *s. m. supply of provisions*
Abate, *s. m. one dressed like a priest in a short cloak*
A'bate, *interj. take care*
Abatidamente, *ad. basely*
Abatido, da, *a. vile, base* || *low in spirit, etc.*
Abatimiento, *s. m. overturning* || *debasing ; casting down*
Abatimiento del rumbo, *ship's deflection*
Abatir, *v. a. to beat down* || *to discourage, etc.*
Abatir la bandera, *to strike the colours*
Abatir, *v. n.* y abatirse, *v. r. to stoop, as a hawk*
Abaxador, *s. m. a groom of the stable in the mines* [*ment*
Abaxamiento, *s. m. abasement*
Abaxar, *v. a. to abase*
Abaxar el halcon, *to bring down a hawk's fat* — la cabeza, *to hang down the head* — los parpados, *to wink* — los brios *to cool a man's courage* — la marea, *to ebb* — las rentas, *to lower the revenues*
Abaxo, *adv. below*
Abdicacion, *s. f. abdication*
Abdicar, *v. a. to abdicate*
Abdomen, *s. m. abdomen*
Abecé, *s. m. the alphabeth the A, B, C*
Abecedario, *s. m. horn-book*
Abeja, *s. f. a bee*
Abejar (uva), *a fort of grape much liked by the bees*
Abejarron, *s. m a horse-fly* [*(a bird)*
Abejaruco, *s. m. bee-eater*
Abejera, *s. f. balm-mint*
Abejero, *s. m. one who takes care of the bee-hives*
Abejeruco, *s. m. V.* Abejaruco [*little bee*
Abejica, illa, uela, *s. f. a*
Abejon, *s. m. a hornet*
Abejonazo, *s. m. a great hornet* [*hornet*
Abejoncillo, *s. m. a litle*
Abejorro, *s. m. may-bug*
Abellacar, *v. a. to despise*
Abellacarse, *v. r. to deprave* or *corrupt one's self*
Abemolar, *v. a. to soften, to supple*
Aberengenado, da, *adj. violet-coloured*
Aberrugado, da, *a. warty*
Abertura, *sub. f. an opening ; hole, etc.*

Abes, *ad. hardly*
Abeterno, *ad. from eternity* [*fir-tree*
Abeto, *s. m. a kind of*
Abetunado, da, *a. like the bitumen*
Abezana, *sub. f. a set of oxen to plough*
Abiertamente, *ad. openly; plainly*
Abierto, ta, *adj. open; frank; free*
Abigarrar, *v. a. to party-colour*
Abigeato, *s. m. the thieving of catle*
Abigeo, *s. m. the thief of catle*
Abigotado, da, *adj. one with long whiskers*
Ab inicio, *adv. from the begining*
Ab intestato, *ad. intestate*
Abismar, *v. a. to throw into an abiss || to ruin*
Abismo, *s. m. an abyss*
Abitaque. *s. m. the fourth part of the measure called viga*
A'bito, *s. m. V.* Hábito
Abizcochado, da, *a. like the sea-bisket*
Abjuracion, *s. f. abjuration*
Abjurar, *v. a. to abjure*
Ablandadura, *s. f.* / Ablandamiento, *s. m.* } *softening*
Ablandar, *v. a. to mollify; to soften*
Ablandar, *v. n. to grow mild; to relent*
Ablativo, *s. m. the ablative case*
Ablacion, *s. f. ablution*
Abnegacion, *s. f. abnegation*
Abobar, abobamiento. *V.* Embobar, etc.

Abobas, *adv. foolishly; sillily* [*rence*
Abocamiento, *s. m. confe-*
Abocar, *v. a. to seize with the mouth*
Abocar la artillería, *to point or aim the cannon* — las tropas, *to post the troop* — las vergas, *to make fast the yards of a ship*
Abocarse, *v. r. to come mouth to mouth to confer*
Abocardado (cañon), *cannon with a mouth like that of a trumpet*
Abochornar, *v. a. to burn; to parch up || to weary; to irritate*
Abofeteador, ra, *s. one that boxes another*
Abofetear, *v. a. to cuff*, or *box*
Abogacía, *s. f. the office of a lawyer; advocateship*
Abogada, *s. f. advocate; patroness* [*advocate*
Abogado, *s. m. lawyer ||*
Abogar, *v. a. to plead as a lawyer does*
Abohetado. *V.* Abuhado
Abolengo, *s.m. genealogy*
Abolicion, *s. f. abolition*
Abolir, *v. a. to abolish*
Abolladura, *s. f. a bruise || a relievo*
Abollar, *v. a. to work in relievo || to vex, to tire*
Abollon. *s. m. the bud of a vine* [llar
Abollonar, *v. a. V.* Abo-
Abollonar, *v. n. to bud*
Abolsado, da, *adj. folded as a purse*
Abominable, *adj. abominable* [*abominably*
Abominablemente, *adv.*

Abominacion, *s. f. abomination*
Abominador, *sub. m. one that abominates*
Abominar, *v. act. to abominate*
Abonado, da, *a. one that is rich*, or *that has got a name, etc.*
Testigo abonado, *an unexceptionable witness*
Abonador, ra, *s. bail; respondent* [Abono
Abonamiento, *sub. m. V.*
Abonanzar, *v. n. to grow calm (the sea); to clear up the weather*
Abonar, *v. a. to approve || to improve || to bail or warrant*
Abono, *s. m. approbation || manure || bail; security || a bailing.*
Abordador, *s. m. he that boards a ship*
Abordage, *s. m. boarding*
Abordar, *v. a. to board; to accost*
Abordo, *s. m. V.* Abordage
Abordo, *ad. aboard*
Abordonar, *v. n. to lean on a walking staff*
Aborrachado, da, *a. brigtred* [*a storm*
Aborrascar, *v. a. to raise*
Aborrecedor, ra, *subst. abhorrer*
Aborrecer, *v. a. to abhor*
Aborrecible, *a. hateful*
Aborreciblemente, *ad. hatefully*
Aborrecimiento, *sub. m. hate; aversion*
Abortamiento, *s. m. V.* Aborto
Abortar, *v. a. to miscarry, to abort*
Abortivo, va, *a. abortive*

Aborto, *s. m. miscarriage*
Aborton, *s. m. an abortive child, etc.*
Aborujarse, *v. r. to wrap one's self up*
Abotagarse, *v. r. to swell as á leather-botle*
Abotinado, da, *a. having the form of a boot*
Abotonador, *s. m. a buttoner*
Abotonar, *v. a. to button*
Abotonar el caballo, *to spur a horse*
Abotonar, *v. n. to bud*
Abovedar, *v. a. to vault* or *arch*
Aboyado (cortijo), *an estate farmed with the necessary catle*
Abra, *s. f. haven, bay, or creek* || *opening; cleft, etc.* [*dently*
Abrasadamente, *adv. ar-*
Abrasador, ra, *sub. y a. that burns*
Abrasamiento, *sub. m. a violent burning; conflagration*
Abrasar, *v. a. to burn; to set on fire* || *to spend* or *squander away* || *to irritate; to incense*
Abrasarse, *v. r. to be inflamed*
Abrasilado, da, *a. brasil-coloured* [*rule*
Abrazadera, *s. f. a fer-*
Abrazador, ra, *s. the person who embraces another*
Abrazar, *v. a. to embrace*
Abrazo, *s. m. an embrace*
A'brego, *s. m. the south-west wind*
Abrenuncio, *int. fy upon! God forbid!*
Abrevadero, *s. m. watering-place*
Abrevado, da, *a. wet*
Abrevador, *s. masc. one who waters catle*
Abrevar, *v. a. to water*
Abreviacion, *s. f. abbreviation* [*viator*
Abreviador, *s. m. abbre-*
Abreviados, *s. m. pl. bastards*
Abreviar, *v. a. to abridge*
Abreviarse, *v. r. to humble one's self*
Abreviatura, *s. f. abbreviation*
En abreviatura, *quickly*
Abribonarse, *v. r. to abandon one's self to idleness, etc.*
Abridero, *sub. m. peach easy to be opened*
Abridero, ra, *a. easy to be opened*
Abridor, *s. m. one that opens* || *an engraver* || *a grafting-knife*
Abrigaño, *s. m. a sheltering-place*
Abrigar, *v. a. to shelter* || *to protect*
Abrigo, *s. m. a shelter*
Abril, *s. m. april*
Abrillantar, *v. a. to cut a diamond into angles*
Abrimiento, *s. m. an opening*
Abrir, *v. a. to open*
Abrir lo sellado, *to open* — mano de una cosa, *to desist from a thing* — portillo, *to make a breach* — en cobre, *to engrave on copper* — el tiempo, *clear up the weather* [*toner*
Abrochador, *s. m. a but-*
Abrochamiento, *s. m. the clasping, buttoning, etc.*
Abrochar, *v. a. to clasp*, or *button*
Abrogacion, *s. f. abrogation*
Abrogar, *v. a. to abrogate*
Abrojo, *s. m. a kind of thistle* || *a caltrop*
Abrojos, *pl. shelves in the sea* [*foggy*
Abromado, da, *a. cloudy*,
Abromarse, *v. r. to be eaten by worms*
Abroquelarse, *v. r. to cover one's self with a buckler*
Abrótano, *s. m. southern-wood* [|| *troublesome*
Abrumador, ra, *a. heavy*
Abrumador, *s. m. a skip-jack*
Abrumar, *v. a. to oppress* — *to molest*
Abrutado, da, *a. besotted*
Absceso, *s. m. an abscess*
Absolucion, *s. f. absolution* [*lutely*
Absolutamente, *ad. abso-*
Absoluto, ta, *a. absolute*
Absolutorio, ria, *a. absolutory*
Absolvederas, *s. f. pl. easiness in a confessor to give absolution*
Absolvedor, *sub. m. one that absolves*
Absolver, *v. a. to absolve*
Absortar, *v. a. to suspend; to astonish*
Absorvencia, *s. f. absorption* [*bent*
Absorvente, *s. m. absor-*
Absorver, *v. a. to absorb*
Abstemio, mia, *adj. abstemious*
Abstenerse, *v. r. to abstain*
Abstergente, *a. 2. abstersive*
Absterger, *v. act. to absterse*, or *absterge*
Abstersivo, va, *a. abstersive* [*nence*
Abstinencia, *s. f. absti-*

te, *a. abstinent*
temente, *ad. with*
ence [*traction*
ion, *sub. f. abs-*
vaménte, *adv.*
ctedly
), ta, *a. abstract*

, *v. a. to abstract*
de... *to abstain*
..
se, *v. r. to retire*
ne's self
, da, *a. retired,*
y
, sa, *a. abstruse*
ad, *s. f.* } *absur-*
s. m. } *dity*
, da, *a. absurd*
, *s. f. puet; lap-*
[narse
rse, *V.* Abocho-
.f. grandmother
. m. grandfather
, da, *adj. big* or

v. a. to make
; to enlarge
v. neut. to grow
[*dance*
ia, *s. f. abun-*
e, *a. abundant*
emente, *adv.*
ntly
v. n. to abound
r, *v. a. to make*
orm of a fritter
. a. to burn
, da, *adj. dark-*

nto, *s. m. te-*
ss; disquiet, etc.
v. a. to vex; to
— to spend
, da, *adj. intri-*

v. a. to squeeze,
g, to wind into
a

Abusar, *v. a. to abuse*
Abusion, *s. f. catachresis* || *augury* or *divination*
Abusivamente, *ad. abusively*
Abusivo, va, *adj. abusive*
Abuso, *s. m. abuse*
Acá, *adv. hither; here*
Acá y acullá, *hither and thiter* — desde un mes acá, *a month ago*
Acabable, *adj. that can be finished*
Acabadamente, *adv. completely; perfectly*
Acabalar, *v. a. to complete* || *to equal; to make even* || *to finish*
Acaballadero, *s. m. the time and place where horses cover the mares*
Acaballado, da, *adj. resembling a horse*
Acaballar, *v. a. to leap the mare; to horse*
Acaballerado, da, *adj. like a gentleman*
Acaballerar, *v. a. to make a one like a gentleman*
Acabamiento, *s. m. end* || *death*
Acabar, *v. a. to end; to finish* || *to perfect* || *to obtain*
Acabar con alguno, *to kill,* or *slay* — con alguna cosa, *to destroy*
Acabar, *v. n. to end* || *to die*
Acabdillamente, *adv. orderly*
Acabellado, da, *adj. chesnut colour*
Acabestrillar, *v. n. to hunt with muzaled oxen*
Acabronado, da, *adj. proud; impudent*
Acacia, *s. f. acacia* || *the juice of the sloes*

Academia, *s. f. academy*
Académico, *s. m. academician* [*mical*
Académico, ca, *adj. academical*
Acaecedero, ra, *adj. that can happen*
Acaecer, *v. neut. imp. to happen*
Acaecerse, *v. r. to be present*
Acaecimiento, *s. m. an accident* or *event*
Acal, *s. m. V.* Canoa
Acalia, *s. f. V.* Malvavisco
Acallar, *v. a. to still; to silent*
Acalorar, *v. a. to warm*
Alcalorarse, *v. r. to hurry one's self*
Acamadas (mieses), *s. f. pl. corn laid down by the rain*
Acamellado, da, *adj. resembling a camel*
Acampamento, *s. m. encampment* || *a camp*
Acampar, *v. a. y n. to incamp*
Acamuzado, *V.* Gamuzado
Acana, *s. f. tree of the west-indies*
Acanalado, da, *ad. passing trough a canal*
Acanalados, *pl. the horse's chine*
Acanalador, *s. m. a sort of plane*
Acanalar, *v. a. to channel* || *to drive through a canal*
Acandilado, da, *adj. made in the shape of the jocket of a lamp*
Acanelado, da, *adj. of a cinnamon colour*
Acanillado, da, *adj. ill-weaved; ill-made*
Acantarar, *v. a. to measure out by pitchers*

Acantilada (costa), *s. f. an easily accessible coast*
Acanto, *s. m. bear's breech*
Acantonamiento, *s. masc. cantoning*
Acantonar, *v. a. to canton*
Acañaverear, *v. a. to pierce*, or *wound with sharp canes*
Acañonear, *v. a. to cannonade*
Acaparrarse, *v. r. to shelter one's self under another's cloak*
Acaparrozado, da, *adj of a copperas colour*
Acapizarse, *v. r. to pluck one another by the hair*
Acaponado, da, *adj. like an eunuch* or *a capon*
Acardenalar, *v. a. to bruise*
Acariciador, ra, *s. a person that makes much of his guests, etc.*
Acariciar, *v. a. to caress; to make much of.....*
Acarrarse, *v. r. to gather*, or *join together*
Acarreadizo, za, *adj. portable* [*rier*
Acarreador, ra, *s. a car-*
Acarreadura, *s. f. y* acarramiento, *s. m. V.* Acarreo
Acarrear, *v. a. to carry*
Acarreo, Acarrete, } *s. m. carriage*
Acaso, *s. masc. accident; chance*
Acaso, *adv. by chance*
Acastillage, *s. m. poop and fore castle*
Acatable, *adj. respectable*
Acatadamente, *adv. respectfully*
Acataléctico, ca, Acátalecto, ta, } *adj. acatalectick*
Acatamiento, *s. m. reverence; respect*

Acatar, *v. a. to respect; to honour — to behold*
Acatarse, *v. r. to mistrust*
Acatarrarse, *v. r. to catch cold*
Acates, *s. m. V.* A'gata
Acaudalado, da, *adj. rich*
Acaudalar, *v. a. to heap up treasures || to get a name, etc.*
Acaudillador, *s. m. a commander; a leader*
Acaudillar, *v. a. to lead; to command*
Acceder, *v. n. to accede*
Accesible, *adj. accessible*
Accesion, *s. f. accession || a fit of an ague*
Acceso, *s. m* Access || *a carnal conjunction || right; claim*
Accesorias, *s. f. pl. accessory buildings*
Accesoriamente, *ad. incidently* [*sory*
Accesorio, ria, *adj. acces-*
Accidentado, da, *adj. sickly* [*tal*
Accidental, *adj. acciden-*
Accidentalmente, *y* accidentariamente, *adv. accidentally*
Accidentarse, *v. r. to be suddenly taken ill*
Accidentazo, *s. m. a dangerous and sudden distemper*
Accidente, *s. m. accident*
Accion, *s. f. action || share in stock*
Accion de gracias, *thanksgiving*
Accionar, *v. n. to use much action in talking*
Accionista, *s. m. actionist; actionary*
Acebadamiento, acebadar, *V.* Encebadamiento, encebadar.

Acebedo, *s. m. a h[...] plot*
Acebo, *s. m. holly*
Acebuchal, *adj. V.* [...]buchено
Acebuchal, *s. m. an ol[...]ter-orchard*
Acebuche, *s. m. oleas[...]*
Acebucheno, na, *adj.* [...] *belongs* or *relates* [...] *the oleaster*
Acebuchina, *s. f. an o[...]ter's fruit*
Acechador, ra, *s. one* [...] *is always watching* [...] *prying*
Acechar, *v. a. to wa[...] to pry*
Aceche, *s. m. a kin[...] black earth*
Acecho, *s. m. the a[...] watching* or *pryin[...]*
Acechon, na, *s. V.* [...]chador [*t*
Acecinar, *v. a. to*
Acecinarse, *v. r. to g[...] lean and dry*
Acedar, *v. a. to sour* [...] *molest*
Acedera, *s. f. sorrel*
Acederilla, *s. f. wo[...] sorrel*
Acedia, *s. f. sour ta[...] acidity || roughn[...] harshness — a flou[...]*
Acedo, da, *adj. sour;*
Acéfalo, la, *adj. ace[...]lous*
Aceleracion, *s. f. acc[...]ration; swiftness*
Aceleradamente, *ad[...] swiftly; hastily*
Aceleramiento, *s. m.* [...] Aceleracion [
Acelerar, *v. a. to acc[...]*
Acelga, *s. f. white-be[...]*
Acemila, *s. f. a sump[...] mule*
Acemilar, *adj. belon[...]*

to the mule-driver, or *to the sumpter-mule*
Acemileria, *s. f. a mules's stable*
Acemilero, *s. m. a mule-driver*
Acemilero, ra, *adj. belonging to the mules's stables*
Acemita, *s. f. bread made wi h bran*
Acemite, *s. m. bran*
Acender, *V.* Encender
Acendrado, da, *adj. pure, clean*
Acendrar, *v. a. to refine || to cleanse, to purify*
Acensuar, *v. a. to lay a rent upon a land*
Acento, *s. m. accent*
Acentuacion; *s. f. the act of accenting*
Acentuar, *v. a. to accent*
Aceña, *s. f. a water-mill*
Aceñero, *s. m. a miller*
Acepcion, *s. f. acception*
Acepcion de personas, *respect of persons*
Acepilladura, *s. f. planing || shavings of wood*
Acepillar, *v. a. to plane the wood || to brush cloaths*
Aceptable, *adj. reasonable*
Aceptacion, *s. f. acceptation*
Aceptador, ra, *s. he that accepts; a receiver*
Aceptar, *v. a. to accept*
Aceptar personas, *to give the preference to persons, without their deserving it*
Acepto, ta, *adj. well received; grateful*
Acequia, *s. f. a canal*
Acequiado, da, *adj. surrounded*, or *divided by canals*
Acequiero, *s. m. one who takes care of canals*
Acer, *s. m. the maple-tree*
Acera, *s. f. the wall in the streets*
Acerado, da, *adj. made with steel*
Acerar, *v. a. to steel*
Acerbamente, *adv. harshly; bitterly*
Acerbidad, *s. f. acerbity*
Acerbo, ba, *adj. acerb*
Acerca de, *prep. concerning*
Acercamiento, *s. m. approach*
Acercar, *v. a. to approach*
Acercen, *adv. close to the root, etc.*
Acerico y acerillo, *s. m. a pillow || a pin-cushion*
Acerino, na, *adj. made with* or *belonging to the steel*
Acero, *s. m. steel || sword courage* [*lar*
Acerola, *s. f. a small med-*
Acerolo, *s. m. the small medlar-tree*
Aceroso, sa, *adj. sharp*
Acérrimamente, *ad. strongly; obstinately*
Acérrimo, ma, *adj. steady; obstinate*
Acertadamente, *adv. dextrously*
Acertado, da, *adj. prudent; discreet || perfect*
Acertador, *s. m. skilful in shooting*
Acertajo, *s. m. V.* Acertijo
Acertar, *v. a to hit a mark || to reach*, or *come at... || to guess || to find*, or *meet || to fit; to size*
Acertar, *v. n. to happen*
Acertijo, *s. m. enigma, riddle*
Aceruelo, *s. m. an instrument, etc. furnished with very litle steel || a litle sword || a kind of english saddle*
Acervo, *s. m. a heap*
Acetábulo, *s. m. acetabulum || a litle measure by apothecaries*
Acetar, *v. a. V.* Aceptar
Acetosidad, *s. f. sourness; acidity* .
Acetosilla, *s. f. wood-sorrel*
Acetre, *s. m. holywater-pot || holywater || sprinkle || one that carries the holywater-pot*
Aceytada, *s. f. an exceeding quantity of oil*
Aceytar, *v. a. to oil || to pour oil into....*
Aceyte, *s. m. oil* [*oil*
Aceytera, *s. f. a cruet for*
Aceyterazo, *s. m. a stroke with a cruet*
Aceytero, ra, *s. an oil man*
Aceytoso, sa, *adj. oily*
Aceytuna, *s. f. an olive*
Aceytunado, da, *adj. olive-coloured*
Aceytunero, *s. m. one that gathers* or *sells the olives*
Aceytuno, *s. m. V.* Olivo
Acha, *V.* Hacha
Achacadizo, za, *adj. cunning; deceitfull*
Achacar, *v. a. to lay to another's charge*
Achacarse, *v. r. to claim to one's self another man's merit, etc.*
Achacosamente, *adv. sickly*
Achacoso, sa, *adj. sickly*
Achaparrado, da, *adj. branchy as a shrub*
Hombre achaparrado, *a shrub.*
Achaque, *s. m. sickness ||*

a woman's monthly terms || *an excuse*, or *pretence* || *an ordinary defect* or *vice* || *a secret accusation* || *a fine*

Achaquero, *s. m. a fines's farmer*

Achaquiento, ta, *adj. V.* Achacoso

Achaquillo, ito, *s. m. a small distemper*

Achicador, *s. m he that lessens*, or *diminishs* || *a scoop*

Achicadura, *s. f. lessening; diminishing*

Achicar, *v. a. to lessen; to diminish* || *to pump*

Achicharrar, *v. a. to toast*, or *fry too much*

Achichinque, *s. m. one employed to dry up the mines*

Achicoria, *s. f. wild-endive*

Achinelado, da, *adj. made in the shape of a slipper*

Achiote, *s. m. a tree growing in America*

Achocar, *v. a. to knock, to strike* || *to hoard up money*

Achuchar, *y* achuchurrar *v. a. to press*, or *squeeze* || *to squash* || *to convict* or *confound; to non plus*

Achulado, da, *adj. jocose; pleasant*

A'cia. *V.* Hácia

Aciago, ga, *adj. unluckly; ominous* || *sad; melancholy*

Acial, *s. m. barnacles*

Acianos, *s. m. V.* Extrellamar

Acibar, *s. m. aloes* || *bitterness; disgust*

Acibarar, *v. a. to make bitter with aloes* || *to vex; to trouble*

Acibarrar, *v. a. to dash against....*

Acicalador, *s. m. a sword-cutler* || *a polisher* || *a polishing-iron*

Acicaladura, *s. f.*, Acicalamiento, *s. m.* } *furbishing; polishing*

Acicalar, *v. a. to furbish; to polish*

Acicate, *s. m. a turkish spur*

Aciche, *s. m. the bricklayer's hatchet*

A'cido, *s. m. acid*

A'cido, da, *adj. acid; sour*

Acierto, *s. m. a good hit* || *a good success* || *skill chance*

Aciguatado, da, *adj. yellow; pale*

Aciguatarse, *v. r. to be seized with the yellow-jaundice*

Acije, *s. m. V.* Aceche

Acimboga, *s. f. a kind of citron-tree*

Acimiento, *s. m. V.* Hacimiento

Acina, *s. f. V.* Hacina

Acion, *s. f. a stirrup-leather*

Acionero, *s. m. a stirrup-leather-maker*

Acipado (paño), *s. m. a close-woven cloth*

Acirates, *s. m. pl. limits* || *platband; border*

Acitara, *s. f. partition made with, brick, and parget* || *a partition-wall*

Acitron, *s. m. a preserved citron*

Aclamacion, *s. f. acclamation* || *epiphonema*

Aclamador, *s. m. applauder*

Aclamar, *v. a. to applaud* || *to proclaim* || *to call back the hawk*

Aclaracion, *s. f. explication*

Aclarar, *v. a. to clear; to explain* || *to thin a licor*

Aclarar, *v. n. to clear up the weather*

Aclocarse, *v. r. to brood*

Acobardar, *v. a. to intimidate; to make one cowardly*

Acobdar, Acobdiciar. *V.* Acodar, Acodiciar

Acoceador, ra, *s. a horse that kicks*

Acoceamiento, *s. m. a kicking*

Acocear, *v. a. to kick* || *to treat with contempt* || *to stamp with one's feet*

Acochinar, *v. a. to assassinate* || *to come to a secret agreement with a criminal*

Acocotar, *v. a. V.* Acogotar

Acodadura, *s. f. the leaning on the elbow* || *the setting layers*

Acodar, *v. a. to lean on one's elbow* || *to set layers; to provine*

Acodillar, *v. a. to bend*

Acodillar con la carga, *to shrink under the burden*

Acodo, *s. m. a layer*

Acoger, *v. a. to receive* || *to protect*

Acogerse, *v. r. to fly to:... for shelter*

Acogida, *s. f.*, Acogimiento, *s. m.* } *reception* || *asylum; refuge*

Acogollar, *v. a. to fence plants from the frost with straw, etc.*

Acogombrar, *v. a. Voyez* Aporcar

Acogotado, da, *adj. pressed, or oppressed*

Acogotar, *v. a. to kill*

low on the neck
. *a. to join two*
f arms
v. a. to quilt
s. m. acolyte
, *s. m. lamier*
o (palomo), *s. m.*
dove
, *v. a. to put the*
to draught-hor-
s.
or, ra, *s. assai-*
gressor
, *v. a. to attack;*
il || *to undertake*
a, *s. f.* } *an at-*
iento, } *tack, an*
} *assault*
ndertaking — a
tion || *a fit of an*

ble, adj. conve-
fit
cion, *s. f. adap-*

lamente, *adver.*
iently || *como-*
,
lo, da, *adj. fit;*
ient || *opulent* ||
ves his own ease
veniencies
lor, ra, *s. he who*
, *etc.* || *he who*
women their
at the playhouse
lora, *s. f. she*
commends wet-

miento, *s. m. ag-*
nt; accommo-
|| *conveniency*
r, *v. a. to fit up;*
order || *to com-*
a difference || *to*
servant, etc. ||
vide for another
r, *v. n. to fit; to*

Acomodarse, *v. r. to conform one's self to....*

Acomodaticio, cia, *adj. figurative*

Acomodo, *s. m. commodity; conveniency* || *employ; place*

Acompañador, ra, *s. companion*

Acompañamiento, *s. m. accompanying* || *retinue* || *musick played to one that sings, etc.*

Acompañar, *v. a. to acompany*

Acompasado, da, *adj. measured by the compass* || *starched*, or *affected*

Acomplexionado, da, *adj. V.* Complexionado

Aconchar, *v. a. to equip a galley*

Acondicionado (género bien), *sub. m. a stanch commodity*

Acondicionar, *v. a. to put into good condicion*

Acongojar, *v. a. to vex; to grieve*

Acónito, *s. m. wolf's-bane*

Aconsejar, *v. a. to counsel*

Aconsejarse, *v. r. to consult*, or *advise with*

Aconsonantar, *v. a. to employ vitious consonances*

Acontar, *v. a. V.* Contar *y* Apuntalar

Acontecer, *v. a. imp. to happen*

Acontecimiento, *s. m. accident; event*

Acopar, *v. n. to grow round like a cup*

Acopetado, da, *adj. curled*

Acopiamiento, *s. m. Voy.* Acopio

Acopiamientos, *pl. assesments of the provisions*

Acopiar, *v. a. to purchase, to heap up corn, etc.*

Acopio, *s. m. purchase*, or *heap of corn, etc.*

Acoplar, *v. a. to join together*

Acoquinar, *v. a. to frighten* [*stifle*

Acorar, *v. act. to kill; to*

Acorcharse, *v. r. to dry; to wither*

Acordablemente, *adv. V.* Acordadamente

Acordacion, *s. f. V.* Recordacion

Acordadamente, *ad. with one accord*

Acordado, da, *ad. made with mature deliberation*

Acordar, *v. act. to determine unanimously* || *to remember* || *to awake* || *to tune*

Acordar, *v. n. to agree together* || *to be undeceived, etc.*

Acorde, *a. agreed; unanimous*

Acordemente, *ad. V.* Acordadamente

Acordonado, da, *a. made, or disposed like a twist*

Acordonar, *v. act. to surround*

Acorneador, *s. m. a bull that butts*

Acornear, *v. a. to butt as horned beasts do — to use ill*

Acoro, *s. m. galingale*

Acorralar, *v. act. to fold cattle* || *to intimidate, or confound* [rugar

Acorrucar, *v. a. V.* Ar-

Acortadizo, *s. m. shreds; fragments*

Acortar, *v a. to shorten*

Acortarse, *v. r. to be stop-*

ped short with fear, etc.
Acorullar, v. a. to draw back the ears
Acosador, ra, s. one that pursues || persecutor
Acosamiento, s. m. close pursuit || persecuting
Acosar, v. a. to pursue close || to persecute, vex, etc.
Acostado, da, a. stipendiary
Acostamiento, s. m. the putting or going to bed
Acostar, v. a. to put to bed
Acostar, v. n. y acostarse, v. r. to incline; to be in decay || to coast along
Acostumbradamente, ad. after the usual manner
Acostumbrar, v. a. to accustom
Acostumbrar, v. n. to use
Acotacion, sub. f. setting bounds || annotation in the margin
Acotar, v. a. to set bounds || to mark || to make annotations
Acotarse, v. r. to put one's self in safety
Acotillo, sub. m. a great hammer [the oxen
Acoyundar, v. a. to yoke
Acre, a. sour; sharp
Acrecencia, s. f. increase
Acrecentador, s. mas. one that increases
Acrecentamiento, s. mas. increase
Acrecentar, } v. a. to in-
Acrecer, } crease
Acrecer, v. n. to augment
Acrecimiento, s. mas. V. Aumento
Acreditar, v. act. to give credit, or esteem || to approve || to bail
Acreedor, ra, s. creditor

Acremente, ad. sharply
Acribadura, s. f. the sifting
Acribaduras, pl. siftings
Acribar, v. act. to sift || to shoot through and through
Acribillar, v. a. to pierce full of holes || to tire, to molest
Acriminacion, sub. f. the action of exaggerating a crime
Acriminador, subs. mas. he that exaggerates a crime
Acriminar, v. act. to amplify, or aggravate a fault, etc.
Acrimonia, s. f. acrimony || asperity || energy; vehemence
Acrisolar, v. act. to refine in a crucible || to cleanse, purify, etc.
Acronicto, ad. acronycal
Acróstico, ca, a. acrostick
Acrotera, s. f. acroteria
Acroy, s. m. gentleman of the king's household
Actas, sub. f. pl. publick acts, or records
Actimo, sub. m. a point's twelfth part
Actitud, s. f. attitude
Activamente, ad. actively
Actividad, s. f. activity
Activo, va, a. active
Acto, s. m. act, action || a carnal conjunction
Actor, s. m. actor || plaintiff, in the law
Actriz, s. f. actress
Actual, a. actual
Actualidad, sub. f. actual state [ly
Actualmente, ad. actual-
Actuar, v. a. to digest || to make a cause ready

Actuario, subs. m. a s
vener
Actuoso, sa, a. dilig
careful
Acubado, da, a. mad
the shape of a tub
Acucharado, da, a. m
in the shape of a sp
Acuchillado, da, a. tr
skilful
Mangas acuchilladas,
shed sleeves
Acuchillador, sub. m
prize-fighter; a
diator [to
Acuchillar, v. a. to sl
Acudimiento, s. m. re
ring to || relief; a
tance
Acudir, v. a. to come
portunely || to suc
|| to have recourse
to frequent || to b
forth plenty of fru
Acuento, ad. on acc
Acuerdo, s. m. a m
deliberation || a
ment; resolution ||
son; judgment
Acuerdo de asesor,
opinion of the c
sellor to the jury
cuerdos de Reyno
resolution taken, i
spanish-courts
Acuernar, v. n. to t
ten, or strike wit
horns
Acuestas, adv. up
man's back
Acular, v. a. to pu
hard to it
Aculebrinado, da, a
a culverin
Acullá, ad. there
Allá y acullá, here
there
Acumulacion, s. f.
mulation

mulador, ra, *sub. one hat accumulates*
mular, *v. a. to accumulate* || *to lay to one's harge*
ñacion, *s. f. the action of coining money*
ñador, ra, *s. a coiner*
ñar, *ver. act. to coin money* || *to cleave with edges* [*wealth*
ñar dinero, *to heap*
rrucarse, *ver. rec. to muffle one's self up*
rrullar, *v. a. to furl he sails* [*tion*
sacion, *s. f. accusa-*
sador, *s. m. accuser*
sar, *v. a. to accuse* || *o notify the receipt of letter* [*sative*
sativo, *s. mas. accu-*
satorio, ria, *a. accuatory*
tángulo, *adj. acutangular* [*goo*
afina, *s. f. a jewish ra-*
agio, *s. m. adage*
ala, *s. f. a gutter, in he ship* [*leader*
alid, *s. m. a chief; a*
amadillo, lla, *a. sparish; beauish* [*effeminate*
amado, da, *adj. nice*,
amarse, *v. r. to become inical, nice. lady-like*
amascado, da, *a. damasked* [*nient*
aptable, *a. fit; conve-*
aptacion, *sub. f. adaping; adaptation*
aptadamente, *ad. fitly*
aptado, da, *adj. fit, or roper for*
aptar, *v. a. to adapt*
arga, *s. f. a short light arget*
argarse, *v. r. to cover one's self with a target*

Adargazo, *s. m. a stroke with a target*
Adarguilla, *sub. f. a litle target* [*dram*
Adarme, *s. mas. an half-*
Adarve, *s. m. the space on the top of the walls of a fortified place*
Adatar, *v. a. to record one his expense, etc.*
Adefina, *s. f. V.* Adafina
Adefesio, *s. mas. V.* Despropósito
Adehala, *sub. f. a present made into the bargain*
Adelantadamente, *ad. before time*
Adelantado, *s. m. president; chief; governor*
Adelantamiento, *sub. m. advancement; increase* || *the dignity and district of the* adelantado
Adelantar, *v. a. to hasten* || *to out-strip* || *to anticipate* || *to increase, enlarge, etc.*
Adelantarse, *v. r. to go forwards* [*behond*
Adelante, *adv. before;*
De hoy en adelante, *from this time forwards*
Adelfa, *sub. f. rose baytree*
Adelfal, *sub. m. a plot of ground planted with rose bay-trees*
Adelgazador, *sub. m. one that makes things slender*
Adelgazamiento, *s. m. lessening, diminution*
Adelgazar, *v. a. to make thin or slender* || *to subtilize, to refine*
Adema, *V.* Ademe [*maker*
Ademador, *s. m. a prop-*
Ademan, *s m gesture; countenance* || *attitude*

Ademar, *v. a. to support, to stay*
Ademas, *ad. moreover*
Ademe, *s. m. prop; support*
Adentellar, *v. a. to bite*
Adentro, *ad. within*
Adequacion, *s. f. adequateness* [*quately*
Adequadamente, *ad. ade-*
Adequado, da, *adj. adequate*
Adequar, *v. a. to equal*, or *proportion*
Aderezar, *v. a. to dress; to adorn*
Aderezar la comida, *to dress meat* — la casa, *to set the house in order*
Aderezo, *s. m. dressing; ornament* || *a set of diamonds, etc.*
Aderezo de caballo, *horse-trappings* — de casa, *furniture* — de espada, *the handle, and hilt, of a sword*
Adeshora, *ad. out of time*
Adestrado, da, *a. on the right hand*
Adestrador, *sub. m. conductor; guide*
Adestrar, *v. a. to guide; to direct* || *to instruct*
Adeudarse, *v. r. to run in debt* [*rence*
Adherencia, *sub. f. adhe-*
Adherente, *a. adherent* || *relation; friend, etc.*
Adherir, *v. n. to adhere*
Adhesion, *s. f. adhesion*
Adiado (dia), *s. m. an appointed day*
Adiamantado, da, *a. adamantine*
Adicion, *s. f. addition*
Adicionador, *sub. m. one who makes a new addition*

Adicionar, *v. a. to add*
Adicto, ta, *a. inclined to*
Adiestrar, *v. a. V.* Adestrar
Adietar, *v. a. to diet one*
Adinas, *s. f. V.* Adivas
Adinerado, da, *adj. V.* Acaudalado
Adintelado (arco), *s. m. an arch ending in a right line.*
Adiposo, sa, *a. adipous*
Adir la herencia, *v. a. to accept an heritage*
Aditamento, *s. m. an addition*
Aditicio, cia, *a. added*
Adiva, ó Adive, *s. m. a beast in Africa*
Adivas, *s. f. pl. vives*
Adivinacion, *s. f. divination*
Adivinador, ra, *s. diviner, divineress*
Adivinamiento, *s. m. divination*
Adivinanza, *s. f. V.* Adivinacion
Adivinar, *v. a. to divine*

A

Adjetivacion, *s. f the art of joining adjectives with substantives*
Adjetivar, *v. a. to construe the adjectives with the substantives*
Adjetivo, *s m. adjective*
Adjudicacion, *s. f. adjudging*
Adjudicar, *v. act. to adjudge* [*tion*
Adjuncion, *s. f. adjunc-*
Adjungir, *v. a. to adjoin*
Adjunto, *s. m. V.* Adjetivo || *assistant adjunct*
Adminicular, *v. a. to aid;* [*minicle*

[Adminicular cont.] *, s. f. administration*
Administrador, ra, *s. administrator, trix*
Administrar, *v. a. to administer; to manage*
Administratorio, ria, *a. belonging to the administrator, etc.*
Admirable, *a. admirable*
Admirablemente, *ad. ad-*

Admirar, *v. a. to cause admiration || to admire*
Admirarse, *v. r. to be taken up with admiration*
Admisible, *a. allowable*
Admision, *s. f. admission*
Admitir, *v. a. to admit || to accept || to permit*
Admonicion, *s. f. V.* Admonestacion
Admonitor, *s. m. adviser*
Ádnata, *s. f. conjunctive, in the eye*
Adobado, *s. m. salt-pork*
Adobar, *v. act. to botch cloaths || to cobble shoes || to put meat into the brine || to dress meat || to tan; to curry || to dispose the minds*
Adobe, *s. mas. brick that is not burnt*
Adoberia, *sub. f. a brick-kiln*
Adobo, *s. m. mending; repairing || brine || dressing of meat; seasoning — women's paint*
Adocenar, *v. a. to make into dozens || to despise*
Adolecer, *v. neut. to fall sick*

Adolecer, *v. a. to hurt*
Adolescencia, *s. f. adol cency*
Adolescente, *s. m. yout*
Adonde, *ad. where; wh her*
Adonio, *a. m. adonick*
Adopcion, *s. f. adoptio*
Adoptador, *s. m. adopt*
Adoptar, *v. a. to adopt to graft*
Adoptivo, va, *a. adopti*
Adorable, *a. adorable*
Adoracion, *s. f. adorati*
Adorador, *s. m. adorer*
Adorar, *v. a. to adore*
Adoratorio, *s. m. a temp of idols*
Adormecedor, *subs. m. thing that causes sle*
Adormecer, *v. act. to lu a sleep*
Adormecerse, *v. r. to fa a sleep*
Adormecimiento, *sub. sleepiness*
Adormidera, *s. f. a popp*
Adornar, *v. a. to adorn*
Adorno, *s. m. ornamen*
Adquiridor, *s. m. acqu rer*
Adquirir, *v. a. to acqui*
Adquisicion, *s. f. acqu sition*
Adrales, *s. m. pl. racks a wain*
Adredo, *ad. purposely*
Adrizar, *v. a. to drim t galley*
Adrubado, da, *adj. V.* G bado
Aduana, *s. f. the custom house || custom*
Aduanar, *v. act. to searc commodities in the cu tom-house || to pay th custom*
Aduanero, *s. m. custom house-officer*

Aduar, *s. mas. village of tents or huts*

Aducar, *s. mas. a coarse silk-stuff* [*hobgoblin*

Aduendado, da, *a. like a*

Adufazo, *s. mas. a stroke on, or with a timbrel*

Adufe, *s. m. a timbrel, or tabor*

Adufero *s. mas. one that plays on a timbrel*

Adujar, *v. act. to coil a cable*

Adujas, *s. f. pl. fakes of a cable coiled up*

Adulacion, *s. f. flattery*

Adulator, *s. m. adulator*

Adular *v. a. to flatter*

Adulatorio, ria, *a. adulatory* [*loud; to howl*

Adulear, *v. neut. to cry*

Adulero, *s. mas. a herdsman—a vociferous fellow* [*teration*

Adulteracion, *s. f. adul-*

Adulterador, *sub. m. one who adulterates*

Adulterar *v. a. to adulterate*

Adulterinamente, *adver. adulterately*

Adulterino, na, *a. born in adultery* || *adulterate*

Adulterio, *s. m. adultery*

Adulto, ta, *a. adult*

Adulzar, *v. a. V.* Endulzar

Adumbracion, *s. f. shadowings in painting*

Adunacion, *sub. f. meeting together*

Adunar, *v. a. to meet togeter; to assemble*

Adustion, *s. f. adustion*

Adustivo, va, *a. burning; inflammatory*

Adusto, ta, *adj. adust; burned up* || *melancholy*

Advena, *subs. m. a foreigner; a stranger*

Advenedizo za *a. a foreigner without estate, nor profession etc.*

Advenimiento, *s. m. V.* Venida

Adventaja, *s. f. jointure*

Adventicia, cia, *adj. adventitious*

Adverbial, *a. adverbial*

Adverbialmente, *ad. adverbially*

Adverbio, *s. m. adverb*

Adversamente, *adv. adversly*

Adversario, *s. m. adversary*

Adversarios, *pl. a collection of notes, extracts, etc.; adversaria*

Adversativo, va, *a. adversative*

Adversidad, *s. f. adversity*

Adverso, sa, *a. adverse*

Advertencia, *s. f. advertency* || *advice; counsel*

Advertidamente, *ad. advertently*

Advertido, da, *adj. prudent; skilfull*

to reflect upon || *to advise; to counsel*

Adviento, *s. m. advent*

Advocacion *sub. fem. the name given to a church*

Advocatorio, ria *adj. V.* Convocatorio

Adyacente, *a. adjacent*

Aechadero, *s. m. the place where corn is sifted*

Aechador, *s. m. a sifter*

Aechaduras, *s. f. pl. the siftings*

Aechar, *v. a. to sift* || *to perfectionnate*

Aéreo, rea, *adj. aerial; ethereal* || *vain; useles*

Aeromancia, *sub. f. aeromancy*

Aeromántico *sub. m. one who forete by the air* [*metry*

Aerometria *subs. f. aero-*

Aerophilacios, *s. mas. pl. cavities in the earth, full of air* [condidas

Aescondidas, etc. *V.* Es-

Afabilidad, *s. f. affability*

Afable, *a. affable*

Afablemente, *ad. affably*

Afaca, *s. f. wild-orobus*

Afamado da *famous*

Afan, *s. m. excessive labour, care, or anxiety*

Afanadamente, *ad. laboriously* || *vexatiously*

Afanador, *s. m. one that takes much pains* || *anxious; solicitous*

Afanar, *v. n. to toil, to labour* | *to be over careful, anxious* *tc.*

Afanoso, sa *a. vexatious*

Afascalar, *v. act. to heap up the sheaves*

Afeador, ra, *adj. he that deforms, etc.*

Afeamiento, *sub. mas. the growing*, or *making ugly* || *aspersion*

Afear, *v. act. to deform; to make ugly* || *to asperse*

Afeccion, *s. f. affection* || *aggregation; union*

Afectacion, *sub. f. affectation*

Afectadamente, *adv. affectedly* [*affects*

Afectador, *s. m. he that*

Afectar, *v. a. to affect* || *to unite; to annex* || *to desire*, or *prosecute anxiously*

Afectito, *s. m. a light affection* –

Afectivo, va, a. affective
Afecto, s. m. affection || the expressing in a picture || harmony of colours
Afecto, ta, a. affectionate || affected || inclined; well disposed [rously
Afectuosamente, ad. amo-
Afectuoso, sa, amorous
Afelio, s. m. aphelium
Afelpado, da, a. hairy
Afeminacion, sub. f. effeminacy
Afeminadamente, ad. effeminately
Afeminado, da, y afeminadillo, lla, a. effeminate
Afeminamiento, s. m. V. Afeminacion
Afeminar, v. a. to effeminate
Aferesis, s. f. aphæresis
Aferrador, ra, s. he that seizes, etc.
Aferrar, v. a. to seize; to lay fast hold of || to furl and make fast the sails
Aferrarse, v. r. to grapple with a ship
Aferravelas, subst f. pl. rope-bands
Afeytadamente, adver. handsomely
Afeytar, v. a. to shave || to paint the face || to trim up a garden || to shear the horses, etc.
Afeyte, s. m. paint
Afianzar, v. a. to bail || to fix with ropes, etc.
Aficion, s. f. affection
Aficionadamente, ad. affectionately
Aficionar, v. a. to gain the affection of
Aficionarse, v. n. to take an affection to

Aficioncilla, s. f. a light affection
Afilar, v. a. to sharpen
Afiligranado, da, a. like a filligreen-work || very thin and nice
Afilon, s. m. iron or steel to sharpen
Afin, s. m. a kinsman
Afinacion, s. f. affinage || perfection || consort; harmony [fectly
Afinadamente, adv. per-
Afinador, s. mas. one that finishes, and perfects || a refiner || a tuner
Afinadura, sub. f. y afinamiento, s. m. V. Afinacion
Afinar, v. a. to perfect || to refine || to tune
Afinidad, s. f. affinity
Afir, s. m. liquor made of juniper berries
Afirmacion, s. fem. affirmation [gly
Afirmadamente, ad. stron-
Afirmador, ra, s. affirmer
Afirmamiento, s. mas. V. Afirmacion
Afirmar, v. a. to strengthen || to affirm
Afirmativamente, ad. affirmatively [mative
Afirmativo, va, a. affir-
Afistolar, v. act. to grow into a fistula
Afixamiento, subs. m. V. Fixacion
Afliccion, s. f. affliction
Aflictivo, va, a. afflictive
Afligidamente, ad. afflictedly
Afligir, v. a. to afflict
Afloxadura, s. f. } slackening;
Afloxamiento, s. m. } relaxation
Afloxar, v, a. to slacken;

to let loose
Afloxar el arco, the bow — e lose courage jetas, to un tr
Afloxar, v. n. t mis. || to un mind. etc.
Afluencia, s. f.
Afluente, a. a. flowing || lo
Afollado, da, made in larg
Afollar, v. a. t fire
Afondar, v. a. dow
Aforador, s. m.
Aforar, v. a. t gauge || to i be made ten mager
Aforisma, sub. vrism in the
Aforismo, s. m
Aforo, s. m. ga
Aforrar, v. a. t
Aforro, s. m. a
Afortunado, da nate
Afortunar, v. fortunate
Afrancesado, d.
Afratelarse, v. come as fan brother
Afremillar, v.
Afrenta, sub. dishonour ||. valour
Afrentar, v. a. to dishonour
Afrentarse, v. hamed [
Afrentosamente
Afrentoso, sa, ful; ignomi
Afretar, v. a. ship

:o, s. m. the south-
it wind
onado (caballo), sub.
horse corpulent, not
l shaped, etc.
tadamente, ad. face
face — over against;
osite
tar, v. act. to con-
unt
, ad. after the man-

a, ad. out; without
ublickly; openly ||
ther; besides
a, afuera, clear the
r; make room
as, s. m. pl. the out-
; the outworks
, s. m. flight; run-
g away
r, v. n. y Afufarse,
. to scamper, to fly
, s. mas. frame of a
non
adiza, s. f. a snipe
arse, v. r. to squat
anado, da, adj. V.
banero
, s. f. a gall nut
de cipres, the cy-
ss nut.
s, s. f. pl. kernels
the neck || gills of
es || swelling in the
oat
n, s. m. a great
l nut
nes, pl. great hol-
silver beads
itar, v. a. to imitate
cry of a small game
nzado, da, adj. of a
moy colour
ado, da, adj. Voyez
boso
arse, v. r. to hide
's self suddenly; to

Agareno, na, adj. any of
the race of ishmael
Agárico, s. m. agarick
Agarradero, s m. ancho-
rage
Agarrador, s. m. one who
grasps || a sergeant; a
bailif's assistant, etc.
Agarrafar, v. a. to lay
fast hold of
Agarrar, v. a. to grasp;
to gripe
Agarro, s. m. the grasping
Agarrochar, } v. a. to
Agarrochear, } prick and
fret the bulls at the bull-
feats
Agarrotar, v. a. to bind
with cords
Agasajador, ra, s. one that
makes much of
Agasajar, v. a. to make
much of; to treat lo-
vingly || to make a pre-
sent
Agasajo, s. m. kind and
loving entertainment
|| a gift || a collation
A'gata, s. f. agate
Agavanza, s. f. arbut-tree
Agavillar, v. a. to bind up
into sheaves
Agavillarse, v. r. to troop;
to get together
Agazapar, v. a. to catch up
Agazaparse, v. r. to squat
down [groan
Agear, v. n. to cry, or
Agencia, s. f. agency ||
care, diligence
Agenciar, v. a. to procure
any thing [illegible]
Agencioso, sa, [illegible]tive;
solicitous
Ageno, na, adj. belonging
to another || contrary
Agente, s. m. an agent
Agenuz, s. m. cockle, or
gith

Agerato, s. m. sweet mau-
dlin [diseases
Ages, s. m. pl. habitual
Agestado, da, adj. coun-
tenanced
Ageste, s. m. V. Cauro
Agi, s. m. guinea pepper
Agible, adj. V. Factible
Agigantado, da, adj. gi-
gantick
A'gil, adj. agile; nimble
Agilidad, s. f. agility
Agilitar, v. a. to make
nimble and active || to
facilitate
A'gilmente, adv. nimbly
Agitacion, s. f. agitation
Agitanado, da, adj. gipsy
like
Agitar, v. a. to agitate
Agnacion, s. f. agnation
Agnado, s. m. the male
issue of the same father
in another line
Agnaticio, cia, adj. belon-
ging to the agnacion,
etc.
Agnicion, s. f. agnition
Agnocasto, s. m. agnus
castus; chaste-tree
Agnus Dei, s. m. An Agnus
Agobiar, v. a. to bend; to
bow || to oppress
Agobiarse, v. r. to bend
as old men do [sails
Agolar, v. a. to furl the
Agolparse, v. r. to troop
Agonalos (fiestas), s. f. pl.
feasts in honour of Ja-
nus
Agone (in), adv. at the
point of death
Agonia, s. f. agony
Agonista, } s. m. a dying
Agonizante, }
Agonizar, v. a. to attend
a dying
Estar agonizando, to be at
the point of death

Agorería, *s. f. auguration*
Agorero, *s. m. augury* || *prophetick*
Agorgojarse, *v. r. to be eaten by weevils*
Agostadero, *s. m. summer-pasturages*
Agostar, *v. a. to dry; to parch* || *to spend; to consume* || *to lead the cattle in freshly-reaped fields*
Agostero, *s. m. one that serves the reapers at harvest time*
Agostizo, za, *adj. born in august* [*harvest*
Agosto, *s. m. august* ||
Hacer su agosto, *to reap*
Agotar, *v. a. to drain; to exhaust* || *to run out an estate* || *to tire one's patience*
Agraceño, ña, *adj. belonging to the verjuice*
Agracera, *s. f. vessel that contains verjuice*
Agraciar, *v. a. to make graceful* || *to make a present* [*pleasing*
Agradable, *adj. agreeable;*
Agradar, *v. a. to please*
Agradecer, *v. a. to give thanks* [*teful*
Agradecido, da, *adj. gra-*
Agradecimiento, *s. m. gratitude*
Agrado, *s. m. agreeableness* || *pleasing, obliging behaviour*
Agradulce, *adj. V.* Agridulce
Agramadera, *s. f. a brake*
Agramar, *v. a. to brake the hemp* [*like*
Agramilado, da, *adj. brick-*
Agramiza, *s. f. the reeds in hemp growing*
Agrandar, *v. a. to enlarge*

Agravacion, *s. f.* / Agravamiento, *s. m.* } *a threatening monitory*
Agravar, *v. a. to overload* || *to aggravate* || *to exaggerate*
Agravatorio, ria, *adj. a writ of execution*
Agraviadamente, *adv. efficaciously* || *with effort*
Agraviador, ra, *s. offender*
Agraviar, *v. a. to wrong; to injure*
Agraviarse, *v. r. to be offended* or *angry at*
Agravio, *s. m. a. wrong*
Agraz, *s. m. verjuice*
En agraz, *adv. unseasonablely*
Agrazada, *s. f. liquor made with verjuice and sugar*
Agrazon, *s. m. vine's grape* || *grief; discontent*
Agregacion, *s. f. heaping together*
Agregado, *s. m. a heap*
Agregar, *v. a. to heap together* || *to associate*
Agresor, *s. m. aggressor*
Agreste, *adj. clownish*
Agrete, *s. m. any thing a little sourish*
Agrete, *adj. V.* Agrillo
Agriamente, *adv. sourly-severely*
Agriar, *v. a. to sour* || *to irritate*
Agricultor, *s. m. a husbandman* [*dry*
Agricultura, *s. f. husban-*
Agridulce, *adj. sour-sweet*
Agrifolio, *s. m. the holly-tree*
Agrillado, da, *adj. bound with fetters*
Agrillo, lla, *adj. taste; sourish*

Agrimensor, *s. m. surveyor*
Agrimensura, *s. f. land-survey* [*wor*
Agrimonia, *s. f. liver-*
Agrio, ia, *adj sour; sharp* || *peevish; ill-natured* || *eager; brittle* || *harsh; inharmonious* || *unpleasant*
Subida agria, *a steep ascent* [*wea*
Agripalma, *s. f. mother*
Agrura, *s. f. sharpness* || *harshness of temper*
Agua, *s. f. water*
Agua ardiente, *brandy* —
acerada, *steel-water* —
bendita, *holy-water* —
de pie, *running-water*
— fuerte, *aqua fortis*
— llovediza, *rain-water*
Aguas vivas, *spring-tide*
— muertas, *neap-tide*
Aguas, *s. f. pl. the watering of mohair, etc.*
Camelote de aguas, *watered camlet*
Agua va, *int. take care below*
Aguacate, *s. m. a fruit growing in new-spain*
Aguacero, *s. m. a storm of rain*
Aguachirle, *s. m. an insipid liquor*
Aguada, *s. f. fresh water* || *a watering place* || *water-colours* || *broa*
Aguaderas, *s. f. pl. vessels to carry water in*
Aguadero, *s. f. V.* Abrevadero
Aguado, *s. m. abstemious*
Aguado (caballo), *s. m. foundered horse*
Aguador, *s. m. a water-carrier*
Aguage, *s. m. the rapidity of currents in the sea*

Aguamanil,

, *s. m. ewer*
, *s. m. water to hands*
), da, *adj. dipt*
s. m. mead
d, *s. f. serosity*
sa, *adj. wate-p*
v. a. to suffer; te
m. strength; courage; pa-
s. m. a water-maker
. f. tart sort of
a. to mix wine er || *to disturb, pleasures*
. r. to be over- to catch cold
it [*tion*
, *s. f. expecta-*
v. a. to expect; for
eria, *s. f. a shop*
ero, *s. m. a bran-hant*
te, *s. m. brandy*
s. m. a close w t for game
s. f. spirit of ine.
, *s. f.* } *á great*
, *s. m.* } *syringe guish fire with*
e, *s. m. gum iac*
r, ra, *s. one that ait for*
iento, *s. m. lying for*
, *v. a. to watch; wait*
. f. watery hu-der the skin

Aguazal, *s. m. a pond; a meer* [*lour*
Aguazo, *s. m. water-co-*
Aguazoso, sa, *adj. Voy.* Aguanoso
Agudamente, *adv. sharply; readly; wittily*
Agudeza, *s. f. sharpness of the edge of a tool* || *quickness of wit* || *piercing of sight* [*pish*
Agudillo, lla, *adj. shar-*
Agudo, da *adj. sharp*
Agüero, *s. m. omen*
Aguerrido, da, *adj. experienced in war*
Aguijada, *s. f. a goad*
Aguijador, ra, *s. one that pricks on*
Aguijadura, *s. f. pricking forward*
Aguijar, *v. a. to prick forward* || *to incite*
Aguijon, *s. m. a sting*, or *prick* || *a spur; an incentive* || *anxiety*
Aguijonazo, *s. m. a pricking; a sting*
Aquijonear, *v. a. Voyez* Aguijar
A'guila, *s. f. an eagle*
Aguileño, ña, *a. hawked*
Aguililla, *s. f. a little eagle*
Aguilucho, *s. m. eaglet*
Aguinaldo, *s. m. a new year's gift.*
Aguja, *s. f. needle* || *bodkin* || *a steeple's spire* || *obelisk* || *hornback*
Aguja de marear, *the sea compass* — de hacer media, *a knitting-needle* — de pastor, *geranium*
Agujazo, *s. m. a prick of a needle*
Agujerazo, *s. m. a large hole*
Agujerear y Agujerar, *v. a. to bore; to pierce*

Agujerico, illo, uelo, *s. m. a little hole*
Agujero, *s. m. a hole* || *a needle-maker* || *a needle-case*
Agujeta, *s. f. a tagged point* [*salary*
Agujetas, *pl. post-boy's*
Agujetería, *s. f. the point-maker's trade*, or *shop*
Agujetero, *s. m. a point-maker* [*needle*
Agujon, *s. m. a great*
Aguosidad, *s. f. a watery humor in the body*
Agustino y Agustiniano, *s. m. an Augustin friar*
Aguzadera, *s. f. whetstone*
Aguzadero, *s. m. a place where wild boars sharpen their tusks*
Aguzaduda, *s. f. a whetting*
Aguzanieve, *s. f. a wagtail*
Aguzar, *v. a. to whet; to sharpen* || *to incite*
Ah! *int. ah!*
Ahembrado, *a. effeminate*
Ahervorarse, *v. r. to be burnt up with heat*
Ahi, *ad. there*
Ahidalgado, da, *a. gentlemanlike*
Ahijada, *s. f. a god-daughter*
Ahijado, *s. m. a god-son*
Ahijar, *v. a. to adopt* || *to impute; to charge with*
Ahijar, *v. n. to bring forth young one's* || *to shoot out again*
Ahilarse, *v. r. to be wore away with hunger — to be fainting*
Ahilo, *s. m. a swoon*
Ahineo, *s. m. earnestness* || *effort*
Ahitar, *v. a. to surfeit*

Ahitarse, *v. r. to be surfeited*
Ahitera, *s. f. a violent indigestion*
Ahito, ta, *a. raw; indigested*
Ahito, *s. m. indigestion*
Ahobachonado, da, *a. supine*
Ahocinarse, *v. r. to grow straiter, narrower*
Ahogadero, *s. m. a hanging rope* || *a great press* or *crowd* || *a woman's necklace* || *the throat-band of a bridle*
Ahogadizo, za, *a. hard to swallow*
Carnes ahogadizas, *things strangled*
Ahogado, da, *adj. very strait*, or *narrow*
Carnero ahogado, *a stewed mutton* — dar mate ahogado, *to give check-mate*
Ahogamiento, *s. m. suffocation*
Ahogar, *v. a. to choak* || *to tire; to vex*
Ahogarse de calor, *to be stifled with heat* — de gente, *to be thronged to death*
Ahogo, *s. m. pain; affliction*
Ahoquijo, *s. m. squinancy*
Ahoguio, *s. m. suffocation*
Ahojar, *v. a. to feed cattle with leaves*
Ahombrado, da, *a. manly*
Muger ahombrada, *a virago*
Ahondar, *v. a. to dig* || *to search to the bottom*
Ahora, *ad. now; this hour*
Ahora, ahora, *just now*
Ahora bien, *well then*
Ahorcador, *s. m. a hangman*
Ahorcajarse, *v. r. to set astride*
Ahorcar, *v. a. to hang*
Ahorcarse, *v. r. to hang one's self* || *to be impatient; to fret*
Ahormar, *v. a. to stretch upon a last* || *to instruct*, or *educate*
Ahornar, *v. a. V.* Enhornar
Ahorquillar, *v. a. to support with a little fork*
Ahorrado, da, *adj. free; disintricated*
Ahorramiento, *s. m. a setting free. V.* Ahorro
Ahorrar, *v. a. to make a slave free* || *to spare*
Ahorrativo, va, *adj. too sparing*
Ahorro, *s. m. savingness; parsimony*
Ahoyar, *v. a. to ditch; to dig holes*
Ahuchador, ra, *s. one who hoards up money in a box*
Ahuchar, *v. a. to hoards money into a box, etc.*
Ahuecamiento, *s. m. a hollowing*
Ahuecar, *v. a. to make hollow* || *to break the clods*
Ahuecarse, *v. r. to grow proud*
Ahumada, *s. f. smoking*
Ahumar, *v. a. to besmoke*
Ahumar, *v. n. to smoke*
Ahusar, *v. a. to shape like a spindle*
Ahusarse, *v. r. to end sharp as a spindle*
Ahuyentador, ra, *s. one that puts to flight*
Ahuyentar, *v. a. to put to flight*
Ainas, *adv. quite near; almost*
Airadamente, *adv. wrathfully*
Aislar, *v. a. to encompass with water* || *to make an opening to a buildi[ng]*
Ajada, *s. f. sauce ma[de] with garlick*
Ajamiento, *s. m. the ha[n]dling so as to spoil [|| an] injury; outrage*
Ajar, *v. a. to handle so [as] to spoil, etc.* || *to inju[re]*
Ajar la hermosura, *to ma[ke] the beauty fade* — vanidad, *to humble; mortify*
Ajazo, *s. m. a. a great g[ar]lick*
Ajero, *s. m. a garlic seller*
Ajete, *s. m. young garli[ck]*
Ajiaceyte, *s. m. sauce m[a]de with garlick and [oil]*
Ajicola, *s. f. glue ma[de] with garlick, etc.*
Agilimoge y Agilimógil[i], *s. m. sauce made wi[th] garlick and pepper*
Ajillo, *s. m. a little ga[r]lick*
Ajo, *s. m. garlick* || *wo[]man's paint*
Ajobar, *v. a. to load, t[o] carry upon the back*
Ajobo, *s. m. the action [of] loading — a burden*
Ajonje, *s. m. bird-lime*
Ajonjera, *s. f. carli[ne] thistle*
Ajónjoli. *V.* Alegria
Ajoqueso, *s. m. ragoo ma[de] with garlick [and] cheese*
Ajorar, *v. a. to drive [by] violence*
Ajorcas. *V.* Axorcas
Ajordar, *v. n. to scream*, *to squeak*
Ajornalado, da, *a. hi[red] by the day*
Ajuagas, *s. f. pl. spavin*
Ajuanetado, da, *a. full [of] corns*
Cara ajuanetada, *a le[an face]*

Axuar
da, *a. jew-like*
.*n. to grow ripe*
ment
ente, *adv. ri-*
ustly
da, *adj. right;*
ingy
, *s. m. under-*
at
nto, *s. m. equa-*
portion || *agree-*
a regular beha-
an account
upon
. *a. to adjust* ||
fit || *to regulate*
e || *to reconcile*
le accounts ||
in any bargain
v. r. to agree in
m. a joining ||
ect, or *bargain*
v. a. to execute
the
wing || *a flank*
fication || *eli-*
e || *V.* Alero
teen sails || *the*
of the heart ||
of a fish
god
alas!
. *m. anthem*
s. m. one that

o, sa, *a. Voy.*
oso
, *s. f. manga-*

s. f. praise
a. to praise
. *r. to boast; to*
[*halberd*
s. f. halbert, or
, *s. m. stroke*
alberd
, *s. m. halber-*

Alabastrado, da, *a. alabaster like*
Alabastrina, *s. f. thin piece of alabaster*
Alabastrino, na, *a. of the colour of alabaster*
Alabastro, *s. m. alabaster*
A'labe, *s. m. a tree's branch bended to the ground*
Alabearse, *v. r. to warp, as wood does; to cast*
Alabega, *s. f. V.* Albahaca
Alabeo, *s. m. the vicious bent of a plank*
Alabesa, *s. f. an old pike*
Alacena, *s. f. a cupboard*
Alacha, *s. f. mackerel*
Alacran, *scorpion*
Alacranado, da, *a. bitten by a scorpion*
Alacranera, *s. f. scorpion-wort* [*wings*
Alada, *s. f. motion of the*
Aladares, *s. m. pl. the hair on the temples*
Alado, da, *a. winged*
Alafia, *s. f. pardon*
A'laga, *s. f. a sort of corn*
Alagarero, ra, *a. Voyez* Algarero
Alagartado, da, *a. coloured like a lizard*
Alaica, *s. f. a winged ant*
Alaja, Alajar, etc. *Voy.* Alhaja, etc.
Alajú, *s. m. paste made with kernels, walnuts, honey, etc.*
Alamar, *s. m. silver* or *silken twist for cloaths*
Alambicar, *v. a. to distill* || *to puzzle*
Alambique, *s. m. alembick*
Alambor, *s. m. convexity of a vault* [*wire*
Alambre, *s. m. copper* ||
Alameda, *s. f. a walk planted with poplars*
Alamin, *s. m. inspector of the weights and measures*
Alamina, *s. f. a tax laid upon potters*
Alamiré, *s. f. a key* or *cliff in musick*
A'lamo, *s. m. poplar-tree*
Alamparse, *v. r. to wish*, or *long for*
Alamud, *s. m. a bolt*
Alanceador, *s. m. one who brandishes a spear*
Alancear, *v. a. to wound with a lance*
Alandal, Alania. *V.* Alandal, Alhania
Alano, na, *s. a bull-dog*
Alanzada. *V.* Aranzada
Alaqueques. *V.* Alfaqueques
Alar, *s. m. net to catch partridges withal*
Alar, *v. a. V.* Halar
Alara (huevo en), *an egg without a shell*
Alaraca, Alaraquiento. *V.* Alharaca, Alharaquiento
Alarbe, *s. m. a cross, rustical man* || *barbarous, ferocious*
Alargador, *s. m. one that lengthens*
Alargamiento, *s. m. lengthening* || *a delay*
Alargar, *v. a. to lengthen* || *to release* || *to yield up* || *to reach* || *to out strip*
Alargar la vela, *to loose the sail* — la rienda, *to give a horse his head* — el tiempo, *to protract time* — la bolsa, *to have money at will*
Alargarse, *v. r. to get far off*
Alarguez, *s. m. eglantine*
Alaria, *s. f. a potter's tool*
Alarida, *sub. f. cries; shouts, etc.*

Alarido, sub. m. *a crying out*

Alarifazgo, s. m. *surveyor ship*

Alarife, s. m. *surveyor, or master builder*

Alarixes, s. f. pl. *grapes of a purplish colour*

Alarma, s. f. *alarm*

Alarmar, v. a. *to give an alarm*

Alastrarse, v. r. *to lay one's self flat on the ground*

Alatron, s. m. *salt-petre*

Alazan, a. *a sorrel horse*

Alazo, s. m. *V.* Aletazo

Alazor, sub. m. *wild safron* [|| *an alb*

Alba, subst. f. *day-break*

Albacea, s. m. *the executor of a will*

Albaceazgo, s. m. *office of the executor of a will*

Albacora, s. m. *a sea fish like the scomber*

Albada, s. f. *morning serenade* [*sil*

Albahaca, s. f. *sweet-ba-*

Albahaquero, s. m. *a flower-pot*

Albahaquilla del rio, s. f. *calamint*

Albalá, s. m. *an acquittance; a pass*

Albanega, s. f. *a net-work coif*

Albañil, s. m. *a mason*

Albañilería, s. f. *masonry*

Albar, a. *white; witish*

Albarazado, da, a. *affected with morphew* || *witish*

Uva albarazada, *a grape of jasper colour*

Albarazo, s. m. *morphew*

Albarca, s. f. *V.* Abarca

Albarda, s. f. *pack-saddle* || *slice of bacon*

Albardar, v. a. *V.* Enalbardar || *to cover with a slice of bacon* || *to ice march-panes, etc.*

Albardería, s. f. *street the pack-saddlers live in*

Albardero, s. m. *pack-saddler*

Albardilla, sub. f. *a little pack-saddle* || *coping of a wall* [*of rush*

Albardin, s. m. *a kind*

Albardon, s. m. *pannel*

Albardoncillo, s. m. *a little pannel*

Albaricoque, s. m. *apricot* || *apricot-tree*

Albarillo, s. m. *a white apricot*

Albarino, subs. m. *white paint*

Albarrada, s. f. *a dry wall* || *an inclosure* || *a cause-way*

Albarrana, (cebolla), s. f. *a wild onion*

Torre albarrana, *a watch-tower in the fields*

Albarraz, s. m. *morphew* || *louse-wort*

Albatara, s. f. *the clitoris*

Albayaldado, da, a. *daubed with ceruse*

Albayalde, s. m. *ceruse*

Albazano, na, adj. *bay-colour*

Albazo, subs. m. *assault made at break of day*

Albear, v. a. *V.* Blanquear

Albedrio, s. m. *free-will*

Albenda, s. f. *hangings made of white linen*

Albengala, s. f. *a fine web woven in silk*

Albéntola, s. m. *a small net*

Alberca, s. f. *fish-pond*

Albérchiga, s. f. } *nectarine* || *nectarine-tree*
Albérchigo, s. m. }

Albercon, s. m. *a gr fish-pond*

Alberengena, s. f. *V.* B rengena

Albergador, s. m. *lodg*

Albergar, v. a. *to lodg*

Albergue, s. m. *an in a publick house a sh ter against bad weat*

Albero, subs. m. *a wh earth* || *dish-clout*

Alberquero, s. m. *the k per of a place for st ping hemp*

Alberquilla, s. f. *a lit fish-pond* [

Albeytar, s. m. *horse-d*

Albeytería, s. f. *the art the horse-doctor*

Albicante, a. *witish*

Albiar, s. m. *ox-eye*

Albilla, sub. f. *a sort white grape*

Albillo, s. m. *wine ma with white grapes*

Albin, s. m. *a blood sto*

Albina, s. f. *a marsh fen* [*neg*

Albino, na, a. *a whi*

Albitana, s. f. *apron (a ship)*

Albo, ba, a. *white*

Albogue, s. m. *a pipe flute* || *a sort of cymb*

Alboguero, s. m. *a pip* || *a pipe-maker*

Albohol, s. m. *bind-we*

Albóndiga, s. f. *force meat-balls*

Albondiguillas, s. f. p *little balls of forc meat* [Albu

Albor, sub. m. *V.* Alba

Alborada, s. f. *the brea of day* || *a morning-s renade*

Alborear, v. n. *to dawn*

Alborga, s. f. *shoes ma of broom*

rnoz, s. m. a coarse
iry cloth || a great
at against the rain
roc, s. m. V. Albo-
que
ronía, s. f. a kind of
ss made with love-
ples, pimento, etc.
roque, s. m. a bottle;
oves or a pair of glo-
s [sorderly
rotadamente, ad. di-
rotadizo, } s. m. unquiet, timorous, etc.
rotado, }
rotador, ra, s. a mu-
ous seditious fellow
rotar, v. a. to trou-
e, disturb, etc. || to
ise a tumult
roto, s. m. mutiny;
mult, etc.
rozador, ra, sub. one
ho excites mirth in
hers
rozar, v. act. to re-
ice [mirth
rozo, subst. m. joy;
icias, sub. f. pl. gift
ade to one that brings
od news
fera, s. f. a pool of
gnant water
gineó, nea, a. like
white of an egg
hera, s. f. a flash; a
ol
r, s. m. a roach
ra, s. f. whiteness
rero, s. m. he that
ys at Albures
res, s. m. pl. a cer-
n game at cards
ala, s. f. duty impo-
l upon things sold
alero, s. m. a collec-
of that duty
us, s. m. V. Arcabuz

Alcacel, } s. m. green barley cut for the horses
Alcacer, }
Alcachofa, s. f. artichoke || a thistle's head
Alcachofado, da, a. artichoke like
Alcachofado, s. m. ragoo made with artichokes
Alcachofal, s. m. the place where artichokes grow
Alcachofazo, s. m. stroke whith an artichoke
Alcacil, V. Arcacil
Alcahaz, s. m. cage
Alcahazada, s. f. a cage-full
Alcahazar, v. a. to shut up in a cage
Alcahuete, s. a pimp; a bawd
Alcahuetar, } v. act. to pimp, or bawd
Alcahuetear, }
Alcahuetazo, s. m. V. Alcahueton
Alcahuetería, s. f. bawding
Alcahuetillo, lla. s. a little pimp, or bawd
Alcahueton y Alcahuetazo, s. m. an infamous pimp
Alcaldada, s. f. a blunder of an Alcalde, etc.
Alcalde, s. m. magistrate; judge || dance leader
Alcaldesa, s. f. wife of an Alcalde
Alcaldiá, sub. f. the office and district of the Alcalde
Alcalizado, da, a. alkaline
Alcam, s. m. coloquintida [spices
Alcamonias, s. f. pl. sweet
Alcance, s. f. the action of reaching || the reach of a gun, etc. || the ba-
lance of an account || cut got by interfering || an express
Alcancía, s. f. earthen money box || a pot-granado || a thin earthen pot full of ashes, etc.
Alcanciazo, s. m. a blow with such a pot
Alcándara, s. f. a perch for a hawk
Alcandia, s. f. a kind of millet
Alcandial, subst. m. the ground where such seed is sown
Alcanfor, s. m. camphire
Alcanforado, da, a. camphorate
Alcántara, s. f. a bridge
Alcantarilla, s. f. a little bridge || a subterranean canal
Alcantarillado, da, adj. ached [reach
Alcanzadizo, za, a. easy to
Hacerse alcanzadizo, to lend a deaf ear
Alcanzador, ra, s. one that reaches, etc
Alcanzar, v. a. to reach || to overtake || to obtain || to understand
Alcanzar, v. n. to concern; to import || to suffice || to carry or reach || to interfere
Alcaparra, s. f. caper-tree
Alcaparrado, s. m. ragoo seasoned with capers
Alcaparral, s. m. a place where capers grow
Alcaparro, s. m. caper-tree
Alcaparron, s. m. caper
Alcaparrosa, s. f. V. Caparrosa
Alcaravan, s. m. a bittern

Alcaravanero (halcon), *s. m. a hawk trained for the bittern*
Alcaravea, *s. f. caraway-seed* [*artichoke*
Alcarcil, *subs. m. a wild*
Alcarovea, *s. f. V.* Alcaravea
Alcarracero, ra, *s. a pitcher-maker*
Alcarraza, *s. f. a sort of pitcher*
Alcatifa, *s. f. carpet* || *a bed of mortar*
Alcatraz, *s. m. onocrotalus* [cil
Alcaucil, *s. m. V.* Alcar-
Alcaudon, *s. m. a sort of long-tailed bird*
Alcayata, *s. f. a hook*, or *peg*
Alcayatazo, *s. m. stroke with a hook*
Alcayde, *s. m. governor of a fort*, etc. || *gaoler*
Alcaydesa, *s. f. the wife of a Governor* or *of a gaoler*
Alcaydía, *s. f. Governement of a fort, etc.* || *keeping of a gaol*
Alcazar, *s. m. fortress* || *palace* || *deck*
Alcedon, *s. m. V.* Alcion
Alchimia, *s. f. V.* Alquimia
Alcino, *s. m. wild basil*
Alcion, *s. m. king's fisher*
Alcoba, *s. f. a bed-chamber* || *an alcove* || *beam of a balance*
Alcobaza, *s. f. a great bed-chamber* or *alcove*
Alcobilla ita *s. f. a little bed-chamber* or *alcove*
Alcohol, *s. m. antimony*
Alcoholado (toro), *s. m. a bull with black eyes*
Alcoholador, ra, *sub. one that colours with antimony*
Alcoholar, *v. a. to colour with antimony* || *to alcoholize*
Alcoholera, *s. f. a vessel for antimony* [*holize*
Alcoholizar, *v. a. to alco-*
Alcomenias, *s. f. pl. Voy.* Alcamonias
Alcon, *V.* Halcon
Alcoran, *s. m. the Coran*
Alcoranista, *s. m. a Mahometan doctor*
Alcornocal, *s. m. a grove* or *wood of cork trees*
Alcornoque, *s. m. cork-tree*
Alcornoqueño, ña, *a. belonging to the cork-tree*
Alcorza, *subst. f. a paste made with sugar and starch*
Alcorzar, *v. a. to cover* or *ice with a such paste* || *to adorn*
Alcotan, *s. m. a lanner*, or *merlin*
Alcotana, *s. f. a mason's hammers*
Alcotancillo, *s. m. a little lanner* or *merlin*
Alcrebite, *s. m. V.* Azufre
Alcucero, ra, *s. one that makes* or *sells oil-bottles* [*bottle*
Alcucilla, *s. f. a little oil-*
Alcuza, *s. f. an oil-bottle* or *pot*
Alcuzada, *s. f. quantity of oil in the Alcuza*
Alcuzazo, *sub. m. a blow with an oil pot*
Alcuzcuz, } *s. m. a paste*
Alcuzcuzu, } *with flour and honey*
Alcuzon, *s. m. a gre[at] pot*
Alda, *s. f. V.* Halda
Aldaba, *s. f. knocke[r] iron bar to shu[t] door, etc.*
Aldabada, *s. f. stroke [with] a knocker*
Aldabazo, *s. m. au[gm.] Aldabada*
Aldabear, *v. a. to [knock] at a door*
Aldabilla, *sub. f. a [little] knocker*
Aldabon, *s. m. a knocker* || *a ha[ndle] ring*, or *hasp*
Aldea, *s. f. a village*
Aldeanamente, *ad. [rusti]cally*
Aldeano, na, *s. a co[untry] man*, or *woman*
Aldeano, na, *a. rust[ic]*
Aldehuela, } *s. f. a*
Aldeilla, } *hamle[t]*
Aldeorrio, *s. m. a vi[llage]* or *little place [...] the inhabitants [...] poor, clownish, [...]*
Aldiza, *subst. f. a [...] brush wood*
Aleacion, *s. f. mixt[ure of] metals*
Alear, *v. a. to mix [...]* || *to beat with wings* || *to beg[in to] show courage* || *[to re]cover one's healt[h]* || *aim at*
Alebrarse, Alebrast[arse]
Alebrestarse, *v. [...] squal* || *to be frigh[tened]*
Alebronarse, *v. r. t[o lose] courage*
Alece, *s. f. ragoo with fish livers*
Alechugar, *v. act. [...] in the form of a [...]*
Alectoria, *sub. f. a [...]*

in the liver of a

ña, *adj. conti-*

as (píldoras), *s*
urging pills
. m. mortise
, *s.f.* } *alle-*
nto, *s.m.* } *gation*
. a. to alledge
s. m. lawyer's
ation
s.f. allegory
mente, *ad. alle-*
ly
, ca, *a. allego-*
[*gorise*
, v. a. to alle-
, *s.m. one that*

. a. to rejoice ‖
he fire
. joyful; merry
nte, *ad. joyfully*
. f. mirth; joy
ne
pl. publick re-
s
subs. m. a great
joy upon any
less news
nto, *sub. m. dis-*
[*a distance*
act. to put at
m. V. Alajú
da, *a. simple,*

n. gilly flower
s. m. [illegible]*lu-*
ioy ‖ [illegible] ‖
orrel
, da, *a. joyful;*

f. the assigned
f water for wa-
fields
sub. f. a sort of

miento, *s. m. a*

paction upon a pasture
Alenguar, *v. a. to contract upon a pasture-ground*
Alentada, *s. f. breathing*
Alentadamente, *ad. courageously*
Alentado, da, *adj. vigorous; courageous*
Alentar, *v. a. to encourage*
Alentar, *v. n. to breath*
Alerce, *s. m. larch-tree*
Alero, *s. m. the eaves of a house*
Aleros, *pl. leather aprons in the coaches*
Alerta, *int. y adv. upon one's guard*
Alertar, *v. act. to make watchful*
Alerto, ta, *a. alert*
Alesna, *s. f. an awl*
Alesnado, da, *a. as sharpas an awl*
Aleta, *s. f, a little wing* ‖ *a fin*
Aletas, *pl. transom knees*
Aletada, *s. f. motion of the wings*
Aletazo, *sub. m. a blow with a wing*
Aletear, *v. a. to move the wings* [*hawk*
Aleto, *s. m. a sparrow-*
Aleton, *s. m. a great wing*
Aleve, *a. traitor* ‖ *traitorous*
Alevosa, *s. f. a swelling under the oxen's tongue*
Alevosamente, *ad. treacherously*
Alevosía, *s. f. treachery*
Alevoso, sa, *a. treacherous*
Alexiphármaco, ca, *adj alexiterical* [*betical*
Alfabético, ca, *a. alpha-*
Alfabetista, *s. m. one that learns the alphabet*

Alfabeto, *s. m. alphabet* —, *a horn-book*
Alfadía, *s. f. present; gift*
Alfahar, Alfaharero, *V.* Alfar, Alfaroro
Alfajor, *s. m. Voy.* Alajú ‖ *a kinf of hypocras*
Alfalfa, *s. f. clover grass*
Alfalfar, *s. m. a field of clover grass*
Alfana, *s. f. a strong bold spiritid horse*
Alfaneque, *s. m. a lanner*
Alfange, *s. m. a cymetar*
Alfangete, *s. m. a little cutlass*
Alfanjazo, *s. m. a blow* or *cut with a cymetar*
Alfanjon, } *s. m. a great*
Alfanjonazo, } *cymetar*
Alfaque, *s. m. a shelf*
Alfar, *subs. m. a potter's shop*
Alfaraces, *adj. the ligt horse*
Alfarda, *s. f. tribute paid for watering*
Alfardero, *s. m. collector of the water tribute*
Alfardon, *s. m. the axle-tree of a coach, etc.*
Alfarero, *s. m. a potter*
Alfarge, *s. m. the under-stone of the oil-mill*
Alfeñicarse, *v. r. to pamper one's self*
Alfeñique, *s. m. a paste made with sugar and almond-oil*
Alferecía, *s. f. epilepsy*
Alferez, *s. m. an ensign*
Alfeya, *s. f. a gap in a wall for a door, etc.*
Alfeyar, *v. act. to make such a gap*
Alficoz, *s. m. a kind of cucumber*
Alfierez, *s. m. V.* Alferez

Alfil, *s. m. a bishop* (*at chess*)
Alfiler, *s. m. a pin*
Alfileres de las señoras, *pin-money*
Alfilerazo, *s. m. pricking of a pin* || *a great pin*
Alfiletero, *s. m. a pin-case*
Alfilete, *s. m. composision of seasoning things*
Alfolí, *s. m. a corn-house* || *a magazine of salt*
Alfombra, *s. f. a carpet* || *the measles*
Alfombrar, *v. a. to cover with carpets*
Alfombraza, *s. f. a great carpet*
Alfombrero, *s. m. a carpet-maker*
Alfombrilla, *s. f. a little carpet* || *the measles*
Alfónsigo, *sub. m. pistachio-tree*
Alfonsina, *s. f. act of the students in the university of* Alcala
Alforja, *s. f. a wallet*
Alforjero, *s. m. a maker* or *seller of wallets* || *a mendicant friar*
Alforjilla, ita, uela, *s. f. a little wallet*
Alforza, *s. f. folding in*
Alga, *s. f. sea-weed*
Algalaba, *s. f. snake-weed*
Algalia, *s. f. civet-cat* || *musk* || *a probe*
Algarabia, *s. f. the arabick tongue* || *gibberish* || *out cries* || *broom*
Algarada, *s. f. a tumult*; *a hurlyburly* || *a sudden attack* || *bailista*
Algarrada, *s. f. bull-feast in the field*
Algarroba, *s. f. a carob-bean*

Algarrobal, *s. m. a place planted with carob-trees*
Algarrobera, *s. f.* } *carob-tree*
Algarrobo, *s. m.* }
Algazara, *s. f. shout of the moors, when in battle* || *any confused noise*
Algebra, *s. f. algebra* || *the art of setting bones*
Algebrista, *s. m. algebraist* || *bone-setter*
Algecería, *s. f. the place where the plaster is made or sold*
Algecero, *s. m. V.* Yesero
Algente, *a. very cold*
Algez, *s. m. plaster*
Algezar, etc. *V.* Yesar
Algibe, *s. m. cistern.*
Algibero, *s. m. cistern-keeper*
Algimifrado, da, *a. painted*
Algo, *s. m. something*; [*aught*
Algo, *ad. a. little*
Algodon, *s. m. cotton* || *a cotton-tree*
Algodonal, *s. m. cotton-tree* || *the ground where cotton grows*
Algodonero, *s. m. one who deals in cotton* [*tick*
Algoritmo, *s. m. arithme*
Algoso, sa, *a. abundant of sea-weeds*
Alguacil, *s. m. a bailiff* or *catchpole*
Alguacil de moscas, *a great spidder*
Alguacilazgo, *sub. m. the office of an alguacil*
Alguarin, *s. m. a pantry*
Alguaza, *s. f. a hinge*
Alguien, *pron. somebody*
Algun, *V.* Alguno
Algun tanto, *ad. a little*
Alguno, na, *pron. some; somebody*

Alguna vez, *adv. sometimes* [*board*
Alhacena, *s. f. a cup-*
Alhadida, *subst. f. burnt brass*
Alhagar, *V.* Halagar
Alhaja, *s. f. toy; household goods; furniture, etc.*
Alhajar, *v. a. to furnish*
Alhajuela, *s. f. toy of little value*
Alhandal, *s. m. coloquintida* [*cry*
Alharaca, *sub. f. an out-*
Alharaquiento, ta, *a. a bawler*
Alhárgama, *s. f. wild rue*
Alhelí, *s. m. V.* Alelí
Alheña, *s. f. privet* || *mildew* [*hair black*
Alheñar, *v. a. to dye the*
Alheñarse, *v. r. to be blasted*
Alhócigo, *s. m. V.* Alfónsigo
Alhoja, *s. f. a lark*
Alholva, *s. f. fenigreek*
Alhóndiga, *s. f. a corn-loft*
Alhondiguero, *sub. m. a corn-house-keeper*
Alhorre, *s. m. a sort of troublesome running titter* || *letter of enfranchisement*
Alhóstigo, *s. m. Voy.* Alfónsigo
Alhucema, *s. f. lavander*
Aliacan, *s. m. the jaundice* [*diced*
Aliacanado, da, *a. jaun-*
Aliacran, *s. m. V.* Aliacan
Aliaga, *s. f. broom*
Alianza, *s. f. alliance* || *treaty*
Aliara, *s. f. a horn-vase*
Aliaria, *sub. f. jack of the hedge*

v. r. to make an
with || to match
lv. otherwise
f. a little wing
da, adj. wing-

a, s. f. a little
ous lizard
s. m. a kind of

a, s. f. wile
, s. m. chequer
of different co-
[nippers
s. m. pl. pliers ||
, s. m. attractive
, v. a. V. Ense-

s. f. crosss-staff
sub. m. breath ||
e || smell
ento, of a stretch
n. a rower
s. m. curbs || an
al sickness
a. to polish
. f. luncheon
, s. f. y Aliga-
, s. m. allaying;
e, etc.
. a. to bind; to
o lay under an
ion
iento, s. m. alle-

v. a. to lighten
celerate
a, a. winged ||

s. m. one that
s [a ship
. act. to lighten
s. the lightening
f. a little wing

sub. f. a brute
tame cattle
cion, s. f feeding
r, v. a. to feed;

to maintain || to culti-
vate — to foment
Alimentario, sub. m. one that has assigned alimony [mentary
Alimenticio, cia, a. ali-
Alimentista, s. m. V. Alimentario
Alimento, s. m. aliment
Alimentos, pl. alimony
Alimentoso, sa, adj. alimental [bounds
Alindar, v. act. to set
Aliñador, s. m. adorner
Aliñar, v. a. to adorn; to dress
Aliño, s. m. ornament; dressing || preparative
Alionin, s. m. a blue titmouse
Aliox, s. m. marble
Alipede, a. foot-winged
Alipte, subst. m. he that anoints and perfumes people in the bagnio
Aliquanta (parte), sub. f. aliquant part
Aliquota (parte), s. f. aliquot part
Alisador, s. m. a polishing — box
Alisadura, s. f. polishing
Alisaduras, pl. chips
Alisar, v. a. to polish; to smooth [plot
Alisar, sub. m. an alder's
Alisma, subs. m. a sort of plantain
Aliso, s. m. alder
Alistado, da, a. striped
Alistar, v. a. to enroll; to list || to prepare
Aliviador, s. m. one that eases another
Aliviar, v. a. to ease; to lighten — to rob
Alivio, s. m. ease
Alivio de luto, second mourning

Alixar, subst. m. fallow ground
Alixarar, v. a. to distribute fallow grounds
Alixarero, s. m. he that grubs up an untilled piece of ground
Alixariego, ga, a. belonging to a fallow ground
Aljaba, s. f. a quiver
Aljama, s. f. synagogue
Aljarfa, } s. f. a tarred
Aljarfe, } net
Aljofar, s. m. seed-pearl || a rough pearl
Aljofarar, v. a. to form like a pearl || to adorn with pearls
Aljofayna, s. f. a dutch-ware-bowl [cloth
Aljofifa, sub. f. a course
Aljofifar, v. act. to rub with a coarse cloth
Aljonge, Aljonjera, Aljónjoli, etc. V. Ajonje, etc.
Aljuba, sub. f. a moorish garment like a short vest
Alkali, s. m. alkali
Alkalino, na, a. alkaline
Alkakengi, } s. m. al-
Alkanquegi, } kekengi
Alkanquengi, }
Alkermes, s. m. alkermes
Allá, ad. thither — there
Allanador, s. m. leveller
Allanamiento, s. m. plaining
Allanar, v. a. to plain || to levell || to quell || to subdue
Allanarse, v. r. to submit; to yield || to tumble down
Allariz, s. m. a kind of linen cloth
Allegadizo, za, a. heaped up without choice

Allegados, s. m. pl. *allies* || *relations*

Allegador, ra, s. *gatherer*

Allegar, v. a. *to gather; to heap up* || *to draw near*

Állende, adv. *beyond; on the other side*

Allende y aquende, *on this side and the other*

Allí, ad. *there* || *then*

Allico, s. m. *linaria*

Alloza, s. f. *a green almond*

Allozo, sub. m. *a wild almond-tree*

Alma, s. f. *the soul* || *the inside of the cannon* || *the sounding — post in a fiddle, etc.*

Alma de cántaro, a. *silly fellow* [*herman*

Almacaero, s. m. *a fis-*

Almacen, s. m. *magazine*

Almacenar, v. a. *to lay in a magazine*

Almáciga, s. f. *gum-mastich* || *seed-plot*

Almacigar, v. a. *to mix with gum-mastich*

Almácigo, s. m. *seeds fit for transplanting*

Almaciguero, ra, a. *belonging to the gum-mastich*

Almadana y Almadena, s. f. *a great iron-sledge*

Almadia, s. f. *canoe* || *raft of timber*

Almadiado, da, a. *giddy*

Almadiero, s. m. *a guide of canoes* or *rafts*

Almadraba, s. f. *the fishing of tunny* || *net to catch tunnies*

Almadrabas, pl. *places into which the fishermen drive the tunny fish*

Almadrabero, s. m. *fisherman of tunny*

Almadraque, sub. m. *pad* (*to stuff chairs, etc.*)

Almadraques, s. m. pl. *embroidered pillow-beers*

Almadreña, s. f. *wooden shoe* [macen

Almagacen, s. m. V. Al-

Almaganeta, s. f. V. Almadana [*gest*

Almagesto, s. m. *alma-*

Almagrar, v. a. *to colour with red ochre, etc.*

Almagre, s. m. *red ochre,* or *lead*

Almaizal, s. m. *a sort of veil,* or *scarf*

Almaizar, s. m. *a long stripped hood of the moorish women*

Almajaneque ó Almajanequis, sub. m. *an antick obsidional machine*

Almalafa, s. f. *a kind of moorish veil,* or *vest*

Almanak, Almanaque, } s. m. *almanack*

Almanaquero, s. m. *almanack-maker,* or *seller*

Almanta, s. f. *seed-plot*

Almarada, s. f. *a triangular poniard; a stilleto*

Almarcha, s. f. *a village situated in a bottom*

Almario, s. m. V. Armario

Almarjal, s. m. *the place where grows the salt-wort*

Almarjo, s. m. *salt-wort*

Almaro, s. m. *marum*

Almarraes, s. m. pl. *tools to card cotton*

Almarraxa y Almarraza, s. f. *a glass watering bottle*

Almártaga, Almártega y

Almártiga, s. f. || *an halter*

Almastigado, da, a *with gum-mast*

Almatrero, s. m. *fishes for shads*

Almatriche, s. m.

Almazarron, s. m. magre

Almea, s. m. *red*

Almea, s. f. V. Al

Almear, s. m. *a* || *stack of straw*

Almeja, sub. f. *a* (*fish*)

Almena, s. f. *batt*

Almenage, s. m. *blage, series of ments*

Almenar, v. a. *t battlements* || *t*

Almenar, s. m. *a iron to suppor torches*

Almenara, s. f. *be*

Almendra, s. f. *al kernel*

Almendrada, s. f. *milk*

Almendrado, da, *mond like*

Almendral, s. m. *chard of almo*

Almendrero, s. m mendro

Almendrero, ra, *son, etc. full of a*

Almendrica, ita, *f. a little almo*

Almendrilla, *an*

Almendro, s. m. *tree*

Almendron, s. m. *almond* || *a fals*

Almendrones, pl. *almonds*

Almendruco, s. m *almond*

Almenilla, sub. f.

ent || an indentelow, etc.
. m. helmet ||
with a helmet
s. f. a sort of old garment
m. lote-tree
f. fruit of the
. m. V. Almez
m. V. Almear
. m. syrup
pl. sweet-meats
v. a. to sweeten
s. m. starch
o, da, a. painrched; affected
, v. a. to starch
, s. m. a mine-
f. waistcoat || of pork || coat || tenon
s. f. the second fleet || Admiè
lgo, } s. m. ad-
go, } miralty
, s. m. admiral
a, s. f. admiè
s. m. a mortar
v. act. to scent sk
s. m. musk
, ña, a. that be musk
, s. f. a watermells the musk
. s. f. V. Al-
, s. m. capfoot
, s. m. a hoe
, s. m. sal am-
, s. m. sauce garlick, chee-

se, etc. || a mingle-mangle
Almofar, s. m. some covering for the head
Almofia, s. f. Voy. Aljofayna
Almofrex, s. m. a case to carry a travelling bed in
Almogama, s. f. the narrow part of a ship towards head and stern
Almogarave, } s. m. experienced
Almogavar, } soldier sent in party
Almogavaría, s. f. a party of such soldiers
Almohada, s. f. a pillow; a cushion || rusticks
Almohadica de olor, s. f. a sweet-bag
Almohadilla, s. f. a little cushion || rusticks || swellings on the horse's withers
Almohadillado, da, adj. like a cushion
Almohadon, s. m. a great cushion
Almohatre, s. m. sal ammoniak
Almohaza, s. f. a curry-comb
Almohazador, s. masc. a groom [horses
Almohazar, v. a. to curry
Almojábana, s. f. a cheese-pie || wafer || a fritter
Almojama, s. f. Voy. Mojama [hatre
Almojatre, s. m. V. Almo-
Almona, s. f. place fit to fish shads
Almóndiga, s. f. Voy. Alhóndiga]tion
Almoneda, s. f. an auc-
Almonedear, v. a. to sell by auction
Almoradux, s. m. sweet marjoram

Almorí, } s. m. a cake
Almurí, } made with honey, dates, etc.
Almoronía, s. f. V. Alboronía
Almorranas, s. f. pl. piles
Almorrefa, s. f. floor made with blue bricks
Almortas, s. f. pl. square peases
Almorzada, s. f. V. Almuerza [fast
Almorzar, v. a. to break-
Almotacen, s. m. a clerk of the market
Almotacenazgo, s. m. } the
Almotazanía, s. f. } office of the clerk of the market
Almoxarifazgo, s. m. custom upon commodities
Almoxarife, s. m. custom-house receiver
Almozarabe, s. m. a christian under the dominion of the moors
Almud, s. m. a measure of half a bushel
Almudada, s. f. as much land as half a bushel of wheat will sow
Almuerza, sub. f. double handful
Almuerzo, s. m. a breakfast
Alnadillo, lla, s. dim. de Alnado, da
Alnado, da, s. a son, or daughter-in-law
Alobado, da, a. that has been bit by wolves
Alobunado, da, a. wolf-like [lessly
Alocadamente, ad. heed-
Alocado, da, adj. hare-brained
Alodial, a. allodial
Aloe, s. m. aloes
Alojamiento, s. m. lodge-

ment || *encampment* || *the deck of a ship*
Alojar, *v. a. y n. to lodge*
Alomado (caballo), *a back-crooked horse*
Alomar, *v. act. to distribute equally the strengh of a horse*
Alomarse, *v. r. to gather strength*
Alon, *s. m. a fowl's wing*
Alon, *int. come* or *come on* [*wing*
Aloncillo, *s. m. a little*
Alondra, *s. f. a lark*
Alongar, *v. a. to prolong; to protract*
Alopecia, *s. f. fox's evil*
Aloque, *subs. m. a pale wine*
Alosna, *s. f. wormwood*
Alotar, *v. a. to reef*
Aloxa, *s. f. metheglin*
Aloxero, *s. m. one that sells* or *makes metheglin*
Alpañata, *s. f. a polishing — leather* [cería
Alparcería, *s. f. V.* Apar-
Alpargata, *subst. f. shoe made of pack-thread* or *rushes*
Alpargatado, da, *a. made in the shape of the* alpargata
Alpargatar, *v. a to make* alpargatas
Alpargatazo, *s. m. a stroke with an* alpargata
Alpargatería, *s. f. a shop where are made* or *sold* alpargatas
Alpargatero, *sub. m. one that makes* or *sells* alpargatas
Alpargatilla, *s. f. dim. de alpargata*
Alpechin, *s. m. the dregs of oil*

Alpino, na, *a. alpine*
Alpiste, *s. m. canary-seed*
Alpistela, } *s. f. a kind*
Alpistera, } *of cake*
Alpistero (harnero), *s. m. sieve for canary-seed*
Alquequenje. *V.* Alkanquegi [*house*
Alquería, *sub. f. farmer's*
Alquez, *s. m. measure of about eighty gallows*
Alquicel, } *s. m. a morish*
Alquicer, } *mantle* or *covering*
Alquiladizo, za, *a. that may be hired*
Alquilador, *s. m. letter*
Alquilar, *v. a. to hire* || *to let out*
Alquiler, *sub. m. letting out* || *hiring* || *hire*
Alquilon, na, *adj. proper to be hired*
Alquimia, *s. f. alchymy*
Alquimila, *sub. f. ladies-mantle*
Alquimista, *s. m. alchymist*
Alquitara, *s. f. alembick*
Alquitarar, *v. a. to distil*
Alquitira, *s. f. gum tragacanth* [*tar*
Alquitran, *s. m. pitch and*
Alquitranar, *v. a. to tar*
Alrededores, *s. m. pl. the avenues round the place*
Alrota, *s. f. tow; hards*
Alsine, *s. f. chickweed*
Alta, *s. f. an old spanish dance* || *a publick exercise of dancing* or *fencing* [*grass*
Altabaquillo, *s. m. knot-*
Altamar, *s. m. the main ocean* [*ly*
Altamente, *ad. egregious-*
Altamisa, *sub. f. V.* Artemisa
Altanería, *subs. f. a high*

soaring || *hau*
prides
Altanero, ra, *a. t*
high || *proud;*
Altar, *s. m. alta*
Altarero, *sub. m*
sets up altar
streets, etc
Altarico, *subs. n*
altar
Alterabilidad, *s.*
bleness
Alterable, *a. alt*
Alteracion, *s. f. c*
|| *popular up.*
Alterador, *s. m.*
alters
Alterar, *v. a. t*
to stir up
Altercacion, *s. f.*
Altercado, *s. m.*
Altercador, ra,
gler
Altercar, *v. n. t*
Alternacion, *s.*
nation
Alternadamente
Alternativame
Alternar, *v. a. t*
Alternar, *v. n.*
nate
Alternativa, *s. f*
Alternativament
ternately
Alternativo, va,
Alterno, na,
Alteza, *s. f. high*
Altibaxo, *s. m.*
right stroke
Altibaxos, *pl. un*
ces || *vicissitu*
fortune
Altillo, lla, *adj*
Altillo, *s. m. a*
Altiloqüo, qüa, *a*
Altimetría, *s. f.*
Altisimo, ma, *a.*
Altisimo, *s. m.*
Altisonante, *a.*

...ono, na, *a. pompous; sublime*
...ivamente, *ad. proudly*
...varse, *v. r. to grow proud*
...vez, *s. f. haughtiness*
...ta, *adj. high || arduous || enormous || profound*
..., *sub. m. highness || a ...ry || hill || the treble halt*
..., *int. halt || stop; silence || cheer up*
...bordo, *s. m. a large ship*
...r, *s. m. V.* Altura
...zanillo, *s. m. dim* altozano
...zano, *sub. m. a little hill*
...amuz, *s. m. lupine*
...amuces, *pl. shells used ... vote*
...ra, *s. f. height || tallness || the latitude of a place*
...ras, *pl. tops of the mountains, etc.*
...ia, *s. f. kidney-bean*
...inar. *v. a. to darken ... dazzle*
...on, *s. m. an owl*
...la, *sub. f. a winged ...*
...lir, *v. n. to allude*
...mbrado, da, *adj. aluminous || one that is ...on the merry pin*
...mbrado, *sub. m. the lights of a church, etc.*
...mbrados, *pl. a kind of aromaticks*
...mbrador, ra, *s. one that lights*
...mbramiento, *sub. m. lighting || illusion*
...mbrar, *v. a. to light; enlighten || to steep in alum-water || to open a vine at the root*

Alumbre, *s. m. alum*
Alumbrera, *s. f. an alum mine*
Aluminoso, sa, *a. aluminous*
Alumno, *sub. m. foster-child*
Alunado, da, *adj. lunatick*
Caballo alunado, *a horse who suffers a contraction of his nerves*
Aluquete, *s. m. a match*
Alusion, *s. f. allusion*
Alusivo, va, *a. allusive*
Alustrar, *v. a. to give a gloss*
Alutacion, *s. f. the first gold found in the mines*
Aluvion, *s. f. overflowing*
Alveario, *s. m. cavity of the ear*
A'lveo, *s. m. the channel of a river*
Alveolo, *s. m. tooth-socket*
Alverja, etc. *V.* Arveja
Alza, *s. f. piece of leather that underlays the shoe*
Alzacuello, *s. m. a clergy man's band*
Alzadamente, *adv. summarily*
Alzado, *s. m. upright; elevation*
Alzados, *pl. laid up things*
Alzadura, *s. f. the action of raising, etc.*
Alzadura de barbecho, *the breaking up the ground*
Alzamiento, *s. m. lifting up || out-bidding*
Alzapaño, *s. m. a hook to raise the hangings*
Alzaprima, *s. f. lever*
Alzaprimar, *v. a. to move, or lift with a lever*
Alzapuertas, *s. m. a mute servant in a comedy*
Alzar, *v. a. to lift; to raise || to take up || to lay up, or keep || to proclaim a king || to cut the cards || to put in order the printed leaves || to break up the ground || to recall a banished person*
Alzar de eras, *to keep up the corn after harvest* — de obra, *to interrupt a work* — el real, *to decamp* — hervor, *to begin boiling* — la mesa, *to take away the table* — la tienda, *to shut up one's shop* — velas, *to sail*
Alzarse, *v. r. to rebel || to give over play*
Alzarse á mayores, *to pretend superiority*
Ama, *s. f. a nurse || mistress*
Ama de llaves, *housekeeper*
Amabilidad, *s. f. amability*
Amable, *adj. amiable*
Amablemente, *adv. amiably*
Amaca, *V.* Hamaca
Amacena, *sub. f. damask prune*
Amador, ra, *s. lover*
Amadrigarse, *v. r. to burrow*
Amadronado, da, *adj. arbutelike*
Amaestrar, *v. a. to instruct; to train up*
Amagar, *v. a. to threaten to strike*
Amago, *s. m. a threatening beck* or *gesture*
A'mago, *s. m. an unpleasant honey's favour*
Amajadar, *v. n. V.* Majadear
Amalgama, *s. f. amalgam*
Amalgamacion, *s. f. amalgamation*

Amalgamar, v. a. to amalgamate
Amamantar, v. a. to suckle
Amancebamiento, sub. m. concubinage
Amancebarse, v. r. to live in the concubinage
Amancillar, v. a. to stain || to wound || to tarnish
Amanecer, v. n. to grow day; to dawn || to arrive at the break of day
Amanecer, v. a. to light
Al amanecer, adv. at the break of day
Amanaceres, s. m. day-break
Amanojar, v. a. to make up in bunches
Amansador, ra, s. tamer
Amansamiento, s. m. taming [|| to pacify
Amansar, v. a. to tame
Amantar, v. a. to cover with a blanket
Amanteniente, ad. forcibly [ropes
Amantes, s. m. pl. ship-
Amantillar, v. act. to rop the lifts
Amantillo, s. m. lift
Amanuense, s. m. amanuensis [tom
Amañarse, v. r. to accus-
Amaños, s. m. pl. tools; instruments; means
Amapola, s. f. wild poppy
Amar, v. a. to love
Amaracino (ungüento), s. m. marjoram-unguent
Amaraco, s. m. marjoram
Amaranto, sub. m. amaranthus
Amargaleja, s. f. a bitter plum [terly
Amargamente, adv. bit-
Amargar, v. n. to taste bitter

Amargar, v. a. to imbitter
Amargo, ga, adj. bitter
Amargon, s. m. wild-endive
Amargo y Amargor, s. m. bitterness || sorrow
Amargoso y Amargosamente, V. Amargo, Amargamente
Amarguillo, s. m. bitterish [gor
Amargura, s. f. V. Amar-
Amaricado, da, a. effeminate [wish
Amarillazo, za, a. yello-
Amarillear, v. n. to grow yellow [wish
Amarillejo, ito, a. yello-
Amarillez, s. f. yellowness; paleness
Amarillo, lla, a. yellow || pale; wan
Amaro, s. m. St. John's-wort
Amarra, s. f. a ship-rope
Amarradero, sub. m. the place for mooring
Amarrar, v. a. to moor a ship
Amarrazon, s. m. the ropes of a ship
Amarrido, da, adj. sad; melancholy
Amartelar, v. a. to fondle
Amartelarse v. r. to fall in love
Amartillar, v. a. to hammer || to cock a gun
Amasadera, s. f. kneading-trough
Amasadijo, s. m. V. Amasijo [der
Amasador, ra, s. knea-
Amasadura, sub. f. kneading
Amasamiento, s. m. union; assemblage
Amasar, v. a. to knead
Amasijo, sub. m. paste; dough || mortar || mingle-mangle

Amatista, s. f. ameth[ist]
Amatorio, ria, a. be[lon]ging to love
Amaynar v. a. to f[url] or to brail up the s[ails] || to cool, or relent
Amaytinar v. a. to [ob]serve narrowly
Amazona, s. f. amaz[on]
Ambages, sub. m. pl. circumlocutions
A'mbar, s. m. yellow [am]ber
A'mbar gris, ambergr[is]
Ambarino, na, a. be[lon]ging to amber
Ambicion, s. f. ambi[tion]
Ambicionar, v. a. to [am]bition; to seek aft[er]
Ambiciosamente, ad. [am]bitiously
Ambicioso sa a. a[mbi]tious desirous of
Ambidextro, tra, a. [am]bidextrous
Ambiente, s. m. the [am]bient air
Ambigú, s. m. ambig[u]
Ambigüamente, adv. [am]biguously
Ambigüedad, s. f. am[bi]guity [gu
Ambigüo, gua, a. am[bi]
A'mbito, s. m. ambit
Ambla, s. f. amble
Amblador, s. m. ambl[er]
Amblar, v. n. to ambl[e]
Amblèo, subs. m. a w[ax] taper
Ambos, pron. both
Ambos á dos, both toge[ther]
Ambrollar, v. a. to in[tri]cate
Ambrosía, s. f. ambros[ia]
Ambular, v. n. to wal[k]
Ambularios, s. m. pl. r[ag]ged clothes

tivo, va, *a. wan-*
g
, *s. m. answering*
ately verses
ntador, *s. m. one*
rights
ntar, *v. a. to fright*
, *s. f. a furrow*
, *v. a. to furrow*
s. m. share-wort
ado, da, *a. melon-*

s. m. y ad. amen
, *s. f. a threat*
ador, ra, *s. threa-*
[*ten*
ar, *v. a. to threa-*
ad, *s. f. amenity*
r, *v. act. to give*
ty || *to adorn*
na, *a. pleasant*
id
s. m. V. Ammi
v. a. to mix wa-
th wine
lear, *v. a. to fa-*
to befriend, etc.
lo, da, *a. of lat-*
lour
. f. V. Bonito
, *s. f.* } *amiantus*
, *s. m.* }
, *sub. m. leather*

subs. f. a female
l; mistress
e, *adj. amiable;*
ly
emente, *adver.*
ly
ga, *sub. friend* ||

ga, *a. friendly*
lo, lla, *s. dim.*
igo
r, *v. a. to frighten*
, *s. f. friendship*
redom || *favour;*
s || *desire*

Amistar, *v. a. to reconcile*
Amistarse, *v. r. V.* Amancebarse
Amistosamente, *adver. friendly*
Amistoso, sa, *a. friendly*
Amito, *s. m. amice*
Ammi, *sub. m. bishop's weed*
Amnestia, } *s. f. amnesty*
Amnistia, }
Amo, *s. m. master; owner* || *a fosther-father*
Amodita, *s. f. a kind of serpent*
Amodorrarse, *v. r. to grow drowsy*
Amodorrido, da, *a. drowsy*
Amohecerse, *v. r. V.* Enmohecerse
Amohinar, *v. a. to anger*
Amojamado, da, *a. lean; thin; lank*
Amojonador, *sub. m. one who sets bounds*
Amojonamiento, *s. m. setting the bounds* || *bounds; limits*
Amojonar, *v. act. to set bounds*
Amoladera (piedra), *s. f. grind-stone*
Amolador, *s. m. a grinder*
Amoladura, *s. f. grinding*
Amolar, *v. a. to grind a knife, etc.*
Amoldar, *v. a. to mould* || *to correct the manners, etc.*
Amollador, ra, *s. one who yields the trick*
Amollar, *v. n. to yield the trick*, or *lift*
Amolletado, da, *a. spungy bread-like*
Amomo, *s. m. a very hot astringent plant*
Amonedar, *v. a. to coin money*

Amonestacion, *s. f. admonishment* || *a ban of matrimony*
Amonestador, ra, *s. admonisher*
Amonestar, *v. a. to admonish* || *to proclaim a matrimony*
Amoniaco, *a. m. ammoniack*
Amontar, *v. n. y* Amontarse, *v. r. to get up into the mountains*
Amontonador, ra, *s. heaper*
Amontonamiento, *s. m.* [*heaping*
Amontonar, *v. a. to heap*
Amontonarse, *v. r. to be angry*
Amor, *s. m. love*
Amor mio, *a. daffodil-like plant* — de hortelano, *burdock*
Amores, *pl. a lewd passion* || *common courtship* || *clotbur*
De mil amores, *ad. very willingly*
Amoradux, *s. m. marjoram*
Amoratado, da, *a. blac-* [*kish*
Amorcillo, *s. m. a weak love*
Amoretado, da, *a. blackish*
Amorgado, da, *adj. half dead*
Amoricones, *s. m. pl. testimonies of love* || *clownish coarse love*
Amorio, *s. m. falling in love*
Amoriscado, da, *a. moor-* [*like*
Amorosamente, *ad. amorously*
Amoroso, sa, *adj. loving;* [*kind*
Amorrar, *v. neut. to bow one's head* || to be silent
Amortajar, *v. a.* to bury
Amortecerse, *v. r.* to swoon

Amortecimiento, *sub. m. swoon*
Amortiguamiento, *s. m. deadening*
Amortiguar, *v. a. to deaden || to darken colours*
Amortizacion, *s. f. amortization*
Amortizar, *v. a. to amortize* [*flies away*
Amoscar, *v. a. to drive*
Amoscarse, *v. r. to go away angry*
Amostachada, da, *a. one that has whiskers*
Amostazarse, *v. r. to be angry*
Amotinador, *s. m. mutinous ; mutineer*
Amotinamiento, *sub. m. mutiny* [*mutiny*
Amotinar, *v. a. to raise a*
Amovible, *a. removeable*
Ampa. *V.* Hampa
Ampara, *s. f. sequestration* [*tector*
Amparador, ra, *sub. pro-*
Amparar, *v. a. to protect ; to defend*
Ampararse, *v. r. to fly to.... for shelter*
Amparo, *s. m. protection; defence*
Amphibio, Amphibología, etc. *Voy.* Anfibio, Anfibología, etc.
Amphisbena ó Amphisibena, *sub. f. a kind of serpent*
Amphiscios, *s. m. pl. amphiscii*
Ampliacion, *s. f. ampliation* [*fier*
Ampliador, ra, *s. ampli-*
Ampliamente, *ad. largely*
Ampliar, *v. a. to amplify*
Ampliativo, va, *a. ampliating*
Amplificacion, *sub. f. enlargement || amplification*
Amplificar, *v. a. to amplify ; to enlarge*
Amplio, ia, *adj. ample ; large*
Amplitud, *s. f. amplitude*
Amplo. *V.* Amplio
Ampo, *s. m. whiteness of snow*
Ampolla, *s. f. a blister || a bubble* [*blisters*
Ampollar, *v. a. to cause*
Ampollarse, *v. r. to blister*
Ampolleta, *sub. f. a little phial || hour-glass*
Amuchachado, da, *adj boyish*
Amufar, *v. a. to attack with roarings*
Amugamiento, *s. m. Voy.* Amojonamiento
Amugerado, da, *adj. woman-like* [*vine*
Amugronar, *v. a. to pro-*
Amulatado, da, *a. tawny*
Amuleto, *s. m. amulet*
Amunicionar, *v. a. to supply with provisions*
Amura, *s. m. main-tack*
Amuradas, *sub. f. pl. the high sides withing the ship*
Amurar, *v. act. to haul aboard the tack of a sail*
Amurca, *s. f. V.* Alpechin
Amurcar, *v. a. to strike with the horns*
Amurco, *subs. m. a blow with the horns*
Amusgar, *v. a. to prick up the ears || to stretch out the snout to bite*
Ana, *s. f. an ell || fathom*
Anabaptista ó Anabatista, *s. m. Anabaptist*
Anacardina, *s. f. confection of* anacardo
Anacardo, *s. m. a sort indian fruit*
Anacefalcosis, *s. f. re- pitulation*
Anacoreta, *s. m. anch*
Anacoretico, ca, *a. bel- ging to the anchor*
Anacreoncio, cia, } *a.*
Anacreóntico, ca, } *acre- tick*
Anacrenismo, *s. m. a- chronism*
Anade, *s. á duck* or *d*
Anadear, *v. n. to wa*
Anadeja, *s. f. a duckl*
Anadino, na, *s. a du- ling* [*d*
Anadon, *sub. m. a li*
Anadoncillo, *s m. a li- tle young duck*
Anafaya, *s. f. a sort cotton-cloth*
Anafe, *s. m. a port stove*
Anáfora, *s. f. repetiti*
Anagalide, *s. f. pimper*
Anagiris, *s. f. bean-tre*
Anaglifos, *s. m. pl. e- bossed vessels* or *pla*
Anagoge, } *s. f. mysti*
Anagogia, } *interpretati*
Anagógicamente, *ad. my- tically*
Anagogico, ca, *a. mysti*
Anagrama, *s. f. anagra*
Analema, *s. m. arm dialing*
Analéptico, ca, *a. a- naleptick*
Anales, *s. m. pl. annal*
Analisis, *s. f. analysis*
Analista, *s. m. annalis*
Analítico, ca, *a. analy- cal*
Análogamente, *ad. a- logically*
Analogía, *s. f. analogy*
Analógicamente, *ad. a- logically*

Analógi

a. *analogical*
. *ananas*
. m. *wolfs*
n. *a sort of* ...es
. *cupboard's*
v. a. *to at-*
oranges
a, a. *orange-*
f. *anarchy*
, *adj. anar*
b. m. hou
uff)
s. f. *anas-*
sub. f. a vision
nnats
f. *anathema*
, v. *act. to* ...ize
receiver of
s. m. *usury*
f. *anatomy*
...nte, *ad. ana-*
...a, *adj. ana-*
s. m. *anatomist*
v. a. *to ana-*
...rse's *buttock*
... las ancas, *to* ...d
. *contraction* ...ves
, *ad. largely;* [*venture*
f. *seaman's*
...ta, *adj. short*

Ancho, cha, *a. broad*
Vida ancha, *licentious life*
Anchoa, *s. f. anchovy*
Anchor, *s. m. V.* Anchura
Anchova, *s. f. anchovy*
Anchuelo, la, *a. a little broad*
Anchura, *s. f. breadth*
Andar á sus anchuras, *to take one's pleasures*
Anchuroso, sa, *adj. very wide* or *broad*
Anchûsa, *s. f. orchanet*
Ancianidad, *s. f.* } *old age*
Ancianismo, *s. m.* }
Anciano, na, *a. old; ancient*
Ancla, *s. f. anchor*
Anclage, *s. m. anchorage*
Anclar, *v. n. to anchor*
Ancon, *s. m. haven; harbour*
A'ncora, Ancorage, Ancorar. *V.* Ancla, etc.
Ancorca, *s. f. an yellow earth*
Ancusa, *s. f. bugloss*
Andabatas, *subs. mas. pl. blind folded gladiators*
Andaboba, *s. f. game at cards*
Andadas, *s. f. pl. traces*
Andaderas, *s. f. pl. a go-cart*
Andadero, ra, *a. accessible; easy to run over*
Andado, *s. m. V.* Alnado
Andado, da, *a. common; usual*
Camino andado, *a beaten road* || vestido andado, *worn out cloth*
Andador, ra, *s. walker*
Andadores, *pl. leading-strings* [*walking*
Andadura, *sub. f. going;*
Caballo de andadura, *a pacing horse*

Andalia, *s. f. V.* Sandalia
Andamio, *s. m. scaffold*
Andana, *sub. fem. row; range, etc.*
Andaniños, *s. m. pl. V.* Andadores
Andante (caballero), *s. m. a knight-errant*
Andar) *v. neut. to go; to walk*
Andar, *s. m. walking*
Andar, *int. well; very well* [*bler*
Andariego, ga, *a. ram-*
Andarin, *s. m. a running footman*
Andario, *s. m. wag-tail*
Andas, *s. f. pl. a kind of litter*
Anden, *s. m. a walk. or galery* || *V.* Vasar y anaquel
Andero, *s. mas. a litter's bearer*
A'ndito, *s. m. a surrounding galery*
Andolas, *s. f. pl. fooleries*
Andolina, ó Andorina, *s. f. swallow*
Andorrero, ra, *s. rambler*
Adosca (res), *s. f. mutton, etc. two years old*
Andrajero, *s. m. a ragman*
Andrajo, *s. m. a rag*
Andrajosamente, *ad. raggedly*
Andrajoso, sa, *a. ragged*
Andriana, *s. f. a woman's morning gown*
Andrina, *V.* Endrina
Androgeno, ó Androgino, *s. m. hermaphrodite*
Andromina, *s. f. artifice; deceit*
Androsaces, *sub. fem. the white herb*
Androsemo, *subst. m. V.* Asciro
Anduar, *s. m. V.* Aduar

Andularios, *s. m. pl. long ragged clouths*
Andullo, *s. m. a roll of tobacco* || *V.* Pandero
Andurriales, *s. m. pl. unfrequented ways*
Anea, *s. f. an aquatick-herb* [*by ells*
Aneage, *s. m. measuring*
Anear, *v. a. to measure by ells — to rock*
Aneblar, *v. act. V.* Anublar || *to blast*
Anegacion, *s. f. drowning* || *over flowing*
Anegadizo, za, *a. subject to be overflowed*
Anegamiento, *s. mas. V.* Anegacion
Anegar, *v. a. to drown* || *to overflow*
Anémone, *s. f. anemony*
Anemoscopio, *s. m. anemoscope*
Aneurisma, *subst. masc. aneurism*
Auexar, *v. a. to annex*
Anexidades, *s. f. pl. annexes*
Anexion, *s. f. annexment*
Anexo, xa, *a. annexed*
Anfibio, ia, *adj. amphibious*
Anfibologia, *s. f. amphibology*
Anfibológico, ca, *a. amphibological*
Anfion, *s. m. opium*
Anfiteatro, *s. m. amphitheater*
Anfracto, *s. mas. anfractuosity*
Angarrillas, *s. fem. pl. a hand-barrow* || *hurdle, etc. to draw goods on*
Angarillon, *s. m. a great hand-barrow*
Angaripola, *s. f. a coarse striped linen cloth*
A'ngaro, *s. m. a signal*
A'ngel, *s. m. an angel* || *chain-shot* || *a maid* (*fish*)
Angélica, *s. f. angelica*
Angélica carlina, *carline*
Angelical, *a. angelical*
Angelicalmente, *ad. angelically*
Angélico, ca, *a. angelical*
Angelote, *s. m. aum. de* A'ngel
Angeo, *s. m. canvass*
Angina, *s. f. angina*
Angla, *s. f. a cape*
Angostamente, *adv. narrowly*
Angostar, *v. act. to narrow ; to streight*
Angostillo, lla, *a. a little narrow*
Angosto, ta, *narrow*
Angostura, *s. f. narrowness* || *streights ; defile*
Angra, *s. f. V.* Ensenada
Anguarina, *a wide coat*
Anguila, *s. f. an eel*
Anguilazo, *subs. m. lash ; lashing*
Anguina, *s. f. vein of the groin*
Angular, *a. 2. angular*
Angularmente, *adv. angulary*
Angulema, *s. f. canvass*
Hacer angulemas, *to be very ceremonious*
A'ngulo, *s. m. angle*
Angurria, *subs. f. water-melon*
Angustia, *s. f. anguish ; pain*
Angustiadamente, *adver. anxiously*
Angustiado, da, *a. covetous* [*afflict*
Angustiar, *v. a. to vex, to*
Angustioso, sa, *a. afflicted*
Anhelar, *v. neut. to cov[eet] earnestly* || *to pant*
Anhélito, *s. m. the brea[th]*
Anhelo, *subs. m. desir[e] covetousness*
Anheloso, sa, *a. earne[s]tely coveted*
Anidar, *v n. y* Anidar[se] *v. r. to nest*
Anidar, *v. a. V.* Abrig[ar]
Anieblar, *v. a. V.* A[nu]blar || *to blast*
Anifala, *s. m. bran-br[ead]*
Anillejo *y* Anilleto, *s.* *a little ring*
Anillo, *s. m. ring* || *tragal*
A'nima, *s. f. the soul*
Animacion, *s. f. ani[ma]tion*
Animador, *sub. mas.* *animates*
Animadversion, *s. f. a[ni]madversion*
Animadvertencia, *s. f.* Advertencia
Auimal, *s. m. anim[al] beast* || *a brutish m[an]*
Animal, *a. 2. animal*
Animalazo, *s. m. aum.* Animal
Animalejo, ico, ito, *s. m. animalcule*
Animalon *y* Animal[ote] *m. a great beast*
Animar, *v. a. to anim[ate]*
Anime, *s. m. gum an[ime]*
Animero, *s. m. one [who] begs for the soul[s in] purgatory*
A'nimo, *subs. m. mi[nd] courage*
A'nimo, ó buen ánim[o] *int. cheer up*
Animosamente, *ad. b[oldly]*
Animosidad, *sub. f. b[old]ness*
Animoso, sa, *adj. b[old] courageous*

nte, ad. chil-
v. r. to grow
:, a. that may
ilated
n, s. f. y Ani-
nto, s. m. an-
n [hilate
v. a. to anni-
, v. r. to hum-
[seed
s. anise || ani-
ub. m. dim. de
o, s. m. anni-
, ria, ad. an-
y
the anus
l. last night
, v. n. to grow
to be at night
:e
cer, ad. at the
ll
se, v. r. to be-
rk
v. a. to apply
s
na, a. anodine
y anomalidad,
maly
la, a. anoma-
. tree that bears
na
f a sort of in-
it
on, s. f. y Ano-
nto, s. m. an-
on || diminu-
ontempt of one's
, v. a. to anni-
to diminish
se, v. r. to hum-
[mous
, ma, a. anony-

Anotacion, s. f. annotation
Anotador, ra, s. annotator
Anotar, v. a. to make annotations
Anotomía, s. f. V. Anatomia
Anquiseco (caballo), sub. m. a buttock-lean horse
A'nsar, s. m. a goose
Ansarería, s. f. a goose-pen [herd
Ansarero, s. m. a goose-herd
Ansarino, s. m. a gosling
Ansarino, no, a. belonging to a goose
Ansaron, sub. m. a great goose
Ansia, s. f. pain; grief || ardent desire
Ansías de muerte, pangs of death
Ansiado, V. Ansioso
Ansiar, v. a. to long; to desire eagerly
Ansiosamente, ad. eagerly; anxiously
Ansioso, sa, a. desirous || anxious
Antas, s. f. pl. pilasters; antes
Antagonista, s. m. antagonist
Antaña (llamarse), to make a recantation
Antaño, ad. the last year
Antañona, sub. f. an old woman [tick
Antártico, ca, a. antartick
Ante, prep. before
Ante, s. m. buff
Anteado, da. a. of a buff colour
Anteanteanoche, ad. three nights ago
Anteanteayer, } ad. three
Anteantier, } days ago
Anteayer, adv. two days since

Antobrazo, s. m. the part of the arm betwixt the elbow and the wrist
Antecama, s. f. carpet before the bed
Antecámara, sub. f. antichamber
Antecedencia, s. f. } the antecedent
Antecedente, s. m. } proposition
Antecedentemente, adver. antecedently
Anteceder, v. a. to precede
Antecesor, ra, s. predecessor
Antecesores, pl. ancestors
Antechinos, s. m. pl. hollow mouldings
Antechristo, s. m. antichrist
Antecoger, v. a. to take, bear, or drive before one
Antecolumna, sub. f. column of a peristile, etc.
Antecoro, s. m. the hall before the choir
Antecos, s. m. pl. antœci
Antedata, s. f. antedate
Antedatar, v. a. to antedate
Antediem, adv. the day before
Anteiglesia, subst. fem. church porch || country-church || a village
Antelacion, s. f. priority || preference
Antemano, subs. mas. a present made beforehand
De antemano, ad. previously
Antemeridiano, na, adj. before noon
Antemulas, sub. mas. the groom of the mules

Antemural, s, m. / Antemuralla, s. f. / Antemuro, s. m. } *a fort, etc. that defends a place*
Antenoche, *ad. the night before last*
Antenombre, *s. m. first-name*
Anteojo, *s. m. glass*
Anteojo de larga vista, *a prospective glass binócle, double prospective* [glass
— de puño, *a spying-*
— poliedro, ó de carrillas, *a multiplying glass*
Anteojos, *p. spectacles || eye-flaps*
Ante-omnia, *adv. before all things*
Antepasado, da, *adj. gone before* [cestors
Antepasados, *s. m. pl. an-*
Antepecho, *s. m. parapet; rail of balcony, etc. || poitrel*
Antepenúltimo, ma, *adj. the last but tow*
Anteponer, *v. a. to prefer*
Antepuerta, *sub. f. a curtain behind a door*
Anterior, *a. 2. precedent || foremost* [dency
Anterioridad, *s. f. prece-*
Anteriormente, *ad. before*
A'ntes, *prep. before*
A'ntes, *ad. rather*
Antesacristía, *s. f. room before the vestry*
Antesala, *s. f. antichamber*
Antestatura, *s. f. intrenchment; fence*
Antevíspera, *s. f. the day before the vigil*
Antia, *s. f. a kind of sea-fish*

Antibaquio, *s. m. a foot of latin verses*
Antibo, *s. m. the force or impulse of the water*
Anticardenal, *s. m. anticardinal* [cipation
Anticipacion, *s. f. anti-*
Anticipadamento, *ad. before time* [cipator
Anticipador, ra, *s. anti-*
Anticipamiento, *s. m. V.* Anticipacion [pate
Anticipar, *v. a. to antici-*
Anticrítico, *s. m. an adverse critick*
Antidotario, *s. m. a dispensatory || the place were the antidotes are kept*
Antídoto, *s. m. antidote*
Antífona, *s. f. anthem*
Antifonal, / Antifonario, } *s. m. book in wich the anthems are noted*
Antifonero, *s. m. he who begins the anthem*
Antífrasis, *s. f. antiphrasis* [guo
Antigo, ga, *a. V.* Anti-
Antigualla, *s. f. an antique || old rubbish* or *stuff* [ciently
Antiguamente, *adv. an-*
Antiguamiento, *s. m. admittance among the veterans*
Antiguar, *v. n. to become veteran* [quate
Antiguar, *v. act. to anti-*
Antigüedad, *sub. f. antiquity*
Antiguo, gua, *a. ancient || veteran* [ancients
Antiguos, *sub. m. pl. the*
Antilogía, *s. f. antilogy*
Antimonial, *a. 2. antimonial* [ny
Antimonio, *s. m. antimo-*
Antinomia, *s. f. antinomy*

Antipapa, *s. m. anti*
Antipara, *s. f. a scre*
Antipatía, *s. f. antip*
Antipático, ca, *a. av*
Antiperístasis, *s. f. a peristasis*
Antipoca, *s. f. reco sance of a rent*
Antipocar, *v. act. t cognize a rent*
Antipoda, *s. m. antip*
Antiquado, da, *a. a quated* [q
Antiquario, *sub. m.*
Antiscorbútico, ca, *a tiscorbutical*
Antispodio, *s. m. a of medicinal ashes*
Antítesis, *s. f.* / Antiteto, *s. m.* } *a t*
Antitipo, *s. m. antit*
Antiyer, *ad. V.* Ante
Antojadizamente, *ad priciously* [c
Antojadizo, za, *a. ca*
Antojado, da, *a. tha sires earnestly, etc*
Antojarse, *v. r. to d earnestly and ca ciously*
Antojera, *s. f. a cas speotacles || eye-fla*
Antojo, *s. m. a longi a fancy || a rash ju ment. V.* Anteojo
Antojuelo, *s. m. dim* Antojo
Antología, *s. f. anthe*
Antoniano, *y* Anton *s. m. Antonian*
Antonomasia, *s. f. a nomasia*
Antonomasticamente *by antonomasia*
Antonomástico, ca, *a longing to antono sia*
Antorcha, *s. f. torch*
Antro, *s. m. den; ca*

opófago, s. m. man-
ter
nejo, s. m. the three
st days of the car-
ival
tvion, s. m. unexpec-
d blow or attack
antuvion, ad. sud-
nly
ar de antuvion, to
event
al, a. annual
alidad, subs. f. state
property of annual
ings
almente, ad. annual-
[bute
bada, s. f. an old tri-
barrado, a. clouded,
stered
blar, v. a. to cloud
blarse, v. r. to fade
vay || to vanish
dar, v. a. to knit
lable, a. that may be
nulled
lar, a. annullar.
ar, v. a. to annul
ativo, va, a. annul-
g
oso, sa, adj. full of
ngs || ring-like
nciacion, s. f. annun-
ation
nciador, ra, s. mes-
nger
nciar, v. a. to make
own || to presage
ncio, s. m. presage
, nua, a. annual
lero, s. m. one that
kes fish-hooks
elito, subs. m. small
h hook
alo, s. m. fish-hook
, s. f. a sort of fox
didura, s. f. addi-
n
dir, v. a. to add || to
amplify || to make ad-
ditions [trumpet
Añafil, sub. f. a moorish
Añafilero, s. m. trumpeter
Añagaza, s. f. bird call ||
allurement
Añal, a. annual || yearling
Añal, s. m. anniversary
|| yearly offering
Añalejo, s. mas. book that
orders the daily divine
service
Añascar, v. a. to heap up
trifles, etc.
Añaza, s. f. annual feast
Añejar, v. a. to make one
grow old
Añejarse, v. r. to grow old
Añejo, ja, a. old
Añicos, s. m. pl. tener sus
añicos, to be in years ||
hacer añicos, to pull to
pieces || hacerse añicos,
tobe in the greatest fury
Añil, s. m. woad || indigo
Añinero, s. m. one works
or deals in skins of
lamb [tow
Añines. s. m. pl. a coarse
Añinos, s. m. pl. a young
lam's skin or fleece
Año, s. m. year
Añojo, s. mas. a yearling
calf
Añublar, v. a. V. Anublar
Añublo, s. mas. mildew;
blasting [knits
Añudador, s. m. one that
Añudadura, s. f. y Añuda-
miento, s. m. kniting
Añudar, v. a. V. Anudar
Añusgar, v. n. to be cho-
ked, or stifled
Aocar, v. a. V. Ahuecar
Aojador, sub. m, one that
fascinates
Aojadura, s. f. } fasci-
Aojamiento, s. m. } nating
Aojar, v. a. to fascinate
Aojo, s. m. fascination
Aorta, s. f. aorta
Aovado, da, a. egg-like
Aovar, v. n. to lay eggs
Aovillarse, v. r. to gather
like a bottom of tread,
etc.
Apabilar, v. a. to dispose
the match or wick
Apabilarse, v. r. to dar-
ken || to consume one's
self by degrees
Apacentador, s. m. herds-
man
Apacentamiento, sub. m.
feeding; grazing || pas-
ture [to graze
Apacentar, v. a. to feed;
Apacibilidad, s. f. affabi-
lity
Apacible, a. 2. mild; af-
fable || sweet; pleasant
Apaciblemente, ad. mil-
dly
Apacignador, ra, pacifier
Apaciguamiento, sub. m.
pacification
Apaciguar, v. a. to pacify
Apagable, a. 2. extinguis-
hable
Apagado, da, a. sluggish;
slow
Apagador, s. m. quencher
Apagamiento, s. m. quen-
ching
Apagapenoles, sub. m. pl.
brails
Apagar, v. a. to quenchs,
or extinguish || to ap-
pease || to kill lime
Apainelado (Arco), s. m.
arch who imitates half
an ellipsis
Apalabrar, v. a. to assign
a rendez-vous || to treat
by word of mouth
Apalancar, v. act. to lift
or move with a lever ||
to supplant

Apaleador, ra, *s. one that cudgels* || *one that ventilates corn*

Apalear, *v. a. to cudgel* || *to beat a cloth, etc,* || *to ventilate corn*

Apanage, *s. m. appanage*

Apancora, *sub. f. a sort of shell-fish* [*a sedition*

Apandillar, *v. act. to raise*

Apantuflado, da, *a. slipper-like* [|| *robber*

Apañador, ra, *s. grasper*

Apañadura, *sub. f. grasping* || *robbery*

Apañamiento, *sub. m. V.* Apaño

Apañar, *v. a. to grasp* || *to lay hold on* || *to rob* || *to dispose*

Apañarse, *v. r. to prepare one's self*

Apaño, *s. m. disposition*

Apañuscador, ra, *sub. one that rumples, etc.*

Apañuscar, *v. a. to rumple; to tarnish*

Apapagayado, da, *a. parrot-like*

Nariz apapagayada, *an hooked nose*

Apapagayarse, *v. r. to put on one's self green clothes*

Aparador, *s. f. side-board table* || *work-shop*

Aparar, *v. a. to hold up* or *forth* || *to weed* || *to dispose*

Aparatado (bien, ó mal), *a. able bodied,* or *in bad health*

Aparato, *s. mas. preparation* || *pomp; splendour* || *means; way*

Aparatoso, sa, *a. pompous; splendid*

Aparcería, *subst. f. partnership*

Aparcero, *s. m. partner* || *coheir* [*couple*

Aparear, *v. a. to pair; to*

Aparearse, *v. r. to walk two by two*

Aparecer, *v. n. y* aparecerse, *v. r. to appear*

Aparejado, da, *a. apt; fit*

Aparejador, ra, *subs. one that prepares* || *he that marks stones that are to be cut*

Aparejar, *v. a. to prepare* || *to rig a ship* || *to saddle,* or *harness* || *to prime the cloth*

Aparejo, *s. m. preparation* || *harness* || *rigging* || *winding tackle*

Aparejos, *pl. necessary toosl,* or *instruments*

Aparejuelo, *s. m. a little preparation*

Aparentado, da, *a. related*

Aparentar, *v. a. to feing*

Aparente, *adj. apparent* || *fit* [*parently*

Aparentemente, *ad. ap-*

Aparicion, *s. f. apparition*

Apariencia, *s. f. appearance* [*a theatre*

Apariencias, *pl. scenes of*

Aparrado, da, *a. winding like the vine*

Aparroquiado, da, *a. parishioner* [*custom*

Aparroquiar, *v. a. to get*

Apartadijo, *s. m. portion; part* || *V.* Apartadizo

Apartadizo, *s. m. a closet; a lodge, etc.*

Apartado, da, *a. remote*

Apartado, *s. m. a remote room*

Apartador, ra, *s. one that parts* or *separates*

Apartador de ganado, *thief of cattle*

Apartamiento, *s. m. separation; division* [...] *sisting*

Apartamiento de ga[...] *the thieving of c*[...]

Apartar, *v. a. to pa*[...] *separate* || *to di*[...] || *to take away*

Apartarse, *v. r. to l*[...] *place* || *to be di*[...] || *to desist*

Aparte, *ad. apart*[...]

Aparte, *s. m. an as*[...]

Aparvar, *v. a. to a*[...] *the seaves up c*[...] *barn-floor* || *to h*[...]

Apasionadamente, *passionately*

Apasionado, da, *a*[...] *sionate* || *affecte*[...]

Apasionar, *v. a. to* [...] *a passion* || *to hu*[...]

Apasionarse, *v. r. t*[...] *a strong passion*

Apastuco, *s. m. orn*[...]

Apaysado, da, *adj*[...] *scape-picture-li*[...]

Apazote, *sub. m. a*[...] *basil*

Apea, *s. f. fetter*

Apeadero, *sub. m.*[...]

Apeador, *s. m. sur*[...]

Apeamiento, *s. m*[...] *tining* || *land-s*[...]

Apear, *v. a. to surv*[...] || *to wedge up* || || *to let down* || [...] *suade* || *to take* [...] *difficulty*

Apear á alguno de[...] pleo, *to give o*[...] *move* — el rio, [...] — un caballo, *t*[...]

Apear, *v. n. y* Ap[...] *r. to alight*

Apechugar, *v. a.* [...] *close* [...]

Apedazar, *v. a. t*[...]

Apedernalado, da[...] *hard as a flin*[...]

readero, *sub. m. the* ice *where boys throw* nes *at one another*
reado, da, *a. marked* 'h *the small pox*
reador, *s. mas. one* 't *throws stones*
reamiento, *s. m. the* wing *of stones*
rear, *v. act. to throw* nes *|| to stone*
rear, *v. n. to hail*
rearse, *v. rec. to be* iled *with hail*
reo, *s. m. V.* Pedrea
amiento, *subst. mas.* ing; *sticking, etc.* *V.* Apego
o, *s. mas. affection;* clination
acion, *s. f. appeal*
ado, da, *adj. of the* me *hair*
ambrar, *v. a. to take* e *hair of skins*
ar. *v. n. to appeal*
ativo, *adj. m. appel-* tive
dar, *v. n. to make an* cape
de, *s. m. escape*
ligrado, da, *a. expo-* d *to the danger*
llar, *v. a. to soften a* in *with oil, etc.*
llidamiento, *s. m. cal-* ng *|| proclaiming*
llidar, *v. a. to call* or ame *|| to proclaim*
llideros, *s. m. pl. sol-* iers *called together*
llido, *s. m. surname*
lmazar, *v. a. to co-* ense *|| to vex*
lo, *ad. fit to a hair;* ust [*much ado*
mas, *ad. hardly || with*
indice, } *s. m. appen-* ndix, } *dix*

Apeñuscar, *v. a. V.* Apañuscar [*|| prop*
Apeo, *s. m. land-survey*
Apeonar, *v. n. to run on the ground*
Aperador, *s. m. farmer || cart wright*
Aperar, *v. act. to make country-carts* [cibir
Apercebir, *v. a. V.* Aper-
Apercibimiento, *sub. m. preparation || warning || order || summons*
Apercibir, *v. a. to prepare || to warn || to summon*
Apercion, *s. f. V.* Abertura
Apercollar, *v. a. to take by the collar || to take clandestinely || to murder*
Aperitivo, va, *a. aperitive*
Apernador, *s. mas. a dog that catches the game by the leg*
Apernar, *v. a. to catch by the leg*
Apero, *s. m. all the furniture for the ploughing || necessary tools* or *instruments*
Aperreador, ra, *s. importunate*
Aperrear, *v. a. to deliver up to devouring dogs*
Aperrearse, *v. r. to ower work one's self* [ura
Apertura, *s. f. V.* Abert-
Apesadumbrar, *v. act. to afflict; to grieve*
Apesaradamente, *adver. grievously*
Apesarar, *v. a. to grieve*
Apesgamiento, *sub. mas. squeezing; weighing*
Apesgar, *v. a. to weigh; to press down*
Apesgarse, *v. rec. to be heavy*

Apestar, *v. a. to infect*
Apotecedor, ra, *s. desirous*
Apetecer, *v. a. to desire*
Apetecible, *a. 2. desirable*
Apetencia, *s. f. appetency*
Apetite, *s. m. a relishing sauce, etc.*
Apetitivo, va, *a. appetive*
Apetito, *s. m. appetite*
Apetitoso, sa, *adj. relishing || desirable*
Apezuñar, *v. n. to lean upon the foot*
Apiadador, ra, *s. compassionate*
Apiadarse, *v. r. to commiserate*
Apiaradero, *s. m. a herd's reckoning* [*gentle*
Apiastro, *sub. mas. balm-*
Apicarado, da, *a. roguish*
A'pice, *s. mas. top; summit || the smallest part || a jot; a little*
Apilador, *s. m. heaper*
Apilar, *v. a. to heap up*
Apilarse la gente, *to run into a throng*
Apiñadura, *s f. y.* Apiñamiento, *s. m. sticking close together*
Apiñar, *v. act. to stick close together*
Apiñarse las berzas, etc. *to cabbage*
Apio, *s. m. celery*
Apio de risa, *ranunculus*
Apio montano, *lovage*
Apiolar, *v. act. to tie by the foot || to string and hang by the beak || to catch,* or *kill*
Apique, *adv. upon the brink*
Apisonar, *v. act. to level with a paving beetle*
Apitonamiento, *s. m. first eruption of the horns || passion; raving*

Apitonar, *v. n. to peep out* || *to bud*
Apitonar, *v. a. to prick* || *to pierce*
Apitonarse, *v. r. to wrangle*
Aplacable, *a. that may be appeased*
Aplacacion, *s. f. appeasing*
Aplacador, ra, *s. pacifier*
Aplacamiento, *s. m. appeasing*
Aplacar, *v. a. to appease*
Aplanador, *s. m. V.* Allanador
Aplanamiento, *s. m. levelling*
Aplanar, *v. a. to level; to smooth* || *to confound; to stupefy*
Aplanarse, *v. rec. to fall down*
Aplanchado, *s. m. ironed linen*
Aplanchadora, *sub. f. ironing woman*
Aplanchar, *v. act. to iron linen*
Aplantillar, *v. a. to fit; to adapt*
Aplastar, *v. a. to flaten; to squash* || *to confound; to non plus*
Aplaudir, *v. a. to applaud*
Aplauso, *s. m. applause*
Aplayar, *v. n. to overflow*
Aplazamiento, *s. m. appointement*
Aplazar, *v. a. to appoint a day*
Aplegar, *v. a. to approach*
Aplicahle, *a. applicable*
Aplicacion, *s. f. application*
Aplicacion de bienes, *ad-judging*
Aplicar, *v. a. to apply* || *to adjudge*
Aplicarse, *v. r. to be diligent, carcful, etc.*
Aplomado, da, *a. of a lead colour*

Aplomar, *v. a. to overload*
Aplomar, *v. n. to stand upright* || *to level a wall*
Aplomarse, *v. r. to fall to the very ground*
Apoca, *s. f. acquittance; discharge*
Apocadamente, *ad. a little* || *meanly; abjectly*
Apocado, da, *adj. mean-spiritided*
Apocador, ra, *s. one that lessens*
Apocalipsis, *s. f. apocalypse*
Apocamiento, *s. m. pusillanimity*
Apocar, *v. to lessen* || *to reduce, abridge, etc.* || *to abate the courage, etc.*
Apocarse, *v. r. to humble*
Apocopar, *v. a. to take a syllable from the end of a word*
Apocope, *s. f. apocope*
Apócrifamente, *adv. falsely*, or *uncertainly*
Apócrifo, fa, *a. apocryphal*
Apodador, *s. m. banterer; jester*
Apodar, *v. a. to nickname* || *to rally* or *banter*
Apcdencado, da, *a. greyhound-like*
Apoderado, *s. m. proxy*
Apoderar, *v. act. to give power*
Apoderarse, *v. r. to seize; to possess*
Apodo, *s. m. nickname* || *a witty jest*
Apofisis, *s. f. apophysis*
Apogeo, *s. m. apogæum; apogee*
Apolillado, da, *a. moth-eaten*
Apolilladura, *s. f. eating of a moth*
Apolillar, *v. a. to cut, as moth does*

Apolillarse, *v. rec. moth-eaten* || *to t.*
Apolinar, } *a. l*
Apolineo, nea, } *g A*
Apologético, ca, *a. logetick*
Apologia, *s. f. apol*
Apológico, ca, *a. b ging to the apolo*
Apologista, *subs. m logiste*
Apólogo, *s. m. apol*
Apoltronarse, *v. r grow lazy and id*
Apomazar, *v. a. to s with the pumice s*
Apoplético, ca, *ap tick*
Apoplegía, *s. f. ap*
Aporcadura, *s. f. r ridges*
Aporcar, *v. a. to ra earth round the c etc.*
Aporisma, *s. m. in mation after be blood*
Aporismarse, *v. r. inflammed*
Aporracear, *v. a. t*
Aporrar, *v. n. to stupefied*
Aporrarse, *v. r. to b importunate*
Aporreamiento, *s.* Aporreo
Aporrear, *v. act. to to cudgel, etc.*
Aporreo, *s. m. beat.*
Aporrillarse, *v. r. to*
Aporrillo, *ad. abund*
Aportaderas, *s. f. pl. niers carried by m etc.*
Aportadero, *s. m. easy to land at*
Aportar, *v. n. to la to arrive*

rtillar, v. a. *to break* »en

sentador, subs. mas. *arbinger || quarter-aster*

sentamiento, sub. m. *dging*

sentar, v. a. *to lodge*

sentillo, s. m. *a little hamber*

sento, s. m. *chamber inn || lodging || box*

sesionarse, v. rec. *to ke possession*

sicion, s. f. *apposition*

siopesis, s. f. *reticence*

spelo, ad. *against the air || the wrong way*

sta y Apostadamente, l. *purposely*

stadero, s. m. *post*

stal, s. m. *a fit place r fishing* [*post*

star, v. a. *to bet || to st*

starse, apostarlas. ó ostárselas, *to strive ho shal work best*

stasia, s. f. *apostacy*

stata, s. m. *apostate*

statar, v. n. *to apostize*

stelar, v. a. V. Apos- llar

stema, s. f. *aposteme*

stemar, v. a. *to cause s aposteme*

stemarse, v. rec. *to postemate*

stemero, s. mas. *incion-knife*

stemilla, s. f. *dim. de postema*

stemoso, sa, adj. *benging to an aposteme*

stilla, s. f. *postscript marginal note*

stillar, v. a. *to write arginal notes*

Apostillarse, v. r. *to grow scurfy, etc.*

Apóstol, s. m. *apostle*

Apostolado, s. m. *apostleship || college, or pictures of the apostles*

Apostólicamente, adver. *apostolically*

Apostólico, ca, a. *apostolical*

Apóstrofe, subs. f. *apostrophe* {*trophe*

Apóstrofo, sub. m. *apos-*

Apote, ad. *abundantly*

Apotegma, subs. m. *apophtegm* [*sis*

Apoteósis, s. f. *apotheo-*

Apoyadero, sub. mas. V. Apoyo

Apoyadura, s. f. *flowing of the milk*

Apoyar, v. a. *to support*

Apoyo, sub. m. *support; prop* [*valuable*

Apreciable, a. *estimable;*

Apreciadamente, ad. *with estimation || commendably*

Apreciador, ra, sub. *appraiser*

Apreciar, v. act. *to appraise || to commend*

Apreciativo, va, adj. *belonging to the appraising* [*|| esteem*

Aprecio, s. m. *appraising*

Aprehender, v. a. *to apprehend*

Aprehension, s. f. *apprehension*

Aprehensivo, va, a. *apprehensive || fearful*

Apremiador, ra, sub. *one that compels*

Apremiar, v. act. *to press or squeeze || to force* or *compel*

Apremio, s. m. *pressing || constraint*

Aprender, v. a. *to learn*

Aprendiz, s. m. *apprentice*

Aprendizage, sub. m. *apprenticeship* [*ser*

Aprensador, s. m. *a pres-*

Aprensar, v. a. *to press || to molest*

Apresador, s. m. *corsair*

Apresamiento, s. mas. *taking* or *prize*

Apresar, v. a. *to take; to catch, etc.*

Aprestar, v. a. *to prepare*

Apresto, s. m. *preparation* [*ning*

Apresuracion, s. f. *haste-*

Apresuradamente, adver. *hastily*

Apresurado, da, a. *hasty || concise*

Apresuramiento, subs. m. *hastening*

Apresurar, v. a. *to hasten*

Apretadamente, ad. *closely; pressingly*

Apretaderas, subst. f. pl. *strings, ropes, etc. || urgent instances, etc.*

Apretadero, s. m. *a truss*

Apretadillo, lla, a. *a little pressed, etc.*

Apretado, da, adj. *mean-spirited || close-fisted*

Apretador, s. m. *presser || pavior || rammer || under waist coat || jumps || a woman's girdle || a press*

Apretadura, s. f. }
Apretamiento, s. m. } *pression*

Apretar, v. a. *to press; to squeeze || to pursue || to molest || to urge*

Apreton, s. m. V. Apretadura || *anguish || urgent necessity || a short swift race*

Apretura, s. f. *a narrow compass* || V. Apriete.

Apriesa, *ad. V.* Aprisa
Aprieto, *s. mas. streightness* || *throng* || *a pressing danger* or *circumstance* || *want; scarcity*
Aprimir, *v. act. V.* Comprimir
Aprisa, *ad. quickly*
Aprisar, *v. act. V.* Apresurar
Apriscadero, *subs. m. V.* Aprisco [*fold*
Aprisco, *s. mas. a sheep-*
Aprisionadamente, *adv. narrowly*
Aprisionado, da, *a. tied*
Aprisionar, *v. a. to imprison*
Aprobacion, *s. f. approbation* || *probation*
Aprobador, ra, *s. approver* [*prove*
Aprobar, *v. act. to ap-*
Aprobativo, va, *a. approving* [*ches*
Aproches, *s. m. pl. approa-*
Aprontar, *v. a. to make ready*
Apronto, *s. mas. a speedy preparation*
Apropiacion, *s. f. appropriation*
Apropiadamente, *ad. fitly*
Apropiar, *v. a. to invest with* || *to appropriate*
Apropiarse, *v. r. to appropriate to one's self*
Apropinquacion, *s. f. approach*
Apropinquarse, *v. rec. to come near* [piar
Apropriar, *v. a. V.* Apro-
Aprovechable, *adj. profitable*
Aprovechadamente, *adv. profitably* [*fisted*
Aprovechado, da, *a. close-*
Aprovechamiento, *s. mas. profit* || *progress*

Aprovechar, *v. n. to profit*
Aprovechar, *v. a. to put to good use*
Aprovecharse, *v. r. to get by a thing*
Aproximacion, *s. f. approximation*
Apsides, *s. m. pl. apsides*
Aptamente, *ad. aptly*
Aptitud, *s. f. aptness*
Apto, ta, *a. apt*
Apuesta, *s. f. a wager*
Apulgarar, *v. a. to press with the thumb*
Apuntacion, *sub. f. pointing; denoting; etc.* || *note*
Apuntador, *s. m. grinder* || *pointer* || *prompter*
Apuntalar, *v. a. to prop*
Apuntamiento, *s. m. annotation* || *a breviate* || *resolution* || *denoting* || *prompting* || *preparation*
Apuntar, *v. a. to point* || *to denote* or *appoint* || *to note* || *to abstrent* or *abridge* || *to sharpen* || || *to prompt* || *to peep. V.* Punctuar
Apuntarse, *v. r. to grow sour*
Apunte, *s. m. V.* Apuntamiento
Apunto, *s. m. prompting*
Apuñadar, } *a. to strike*
Apuñear, } *with the fist*
Apuñetear, *v. a. to beat with the fits*
Apuradamente, *ad. exactly* || *seasonably*
Apurado, da, *adj. poor* || *clear; manifest* || *excellent*
Apurador, *s. m. one that purifies, examines, etc.*
Apuramiento, *s. m. examination*

Apurar, *v. a. to p*
|| *to clear; to v*
|| *to consume; to*
haust
Apurar la paciencia
try a man's paci
— un hombre, *to pr*
man hard
Apurarse, *v. r. to b*
flicted
Apuro, *s. m. want;*
city || *affliction*
Apurrir, *v. a. to giv*
reach
Aquadrillar, *v. a. to*
duct a squadron of
diers
Aquario, *s. m. aqua*
Aquartelado, da, *ad*
quartered
Aquartelamiento, *s. n*
quartering || *quart*
Aquartelar, *v. a. to q*
ter soldiers
Aquartillar, *v. n. to l*
the houghs
Aquático, ca, } *a. a*
Aquatil, } *tic*
Aqüeducto, *s. m. aque*
Aquejar, *v. a. to gri*
to molest
Aquel, aquello, aqu
pron. that
A'qüeo, ea *adj. aqu*
Aquerenciarse, *v. r.*
light in a place
Aquese, sa, so, *pron.*
Aqueste, ta, to, *pron*
Aquí, *adv. here* || *n*
De aquí á tres d
three days hence
aquí ó ves aquí,
re is [*pli*
Aquiescencia, *s. f.*
Aquietar, *v. a. to q*
Aquila alba, *s. f.*
mate
Aquilatar, *v. a. to*
or try silver, etc

ullea, s. f. milfoil
ullifero, s. m. an ancient roman ensign
ailino, na, adj. Voy. guileño
uilon, s. m. north || north-wind
uilonal y Aquilonar, a. northern
iosidad, sub. f. wateriness
ioso, sa, adj. waterish
a, s. f. altar || altar-stone
bigo, ga, y Arábico, a, adj. arabian; arabick
ada, s. f. a ploughed field.
do, s. m. a plough
dor, s. m. a plougsan || a hand-worm.
dorcico, s. m. a little hand-worm
dura, s. f. tillage
mbel, s. m. an old-ragged-cloth
na, s. f. deceit; craft
ncel, s. m. a custom book; a book of rates
- rule, method
ndano, s. m. a wild service-tree
ndela, s. f. candlestick-socket || halfports in a ship
niego (gavilan), s. m. sparrow-hawk taken in net
nzada, s. f. an acre
ña, s. f. spidder || sea-dragon || a crab || a branched candlestick || the crow-feet of the tops
ñador, s. m. scratcher
ñamiento, s. m. scratching
ñar, v. a. to scratch
ñazo, s. m. aum. de raño

Araño, s. m. a scratch
Arañon, s. m. V. Endrina
Arañuela, s. f. a little spidder
Arañuelo, s. m. a net to catch birds in || a little spidder
Arar, v. a. to plough
Aratorio, ria, adj. belonging to the tillage
Arbelo, s. m. a kind of curvilineal figure
Arbitana, s. f. V. Albitana
Arbitrable, } adj. Voy. Arbitrario
Arbitradero, ra,
Arbitrador, s. m. arbitrator
Arbitrage, s. m. arbitrage
Arbitral, a. V. Arbitrario
Arbitramento, arbitrage
Arbitrar, v. a. to arbitrate || to act or decide arbitrarily || to imagine expedients, etc.
Arbitrariamente, adv. arbitrarily
Arbitrario, ria, y Arbitrativo, va, a. arbitrary || projector
Arbitreria, s. f. a troop of projectors
Arbitrio, s. m. free will || way; expedient || project
Arbitrios, plur. passage-penny
Arbitrista, s. m. projector
A'rbitro, s. m. arbiter; arbitrator
A'rbol, s. m. a tree || a mast || the body of a shirt, etc.
Arbolado, da, adj. full of trees
Arboladura, s. m. the mast of a ship
Arbolar, v. a. to mast a ship || to set upright

Arbolarse el caballo, to prance
Arbolazo, s. m. a great tree
Arbolecico, cillo, y Arbolcillo, s. m. a small tree; a shrub
Arboleda, s. f. a grove of trees
Arbolete, s. m. a lime-twig
Arbolista, s. m. dresser or planter of trees
Arbollon, s. m. dam; sluice
Arbóreo, rea, adj. belonging to the tree
Arbotante, s. m. buttress
Arbustillo, s. m. a small shrub
Arbusto, s. m. a shrub
Arca, s. f. a trunk; a chest || a tomb
Arca de agua, water-house — del pan, the belly — del testamento, the ark of the covenant — de Noé, Noah's ark
Arcas, plur. the king's coffers
Arcabucear, v. a. to shoot a gun or a soldier
Arcabucería, s. f. a body of musketeers || discharge of muskets || gun-smith's shop
Arcabucero, s. m. a musketeer || gun-smith
Arcabuco, s. m. a great thick wood of trees
Arcabuz, s. m. a musket
Arcabuzazo, s. m. a musket-shot
Arcacil, s. m. artichoke
Arcada, s. f. reaching to vomit || vault || arch
Arcador, s. m. Voy. Arqueador
Arcaduz, s. m. conduct for water; aqueduct, etc. || flatterer; pimp

Arcaduzar, *v. a. to conduct water by canals, etc.*
Arcaismo, *s. m. archaism*
Arcángel, *s. m. Archangel*
Arcanidad, *s. f.* } *a secret*
Arcano, *s. m.* }
Arcano, na, *adj. secret mysterious*
Arcar, *v. a. to beat wool*
Arcaz, *s. m. a great chest* || *coffin*
Arcaza, *s. f. V.* Arcon
Arce, *s. m. the maple-tree* || *tower in the field*
Arcedianato, *s. m. archdeaconship* || *archdeaconry*
Arcediano, *sub. m. archdeacon*
Archero, *s. m. archer* || *yeoman of the guard*
Archiducado, *s. m. Archdukedom*
Archiducal, *a. 2. belonging to the archduke, etc.*
Archiduque, esa, *s. Archduke, Archdutchess*
Archilaud, *s. m. a large lute*
Archimandrita, *s. m. a superior of religious men*
Archipiélago, *s. m. archipelago*
Archisinagogo, *s. m. chief of the synagogue*
Archivar, *v. a. to put*, or *keep in the archives*
Archivero, } *s. m. keeper of the records*
Archivista, }
Archivo, *s. m. archives*
Arcilla, *s. f. white clay*
Arcilloso, sa *adj. clayed*
Arciprestazgo, ó Arciprestadgo, *s. m. dignity of an archpriest*
Arcipreste, *s. m. archpriest*
Arco, s. m. an arch || *a brow*
Arcos, *pl. eye-brows*
Arcola, *s. f. a coarse canvass*
Arcon, *s. m. a great trunk* or *chest*
A'rctico, ca, *adj. arctick*
Arcuado, da, *adj. V.* Arqueado
Arda, *s. f. a squirrel*
Ardalear, *v. n. V.* Ralear
Ardentia, *s. f. ardor* || *light caused by the waves*
Arder, *v. n. to burn; to flame*
Ardid, *s. m. stratagem*
Ardido, da, *a. heated* or *burnt*
Ardiente, *a. hot; burning* || *ardent; vehement* || *eager; earnest*
Ardientemente, *adv. ardently*
Ardilla, *s. f. a squirrel*
Ardimiento, *s. m. boldness; courage*
Ardite, *s. m. an old brass coin worth three maravedies*
Ardor, *s. m. ardor*
Arduamente, *adv. difficultly*
Arduidad, *s. f. arduousness*
Arduo, dua, *a. arduous*
Area, *s. f. area*
Arena, *s. f. sand*
Arenas, *pl. gravel*
Arenal, *s. m. a sandy place*
Arenalejo, illo, *s. m. dim. de* Arenal
Arencon, *s. a great herring*
Arenga, *s. f. speech; oration* [*rangue*
Arengar, *v. n. to ha-*
Arenica, illa, *s. f. small sand*
Arenisco, ca, y Arenoso, sa, *adj. sandy*
Arenque, *s. m. herrin*
Areopagita, *s. m. ar pagite*
Areopago, *s. m. areopa*
Arestin, *s. m. scratch*
Arestinado, da, *a. affe with scratches*
Arfada, *s. f. pitching*
Arfar, *v. n. to pitch sond*
Arfil, *s. m. V.* Alfil
Argadillo, y Argadyso, *s a reel* || *a busy-body a great hamper*
Argado, *s. m. a shuff a trick*
Argalia, *s. f. V.* Alg
Argallera, *s. f. a hand-*
Argamandel, *s. m. a tat red rag*
Argamandijo, *s. m. h of bawbles, etc.*
Argamasa, *s. f. morta*
Argamasar, *v. a. to the mortar*
Argamason, *s. m. rubb*
Argamula, *s. f. share-w*
Argana, *s. f. V.* A'rg
Arganas, *pl. a sort panniers*
Arganel, *s. m. a lit brass ring* [*ri*
Arganeo, *s. m. anch*
Argano, *s. m. a cr (engine)*
Argel, *a. m. a horse w a white spot in his ri foot* [*the*
Argema, *s. f. a web*
Argemone, *s. m. a th ny-poppy*
Argen, *s. m. argent*
Argentado, da, *a. of clear sound*
Argentador, *s. m. one th silvers over*
Argentar, *v. a. to sil over* || to adorn w over

ría, s. f. embroi-
with gold or silver
[illegible]odina, s. f. sil-
ine
, s. m. silver
vivo, quick-silver
, s. f. V. Arcilla
, s. f. a great iron

ta, ica, ita, sub. f.
de Argolla
a, s. m. aum. de
a
a, s. f. a linden-tree
l, s. m. a grove of
n-trees
re, s. f. the ship
; constellation.
itas, s. m. pl. Ar-
uts
aque, s. m. [illegible]
oniack
a, s. f. quirk; cavil
s. m. a capstan
lar, v. a. to lessen
arse, v. r. to grow

lo, s. m. leanness;
ying
ias, s. f. pl. Voy.
illas
, v. n. to argue
a. V. A'rgoma
entacion, s. f. ar-
g || argument
entador, s. m. ar-

entar, v. n. Voy.
r
ento, s. m. argu-
t
entoso, sa, a. in-
ous; diligent
s. f. arietta
, s. f. aridity
, da, adj. arid;
en
s. m. aries
, s. f. arietta

Ariete, s. m. batteringram
Arija s. f. V. Harija
Arija (tierra), s. f. ligth land
Arillo, s. m. a little ring
Arillos, pl. ear-rings
Arimez, s. m. a projecture; a leaning out
Arisaro, s. m. an herb so called
Arisco, ca, a. wild; savage; fierce
Arisnegro, } s. f. buck-
Arisprietro, } wheat
Arista, s. f. the beard of the ear of corn
Aristarco, s. m. a severe critick
Aristino, s. m. V. Arestin
Aristocracia, s. f. aristócracy
Aristocratico, ca, a. aristocratical
Aristoloquía, s. f. hart-wort
Aristosa (espiga), a very bearded ear of corn
Aristotélico, ca, a. belonging to aristotle
Aritmética, s. f. arithmetick
Aritmético, s. m. arithmetician
Arithmético, ca, a. arithmetical
Arlequin, s. m. harlequin
Arlequinillo, s. m. a little harlequin
Arlo, s. m. a shrub used to dye the hair yellow
Arlota, s. f. tow of flax
Arma, s. f. weapon; arm
Arma arrojadiza, dart, arrow, etc. — do fuego, fire-arms — falsa, a false alarm
Armas, pl. arms; army || coat of arms
Armacion, s. f. a sort of military tune

Armada, s. f. armada fleet
Armadía, s. f. a raft
Armadijo, s. m. a snare; a pit fall, etc.
Armadillo, s. m. a sort of scaly lizard
Armador, s. m. a privateer
Armadura, s. f. armour || bed-stead, etc. || skeleton
Armamento, s. m. armament
Armandijo, sub. m. Voy. Armadijo
Armar, v. a. y n. to arm
Armar á los paxaros, to let snares for birds — navíos, to equip ships — una ballesta, to bend a cross-bow — una casa, to set up the wooden frame of a house — en el jugo, to cheat at play — un lazo, to lay a snare — una cama, to set up a bed-stead
Armario, s. m. cup-board || chest of drawers
Armatoste, s. m. a coarse massive work
Armazon, s. f. arming or equipping || any frame work || bed-stead
Armella, s. f the staple of a lock, etc.
Armelluela, s. f. dim. de armella
Armería, s. f. armoury
Armero, s. m. armourer
Armígero, ra, a. martial
Armilla, s. f. torus
Armiñado, da, a. ermined
Armiño, s. m. ermine
A'rmipotente, a. powerful in arms
Armisticio, s. m. armistice
Armonía, s. f. harmony
Armoniaco, s. m. gum ammoniack

Armónico, ca, *adj. harmonious*
Armuelle, *s. m. orache*
Arna, *s. f. V.* Colmena
Arnes, *s. m. armour*
Arneses, *pl. implements for hunting, fishing, etc.*
Arnilla, *s. f. dim. de* Arna
Aro, *s m. a hoop*
Aroca, *s. f. a web of fine texture* [aromo
Aroma, *s. f. flower of the*
Aroma, *s. m. aroma*
Aromaticidad, *s. f. aromatical perfume*
Aromático, ca, *adj. aromatical*
Aromatizar, *v. a. to spice*
Aromo, *s. m. a spice-tree*
Aroza, *s. m. the chief among the black smiths*
Arpa, *s. f. harp* || *claw; clutch* || *hook; grapling*
Arpador, *s. m. harper*
Arpar, *v. a. to tear* || *to scratch*
Arpella, *s. f. a sort of sparrow-hawk*
Arpía, *subs. f. harpy* || *a shrew* [cloth
Aapillera, *s. f. packing-*
Arpista, *s. m. harper*
Arpon, *s. m. harpoon*
Arqueada, *s. f. the playing on a violin with the bow*
Arqueador, *s. m. one who beats wool with a bow*
Arqueage, *s. mas. V.* Arqueo
Arqueamiento, *s. m. gauging of a ship*
Arquear, *v. a. to bow; to arch* || *to beat wool with a bow* || *to gauge a ship*
Arquear las cejas, *to frown*
Arqueo, s. m. bowing || *gauging of a ship*

Arqueria, *subs. f. arched work*
Arquero, *s. m. a bow-maker* || *a hoop maker* || *a chest-maker* || *a cashier*
Arqueta, *subs. f. a small chest* [chest
Arqueton, *s. m. a great*
Arquetoncillo, *s. m. a very little chest*
Arquibanco, *s. m. a bench with chests* or *drawers*
Arquiepiscopal, *V.* Arzobispal [bow
Arquillo, *s. mas. a little*
Arquimesa, *s. f. a burse*
Arquitecto, *subs. m. architect*
Arquitectónico, ca, *adj. architectonick*
Arquitectura, *s. f. architecture* [trave
Arquitrabe, *s. m. archi-*
Arrabal, *s. m. suburb*
Arracada, *s. f. ear-bob*
Arracadilla, *s. f. dim. de* Arracada [recife
Arracife, *s. m. Voy.* Ar-
Arracimar, *v. a. to heap up like grapes*
Arraez, *s. m. master of a moorish ship*
Arramblar, *v. a. to gravel over*
Arranca, *s. f. grubbing up*
Arrancada (boga) *a strong hasty rowing*
Arrancadero, *s. m. the breech of a gun*
Arrancador, ra, *one that roots hup*
Arrancar, *v. a. to grub up; to root up* || *to pull, or draw* || *to take away by force* || *to hawk up phlegm* || *to start for a race* || *to fly out on a sudden*
Arrancasiega, *s. f.* the roo-

ting up corn, oats, etc.
Arrancharse, *v. r. to lodge together*
Arranciarse, *v. r. V.* Enranciarse
Arranque, *s. m. pulling out; rooting out* || *impetuous motion*
Arrapar, *v. a. Voy.* Arrebatar
Arrapiezo y Arrapo, *s. m. rag; tatter*
Arras, *s. f. pl. earnest* || *jointure* [sad-
Arrasadura, *s. f. Voy.* Ra-
Arrasar, *v. a. to smooth or level* || *to raze* || *to beggar* || *to fill to the brim* || *V.* Rasar
Arrasar *v. n. y* Arrasarse *v. r. to clear up*
Arrastradamente, *adv. imperfectly* || *painfully* || *unluckily*
Arrastrado, da, *a. painful; unhappy*
Arrastramiento, *s. m. drawing; dragging*
Arrastrar, *v. a. to draw, to drag along* || *to tire, to molest* || *to trump*
Arrastre, *s. m. trumping at cards*
Arraxaque, *s. m. V.* Arrexeque [tre
Arrayan, *s. m. a myrtle*
Arrayanal, *s. m. a myrtle grove*
Arraygar, *v. n. to take* or *strike root*
Arraygarse, *v. r. to settle somewhere*
Arraygo, *s. m. immoveable goods*
Arre, *word used to make horses go* [horse
Arrear, *v. a. to hasten*
Arrebañadura, *sub. f. raking; scraping*

a. to rake ;
te, *ad. pre-*
, *a. rapid ;*
ada, *a sud-*
iombre ar-
hasty pas-
;
a, *s. ravis-*
, *s. m. a*
ness ; pas-
a. to sna-
away vio-
atch sud-
ttract
. *r. to fly*
on || *to be*
it || *to be*
dried with
f. a cat-
atching ||
r *scram-*
V. Rebato
redness of
red paint
. *to redden*
r. to paint
[*of paint*
a little box
f. swarm
to ice com-
r. V. Em-
warm
V. Emboso
te, *a. con-*
. *to mix ,*
confusedly
. *to muffle*
a thorny

Arreciar, *v. n. to grow* or *increase*

Arreciarse, *v. r. to recover one's health*

Arrecife, *s. m. a causeway* || *a rock ; sand*

Arrecirse, *v. r. to grow stiff*

Arredondear, *v. a. V.* Redondear

Arredramiento, *s. m. putting* or *removing back*

Arredrar, *v. a. to put , force* or *drive back* || *to intimidate*

Arredro, *adv. behind*

Arregazada (nariz), *s. f. a nose that turns up*

Arregazarse, *v. r. to tuck up one's coats*

Arreglar, *v. a. to regulate*

Arregostarse, *v. r. to delight in...*

Arrejacar, *v. a. to roll the ground to cover the seed*

Arrejada, *s. f. the plough-staff*

Arrelde, *sub. m. a four pound weight*

Arrellanarse, *v. r. to sit down at one's full ease*

Arremangado de nariz, *a. who has a nose that turns up*

Arremangar, *v. a. to tuck up the sleeves, etc.* || *to rob*

Arremango, *s. m. tucking up of sleeves* || *folding in*

Arremedador, ra, *s. imitator, trix* [*lant*

Arremetedor, *s. m. assai-*

Arremeter, *v. a. to attack; to assault* || *to offend the eye* || *to put on a horse* [*dle in*

Arremeterse, *v. r. to med-*

Arremetida, *s. f. assault ; attack* || *gallop*

Arremolinarse, *v. r. V.* Remolinarse

Arrempujar, *v. a. V.* Empujar [maco

Arremueco, *s. m. V.* Arru-

Arrendable, *a. a. rentable*

Arrendadero, *s. m. an iron hook* or *ring*

Arrendador (caballo), *s. m. a docile horse*

Arrendador, *s. m. farmer* || *V.* Arrendadero

Arrendadorcillo, *s. m. a little farmer*

Arrendajo, *s. m. a mocking bird — a mimick person*

Arrendamiento, *s. m. renting out ; lease, etc.*

Arrentar, *v. a. to let out ; to rent* || *to tie by the bridle* || *to mimick ; to ape*

Arrendatario, *s. m. farmer*

Arreo, *s. m. ornament ; dress* || *horse-trappings*

Arreos, *pl. accessories*

Arreo, *adv. successively* || *upon a man's back*

Arrepápalo, *s. m. a kind of fritter*

Arrepasar, *v. n. to pass and repass*

Arrepentidas, *s. f. pl. the penitent nuns*

Arrepentimiento, *s. m. repentance*

Arrepentirse, *v. r. to repent*

Arrepistar, *v. a. to grind* or *pound again*

Arrepisto, *s. m. a second grinding*

Arrepticio, cia, *a. possessed with the devil*

Arrequife, *s. m. a little iron point*

Arrequives, *s. m. pl. dress, furnitures, etc.*

Arrestado, da, *a. bold*

Arrostar, *v. a. to arrest*

Arrestarse, *v. r. to be bold or enterprizing*

Arresto, *s. m. arrest* || *boldness*

Arrexaco, Arrexaque, } *s. m. a trident* || *a martlet*

Arrezafe, *s. m. a place full of briars*

Arriano, na, *a. y s. arian*

Arriar, *v. a. to strike (sea-term)*

Arriate, *s. m. y* Arriata, *s. f. border for flovers* || *causeway*

Arriba, *adv. above* || *heretofore*

Arribada, *s. f.* Arribage, *s. m.* } *arrival*

Arribar, *v. n. to land* || *to arrive* || *to recover one's health, etc.*

Arribo, *s. m. V.* Llegada

Arricises, *s. m. a stirrup-leather*

Arriedro, *adv. behind*

Arriendo, *s. m. V.* Arrendamiento

Arriería, *s. f. the office of a muleteer*

Arrierico, llo, to, *s. m. a sorry muleteer*

Arriero, *s. m. muleteer*

Arriesgadamente, *ad. hazardously*

Arriesgado, da, *a. dangerous* || *bold, daring*

Arriesgar, *v. a. to hazard; to venture*

Arrimadero, *s. m. a leaning-place*

Arrimadillo, *s. m. mat, etc. to cover the walls with*

Arrimadizo, za, *adj. fit to be applyed* || *parasite; flatterer, etc.*

Arrimado ó arrimados (tener), *to be possessed by the devil* [*ching*

Arrimadura, *s. f. approa-*

Arrimar, *v. act. to approach; to draw near* || *to give over; to abandon*

Arrimar á uno, *to turn out of a place* — el clavo, *to nail up* — las espuelas, *to clap spurs to a horse* — un delito, *to add one crime more*

Arrimarse, *v. r. to lean; to rest*

Arrimo, *s. m. a leaning staff*, or *wall, etc.* || *protection* || *support; prop* || *a new accusation* || *approaching*

Arrinconar, *v. a. to thrust into a a corner* || *to depose, etc.*

Arrinconarse, *v. r. to live in private*

Arriscadamente, *ad. boldly* [*audacious*

Arriscado, da, *adj bold;*

Arriscador, *s. m. one that gathers olives*

Arriscarse, *v. r. to swell; to grow proud*

Arritranca, *s. f. Voy.* Retranca

Arrizar, *v. a. to reeve* || *to fasten the anchor, etc.* || *to tie*

Arroba, *s. f. a twenty-five pounds weight* || (*in liquid,*) *about twelve english quarts*

Arrobadizo, za, *adj. who counterfeits extasy*

Arrobamiento, *s. m. extasy; rapture*

Arrobarse, *v. r. to fall in to an extasy* || *to be in rapture*

Arrobita, *s. f. dim* roba

Arrobo, *s. m. V.*

Arrocero, *s. m. ri*

Arrocinado (caball *ry horse*

Arrocinarse, *v.* *come brutish*

Arrodelarse, *v. r.* *one's self with c*

Arrodillamiento, Arrodilladura, *ling*

Arrodillar, *v. n.* dillarse, *v. r.*

Arrodrigonar, *v.* *a vine*

Arrogacion, *s. f. t* *arrogating* ||

Arrogador, *s. m.* *arrogates*

Arrogancia, *s. f.*

Arrogante, *a. a.* || *couragious*

Arrogantemente, *rogantly*

Rrrogarse, *v. r.* *gate*

Arrojadamente,

Arrojadizo, za, || *V.* Arrojado

Arrojado, da, *a. l* *dacious*

Arrojar, *v. a. to* *throw* || *to ve* *shoot* or *bud*

Arrojarse, *v.* *one's self vic*

Arrojo, *s. m. l* *audacity*

Arrolar, *v. a. to* *root* or *defea*

Arromadizar, *v* *se a cold*

Arromadizarse *catch cold*

Arromanzar, *v.* *late into spa* *gue*

v. a. to blunt
. a. to grub up
.m. new plan-
nto, *s. m. grub*
. n. to weigh
r
o, *s. m. clo-*
act. to clothe
. must
noras, *sirup*
ries
f. irons; fet-
. a. to allow;
o face
v. r. to face
. to overflow
. r. to divide
small chan-
e mildewed
b. m. a little
. brook
s. m. a little
. rice
n. a rice-field
a. to congeal
n. to grunt
, s. f. sheer of
ecks
, da, *a. tuc-*
a. to bend
, da, *adj. ruf-*
f. a wrinkle ||
to, *sub. m. a*
g
. a. to wrinkle
it or fold
rente, *to frown*
v. r. to die

L E INGLES,

Arrugia, *s. f. a very deep gold-mine*
Arruinamiento, *s. m. ruin*
Arruinar, *v. a. to ruin; to destroy*
Arrullador, ra, *s. a flatterer*
Arrullar, *v. a. to rock; to lull* || *to coo*
Arrullarse, *v. r. to fall asleep* || *to project a secret attempt*
Arrullo, *sub. m. cooing* || *lulling*
Arrumaco, *s. m. kindness; fair words, etc.*
Arrumage, *s. m. stowing*
Arrumar, *v. a. to stow*
Arrumazon, *s. m. stowing* || *the gathering of clouds in the horizon*
Arrumbadas, *s. f. pl. two platforms in the fore part of a galley*
Arrumbar, *v. a. to lay aside* || *to convince; to confound — to decant*
Arrumbarse, *v. r. to stand on the course*
Arrumblar, *v. a. V.* Arramblar
Arrumucco, *s. m. V.* Arrumaco
Arsenal, *s. m. dock-yard*
Arsenical, *a. 2. arsenical*
Arsénico, *s. m. arsenick*
Artalejo y Artalete, *s. m. a little tart*, or *pye*
Arte, *s. m. y f. art*
De arte, *ad. so that*
Artecillo, *s. m. a mean art*
Artefacto, *sub. m. work made with art*
Artejo, *s. m. a joint of the finger* [*f. mugwort*
Artemisa, ó Artemisia, *s.*
Artemon, *s. m. mizen-mast*

Arteria, *s. f. artery*
A'spera arteria, *the tracheal artery*
Arterial, *a. arterial*
Arteriola, *sub. f. a little artery*
Arterioso, sa, *a. arterial*
Arteriotomía, *s. f. arteriotomy*
Artesa, *s. f. a trough* || *a canoe*
Artesano, *s. m. artisan*
Artesilla, *subs. f. a little trough*
Arteson, *s. m. a sink to wash dishes in* || *ceiling*
Artesonado, da, *a. ceiled*
Artesoncillo, *s. m. a little sink* [*trough*
Artesuela, *sub. f. a little*
Artética, *s. f. the articular disease*
Artético, ca, *a. gouty*
A'rtico, ca, *a. V.* A'rctico
Articulacion, *s. f. articulation* || *an articulate pronunciation*
Articular, *v. a. to articulate*
Articular, *a. 2. articular*
Articulo, *sub. m. article* || *joint*
Artífico, *s. m. artificer* || *artist* || *forger* or *contriver*
Artificial, *a. artificial*
Artificialmente, *adv. artfully*
Artificiar, *v. a. to make with art*
Artificio, *s. m. art; industry* || *artifice; craft*
Artificiosamente, *ad. artfully* || *craftily*
Artificioso, sa, *a. artful* || *crafty* [*hed land*
Artiga, *s. f. new plough-*
Artillar, *v. a. to furnish with artillery*

D

Artillería, *s. f. artillery ; ordnance*
Artillero, *s. m. matross ; gunner*
Artimaña, *sub. f. snare ; net, etc.* || *craft; deceit*
Artista, *s. m. artist* || *one that studies the arts*
Artizado, da, *a. learned in some art*
Artrodía, *s. f. a kind of articulation*
Arula, *s. f. a little altar*
Aruñar, *v. a. to scratch*
Aruñon, *s. m. scratcher* || *a cut-purse*
Arúspice, *s. m. a soothsayer*
Aruspiciua, *s. f. divination by bowels of beasts*
Arveja, *s. f. vetch*
Arvejal, *s. m. a place sowed with vetches*
Arvejon, *sub. m. a great vetch*
Arvela, *s. f. king's-fisher (bird)*
Arytena, *s. f. larynx*
Arza, *s. f. a great rope wich serves to heave goods into the ships*
Arzobispado, *s. m. archbishoprick*
Arzobispal, *adj.* 2. *archiepiscopal* [*hop*
Arzobispo, *s. m. archbis-*
Arzolla, *s. f. a green almond*
Arzon, *s. m. saddle-bow*
As, *s. m. ace*
Asa, *s. f. ear* or *handle* || *benjamin*
Asa fetida, *devils's dung*
Asabiendas, *ad. knowingly ; purposely*
Asacion, *s. f. roasting*
Asadero, ra, *adj. fit to be roasted*
Asado, *s. m. roast meat*
Asador, *s. m. a spit* || *a jack*
Asadorazo, *s. m. a blow with a spit* [*spit*
Asadorcillo, *s. m. a little*
Asadura, *sub. f. pluck* || *a duty upon beasts*
Asadurilla, *sub. f. a little pluck* [*man*
Asaetcador, *s. m. a bow-*
Asaetear, *v. act. to shoot with arrows*
Asalariar, *v. a. to allow a salary* or *wages*
Asaltador, *s. m. assaulter* || *highway man*
Asaltar, *v. a. to assault ; to storm*
Asalto, *sub. m. assault ; attack* [|| *a call*
Asamblea, *s. f. assembly*
Asar, *v. a. to roast*
Asarabácara, *s. f. asarabacca* [*like*
Asargado, da, *adj. serge-*
A'saro, *s. m. asarabacca*
Asbestino, na, *a. asbestine*
Asbesto, *s. m. asbestos*
Ascalonia, *s. f. eschalot*
Ascendencia, *s. f. ancestry* [*dant*
Ascendente, *s. m. ascen-*
Ascender, *v. n. to ascend*
Ascendiente, *s. m. ascending* || *ascendant*
Ascension, *s. f. ascension*
Ascensional, *a.* 2. *ascensional*
Ascenso, *s. m. rise ; advancement*
Ascético, ca, *a. ascetick*
Ascios, *s. m. pl. ascii*
Asciro, *sub. m. St. John's wort* [*piad*
Asclepiadeo, *s. m. ascle-*
Asco, *s. m. loathing*
Ascondido (en), *adv. secretly*
Ascua, *s. f. live coal*
Aseadamente, *adv. nea[tly] ; finely*
Aseado, da, *adj. work[ed] artfully ; finely*
Asear, *v. a. to adorn ;* [...] *compose neatly*
Asechamionto, *subst* [...] *snares*
Asecla, *s. m. a page,* [...] *lacquey* [...]
Asecucion, *s. f. asse*[...]
Asedado, da, *a. silk*[...] *soft*
Asedar, *v. act. to ma*[...] *like silk*
Asediar, *v. a. to besieg*[...]
Asedio, *s. m. siege*
Aseglarado, da, *a. laym*[...] *like*
Asegundar, *v. a. to re*[...] *rate* [...]
Aseguracion, *s. f.* [...]
Aseguradamente, *adv.* [...] *suredly*
Asegurador, *s. m.* [...] *rer ; insurer*
Asegúramiento, *s. m.* [...] *surance* || *insurance*
Asegurar, *v. a. to ass*[...] || *to secure* || *to insu*[...]
Asemejar, *v. a. to lik*[...] || *to copy* or *imitate*
Asemejarse, *v. r. to* [...] *semble*
Asendereado (camino), [...] *beaten road*
Asenderear, *v. a. to* [...] *a path* || *to* [...] *through paths*
Asengladnra, *s. f. V.* [...] gladura
Asenso, *sub. m. asse*[...] *consent*
Asentada (de una), [...] *all at once* [*butto*[...]
Asentaderas, *s. f. pl.* [...]
Asentadillas (cabalgar á) [...] to ride sitting

m. brick-
arter-mas-
f. } settling
s. } || con-
tract
to set ; to
esuppose ||
confirm ||
| to annote
, to encamp
to lay sto-
ro , to book-
mano , ó el
chastise or
el licor , to
aza , to list
r a soldier
to suit ; to
ttle
uclillas , to
hams
to assent ;
m. an un-
contractor
us , etc.
eatness
2. that may
l
assertion
s. m. saw-
a , adj. fit to
m. sawyer
.f. sawing
, pl. saw-
. to saw
, a. assertive
assertion
to grow wise
a. to mur-
till treache-
. m. an as-
n. assassin

Asesor , s. m. *assessor*
Asesor , ra , s. *counsellor*
Asesorarse , v. r. *to take an assessor*
Asesoría , s f. *the assessor's office*
Asestadura , s. f. *aiming*
Asestar , v. a. *to aim ; to point* [*ration*
Aseveracion , s. f. *asseveration*
Aseveradamente , adv. *affirmatively*
Aseverar , v. a. *to affirm*
Así , adv. *so*
Asidero , s. m. } *ear ; handle || occasion ; opportunity*
Asidilla , s. f. }
Asido , da , a. *knit ; addicted*
Asiduo , dua , a. *assiduous*
Asiento , s. m. *seat || sitting ; place || situation || foot of a table , etc. || bottom ; ground || sediment ; dregs || contract lease , etc. || annotation*
Asientos , pl. *pearls that are flat on one side || wrist-bands , etc. || the bit*
Asiento de estómago , *surfeit* — de los pies , *the soles* — de paz , *treaty of peace* — de molino , ó de atahona , *a mill-stone*
Asignable , a. 2. *assignable* [*ment*
Asignacion , s. f. *assign-*
Asignar , v. a. *to assign*
Asignatura , s. f. *notice , or bill of any treatise to be read by a professor*
Asilla , s. f. *a little handle || a light pretext*
Asillas , pl. *the collar-bones* [*shelter*
Asilo , subs. m. *asylum ;*

Asimesmo , adv. V. Asimismo
Asimiento , s. m. *catching — proneness ; inclination* [*ble*
Asimilar , v. n. *to resem-*
Asimilativo , va , adj. *that makes like*
Asimismo , adv. *likewise*
Asimplado , da , a. *simple ; silly*
Asimptotos , s. f. pl. *asymptotes*
Asinino , na , a. *belonging to an ass*
Asir , v. a. *to catch ; to lay hold of*
Asir , v. n. *to take root*
Asirse , v. r. *to have high words together*
Asistencia , s. f. *presence || assistance*
Asistencias , pl. *alimony*
Asistenta , s. f. *wife of the Governor || a maid servant* [|| *assistant*
Asistente , s. m. *Governor*
Asistir , v. n. *to assist || to haunt*
Asistir , v. a. *to assist ; to help || to protect || to have a patient under one's hands*
Asma , s. m. *asthma*
Asmático , ca , a. *asthmatick*
Asna , s. f. *she ass*
Asnas , pl *rafters ; joists*
Asnado , s. m. *a prop in the mines* [*an ass*
Asnal , a. 2. *belonging to*
Medias asnales , *coarse stockings*
Asnalmente , adv. *ass like*
Asnazo , subs. m. *a great ass* [*asses*
Asnería , s. f. *a drove of*
Asnero , s. m. *ass-driver*
Asnico , illo , s. m. *ass-colt*

Asnilla, s. f. *a kind of prop*
Asnino, a. *belonging to an ass*
Asno, s. m. *an ass*
Asobarcado, s. m. *street-porter*
Asobarcar, v. a. *to lift up a weight*
Asocarronado, da, adj. *crafty*
Asociacion, s. f. *association*
Asociado, s. m. *partner*
Asociar, v. a. *to associate*
Asolacion, s. f. V. Desolacion
Asolador, ra, s. *destroyer*
Asolamiento, s. m. *waste; ravage*
Asolanar, v. a *to spoil with easterly wind*
Asolar, v. a. *to ravage; to destroy*
Asolarse, v. r. *to settle*
Asolear, v. a. *to sun*
Asolearse, v. r. *to be sunburnt*
Asolvamiento, sub. m. *a being choaked up*
Asolvarse, v. r. *to be choaked up* [*pearance*
Asomada, s. f. *a short ap-*
Asomado, da, a. *drunkish*
Asomar, v. n. *to peep*
Asomar, v. a. *to shew; to let see*
Asomarse, v. r. *to look out at window, etc.* || *to make one's self drunk*
Asombradizo (caballo), s. m. *a starting horse*
Asombrador, s. m. *one that frights others*
Asombrar, v. a. *to fright* || *to astonish* || *to shadow*
Asombro, s. m. *fright* || *amazement* || *prodigy*

Asombroso, sa, a. *amazing*
Asomo, s. m. *mark; sign* || *suspicion*, or *conjecture*
Asonancia, s. f. *assonance*
Asonantar, v. a. *to make assonant verses*
Asonante, a. *assonant*
Asonar, v. n. *to sound like*
Aspa, s. f. *St. Andrew's cross* || *spindle*
Aspas de molino, *the sweeps of a windmill*
Aspalato, s. m. *aspalathus*
Aspamiento, s. m. V. Aspaviento
Aspar, v. a. *to reel* || *to tie on a St. Andrew's cross* || *to plague; to molest*
Aspaviento, s. m. *fright; amazement*
Aspavientos, pl. *braggings*
Aspecto, s. m. *aspect*
A'speramente, adv. *harshly; severely*
Asperear, v. n. *to be sharp*
Asperete, s. m. V. Asperillo
Aspereza, s. f. *asperity; sharpness*
Asperges, s. m. *aspersion*
Asperiega, s. f. *an apple of a sourish taste*
Asperillo, s. m. *a sourish taste*
A'spero, s. m. *a coin used in the levant*
A'spero, ra, adj. *harsh; sharp.* || *rugged; uneven* || *rough; austere*
Asperon, s. m. *whetstone*
Aspersion, s. f. *aspersion*
Aspersorio, s. m. *holy water stick*
Asphalto, s. m. *asphaltos*
A'spid, s. m. *aspick*
Aspiracion, s. f. *aspiration* || *a minim, in musick*

Aspiradamente, adv. *a*
aspiration
Aspirar, v. a. *to d*
breath || *to aspirat*
to aspire to...
Asquear, v. a. *to loa*
to nauseate
Asquerosamente, adv.
thily [
Asquerosidad, s. f. *fil*
Asqueroso, sa, a. *lo*
some || *loathing* ||
dainfull
Asta, s. f. *the staff*
lame, etc. || *a pike* ||
branch of a stag's h
Astas, pl. *a bull's hor*
Astaco, s. m. *a kind*
crab-fish
Asterisco, s. m. *asteri*
Asterismo, s. m. *aster*
A'stil, s. m. *handle o*
axe, etc. || *staff of a*
velin, etc. || *beam*
balance
Astilla, s. f. *a chip*
Astillar, v. a. *to chip*
Astillazo, s. m. *a blo*
wound with a chip
Astillejos, s. m. pl. *or*
Astillero, s. m. *a rac*
place arms on || *doc*
Astrágalo, s. m. *astrag*
Astral, a. 2. *astral*
Astriccion, s. f. *astrict*
Astringente, a. *astrin*
Astringir, v. a. *to astr*
Astro, s. m. *star* || *co*
tellation
Astrolabio, s. m. *cr*
staff
Astrología, s. f. *astrol*
Astrológico, ca, a. *as*
logical
Astrologo, s. m. *astrolo*
Astronomía, s. f. *astrono*
Astronómico, ca, a. *as*
nomical [
Astrónomo, s. m. *astro*

trosamente, ad. *loathsomely* [*poor* || *unlucky*
troso, sa, a. *loathsome;*
tucia, s. f. *wile*
urion, s. m. *a fit*
utamente, ad. *craftily*
uto, ta, a. *crafty; cunning*
biar, v. n. *to shelter one's self against the rain*
eto, s. m. *play-day*
lcar, v. a. V. Surcar
mirse, v. r. *to arrogate*
mcion, s. f. *raising; advancing* || *assumption* [*ject*
nto, s. m. *matter; subject*
ramiento, s. m. *burning* [*parch*
rarse, v. r. *to burn; to parch*
rcar, v. a. *to furrow*
star, v. a. *to frighten*
bacado, da, a. *snuff coloured* [*drum*
bal, s. m. *a kettle-drum*
balear, v. n. *to make a clattering with the feet*
balejo, illo, s. m. *a little kettle-drum*
balero, ra, s. *kettle-drummer*
banado (caballo), *a bee-bitten horse*
bardillado, da, a. *belonging to the spotted fever*
be, s. m. *vent-hole*
blar, v. a. *to harrow*
cado, da, a. *irresolute* || *pusillanimous* || *niggardly*
mbre de calzas atacadas, *a man of the old stamp*
cador, s. m. *assailant* || *troublesome man* || *a ...ce* || *cannon-rammer*
adura, s. f. y Atacamiento, s. m. *lacing; tying*

Atacar, v. a. *to lace; to tie up* || *to ram in* || *to attack* || *to teaze*
Ataderas, s. f. pl. *garters*
Atadero, s. m. *string; tie; bond, etc.*
Atadijo, s. m. *a little-bundle*
Atadito, ta, a. *tied genteely*
Atado, s. m. *bundle*
Atado, da, a. *tied* || *pusillanimous*
Atador, s. m. *reaper who ties the sheaves*
Atadura s. f. *tying* || *union*
Ataduras, pl. *ligaments*
Atafagar, v. a. *to stun* || *to tire* or *teaze* [*like*
Atafetanado, da, a. *taffety-like*
Ataharre, s. m. *crupper*
Atahorma, s. f. *ospray*
Atairar, v. a. *to adorn with mouldings*
Ataire, s. m. *moulding*
Atajadizo, s. m. *partition* || *lodge*
Atajador, s. m. *one that stops other's way*
Atajar, v. n. *to take the shortest way*
Atajar, v. a. *to stop one's way* || *to straiten with a partition*
Atajar la tierra, *to scour the country* — el enemigo, *to cut off an enemis retreat* — ganado *to drive away cattle* — pleyto, *to withdraw one's plea* — razones, *to make few words*
Atajarse, v. r. *to be at a stand; to be mum*
Atajo, s. m. *a short path* || *stop in the way* || *portion of cattle* || *parrying*
Atalantar, v. a. V. Aturdir

Atalantar, v. n. *to please*
Atalaya, s. f. *a watch-tower*
Atalaya, s. m. a. *centinel*
Atalayador, ra, s. *centinel, spy, etc.*
Atalayar, v. a. *to be upon the watch*
Atanasia, s. f. *tansy*
Atancar, v. a. *to press*, or *squeeze*
Atancarse, v. r. *to be at a stand*
Atanquia, s. f. *depilatory* || *a gross sort of silk*
Atañer, v. imp. *to belong*
Ataque, s. m. *attack* || *fit of a disease*
Ataquiza, s. f. *a planting of new vines*
Ataquizar, v. a. *to plant new vines*
Atar, v. a. *to tie* || *to make a coherent discourse* || *to stop*
Atarse, v. r. *to confine one's self* || *to be beside one's self*
Ataracea, Ataracear, V. Taracea, etc.
Atarantado, da, a. *bitten by the tarantula*
Atarazana, s. f. *dock; arsenal* || *a rope-yard* || *wine-cellar* [*tear*
Atarazar, v. a. *to bite-to tear*
Atarear, v. a. *to set a task*
Atarquinar, v. a. *to dirt*
Atarragar, v. a. *to fit shoes on the horse*
Atarrajar, v. a. *to work a screw*
Atarugamiento, s. m. *wedging*
Atarugar, v. a. *to wedge* || *to peg* || *to bung* || *to confound*, or *puzzle*
Atarxéa, s. f. *a case of bricks* || *canal*

Atasajado, da, *a. lying on a horse* [*pieces*
Atasajar, *v. a. to cut in*
Atascadero, *s. m. a marshy place* || *obstacle*
Atascar, *v. a. to stop; to calk* || *to hinder*
Atascarse, *v. r. to be mired* or *choked* || *to be at a stand*
Ataud, *s. m. a coffin*
Ataudado, da, *a. coffin like* [*work*
Atauxía, *s. f. damask-*
Atauxiado, da, *a. damasked*
Ataviar, *v. a. to adorn*
Atavillar, *v. a. to unline*
Atavío, *s. m. ornament; dress*
Ataxia, *s. f. V.* Ataxy
Atediarse, *v. r. to grow cool*
Ateismo, *s. m. atheism*
Ateista, *s. m. atheist*
Atemorizar, *v. a. to intimidate*
Atemperar, *v. a. to temper; to moderate*
Atenacear, } *v. a. to tear*
Atenazar, } *off the flesh with red hot pincers*
Atencion, *s. f. attention* || *regard; respect*
Atender, *v. n. to attend* || *to consider* or *regard*
Atenerse, *v. r. to stick to one, etc.*
Atentado, *s. m. outrage; incrouchment*
Atentado, da, *a. prudent — made without noise*
Atentamente, *adv. attentively* || *respectfully*
Atentar, *v. a. to attempt* || *to grope*
Atentarse, *v. rec. to do things with deliberation, etc.*

Atento, ta, *a. attentive* || *polite*
Atento, *prep. considering*
Atenuacion, *s. f. attenuation*
Atenuar, *v. a. to attenuate*
Ateo, *s. m. V.* Ateista
Atercianado, da, *a. troubled with a tercian day ague*
Aterciopeledo, da, *a. velvet; velvet-like*
Aterillado, da, *a. broken to pieces* [*ness*
Aterimiento, *s. m. numb-*
Aterirse, *v. r. to grow stiff*
Aterramiento, *s. m. pulling down* || *consternation*
Aterrar, *v. act. to pull dow* || *to dismay; affright, etc.*
Aterrarse, *v. r. to come near the land; to land-fall*
Aterronarse, *v. r. to clod*
Aterrorizar, *v. a. to frighten*
Atesar, *v. a. to harden* || *to stretch a rope, etc.*
Atesorar, *v. a. to treasure up* [*tion*
Atestacion, *s. f. attesta-*
Atestado, da, *a. headstrong* [*timonial*
Atestados, *s. m. pl. a tes-*
Atestadura, *s. f. y* Atestamiento, *s. m. stuffing*
Atestar, *v. a. to stuff* || *to attest*
Atestiguacion, *s. f. y* Atestiguamiento, *s. m. testifying*
Atestiguar, *v. a. to testify*
Atetar, *v. a. to suckle*
Atetillar, *v. a. to dig the ground*
Atezamiento, *s. m. blacking* || *blackn*

Atezar, *v. a. to b*
Atiborrar, *v. a. t*
A'tico, *s. m. atti*
A'tico, ca, *a. att*
Aticurga (baza),
of an attick p
Atiesar, *v. a. to*
Atildadura, *s. f. o*
elegance
Atildar, *v. a. to*
remark, or *c*
to adorn; to a
Atinadamente, *a*
terously
Atinar, *v. n. t*
mark || *to gue*
Atincar, *s. m. b*
Atiplar, *v. a. t*
the sound
Atiplarse, *v. r*
from a grave t
note
Atiriciarse, *v.*
jaundiced
Atisbador, ra, *s.*
Atisbadura, *s. f.*
Atisbar, *v. a. t*
to spy
Atizador, *s. m.*
stirs the fire
Atizar, *v. a. to s*
|| *to heighte*
rel, etc. || *to*
candle
Atizonar, *v. a.*
with brick, *c*
Atlante, *s. m. a*
Atlantes, *pl.*
(*in building*
Atlántico, ca, *a*
Atlántides, *s. f. p*
Atlas, *s. m. an*
Atleta, *s. m. at*
Atmósfera, *s. f. a*
Atmosférico, ca
pherical
Atoar, *v. a. to*
Atobar, *v. a. t*
Atocha, *s. f.*

tochar ; s. m.
eld
, a. fat like
a. to make
kill
. r. to be in a
[drink
a mexican
. m. mire ;
o stick in the
. to entangle
n a business
. a. to stun
n. atomist
, a. atomical
atom
a. to spur a
. astonished
ad. rashly
, s. m. stun-
. to stun
nente , adv.
, s. m. tor-
[ment
v. a to tor-
a. to intimi-
a. to squat,
. r. to be gri-
[soner
. m. a poi
o, s. m. poi-
[|| to vex
a. to poison
. a. to hurry
m. hurrying
ia, } a. atra-
a, } bilarious
f. black cho-
to draw the

ship close to land, etc.
Atracarse , v. r. *to grapple with a ship* || *to glut one's self*
Atraccion , s. f. *attraction*
Aattractivo , va , a. *attractive* [*ment*
Atractivo , s. m. *allure-*
Atractiz , s. f. *attractiveness*
Atraer, v. a. *to attract*
A ragantarse , v. r. *to be choked* || *to be at a stand*
Atraidoramente, adv. *treacherously*
Atraidorado , da , a. *traitor-like ; treacherous*
Atraillar , v. a. *to tie with a leash* [*ting*
Atraimiento , s. m. *attrac-*
Atramparse , v. r. *to fall into the snare* || *to be choked up*
Atrancar , v. a. *to bar* || *to take large steps*
Atrapar , v. a. *to overtake*
Atras , adv. *behind*
De tiempos atras , *of former times*
Atrasados, s. m. pl. *arrears*
Atrasado de medios , adj. *grown poor*
Atrasar , v. a. *to leave behind* || *to stop one's way* || *to put off*
Atrasarse , v. r. *to stay behind* || *to run in debt*
Atrasmano , adv. *too late* || *out of the reach*
Atraso , s. m. *delay* || *loss of wealth, etc.*
Atravesado , da , a. *squint-eyed* || *ill affected* || *mongrel*
Atravesar , v. a. *to cross* || *to run a man through* || *to ruff (at cards)*
Atravesarse , v. r *to bar the way* || *to interrupt*

|| *to interpose* || *to fall cross*
Atreverse , v. r. *to dare*
Atrevidamente , adv. *boldly*
Atrevidillo , lla , a. *a little bold-hot-headed fellow*
Atrevido , da , a. *bold* || *saucy* [*ness*
Atrevimiento , s. m. *bold-*
Atribucion , s. f. *allowance*
Atribuir , v. a. *to attribute*
Atribular , v. a. *to trouble ; to grieve*
Atribularse, v. r. *to grieve ; to mourn*
Atributo , s. m. *attribute*
Atriceses , s. m. pl. *eyes of the stirrup*
Atricion , s. f. *attrition*
Atril , s. m. *a reading-desk*
Atrilera , s. f. *the cover of a desk*
Atrincheramiento , s. m. *entrenchment*
Atrincherarse , v. r. *to intrench one's self*
Atrio , s. m. *porch ; portico*
Atro , tra , a. *black*
Atrochar , v. n. *to go by cross ways*
Atrocidad , s. f. *atrocity*
Atrofia , s. f. *atrophy*
Atrófico , ca , a. *affected with an atrophy*
Atrompetado , da , a. *shaped like a trumpet*
Atronadamente, ad. *rashly*
Atronado , da , a. *rash ; heedless*
Atronador , ra , s. *bawler*
Atronamiento , s. m. *stunning with noise*
Atronar , v. a. *to make a thundering noise* || *to stun*
Atronarse , v. r *to be killed*

by the noise of thunder
Atronerar, *v. a. to make loop-holes* [*ther*
Atropar, *v. a. to get toge-*
Atropelladamente, *adv. in haste; disorderly*
Atropellado, da, *a. hasty; inconsiderate*
Atropellador, ra, *s. one that treads under foot*
Atropellamiento, *s. m. treading under foot*
Atropellar, *v. a. to tread under foot*
Atropellarse, *v. r. to do things in a hurry*
Atroz, *a. 2. atrocious*
Atrozar, *v. a. to tie the yard to the mast*
Atrozmente, *adv. atrociously*
Atruhanado, da, *a. buffoon like* [*grily*
Atufadamente, *adv. an-*
Atufar, *v. a. to put into a passion*
Atufarse, *v. r. to take wind*
Atun, *s. m. tunny*
Atunara, *s. f. the place where tunnies are caught*
Atunera, *s. f. hook to catch tunnies with*
Atunero, *s. m. tunny-fisher*, or *seller*
Aturdimiento, *s. m. stunning — stupefaction*
Aturdir, *v. a. to stun* || *to stupefy*
Aturrullar, *v. a. to confound; to puzzle; to non plus*
Atusador, *s. m. one that cuts the hair*
Atusar, *v. a. to cut the hair* || *to shear an hedge, etc.* || *to whet the wit*

Atusarse, *v. r. to dress affectedly*
Atutía, *s. f. tutty*
Atutiplen, *adv. abundantly* [*ness*
Audacia, *s. f. audacious-*
Audaz, *a. 2. audacious*
Audiencia, *s. f. audience* || *court*
Auditivo, va, *a. auditory*
Auditor, *s. m. auditor*
Auditorío, *s. f. the auditor's office*
Auditorio, *s. m. auditory*
Auditorio, ria, *a. V.* Auditivo
Augo, *s. m. apogdum* || *height*
Auguracion, *s. f. augueration*
Augural, *a. 2. augurial*
Augures, *s. m. pl. augurs*
Augusto, ta, *a. august*
Aula, *s. f. a form in a school* || *a hall* || *a court*, or *palace*
Aulaga, *s. f. broom*
Aúlico, ca, *a. aulick*
Aulladero, *s. m. a place where wolves howl*
Aullador, ra, *s. he that howls*
Aullar, *v. n. to howl*
Aullido, } Aullo, } *s. m. a howl*
Aumentacion, *s. f. augmentation* [*menter*
Aumentador, ra, *s. aug-*
Aumentar, *v. a to augment*
Aumentativo, va, *a. augmentative*
Aumento, *s. m. augmentation*
Aun, *adv. yet — also*
Auna, *adv. together*
Aunar, *v. a. to unite*
Aunque, *prep. although*
Aura, *s. f. gale, breeze*

Aura popular, *p favour*
Aureo, a, *a. golden*
Aureola, *s. f. a glor*
Auricalco, *s. m. lat*
Aurícula, *s. f. the a of the heart*
Auricular, *a. 2. aur*
Aurífero, ra, *a. auri*
Auriga, *s. m. coach*
Aurora, *s. f. aurora*
Aurragado, da, *a. il ghed*
Ausencia, *s. f. abs*
Ausentarse, *v. r. to one's self*
Ausente, *a. 2. abs*
Auspicio, *s. m. aus*
Auspicios, *pl. pat*
Austeramente, *adv rely*
Austeridad, *s. f. au*
Austeró, ra, *a. aus*
Austral, *y* Austrin *a. austral*
Austro, *s. m. the wind*
Auténtica, *s. f. auth*
Autenticacion, *s. making authenti*
Auténticamente, *au thentically*
Autenticar, *v. a. to authentick*
Autenticidad, *s. aut city*
Auténtico, ca, *a. a.*
Autillo, *s. m. an*
Auto, *s. m. a public a decree, etc.*
Autos, *pl. papers re to a suit in law*
Autógrafo, *s. m. auto*
Autógrafo, fa, *a. au phical*
Autómato, *s. m. au*
Autor, ra, *s. autho* rector of a comp players

direction of a
of players
. f. authority
mente, adv.
ively
a. 2. that may
zed
, s. f. autho-
ente, adv.
ority
da, adj. res-
s. m. one that
[thorizing
to, s. m. au-
. a. to autho-
ake a writing
k || to prove,
| to give cre-
dable author
n. a commen-
a. 2. autum-
[rer
ra, s. succou-
a. to help; to
to attend a
2. auxiliary
n. help; asis-
, a. cow-like
, a. fordable
. y Avadarse,
ome fordable
to warm with
|| to dry up
da, a. brag-
a. to palisade
a. to value ||
he price || to
edition
. attack; as-
Avanzo
n. apron
s. m. a little

Avantren, *s. m. the fore wheels of a carriage*
Avanzar, *v. a. y n. to advance || to overbalance in an account*
Avanzo, *s. m. remainder || benefit of a merchant*
Avaramente, *a. covetously*
Avaricia, *s. f. covetousness*
Avariento, ta, } *a. covetous*
Avaro, ra, }
Avarraz, *V.* Albarraz
Avasallar, *v. a. to subdue*
Ave, *s. f. a bird || poultry*
Avechucho, *s. m. an useless bird || an ugly man*
Avecica, cilla, *s. f. a little bird*
Avecinar, *v. a. to bring, or draw near*
Avecinarse, *v. r. to approach || to knit friendship with one*
Avecindamiento, *s. m. settling in a place || dwelling-house*
Avecindar, *v. a. to make one a freeman*
Avecindarse, *v. r. to settle in a place*
Avejentar, *v. n. y* Avejentarse, *v. r. to grow, or appear old*
Avellana, *s. f. hazel-nut*
Avellanado, da, *a. of a hazel-nut colour*
Avellanar, *s. m. hazel-grove*
Avellanarse, *v. r. to grow old and tough*
Avellanera, *s. f. hazel-tree*
Avellanero, ra, *s. one that sells hazel-nuts*
Avellanica, *s. f. a little hazel-nut*
Avellano, *s. m. hazel-tree*
Ave Maria, *s. f. Ave Mary*

Avena, *s. f. oats || a reed*
Avenado, da, *adj. lunatick*
Avenal, *s. m. oats-field*
Avenar, *v. n. to make a passage for water*
Avenate, *s. m. drink with oats*
Avenenar, *v. a. to poison*
Avenencia, *s. f. agreement*
Aveniceo, cea, *a. belonging, to the oats*
Avenida, *s. f. inundation || concurse*
Avenidas, *pl. avenues*
Avenir, *v. a. to adjuste; to agree*
Aventador, *s. m. a kind of winnowing fork || winnower || a great rush-fan*
Aventaja, *s. f. jointure*
Aventajadamente, *adv. advantageously || excellently* [lent
Aventajado, da, *a. excel-*
Aventajar, *v. a. to excel || to out-go || to improve*
Aventar, *v. a. to fan || to winnow*
Aventarse, *v. r. to take a fright || to run headlong*
Aventura, *s. f. adventure*
Aventura, *adv. by chance*
Aventurado, da, (bien, ó mal), *a. happy, or unhappy* [ture
Aventurar, *v. a. to adven-*
Aventurero, *s. m. adventurer || spunger*
Aver. *V.* Haber
Averamia, *s. f. a sort of wild duck*
Avergonzar, *v. a. to put to the blush*
Avergonzarse, *v. r. to be ashamed*
Avería, *s. f. average* [ged
Averiarse, *v. r. to be avera-*

by the noise of thunder
Atronerar, *v. a. to make loop-holes* [*ther*
Atropar, *v. a. to get toge-*
Atropelladamente, *adv. in haste; disorderly*
Atropellado, da, *a. hasty; inconsiderate*
Atropellador, ra, *s. one that treads under foot*
Atropellamiento, *s. m. treading under foot*
Atropellar, *v. a. to tread under foot*
Atropellarse, *v. r. to do things in a hurry*
Atroz, *a. 2. atrocious*
Atrozar, *v. a. to tie the yard to the mast*
Atrozmente, *adv. atrociously*
Atruhanado, da, *a. buffoon like* [*grily*
Atufadamente, *adv. an-*
Atufar, *v. a. to put into a passion*
Atufarse, *v. r. to take wind*
Atun, *s. m. tunny*
Atunara, *s. f. the place where tunnies are caught*
Atunera, *s. f. hook to catch tunnies with*
Atunero, *s. m. tunny-fisher*, or *seller*
Aturdimiento, *s. m. stunning — stupefaction*
Aturdir, *v. a. to stun* || *to stupefy*
Aturrullar, *v. a. to confound; to puzzle; to non plus*
Atusador, *s. m. one that cuts the hair*
Atusar, *v. a. to cut the hair* || *to shear an hedge, etc.* || *to whet the wit*
Atusarse, *v. r. to dress affectedly*
Atutía, *s. f. tutty*
Atutiplen, *adv. abundantly* [*ness*
Audacia, *s. f. audacious-*
Audaz, *a. 2. audacious*
Audiencia, *s. f. audience* || *court*
Auditivo, va, *a. auditory*
Auditor, *s. m. auditor*
Auditorío, *s. f. the auditor's office*
Auditorio, *s. m. auditory*
Auditorio, ria, *a. V.* Auditivo
Auge, *s. m. apogdum* || *height*
Auguracion, *s. f. augucration*
Augural, *a. 2. augurial*
Augures, *s. m. pl. augurs*
Augusto, ta, *a. august*
Aula, *s. f. a form in a school* || *a hall* || *a court*, or *palace*
Aulaga, *s. f. broom*
A'ulico, ca, *a. aulick*
Aulladero, *s. m. a place where wolves howl*
Aullador, ra, *s. he that howls*
Aullar, *v. n. to howl*
Aullido, } *s. m. a howl*
Aullo, }
Aumentacion, *s. f. augmentation* [*menter*
Aumentador, ra, *s. aug-*
Aumentar, *v. a to augment*
Aumentativo, va, *a. augmentative*
Aumento, *s. m. augmentation*
Aun, *adv. yet — also*
Auna, *adv. together*
Aunar, *v. a. to unite*
Aunque, *prep. although*
Aura, *s. f. gale, breeze*
Aura popular, *popul favour*
Aureo, a, *a. golden*
Aureola, *s. f a glory*
Auricalco, *s. m. latten*
Aurícula, *s. f. the auri of the heart*
Auricular, *a. 2. auricul*
Aurífero, ra, *a. aurifero*
Auriga, *s. m. coachma*
Aurora, *s. f. aurora*
Aurragado, da, *a. ill pl ghed*
Ausencia, *s. f. absence*
Ausentarse, *v. r. to abs one's self*
Ausente, *a. 2. absent*
Auspicio, *s. m. auspice*
Auspicios, *pl. patrona*
Austeramente, *adv. sev rely*
Austeridad, *s. f. austeri*
Austeró, ra, *a. austere*
Austral, y Austrino, *a. austral*
Austro, *s. m. the so wind*
Auténtica, *s. f. authenti*
Autenticacion, *s. f. t making authentick*
Auténticamente, *adv. a thentically*
Autenticar, *v. a. to ma authentick*
Autenticidad, *s. authen city* [*ti*
Auténtico, ca, *a. authe*
Autillo, *s. m. an howl*
Auto, *s. m. a publick ac a decree, etc.*
Autos, *pl. papers relati to a suit in law*
Autógrafo, *s. m. autogra*
Autógrafo, fa, *a. autogr phical* [*ti*
Autómato, *s. m. autom*
Autor, ra, *s. author* || *d rector of a company players*

ria, s. f. direction of a
mpany of players
ridad, s. f. authority
ritativamente, adv.
'horitatively
rizable, a. 2. that may
authorized
rizacion, s. f. autho-
ation
rizadamente, adv.
th authority
rizado, da, adj. res-
table
rizador, s. m. one that
'horizes [thorizing
rizamiento, s. m. au-
rizar, v. a. to autho-
e || to make a writing
thentick || to prove,
justify || to give cre-
[dable author
ron, s. m. a commen-
mnal, a. 2. autum-
l [rer
liador, ra, s. succou-
liar, v. a. to help; to
:cour || to attend a
ing
liar, a. 2. auxiliary
lio, s. m. help; asis-
ice
ado, da, a. cow-like
lado, da, a. fordable
lar, v. n. y Avadarse,
r. to become fordable
ar, v. a. to warm with
breath || to dry up
ntado, da, a. brag-
g
ar, v. a. to palisade
rar, v. a. to value ||
raise the price || to
courage
ıte, s. sedition
ce, s. m. attack; as-
ılt || V. Avanzo
ıtal, s. m. apron
ıtalillo, s. m. a little
ew

Avantren, s. m. the fore wheels of a carriage
Avanzar, v. a. y n. to advance || to overbalance in an account
Avanzo, s. m. remainder || benefit of a merchant
Avaramente, a. covetously
Avaricia, s. f. covetousness
Avariento, ta, } a. covetous
Avaro, ra, }
Avarraz, V. Albarraz
Avasallar, v. a. to subdue
Ave, s. f. a bird || poultry
Avechucho, s. m. an useless bird || an ugly man
Avecica, cilla, s. f. a little bird
Avecinar, v. a. to bring, or draw near
Avecinarse, v. r. to approach || to knit friendship with one
Avecindamiento, s. m. settling in a place || dwelling-house
Avecindar, v. a. to make one a freeman
Avecindarse, v. r. to settle in a place
Avejentar, v. n. y Avejentarse, v. r. to grow, or appear old
Avellana, s. f. hazel-nut
Avellanado, da, a. of a hazel-nut colour
Avellanar, s. m. hazel-grove
Avellanarse, v. r. to grow old and tough
Avellanera, s. f. hazel-tree
Avellanero, ra, s. one that sells hazel-nuts
Avellanica, s. f. a little hazel-nut
Avellano, s. m. hazel-tree
Ave Maria, s. f. Ave Mary

Avena, s. f. oats || a reed
Avenado, da, adj. lunatick
Avenal, s. m. oats-field
Avenar, v. n. to make a passage for water
Avenate, s. m. drink with oats
Avenenar, v. a. to poison
Avenencia, s. f. agreement
Aveniceo, cea, a. belonging, to the oats
Avenida, s. f. inundation || concurse
Avenidas, pl. avenues
Avenir, v. a. to adjuste; to agree
Aventador, s. m. a kind of winnowing fork || winnower || a great rush-fan
Aventaja, s. f. jointure
Aventajadamente, adv. advantageously || excellently [lent
Aventajado, da, a. excel-
Aventajar, v. a. to excel || to out-go || to improve
Aventar, v. a. to fan || to winnow
Aventarse, v. r. to take a fright || to run headlong
Aventura, s. f. adventure
Aventura, adv. by chance
Aventurado, da, (bien, ó mal), a. happy, or unhappy [ture
Aventurar, v. a. to adven-
Aventurero, s. m. adventurer || spunger
Aver. V. Haber
Averamia, s. f. a sort of wild duck
Avergonzar, v. a. to put to the blush
Avergonzarse, v. r. to be ashamed
Avería, s. f. average [ged
Averiarse, v. r. to be avera-

Averiguable, *a. that may be verifyed*
Averiguacion *f. verification* [*miner*
Averiguador, ra, *s. exa-*
Averiguamiento, *s. m. verification*
Averiguar, *v. a. to verify*
Averío, *s. m. a beast of burden* || *a flock of birds*
Averno, *s. m. hell*
Aversion, *s. f. aversion*
Averso, sa, *a. perverse*
Avestruz, *s. m. ostrich*
Aviador, *s. m. one that disposes for a journey* || *a small wimble*
Aviar, *v. a. to dispose for a journey* || *to hasten*
Aviciar, *v. a. V.* Enviciar
A'vido, da, *adj greedy; eager*
Aviejarse, *v. r. Voy.* Avejentarse [*fork*
Aviento, *s. m. a sort of*
Aviesamente, *adv. crossly* || *perversely*
Avieso, sa, *a. cross; crooked* || *perverse*
Avigorar, *v. a. to give vigour* || *to encourage*
Avilantez, *s. f. arrogance*
Avillanado, da, *adj. plebeian*
Avillanarse, *v. r. to degenerate* [*natured*
Avinagrado, da, *adj. ill-*
Avinagrar, *v. a. to sour*
Avio, *s. m. preparation*
Avion, *s. m. a martlet*
Avisadamente, *adv. prudently*
Avisado, da, *a. prudent*
Avisador, *s. m. advertiser*
Avisar, *v. a. to warn; to advise* [*prudence*
Aviso, *sub. m. advice* ||
Aviso ó navío de aviso, advice-boat

Avison, *int. take care*
Avispa, *s f. a wasp*
Avispado, da, *a. lively; brisk*
Avispar, *v. a. to whip* or *spur* || *to examine*
Avisparse, *v. r. to grow uneasy*
Avispero, *s. m. wasp's nest* [*wasp*
Avispon, *sub. m. a great*
Avistar, *v. a. to see, to look at*
Avistarse, *v. r. to speak mouth to mouth*
Avitar, *v. a. to heave the capstern* [*tual*
Avituallar, *v. a. to vic-*
Avivadamente, *adv. briskly*
Avivador, *s. m. exciter*
Avivar, *v. a. to excite; to hearten* || *to heat; to inflamme* || *to enliven* || *to hatch*
Avivar, *v. n. to be hatched*
Avizor, (ojo), *adv. take care*
Avizorar, *v. a. to watch; to spy*
Avocacion, *s. f.* } *the bringing of a cause before a higher court*
Avocamiento, *s. m.* }
Avocar, *v. act. to bring before a higher court*
Avos, *s. m. fraction*
Avucasta, *s. f. a kind of duck*
Avutarda, *s. f. a bustard*
Avutardado, da, *a. bustard-like*
Axaqueca, *s. f. V.* Xaqueca
Axe, *s. m. habitual sickness*
Axedrea, *sub. f. the herb savory*
Axedrez, *s. m. the game of chess*

Axedrezado, da, *a. ...kcred*
Axenabe, *s. m. wi...*
Axenjo, *s. m. wo...*
Axenuz, *s. m. V.*
Axerquía, *s. f. V...* bal
Axí, *s. m. red pep...*
Aximez, *s. m. a ... fashioned win...*
Axioma, *s. m. axi...*
Axorcas, *s. f. bra...*
Axuar, *s. m. a bri... thes* || *househol...*
Ay! *int. alas*
Aya, *V.* Haya
Ayanque, *s. m. h... gears*
Ayer, *adv. yeste...*
Ayo, ya, *s. tutor ... nor of youth*
Ayrazo, *s. m. sto...*
Ayre, *s. m. air* || *song*
Ayrearse, *v. r. to...*
Ayrecico, } *s. m... bre...*
Ayrecillo, }
Ayron, *s. mas. a ... egret* || *a topp... tuft*
Ayrosamente, *ad... gantly; gentee...*
Ayrosidad, *sub. f. ... fulness*
Ayroso, sa, *a. lyi... to the wind* || *n... teel*
Ayuda, *s. f. aid* || *syringe* || *hel... sistant* || *subsid...*
Ayuda de cámara, *de chambre — a gift above w...*
Ayudador, ra, *s.*
Ayudante, *s. m. a...*
Ayudar, *v. a. to h...*
Ayudar á misa, *at mas...*
Ayunador, ra, *s...*

, v. n. to fast
nas, adv. fasting
s. m. fast; fasting
na, a. fasting
, s. m. V. Yun-
[council
niento, s. m. city-
ayuntamiento,
all
, V. Haz, haza
ado, da, a. jetty
, s. m. jet
s, pl. jet-works
. f. hoe
dos dientes, hoe
wo forks
dilla, subst. f. a
hoe
s. m. pick-axe
da, } a stroke of a hoe or pick-axe
zo,
r, v. act. to dig
pick axe
illo, s. m. dim. de
n
ro, s. m. one that
with a pick-axe ‖
er
s. f. a tire-wo-
o the queen
sub. m. a work-

, s. m. saffron
romin, bastard
n
ado, da, a. of saf-
olour
l, s. mas. a field
saffron grows
ar, v. a. to saffron
, s. f. a zagaye
da, sub. f. a blow
a zagaye
subs. m. orange-

ravo, a sort of

Azamboo, s. m. a kind of quince-tree [ria
Azanoria, s. f. V. Zanaho-
Azanoriate, s. m. pickled carrots
Azaña, etc. V. Hazaña
Azar, s. m. ill luck
Tener azar con... to have an aversion to...
Azarbe, subs. m. trench; gutter
Azarcon, s. m. ashes of the burnt lead
Azarnefe, s. mas. a kind of poison [luckly
Azarosamente, adv. un-
Azaroso, sa, a. unlucky
Azarote, s. m. sarcocele
Azaynadamente, ad. treacherously
Azconilla, sub. f. a small dart [ned
A'zimo, ma, a. unleave-
Azimuth, s. m. azimuth
Azimuthal, a. 2. azimuthal
Aznacho, s. m. pine-tree of scotland
Azófar, s. m. latten
Azofayfa, Azofayfo, V. Azufayfa, etc.
Azogadamente, adv. hastily
Azogado, da, a. restles
Azogamiento, s. m. an excessive hastiness or agitation
Azogar, v. act. to mix or rub with quicksilver
Azogar la cal, to kill lime
Azogarse, v. rec. to be infected with quicksilver ‖ to be unquiet, restless
Azogue, s. m. quicksilver
Azoguería, s. f. a place where the quicksilver is prepared
Azoguero, s. m. one that prepares, buys or sells quicksilver
Azolar, v. a. to plane
Azor, s. m. goss-hawk
Azoramiento, s. m. trouble; fear
Azorar, v. a. to trouble; to fright — to excite
Azorramiento, s. m. heaviness of the head
Azorrarse, v. rec. to grow heavy, or dull
Azotado, s. m. a whipped malefactor
Azotador, ra, f. whipper
Azotamiento, s. m. whipping
Azotar, v. a. to whip
Azotar calles, to ramble about the streets; to saunter
Azotayna, sub. f. a whipping
Azotazo, s. mas. a lash or jerk
Azote, s. m. whip; lash
Azotea, s. f. terrass flat-roof
Azotina, s. f. V. Azotayna
Azoton, s. m. V. Azotazo
Azua, sub. f. drink made with meal of maiz
Azúcar, s. m. sugar
Azúcar piedra, ó cande, sugar candy
Azucarado, s. m. a sort of women's paint
Azucarado, da, a. gentle; mild
Azucarar, v. a. to sugar ‖ to sweeten [box
Azucarero, s. mas. sugar-
Azucena, s. f. a lily
Azud, sub. fem. the place where water begins to run into the channels
Azuda, s. f a large wheel used to draw water
Azuela, s. f. adze; addice

Azufayfa y Azufeyfa, s. f. jujube

Azufayfo y Azufeyfo, s. m. jubube-tree

Azufrado, da, a. sulphurous

Azufrar, v. a. to smoke with brimstone

Azufre, s. m. brimstone

Azufroso, sa, a. sulphurous

Azul, a. 2. blue [blue

Azular, v. act. to colour

Azulear, v. n. to be bluish

Azulejo, s. mas. a glazed tile || the blue-linnet

Azumbrado, da, a. measured by azumbres

Azumbre, s. m. a measure for liquors, about half a gallon

Azur, a. azure

Azutea, s. f. V. Azotea

Azuzador, ra, s. exciter

Azuzar, v. act. to excite, provoke, etc.

B.

Baba, s. f. foam; slaver

Babada, s. f. bone of the ilia

Babador, } s. m. a bib
Babadero, }

Babara, s. f. a berlin || a sort of country-dance

Babaza, subst. f. a thick abundant slaver || snail

Babazorro, s. mas. blockhead

Babear, v. n. to slaver

Babeo, s. m. slabbering

Babera, s. f. y Baberol, s. m. the part of the helmet that covers the chin — a fool

Babero, s. m. V. Babador

Babia (estar en), to stand gaping into the air

Babieca, s. m. a lazy foolish fellow

Babilla, s. f. a thin skin

Babilonia, s. f. great concourse of people; confusion, noise, etc.

Babor, s. m. larboard

Babosa, s. f. a slug-snail

Babosear, v. a. to slaver any thing

Babosilla, sub. f. dim. de Baboza [slaverer

Babosillo, lla, a. a little

Baboso, sa, a. slaverer

Bacallao, s. m. stock-fish

Bacanal, adj. belonging to Bacchus || drinker; guttler [chanals

Bacanales, sub. f. pl. bac-

Bácara, s. f. throat-wort

Bacarí, adj. covered with leather

Bacaris, s. f. V. Bácara

Bacera, s. f. obstruction in the melt || swelling in the belly

Baceta, s. f. the stock at cards [ness

Bache, s. m. a way's deep-

Bachico, ca, a. belonging to Bacchus

Bachiller, s. m. batchelor of arts, etc.

Bachiller, ra, s. talkers, chatterer [chelorship

Bachillerato, s. mas. bat-

Bachillerear, v. neut. to chate; to prate

Bachillerejo, s. m. prattler [veness

Bachilleriá, s. f. talkati-

Bachillerillo, lla, s. prattler

Baciá, s. f. bason || barber's bason || vase of a fountain

Báciga, s. f. a certain game at cards [pan

Bacin, s. m. a close-stool

Bacinada, s. f. excreme[nt] in a close-stool-pan

Bacinejo, s. mas. dim. Bacin

Bacinero, s. m. one w[ho] makes a gathering

Bacineta, ica, illa, s. a little bason

Bacinete, s. m. a kind head piece

Báculo, s. m. staff || su[p]port [cro[sier]

Báculo pastoral, a bisho[p]

Bada, s. f. V. Abada

Badajada, s. f. stroke of clapper || a foolish e[x]pression [clap[per]

Badajazo, sub. m. a gre[at]

Badajo, s. m. clapper a bell || a dull pratt[ling] fellow [clapp[er]

Badajuelo, s. mas. a lit[tle]

Badab, s. m. a muzzle

Badana, s. f. sheep's lea[ther]; basil

Badazas, s. f. pl. the rop[es] by wich the bonnets [are] laced to the sails

Badea, s. f. water-mel[on] || a worthless fellow

Baden, sub. mas. a gu[tter] caused by a flood

Badil, s. m. } a shovel
Badila, s. f. }

Badilazo, sub. m. a stro[ke] with a shovel

Badina, s. f. a sort of p[ool]

Badulaque, subs. m. me[at] hashed with thick sa[u]ce || a worthless m[an]

Bafanear, v. a. to boast

Bafanería, s. f. boastin[g]

Bafanero, s. m. boaster

Baga, sub. f. a cord wh[ich] ties the packs up horses

Bagage, s. m. baggage beast for carriage

ero, *sub. m. a bag-*
e-carrier
ela, *sub. f. a trifling*
ig [*grapes, etc.*
), *s. m. the husks of*
a, *s. f. dishes and*
tes [*hawk*
l, *sub. m. sparrow-*
s. f. a bay
rina, *subst. f. swee-*
gs, etc. || *the mob*
io, na, *a. low; vile*
s. f. a bullet || *a bale*
vares [*shot*
nramada, *cross-bar*
, *plur. a printer's*
ls; pompets
l, *a. slight; vile*
or, ra, *s. bleating*
ron, *s. m. a bragga-*
io
ronada. *s. f. rodo-*
ntado [*ger*
ronear, *v. n. to swag*
ar, *s. m. hay-rick*
o, *subst. m. hay*, or
w || *foam of the soap*
V. Balaguero [*straw*
uero, *s. m. an heap of*
ice, *s. m. balancing*
eeling of a ship ||
lance of an account
icear, *v. n. to be ba-*
nced || *to waver* || *to*
l or seel
icear, *v. a. to balance*
icia, *subst. f. water-*
lon [*balance*
icica, *subs. f. a little*
icin, *s. m. a spring-*
e - bar || *a pay*, or
le || *a coiner's stamp*
icines, *pl. lifts*
adra, *s. f. bylander*
ndran, *sub. m. large*
arse cloak
nza, *s. f. balance* ||
ale [cear
nzar, *v. a. V* Balan-

Balanzario, *s. m. one that sizes the blanks*
Balanze, *s. m. V.* Balance
Balar, *v. n. to bleat*
Balaustra, *s. f. blossoms of pomegranate-trees*
Balaustrada, *s. f. balustrade*
Balaustrado y Balaustriado, da, *a. ballistred*
Balaustre, *s. m. ballister; rail*
Balaustrería, *s. f. rails*
Balaustría, *sub. f. V.* Balaustra [*rail*
Balaustrillo, *s. m. a little*
Balax, *s. m. a balass ruby*
Balazo, *s. m. a bullet-shot*
Balbucencia, *s. f. stammering*
Balbuciente, *a. 2. stammerer*
Balcon, *s. m. balcony*
Balconage, *s. m. a row of balconies* [*balcony*
Balconazo, *s. m. a great*
Balconcillo, *s. m. a little balcony* [conage
Balconería, *s. f. V.* Bal-
Baldado, da, *a. gratuitous*
Baldaquí, *s. m. canopy*
Baldar, *v. a. to maim; to make impotent* || *to cut at cards*
Balde. *s. mas. a leathern bucket*
Debalde, *adv. for nothing*
En balde, *adv. vainly*
Baldes. *s. m. tawed skin*
Baldío, día, *a. untilled*
Baldo, *s. m. renouncing at cards* [*affront*
Baldon, *s. m. reproach;*
Baldonar, *v. act. to reproach* || *to call one names*
Baldosa, *s. f. a square tile*
Baldraque, *s. m. a worthless man* or *thing*

Baldres, *s. m. V.* Baldes
Balería, *subst. f. heap of bullets* [*pack*
Baleta, *s. f. a little bale* or
Balido, *s. m. bleating*
Balija, *s. f. cloak-bag* || *mail* [Balija
Balijon, *sub. m. aum. de*
Baliladera, *s. f. deer-call*
Ballena, *s. f. whale*
Ballenato, *sub. m. young whale*
Ballener, *s. m. ship shaped like a whale*
Ballesta, *sub. f. ballist* || *cross-bow*
Ballestazo, *s. m. a shot of a steelbow* [*bow-man*
Ballesteador, *s. m. cross-*
Ballestear, *v. a. to shoot with a cross-bow* || *to watch; to wait for*
Ballestera, *sub. f. a loop-hole*
Ballestería, *s. f. the art of using the bow, etc.* || *heap of cross-bows* || *body of cross-bow-mans*
Ballestero, *sub. m. cross-bow-man* || *cross-bow-maker* [*terwort*
Hierba de ballestero, *set-*
Ballestilla, *sub. f. a little cross-bow* || *fleam* || *cross-staft*
Balleston, *s. m. aum. de* Ballesta
Ballico, *s. m. darnel; tares*
Balon, *s. m. bale; pack* || *fool-ball*
Balota, *s. f. ballot*
Balotar, *v. a. to ballot*
Balsa, *s. f. a pool; a meer* || *raft of timber*
Balsamerita, *s. f. a vase to put balsam into*
Balsámico, ca, *a. balsamick* [mina
Balsamina, *sub. f.* balsa-

Balsamita mayor, *s. f. a sort of mint*
Bálsamo, *s. m. balsam*
Balsar, *sub. m. a marshy bushy place*
Balsear, *v. a. to cross the river on a raft*
Balsero, *sub. m. one that drives a raft*
Balsilla, *s. f. a little raft*
Balsopeto *s. m. a wallet*
Baluarte, *s. m. a bulwark*
Balumba, *sub. f. a great bulk*
Balumbo, *s. mas. a bulky cumbersome thing*
Balza, *s. f. banner of the knights templars*
Bambalear, *v. n. to stagger*
Bambalina, *s. f. canvas on wich are represented the skies, etc.*
Bambarotear *v. n. to cry out to bawl*
Bambarotero, *s. m. bawler*
Bambarria *s. m. a fool or idiot*
Bambarria, *s. f. a meer chance at billiards*
Bambarrion, *s. m. aum. de* Bambarria
Bambocho, *s. m. a landscape*
Bambolear, *v. n. y* Bambolearse, *v. to swing one's body*
Bamboléo, *s. m. swinging*
Bambolla *s. f. pride; ostentation*
Bambóneo, *s. m. swinging*
Banasta, *s. f. basket; pannie*
Banastero *s. m. basket-seller maker*
Banasto, *subs. m. a great round basket* [bank
Banca, *s. f. a bench — a*
Bancal, *s. m. a carpet to cover a bench || the sands || a bed in a garden*
Bancalero, *s. m. one that makes carpet. V.* Bancal [tey
Bancarrota, *s. f. bankrup-*
Bancaza, *s. f.* } *a great*
Bancazo, *s. m.* } *bench*
Banco, *sub. mas. bench || thwart || bank || banker*
Banco de arena, *the sands*
Bancos, *pl. the branches of a bridle*
Banda, *s. f. scarf || side || bend || band*
Bandada, *s. f. company of birds*
Bandarria, *s. f. hammer in a ship*
Bandear, *v. a. to go from side to side*
Bandearse, *v. r. to behave one's self wisely, etc.*
Bandeja, *s. f. a silver dish*
Bandera, *s. f. colours || flag*
Bandereta, ica, illa, *s. f. dim. de* Bandera || *a fan shaped like a banner*
Banderizar *ver. act. V.* Abanderizar
Banderizo za, *a. factious*
Banderola, *s. f. streamer*
Bandibula, *s. f. mandible*
Bandido, *s. mas. higwayman*
Bandines, *s. m. pl. benches and balustrades in a galley*
Bandita, *s. f. a little fillet*
Bando, *s. m. a ban || faction*
Bandola, *s. f. mandore*
Bandolera, *s. f. bandoleer*
Bandolero, *s. m. highwaiman* [the guts
Bandullo, *s. m. the belly;*
Bandurria, *s. f. mandore*
Bánova, *s. f. counterp*
Banquera, *s. f. an un vered bee-hive*
Banquero *s. m. bank*
Banqueta, *s. f. a stool raised way*
Banquete, *s. m. a banq* || *V.* Banquillo
Banquetear, *v. n. to b quet* [be
Banquillo, *s. m. a l*
Baña, *s. f. V.* Bañado
Bañadera, *s. f. a scoo*
Bañadero, *s. m. soil wild boar*
Bañador, ra, *s. one bathes*
Bañar, *v. a. to bathe ice comfits, etc. glaze earthenware*
Bañero, *s. m. bath-ke*
Bañil, *s. m. soil of a boar*
Baño, *s. m. bath || a p where the slaves kept*
Baños, *pl. hot baths*
Baos, *s. m. pl. beams*
Baptismal, Baptismo *V.* Bautismal
Baqueta, *s. f. a gun- — a switch*
Baquetas, *pl. drum-st —gantlope*
Baquetear, *v. a. to run gantlope*
Barahunda, *s. f. tum confusion*
Barahuste, *s. m. bal*
Barahustillos, *sub. m little rails* [c
Baraja, *s. fem. a pac*
Barajaduras, *s. f. pl. tercations*
Barajar, *v. a. to shuffl cards || to bar the || to mix; to confo || to intangle*
Baranda, *s. f. balust*

…lar de baranda, *to exaggerate*

…andilla, *sub. f. a little balustrade*

…ngay, *s. m. indian …ip* [*ground*

…ar, *v. neut. to run a…*

…ata, *s. f. a low price*

…tijas, *s. f. pl. trifles; mean goods*

…tillo, *s. m. a market where, mean goods are sold*

…tillo, lla, *adj. very cheap*

…to, *s. m. money given to standers by at play by the winner*

…to, ta, *a. cheap*

…to, *adv. cheap*

…tro, *s. m. hell*

…tura, *subs. f. a mean price*

…a, *sub. f. beard || the chin || the first swarm*

…as, *pl. small strings of the roots || barbles*

…a cabruna, *goat's beard* — de ballena, *whale-bone*

…cana, *s. f. barbacan*

…da, *s. f. a curb—a dab*

…damente, *adv. man…* [*bearded*

…dillo, lla, *a. a little*

…do, da, *a. bearded*

…do, *s. m. a man || a plant or set with roots*

…ja, *s. f. goat's beard*

…jas, *sub. f. pl. fibres about the roots*

…lla, *s. f. V.* Barbaja

…nca, *s. f. confusion; noise, etc.*

…r, *v. n. to begin, to have a beard || to swarm || to soot roots*

…ramente, *adv. barbarously*

Bárbara (santa), *s. f. gun-room*

Barbaresco, ca, *a. barbarous*

Barbarica, *subs. f. goat's beard* [*barously*

Barbáricamente, *adv. bar-*

Barbárico, ca, *a. barbarous*

Barbaridad, *s. f. barbarity || audaciousness || absurdity* [*ness*

Barbarie, *s. f. barbarous-*

Barbarismo, *s. m. barbarism || all barbarous nations*

Barbarizar, *v. a. to make barbarous*

Bárbaro, ra, *adj. barbarous || audacious*

Bárbaro, *s. m. a barbarian* [*barous man*

Barbarote, *s. m. a very bar-*

Barbaza, *s. f. a great beard*

Barbear, *v. neut. to reach with the chin*

Barbechar, *v. a. to break up the ground*

Barbechazon, *sub. m. the season of ploughing*

Barbechera, *s. f. a ploughing || the season of ploughing*

Barbecho, *s. m. the breaking up the ground || a ploughed ground*

Barbera, *subs. f. barber's wife*

Barbería, *s. f. barber's shop || shaving and trimming*

Barberillo, ito, *s. m. dim. de* Barbero

Barbero, *s. m. a barber*

Barbeta, *sub. f. a kind of uncovered platform*

Barbiblanco, ca, *adj. grey bearded*

Barbica, *s. f. a little beard*

Barbicacho, *s. m. ribbon, etc. that comes under the chin* [*bearded*

Barbicano, na, *adj. grey*

Barbihecho, cha, *a. newly shaved*

Barbiespeso, sa, *a. thick bearded*

Barbilampiño, ña, *a. rare-bearded*

Barbilindo, da, *adj. close shaved || a beau*

Barbilla, *s. f. a little beard || a chin || barbles*

Barbillera, *sub. f. flock of tow, etc.*

Barbilucio, cia, *a. pretty*

Barbinegro, gra, *a. black-bearded*

Barbiponiente, *adj. that begins to have a beard || novice*

Barbiroxo, Barbirubio } *a. red bearded*

Barbita, *s. f. a little beard*

Barbiteñido, *adj. with a painted beard*

Barbizaeño, ña, *a. rough-bearded*

Barbo, *s. m. barbel*

Barbon, *s. m. a bearded man*

Barboquejo, *s. m. halter || the fore stay*

Barbotar, *v. a. to mutter*

Barbote, *s. m. V.* Babera

Barbudo, da, *a. that has a great beard*

Barbudo, *s. m. V.* Barbado

Barbulla, *s. f. an undistinguishable noise, etc.*

Barbullar, *v. a. to cry or speak tumultuously*

Barbullon, na, *adj. a tumultuous speaker*

Barca, *s. f. bark; boat*

Barcada, *s. f. a boat full*

Barcage, *s. m. fare; waterage*

Barcaza, s. f. } a great bark or boat
Barcazo, s. m. }

Barceno, na, a. V. Barcino

Barceo, s. m. dry rush

Barcina, s. f. a sort of frail || a great bundle of straw

Barcino, na, a. reddish

Barco, s. m. a boat

Barcon s. m. a great boat

Barcote s. mas. a kind of bark

Barda, s. f. horse armour the covering on the top of a wall

Bardado, da, a. barbed

Bardago, sub. m. a sort of rope

Bardal, s. m. enclosure

Bardana, s. f. burdock

Bardar, v. a. to lay boards, a wall

Bardoma s. f. dirt; clay

Barga s. f. high beach

Barítono, s. mas. a voice between tenor and a base

Barjuleta, s. f. a travelling-bag || a pouch

Barloar, v. n. to grapple with a ship

Barloventear, v. neut. to laveer [ward

Barlovento, s. mas. wind-

Barniz, sub. mas. varnish || printing-ink

Barnizar, v. a. to varnish

Barómetro, s. mas. barometer

Baron, s. m. a Baron

Baronesa, s. f. Baroness

Baronía, s. f. barony

Barquear, v. n. to cross a river in a bark

Barquero, s. m. waterman

Barqueta, illa, subs. f. a small boat

Barquichuelo, s. m. a little bark [man

Barquillero, s. m. a wafer-

Barquillo, s. f. wafer

Barquin, s. m. } bellows
Barquineta, s. f. }

Barquito, subs. m. a little bark

Barra, s. f. bar || a wedge of gold, etc. || the port at billiards — stripe || line [bows

Barras, pl. pack-saddle-

Barraca, s. s. f. barrack

Barrachel, s. m. the captain of the alguaciles

Barraco, s. m. V. Verraco

Barrado, da, a. striped || barred

Barragan, s. m. barracan

Barraganería, s. f. concubinage

Baraganetes, s. m. pl. futtocks [ge

Baragania s. f. concubina-

Barral, s. m. a large bottle [mire

Barranca, s. f. bog; quag-

Barranco, s. m. bog || obstacle

Barrancoso, sa, a. boggy

Barranquear, v. n. to hop, like a top

Barranquero, ra, a. hopping about

Barraquear, v. n. V. Verraquear

Barraquilla, s. f. a little barrack || cabbin

Barrar, v. a. V. Embarrar

Barrear, v. a. to bar

Barrearse, v. r. to barricade one's self || to tumble

Barreda, s. f. clay-pit

Barrederas, s. f. pl. studding sails

Barredero, s. m. maulkin

Barredor, s. m. a sweeper

Barredura, s. f. sweepi[ng]

Barreduras, pl. sweepi[ngs] || siftings, pickings, [...]

Barrena, sub. f. auge[r] piercer [dy brain[...]

Barrenado de cascos, [...]

Barrenar, v. a. to pierce to bore || to travers[e] or cross

Barrendero, ra, s. sweep[er]

Barreno, s. m. auger || [ho]le || vanity [...]

Barreño, s. m. an earth[...]

Barreño, s. m. a great ea[r]then pan

Barreñoncillo, s. m. dim. de Barreño

Barrer, v. a. to sweep

Barrera, s. f. clay-pit || cup-board || barrier

Barreta, s. f. a little ba[r]

Barretear, v. a. to bar

Barretero, s. m. miner th[at] uses of iron bars, [...]

Barreton, s. m. a great ba[r]

Barretoncillo, s. m. a li[t]tle bar

Barriada, s. f. V. Barri[...]

Barrica, s. f. hogs head french barrel

Barrido, s. m. sweping

Barriga, s. f. belly

Hacer barriga, to bell[y] out [chi[...]

Traer barriga, to be wi[th]

Barrigon, s. m. a big bel[ly]

Barrigudo, da, adj. bi[g] bellied

Barriguillo, s. m. a li[t]tle belly

Barril, s. m. barrel || [...] earthen vessel with great belly and na[r]row neck [barr[...]

Barrilejo, s. m. a lit[...]

Barrilería, s. f. colle[c]tion of barrels

Barrilete, s. m. hold-fa[st] || V. Barrilejo

, to , s. m. a
el
f. salt-wort
m. a ditch to
salt-wort into
. ward ; quar-
[sour
da, a. sharp ;
a little bar
s. clayish spot
l
. clay
pimples
n. a great bar
, a. clayish ||
reddish
m. a great bar
s. m. a scotch
, s. f. exces-
expense
r, ra, s. con-
ento, sub. m.
ing
v. a. to con-
. m. conjectu-
[ness
. m. pl. basi-
m. rolled stoc-
m. a ring to
lough-share in
v. n. to wander
base ; basis
n. to be trou-
h qualms .
f. pl. qualm ;
, s. f. nastiness
a, a. qualmish
base
istincion (en la
focus
s. f. Royal hou-
great church
silica , the ba-
cis

Basilicon , s. m. basilicon
Basilio , s. m. basilian
Basilisco , s. m. basilisk
Basquear , v. n. to reach for vomiting
Basquiña , s. f. a petticoat
Basta , s. f. basting
Bastas , pl. distant stitches in a mattress
Bastante , a. 2. sufficient
Bastantemente , adv. sufficiently
Bastantero , s. m. one who verifies the powers, etc.
Bastar , v. n. to suffice
Bastar , v. a. to give ; to supply
Bastarda , s. f. a small latin sail [nerate
Bastardear , v. n. to dege-
Bastardelo , s. m. book of memorandum
Bastardia , s. f. bastardy
Bastardo , da , a. bastard
Bastardo , s. m. a kind of serpent
Bastear , v. a. to baste
Bastero , s. m. maker of pack saddles
Bastidor , s. m. a frame for embroidering || scene of a play-house
Bastilla , s. f. a hem
Bastimentar , v. a. to supply with provisions
Bastimento s. m. victuals ; provisions
Bastion , s. m. bastion
Basto , s. m. pack-saddle || baste
Bastos , pl. clubs at cards
Basto , ta , adj. coarse
Baston , s. m. staff ; stick
Bastones , pl. pales , in heraldry
Bastonada , s. f. } bastinade
Bastonazo , s. m. }
Bastoncillo , s. m. a little staff

Bastonero , s. m. the guider of the dancers in a ballet — a turnkey
Basura , s. f. the sweepings || dung of horses
Basurero , s. m. scavenger
Bata , s. f. a nigth-gown || a course silk
Batacazo , s. m. a stroke given on the ground
Batahola , sub. f. noise ; clamours , etc.
Batalla , s. f. a battle ; a fight || fencing
Batallador , s. m. a fencing-master || a gladiator
Batallador , ra , s. a combattant
Batallar , v. n. to fight || to fence
Batallon , s. m. battalion
Batan , s. m. a fulling-mill
Batanar , v. a. to full clothes
Batanear , v. a. to beat one
Batanero , s. m. fuller of clothes
Batata , s. f. a potatoe-root
Batea , s. f. a tea-table or equipage — kneading-trough [tea
Bategüela , s. f. dim. de Ba-
Batel , s. m. a ship-boat
Batelejo lico , lillo , lito , s. m. a little boat
Bateo , s m. V. Bautizo
Bateria , s. f. battery || beating || kitchen-tackling
Batero , ra s. one that makes night-gowns
Batida , s. f. the act of beating bushes || a violent rain
Batidera , s. f. a plaisterer's beater
Batidero , s. m. beating , striking

Batidero de agua, *a great fall of water*
Batideros, *pl. the lowest part of a ship's cut-water*
Batido, *s. m. paste for biscuits*
Batidor, *s. m. a scout* || *one that beats bushes*
Batidor de oro, *gold-beater*
Batiente, *s. m. fold* or *leaf of a double door*
Batioja, *s. m. gold-beater*
Batiportes, *s. m. port-sells*
Batir, *v. a. to beat*
Batir banderas, *to strike the flag* — el campo, *to scout*—el cobre, *to hammer copper* — la muralla, *to batter walls* — los dientes, *to chatter the teeths* — las alas, *to clap the wings*, — los hijares, *to spur* — moneda, *to coin money*
Batista, *s. f. cambrick*
Batología, *s. f. battólogy*
Batueco, *s. m. a clownish, brutal fellow*
Baturillo, *s. m. a hotchpotch*
Baul, *s. m. trunk*
Baulillo, *s. m. a little trunk*
Bauprés, *s. m. bowsprit*
Bausan, na, *s. a figure made like a man stuffed with straw*
Bautismal, *a. 2. baptismal*
Bautismo, *s. m. baptism*
Bautisterio, *s. m. the font* or *place of baptism*
Bautizar, *v. a. to baptise*
Baxa, *s. m. a turkish bashaw*
Baxa, *s. f. abatement* || *an old dance*
Baxada, *s. f. a descent*
Baxamar, *s. f. low-water*
Baxamente, *adv. lowly*
Baxamiento, s. m. descending
Baxar, v. n. to descend || *to fall, decrease, etc.*
Baxar, *v. a. to bring* or *let down* || *to bate, to abate* || *to humble*
Baxarse de la querella, *to desist*
Baxel, *s. m. ship; vessel*
Baxelero, *s. m. the master of a ship*
Baxero, ra, *a. that is below*
Baxete, *s. m. V.* Barítono || *man of a low stature*
Baxeza, *s. f. lowness* || *a base action*
Baxío, *s. m. a flat* || *decline; decay* || *lowering in price, etc.*
Baxío, xía, } *adj. low* ||
Baxo, xa, } *deep*
Hombre baxo, *a mean man* — Mar baxa, *a shallow sea*
Baxo, *adv. donn; low*
Baxo, *s. m. the bass in musick* || *V.* Baxío || *a horse's hoof*
Baxos, *pl. under-clothes* || *horse's foots*
Baxon, *s. m. bassoon*
Baxoncillo, *s. m. dim. de* Baxon
Baxuelo, la, *adj. dim. de* Baxo
Baya, *s. f. berry* || *sham; stam*
Bayal, *s. m. a frame used in shifting mill-stones*
Bayeta, *s. f. a kind of woollen stuff*
Bayla, *s. f. a sea-trout*
Baylador, ra, *s. dancer*
Bayladorcillo, la, *s. dim. de* Baylador
Baylar, *v. n. to dance*
Baylarin, na, *s. dancer*
Bayle, *s. m. dance* || *a ball* || *a bailiff*
Baylecito, s. m. dim. de Bayle
Baylía, *s. f.* } *b*
Bayliazgo, *s. m.* } *s*
Bayliage, *s. m. a ben[efice] among the knight[s of] Malta*
Baylío, *s. m. knigh[t of] Malta that obtai[ns a] benefice*
Bayo, ya, *a. of a bay*
Bayoco, *s. m. a little [ita]lian coin*
Bayoneta, *s. f. bayon[et]*
Bayonetazo, *s. m. a wo[und] made with a bayo[net]*
Bayoque, *s. m. V.* Ba[yoco]
Bayuca, *s. f. a taver[n]*
Bayvel, *s. m. bevel*
Baza, *s. f. trick at ca[rds]*
Bazo, *s. m. the splee[n]*
Bazo, za, *adj. brown*
Bazofia, *s. f. remna[nts;] scraps*
Bazucar, *v. a. to mix [ag...]*
Bazuqueo, *s. m. mixi[ng]*
Bé, *the cry of a sheep*
Beata, *s. f. a sort of [reli]gious woman* || *an [hy]pocrite female*
Beatería, *s. f. bigotry*
Beaterio, *s. m. a h[ouse] where the* beatas *li[ve]*
Beatico, ca, *s. a big[ot]*
Beatificacion, *s. f. b[eati]fication*
Beatificar, *v. a. to be[atify]*
Beatífico, ca, *a. beat[ific]*
Beatilla, *s. f. a sort o[f li]nen wove*
Beatitud, *s. f. beatit[ude]*
Beato, ta, *a. happy; [bles]sed* || *devout* || *big[ot]*
Bebedero, *s. m. dra[wer of] a bird-cage* || *a [place] for beasts to drin[k]*
Bebedero, ra, *a. po[table]*
Bebedizo, *s. m. a dr[ink]* || *love-potion*
Bebedizo, za, *a. drin[kable]*
Bebedor, ra, *s. dri[nker]*

a. to drink
f. drink || *po-*
[*ken*
ien), *a. drun-*
ır, *v. n. to sip ;*
e
s. m. a draught
ension in a col-
ɛll of cloth worn
students, etç.
f. a woodcock
s. m. beccafigo
, lla, *s. young*

-a, *s. calf*
. *m. calves-lea-*

arino, *sea-calf*
s. m. Voy. Pa_

n. beadle
s. f. a beadle's

s. m. hangman
f. a flock of wool
ra, *s. one that*
the fallen wool
. *m. V.* Bequa-

a scoff ; a jest
s. m. S, (*in*
)
a. to scoff ; to

s. a horse's lip
da, *s. a sort of*
;
m. a puff-ball
ssionate man
na, *s. a sort of*
;
s. f. a city, etc.
m the subjec-
any lord || *con-*
disorder
s. m. a rushy
[*rush*
. *m. a kind of*
, *s. m. a little*

golden chain || *ipeca-cuanha*
Beldad, *s. f. beauty*
Beleño, *s. m. hen-bane* || *V.* Veneno
Belerico, *s. m. V.* Mirabolano [*der-lip*
Belfo, *s. m. a horse's un-*
Belfo, fa, *a. one who has a hanging under-lip*
Belhez, *s. f. y* Belhezo, *s. m. a great jar*
Bélico, ca, *a. warlike*
Belicoso, sa, *a. martial*
Belígero, ra, *a. belligerous*
Belitre, *adj. a beggar ; a scoundrel* [*vishly*
Bellacamente, *adv. kna-*
Bellaco, *s. m. a knave*
Bellaco, ca, *a. ill ; wicked* || *cunning*
Bellacon *y* Bellaconazo, *s. m. aum. de* Bellaco
Bellamente, *adv. fairly ; finely* [*the knave*
Bellaquear, *v. n. to play*
Bellaquería, *s. f. knavery*
Belleza, *s. f. beauty*
Decir Bellezas, *to speak with particular graces*
Bello, lla, *a. fair, beautiful*
Bellorio (caballo), *s. m. a horse of a mouse colour*
Bellorita, *s. f. cowslip ; primrose*
Bellota, *s. f. acorn*
Bellote, *s. m. a round-headed nail*
Bellotear, *v. n. to eat acorns*
Bellotera, *s. f. forest-mast*
Bellotero, *s. m. time* or *place where acorns are gathered*
Bellotero, ra, *s. one that gathers* or *sells acorns*
Bellotica, *s. f. a small acorn*

Belortas, *s. f. pl. iron-rings in the plough*
Bemol, *s. m. a B flat in musick*
Bendecir, *v. a. to bless*
Bendicion, *s. f. a blessing*
Bendito, ta, *adj. blessed* || *silly*
Benedicta, *s. f. a stomachick electuary*
Benedictino, na, *a. benedictine* [*tor*
Benefactor, *s. m. benefac*
Beneficencia, *s. f. beneficence*
Beneficiado, *s. m. incumbent ; beneficed*
Beneficiador, ra, *s. a careful administrator*
Beneficial, *adj.* 2. *belonging to a benefice*
Beneficiar, *v. a. to benefit ; to improve* || *to collate a benefice* || *to make the best of an estate, etc.* || *to refine gold, etc.*
Beneficiario, *s. m. beneficiary*
Beneficio, *s. m. benefit* || *benefice* || *improving*
Beneficioso, sa, *a. beneficial* [*cent*
Benéfico, ca, *adj. benefi-*
Benemerencia, *s. f. good turns ; service*
Benemérito, ta, *a. well deserving*
Beneplácito, *s. m. permission ; approbation*
Benevolencia, *s. f. good-will* [*her*
Benévolo, la, *a. well-wis-*
Benignamente, *ad. kindly*
Benignidad, *s. f. benignity*
Benigno, na, *a. benign*
Benito, ta, *s. a benedictine monk or nun*
Benjui, *s. m. benjamin*

Bequadrado, *subs. m. a B sharp (in musick)*
Beque, *s. m. a privy in a ship* [*ker*
Bequebo, *s. m. wood-pec-*
Bérberis } *s. m. barberry*
Berbero }
Berbiquí, *s. m. a wimble*
Bercero, ra, *s. V.* Verdulero
Berengena, *s. f. a kind of pumpion*
Berengenado, da, *adj. V.* Aberenjenado
Berengenal, *s. m. a field where* berengenas *grow*
Berengenazo, *s. m. a blow with a* berengena
Bergamota, *s. f. bergamot pear*
Bergamote, } *s. m. bergamot tree*
Bergamoto, }
Bergante, *s. m. a rogue ; a rascal* [*tine*
Bergantin, *s. m. brigan-*
Bergantinejo, *s. m. a little brigantine*
Berganton y **Bergantonazo**, *s. m. a great rogue*
Berilo, *s. m. beryl*
Berlína, *s. f. a berlin*
Berlinga, *s. f. a perpendicular stake*
Berma, *s. f. a berm*
Bermejear, *v. n. to be reddish* || *to blush*
Bermejizo, za, *a. reddish*
Bermejo, ja, *adj. red*
Bermejon, na, *a. reddish*
Bermejuela, *s. f. a reddish fish* [*dish*
Bermejuelo, la, *a. red-*
Bermejura, *s. f. redness*
Bermellon, *s. m. vermilion* [*montados*
Bernandinas, *s. f. pl. ro'o-*
Bernado, da, s. Bernardin, ine
Bernegal, s. m. a flat cup

Bernia, *s. f. a coarse cloth*
Berra, *s. f. cresses*
Berraza, *s. f. over-grown water-cresses*
Berrear, *v. n. to bellow*
Berreguetar, *v. n. to cheat at cards*
Berrinchin, *s. m. wild-boar's odour* || *spite ; anger*
Berrendearse, *v. r. to grow vary-coloured*
Berrendo, da, *adj. party-coloured*
Berrera. *s. f. V.* Berraza
Berrido, *s. m. bellowing*
Berrin, *s. m. a peevish child*
Berro, *s. m. water-cresses*
Berrocal, *s. m. a place full of rocky hillocks*
Berroqueña, *s. f. a sort of speckled coarse marble*
Berrueco, *s. m. an uneven hillock* || *tumour in the eye. V.* Barrueco
Berruga, *s. f. a wart*
Berrugaza, *s. f. aum. de* Wart [*ty*
Berrugoso, sa, *adj. war-*
Berza, *s. f. a cabbage*
Berza perruna, *wild mercury* -- crespa, *curled cabbage*—colorada, *red cabbage* — florida, *colly flower*
Berzaza, *s. f. aum. de* Berza
Besamanos, *s. m. a kissing of the hand*
Besana, *subs. f. the first furrow*
Besar, *v. a. to kiss*
Besico, ito, *s. m. dim. de* Beso
Beso, *s. m. a kiss* [*beast*
Bestezuela, *s. f. a little*
Bestia, *s. f. beast*
Gran bestia, *elk*
Bestial, *a. 2. beastly*

Bestialidad, *sub. f. beast-liness* [*tially*
Bestialmente, *adv.* [illegible]
Bestecica, cilla, cita, [illegible]la, *s f. a little beast*
Bestion, *subs. m. a great beast* || *V.* Bastion
Besucador, *s. m.* [illegible]
Besucar, *v. a. to ki*[illegible] *often*
Besucada, *s. f.* [illegible] *made with sea-*[illegible]
Besugo, *s. m. sea* [illegible]
Besuguero, *s. m.* [illegible] *sells sea-bream*.
Besuguete, *s. m. a* [illegible] *little sea-bream*
Beta, *s. f. rigging* · *cordage*
Betarraga, *s. f. beet-root*
Betónica, *s. f. betony*
Betun, *s. m. bitumen*
Betunar, *v. a. V.* Embetunar
Beuna, *s. f. a sort of* [illegible]*dish grape* [illegible]
Beud, *s. m. a kind of* [illegible]
Bezaar, *s. m. V.* Bezar
Bezaartico, ca, *a. V.* Bezoardico
Bezante, *s. m. besant*
Bezar, *s. m. bezoar-stone*
Bezo, *s. m. a thick lip*
Bezoar, *s. m. V.* Bezar
Bezoárdico, ca, *a. belonging to the bezoar-stone*
Bezon, *s. m. V.* Ariete
Bezole, *s. m. a ring i*[illegible] *the under-lip*
Bezudo, da, *adj. having thick lips*
Biazas, *s. f. pl. V.* Bizazas
Bíbaro, *s. m. a beaver*
Biblia, *s. f. the bible*
Bíblico, ca, *adj. belonging to the bible*
Biblioteca, *s. f. library*
Bibliotecario, *sub. m. librarian*
Bicerra, *s. f. chamois*

a, s. any insect
:ral
f. centry-box ||
paltry town ||
etc.
, s. m. a sort of
a. 2. bicornous
m. pl. a little
tuft [ged hoe
:. m. a two-pron-
f. a kind of fork
'. a. to winnow
s. m. a sort of fork to win-now corn with
:. good
l. estate; means
'. well; right ||
ly || very
dj. 2. biennial
za, s. f. happi-
[happily
uradamente, ad.
urado, da, adj.
|| happy
uranza, s. f. bea-
| happiness
iado, da, a. hap-
[jerusalem
da, s. f. oak of
lo, da, a. who
well
r, s. m. bene-
ub. m. the space
years
r, v. a. to belove
teem
r, s. m. good-
affection
, ta, a. beloved
a, s. f. a welco-
cloth
a. a sort of linen
s. 2. biformed
adj. 2. that has
f. bigamy

Bigamo, s. m. twice married || bigamist
Bigardía, s. f. dissimulation; fraud
Bigardo, s. m. an unruly monk
Bigarrado, da, a. V. Abigarrado
Bigorda, s. f. bind-weed
Bigorneta, s. f. dim de Bigornia
Bigornia, s. f. a rising anvil || a vice
Bigotazo, s. m. a great whisker
Bigote, s. m. whisker
Bigotera, s. f. a little bag to put the whisker into || a knot of riband || stool; cricket
Bija, s. f. V. Achiote
Bilioso, sa, a. bilious
Bilis, s. f. choler
Billete, s. m. billet; note || a bill of exchange, etc.
Billetico, s. m. a little note || a billet-doux
Bilmador, s. m. bone-setter
Bilorta, s. f. an iron ring
Biltrotear, ver. n. to gad about the streets
Biltrotera, s. f. a gadding woman
Bimestre, s. m. the space of two months
Bimestre, a. 2. two months old [again
Binador, s. m. one that digs
Binar, v. a. to dig again
Binario, adj. m. binary
Binazon, s. f. diggin again
Binóculo, sub. m. double prospective
Binza, s. f. pellicle
Biombo, s. m. folding-screen
Bipartid[illegible]da, a. bipartite
Birar[illegible] a. to put about a ship || to heave the capstern

Biribis, s. m. a kind of play or lottery
Biricú, s. m. a belt
Birilla, s. f. edge; border
Birlador, s. m. one that tips [pins
Birlar, v. a. to tip at nine-
Birlocha, s. f. a kite
Birlonga, s. f. a game so called
Birola, s. f. a ferrule
Birlos, s. m. pl. nine-pins
Birreta, s. f. a cardinal's cap
Birrete, s. m. a cap
Birretina, s. f. a grenadier's cap
Bisabuelo, la, sub. great grandfather; or mother
Bisagra, s. f. hinge
Bisalto, s. m. green pease
Bisbis, s. m. V. Biribis
Bisel, s. m. any thing done sloping
Bisextil, } a. bissextile
Bisiesto, }
Mudar bisiesto, to turn over a new leaf
Bisílabo, adj. dissyllable
Bisojo, ja, a. squint-eyed
Bisoñada y Bisoñería, s. f. a blunder, etc.
Bisoño, adj. a new raised soldier [fle
Bisonte, s. m. a wild buf-
Bistorta, s. f. snake-weed
Bitácora, s. f. the bittacle
Bitas, s. pl. bitto
Bitor, s. m. a rayle
Bitumen, s. m. V. Betun
Bituminoso, sa, adj. bituminous
Bivar, s. m. a goose
Biza, s. f. V. Bonito
Bizarramente, adv. courageously [courage
Bizarrear, v. n. to act with

Bizarria, s. f. *courage; magnanimity* || *generosity; sumptuousness*
Bizarro, ra, a. *courageous* || *generous; magnificent* [*bags*
Bizazas, s. f. pl. *knapsack;*
Bizco, ca, a. *squint-eyed*
Bizcochada, s. f. *soup made with biscuit, etc.*
Bizcochillo, ito, uelo, s. *a fine small biscuit*
Bizcocho, s. m. *biscuit*
Bizcotela, s. f. *a kind of sugared biscuit*
Bizma, s. f. *a poultice*
Bizmar, v. a. *to poultice*
Biznaga, s. f. *wild fennel*
Biznieto, ta, s. *a great-grand-son* or *daughter*
Bizuejo, ja, adj. *squint-eyed*
Blanca, s. f. *blank, (a coin) minum (in musick)*
Blanco, ca, a. *white*
Blanco, s. m. *white* || *mark to shoot at* || *a break; a blank*
Blancor, s. m. } *whiteness* || *a web in the eye*
Blancura, s. f. }
Blandales, s. f. pl. *cross-trees* [*gently*
Blandamente, adv. *softly;*
Blandeador, ra, s. *wavering*
Blandear, v. n. *to waver* || *to yeld*
Blandear, v. a. *to dissuade* || V. Blandir
Blandearse, v. r. *to shake*, or *jog*
Blandiente, a. 2. *shaking*
Blandillo, lla, a. *softish*
Blandir, v. a. *to brandish*
Blandirse, v. r. V. Blandearse
Blando, da, adj. *soft; tender* || *gentle; mild*

Blandon, s. m. *taper* || *candlestick*
Blandoncillo, s. m. *a little candlestick*
Blandura, s. f. *softness* || *gentleness* || *an emollient poultice, etc.* || *mildness of the weather, etc.*
Blandurilla, s. f. *paste used by the for their hands, etc.* [quicion
Blanqueacion, s. f. V. Blan-
Blanqueador, ra, s. *whitener*
Blanqueadura, s. f. y Blanqueamiento, s. m. Voy. Blanqueo
Blanquear, v. a. *to whiten*
Blanquecedor, s. m. *whitener*
Blanquecer, v. a. *to whiten silver, etc.* [*white*
Blanquecer, v. n. *to grow*
Blanquecino, na, a. *whitish*
Blanqueo, s. m. *whitening*
Blanqueria, s. f. *a bleaching ground*
Blanquicion, s. f. *wash to whiten silver*
Blanquilla, s. f. *a small silver coin* [*tish*
Blanquillo, izco, a. *whi-*
Blao, s. m. *azure*
Blasfemable, adj. 2. *blameable* [*phemer*
Blasfemador, ra, s. *blas-*
Blasfemamente, adv. *blasphemously* || *outrageously* [*pheme*
Blasphemar, v. a. *to blas-*
Blasfematorio, ria, a. *blasphemous*
Blasfemia, s. f. *blasphemy*
Blasfemo, ma, s. *blasphemer*
Blasfemo, ma, a. *blasphe-mous*
Blason, s. m. *blazon* || *honour; glory* [illegible]

[illegible] Hacer blason. *t*
Blasonador, ra, [illegible] *ting*
Blasonar, v. a. *t*
Blasonar, v. n. [illegible] *to swag*
Bledo, s. m
Blonda, s. f. *blo*
Blondina, sub. f Blonda
Blondo, da, a. *fal*
Bloquear, v. a. *to*
Bloqueo, s. m.
Boa, s. f. *a n serpent*
Boato, s. m. *oste*
Bobada, s. f. V. I
Bobalias, Bobali barron, s. m. I
Bobamente, adv. || *carelessly*
Bobáticamente, a
Bobático, ca, adj
Bobazo, s. m. *a g*
Bobear, v. n. *to do foolishly*
Boberia, s. f. *foll pery*
Bobicalto, adj. *a plays the man* || *a silly bu style*
Bóbilis bóbilis (*without pain*
Bobillo, s. m. *modesty bit*
Bobillo, ito, s. *m fool*
Bobina, s. f. *a bo*
Bobo, ba, s. *a f*
Bobo, s. m. *buff*
Bobon, na, s. *a g*
Boboncillo, lla, s *fool*
Bobote, s. m. V.
Boca, s. f. *the an opening* || edge || taste;
Boca de calle, tl

ance into a street
aego, any sort of
ns — de noche,
fall — de lobo,
t darkness
s. m. an opening
inal
Bocacin, sub. m.
ne
s. f. a mouthful
, v. a. to bite
, s. m. a small
nouthful || a sort
linen
s. m. bit; mor-
biting || poison
bit of a bridle || a
bit
m. a jug || strait
ce of a port ||
-piece
pozo, the mouth
ell
. V. Vocal
ga, s. f. extremity
eeve
, s. f. a mouth-
liquor
de gente, a crowd
ple — de viento,
of wind
v. n. V. Bocezar
m. the brim of a
tc. || torus; moul-
[mouldings
, v. a. to make
, sub. m. a little
ling [moulding
subs. m. a great
s. f. fragments
the lips
, v. n. to gape,
m
s. m. gaping
.f. a bowl
bocha, spungy
v. a. to drive out
l with another

Bochazo, sub. m. a stroke with a bowl
Boche, s. m. cherry-pit
Bochista, s. m. a dextrous player at bowls
Bochorno, s. m. hot weather || shame; blush, etc.
Bocina, subs. f. hunter's horn || speaking-trumpet || the little bear
Bocinero, s. m. one that winds a cornet
Bocinilla, subst. f. a little cornet
Bocolica, s. f. an exquisite meat
Bocon, subst. m. a great mouth || a braggadocio
Boda, s. f. a wedding
Bode, s. m. he-goat
Bodega, s. f. cellar-warehouse — hold, in a ship
Bodego, } s. m. paltry-eating-house
Bodegon, }
Bodegoncillo, s. m. dim de Bodegon
Bodegonear, v. n. to sit sotting in a tavern, etc.
Bodegonero, ra, s. paltry victualler
Bodeguero, s. m. a cellar man [cellar
Bodeguilla, s. f. a little
Bodigo, sub. m. bread of flower; manchet
Bodijo, s. m. a ridiculous wedding
Bodocazo, s. m. the stroke of a pellet [knife
Bodollo, s. m. pruning-
Bodomaría, s. f. bottomry
Bodoque, s. m. a pellet of clay
Bodoquera, s. f. a mould to make pellets in
Bodoquillo, s. m. dim. de Bodoque

Bodorrio, s. m. a mean, ill-sorted marriage
Bodrio, s. m. a soup made with remnants
Boezuelo, s. m. an artificial ox to chasing partridges with
Bofe, s. m. the lungs
Bofeta, s. m. a fort of fine linen [ear
Bofetada, s. f. box on the
Bofotan, s. m. V. Bofeta
Bofeton, sub. m. aum. de Bofetada
Bofetoncillo, s. m. dim. de Bofetada
Boga, s. f. rowing
Estar en boga, to be in vogue
Boga, s. m. rower
Bogada, s. f. rowing
Bogador, s. m. rower
Bogar, v. n. to row
Bogavante, s. m. fore-rower [mish cloke
Bohemio, s. m. a bohe-
Bohordo, s. m. a small rod || a round-headed rush
Boil, s. m. an ox-stall
Boitrino, s. m. a kind of fishing-net
Bol, s. m. bole
Bola, s. f. bowl; ball || a fib; a lye
Bolada, s. f. V. Bolazo
Bolado, s. m. a cake made with sugar, etc.
Bolantin, subs. m. a fine thin packthread
Bolarménico, s. m. bole armeniak
Bolazo, s. m. a stroke of a bowl
Bolchaco, ca, sub. a great purse or pocket
Bolea, s. f. a spring-tree-bar
Bolcar, v. n. to play a

billiards || *to throw a bowl, etc.*

Bolero, *s. m. a child that flies from his parents*

Boleta, *s. f. ticket* || *a billet for quarters* || *pass* || *a cornet* or *coffin of paper*

Boletar, *v. a. to wrap in cornets*

Boletin, *s. m. an order for paying money* || *a billet for quartering*

Boliche, *s. m. a jack to bowl at* || *small fish*

Juego del boliche, *nine holes*, or *troll-madam*

Bolichero, ra, *s. a gaming house-master*

Bolilla, *s. f. a little bowl*

Bolillo, *s. m. a little nine-pin* || *a bobbin to make lace* || *the port, at billiards*

Bolillos, *pl. a sort of march-panes*

Bolin, *sub. m. a jack to bowl at*

Bolina, *s. f. sounding line* || *bowline* || *tumult; confusion* [*about*

Ir á la bolina, *to tack*

Bolinete, *s. m. the vice of a capstan*

Bol'sa, *s. f. ashes*

Bolla, *sub. f. a duty upon the clothes*

Bollar, *v. a. V.* Abollar

Bollico, *subs. m. dim. de* Bollo

Bollido, da, *a. boiled*

Bollo, *s. m. bread with milk, eggs, sugar, etc.* || *bruise* || *relievo*

Bollos, *pl. buckles of hair*

Bollon, *s. m. stud* || *bud*

Bollonado, da, *a. studded*

Bolluelo, s. m. dim. de Bollo

Bolo, *s. m* [illegible] || *cushion* [illegible] || *newel* [illegible] || *a gig* [*meniak*

Bolo arménico, *bole armeniak*

Bolonio, *s. m. an ignorant man* [*bag*

Bolsa, *s. f. a purse* || *a*

Bolsas, *pl. the scrotum* || *rumples; folds*

Bolsa de corporales, *corporal box*

Bolsear, *v. n. to pucker*

Bolsica, *s. f. a little purse*

Bolsicalávera, *subs. f. an empty purse*

Bolsico, *s. m. V.* Bolsillo

Bolsilla, ita, *s. f. a little purse*

Bolsillo, *s. m. a purse* || *money* || *a coat-pocket*

Bolso, *s. m. purse*

Bolson, *s. m. a great purse*

Bomba, *s. f. a pump* || *a bomb* [*spout*

Bomba marina, *a water*

Bombarda, *s. f. bombarde* || *a bomb-vessel*

Bombardear, *v. a. to bombard* [*bardment*

Bombardeo, *s. m. bom-*

Bombardero, *s. m. bombardier*

Bombasi, *s. m. bombasin*

Bombazo, *s. m. the noise of a cracking bomb*

Bombear, *v. a. to bombard*

Bonancible, *a. fair, calm*

Bonanza, *subs. f. calm; calmness*

Bonazo, za, *a. very good natured* [*kindness*

Bondad, *s. f. goodness;*

Bondadoso, sa, *a. bountiful*

Boneta, *s. f. bonnet of a sail; drabler*

Bonetada, *s. f. cap; capping*

Bonete, *sub. m. a cap;* [illegible] || [illegible]

Bonetería, *s. f. a cap-maker's shop*

Bonetero, *s. m. cap maker* || *spindle-tree*

Bonetillo, *s. m. a little cap*

Bonicamente, *adv. tolerably; so, so* || *prudently* || *secretly* [*good*

Bonico, ca, *a. tolerably*

Bonificar, *v. a. to allow* || *to improve*

Bonificativo, va, *adj. improving*

Bonina, *s. f. camomile*

Bonitalo, *s. m. V.* Benito

Bonitamente, *adv. V.* Bonicamente [*sea-fish*

Bonito, *s. m. a kind of*

Bonito, ta, *a. passable* || *pretty* || *effeminate*

Bonvaron, *s. m groundsel*

Boñiga, *s. f. cow-dung*

Boñigar (higo), *sub. m. a great white fig*

Bootes, *s. m. bootes*

Boque, *s. m. he goat*

Boqueada, *s. f. a gaping* or *yawning*

A' la primera boqueada *immediately* — la última boqueada, *the last gasp*

Boquear, *v. n. to open the mouth* || *to expire*

Boquear, *v. a. to utter*

Boquera, *s. f. opening on the side of a canal* || *pimple in the mouth*

Boqueron, *s. m. a great opening* || *anchovy*

Boquete, *s. m. a narrow entrance, etc.*

Tomar boquete, *to escape*

Boquiabierto, ta, *a. open mouthed*

Boquiancho, cha, *a. with a large mouth*

[illegible] *a. with* [illegible]

[illegible]

[illegible] *adj.* [illegible]

[illegible], da, *adj.* [illegible]

Boquihendido, *adj. with a large mouth*

Boquihundido, da, *a. that has the mouth sunk in*

Boquilla, *subst. f. a little mouth*, or *opening — hole*

Boquimuelle, *adj. tender-mouthed || credulous, etc.*

Boquin, *s. m. the coarsest sort of bays*

Boquinegro, *s. m. a sort of snail*

Boquinveli, *subst. m. an unexperienced person*

Boquirasgado, da, *a. with a very large mouth*

Boquiroto, ta, *a. talker; romancer*

Boquirubio, bia, *a. simpleton; credulous*

Boquiseco, ca, *adj. dry-mouthed* [hundido

Boquisumido, *V.* Boqui-

Boquita, *subst. f. a little mouth*

Boquituerto, ta, *awry-mouthed*

Borbollar, *v. n. to bubble up*

Borbollon, *s. m. bubbling up; gushing out || flow of words* [lar

Borbotar, *v. n. V.* Borbol-

Borcegui, *s. m. buskin*

Borceguineria, *s. f. a buskin-maker's shop*

Borceguinero, ra, *s. buskin-maker*

Borda, *s. f. the main sail of a galley*

Bordado, *s. m. embroidery*

Bord[illegible]ra, *s. embroiderer*

Bordadura, *s. f. embroidery || bordure*

Bordar, *v. a. to embroider*

Borde, *s. m. edge; brim || a bastard son*

Bor[illegible] (árboles), *wild ungrafted trees*

Bordear, *v. n. to ply to windward by boards*

Bordo, *s. m. board*

Bordon, *s. m. pilgrim's staff || the base string of an instrument || burden of a song, etc.*

Bordoncico, cillo, *s. m. dim. de* Bordon

Bordonear, *v. n. to feel*, or *strike with a walking staff || to wander || to to play upon the base strings*

Bordonería, *s. f. a wandering life* [bond

Bordonero, *s. m. a vaga-*

Bordura, *s. f. bordure*

Boreal, *a. 2. northern*

Boreas, *s. m. north-wind*

Borgoñota, *s. f. burganet*

Borla, *s. f. a tuft*

Borlilla, ita, *s. f. a little tuft* [*tuft*

Borlon, *subs. m. a great*

Borne, *s. m. a sort of oak*

Borneadizo, za, *a. flexible*

Bornear, *v. a. to bend; to warp || to turn up*

Bornearse, *v. r. to warp; to cast*

Borneo, *s. m. bending || turning up*

Bornera, *subs. f. a black mill-stone*

Bornero, *a. ground with the* bornera

Borni, *subs. m. a sort of hawk* [*maiz*

Borona, *s. f. a kind of*

Boronía, *s. f. V.* Alboronía

Borra, *sub. f. a sheep of a year old || cow's hair, etc. || tax on sheep || dregs; grounds*

Borra, *int. o! pho!*

Borracha, *s. f. a leather bottle* [rachera

Borrachada, *s. f. V.* Bor-

Borrachear, *v. n. to fuddle*

Borrachera, } *s. f. drunkenness*
Borrachería, }

Borrachez, *s. f. ebriety || the intoxication of the passions*

Borracho, cha, *a. drunk, drunken || preyed upon by pride, etc.*

Borrachon, } *s. m. a great drunkard*
Borrachonazo, }

Borrachuelo, *s. m. a little drunkard*

Borrador, *s. m. foul copy || day book*

Borragear, *v. a. to scribble; to scrawl*

Borrar, *v. a. to bar; to strike out || to darken*

Borrasca, *s. f. a storm || a broil; a fray*

Borrascoso, sa, *adj. tempestuous*

Borrax, *s. m. borax*

Borraxa, *s. f. borage*

Borregada, *s. f. a flock of lambs*

Borrego, ga, *s. a lamb || an unexperienced person* [*nest man*

Borregon, *s. m. a good ho-*

Borreguero, *s. m. shepherd* [Borrego

Borreguillo, *s. m. dim. de*

Borren, *s. m. pannel of a saddle*

Borricada, *s. f. a drove of asses || foolishness*

Borrico, ca, *s. an ass*
Borricon, **Borricote**, *s. m. a great ass*
Borriqueño, ña, *a. belonging to an ass*
Borriquero, *s. m. ass-driver*
Borriqnillo, ito, *s. m. a little ass*
Borro, *s. m. a lamb of a year old* || *a stupid ignorant fellow* || *tax on sheeps*
Borron, *s. m. erasement* || *a blot* || *default* || *dishonour* || *a sketch*
Borronazo, *s. m. aum. de* Borron
Borroncillo, *s. m. dim. de* Borron
Borroso, sa, *adj. full of dregs*
Borrufalla, *s. f. a trifle*
Borrumbada, *s. f. a rash, inconsiderate action*
Borujon, *s. m. V.* Burujon
Borusca, *s. f. V.* Seroja
Boscage, *s. m. boscage* || *landscape (in painting)*
Boscar, *v. a. V.* Buscar
Bósforo, *s. m. bosphorus; streights*
Bosque, *subs. m. wood; grove*
Bosquecillo, ito, *s. m. a little grove*
Bosquejar, *v. a. to sketch*
Bosquejo, *s. m. a sketch*
Bostezador, *s. m. yawner*
Bostezar, *v. n. to yawn; to gape*
Bostezo, *s. m. yawning*
Bota, *s. f. a leather bottle* || *a butt* || *a boot*
Botador, *s. m. one that drives out* || *an iron to drive nails* || *a dentist's pincer* || *a boat hook*
Botafuego, *s. m. lintstock*
Botámen, *s. m. number of barrels for a ship*
Botana, *s. f. a leather-bottle's stopple* || *a plaister* || *a scar*
Botánica, *s. f. botany*
Botánico, ca, *a. botanick*
Botanista, *s. m. botanist*
Botanomancia, *s. f. divination by herbs*
Botar, *v. act. to turn or drive out* || *to steer* || *to launch a ship*
Botar, *v. n. to rebound*
Botarate, *s. m. an ignorant senseless fellow*
Botarel, *s. m. prop; shore*
Botarga, *sub. f. a kind of pantaloons* || *the dress of harlequin* || *harlequin himself* || *a sort of sausage; botargo*
Botasela, *s. f. the sound to horse*
Botavante, *s. m. boom*
Bote, *s. m. thrust; blow* || *rebound* || *a ship's boat* || *a gallipot* || *cherry-pit* || *launching* || *repertory, etc.*
Botecico, cillo, *s. m. a little gallipot*
Botella, *s. f. a bottle*
Botequin, *sub. m. a little boat*
Botero, *s. m. a leather-bottle-makers*
Botica, *s. f. apothecary's shop* || *purge; physick*
Boticario, *s. m. apothecary*
Botiga, *s. f. shop*
Botiguero, *sub. m. shopkeeper*
Botiguilla, *sub. f. a little shop*
Botija, *sub. f. an earthen jar*
Botijero, *s. m. an earthen-wareman*
Botijilla, uela, *s. j... tle jar*
Botijon, *subst. m.*
Botilla, *s. f. a li... ther-bottle*
Botilleria, *s. f. a ... house where th... frozen drinks*
Botillero, *s. m. o... sells frozen drin...*
Botillo, *s. m. V.* B...
Botin, *s. m. jock...* || *spatterdash* ||
Botinero, *sub. m. who keeps or s... booty*
Botinico, illo, *s. m... tle jockey-boot*
Botiquin, *s. m. box*
Botivoleo, *s. m. king a ball at ... rebound*
Boto, ta, *a. blunt*
Boton, *s. m. a bu... bud* || *a pimple*
Boton de fuego, *a ...*
— **de buba**, *a po...*
Botonadura, *s. f. sc... tons*
Botonazo, *s. m. a... with a foil*
Botoncico illo, ito *dim. de* Boton
Botonero, *s. m. ... maker*
Botryite, *s. m. a*
Bóveda, *s. f. a va...*
Bóveda de jardin, ...
Bovedilla, *s. f. vault*
Box, *s. m. box, b...* || *V.* Boxeo
Boxar, *v. act. to c... about*
**Boxar tantas leg... contain so ma... gues around*
Boxear, *v. a. y n.*

a grove of
s. m. com-
pass
toy
of
Boyuno
ing before
buoy up
a great ox
a ox-stall
cow-herd
m. a little
belonging
uzzle
al, *a mere*
ballo bozal,
med horse
m. a little
wn; downy
er
. a kind of
rize
motion of
. coining
to move the
esist — to
rds
brassets
a gentle-
|| *a day-*
strong dar-
small arm
f. laconism
he fore part
[*arm*
m. a small
j. a short-
dog || *flat-*
[*clouts*
children's

Bragas, *pl. breeches*

Bragada, *s. f. thigh in a quadruped*

Bragado, da, *a. that has thighs a different colour from his body*

Bragadura, *s. f. the twist of a man*

Bragazas, *s. f. pl. great large breeches* || *a coward, etc.*

Braguero, *s. m. a truss-span* [*piece*

Bragueta, *sub f. the cod-*

Braguetero, *s. m. a debauchee*

Bragueton, *s. m. a great cod-piece*

Braguillas, *s. f. pl. small breeches* || *a child in breeches* || *an ugly short man*

Brama, *s. f. rutting-time*

Bramadero, *s. m. the place where the stags bray at rutting-time*

Bramador, ra, *a. roarer*

Bramante, *subs. m. pack-thread*

Bramar, *v. n. to bray; to roar; to bellow, etc.*

Bramido, *sub. m. bellow; roar* [*tool*

Bramil, *s. m. a joiner's*

Bramona (soltar la), *to abuse one*

Bran de Inglaterra, *s. m. an old spanish dance*

Brancada, *s. f. a drag-net*

Branca ursina; *sub. f. set-wort* [*of fishes*

Branchas, *s. f. pl. gills*

Brandales, *subst. m. pl shrouds of the masts*

Brandis, *s. m. a great uppercoat*

Brando, *s. m. brawl*

Branza, *sub. f. a galley-slave's chain*

Braquillo, *s. m. dim. de* Braco

Brasa, *s. f. live coal*

Braserico, illo, ito, *s. m. dim. de* Brasero

Brasero, *sub. m. pan for coals* || *the place where they burn malefactors*

Brasil, *s. m. brasil-wood*

Brasilado, da, *adj. of the brasil colour*

Brasilete, *s. m. a kind of brasil*

Bravamente, *adv. bravely* || *fiercely* || *perfectly abundantly*

Bravata, *s. f. hectoring*

Bravear, *v. n. to brave, to bully*

Braveza, *s. f. fierceness*

Bravillo, lla, *a. dim. de* Bravio [*wild*

Bravio, via, *adj. savage,*

Bravio, *s. m. fierceness*

Bravo, va, *adj. brave* || *swaggerer* || *ferocious, wild* || *terrible* || *good; excellent*

Bravosidad, *s. f. bravery*

Bravura, *s. f. fierceness; wildness* || *valour; courage* || *hectoring*

Braza, *s. f. a fathom*

Brazada, *s. f. V.* Braza *y* Brazado

Brazado, *s. m. an arm-full*

Brazage, *s. m. measuring by fathoms. V.* Braceage

Brazal, *sub. m. brachial muscle* || *brassets* || *a wooden cuff worn by balloon players — a trench*

Brazalete, *s. m. a bracelet. V.* Brassal

Brazazo, *s. m. a great arm*

Brazo, *s. m. arm* || *branch* || *strength; power*

Brazo eclesiástico, *the clergy* — seglar, ó real, *the laity* — militar, *the soldiery*

Brazos de rayno, *the estates of the kingdom* — de la entena, *braces* — de cangrejo, *the claws of a crab*

Brazuelo, *sub. m. a little arm* || *shoulderblade* || *a skin of beef*

Brea, *s. f. pitch and tar* || *a coarse canvas*.

Breadura, *s. f. daubing with tar*

Brear, *v. a. to tar a ship* || *to plague; to molest*

Brebage, *s. m. beverage* || *a potion* || *a drench*

Breca, *s. f. blay* or *bleak fish*

Brecha, *s. f. breach*

Bredo, *s. m. blit*

Brega, *s. f. fray; strife*

Dar brega, *to geer; to laugh at*

Bregar, *v. n. to quarrel; to contend* || *to struggle against fortune, etc.*

Bregar, *v. act. to knead with a rolling-pin* || *to bend a bow*

Brenca, *s. f. maiden-hair*

Brencas, *pl. the bars of a sluice*

Breña, *s. f. a place full of shrubs, etc.* || *a crag of a mountain*

Breñar, *s. m. a craggy, bushy place*

Breñoso, sa, *a. thorny cragged, etc.*

Breque, *s. m. V.* Breca

Bresca, *s. f. a honey-comb*

Brescadillo, *s. m. purl*

Brescado, da, *a. embroidered with purls* [*linen*

Bretaña, *sub. f. a sort of*

Brete, *s. m. fetters* || *distress* || *a bolt* || *a sort of rack*

Breton, *s. m. sprout*

Breva, *s. f. an early fig* or *acorn*

Breve, *sub. m. the pope's brief*

Breve, *a. 2. brief; short*

Breve, *adv. in short*

Brevecico, illo, ito, *a. a little brief*

Brevedad, *s. f. brevity*

Brevemente, *adv. briefly*

Breveto, *s. m. a little bill,* or *note*

Breviario, *s. m. breviary*

Brezo, *s. m. a sort of rosemary*

Briaga, *s. f. a rope made with rushes*

Brial, *s. m. a sort of garment worn by queens, etc.* [*begging*

Briba, *sub. f. mumping;*

Bribia, *s. f. V.* Briba

Bribiático, ca, *a. belonging to the mumping*

Bribion, *s. m. V.* Bribon

Bribon, na, *sub. beggar; mumper; vagabond*

Bribonada, *s. f. knavery*

Bribonazo, *s. m. aum. de* Bribon || *a crafty knave*

Briboncillo, *sub. m. dim. de* Bribon

Briboncar, *v. n. to mump; to wander up and down*

Bribonería, *s. f. beggary; vagrancy*

Bribonzuelo, *s. m. V.* Briboncillo

Bricho, *s. m. a thin plate of gold, etc.*

Brida, *s. f. a bridle*

Andar á la brida, *to ride long in the stirrups*

Bridar, *v. a.* to bridle

Bridon, *sub. m.* one that *rides long in the* [*stir*]*rups*

Brigada, *sub. f. b*

Brigadier, *s. m. b*

Brillador, ra, *a. s*

Brilladura, *s. f. V.*

Brillante, *s. m. a br*

Brillantez, *s. f. V.*

Brillar, *v. n. to shi*

Brillo, *s. m. brigh*[*t*] *splendor*

Brincador, *s. m.*

Brincar, *v. n. to lea*[*p*] *skip*

Brincho, *subst. m.* (*at cards*)

Brincia, *s. f. onion's*

Brinco, *s. m. a leap; skip*

Brindar, *v. n. to drink* || *to offer* || *to engage*

Brindis, *s. m. a health drinking*

Brinquillo, } Brinquiño, } *s. m. a little joy*

Brio, *s. m. strenght; vigour* || *courage* || *liveliness*

Hombre de brio, *a man of mettle*

Briol, *s. m. bunt-line*

Briosamente, *adv. strenuously*

Brioso, sa, *a. strenuous; mettlesome* || *lively*

Brisa, *sub. f. north-east wind*

Brisca, *s. f. a breeze*

Briscado (hilo), *silver* or *gold wire*

Briscar, *v. a. to twist silver* or *gold*

Briso, *s. f. a breeze*

Británica, *s. f. spoon wort*

Brizna, *subst. f. splent; splinter*

Briznoso, sa, *adj. full of* splinters, etc.

Broca, *s. f.* bobbin || pier-

|| [illegible] shoemaker's k[illegible]
[illegible]dillo, s. m. dim. de [illegible]ado
[illegible]do, s. m. brocade
[illegible] s. brim of a [illegible]k, verrel of a [illegible]
[illegible]ta, the mouth [illegible]her bottle
[illegible]on, s. m. clasp, [illegible]tc.
[illegible]co, s. m. axiom
[illegible], s. m. lindsey-[illegible]y
[illegible] s. m. V. Brocado
[illegible] s. f. a painter's [illegible] || cogged dice || [illegible] Broche
[illegible]lo, da, a. worked [illegible] gold, silk, etc.
[illegible]dura, s. f. suit of [illegible]ps, etc.
[illegible]he, s. m. clasp || loop [illegible] a coat
[illegible]hica, uela, s. f. a lit[illegible] clasp
[illegible]hon, sub. m. a great [illegible]asp || a great pain[illegible]r's brush
[illegible]uli, s. m. brocoli
[illegible]lio, s. m. V. Bodrio || [illegible]y odd confused mix[illegible]re
[illegible]lista, s. m. one that [illegible]pairs to the monaste[illegible]es to dine upon pot[illegible]ge
[illegible]na, s. f. a worm that [illegible]t wood || ragged sto[illegible]s || soup of oat-meal [illegible]an heavy thing
[illegible]nado, da, a. worm-[illegible]ten || heavy; bad sai[illegible]r
[illegible]no, s. m. wild oats
[illegible]ce, sub. m. bronze; [illegible]ass || trumpet; cla[illegible]

Broncear, v. a. to bronze || to adorn with bronze
Broncería, sub. f. brazen works
Bronchial, a. 2. bronchial
Bronchios, s. m. pl. bronchos
Bronco, ca, adj. coarse; rough hoarse
Bronquedad, s. f. roughness; hourseness
Bronquina, s. f. a quarrel
Broquel, s. m. buckler; target
Broquelazo, s. m. a stroke with a buckler
Broquelero, s. m. target maker || shield-bearer || a quarrelsome fellow
Broquelillo, lete, s. m. a little buckler || ear-bob
Brosquil, s. m. a sheep-fold
Brotadura, s. f. budding
Brotano, s. m. V. Abrótano
Brotar, v. n. to bud; to shoot out
Broton, s. m. clasp of the sayo || sprout
Broza, s. f. dust that falls from worm-eaten vood || chips, shards, etc || stuff of no value || printer's brush
Brozar, v. a. to brush
Brozoso, sa, adj. full of wastes, of chips, etc.
Bruces, s. m. pl. the lips De ó á bruces, with the mouth downwards
Brugidor, sub. m. tool to grind glass with
Brugir, v. act. to grind glass
Brulote, s. m. a fire-ship
Bruma, s. f. V. Broma || a fog at sea
Brumal, a. 2. winterly

Brumar, v. a. to beat one soundly [Bruma
Brumazon, s. m. aum. de
Brumo, s. m. a very pure wax
Brunete, a. 2. brownish
Bruno, na, a. brown
Bruno, sub. m. a kind of plum
Bruñidor, s. m. burnishing-stick
Bruñir, v. a. to burnish
Bruscate, s. m. an old ragoo
Brusco, sub. m. butcher's broom || loose corn at harvest
Brutal, a. 2. brutish
Brutalidad, s. f. brutishness || brutality
Brutalmente, adv. brutishly
Brutesco, V. Grutesco
Bruteza, s. f. roughness
Bruto, subs. m. a brute beast || a brutish man
Bruto, ta, a. rough; unpolished, etc.
Bruxa, s. f. a witch
Bruxear, v. n. to make sorceries || to walk all the night
Bruxería, s. f. witchcraft
Bruxo, s. m. a wizzard
Brúxula, s. f. sea compass || aim (in the gun)
Bruxulear, v. a. to discover one's cards by degrees || to conjecture
Bruxuleo, s. m. discovering by degrees || conjecture
Bruxa, s. f. curry-comb
De bruzas, adv. V. De bruces
Bua, s. f. pimple; pustule || border; limit
Buas, pl. V. Bubas
Buar, v. a. to set limits

Buaro, y Buarillo, s. m. a sort of kestrel
Bubas, s. f. pl. the french pox [ple
Bubilla s. f. little pim-
Bubon, s. m. bubo
Buboso sa a. pocky
Bucaran, s. m. buckram
Bucarito, sub. m. dim. de Búcaro [red cup
Búcaro, s. m. a sort of
Bucear, v. a. to dive under the water
Buceo, s. m. diving
Buces (de), V. De bruces
Bucha, s. f. V. Hucha
Buchar, v. a. to hide or conceal
Buche, subs. m. a bird's crop || ventricle || stomach || a mouthful of liquor [crop, etc.
Buchecillo, s. m. a little
Buchete, subs. m. a cheek puffed up with wind
Bucle, subs. m. buckle; hair-curl
Buco, s. m. V. Buque
Bucólica, s. f. bucolick || food
Bucólico, ca, a. bucolick
Budion, s. m. miller's-thumb
Buega, s. f. limit
Buen, a. good
Buena-boya f. a voluntary rower
Buenamente, adv. well; easily
Bueno, na, a. good || useful; convenient || in good health || great
Bueno, ad well || enough
Bueras, s. f. pl. pimples

Buey, s. m. an ox
Bueyazo, s. m. a great ox
Bueyecillo, s. m. a little ox

Bueyezuelo, s. m. an artificial ox for chasing partridges
Bueyuno, na, a. Voyez Boyuno
Buf! int. fy upon!
Bufa, s. f. jest; derision
Bufado (vidrio), sub. m. glass made into small empty bubbles
Búfalo, la, s. buffalo
Bufar, v. n. to bellow || to puff to blow
Bufete, s. m. a table for writing; scrutoire, etc.
Bufetillo, s. m. dim. de Bufete
Bufido, s. m. bellowing || puffing or blowing
Bufo, fa, s. buffoon
Bufon, s. m. a jester
Bufonada, s. f. buffoonry || a nipping jest
Bufonazo, s. m. aum. de Bufon [Bufon
Bufoncillo, s. m. dim. de
Bufonearse, v. r. to buffoon [nada
Bufonería, s. f. V. Bufo-
Bufonicista, s. m. V. Bufon [nearse
Bufonizar, v. n. V. Bufo-
Bufos, s. m. pl. an ancient head-dress
Bugalla, s. f. a gall-nut
Buge, s. m. an iron ring in the stock of a wheel
Bugía, s. f. a wax candle || flat wax-candlestick
Bugier, s. m. V. Uxier
Buglosa, s. f. bugloss.
Bugula, subs. f. bugle (a plant)
Buharda, s. f. dormer-window
Buhardilla, s. f. dim. de Buharda [mire
Buhedal, s. m. bog; quag-
Buhera, s. f. a loop-hole

Buhero, sub. m. on breeds owls
Buho, s. m. an ow
Buhonería s. f. ped
Buhonero, s. m. pe
Buido, da, adj. l scraggy
Bujarasol, s. m. a re
Bula, s. f. a bull
Bulario, s. m. coll of bulls
Bulbo, s. m. a bul scallion
Bulboso, sa, a. bul
Bulda, s. f. V. Bul
Bulero, s. m. distr of bulls
Buleto, sub. m. a p bull; a brief
Bulla, sub. f. humm murmur || cro throng
Bullador, s. m. mo bank [t
Bullage, s. m. conc
Bullebulle, s. m. a body
Bullicio, s. m. humr buzzing || tumult dition [mult
Bulliciosamente, ad
Bullicioso, sa, a. less; turbulent || tions
Bullidor, ra, s. V. B cioso
Bullir, v. n. to boil bubble up || to b ways stirring
Bullon, s. m. a boilir
Bultillo, sub. m. di Bulto
Bulto, s. m. bulk || ling; bruise, etc. || tomb || a pi case
A' bulto, adv. b great; in genera
Bunio, s. m. wild

s. *one that*
's buñuelos
. *a sort of*
. *a sort of*
'*he bulk* or
ship || *a*
s. *a coarse*
r || *a trans-*
'*rican coin*
. *a kind of*
bubble
n. to bub-
[*bubble*
. *f. a little*
. *a kind of*
t
ay
a bawdy-
coarse
l. binding
deck
. *a mulat-*
. *assembly*
nent of the
hold || *en-*
; *merry-*
t waters
an ancient
erate gold
s. m. bur-
[*cloth*
. *a coarse*
aver; bu-
f. a touch
r
f. engra-
o engrave
great lea-
knapsack

Burla, *s. f. jest; banter; trick*
Burlas, *pl. idle stories*
De burlas, *in jest* — dexadas las burlas, *jesting aside*
Burlador, ra, *s. a jester*
Burlar, *v. a. to jest* || *to impose upon* || *to despise*
Burlería, *s. f. jesting* || *an idle silly story*
Burlesco, ca, *a. burlesque*
Burleta, illa, ita, *s. f. a little jest*
De burlitas, *V.* de Burlas
Burlon, na, *s. a merry jesting companion*
Burra, *s. f. she ass*
Burra de palo, *a ship*
Burrada, *s. f. a company of asses* || *soppery; impertinence*
Burragear, *v. a. V.* Borragear
Burrajo, *s. m. a dry horse-dung*
Burrazo, za, *sub. a great ass*
Burrero, *s. m. ass-driver*
Burrillo, *s. m. V.* Añalejo
Burro, *s. m. an ass* || *a sawing horse* || *a game at cards like beast*
Burros de la mesana, *the fore tackles*
Burrucho, *s. m. a young ass*
Burrumbada, *s. f. V.* Barrumbada
Burujo, *s. m. the husk of grapes, etc.* || *a little tight packet*
Burujon, *s. m. a great packet* || *bruise; swelling*
Burujoncillo, *s. m. a little swelling*
Busca, *s. f. search; quest* || *a questing dog*

Buscador, ra, *s. seeker*
Buscapies, *s. m. serpent; a fire-work*
Buscar, *v. a. to seek; to search*
Buscarruidos, *s. m. a quarrelsome man*
Buscavidas, *s. m. one that pries into the life of others*
Buscon, na, *s. seeker a cunning thief*
Busilis, *s. m. knot, stress, difficulty of a business*
Busto, *s. m. a bust*
Butifarra, *s. f. a sort of pudding* || *a rumpled stocking*
Butillo, lla, *a. yellowish*
Butrino, } *s. m. a net to*
Butron, } *catch birds in*
Buxeda, *s. f.* } *a grove*
Buxedal, *s. m.* } *of box-*
Buxedo, *s. m.* } *trees*
Buxería, *s. f. toy; triffle*
Buxeta, *s. f. a box* || *a perfuming pan*
Buxetilla, *s. f. dim.* de Buxeta
Buytre, *s. m. vulture*
Buytrera, *s. f. a place fit to shoot at vultures*
Buytrero, *s. m. one that catches vultures*
Buytrero, ra, *a. vulturine*
Buytron, *s. m. a weel* || *a net to catch birds* || *a stove to resine silver, etc.*
Buz (hacer el), *to pay a respect; to do honour*
Buzano, *s. m. an ancient cannon*
Buzo, *s. m. diver; plunger* || *a herring buss*
De Busos, *adv. with the mouth downwards*
Buzon, s. m. a conduit-pipe || a post-office's hole || bung; stopple

C.

CABACO, *s. m. fragment of a timber* ||

Cabal, *a. 2. just; exact* || *perfect*

Cabal, *s. m. a natural quality* || *quota*

Al cabal, *adv. V.* Cabalmento

Cabala, *s. f. cabala* || *cabal*

Cabalgada, *s. f. scouts* | *booty; spoil* || *cavalcade*

Cabalgador, *s. m. a horseman*

Cabalgadura, *s. f. a beast of burden*

Cabalgar, *v. n. to ride* || *to leap*

Cabalista, *s. m. cabalist*

Cabalistico, ca, *a. cabalistick*

Caballa, *s. f. a mackerel*

Caballada, *s. f. a. drove of horses*, or *mares*

Caballago, *s. m leaping*

Caballar, *a. 2. belonging to a horse* [*way*

Caballejo, *s. m. tit; galto-*

Caballerato, *s. m. knighthood* || *the right enjoyed by a knight*

Caballerear, *v. n. to live like a knight*, or *gentleman*

Caballerosco, ca, *a. belonging to a knight*

Caballerete, *s. m. a young proud knight*

Caballería, *s. f. any beast to ride upon* || *cavalry* || *military order of knight* || *knight-hood* || *chivalry* || *the nobility and gentry*

Caballerito, *s. m. a young knight*

Caballeriza, *s. f. stable* || *equipage*

Caballerizo, *s. m. master of the horse*

Caballero, *s. m. a knight* || *cavalier*, (*a high platform*) || *an ancient spanish dance* || *a kind of balance*

Caballero andante, *a knight-errant*

A caballero, *adv. above*

Ir caballero, ra, *to ride*

Caballerosamente, *adv. nobly*

Caballeroso, sa, *a. noble; generous*, etc. || *gentleman-like*

Caballerote, *s. m. petty-country-squire*

Caballeta, *s. f. a sort of locust*

Caballete, *s. m. roof-timber* || *the wooden-horse* || *a painter's stand* || *the gallows of a printer's press* || *a brake*

Caballico, ito, *s. m. a tit* || *a hobby-horse*

Caballo, *s. m. a horse* || *a knight* (*at chess*) || *a bubo in the groin* || *the queen* (*at cards*) || *a trestle* || *a mackerel*

Caballo aguabo, *a foundered horse* — albardon, *a pack-horse* — amormado, *glandered horse* — de carro, *a cart-horse* — de silla, *a saddle horse* — arroncinado, *a worthless nag* — corredor, *a fleet horse* — morisco, *a barb* — garañon, *a stallion* — frison, *a great flanders horse* — entero, *a stone-horse* — castrado, *a gelding horse* — de brida, *a running horse* — [...]zado, *a horse tha[t] one w[h]ite fo[o]t* — [...]ñado, *a white ho[rse]* [...]bito, or morcill[o] *black horse* — quat[...] *a horse that h[...] white feet*

Caballos, *pl. horse*, [ca]*val*[r]*y*

Caballos de frisia, *ch*[*evaux*] *de frise* — ligeros, *horses; troopers*

Caballon, *s. m. a horse* || *a ridge be*[*tween*] *furrow and furro*[*w*]

Caballona, *s. f. the* [...] *at chess*

Caballuelo, *s. m. a* [...] *horse* [*com*[...]

Cabalmente, *adv. ju*[*st*...]

Cabaña, *s. f. cot; c*[...] || *a drove of two* [*hun*]*dred sheeps, asse*[...] || *a landscape*

Cabañal, | Cabañero, ra, | Cabañil, } *a. b*[...] *ging* [...] *dro*[...] Cab[...]

Cabañuela, *s. f. a litt*[...]

Cabaya, *s. f. a great* [...] or *loose coat*

Cabe, *s. m. a strok*[*e*...] *bowl on another*

Cabe de paleta, *a de*[...] *blow* [*of a*

Cabeceado, *s. m. th*[...]

Cabecear, *v. n. to s*[...] or *wag the head* || [...] || *to toss* || *to pitc*[*h*...] *sond* [

Cabecear las viga[s...]

Cabecear, *v. a. to* [...] *the full of a lett*[*er*...] *make head-band*[*s*...] *books* || *to edge* [...] *der*, etc. || *to* [...] *an open* [...]

Cabeceo,

a nodding of the

s. f. the upper the table, etc. ||
ead || bolster
cabecera, the
ity
ho, cha, a. large

, ita, s. f. a little
a giddy brain ||
[V. Cabelluelo
, ico, ito, s. m.
, s. f. long hairs
iwig
s. m. hair
le ángel, a pre-
f citron — de car-
large sinews in

, da, a. hairy
ous
o, s. m. short hair
n. to be contai-
to fall to one's
turn
s. to comprehend
ro, s. m. halter;
ng [brestante
ato, s. m. V. Ca-
, v. a. to put a

r, v. n. to hunt
muzzled ox
ar, v. n. to be
by a halter
ria, s. f. the shop
halters are sold
ro, s. m. halter-

lo, s. m. a sling
hurt arm)
, s. m. a. halter
bell-weather || a
to his own wife
s. f. head || begi-
| chief
, s. f. a blow with
d || head-stall ||

pitching || heat-band || foot-leather of a boot

Dar cabezadas, to nod

Cabezal, s. m. a pillow || a bolster

Cabezales, pl. standards of a coach

Cabezalejo, ico, illo, ito, s. m. a little pillow

Cabezo, s. m. hillock || top of a mountain || V. Cabezon y Cuello

Cabezon, s. m. roll of the impositions || neck-band || collar || caves-son [mous head

Cabezorro, s. m. an enor-

Cabezudo, s. m. pollard

Cabeздudo, da, a. who has a great head || head-strong

Cabezuela, sub. f. a little head || a coarse meal || thistle; eringo || a bud of a rose || giddy-brain

Cabezuelo, s. m. top of a hill

Cabial, s. m. caviare

Cabida, s. f. admittance; room

Cabildo, s. m. chapter || chapter-house || council

Cabillo, ito, s. m. a little end

Cabimiento, s. m. V. Cabida

Cabio, s. m. lintel

Cabizbaxo, xa, a. hanging down the head || pensive; melancholy

Cabistuerto, ta, adj. turning the head down || hypocrite

Cable, s. m. cable

Cabo, s. m. end; extremity || a knife-haft || a little piece of a ribbon, etc. || a cape

Cabo de esquadra, a cor-poral — de año, anniversary — de agujeta, a tag — de fila, bringer up

Cabos, pl. rigging; cordage || points; heads

Cabra, s. f. she goat || a crab or gin

Cabra montes, a wild goat

Cabrahigal, } subs. m. the
Cabrahigar, } place where the wild figs grow

Cabrahigo, s. m. a wild fig [goat-herd

Cabrero, rizo, s. m. a

Cabrestante, s. m. capstan [a crab

Cabria, s. f. axle-tree ||

Cabrilla, subs. f. a little goat || a sort of fish

Cabrillas, pl. the pleiades || reddish spots in one's legs [joist

Cabrio, subs. m. rafter;

Cabrío, ía, a. belonging to goats

Cabriola, s. f. a capriol

Cabriolar, } v. n. to ca-
Cabriolear, } per

Cabrita, s. f. she-kid

Cabritero, s. m. one who sells kids

Cabritilla, s. f. kid's skin

Cabritillo, s. m. a little kid

Cabrito, s. m. a kid

Cabron, s. m. he goat || a patient cuckold

Cabronada, s. f. prostitution that a man makes of his own wife

Cabronazo, s. m. a pimp to his own wife

Cabroncillo, cito, zuelo, s. m. a little dirty cuckold

Cabruno, na, a. goatish

Cabujon, s. m. a ruby polished but not cut

Cabuya, *s. f. an indian thread* [*ting*

Caca, *s. f. Ah-ah; shi-*

Cacalia, *s. f. colt's-foot*

Cacao, *s. m. cacao-nut-tree* || *cacao-nut*

Cacaotal, *s. m. the place where the cacao-nut-trees grow*

Cacareador, ra, *s. cackler* || *bragger* [*to brag*

Cacarear, *v. n. to cackle* ||

Cacareo, *s. m. cackling* || *bragging*

Cacear, *v. a. to stir* or *mix in a stew-pan*

Cacera, *s. f. canal; trench*

Cacería, *s. f. a hunting-match* [cera

Cacerilla, *s. f. dim.* de Ca-

Cacerina, *s. f. a cartouch-box*

Caceta, *s. f. a little skillet*

Cacha, *s. f. a knife-haft*

Cachada, *s. f. a blow of a gig on another*

Cachar, *v. a. to bruise to pieces*

Cacharro, *s. m. a potsherd*

Cachaza, *sub. f. dulness; heaviness*

Cachera, *sub. f. a coarse sort of blanket*

Cachetas, *s. f. pl. teeth made in a lock*

Cachete, *s. m. the cheek* || *a cuff on the ear*

Cachetero, *s. m. a short broad knife*

Cachetudo, da, *a. chubbed* [*overseer*

Cachican, *s. m. intendant,*

Cachicuerno, na, *a. horn-hafted*

Cachidíablo, *s. m. an hobgoblin* || *a man of bad inclinations*

Cachigordete, dito, *adj. squat; stubbed*

Cachillada, *s. f. litter*

Cachipolla, *s. f. a sort of butterfly* [*gel*

Cachiporra, *s. f. club; cud-*

Cachivache, *s. m. old broken trumpery* || *a despicable fellow*

Cachbo, *subs. m. a bit; a piece* || *a kind of barbel*

Cacho, cha, *a. V.* Gacho

Cachones, *sub. m. pl. the foam of the sea*

Cachonda (perra), *s. f. a proud bitch*

Cachopo, *subst. m. a dry trunk of tree*

Cachorrillo, ito, *s. m. a little whelp, etc.*

Cachorro, *s. m. a whelp; a bear's cub, etc.* || *a chub-child* || *a little pistol*

Cachuelas, *sub. f. pl. the heart, kidneys, and liver of a rabbit*

Cachuelo, *subs. m. a little fish* [*cave*

Cachulera, *s. f. a den* or

Cachumbo, *s. m. a kind of cocoa-nut-tree*

Cachunde, *s. m. cashoo*

Cachupin, *s. m. spaniard that goes to the west-indies, and settles there*

Cacicazgo, *s. m. dignity of* Cacique

Cacillo, ito, *s. m. a little stew-pan*

Cacique, *s. m. a Prince in the west Indies*

Caco, *sub. m. a cunnin thief* || *a coward* *g*

Cacochímia, *sub. f. cacochymy*

Cacochímico, ca, *a. cacochymical*

Cacochímio, *s. m. ill-complexioned*

acofonía, *s. f.* cacophony

Cacodemon, *sub. m.* [...] *mon; devil*

Cada, *a. every*

Cada que, Cada *y* Q[...] *whensoever*

Cada uno, Cada qual [...] *ry one*

Cadalecho, *sub. m.* [...] *made with bou*[...] *trees*

Cadalso, *s. m. a sc*[...]

Cadañero, ra, *a.* [...]

Muger cadañera, *a*[...] *that breeds every*[...]

Cadarzo, *subs. m.* [...] *silk; ferret, etc.*

Cadáver, *sub. m. co*[...] *carcass*

Cadavérico, ca, *a.* [...] *verous*

Cadejo, *s. m. a ska*[...]

Cadena, *s. f. a chai*[...]

Cadencia, *s. f. cade*[...]

Cadenata, *s. f. a fi*[...] *of needle work*

Cadenilla, ita, *s. f.* [...] *tle chain*

Cadente, *adj.* 2. *rea*[...] *fall — cadenced*

Cadera, *s. f. the hi*[...]

Caderillas, *s. f. pl.* [...] *tle hoop*

Cadete, *s. m. a ca*[...]

Cadillar, *s. m. the* [...] *where the burdock*[...]

Cadillo, *s. m. burd*[...]

Cadillos, *pl. the first*[...] *of a weaver's war*[...]

Cadis, *s. m. caddis*

Cadmía, *s. f. cadmi*[...]

Caducamente, *adv.*[...]

Caducar, *v. n. to d*[...] *to fall to ruin*

Caduceo, *s. m. mer*[...] *wand* || *tip staff*

Caducidad, *s. f.* [...] *of the conditio*[...] *wich an intail w*[...]

Caduco, ca, *a. de*[...]

crazy || *frail; perishable*
egado caduco, *caduke legacy* — mal caduco, *falling-sickness*
laquez, *s. f. weakness; craziness*
dizo, za, *a. ruinous; falling to decay*
r, *v. n. to fall*
áreo, *s. m. a deep gulf*
é, *s. m. coffee* || *coffee house*
étan, *s. m. caftan*
etera, *s. f. coffee-pot*
ila, *s. f. a caravan of travellers, etc.*
re, *s. m. cruel; barbarous* [*of bird*
gaceyte, *s. m. a sort*
gachin, *s. m. a gnat*
gada, *s. f. shiting* || *a turd*
gadero, *subst. m. house of office*
gadillo, ito, *s. m. dim.* de Cagado
gado, *s. m. a simpleton; a silly oaf*
gador, *s. m. sea-hare*
gafierro, *s. m. dross of iron*
gajon, *sub. m dung of beasts*
galar (tripa del), *s. f. the arse gut*
galera, *s. f. diarrhœa*
gamelos, *s. m. a sort of mushroom*
gar, *v. a. to skite* || *to foul* [*of gnat*
garopa, *sub. m. a sort*
garrache, *s. m. a staring* || *one that washes the olives*
garria, *s. f. a mushroom like a pine-apple*
garrpta, *s. f. goat's or sheep's treads*

Cagatorio, *s. m. V.* Cagadero
Cagon, na, *subs. a loose man, etc.* || *a coward*
Cahiz, *s. m. a measure of corn*
Cahizada, *s. f. as much land as may be sown with a cahiz of wheat*
Caida, *sub. f. a fall* || *the depth of hangings, etc.*
Caidos, *s. m. pl. arrears*
Caimiento, *s. m. weakness* || *a fall*
Cal, *s. f. lime*
Cal viva, *unslacked lime*
Cala, *sub. f. a bit cut for tasting* || *a creek* || *a suppository*
Calabacero, *subs. m. one who sells pumpions*
Calabacica, illa, ita, *s. m. a little pumpion*
Calabacillas, *pl. ear-bobs like pears*
Calabacin, *s. m. a tender delicate pumpion*
Calabacino, *s. m. a gourd bottle*
Calabaza, *s. f. pumpion; gourd*
Calabazada, *sub. f. a blow with the head*
Calabazar, *s. m. a pumpion-bed*
Calabazate, *s. m. conserve made with pumpkins*
Calabazona, *s. f. winter-pumpkins*
Calabobos, *s. m. a little rain* [*fees*
Calabozage, *s. m. prison*
Calabozo, *s. m. a dungeon* || *hell* [*cable*
Calabrote, *s. m. a little*
Calacanto, *sub. m. herb wich kills fleas, etc.*
Calada, *s. f. the flight of a hawk*

Calado, *subst. m. a bored through work*
Calados, *pl. laces of the stays*
Calador, *s. m. one that pierces, etc.* || *probe*
Calafate, } *s. m. a calker*
Calafateador, }
Calafatería, *s. f. calking*
Calafatear, *v. act. to calk ships*
Calafraga, *s. f. saxifrage*
Calagozo, *s. m. hedging-bill*
Calahorra, *s. f. a store-house where provision is laid up in time of famine* [*boat*
Calaluz, *s. m. an indian*
Calamaco, *subs. m. callimanco*
Calamar, *s. m. calamary*
Calambre, *s. m. cramp*
Calambuco, *s. m. an odoriferous kind of aloes*
Calamento, *s. m. calamint*
Calamidad, *s. f. calamity*
Calamina, *o* piedra calaminar, *s. f. calamine-stone*
Calaminta, *s. f. calamint*
Calamita, *s. f. load-stone* || *a sort of frog*
Calamite, *s. f. a very little frog*
Calamitoso, sa, *a. calamitous*
Cálamo, *s. m. a reed*
Cálamo aromático, *sweet calamus*
Calamocano, *adj. m. hot with wine*
Calamoco, *s. m. icicle*
Calamon, *s. m. a sort of moor-hen* || *a round-headed nail*
Calamorra, s. f. the head
Calamorrada, s. f. V. Cabezada

Calandra, s. f. calender
Calandrajo, s. m. old rag || a ridiculous man
Calandria, s. f. calender (a lark) [ass
Calandria de aguador, an
Calanis, s. m. sweet calamus
Calar, v. act. to pierce through || to penetrate or understand || to let, or bring down
Calar el can, to cock a gun — el melon, to cut a bit of a melon, to taste it — el sombrero, to press the hat on the head — las cubas, to gage
Calarse, v. r. to introduce, to insinuate one's self into || to stoop down
Calar, a. 2. belonging to the lime
Calavera, s. f. a skull || a shallow-brains
Calaverada, s. f. extravagance [travagances
Calaverear, v. n. to do ex-
Calaverilla, ita, sub. f. a little skull
Calcanto, s. m. copperas
Calcañar, s. m. the heel
Calcar, v. act. to press, or thrust together || to trample on
Calce, s. m. band of iron
Calcedonia, s. f. chalcedony
Calces, s. m. mast-head
Calceta, s. f. under-stocking [shop
Calcetería, s. f. a stocking-
Calcetero, ra, s. a botcher
Calceton, s. m. stocking worn under boots
Calcilla, s. f. a little breeches [brat
Calcillas, pl. a fearful,

Calcina, s. f. mixture of lime, sand, gravels, etc.
Calcinacion, s. f. calcination
Calcinar, v. a. to calcine
Calcites, s. f. a mineral like the brass
Calculacion, s. f. calculation
Calculador, s. m. calculator
Calcular, v. a. to calculate
Cálculo, s. m. calculation || stone in the bladder
Calda, s. f. heating; heat
Caldas, pl. hot-waters
Caldaria (ley), s. f. ordeal by hot water
Caldear, v. act. to make iron hot || to heat || to scald [dron
Caldera, s. f. kettle; cal-
Caldera de xabon, a soap-house — de pero botero, the hell
Calderada, s. f. kettle full
Caldereria, s. f. a brazier's shop
Calderero, s. m. a brazier
Caldereta, s. f. a little kettle || holy water-pot || ragoo made with fish
Calderico, s. m. a little kettle
Calderilla, s. f. holywater-pot Voy. Calderico || a sort of coin
Caldero, subs. m. a brass bucket [kettle
Calderon, s. m. a great
Calderuela, s. f. a little kettle
Caldibaldo, s. m. poor thin broth
Caldillo, ito, s. m. sauce
Caldo, s. m. broth
Calducho, s. m. bad broth

Calefaccion, s. f. cale-
tion [fa
Calefactorio, ria, a.
Calefactorio, s. m. a
ming-place
Calefetear, v. a. V. C
fatear
Calenda, subs. f. a
lesson of the mart
logy || catalogue
Calendas, pl. calends
A las calendas gri
at latter lammas;
ver
Calendario, s. m. a c
lendar [ming
Calentador, s. m. a w
Calentador, ra, a. h
warming [
Calentamiento, s. m. h
Calentar, v. a. to heat;
warm
Calentarse, v. r. to gr
hot or angry
Calentarse la perra,
grow proud
Calenton, s. m. a sudd
or quick heat
Calentura, subs. f. fev
ague
Calenturiento, ta, a
troubled with an a
Calenturilla, s. f. li
fever [f
Calenturon, s. m. a gr
Calera, s. f. a lime-kil
Calería, subst. f. a pl
where the lime is m
or sold [
Calero, s. m. a lime-
Calero, ra, a. belong
to the lime
Calesa, s. f. a calash
Calesero, s. m. the
ver of a calash
Calesin, s. m. a very li
calash
Caleta, s. f. a little cr
Caletre, s. m. noddl

. *a. to dispart*
n. bore || *size*
bst. m. gravel
ith brick
f. quality
pl. the laws of

f. heat
a. hot || *cun-*

a. warm ; hot
e, out of hand
aliente, *to be*
· hierro calien-
on
. *Caliph*
, *s. f. qualifi-*
judgment ;
a proof
s. m. quali-

a. to qualify
ove || *to make*
lustrious, etc.
v. r. to prove
ility
a sort of an-
kin
, *s. f. darkness*
sa, *a. dark*
a little sup-
[maco
s. m. V. Cala-
a thick hot

ub. m. a little
o called
m. the great
[*calix*
m. chalice ||
a. belonging
[*tly*
lo, *adv. secre-*
y Calladamen-
silently
, *adj. silent ;*

n. a man of

Callandico, ito, *adv. stilly ; silently*
Callar, *v. a. to conceal*
Callar, *v. n. to be silent*, or *still*
Calle, *sub. f. a street* || *a motive*, or *pretence* || *gullet*
Calle de árboles, *an alley, a walk* [*street*
Calleja, *s. f. a narrow*
Callejear, *v. n. to gad about the streets*
Callejero, ra, *s. an idle gadding fellow*
Callejo, *s. m. a covered ditch to catch beasts in*
Callejon, *s. m. a lane ; a path* [*de* Callejon
Callejoncillo, *s. m. dim.*
Callejuela, *s. f. a narrow street* || *a come-off*
Callo, *s. m. callosity*
Callo de herradura, *a piece of an old broken horseshoe*
Callos de vaca, *tripes*
Callon, *s. m. aum. de* Callo
Callosidad, *s. f. callosity*
Calloso, sa, *a. callous*
Calma, *s. f. calm at sea* || *calmness*
Tierras calmas, *ground without any tree*
Calmar, *v. a. to calm*
Calmar, *v. neut. to be or fall calm*
Calmoso, sa, *a. calm ; quiet*
Calofriado, da, *a. troubled with shivering fits*
Calofriarse, *v. r. to shiver, in an ague*
Calofrio, *s. m. a shivering fit*
Calomar, *s. m. the cry of sailors when they haie a rope all together*

Calor, *subst. m. heat ; warmth* || *zeal*
Caloroso, sa, *a. V.* Caluroso [*frio*
Calosfrio, *s. m. V.* Calo-
Calostro, *s. m. beestings* or *biestings*
Calpisque, *s. m. a gatherer of rents*
Calumnia, *s. f. calumny*
Calumniador, ra, *s. calumniator, trix*
Calumniar, *v. a. to calumniate*
Calumniosamente, *adv. slanderously*
Calumnioso, sa, *a. slanderous*
Calunia, } *s. f. V.* Calumnia
Caluña, }
Calurosamente, *adv. hotly*
Caluroso, sa, *adj. hot, ardent* || *that has a great stock of natural warm*
Calva, *s. f. a bald head*
Calvar, *v. n. to grow bald*
Calvar, *v. a. to cheat ; to deceive*
Calvario, *s. m. calvary* || *a debt* || *a charnel-house*
Calvatrueno, *s. m. a totally bald head* || *hair-brained* [va
Calvaza, *s. m. aum. de* Cal-
Calvero, *s. m. a heath*
Calvete, *s. m. half-bald*
Calvez, *s. f. baldness*
Calvijar, itar, *s. m. Voy.* Calvero
Calvilla, *s. f. dim. de* Calva
Calvinista, *s. m. calvinist*
Calvo, va, *adj. bald*
Terreno calvo, *ground without grass, etc.* || paño calvo *a bare cloth*
Calya, *s. f.* orchanet
Calzas, *s. f.* pl. breeches || stockings
Calzada, *s. f. a causeway*

Calzadera, *s. f. a string to fasten the* — abarcas, *to the feet*
Calzadillo, ito, *s. m. dim. de* Calzado
Calzado *s. m. any cover of the leg and foot*
Calzador *s. m. shoeing-leather* or *horn*
Calzadura, *s. f. a shoeing* || *a present for new shoes*
Calzar, *v. act. to put on shoes* or *stockings* || *to make shoes* || *to quoin* or *wedge up a wheel, etc.*
Calzar las herramientas, *to put steel-edges to tools*
Calzar, *v. n. to wear a shoe of such a size*
Calzo, *s. m. V.* Calce.
Calzones, *s. m. pl. breeches*
Calzonazos, *s. m. pl. great breeches* || *a lumpish heavy fellow* [*wers*
Calzoncillos, *s. m. pl. dra-*
Cama, *s. f. a bed*
Cama de arado, *furrow* — de freno, *cheek* — de liebre, *form* — de ropá, *a quarter-piece*
Camada, *s. f. a litter* || *a gang of thieves*
Camafeo, *s. m. cameo*
Camal, *s. m. a halter*
Camaleon, *s. m. cameleon*
Camamilla, *s. f. camomile*
Camándula, *sub. f. a sort of chaplet*
Camandulero, ra, *adject. cheating; hypocrite*
Cámara *sub. f. chamber; room a turd*
Cámaras, *pl. looseness; lask rade; fellow*
Camarada, *subst. m. com-*
Camarage, *s. m. granary's rent* [*ret*
Camaranchon, *s. m. a gar-*

Camarería, *s. f. a chamberlain's office*
Camarero, *s. m. chamberlain* || *a first valet-de-chambre* || *a public granary-keeper*
Camariento, ta, *adj. loose*
Camarilla, *s. f. a little chamber*
Camarin, *s. m. a closet*
Camarista, *s. m. a member of the King's council, etc.*
Camarista, *s. fem. the woman who waits in the queen's chamber* [la
Camarita, *s. f. V.* Camaril-
Camarlengo, *s. m. great chamberlain*
Camaron, *s. m. a shrimp; a prawn*
Camaronero, *s. m. one that fishes or sells shrimps*
Camarote, *s. m. cabbin*
Camarroya, *s. f. dandelion*
Camarroyero, *sub. m. one that sells dandelion*
Camastron, *sub. masc. a dissembling, deceitfull man*
Camastronazo, *s. m. aum. de* Camastron
Cambalachar, *v. a. Voyez* Cambalachear [*ge*
Cambalache, *s. m. exchan-*
Cambalachear, *v. a. to exchange; to batter*
Cambas, *s. f. V.* Camas de ropa
Cambiable, *adject. a. that can be exchanged*
Cambiador, *s. m. swapper*
Cambiamiento, *s. m. changing; inconstancy*
Cambiante, *s. m. variety of colours in a changeable stuft*
Cambiante de le[illegible] *Voy.* Cambista

Cambiar, *v. a. to exch-ge; to change* || *to turn money by bills*
Cambiar la vela, *to tri- sail*
Cambija, *s. f. a water- se* || *a perpendicula*
Cambio, *s. m. exchang- trad- change*
Cambista, *s. m. bank-*
Cambray, *s. m. cambr-*
Cambrayado da, *adj. the cambrick*
Cambrayon, *s. m. a li- like cambrick* [*b*
Cambron *m. brambl-*
Cambronal *s. m. a pl- full of brambles*
Cambronera, *s. f. hedg- thorns* [|| *am*
Cambux, *s. m. a stay-*
Camedafne, *sub. f. p- winkle* [
Camedris, *s. m. germ-*
Cameleon, *s. m. camel-*
Cameleuca, *s. f. colts-*
Camella, *s. f. she cam- a kind of wooden ve-* || *Yoke* || *a bedin- den* *co*
Camellejo *sub. m. a*
Camellería, *s. f. the q- of a camel-keeper stable for the came-*
Camellero, *s. m. ca- driver* [*c*
Camello, *s. m. cam-*
Camellopardal, *s. m. meleopard*
Camellon, *s. m. a bed garden* || *a ridge wen two furrows*
Camelote, *s. m. caml-*
Cameral, *adj. a. belon- to the King's treas-*
Camero, *s. m. one th- r-s beds* [*to*
Camero, ra, *adj. bel-*

esyse, s. f. *tithymal*
lla, s. f. *a little bed*
nador, ra, s. *walker*
nante, s. m. *traveller*
nar, v. n. *to travel; go; to walk*
nata, sub. f. *a great lk*
nillo, ito, sub. m. *a tle narrow way*
no, s. m. *way; road voyage; travel*
no de santiago, *the lky way*
sa, s. f. *a shirt; a ock || the pellicle of its || a snake's slough the lining with stone rampire, etc. || rough st || a stake at play*
isilla, ita, s. f. *dim.* Camisa
isola, s. f. *a fine shirt th ruffles || a galley-ve's waistcoat*
ison, sub. m. *a great irt* [*mail*
isote, s. m. *a coat of*
ita, s. f. *a little bed*
on, s. m. *a large bed*
ones, plur. *bands of lme* [*stool*
oncillo, s. m. *a little*
orra, s. f. *a quarrel*
orrista, s. m. *a quar-lsome man*
ote, subs. m. *a sort of dian potatoe*
pal, adj. 2. *belonging the field* [*battle*
alla campal, a. *field-*
pamento, s. m. *Voyez* campamento
pana, sub. f. *a bell || a hurch*
pana de queda, *cur-w-bell*
panada, s. f. *the rin-g of a bell*

Campanario, s. m. *steeple; belfry*
Campanear, v. n. *to ring the bells; to chime*
Campanela, s. f. *the turning on one's leg*
Campaneo, s. m. *chime || V.* Contoneo
Campanero, s. m. *a ringer of bells || a bell-founder*
Campaneta, sub. f. *a. little bell* [*a bell*
Campanil, a. *belonging to*
Campanilla, s. f. *a little bell || a bubble || the uvula || bind weed || a tuff*
Campanillazo, s. m. *signal given with a little bell*
Campanillear, v. n. *to ring a little bell*
Campanita, s. f. *a little bell*
Campanudo, da, adj. *bell-fashioned || turgid*
Campaña, s. f. *the country || the field for armies || a cruize at sea*
Campar, v. n. *to encamp || to shine; to excel over*
Campear, v. n. *to take* or *keep the field || to excel; to overtop*
Campeche, s. m. *campechy-wood*
Campeon, s. m. *a famous warriour || a champion*
Campero, ra, adj. *exposed to the air* [*fields*
Campero, s. m. *a keeper of*
Campesico, sub. m. *a little field*
Campesino, na, y Campestre, adj. *rural || rustick, savage* [*field*
Campillo, sub. m. *a little*
Campiña, s. f. *champaign*
Campio, ia, ad. *rambling cross the fields || disordered; unruly*

Campo, subs. m. *a field || camp; list*
Camuesa, s. f. *calville*
Camueso, s. m. *calville-tree || an ignorant-stupid fellow*
Camuñas, s. f. pl. *smaller corn*
Camuza, s. f. *V.* Gamuza
Camuzon, sub. m. *a large shammy leather*
Can, s. m. *a. dog*
Canes, pl. *corbels*
Cana, s. f. *a measure containing two ells*
Canas, pl. a. *hoary head*
Canal, s. f. *canal; channel || a trough || the stay of a weaver's loom*
Canales, pl. *channellings*
Canal, subs. m. *channel; streights*
Canalado, da, adj. *Voyez* Acanalado
Canaleja, s. f. *a little trough*
Canalera, s. f. *a pipe to convay rain water from the gutters*
Canalete, s. m. *a little indian oar*
Canalita, s. f. *a little canal*
Canalizo, sub. m. *narrow streights* [*rabble*
Canalla, s. f. *the mob*, or
Canalon, s. m. *gutter*
Canapé, s. m. *a. canopy-bed* [|| *a sort of dance*
Canario, s. m. *canary-bird*
Canasta, s. f. *a great basket*
Canastilla, s. f. *a little basket || child-bed clothes*
Canasto, sub. m. *basket; hamper*
Cancamo, s. m. *gum anime || a sort of iron ring*
Cancamurria, s. f. *Voyez* Murria
Cancamusa, s. f. *a cheat*
Cancel, s. m. *tambour*

[illegible]cion, } *s. f. cancelling*
Canceladura, }
Cancelar, *v. a. to cancel*
Cancelaria, *s. f. chancery*
Cancelario, *sub. m. chancellor of an university*
Cancer, *s. m. cancer*
Cancerado, da, *adj. that has a cancer*
Cancerarse, *v. r. to cancerate*
Canceroso, sa, *ad. cancerous*
Cancilla, *s. f. a gate made with bars across each other*
Canciller, *s. m. chancellor*
Cancilleresco, ca, *adj. belonging to the chancery*
Cancion, *s. f. a song*
Cancioncilla, *s. f. a little song*
Cancionero, *s. m. collection of songs*
Caucro, *s. m. V.* Cancer
Candadillo, ito, *s. m. a little padlock*
Candado, *s. m. a padlock*
Candeal. *V.* Candial
Candela, *s. f. a candle || flower of the chesnut-tree || fire*
Candelabro, *s. m. candlestick*
Candelada, *s. f. an illumination || V.* Hoguera
Candelaria, *s. f. candlemas*
Candelera, *s. f. woman that lights the wax-tapers*
Candelerazo, *s. m. a great candlestick || a blow with a candlestick*
Candeleria, *s. f. a tallow-chandler's shop*
Candelero, *s. m. candlestick*
Candeleton, *s. m. a tackle used on board ships*
Candelica, ita, *s. f. a little candle || flower of the poplar-tree, etc.*

Candelizas, *s. f. pl. clue-garnets*
Candial, *adj. of the best wheat*
Candial, *s. m. the finest white bread*
Candidamente, *adv. sincerely*
Candidato, *s. mas. a candidate*
Candidez, *s. m. whiteness || sincerity || silliness*
Candido, da, *a. white || sincere || silly*
Candiel, *s. m. a sort of sauce*
Candil, *s. m. a lamp hanging in the kitchen*
Candilada, *s. f. a spot of lamp-oil*
Candilazo, *s. m. a stroke with a lamp*
Candilejo, *s. mas. a little lamp*
Candilon, *s. mas. a great lamp*
Candiota, *sub. m. a little tun* or *barrel*
Candiotero, *s. m. a cooper*
Candonga, *s. f. a deceitful flattery, etc. || jest; scoffing || an old mule*
Candonguear, *v. a. to jest; to laugh at*
Candonguero, ra, *a. cajoler || jester; scoffer*
Candor, *s. m. whiteness || candour*
Canecer, *v. neut. to grow grey-haired*
Canela, *s. f. cinnamon*
Canelado, da, *a. V.* Acanaledo
Canelon, *s. m. sugar cinnamon || gutter || icicle*
Cange, *s. m. exchange of prisoners*
Cangear, *v. a. to exchange prisoners*
Cangilon, *s. m. a pitcher*
Cangreja (vela), *s. f. sail of a bylander*

Cangrejo, *s. m. a crab || a cray-fish*
Cangrejuelo, *s. mas. dim. de* Cangrejo
Cangrena, *s. f. gangrene*
Cangrenarse, *v. r. to gangrene*
Cania, *s. f. the greek nettle*
Canicula, *s. f. dog-star || dog-days*
Caniculares (dias), *s. m. pl. the dog-days*
Canijo, ja, *a. weak; languishing*
Canil, *s. m. bread made for dogs*
Canilla, *s. f. the shin-bone || the radius || a tap or cock || a weaver's quill*
Canillado, da, *a. V.* Acanillado
Canillazo, *s. mas. a blow upon the shin-bone*
Canillera, *s. f. armour for the legs*
Canillero, *s. m. the hole of a tap*
Canina, *s. f. dog's dung*
Caninamente, *adv. like a mad dog*
Canino, na, *a. canine*
Caninero, *s. m. one that gather dog's dungs*
Caninuez, *s. m. a canine appetite*
Canique, *s. m. a very fine muslin*
Cano, na, *a. grey-hai[red] || judicious, wise*
Canoa, *s. f. canoe*
Canoero, *s. m. one th[at] guides a canoe*
Canoita, *s. f. a little c[anoe]*
Canon, *s. m. canon*
Canonesa, *s. f. a canoness*
Canongia, *s. f. canonship, prebend*
Canongible, *a. 2. canoni[cal]*
Canonicamente, *adv. canonically*
Canónico, ca, *a.* [illegible]

aigo, s m. a canon, prebendary
nista, s. m. a canonist
nizable, a. deserving canonization
nizacion, s. f. canonization [nize
nizar, v. a. to cano-
ro, ra, a. melodious; rmonious
o, sa, a. hoary
damente, adv. importunately [Cansado
dazo, s. m. aum. de
do, s. m. a troublese man
ncio, s. m. weariis [to tire
ar, v. a. to weary;
era, s. f. weariness
vexation; plaguing
able, a. 2. which may sung
ada, s. f. cantata
ador, s. m. a singer
aleta, s. f. a nipping st; a scoff, etc.
tar, s. m. a song
tar, v. a. to sing || creak or screak || to ublish || to call one's game
ntara, s. f. a pitcher
ntarcico. cillo, s. m. a little song
ntarera, s. f. a shelf to set pitchers on
ntárida, s. f. spanish fly
ntarillo, s. m. a little itcher
ntarin, s. m. a contil singer
ña, s. f. a singing n
: m. a pitcher
- f. V. Canta-
ub. m. a blow
one

Canteado, da, a. placed obliquely
Canteles, s. mas. pl. ropes used among sailors
Cantera, sub. f. quarry || talent; capacity
Canteria, s. f. the art of cutting stones
Cantero, s. m. stone-cutter || angle; corner || cantle
Canteron, s. mas. a great corner or cant e
Canticio, s. m. a frequent singing
Cántico, s. m. canticle
Cantidad, s. f. quantity
Cantilena, s. f. a little song
Cantillo, sub. m. a little stone
Cantimplora, s. f. siphon || a vessel to cool wine, etc.
Cantina, subs. f. a wine-cellar
Cantinas, pl. bottle-case
Cantinela, s. f. a little song
Cantinero, s. m. the butler
Cantiña, s. f. a song
Cantizal, sub. m. a stony ground
Canto, s. m. stone || the side of a bed, etc. || hem; skirt || singing || musick or poetry || canto || thickness, depth
Canton, sub. m. corner || canton
Cantonada (dar), to slip away at the corner of a street || to jest; to play a trick
Cantonar, v. a. to canton
Cantonearse, v. rec. V. Contonearse
Cantonera, sub. f. an iron plate at the corners of chests, etc.
Cantor, ra, s. a singer

Cantorcillo, s. m. a paltry singer
Cantorral, s. m. a stony place
Cantueso, s. m. lavender
Canturia, s. f. musick || method or manner of singing, etc.
Cantusar, v. a. to deceive
Caña, s. f. a cane, a reed | the shin-bone or radius || marrow
Caña de vaca, a marrow-bone — de columna, shaft; shank — del timon, tiller — depescar, fishing-rod — dulce, a sugar cane
Cañada, s. f. streight between hills
Cañafístola, s. f. cassia
Cañafistolo, s. m. a cassia-tree
Cañaheja, } s. f. hercules's all-heal
Cañaheria, }
Cañal, s. m. a place enclosed with reeds || a letting out the water || || V. Cañaveral
Cañama, s. f. assessment
Cañamar, s. m. hemp-field
Cañamazo, s. mas. coarse hempen cloth || canvass
Cañameño, ña, a. made of coarse hemp
Cañamiel, s. mas. a sugar cane [dian ship
Cañamiz, s. m. a little in-
Cañamiza, s. f. V. Agramiza
Cañamo, s. m. hemp
Cañamon, s. m. hemp-seed
Cañar, s. m. an enclosure of reeds || V. Canaveral
Cañariegos (pellejos), s. mas. pl. skins of sheep that died in their walks
Cañarroya, s. f. V. Parietaria

Cañavera, *sub. f. a wild cane*

ñaverear

Cañaveral, *s. m. a place where reeds grow* || *an intangled affair*

Cañavete, *s. mas. a little knife* || *a sort of locust*

Cañazo, *s. m. a blow with a cane*

Cañería, *s. f. water-pipes*

Cañerla, *s. f. V.* Cañaheja

Cañero, *s. m. fisher with a rod*

Cañilavado, da, *a. that has no calves to his legs*

Cañilla, ita, *s. f. a little cane*

Cañillera, *s. f. V.* Canillera [*nen*

Cañiza, *s. f. a coarse linen*

Cañizo, *s. m. hurdle of reeds*

Caño, *s. m. conduit; pipe* || *a vessel to cool water, etc.* || *the pipe of the lungs*

Caños de barquillas, *wafers* — de Organo, *organ-pipes*

Cañon, *s. m. barrel of a gun* || *pipe* || *a sleeve* || *a hollow fold* || *pipe of a quill* || *the reed of corn* || *a cannon*

Cañon de chimenea *tunnel*—de cruxia, *a bow-chase*

Cañonazo, *s. m. aum. de* Cañon || *cannon-shot*

Cañoncico, illo, ito, *s. m. dim. de* Cañon [*nade*

Cañonear, *v. a. to cannonade*

Cañoneo, *s. m. cannonade*

Cañonera, *sub. f. a loop-hole* || *a sort of tent*

Cañonería, *s. f. the row of pipes of an organ*

Cañonero, *s. m. cannoneer* [*little cane*

Cannela, *s. f. a little cane*

Cañutazo, *s. m. thing said in a whisper*

Cañutería, *subst f. work made with little glass-pipes, etc.* || *V.* Cañonería

Cañutillo, *s. mas. a little pipe of glass, etc.*

Cañuto, *sub. m. a joint of reed or cane* || *case for pens, etc.* || *V.* Cañutazo

Caoba, Caobana, } *s. f. a great tree of the west-indies*

Caos, *s. m. chaos*

Capa, *s. f. a cloak* || *a cover* || *plaistering a horse's hair* || *a churchman's cope*

Capacete, *s. m. helmet*

Capacha, *s. f. a frail*

Capachazo, *s. m. a stroke with a frail*

Capacho, *s. m. a frail* || *a great basket* || *a night-crow*

Capacidad, *s. f. capacity* || *opportunity*

Capada, *s. f. the slap of a cloak full of any thing*

Capador, *s. m. a gelder* || *a gelder's whistle*

Capadura, *s. f. gelding*

Capar, *v. a. to geld* || *to diminish*

Caparazon, *s. m. caparison* || *cover*

Caparra, *s. f. earnest*

Caparrilla, *s. f. a little tick*

Caparrosa, *s. f. copperas*

Capataz, *s. m. overseer; chief; warden*

Capaz, *adj.* 2. capable || *capacious*

Capazo, *s. m. V.* Ca

Capazon, *subs. m. a basket or frail*

Capcioso, sa, *a. cap*

Capeador, *sub. m. that steals cloaks night*

Capear, *v. act. to cloaks in the ni to give signals cloak* || *to try or l*

Capear el toro, *to t cloak over a bull*

Capelardente, *s. f.* pilla ardiente

Capellada, *sub. f. a wich a cobler set shoes*

Capellan, *s. m. a ch*

Capellania, *sub. f. plain's living*

Capellar, *s. m. a moorish cloak*

Capellina, *s. f. a m*

Capelo, *s. m. a car cap*

Capeo, *s. m. the p with the bull, n a cloak*

Capero, *s. m. cope-*

Caperoles, *s. m. pl nels*

Caperuceta, cilla, *s. de* Caperuza

Caperuza, *s. f. cap*

Caperuzon, *s. m. a* Caperuza

Capialzado, *sub. n constructed obli*

Capigorrista, Capigorron, } *s. n vite uni*

Capilar, *adj.* 2. *ca*

Capilla, *sub. f. a a capouch* || *a f chapel* || *a proo printing*

Capilla ardiente, t *where, a dea*

ies in state—de horno, an oven's vault

apilleja, subs. f. a little chapel

apillejo, s. m. a little bigging || a thrown silk

apiller, } apillero, } s. mas. a chapels keeper

apillera, sub. m. nich || hood [pel

apillita, s. f. a little chapel

apillo, s. m. bigging || Chrisom-cloth || V. Rocadero || the inside leather in a shoe || hawk's hood || bud of a flower

apillo de hierro, a helmet [like

apilludo, da, adj. hoodlike

apion de popa, the stern-post—de proa, the stem

apingot, s. m. a sort of riding-coat with a hood

apirotada, s. f. a sauce made with oil, cheese, eggs, etc.

apirote, s. m. hood || a fillip

apisayo, s. m. a sort of short garment

apisayuelo, dim. de Capisayo

apiscol, s. m. a chanter or head of a choir

apiscolia, s. f. the dignity of a chanter

apita, s. f. a little cloak

apitacion, s. f. poll-tax

apital, s. m. the principal of a sum || inventory of a man's substance, when about marrying

apital, a. 2. capital; chief || belonging to the head

apitalmente, adv. deadly

apitan, s. m. a captain

apitana, s. f. the Admiral's ship || the chief galley

Capitanazo, s. a great General

Capitanear, v. a. to Command; to lead

Capitanía, s. f. Captainship || military government of a province || a company of soldiers

Capitel, s. m. chapiter—V. Chapitel

Capitolino Júpiter), Jupiter Capitolinus

Capitolio, s. m. Capitol

Capiton, sub. m. a sort of mullet

Capítula, s. f. a portion of scripture read at the vespers

Capitulacion, s. f. capitulation agreement

Capitulaciones, pl. articles of marriage

Capitular, s. m. member of a chapter

Capitular, v. act. to capitulate; to covenant—to impeach, or accuse

Capitular, v. n. to read or sing the capitulas

Capitulario, s. m. a book containing the capitulas

Capitularmente, adv. chapterly (|| article

Capítulo, s. m. a chapter

Capnitis, s. f. tutty

Capolar, v. a. to mince || to cut off the head, etc.

Capon, s. m. an eunuch || a capon || a fillip upon the head || the cat-tackle nish dance

Capona, s. f. a sort of spa-

Caponera, sub. f. mew or coop || a sort of trench or lodgement

Caporal, s. m. chief; leader || corporal

Capota, s. f. the head of a fuller's thistle

Capote, s. m. a loose upper coat || a crabbed look

Dar capote, to capot

Capotillo, s. m. mantelet

Capoton, sub. m. aum. de Capote

Capotudo, da, a. V. Ceñudo

Capricho, s. m. caprice; whim || whimsical start

Caprichosamente, adv. capriciously

Caprichoso, sa, adj. capricious || obstinate || made by caprice

Caprichudo, da, a. headstrong

Capricornio, s. m. capricorn || a cuckold

Caprino, na, a. belonging to a goat

Capsario, s. m. keeper of the clothes in a washing-place, etc.

Captar la benevolencia, to curry favour

Captivar, etc, V. Cautivar

Captura, s. f. capture

Capucha, s. f. a circonflex || a mantelet's hood

Capuchino, s. m. a capuchin friar [cowl

Capucho, subs. m. hood;

Capullito, sub. m. dim de Capullo

Capullo, s. m. the cod of a silk-worm || a rose bud

Capuz, s. m. a long mourning cloak

Cara, s. f. face, visage || presence—front; forefront || surface

Cara á cara, face to face

Cáraba, s. mas. a sort of large ship

Carabe, s. m. amber

Carabela, s. f. caravel

Carabelon, s. m. brigantine

Cárabina, *s. f. carbine*

Carabinazo, *s. m. carbine-shot* [*neer*

Carabinero, *s. m. carbi-*

Carabo, *s. m. an howlet*

Caracia, *s. f. balsalmine*

Caracoa, *subs. f. a sort of large indian boat*

Caracol, *s. m. a snail* || *his shell* || *cockle-stairs* || *caracol* [*col*

Caracolear, *v. n. to cara-*

Caracolejo, *s. m. a little snail* [*snails*

Caracolero, ra, *s. seller of*

Caracolillo, *s. m. a little snail* || *a flower so called*

Caracolillos, *pl. a sort of twisted golden* or *silver wire* [*snail*

Caracolito, *s. m. a little*

Carácter, *s. m. character*

Caracteristicamente, *adv. in a characteristick manner*

Característico, ca, *a. characteristick*

Caracterizar, *v. a. to characterize* [*ret*

Caramanchon, *s. m. a gar-*

Carámbano, *s. m. a flake of ice*

Carambola, *s. f. a manner of playing at billiards* || *a trick; a cheat* || *a fruit growing in India*

Caramel, *s. mas. a sort of small pilcher*

Caramelo, *sub. m. sugar melted and crusted*

Caramente, *adv. dearly* || *rigorously*

Caramiello, *s. m. a kind of hat used by women*

Caramillo, *s. m. a sort of flagelet* || *a confused heap* || *a cheat* or *trick*

Caramuzal, *s. m. caramosil*

Carancia, *s. f. balsamine*

Carantamaula, *s. fem. an ugly mask*, or *face*

Carantoña, *s. f. an ugly mask* || *an old ugly painted woman*

Carantoñas, *pl. flatteries*

Carantoñero, *s. m. flatterer*

Caraña, *s. f. a sort of aromatical gum*

Caraos, *sub. m. health in drinking supernaculum*

Carátula, *s. f. a mask*

Caratulero, *s. m. one that makes* or *sells masks*

Caravana, *s. f. caravan*

Caravero, *s. m. one who frequents all publick companies*

Caray, *s. m. a tortoise's shell*

Caraza, *s. f. a large face*

Carbon, *s. m. charcoal*

Carbonada, *s. f. a carbonado* [Carbonada

Carbonadilla, *s. f. dim. de*

Carboncillo, *s. m. a bit of charcoal*

Carbonera, *s. fem. a coal-hole* || *a coal-pit*, or *colliery* [*shop*

Carbonería, *s. f. a collier's*

Carbonero, *s. m. a collier*

Carbonizar, *v. act. to reduce into coals*

Carbunclo, } *s. m. carbuncle*
Carbunco, }

Carbuncoso, sa, *a. like the carbuncle*, or *plague-sore*

Carcajada, *s. fem. a fit of laughing*

Reir á carcajadas, *to laugh out-right* [*name*

Carcamal, *s. m. a nick-*

Carcañal, ñar, *s. m. heel*

Carcasa, *s. f. carcass*

Carcava, *s. f. a grave quagmire*

Carcavon, *s. m. a deep pit*

Carcax, *s. m. a quiv*

Cárcel, *s. m. a pris list to fight in* || *a in a printing-hou*

Carcelage, *sub. m. fees*

Carcelería, *s. f. ment* || *the enter the gaoler's boo*

Carcelero, *s. m. a*

Fiador carcelero, *a for a prisoner*

Carchesia, *s. f.* } *a*
Carchesio, *s. m.* } *deep*

Carcoa, *s. f. a large dian canoe* [*treas*

Cárcola, *s. f. a wea*

Carcoma, *s. f. a worm in wood* || *worm-hole* || *a great trouble of mind*

Carcomer, *v. a. to worm-eat*

Carda, *s. f. the head of a fuller's thistle* || *a card* || *reprimand*

Cardador, *s. m. carder*

Cardadura, *s. f. carding*

Cardamomo, *s. m. cardamomum* [*to nap*

Cardar, *v. act. to card* ||

Cardenal, *s. m. a cardinal* || *a bruise* [*nalship*

Cardenalato, *s. m. cardi-*

Cardenalicio, cia, *a. belonging to a cardinal*

Cardencha, *s. f. a fuller's thistle* || *a card*

Cardenchal, *s. m. a thistly place* [*grise*

Cardenillo, *s. mas. verdi-*

Cardeno, na, adj. livid bluish

iaca, *sub. f. mother-rt*
aco, ca, *a. cardiack*
algía, *s. f. cardialgy*
algico, ca, *a. belong to the cardialgy*
co, *subs. m. a little stle* [dillo
llo, *s. m. V.* Escar-
nal, *ad.* 2. *cardinal*
ne, *s m. hinge*
nes, *pl. the poles of world*
to, *s. m. V.* Cardico
nal, *s. mas. a thistly ce* [cardoon
, *s. mas. a thistle* ||
bendito, santo, le-
ro, lechar, *the holy stle* — espinoso, *our lies thistle* — corre-
, *sea-holm* — huso, *ld bastard saffron*
, da, *a. cheating; fty*
m, *s. m. a fuller's stle*
ncillo, *s. m. a wild ichoke*
cha, *s. f. a large card*
ume, }*s. m. a shoal*
umen, }*of fishes*
ador, *s. m. a carder*
ar, *v. a. to card* || *scratch*
r, *v. a. to confront to compare*
rse, *v. r. to meet face face* *to lack*
er, *v. n. to want;*
a, *s. f. careen* || *ca-ning* || *a ship*
ar, *v. a. to careen*
cia, *s. f. want*
ero, *sub. m. careeng-place*
, *s. m. confronting*
o, ra, *a. selling at ar price*

Carestía, *s. f. want; scarcity* || *dearth*
Careta, *s. f. a mask*
Careto (caballo), *a horse with a white forehead*
Carey, *s. mas. a tortoise s shell*
Carga, *s. f. load* || *charge* || *cargo* || *employment* || *shot* || *poultice*
Cargada, *a. fem. big with child*
Cargadero, *s. m. a place where ships take in or discharge their goods*
Cargadilla, *s. fem. the increase of a debt*
Cardagor, *sub. m. a merchant that loads ships* || *a street-porter*
Cargar, *v. act. to load; to burden* || *to impose taxes* || *to charge*
Cargar, *v. n. to carry; to bear; to rest* || *to take upon one's self*
Cargazon, *s. f. a cargo* || *a heap* || *heaviness in the head, etc.*
Cargo, *s. mas. loading* || *burden — charge*
Cargos, *pl. articles of impeachment*
Cargoso, sa, *adj. heavy; grievous*
Cargue, *s. m. V.* Cargazon
Carguero, ra, *adj. that bears a load, etc.*
Carguilla, ita, *s. f. dim. de* Carga
Carguío, *subst. m. goods ready to ship*
Cariacedo, da, *a. looking severely*
Cariacontecido, da, *adj. looking gloomily*
Cariado, da, *adj. rotten; curious*
Cariaguileño, ña, *a. long-faced with a hook nose*
Cariampollar, }*a. full chee-*
Cariampollado, da, }*ked*
Cariancho, cha, *a. broad-faced*
Cariátide, *s. f. caryatide*
Caribe, *sub. m. a cruel, barbarous man*
Cariboɔo, *s. mas. looking stupidly*
Caricia, *s. f. caress; making much of*
Caricioso, *V.* Cariñoso
Caricuerdo, da, *a. sober-looking*
Caridad, *s. f. charity*
Caridoliente, *a. sorrow-full*
Cariescrito, *adj. a melon the rind of wich is full of warts*
Cariexento, ta, *a. brazen-faced* [kled
Carifruncido, da, *a. wrin-*
Carigordo, da, *a. plump-faced* [cheeked
Cariharto, ta, *adj. full-*
Carilargo, da, *adj. long-faced*
Carilla, *s. f. a little face* || *a mask* || *a small silver coin* [faced
Carilleno, na, *a. plump-*
Carillo, lla, *adj. dim. de* Caro
Carilucio, cia, *a. having a shining face* [faced
Carinegro, gra, *a. tawny-*
Cariño, *s. m. kindness; affection*
Cariñosamente, *adv. lovingly* *nate; kind*
Cariñoso, sa, *a. affectio-*
Cariota, *s. f. a wild carrot*
Caripando, da, *a. foolish; idiot like*
Cariraido, da, *a. brazen-faced*

Cariredondo, da, *a. round-faced*
Carisma, *s. m. a heavenly favour* or *gift*
Carita, *s. f. dim. de* Cara
Caritativamente, *adver. charitably*
Caritativo, va, *a. charitable*
Carlanca, *s. f. a dog's collar full of points*
Carlear, *v. n. to pant*
Carlin, *s. m. a sort of coin*
Carlina, *s. fem. carline-thistle*
Carlinga, *s. f. keelson*
Carmel, *s. m. a plantain with large leaves*
Carmelita, *s. 2. a carmelite friar* or *nun*
Carmelitano, na, *a. belonging to the carmelite friars*
Cármen, *sub. mas. order of carmelite friars* || *a pleasure-garden, etc.*
Carmenador, *s. m. a carder* [*ding*
Carmenadura, *sub. f. car-*
Carmenar, *v. a. to card* || *to lug a man by the hair*
Carmesí, *a. crimson*
Carmesí, *s. m. cochineal*
Carmin, *s. m. carmine* || *a crimson colour* || *a sort of wild rose* [peler
Carminar, *v. act. V.* Ex-
Carnada, *s. fem. the bait made of flesh*
Carnage, *s. m. provision of flesh* [*nal*
Carnal, *a. 2. fleshly; car-*
Carnal, *s. m. flesh-time*
Carnalidad, *s. f. carnality*
Carnalmente, *adv. carnally*
Carnaval, *s. m. carnival*
Carnaza, *s. fem. the fleshy side of a leather* || *a great lump of flesh*
Carne, *s. f. flesh* || *meat* || *the pulp of fruit*
Carnecica, *sub. f. dim. de* Carne
Carnecilla, *s. f. a pimple*
Carnerada, *sub. f. a large flock of sheep*
Carnerage, *sub. m. a tax upon sheep*
Carnerero, *s. m. a shepherd* [*to sheep*
Carneril, *a. 2. belonging*
Carnero, *s. mas. mutton; sheep* || *sheep's leather* || *a large burying-pit* || *a charnel-house* || *a tomb*
Carneruno, na, *a. belonging to sheep*
Carnestolendas, *s. f. pl. shrovetide*
Carnicería, *s. f. the shambles* || *butchery*
Carniceril, *adj. 2. belonging to the stambles*
Carnicero, *s. m. a butcher*
Carnicero, ra, *a. carnivorous*
Carnicol, *s. m. hoof of the cloven-footed beasts*
Juego de los carnicoles, *cockal* [*vorous*
Carnívoro, ra, *a. carni-*
Carniza, *sub. f. a tainted meat*
Carnosidad, *s. f. carnosity* || *fleshiness*
Carnoso, sa, } *a. fleshy* || *pulpous* ||
Carnudo, da, } *full of marrow*
Caro, ra, *a. dear*
Carocas, *s. f. pl. flatteries; deceitful praises, etc.*
Carocha, *s. f. an egg of the queen bee* [coin
Carolus, *sub. m. a sort of*
Carona, *s. f. a horse's* [...] *on the back and wi*[...]
Caroñoso, sa, *adj.* [...] *galled*
Caroquero, ra, *a. fl*[...]*ring*
Carotidas, } *s. f. p.* [...]
Carotides, } *rotidas* [...]
Carozo, *s. m. pellicla* [...] *pomegranate's gr*[...]
Carpa, *subst. f. a carp* [...] *bunch of grapes*
Carpanel, *a. V.* Ap[...]lado [...]
Carpe, *s. m. hornbe*[...]
Carpedal, *s. mas. a gr*[...] *of hornbeam-trees*
Carpentear, *v. a. V.* [...]rejacar
Carpentería, *s. f. V.* C[...]pintería
Carpeta, *s. f. a carpe*[...] *a port-folio*
Carpintear, *v. n. to w*[...] *at the carpenter's b*[...]*siness*
Carpintería, *s. f. carpe*[...]*try* || *a carpenter's sh*[...]
Carpintero, *s. m. carpent*[...]
Carpobálsamo, *s. mas. t*[...] *fruit of the balsam-tr*[...]
Carraca, *sub. f. carack* [...] *rattle*
Carraco, ca, *a. infirm* [...] *old; weak* [ra
Carracon, *s. m. V.* Ca[...]
Carral, *s. mas. a cask* [...] *barrel*
Carralero, *s. m. make*[...] *barrels, etc.*
Carrancudo, da, *a.* [...] *affected in walking*[...]
Carrasca, *s. f. holme*
Carrascal, *s. m. a g*[...] *of holme-oaks*
Carrasco, *s. m. V.* Car[...]
Carrascon, *s. m. a gr*[...] *old holme-oak*
Carraspada, *s. mas. d*[...]

ade with honey, red ine and spices

aspante, adj. sour; rsh [ness

aspera, s. f. hoarse-

asqueño, ña, a. benging to the holmet

rra, s. f. a course; a ce || career || highy || street || alley; lk || a row || the seam he hair || behaviour; y

rilla, ita, s. f. dim. Carrera

ta, s. f. a cart

tada, s. f. a cart-load

te, sub. m. a sort of bin for the fishinge, etc.

carrete, to delay; to ffer

etear, v. a. to carry a cart || to drive a rt

etel, s. m. V. Carrete a turning engine in ship

etera, s. f. highway

reteria, s. f. a quantity f carts || carriage || art-wright's shop

retil, a. 2. belonging to a cart

rretero, s. m. carter || a cart-wright

rretilla, sub. f. a little cart || a go-cart || V. Buscapies

a carretilla, adver. by custom; thougthlessly

rreton, s. m. tumbrel || wheel-barrow || a gort

ton de lámpara, a ey

ncillo, s. m. dim. reton

Carretoncillo, de una rueda, *wheel-barrow*

Carricoche, s. m. *a covered cart || a bad old coach || a dung-cart*

Carril, s. m. *a wheel-rut || a cart-way || a furrow*

Carrillada, s. f. *the grease of a hog's cheek*

Carrillado, da, a. *chub-cheeked*

Carrillo, s. m. *a cheek || a little cart || a pulley*

Carrilludo, da, a. *chub-cheeked* [*bed*

Carriola, s. f. *a truckle-*

Carrizal, sub. m. *a sedgy place*

Carrizo, s. m. *sedge*

Carro, s. mas. *cart; chariot, etc. || the carriage of a coach, etc. || the greater bear*

Carrochar, v. n. *to lay eggs (said of the bees)*

Carrocilla, sub. f. *a little coach*

Carrozin, s. m. *a chaise*

Carromato, s. m. *a sort of very light cart*

Carroña, s. f. *rotten flesh*

Carroñar, v. a. *to infect a flock*

Carroño, ña, a. *rotten; corrupted*

Carroza, s. f. *a coach || a quarter-deck*

Carruage, s. m. *a number of carts, coaches, etc.*

Carrucha, s. f. *a pulley*

Carruco, s. m. *a little cart used in the mountains*

Carrujado, da, a. *plaited, gathered very small*

Carta, s. fem. *a letter || a deed; an act || a map*

Carta de venta, *a bill of sale*—de pago, *an acquittance*—de marear, *a sea-chart*—de horro, *a discharge to a slave*—de concejos, de chancillería, *order, decree*—de amparo, ó de seguro, *safe-conduct*—de dote, *articles of marriage*—de guia, *passport*—cuenta, *a bill*, or *account*—nueva, *an y paper of news*—blanca, *cart blanch*

Cartas, pl. *playing cards*

Cartabon, s. m. *a carpenter's square*

Cártamo, s. m. *wild saffron*

Cartapacio, s. m. *a book of accounts, etc. || a school boy's copy-book*, or *port-folio*

Cartapacios, pl. *waste papers*

Cartapazuelo, s. m. *dim.* de Cartapacio

Cartapel, s. m. *a paper full of foolish conceits, etc.*

Cartazo, s. m. *a letter full of reproaches, etc.*

Cartearse, v. rec. *to keep correspondence by letters*

Cartel, s. m. *a bill posted up || a challenge || a cartel*

Cartela, s. f. *a sort of pocket-book || a bracket*

Cartelon, s. m. *aum.* de Cartel, *and* Cartela

Cartera, s. f. *a letter case || a port-folio* [*rier*

Cartero, s. m. *letter-car-*

Cartesiano, na, a. *cartesian* [*cards*

Cartela, s. fem. *a game at*

Cartica, s. f. *a little letter*

Cartilagine, } sub. mas. *a*
Cartilagen, } *gristle*

Cartilaginoso, sa, *adj. gristly*
Cartilago, *s. m. a gristle*
Cartilla, ita, *s. f. a little letter* || *criss-cross-row*
Carton, *s. m. paste-board* || *volute* [*box*
Cartuchera, *s. f. cartouch-*
Cartucho, *s. m. cartouch; cartridge*
Cartulario, *s. m. register book of a monastery*
Cartulina (encaxe de), *vellum-lace*
Cartuxa, *s. f. the carthusian order*
Cartuxano, na, *a. belonging to the carthusian order*
Cartuxo, *s. m. a carthusian friar*
Carúncola, *s. f. caruncle*
Carvallo, *s. m. a sort of oak* [*seed*
Carví, *s. mas. carraway-*
Casa, *s. f. house* || *a lurking hole, a den* || *square in a draught board* [*coat*
Casaca, *s. f. a great loose*
Casacion, *s. f. repeal*
Casacon, *s. mas. aum. de* Casaca
Casadero, ra, *a. marriageable*
Casadilla, *s. f. a young new married woman*
Casamata, *s. f. casemate*
Casamentero, ra, *subs. a match-maker*
Casamiento, *s. m. a wedding; a match* || *a toy or stake, at play*
Casamuro, *s. m. a rampart without platform*
Casapuerta, *s. f. a porch*
Casaquilla, *s. f. dim. de Casaca*
Casar, *s. m. a villa*

Casar, *v. act. to marry; to match* || *to reverse, annul, etc.* || *to redeem a rent-charge*
Casar, *v. n. y* Casarse, *v. r. to marry*
Casatienda, *s. f. a shop*
Casca *sub. f. the husks of grapes* || *tan of oak* || *a kind of march-pane*
Cascabel, *s. m. a hawk's bell*
Cascabelada, *s. fem. a jingling with little bells* || *a blunder*
Cascabelear, *v. a. to fool one with fair promises*
Cascabelear, *v. n. to talk or act idly*
Cascabelillo, *s. m. a little mirabelle plum*
Cascabillo, *s. m. V.* Cascabel || *the chaff or refuse of corn*
Cascaciruelas, *s. m. a good for nothing fellow*
Cascada, *s. f. cascade*
Cascadas, *pl. the folds of a drapery*
Cascado, da, *adj. broken through age, etc.*
Cascadura, *s. f. breaking*
Cascajal, } *s. m. a gravel-*
Cascajar, } *pit the place where they throw out the husks of grapes*
Cascajo, *s. mas. gravel* || *potsherd* || *old rubbish heap of winter fruits any brass coin*
Cascajoso sa *a. gravelly*
Cascamajar, *v. a. to pound*
Cascamiento, *s. m. breaking*
Cascanueces, *s. m. a nutcracker*
Cascar, *v. a. to break in pieces; to crack, etc.* || *to cudgel, etc.*

Cáscara, *s. f.* ... *cod, etc.* ||
Cáscaras! *a w*... *ration*
Cascarela, *s.* ... *play at car*...
Cascarilla, ita ... Cáscara || *je*...
Cascaron, *s.* ... *shell* || *a so*...
Cascaron, na, ... *coarse, etc*
Cascarudo, da ... *a thick she*...
Casco, *s. m.* ... *potsherd* || ... || *the peel* ... *the carcas*... *a horse's h*...
Cascos, *pl. a* ... *without th*... *tongue* || *brains*
Cascote, *s. m*...
Casera, *s. f.* ...
Caseramente ... *ly; famili*...
Casería, *s. f.* ... *farm*
Caserio, *s. m* ... *of a town*
Caserna, *s. f*...
Casero, *s. m.* ... *house*
Casero, ra, *a*... || *plain;* Pan casero ... *bread* || li... *home-spu*... ger casei... *that keeps*
Caseta, *s. f.* ...
Casi, *adv. a*...
Casia, *s. f.* ...
Casica, illa ... *V.* Caseta ... *house*
Casillas, pl. ... draught...

a servant
'he close-
n. de Caso
ıccident ;
e || mat-
|| hand,
ʒ
hasty in-
narriage
ındruff ||
n. a blow
d
. a head-
ather-cap
or a scald
[hoofed
,a. tender-
o, da, *adj.*
rubbish
the cell
. dim. de
ule in the
a pike ,
ead of an
[brained
, a. hare-
, adj. gid-
; lineage
v. chastly
chesnut
. chesnut-
-chard
. a blow
ut
. one who
s
castanet
ing of the
n. the noi-
the casta-
snapping
m. an air
case.

played on the castanets

Castañetear, *v. n. to play on the castanets || to make one's fingers snap*

Castañeton, *s. m. V.* Castañetazo [*tree*

Castaño, *s. m. a chesnut-*

Castaño, ña, *a. of a chesnut-colour*

Castañuela, *s. f. castanet*

Castañuelo, la, *adj. of a chesnut-colour*

Castellan, *s. m. castellain*

Castellanía, *s. f. castellany*

Castellano, *sub. m. an ancient coin of gold || the fiftieth part of a mark of gold || V.* Castellan

Castellano, na, *adj. generated between a he ass and a mare*

Castidad, *s. f. chastity*

Castificador, *s. m. he that makes chaste*

Castificar, *v. a. to make chaste*

Castigacion, *s. f. correction; amendment*

Castigadamente, *adv. correctly* [*string*

Castigadera, *s. f. a little*

Castigador, ra, *s. a chastiser || a severe censor*

Castigar, *v. a. to chastise || to correct amend, etc.*

Castigo, *s. m. chastisement || amendment ; correction*

Castillage, *s. m. V.* Castillería

Castillejo, *s. m. a little castle || a go-cart*

Castillería, *s. f. a tribute paid in the district of a castle* [*castle*

Castillete, *s. m. a little*

Castillo, *s. m. a castle || a fortress || a cell of the queen of bees*

Castillo de proa, *the fore castle* de proa, *quarter-deck*

Castillo ó leon, *cross or pile* [*castle*

Castilluelo, *s. m. a little*

Castizo, za, *adj. of a good race*

Estilo castizo, *a pure and correct style*

Castor, *s. m. a beaver ; a castor*

Castoreo, *s. m. castoreum*

Castra, *s. f. the pruning*

Castracion, *s. f. V.* Castradura [*knife*

Castradera, *s. f. a gelding-*

Castrador, *s. m. a gelder*

Castradura, *s. f. castration ; gelding*

Castrapuercas, *s. m. a gelder's whistle*

Castrar, *v. a. to geld ; to castrate || to deterge a wound || to lop* or *prune*

Castrar colmenas, *to take the honey away*

Castrazon, *s. m. the season for taking honey away* [*a camp*

Castrense, *a. belonging to*

Castro, *s. m. merils || V.* Campo *|| the reliques of a demolished fortress, etc.*

Castron, *s. m. a gelt goat*

Casual, *adj. casual*

Casualidad, *s. f. casualty*

Casualmente, *adv. casually* [*tage*

Casucha, *s. f. hutt ; cot-*

Casuista, *s. f. a casuist*

Casulla, *s. f. chasuble*

Casullero, *s. m. a maker of eclesiastical ornaments*

Cata, s. f. an essay ; a taste ; a search

Cata, int. take care

G

(*a rope*)
Catábulo, *s. m. a stable*
Cataclismo, *s. m. deluge; inundation*
Catacumbas, *s. catacombs*
Catador, *s. m. one that tastes the wines, etc.*
Catadura, *s. f. tasting; palating* || *air; look*
Catalejo, *s. m. a prospective-glass*
Catalicon, *s. m. catholicon*
Catalina, *s. f. the french-pox*
Catalnica, *s. f. V.* Cotorra
Catálogo, *s. m. a catalogue*
Catan, *s. m. a large broad sword called*
Catanance, *s. f. a plant so called*
Cataplasma, *s. f. cataplasm*
Catapocia, *s. f. a pill*
Catapucia, *s. f. catapuce*
Catapulta, *s. f. catapult*
Catar, *v. a. to taste* || *to behold; to observe* || *to think* || *to search* || *to respect*
Cataraña, *s. f. shell-drake* || *smallage*
Catarata, *s. f. cataract*
Cataribera, *s. m. an inquisitor* or *examiner* || *an idle strolling fellow*
Catarrals, *a. a. catarrhou[s]*
Catarro, *s. m. a catarrh*
Catarroso, sa, *a. subject to a catarrh*
Catastro, *s. m. a general tax*
Catástrofe, *s. f. catastrophe*
Cataviento, *s. m. vane*
Catavino, *s. m. a cup used to taste wine*
Catavinos, *pl. drunkards*
Catear, *v. a. to seek; to search*
Catechizar, etc. *V.* Catequizar, *etc.*

Catecúmeno, na, *s. catechumen*
Cátedra, *s. f. a pulpit* || *episcopal see*
Catedral (iglesia), *s. f. a cathedral*
Catedralidad, *s. f. the dignity of a cathedral church*
Catedrático, *s. m. professor in an university*
Catedrilla, *s. f. dim. de* Cátedra [*class*
Categoría, *s. f. category;*
Categóricamente, *adv. categorically*
Categórico, ca, *adj. categorical* [*chism*
Catequismo, *s. m. cate-*
Catequista, *s. m. catechist*
Catequizar, *v. a. to catechize* [*troop*
Caterva, *s. f. a crew; a*
Cateto, *s. m. a perpendicular line*
Catite, *s. m. a little lump of sugar*
Cato, *s. m. cashoo*
Catoblepa, *s. f. a kind of ferocious beast*
Católicamente, *adv. like a catholick*
Catolicismo, *s. m. catholicism*
Católico, ca, *adj. catholick* || *good; pure*
Católico, *s. m. a catholick*
Catolicon, *s. m. catholicon*
Catóptrica, *sub. f. catoptricks*
Catorce, *adj. fourteen*
Catorceno, na, *adj. fourteenth*
Catre, *s. m. a couch*
Cauce, *s. m.* **Caucera**, *s. f. Voy.* Cacera
Cauchil, *s. m. a little reservoir*

rity || *precaut*
Caucionar, *v. a. t*
Caucionero, *s. m. man*
Cauda, *s. f. tail*
Caudal, *sub. m. means; stock dance*
Hacer caudal de *much of*
Caudalejo, *s. m.* Caudal
Caudaloso, sa, *a thy; wel stoc*
Rio caudaloso, *river*
Caudatario, *s. n*
Caudato (comet *a tailed come*
Caudillo, *s. m. chief; head*
Caudon, *s. m.* caudon
Causa, *s. f. a ca*
Causador, ra, *s.*
Causal, *s. f. rea tive*
Causar, *v. a. to*
Causídico, *s. m.*
Causon, *s. m. a fever*
Caústico, ca, *a.*
Causto, ta, *a. ca*
Cautamente, *a tiously*
Cautela, *s. f. ca fraud* or *che*
Cautelar, *v. a. t tious; to pro*
Cautelosamente, *tiously* || *dece*
Cauteloso, sa, *a.* || *crafty; dec*
Cauterio, *s. m.*
Cauterizacion, *terizing*
Cauterizador, *s that cauteriz*

auterizar, v. a. to cauterize

autivar, v. a. to captive || to captivate

autiverio, s. m. } captivity
autividad, s. f. }

autivo, va, a. captive

auto, ta, adj. cautious; prudent

va, s. f. the grubbing with a hoe, etc. || cellar

ena cava, the hollow vein

vadiza (arena), s. f. sand taken out by digging [deep

vado, da, adj. hollow;

vador, s. m. a digger

vadura, s. f. digging || ditch; pit

vallillo, s. m. a trench between two beds of a garden

var, v. a. to dig || to examine thoroughly

var la materia, to eat down into the flesh

verna, s. f. cavern; den || cavity

vernoso, sa, a. cavernous

vidad, s. f. cavity

vilacion, s. f. cavillation

vilar, v. a. to cavil

villas, s. f. pl. iron pins

vilosamente, adv. captiously

viloso, sa, a. captious

xa, s. f. a box, a chest, etc. || a sheath; a case || a coffin || a drum || a cash

xa de arcabuz, etc. stock — de las cartas, a general post-office — de las muelas, the gums

xcara, Caxco, V. Cáscara, Casco

Caxeras, s. f. pl. particular hollows in a ship

Caxero, s. m. a cash-keeper || a box-maker

Caxeta, s. f. a little box || a money-box

Caxetin, s. m. dim. de Caxeta [box

Caxilla, ita, s. f. a little

Caxista, s. m. a compositor [or chest

Caxon, s. m. a great box,

Caxuela, s. f. a little box

Cayadilla, s. f. a little crook

Cayada, s. f. } a crook || a bishop's staff
Cayado, s. m. }

Cayman, s. m. a cayman

Cayo, s. m. a jay

Cayos, pl. shelves

Cayque, s. m. a ketch

Cayrel, s. m. periwig || a sort of fringes || the dandruff

Cayrelar, v. a. to adorn with fringes

Caz, s. m. channel; trench || reservoir; sluice

Caza, s. f. hunting; fowling, etc. || game; venison

Cazabe, s. m. a kind of bread eaten in America

Cazador, ra, s. an hunter

Cazar, v. a. to hunt; to fowl, etc. || to curry favour, etc.

Cazcalear, v. n. to apply a great but unprofitable diligence

Cazcarria, s. f. dirt

Cazcarriento, ta, a. dirty

Cazo, sub. m. stew-pan; sauce-pan, etc. || a great spoon

Cazoleja, s. f. a little sauce-pan || pan of a gun

Cazoleta, s. f. V. Cazoleja || hilt of a sword || a relievo in a shield || a burnt perfume || the pan of a gun

Cazolilla, s. f. dim. de Cazuela [zuela

Cazolon, s. m. aum. de Ca-

Cazon, s. m. a sea-lamprey

Cazonetes, s. m. pl. a sort of blocks

Cazuela, s. f. an earthen sauce-pan || the meat dressed in it || a separate place for women in the play-house

Cazumbrar, v. a. to splice the hoops of a cask, etc.

Cazumbre, s. m. the rope with wich the cask is spliced

Cazumbron, s. m. a cooper [ivy

Cazur, sub. m. a kind of

Cazurro, ra, adj. silent; melancholy

Ce, a soft way of calling

Cea, s. f. spelt — V. Cia

Ceática, s. f. V. Ciática

Cebada, s. f. barley

Cebadal, s. m. a field sowed with barley

Cebadera, s. f. a sort of bag to feed mules as they go along || the sprit-sail

Cebadero, s. m. a falconer || a beast who bears the barley || a seller of barley || a picture of domestick birds

Cebadilla, s. f. powder of hellebore

Cebador, s. m. one that crams fowls, etc.

Cebadura, s. f. feeding

Cebar, v. a. to feed || to cram poultry, etc. || to bait; to allure || to prime a gun

Cebellina, s. f. a sable

Cebo, s. m. *food; aliment* || *a bait* || *prime*
Cebolla, s. f. *onion* || *any bulbous root* || *a lamp's belly*
Cebollar, s. m. *a place where onions grow*
Cebollero, ra, s. *one that sells onions* || *rustick; clownish* [*sucker*
Cebolleta, s. f. *cibol* || *a*
Cebollino, s. m. *a young onion* [*onion*
Cebollon, sub. m. *a great*
Cebollndo, da, adj. *belonging to an onion*
Cebon, s. m. *a fated ox* or *hog* [Cebon
Ceboncillo, s. m. *dim. de*
Cebra, s. f. *a zebra*
Cebratana, s. f. *V.* Cerbatana || *a sort of culverin*
Cecear, v. a. *to lisp*
Ceceo, s. m. *lisp; lisping*
Ceceoso, sa, adj. *one that lisp*
Cecial, s. m. *a cod dried up* || *a very lean man*
Cecias, s. m. *the north east wind* [*pent*
Cecilia, s. f. *a kind of ser-*
Cecina, s. f. *salt meat; hung-beef, etc.*
Cecinar, v. a. *to salt meat*
Cedacería, s. f. *a sieve-maker's shop*
Cedacero, s. m. *a sieve-maker* [*sieve*
Cedacillo, ito, s. m. *a little*
Cedazo, s. m. *a sieve*
Cedazuelo, s. m. *a little sieve* [*give up*
Ceder, v. a. *to yeld; to*
Ceder, v. n. *to yeld; to submit* || *to turn to one's avantage, etc.* || *to remiss* or *abate*
Cedilla, s. f. *cerilla*
Cedizo, za, a. *tainted*

Cedria, s. f. *the gum of the cedar tree*
Cedride, s. f. *the fruit of the cedar tree*
Cedrino, na, a. *cedrine*
Cedro, s. m. *a cedar-tree*
Cédula, s. f. *bill; note, schedule* || *warrant; writ, etc.*
Cedulilla, sub. f. *a little bill, etc.*
Cedulon, s. m. *a great bill, etc.* || *satire, lampoon, etc.* [*vein*
Cefálica, s. f. *the cephalick*
Céfalo, s. m. *a sort of fish*
Céfiro, s. m. *western-wind* || *zephir*
Cefo, s. m. *a kind of ape*
Cegajo, s. m. *he goat two years old*
Cegajoso, sa, a. *blear-eyed*
Cegar, v. n. *to grow blind*
Cegar, v. a. *to blind* || *to choak up* [*ted*
Cegarrita, s. m. *short-sigh-*
A cegarritas, adv. *with the eyes shut*
Cegato, ta, adj. *purblind*
Cegatoso, sa, adj. *V.* Cegajoso [Ciego
Ceguecillo, s. m. *dim. de*
Ceguedad, s. f. *blindness*
Ceguera, s. f. *ophthalmy*
Ceguezuelo, s. m. *dim. de* Ciego
Ceguiñuela, s. f. *the whip-staff of a helm*
Ceja, s. f. *eye-brow* || *chain-lace; edging* || *edge of a mountain*
Cejadero, sub. m. *a leather-strap put behind a coach-box*
Cejar, v. n. *to draw back*
Cejijunto, ta, a. *that has his eye-brows joined*
Cejo, s. m. clouds upon *a river*

Cejuela, s. f. *a little ey-brow*
Celada, s. f. *a head pi-* || *ambuscade* || *amb-*
Celadilla, s. f. dim. Celada
Celage, s. m. *variety colours in the cloud heaven painted in picture* || *presage* || Claraboya y Ventana.
Celar, v. a. y n. *to gr-* || *to conceal*
Celda, s. f. *a cell*
Celdilla, ita, s. f. *a li-tle cell* [
Celebracion, s f. *celeb-*
Celebrador, s. m. *one th- celebrates*
Celebrante, s. m. *a pri- that celebrates the ma-*
Celebrar, v. a. *to celebra-*
Célebre, a. *celebrious renowned* || *chearfu- pleasant*
Célebremente, adv. *f-mously* || *pleasantly*
Celebridad, s. f. *celebri-* || *solemnity* [b-
Celebrillo, s. m. *V.* Ce-
Celebro, s. m. *the brain judgment* || *imagin-tion*
Celemin, s. m. *a dry me-sure answerable to peck*
Celeridad, s. f. *celerity*
Celeste, a. *celestial; he-venly*
Azul celeste, *sky-blue*
Celestial, a. *celestial perfect; excellent*
Celestialmente, adv. *e-cellently*
Celfo, s. m. *V.* Cefo
Celiaca, s. f. *a celiack -tery*
Celiaco, ca, adv. *celia-*
Celibato, s. m. *celiba-*

be, s. m. celibate
co, ca, a. celestial
cola, s. m. an inhabitant of heaven.
donia, s. f. celandine
ta, s. f. a kind of great ...
a, s. f. V. Celda
mca, s. f. a whore
mco, ca, adj. old; weak; decrepit
isca, s. f. a sudden storm
ro, sa, a. that sails very swiftily
sia, s. f. lattice for window
itud, s. f. highness
la, s. f. a little cell
lario, ria, a. cellular
llilla, s. f. dim. de Célula
menterio, s. m. V. Cimenterio
a, s. f. a supper
acho, s. m. a pannier, hamper
áculo, s. m. the room where our saviour celebrated his last supper
adero, s. m. a supping room
ador, s. m. one who sups much || an arbour
agal, subs. m. mire; slough
agoso, sa, a. muddy
ar, v. n. to sup
ceño, ña, a. lean; thin
n cenceño, unleavened bread
cerra, s. f. V. Cencerro
cerrada, s. f. mock-music of kettles, frying-pans, etc.
cerrear, v. n. to ring little bells || to creak, or sereak
cerreo, s. m. sound of any little bells

Cencerril, a. belonging to the bells
Cencerrilla, s. m. } dim. de Cencerro
Cencerrillo, s. f. }
Cencerro, s. m. a bell hung to the neck of a cow, etc.
Cencerron, s. m. aum. de Cencerro
Cencerruno, na, a. belonging to a little bell
Cencido, da, a. uncultivated
Cencro, s. m. a kind of serpent
Cendal, s. m. a fine linen, or silk || a garter
Cendra, s. f. ashes to refine silver with
Cendrar, v. a. V. Acendrar
Cenefa, s. f. edge; border || the valance of a bed, etc.
Cenicero, s. m. ash-pan
Ceniciento, ta, a. ash-coloured
Cenit, s. m. zenith
Ceniza, s. f. ashes
Cenizo, s. m. savory
Cenizo, za, a. V. Ceniciento
Cenizoso, sa, a. ashy; full of ashes || V. Ceniciento
Cenobita, s. m. a monk
Cenobitico, ca, monastick
Cenogil, s. m. a garter
Cenotáfio, s. m. cenotaphium
Censatario, s. m. a copyholder
Censo, s. m. quit-rent — a roll of the inhabitants, etc.
Censo de por vida, a life-rent
Censor, s. m. censor || censure || a list, or roll
Censual, a. 2. feudal
Censual[illegible], } s. m. the lord of a mannor
Cen[illegible]neo, }
C[illegible]ura, s. f. censorship

Censurable, a. 2. censurable
Censurar, v. a. to censure || to number
Centaurea, s. f. centaury
Centauro, s. m. a centaur
Centella, s. f. a spark — a thunder-bolt
Centellador, ra, a. sparkling
Centellar, } v. neut. to sparkle
Centellear, }
Centellica, ita, s. f. dim. de Centella
Centellon, s. m. a great spark
Centena, s. f. an hundred
A' centenadas, ó á centenares, adv. in great number
Centenario, ria, a. centenary
Centenaza (paja), s. f. straw of the rye
Centeno, s. m. rye
Centenoso, sa, a. mixed with rye
Centésimo, ma, a. hundredth
Centiloquio, s. m. a work divided into hundred parts, etc.
Centimano, a. that has hundred hands
Centinela, s. f. a centinel
Centinodia, s. f. knot-grass
Centiplicado, da, a. centuple
Centipetalo... holder?
Centolla, s. f. a sort of sea-fish
Centon, s. m. a great cover, or blanket || a rhapsody
Central, } a. 2. central
Centrical, }
Céntrico (punto), the central point
Centrifugo, ga, a. centrifugal
Centripeto, ta, a. centripetal

Centro, *s. m. center*
Estar en su centro, *to be in on'es element*
Centuplicado, da, *a. centuple* [*hundred*
Centuria, *s. f. century ;*
Centurion, *s. m. a centurion*
Cenzaya, *s. f. a girl kept to look after childrens*
Ceñar, *v. n. to frown*
Ceñido, da, *a. moderate ; sober*
Ceñidor, *s. m. a girdle*
Ceñir, *v. a. to gird* || *to compass about* || *to reduce, abridge, etc.*
Ceñirse, *v. rec. to lessen one's expences*
Ceño, *s. m. frown ; frowning* || *a ferrule*
Ceñoso, sa, } *a. frowning*
Ceñudo, da, }
Ceo, *s. m. a kind of sea-fish*
Cepa, *s. f. log ; stump* || *a vine* || *stock ; head of a house* || *the pier of a bridge* || *spring ; begining* [*tle*
Cepa caballo, *carline this-*
Cepejon, *s. m. the thickest part of a branch lopt from a tree*
Cepilladuras, *s. f. pl. chips*
Cepillar, *v. a. V.* Acepillar
Cepillo, *s. m. a plane* || *a brush* || *a little church-box*
Cepo, *s. m. stock of an anvil, etc.* || *stocks ; fetters* || *a sort of spinning-wheel* || *a trap* || || *a church-box*
Cepo del ancla, *the anchor-stock*
Cepon, *s. m. a great stump*
Ceporro, *s. m. an old vine*
Cequí, *s. m. zechin*

Cera, *s. f. wax*
Cerafolio, *s. m. chervil*
Cera pez, *s. f. ointmen made with wax and pitch*
Cerasta, }
Ceraste, } *s. f. cerastes*
Cerastes, }
Cerástico, ca, *a. belonging to the cerastes*
Cerbatana, *s. f. a shooting-trunk* || *any thing like a tube*
Cerca, *s. f. an inclosure*
Cerca, *adv. about ; near ; close by* [*sure*
Cercado, *s. m. an inclo-*
Cercador, *s. m. besieger*
Cercanamente, *adv. nearly*
Cercanía, *s. f. nearness*
Cercano, na, *a. next ; near*
Cercar, *v. a. to enclose* || *to besiege* || *to encompass ; to wall, etc.*
Cercenador, *s. m. a clipper*
Cercenadura, *s. f. clipping* || *shreds ; parings*
Cercenar, *v. a. to clip, pare*, or *shred* || *to diminish*, or *retrench* || *to cut one's hair*
Cercera, *s. f. vent-hole*
Cerceta, *s. f. a teal*
Cercetas, *pl. antlers*
Cercha, *s. f. a wooden flexible rule*
Cerchon, *s. m. a mould for an arch*
Cercillo, *s. m. tendril of a vine* [*the indies*
Cercio, *s. m. a bird of*
Cerciorar, *v. a. to certify ; to assure*
Cerco, *s. m. compass ; circuit* || *siege*
Cerco de cuba, *hoop* — de hombres, *a knot* [illegible] *ple* — de puerta, [illegible] tana, *frame*

Cercopiteco, *s.*
tailed ape
Cerda, *s. f. a h*
|| *the strong*
horse, etc. ||
Cerdamen, *s. m*
of hog's brist
Cerdana, *s. f.*
dance
Cerdazo, *s. m.*
Cerdear, *v. n.*
(*said of hor*
Cerdillo, ito, *s*
hog
Cerdo, *s. m. a*
Cerdoso, sa, *a.*
Cerdudo, da,
hairy
Cerdudo, *s. m.*
Cerebelo, *s. m.*
of the brain
Cerebro, *s. m.*
Cerecita, *s.*
cherry
Ceremonia, *s. f*
Ceremonial, *s.*
monial
Ceremonial, *a*
Ceremoniátican
ceremonious
Ceremoniático,
remonious
Ceremoniosamc
ceremonious
mally
Ceremonioso, *s*
monious ; fo
Cerería, *s. f. a w*
ler's shop
Cerero, *subs. m*
chandler
Cereza, *s. f. a*
Cerezal, *s. m.*
chard
Cerezo, *s. m.*
Ceribon, } *s.*
Ceribones, } *s*
our goods t
tors

rífico, ca, *a. belonging to wax*
rilla, *s. f. a little wax-candle* || *a wax-tablet*
rillas, *pl. lip-salve*
meña, *s. f. a muscatine pear*
meño, *s. m. a muscatine-pear-tree*
nada, *s. f. buck-ashes* || *an ashy plaister*
nadero, *s. m. bucking-cloth*
naedero, *s. m. the bolting-room* || *a bolting maker's apron*
nejas, *s. f. pl. fetlock*
ner, *v. a. to bolt meal*
ner, *v. n. to begin to blossom* || *to drizzle*
nerse, *v. r. to swing one's body*
nerse las aves, *to hover*
nícalo, *s. m. kestrel*
nidillo, *s. m. a drizzing rain*
nido, *s. m. the bolting* || *bolted meal*
nidura, *s. f. bolting*
nír, *v. a. V.* Cerner
ro, *s. m. a cypher; nought*
roferario, *s. m. a wax-taper's bearer*
ron, *s. m. a coarse wax*
rote, *s. m. shoe-maker's wax*
roto, *s. m. cerate*
rquillo, *s. m. a little circle, or ring* || *a monk's shaven crown*
rquita, *s. f. little inclosure* [*hand*
rquita, *adv. near at*
rrada, *s. f. the thickest part of a beast's skin*
rradera, *s. f.* } *the staple of*
rradero, *s. m.* } *lock* || *obstacle*

Cerrado, *s. m. V.* Cercado
Cerrado, da, *a. silent; dissimbling*
Cerrado de barba, *strong-bearled* — de mollera, *peevish; obstinate*
Cerrador, *s. m. a door-keeper* || *any thing used to shut with*
Cerradura, *s. f. shutting* || *a lock*
Cerradurilla, *s. f. a little lock*
Cerraja, *s. f. a lock* || *sow-thistle* [*locks, etc.*
Cerrajear, *v. n. to make*
Cerrajería, *s. f. the lock-smith's trader*, or *shop*
Cerrajero, *s. m. a lock-smith*
Cerramiento, *s. m. shutting* || *an inclosure* || *roof of a house* || *a by-place*
Cerrar, *v. a. to shut; to lock* || *to close up* || *to contain* || *to set bounds to* || *to finish* || *to stop* || *to forbid; to hinder*
Cerrar con alguno, *to run upon any one with violence* [*stand out*
Cerrarse, *v. r. to hold*, or
Cerrazon, *s. m. a close, gloomy weather*
Cerrejon, *s. m. a little hill*
Cerrero, ra, *a. wandering from hill to hill* || *haughty*
Cerril, *a. 2. rugged; uneven* || *untamed; wild* || *unpolished; intractable*
Cerrillo, *s. m. a little hill*
Cerrion, *s. m. an icicle*
Cerro, *s. m. a hill* || *the neck of a beast* || *the back-bone* || *the loins* || *hackled hemp*, or *flax* [*tle bolt*
Cerrojillo, ito, *s. m. a lit-*
Cerrojo, *s. m. a bolt*
Cerron, *s. m. a sort of coarse linen*
Cerrumado, da, *a. affected with a spavin, etc.*
Cerrumas, *s. f. pl. the horse's hams, when affected with a spavin, etc.*
Certámen, *s. m. a litterary dispute*
Certero, ra, *adj. a good marksman*
Certeza, *s. f. certainty*
Certidumbre, *s. f. certainty*
Certificacion, *s. f. certification* || *a certificate*
Certificado, *s. m. a certificate*
Certificador, *subs. m. one who certifies*
Certificar, *v. a. to certify*
Cerúleo, lea, *a. sky-coloured*
Cerusa, *s. f. white lead*
Cerval, } *a. belonging*
Cervario, ria, } *to a stag*
Cervatico, illo, *s. m. a fawn*
Cervato, *s. m. a brocket*
Cervecería, *s. f. brew-house*
Cervecero, *s. m. a brewer*
Cerveza, *s. f. beer*, or *ale*
Cervicabra, *s. f. a doe*
Cervigudo, da, *a. thick-necked* || *obstinate*
Cervino, na, *adj. Voy.* Cervuno
Cerviz, *s. f. the nape of the neck* [*to a stag*
Cervuno, na, *a. belonging*
Cesacio, ó Cesacion a divinis, *s. f. interdiction; suspension*
Cesacion, *s. f.* } *cessa-*
Cesamiento, *s. m.* } *tion*

Cesar, *v. n. to cease.*
César, *s. m. Cesar; Emperor*
Cesáreo, rea, *a. imperial*
Operacion cesárea, *the cesarian operation*
Cesion, *s. f. cession; yielding up*
Cesionario, *s. m. cessionary; grantee*
Césped, } *s. m. a turf of*
Céspede, } *sod*
Cespedera, *s. f. a field from whence turfs are taken away*
Cesta, *s. f. a basket*
Cestería, *s. f. a basket-maker's shop*
Cestero, *s. m. a basket-maker* [*basket*
Cestica, illa, *s. f. a little*
Cestico, illo, *s. m. dim. de* Cesto
Cesto, *s. m. a great basket; a hamper, etc.*
Ceston, *subs. m. aum. de* Cesto || *gabion*
Cestonada, *s. f. intrinchment fortified with gabions*
Cestreo, *s. m. a sort of mullet*
Cesura, *s. f. pause, rest, in a verse*
Cetáceo, cea, *a. cetaceous*
Ceto, *s. m. any great sea-fish*
Cetra, *s. f. a buckler made of the buffalo's hide*
Cetre, *s. m. V.* Acetre
Cetrería, *s. f. falconry; hawking*
Cetrero, *s. m. the verger of a church*
Cetrífero, *a. m. that bears the sceptre*
Cetrino, na, *a. lemon-coloured*
...tro, *s. m. a sceptre*

Ceyba, *s. f. a sort of tall thorny tree*
Cha, *s. m. tea*
Chabacanamente, *adv. without art*, or *regularity*
Chabacanería, *s. f. a bad composition; coarseness, etc.* || *niggardliness*
Chabacano, na, *a. coarse; unwrought*
Chabeta, *s. f. a peg*, or *pin* || *a little bolt*
Chabo, *s. m. a small copper coin*
Chabrana, *s. f. door-cass*
Cháchara, *s. f. empty talk*
Chacharear, *v. a. to talk emptily*
Chacharero, } *s. m. an emp-*
Chacharon, } *ty talker*
Chacho, *s. m. vole*, or *flam*
Chacolí, *s. m. a poor small wine*
Chacolotear, *v. n. to crak, an horse-shoe, when loose*
Chacoloteo, *s. m. cracking*
Chacona, *s. f. chacoon*
Chaconista, *s. m. a dancer*
Chacota, *s. f. a noise made by way of jest, etc.*
Chacotear, *v. n. to make a noise of merriment, etc.*
Chacotero, ra, *adj. gay, merry; frolick-some*
Chacra, *s. f. hut; cottage*
Chacuaco, *s. m. a clownish sloven fellow*
Chafaldetes, *subs. m. pl. clue-lines*
Chafallar, *v. a. to patch; to botch* [*garment*
Chafallo, *s. m. a patched*
Chafallon, *s. m. a botcher*
Chafar, *v. a. to take away the gloss of a cloth* || *to spoil*, or *destroy*

Chafarote, *s. m. a* [illegible] *broad crooked sw*[illegible]
Chafarrinada, *s. f. a* [illegible] *of ink*
Chafarrinar, *v. a. to* [illegible] *to spot.*
Chafarrinon, *s. m.* [illegible] Chafarrinada
Chaflan, *s. m. an* [illegible] *angle*
Chaflanar, *v. a. to* [illegible] *angle, so as to* [illegible] *obtuse*
Chalan, na, *s. a trad*[illegible] *wo allures the custom*[illegible]
Charlancar, *v. a. to* [illegible] *the customers, etc.*
Chalon, *s. m. a sort* [illegible] *woolen stuff*
Chalupa, *s. f. great* [illegible]
Chamaleon, *s. m. V.* [illegible]maleon.
Chamarasca, *s. f.* [illegible] *wood wich gives* [illegible] *short flame*
Chamarillero, *s. m. a seller of pictures, old cloaths, etc.* || *V.* Tahur
Chamarillon, *s. m. a silly, ignorant gamester*
Chamaris, *s. m. a green-finch* [*long coat*
Chamarra, *s. f. a sort of*
Chamarreta, *s. f. dim. de* Chamarra
Chamberga, *s. f. a kind of great coat*
Chambergo, *s. m. an officer called so from* Chamberga [*lete*
Chameloto, *s. m. V.* Came-
Chamelote de aguas, *watered camlet*
Chamerluco, *s. m. a sort of long woman's gown*
Chamicera, *s. f. a wood that is half burnt*
Chamicero, ra, *a.* belonging to burnt wood

s. f. a reed gro-
ı lakes
, *s. m. brand;*
ınd [*head*
, *s. f. a sheared*
r, *v. a. to shear*
, ra, *a. bald;*
t hair
ımorro, *corn that*
without beards
'ar, *v. a. to mix*
, *etc.*
do, da, *a. half*
r, *v. a. to singe*
, *s. m. shinging*
n, *s. m. aum. de*
ıco
uina, *s. f. singing*
rel
, *v. neut. to jest*
[lar
r, *v. a. V.* Cance-
, ra, *a. merry;*
ts
, illa, ita, *s. f. a*
st
ría, *s. f. the court*
ıcery
, *s. f. an old shoe*
t straps, etc.
s. m. a wooden
ı, *s. f. a dish of*
| *a thing of no*
[*unpolished*
, na, *a. coarse;*
á uno alguna co-
hrow a thing in
ish
ı, *s. m. a rule,*
ıure
s. m. chanter;
nger
s. f. the chan-
nity
f. a jest
ı, *s. f. a little*
ttle song

Chanzonetero, *s. m. ballad-maker* || *a jester*
Chaos, *s. m. V.* Caos
Chapa, *s. f. a thin plate* || *colour in the cheeks* || *a little strap*
Hombre de chapa, *a man of parts*
Chapas de freno, *the bosses of a bridle*
Chapadanza, *s. f. a nipping jets*
Chapaleta, *s. f. the sucker of the lower pump-box*
Chaparra, *s. f. V.* Chaparro || *a sort of great coach*
Chaparrada, *s. f. V.* Chaparron
Chaparral, *s. m. a grove of holme-oaks*
Chaparro, *s. m. holme oak*
Chaparron, *s. m. a sudden and violent shower*
Chapear, *v. a. to plate*
Chapellina, *s. f. an ancient gold coin*
Chapería, *s. f. any thing adorned with plates*
Chapeta, *s. f. a little plate*
Chapeton, *s. m. an European new arrived in Spanish America*
Chapilla, *s. f. V.* Chapeta
Chapin, *s. m. a sort of sandal the women wear under their shoes*
Chapina, *s. f. a shell*
Chapinazo, *s. m. a blow with a* Chapin
Chapinería, *s. f. the place where the* Chapines *are sold*
Chapinero, *s. m. one that makes the* Chapines
Chapinito, *s. m. dim. de* Chapin
Chapita, *s. f. a little plate*
Chapitel, *s. m. the top of a tower* || *chapiter*

Chapodar, *v. a. to prune the trees*
Chapotear, *v. a. to moisten* [*dle*
Chapotear, *v. n. to pad-*
Chapuceramente, *adver. coarsely*
Chapucería, *s. f. a coarse piece of work*
Chapucero, *s. m. a nail-smith* || *an iron-monger* || *an ill workman*
Chapuz, *s. m. a diving under water* || *a work ill done*
Chapuces, *pl. fishes of the masts*
Chapuzar, *v. a. y n. to sink,* or *dive under water*
Chaquete, *s. m. the game at ame's ace*
Charadrio, *s. m. loriot*
Charca, *s. f.* } *a puddle of standing water*
Charco, *s. m.* }
Charla, *s. f. an empty talk*
Charlador, ra, *s. prattler*
Charlar, *v. neut. to talk emptily*
Charlatan, na, *s. an empty talker* || *a mountebank*
Charlatanear, *v. n. Voy.* Charlar
Charlatanería, *s. f. Voy.* Charla [*tree*
Charneca, *s. f. turpentine-*
Charnecal, *s. m. grove of turpentine-trees*
Charnela, *s. f. a turning-joint,* or *hinge*
Charol, *s. m. varnish; japan*
Charolear, *v. a. to japan*
Charolista, *s. m. a varnisher* [*shoulder-belt*
Charpa, *s. f. a sort of*
Charquillo, s. m. a little puddle [ness
Charrada, s. f. clownishle

Charro, ra, *s. a rustick clownish fellow, etc.*
Charro, ra, *a. rustick*
Chasco, *s. m. a banter; a trick* || *whip-cord* || *check; fatal blow, etc.*
Chasquear, *v. a. to make a noise with a whip*
Chasquear, *v. n. to snap to play a trick*
Chasqui, *s. m. a messenger sent on foot*
Chasquido, *s. m. the sound of a snaping whip, etc.*
Chasquista, *s. m. a sharper; a pilferer* [*ter*
Chata, *s. f. a sort of ligh-*
Chato, ta, *a. flat* || *flat-nosed* [*stuff*
Chaul, *s. m. a sort of silk-*
Chaza, *s. f. chase, at tennis*
Chazas, *pl. spaces between the cannons of a ship*
Chazador, *s. m. a marker of the chases*
Chazàr, *v. a. to push back the ball* || *to mark the chases*
Cheno, na, *a. V.* Lleno
Cherna, *s. f. a kind of sea-fish*
Chêrubin, *s. m. V.* Querubin [*sperage*
Cherva, *subst. f. the herb*
Chevron, *s. m. chevron*
Chevronado, da, *adj. chevronny*
Chia, *s. f. a short mourning cloak* || *a kind of head-dress* || *a whitish medicinal earth*
Chiba, *s. f. a she-goat*
Chibalete, *s. m. a bench used among printers*
Chibata, *s. f. a crook*
Chibato, *s. m. a young kid*
Chibetero, *s. m. a house for kids*

Chibital, *s. m. V.* Chibetero
Chibo, *s. m. a kid*
Chibon, *sub. m. a young goldfinch*
Chibor, *s. m. a kind of monkey*
Chicada, *s. f. a flock of sick lambs*
Chicarrero, *s. m. a shoe-maker for children*
Chicha, *s. f. the name children give to meat* || *a drink made with maiz*
Chicharo, *s. m. cook*
Chicharra, *s. f. V.* Cigarra
Chicharrar, *v. a. Voyez* Achicharrar
Chicharrero, *sub. m. any hot place*
Chicharron, *s. m. a hard knob left in frying of suet, etc.*
Chicheria, *s. f. the place where* chicha *is drunk or sold*
Chichisveo, *s. m. a courteous gallant*
Chichon, *s. m. a bump in the head*
Chichoncillo ito, *sub. m. dim. de* Chichon
Chichota, *s. f. a jot*
Chico, ca, *adject. little; small* [*to jest*
Chicolear, *v. n. to joke;*
Chicoleo, *s. m. a merry* or *nipping jest*
Chicoria, *s. f. sucorry*
Chicorrotico, ito, *adj. very little*
Chicote, ta, *s. a person who is short and thick*
Chicote, *s. m. the end of a rope or cable*
Chicozapote, *s. m. a fruit of the west-indies*
Chicuelo, la, *adj. a young child*
Chifla, *s. f. a sort of whisel*

|| *a book-binder's scraper*
Chifladera, *s. f. a whistle*
Chifladura, *s. f. whistling; hissing*
Chiflar, *v. a. to scrape*
Chiflar, *v. n. to whistle* || *to hiss* || *to drink hard*
Chiflato, *s. m. whistling*
Chifle, *s. m. a whistle* || *a bird-call*
Chiflete, *s. m. V.* Chifla
Chiflido, *s. m. a whistling, or hissing*
Chiflo, *s. m. V.* Chifla
Chilacayote, *s. m. Voyez* Cidracayote
Chilindrina, *s. f. a thing of no value*
Chilindron, *s. m. a sort of game at cards* || *collection of different things* || *flask on the head*
Chilla, *s. f. a bird-call*
Tabla de chilla, *a very thin board* || clavo de chilla, *a tack*
Chillado, *s. m. a roof made with thin boards, etc.*
Chillador, *s. m. a whistler* || *a scold*
Chillador, *s. m. a common crier*
Chillar, *v. n. to scold; to bawl; to squeak* || *to trepan birds with a bird-call* || *to crackle* || *to creak or screak*
Chillido, *s. m. a bawling or scolding*
Chillo, *s. m. V.* Chilla
Chillon, *s. m. a bawler* || *a common crier*
Chilo, *s. m. V.* Quilo
Chimenea, *s. f. a chimney*
Chimera, Chimerista. *V.* Quimera, etc.
Chimia, } *s. f. chimistry*
Chimica, }

rista, s. m. a chymist
a, s. f. a pebble || a
rt of china-root || a
ina-ware
arro, s. m. a pebble
rteado, s. m. bed of
all pebbles
azo, s. m. a pebble
charrazo, subst. m. a
rust with a sword
charrero, s. m. a place
ll of bugs
che, s. m. a bug
chero, s. m. a bug-
p [squirrel
chilla, s. f. a sort of
chorrero, s. m. Voy.
incharrero
chon, s. m. V. Chi-
on
chorro, s. m. a fis-
ng-boat, or net
ela, s. f. a slipper
illa, ita, s. f. a little
bble
chio, s. m. the chir-
ng of sparrows
iero, s. m. a hog-sty
ichaque, subs. m. a
wyer || clashing
iillo, lla, s. an young
ild
uitico, llo; Chiquir-
ico, llo, to; Chiquir-
in, adj. very little
uito, ta, adj. Voyez
iquitico
bitil, subs. m. a very
all passage
gayta, s. f. a kind of
ard
mía, sub. f. hautboy
strument)
mía, s. m. hautboy
layer)
moya, sub. f. a pear
owing in America
ola, s. f. a play like
ine-pins

Chirivía, s. f. skirret — a wagtail
Chirla, s. f. V. Almeja
Chirlador, ra, s. bawler
Chirlar, v. n. to cry; to bawl [wound
Chirlar, v. a. to strike; to
Chirle, s. m. wild grapes || a thing of no value
Chirlo, s. m. a gash; a slash [mancy
Chiromancia, s. f. chiro-
Chirriadero, ra, adj. crackling [rido
Chirriado, s. m. V. Chir-
Chirriador, adject. crackling, etc.
Chirriar, v. n. to crackle || to creak || to chirp or sing untunably || to drink hard
Chirrido, s. m. an untunable chirping
Chirrio, s. m. the noise of a creaking wheel
Chirrion, s. m. a creaking dung-cart
Chirrionero, s. m. a carter
Chirumbela, s. f. V. Charumbela
Chirúrgico, adj. V. Quirúrgico
Chis, int. ho!
Chis-chas, s. m. an incessant knocking [body
Chisgaravis, s. m. a busy-
Chisguete, s. m. a small draught of wine
Chisme, s. m. false-report; tale
Chismes, pl. effects, moveables of little value
Chismear, v. act. to make false reports
Chismoso, sa, adj. a tale-carrier
Chispa, s. f. a spark — a very short gun || a very small diamond

Echar chispas, to fly in passion
Chispas! int. udsbudikins
Chispazo, s. m. the blow given by a spark || false report
Chispear, v. n. to sparkle || to shine || to drizzle
Chispero, sub. m. a smith who makes shovels, tongs, etc.
Chispero (cohete), sub. m. a sparkling squib
Chispo, s. m. V. Chisguete
Chisporrotear, v. neut. to throw a multitude of sparks || to crack
Chisporroteo, s. m. sparkling || cracking
Chisposo, sa, adject. that throws many sparks
Chistar, v. n. to mutter; to mumble
Chiste, sub. m. a jest || a pleasant adventure
Dar en el chiste, to hit the mark
Chistera, s. f. a sort of a fisherman's hamper
Chistoso, sa, adj. facetious
Chita, s. f. a bone in the sheep's or cow's foot
Chiticalla, s m. silent
Chiticallar, v. neut. to be silent [quoits
Chito, subs. m. the but at
Chito y Chiton, int. hush!
Cho! int. used to stop horses [reward
Choca, sub. f. the hawk's
Chocador, ra, s. one that strikes against
Chocante, adj. 2 offensive unpleasant
Chocar, v. n. to strike or dash against... || to engage or encounter
Chocar, v. a. to offend
Chocarrear, v. n. to jest

Chocarrería, *s. f. jesting*
Chocarrero, *s. m. jester*
Chocarrero, ra, *a. pleasant*
Chocha y chocha perdiz, *s. f. a woodcock*
Chochear, *v. n. to dote*
Chochera, } *s. f. dotage*
Chochez, }
Chocho, *sub. m. lupine* || *sugar cinnamon*
Chochos, *pl. dainties for children*
Chocho, cha, *adj. doting*
Chocilla, *s. f. a little cottage*
Choclar, *v. neut. to bolt into a place*
Choclo, *s. m. V.* Chanclo
Choclon, *subs. m. bolting through a ring, etc.*
Choco, *s. m. a little cuttle-fish*
Chocolate, *s. m. chocolate*
Chocolatera, *s. f. a chocolate-pot*
Chocolatero, *s. m. chocolate-maker*
Chocolatear, *v. n. Voyez* Chacolotear
Chofes, *s. m. pl. the lungs*
Chofeta, *s. f. a little chafing-dish*
Chofista, *sub. m. one who eats lungs*
Cholla, *s. f. the top of the head* || *judgment*
Chopa, *s. f. a little sea-fish* || *the steersman's cabbin*
Chopo, *s. m. alder*
Choque, *s. m. dashing or striking against* || *shock*
Choquezuela, *s. f. the knee-ball*
Chorcha, *s. f. V.* Chocha
Chordon, *s. m. V.* Churdon
Choricero, *s. m. sausage-maker*
Chorizo, *s. m. sausage*

Chorlito, *s. m. a curlew* || *a plover*
Chorrear, *v. neut. to drop down* || *to come slowly*
Chorrera, *s. f. a place from whence water drops* || *a shirt's bosom*
Chorretada, *s. f. impetuosity of a running stream*
Chorillo, ito, *s. m. dim. de* Chorro || *continual expences*
Chorro, *sub. m. spouting out, running of water, etc.* || *the sound of the voice* || *bloody-flux*
A' chorros, *adv. abundantly*
Chorron, *sub. m. hackled again hemp*
Chotacabras, *s. m. goat-milker*
Chotar, *v. a. to suck*
Choto, *s. m. a sucking kid*
Chotuno, *a. lean; weak; sickly* [*daw*
Chova, *s. f. a kind of jack*
Choya, *s. f. a crow (bird)*
Choz, *s. m. a blow given*
Choza, *s. f. a hut; a cottage*
Chozno, *s. m. the great-grand-son of one's grand-son*
Chozuela, *s. f. a little hut*
Christianamente, *adver. christianly*
Christianar, *v. a. to christen* [*tendom*
Christiandad, *s. f. Chris-*
Christianesco, ca, *adj. belonging to a christian*
Christianillo, lla, *s. dim. de* Christiano
Christianismo, *s. m. christianism* || *christendom*
Christianizar, *v. a. to make christian*
Christiano, na, *s. y adj. christian*

Christo, *s. m. Christ*
Chrisma, *s. m. c*
row
Chubarba, *sub. f.*
Chubasco, *s. m. a*
a violent rain
Chuca, *s. f. the*
part of a ball,
Chucero, *s. m. a*
armed with a
Chuchear, *v. n.*
birds || *to whi*
Chuchería, *s.*
gew' gaw ||
way of catching
Chuchero, *s. m. a*
catcher
Chucho, *sub. m. a*
Chucho! *int. used to*
dogs
Chuchumeco, *subs. m*
ugly contemptible
low [*to beat*
Chuchurrar, *v. a. to grind*
Chueca, *s. f. the hollow of*
a joint where the bones
play || *cricket*
Chuecazo, *s. m. a stroke*
with a goff-stick
Chufa, *s. f. pignut*
Echar chufas, *to boast*
Chufeta, *s. f. a jest*
Chufleta, *s. f. a nipping*
jest [*to scoff*
Chufletear, *v. n. to jest;*
Chufletero, ra, *adj. jester*
Chulada, *subs. f. genteel*
way; good grace || *obscenity; smuttiness*
Chulear, *v. n. to jest merrily*
Chulería, *s. f. V.* Chulada
an apish trick
Chuleta, *s. f. scotch-collops* [Chulo
Chulillo, ito, *s. dim. de*
Chulla, *s. f. a gammon's*
cut || mutton-chop
Chulo, la, sub. a gracefu

'oman || a mer-
'ar de), to be in
ımour
the waist coat
, ra, a. sucking
ɑpadera, the
t vein
la, adj. lean;
ed
ra',s. a sucker
s. m. a child's
, s. f. sucking
a. to suck
va, adj. ab-
lla, ita, sub. a
istcoat
s. m. under-
it
s. m. suction;
m. a red spot
the skin by su-
sub. f. a whore
ces her gallant
sub. m. a paste
'ith rasberries
ar
f. } bag of cin-
m. } namon
ıb. m. running
i, s. m. rasca-
ıb
, ta, a. greasy
s. m. a deserter
, s. m. a pra-
ow [wine
r, v. n. to sip
'se, v. r. to be
ɔarched, etc.
, sub. m. half-
'ead [pipe
la, s. f. a reed or
s. m. juice
's (no decir),

not to speak a syllabe
Chusco, ca, s. *a genteel speaker, etc.*
Chusma, s. f. a. *galley's crew || the mob*
Chutear, v. n. *to whisper*
Chuzazo, s. m. *a long dart || a blow with a dart*
Chuzo, s. m. *a dart*
Chuzon, s. m. aum. de Chuzo
Chuzon, na, adj. *cautious || cunning || merry; jocular*
Cia, s. f. *the hip-bone*
Ciaboga, s. f. *the tacking about of a galley*
Ciaescurre, s. m. *to wing of a ship*
Cianco, s. m. *the hip-bone*
Ciar, v. n. *to hold water || to cease* or *suspend*
Ciática, s. f. *sciatica*
Ciático, ca, adj. *sciatical*
Cibario, ria, adj. *belonging to the food*
Cibera, s. f. *quantity of corn thrown into the hopper || corn || dregs; dross || a mill-hopper*
Ciberuela, s. f. dim. de Cibera
Cibica, s. f. *an iron bar in the axle-trees*
Cibicon, sub. m. aum. de Cibica [*didly*
Cicatear, v. n. *to spare sor-*
Cicatería, s. f. *covetousness*
Cicaterillo, uelo, a. dim. de Cicatero
Cicatero, ra, a. *covetous*
Cicatricilla, s. f. *a little scar*
Cicatriz, s. f. *a scar*
Cicatrizacion, s. f. *cicatrizing*
Cicatrizal, adj. *belonging to a scar*
Cicatrizar, v. a. *to cicatrize*

Cicatrizativo, va, adj. *cicatrizing* [*ting fever*
Cicion, s. f. *an intermit-*
Ciclada, s. f. *a sort of woman's morning-gown*
Ciclan, s. m. *he that has but one testicle*
Ciclo, s. m. *cycle*
Cicloide, s. *cycloid*
Ciclope, s. m. *a cyclop*
Cicuta, s. f. *hemlock*
Cidia, s. f. *a citron*
Cidracayote, s. f. *a gourd growing in America*
Cidral, s. m. *an orchard of citron-trees || Voyez* Cidro
Cidria, s. f. *rosin of cedar*
Cidro, s. m. *citron-tree*
Cidronela, s. f. *balm-gentle*
Ciegamente, adv. *blindly*
Ciego, ga, adj. *blind*
Noche ciega, *a dark night*
A' ciegas, adv. *blindfold*
Cielo, s. m. *the h aven || the sky || climate*
Cielo de la boca, *the palate* [*a bed*
— de la cama, *tester of*
— del coche, *the roof of a coach* —raso, *the ceiling*
Cien, adj. *hundred*
Cienaga, s. f. *a quagmire*
Ciencia, s. f. *science*
Cieno, s. m. *mud; mire*
Científicamente, adver. *scientifically*
Científico, ca, adj. *scientifical || skilful; knowing*
Ciento, adj. *hundred*
Ciento, s. m. *an hundred*
Juego de los cientos, *the game of piquet*
Cientopies, sub. m. *millepedes*
Cierne, s. f. *the blossom of the vines* [*ly*
Ciertamente, adv. *certain-*

Cierto, ta, *a. certain*
Cierto, *adv. certainly*
Cierva, *s. f. a hind*
Ciervo, *s. m. a stag; a hart*
Ciervo volante, *s. m. the great horn-beetle*
Cierzo, *s. m. the north-wind*
Cifra, *s. f. cypher* || *figure*
Cifrar, *v. a. to cypher* || *to epitomise*
Cifrarse, *v. r. to be made concise*
Cigarra, *s. f. chirping kind of grashopper; langosta*
Cigarral, *s. m. an orchard enclosed with walls*
Cigarro, *s. m. leaves of tobacco folded like a roll*
Cigarron, *s. m. aum. de* Cigarra
Cigoñal, *s. m. a crane to draw up water*
Cigoñino, *s. m. a young stork*
Cigoñuela, *s. f. dim. de* Cigueña
Ciguatera, *s. f. a sort of jaundice*
Ciguato, ta, *a. jaundiced*
Cigüente (uva), *sub. f. a kind of white grapes*
Cigüeña, *s. f. a stork* || *a handle*
Cigüeñal, *s. m. swing-gate*
Cigüeñear, *v. n. to make a noise like a stork*
Cigüeño, *s. m. a he stork*
Cija, *sub. f. granary* || *a dungeon*
Cilantro, *s. m. coriander*
Cilicio, *s. m. hair-cloth*
Cilíndrico, ca, *adj. cylindrical*
Cilindro, *s. m. cylinder*
Cilla, *s. f. granary*
Cillazgo, *s. m. duty for stowing corn in the granaries*
Cillerero, *s. m. a caterer*
Cilleriza, *s. f. a house-keeper*
Cillero, *s. m. a store-keeper* || *a granary*
Cima, *s. f. the top*
Cimacio, *s. m. ogee*
Cimarron, na, *adj. wild; untamed*
Cimbalaria, *s. f. a plant so called*
Cimbalillo, *s. m. a little bell*
Cimbalo, *s. m. cymbal*
Cimbara, *s. f. a scythe*
Cimborio, *s. m. lantern; cupola*
Cimbra, *s. f. a mould for an arch*
Cimbrar, *v. a. to vibrate; to brandish*
Cimbrar á alguno, *to lash or switch*
Cimbrarse, ó Cimbrearse, *v. r. to bend*
Cimbreño, ña, *a. flexible*
Cimbria, *s. f. V.* Cimbra
Cimbronazo, *s. m. a blow with a fencing-foil*
Cimentar, *v. act. to lay foundations*
Cimenterio, *s. m. a church-yard*
Cimera, *s. f. a helmet's crest*
Cimero, ra, *adj. put in the top*
Cimiento, *s. m. foundation*
Cimillo, *s. m. a snare to catch pigeons*
Cimitarra, *s. f. a cimeter*
Cimorra, *s. f. cold upon heat*
Cinabrio, *s. m. dragons blood* || *cinnabar*
Cinamomino, *sub. m. an aromatick ointment*
Cinamomo, *s. m. cinnamon*
Cincel, *s. m. a chisel*
Cincelador, *s. m. a* [illegible] *ser; a carver*
Cincelar, *v. a. to* [illegible] *to engrave*
Cincha, *s. f. a girth*
Cinchadura, *s. f. gird*[illegible]
Cinchar, *v. a. to gir*[illegible]
Cinchera, *s. f.* [illegible] *a horse who is bi*[illegible] *with the girth*
Cincho, *s. m. a broad* [illegible] *dle of leather,* [illegible] *verrel* || *a cheese-*[illegible] *a plinth or fascia* [illegible] *swelling about the* [illegible]
Cinchon, *s. m. aum.* Cincho
Cinchuela, *sub. f. a li*[illegible] *girth*
Cinco, *s. m. five*
Cinco en rama, *s. f. ci*[illegible] *quefoil*
Cincomesino, na, *a.* [illegible] *months old*
Cincuenta, *s. m. fifty*
Cincuenteno, na, *a. belon*[illegible] *ging to the number* [illegible] *fifty*
Cincuesma, *s. f. whitsun*[illegible]
Cíngaro, ra, *s. a gyps*[illegible]
Cíngulo, *s. m. a girdle*
Cínico, ca, *a. cynick*
Cinife, *s. m. a midge*
Cinocéfalo, *s. m. a kin*[illegible] *of monkey*
Cinosura, *s. f. the pole star*
Cinqueno, na, *a. fifth*
Cinqueño, Cinquillo, } *s. m. the hom*[illegible] *bre wh*[illegible] *played by five person*[illegible]
Cinta, *s. f. any sort of ribbon* || *a girdle* || *a net* [illegible] *catch tunnies into*
Estar en cinta, *to be wi*[illegible] *child*
Cintadero, *s. m. that pa*[illegible] *of the cross-bow whe*[illegible] *the string is fixed*

, *a. adorned*
ons
ub. m. a blow
lat side of a
. a. to strike
ord
ribbon-trade
. ribbon-wea-
e made with
[bon
. a little rib-
. a hat-band
. a girdle ||
k
the waist ||
la, ita, *s. f. a*
le
m. a belt
. cypress
n. a grave of
es
, *a. of cypress*
. f. caresses ;
lj. 2. belon-
e circus
circus
to surround;
ass
n. circuit
s. f. circula-
[late
n. to circu-
a. to encom-
. circular
, *adv. circu-*
. a circle
, *a. 2. that is*
pole
, *v. a. to cir-*
, *s. f. circum-*
sa, *adj. cir-*

Circundar, *v. a. to compass round*
Circunferencia, *s. f. circumference* || *concourse of people*
Circunferencial, *a. 2. belonging to the circumference*
Circunferencialmente, *ad. circularly* || *about*
Circunflexo, *a. circumflex*
Circunlocucion, *s. f. circumlocution*
Circunloquio, *s. m. a great compass of words*
Circumscribir, *v. act. to circumscribe*
Circunscripcion, *s. f. circumscription*
Circunspeccion, *s. f. circumspection*
Circunspecto, ta, *a. circumspect*
Circunstancia, *sub. f. circumstance*
Circunstanciado, da, *adj. circunstanciated*
Circunstantes, *a. pl. presents; assistants*
Circunvalacion, *s. f. circumvallation*
Circumvalar, *v. a. to compass* or *entrench round*
Circunvecino, na, *a. neighbouring*
Circunvenir, *v. a. V.* Rodear
Circunvolucion, *s. f. circumvolution*
Cirial, *s. m. a church-candelistick*
Ciriales, *pl. the clerks who bear the candelisticks*
Cirineo, *s. m. an helper; an assistant* [*dle*
Cirio, *s. m. a wan-candle*
Cirio pascual, paschal candle

Cirro, *s. m. schirrhus*
Cirroso, sa, *a. schirrhous*
Ciruela, *s. f. a plum*
Ciruelica, illa, ita, *sub. f. a little plum*
Ciruelico, illo, ito, *s. m. dim. de* Ciruelo
Ciruelo, *sub. m. a plum-tree*
Cirugia, *s. f. surgery*
Cirujano, *s. m. a surgeon*
Ciscar, *v. a. to foul; to stain*
Ciscarse, *v. r. to bewray one's self*
Cisco, *s. m. charcoal-dust*
Cision, *s. f. cutting; incision*
Cisma, *s. m. schism*
Cismático, ca, *a. schismatick* || *unquiet; seditious*
Cismontano, na, *adj. of this side of the mountain*
Cisne, *s. m. a swan*
Cisquero, *sub. m. a little linen bag full of small coal*
Cistel, ó Cister, *sub. m. order of the Cistercians*
Cisterciense, *a. 2. belonging to* Cister
Cisterna, *s. f. a cistern*
Cisternica, illa, ita, *s. f. a little cistern*
Cisura, *s. f. breathing of a vein*
Cita, *s. f. a rendez-vous* || *citation; quoting*
Citacion, *sub. f. citation; summous*
Citano, *V.* Zutano
Citar, *v. a. to cite*
Citara, *s. f. mandore* || *a partition of bricks*
Citarista, *s. m. one who plays upon the mandore*

moning
Citerior, *a. 2. citerior*
Citiso, *s. m. citisus*
Cito, *int. used to call a dog*
Citocredente, *a. 2. credulous*
Citola, *s. f. the clapper of a mill* [*summoner*
Citote, *s. m. summons* ||
Citramontano, na, *a. of this side of the mountain*
Citrino, na, *a. citrine*
Ciudad, *s. f. a city*
Ciudadano, na, *s. a citizen*
Ciudadela, *s. f. a citadel*
Cívico, ca, *a. civick*
Civil, *a. 2. civil*
Civilidad, *s. f. civility*
Civilmente, *adv. civilly*
Muerto civilmente, *dead in law*
Cizalla, *sub. f. shearings; clippings*
Clamador, *s. m. a bawler*
Clamar, *v. n. to cry; to bawl* || *to complain*
Clamor, *s. m. cry; clamour* || *complaint; lamentation* || *V.* Clamoreo
Clamorear, *v. a. to implore; to call upon*
to ring a peal for the dead
Cla
Clamoroso, sa, *a. doleful*
Clandestinamente, *adv. clandestinely*
Clandestino, na, *a. clandestine*
Clangor, *s. m. clangor*
Clara, *s. f. a short intermission of the rain* || *the white of an egg*
A la clara, adv. publickly

a gallery in a church
Claramente, *adv. clearly; plainly*
Clarea, *subs. f. a liquor made with white-wine, sugar, etc.*
Clarear, *v. n. to dawn*
Clarearse, *v. r. to grow transparent* || *to clear*
Clarecer, *v. neut. to grow day*
Clarete, *a. claret*
Claridad, *subs. f. light* || *clearness* || *upbraiding*
Clarificacion, *s. f. clarifying*
Clarificar, *v. a. to clear* || *to clarify* || *to purify*
Clarificativo, va, *a. clarifying*
Clarin, *s. m. clarion* || *a sort of very fine linen*
Clarinero, *s. m. one who plays upon the clarion*
Clarinete, *s. m. a sort of hautboy* [*crayon*
Clarion, *sub. m. a white*
Clarisa, *sub. f. a nun of* santa Clara
Claro, ra, *a. clear* || *thin*
Claro, *s. m. an oval* || *a vacant space in a book, etc.* || *intercolumnation* || *glade*
Clase, *s. f. class* || *a form in a school*
Clásico, ca, *a. classical*
Claudicacion, *s. f. halting*
Claudicar, *v. n. to halt; to go lame*
Claustral, *a. 2. claustral*
Claustrico, *s. m. a little cloister*
Claustro, *s. m. a cloister*
Claúsula, *s. f. a sentence* or *period* || *a clause*
Clausular, *v. a.* to end a *period*

Clausula
Clausura, *s. f*
closure
Clava, *s. f. a*
per-hole
Clavado, da,
Clavadura, *s.*
a horse's fo
Clavar, *v. a.*
enchase || *to*
Clavar el coraz
the heart —
to nail up
Clavazon, *s.*
Clave, *s. f. key*
or *cliff* || *k*
pher, etc.
Clave, *s. m. a*
Clavel, *s. m.*
Clavellina, *s.*
Clavelon, *s.*
Clavel || *an*
Claveque, *sub*
like a dia
of less val
Clavera, *sub.*
for forging
hole a nail
place wher
Clavería, *s.*
of knight-h
Clavero, *s. m*
of note in t
knight-hoo
Clavero, ra,
rer || *clove-*
Clavete, *s. m.*
Clavetear, *v.*
to tag
Clavicordio, *s*
sicord
Clavícula, *s. f.*
Clavigera, *s.*
Clavija, *s. f.*
Clavillo, ito,
nail
Claviórgano,
instrumen

! and an or-
s. a nail || *a*
edget || *clove*
udder
a spot in the
he eye — de
e tongue of a

. f. perwinkle
imber
. f. clemency
. 2. clement
nte, *adv. cle-*

, s. f. pl. the
ons of Pope
he fifth
. f. clepsydre
f. the clergy
2. clerical
te, *adv. cler-*
ike
. m. clerkship
s. f. clerkship
m. a clergy-
[tling
s. m. a pries-
m. a singing-

s. m. a lay-
h the clergi-
othes
the clergy
m. a client
. f. clientship
s. m. a little

: a climate
, ca, *a. cli-*
k
ca, *a. incons-*

. m. water-be-

horse-hair
, s. m. horse-

m. a clyster

Clistelera, *s. f. a woman that gives clysters*
Clister, *s. m. a clyster*
Clisterizar, *v. a. to give a clyster*
Clivoso, sa, *a. bending downward*
Clo, clo, *s. m. clucking*
Cloaca, *s. f. a common shore* || *a stinking place*
Clocar, *v. n. V.* Cloquear
Cloque, *s. m. grappling-iron* || *V.* Cócle
Cloquear, *v. n. to cluck*
Cloquero, *s. m. one that fishes with a harpoon*
Clueca (gallina), *a brood-hen*
Clueco, ca, *adj. weak; impotent* || *hoarse*
Coaccion, *s. f. coaction*
Coacervar, *v. a. to heap up together*
Coactivo, va, *a. coactive*
Coadjutor, ra, *s. a helper*
Coadjutor, *s. m. a coadjutor*
Coadjutoría, *s. f. coadjutorship* [*trix*
Coadjutriz, *s. f. coadju-*
Coadministrador, *s. m. a bishop's vicar*
Coadunacion, *s. f.* } *union;*
Coadunamiento, *s. m.* } *mixture*
Coadunar, *v. a. to unite; to incorporate*
Coadyuvador, *s. m. a helper*
Coadyuvar, *v. a. to help; to assist* [*lation*
Coagulacion, *s. f. coagu-*
Coagular, *v. a. to coagulate*
Coagulo, *sub. m. clotted blood*
Coalla, *s. f. a wood-cock*
Coapóstol, *s. m. apostle with another*

Coaptacion, *s. f. adapting*
Coaptar, *v. act. to adapt; to fit*
Coarrendador, *s. m. one who takes at a rent, with another*
Coartar, *v. a. to bound or limit* [*basket*
Cobanillo, *s. m. a little*
Cobarde, *a. 2. cowardly* || *idle; lazy*
Cobardear, *v. n. to be a coward* [*dly*
Cobardemente, *adv. coar-*
Cobardía, *s. f. cowardice*
Cobertera, *s. f. a cover* || *a bawd*
Coberteras, *pl. two large feathers in the hawk's tail*
Cobertizo, *subs. m. a pent-house* || *a covered passage*
Cobertor, *s. m. V.* Colcha
Cobertura, *s. f. covering*
Cobija, *s. f. a gutter-tile* || *a short sort of mantle*
Cobijar, *v. a. to cover*
Cobrador, *s. m. a receiver*
Perro cobrador, *a dog that fetches and carries well*
Cobranza, *s. f. receiving; recovering*
Cobrar, *v. a. to receive* || *to reave* || *to acquire*
Cobrar el halcon, *to retrieve the hawk* — fuerzas, *to gather strength* — ánimo, *to take courage*
Cobrarse, *v. r. to recover one's self*
Cobre, *s. m. copper*
Cobre de cebollas, *a rope of onions* — de bestias, *a herd of cattle* — de cecial, *two stock-fishes tied together*

Cobrizo, za, *adj. mixed with copper*
Cobro, *s. m. V.* Cobranza
Coca, *subs. f. a small tree growing in the meridional America*
Cocar, *v. act. to make mouths like a monkey || to coax*
Cocarar, *v. n. to lay up corn, etc. in a granary*
Coccíneo, nea, *a. purple coloured*
Coccion, *s. f. coction*
Coceador, ra, *s. kicker*
Coceadura, *s. f.* } *kicking*
Coceamiento, *s. m.* }
Cocear, *v. a. to kick || to reluct* [*boil*
Cocedero, dizo, *a. easy to*
Cocedero, *s. m. a kneading-room*
Cocedra, *s. f. a feather-bed* [Cocedra
Cocedron, *s. m. aum. de*
Cocedura, *s. f. boiling*
Cocer, *v. a. to boil; to bake || to digest, discuss*
Cocer, *v. n. to boil*
Cocerse, *v. r. to fret one's self*
Cochambre, *s. m. a greasy filthy smell*
Cochambrería, *s. f. filth*
Cochambroso, sa, *adj. filthy* [*cup*
Cocharro, *s. m. a wooden*
Coche, *s. m. a coach*
Coche deagua, *a passage-boat*
Cochear, *v. n. to drive a coach*
Cochecillo, ito, *s. m. a little coach*
Cochera, *sub. f. a coach-house || a coachman's wife*
Cocheril, *adj. 2. belonging to a coachman*

Cocherillo, *s. m. dim. de* Cochero [*man*
Cochero, *s. m. a coach-*
Cochifrito, *s. m. a particular stewed dish*
Cochinata, *s. f. rider (in a ship)*
Cochinilla, *s. f. cochineal || a wood-louse || a young sow*
Cochinillo, lla, *s. a sucking-pig* or *sow*
Cochino, *s. m. a pig; a hog*
Cochino, na, *a. slovenly*
Cochite hervite, *adv. hastily*
Cochura, *s. f. boiling || an ovenfull*
Cocido, *subs. m. boiled-meat*
Cocimiento, *s. m. coction || decoction*
Cocina, *s. f. kitchen || a soup of legumes*
Cocinar, *v. a. to cook*
Cocinero, ra, *s. a cook*
Cocinilla, ita, *s. f. dim. de* Cocina
Cocle, *s. m. a grapple; a hook || a harpoon*
Coclear, *v. a. to harpoon*
Coclear, *v. n. to cluck*
Coco, *s. m. cocoa || a cocoa-tree || a worm that eats the vines, etc. || bug-bear*
Hacer cocos, *to caress; to coax*
Cocobolo, *s. m. a tree in the west-indies*
Cocodrilo, *s. m. a crocodile*
Cocoliste, *s. m. a sicknes like the spotted fever*
Cocoso, sa, *a. worm-eaten*
Cocote, *s. m. V.* Cogote
Cocotriz, *s. m. V.* Cocodrilo

Cocuyo, *s.* ... *worm*
Coda, *s. f. V*
Codadura, *s.* ... *a vine*
Codal, *s. m* ... *the elbow* | ... *taper || la*... *|| a cubit*
Codal, *a. 2.* ... *|| that ma*...
Codales, *s.* ... *penter's sq*...
Codaste, *s. m* ... *post*
Codazo, *s. m*
Codear, *v. n* ... *with one's*
Codera, *s. f.* ... *the elbow*
Códice, *s. m* ... *cript*
Codicia, *s.*
Codicilar, *a.* ... *in a codici*...
Codicilo, *s.* ...
Codiciosamen... *sirously*
Codiciosito, t... Codicioso
Codicioso, sa ... *eager — la*...
Código, *s. m*
Codillo, *s. m.* ... *|| an elbo*... *|| codille*
Codo, *s. m.* ...
Codon, *s. m.* ... *up a horse*
Codorniz, *s.* ...
Coeficiente, ... *cient*
Coepíscopo, *s.*
Coequal, *a.* ...
Coercion, *s.* ...
Coetáneo, nea ... *neous*
Coeterno, na ...
Coevo, va, ...

existencia, s. f. coexistence [exist
existir, v. n. to co-
extenderse, ver. r. to stretch out together and equally
fia, s. f. a coif
fiemela, sub. f. a little coif [nier, etc.
fin, s. m. basket, pan-
frade, s. m. brother || fellow
fradía, sub. f. brotherhood || society; partnership [chest
fre, s. m. a trunk; a
frecico, illo, ito, s. m. a little chest
frero, s. m. a trunkmaker
gedero, ra, s. gatherer
gedizo, za, a. that may be gathered
gedor, s. m. gatherer || a chest to put sweepings in
gedura, s. f. gathering
ger, v. a. to gather || to catch || to contain || to quoil a rope || to fold linen
gimiento, s. m. gathering or catching
gitabundo, da, adject. thoughtful [king
gitativo, va, a. thin-
gnacion, s f. cognation
gnado, da, a. kindred
gnomento, s. m. a surname [name
gnominar, v. a. to sur-
gnoscitivo, va, a. having the power of knowing
gollico, ito, s. m. dim. de Cogollo
gollo, sub. m. the close part of a lettice, etc. || a tree's shoot or top

Cogombradura, sub. f. V. Aporcadura
Cogombro, s. m. V. Cohombro
Cogote, s. m. the nape of the head
Cogucho, s. m. the coarsest sort of sugar
Cogujada, s. f. the copped lark
Cogujon, s. m. the cornet of a quilt, etc.
Cogujonero, ra, a. angular [cowl
Cogulla, sub. f. a monk's
Cogullada, subs. f a part full of kernels in the neck of swine
Cohabitacion, s. f. cohabitation [bit
Cohabitar, v. n. to coha-
Cohechador, s. m. briber
Cohechar, v. act. to bribe- to plough [hing
Cohechazon, s. f. ploug-
Cohecho, s. m. a bribe
Coheredero, ra, s. a coheir
Coherencia, s. f. coherence
Coherente, a. 2. coherent
Cohete, s. m. a squib
Cohetero, s. m. fire-worker
Cohibicion, s. f. coercion
Cohibir, v. a. to coerce, restrain, etc.
Cohol, s. m. antimony
Cohombral, s. m. a bed of cucumbers
Cohombrillo, s. m. dim. de Cohombro || wild cucumber
Cohombro, s. m. cucumber
Cohorte, s. f. cohort
Coincidencia, s. f. coincidence
Coincidir, v. n. to coincide [char
Coinquinar, v. a. V. Man-

Coitivo, va, a. belonging to the coition
Coito, s. m. coition
Cojon, s. m. a testicle
Cojudo, da, a. that is not gelt
Col, s. m. a colewort
Cola, s. f. a tail || glue, size || a long note in musick [pez
Cola de pescado, V. Cola-
Colacion, s. f. collation
Colacionar, v. a. to collate
Colada, s. f. buck for linen || the collacion of a benefice
Coladera, s. f. } a strainer; a cullender || a narrow passage
Coladero, s. m. }
Colador, s. m. a strainer || collator || a trough, in a printing-house
Coladura, s. f. straining || bucking
Colanilla, s. f. snacket
Colaña, sub. f. a sort of timber
Colapez, } s. f. isinglass
Colapiscis, }
Colar, v. a. to strain || to collate a benefice || to buck linen
Colar, v. n. to go through a narrow way || to succeed; to prosper
Colarse, v. r. to slip; to creep
Colateral, a. 2. collateral
Colativo, va, a. collative
Colcedra, s. f. a featherbed [Colcedra
Colcedron, s. m. aum. de
Colcha, s. f. counterpane
Colchadura, s. f. quilting
Colchar, v. a. to quilt
Colchero, s. m. one who makes counter-panes

Colchico, *sub. m. hermodactyl*

Colchon, *s. m. mattress*

Colchoncico, **llo**, *s. m a little mattress*

Colchonero, **ra**, *s. quilt-maker*

Coleada *subs. f. a stroke with the tail*

Coleadura, *s. f. wagging of the tail* [*tail*

Colear, *v. n. to wag the*

Coleccion, *s. f. collection*

Colecta *s. f. a levy of a tax* || *a collect*

Colectacion, *s. f. V.* Recaudacion

Colectar, *v. a. V.* Recaudar

Colecticio, **cia**, *a. of the common stock or sort*

Colectivamente, *adv. collectively*

Colectivo, **va**, *a. collective*

Colector *s m. collector*

Colecturía, *s. f. the office of a collector*

Colega *s. m. colleague*

Colegial, **la**, *s. a collegiate; a fellow*

Colegial, *a.* 2. *collegial*

Colegialmente, *adv. collegiate-like; in common*

Colegiata, *sub. f. a collegiate church*

Colegiatura, *s. f. a pension in a college*

Colegio, *s. m. a college*

Colegir, *v. a. to infer, or deduce*

Coleo, *s. m. V.* Coleadura

Cólera, *s. f. choler* || *anger*

Colera, *s. f. ornament in a horse's tail*

Colérico **ca** *a. cholerick*

Coleta, *sub. f. the hair of the head cut round* || *a little cue* || *a small skull-cap* || *a sort of canvass*

Coletero, *s. m. one that makes buff coats*

Coletilla, *sub. f. dim. de* Coleta

Coleto, *s. m. a buff coat*

Colgadero, *s. m. a thing to hang another by*

Colgadizo, *sub. m. pent-house*

Colgadizo, **za**, *a. that is, or may be hung*

Colgadura, *s. f. a suit of hangings* || *a suit of bed curtains*

Colgar, *v. a. y n. to hang*

Colgajo, *s. m. a hanging tatter*

Colgajo de uvas, *a bunch of grapes*

Cólica, *s. f. a colick*

Colicano, *a. m. rubican*

Cólico (**dolor**), *s. m. V.* Cólica

Colidir, *v. n. to collide*

Coliflor, *s. m. a cauliflower* [*alliance*

Coligacion, *s. f. union;*

Coligado, **da**, *a. allied*

Coligadura, *s. f. entangling* || *connexion*

Coligarse, *v. r. to confederate*

Colilla, *s. f. a little tail*

Colina, *s. f. a hill*

Coliquacion, *s. f. colliquation*

Coliquar, *v. act. to colliquate*

Colirio, *s. m. collyrium*

Coliseo, *s. m. colyseum* || *a play-house*

Colision, *s. f. collision*

Colitigante, *s. m. adverse party* [*wind*

Colla, *sub. f. a gale of*

Collacion, *s. f. V.* Colacion

Collado, *s. m. a hillock*

Collar, *sub. m. a collar* [...] *iron-collar*

Collarejo, **ico**, **ito**, *s.* [...] *a little collar*

Collarin, *s. m. the ca*[...] *of a coat*

Collarino, *s. m. coller*[...]

Colleja, *s. f. cornsalla*[...]

Collejas, *pl. sweet-brea*[...] || *hollyhock*

Collera, *s. f. the collar* [...] *a draught horse* || [...] *chain for the galley slaves*

Colleta, *s. f. a small* [...] *lewort*

Colmadamente, *adv. abu*[...]*dantly; completely*

Colmar, *v. a. to heap,* [...] *fill up*

Colmena, *s. f. a bee-h*[...]

Colmenar, *s. m. a pla*[...] *to keeps bee-hives*

Colmenero, *s. m. one th*[...] *keeps bee-hives*

Colmillazo, *s. m. a gre*[...] *tusk* || *a wound made* [...] *a tusk* [*a fa*[...]

Colmillejo, *s. m. a tus*[...]

Colmillos de jabalí, *s.* [...] *pl. razers*

Colmilludo, **da**, *a. fang*[...] *— prudent*

Colmo, *subs. m. the to*[...] *height; heaping*

Colocacion, *s. f. placin*[...] || *situation* || *office* [...] *employment*

Colocar, *v. a. to place,* [...] *settle* [*call*[...]

Colocasia, *s. f. a plant* [...]

Colocutor, *s. m. confer*[...]

Colodra, *s. f. a deep p*[...] *to milk cows in* || [...] *leathern jack*

Colodrillo, *s. m. the na*[...] *of the head*

Colodro, *sub. m. a sort* [...] *wooden shoes*

…fonia, *s. f. colophony*
…mbroño, *s. m. name-…ke*
…n, *s. m. a member of … period*
…stino colon, *the colon*
…nia, *s. f. a colony* || *a … oad silk ribbon*
…no, *s. m. a planter* || *… husbandman*
…quíntida, *s. f. colo-… intida*
…quio, *s m. colloquy*
…, *s. m. colour* || *wo-… n's paint* || *the suit, … cards*
…acion, *s. f. blushing … colouring*
…ado, da, *a. red*
…rse colorado, *to blush*
…ar, *v. a. to colour*
…ativo, va, *adj. that … y colour*
…ear, *v. a. to colour … palliate*
…ear, *v. n. to grow red*
…ido, *s. m. colouring … colour; pretence*
…in, *s. m. goldfinch*
…ir, *v. a. to set out in … ours*
…ista, *s. m. colourist*
…al, *a. 2 colossean*
…o, *s. m. colossus*
…tro, *s. m. V.* Calostro
…nbino, na, *a. colum-… ne*
…nbrar, *v. a. to disco-… at a distance* || *to … jecture*
…una, *s. f. V.* Coluna
…apiar, *v. a. to swing … a rope*
…apiarse, *v. r. to swing*
…npio, *s. m. a swing*
…na, *s. f. a column* || *a … k of ships*
…ario, *s. m.* } *colo-*
…ta, *s. f.* } *nade*

Colunica, illa, ita, *s. f. a little column*
Coluros, *s. m. pl. colures*
Colusion, *s. f. collusion*
Coma, *s. f. coma*
Comadre, *s. f. a midwife* || *a gossip*
Comadreja, *s. f. a weasel*
Comadrero, *s. m a man that is always among the women*
Comadron, *s. m. man-mid-wife*
Comandancia, *s. fem. the government of any province, etc.*
Comandante, *s. mas. commander* [*mand*
Comandar, *v. a to com-*
Comando, *s. m. command*
Comarca, *s. f. territory; precinct* || *the borders* or *confines*
Comarcano, na, *a. neighbouring*
Comarcar, *v. n. to border*
Comarcar, *v. act. to plant in quincunx*
Comaya, *s. f. scritch-owl*
Comba, *s. f. curvity; bending* [*vault*
Combar, *v. a. to bend; to*
Combate, *s. m. combat; fight* || *conflict*
Combatidor, } *s. m. a com-*
Combatiente, } *battant*
Combatir, *v. act. y n. to combat*
Combeneficiados, *s. m. pl. incumbents in a same church*
Combés, *s. m. the deck of a ship*
Combinable, *adj. 2. that may be combined*
Combinacion, *s. f. combination* [*bine*
Combinar, *v. act. to com-*
Combinatorio, ia, *a. be-longing to the combinations*
Combo, ba, *a. bended*
Combos, *s. m. pl. gawn-tree*
Comboy, etc. *V.* Convoy
Combustible, *a. 2. combustible,* [*tion*
Combustion, *s. f. combus-*
Combusto, ta, *a. burnt*
Comedero, *s. m. a dining-room* || *a manger*
Comedero, ra, *a. eatable*
Comedia, *s. f. a comedy*
Comediante, ta, *s. a comedian*
Comediar, *v. a. to divide into two halves*
Comédico, ca, *a. comical*
Comedidamente, *a. courteously* [*teous*
Comedido, da, *adj. cour-*
Comedimiento, *s. m. courteousness*
Comedio, *s. mas. center; middle*
Comedirse, *v. r. to refrain one's self*
Comedor, ra, *sub. a great eater* [*room*
Comedor, *s. m. a dining-*
Comendador, *s. m. commander of an order*
Comendatario, *s. m. commendatary*
Comendaticia (carta), *s. f. commendatory letters*
Comendero, *s. m. commendatary*
Comentador, *s. m. commentator* [*ment*
Comentar, *v. act. to com-*
Comentario, *s. mas. commentary*
Comento, *s. m. comment*
Comenzar, *v. act. y n. to begin*
Comer, *v. act. to eat* || *to spend* — to itch

Comerciable, *a.* 2. *negociable* || *sociable* [*der*
Comerciante, *s. m. a tra-*
Comerciar, *v. n. to trade* || *to commerce*
Comercio, *s. m. trade* || *commerce; intercourse*
Comeres, *s. m. pl. eatables*
Comestible, *a.* 2. *eatable*
Comestibles, *s. m. pl. victuals; eatables*
Cometa, *s. m. a comet* || *a paperkite* [*ter*
Cometedor, *s. m. commi-*
Cometer, *v. a. to commit*
Comezon, *s. f. itching*
Cómicamente, *adv. comically*
Comicios, *s. m. pl. the comitia*
Cómico, ca, *a. comical*
Cómico, ca, *s. a comedian*
Comida, *s. f food, meat* || *dinner*
Comidilla, *s. fem. a little dinner* [*ger*
Comiliton, *s. m. a spun-*
Comilitona, *s. f. a banquet*
Comilon, na, *sub. a great eater*
Comino, *s. m. cummin*
Comisaria, *s. f.* } *the office of a commissary*
Comisariato, *s. m.* }
Comisario, *s. m. a commissary* [*sion*
Comision, *s. f. commis-*
Comisionado, } *s. m. a deputy of a community, etc.*
Comisionario, }
Comisionar, *v. a. to depute*
Comisionista, *s. m. a commissioner*
Comiso, *s. mas. confiscation of prohibited goods*
Comistion, *s. f. V.* Comicion

Comistrajo, *s. m. a hotchpotch*
Comisuras, *s. fem. pl. the sutures of the cranium*
Cómite, *s. m. V.* Conde
Comitiva, *s. f. a retinue*
Cómitre, *s. m. a boatswain of a galley*
Comiza, *sub. m. a sort of barbel*
Como, *conj. as; like; how; why*
Cómoda, *s. f. a commode*
Comodable, *adj.* 2. *that may be lent*
Cómodamente, *adv. commodiously*
Comodato, *s. mas. a thing lent to be restitued in kind* [*dity*
Comodidad, *s. f. commo-*
Comodista, *s. mas. a man studious of his own conveniency*
Cómodo, *s. m. conveniency*
Como quiera, *adv. however it be* [*though*
Como quiera que, *adv. al-*
Compadecerse, *v. rec. to commiserate*
Compadrar, *v. n. to ally as gossips*
Compadrazgo, *s. m. gossipship* [*gossip*
Compadre, *s. mas. a man*
Compadrería, *s. fem. any thing treated between gossips*
Compage, } *s. f. connexion*
Compaginacion, }
Compaginador, *s. m. one that connects* [*nect*
Compaginar, *v. a. to con-*
Compaña, *s. f. family*
Compañero, ra, *sub. companion, fellow* || *colleague* || *partner*
Compañía, *s. f. company*

|| *fellowship i*
etc. || *the hu*
wife
Compañon, *s. m*
Compañon de per
der-grass
Compañoncico, i
dim. de Comp
Comparable, *a.*
parable
Comparacion, *s.*
Comparador, *s.*
parer
Comparanza, *s.*
Comparacion
Comparar, *v. a*
pare [*comp*
Comparativamen
Comparativo, *v*
parative
Comparecencia,
pearence
Comparecer, *v.*
Comparendo, *s.*
mons
Comparicion, *s.*
rance || *sumn*
Comparsa, *s. f.*
Compartimiento
compartition
Compartir, *v. a*
tribute
Compas, *s. m.*
|| *measure*,
|| *motion of fencing*
Echar el comp
time
Compasadament
with order a
Compasar, *v. a*
sure with th
ses || *to propo*
Compasible, *a.*
Compasillo, *s. n*
of two times
Compasion, *s.*
sion
Compasivo,

...mpaternidad, *s. f. compaternity*
...mpatia, *s. f. sympathy*
...mpatibilidad, *s. f. compatibility*
...mpatible, *adj. 2. compatible*
...mpatriota, *s. 2. compatriot*
...mpatron, na, *s. a patron with another*
...mpatronato, *subs. m. a common right of patronage* [Compatron
...mpatrono, *subs. m. V.*
...mpeler, *v. a. to compel*
...mpendiador, *s. m. abreviator* [*tomize*
...mpendiar, *v. a. to epi-*
...mpendiariamente, *adv. compendiously*
...mpendio, *s. m. compendium*
...mpendiosamente, *adv. compendiously*
...mpendioso, sa, *a. compendious*
...mpendizar, *v. act. V.* compendiar
...mpensable, *a. 2. compensable*
...mpensacion, *s. f. compensation*
...mpensar, *v. a. to compensate* [*tence*
...mpetencia, *s. compe-*
... competencia, *adver. with emulation*
...mpetente, *a. 2. competent*
...mpetentemente, *adver. competently*
...mpeter, *v. n. to belong*
...mpeticion, *s. f. competence* || *competition*
...mpetidor, ra, *s. competitor*
...mpetir, *v. n. to stand* ...*competition*

Compilacion, *s. f. compilation*
Compilar, *v. a. to compile* [*comrade*
Compinche, *s. m. friend;*
Complacencia, *s. f. complacency*
Complacer, *v. n. to please; to humour*
Complacerse, *v. r. to delight in*
Complemento, *s. m. complement* [*pletely*
Completamente, *adv. com-*
Completar, *v. a. to complete* [*plines*
Completas, *s. f. pl. com-*
Completo, ta, *a. complete*
Complexîon, *sub. f. complexion*
Complexîonado, da, *a. complexioned* [*plexional*
Complexîonal, *a. 2. com-*
Complexo, *s. m. a complex* [*plex*
Complexo, xa, *adj. com-*
Complicacion, *s. f. complication*
Complicar, *v. a. to complicate*
Cómplice, *s. 2. complice*
Complicidad, *s. fem. the being an accomplice*
Componedor, ra, *subs. a composer* || *an adjuster, etc.*
Componedor, *s. m. arbitrator; compounder* || *a composing-stick*
Componenda, *s. f. a composition with the court of Rome.*
Componer, *v. a. to compose* || *to compound* || *to adjuste* || *to reconcile*
Componer discordias, *to make up differences* — lo desconcertado, *to order*

Componerse con la parte, *to compound; to agree* — una muger, *to dress herself*
Componible, *adj. 2. that may be adjusted*
Comporta, *s. f. V.* Cuébano
Comportable, *a. 2. tolerable* [*to bear*
Comportar, *v. a to suffer;*
Comportilla, *s. f. dim. de* Comporta
Composible, *a. 2. V.* Componible
Composicion, *s. f. composition* || *order; ordering* || *agreement* || *modesty* || *the exercise of a school boy*
Compositor, *s. m. a composer (in musick)*
Compostura, *s. f. composition* || *repair; reparation* || *ornament; attire* || *modesty; decency*
Compota, *s. fem. stewed fruit*
Compotera, *s. f. a vessel to put stewed fruits in*
Compra, *s. f. purchase*
Comprable, *a. that can be bought* [Comprado
Compradillo, *subs. m. V.*
Compradizo, za, *adj. V.* Comprable
Comprado, *s. m. a game at cards*
Comprador, ra, *s. purchaser* [*veyor*
Comprador, *s. m. a pur-*
Comprar, *v. a. to buy; to purchase*
Comprar fiado, *to tick*
Comprehendedor, ra, *sub. one that comprehends*
Comprehender, *v. act. to comprehend* || to understand

the being comprehensible
Comprehensible, *adj.* 2. *comprehensible*
Comprehension, *s. f. comprehension*
Comprehensivo, va, *adj. comprehensive*
Comprehensor, *s. m. one that comprehends*
Comprehensor, ra, *s. happy; blessed*
Compresbítero, *s. m. colleague in the priesthood*
Compresion, *s. f. compression*
Compresivamente, *adver. narrowly* [*pressing*
Compresivo, va, *a. com-*
Compreso, sa, *adj. compressed*
Comprimir, *v. a. to compress — to repress*
Comprobacion, *s. f. comprobation*
Comprobar, *v. a. to prove, to confirm*
Comprometer, *v. act. to compromise* [*ferree*
Compromisario, *s. m. re-*
Compromision, *s. f. compromising*
Compromiso, *s. m. a compromise*
Comprovincial, *adj. m. of the same province*
Compuerta, *s. f. a sluice* || *a portcullis*
Compuertas, *pl. the eyelyds* [*derly*
Compuestamente, *adv. or-*
Compuesto, *s. m. a compound* [*pounded*
Compuesto, ta, *adj. com-*
O'rden compuesto, *composite order*
Compulsa, *s. f. the copy of an original writing*

pel [*sion*
Compulsion, *s. f. compul*
Compulsorio, *s. m. a warrant*
Compulsorio, ria, *a. compulso y* [*punction*
Compuncion, *sub. f. com-*
Compungirse, *v. r. to be penitent*
Compungivo, va, *a. compunctive* [*purgation*
Compurgacion, *s. f. com-*
Compurgador, *s. m. compurgator*
Compurgar, *v. a. to clear one's self from a crime*
Computacion, *s. f. computation*
Computar, *v. act. to compute* [*putist*
Computista, *s. mas. com-*
Cómputo, *s. m. a compute*
Comulacion, *s. f. V.* Acumulacion
Comulgar, *v. a. y n. to administer* or *receive the sacrament*
Comulgatorio, *s. m. the place where the sacrament is received*
Comun, *a.* 2. *common*
Comun, *s. m. commonalty*
Comunal, *s. m. V.* Comun
Comunero, ra, *a. popular* || *seditious*
Comunero, *s. m. coheir, etc.* || *a factious fellow*
Comunicabilidad, *s. f. the being communicable*
Communicable, *a.* 2. *communicable* || *sociable*
Comunicacion, *s. f. communication*
Comunicar, *v. a. to communicate* || *to produce* || *to confer* or *consult* || *to have* correspondence

in alliance
Comunicativo
communica
Comunicatorio
be comunic
Comunidad, s
nity || *cor*
corporation
ny; society
Comunidades
tions
Communion, s
Comunmente,
monly
Con, *prep. wi*
Conato, *s. m.*
|| *attempt*
Concadenar,
catenate
Concanónigo,
low preben
Concatenacion
s. f.
Concatenamie
s. m.
Concatenar,
catenate
Cóncava, *s. f.*
Concavidad, *s*
Cóncavo, *s. m*
Cóncavo, va,
Concebir, *v.*
ceive
Conceder, *v.*
Concejal, *s. m*
sellor
Concejal, *a.* 1
Concejeramen
blickly
Concejil, *a.* 2
to the publi
Concejo, *s. m*
cil of a tou
house
Concento, *s. n*
consort
Concentrado,
centered

, ca, a. con-

!

it

man || a pro-

. m.
cept

; judgment
v. a. to think;

mente, adv.

, sa, a. sen-
ingenious
a, s. f. rela-

v. n. to be-
concern
iente, adver.
by agreement
hombre), s.
r, staid man
, s. mas. me-
djuster
. act. to set in
concert || to
adjust || to re-
to contract ||
to compare
. n. to square;

, v. rec. to go
hand in a bu-

s. f. a grant
io, subs. m. a

:

tisfying one's self in a

shell

|| cautious; circums-
pect [shell
Conchuela, subs. f. a little

Concepto
Conciencia, s. f. the conscience

scientious
Concierto, s. m. order; dis-
position || agreement;
contract || concert; con-
sort [one accord
De concierto, adv. with
Conciliábulo, s. m. con-
venticle [liation
Conciliacion, s. f. conci-
Conciliador, ra, s. conci-
liator [liate
Conciliar, v. a. to conci-
Conciliar, s. m. a bishop
member of a council
Conciliar, a. 2. belonging
to a council
Concilio, s. m. a council
of bishops [nity
Concinidad, s. f. concin-
Concino, na, a. concin-
nous [cisely
Concisamente, adv. con-
Concision, s. f. concision
Conciso, sa, a. concise
Concitacion, s. f. instiga-
tion || trouble; sedition
Concitador, s. m. instigator
Concitar, v. a. to stir up;
to excite
Concitativo, va, a. that
excites, etc.

fel-
low-citizen

conclave

Conclavista, s. m. atten-
dant on a cardinal du-
ring a conclave
Concluir, v. a. to conclude
|| to convince
Conclusion, s. f. conclu-
sion || thesis
Concluso, sa, a. conclu-
ded || contained [last
En conclusion, adv. at
Concluyentemente, adv.
conclusively
Concolega, s. m. a fellow-
collegian
Concomerse, v. r. to shrug
as one that has the itch
Concomiento, mio s. m.
a rubbing of the body
Concomitancia, s. f. con-
comitancy
Concomitar, v. a. to ac-
company || to act with
another
Concordable, a. 2. agreea-
ble
Concordacion, s. f. agree-
ment; concord
Concordador, s. m. one
that agrees
Concordancia, s. f. con-
cordance
Concordar, v. a. to agree;
to accord; to tune
Concordar, v. n. to concord
Concordata, s. f. } concor-
Concordato, s. m. } date
Concorde, a. 2. agreeing;
of one mind
Concordemente, adv. una-
nimously
Concordia, s. f. concord
Concorpóreo, rea, a. con-
corporal
Concretar, v. a. to concrete
Concreto, ta, a. concrete
Concubina, s. f. a concu-
bine
Concubinario, s. m. one
who keeps a concubine.

Concubinato, s. m. concubinage
Concubio, s. m. the common hour of going to bed [encounter
Concubito, s. m. carnal

ple on
Concuñado, da, s. brother-

rente; concourse
Concurrente cantidad, odd money
Concurrir, v. n. to concur || to be in competition
Concursar, v. a. to deliver up the goods of a debtor
Concurso, s. m. concourse || concurrence || competition
Concusion, s. f. concussion; shaking
Condado, s. m. earldom; county
Condadura, s. f. the dignity of a count
Condal, a. 2. belonging to a count
Conde, s. m. a count, or earl || king of the gypsies
Condecente, a. 2. convenient || correspondent
Condecoracion, s. f. decoration [rate
Condecorar, v. a. to deco-
Condenable, a. 2. condemnable
Condenacion, s. f. condemnation || a fine, or penality || damnation
Condenado, s. m. a damned
Condenador, ra, s. one who condemns

Condenar, v. a. to condemn
Condenar una puerta, to nail, or wall up a door
Condenarse, v. r. to damn one's self
Condenatorio, ria, a. condemning
Condensacion, s. f. condensation [dense
Condensar, v. a. to con-
Condensativo, va, a. condensing
Condesa, s. f. a countess
Condesado, s. m. a county
Condescendencia, s. f. condescendence
Condescender, v. neut. to condescend
Condesico, ito, s. m. dim. de Conde
Condestable, s. m. constable [tableship
Condestablia, s. f. cons-
Condicion, s. f. condition || character; genius || quality || constitution
Condicionado, da, } a. conditional
Condicional, }
Condicionalmente, adv. conditionally
Condicionarse, v. r. to be of the same condition, or nature
Condicionaza, s. f. great genius. etc. || moroseness; hardness
Condicioncilla, ita, s. f. moroseness; peevishness [dignedly
Condignamente, adv. con-
Condignidad, s. f. condignity
Condigno, na, a. condign
Condimentar, v. a. to season [ning
Condimento, s. m. seaso-
Condiscipulo, s. m. schoolfellow

Condistinguir,
tinguish
Condolecerse, v
Condoler, v. n.
Condolerse, v.
Condonacion, .
Condonar, v. a
Condrila, s. f. c
the wild enc
Conduccion, s.
ting
Conducidor, s. 1
Conducir, v. a.
Conducta, s. f.
convoy of n
vernment || c
sion to raise
cruit
Conductivo, v
Conducto, s. .
Conductor, s. m
Condumio, s. m
to be eaten s
Condutal, s. m
for the rain-
Conejal, } s. :
Conejar, } b
Conejera, subs
warren || ab
Conejero, ra,
sells rabbits
Conejero (per
for the rabb
Conejillo, ito,
Conejo
Conejo, s m. c
cony
Conejuelo, s. r
rabbit
Conejuna, s.
hair
Conejuno, na
ging to a ra
Conexidades,
sories; depe
Conexion, s. f
Conexivo, va,
ting
Conexò, xa.

ulacion, *s. f. confabulation* [*bulate*
ular, *v. a. to confa-*
on, *s. m. a banner, standard*
onier, ionero, } *sub. m. a standard-bearer*
cion, *s. f. confection*
ccionador, *s. m. one t makes confections*
ccionar, *v. a. to make fections*
deracion, *s. f. confeacy* [*federate*
derado, *s. m. a con-*
derarse, *v. r. to con-erate* [*ference*
rencia, *s. f. a con-*
renciar, *v. a. to con-; to discourse*
rir, *v. a. to confer*
sado, da, *s. a penit*
sar, *v. a. to confess*
sion, *s. f. confession*
sionario, *s. m. a med for confessing well t confessionary*
so, sa, *s. a convert*
sonario, *s. m. a consionary* [*sor*
sor, *s. m. a confes-*
able, *adj. 2. trusty; thful*
adamente, *adv. confently*
ado, da, *a. sanguine*
ador, *s. m. bail; sur*
anza, *s. f. confidence a secret contract, etc.*
ar, *v. n. to trust; to fide*
ar, *v. a. to trust; to mmit* || *to flatter; to e hope*
iente, *a. acting in unction with*

Confidencia, *s. f. confidence*
Confidencial, *a. 2. that gives confidence*
Confidencialmente, *adv. confidently*
Confidente, *s. m. confident*
Confidente, *a. 2. trusty; faithful* [*confidence*
Confidentemente, *adv. in*
Configuracion, *s. f. configuration*
Configurado, da, *a. of the same figure*
Configurar, *v. a. to shape; to figure*
Confin, *s. m. confine; limit*
Confin, *a. bordering on*
Confinar, *v. n. to confine* || *to compare*
Confirmacion, *s. f. confirmation*
Confirmadamente, *adver. surely; certainly*
Confirmador, *s. m. confirmer* [*firm*
Confirmar, *v. a. to con-*
Confirmatorio, ria, *a. confirmatory* [*cation*
Confiscacion, *s. f. confis-*
Confiscar, *v. a. to confiscate* [*to preserve*
Confitar, *v. a. to candy;*
Confito, *s. m.* } *sweet*
Confites, *pl.* } *meats; sugar plums, etc.*
Confitera, *s. f. a box to keep sweet meats in*
Confitería, *s. f. a confectioner's shop*
Confitero, *s. m. a confectioner* [Confite
Confiton, *s. m. aum. de*
Confitura, *s. f. confiture*
Conflacion, *s. f. the melting of a metal*
Conflagracion, *s. f. conflagration*

Conflatil, *a. 2. fusible*
Conflicto, *s. m. conflict*
Confluencia, *s. f. conflux*
Confluir, *v. n. to flow together*
Conformacion, *s. f. conformation*
Conformar, *v. a y n. to conform*
Conformarse, *v r. to conform on'es self* || *to resign*
Conforme, *a. 2. conformable* || *resigned; submissive* [*mably*
Conforme, *adv. confor-*
Conformemente, *adv. unanimously*
Conformidad, *s. f. conformity* || *concord* || *symmetry* || *resignation*
Confortacion, *s. f. corroboration* || *comfort*
Confortador, ra, *s. one that corroborates, etc.*
Confortar, *v. a. to corroborate* || *to confort*
Confortativo, va, *a. corroborative*
Confraccion, *s. f. fracture*
Confraternidad, *s. f. confraternity*
Confricacion, *sub. f. friction; rubbing*
Confricar, *v. a. to rub*
Confrontacion, *s. f. confronting* || *comparing* || *sympathy* [*front*
Confrontar, *v. a. to con-*
Confrontar, *v. n. to sympathize* || *to border upon*
Confugio, *s. m. V.* Refugio
Confundir, *v. a. to confound* [*fusedly*
Confusamente, *adv. con-*
Confusion, *s. f. confusion*
Confuso, sa, *a.* confused
En confuso, *adv.* confusedly

Confutacion, *s. f. confutation*
Confutar, *v. a. to confute*
Congelacion, *s. f.* } *congealation*
Congelamiento, *s. m.* }
Congelar, *v. a. to congeal*
Congelarse, *v. r. to coagulate*
Congelativo, va, *a. congealing*
Congeniar, *v. a. to be of the same genius, etc.*
Congerie, *s. m. heap*
Congestion, *s. f. congestion*
Congiario, *s. m. congiary*
Congio, *s. m. congius*
Conglobacion, *s. f. conglobation* [*globe*
Conglobar, *v. a. to con-*
Congloriar, *v. a. to give glory to*
Conglutinacion, *s. f. conglutination*
Conglutinar, *v. a. conglutinate*
Conglutinativo, va, } *a glutinous*
Conglutinoso, sa, }
Congoja, *s. f. anguish; grief* [*grieve*
Congojar, *v. a. to vex; to*
Congojosamente, *adv. grievingly*
Congojoso, sa, *a. grievous* || *grieved* [*terer*
Congraciador, *s. m. a flat-*
Congraciamiento, *sub. m. flattery coaxing*
Congraciarse, *v. r. to insinuate one's self into another's favour*
Congratulacion, *s. f. congratulation*
Congratular, *v. a. to congratulate*
Congratulatorio, ria, *adj. congratulatory*

Congregacion, *s. f. congregation*
Congregante, *s. member of a congregation*
Congregar, *v. a. to congregate*
Congreso, *s. m. a congress*
Congrio, *s. m. a conger*
Congrúa, *s. f. the ecclesiastical revenue belonging to any priest*
Congruamente, *adv. Voy.* Congruentemente
Congruencia, *s. f. congruence* [*gruent*
Congruente, *adj.* 2. *con-*
Congruentemente, *adver. congruously*
Congruo, grua, *adj. congruous*
Cónico, ca, *a. conick*
Coniza, *s. f. flea-bane*
Conjetura, *s. f. conjecture*
Conjeturable, *a.* 2. *that may be conjectured*
Conjeturador, ra, *s. conjector* [*tural*
Conjetural, *a.* 2. *conjec-*
Conjeturalmente, *adver. conjecturally*
Conjeturar, *v. a. to conjecture*
Conjuez, *s. m. a fellow-judge* [*gation*
Conjugacion, *s. f. conju-*
Conjugal, *a.* 2. *conjugal*
Conjugalmente, *adv. conjugally* [*gate*
Conjugar, *v. a. to conju-*
Conjuncion, *s. f. conjunction*
Conjuntamente, *adv. conjunctively*
Conjuntivo, va, *adj. conjunctive* [tantivo
Conjuntivo, *s. m. V.* Subs
Conjunto, ta, *a. conjoined*
Conjuracion, *s. f.* conju*ration*

Conjurado, da, *s* … *pirator; a pl*…
Conjurador, *s. m.* …
Conjuramentar, … *bind by an oa*…
Conjurar, *v. a. t*…
Conjuro, *s. m. ex*… *conjuring*
Conllevador, *s. m* … *assistant*
Conllorar, *v. n. t*… *with another*
Conmemoracion, … *memoration*
Conmemorar, *v.* … *memorate*
Conmensal, *s. n*…
Conmensalía, *s.* … *mensality*
Conmensuracion … *commensurati*…
Conmensurar, *v* … *commensurate*
Conmensurativo, … *commensurati*…
Conmigo, *adv. u*…
Conmiliton, *s. m.* … *soldier*
Conminacion, *s. f*…
Conminar, *v. a.* … *ten*
Conminatorio, ria … *minatory*
Conmiseracion, *s* … *miseration*
Conmistion, Com… *s. f. commixtio*…
Conmisto, Conmi… *a. commixed*
Conmocion, *s. f.*…
Conmonitorio, *s.* … *monition*
Conmover, *v. a. to* … *to move*
Conmutacion, *s.* … *mutation*
Conmutable, *adj.* … mutable
Conmutar, *v. a*…

a, a. com-
2. conna-
e, v. r. to
ne's self
te, adver.
:. V. Co-
f. conni-
.f. } a re-
n. } mote
Relacion
to relate
a, a. rela-
[novice
s. a fellow-
connubial
m. matri-
[among
a. to count
. with us
:one
m. a con-
ne that exa-
se
o know || to
nce of
. knowable
, adver.
wingly
s. an ac-
s. m. know-
nizance ||
e
conoid
condition
a conquest
s. m. con-
. a. to con-
adj. who
another
n. to reign
r

Consabido, da, *a. known*
Consabidor, *s. m. one who is conscious of any thing*
Consagracion, *s. f. consecration* [*crator*
Consagrador, *s. m. consecrator*
Consagrar, *v. a. to consecrate*
Consanguineo, nea, *adj. consanguineous*
Consanguinidad, *s. f. consanguinity*
Consecracion, etc. *V.* Consagracion [*tary*
Consectario, *s. m. consectary*
Consecucion, *s. f. the obtaining one's desires*
Consecutivamente, *adv. consecutively*
Consecutivo, va, *a. consecutive*
Conseguimiento, *s. m. V.* Consecucion
Conseguir, *v. a. to obtain*
Conseja, *s. f. a fable; an apologue* [*lor*
Consejero, *s. m. counsellor*
Consejo, *s. m. counsel* || *council*
Consentido (muchacho), *s. m. a spoiled child*
Marido consentido, *a consentient cucklod*
Consentidor, *s. m. consentient* [*sent*
Consentimiento, *s. m. consent*
Consentir, *v. a. to consent* || *to hope*, or *think firmly* || *to agree*
Conseqüencia, *s. f. consequence*
Conseqüente, *a. 2. s. m. consequent*
Conseqüentemente, *adv. consequently*
Conserge, *s. m. a keeper of a palace, etc.*
Consergería, *s. f. a keeper's office*

Conserva, *s. f. conserve* || *convoy of ships*
Navegar, ó caminar en conserva, *to go in company* (*as ship at sea*)
Conservacion, *s. f. conservation* [*vator*
Conservador, *s. m. conservator*
Conservaduría, *sub. f. the office of a judge-conservator*
Conservar, *v. a. to conserve*
Conservativo, va, *a. conservatorio*
Conservatoría, *s. f. court of conservancy*
Conservatorio, ria, *adj. conservatory*
Conservero, ra, *s. a confectioner*
Conseso, *s. m. V.* Junta
Considerable, *a. 2. considerable*
Considerablemente, *adv. considerably*
Consideracion, *s. f. consideration*
Consideracioncilla, *s. f. dim. de* Consideracion
Consideradamente, *adver. considerately*
Considerado, da, *a. considerate* [*siderer*
Considerador, ra, *s. considerer*
Considerar, *v. a. to consider*
Consiervo, *s. m. a fellow-slave*, or *servant*
Consignacion, *s. f. consignment*
Consignador, *s. m. one that consigns*
Consignar, *v. a. to consign* || *to destine*
Consignatario, *subst. m. a trustee*
Consigo, *ad. with himself*
Consiguiente, *a. 2. s. m. consequent*

… consiguiente , adv. by consequence
Consiguientemente , adv. consequently
Consiliario , s. m. a counsellor [tence
Consistencia , s. f. consis-
Consistente , a. 2. consistent
Consistir , v. n. to consist
Consistorial , a. 2. consistorial
Consistorialmente, adv. in consistory
Consistorio , sub. m. consistory || a municipal council || the town-house
Consocio , s. m. consociate
Consolable , a. 2. comfortable [fortably
Consolablemente, ad. com-
Consolacion , s. f. consolation ; comfort
Consolador , ra , s. comforter [latory
Consolador , ra , a. conso-
Consolar , v. a. to console [solatory
Consolatorio , ria , a. con-
Consólida , s. f. comfrey
Consolidacion , s. f. consolidation [lidate
Consolidar , v. a. to conso-
Consolidativo , va , a. consolidating
Consonancia , s. f. consonance
Consonante , a. 2. consonant
Consonante , s. m. a word ending like another
Consonantemente , adv. consonantly
Consonar , v. n. to agree in sound , etc.
Cónsone , a. 2. consonant
Cónsono , na , a. consonous

Consorcio , s. m. society ; partnership
Consorte , s. m. consort || complice
Conspicuo , cua , a. conspicuous [racy
Conspiracion , s. f. conspi-
Conspirado) s. m. a cons-
Conspirador , } pirator
Conspirar , v. n. to conspire
Conspirar , ver. a. to invoke ; to call upon
Constancia , s. f. constancy
Constante , a. 2. constant
Constantemente , adver. constantly
Constar , v. n. to be certain , plain , etc. || to consist [tellation
Constelacion , s. f. cons-
Consternacion , s. f. consternation
Consternar , v. a. to dismay , affright , etc.
Constipacion , sub. f. obstruction of the pores || constipation
Constipar , v. a. to obstruct the pores || to constipate
Constitucion , s. f. constitution
Constituir , ver. act. to constitute || to settle a rent , etc.
Constitutivo , va , a. constitutive
Constituyente , s. m. one that settles a rent
Constreñidamente , adv. constrainedly
Constreñimiento , sub. m. constraint
Constreñir , v. a. to constrain || to constrict
Constriccion , s. f. constriction [tringent
Constrictivo , va , a. as-
Construccion , s. f. cons

… ding
Constructor , s.
Construir , v. … truct || to c… build ships
Construpador , … lator ; ravis…
Construpar , v. … prate [
Consubstancial
Consubstancial … consubstant…
Consuegrar , v … come joint … mothers in l… suegro
Consuegro , gr… ther and … marry thei… together
Consuelda , su…
Consuelda ma… frey
Consuelo , s. … gladness || …
Consueta , s. … perer ; a p…
Consuetudinar… used ; accus…
Cónsul , s. m. …
Consulado , s. … ship
Consular , a. 2
Consultat ,
Consultacion ,
Consultante , a … ter
Consultar , v.
Consultísimo , … very prud… wise
Consultor , s. … gives advic…
Consultor del … counsellor o… sition
Consumacion , … summation

lamente , *adv.*
y
lo , da , *a. con-*
te [*broth*
lo , *s. m. jelly-*
lor , ra , *s. finis-*
[*summate*
, *v. a. to con-*
ion, *s. f. expence*
o , da , *a. lean ;*
ted || *sorrowful*
or , ra , *s. con-*
[*suming*
niento, *s. m. con-*
, *v. act. to con-*
[*sume away*
rse, *v. r. to con-*
s. m. consump-
vasting
n, *s. f. consump-*
[*med*
, ta , *a. consu-*
, *s. m. contact*
, ra , *a. that is*
counted
, *s. m. a nar-*
ssage
da , *a. rare ; un*
n [*hand*
ido , *adv. out of*
, ra , *s. calcula-*

, *s. m. a coun-*
ard || *a counter*
with || *teller of*
hequer
ito , *s. m. dim.*
tador
a , *s. f. chamber*
unts
, *v. a. to infect*
, *s. m. contagion*
, *s. f. the pro-*
he gangrene, etc.
o , sa , *adj. con-*

cuentas , *a set*
ters to cast ac-
with

Contaminacion , *s. f. contamination*
Contaminar , *v. a. to contaminate* || *to infect*
Contante , *s. m. ready money*
Contatejo , *s. m. a small sum in ready money*
Contar , *v. act. to count ; to reckon* || *to relate ; to report*
Contemperar , *v. a. to contemper*
Contemplacion , *s. f. contemplation* || *condescendence* [*templator*
Contemplador , *s. m. con-*
Contemplar , *v. a. to contemplate* || *to please ; to flatter* || *to condescend*
Contemplativamente, *adv. contemplatively*
Contemplativo , va , *a. contemplative*
Contemplativo, *s. m. a contemplative* || *a flatterer*
Contemporaneo , nea , *a. y s. contemporary*
Contemporizar , *v. n. to conform one's self to the times*
Contencion, *s. f. contention*
Contencioso , sa , *adj. contentious* [*tending*
Contendedor , *s. m. con-*
Contender , *v. n. to contend* [*ding*
Contendor , *s. m. conten-*
Contendoso , sa , *a. V.* Contencioso
Contenedor , ra , *sub. one that contains*
Contenencia , *s. f. the hovering of a bird* || *the balance , in dancing*
Contener , *v. a. to contain*
Contenerse , *v. r. to moderate one's self*
Contenido , *s. m. contents*

Contenido , da , *a. staid ; sober* [*ment*
Contenta , *s. f. endorse-*
Contentadizo (bien) , *a. m. easy to be contented*
Contentamiento, *s. m. contentment*
Contentar , *v. a. to content* || *to endorse a bill of exchange*
Contentible , *adj. a. contemptible* [*ning*
Contentivo , va , *a. contai-*
Contento , ta , *a. content*
Contento , *s. m. contentment* || *receipt ; acquittance*
A' contento , *adv. to the satisfaction of*
Contera , *s. f. the chape of a scabbard* || *cascabel*
Contérmino , na , *a. bordering on* [*try-man*
Conterraneo , nea , *s. coun-*
Contestacion , *s. f. deposition ; evidence* || *defence ; plea* || *contestation*
Contestar , *v. a. to depose* || *to prove* or *confirm* || *to answer*
Contestar la demanda , *to plead*
Conteste , *adj. a witness declaring just the same as another*
Contexto , *s. m. context ; contexture*
Contextura , *s. f. contexture* [*bate*
Contienda , *s. f. strife ; de-*
Contignacion , *s. f. contignation*
Contigo , *adv. with thee*
Contiguamente , *adv. contiguously*
Contigüidad, *s. f. contiguity*
Contiguo , gua , *a. contiguous*

Continencia, *s. f. continence* || *soberness* || *capacity; capaciousness*

Continente, *s. m. container* || *countenance* || *continent* [*nent*

Continente, *adj.* 2. *conti-*

En continente, *adv. immediately*

Continentemente, *ad. continently* [*gency*

Contingencia, *s. f. contin-*

Contingente, *a.* 2. *contingent*

Contingente, *s. m. quota*

Contingentemente, *adv. contingently*

Contino, *adv. continually*

Continuacion, *s. f. continuation* || *continuity*

Continuadamente, *ad. continually*

Continuador, *s. m. continuator*

Continuamente, *adv. continually*

Continuar, *v. a. to continue* [*nuity*

Continuidad, *s. f. conti-*

Continuo, nua, *a. continuous* || *continual*

Continuo, *sub. m. a close body*

Contonearse, *v. r. to walk affectedly*

Contoneo, *s. m. a proud conceited gait, etc.*

Contorcerse, *v. r. to be distorted* [*sion*

Contorcion, *s. f. contor-*

Contornar, *v. a. to turn round; to go about*

Contornear, *v. a. V.* Contornar

Contorno, *s. m. compass; circumference* || *winding* || *contour*

Contorsion, s. f. contorsion

Contra, prep. against

En contra, *adv. in a contrary sense*

Contras, *s. m. pl. the drones of an organ*

Contraamura, *s. f. a particular rope in a ship*

Contraaproches, *s. m. pl. counter-approaches*

Contraarmiños, *s. m. pl. the black colour spotted with white in blazon*

Contraataques, *sub. m. pl. counter-attacks*

Contrabalanza, *s. f. Voy.* Contrapeso

Contrabandista, *subs. m. smuggler*

Contrabando, *s. m. contraband* || *smuggled goods*

Contrabateria, *s. f. counter-battery*

Contrabatir, *v. a. to shoot off a cannon againts a battery* [*bass*

Contrabaxo, *s. m. counter-*

Contracambio, *s. m. re-exchange* || *counter-change* [*tion*

Contraccion, *s. f. contrac-*

Contracebadera, *s. f. the sprit-top sail*

Contracédula, *s. f. a defeasance*

Contracifra, *s. f. the key of a cypher*

Contracosta, *s. f. a coast opposite to another*

Contraculto, *s. m. one who speaks without affectation*

Contradanza, *s. f. countrydance* [*tradict*

Contradecir, *v. a. to con-*

Contradiccion, *s. f. contradiction*

Contradictor, *s. m. contradictor*

Contradictoriamente, *adv. contradictorily*

Contradictorio, [illegible] *contradictory*

Contradique, *s. m* [illegible] *terdike*

Contraemboscada [illegible] *ambuscade op*[illegible] *another*

Contraer, *v. a. to* [illegible]

Contraer deudas [illegible] *in debt* — enf[illegible] *to get a distem*[illegible] trimonio, *to m*[illegible]

Contraescarpa, *s* [illegible] *terscarp*

Contraescritura, [illegible] *instrument o*[illegible] *to reject a for*[illegible] *ting*

Contraestay, *s.* [illegible] *venter stay*

Contrafoso, *s. m.* [illegible]

Contrafuerte, *s.* [illegible] *ter-fort* || *a gir*[illegible]

Contrafuga, *s. f.* [illegible] *fuge* [[illegible]

Contraguardia, *s* [illegible]

Contrahacer, *v.* [illegible] *terfeit* || *to ap*[illegible]

Contrahacerse, [illegible] *guise one's se*[illegible]

Contrahaz, *s. f.* [illegible] *side*

Contrahecho, c[illegible]

Contraindicar, *v.* [illegible] or *teach the* [illegible]

Contralor, *s. m.* [illegible]

Contralto, *s. m* [illegible] *tenor* [*te* ||

Contramaestre, *s* [illegible]

Contramalla, *s.* [illegible] *stitch in a ne*[illegible]

Contramallar, *v* [illegible] *ke double sti*[illegible]

Contramandar, [illegible] *counter-man*[illegible]

Contramangas, [illegible] *sort of cuffs*

Contramarca, *s* [illegible] *ter-mark*

C[illegible]

rear, v. act. to
–mark
rcha, s. f. coun-
rch
rchar, v. n. to
–march
rco, s. m. a fra-
a window
rea, s. f. ebb;
[mine
na, s. f. counter-
nar, v. a. to coun-
te
ralla, } counter-
ro, } mure
ural, a. 2. con-
o the nature
len, s. f. counter-

sar, v. n. to go
he adverse party
so, s. m. a cross
dancing || firts
cond part in mu-

lo (á), ad. againts
ir, or grain
sar, v. a. to coun-
se [poise
so, s. m. counter-
ste, s. m. a reme-
ainst the plague
mer, v. a. to op-

sicion, s. f. opo-

ueba, s. f. coun-
oof [ton
erta, s. f. V. Por-
ntante, s. m. one
ings in counter-

ntear, v. act. to
er-point || to com-
| to contradict
nto, s. m. coun-
int

Contrapunzon, s. m. matrix of mint-men, etc.
Contraquilla, s. f. keelson
Contrareparo, s. m. a counter-prop
Contraréplica, s. f. an answer to a reply
Contrarestar, v. a. to stand against || to push back the ball
Contraresto, subs. m. the player who is so placed as to stop and push back the ball || opposition
Contrariamente, adv. contrarily [riety
Contrariedad, s. f. contra-
Contrario, s. m. adversary
Contrario, ria, a. contrary
Al, ó por el contrario, ad. on the contrary
Contraroda, s. f. apron
Contraronda, s. f. counter-round
Contraseña, s. f. the watch-word || a sign agreed on
Contrastar, v. a. to oppose; to resist || to oppugn || to verify
Contraste, s. m. an officer who weighs gold, silver, pearls, etc. || contention, opposition || trouble; obstacle
Contrata, s. f. contract
Contratacion, s. f. trade; commerce
Contratar, v. a. to trade
Contratela, s. f. a second enclosure made of spread canvass
Contratiempo, s. m. mischance; disappointment
Contrato, s. m. contract
Contrarota, s. f. counter-plot
Contravalacion, s. f. contravallation

Contravalar, v. a. to intrench with lines of contravallation
Contravencion, s. f. contravention || precaution [ter-poison
Contraveneno, s. m. coun-
Contravenir, v. n. to contravene || to oppose; to withstand
Contraventana, s. f. an outside shutter
Contraventor, ra, s. contravener; transgressor
Contravidriera, s. f. a double casement
Contray, s. m. a fine cloth of Flanders
Contrayerba, s. f. a sort of antidote
Contribucion, s. f. contribution
Contribuidor, s. m. contributor [tribute
Contribuir, v. a to con-
Contributario, s. m. contributary
Contricion, s. f. contrition
Contrincante, s. m. competitor
Contristar, v. a. to grieve
Contrito, ta, a. contrite
Controversia, s. f. controversy
Controversista, s. m. controversist
Controvertible, a. 2. controvertible
Controvertido, da, a. controverted [trovert
Controvertir, v. a. to con-
Contubernio, s. m. fellowship in one house || concubinage [macy
Contumacia, s. f. contu-
Contumaz, a. 2. contumacious
Contumazmente, adv. contumaciously

Contumelia, *s.f. contumely*
Contumeliosamente, *adv. contumeliously*
Contumelioso, **sa**, *a. contumelious* [*sing*
Contundente, *a.* 2. *contu-*
Contundir, *v. a. to contuse*
Conturbacion, *s.f. trouble; disquiet* [*ber*
Conturbador, *s. m. distur-*
Conturbar, *v. a. to trouble; to disturb*
Contusion, *s.f. contusion; bruise*
Contuso, **sa**, *a. bruised*
Contutor, *s. m. a fellow-guardian*
Convalecencia, *s. f. convalescence*
Convalecer, *v. n. to recover health*
Convaleciente, *s. m. convalescent*
Convalecimiento, *sub. m. convalescence*
Convalescer, *v. n. to grow up; to gather strength*
Convalidacion, *s.f. confirmation*
Convecino, **na**, *a. neighbouring; near*
Convelerse, *v. r. to be irritated, contracted, etc.*
Convencedor, **ra**, *a. convictive* [*vince*
Convencer, *v. a. to con-*
Convencible, *a.* 2. *convincible* [*conviction*
Convencimiento, *sub. m.*
Convencion, *s.f. convention; convenant* || *convenience*
Convencional, *a.* 2. *convencional*
Convencionalmente, *adv. by convention*
Convenible, *a.* 2. *easy to deal with*

Conveniencia, *s.f. convenience* || *expediency* || *employment; service* || *agreement*
Conveniencias, *pl. goods; ability* [*nient*
Conveniente, *a.* 2. *conve-*
Convenientemente, *adv. conveniently*
Convenio, *subs. m. agreement; convention*
Convenir, *v. n. to agree* || *to convene* || *to be fit, expedient*
Convenirse, *v. r. to agree*
Conventazo, *s. m. a great convent*
Conventicula, *s.f.* } *conventicle*
Conventiculo, *s. m.* }
Conventico, **illo**, **ito**, *s. m. a little convent*
Conventillo, *s. m. a little bawdy house*
Convento, *s. m. a convent*
Conventual, *a.* 2. *conventual* [*tual*
Conventual, *s. m. conven-*
Conventualidad, *s. f. the living in a convent*
Conventualmente, *adver. conventually*
Convergente, *a.* 2. *converging* [*sable*
Conversable, *a.* 2. *conver-*
Conversacion, *s.f. conversation* || *society* || *concubinage*
Conversar, *v. n. to converse* || *to live*, or *deal with* [*sion*
Conversion, *s. f. conver-*
Conversivo, **va**, *a. that may convert*
Converso, **sa**, *a. converted* || *laybrother*, or *sister*
Convertible, *a.* 2. *convertible* [*ter*
Convertidor, *s. m. conver-*

Convertir, *v. a. t*
Convexidad, *s.f. c*
Convexô, **xâ**, *a.*
Conviccion, *s.f. co*
Convictor, *s. m.*
Convictorio, *s. m ding school*
Convictorista, *s.* Convictor
Convidado, *s. m.*
Convidador, *s. m*
Convidar, *v. a. t*
Convincente, *a.* 2 *tive*
Convincentemen *convincingly*
Convite, *s. m. i* || *a feast*, or
Convocacion, *s. cation*
Convocadero, **ra** *is to be convol*
Convocador, *s. m convokes*
Convocar, *v. a. to* || *to proclaim*
Convocatoria, *s. of convocation*
Convoy, *s. m. a a retinue*
Convoyar, *v. a.*
Convulsar, *v. n.*
Convulsarse, *v. r*
Convulsion, *s. f. sion*
Convulsivo, **va**, *a*
Convulso, **sa**, *bled with con*
Conyuges, *s. m. ses*
Cooperacion, *s. f*
Cooperador, **ra**, *rator*
Cooperar, *v. n. t*
Cooperario, *s. m rator*
Cooperativo, **va**,
Coopositor, *s. m titor*

s. f. } co-or-
to, } dina-
} tion
nte, adver.
[dinate
a. to co-or-
cup || the
l of a tree ||
of a hat || a
ls || the mid-
ickler || the
oven
e hearts at
ls in a bridle
the copped
[like a cup
adj. round,
opal [tree
f. a kind of
great broad
m. aum. de
coppel
to refine sil-
.
cup-board
m. dim. de
[rer
a cup-bea-
a little cup
a toupee || a
bet || the top
tain
, a. copped
of birth, etc.
n. a tree so
copy || co-
m. copist
to copy
im. de Copa
lim. de Copo
f. compila-
[ler
m. compi-
to compile

Copilla, s. f. V. Copica
Copillo, s. m. V. Copico
Copiosamente, adv. copiously
Copioso, sa, a. copious
Copista, s. m. copist
Copita, Copito, V. Copica, etc,
Copla, s. f. a staff; a stanza || a smart saying
Coplear, v. n. to make or sing staffs
Coplero, sub. m. a paltry rhymer
Coplero, s. m. one who sells songs, etc.
Coplica, illa, s. f. dim. de Copla [plero
Coplista, s. m. Voy. Co-
Coplon, s. m. a low witless staff
Copo, s. m. distaff-full || a flake of snow
Copon, s. m. a great cup || a holy pyx
Copon de cuero, a leather jack
Coposo, sa, adj. Voy. Copado
Copra, s. f. the marrow of a cocoa nut
Cópula, s. f. copulation || key-stone
Copular, v. a. to join
Copularse, v. r. to copulate
Copulativamente, ad. jointly [lative
Copulativo, va, a. copu-
Coquillo, sub. m. a little worm || a little cocoa-nut
Coquina, s. f. V. Almeja
Coquito, subs. m. a little worm || a ridiculous gesture, etc.
Coracero, s. m. cuirassier
Coracha, s. f. a leather sack
Coracilla, s. f. a little cuirass

Coracina, s. f. a kind of ancient cuirass
Corada, s. f. pluck
Corage, s. m. courage || wrath; passion
Corajudo, da, a. angry; passionate
Coral, s. m. coral || apron
Coral, a. 2. choral
Coralina, s. f. coraline
Corambre, s. m. leather
Corambrero, s. m. one who deals with leather
Coramvobis, s. m. mien; carriage
Corascora, s. f. a sort of boat, or ship
Coraza, s. f. a cuirass
Corazonada, s. f. the heart of a pine tree || a ragoo made with hearts
Corazon, s. m. heart
Carazonada, s. f. the beating of the heart || pluck
Carazonazo, s. m. aum. de Corazon
Corazoncico, illo, ito, s. m. dim. de Corazon
Corazoncillo, sub. m. St.-John's wort
Corbachada, s. f. a blow with a bull's pizzle
Corbacho, s. m. a bull's pizzle
Corbas, subs. f. pl. small feathers in the hawk's wings
Corbata, s. f. a cravat
Corbata, s. m. a layman that is not a gown-man
Corbatin, s. m. neck cloth
Corbato, s. m. a pipe used in the distillations
Corbaton, s. m. small knee
Corcel, s. m. a courser
Corcha, s. f. a vessel made with cork
Corcho, s. m. a kind of sandal

Corchea, *s. f. a quaver*

Corchera, *s. f. a vessel of cork to keep ice in*

Corchete, *s. m. a hook; a claps || catch-pole || a crotchet, in printing*

Corcho, *s. m. cork*

Corchos, *pl. V.* Chapin

Corcillo, ino, *s. m. a little roe-buck*

Corcova, *s. f. a bunch in the body || crookedness*

Corcovado, da, *a. bunch-backed* [*to skip*

Corcovear, *v. n. to bound;*

Corcovete, *s. m. a bunch-backed man*

Corcovilla, ita, *s. f. dim. de* Corcova

Corcovo, *s. m. a bound* or *skip || unevenness; curvity* [*to patch*

Corcusir, *v. a. to mend;*

Corda (estar el navió á la), *to lye to* [*ropes*

Cordage, *s. m. cordage;*

Cordal, *sub. f. the hinder most tooth*

Cordel, *s. m. a line*

Cordelado, da, *a. twisted*

Cordelazo, *s. m. a lash with a line*

Cordelejo; *s. m. a small line* or *cord || a nipping jest*

Cordeleria, *s. f. a rope-yard || V.* Cordage

Cordelero, *s. m. a rope-maker*

Cordelico, illo, ito, *s. m. a little line*

Cordellate, *s. m. a sort of coarse cloth*

Corderia, *s. f. assemblage of cords*

Corderico, illo, ito, *s. m. a young lamb*

Corderillo, *s. m. a lamb-skin with the wool*

Corderina, *s. f. a lamb-skin*

Corderino, na, *a. belonging to lambs*

Cordero, ra, *s. a lamb — a lamb-skin*

Corderuelo, la, *a. V.* Corderico [*skin*

Corderuna, *s. f. a lamb-*

Corderuno, na, *a. V.* Corderino

Cordezuela, *sub. f. a little rope* or *cord*

Cordiaco, ca, *a. V.* Cardiaco

Cordial, *a. 2. cordial*

Cordial, *s. m. a cordial*

Cordialmente, *adv. cordially* [*tunny*

Cordila, *s. f. a new-born*

Cordilla, *s. f. a twist of the intestines of sheep*

Cordillera, *s. f. a long range of mountains*

Cordilo, *s. m. a kind of lizard* [*leather*

Cordoban, *s. m. cordovan*

Cordobana (andar á la), *to go naked*

Cordojo, *s. m. sorrow; grief*

Cordon, *s. m. a twist || a lace || a string || a girdle worn by friars || stone-plinth || ring-edge of coin*

Cordonazo, *s. m. a stroke* or *lash with a rope*

Cordoncico, illo, ito, *sub. m. dim. de* Cordon

Cordoncillo, *s. m. a sort of embroidery-milled-edge of a coin*

Cordoneria, *s. f. the place where lace is made* or *sold*

Cordonero, *s. m. one that makes silk cords* or *laces || a rope-maker*

Cordovan, *s.* ... *van leather*

Cordula, *s. f.*

Cordura, *s. f.* ... *wisdom*

Corea, *s. f. a* ...

Coreada (músi... *church musi*...

Corear, *v. a.* ... *the musick* ...

Corecico, *s. m.* ... *leather*

Coreo, *s. m.* ... *consort; ha*... *choral musi*...

Corezuelo, *s.* ... *leather || a* ... *king-pig*

Cori, *s. m. gr*...

Coriandro, *s.* ... *der*

Corifeo, *s. m.* ...

Corillo, *s. m. d*...

Corintio, tia, ...

Corintico, ca, ...

Corion, *s. m.* ...

Corista, *s. m.* ...

Coriza, *s. f. a* ... *ther shoe us*... *rias*

Corladura, *s.* ... *gold-varnis*...

Corma, *subst.* ... *shackles*

Cormano, *s. m* ... *of a differen*... *mother*

Cornada, *subs.* ... *with a beas*...

Cornadillo, *s.* ... Cornado

Cornado, *sub.* ... *used ancien*...

Cornadura, *s.* ... namenta

Cornal, *s. m.* ... *yoke the oxe*...

Cornamenta, ... horns of an ...

ı, *s. f. a horn-*
[*of olive*
, *s. m. a kind*
. *f. cornea of*

, ra, *s. a beast*
ts with the horn
v. neut. to butt
horn
. illo, ito, *s. m.*
horn
. *f. a rook*
s. m. corner;

o, *sub. m. cod;*
shell
, *s. f. a young-*
[*tree*
ub. m. cornil-
, *s. f. cornelian-*

s. m. a cantle
l
. a. *a cornet* ||
ndard or *cornet*
op of horse || *a*
endent
monte, *a hun-*
n — de posta,
oy's horn
s. m. V. Corne-

, illa, ita, *s. f. a*
rnet [*horn*
o, *s. m. a little*
. *m. horn like*
a, *s. f. turpen-*
e || *a sort of oli-*
onsentient cuc-

ta (luna), *s. f.*
moon
ie (cometa), *s.*
met with a croo-
l
, ra, *a. horned*
s. f. V. Cornisa
sub. m. corner;

Cornijamiento, *s. m. V.* Cornijon
Cornijon, *s. m. the architrave, freese and cornice* || *the corner of a house* [*stone*
Corniola, *s. f. cornelian-*
Cornisa, *s. f. cornice*
Cornisamiento, *s. m. Voy.* Cornijon
Cornisica, illa, ita, *s. f. a little cornice*
Cornison, *s. m. V.* Cornijon [*tree*
Corno, *s. m. wild cherry-*
Cornucopia, *s. f. cornucopia*
Cornudazo, *s. m. aum. de* Cornudo
Cornudico, illo, ito, *sub. m. dim. de* Cornudo
Cornudo, da, *a. horned*
Cornudo, *s. m. cuckold*
Cornupeta, *s. m. a bull that butts with the horn*
Coro, *s. m. choir* || *chorus*
De coro, *adv. by heart*
Corocha, *s. f. a sort of caterpillar*
Corografia, *s. f. chorography*
Corográficamente, *adver chorographically*
Corográfico, ca, *a. chorographical*
Corógrafo, *s. m. chorographer* [*lary*
Corolario, *sub. m. corol-*
Corona, *s. f. a crown* || *a garland* || *a glory*
Corona de rey, *the herb melilot* [*tion*
Coronacion, *s. f. corona-*
Coronada (obra), *s. f. a crowned-work*
Coronado, *s. m. one with a shaven crown*
Coronador, ra, *s. one that crowns another*

Coronal, *a. m. coronal*
Coronamiento, *s. m. crowning*, (*in building*)
Coronar, *v. a. to crown*
Coronaria, *a. f. coroner*
Coronario, ria, *a. belonging to the crown*
Oro coronario, *the purified gold*
Corondel, *s. m. a reglet*
Coronel, *s. m. colonel* || *coronet*
Coronela, *s. f. the colonel's company* or *wife*
Coronelía, *s. f. a regiment*
Coronica, illa, *s. f. a little crown*
Corónica, *s. f. a chronicle*
Coronilla, *s. f. the crown of the head*
Coronilla real, *melilot*
Coronista, *s. m. chronicler*
Coroza, *sub. f. a painted cap like a mitre*
Corpanchon, *s. m. a great body* [*body*
Corpecito, *s. m. a little*
Corpezuelo, *s. m. a waistcoat without sleeves* || *V.* Corpecito
Corpiñejo, *s. m. dim. de* Corpiño
Corpiño, *sub. m. a little waist-coat worn by women*
Corporal, *a. 2. corporal*
Corporal, *s. m. corporal*
Corporalidad, *s. f. corporality*
Corporalmente, *adv. corporally*
Corporeidad, *s. f. corporeity*
Corporeo, rea, *adj. corporal*
Corps, *s. m. V.* Cuerpo
Sumiller de corps, *the lord great chamberlain*

— guardias de corps, *the life-guard-men*
Corpudo, da, *a. corpulent*
Corpulencia, *s. f. corpulency* [*pulent*
Corpulento, ta, *adj. cor-*
Corpus, *sub. m. Corpus-Christiday*
Corpuscular, *a.* 2. *corpuscular* [*cle*
Corpúsculo, *s. m. corpus-*
Corral, *s. m. a yard; a court* || *a poultry-yard*
Hacer corrales, *to absent one's self from school*
Corralero, *s. m. one who feeds fowls in a poultry-yard*
Corralillo, ito, *s. m. dim. de* Corral
Corraliza, *s. f. V.* Corral
Correa, *s. f. leather strap*
Correage, *s. m. straps, harness, etc.*
Correal (coser), *to stitch with thin straps*
Correar, *v. a. to prepare the wool*
Correccion, *s. f. correction*
Correctamente, *adv. correctly*
Correctivo, va, *a. corrective* [*rective*
Correctivo, *s. m. a cor-*
Correcto, ta, *a. correct*
Corrector, *s. m. corrector*
Corredentor, *subs. m. the person who with another redeems a third*
Corredera, *sub. f. a place for horses to run* || *the upper stone of a mill* || *a cricket* || *a bawd*
Corredilla, *s. f. a short running*
Corredizo (nudo), *s. m. a running knot*
Corredor, ra, *s. runner*
Corredor, *s. m. corridor; gallery* || *a broker* || *a common crier*
Corredor de bestias, *a jockey* — de culpas, *a pimp*
Corredorcillo, *s. m. a little corridor*
Correduría, *s. f. brokerage* || *pimping*
Correería, *s. f. the trade of a strap-maker*
Correero, *s. m. a strap-maker* [*lity*
Corregibilidad, *s. f. doci-*
Corregible, *adj.* 2. *corrigible*
Corregidor, *s. m. corregidor* || *corrector*
Corregidora, *s. f. the wife of a corregidor*
Corregimiento, *s. m. the office* or *district of a corregidor*
Corregir, *v. a. to correct*
Corregüela, *s. f. a little leather strap* || *bloodwort*
Correlacion, *s. f. correlativeness*
Correlativamente, *adver. correlatively*
Correlativo, va, *adj. correlative* [*seness*
Correncia, *s. f. flux; loo*
Correndilla, *s. f. V.* Correría
Correntía, *s. f. an artificial inundation*
Correntiar, *v. a. to overflow a new-reaped field*
Correntío, tía, *a. running*
Correnton, na, *a. going from one feast to another*
Correo, *s. m. a courier* || *a post-office* || *a complice*
Correon, *sub. m. a great leather strap*
Correoso, sa, *a. flexible*
Correr, *v. a.* ;
Correr la post *post* — la mo *current* — la *bleed* — tal *blow*
Correrse, *v. r.*
Correrse la vel
Correría, *s. f. excursion of*
Correspondenci *correspondei*
Corresponder, *correspond*
Correspondient *respondent*
Correspondient
Corresponsal, *pondent*
Corresponsio,
Corretage, *s. m.* || *pimping*
Corretear, *v. about; to ra*
Correvedile, *s. bearer* || *a pi*
Corrida, *s. f. race*
Corrida de tiem
De corrida, *a ly; running*
Corridamente, Corrientemen
Corridita, *subs race* or *cours*
Corrido, da, *a.*
Zorra corrida, *dent saucy w*
Corriente, *s. m.*
Corriente, *a.* 2. *running*
Corrientemente, *rently*
Corrillero, *s. m goes from one to another*
Corrillo, *s. m. a of news-mon*
Corrimiento, *s*

n || stream ;
|| fluxion
, s. m. a compa-
ean people
on , s. f. the run-
f waters together
e stream
. m. a company
ing in a ring
racion , s. f. cor-
ation.
oranto , a. 2. s. m.
borant ; corrobo-
[borate
e
orar , v. a. to corro-
ra , s. f. a reward
n to a broker
er , v. a. to corrode
mpedor , ra , s. cor-
pter
omper , v. a. to cor-
pt || to bribe || to de-
auch
romper , v. n. to stink
rromperse , v. r. to cor-
rupt
rrompidamente , adv.
corruptly
rrompimiento , sub. m.
corrupting
orrosion , s. f. corrosion
orrosivo , va , a. corro-
sive [kling
Corrugacion , s. f. wrin-
Corrugar , v. a. to corru-
gate
Corrugo , s. m. canal
Corrulla , s. f. a particular room , in gallies
Corrupcion , s. f. corrup-
tion || bribery || loose-
ness
Corruptamente , adv. cor-
ruptely
Corruptela , s. f. corrup-
tion || bribery
Corruptibilidad , s. f. cor-
ruptibility [tible
Corruptible , a. 2. corrupt

Corruptivo , va , adj. cor-
ruptive
Corrupto , ta , a. corrupt
— bribed
Corrupta , a deflowred girl
Corruptor , s. m. corrupter
Corsa , s. f. a sailing , or
cruizing of ships
Corsario , s. y a. corsair
Corsé , s. m. jumps
Corsear , v. a to cruize at
sea
Corso , s. m. cruize , crui-
zing [trees
Corta , s. f. the felling of
Cortabolsas , s. m. a cut-
purse
Cortadera , s. f. a tool to
cut-iron with
Cortadillo , s. m. a cylin-
drical drinking glass
|| a studied talking
Cortador , s. m. a sort of
capriol
Cortador , ra , a. cutting
Cortador , s. m. a butcher
Cortadores , pl. the inci-
sors
Cortadura , s. f. a cut
Cortaduras , pl. shreds ;
parings ; clippings ||
cut-paper-works
Cortafrio , s. m. a tool to
cut iron with
Cortamente , adv. shortly
|| soberly
Cortamiento , sub. m. the
cutting
Cortante , s. m. a butcher
Cortapies , subs. m. a cut
upon the legs with a
sword [knife
Cortaplumas , s. m. a pen-
Cortar , v. a. to cut
Cortarse , v. r. to be daun-
ted ; to be at a stand
Corte , s. m. the edge of a
sword , etc. || a cut || a
felling of trees || means

way || a court || a yard
Corte de vestido , the ne-
cessary quantity of stuff
Córtes , pl. the assembly
of the states of spain
Cortecica , illa , ita , s. f.
dim. de Corteza
Cortedad , s. f. shortness ;
brevity || bashfulness
Cortejador , s. m. courtier
Cortejar , v. a. to court
Cortejo , s. m. a retinue
|| a present || a gal-
lant ; a spark
Cortes , a. 2. courteous
Cortesanamente , adverb.
courteously
Cortesanazo , za , a. cere-
monious , etc.
Cortesanía , s. f. courtli-
ness
Cortesano , na , adj. cour-
teous || prudent || belon-
ging to the court
Dama cortesana , a cour-
tesan [tier
Cortesano , s. m. a cour-
Cortesía , s. f. courtesy
Cortesmente , adv. courtly
Corteza , s. f. bark ; rind
|| crust || the out side
Cortezon , s. m. aum. de
Corteza [Corteza
Cortezoncito , s. m. dim. de
Cortezudo , da , adj. corti-
cose || rustick
Cortezuela , sub. f. a little
bark
Cortico , ca , a. very short
Cortijo , s. m. a farm
Cortina , s. f. curtain
Cortinage , s. m. a set of
curtains
Cortinal , s. m. a field en-
closed with walls
Corto , ta , a. short || bash-
ful
Corto de entendimiento
half-witted — de ra-

de corazon, *cow-hearted* — de manos, *backward* [*worm*
Corton, *s. m. a sort of*
Coruscante, } *adj. coruscant*
Corusco, ca, }
Corva, *s. f. the ham* || *V.* Corvaza
Corvadura, *s. f. curvity*
Corvar, *v. a. to bend*
Corvaza, *s. f. curbs*
Corvecito, *s. m. a young raven*
Corvejon, *s. m. the joint wich bows the foot of any beast* || *a cok's spur* || *a sea-raven*
Corveta, *s. f. curvet*
Corvillo (miércoles), *sub. m. ash-wednesday*
Corvina, *subs. f. a sort of conger*
Corvo, va, *a. crooked*
Corvo, *s. m. a sort of fish* || *hook*
Corzo, za, *s. a roe-buck*
Corzuelo, *sub. m. dim. de* Corzo
Cosa, *s. f. a thing*
Cosario, *s. m. corsair* || *a carrier* || *a hunter*
Cosario, ria, *a. belonging to a corsair*
Camino cosario, *a beaten road*
Coscoja, *s. f. holme-oak* || *the dry pickly leaves of the oak*
Coscojo, *subs. mas. a red grain that grows on the holme-oak*
Coscojos, *plur. prickly wheels put to the bridles*
Coscojal, } *s. m. a grove of holme-oaks*
Coscojar, }
Coscorron, *s. m. bruise; blow*
Coseclia, *s. f. harvest of a harvest*
Cosedura, *s. f. sewing*
Coselete, *s. m. a corslet* || *armour*
Coser, *v. a. to sew*
Cosera, *subs. f. a watered field*
Cosetada, *s. f. a quick run*
Cosica, illa, ita, *s. f. a trifle* [*clothes*
Cosido, *s. m. sewed linen-*
Cósmico, ca, *a. cosmical*
Cosmogonía, *s. f. cosmogony*
Cosmografía, *sub. f. cosmography*
Cosmógrafo, *s. m. cosmographer*
Cosmología, *s. f. cosmology*
Coso, *s. m. the place for the bull feasts* || *a little worm in wood*
Cosquillas, *s. f. tickling*
Hacer cosquillas, *to tickle*
Cosquillaza, *s. f.* } *a violent and sudden tickle*
Cosquillon, *s. m.* }
Cosquilloso, sa, *a. ticklish*
Costa, *s. f. cost; price* || *a sea-coast* || *a wedge used by shoe-makers*
Costado, *s. m. side* || *back*
Costados, *pl. descents* (*in genealogy*)
Costal, *s. m. a sack* || *a rammer*
Costalada, *s. f. a fall upon the side*, or *upon the back*
Costalazo, *sub. m. a great sack* || *a blow with a sack* [*porter*
Costalero, *sub. m. street-*
Costalico, illo, ito, *s. m a little sack*
Costaneras, *s. f. joists* ...
ning; shelvin[g]
Costar, *v. n. to [...]*
Coste, *s. m. cost*
Costear, *v. a. to [...] defray*
Costera, *s. f. sid[e]*
Costero, *s. m. a [...] slab of timber*
Costilla, *s. f. a r[...]*
Costillas, *pl. all knees*
Costillage, } *s. m. [...]ture [...]*
Costillar, }
Costiller, *s. m. a[n] officer of the h[...]*
Costillica, ita, *s[...] de* Costilla
Costilludo, da, *[...] rough hewn, [...] clownish*
Costo, *subst. m. [...] indian tree*
Costosamente, *pensively*
Costoso, sa, *a. [...]*
Costra, *s. f. a cr[...]*
Costrada, *sub. f. [...] cake*
Costrilla, *sub. f [...]* Costra
Costringimiento [...] *constraint*
Costringir, *v. a[...] train*
Costroso, sa, *a.[...]*
Costumbre, *s. f. [...]* || *a woman's [...]*
Costumbres, *pl.[...]*
Costura, *s. f. s[e]wing*
Costurera, *s. f. [...]*
Costuron, *s. m [...] coarse seam [...] scar*
Cota, *s. f. a co[...]* || *a coat of ar[...]* || *quotation*
Cotana, *s. f. m[...]*

f. a kind of
i
ub. f. a mean woman
n. hospital || *a*
use
z. to compare
s. comparison
ento, *adverb.*

ia, *a. daily*
stays; bodice
ub. m. a stay-

a back-stroke
s. f. a certain
coat of arms
full of bands
nt colours
m. a park, a
etc. || *the price*
any commo-
bound || *the*
eath || *miller's*

s. printed cal-

s. f. a sort of

s. m. a little
at top of the
b
f. dimity
f. paroquet ||

f. ashe-parrot
z. an old ox
a certain in-
t || *a dainty*
m. a buskin
f. a little oa-
s
, sub. f. a very
s || *the office of*
ry of state
s. f. } *a little*
. m. } *basket*
s. f. dim. de

Cox cox (á) **á cox coxita**, *adv. upon one foot*
Coxear, *v. n. to halt* || *to shuffle*
Coxedad, *s. f. lameness*
Coxendico, *s. m. the hip bone*
Coxera, *s. f. lameness*
Coxijo, *sub. m. contest on trifles*
Coxijoso, sa, *a. that complains at every thing*
Coxin, *s. m. a cushion; a pillow*
Coxinete, nillo, *sub. m. a little cushion*
Coxitranco, ca, *a. a lame that is never still*
Coxixo, *s. m. a vermin*
Coxo, xa, *a. lame*
Coxo, *s. m. the time*
Coxquear, *V.* Coxear
Coxquearse, *v. r. to be offended* [*lame*
Coxuelo, la, *adj. a little*
Coyma, *s. f. a sum paid to the keeper of a gaming house*
Coyme, *sub. m. one that keeps a publick gaming house*
Coyunda, *s. f. a strap to tie oxen to the yoke*
Coyundado, da, *a. tied to the yoke*
Coyundilla, *s. f. a little strap*
Coyuntura, *s. f. a joint* or *articulation* || *juncture, opportunity*
Coz, *s. f. a kick* || *the but-end of a musket* || *the recoiling of it*
Crabron, *s. m. a hornet*
Craneo, *s. m. a skull*
Crápula, *s. f. gross intemperance*
Crascitar, *v. n. to croak*
Crasicie, *s. f. thickness*

Crasiento, ta, *a. greasy*
Crasitud, *s. f. fatness*
Craso, sa, *a. fat; thick* || *gross* [*cloth*
Crea, *s. f. a sort of linen*
Creacion, *s. f. creation*
Crear, *v. a to create*
Crear, *v. n. to grow up*
Creatura, *s. f. a creature*
Crebol, *s. m. holly*
Crecedero, ra, *a. apt to grow* or *increase*
Crecer, *v. n. to grow up to increase*
Creces, *s. f. plu. the over plus in measures of corn, etc.* || *increase*
Crecida, *s. f. growing; increase*
Crecidamente, *adv. abundantly*
Crecidito, ta, *a. a little increased*
Crecido, da, *adj. great* || *abundant*
Creciente, *s. mas. the increase of rivers* || *crescent* || *flood*
Crecimiento, *s. mas. increase*
Credencia, *s. fem. a little cup-board near the altar* [*tial*
Credencial, *a. a credential*
Credibilidad, *s. f. credibility*
Crédito, *s. mas. credit* || *active debt*
Credo, *s. m. creed*
Credulidad, *s. f. credulity*
Crédulo, la, *a. credulous*
Creederas (tener buenas), *to be very credulous*
Creedor, ra, *a. credulous*
Creencia, *s. f. belief*
Creendero, ra, *s. a person recommended to another*
Creer, *v. a. to believe*

Cregüela, *sub. f. a sort of linen cloth*
Creible, *a.* 2. *credible*
Creiblemente, *adv. credibly* [*diæresis*
Crema, *sub. f. cream* ||
Cremásteres, *s. m. pl. two muscles so called*
Cremor, *s. m. cream; the best of a thing*
Crencha, *s. f. the partition of the hair*
Crepusculino, na, *a. belonging to the crepuscule* [*cule*
Crepúsculo, *s. m. crepus-*
Cresa, *s. f a little worm* || *eggs of bees*
Crespar, *v. a. to curl*
Cresparse, *v. r. to be angry* [*tree*
Crespino, *s. m. a sort of*
Crespo, pa, *adj. crisped; curled* || *entangled* || *angry*
Crespon, *s. m. crape*
Cresta, *s. f. a cockscomb* || *a cop* or *tuft* || *a crest*
Cresta de la explanada, *land-walk*
Crestado, da, *a. crested*
Crestica, illa, ita, *s. fem. dim. de* Cresta
Creston, *s. m. crest of a helmet*
Creyente, *s. m. believer*
Cresneja, *s. f. a rush-lace*
Cria, *s. f. a litter* || *the young of any animal*
Criada, *s. f. a maid servant* || *a beetle*
Criadero, *s. m. nursery; seed-plot*
Criadero, ra, *a. teeming; fecund*
Criadilla, *s. f. testicle* || *a little servant wench*
Criadillas de tierra, truffles

Criado, *s. m. a servant*
Criado (bien ó mal), *well* or *ill-bred*
Criador, ra, *s. one that educates* or *breeds up*
Criador, *s. m. creator*
Criaduela, *sub. m. a little maid servant*
Crianza, *s. f. breeding; education* || *courtesy*
Criar, *v. a. to create* || *to produce* || *to nurse* || *to breed; to educate*
Criatura, *s. f. a creature* || *a child*
Criaturica, illa, ita, *s. f. a little child*
Criba, *s. f. a sieve*
Cribar, *v. a. to sift*
Cribo, *s. m. V.* Criba
Crimen, *s. m. a crime*
Criminacion, *s. f. crimination*
Criminal, *a.* 2. *criminal*
Criminalidad, *s. f. criminalty*
Criminalmente, *adv. criminally*
Criminar, *v. a. to accuse*
Criminosamente, *adv. criminously* [*nous*
Criminoso, sa, *a. crimi-*
Crimno, *s. mas. a coarse sort of meal*
Crin, *s. f. horse* or *lion's mane* [*haired*
Crinado, da, *adj. long-*
Crinito, ta, *adj. V.* Crinado || *ominous*
Criollo, *s. m. a creole*
Criptas, *s. f. pl. cryptæ*
Crisis, *s. f. crisis* || *judgment*
Crisma, *s.* 2. *chrism*
Crismar, *v. a. to anoint with chrism; to confirm*
Crismera, *s. f. a bottle in wich the chrism is kept*

Crisoberilo, *s. m*
beryl
Crisol, *s. m. cru*
Crisolada, *s. f.*
full
Crisolito, *s. m.*
Crisopasio, *s. m*
phrasus
Crisopeya, *s. f.*
Crispatura, *s. f. c*
Crista, *s. f. cres*
of arms
Cristal, *s. m. cr*
Cristal tártaro,
tartar
Cristalino, na,
line
Cristalizacion, *s.*
Cristalizar, *v. a*
tallize
Cristel, *s. m. a*
Crítica, *s. f. cri*
Criticar, *v. a. t*
Crítico, *s. m. a*
a purist
Crítico, ca, *a. c*
Critiquizar, *v.*
cise
Crizneja, *sub. f*
wattle
Croaxar, *v. a. t*
Crocino, *s. mas.*
ment made wi
Crocodilio, *s. m*
like a thistle
Crocodilo, *s. m*
dile
Crocomagna, *s.*
of the oil of s
Crocuta, *s. f.*
beast suppose
a hyena and
Cromático, ca, *a*
tick
Crónica, *s. f.*
Crónico, *s. m.*
Crónico, ca, *a.*
Cronicon, *s. m*
annals

z chronicler
..f. chrono-
. m. anna-
[logy
. f. chrono-
ente, adver.
lly
a, a. chro-
Cronólogo,
ologist
s. a muscle
le
bittern
the withers
: a gothick
. cross-bar
am || cross-
-bearer
cross-wort
Crucífero,
bearer
a. crucife-
t. to crucify
ub. f. cruci-
n. crucifix
m. one who
a. crucife-
. pushpin
dv. bluntly
f. asperity;
roughness
rudities
aw || sharp
rogant
iempo cru-
recise mo-
nto crudo,
ly
el
uelty

Cruelmente, *adv. cruelly*

Cruentamente, *adv. bloodily*

Cruentar, *v. a. V.* Ensangrentar

Crural, *a.* 2. *crural*

Crureo, *s. m. one of the muscles of the leg*

Crústico, ca, *a. V.* Pulsatil

Cruxía, *s. f. gang-way || a bow-chase || a corridor* or *gallery || dormitory*

Cruxía de piezas, *a ribble-row of rooms* — pasar cruxía, *to run the gauntlet*

Cruxida, *s. f. deck*

Cruxido, *s. m. a crack*

Cruxir, *v. n. to crack*

Cruz, *s. m. a cross || horse's withers*

Cruzada, *s. f. crusade*

Cruzado, *s. m. a croise || cruzado*

Cruzador, *s. m. cruiser*

Cruzar, *v. a. to cross*

Cruzar, *v. n. to cruise*

Cruzarse, *v. rec. to take upon one the cross for the holy war*

Cuaderviz, *s. f. a quail*

Cuajada, *s. fem. curds of milk*

Cuajadillo, *s. m. a woven piece of silk intermixt with flowers*

Cuajamiento, *s. m. coagulation*

Cuajar, *s. m. runnet-bag*

Cuajar, *v. a. to coagulate || to please*

Cuajareo, *s. m. runnet*

Cuajaron, *s. m. a clod of blood*

Cuajo, *s. m. curdled milk*

Yerba de cuajo, *cheese-wort*

Cuatequil, *s. m. millet*

Cuba, *s. fem. cask; tun; pipe || a great drinker || a paunchbelly*

Cubazo, *sub. mas. a blow against a cask*

Cubeba, *s. f. a small indian fruit* or *berry*

Cubero, *s. m. a cooper*

Cubertado, da, *a. covered*

Cubertura, *s. f. a covering*

Cubeta, *s. f. a little cask || a sort of pail*

Cubetilla, *s. f. dim. de* Cubeta

Cubeto, *s. f. dim. de* Cuba

Cubichetes, *s. m. pl. fillingpieces (in a ship)*

Cúbico, ca, *a. cubical*

Cubiculario, *s. m. a valet de chamber*

Cubículo, *s. mas. a bed-chamber*

Cubierta, *s. f. any covering || deck*

Cubiertamente, *adv. secretly*

Cubierto, *s. m. a cover || a lodging-roof || a set of dishes, etc.*

Cubierto, ta, *a. covered*

Cubil, *s. m. hare's form; wild boar's hold, etc.*

Cubilete, *s. m. a pattee-pan || a litle-pie || a goblet || a juggler's box || a dice-box*

Cubiletero, *s. m. a pattee-pan || a great drinking cup*

Cubillo, *s. m. a little pail || a sort of spanish fly*

Cubital (Medida), *s. f. a cubit*

Cubito, *s. m. a little pail*

Cubo, *s. m. a cube || a pail || a nave or stock of a wheel || a round tower*

Cuboydes, *s. m. the foot-bone*

Cubrepan, *s. m. a sort of oven-fork*

Cubrir, *v. a. to cover*

Cubrir faltas, *to conceal faults* — cubrir á la yegua, *to leap the mare*

Cubrirse el cielo, *to grow cloudy*

Cuca, *s. f. pignut* || *a sort of caterpillar*

Cucaña, *s. f. a profit gained by another's cost*

Tierra de cucaña, *a land of milk and honey*

Cucañero, *s. m. one who gains at another's cost*

Cucar, *v. a. to jest*

Cucaracha, *s. f. a wood-louse*

Cuchar, *s. m. a tax upon corn*

Cuchara, *s. f. a spoon* || *a ladle* || *a scoop*

Cucharada, *s. f. a spoonful*

Cucharal, *s. m. a little bag to put the spoons into*

Cucharazo, *s. m. a blow with a spoon*

Cucharero, *s. m. one who makes or sells spoons*

Cuchareta, *sub. f. a little spoon*

Cucharetear, *v. a. to stir with a spoon* || *to intermeddle with other persons matter*

Cucharetero, *s. m. V.* Cucharero || *case of spoons*

Cucharica, illa, ita, *s. f. a tea-spoon*

Cucharon, *s. m. a ladle*

Cuchichear, *v. n. to whisper*

[ring

Cuchicheo, *s. m. whispe-*

Cuchichiar, *v. n. to chirp, like the partridges*

Cuchilla, *s. f. cleaver* || *sword* || *a book binder's knife*

Cuchillada, *sub. f. slash; gash; cut*

Cuchilladas, *pl. strifes; squabbles*

Cuchilladica, illa, ita, *s. f. a little slash, etc.*

Cuchillar, *a. 2. belonging to a knife*

[*knife*

Cuchillazo, *s. m. a great*

Cuchillejo, *s. m. a little knife*

Cuchillería, *s. f. the making of knives* || *a cutler's shop*

Cuchillero, *s. m. a cutler*

Cuchillico, ito, *sub. m. a little knife*

Cuchillo, *p. a knife*

Cuchillos, *plu. studding sails* || *six principal feathers in the hawk's wings* || *gores put to garments, etc.*

Cuchillon, *s. m. a great knife*

Cuchuchear, *v. n. to whisper* || *to report; to tell*

Cuchufleta, *s. f. a quibble; a joke*

Cucita, *s. f. a little dog*

Cuclillas (sentarse de ó en), *to sit on one's hams*

Cuclillo, *s. m. a cuckow* || *a cuckold*

Cuco, *s. m. a caterpillar*

Cuculla, *s. f. a hood*

Cucurucho, *s. m. a cornet of paper*

Cudria, *s. f. a rope made with rushes*

Cuébano, *V.* Cuévano

Cuelga, *sub. f. a present given on one's birth day*

Cuellierguido, da, *adj. haughty; stiffnecked*

Cuello, *s. m. neck* || collar || *ruff* || instep

Cuelmo, *s. m.* [illegible]

Cuenca, *sub. f.* [illegible] *porringer* || [illegible] *the eye*

Cuenco, *s. m. a* [illegible]

Cuenda, *subst.* [illegible] *thread of a s*[illegible]

Cuenta, *s. f. a*[illegible] || *a bead*

Cuentecica, ill[illegible] *dim. de* Cuen[illegible]

Cuentecico, ill[illegible] *m. dim. de* C[illegible]

Cuentista, *s. m* [illegible] *teller*

Cuento, *s. m.* [illegible] *million* || *a p*[illegible] || *a quarrel*

Cuera, *s. f. a le*[illegible]

Cuerda, *s. f. cor*[illegible] *string* || *matc*[illegible] || *a watch's c*[illegible]

Cuerdas, *pl. sin*[illegible]

Cuerdamente, *a*[illegible]

Cuerdecica, illa [illegible] *a little cord*

Cuerdecito, ta, [illegible]

Cuerdo [*se*[illegible]

Cuerdo, da, *a. s*[illegible]

Cuerecico, ito, [illegible] *little thin ski*[illegible]

Cuerezuelo, *s. m* [illegible] recico || *a suck*[illegible]

Cuerna, *s. f. a s*[illegible] || *a hunter's h*[illegible]

Cuernecico, ill[illegible] *m. a little ho*[illegible]

Cuernezuelo, *su*[illegible] Cuernecico || [illegible] *of a wild boa*[illegible]

Cuerno, *s. m. h*[illegible]

Cuernos de anten[illegible] — de altar, *co*[illegible]

Cuero, *s. m. ski*[illegible] *leather* || *leat*[illegible] *a drunkard*

Estar en cuer[illegible] stark naked

Cuerpecico, [illegible]

s. mas. a little

s. m. body || *the*
|| *dead body;*
|| *a volume* || *a*
ration
de guardia, *corps*
rd || *guard-house*
s. f. the hen crow
ico, cillo, cito, *s.*
a little or *young*

s. m. a crow
calvo, *a cormo-*
| *marino, a plun-*

s. m. the stone of
t || *a fart*
llo, *s. m. dim. de*
o
, *s. f. a hill*
stas, *adv: on one's*
lders or *back*
ica, cilla, cita,
, *s. f. a little hill*
s. f. den; cavern ||
r; cave
o, *s. m. a great*
et to gather the gra-
n
ica, cilla, cita. *s.*
n. de Cueva
o, *s. m. one who*
s caves
s. m. a brick layer's

da, *s. f. the cop-*
ark
, *s. f. a monk's*

co, illo, ito, *s. m.*
de Cuidado
o, *s. m. diligence;*
|| *fear; suspicion*
osamente, *adv. ca-*
ly
oso, sa, *a. careful;*
ent
v. a. to take care

Cuita, *subs. f. anguish; anxiety*

Cuitadico, illo, ito, *adj. dim. de* Cuitado

Cuitado, da, *a. anxious; miserable* || *faint-hearted*

Culada, *s. f. a fall on the backside*

Culantrillo, *s. mas. maiden-hair*

Culantro, *s. m. coriander*

Cular, *s. m. the gut of the fundament*

Culata, *s. f. the breech of a gun* || *the back-side of a coach*

Culatazo, *sub. m. a blow with the breech of a gun*

Culazo, *s. m. a great breech*

Culcusido, *s. m. patched works*

Culebra, *s. f. an adder* || *a sham*, or *stam*

Culebrazo, *s. m. lash; lasking*

Culebrear, *v. n. to move from one side to another*

Culebrica, illa, ita, *s. f. a little adder*

Culebrilla, *s. f. a tetter* || *a chap in a gun's barrel*

Culebrina, *s. f. culverin*

Culebro, *s. m. a he adder*

Culebron, *s. m. a great adder* || *a cunning, crafty man*

Culera, *s. f. a foul clout*

Culero, *sub. m. clout for children*

Culero, ra, *a. that comes the last to an appoin- the place*

Culito, *s. m. a little breech*

Culo, *s. m. breech; arse* || *bottom*

Culon, *s. m. a great breech*

Culpa, *s. f. a fault*

Culpable, *a. culpable*

Culpablemente, Culpadamente, *adv. culpably*

Culpado, da, *a. culpable; guilty*

Culpar, *v. a. to accuse of a fault*

Cultamente, *adver. elegantly* || *affectedly*

Cultedad, *s. f. affectation in speaking*

Culteranismo, *sub. m. the sect of the purists*

Culterano, na, *s. a purist*

Culterano, na, *a. belonging, to the purists*

Cultería, *s. f. V.* Cultedad

Cultero, *s. m. purist*

Cultiparlar, *v. n. to speak with affectation*

Cultiparlista, *s. m. one who speaks with affectation*

Cultipicaño, ña, *a. who speaks with affectation and malignity*

Cultivacion, *s. f. cultivation*

Cultivador, *s. m. husbandman*

Cultivar, *v. a. to cultivate*

Cultivo, *s. m. culture*

Culto, *s. m. worship*

Culto, ta, *a. pure; clean; correct* || *affected* || *cultivated*

Cultor, *s. m. husbandman*

Cultura, *s. f. culture*

Culturar, *v. a to cultivate*

Cumbé, *s. m. a moorish dance*

Cumbre, *s. m. the top*

Cumpleaños, *s. m. birthday*

Cumplidamente, *adv. completely*

Cumplidero, ra, *adj. fit; becoming*

Cumplido, da, *a. large* || *abundant* || *complete; perfect* || *respectful*

Cumplido, *s. m. compliment*

Cumplidor, *s. m. accomplisher* || *executor of a will*

Cumplimentar, *v. act. to compliment*

Cumplimentero, ra, *adj complimentar*

Cumplimiento, *s. m. accomplishment* || *compliment* || *complement*

Cumplir, *v. a. to accomplish; to perform*

Cumplir años, *to be come to one's birth day*

Cumplir, *v. n. to be convenient* || *to suffice*

Cumular, *v. a. to heap up*

Cumulativamente, *adver. accumulatively*

Cúmulo, *s. m. an heap*

Cuna, *s. f. a cradle*

Cundido, *s. m. the meat, etc. that is given to a child, to eat with his bread*

Cundir, *v. n. to spread* || *to increase*

Cunera, *s. f. rocker*

Cuneta, *subs. f. a deeper trench cut along the middle of a dry ditch*

Cunica, illa, ita, *s. f. a little cradle*

Cuña, *s. f. a wedge*

Cuñada, *s. f. a sister-in-law*

Cuñaderia, *s. f. a spiritual affinity*

Cuñadía, *s. f. affinity by marriage*

Cuñadico, illo, ito, *sub. m. dim. de* Cuñado

Cuñadío, *s. m. V.* Cuñadía [*in law*

Cuñado, *s. m. a brother*

Cuñar, *v. a. V.* Acuñar

Cuñete, *s. m. V.* Cubeta

Cuño, *s. m. a die* || *the die's stamp*

Cupé, *s. m. a chariot*

Cupresino, na, *a. of cypress*

Cupula, *s. f. cupola*

Cupulino, *s. m. lantern*

Cuquillero, *s. m. a baker's servant*

Cuquillo, *s. m. a cuckow*

Cura, *s. m. a parson*

Teniente cura, *vicar, curate*

Cura, *s. f. a cure* || *care; diligence* [*souls*

Cura de almas, *cure of*

Curable, *a. 2. curable*

Curacion, *s. f. curation*

Curadillo, *subs. m. poor-jack*

Curado (beneficio), *s. m. a benefice with cure of souls*

Curador, ra, *s. administrator; manager*

Curador, *sub. m. curator; guardian* || *a physician*

Curaduría, *s. f. guardianship*

Curalle, *s. m. casting* (*in falconry*)

Curandero, *s. m. an empirick; a quack*

Curar, *v. act. to cure* || *to dress a wound* || *to whiten linen*

Curar, *v. neut. to recover one's health*

Curativo, va, *a. curative*

Curato, *s. m. living* || *parsonage* || *parish*

Curcuma, *s. f. the indian saffron*

Cureña, *s. f. a carriage for cannon* || *stock of a cross-bow*

Curia, *s. f. a court of justice*

Curial, *a. 2. belonging to a court of justice* || *intelligent, skilful*

Curial, *s. m. a.*
the pope's co
licitor

Curiana, *s. f. a*

Curiosamente,
riously || *car*

Curiosidad, *s. f*
|| *care*

Curioso, sa, *a*
|| *careful*

Currpea, *s. f. h*
row

Cursado, da,
experienced

Cursar, *v. a. t*
|| *to follow t*

Cursillo, *sub.*
Curso

Cursivo, va,

Curso, *s. m. co*
seness

Curtacion, *s.*

Curtidos, *s. m.*
leathers

Curtidor, *s. m*

Curtiduría, *s. f.*
shop or trade

Curtir, *v. a. to*
tan

Curuca, ja, *s.*

Curva, *s. f. a*
knee

Curvaton, *sub.*

Curvatura, } *s. f*
Curvidad, }

Curvilineo, nea
vilinear

Curvo, va, *a. c*

Cuscuta, *s. f. w*

Cusir, *v. a. to*
sely

Custodia, *s. f.*
the remonstr
tabernacle –
trict of a Cus

Custodio, *s. m.*
tual governo
ber of conve
dian

, nea, *adj. cuta-*

, *s. f. cuticle*

r, *a. 2. cuticular*

. *a. to shake ; to*

2. *the skin*

. *m. V.* Miserable

. *f. a rest for a*

, *etc.*

a word used to
logs by

zarina, *V.* Zar,
a

D

s, *a. 2. easy to be*
or made

. *defect. give hi-*
give it me

a las pajas, *in a*
nt

. *m. tax; custom;*

, *s. m. a dactyle*

. *f. enjoyment of*
thing given

, *s. f. a gift*

lo, da, *a. bribed*

amente, *adv. li-*
ly [*lily*

idad, *s. f. libera-*

o, sa, *a. liberal*

. *m. a die*

, *s. a giver*

s. m. a liberal gi-
| *the drawer of a*
f exchange

. *f. a dagger* || *a*
bricks in the oven

s. m, *a great dag-*

f. pump-dale

r, *s. m. a mower*

. *m. a scythe*

ica, *s. f. dalmatick*

s. f. a lady || *the*
(*at chess*) ||

mistress ; love || *concu-*
bine || *a doe*

Juego de damas, *the game*
of draughts

Damascena, *s. f. damask-*
prune

Damasco, *s. m. damask* ||
a sort of apricots

Damasquillo, *s. m. wors-*
ted damask

Damasquino, na, *a. da-*
masked

Damaza, *sub. f. a great*
handsome lady

Damería, *s. f. delicacy ;*
niceness [*board*

Damero, *s. m. a draught-*

Damisela, *s. m. a damsel*
|| *a courtesan*

Damnacion, *s. f. damna-*
tion [*nify*

Damnificar, *v. a to dam-*

Danchado, da, *a. denti-*
culated

Danta, *s. f. an animal of*
the east-indies

Dantelado, da, *a. denti-*
culated

Danza, *s. f. a dance*

Danzador, *s. m. a dancer*

Danzante, ta, *s. a dancer*
in the processions

Danzar, *v. n. to dance*

Danzarin, *s. m. a genteel*
dancer [*damnifies*

Dañador, *s. m. one that*

Dañados, *sub. m. pl. the*
damneds

Dañar, *v. a to damnify ;*
to hurt [*hurtful*

Dañino, na, *a noxious ;*

Daño, *s. m. hurt ; detri-*
ment [*fully*

Dañosamente, *adv. hurt-*

Dañoso, sa, *a. hurtful*

Dar, *v. a. to give, to bes-*
tow [*yield*

Darse, *v. r. to submit ; to*

Darse á las letras, *to ap-*
ply to learning || por
contento, *to rest satis-*
fied

Dardazo, *s. m. a stroke or*
wound of a dart

Dardo, *s. m. a dart*

Data, *sub. f. a date* || *ex-*
pence [*office*

Dataría, *s. f. the datary's*

Datario, *s. m. datary*

Dátil, *s. m. date* (*fruit*)

Datilado, da, *a. date like*

Datilillo, *sub. m. dim. de*
Dátil

Dativo, *s. m. dative*

Dauco, *s. m. daucus*

Daysa, *s. f. a guest* || *a con-*
cubine

De, *prep. of* || *from* || *out*
of || *for, etc.* || *some*

Dea, *s. f. a goddess*

Dean, *s. m. a dean*

Deanato / Deanazgo } *s. m. deanery*

Debate, *s. m. debate*

Debatir, *v. a to debate*

Debaxo, *adv. under*

Debelacion, *s. f. conquest ;*
overthrow

Debelar, *v. a. to vainquish ;*
to overthrow

Deber, *v. a. to owe*

Deber, *s. m. duty*

Debidamente, *adv. duly*
|| *completely*

Débil, *a. 2. feeble ; weak*

Debilidad, *s. f. debility*

Debilitacion, *s. f. debili-*
tation [*litate*

Debilitar, *v. act. to debi-*

Debilmente, *adv. weakly*

Débito, *s. m. debt*

Débito conjugal, *a con-*
jugal duty

Década, *s. f. decade*

Decadencia, *s. f. decay*

Decaer, *v. n. to decay*
|| *to deflect from the*
course

Decanato, s. m. *the office of the senior*

Decano, s. m. *eldest; senior* [*ting*

Decantacion, s. f. *decan-*

Decantar, v. a. *to decant* || *to praise; to exalt* || *to bend*, or *bow down*

Decena, s. f. *ten*

Decenal, a. 2. *decennial*

Decenario, s. m. *a chaplet of ten beads*

Número decenario, *the number of ten*

Decencia, s. f. *decency*

Decender, etc. *V.* Descender (*of ten years*

Decenio, s. m. *the space*

Deceno, na, a. *tenth*

Decentar, v. a. *to make the first cut; to broach, etc.* [*make sore*

Decentarse, v r. *to fret to*

Decente, a. 2. *decent*

Decentemente, adv. *decently*

Decepcion, s. f. *deception*

Dechado, s. m. *a pattern*

Decible, a. 2. *that can be said*

Decideras, s. f. pl. *easiness and elegance in expression*

Decidero, ra, a. *fit to be said*

Decidir, v. a. *to decide*

Decidor, ra, sub. *one who speaks elegantly*

Deciembre, s. m. *V.* Diciembre

Décima, s. f. *a stanza of of ten verses* || *a tenth part* || *a tithe*

Decimal, a. 2. *decimal*

Decir, v. a. *to tell; to say* || *to affirm* || *to call* || *to speak; to preach, etc.*

Decires, s. m. pl. *slanders; murmurs, etc.*

Decision, s. f. *decision*

Decisivamente, adv. *decisively*

Decisivo, va, a. *decisive*

Deciso, sa, a. *decided*

Decisorio, ria, a. *decisory*

Declamacion, s. f. *declamation* [*mer*

Declamador, s. m. *declai-*

Declamar, v. a. *to declaim*

Declamatorio, ria, a. *declamatory*

Declaracion, s. f. *declaration*

Declaradamente, adverb. *clearly; openly*

Declarador, s. m. *declarer*

Declarar, v. a. *to declare*

Declarativa, s. f. *easiness and elegance in expression* [*claratory*

Declaratorio, ria, a. *de-*

Declinable, a. 2. *declinable*

Declinacion, s. f. *declination* || *declining; decay*

Declinar, v. a. y n. *to decline* [*natory*

Declinatorio, s. m. *decli-*

Declive, vio, s. m. *declivity; shelving*

Decoccion, s. f. *coction* || *decoction*

Decorar, v a. *to decorate* || *to learn by heart*

Decoro, s. m. *respect; honour* || *decorum; decency* [*cently*

Decorosamente, adv. *de-*

Decoroso, sa, a. *decent*

Decremento, s. m. *decrement*

Decrepitar, v. n. *to dry any thing by the fire*

Decrépito, ta, a. *decrepit* [*pitude*

Decrepitud, s. f. *decre-*

Decretal, s. f. decretal

Decretal, a. 2. decretal

Decretalista, s.
poser or *int*
the Pope's d

Decretar, v. a.

Decreto, s. m.
warrant || *a*
the canon la

Decretorio, ri
cretory

Decúbito, s. m.
sition made
mour in an
the body

Decumana, s. f
thing in the
order

Decuria, s. f. *a*

Decurion, s. m
rion

Decursas, s. f.

Decurso, s. m

Dedada, subst.
with a fing
ger's length ||

Dedal, s. m. *a*
a case of lin
put lover a
little drinki

Dédalo, s. m.

Dedalísimo, s.
great thimbl

Dedicacion, s.

Dedicar, v. a.

Dedicarse, v. r
to fix the mi

Dedicatoria, s.
le dedicatory

Dedignar, v. a.

Dedignarse, v.

Dedil, s. m. *V*

Dedillo, sub.
Dedo

Dedo, s. m. *a*

Dedo pulgar,
—indice, *the*
—de en medi
dle finger—
anillo, del
ring-finge

ager — del
deduction
to deduce
defection
. defectible
adj. defec-
[want
s. defect ||
te, adver.
, a. defec-
a, a. defen-
[der
m. a defen-
. to defend
or prohibit
, s. m. de-
, s. m. an
eed upon
defence ||
|| fence
nao, fan-
[sible
2. defen-
. f. defen-
a discharge
n. defence,
a defensa-
, a. defen-
fensiva, to
vely
. defender,
f. the office
der or ad-
. m. apolo-
zation, etc.
m. deferent
. to defer;
nd
. deficient
definition
NOLES.

Definidor, *s. m. definer* || *definitor*

Definir, *v. a. to define*

Definitivamente, *adv. definitively* [nitive

Definitivo, **va**, *adj. defi-*

Définitorio, *sub. m. the chapter or assembly of the* **Definidores**

Defluxo, *s. m. defluxion*

Deformacion, *s. f. deformation*

Deformador, *subs. m. one who deforms*

Deformar, *v. a. to deform*

Deformatorio, **ria**, *a. deforming*

Deforme, *a. 2. deformed*

Deformidad, *s. f. deformity* || *a blunder*

Defraudacion, *s. f. usurpation; defrauding*

Defraudador, *s. m. usurper* || *defrauder*

Defraudar, *v. a. to usurp* || *to defraud* [thout

Defuera, *adv. out; wi-*

Defunsion, *s. f. obsequies*

Degeneracion, *s. f. degeneracy*

Degenerar, *v. a. to degenerate* [ding

Degollacion, *s. f. behea-*

Degolladero, *s. m. throat; gullet* || *a scaffold*

Degollador, *s. m. executioner* || *a murderer* || *a butcher*

Degolladura, *s. f. a wound in the throat* or *neck*

Degollar, *v. a. to behead* || *to kill* or *slay*

Degradacion, *s. f. degrading; degradation*

Degradar, *v. a. to degrade*

Degüello, *sub. m. beheading* || *slaying*

Dehender, *v. a. to cleave asunder*

Dehendimiento, *subs. m. cleaving* [ground

Dehesa, *s fem. a pasture*

Dehesa concejil, *a common pasture*

Dehesar, *v. a. to convert a piece of ground to a pasture*

Dehesero, *s. m. a keeper of the pasture*

Deicida, *s. m. deicide*

Deicidio, *s. m. deicide*

Deidad, *s. f. deity*

Deificacion, *s. f. deification*

Deificar, *v. a. to deify*

Deifico, ca, } *a. divine*
Deiforme }

Deismo, *s. m. deism*

Deista, *s. m. a deist*

Deístico, **ca**, *a. deistical*

Del, *art. of him* or *of it*

Del, **della**, **dello**, *of him, of her, of it*

Delacion, *s. f. delation*

Delantal, *s. m. apron*

Delante, *adv. before*

Delantera, *s. f. the fore part*

Delantero, **ra**, *adj. that is before another*

Relox delantero, *a clock that goes too fast*

Delatable, *a. 2. worthy of accusation*

Delatar, *v. a. to accuse; to impeach* [man

Delate, *s. m. an higway-*

Delator, *s m. delator*

Delectable, **Delectacion**, **Delectar**, *V.* **Deleytable**, etc.

Delecto, *s. m. election; choice* [tion

Delegacion, *s. f. delega-*

Delegado, *s. m. a delegate*

Delegar, *v. a. to delegate*

Deletrear, *v. a. to spell* || *to guess at*

K

Deleytable, *a.* 2. *delectable* [*tation*
Deleytacion, *s. f. delec-*
Deleytar, *v. a. to delight*
Deleyte, *s. m. delight; pleasure*
Deleytosamente, *adv. delightfully* [*ful*
Deleytoso, sa, *a. delight-*
Deleznable, *a.* 2. *slippery*
Deleznadero, *s. m. a slippery place* [*ping*
Deleznamiento, *s m. slip-*
Deleznarse, *v. r. to slip*
Delfa, *s. f. the rose-laurel*
Delfin, *s. m. dolphin*
Delfinio, *s. m. a purple-coloured flower*
Delgadamente, *adv. slenderly* || *ingeniously*
Delgadeza, *s. f. thinness; slenderness* || *delicacy of wit*
Delgadito, ta, *a. dim. de* Delgado
Delgado, da, *a. thin; slender* || *subtil; ingenious*
Deliberacion, *s. f. deliberation* || *emancipation*
Deliberadamente, *adver. deliberately* [*rer*
Deliberador, *s. m. delive-*
Deliberamiento, *s. m. delivery*
Deliberar, *v. a. y n. to deliberate* || *to emancipate* [*berative*
Deliberativo, va, *a. deli-*
Delicadamente, *adv. delicately*
Delicadez, *s. f. delicacy*
Delicadeza, *s. f. delicacy* || *slenderness*
Delicado, da, *a. delicate* || *nice* || *slender*
Delicia, *s. f. delight*
Deliciarse, *v. r. to delight*
Deliciosamente, *adv. deliciously*

Delicioso, sa, *a. delicious*
Delineacion, *s. f. delineation*
Delineamento, } *s. m. delineation* || *a laying out by a line*
Delineamiento, }
Delinear, *v. a. to delineate* || *to lay out by a line*
Delinquente, *s. m. a delinquent*
Delinquimiento, *s. m. delinquency*
Delinquir, *v. n. to commit a crime*
Deliñar, *v. a. to adorn; to dress*
Deliquio, *s. m. deliquium*
Deliramento, *s. m. Voy.* Delirio
Delirar, *v. n. to delirate*
Delirio, *s. m. delirium*
Delito, *subs. m. crime; offence* [*idol*
Delubro, *s. m. temple* ||
Delusor, *s. m. deluder*
Demanda, *s. f. demand* || *a gathering* || *search; perquisition* || *enterprise*
Demandadera, *s. f. a maid the nuns keep out of the monastery*
Demandadero, *s. m. one that goes about begging for pious uses*
Demandador, *sub. m. one who makes a gathering* || *a demandant*
Demandar, *v. a. to demand* || *to ask* || *to require* || *to rob*
Demanial, *a.* 2. *proceeding*
Demarcacion, *s. f. the marking out* [*out*
Demarcar, *v. a. to mark*
Demas, *adv. besides; moreover* [remainder
Demas, *s. m.* overplus;

Demas, *a. p*
Demasía, *s. abundan* || *superfl wrong* || *rashness*
Demasiadam *cessively*
Demasiado, *sive* || *sup dacious*
Demasiado, || *too mu*
Demediar, *into halv*
Demencia,
Dementar, *tate*
Demente, *a*
Demérito,
Demision, *sion; hu*
Demo, *s. m*
Democracia *cracy*
Democratic *mocratic*
Demoler, *v.*
Demolicion *tion*
Demoniaco, *niack* || *d*
Demonichu *ugly dem*
Demonio, *s*
Demora, *s.*
Demorar, *v to stay*
Demostrable
Demostracio *monstrati*
Demostrado *monstrat*
Demostrar, *monstrat*
Demostrativ *monstrati*
Demudacion *ging; al*

r, *v. a. to change;* *er*

rse, *v. r. to change* *enance*

, *s. m. denarius* || *nth in number* || *in numeration* || *alary for a day's*

adv. V. Desde

cion, *s. f. denial*

r, *v. a. to deny*

cer, *v. a. to de-* *te*

ido da, *a. belon-* *to the negros*

ir, *v. a. to deni-* || *to asperse*

a, *s. f. V.* Denguera

, *s. m. coyness;* *ning* || *a very short* *elet*

ra, *subs. f. a coy,* *woman*

ar, *v. a to asperse*

ativo, va, *a. defa-* *ry*

do, da, *a. bold*

damente, *adv. bol-*

inacion, *s. f. deno-* *tion* [*minator*

inador, *s. m. deno-*

inar, *v. a. to de-* *inate*

ar, *v. a. to call* *names*

r, *v. a. to denote* *explain*

iente, *adv. thickly*

, *v. a. to condense*

ad, *s. f. density*

, sa, *a. dense*

o, da, *a. dented;* *hed* [*of teeth*

lura, *s. f. the set*

, *s. m. the beam of* *plough* || *a great*

Dentar, *v. act. to make teeth to any thing* || *to sharpen teeth.*

Dentecer, *v. n. to breed teeth; to teeth*

Dentellada, *s. f. chattering of the teeth* || *bite*

Dentellado, da, *a. jagged*

Dentellar, *v. n. to chatter with teeth*

Dentellones, *subs. m. pl. denticles*

Dentera, *sub. f. a setting on edge*

Dar dentera, *to set the teeth on edge*

Dentezuelo, *s. m. a little tooth*

Denticular, *a.* 2. *in the shape of teeth*

Dentivano, na, *a. having teeth long and broad, and some of them hollow*

Denton, na, *a. that has great teeth*

Denton, *s. m. a sea-bream*

Dentro, *adv. within*

Dentuda, *s. f. a sort of sea-fish*

Dentudo, da, *a. that has great teeth*

Denuedo, *s. m. boldness*

Denuesto, *s. m. affront; reproach* [*ciation*

Denunciacion, *s. f. denun-*

Denunciador, *s. m. denouncer*

Denunciar, *v. a. to denounce* || *to warn* || *to foretell*

Denunciatorio, ria, *a. belonging to a denunciation* [*God*

Deo gracias, *thanks to*

Deparar, *v. act. to give, offer* or *send*

Departidamente, *adv. distinctly*

Departimiento, *s. m. division; separation*

Departir, *v. a. to distinguish* || *to define*

Departir, *v. n. to discourse* || *to debate*

Depauperar, *v. a. to impoverish* || *to weaken*

Dependencia, *s. f. dependence* || *affair; business*

Depender, *v. n. to depend*

Deplorable, *a.* 2. *deplorable*

Deplorar, *v. a. to deplore*

Deponente, *a. m. deponent*

Deponer, *v. a. to depose* || *to lay down* || *to deposite*

Deportacion, *s. f. transportation* [*port*

Deportar, *v. a. to trans-*

Deportarse, *v. r. to walk; to divert one's self*

Deporte, *s. m. diversion; pastime*

Deposicion, *s. f. deposition; deposing*

Depositador, *sub. m. one who deposites*

Depositar, *v. a. to deposite*

Depositaría, *s. f. depositum* [*tary*

Depositario, *s. m. deposi-*

Depósito, *s. m. deposite; depositum* || *grave, sepulchre* [*vation*

Depravacion, *s. f. depra-*

Depravadamente, *adver. corruptly*

Depravado, da, *a. depraved* [*ter*

Depravador, *s. m. corrupter*

Depravar, *v. a. to deprave*

Deprecacion, *s. f. deprecation* [*cate*

Deprecar, *v. a.* to depre-

Deprecativo, va, *a.* deprecative

Depreuder, *v. a. to learn*
Depresion, *s. f. depression*
Depresor, *s. m. depressor*
Depretericion, *sub. f. V.* Pretericion
Deprimir, *v. a. to depress*
Depurar, *v. a. to depurate*
Deputar, *v. a. V.* Diputar
Derechamente, *adv. directly* || *rightly* || *prudently*
Derechero, *s. m. a receiver of the duties*
Derechez, *s. f. uprightness*
Derecho, cha, *a. right*. A'derechas, *to the purpose; well* — á la derecha, *on the right hand* — á las derechas, *uprightly*
Derecho, *subs. m. law* || *equity; right* || *claim* || *the right side of a stuff*
Derechos, *plur. duties, taxes, etc.*
Derechura *s. f. rightness*
Derivacion, *s. f. derivation* [*rive*
Derivar, *v. a. y n. to de-*
Derivativo, va, *a. derivative*
Derogacion, *s. f. derogation* || *deterioration; diminution*
Derogar, *v. a. to derogate* || *to lessen; to take from* [*rogatory*
Derogatorio, ria, *a. de-*
Derrabadura, *s. f. the acting off the tail*
Derrabar, *v. a. to cut off the tail*
Derrama *s. f. repartition; assessment*
Derramadamente, *adv. profusely*
Derramador, *s. m. a prodigal man*

Derramamiento, *subs. m. effusion* || *profusion*
Derramar, *v. a. to divide; to assess* || *to shed; to pour out* || *to scatter* || *to discharge* or *disembogue* || *to dissipate to waste*
Derramo, *s. m. dissipation; wasting* || *the chamfering of a door, etc.*
Derranchar, *v. n. to quit one's rank*
Derredor (al *ó* en), *adv. about; round*
Derrenegar, *v. a. to abhor*
Derrengada, *s. f. a certain contorsion, in dancing*
Derrengado, da, *a. crooked*
Derrengadura, *s. f. breaking the back*
Derrengar, *v. a. to break the back*
Derreniego, *s. m. abhorrence* [*melting*
Derretimiento, *sub. m. a*
Derretir, *v. a. to melt*
Derribar, *v. a. to demolish; to throw down*
Derribar el caballo, *to make a horse supple* || la capa, *to throw the cloak off the shoulders*
Derribo, *s. m. demolition — rubbish*
Derrocar, *v. a. to throw down*
Derrocar, *v. n. to fall; to tumble*
Derrostrarse, *v. r. to hurt one's self on the face*
Derrota, *s. f. the course of a ship* || *road; way* || *rout*
Derrotar, *v. a. to drive to leeward* || to ruin; to undo || to rout or defeat

Derrotar, *v. n.*
sordered, etc
Derrotero, *s. m*
Derruir, *v. a. to*
Derrumbadero,
cipice
Derrumbamien
throwing or fa
long
Derrumbar, *v.*
cipitate || *to*
of light
Derruviar, *v. a*
mine
Desabarrancar,
take out of t
Desabastecer, *v*
ry off the pro
leave withou
Desabollar, *v.*
bruises out o
Desabono, *s. m*
Desabor, *s. m.*
|| *distaste*
Desabotonar, *v.*
botton || *to*
open
Desabridament
Desabrido, da,
Desabrigado, d
heltered
Desabrigar, *v.*
Desabrigo, *s.*
ness
Desabrimiento,
savouriness ||
|| *trouble; v*
Desabrir, *v. n.*
voury || *to d*
offend
Desabrochar, *v*
clasp
Desabrocharse,
blow; to op
Desacabalar, *v.*
cabalar [
Desacalorarse,
Desacatadamen
disrespectfu

', da, a. disres- [respect
iento, s. m. dis-
v. a. to disres-
s. m. disrespect
', v. a. to tem-
e sourness
amente , adv.
edly
o, da, a. unad-
, v. a. to err; to
, s. m. mistake
lar, v. a. to en-
, v. a. to open
t the root
adamente , ad.
iently
ado, da, adj.
the necessary
ncies || without
ent or place
ar, v. a. to in-
arse , v. r. to
's employment
fiamiento, s. m.
company
fiar, v. act. to
ne.
ado, da, adjec.
d [suade
ar, v. a. to dis-
damente, adv.
erately
, v. a. to un-
se, v. r. to for-
disagree
a. 2. out of
r, v. a. to take
of the fold ||
den
rradamente ,
customedly

Desacostumbrado, da, a. unusual

Desacostumbrar, v. a. to wean from a custom

Desacotar, v. a. to take away the inclosures || to permit || to suppress a tax || to break off a bargain

Desacoto, s. m. taking off the prohibition, etc.

Desacreditar, v. a. to discredit

Desacuerdo, s. m. forgetfulness || the loss of one's witts || mistake

Desaderezar, v. a. to undress

Desadeudar, v. a. to free from debt

Desadorar, v. a. to leave off the love

Desadormecer, v. act. to awake || to quicken

Desadornar, v. a. to strip of ornaments

Desadorno, s. m. want of ornaments, etc.

Desadvertidamente, adv. inadvertently

Desadvertido, da, a. inconsiderate

Desadvertimiento, s. m. inadvertency

Desadvertir, v. a. to act inconsiderately

Desafear, v. a. to make ugly

Desafectacion, s. f. reserve; moderation

Desafecto, s. m. disaffection [ted

Desafecto, ta, a. disafec-

Desaferrar, v. a. to weigh anchor || to unhook || to dissuade

Desafiadero, s. m. the place appointed for a challenge

Desafiador, s. m. a challenger

Desafiar, v. a. to challenge

Desaficion, s. disaffection

Desaficionar, v. a. to disaffect

Desafinar, v. n. to go out of tune

Desafio, s. m. a challenge

Desaforadamente, adv. disorderly || excessively || impudently

Desaforado, da, a. rash; impudent || excessive

Desaforar, v. a. to deprive of the privileges

Desaforrar, v. a. to unline

Desafortunado, da, a. unhappy [injury

Desafuero, s. m. wrong;

Desagarrar, v. a. to loosen; to untie

Desagraciar, v. a. to make ugly [pleasant

Desagradable, a. 2. unpleasant

Desagradablemente, adv. unpleasantly

Desagradar, v. a. to displease

Desagradecer, v. a. to be unthankful [grateful

Desagradecido, da, a. un-

Desagradecimiento, s. m. ingratitude

Desagrado, s. m. roughness || disgust; trouble

Desagraviar, v. a. to redress wrongs

Desagravio, s. m. righting of wrongs [nite

Desagregar, v. a. to disu-

Desaguadero, s. m. drain, channel, gutter, etc. || occasion of expence

Desaguar, v. a. to draw off water

Desague, s. m. V. Desaguadero

Desaguisado, *s. m. disgust; wrong, injury*
Desahijar, *v. a. to wean*
Desahogadamente, *adver. freely; clearly* || *impudently*
Desahogado, da, *a. impudent* || *lewd*
Desahogar, *v. a. to ease; to relieve*
Desahogarse, *v. r. to unload one's heart*
Desahogo, *s. m. ease; relief* || *enlarging; widening* || *impudence*
Desahuciadamente, *adv. desperately*
Desahuciar, *v. a. to give* or *have no hopes* || *to dismiss from a pasture*
Desahucio, *s. m. dismission from a pasture*
Desahumar, *v. a. to free from smoke*
Desajustar, *v. a. to discompose*
Desajustarse, *v. r. to break off a treaty, etc.*
Desalabar, *v. a. to dispraise*
Desalabear, *ver. act. to make straight a warped board, etc.*
Desalar, *v. a. to cut off the wings* || *to unsalt*
Desalarse, *v. r. to run with open arms*
Desalbardar, *v. a. to take off the pack-saddle*
Desalentar, *v. a. to put out of breath* || *to discourage*
Desalforjar, *v. a. to take off a wallet*
Desalforjarse, *v. r. to let the clothes hang loose*
Desaliento, *s. m. decay of spirits* or *courage*
Desaliñadamente, *adver. slovenly; ungenteelly*
Desaliñar, *v. a. to disorder; to discompose*
Desaliño, *s. m. slovenliness; ungenteelness*
Desaliños, *pl. a sort of ear-bobs*
Desalmadamente, *adv. impiously*, or *cruelly*
Desalmado, da, *a. impious* || *inhuman, etc.*
Desalmamiento, *subs. m. want of conscience*
Desalmar, *v. a. to kill* || *to unbosom one's self*
Desalojar, *v. a. to dislodge*
Desalojar, *v. n. to go from one's lodging*
Desalumbradamente, *adv. blindly*
Desalumbramiento, *s. m. blindness*
Desamable, *a, 2. unworthy of love*
Desamar, *v. a to hate*
Desamarrar, *v. a. to unbind; to unmoor*
Desamistarse, *v. r. to break off friendship*
Desamoldar, *v. a. to defigure the form of the mould*
Desamor, *s. m. hatred; aversion*
Desamoradamente, *adver. roughly; disdainfully*
Desamorado, da, *a. rough; disdainful, etc.*
Desamoroso, sa, *a. disaffectionate*
Desamorrar, *v. a. to bid one lift up the head*
Desamotinarse, *v. r. to renounce sedition*
Desamparador, *s. m. forsaker*
Desamparar, *v. a. to forsake*
Desamparo, *s. m.* distress; *abandonment*
Desancorar, *v.* ... *anchor*
Desandar, *v. a* ...
Desandrajado, ... *tered*
Desangrar, *v.* ...
Desanidar, *v.* ... *the nest*
Desanidar, *v. a.* ...
Desanimar, *v.* ... *one's life* || ... *mate* [...
Desanudar, *v.* ...
Desapacibilida... *roughness;* ...
Desapacible, *a* ... *sharp*
Desapacibleme...
Desaparear, *v* ... *match*
Desaparecer, ... *away from* ...
Desaparecer, ...
Desaparecerse, ...
Desaparecimie... *disappearin...*
Desaparejar, ... *off the pack...*
Desaparroquia... *change one* ... *merchant*
Desapartar, *v.* ...
Desapasionada... *without pa...*
Desapasionar, ... *out a passio...*
Desapegar, *v.* ...
Desapego, *s.* ... *gement* || *di...* *ness*
Desapercebida... *unprovided...*
Desapercebido ... *provided*
Desapercebimi... *want; penu...*
Desapestar, *v* ... from infec...

mente, *adver.*
ally
, da, *a. mer-*

v. a. to untie;
[*plication*
n, *s. f. inap-*
, da, *adj. un-*
careless
lamente, *adv.*
sly
lo, da, *furious;*
excessive
niento, *s. m.*
ned audaci-
.
, *v. a. to dis-*
to turn away

, *v. a. to clear*
the
r, *v. a. to turn*
lodging
nar, *v. a. to*
s
v. a. to take
support
, *v. a. to un-*

r, *v. a. to forget*
, *v. a. to take*
gloss
se, *v. r. to slip*
ck out of the

v. a. to loosen
ar, *v. a. to de-*
of prison
ion, *s. f. di-*
tion
, *v. a. to disa-*
[*divesture*
niento, *s. m.*
rse, *v. r. to di-*
's self
, *s. m. giving*
own property
badamente, *ad.*
bly

Desaprovechado, da, *adj. fruitless* || *that makes not progress*
Desaprovechamiento, *s. m. want of progress*
Desaprovechar, *ver. a. to put to not use*
Desaprovechar, *ver. a. to make not progress*
Desapuntalar, *v. a. to take down the props*
Desapuntar, *ver. a. to unsew* || *to un cock a gun, etc.* [*mast*
Desarbolar, *v. a. to dis-*
Desarenar, *v. a. to clear from sand*
Desareno, *s. m. clearing from sand*
Desarmar, *v. a. to disarm* || *to uncock a gun* || *to unstock, etc.*
Desarraygar, *v. a. to root up* || *to banish*
Desarrebozar, *v. a. to un mufle* [*fold*
Desarrebujar, *v. a. to un*
Desarrimar, *v. a. to remove* || *to dissuade*
Desarrimo, *s. m. want of support* [*roll*
Desarrollar, *v. a. to un-*
Desarropar, *v. a. to pull off the clothes, etc.*
Desarrugardura, *s. f. unrumpling*
Desarrugar, *v. a. to unrumple*
Desasado, da, *a. without handles*
Desaseadamente, *a. without ornament, etc.*
Desasear, *v. a. to take off the ornaments, etc.*
Desasentarse, *v. r. to rise; to get up*
Desaseo, *s. m. want of ornament, etc.*
Desasimiento, *s. m. disseizing* || *disinterestedness*
Desasir, *v. a. to loosen; to let go hold*
Desasirse, *v. r. to disseize*
Desasnar, *v. a. to rob an ass* || *to teach wit*
Desasociable, *a. 2. unsociable*
Desasosegadamente, *adv. unquietly*
Desasosegar, *v. a. to disquiet; to trouble*
Desasosiego, *sub. m. unquietness*
Desastradamente, *adv. unfortunately*
Desastrado, da, *a. unfortunate*
Desastre, *s. m. disaster*
Desatacar, *v. a. to untie* || *to unload a gun*
Desatadamente, *adv. disjointly* [*unties*
Desatador, *s. m. one who*
Desatadura, *s. f. untying*
Desatamiento, *s. m. untying* || *dissolution*
Desatancar, *v. a. to clean a canal, etc.*
Desatapadura, *s. f. uncovering* [*ver*
Desatapar, *v. a. to unco-*
Desatar, *v. a. to untie* || *to dissolve* || *to undo* || *to disunite* [*resolve*
Desatar la duda, etc. *to*
Desatascar, *v. a. to take out of the mire*
Desataviar, *v. a. to take off the ornament*
Desatavio, *s. m. want of ornament, etc.*
Desatencion, *s. f. want of attention* || *disregard*
Desatender, *v. a. to be inattentive* || *to despise*
Desatentadamente, *adv. unadvisedly*

considerate [*civilly*
Desatentamente, *adv. un*
Desatentar, *v. a. to trouble the mind*
Desatento, ta, *adj. inattentive* || *uncivil*
Desatesado, da, *a. feeble*
Desatiento, *s. m. alienation of mind*
Desatinadamente, *ad. madly* || *excessively* || *obstinately* [*sive*
Desatinado, da, *a. exces*
Desatinar, *v. a. to make mad* || *to put out; to confound* || *to rave; to dote* || *to totter*
Desatino, *s. m. tottering* || *extravagance*
Desatollar, *v. a. to take out of the mire*
Desatolondrarse, *v. r. to come to one s self*
Desatraer, *v. a. to separate; to remove*
Desatraillar, *v. a. to uncouple dogs*
Desatrampar, *to cleanse a pipe* [*bolt*
Desatrancar, *v. a. to un-*
Desatravesar, *v. a. to remove from lying across*
Desatufarse, *v. r. to appease one's anger*
Desaturdir, *v. a. to get one out of stunning*
Desautoridad, *s. f. want of authority*
Desautorizar, *v. a. to disauthorise*
Desavahar, *v. a. to open; to uncover*
Desavaharse, *v. r. to divert one's self*
Desavecindado, da, *a. left by the inhabitants*
Desavecindarse, *v. r. to go from one's lodging*

Desavenido, da, *a. disagreeing* [*gree*
Desavenir, *v. a. to disa-*
Desaventajadamente, *adv. disadvantageously*
Desaventajado, da, *adj. disadvantageous*
Desaviar, *v. a. to lead out of the way*
Desavió, *s. m. straying* || *want of any thing necessary* [*vised*
Desavisado, da, *a. unad-*
Desavisar, *v. a. to send an advice contrary to the first*
Desaynar, *v. a. to scour* || *to extenuate* || *to waste; to spend away*
Desayradamente, *adv. without elegance*
Desayrado, da, *a. ill rewarded* || *awkward; inelegant, etc.*
Desayrar, *v. a. to despise*
Desayre, *sub. m. scorn; contempt* || *inelegance*
Desayudar, *v. a. to disserve* [*fast*
Desayunarse, *v. r. to break*
Desayuno, *s. m. breakfast*
Desazogar, *v. a. to take away the quick silver*
Desazon, *s. m. sharpness of an unripe fruit* || *disgust* || *illness*
Desazonado, da, *a. hard to be pleased* || *distempered*
Desazonar, *v. a. to make unsavory* || *to disgust*
Desbabar, *v. n. to slabber*
Desbalijar, *v. a. to rob; to strip*
Desballestar, *v. a. to unbend a cross-bow*
Desbancar, *v. a. to take away the benches* || *to*

of the l
Desbandar
from on
Desbaratac
disordr
Desbaratac
*lewd; *
Desbaratar
down ||
waste
Desbaratar
Desbaratar
found o
Desbarato
Desbarato
defeat ||
Desbarbar
the bea
quills,
Desbarrar
to fall
sense
Desbarreta
away th
Desbarriga
paunch
Desbarro,
fall
Desbastadu
ning, et
Desbastar,
to polish
Desbautiza
curse th
Desbeber,
Desblanque
whitish
Desbocar,
the gulle
Desbocarse
on the b
Desbombar
Desbonetar
one's ca
Desbordar,
flow
Desbozar,
a relie

dj. [illegible]wi-
ies
a. to ta[illegible]
. r. to ex-
ss
a. to hash;
a. to take
dust, etc.
s. to unbo-
lf; to tat-
a. to make
|| to bate
n. to alight
. a. to dis-
nnon
la, a. dishe-
l-strong ||
v. a. to un-
[brained
a, a. hare-
. to behead
the top || to
ficulties ||
sueño, to
ver. r. to
[the hips
a. to break
s. to decay
, a. feeble;
, sub. m.
meanness
V. Decaer
sub. mas.
niento
, ver. r. to
brains
, sub. f. a
uise on the
. to break

the head || to wound one's reputation || to publish the bans of matrimony

[illegible]labro, *sub. m. loss;* [illegible]*rtune* [*tear*

Des[illegible]rajar, *v. a. to*

Descalc[illegible], *s. f. nakedness of the feet* [*cool*

Descalorarse, *v. r. to grow*

Descalzar, *v. a. to pull off one's shoes* or *stockings*

Descalzarse de risa, *to break one's side with laughing*

Descalzo, za, *adj. barefooted*

Descaminar, *v. a. to put out of the way || to seize contraband*

Descamino, *s. m. straying || seizure of prohibited goods* [*cessitous*

Descamisado, da, *adj. ne-*

Descampado, da, *a. open; plain*

Descansadamente, *adver. easily; quietly*

Descansadero, *sub. m. a resting-place*

Descansado, da, *a. easy; quiet*

Vivir descansado, *to live at one's ease*

Descansar, *v. n. to rest*

Descanso, *sub. m. rest; quiet; repose || a landing place*

Descantillar, *v. a. to break the corners || to curtail; diminish*

Descañonar, *v. a. to pick,* or *plume || to fleece*

Descapar, *v. a. to rob the cloak*

Descaperuzarse, *v. r. to pull off one's hat*

Descaperuzo, *s. m. pulling off the hat*

Descapillar, *v. a. to take off the cowl*

Descapirotar, *v. a. to unhood* [*pudently*

Descaradamente, *adv. im-*

Descararse, *v. r. to grow impudent*

Descarga, *s. f. unloading || discharge; shooting*

Descargadero, *s. m. the place where goods are unladen*

Descargadura, *sub. f. unboning*

Descargar, *v. a. to unload; to unbone || to discharge; to shoot*

Descargarse, *v. r. to clear one's self from a crime*

Descargo, *s. m. unloading || discharge*

Descariñarse, *v. r. to withdraw affection,* or *esteem*

Descariño, *s. m. the withdrawing affection*

Descarnador, *s. m. a fleam*

Descarnár, *v. a. to pick off the flash*

Descaro, *s. m. impudence*

Descarriamiento, *sub. m. straying*

Descarriar, *v. a. to put out of the way*

Descarrilladura, *s. f. tearing of the jaws*

Descarrillar, *v. a. to tear away the jaws*

Descartar, *v. a. to lay out (at cards) || to discard || to cashïer* [*ne*

Descartarse, *v. r. to decli-*

Descarte, *s. m. discarded cards || excuse*

Descasar, *v. a. to unmarry*

Descascar, *v. a. V.* Descascarar

Descascarse, *v. r.* to break

Descascarar, *v. a.* to shell || to pare; to peel

Descascararse, *v. r. to peel off; to scale*
Descendencia, *s. f. descent*
Descendente, *adj. 2. V.* Descendiente
Descender, *v. n. to descend*
Descender, *v. a. to take* or *bring down*
Descendida, *s. f. descent*
Descendiente, *a. y s. 2. descendant*
Descendimiento, *s. m. taking down*
Descension, *s. f. descension* [*sional*
Descensional, *a. 2. descen-*
Descenso, *s. m. descent; going down* || *declivity* || *decay* [*landing*
Descenta, *s. f. descent;*
Desceñir, *v. a. to ungird*
Descepar, *v. a. to root up* || *to pull down*
Descercado, da, *adj. open*
Descercador, *s. m. one that raises a siege*
Descercar, *v. a. to raise a siege* || *to dismantle, etc.*
Descereo, *s. m. raising of a siege*
Descerrajar, *v. a. to take away the lock*
Descervigar, *v. a. to wring one's neck*
Descetranar, *v. a. to eat,* or *gnaw the wood*
Deschrismar, Deschristianar, *v. a. to raise into a violent passion*
Descifrador, *s. m. a decipherer* [*pher*
Descifrar, *v. a. to deci-*
Descimentar, *v. a. to pull down*
Desclavar, *v. a. to unnail*
Descoagular, *v. a. to make liquid* [*vering*
Descobertura, s. f. unco-
Descobijar, v. a. to uncover || *to reveal* || *to undress* or *strip*
Descocadamente, *adv. impudently*
Descocar, *v. a. to clear of caterpillars*
Descocarse, *v. r. to speak impudently*
Descocer, *v. a. to digest food*
Descoco, *s. m. impudence*
Descoger, *s. m. to unfold,* or *un roll*
Descogotado, da, *adj. who has a very short neck*
Descogotar, *v. a. to kill with a blow on the neck* || *to cut off the horns of a deer*
Descolar, *v. a. to cut off the tail* [*cable*
Descolchar, *v. a. to undo a*
Descolgar, *v. a. to unhang*
Descolgarse, *v. r. to slip down by a rope*
Descoligado, da, *a. breaking off an alliance*
Descolladamente, *ad. boldily; haughtily*
Descollar, *v. n.* } *to over-*
Descollarse, *v. r.* } *top* || *to surpass* or *excel*
Descolmar, *v. a. to take away the over-measure*
Descolmillar, *v. a. to pull out the tusks*
Descoloramiento, *s. m. discolouring*
Descolorar, *v. a. to discolour* [*pale*
Descolorido, da, *a. wan;*
Descolorimiento, *s. m. paleness* [*lour*
Descolorir, *v. a. to disco-*
Descombrar, *v. a. to lay open; to cleanse*
Descomedidamente, *adv. uncivilly*
Descomedido, da, *a. un-civil* || *huge*
Descomedimien[...] *unmannerli[...]*
Descomedirse, [...] or *speak un[...]*
Descomer, *v. a[...] rate the bell[...]*
Descomimiento [...] *feigned disd[...]*
Descomodado, [...] *convenient*
Descomodidad, [...] *venience*
Descompadrar, [...] *out with on[...]*
Descompasadan[...] *excessively*
Descompasado, [...]
Descompasarse [...] *out of meas[...]*
Descomponer, [...] *compose* || *to [...] riance*
Descomponerse [...] *fly into a p[...]*
Descomposicio[...] *sorder*
Descompostura [...] *composure* | [...] *ce* || *indecen[...]*
Descompuestan[...] *uncivilly* || *i[...]*
Descompuesto, [...] *pudent*
Descomulgar, [...] colmugar
Descomunal, [...] *measurable*
Descomunalme[...] *unmeasurab[...]*
Descomunion, [...] *munication*
Desconcertadar[...] *disorderly*
Desconcertado, [...] *glectful*
Desconcertar, [...] *sorder* || *to* [...]
Desconcertar[...]

ι.*f. discord*
ıte, *ad. dis-*
lla, *a. dim.*
do
a , *a.*
.f.
n. to mis-
[sagree
v. n. to di-
a. 2. disa-
equal
l, *s.f. dis-*
|| *unequa-*
a. not to
rget one's
tc. || *to be*
ι, *a. ungra-*
nbling
to, *s. m. im*
ı. *n. not to*
to dissent
, da, *a. in-*
, *s. f. dis-*
ente , *adv.*
da, *a. sor-*
rvous
. *a. to dis-*
m. discom-
ess through
ishment
to discount

, *s. m.*
, *v. a. to dis-*
content [*tent*
Descontento, *s. m. discon-*
Descontento, ta, *adj. dis-*
contented
Descontinuar, *v. a. to dis-*
continue
a. 2. that
will not agree
Desconveniencia, *s. f. dis-*
convenience || *inconve-*
niency || *discord*
Desconvenir, *v. n. to dis-*
, *a. 2. un-*
tractable
Desconversar, *v. n. to shun*
the society
Descorazonar, *v.*
out the heart |
courage
Descorchador, *s. m. one*
that takes off the cork
Descorchar, *v. a. to pull*
off the cork or *bark*
Descorderar, *v. a. to wean*
lambs
Descornar, *v. a. to break*
the horns
Descorregido, da, *a. in-*
corrigible
Descortes, *a. 2. discour-*
teous [*tesy*
Descortesía, *s. f. discour-*
Descorteamente *adv. dis-*
courteously
Descortezador *s. m. one*
that takes off the bark
Descortezadura, *s. decor-*
tication
Descortezar, *v. a. to take*
off the bark [*sewing*
Descosedura, *subs. f. un-*
Descoser, *v. a. to unsew;*
to rip up

Descosidamente, *adv. im-*
moderately
Descostillar, *v. a. to break*
the ribs
Descostrar, *v. a. to cut*
disuse
s. m.
Descoyuntar, *v. a. to dis-*
locate, to disjoint || *to*
, *to*
th
se [*crease*
Descrecimiento, *s. m. de-*
Descrédito, *s. m. discredit*
v. a. to
weaken;
to emaciate
Describir, *v. a. to describe*
Descripcion, *s. f. descrip-*
tion
Descriptivo, va, *adj. des-*
cribing
Descripto, ta, *a. described*
Descruzar, *v. a. to uncross*
Descuajar, *v. a. to make*
liquid || *to disanimate*
Descubiertamente, *adv.*
very || *the remainder of*
an account
Descubridero, *s. m. a ri-*
sing piece of ground;
a turret, etc.
Descubridor, *s. m. a dis-*
. dis-
covery
Descubrir, *v. a. to unco-*

Descuidadamente, ad. carelessly
Descuidado, da, adj. neglectful; careless
Descuidar, v. n. to neglect; to be careless
Descuidar, v. a. to help; to ease
Descuidarse, v. r. to forget one's self
Descuido, s. m. negligence; carelessness || forgetfulness; inadvertency || unmannerliness
Descular, v. a. to break the bottom
Descumplir, v. a. to fail in one's duty
Desdar, v. a. to give back
Desde, prep. from || since
Desdecir, v. a. to disown
Desdecir, v. n. to degenerate || to differ || to decay || to lean, or bow down
Desdecirse, v. r. to unsay; to recant
Desden, s. m. disdain; scorn
Desdentar, v. a. to draw the teeth
Desdeñable, adj. 2. contemptible
Desdeñadamente, ad. disdainfully
Desdeñador, ra, sub. one that disdains
Desdeñar, v. a to disdain; to scorn
Desdeñarse, v. r. to scorn
Desdeño, s. m. disdain
Desdesoñamente, adv. disdainfully [ful
Desdeñoso, sa, a. disdain-
Desdevanar, v. a. to unwind silk, etc.
Desdicha, s. f. misfortune
Desdichadamente, ad. unfortunately
Desdichadico, illo, adj. dim. de Desdichado
Desdichado, da, adj. unfortunate
Desdoblar, v. a. to unfold
Desdon, s. m. clownishness [nishly
Desdonadamente, ad. clow-
Desdonado, da, adj. clownish; unpleasant
Desdonar, v. act. to take back what was given
Desdorar, v. a. to ungild || to blemish
Desdormido, da, a. lying awake
Desdoro, s. m. blemish
Deseable, a. 2. desirable
Deseador, s. m. he who desires
Desear, v. a. to desire
Desecar, v. a. to dry up
Desecativo, va, adj. desicative
Desechar, v. a. to despise; to reject
Desecho, s. m. out-cast; trash, etc.
Desedificacion, s. f. demolishing || scandal
Desedificar, v. a. to demolish [titute
Deseguida, s. f. a pros-
Desellar, v. a. to unseal
Desembanastar, v. a. to take out of a basket || to talk inconsiderately
Desembarazadamente, ad. freely
Desembarazado, da, a. free
Desembarazar, v. act. to disencumber || to clear; to free
Desembarazo, s. m. clearness || casiness; freedom
Desembarcacion, s. f. landing
Desembarcadero, s. m. a landing place
Desembarcar, ... sembark
Desembarcar, ... || to alight
Desembarco, s. ...
Desembargar, ... off an em... clear or fr...
Desembargo, ... off the emb...
Desembarrar, ... cleanse a ...
Desembaular, ... out of a che...
Desembeber, ... v. n.
Desembebeerse, v. r.
Desembelesarse, v. r.
Desembocader... mouth of a ...
Desembocar, ... sembogue
Desembolsar, ... burse
Desembolso, s...
Desemborrach... remove dru...
Desemboscarse ... out of a wo...
Desembozar, ... muffle || to ...
Desembozo, s. ... fling || liber...
Desembravece... tame
Desembravecir... m. making tame
Desembrazar, ...
Desembriagars... sleep one's ...
Desembuchar, ... out of the m...
Desembudar, v... out trough a...
Desemejable, ...
Desemejante ...

ejanza, s. f. unlike- [guise

ejar, v. a. to dis-

acarse, v. r. to ap- s one's self

acharse, v. r. to ta- urage

pacho, s. m. daring- ; confidence

padrar, v. a. to de- e of a father

palagar, v. a. to ta- way loathing

pañar, v. a. to uns- ke and dress a child o clear a looking- s

papelar, v. a. to un- any thing covered h paper

parejar, v. a. to re- ve from joining to ther

parvar, v. a. to ga- in heap the trashed s

patar, v. a. to make qual || to facilitate

pedrador, s. m. one unpaves

pedrar, v. a. to un- e

pegar, v. a. to take the pitch

peñar, v. a. to fetch of pawn || to clear m debts || to perfom 's promise, etc.

peño, s. m. r. dee- g out of pawn || pay- t of a debt || perfor- nce

peorarse, ver. r. to w better

perezar, v. a. to sha- off sloth

polvorar, v. a. to an from dust

ponzoñar, v. act. to heal one that is poisoned || to expel any violent passion

Desempotrar, v. a. to take off the props, etc.

Desempulgadura, s. f. unbending

Desempulgar, v. a. to unbend a cross-bow

Desenalbardar, v. act. to pull off the pack-saddle

Desenamorar, v. a. to extinguish the love

Desenamorarse, v. r. to desist; to leave off

Desencabalgar, v. a. to dismount the cannon

Desencabestrar, v. a. to unhalter; to disentangle [chain

Desencadenar, v. a. to un-

Desencalabrinar, v. a. to settle the head

Desencalcar, v. a. to loosen

Desencallar, v a. to bring a ship a float

Desencaminar, v. a. V. Descaminar

Desencantar, v. a. to disenchant

Desencanto, s. m. disenchanting

Desencapotadura, s. f. the taking off a cloak

Desencapotar, v. act. to take off the cloak || to unveil

Desencapotarse, v. r. to clear one's looks from frowns

Desencaprichar, v. act to work one out of his conceit

Desencarcelar, v. a. to free from a prison

Desencarnar, v. a. V. Descarnar [out a castle

Desencastillar, v. a. to beat

Desencaxamiento, s. m. disjointing [joint

Desencaxar, v. a. to dis-

Desencaxonar, v. a. to take out of chest or box

Desencerrar, v. a. to let loose what has been locked up || to reveal or declare

Desincintar, v. a. to unbind, to untie

Desinclavar, v. a. to unnail [peg

Desenclavijar, v. a. to un-

Desincoger, v. a. to extend; to unfold, etc.

Desencogerse, v. r. to lay aside bashfulness

Desincogimiento, sub. m. freedom; easiness

Desincolar, v. a. to unglue

Desencolerizarse, v. r. to appease one's anger

Desenconar, v. a. to take away the rankling of a sore || to appease one's anger

Desencono, s. m. an appeasing of anger

Desencordar, v. a. to unstring [tie

Desencordelar, v. a. to un-

Desencorvar, v. a. to make straight [curl

Desencrespar, v. a. to un-

Desendiablar, v. act. to cast out devils

Desendiablarse, v. r, to lay a side wrath

Desendiosar, v. a. to humble, to pull down the pride

Desendueñarse, v. r. to be free from a dueña

Desenfadado, da, a. gay; merry

Desenfadar, v. a. to appease, or recreate

Desenfado, sub. m. easi-

ness; freedom of behaviour

Desenfaldarse, *ver. r. to untuck one's gown, etc.*

Desenfardelar, *v. a. to unpack*

Desenfrenadamente, *adv. unrulily*

Desenfrenamiento, *s. m unruliness*

Desenfrenar *v. a. to unbridle*

Desenfrenarse *v. r. to grow unruly*

Desenfreno, *s. m. unruliness*

Desenfundar, *v. a. to pull out of the holster, etc.*

Desenfurecerse, *ver. r. to lay aside rage*

Desengañadamente, *adv. ingenuously || wickedly*

Desengañado, da, *a. desabused || bad*

Desengañador, *s. m. who undeceives another*

Desengañar, *v. a. to undeceive*

Desengaño, *s. m. undeceiving || a reproach*

Desengarzar, *v. a. to take off from the string, etc*

Desengastar, *v. a. to take stone out of ring*

Desengrasar, *v. a. to scour*

Desengrosar, *v. a. to make thin and slender*

Desengrudamien *ungluing*

Desengrudar, *glue*

Desenhebrar, *v. a. to unthread || to explain*

Desenjaezar, *v. a. to unharness*

Desenjaular, *v. a. to take out of a cage*

Desenlabonar, *v. a. to unchain*

Desenladrillar, *v. act. to pull off the bricks*

Desenlazar, *v. a. to unlace*

Desenlosar, *v. a. to unpave*

Desenlutar, *v. a. to go out of mourning*

Desenmarañar, *v. act. to disentangle*

Desenmohecer, *v. a. to rub off the rust*

Desenmudecer, *v. act. to make one speak*

Desenmudecer, *v. neu. to cease to be dumb; to speak*

Desenojar, *v. act. to appease the anger*

Desenojo, *s. m. appeasing of anger*

Desenquadernar, *v. a. V.* **Desquadernar**

Desenrazonado, da, *adj unreasonable*

Desenredar, *v. a. to disentangle*

Desenrollar, *v. a. to unroll*

Desensabanar, *v. act. to take off the sheets || to disentangle*

Desensañar, *v. a. to appease the wrath*

Desensartar, *v. a. to unthread*

Desensebar, *v. a. to take away the fat*

Desenseñar, *v. a. to take out of the bosom*

Desenseñar, *v. a. to unteach*

Desensillar, *v. a. to unsaddle*

Desensoberbecerse, *v. r. to lay aside pride*

Desentablar, *v. a. to unboard || to disorder*

Desentender, *v. n.* / **Desentenderse**, *v. r.* } *to feign one's self ignorant*

Desenterrador, *s. m. one who digs out of the ground*

Desenterrar, *v. a. to dig out of the ground*

Desentoldar, *v. a. to* [...] *down a silk*

Desentonadamente, [...] *out of tune*

Desentonamiento, *s.* [...] *being out of tune*

Desentonar, *v. n.* [...]

Desentonarse, *v. r.* [...] *tune || to speak* [...]

Desentono, *s. m.* [...] *out of tune or* [...] *loud*

Desentorpecerse, [...] *to grow supple || to* [...] *wit*

Desentrañar, *v. a.* [...] *bowel || to extric*[...] *affair*

Desentumecer, *v. a.* [...]

Desenvaynar, *v.* [...] *draw out of the* [...] *bard*

Desenviolar, *v. a.* [...] *rify or expiate*

Desenvoltura, *s. f.* [...] *ness; readiness;* [...] *terity, etc. || effr*[...] *|| grace in speak*[...]

Desenvolvedor, *s. m.* [...] *cher*

Desenvolver, *v. a.* [...] *roll || to disentan*[...]

Desenvolverse, *ver.* [...] *grow bold or imp*[...]

Desenvuelta, *s. f.* [...] *man too free with*

Desenvueltamente [...] *boldly; impuden*[...]

Desenxalmar, *v.* [...] *take off the pack*[...]

Deseo, *s. m. desire*

Deseoso, sa, *a. des*[...]

Desequido, da, *a.* [...]

Desercion, *s. f. des*[...]

Desertado, da, *a. st*[...]

Desertar, *v. a. to d*[...]

Desertor, *s. m. a d*[...]

Deservicio, *s. m. d*[...] *vice offence*

. to disserve
, s. } despair || anger ; fury
nto, }
ente , adv.
ly
. act. to put
opes
. n. to des-
v. r. to kill
| to be mad
a. to unmat
m. the ta-
ats
, s. f. dises-
, ra, s. one
ems
. a. to di-
a. to defal-
suade
nto, sub. m.
. n. to faint
r, s. m. one
ves
v. a. to put
ur || to dis-
ejudice, etc.
. to ungird
. a. to disfi-
. a. V. Des-
. m. a defile
. to file off
e , v. r. to
ht
iento, s. m.
ght
a. to purge

Desflocar, *v. a. to ravel out the ends of any thing like fringes*

Desfloramiento, *s. m. defloration*

Desflorar, *v. a. to cut off the flowers || to deflower*

Desfogar, *v. act. to give vent to fire || to vent one's passion*

Desfogonar, *v. a. to spoil the touch-hole of a cannon*

Desfogue, *s. m. vent given to anger, etc.*

Desformar, *v. a. to deform*

Desfortalecer, *v. a. to dismantle*

Desfrenar, *v. a. V.* Desenfrenar

Desfrutar, *v. a. to gather all the fruit || to enjoy*

Desgajadura, *s. f. a tearing*

Desgajar, *v. a. to tear off || to rend*

Desgajarse, *v. r. to break off friendship*

Desgalgar, *v. a. to precipitate*

Desgana, *s. f. loathing of meat || dislike*

Desganarse, *v. r. to lose one's stomach*

Desganchar, *v. a. to lop off the branches*

Desgañifarse, } *v. r. to make one's throat sore by vociferation*
Desgañitarse, }

Desgargamillado, da, *a. weak ; feeble ; without grace, etc.*

Desgargantarse, *v. r. V.* Desgañifarse

Desgargolar, *v. a. to beat the bark out of hemp*

Desgaritarse, *v. r. to fall to leeward || not to follow the first scheme*

Desgarradamente, *adver. impudently*

Desgarrar, *v. a. to rend; to tear*

Desgarrarse, *v. r. to escape ; to go away || to grow impudent*

Desgarro, *s. m. a rent || impudence || a bravado or boasting*

Desgarron, *s. m. a great rent || a rag*

Desgastar, *v. a. to lessen any thing by degrees*

Desgastarse, *v. r. to squander away one's estate*

Desgatar, *v. a. to pursue or kill cats*

Desgayre, *s. m. inelegance ; ungenteelness*

Al desgayre, *adv. negligently || inelegantly || disdainfully*

Desglosar, *v. a. to blot out remarks*

Desglose, *sub. m. blotting out remarks*

Desgobernadura, *s. f. knitting. V.* Desgobernar

Desgobernar, *v. a. to unsettle the government || to dislocate || to knit fast a horse's vein || to steer ill*

Desgobierno, *s. m. disorder || knitting*

Desgolletar, *v. a. to break the gullet of a pot, etc.*

Desgorrarse, *v. r. to pull off the hat*

Desgotar, *v. a. V.* Agotar

Desgoznar, *v. a. to unhinge*

Desgracia, *s. f. misfortune || disgrace || enmity*

Desgraciadamente, *adv. unfortunately*

Desgraciado, da, *a. unpleasant ; inelegant*

Desgraciar, *v. a. to offend*

Desgraciarse, *v. r. to fall out with one || to be not well in health || to degenerate*

Desgraduado, da, *a. degraded*

Desgramar, *v. a. to pluck up the grass*

Desgranar, *v. a. to shake out the grain || to kill*

Desgranzar, *v. a. to take away the siftings*

Desgreñar, *v. act. to pull off* or *dishevel the hair — to disorder*

Desguarnecer, *v. a. to unfurnish || to strip, etc.*

Desguindar, *v. a. to take* or *bring down*

Deshabitar, *v. a. to quit the house, etc. || to dispeople*

Deshabituar, *v. a. to disaccustom*

Deshacer, *v. a. to undo; to d stroy || to defeat || to digest || to blot out || to annihilate || to waste || to melt || to break off a treaty, etc. || to lessen || to disband*

Deshacer agravios, *to revenge injuries*

Deshacerse, *v. r. to afflict one's self*

Desharrapadillo, *a. dim.* de Desharrapado

Desharrapado, da, *adj. poor; all in rags*

Deshebillar, *v. a. to unbuckle* [*ravel*

Deshebrar, *v. a. to un-*

Deshecha, *s. f. shift; evasion || a pass in a road || a civil farewell || a song's burden*

Deshechizar, *v. a. to unbewitch*

Deshecho, cha, *adj. undone.*

Borrasca deshecha, *a violent storm*—fuga deshecha, *a hurried flight*

Deshelar, *v. a. to thaw*

Desheredacion, *s. f. disinheriting*

Desheredar, *v. a. to disinherit* [*generate*

Desheredarse, *v. r. to de-*

Deshermanar, *v. a. to break brootherly friendship || to unpair*

Desherradura, *s. f. a sore in the hoof of a horse*

Desherrar, *v. a to unfetter || to unshoe*

Deshilachar, *v. a. to make lint out of linen*

Deshilado, *s. m. a sort of embroidery*

Deshilar. *v. a. to unweave; to unravel*

Deshinchar, *v. a. to unbosom one's self*

Deshincharse, *v. r. to unswell*

Deshojador, *sub. m. one who strips of leaves*

Deshojadura, *s. f. tearing off the leaves*

Deshojar, *v. a. to strip of leaves* [*to peel*

Deshollejar, *v. a. to pare;*

Deshollinador, *subs. m. a chimney-sweeper*

Deshollinar, *v. a. to sweep a chimney*

Deshombrecerse, *v. r. to shrug up the shoulders*

Deshonestamente, *adver. dishonestly*

Deshonestar, *v. a. to disgrace || to disfigure*

Deshonestico, ca, *a. dim.* de Deshonesto

Deshonestidad, *s. f. dishonesty*

Deshonesto, t
nest

Deshonor, *sub*
nour

Deshonorar,

Deshonra, *s. f*

Deshonradame
dishonoura

Deshonrador,
that dishon

Deshonrar, *v.*
grace; to d
to ruin a vi

Deshonroso, s
nourable

Deshora, *s. f.*

Deshorado, da
sonable || u

Deshornar, *v.*
out of the o

Deshospedado
wants lodg

Deshospedami
inhospitali

Desiderable,
ble

Desidia, *s. f.*

Desidioso, sa
ful; idle

Desierto, *s. m.*
dernes

Desierto, ta,

Designacion,
gnation

Designar, *v. a*

Designio, *s. n*

Desigual, *a.*
|| uneven ||
inconstant

Desigualar, *v.*
unequal

Desigualarse,

Desigualdad,
lity || wron

Desigualment
qually

Desimaginar,
out of the i
|| to disan

D

Deslazar, *v. a. to untie*
Deslazo, *s. m. untying*
Desleal, *a. 2. disloyal*
Deslealmente, *adv. disloyally*
Deslealtad, *s. f. disloyalty*
Deslechugador, *sub. m. a pruner*
Deslechugar, *v. a. to prune*
Desleidura, *s. f. diluting*
Desleir, *v. a. to dilute*
Deslendrar, *v. a. to clear from nits*
Deslenguado, da, *a. that has lost the tongue* || *evil-speaker*
Deslenguamiento, *s. mas. lewdness of the tongue*
Deslenguarse, *v. rec. to speak insolently, etc.*
Desliar, *v. a. to unbind; to untie*
Desligar, *v. a. to unbind* || *to explain; to clear*
Deslindador, *s. m. one that marks out the bounds*
Deslindadura, *s. f.*, **Deslindamiento**, *s. m.* } *marking out bounds*
Deslindar, *v. a. to mark out the bounds*
Desliz, *s. m. slipping*
Deslizadero, *s. m. a slippery place*
Deslizadizo, za, *a. slippery*
Deslizar, *v. n. to slip; to slide*
Deslizo, *s. m. V.* Desliz
Desloar, *v. a. to dispraise*
Deslomadura, *s. fem. the breaking the back*
Deslomar, *v. act. to break the back*
Deslucidamente, *adv. inelegantly*
Deslucimiento, *s. m. obscurity* || *disgrace*
Deslucir, *v. a. to obscure, to darken* || *to blemish*
Deslumbramiento, *s. m. dazzling* || *blindness of the mind*
Deslumbrar, *v. a. to dazzle*
Deslustrador, *s. mas. one that takes away the lustre*
Deslustrar, *v. a. to take away the lustre* || *to blast one's reputation*
Deslustre, *s. m. the loss of the lustre*
Deslustroso, sa, *a. unbecoming disgraceful*
Desmadexado, da, *a. slow; dull; faint* || *inelegant*
Desmadexamiento, *s. m. slowness; dulness; faintness* || *inelegance*
Desmajolar, *v. a. to grub up a vine* || *to untie the shoes*
Desmallar, *v. a. to unmall*
Desman, *s. m. misbehaviour* || *misfortune*
Desmanarse, *v. r. to go astray*
Desmancebar, *v. act. to hinder the living with a concubine*
Desmandar, *v. a. to countermand* || *to revoke a legacy*
Desmandarse, *v. r. to be disordered* || *to disband* || *to go astray*
Desmanear, *v. a. to unfetter*
Desmangar, *v. a. to unhaft*
Desmanotado, da, *a. slow, or unhandy*
Desmantelar, *v. a. to dismantle* || *to abandon*
Desmaña, *s. f. unskilfulness* || *laziness*
Desmañado, da, *a. unhandy* || *lazy*
Desmarañar, *v. a. V.* Desenmarañar

Desmarrido, da, *a. weak; fallen away* || *faded*

Desmayadamente, *adver. faintly*

Desmayado, da, *a. faint-hearted*

Color desmayado, *a light colour*

Desmayar, *v. n. to want strenght and courage*

Desmayarse, *v. r. to faint;*

Desmayo, *s. m. fainting; swoon* || *discouragement*

Desmayuelo, *s. m. dim. de* Desmayo

Desmazalado, da, *a. slow; feeble; without briskness*

Desmedidamente, *adv. out of measure*

Desmedido, da, *a. unmeasurable*

Desmedrar, *v. neut. to decrease to decay*

Desmedro *s. m. decreasing decaying*

Desmejorar *v. a. to make worse*

Desmelancolizar, *v. a. to rejoice* . [*vel*

Desmelenar, *v. a. to dishe-*

Desmembracion, *s. f.* / Desmembramiento, *s. m.* } *dismembering*

Desmembrar, *v. a. to dismember* [*forget*

Desmemoriarse, *v. r. to*

Desmenguar, *v. a. to diminish*

Desmentida, *s. f. a lie*

Desmentidor, *s. m. one that gives the lie*

Desmentir, *v. a. to give one the lie* || *to conceal or dissemble*

Desmentir el camino, to go out of the road

Desmentirse el edificio, *to be ready to fall*

Desmenuzable, *a. 2. friable; brittle*

Desmenuzador, *s. m. one that scans*

Desmenuzar, *v. a. to break into small bits* || *to scan; to examine*

Desmeollamiento, *sub. m. taking out the marrow, etc.*

Desmeollar, *v. a. to take out the marrow*, or *kernel*

Desmerecedor, *s. m. unworthy of praise, etc.*

Desmerecer, *v. n. to do amiss* [*merit*

Desmerecimiento, *s. m. de-*

Desmesura, *s. f. unmeasurableness* || *impudence*

Desmesuradamente, *adv. out of measure* || *impudently* [*measurable*

Desmesurado, da, *a. un-*

Desmesurarse, *v. rec. to speak* or *act impudently, etc.*

Desmigajar, *v. a. to crumble* [minuir

Desminuir, *v. a. V.* Dis-

Desmirriado, da, *a. feeble; fallen away* || *sad*

Desmocha, / Desmochadura, } *s. f. maiming; lopping, etc.* || *diminution*

Desmochar, *v. a. to maim; to mutilate* || *to lop*, or *prune* || *to cut off the horns* [mocha

Desmoche, *s. m. V.* Des-

Desmocho, *s. m. the lopping of trees*

Desmolado, da, *a. that has no grinders*

Desmoler, *v. a.* to digest

Desmontar, *v. a.* to grup

up; to
horse || *i*
Desmontar
dismoun
Desmontar
Desmonte,
up
Desmorona
Desmorona
troy by
Desmotade
man th
tufts, e
Desmotado
pulls of
Desmotar,
the clot
the tufts
Desmuelo
want of
Desmuger
prive o
Desnariga
the nos
Desnatar,
Desnatura
unnatu
Desnecesa
necessa
Desnervar
Desnevar
lar
Desnivel,
Desnoviar
rate nes
ple
Desnucar,
the nap
Desnudado
strips
Desnudam
Desnudar
naked
Desnudars
dress on
Desnudez
Desnudo,
plain
Desnudo

r, v. a. to diso- [bedience
eia, s. f. diso-
temente, adv.
ently
, v. a. to disen-
disoblige
ado, da, a. un-
le
on, s. f. leisure
amente, adver.
business
o, da, a. unem-

, v. a. to clear
s place
e, v. r. to free
lf from a bu-

act. to endea-
to hear
v. rec. to wear
s eyes
, s. f. desola-
treme grief
da, a. discon-

. a. to desolate
mente, adv. in- [dent
da, a. impu-
, s. m. flayer ||
| flaying-house
a, s. f. excoria-

v. a. to flay || to
oon
v. a. to deop-

ro, va, a. deop-
s [dit
, v. a. to discre-
r, v. a. to free
pression
, s. 2. } disor-
cion, } der
damente, adv.
y || excessively

Desordenamiento, s. mas. disorder
Desordenar, v. act. to disorder [out of order
Desordenarse, v. r. to be
Desorejar, v. a. to cut off the ears
Desosar, v. a. to unbone
Desovar, v. n. to spawn
Desove, s. m. the time in wih fishes east their spawn
Desovillar, v. a. to wind off bottoms || to disentangle || to encourage
Despabiladeras, sub. f. pl. snuffers
Despabiladura, sub. f. the snuff of a candle
Despabilar, v. a. to snuff || to dispatch
Despabilar el ingenio, to sharpen the wit — los ojos, to be very careful
Despachada, s. f. an office in the Spanish exchequer
Despachar, v. act. to dispatch || to sell
Despacho, s. m. dispatch resolution || warrant; commission, etc.
Despachurrado, sub. m. a silly contemptible fellow
Despachurrar, v. act. to squash; to crush
Despachurro, sub. m. an awkward motion of the body
Despacio, adv. leisurely
Despacio! int. softly
Despacito, adv. dim. de Despacio
Despagamiento, s. m. displeasure [please
Despagar, v. act. to dis-
Despajadura, sub. f. clearing from straw

Despajar, v. act. to clear from straw
Despaldarse, } v. r. to
Despaldillarse, } disjoint the shoulder bone
Despalmador, s. m. a careening place
Despalmar, v. a. to grave a ship; to careen || to pare a horse's hoof
Despampanador, s. m. one that unleaves
Despampanadura, subs. f. unleaving
Despampanar, v. a. to unleave vines
Despanado, da, adj. that has not bread to eat
Despancijar, } v. act. to
Despanzurrar, } burst the belly
Despapar, v. n. to bridle up [eir
Desparcir, v. a. V. Espar-
Desparecer, v. n. to disappear
Desparecerse, v. r. to be unlike
Desparejar, v. act. to unmatch
Desparpajar, v. a. to overthrow || to scatter || to prattle
Desparramar, v. act. to scatter [ciler
Despartidor, s. m. recon-
Despartir, v. a. to part; to dispart
Desparvar, v. act. to lay open the sheaves to thrash them
Despasionarse, v. a. to get rid of a passion
Despatarrada, s. f. a step made in a dance by opening the legs excessively
Despatarrar, v. a. to confound, to puzzle

Despatarrarse, *v. r. to fall down by slipping*

Despavesadura, *s. f. snuffing* [*candles*

Despavesar, *v. a. to snuff*

Despavorirse, *v. r. to be frightened*

Despeadura, *s. f. foundering*

Despearse, *v. r. to be foundered with much going*

Despechador, *s. mas. one who vexes* || *exacter*

Despechar, *v. act. to vex; to oppress*

Despecharse, *v. r. to fret* || *to despair*

Despecho, *s. m. despite; anger* || *sorrow* || *vexation* || *fainting* || *insolence* || *misfortune* || *jesting*

A' despecho, *adv. to spite*, or *despite*

Despechugadura, *s. f. taking off the flesh, etc.*

Despechugar, *v. a. to take off the flesh from the breast of a fowl*

Despechugarse, *v. rec. to open one's breast*

Despedazadura, *s. f.*, Despedazamiento, *s. m.* } *tearing to pieces*

Despedazar, *v. act. to tear to pieces*

Despedida, *s. f.*, Despedimiento, *s. m.* } *a farewell*

Despedir, *v. a to cast or throw* || *to dimiss* || *to turn off* || *to deny*

Despedirse, *v. rec. to take leave*

Despedrar, Despedregar, } *v. a. to clear of stones*

Despegamiento, *s. m. V.* Desapego

Despegar, *v. a. to unglue*

Despegarse, *v. r. to fall out with a friend*

Despego, *s. m. falling out*

Despejadamente, *adver. freely; easely; quickly*

Despejado (hombre), *a forward, bold*, or *airy man*

Lugar despejado, *a place that is cleared or voided*

Despejar, *v. a. y n. to clear or void a place*

Despejarse, *v. r. to divert one's self*

Despejo, *s. m. clearing or voiding* || *airiness; gayety* || *boldness*

Despelotar, *v. a. to tangle the hair*

Despeluzarse, Despeluznarse, } *v. r. to stand on end*

Despeluzo, *s. m. the standing of the hair on end*

Despenar, *v. a. to put out of pain*

Despendedor, *s. m. an expensive man*

Despender, *s. m. to spend*

Despensa, *sub. f. buttery — provisions*

Despensado, da, *a. starved*

Despensar, *v. a. to repent of one's thoughts*

Despensero, *s. m. a steward; a purveyor; a manciple*

Despeñadero, *s. m. a precipice*

Despeñamiento, *s. m. V.* Despeño

Despeñar, *v. a. to precipitate*

Despeño, *s. m. falling from a high place* || *ruin — looseness*

Despepitarse, *v. r. to speak or act rashly*

Despercudir, *v. a. to clean or wash*

Desperdiciadamente, *ad[illegible] profusely*

Desperdiciador, do, *s.* [illegible] *a spendthrift*

Desperdiciar, *v. a. to* [illegible] [illegible]

Desperdicio, *s. m. lavi*[illegible]

Desperdigar, *v. a. to se*[illegible] *parate* || *to disperse*

Desperecerse, *v. r. to lo*[illegible] *to pant after*

Desperecerse de risa, [illegible] *laugh heartily*

Desperezar, *v. a. to shake off sloth; to yawn o*[illegible] *sleeping*

Desperezo, *s. m. shaking off sloth*

Desperfilar, *v. a. to soft*[illegible] *the profile*

Despernada, *s. f. motion of the legs in a country dance*

Despernado, da, *a. weary*

Despernar, *v. a. to break or cut off the legs*

Despertador, *s. m. he that awakes others* || *alarm-clock, larum*

Despertamiento, *s. m. awaking* [*awak*[illegible]

Despertar, *v. a. y n. to* [illegible]

Despesar, *s. m. displeasure*

Despestañarse, *v. r. to look stedfastly*

Despeynar, *v. a. to tangle the hair*

Despezar, *v. n. to end at in a point*

Despezo, *s. m. diminution of a pipe*

Despezonar, *v. a. to take off the stalk of a fruit* || *to divide*

Despicarse, *v. r. to take revenge*

Despicarar, *v. a. to* [illegible] *from rogues* [illegible]

Despiertamente, *adv.* [illegible]

to, ta, a. *awake*
ely, brisk
arrado, da, a. *rag-*
tattered
urro, s. m. *abuse*
venliness
tar, v. a. *to blot out*
ting
tar, v. a. *to pluck*
ith pincers
ar, v. a. *to louse*
te, s. m. *satisfac-*
revenge
ar, v. a. *to mince;*
umble, etc.
er, s. m. *displea-*
[*please*
er, v. a. *to dis*
itar, v. a. *to des-*
t
ito, s. m. *an obli-*
posture in fencing
ar, v. a. *to sepa-*
silver from other
ls
s, s. m. *separation*
ilver from other
ls
gar, v. a. *to unfold*
explain
gar las velas, *to*
ad the sails [*tion*
go, s. m. *explana-*
marse, v. r. *not to*
d upright || *to fall*
a
mo, s. m. *the defect*
ot being perpendi-
r [*to fleece*
mar, v. a. *to pick;*
lacion, s. f. *depo-*
tion
lado, s. m. *desert*
lar, v. a. *to dispeo-*
[*a place*
lar, v. n. *to leave*
ador, s. m. *one who*
r [*dispossess*
, v. a. *to strip; to*

Despojarse, v. rec. *to undress, or deprive one's self*

Despojo, s. m. *stripping; dispossessing* || *booty;* || *spoil* || *garbage*

Despojos, pl. *the meat with comes from the table*

Despolvorear, } v. a. *to dust; to brush, etc.*
Despolvorizar, }

Desportillar, v. a. *to break the gullet of a pot, etc.*

Desposada, s. f. *a bride*

Desposado, s. m. *a bridegroom* [*fettered*

Desposado, da, a. *hand-*

Desposar, v. a. *to betroth; to marry*

Desposarse, v. r. *to betroth or marry* [*sess*

Desposeer, v. a. *to dispo-*

Desposorio, s. m. *betrothing* [*potically*

Despóticamente, adv. *des-*

Despótico, ca, a. *despotick*

Despotismo, s. m. *despotism*

Despoto, s. m. *a despot*

Despotricar, v. n. *to speak rashly; to prattle*

Despreciable, a. 2. *despisable* [*pizer*

Despreciador, s. m. *des-*

Despreciar, v. a. *to despise*

Despreciarse, v. r. *to scorn*

Desprecio, s. m. *contempt*

Desprender, v. a. *to part; to loosen*

Desprenderse, v. r. *to fall down* || *to extricate one's self*

Desprevencion, s. f. *want of preparation*

Desprevenido, da, *unprovided* [*proportion*

Desproporcion, s. f. *dis-*

Desproporcionadamente, adv. *disproportionably*

Desproporcionar, v. a. *to disproportion*

Despropositado, da, adj. *nothing to the purpose*

Desproposito, s. m. *folly; extravagance*

Desproveer, v. a. *to unfurnish*

Desproveidamente, adv. *at unwares*

Despueblo, s. m. V. Despoblacion

Despues, adv. *after; afterward* [*wing*

Despues, a. *next; follo-*

Despulsar, v. a. *to take away the pulse; to stupefy, etc.*

Despuntar, v. a. *to blunt*

Despuntar, v. n. *to double the cape* || *to shew wit*

Al despuntar del dia, *at the dawn*

Desquadernar, v. a. *to unbing a book — to disorder*

Desquadrillado (caballo), s. m. *a hipshot horse*

Desquartizar, v. a. *to quarter* || *to cut or carve meat* [*hinge*

Desquiciar, v. a. *to un-*

Desquilatar, v. a. *to lower the value of gold, etc.*

Desquitar, v. act. *to win one's money back again*

Desquitar, v. n. *to retaliate*

Desquite, s. m. *revenge at play* || *retaliation*

Desquixarar, v. a. *to tear the jaws* [*the tail*

Desrabotar, v. a. *to cut off*

Desranchar, v. n. *to part from chamber-fellows*

Desrazonable, a. *unreasonable*

Desregladamente, *adver. unruly*

Desreglado, da, *adj. of a disorderly life*

Desreglarse, *v. r. to go out of order* || *to grow lewd, etc.*

Desriscarse, *v. r. to fall down from a precipice*

Desrizar, *v. a. to uncurl*

Destacamento, *s. m. detachment*

Destacar, *v. a. to detach*

Destajar, *v. a. to undertake by the great*

Destajero, *s. m. undertaker by the great*

Destajo, *s. m. undertaking by the great* || *partition*

Vender por destajo, *to sell by retail*

Destapada, *s. f. uncovering*

Destapar, *v. a. to unstop; to uncover*

Destaparse, *v. r. to unveil* or *unmuffle one's self*

Destapiar, *v. a. to pull dawn a mudwall*

Destapo, *s. m. unstopping; uncovering*

Deste, *instead of* de este, *of this* [*the roof*

Destechar, *v. a. to take off*

Destejar, *v. a. to untile*

Destellar, *v. a. to pour by little and little*

Destello, *s. m. dropping* || *sparkling*

Destempladamente, *adv. intemperately*

Destemplado, da, *a. discordant*

Destemplanza, *s. f. intemperance* || *intemperature* || *disorderly life* || *inconstanly* || *alteration in the pulse*

Destemplar, *v. a. to distemper; to disorder*

Destemplarse, *v. r. to put one's self out of order* || *to blunt*

Destemple, *sub. m. dissonance* || *distemper*

Destentar, *v. a. to take away the temptation*

Desteñir, *v. a. to discolour*

Desterradero, *s. m. a distant country, etc.*

Desterrar, *v. a. to banish*

Desterronar, *v. a. to break the clods*

Destetar, *v. a. to wean*

Destetarse, *v. r. to break ill habits, etc.*

Destete, to, *s. m. weaning*

Destexer, *v. a. to unweave*

Destiempo, *s. m. an unfit* or *improper time*

Destierro, *s. m. banishment* [*tion*

Destilacion, *s. f. distilla-*

Destiladera, *s. f. alembick*

Destilador, *s. m. distiller*

Destilar, *v. a. y n. to distil*

Destilatorio, *s. m. a place to distil in* [*tion*

Destinacion, *s. f. destina-*

Destinar, *v. a. to destine*

Destino, *s. m. destiny* || *destination*

Destirar, *v. a. to unbend; to loosen* [*tion*

Destitucion, *s. f. destitu-*

Destituir, *v. a. to destitute*

Destocar, *v. a. to uncoif* || *to pull off one's hat*

Destorcer, *v. a. to untwist* || *to make straight* || *to set in order*

Destoserse, *v. r. to feign a cough*

Destotro, tra, *of the other*

Destrabar, *v. a. to unfetter* || *to untie or separate* || *to cut the band of the tongue*

Destral, *s. m. an axe*

Destraleja, *s. f. a small axe* [r

Destramar, *v. a. to unre-*

Destrenzar, *v. a. to untwist* [*fencir*

Destreza, *s. f. dexterity*

Destripar, *v. a. to embowel* || *to trample on*

Destripaterrones, *s. m. a clod-beater; a bumpkin, etc.* [*small pieces*

Destrizar, *v. a. to cut in*

Destrizarse, *v. r. to pine away* [*agoa*

Destrocar, *v. a. to change*

Destron, *sub. m. a blind man's leader*

Destronar, *v. a. to dethrone*

Destroncamiento, *sub. m. cutting off from the trunk*

Destroncar, *v. a. to cut off from the trunk* || *to mutilate* || *to cross* or *thwart*

Destrozador, *sub. m. destroyer*

Destrozar, *v. a. to break; to destroy* || *to rout; to defeat*

Destrozo, *s. m. destruction, havock* || *slaughter; defeat*

Destruccion, *s. f. destruction* [*tructive*

Destructivo, va, *adj. des-*

Destrueco, } *s. m. reci-*
Destrueque, } *procal restitution of the exchanged things*

Destruccion, *s. f. destruction* [*troyer*

Destruidor, *s. m. a des-*

Destruir, *v. a. to destroy*

Desturbar, *v. a. to put out; to turn away*

pello, s. m. flaying ; kinning || impudence | exaction
uncir, v. a. to unyoke
unidamente, adv. separately
union, s. f. disunion
unir, v. a. to disunite
ñar, v. a. to pluck off the nails
usadamente, adv. unusually
usar, v. a. to wean from a custom
uso, s. m. disuse
uso, adv. V. Suso
aido, da, a. languid, dull
alia, s. f. V. Desvalimiento
svalido, da, a. forsaken out of favour, etc. || eager ; zealous
svalimiento, s. m. the condition of a forsaken man
svalor, s. m. cowardise
svan, s. m. a garret
svanar, v. a. to wind to a skain
svanecer, v. act. to reduce to atoms || to take away from the sight || to make proud
esvanecerse, v. r. to evaporate || to be giddy
esvanecidamente, adv. proudly
esvanecimiento, s. m. pride || giddiness
esvariadamente, adv. diversly
Desvariado, da, a. delirious
Desvariar, v. n. to delirate ; to rave
Desvario, s. m. delirium || raving ; impertinence

Desvaynar, v. a. to unsheath || to shell
Desveladamente, adverb. watchfully
Desvelamiento, s. m. V. Desvelo
Desvelar, v. act. to keep awake [watchful
Desvelarse, v. r. to be
Desvelo, s. m. want of sleep || watchfulness
Desvenar, v a. to cut or take off the veins
Desvencijarse, v. r. to burst
Desvendar, to pull off the bandage
Desventar, v. a. to extract the wind out of. . .
Desventura, s. f. misfortune
Desventuradamente, adv. unfortunately
Desventurado, da, a. unfortunate || silly || covetous
Desvorgonzadamente, ad. impudently
Desvergonzarse, v. r. to grow impudent
Desvergüenza, s. f. impudence
Desviar, v. a. to turn aside ; to avert || to dissuade || to put by
Desvío, s. m. turning aside || going about || despising
Desvirar, v. a. to cut even shoes [love, etc.
Desvivirse, v. r. to die for
Desvolver, v. a. to unfold || to plough
Desxugar, v. a. to squeeze ; to press close
Desyuncir, v. a. to unyoke
Deszumar, v. a. V. Desxugar
Detencion, s. f. a delay

Detener, v. a. to detain
Detenerse, v. r. to tarry ; to stay
Detenido, da, a. slow ; irresolute || covetous
Detenidamente, adver. slowly [ning
Detentacion, s. f. detai-
Detentador, s. m. detainer [injustly
Detentar, v. a. to detain
Deterior, a. 2. worse
Deterioracion, s. f. deterioration
Deteriorar, v. a. to make worse
Determinacion, s. f. determination || boldness
Determinadamente, adv. determinately || boldly
Determinado, da, a. bold; resolute [termine
Determinar, v. a. to de-
Determinativo, va, a. determinative
Detestable, a 2 detestable
Detestacion, s. f. detestation
Detestar, v. a. to detest
Detienebuey, s. m. rest-harrow
Detraccion, s. f. detraction [tract
Detractar, v. act. to de-
Detractor, s. m. detracter
Detraer, v. act. to draw back || to detract
Detras, adv. behind
Detravès, adv. V. Travès
Detrimento, s. m. detriment
Deturpar, v. a. to foul ; to soil
Deuda, s. f. a debt
Deudo, da, s. relation
Deudo, s. m. kindred
Deudor, s. m. debtor
Devalar, v. n. to fall leeward

Devanadera, *s. f. a reel; a spindle* [*der*

Devanador, *s. m. a win-*

Devanar, *v. a. to wind to a skain* || *to reel*

Devanear, *v. n. to rave; to dote*

Devanéo, *s. m. raving*

Devantal, *s. m. apron*

Devastacion, *s. f. devastation* [*waste*

Devastar, *v. act. to lay*

Devengar, *v. a. to deserve*

Devocion, *s. f. devotion*

Devocionario, *s. m. a book of devotion*

Devocioncilla, cita, *s. f. dim. de* Devocion

Devolucion, *s. f. devolution*

Devolver, *v. a. to refer a cause to the first judge*

Devolverse, *v. r. to devolve* [*ret*

Devorador, *s. m. devou-*

Devorar, *v. a. to devour*

Devoraz, *a. 2. voracious*

Devotamente, *adv. devoutly*

Devoto, ta, *a. devout*

Dexacion, *s f. resigning, giving up*

Dexado, da, *adj. lazy; idle* || *languid*

Dexamiento, *s. m. abdication; cession* || *laziness* || *meanness of spirit* [*forsake*

Dexar, *v. v. to leave; to*

Dexarse, *v. r. to neglect one's self*

Dexativo, va, *adj. slothfull; dull*

Dexenxo, *s. m. a. rcum*

Dexo, *s. m. V.* Dexacion || *end* || *laziness* || *the last relish that a mess or drink leaves in the mouth*

Dezmar, *v. a. to tithe* || *to pay the tithe*

Dezmeño, ña, *a. titheable*

Dezmería, *s. f. the territory out of which a church receives tithes*

Dezmero, *s. m. tither* || *he that pays the tithes*

Dezmero, ra, *a. V.* Dezmeño

Dia, *s. m. day*

Dia de años, *the birthday* — de fiesta, *a holy day* — diado, *a. day appointed for. . .* y victo. *daily sustenance*

Buenos dias, *good-morrow*

Diaambra, *s. f. a medicinal mixture so called*

Diabetes, *sub. m. an hydraulick engine*

Diabetica, *s. f. diabetes*

Diabla, *s. f. she devil*

Diablar, *v. a. to infuse diabolical notions*

Diablazgo, *s. m. the devil's territory*

Diablazo, *sub. m. a huge devil*

Diabledad, Diablencia, *s. f. the quality of the devil*

Diablesa, *s. f. she devil* || *a shrew* [*moment*

Diabliamen, *s. m. short*

Diablillo, *s. m. a little devil*

Diablo, *s. m. the devil*

Diablo marino, *an ugly sea-fish* [*trick, etc.*

Diablura, *s. f. a devilish*

Diabólicamente, *adv. diabolically*

Diabólico, ca, *a. diabolical* [*licon*

Diacatalicon, *s. m. catho-*

Diacitron, *s. m. preserved citron*

Diacodion, *s. m.* ...*dium*

Diaconal, *a. 2. bel*... *to a deacon*

Diaconato, *s. m. dea*...

Diaconía, *s. f. the d*... *of a deacon*

Diaconisa, *s. f. deac*...

Diácono, *s. m. dea*...

Diadema, *s. 2. diad*...

Diademado, da, *adj*... *has a diadem*

Diadocos, *s. m. a*... *like a beryl*

Diafanidad, *s. f. di*... *neity*

Diáfano, na, *a. di*...

Diafenicon, *s. m. a*... *tuary made with*

Diaforético, ca, *adj*... *phoretick*

Diafragma, *sub. m*... *phragm*

Diafragmático, ca, ... *longing to the*... *phragm* [

Diagonal, *a. 2. s. f*...

Diagonalmente, *adv*... *gonally*

Diagráfica, *s. f. the*... *sketching*

Diagridio, *s. m. a*... *purgative*

Dialéctica, *s. f. d*...

Dialécticamente, *ad*... *lectically*

Dialéctico, *s. m. a*...

Dialéctico, ca, *a. d*... *tical*

Dialecto, *s. m. dial*...

Dialogal, *a. 2. belo*... *to a dialogue*

Dialogía, *s. f. a fig*... *rhetorick so call*...

Dialogismo, *s. m. a*... *prosopopeia*

Diálogo, *s. m. dialo*...

Dialoguito, *s. m. d*... Dialogo

ido, da, a. like a
nd
no, s. m. aum.
mante
, s. m. a dia- [diamond
no, na, adj. of
n, s. m. a large
nd
riton, s. m. a
ment made with
l, a. 2. diame
lmente, ad. dia-
ally
, s. m. diameter
, s. m. a medi-
composition of
berries, etc.
, s. m. a medi-
made with musk
diantre, s. m. the
, s. f. a dessica-
ster
, s. f. diapasm
, s. m. diapason
s, s. f. eruption
lood through the
, s. m. a fifth in
sub. f. a sort of
[pered
, da, adj. dia-
, , } s. m. an electuary made with plums
, s. m. a plas-
de of juices and
nte, adv. daily
a, a. daily
s. f. looseness
, s. f. a sort of
ation
m. an electuary
ith sena, etc

Diáspero, Diaspro, } s. m. jasper
Diástole, s. m. diastole
Diatesaron, s. m. diatessaron
Diatónico, a. m. diatonick
Diatragauto, subst. m. an electuary so called
Dibuxador, s. m. a drawer [to design
Dibuxar, v. a. to draw,
Dibuxo, s. m. draught; drawing
Dicacidad, s. f. dicacity
Diccion, s. f. diction
Diccionario, s. m. dictionary
Dicha, s. f. happiness
Por dicha, ad. by chance
Dicharacho, s. m. an unmannerly expression
Dichido, sub. m. a hard word
Dicho, s. m. a saying || promise of matrimony
Dicho, cha, a. said
Dichosamente, adv. happily
Dichoso, sa, a. happy
Diciembre, s. m. december [plina
Diciplina, etc. V. Disci-
Dicotomía, s. f. dichotomy
Dictado, s. m. title of dignity, etc.
Dictador, s. m. dictator
Dictadura, s. f. dictatorship [men
Dictámon, sub. m. dicta-
Díctamo, s. m. dittany
Dictar, v. a. to dictate
Dicterio, sub. m. taunt; scoff; jest
Didascalico, ca, adj. didactick
Diente, s. m. a tooth
Diente de ajo, a clove of garlick—de leon, dandeleon

Dientes de sierra, the ridge of a mountain
Dientecillo, s. m. a little tooth
Diéresis, s. f. dieresis
Diesi, s. f. diesis
Diestra, subs. f. the right hand
Diestramente, adv. dexterously
Diestro, tra, adj. right || dexterous; skilful || cunning || deceitful || propitious; kind
Diestro, sub. m. a skilful fencer
Dieta, s. f. diet || a day's journey || a daily allowance
Dieteutica, s. f. dietetick
Diez, s. m. ten
Diezmar, etc. Voy. Dezmar, etc.
Diezmo, s. m. a tenth part || tithe
Difamacion, etc. V. Disfamacion
Diferencia, s. f. difference
Diferenciar, v. a. to difference || to diversify
Diferenciarse, v. r. to differ || to make one's self eminent, etc.
Diferente, a. 2. different
Diferentemente, adv. differently [to delay
Diferir, v. act. to defer;
Diferir, v. n. to differ
Difícil, a. 2. difficult
Difícilmente, adv. difficultly
Dificultad, s. f. difficulty
Dificultador, sub. m. one who raises difficulties
Dificultar, v. a. to raise difficulties
Dificultosamente, adv. difficultly [cult
Dificultoso, sa, adj. diffi-

Difidacion s. *f. manifesto*
Difidencia, s. *f. diffidence || infidelity*
Difidente, *a.* 2. *unfaithful*
Difinir, etc, *V.* Definir
Difrigo, s. *m. the dross of metal, when refined*
Difundir *v. a. to diffuse*
Difunto, *s. m. corpse*
Difunto, ta, *a. dead*
Difusamente, *adv. diffusely*
Difusion, s. *f. diffusion*
Difusivo, va, *a. diffusive*
Difuso, sa, *a. diffuse*
Diganma, *s. m.*
Digástricos, *adj. m. pl. certain muscles of the human body*
Digerir, *v. a. to digest*
Digestion, *s. f. digestion*
Digestivo, va, *a. digestive*
Digesto, *s. m. digests*
Digito, *s. m. digit || the twelth part of the diameter of the sun or moon*
Dignacion, *s. f. condescendence*
Dignamente, *adv. worthily*
Dignarse, *v. r. to deign*
Dignidad, *s. f. dignity*
Dignificar, *v. a. to dignify || to make worthy*
Digno, na, *a. worthy*
Digresion, *s. f. digression*
Dilacion, *s. f. delay*
Dilapidacion, *s. f. dilapidation*
Dilapidar, *v. a. to dilapidate*
Dilatacion, *s. f. dilatation || magnanimity*
Dilatadamente, *ad.* [*exten*]*sively : widely*
Dilatado, da, *adj. great ; spacious || numerous*
Dilatar, *v. a. to dilate || to delay*
Dilatarse, *v. r. to be prolix in speaking, etc.*
Dilatorio, ria, *a. dilatory*
Dileccion, *s. f. love ; affection*
Dilecto, ta, *a. beloved*
Dilema, *s. m. dilemma*
Diligencia, *s. f. diligence || affair ; business*
Diligenciar, *v. a. to be diligent in the prosecution of affairs*
Diligenciero, *sub. m. an agent*
Diligente, *a.* 2. *diligent*
Diligentemente, *adv. diligently*
Dilucidacion, *s. f. dilucidation*
Dilucidar, *v. a. to dilucidate*
Dilucidario, *s. m. commentary*
Dilusivo, va, *a. delusive*
Diluvio, *s. m. deluge*
Dimanar, *v. n. to spring or flow from*
Dimension, *s. f. dimension || measure, time*
Dimidiar, *v. a. V.* Demediar
Diminucion, *s. f. diminution*
Diminuir, *v. a. V.* Disminuir
Diminutivo, va, *a. diminutive*
Diminutivo, *s. m. diminutive*
Diminuto, ta, *a. diminished ; defective*
Dimision, *s. f. resigning ; laying down*
Dimisorias, *s. f. pl. dimissory letters*
Dimitir, *v. a. to resign ; to abdicate*
Dimoño, *s. m. V.* Demonio
Dinerada, *s. f. a great quantity of money*
Dinérano, *s. m. V* [...]rista [
Dinerillo, *sub. m.*
Dinerismo, *s. m.* [...] *money*
Dinerista, *s. m.* [...] *hunter*
Dinero, *s. m.* [...] *brass coin ||* [...] *weight*
Dinero contante [...] contado, *ready*
Dineroso, sa, *a. m*[...]
Dineruelo, *s. m.* [...] *sum of money*
Dintel, *s. m. lint*[...]
Dintorno, *s. m.* [...] *delineated wit*[...] *outline*
Diocesano, na, *a* [...]*cesan*
Diócesis, *s. f. dio*[...]
Dionisia, *subs. f.* [...] *stone with red* [...]
Dioptra, *s. f. qua*[...]
Dióptrica, *s. f. di*[...]
Dióptrico, ca, *a.* [...]*trical*
Dios, *s. m. God*
A' dios, *adv. a*[...]
Diosa, *s. f. godd*[...]
Diosear, *v. n. to* [...] *god* [*l*
Diosecillo, ito, *s.* [...]
Diosecita, *sub. f.* [...] *goddess*
Dioso, sa, *adj.* [...]
Dioso, *s. m. V.* [...]
Diploe, *s. m. di*[...]
Diploma, *s. m. d*[...]
Dipsas, *s. f. a ki*[...] *pent*
Dipsaco, *sub. m* [...]
Diptico, *s. m. ch*[...]*gister*
Diptongar, *v. a.* [...] *two vowels int*[...] *labe*
Diptongo, *s. m* [...]

ptacion, s. f. deputa-on

tado, s. m. deputy

tar, v. a. to depute

e, s. m. a dike

ecillo, s. m. dim. de ique

ccion, s. f. direction

ctamente, adv. direc-

cto, adv. directly

ctivo, va, adj. direc-e

cto, ta, a. direct

ctor, s. m. director

ctorio, ria, a. direc-tory

ctorio, s. m. direc-

gir, v. a. to direct

nente (impedimento), m. an impediment at invalidates a mar-age

nir, v. a. to divide; disunite || to decide difference || to free; enfranchise

nir el matrimonio, to ssolve a marriage

ir, v. a. to destroy

ato, s. m. a holy day

ntar, v. a. to sing || compose or recite ver- || to descant

nte, s. m. a sort of itar || descant, in mu k

ptacion, s. f. a con-versy

ptar, v. n. to con-vert

rnimiento, s. m. dis-rnment || nomina-on of a guardian

rnir, v. a. to discern o appoint a guardian

plina, s. f. discipline

plinable, adj. 2. dis-inable

Disciplinado, da, a. streaked

Disciplinar, v. a. to discipline

Discipulado, s. m. an assembly of scholars || doctrine

Discípulo, s. m. disciple

Disco, s. m. disk || quoit

Díscolo, a. peevish; froward

Discolor, adj. 2. of many colours

Disconforme, a. 2. V. Desconforme

Discontinuar, v. a. V. Descontinuar

Disconvenir, v. n. Voy. Desconvenir

Discordancia, s. f. discordance

Discordar, v. n. to disagree || to jar

Discorde, a. 2. disagreeing || disonant

Discordia, s. f. discord

Discrecion, s. f. discretion || ready wit || smart repartee

Discrepancia, s. f. discrepance

Discrepar, v. n. to differ, or disagree

Discretamente, adv. discreetly

Discretear, v. n. to converse with wit, agreeableness, etc.

Discretivo, va, a. discretive

Discreto, ta, adj. discreet — witly

Quantidad discreta, a discrete quantily

Discrimen, subs. m. risk; danger

Disculpa, s. f. excuse

Disculpable, a. 2. excusable

Disculpacion, s. f. justification

Disculpar, v. a. to exculpate

Discurrir, v. neu. to run about; to wander || to discourse

Discursar, v. a. to discourse

Discursista s. m. discourser

Discursivo, va a. discoursive || pensive

Discurso, s. m. way; running || reason; judgment || space of time

Discusion, s. f. discussion

Discutir, v. a. to discuss

Disecacion, s. f. V. Disseccion

Disecar, v. a. to dissect

Diseccion, s. f. disection

Disector, s. m. dissector

Diseminar, v. a. dissemi nate

Disension, s. f. dissention

Disenteria, s. f. bloody flux

Disentérico, ca, a. belonging to, or troubled with a bloody flux

Disentimiento, s. m. dissent

Disentir, v. n. to dissent

Diseñar, v. a. to draw, or mark out

Diseño, subs. m. design; draught

Disertacion, s. f. dissertation

Disertar, v. n. to discourse, to make a dissertation

Diserto, ta, a. well spoken; eloquent

Disfamacion, s. f. defamacion

Disfamador, s. m. defamer

Disfamar, v. a. to defame

Disfamatorio, ria, a. defamatory

Disfamia, s. f. infamy

Disfavor, s. m. disfavour || despising

Disforme, a. 2. deformed || monstrously big

Disformidad, *s. f. deformity* || *monstrous bigness*
Disfraz, *s. m. disguise*
Disfrazar, *v. a. to disguise*
Disgregacion, *s. f. separation; division*
Disgregar, *v. a. to part; to separate*
Disgustar, *v. a. to disgust*
Disgutarse, *v. r. to fall out with one*
Disgustillo, *s. m. dim. de* Disgusto
Disgusto, *s. m. disgust; distate*
A' disgusto, *adv. grudgingly*
Disílabo, *s. m. dissyllable*
Disímbolo, la, *a. unlike*
Disímil, *a. 2. unlike*
Disimilar, *a. 2. dissimilar*
Disimilitud, *s. f. unlikeness*
Disimulacion, *s. f. dissimulation*
Disimuladamente, *ad. dissemblingly*
Disimulado, da, *adj. dissembling*
Disimular, *v. a. to dissemble*
Disimulo, *s. m. dissembling*
Disipacion, *sub. f. dissipation*
Disipador, *s. m. a spendthrift*
Disipar, *v. a. to dissipate*
Dislate, *s. m. V.* Disparate
Dislocacion, *s. f. dislocation*
Dislocar, *v. a. to dislocate*
Disminucion, *s. f. diminution*
Disminuir, *v. a. to diminish*
Disoluble, *adj. 2. dissoluble*
Disolucion, *s. f. dissolution* || *dissoluteness*
Disolutamente, adv. dissolutely
Disoluto, ta, a. dissolute

Disolvente, *a. y s. m. dissolvent*
Disolver, *v. a. to dissolve*
Dison, *s. m. a harsh disagreable sound*
Disonancia, *subs. f. dissonance*
Disonante, *a. 2. dissonant*
Disonar, *v. n. to jar* || *to disagree*
Disono, na, *a. dissonant*
Dispar, *adj. 2. unequal; different*
Disparador, *s. m. shooter* || *trigger*
Disparar, *v. a. to shoot* || *to talk nonsense*
Dispararse, *v. r. to unbend* || *to fall upon the enemy, etc.*
Disparatadamente, *adv. foolishly*
Disparatado, da, *adj. foolish; hare-brained, etc.*
Disparatar, *v. n. to talk* or *act foolishly*
Disparate, *s. m. an extravagant, foolish action* or *expression*
Disparaton, *s. m. aum. de* Disparate
Disparatorio, *s. m. a foolish nonsensical discourse*
Disparcialidad, *s. f. dissociation; disjunction*
Disparidad, *s. f. disparity*
Dispendor, *v. a. to spend*
Dispendio, *s. m. profuseness*
Dispensa, *s. f. dispensation*
Dispensable, *a. 2. dispensable*
Dispensacion, *s. f. dispensation*
Dispensador, *s. m. dispensator; dispenser*
Dispensar, *v.* act. to dispense
Dispersion, *s. f.* dispersion

Disperso, sa, *a. dis*[...]
Dispertar, etc. *V.* D[...]tar
Displacer, *v. a. V*[...]
Displicencia, *s. f. d*[...]*sure*
Disponedor, ra, *s.* [...]
Disponer, *v. a. y n.* [...]*pose*
Disponerse, *v. r.* [...]
Disposicion, *s. f. di*[...]*tion* || *disposal* || *resolution*
Dispositiva, *s. f. d*[...]*tion; inclination*[...]*nes*
Dispositivamente, *a*[...]
Dispositivo, va, *a.* [...]*ratory*
Dispuesto, ta, *adj.* [...]*sed; ordered* || [...]*some*
Bien, *ó* mal disp[...] *well* or *ill affect*[...]
Disputa, *s. f. dispu*[...]
Disputable, *a. 2.* [...]*table*
Disputador, *s. m.* [...]
Disputar, *v. a. y n.* [...]*pute*
Disquisicion, *s. f. d*[...]
Distancia, *s. f. dist*[...]
Distante, *a. 2. dista*[...]
Distantemente, *adv*[...] *distance*
Distar, *v. n. to be d*[...] || *to differ*
Disterminar, *v. a. t*[...]*terminate*
Dístico, *s. m. distic*[...]
Distilar, *v. a. V.* De[...]
Distincion, *s. f. di*[...]*tion*
Persona de distinci[...] *man of note*
Distinguir, *v. act. t*[...]tinguish
Distintamente, *ad*[...]tinctly

, va, *adj. dis-*
s. m. a distinc-
ibute, etc.
a, *a. distinct*
. *m. instinct*
ı, *s. f. distrac-*
sence of mind
ess
. *a. to distract*
upt [*dly*
ente, *adv. lew-*
da, *a. distrac-*
d
ıto, *s. m. Voy.*
on [*bution*
n, *s. f. distri-*
r, *s. m. distri-*
[*bute*
v. a. to distri-
o, va, *a. dis-*

m. district
v. a. to disturb
s. m. distur-

. *a. to dissuade*
s. f. dissuasion
f. dysury
, *s. f. disjunc-*

ı. *f. in musick*
of the voice
mente, *ad. dis-*
ly
, va, *adj. dis-*

s. m. the neces-
h of one of two
ctory proposi-

curity; pledge
ı, *s, f. a short*
nciently sung
ced at once
o, ca, *adj. di-*
le
, *s. m. dithy-*

Ditono, *s. m. second* (*in musick*)
Diurético, ca, *a. diuretick*
Diurnal, } *s. m. diurnal*
Diurno, }
Diurno, na, *a. diurnal*
Diuturnidad, *sub. f. long continuance; lastingness*
Diuturno, na, *a. lasting*
Divan, *s. m. divan*
Divergencia, *s. f. tending to various parts from one point*
Divergente, *a. 2. divergent*
Diversamente, *adv. diversly* [*sity*
Diversidad, *sub. f. diver-*
Diversion, *s. f. diversion*
Diverso, sa, *a. divers*
Diversos, *pl. many*
Diversorio, *s. m. inn*
Divertimiento, *s. m. diversion* || *absence of mind*
Divertir, *v. a. to divert* || *to recreate*
Dividir, *v. a. to divide*
Divieso, *s. m. a boil* [*tion*
Divinacion, *s. f. divina*
Divinal, *a. 2. V.* Divino
Divinamente, *adv. divinely*
Divinatorio, ria, *a. belonging to divinacion*
Divinidad, *s. f divinity*
Divinizar, *v. a. to deify*
Divino, na, *a. divine*
Divisa, *s. f. patrimony; inheritance* || *device* || *motto; posy*
Divisar, *v. a. to see* or *discover at distance*
Divisero, *subs. m. heir; coheir* [*bility*
Divisibilidad, *s. f. divisi-*
Divisible, *a. 2. divisible*
Division, *s. f. division* || *hyphen*

Divisivo, va, *a. Voy.* Divisible
Diviso, sa, *a. divided*
Divisor, *s. m. divisor*
Divisorio, ria, *adj. that divides*, or *parts*
Divo, *s. m. divine*
Divorciar, *v. a. to divorce*
Divorcio, *s. m. divorce*
Divulgacion, *s. f. divulging* [*ger*
Divulgador, ra, *s. divul-*
Divulgar, *v. a. to divulge*
Dix, } *s. m. any toy for children*
Dixe, }
Dixes, *pl. jewels, etc.*
Dizque, *instead of* dicen que, *they say that*
Do, *adv. V.* Donde
Dobla, *subs. f. a spanish gold-coin*
Dobladamente, *adv. doubly* || *deceitfully*
Dobladillo, lla, *a. thick and short*
Dobladillo, *s. m. a hem in sewing* [*bly*
Dobladamente, *adv. dou-*
Doblado, da, *a. double* || *strong-limbed* || *deceitful* [*fold*
Dobladura, *sub. f. plait;*
Doblar, *v. a. to double* || *to fold* || *to bend*
Doblar campanas, *to ring a peal for the deads*
Doblarse, *v. r. to bow; to bend* || *to yeld to others*
Doble, *adj. 2. double* || *strong-limbed* || *deceitful*
Doblegar, *v. a. to bend* || *to prevail upon; to make yeld* [*fully*
Doblemente, *adv. deceit-*
Doblero, *s. m. a little loaf*
Doblete, *a. 2. made between double and single*
Doblete, *s. m. false stone*

Doblez, s. m. a fold, or plait || duplicity
Doblo, s. m. double; two fold [pistole
Doblon, sub. m. a spanish
Doblon de vaca, double tripe
Doblonada, sub. f. a great quantity of pistoles
Doce, s. m. twelve
Docena, s. f. a dozen || the weight of twelve pounds
Doceno, na, adj. twelfth
Docientos, adj. two hundred
Dócil, adj. 2. docible || tractable [ness
Docilidad, s. f. docible-
Dócilmente, adv. docilely
Doctamente, adv. learnedly
Docto, ta, a. learned
Doctor, s. m. doctor
Doctoral, a. 2. doctoral
Doctoramiento, s. m. the making a doctor
Doctorar, v. a. to give the degree of doctor
Doctorcillo, s. m. dim. de Doctor
Doctorismo, sub. m. the collective body of the doctors
Doctrina, s. f. doctrine
Doctrinal, a. 2. doctrinal
Doctrinar, v. a. to teach; to instruct
Doctrinar caballos, to manage
Doctrinero, s. m. he that explains or teaches doctrine [ment
Documento, s. m. docu-
Dodecaedro, s. m. dodecaedron
Dodrante, s. m. nine parts out of twelve
Dogal, sub. m. a hempen halter

Dogma, s. m. dogma
Dogmáticamente, adver. dogmatically
Dogmático, ca, a. dogmatical [tist
Dogmatista, s. m. dogma-
Dogmatizador, } s. m. dogmatist
Dogmatizante, }
Dogmatizar, v. a. to dogmatize
Dogo, s. m. a band-dog
Dolames, s. m. pl. secret vices or infirmities in a horse
Dolencia, s. f. sickness; disease || crime; infamy
Doler, v. n. to ake — to act with reluctancy
Dolerse, v. r. to repent || to compassionate
Doliente, a. 2. sick
Dolo, s. m. fraud
Dolor, s. m. pain; ake || grief || anger; wrath
Dolores de parto, labour
Dolorido, da, a. afflicted; sorrowful
Dolorido, s. m. the chief mourner
Dolorioso, sa, a. V. Doloroso
Dolorosamente, adv. grievously
Doloroso, sa, adj. grievous; sorrowful
Dolosamente, adv. fraudulently [lent
Doloso, sa, a. fraudu-
Domable, a. tameable
Domador, s. m. tamer || conqueror
Domadura, s. f. taming
Domar, v. a. to tame || to subdue
Domeñar, v. a. to submit
Domésticamente, adv. familiarly
Domesticar, v. a. to tame

lly ; *wittily ;*
gly
, sa , *a. grace-*
asing ; *witty*
m. a page || *a*
sub. f. a maid ;
|| *a waiting-*
a, } *s. f. virgi-*
, } *nity ; mai-*
d
, ita , *sub. f. a*
maid
eña, *s. f. an old*
at gets married
a , *s. f. a ma-*
all grown maid
a , *s. f. dim. de*
v. where ; whit-
[*soever*
iera , *where-*
s. m. a little
[*at play*
s. m. a sharper
ate, *adv. plea-*
wittily
, *s. f. V.* Dono-
a, *a. pleasant ;*
graceful
, *s. f. graceful-*
on. f. the title
er for a lady
f. } *a gilt-*
s. f. } *head*
m. }
s. fem. mule's
s. m. gilder
, *s. f. gilding*
b. m. a bird all
a. to gild
, *a. dorick*
s. f. sleep ; slee-

Dormideras , *s. f. pl. disposition to sleep*
Dormidero, ra , *a. somniferous*
Dormidor , *s. m. a sleeper*
Dormidura, *s. f. sleeping*
Dormilon , na , *s. a great sleeper*
Dormir , *v. n. to sleep*
Dormir el lobo, ó la zorra , *to sleep one's self sober*
Dormirlas , *s. m. hide and seek* [*ber*
Dormitar , *v. n. to slum-*
Dormitivo , *s. m. a soporifick*
Dormitorio , *s. m. dormitory* || *bed-chamber*
Dornajo , *s. m. a trough*
Dorso , *s. m. the back*
Dos , *s. m. two*
Dosel , *s. m. a canopy*
Doselera , *sub. f. the hanging of a canopy*
Dósis , *s. f. dose*
Dotacion , *s. f. a foundation ; a revenue settled for ....*
Dotacion de navios , *the seamen ; rigging , victuals , etc. necessary for a ship*
Dotador , *s. m. one who endows*
Dotal , *a. 2. dotal*
Dotar , *v. a. to endow* || *to jointure*
Dote , *s. 2. dowery ; portion*
Dotes de naturaleza , *endowments of nature*
Doter , Dotrina , etc. *V.* Doctor
Dovelas , *s. f. pl. the two surfaces of an arch*
Dozavo , *s. m. twelfth part*
Draba , *s. f. yellow cress*
Dracma , *s. f. a dram*
Dragante , *s. f. dragant*

Drago , *s. m. a tree in the east and west-indies*
Dragon , *s. m. a dragon*
Dragon marino , *sea-dragon*
Dragones , *pl. dragoons*
Dragona , *s. f. a shoulder-knot* [*wort*
Dragontea , *s. f. dragon-*
Drama , *s. m. drama*
Dramático, ca , *adj. dramatick*
Driades , *s. f. l, dryads*
Driza , *s. f. haliard ; gear*
Drizar , *v. a. to hoist the yards*
Droga , *sub. f. a drug* || *fraud ; deceit*
Drogueria , *s. f. a druggist's shop*
Droguero , *s. m. druggist*
Droguete , *s. m. drugget*
Droguista , *s. m. a cheat ; an impostor*
Dromedal , } *s. m. dro-*
Dromedario , } *medary*
Duan , *s. m. V.* Divan
Dubiedad , *s. f. doubt*
Dubio , *s. m. a doubtful thing* [dable
Dubitable , *a. 2. V.* Du-
Ducado , *s. m. dukedom* || *ducat*
Ducal , *a. 2. ducal*
Ducha , *s. f. so much of a meadow as is mowed in a straight line by a number of mowers in a given tim.*
Ducho , cha , *a. accustomed* [*hundred*
Ducientos , tas , *a. pl. two*
Ducir , *v. a. to lead ; to guide*
Ductor , *s. m. conductor*
Ductriz , *s. f. conductress*
Duda , *s. f. doubt*
Dudable , *a. 2.* dubitable
Dudar , *v. a.* to doubt

fully
Dudoso, sa, *a. doubtful; uncertain*
Duela, *sub. f. pipe-staff; sideboard*
Duelista *s. m. duellist*
Duelo *s. m. duel* || *mourning* [*bles*
Duelos, *pl. sorrows; trou-*
Duende, *s. m. hobgoblin*
Duendecillo, *s. m. dim. de* Duende
Duenderia, *s. f. the tricks of hobgoblins*
Duendo, da, *a. tame*

D

Dueñesco, ca, *a. belonging to dueñas*
Dueño, *s. m. master; owner; proprietor*
Duerno *s. m. two sheets of paper, one into the other*
Dula, *sub. f. a common herd*, or *flock*
Dulce, *a.* 2. *sweet*
Dulce, *s. m. sweet-meat*
Dulcedumbre, *s. f. sweetness*
Dulcemente, *adv. sweetly*
Dulcisono na *a. that has a sweet sound*
Dulero, *sub. m. the shepherd of a* dula
Dulía, *s. f. dulia*
Dulzayna, *sub. f. a sort of musical pipe*
Dulzor, *s. m.* } *sweetness*
Dulzura, *s. f.* }
Dulzurar, *v. a. to sweeten* || *to edulcorate* || *to mitigate*
Dunas, *s. f. pl. downs*
Duneta, *s. f. poop*
Duodécimo, ma, *a. twelfth*
Dupla, *s. f. a double allowance of provision*
Duplicacion, *s. f. duplication* [*bly*
Duplicadamente, *ad. dou-*
Duplicado, *s. m. a duplicate*
Duplicar, *v. a. to double; to duplicate*
Duplicidad, *s. f. duplicity*
Duplo, pla, *a. double*
Duplo, *s. m. two fold*
Duque, *s. m. a duke*
Duquecito, *s. m. dim. de* Duque
Duquesa, *s. f. dutchess*
Dura, *s. f. duration*
Durable, *a.* 2. *durable*
Duracion, *s. f. duration*
Duraderamente, *adv. durably* [*durably*
Duradero, ra, *a. durable;*
Duramente, *adv. hardly*
Durando, *s. m. a kind of cloth*
Durante, *prep. during*
Durar, *ver. n. to last; to dure* or *endure*
Duraznito, *s. m. dim. de* Durazno
Durazno, *s. m. a sort of peach* || *a peach-tree*
Dureza, *s. fem. solidity; hardness* || *obstinacy* || *harshness* || *stiffnes of one's pencil*
Durezas, *pl. callosities*
Dureza de estilo, *roughness of style* — de oido, *dulness of hearing* — de vientre, *constipation*
Durillo, lla, *a. hardish*
Durillo relevante, *an affected manner of writing*
Duro, ra, *a. hard; firm;*
|| *harsh*
close-fist
Dura madr
Dux, *s. m.*

Ea, *int.*
Ea pues, *ó then*
Ebanificar
as smoo
Ebanista, *s*
E'bano, *s.*
Ebrancado
Ebriedad, *ness*
Ebrio, bria
Ebullicion,
Ebúrneo, *of ivory* ||
Echa, *s. f.*
Echacantos *picable*
Echacuervo *pimp* || *low*
Echada, *s throw*
Echadizo, or *laid signedly*
Echador, *casts*
Echadura, *throwin* || *brood*
Echar, *v. throw;*
Echarse, *v*
Echarse lo *lodged b etc.*
Eclesiastes
Eclesiástic *siasticus*
Eclesiastic *siasticl*

a. 2. that may
ed
. a. to eclipse
m. eclipse
f. ellipsis (in
-)
. f. eclipticк
: V. E'gloga
cho
. f. œconomy
nente, *adver.*
nomy
, ca, *a. œco-*
| *stingy*
s. m. œcono-

m. a wooden-
nstrument of

, ca, *a. œcu-*

age
f. œdema
, sa, *a. belon-*
edema
. f. edition
m. edict || *pro-*
on [*tion*
, *s. f. edifica-*
, *s. m. edifier*
. a. to edify
, va, *adj. edi-*

o, ria, *adj. be-*
to edifices
. m. edifice
. edile
. f. the office of

, *s. f. education*
. a. to educate
, *s. f. eduction*
. a. to educe
ente, *adv. effec-*

va, *a. effective*
. m. effect
l. effects; goods,

Efectual, *a. 2. effectual*
Efectualmente, *adv. effectually* [*tuate*
Efectuar, *v. act. to effec-*
Efemérides, *s. f. pl. a day book* [*ephemeris*
Efemérides astronómicas,
Efémero, *s. m. wild iris*
Efémero cólchico, *hermodactyl*
Efeminar, *v. act. to effeminate*
Eficacia, } *s. f. efficacy*
Eficacidad, }
Eficaz, *a. 2. efficacious*
Eficazmente, *adv. efficaciously* || *effectively*
Eficiencia, *s. f. efficiency*
Eficiente, *a. 2. efficient*
Eficientemente, *adv. effectually*
Efigie, *s. f. effigy*
Efimera, *s. f. an ephemeral ague*
Efluvio, *s. m. efflux*
Efluxion, *s. f.* } *effluxion*
Efluxo, *s. m.* }
Efugio, *s. m. subterfuge; shift* [*gence*
Efulgencia, *sub. f. efful-*
Efundir, *v. a. to effuse*
Efusion, *s. f. effusion*
Egilope, *s. f. wild oats*
Egipciano, na, *s. gipsy*
Egira, *s. f. hegira*
E'gloga, *s. f. eclogue*
Egregio, gia, *adj. egregious*
Egresion, *s. f. egression*
El, *art. the*
Ela, ela aquí, *adv. behold her*
Elaborado, da, *a. elaborate*
Elacion, *sub. fem. pride; haughtiness* || *magnanimity* || *sublimity of style* [*note*
Elami, *s. m. a*, (*musical*

Elasticidad, *s. f. elasticity*
Elástico, ca, *a. elastick*
Elaterio, *s. mas. a strong purge* [*buckwort*
Elatine, *sub. f. running*
Elato, ta, *adj. proud; haughty*
Eléboro, *s. m. hellebore*
Eleccion, *s. f. election*
Electivo, va, *a. elective*
Electo, *a.* y *s. elected; elect*
Elector, *s. m. elector*
Electorado, *s. m. electorate*
Electoral, *a. 2. electoral*
Electriz, *s. f. electoress*
Electro, *s. m. electrum*
Electuario, *sub. m. electuary* [*tiasis*
Elefancia, *s. f. elephan-*
Elefante, *s. mas. an elephant* [*phantine*
Elefantino, na, *adj. ele-*
Elegancia, *s. f. elegance*
Elegante, *a. 2. elegant*
Elegantemente, *adv. elegantly*
Elegía, *s. f. elegy*
Elegiaco, ca, *a. elegiack*
Elegible, *a. 2. eligible*
Elegido, *s. m. an elect*
Elegir, *v. a. to elect*
Elementado, da *a. compounded with elements*
Elemental, tar, *a. 2. elemental; elementary*
Elemento, *s m. element*
Elenco, *s. m. index; table*
Elevacion, *s. f. elevation* || *lifting up* || *raising* || *extasy* || *pride*
Elevado, da, *adj. high; lofty; sublime*
Elevamiento, *s. m. rapture; extasy*
Elevar, *v. a.* to elevate—to raise || to exalt
Elevarse, *v. r.* to be in

rapture || *to grow proud*
Elidir, *v. a. to weaken; to debilitate*
Eligir, *v. a. V.* Elegir
Elipse ó elipsi, *s. f. ellipsis (in geometry)*
Elipsis, *s. f. V.* Eclipsis
Elíptico, ca, *a. elliptical*
Eliseos campos, *s. m. pl. elysian fields*
Elixir, *s. m. elixir*
Elocucion, *s. f. elocution*
Elogiar, *v. a. to praise*
Elogio, *s. m. elogy*
Elogista, *s. m. panegyrist*
Elongacion, *s. f. elongation*
Eloqüencia, *s. f. eloquence*
Eloqüente, *a. 2. eloquent*
Eloqüentemente, *adv. eloquently*
Elucidacion, *s. f. elucidation*
Eludir, *v. a. to elude*
Emanacion, *s. f. emanation* [*origin*
Emanadero, *s. m. spring;*
Emanar, *v. n. to issue from*
Emancipacion, *s. f. emancipation*
Emancipadamente, *adver. with emancipation*
Emancipar, *v. a. to emancipate*
Embabiamiento, *s. m. stupidity* || *thoughtlessness*
Embadurnar, *ver. act. to dawb; to anoint*
Embaidor, *s. m. cheater*
Embaimiento, *s. m. cheating; deceiving*
Embair, *v. a. to cheat; to deceive*
Embalar, *v. a. to pack up*
Embalijar, *v. act. to pack up in a portmanteau*
Emballenador, *sub. m. a stay-maker* [*stays*
Emballenar, *v. a. to make*

Embalestado, *s. m. contraction of the nerves in the horses, etc.*
Embalsadero, *sub. mas. a pond; a pool*
Embalsado, da. *a. emballed*
Embalsamador, *s. m. one that embalms*
Embalsamar, *v. a. to embalm*
Embalsar, *v. act. to put cattle in ponds*
Embalumar, *v. a. to load any beast with inequality*
Embanastar, *v. a. to put in a basquet*
Embanastarse, *ver. r. to throw the one's cards on the stock*
Embaracillo, *s. m. dim. de* Embarazo
Embarazadamente, *adver. difficultly* || *awkwardly*
Embarazadillo, lla, *a. a little encumbered, etc.*
Embarazada, *a. fem. with child*
Embarazador, *s. m. a troublesome man*
Embarazar, *v. a. to encumber* || *to perplex; to intricate* || *to stop; to hinder*
Embarazarse, *v. r. to intangle,* or *confound one's self* [*rassment*
Embarazo, *s. m. embar-*
Embarazosamente, *adver. V.* Embarazadamente
Embarazoso, sa, *a. troublesome; intangling*
Embarbascado, da, *a. difficult; intangled*
Embarbascarse, *v. rec. to stick in the ground, as the plough does against any root*
Embarcacion, *s. f. embar-*

catio
vesse
Embarca
place
goods
Embarca
who e
chana
Embarca
bark;
Embarca
bark
Embarcc
king;
Embarga
trator
Embarga
queste
Embarg
tion ||
feit
Sin em
verthe
Embarn
fat, l
Embarni
nish
Embarra
geter;
Embarra
ting;
Embarra
to dau
clay)
Embarril
in a b
Embastar
Embastar
genera
Embate,
of the
Embate d
sness c
Embauca
ter wh
Embauca
ceitful
Embauca
cheat

v. a. to cheat;
lle [*ceit*
s. m. cheat; de-
v. act. to put
runk || *to eat*

iento, *sub. m.*
ent
, *s. f. embassy*
', *s. m. ambas-*

a, *s. f. ambas-*

, *s. m. one that*
kings brown
a, *s. f. making*

v. act. to make
dark || *to ato-*
stop or detain
, *v. a. to stun;*
e
amente, *adver.*
stupid amaze-

miento, *s. mas.*
ent; stunning
v. a. to imbibe
ntain || *to in-*
|| *to press or*

, *v. r. to be very*
eased with one
to be in rapture
or, etc. *V.* Em-
r, etc.
lo, da, *a. out of*
es, etc.
miento, *s. m. V.*
o
, *v. a. to amaze*

s. m. amaze-
rapture
ecerse, *v. r. to*
cious
, *v. a. to make*
[*redden*
cer, v. act. to

Embermejecer, *ver. n. to blush*

Embero, *s. m. the colour of the grapes, when ripe*

Emberrincharse, *v. r. to fall in a passion*

Embestida, *s. f. attack; assault*

Embestidor, *s. m. a troublesome dun, etc.*

Embestidura, *s. f.*, Embestimiento, *s. m.* } *V.* Embestida

Embestir, *v. a. to attack; to assail* || *to beg earnestly; to dun, etc.*

Embetunar, *v. a. to daub with pitch*

Embicar, *v. a. to bend the yards*

Embion, *sub. m. a stroke that sends any thing from its place*

Embioncito, *s. m. dim.* de Embron

Embixar, *v. act. to paint with vermilion*

Embizarrarse, *v. rec. to boast of courage, etc.*

Emblandecer, *v. a. to soften*

Emblanquecer, *v. act. to whiten*

Emblanquecerse, *v. r. to grow white*

Emblanquimiento, *s. m. making* or *growing white*

Emblema, *s. 2. emblem* || *mosaik-work*

Emblemático, ca, *a. emblematical*

Embobamiento, *subs. m amazement*

Embobar, *v. a. to amaze; to stupify*

Embobarse, *ver. r. to be stupified*

Embobecer, *v. n.* } *to turn*
Embobecerse, *v. r.* } *stupid* or *fool*

Embobecimiento, *sub. m. stupidity; madness*

Embocadero, *s. m. of a river's mouth*

Embocadura, *s. f. the entering into a narrow passage* || *the bit of a bridle*

Embocar, *v. a. to get into the mouth of a passage* || *to pass through a narrow place* || *to eat much, and in a hurry* || *to lay a bowl into the post, at billiards* || *to disembogue* || *to catch* || *to cheat; to impose upon*

Embodarse, *v. r. to marry*

Embolar, *v. act. to put balls on the top of a bull's horns* || *to lay the bole on any thing to be gilt*

Embolismal, *a. 2. intercalary*

Embolismo, *s. m. embolism*

E'mbolo, *s. m. the sucker of a pump*

Embolsar, *v. a. to put into a purse*

Embolso, *s. m. putting in a purse*

Embon, *s. m. sheathing of a ship*

Embonada, *s. f. refitting of a ship*

Embonar, *v. a. to improve* || *to sheath to fur a ship* || *to refit*

Embono, *s. m. a piece of cloth that serves to fortify a coat*

Emboque, *s. m. entering of a bowl into the port, etc.*

Embornales, *s. m. pl. scupper-holes*

Emborrachador, ra, *adj. that makes drunk*

Emborrachar, *v. act. to make drunk*

Emborrar, *v. a. to stuff*

Emborrascar, *v. a. to irritate*

Emborricarse, *v. r. to become brutish, stupid*

Emborrizar, *v. a. to card the wool*

Emborrullarse, *ver. r. to wrangle; to quarrel*

Emboscada, *s. f. ambuscade* [*an ambush*

Emboscar, *v. a. to lay*

Emboscarse, *v. r. to lie in ambush*

Embotador, *s. m. one that blunts* [*ting*

Embotadura, *s. f. blun-*

Embotamiento, *s. m. blunting || stupidity*

Embotar, *v. a. to blunt, to dull*

Embotijarse, *v. r. to swell with anger, etc.*

Emboxar, *v. a. to lay the branches that the silk-worms may climb*

Embozar, *v. a. to muffle up one's self*

Embozo, *subst. m. any thing to muffle up one's self with*

Embracilado, da, *a. carried in the arms*

Embravecer, *v. a. to irritate*

Embravecimiento, *s. m. fierceness; fury*

Embrazadura, *sub. f. the hold of a shield*

Embrazar, *v. act. to hold and fix the buckler to the arm*

Embreadura, *s. f. tarring-tar* [*ship*

Embrear, *v. a. to tar a*

Embregarse, *ver. r. to quarrel*

Embreñarse, *v. r. to hide one's self into the briars*

Embriagar, *v. a. to make drunk*

Embriago, ga, *a. drunk*

Embriaguez, *s. f. drunkenness || rapture; extasy*

Embridar, *v. a. to bridle*

Embrion, *s. m. embryo*

Embrocar, *v. a. to pour on || to wind silk on bobbins || to nail a shoe*

Embrollador, *s. m. entangler* [*gle*

Embrollar, *v. a. to entan-*

Embrollo, *s. m. entangling; embroiling*

Embrutecer, *v. a. to besot*

Embuchar, *v. act. to put into the maw; to cram, etc.*

Embudar, *v. act. to pour through a funnel*

Embudo, *s. m. funnel || cheat; deceit*

Emburujar, *v. a. to heap up and mix confusedly*

Embuste, *s. m. a sly lie; a cheat || a witty saying etc. of a young child*

Embustes, *pl. toys; jewels*

Embusterazo, *sab. m. an arrant liar*

Embustero, ra, *s. a liar; a cheating fellow || hypocrite || a witty child*

Embutido, *s. m. in laid work*

Embutir, *v. a. to stuff || to inlay wood, etc.*

Emelga, *s. f. a large furrow*

Emendacion, *s. f. emendadation*

Emendadamente, *adver. correctly*

Emendad
that co
Emendar
Emergen
geney
Emergent
Emérito,
worthy
Emersion
Emético,
Emienda
|| *anne*
Emienda
mendn
Emigraci
Emigrar,
Eminenci
Eminenci
Eminenci
eminer
Eminente
Eminente
nently
Eminenti
eminer
Emisario
Emision,
Emitir,
Emolient
Emolume
lument
Empacar,
into a
Empacars
a passi
Empacha
med w
Empachar
|| *to tr*
Empacho,
|| *bash*
Empacho
surfeit
Empacho:
Empadro
that re
Empadro
a roll
Empadr

ter people to pay
me
lagar, v. a. to disgust
lagarse, v. r. to be
of conceit with
lago, s. m. loathing
lar, v. a. to empale
liada, s. f. the han-
g of a church, etc.
liar, v. a. to hang a
rch, etc.
liada, s. f. palisade
liar, v. a. to pali-
le
madura, s. f. a joi-
g together
mar, v. a. to join
ther two things
lomar, v. a. to fas-
the sails to the yards
nada, s. f. a pie; a
ty
nadilla, s. f. a little
|| a stool or cricket
nado, s. m. a dark
m, etc.
nar, v. act. to put
o a pie
narse los sembrados
trigo, etc. to grow
thick
adillar, v. a. to rob
ntanar, ver. act. to
wn; to submerge ||
put into the mire ||
ntangle
ñar, v. a. to swathe
dull a looking-glass
h the breath
par, v. a. to soak;
imbibe
pelar, v. a. to wrap
in paper || to waste
per; to scribble
pirotado, da, a. puf-
up [up
pujar, v. act. to fill
retar, v. a. to pack

Emparamentar, v. act. to adorn, to hang a room
Emparchar, v. a. to lay on plasters
Emparedamiento, s. m. shutting up betwixt walls
Emparedar, v. a. to shut up betwixt walls
Emparejar, v. a. to match
Emparentado (estar uno muy), to have goods relations
Emparentar, v. n. to contract kindred
Emparrado, s. m. a vine-arbour
Empastar, v. a. to fill or make with paste
Empatar, v. act. to make equal or even || to detain
Empate, s. m. equality of suffrages || suspension
Empavesada, s. f. netting
Empavesar, v. a. to barricade a ship
Empecer, v. a. to hurt
Empecible, a. 2. hurtful; prejudicial
Empedernirse, } v. r. to
Empedernecerse, } petrify
Empedrado, s. m. pavement
Empedrado, da, a. full of pock-holes
Empedrador, s. m. paver
Empedrar, v. a. to pave
Empegadura, s. f. pitching
Empegar, v. a. to pitch
Empelar, v. n. to begin to be hairy
Empellar, v. a. V. Empujar [with skin
Empellejar, v. a. to cover
Empeller, v. a. V. Impeler [a thrust
Empellon, s. m. a push;

Empelotarse, ver. r. to quarrel
Empenta, s. f. a prop
Empentar, v. a. to prop
Empeñadamente, adver. stoutly
Empeñamiento, subs. m. pawning || takingpledges [|| to engage
Empeñar, v. a. to pawn
Empeñarse, v. r. to run in debt || to engage, or oblige one's self || to be absolutely bent || to dare dangers, etc.
Empeño, s. m. pawning || pledge || engagement || stoutness || protector
Empeoramiento, subs. m. making worse
Empeorar, v. a. to make worse [lessen
Empequeñecer, v. a. to
Emperador, s. m. an emperor
Emperadora, ratriz, s. f. an empress
Emperdigar, v. a. V. Perdigar
Emperegilarse, ver. r. to adorn, or paint one's self
Emperezar, v. n. to be or grow flothful
Emperezar, v. a. to retard; to stop
Empericado, da, a. who wears a periwig
Empero, conj. nevertheless
Emperrada, s. f. a peculiar game at cards
Emperrarse, v. r. to grow mad, as a dog
Empetro, s. m a plant so called
Empeyne, s. m. the lower belly || the instep || the wamp of a shoe || a

horse's hoof || *tetter; ring worm*
Empeynoso, **sa**, *a. full of tetters*
Empezar, *v. a. to begin*
Empicotadura, *s. f. setting on the pillory*
Empicotar, *v. a. to set on the pillory*
Empinadura, *s. f. raising*
Empinar, *v. a. to raise; to lift up*
Empinarse, *v. r. to stand a tip-toe* || *to prance*
Empiño, *s. m. elevation; height*
Empiolar, *v. a. to put on the jesses*
Empireo, *s. m. empyrean*
Empireo, **rea**, *a. empyreal*
Empírico, *s. m. empirick*
Empizarrar, *v. a. to slate*
Emplastar, *v. a. to lay on plasters*
Emplasto, *s. m. a plaster*
Emplástrico, ca, *a. suppurative*
Emplazador, *s. m. a plaintiff or petitioner* || *summoner*
Emplazamiento, *subs. m. summons* [*mon*
Emplazar, *v. a. to sum-*
Emplear, *v. a. to employ*
Empleo, *s. m. a buying of any goods* || *employ; employment* || *trade* || *mistress; love*
Emplomar, *v. a. to lead*
Emplumar, *v. a. to feather*
Emplumar, emplumecer, *v. n. to begin to have feathers*
Empobrecer, *v. a. to impoverish* [*poor*
Empobrecer, *v. n. to grow*
Empollar, *v. a. to brood*

Empolvoramiento, *sub. m. bedusting*
Empolvorar, } *v. a. to be-*
Empolvorizar, } *dust* || *to powder*
Emponzoñar, *ver. a. to poison* || *to infect*
Emponzoñoso, **sa**, *a. poisonous*
Emporcar, *v. a. to foul; to dirt* [*bet-towen*
Emporio, *sub. m. a mar-*
Emposta, *s. f. impost*
Empotrar, *v. a. to shut* or *set in a wall*
Empozar, *v. a. to put* or *throw into a well*
Emprendedor, *s. m. undertaker*
Emprender, *v. a. to undertake*
Emprensar, *v. a. V.* Aprensar
Empresa, *s. f. enterprize emblem; device*
Emprèstido, *s. m. borrowing* || *lending* || *the thing lent* || *tax; duty*
Emprestillador, *s. m. one who borrows money with a design to cheat*
Emprèstito, *s. m. V.* Emprèstido
Emprimar, *v. a. to prime the cloth* || *to card the wool*
Emprimerar, *v. a. to give the first place*
Empuchar, *v. a. to wash with lye*
Empujamiento, *sub. m. a thrusting* or *pushing*
Empujar, *v. a. to thrust; to push* || *to excite* || *to turn out; to supplant*
Empujo, *s. m. the flying* out of *a vault*, etc.
Empujon, s. m. *a push; a thrust*

Empulgadu
bending
Empulgar,
bow
Empulguer
notches
the bow
Apretar á
gueras, *t*
the rack
Empuñador
who gra
Empuñadu
handle
Empuñar,
to gripe
Empuñir,
sheets
Emulacion
tion
Emulador,
Emular, *v*
E'mulo, *s.*
competi
Emulo, la
Emulsion,
Emunctori
emunct
En, *prep.*
Enagenabl
ble
Enagenaci
tion || *r*
out
Enagenam
alienati
mind ||
Enagenar
te || *to*
|| *to p*
himself
Enagenars
out wit
besides
Enaguarch
of wate
Enaguas,
pettic
Enagua

r, *v. a. to have*
d of grand chil-

s. f. enallage
v. act. to heat
to make it look

r, *v. a. to saddle*
pack-saddle
lado, da, *a. m.*
ike [nable
le, *a. unalie-*
ar, *v. a. to mark*
r with red oker
amente, *adver.*
r
illo, lla, *a. dim.*
norado
izo, za, *a. ea-*
ove [moured
o, da, *a. ena-*
or, *sub. m. he*
amours
, *v. a. to ena-*
[fall in love
arse, *ver. r. to*
, *v. a. V.* En-

, *s. y a. dwarf*
, *v. a. to set up*
, *v. a. to inflame*
, *v. a. to cover*
and
r, *v. a. to erect;*
[prance
arse, *ver. r. to*
co, *a. m. enhar-*
[tion
n, *s. f. enarra-*
s, en balde, *adv.*
mas, balde
ar, *v. n. to ride*
ar, *v. a. to re-*
the troopers
r, *v. n. to take*
r a periwig
cer, *v. n. to grow*
[ter a beast
r, *v. a. to hal-*

Encabestrarse la bestia, *to put its foot over the halter*
Encabezamiento, *sub. m. the roll of the impositions*
Encabezar, *v. a. to register; to inrol*
Encabezarse, *v. r. to compound for taxes, etc.*
Encabriar, *v. a. to place* or *dispose a roof*
Encabritarse, *ver. act. to prance*
Encachar, *v. a. to fix any thing in a wall*
Encadenadura, *s. f.* / Encadenamiento, *s. m.* } *chaining || concatenation*
Encadenar, *v. a. to chain || to concatenate*
Encalabriar / Encalabrinar } *v. a. to disturb the head*
Encaladura, *s. f. whitening with lime*
Encalar, *v. a. to whiten with lime || to put in a tube [sands*
Encalladero, *s. m. shelf,*
Encallar, *v. n. to run aground [corns, etc.*
Encallecer, *v. n. to have*
Encallecido en astucias, *a cunning crafty fellow*
Encalletrar, *v. a. to be master of a language, etc.*
Encalmadura, *s. f. foundering; suffocating*
Encalmarse, *v. r. to be suffocated with heat, etc.*
Encalvar / Encalvecer } *ver. n. to grow bald*
Encamarar, *v. a. to lay up corn in a granary*

Encamarse, *v. r. to put one's self in bed*
Encambronar, *v. a. to inclose with thorns || to strengthen with iron, etc. [ting*
Encaminadura, *s. f. direc-*
Encáminar, *v. a. to direct; to lead*
Encaminarse, *v. r. to take the road to*
Encamisada, *s. f. Camisade*
Encamisarse, *v. r. to put on a shirt over one's cloaths*
Encanalar, *v. a. to convey through a canal*
Encanarse, *v. r. to grow stiff by surprise, etc.*
Encanastar, *v. a. to put into a basket*
Encancerarse, *ver. r. to grow to a cancer*
Encandiladera / Encandiladora } *s. f. a bawd*
Encandilar, *ver. act. to dazzle*
Encanecer, *v. n. to grow grey headed*
Encanijamiento, *s. m. extenuation*
Encanijarse, *v. r. to grow lean; to fall away*
Encantacion, *subs. f. enchantment*
Encantadera, *subs. f. enchantress*
Encantador, ra, *adject. charming*
Encantador, *s. enchanter*
Encantamento, *s. m. enchantment*
Encantamiento, *s. m. enchantment*
Encantar, *v. a. to enchant to charm*
Encantarar, *v. a.* to put in a pitchet

Encanto, s. m. *enchantment* || *rapture*

Es un encanto, *it is a wonder*

Encantorio, s. m. V. Encanto

Encantusar, v. a *to cheat with flattering words*

Encañado, s. m. *a water-duct* || *reed-arbour*

Encañadora, s. f. *a woman who winds silk on canes*

Encañadura, s. f. V. Encañado || *the reeds* or *straw of rye*

Encañar, ver. act. *to make cane hedges, etc.* || *to convey the water through pipes* || *to wind silk on canes*

Encañonado (Viento), s. masc. *a wind blowing through a narrow passage*

Encañonar, v. a. *to plait; to fold* || *to wind silk on canes*

Encañonar, v. n. *to begin to have feathers*

Encañutar, v. a. *to plait; to fold*

Encapacetado, da, adj. *armed with a helmet*

Encapachadura, subs. f. *quantity of frails placed upon one another*

Encapachar, v. a. *to put in a frail*

Encapirotado, da, adject. *that has a hood on*

Encapotadura, s. f. *a dogged, sullen look*

Encapotamiento, s. m. *a sullen look*

Encapotar, v. a. *to hide; to conceal* || *to frown*

Encapricharse, v. r. *to be prepossessed*, or *fond*

Encapuzado, da, adj. *covered with a mourning cloke*

Encarado, da, adj. *opposite*

Bien, ó mal encarado, *that has a good* or *ill countenance*

Encaramadura, s. f. *raising* || *a hill*

Encaramar, v. a. *to raise* || *to extol*

Encaramiento, s. m. V. Encaro

Encaramillotado, da, adj. *raised*

Encarar, v. n. *to set face to face*

Encarar la arcabuz, etc. *to take one's aim at one*

Encaratulado, da, adject. *masked*

Encarcavinar, v. act. *to stink*

Encarcaxado, da, adj. *armed with a quiver*

Encarceladito, ta, adject. *dim. de* Encarcelado

Encarcelado, da, a. y s. *prisoner*

Encarcelar, v. a. *to imprison*

Encarecedor, s. m. *amplifier*

Encarecer, v. a. *to raise the price* || *to extol; to magnify*

Encarecidamente, adver. *with exaggeration*

Encarecimiento, s. m. *rising in price* || *exaggeration*

Encargadamente, adver. *earnestly; carefully*

Encargar, v. a. *to give in charge*

Encargarse, v. r. *to take a thing upon one's self*

Encargo, s. m. *charge; commission* || *office; employment*

Encariñarse, v. r. *to be affectionnate* to one

Encarna, s. f. *a bait*

nation || *c*
Encarnadino
carnadine
Encarnado, d
coloured
Encarnadura
Encarnar, v.
|| *to stick*
Encarnar la
grow up,
new flesh
Encarnativo,
carnative
Encarnecer,
or *increas*
Encarnizado
red; infla
Encarnizami
devouring
Encarnizar,
Encarnizarse
cruelly b
one; to f
him
Encaro, s. n
upon atte
Encaro de e
ming
Encarrillar,
duct a c
proper tra
Encarrillarse
be choake
Encarroñar,
fect; to c
Encarrujarse
ne or *winc*
Encartacion,
padronami
sallage
Encartamien
outlawry
Encartar, v.
claim an
register
Encasamento
Encasamien
pair; r

a. to set a bone
ado, da, *adj.*
with little bells
r, *v. a. to fas-*
at on the head
uade
rse, *v. r. to be*
t
o, da, *adj. for-*
h many cast-
d
o, *v. r. to get*
astle — to be
t
, *s. m. one that*
[*sing*
, *s. f. encha-*
. a. to enchase
in a box, etc.
t, or *thrust in*
ose upon
v. r. to intru-
self || *to en-*
s business
m. enchasing
g together ||
|| *inlaid work*
ncaxe, *arbi-*
|| salto y en-
oss-caper
o, *s. m. mud-*

, *v. a. to lay*
trunck
iento, *s. m. a*
caused by oats
ter
se, *v. r. to eat*
t a quantity of
nd drink water
y after
lo, *s. m. a sort*
with onions,

s. f. cheese vat
v. a. to make

niento, subs. m.
in the dirt

Encenagarse, *v. r. to tumble in the dirt*

Encencerrado, da, *adj. with a bell hanging about the neck*

Encender, *v. a. to kindle* || *to light candles* || *to heat*, or *burn* || *to incense* || *to foment a quarrel*

Encenderse, *v. r. to burn with anger*

Encendidamente, *adv. ardently*

Encendidillo, lla, *adj. somewhat hot* or *ardent*

Encendido de color, *high-coloured*

Encendimiento, *subs. m. kindling*

Encenizar, *v. a. to cower with ashes*

Encensar, Encensuar } *v. a. to rent* || *to take at a rent*

Encentadura, *subs. f.*, Encentamiento, *s. m.* } *assaying*

Encentar, *v. a. to assay; to taste; to broach, etc.*

Encepar, *v. a. to set a man in the stocks*

Encerado, da, *adj. of wax-colour* || *dense; thick*

Huevos encerados, *soft boiled eggs*

Encerado, *s. m. cere-cloth* || *a window of waxed paper, etc.* || *cerate*

Encerar, *v. a. to wax*

Encerotar, *v. a. to wax a thread*

Encerradero, *s. m. V.* Encierro

Encerrado, da, *adj. short; concise*

Encerrador, *s. m. he who shuts* || *cow-herd*

Encerramiento, *s. m. shutting* || *inclosure* || *dungeon*

Encerrar, *v. a. to shut; to lock up* || *to inclose* || *to contain*

Encerrona, *s. f. retirement*

Encestar, *v. a. to put into a basket*

Enchancletar, *v. a. to put on slippers* || *to slip one's shoes on*

Encharcado, da, *adject. stagnant*

Encharcarse, *v. r. to be full of puddles*

Encias, *s. f. pl. the gums*

Enciclopedia, *s. f. Encyclopedia*

Encierne, *adv. just ready to ripen*

Encierro, *s. m. shutting; locking up* || *inclosure* || *retirement* || *dungeon*

Encima, *adv. upon* || *on the top* || *besides*

Encimar, *v. a. to raise up*

Encina, *s. f. holm oak*

Encinal, Encinar, } *s. m. a grove of holm oaks*

Encintar, *v. a. to adorn with ribands*

Enclaustrado, da, *adject. cloistered up*

Enclavacion, *s. f. nailing*

Enclavado, da, *adj. inclosed*

Enclavadura, *s. f. nailing*

Enclavar, *v. a. to nail*

Enclavijar, *v. a. to join* or *fasten with pins* || *to stick pins in a musical instrument*

Enclenque, *s. m. sick; fallen away; extenuated*

Enclocarse, *v. r. to cluck*

Encobertado, da, *adject. wrapped up in a carpet*

Encobijar, *v. a. to cover; to shelter*

Encoger, *v. a. to shrink*

Encogerse, *ver. r. to be bashful* || *to humble one's self*

Encogido, da, *adj. bashful; mean-hearted*

Encogimiento, *s. m. shrinking* || *pusillanimity* || *submission* [*of squibs*

Encohetado, da, *adj. full*

Encoladura, *s. f. gluing*

Encolar, *v. a. to glue*

Encolerizarse, *v. r. to fall into a passion*

Encomendar, *v. a. to recommend* || *to commend*

Encomendar, *v. n. to obtain a commandry*

Encomendero, *s. m. a factor, etc.* [*comiastick*

Encomiástico, ca, *adj. en-*

Encomienda, *s. f. recommandation* || *commission* || *compliment* || *commandry* || *care; protection*

Encomio, *s. m. encomium*

Enconamiento, *s. m. inflammation*

Enconar, *v. a. to inflame; to rankle*

Enconoso, sa, *adj. inflammatory* || *hurtful*

Encontra, *adv. V.* Contra

Encontradamente, *adv. in a contrary sense*

Encontradizo,za (Hacerse), *to go to meet one*

Encontrar, *v. a.* y *n. to meet*

Encontrarse con las lanzas, *to tilt with lances*—en palabras, *to come to hard words* — en las opiniones, *to differ in opinion*

Encontron, *s. m. a push; a jostling, etc.*

Encorajado, da, *adj. angry*

Encorar, *v. a. to cover with leather*

Encorazado, da, *adj. armed with a cuirass* || *covered with leather*

Encorchar, *v. a. to put the bees in the hive*

Encordar, *v. a. to string a musical instrument*

Encordelar, *v. a. to cord a bed*

Encordio, *s. m. a bubo*

Encordonar, *v. a. to tie* or *adorn with strings* or *braids* [rar

Encorecer, *v. a. V.* Enco-

Encornijamiento, *s. m. V.* Cornijon

Encornudar, *v. n. to have the horns sprout out*

Encornudar, *v. a. to cornute*

Encorozar, *v. a. to put a paper cap like a mitre on an offender's head*

Encortinar, *v. a. to hang curtains about a bed*

Encorvada, *s. f. bowing down* || *an ancient sort of dance* || *axe-wort*

Encorvadura, *s. f* } *bowing;*
Encorvamiento, *s. m.* } *bending*

Encorvar, *v. a. to bow; to bend*

Encostarse, *v. r. to come near the coast*

Encostradura, *s. f. crust*

Encostrar, *v. a. to cover with a crust*

Encovar, *v. act. to shut up in a cellar*

Encoxarse, *v. r. to grow lame* [*greasy*

Encrasár, *v. a. to make*

Encrespadillo, lla, adj. *crisped; curled*

Encrespador, ... *ling iron*

Encrespadura ... *s. f.*

Encrespamiento, *s. m.*

Encrespar, *v.*

Encresparse ... *foam, to f*

Encrespo, *s.* ... *of hair*

Encrestado, d

Encrestarse, ... *up the com*

Encrisnejado,

Encrucijada, ... *way*

Encrudecer, ... *kle* || *to ca*

Encrudecerse ... *into a pas*

Encruelecer, ... *cruel*

Encubar, *v. a* ... *a tub*, or *c*

Encubertar, ... *horses with*

Encubierta, ... *cheat*

Encubiertame ... *cretly* || *fra*

Encubredizo, ... *may be con*

Encubridor, ... *cealer*

Encubrimient

Encubrir, *v. a*

Encucar, *v.* ... *nuts, etc.*

Encuentro, *s* ... *knocking* || ... *encounter* || ... *difficulty*

Encumbrado, ... *high; lofty*

Encumbramie ... *height; ele*

Encumbrar, ... to get up

...utir, *v. a. to season ...umbers*
...ble, *adj. weak; feeble*
...ágono, *s. m. ende...gon*
...silabo, ba, *adj. of ...en syllables*
...cha, *s. f. a dirge; a ...rning song* [ner
...hadera, *s. f. a mour...*
...har, *v. a. to mourn ... funerals*
...chilla, *s. f. dim. de ...decha*
...moniado, da, *adjec. ...vilish; mishievous*
...moniar, *v. a. to pos...s with devil || to put ...an in a great fury*
...ntado, da, *adj. in...ted*
...ntar, *v. a. to enchase*
...ntecer, *v. n. to cut teeth* [rightly
...rezadamente, *adver.*
...rezadera, *subs. f. a ...aight way*
...rezador, *s. m. one ...o guides or directs*
...rezamiento, *s. m. ma...g straight, etc.*
...rezar, *v. a. to make ...ight || to compound; ...ut in order || to di...' || to send*
...rerezarse, *v. r. to get ... again*
...rezo, *s. m. sending; ...reeting* [redor
...rredor, *adv. V.* Der...
...eudarse, *v. r. to con...act debts*
...iablada, *s. f. masque...ade in which people ...isguises themselves li...e devils*
...iablar, *v. a. to possess ...ith devil—to corrupt; ...pervert*

Endibia, *s. f. endive*
Endilgador, ra, *s. a pimp; a bawd*
Endilgar, *v. a. to direct || to make easy || to persuade*
Endiosamiento, *subs. m. pride || rapture; extasy*
Endiosar, *v. a. to deify*
Endiosarse, *v. r. to grow proud || to be in rapture*
Endosar, *v. a. to endorse*
Endoso, *sub. m. endorsement*
Endragonarse, *v. r. to fly into a passion*
Endriago, *s. m. a strange monster, a dragon, etc*
Endrina, *s. f. damson*
Endrino, *s. m. damson-tree*
Endulzar, *v. a. to sweeten*
Endurador, *s. m. a sparing stingy fellow*
Endurar, *v. a. to harden || to spare || to be covetous || to endure || to use delays*
Endurecer, *v. a. to harden || to inure*
Endurecimiento, *s. m. V.* Dureza
Ene de palo, *a gallows*
Eneágono, *s. enneagon*
Eneático, ca, *adj. belonging to the number nine* [terick-days
Dias eneáticos, *climac-*
Enebral, *sub. m. a place where juniper-trees grow* [tree
Enebro, *sub. m. juniper-*
Eneldo, *s. m. dill*
Enemiga, *s. f. enmity || an unkind mistress*
Enemigamente, *adv. like an enemy*
Enemigarse, *v. r. V.* Enemistarse

Enemigo, *s. m. an enemy*
Enemigo, ga, *a. contrary; adverse*
Enemistad, *s. f. enmity*
Enemistar, *v. a. to make an enemy*
Enemistarse, *v. r. to be at enmity with another*
Energía, *s. f. energy*
Enérgicamente, *ad. energically* [gumenus
Energúmeno, *s. m. ener-*
Enerizarse, *v. r. to stand up on end*
Enero, *s. m. january*
Enervar, *v. a. to enervate*
Enexar, *v. a. to put the axle-tree to a cast*
Enfadar, *v. a. to weary; to tire* [disquiet
Enfado, *s. m. weariness;*
Enfadosamente, *adv. tediously*
Enfadoso, sa, *a. tedious; troublesome*
Enfaldarse, *v. r. to tuck up one's gown, etc.*
Enfaldo, *s. m. tucking up*
Enfardelar, *v. a. to make up into a bandle*
E'nfasis, *s. f. emphasis*
Enfastiar, enfastidiar, *v. a. V.* Enfadar
Enfáticamente, *adv. emphatically* [tick
Enfático, ca, *adj. empha-*
Enfermar, *v. n. to grow sick*
Enfermar, *v. a. to make sick || to hurt || to enfeeble*
Enfermedad, *s. f. sickness || hurt* or *danger*
Enfermería, *s. f. infirmary*
Enfermero, ra, *s. overseer of an infirmary*
Enfermizar, *v. a. V.* Enfermar

Enfermizo, za, *adj. sickly* || *unwholesome*
Enfermo, ma, *adj. sick* || *unhealthy* || *weak*
Enfervorizar, *v. a. to stimulate* [*ment*
Enfeudacion, *s. f. enfeoff-*
Enfeudar, *v. a. to enfeoff*
Enfilar, *v. a. to enfilade* || *to go on; to pursue*
En fin, *adv. in fine; at last*
Enfitéosis } *subs. f. a lease*
Enfitéusis } *from ten to a hundred years*
Enflaquecer, *v. a. to make lean* [*lean*
Enflaquecer, *v. n. to grow*
Enflautador, ra, *s. one who allures to vice*
Enflautar, *v. a. to entice or allure to wickedness*
Enfosado, *s. m. a foundered horse* [*plexed*
Enfoscado, da, *adj. per-*
Enfoscarse, *v. r. to raise into a passion; to look angry* [*tangling*
Enfrascamiento, *s. m. en-*
Enfrascarse, *v. r. to be entangled*
Enfrenamiento, *s. m. bridling* || *moderation*
Enfrenar, *v. a. to bridle* || *to refrain*
Enfrente, *adver. over-against*
Enfriadera, *s. f.* } *a vessel*
Enfriador, *s. m.* } *to cool drink in ice, etc.*
Enfriamiento, *s. m. cooling*
Enfriar, *v. a. to cool*
Enfriarse, *v. r. to slacken; to grow cold*
Enfroscarse, *v. r. V.* Enfrascarse
Enfundadura, *s. f. Putting into a case*

Enfundar, *v. a. to put into a case* || *to fill*, or *stuff* || *to contain*
Enfurecer, *v. a. to make furious* [*furious*
Enfurecerse, *v. r. to grow*
Enfurtir, *v. a. to thicken cloth at the fulling-mill*
Engabanado, da, *adj. covered with a great loose coat*
Engace, *s. m. V.* Engarce
Engafar, *ver. a. to cock a gun, etc.*
Engalanar, *v. a. to adorn; to set off*
Engallado, da, *adj. erect; standing up*
Enganchador, *subs. m. a cunning recruiter*
Enganchamiento, *s. m. decoying of people to enlist themselves*
Enganchar, *v. a. to catch by a hook* || *to decoy; to allure*
Engañadizo, za, *adj. easy to be deceived*
Engañador, *s. m. deceiver*
Engañar, *v. a. to deceive*
Engañarse, *v. r. to err; to mistake*
Engañifa, *sub. f. deceit; trick*
Engaño, *sub. m. deceit; fraud* [*ceitfully*
Engañosamente, *adv. de-*
Engañoso, sa, *adj. deceitful*
Engarabatar, *v. act. to catch by a hook*
Engarabitarse, *ver. r. to climb up*
Engarbarse, *v. r. to perch on the top of a tree*
Engarbullar, *v. a. to entangle*; to confound
Engarce, *s. m.* connexion
Engargantar, *v. a.* to run

the foot step into
Engaritado, *nished boxes*
Engaritar, ·
Engarrafar, *with a ho claws*
Engarrotar *with cor*
Engarzador *who stri pimp*, or
Engarzar, *beads in*
Engastar, *stone in*
Engaste, s. *of stones*
Engatado,
Engatar, *v.* or *catch*
Engatusar, *in a ban*
Engavillar, *up into s*
Engaytador
Engaytar, *v by promi*
Engazar, etc
Engendrabl *can be e*
Engendradc *ter*
Engendrar,
Engendro, *bryon*
Mal engen
Englandado
Englantado *with acor*
Engolado, d *lowed do*
Engolfar, *v out to se*
Engolfarse, one's sel ness, e

o, da, *adject. in a ruf*
lo, da, *adject. haughty*
·inarse, *v. r. to* ... *roud and im-* ... *nt || to fall in*
ar, *v. a. to al-*
·ro, ra, *adject.* ... *ay be gummed*
ıra, *s. f. gum-*
, *v. a. to gum*
or, *s. m. he that* ... *nothing but good* ... *[fatten*
, *v. a. y n. to*
s. m. hindran- ... *stacle*
o, sa, *adj. trou-* ... *se*
v. a. to hinge
ecer, *v. a. to ag-* ... *ise || to exagge-*
ecimiento, *s. m.* ... *ndising || exag-* ... *on*
r, *v. a. to fatten* ... *rease*
dar, *v. a. to af-* ... *ravity*
iento, *s. m. va-* ... *pride*
se, *v. r. to grow* ... *|| to dress one's*
rse, *v. r. to stand* ... *end || to swell*
r, *v. a. to make* ... *r; to enlarge, etc.*
ır, *v. n. to grow* ... *r*
lador, *s. m. gluer*
lamiento, *sub. m.* ... *g*
ır, *v. a. to glue*

Engrudillo, *s. m. dim. de* Engrudo
Engrudo, *s. m. a glue or paste made of flour and water*
Engualdrapar, *v. a. to caparison*
Enguantado, da, *adject. with gloves on*
Enguedejar, *v. a. to put in locks; to dress the hair*
Enguijarrar, *v. a. to pave with pebbles*
Enguirnaldado, da, *adj. adorned with garlands*
Enguizgar, *v. a. to excite*
Engullidor, ra, *s. glutton*
Engullir, *v. a. to swallow up; to devour*
Enhambrecer, *v. n. to be hungry*
Enharinar, *v. a. to sprinkle with meal*
Enhastiar, *v. a. to disgust*
Enhastío, *s. m. loathing*
Enhebrar, *v. a. to thread*
Enhenar, *v. a. to cover,* or *pack up with hay*
Enherbolar, *v. a. to poison with herbs*
Enhestador, *sub. m. one that rears up*
Enhestadura, *s. f. rearing*
Enhestar, *v. a. to rear up*
Enhiesto, ta, *adj. standing upright*
Enhilar, *v. a. to thread || to string*
Enhorabuena, *s. f. congratulation*
Enhorabuena, *adv. well and good*
Enhoramala, *adv. in an ill hour*
Enhornar, *v. a. to put in the oven*
Enhuerar, *v. a. to make eggs addle*
Enigma, *s. m. enigma*

Enigmático, ca, *adject. enigmatical*
Enjaezar, *v. a. to harness; to furnish a horse*
Enjaguar, etc. *V.* Enjuagar
Enjalbegador, *s. m. plaisterer*
Enjalbegar, *v. a. to whitewash the walls*
Enjaular, *v. a. to cage*
Enjordanar, *v. a. to make look younger*
Enjorginarse, *v. r. to black one's face with soot*
Enjoyado, da, *adj. having a great quantity of jewels*
Enjoyar, *v. a. to adorn with jewels*
Enjuagadientes, *s. m. the washing of the mouth with water*
Enjuagadura, *s. f. water made use of for rinsing*
Enjuagar, *v. a. to wash one's mouth || to water,* or *soak*
Enjuague, *s. m. the water put into the mouth to wash it || ostentation*
Enjuiciar, *v. n. to make a cause ready*
Enjuncar, *v. a. to bind with rush-strings*
Enjuncar la vela, *to lash fast the sail*
Enjunque, *sub. m. heavy matters put at the bottom of a ship*
Enlabiar, *v. a. to deceive with fair words*
Enlabio, *s. m. fawning || persuasion*
Enlace, *s. m. interlacing || connexion*
Enladrillador, *s. m. one that paves with square tiles*
Enladrillar, *v. a.* to pave with square tiles

with mud or *slime*
Enlardar, *v. a. to lard*
Enlazable, *a.* 2. *that may be interlaced, etc.*
Enlazador, ra, *a. that ties, binds, connects, etc.*
Enlazadura, *s. f.* / Enlazamiento, *s. m.* } *interlacing, etc.* || *connexion* || *union; friendhip*
Enlazar, *v. a. to tie; to knot* || *to interlace* || *to connect*
Enligarse, *v. r. to be daubed with bird-lime*
Enllenar, *v. a. to fill*
Enlodar, *v. a. to dirt*
Enloquecer, *v. a. to make mad* [*mad*
Enloquecer, *v. n. to grow*
Enlosar, *v. a. to pave with broad stones*
Enlozanarse, *v. r. to boast; to presume*
Enlucimiento, *s. m. white-washing* || *polishing*
Enlucir, *v. a. to white-wash the walls* || *to polish; to brighten*
Enlustrecer, *v. a. to give a gloss* || *to illustrate*
Enlutar, *v. a. to put into mourning* || *to cover with a veil, etc.*
Enmaderamiento, *sub. m. timber work; wainscot, etc.*
Enmaderar, *v. a. to make timber-works; to wainscot, etc.*
Enmagrecer, *ver. neut. to grow lean*
Enmalecer, *v. n. to be* or *to fall sick* [*chased*
Enmalletado, da, *adj. en-*
Enmantar, *v. a. to cover with a mantle, etc.*

sails [*tangle*
Enmarañar, *v. a. to en-*
Enmararse, *v. r. to put out to sea*
Enmaromar, *v. a. to tie with a rope*
Enmascarar, *v. a. to mask*
Enmechar, *v. a. to mortise* [*dle*
Enmedio, *adv. in the mid-*
Enmelar, *v. a. to sweeten with honey*
Enmohecerse, *v. r. to grow mouldy* [*ten*
Enmollecer, *v. a. to sof-*
Enmudecer, *v. a. to bid one hold his tongue*
Enmudecer, *v. n. to grow dumb* [*ken*
Ennegrecer, *v. a. to blac-*
Ennoblecer, *v. a. to ennoble* [*nobling*
Ennoblecimiento, *s. m. en-*
Ennoviar, *v. n. to marry*
Enodrida, *adj. fem. the hen when she has done laying eggs*
Enojadizo, za, *adj. passionate*
Enojar, *v. a. to anger* || *to vex; to tire* || *to hurt*
Enojarse, *v. r. to be raging*
Enojo, *s. m. anger* || *disquiet* || *hurt*
Enojosamente, *adv. angrily*
Enojoso, sa, *adj. troublesome* || *hurtful*
Enorme, *a.* 2. *enormous*
Enormemente, *adv. enormously* [*mity*
Enormidad, *s. f. enor-*
Enpos, *prep. after*
Enquadernacion, *sub. f. a binding of a book*
Enquadernador, *sub. m. a book binder* || *a pimp*

books — t
agree
Enquiciado, d
upon the hi
Enquillotrarse
transformed
love
Enramada, *s. f*
de of bough
Enramar, *v. a*
or *adorn w*
Enranciarse, *v*
rancid
Enrarecer, *v.*
fy; to make
Enrasar, *v. a*
even or *smo*
Enrasar, *v. n. t*
bare
Enrayar, *v. a*
spokes into
Enredadera, *s.*
sort of gras
Enredador, *s.*
dy; inter m
Enredamiento
tangling
Enredar, *v. a.*
the net || *to*
to set toget
ears
Enredo, *s. m.*
|| *an intric*
chievous lie
of a stage-p
Enredoso, sa
gled
Enrehojar, *v.*
wax into a
Enrejado, *s. m*
ge or *arbou*
Enrejar, *v. a.*
|| *to make p*
etc. || *to set*
the plough
Enriar, *v. a. to*
Enriquecer, *v*
make or *g*

da, *a. rocky ;*
c.
nto, *s. m. get-*
ong the rocks
v. act. to get
the rocks and
s || to put on
[the lance
v. a. to couch
. m. curling
. a. to curl the

v. a. to castle
at chess
. a. to break on
l
ar, *v. act. to*
ine
. a. to blunt
er, *v. a. y n. to*
grow hoarse
imiento, *s. m.*
ss
a. to dye of the
ur
ra, *sub. f. ben-*
and
v. a. to bend or
d || to make red
v. a. to make
fair
, *v. a. to besot*
a, *s. f. camisade*
, *v. a. to wrap*
et
s. f. a sallad
, *s. f. sweet-*
ixt together
. f. V. Enxalma
ra, *s. f. a wo-*
it says prayers
k people
r, *sub. m. one*
s prayers, etc.
lmar
v. a. to attempt
by saying cer-
ayers over sick

Ensalmo, *s. m. a cure made by saying strange words, etc.*
Ensalzador, *s. m. praiser*
Ensalzamiento, *s. m. praising*
Ensalzar, *v. a. to praise ; to magnify*
Ensalzarse, *v. r. to boast*
Ensambenitar, *v. a. to put on a sambenito*
Ensamblador, *s. m. a joiner*
Ensambladura, *s. f.* } *joining*
Ensamblage, *s. m.* }
Ensamblar, *v. a. to join ; to enchase ; to inlay*
Ensancha, *s. f. enlarging; widening || a widening piece* [*widens*
Ensachador, *s. m. one that*
Ensanchamiento, *s. m. widening*
Ensanchar, *v. a. to widen*
Ensancharse, *ver. r. to grow stately and require much courtship*
Ensanche, *s. m. V.* Ensancha [*mad*
Ensandecer, *v. n. to run*
Ensangostar, *ver. act. to straiten*
Ensangrentamiento, *s. m. daubing with blood*
Ensangrentar, *ver. a. to daub with blood*
Ensañar, *v. a. to anger ; to enrage*
Ensarnecer, *v. n. to have the itch*
Ensartar, *v. a. to string beads, etc. to enter upon a long story, etc.*
Ensay, *s. m. essay*
Ensayador, *s. m. essayer*
Ensalayado, da, *adj. covered with a bag, etc.*
Ensayar, *v. a. to assay ; to try || to rehearse || to train* or *bring up*

Ensaye, *s. m. essay*
Ensayo, *s. m. assaying ; trial || rehearsing*
Ensenada, *s. f. a bay in the sea* [*the bosom*
Ensenar, *v. a to put into*
Enseñable, *a. 2. easy to be taught*
Enseñadero, ra, *a. docible* [*ned*
Enseñado, da, *adj. lear-*
Enseñador, ra, *s. teacher*
Enseñamiento, *s. m. instruction*
Enseñanza, *s. f. teaching ; instruction*
Enseñar, *v. a. to teach || to shew ; to point out*
Enseñarse, *v. r. to accustom one's self*
Enseñoreador, *s. m. lord*
Enseñorear, *v. a. to be lord of ; to command*
Enserpentado, da, *a. enraged as a serpent*
Ensevar, *v. a. to tallow*
Ensilar, *v. a. to put into a granary || to eat voraciously*
Ensilladura, *s. f. saddling*
Ensillar, *v. a. to saddle*
Ensoberbecer, *v. a. to make proud*
Ensoberbecerse, *v. r. to grow proud || to be raging*
Ensogar, *v. a. to cord*
Ensolver, *v. a. to mix ; to confound*
Ensolverse, *v. r. to come* or *amount*
Ensopar, *v. a. to dip the bread in the soup, etc.*
Ensordamiento, *s. m. deafness*
Ensordar } *v. a. to make deaf*
Ensordecer }
Ensordecer, *v. n.* to grow *deaf*

like a ring || *to curl the hair* || *to link together with rings*
Ensotarse, *v. r. to get into a wood* [*ling*
Ensuciamiento, *s. m. fou-*
Ensuciar, *v. a. to foul*
Ensueño, *s. m. V.* Sueño
En suma, *adv. V.* Suma
Entablacion, *sub. f. a register*
Entablado, *s. m. floor*
Entablamento. *s. m. boarding*
Entablar, *v. a. to board* || *to set the men at tables, etc. to dispose business into method* || *to register*
Entalamado da, *adj. covered with cloth*
Entalegar *v. a. to put in a bag*
Entalingadura, *s. f. clinch*
Entalingar, *v. a. to clinch a cable*
Entallador, *s. m. carver* || *engraver*
Entalladura, *s. f. carving* || *engraving*
Entallar *v. a. to carve* || *to engrave* || *to make cloaths shapeable to the body*
Entalle, *s. m. the work done by the carver, etc.*
Entallecer *v. n. to shoot; to sprout out* [*while*
Entanto *adv. in the mean*
Entapizar *v. a. to hang with tapestry*
Entarimar, *a. to floor*
Entarquinar, *v. a. to dirt*
Ente, *s. m. a being*
Entecado, da, *a. impotent*
Enteco, ca, *adj. V.* Entecado *y* Enetenque
Entejado, da, *a. like a tile*

Entena, *s. f. yard*
Entenada, *s. f. a daughter-in-law* [*law*
Entenado, *s. m. a son-in-*
Entendederas, *s. f. pl. undestanding*
Entendedor, *s. m. one who understands*
Entender, *v. a. to understand — to hear*
Entender, *v. n. to be busy or employed about something* || *to mean or expect*
Entenderse, *v. r. to agree with one*
Entendidamente, *adv. wisely; judiciously*
Entendido, da, *adj. understanding*
Entendimiento, *s. m. understanding*
Entenebrecer, *ver. a. to darken*
Enteramente, *adv. entirely; wholly*
Enteramiento, *s. m. entireness*
Enterar, *v. a. to pay the whole* || *to inform thoroughly*
Entereza, *s. f. entireness* || *integrity* || *constancy* || *perfection* || *pride; obstinacy*
Entereza corporal. *a good health* || *virginity*
Enternecer, *v. a. to make tender* || *to move to pity, etc.*
Enternecerse, *v. r. to be moved to pity, etc.*
Enternecimiento, *sub. m. compassion; pity, etc.*
Entero, ra, *adj. entire; whole* || *perfect; complete* || *obstinate* || *understanding*

horse || lier
coarse linen
Por entero, *a*
Enterrador, *s.*
digger
Enterramiento
Enterrar, *v. a*
Entesadamente
gorously;
Entesamiento
sion; stiffe
Entesar, *v. a.*
Entibador, *s.*
props
Entibar, *v. a.*
Entibar, *v. n.*
or lean
Entibiadero, *s*
to make an
kewarm in
Entibiar, *v. a. t*
Entibiarse, *v.*
to slacken
Entibiecer, *v*
Entibo, *s. m.*
prop in the
Entidad, *s. f.*
lue; estim
Entierro, *s.*
funeral ||
grave
Entigrecerse,
furious, as
Entimema, *s. m*
Entintar, *v.*
with ink ||
Entiznar, *v. a.*
with soot ||
one's reput
Entoldar, *v.*
with a til
hang a ch
Entoldar la na
the awning
Entoldarse el
gloomy, o
Entomecer,
tumecer

izar, v. a. to tie rush-ropes
cion, s. f. intonation wing || pride; pretion
dor, s. m. he that the tune || a blower gans
r, v. a. to set the || to blow the or-
rse, v. r. to grow d
e } adv. then
es }
, s. m. intonation-; arrogance
ecerse, v. r. to grow k
hado, s. m. a sort visted fringe
hados, pl. strings red with wire
har, v. a. to twist over a string with [up
ar, v. a. to turn
o, s. m. contour
cer, v. a. to benum
cimiento, s. m. benedness
dura, s. f. crooking
r, v. a. to crook || ke blind of one eye
ar, v. a. to poison
, s. f. entry; ene || access; admit- || custom; duty
s, pl. the temples
ro, s. m. a wicket
la, sub. f. dim. de da
sos, bas, pron. both
gar, v. act. to en- to insnare || to gle
e, s. m. angle
ble, a. 2. hearty;

Entrañablemente, adver. heartily
Entrañar, v. a. to receive with affection, etc.
Entrañarse, v. r. to knit an intimate friendship
Entrañas, sub. f. pl. entrails; bowels
Entranizar, v. a. to love heartily
Entrapada, s. f. a coarse red cloth
Entrapajar, v. a. to wrap in rags
Entraparse, v. r. to be daubed with dust
Entrar, v. a. to introduce; to insert, etc.
Entrar, v. n. to enter; to go or come in || to begin
Entrar en juego, to make one at play — de por medio, to part a fray, or to mediate
Entrarse, ver. r. to gain ground upon...
Entre, prep. between
Entreabrir, ver. to open half way
Entrecano, na, adj. grey-headed [slightly
Entrecavar, v. a. to dig
Entrecejo, s. m. the space between the eye brows || frowning countenance [do
Entrecielo, s. m. V. Tol-
Entrecogedura, s. f. seizing, etc.
Entrecoger, v. a. to seize upon one between many others || to gather here and there
Entrecortadura, s. f. intersection
Entrecortar, v. a. to cut or divide by halves
Entrecubiertas, sub. f. pl. between decks

Entrecuesto, sub. m. the back-bone
Entredecir, v. a. to interdict [diction
Entredicho, s. m. inter-
Entredoble, a. 2. between thick and thin
Entrefino, na, adj. between coarse and fine
Entrega, s. f. } delivery
Entregamiento, s. m. }
Entregadamento, adver: wholly [ver up
Entregar, v. a. to deli-
Entrego, s. m. delivery
Entrejuntar, v. a. to join together
Entrelazar, v. a. to interlace [mer
Entrelucir, v. a. to glim-
Entremedias, ad. betwixt
Entremes, s. m. interlude, in a play
Entremesado, da, adj. belonging to an interlude
Entremescar, v. a. to play a part in an interlude
Entremesista, s. m. player in the interludes
Entremeter, v. a. to intermix || to unswhate and dress a child
Entremeterse, v. r. to intermeddle
Entremetido, s. m. intermeddler
Entremetimiento, s. m. intermixing || intermeddling
Entremezcladura, s. f. intermixture
Entremezclar, v. act. to intermix
Entremorir, v. n. to be almost expiring
Entremuerto, ta, a. half dead [hear
Entreoir, v. a. to over-

Entreordinario, ria, *adj middle; mean*

Entrepalmadura, s. f. *a swelling in the hollow of a horse's pastern*

Entrepañado, da, a. *made of several panes*

Entrepaño, s. m. *pane (in joinery)*

Entreparecerse, v. r. *to be seen obscurely*

Entrepiernas, s. f. pl. *the space between the legs || pieces put to mend a pair of breeches between the thigs*

Entreponer, v. a. *interpose* [*position*

Entrepostura, s. f. *inter-*

Entrepuentes, s. f. V. Entrecubiertas [*king*

Entrepunzadura, s. f. *pric-*

Entrepunzar, v. n. *to prick*

Entrerenglonadura, s. f. *interlineary note, etc.*

Entrerenglonar, v. a. *to interline*

Entresaca, s. f. *lopping; cutting off boughs, etc.*

Entresacadura, s. f. *picking; culling || lopping*

Entresacar, v. a. *to pick; to chuse, or cull || to lop off* [*tery*

Entresijo, s. m. *mesen-*

Entresijos, pl. *recesses*

Entresuelo, s. m. *a little room between two floors*

Entretalladura, s. f. *basso relievo; bass-relief*

Entretallamiento, sub. m. *pinking*

Entretallar, v. a. *to make a bass-relief || to pink cloth || stop one's way*

Entretela, s. f. *buckram. etc. to put between the lining and the cloth*

Entretelar, v. a. *to put buckram, etc. between the lining and the cloth*

Entretenedor, s. m. *one who entertains, etc.*

Entretener, v. a. *to entertain — to delay || to give some allowance*

Entretenerse, v. r. *to stand playing || to jest || to trifle*

Entretenido, da, a. *merry*

Entretenimiento, s. m. *diversion; pastime || delay* [*terweaving*

Entretexedura, sub. f. *in-*

Entretexer, v. a. *to interweave*

Entretiempo, s. m. *the middle season*

Entreuntar, v. a. *to anoint slenderly*

Entrevenarse, v. r. *to be poured into the veins*

Entreverado, da, adj. *interladed* [*mix*

Entreverar, v. a. *to inter-*

Entrexerir, v. a. *to insert; to intermix*

Entricamiento, s. m. *entangling* [*gle*

Entricar, v. a. *to entan-*

Entrincado, da, adj. *entangled; perplexed*

Entrincamiento, s. m. *entangling*

Entripado, da, a. *intestine; inward*

Entripados, s. m. pl. *inveterate rancour, etc.*

Entristecer, v. a. *to grieve*

Entristecerse las plantas, *to wither; to fade away*

Entrometer, v. a. V. Entremeter [*ne*

Entronar, v. a. *to enthro-*

Entroncar, v. n. *to be a descendant from a race*

Entronerar, v. a. *to throw a ball into the hazard*

Entronizacion *throning*

Entronizar, v. *ne || to rais*

Entronizarse, *proud*

Entroxar, v. *into the ba*

Entruchada, *contrivanc*

Entruchar, v. *to intice,*

Entullecer, *impotent*

Entullecer, v *to suspena*

Entumecer, v *to benum a*

Entumecerse *swell; to b*

Entumecimie *swelling;*

Entupir, v.

Enturbiar, v

Entusiasmo, *siasm*

Enunciacion

Enunciar, v. *ciate*

Enunciativo *ciative*

En uno, *adv*

Envalentonar *bolden*

Envanecer,

Envano, *adv*

Envaramient *traction; crew of ca*

Envarar, v.

Envaronar, *manlike*

Envasador, *puts into || funnel*

Envasar, v. *vessels || run a ma*

Envayar,

v. r. to be
| to fall to-
le ears
a. to make
'd
.to grow old
v. r. to grow
lasting
a, a. used;
, s. m. poi-
[son
. a. to poi-
v. n. to grow
a. to fasten
the yards
. m. pl. the
wich the sail
to the yard
the wrong
back
s. f. inves-
ict. to invest
v. r. to ac-
's self to any
instead
f. sending;
n. an envoy
to send || to
a. to depra-
upt
v. r. to give
ver
. m. inviter
a. to invite
s. envy
s. m. envier
a. to envy
a, a. envious
. a. to aba-
race [vile
v. r. to grow
, a. vinous

Envinar, *v. act. to mix wine with water*

Enviperado, da, *adj. furious*

Enviscar, *v. a. to daub with bird-lime*

Envite, *s. m. invitation || offer*

Enviudar, *v. n. to be a widow*, or *a widower*

Envoltorio, *s. m. a bundle*

Envolturas, *s. f. pl. swaddling clothes*

Envolvedero } *subs. m. a*
Envolvedor } *wrapper*

Envolver, *v. a. to wrap up*

Envolverse, *v. r. to be involved*

Enxabonadura, *s. f. soaping of linen*

Enxabonar, *v. a. to soap linen || to reprimand*

Enxalma, *s. f. a moorish pack-saddle*

Enxalmero, *s. m. one who makes, or sells packsaddles*

Enxambrar, *v. a. to gather the bees in the hive*

Enxambrar, *v. n. to swarm*

Enxambre, *s. m. a swarm of bees || a croud of people* [*lye*

Enxebar, *v. a. wash with*

Enxebe, *s. m. a sort of lye*

Enxergar, *v. a. to commence a business*

Enxeridor, *s. m. grafter*

Enxerimiento, *s. m. grafteng*

Enxerir } *v. a. to graft ||*
Enxertar } *to insert*

Enxerto, *s. m. a graft* or *graff*

Enxugar, *v. a. to dry*

Enxugarse, *v. r. to grow lean*

Enxundia, *s. f. fat; suet; grease || the lump of fat in a hen's bel'y*

Enxuto, ta, *adjec. dry || stingy || silent*

Enyesadura, *s. f. plastering*

Enyesar, *v. a. to plaster*

Enzamarrado, da, *a. covered with a sheep-skin*

Enzarzar, *v. a. to put in the briars || to set together by the ears*

Enzarzarse, *v. r. to be involved in troubles, etc.*

Enzurdecer, *v. n. to become left-handed*

Eolípila, *s. m. colipile*

Epacta, *s. f. epact*

Epactilla, *s. f. V.* Añalejo

Epicedio, *s. m. epicedium*

Epiceno, na, *a. epicene*

Epicíclico, ca, *a. belonging to the epicycle*

Epiciclo, *s. m. epicycle*

E'pico, ca, *adj. epick*

Epidemia, *s. f. epidemical disease*

Epidemial } *a. epide-*
Epidémico, ca, } *mical*

Epidermis, *s. m. epidermis*

Epifanía, *s. f. Epiphany*

Epifonema, *s. f. epiphonema* [*tis*

Epiglotis, *s. f. epiglot-*

Epigrafe, *s. m. epigraphe*

Epigrama, *s. 2. epigram*

Epigramático, ca, *adjec. epigrammatick*

Epigramatista, *s. m. epigrammatist*

Epilepsia, *s. f. epilepsy*

Epiléptico, ca, *adj. epileptick*

Epilogar, *v. a. to sum up the matter*

Epilogismo, *s. m. calculation*

Epílogo, s. m. epilogue || summing up

Episcopal, a. 2. episcopal

Epistolilla, *s. f. dim. de*
Epitafio, *s. m. epitaph*
Epitalamio, *s. m. epithalamium*
Epíteto, *s. m. epithet*
Epitima, *s. f. epithem*
Epitimbra, *s. f. flower of savory* [*thyme*
Epitimo, *s. m. flower of*
Epitomar, *v. a. to epitomise*
Epítome, *s. m. epitome*
E'poca, *s. f. epoch; epocha*
E'poda, *s. f. epode* [*song*
E'podo, *sub. m. a kind of*
Epopeya, *s. f. epopee*
Equable, *a. 2. equable*
Equacion, *s. f. equation*
Equador, *s. m. equator*
Equanimidad, *s. f. equanimity*
Equante, *a. 2. igual*
Equator, *s. m. equator*
Eqüestre, *a. 2. equestrian*
Equiángulo, la, *a equiangular.*
Equidad, *sub. f. equity* || *abatement made in the*

Equiparacion, *s. f. comparison* [*pare*
Equiparar, *v. a. to com-*
Equiponderar, *ver. n. to weigh equally*
Equis, *s. f. the letter* X
Equite, *s. m. V.* Caballero *y* Noble
Equivalencia, *s. f equivalence* [*valent*
Equivalente, *a. 2. equiva-*
Equivalentemente, *adver. equivalently*
Equivaler, *v. n. to be of equal value*
Equivocacion, *s. f. equivocation* [*sly*
Equivocadamente, *adv. fal-*
Equivocamente, *adv. equivocally*
Equivocar, *v. a. y* Equivocarse, *v. r. to equivocate*
Equivocarse una cosa con otra, *to be much alike*
Equívoco, *s. m. equivocal — equivoque*
Equívoco, ca, *adj. equi-*

Eriazo,
Erigir,
Erisimo
must
Erisipel
Erisipel
erysi
Eritreo
Erizar,
end;
Erizarse
Erizo,
echin
husk
Ermado
a spo
Ermadu
spoil
Ermar,
Ermita,
|| *ta*
Ermitañ
Ermitor
Erogar,
Erogato
pipe
Erótico
Erotism

–el golpe, *to*
aim
rrata
a. errant;
wavering
a coal made
of the olives
he letter R
adv. obsti–
adv. erro–
adj. erro–
error
s. f. eru–
s. f. eructa–
to belch
f. erudition
adv. lear–
s. learned
s. m. sha–
inting)
a fine pro–
of a fine size
a catch-pole
a sketch
d || bait
a. to mari–
ckle
m. pickle
m. dim. de
m. a foot–
f. scabious
the scab in
v. r. to fall
ion
a. rough;
sub. m.
y

Ecabullirse, *v. r. to slip away* [queado
Escacado, da, *a. V.* Esca–
Escala, *s. f. ladder || scale || sea-port town*
Escalada, *s. f. escalade*
Escalador, *s. m. one that scales*
Escalamatus, *s. m. a venemous distemper in beasts* [lade
Escalamiento, *s. m. esca–*
Escalamos, *s. m. pl. tholes*
Escalar, *v. a. to scale*
Escaldada, *adj. f. lewd; prostitute*
Escaldar, *v. a. to scald*
Escaldrantes, *sub. m. pl. levels*
Escaldufar, *v. a. to take any liquor out of a pot*
Escaleno, *adj. m. scalene*
Escalera, *s. f. stair || leader*
Escalerilla, *s. f. dim. de* Escalera
Escalfador, *s. m. boiler || chafing-dish*
Escalfar, *v. a. to warm*
Escalfarotes, *s. m. pl. a sort of boots*
Escalimarse, *v. r. to get into the leaks of a ship*
Escalofrio, etc. *V.* Calofrio, etc.
Escalon, *s. m. step || degree*
Escamas, *s. f. pl. scales of fish*
Escamochos, *s. m. pl. fragments; scraps*
Escamondar, *v. a. to prune || to cleanse* [mony
Escamonea, *subs. f. scam–*
Escamoneado, da, *adj. belonging to scammony*
Escamonearse, *v. r. to refuse; to reluct*
Escamoso, sa, *adj. scaly*
Escampar, *ver. n. to give over raining*

Escampar, *v. a. to clear a passage, etc.*
Escamujar, *v. a. to prune an olive-tree*
Escamujo, *s. m. a branch cut off from an olive tree* [wheat
Escanda, *sub. f. the finest*
Escandalizador, *s. m. one that scandalizes*
Escandalizar, *ver. act. to scandalize*
Escandallo, *s. m. sounding plummet*
Escándalo, *s. m. scandal*
Escandalosamente, *adver. scandalously*
Escandaloso, sa, *a. scandalous* [passion
Escandecencia, *s. f. anger;*
Escandecer, *v. a. to anger*
Escandelar, *s. m. a cabbin in the midst of a galley* [de Escandelar
Escandelarete, *s. m. dim.*
Escandir, *v. a. to scan*
Escaño, *s. m. a bench* or *form || waist rail*
Escapada, *s. f. escape*
Escapar, *v. n. to escape*
Escapar, *v. a. to save; to rid of* [of the memory
Escapar, *v. imp. to slip out*
Escaparse alguna palabra, *to slip out*
Escaparate, *s. m. a kind of wooden case* or *frame*
Escapatoria, *s. f. a come off; a shift*
Escape, *s. m. escape*
Escapo, *s. m. the shaat of a pillar* [lary
Escapulario, *s. m. scapu–*
Escaqueado, da, *a. checkered*
Escaques, *s. m. pl. squares*, (in a chess-board)
Escara, *s. f. eschar*
Escarabajear, *v. n. to be*

always in motion || *to write very bad*

Escarabajo, *s. m. a beetle* || *a short ugly person*

Escarabajos, *plur. flaws; cracks—pot-hooks and hangers (in writing)*

Escarabajuelo, *s. m. a little insect that destroys the vine yards*

Escaramujo, *s. m. wild eglantine* || *heps*

Escaramuza, *s. f. skirmish*

Escaramuzador, *s. m. skirmisher*

Escaramuzar, *v. n. to skirmish*

Escarapela, *sub. f. a fray among women, etc.* || *a cockade*

Escarapelarse, *ver. r. to quarrel*

Escarba, *s. f. scarf*

Escarcela, *s. f. a large purse* || *the tasses of a cuirass*

Escarcelon, *s. m. aum. de* Escarcela

Escarceos, *s. m. pl. volts; bounding-turns*

Escarcha, *s. f. hoar-frost*

Escarchar, *v. n. to nip with hoar-frost*

Escarchar, *v. a. to curl*

Escarcho, *s. m. a red fish with a large head*

Escarcina, *subs. f. a short broad, crooked sword*

Escarcinazo, *s. m. a blow given with the escarcina*

Escarda, *s. f. weeding-hook — weeding*

Escardadora, *s. f. she weeder*

Escardador, *s. m. a weeder*

Escardar, *v. a. to weed*

Escardillo, *subs. m. weeding-hook*

Escarizar, *v. a. to take off the eschar*

Escarlata, *s. f. scarlet*

Escarlatin, *s. m. a sort of scarlet*

Escarmenador, *s. masc. a great-toothed comb*

Escarmenar, *v. act. to comb* || *to fine*

Escarmentar, *v. n. to take warning by experience, etc.*

Escarmentar, *v. a. to reprimand severely*

Escarmiento, *s. m. warning taken by experience, etc.* || *punishment; fine*

Escarnecedor, *s. m. scoffer*

Escarnecer, *v. a. to scoff*

Escarnio, *s. m. scoffing*

Escaro, *s. m. a sea fish so called*

Escarola, *s. f. endive* || *ruff*

Escarolado, da, *adj. of the endive colour* || *curled*

Escarpa, *s. f. scarp (of a ditch)*

Escarpado, da, *adj. steep*

Escarpia, *s. f. a tenter-hook*

Escarpiar, *v. a. to fasten with tenter-hooks* || *to strike to the very heart*

Escarpidor, *s. m. a great-toothed comb.*

Escarpin, *s. m. a sock*

Escarvadero, *s. masc. the place where the wild boars whet their tusks*

Escarvadientes, *s. mas. a tooth-pick*

Escarvaorejas, *s. m. ear-picker*

Escarvar, *v. act. to rake into; to scratch, etc.*

Escarza, *s. f. a wound made in horse's feet with a thorn*

Escasamente, || *niggard.*

Escasear, *v. sparingly,*

Escasear, *v.* ... *se; to fall*

Escasez, *s.* ... *niggardlin*

Escaso, sa, ... *frugal, etc*

Escatimar, *v* ... *and lesse. designs to terpret ill attentivel*

Escatimosam ... *malicious*

Escaupil, *s.* ... *armour m*

Escava, *s.* ... *open of th*

Escena, *s. f.*

Escénico, ca

Escenografía ... *graphy*

Esclarecer, *v* ... *ten to enn*

Esclarecidam ... *nobly; ill*

Esclarecido, ... *lustrious*

Esclarecient ... *trious*

Esclarecimie ... *clearness*

Esclavillo, ... *slave*

Esclavina, ... *mantle, w wear*

Esclavitud, || *brother*

Esclavo, va ... *brother*

Esclirótica, ... or *coat o*

Esclusa, *s.*

Esclusilla, ... *sluice*

ma, *s. f. broom ; be-* n

mada, *s. f. sweeping*

bajo, *s. m. an old be- n* || *stalk of a bunch grapes*

mar, *s. m. the place ere the broom grows*

mar, *v. a. to sweep*

mazo, *s. mas. a blow th a broom*

benes, *s. m. pl. the wse holes*

billa, *s. f. a brush* || *e dross or filings of etal*

billa de ámbar, *am- et*

bon, *s. masc. an old rch-broom*

bos, *s. m. pl. briars ; orns*

cer, *v. a. to smart*

cia, *s. f. striæ*

cimiento, *s. m. smart*

da, *s. f. a mason's isel* [*nes*

dar, *v. a. to hew sto-*

fia, *s. f. a coif*

fiado, da, *adj. that s a net-coif on*

fieta, *s. f. a little coif*

fina, *s. f. a raspatory*

finar, *v. a. to smooth ith a raspatory*

ger, *v. a. to choose*

gidamente, *adv. by hoice* || *perfectly ; ni- ly*

gimiento, *s. m. choice*

lar, *s. m. scholar*

lar, *a. 2. scholastick*

lasticamente, *adver. cholastically*

lástico, ca, *adj. scho- astick*

oliador, *s. m. scholiast*

oliar, *v. act. to make holions*

Escolimoso, sa, *adj. rough ; intractable*

Escolio, *s. m. scholion*

Escollo, *s. m. shelf* (*in the sea*)

Escolopendra, *s. f. scolopendra*

Escolta, *s. f. escort*

Escoltar, *v. a. to escort*

Escombrar, *v. a. to clear ; to cleanse*

Escombro, *s. mas. sweepings, etc. rubbish ; riff-raff* || *a small sea-fish*

Escomerse, *v. r. to be consumed by degrees*

Esconce, *s. m. a corner ; an angle*

Escondedero, *s. m. lurking-hole*

Escondedijo, *s. m. a hiding-place*

Esconder, *v. a. to hide*

Escondidamente, *adv. secretly* [*cretly*

Escondidas (á), *adv. se-*

Escondidijo, *s. m. Voy.* Escondrijo

Escondidillo, lla, *adj. dissembling*

Escondido (en), *adv. secretly* [*ding*

Escondimiento, *s. m. hi-*

Escondite, *s. m. hiding-place*

Juego del escondite, *hide and seek* [*place*

Escondrijo, *s. m. hiding-*

Esconzado, da, *adj. angular ; oblique*

Escopeta, *s. f. a gun*

Escopetazo, *s. m. a shot of a gun* [*with a gun*

Escopetear, *v. a. to shoot*

Escopetearse, *v. rec. to wrangle with animosity*

Escopetería, *s. f. a body of fusiliers*

Escopetero, *s. m. a fusilier*

Escopleadura, *s. f. the hole made with a chisel*

Escoplo, *s. m. chisel*

Escopo, *s. m. scope*

Escorar, *v. a. to belay a rope*

Escorbúto, *s. m. scurvy*

Escorchapin, *s. m. a sort of bark*

Escorche, *s. masc. fore-shortening*

Escordio, *s. masc. water-germander*

Escoria, *s. f. scoria*

Escorial, *s. m. an exhausted mine*

Escorpina, *s. f. a sea-fish like a scorpion*

Escorpion, *s. m. scorpion* || *scorpio* || *scourge*

Escorpioyde, *s. fem. scorpion-wort*

Escorrozo, *s. m. pleasure ; satisfaction*

Escorzado, *s. m. what is fore-shortened*

Escorzar, *v. act. to fore-shorten* [*tening*

Escorzo, *s. f. fore-shor-*

Escorzonera, *s. f. scorzonera*

Escoscarse, *v. r. to scratch one's self by shrugging up the shoulders*

Escota, *s. f. sheet of a sail*

Escotado, *s. m. a cut sloping gown*

Escotadura, *s. f. a slope* || *a trap-door*

Escotar, *v. a. to slope, to hollow a garment about the neck* || *to pay one's shot*

Escote, *s. m. slope ; hollowing* || *shot*

Escotero, ra, *adj. free ; without embarrasment*

Escotilla, *s. f. hatches*

door on a theatre
Escotines, *s. m. pl. sheets of the main top-sail*
Escotomia, *s. f. giddiness*
Escozor, *s. masc. smart; smarting*
Escriba, *s. m. scribe*
Escribania, *s. f. the scrivener's office* || *scritory* || *ink-horn*
Escribano, *s. m. scrivener*
Escribiente, *s. m. amanuensis*
Escribir, *v. a. to write*
Escribirse, *v. r. to enrol one's self*
Escriño, *s. m. a large basket* or *hamper*
Escrito, *s. m. a writing*
Escritor, *s. m. a writer* || *a copist*
Escritorillo, *s. m. dim.* de Escritorio
Escritorio, *s. m. a scrutoire* || *a scrivener's study*
Escritura, *s. f. writing*
Escritura publica, *an act or instrument in law* — sagrada, *the holy scripture*
Escriturar, *v. a. to make deeds, instruments, etc.*
Escriturario, ria, *adj. scriptural*
Escriturario, *s. masc. one that professes reading holy writ*
Escrudiñar, *v. act. Voy.* Escudriñar
Escrupulear, *v. neut. Voy.* Escrupulizar {*scruple*
Escrupulete, *s. m. a slight*
Escrupulizar, *v. n. to be full of scruples*
Escrupulo, *s. m. scruple*
Escrupulos, *pl. minutes (of a degree)*

scrupulously
Escrupulosidad, *s. f. scrupulousness*
Escrupuloso, sa, *adj. scrupulous*
Escrutinio, *s. m. scrutiny*
Escrutiñador, *s. m. scrutator*
Escucha, *s. f. a centinel; a scout* || *scouting* || *a nun that attends another to the parlour*
Escuchador, *s. m. hearkener*
Escuchar, *v. a. to hearken*
Escucharse, *v. r. to hear one's self speak*
Escudar, *v. a. to shield*
Escuderage, *s. m. the service of a gentleman-usher*
Escuderear, *v. a. to serve as a gentleman-usher*
Escuderia, *s. f. Voy.* Escuderage
Escuderil, *adj. belonging to an esquire, etc.*
Escuderiles, *s. f. pl. close breeches*
Escuderilmente, *adver. esquire like*
Escudero, *s. m. esquire* || *a lady's gentleman-usher*
Escudero trinchante, *a carver* or *sewer*
Escuderon, *s. m. aum.* de Escudero
Escudete, *s. mas. a little shield* || *escutcheon* || *waterlily*
Enxerir de escudete, *to graft by a scutcheon*
Escudilla, *s. f. a porringer*
Escudillar, *v. a. to take out pottage in porringers*

shield
Escudo, *s. m* ...
escutcheon ...
piece
Escudrinado...
Escudriñami...
searching
Escudriñar, ...
to inquir...
Escuela, *s. f* ...
Esquerzo, *s.* ...
Escueto, ta, ...
open, *wi*...
cumbran...
Esculirse, ...
Esculpir, *v.* ...
Esculto, ta, ...
Escultor, *s.* ...
Escultura, ...
Escupidera, ...
Escupidero, ...
Escupidor, ...
Escupidura, ...
spitting || ...
Escupir, *v. a.* ...
Escurar, *v.* ...
cloth fr...
Escurredizo ...
easy to sl...
Lazo escur...
knot
Escurriband...
|| *loosens*...
Escurridura...
dregs; g...
Escurrir, *v.* ...
to empty
Escurrir, *v.* ...
to slip
Escusalin, ...
short; ap...
Escutas, ...
pl. hatch...
Esdruxulam...
with dact...
Esdruxulo, ...
|| *a ver*...
with a ...

lo, la, *adj. belon-*
to a dactyle, etc.
, eso, *pron. this;*
it
, *s. f. essence*
esencia, *quintes-*
, *a. 2. essential*
mente, *a. esen-*
se, *v. r. to incorporate*
s. f. a sphere
lad, *s. f. spheri-*
, ca, *adj. spherical*
., *s. f. astrono-*
or *astrologer*
le, *s. f. spheroid*
, *s. m. sphinx*
inos, *s. m. plur.*
hes of vine that
out of a twist
amente, *a. boldly;*
ly
o, da, *adj. bold;*
esforzado, *jelly-broth*
, *v. a. to encou-*
to strengthen
se, *v. r. to strive;*
one's endeavours
, *s. m. strenuous-*
endeavour
o, *s. m. a sketch*
with a black-
encil
te, *s. m. a parti-*
step in dancing
, *s. f. fencing*
de esgrima, *a*
g-master
or, *s. m. fencer*
liator
, *v. a. to fence*
le, *a. 2. fordable*
, *v. a. to ford a*
s. m. fording

Esgucio, *s. m. ogee*
Esguince, *s. the motion of the body in slipping away from a blow*
Esguizaro, *s. m. a mean, contemptible fellow*
Eslabon, *s. m. a link* || *a steel to strike fire, etc.* || *spavin*
Eslabonador, *s. masc. one that links*
Eslabonar, *v. a. to link*
Eslinga, *s. f. slings*
Eslora, } *s. f. the length of a ship upon the deck*
Esloria, }
Esmaltar, *v. a. to enamel*
Esmalte, *s. m. enamel*
Esmarchazo, *s. m. a ruffian, a bravo*
Esmarido, *s. m. a sea-fish so called*
Esmeralda, *s. f. emerald*
Esmerar, *v. a. to polish; to brighten*
Esmerarse, *v. r. to carry one's self above others*
Esmerejon, *s. m. merlin*
Esmeril, *s. m. emeril*
Esmerillado, da, *adj. polished with emeril*
Esmero, *s. m. care, diligence*
Esófago, *s. m. oesophagus*
Esotro, tra, *pron. that other*
Espabiladerar, *s. f. plur. snuffers*
Espabilar, *v. a. to snuff a candle*
Espaciar, *v. a. to dilate; to expand* || *to spread* || *to divulge*
Espaciarse, *v. r. to walk; to take the air*
Espacio, *s. m. space* || *slowness*
Espaciosamente, *a. slowly*
Espaciosidad, *s. fem. spaciousness*

Espacioso, sa, *adj. spacious* || *slow.*
Espada, *s. f. sword* || *spadille* || *the sword-fish*
Espada negra, *a foil* — blanca, *a common sword*
Espadas, *pl. spade, at cards*
Espadachin, *s. m. a bully; a ruffian*
Espadado, da, *adj. girt with a sword*
Espadador, *s. m. one who beats hemp*
Espadaña, *s. f. flag (rush)*
Espadañada, *s. f. a blow given by the violence of water*
Espadañar, *v. a. to separate, to expand like flags*
Espadar, *v. a. to beat hemp*
Espadarte, *s. m. the sword-fish*
Espadería, *s. f. a sword-cutler's shop*
Espadero, *s. m. sword-cutler*
Espadilla, *s. fem. a little sword* || *a sort of beetle to beat hemp with* || *spadille* || *kue, at billiards*
Espadillar, *v. a. to beat hemp*
Espadillazo, *s. m. a term in the game of* hombre
Espadin, *s. masc. a little short sword*
Espadon, *s. masc. a two-handled sword* || *an eunuch*
Espadrapo, *s. m. sparadrap*
Espalda, *s. f. shoulder* || *the flank of a bastion*
Espaldas, *pl. the back*
Espaldar, s. m. a shoulder-piece || the back of a chair, etc.

Escotillon, s. m. a trap-door on a theatre
Escotines, s. m. pl. sheets of the main top-sail
Escotomia, s. f. giddiness
Escozor, s. masc. smart; smarting
Escriba, s. m. scribe
Escribanía, s. f. the scrivener's offices || scritory || ink-horn
Escribano, s. m. scrivener
Escribiente, s. m. amanuensis
Escribir, v. a. to write
Escribirse, v. r. to enrol one's self
Escriño, s. m. a large basket or hamper
Escrito, s. m. a writing
Escritor, s. m. a writer || a copist
Escritorillo, s. m. dim. de Escritorio
Escritorio, s. m. a scrutoire || a scrivener's study
Escritura, s. f. writing
Escritura pública, an act or instrument in law — sacrada, the holy scripture
Escriturar, v. a. to make deeds, instruments, etc.
Escriturario, ria, adj. scriptural
Escriturario, s. masc. one that professes reading holy writ
Escrudiñar, v. act. Voy. Escudriñar
Escrupulear, v. neut. Voy. Escrupulizar [scruple
Escrupulete, s. m. a slight
Escrupulizar, v. n. to be full of scruples
Escrúpulo, s. m. scruple
Escrupulos, pl. minutes (in a degree)

Escrupulosamente, adver. scrupulously
Escrupulosidad, s. f. scrupulousness
Escrupuloso, sa, adj. scrupulous
Escrutinio, s. m. scrutiny
Escrutiñador, s. m. scrutator
Escucha, s. f. a centinel; a scout || scouting || a nun that attends another to the parlour
Escuchador, s. m. hearkener
Escuchar, v. a. to hearken
Escucharse, v. r. to hear one's self speak
Escudar, v. a. to shield
Escuderage, s. m. the service of a gentleman-usher
Escuderear, v. a. to serve as a gentleman-usher
Escudería, s. f. Voy. Escuderage
Escuderil, adj. belonging to an esquire, etc.
Escuderiles, s. f. pl. close breeches
Escuderilmente, adver. esquire like
Escudero, s. m. esquire || a lady's gentleman-usher
Escudero trinchante, a carver or sewer
Escuderon, s. m. aum. de Escudero
Escudete, s. mas. a little shield || escutcheon || waterlily
Enxerir de escudete, to graft by a scutcheon
Escudilla, s. f. a porringer
Escudillar, v. a. to take out pottage in porringers

shield
Escudo, s. m. cutcheon || piece
Escudrinador,
Escudriñamien searching
Escudriñar, v. to inquire
Escuela, s. f.
Escuerzo, s. m
Escueto, ta, open, with cumbrance
Escullirse, v.
Esculpir, v. a
Esculto, ta, a
Escultor, s. n
Escultura, s.
Escupidera, s.
Escupidero, s. m
Escupidor, ra
Escupidura, s spitting ||
Escupir, v. a.
Escurar, v. a. cloth from
Escurredizo, easy to slip
Lazo escurre knot
Escurribanda, || looseness
Escurriduras, dregs; grou
Escurrir, v. a to empty
Escurrir, v. n to slip
Escusalin, s. short; apro
Escutas, escu pl. hatches
Esdrúxulamen with dactyl
Esdrúxulo, s. || a verse with a da

ǵrxulo, la, *adj. belonging to a dactyle, etc.*
esa, eso, *pron. this; that; it*
ncia, *s. f. essence*
inta esencia, *quintessence*
ncial, *a. 2. essential*
ncialmente, *a. essentially*
nciarse, *v. r. to incorporate*
ra, *s. f. a sphere*
ricidad, *s. f. sphericity*
rico, ca, *adj. spherical*
rista, *s. f. astronomer, or astrologer*
royde, *s. f. spheroid*
nge, *s. m. sphinx*
rocinos, *s. m. plur. branches of vine that grow out of a twist bough*
rzadamente, *a. boldly; strongly*
rzado, da, *adj. bold; strong*
ldo esforzado, *jelly-broth*
rzar, *v. a. to encourage* || *to strengthen*
rzarse, *v. r. to strive; to do one's endeavours*
rzo, *s. m. strenuousness* || *endeavour*
mado, *s. m. a sketch made with a black-lead pencil*
mbete, *s. m. a particular step in dancing*
ima, *s. f. fencing*
stro de esgrima, *a fencing-master*
imidor, *s. m. fencer gladiator*
imir, *v. a. to fence*
azable, *a. 2. fordable*
azar, *v. a. to ford a river*
zo, *s. m. fording*

Esgucio, *s m. ogee*
Esguince, *s the motion of the body in slipping away from a blow*
Esguizaro, *s. m. a mean, contemptible fellow*
Eslabon, *s. m. a link* || *a steel to strike fire, etc.* || *spavin*
Eslabonador, *s. masc. one that links*
Eslabonar, *v. a. to link*
Eslinga, *s. f. slings*
Eslora, } *s. f. the length*
Esloria, } *of a ship upon the deck*
Esmaltar, *v. a. to enamel*
Esmalte, *s. m. enamel*
Esmarchazo, *s. m. a ruffian, a bravo*
Esmarido, *s. m. a sea-fish so called*
Esmeralda, *s. f. emerald*
Esmerar, *v. a. to polish; to brighten*
Esmerarse, *v. r. to carry one's self above others*
Esmerejon, *s. m. merlin*
Esmeril, *s. m. emeril*
Esmerillado, da, *adj. polished with emeril*
Esmero, *s. m. care, diligence* [gus
Esófago, *s. m. oesophagus*
Esotro, tra, *pron. that other* [snuffers
Espabiladeras, *s. f. plur. snuffers*
Espabilar, *v. a. to snuff a candle*
Espaciar, *v. a. to dilate; to expand* || *to spread* || *to divulge*
Espaciarse, *v. r. to walk; to take the air*
Espacio, *s. m. space* || *slowness*
Espaciosamente, *a. slowly*
Espaciosidad, *s. fem. spaciousness*

Espacioso, sa, *adj. spacious* || *slow.*
Espada, *s. f. sword* || *spadille* || *the sword-fish*
Espada negra, *a foil* — blanca, *a common sword*
Espadas, *pl. spade, at cards*
Espadachin, *s. m. a bully; a ruffian*
Espadado, da, *adj. girt with a sword*
Espadador, *s. m. one who beats hemp*
Espadaña, *s. f. flag (rush)*
Espadañada, *s. f. a blow given by the violence of water*
Espadañar, *v. a. to separate, to expand like flags*
Espadar, *v. a. to beat hemp*
Espadarte, *s. m. the sword-fish*
Espadería, *s. f. a sword-cutler's shop*
Espadero, *s. m. sword-cutler*
Espadilla, *s. fem. a little sword* || *a sort of beetle to beat hemp with* || *spadille* || *kue, at billiards*
Espadillar, *v. a. to beat hemp*
Espadillazo, *s. m. a term in the game of* hombre
Espadin, *s. masc. a little short sword*
Espadon, *s. masc. a two-handled sword* || *an eunuch* [drap
Espadrapo, *s. m. sparadrap*
Espalda, *s. f. shoulder* || *the flank of a bastion*
Espaldas, *pl. the back*
Espaldar, *s. m. a shoulder-piece* || *the back of a chair, etc.*

stroke

ders

Espalder, s. m. the hindmost rower in a galley

Espaldilla, s. f. shoulder-blade

Espalmar, v. a. to grave a

Espalto, s. m. a transparent colour

adver.

adject.

, s.

s.

Espantalobos, s. m. scare-

Espantar, v. a. to fright; to scare

Espantarse, v. rec. to be amazed

Espantavillanos, s. m. a garment adorned with tinsel

Espanto, s. m. fright || threat || amazement

or.

Españolizar, v. a. to late into Spanis

Españolizarse, v. r. like a spaniard

Espar, s. m. a sweet ling drug

Esparavan, s. m. a || spavin

Esparavel, s. m. a sweep- [net

Esparcidamente, ad. scatteringly

Esparcido, da, adj. free; easy; ready

Esparcimiento, s. m. scattering || free way; easiness || magnanimity

Esparcir, v. a. to scatter; to spread

Esparcirse, v. r. to

s. m. a

belon-

the asparagus

Esparragado, s. m. made with asparagus

Espárrago, s. m. asparagus

Esparra stalk

Esparra one's

Espasmo, s.

Espátula, s.

Espaviento, amazeme

Especería, s. shop || spi

Especia, s. f.

Especias, p drugs

Especial, a.

En especial cially

Especialidad cation

Especialmen

Especie, s.

Especiero, spicer

Especificaci fication

Especificada specifica

Especificar,

Especificati specifick

Específico, of one sp tance

Específico, substanc

Espécimen,

Especioso, formed s or art || s

Espectácul cle

Espectator

Espectro, ghost

Especulaci

Especulado lator

to clear
r. to look in
[*glass*
. *a looking-*
, a burning-

m. a little
ss || *talk* (*a*
t stone)
l. spectacles
spelt
. *f. a cave* ;

v. r. to stand
[*spike*
mas. a hand-
a bomba, *the*
ke
expectation
ment || *a sort*

. 2. *that is to*
or
. *m. who ho-*
ects
. *f. hope*
v. a. to give

a. to hope || *to*

, *v. r. to shake*
iness
. *m. shaking*
iness
s. f. exposi-
lanation
, *adj. lean* ;
[rioga
. *f. Voy.* Aspe-
m. sperm
ti, *spermaceti*
, ca, *adject.*
cal
s. f. the last
ny chain
m. the beak of

. *to thicken* ;

Espeso, sa, *adj. thick* || *dirty* ; *nasty*

Espesor, *s. m. thickness of a wall*

Espesura, *s. f. thickening* || *thickness* || *the thick of a forest* || *nastiness*

Espetar, *v. a. to spit* ; *to run trough*

Espetarse, *v. r. to carry one's self stiff*

Espetera, *s. f. kitchen-tackling* || *a rack, to lay the spit on*

Espeto, *s. m. a spit*

Espeton, *s. m. a little spit* || *a long pin* || *a spit-fish*

Espia, *s. f. a spy*

Espiar, *v. a. to spy* || *to bring a ship a float*

Espibio, } *s. m. disloca-*
Espibion, } *tion of the neck's nape, in a horse*

Espicanardi, *s. m. spike-nard*

Espichar, *v. a. to wound with the point*

Espiche, *s. m. any pointed arm*

Espiga, *s. f. an ear of corn* || *tenon* || *a wooden pin* || *a sprig.* || *V.* Espoleta

Espigadera, } *s. f. a woman-*
Espigadora, } *gleaner*

Espigar, *v. n. to ear* || *to grow* || *to glean*

Espigar, *v. a. to give a present to the bride*

Espigon, *s. m. the sting of a wasp, etc.* || *point* || *sharp top* || *thistle*

Espigon de ajo, *a clove of garlick*

Espilorcheria, *s. f. stingi-ness*

Espilorcho, *s. m. a sordid, niggardly fellow*

Espin, *s. m. porcupine*

Espina, *s. f. thorn* || *prickle*

Espinas, *pl. fish-bones*

Espinaca, *s. f. spinage*

Espinal, *s. m. a place full of thorns*

Espinal, *a.* 2. *spinal*

Espinar, *s. m. a place full of briars*

Espinar, *v. a. to prick* || *to surround with thorns* || *to nettle*

Espinazo, *s. m. back-bone*

Espinel, *s. masc. angling-line.*

Espinela, *s. f. a stanza of ten verses* || *spinel ruby*

Espineo, nea, *adj. thorny*

Espineta, *s. f. spinet*

Espingarda, *s. f. a small piece of artillery*

Espingardero, *s. m. gunner*

Espinilla, *s. f. the shin-bone* || *brisket*

Espinita, *s. m. dim. de* Espina

Espino, *s. m. white-thorn*

Espinoso, sa, *adj. thorny* || *hard* ; *arduous*

Espion, *s. m. a spy*

Espiote, *s. m. V.* Espiche

Espira, *s. f. spiral line.*

Espirable, *a.* 2. *that can breathe*

Espiracion, *s. f. breathing* || *expiration*

Espiráculo, *s. masc. vent-hole* || *breathing*

Espirador, *s. m. one who breathes*

Espiral, *a.* 2. *spiral*

Espirar, *v. n. to expire* || *to breathe* || *to blow* || *to exhale* || *to inspire*

Espirativo, va, *adj. expi-ring*

Espiritual, *a.* 2. *spiritual*

Espiritarse, *v. r. to be pos-sessed with an evil spi-rit*

Espiritillo, *s. mas. dim. de* Espíritu
Espiritosamente, *a. boldly*
Espiritoso, sa, *adj. bold; strenuous* || *spiritous*
Espíritu, *s. masc. spirit* || *ghost* [*ghost*
Espíritu santo, *the holy*
Espiritual, *a.* 2 *spiritual*
Espiritualidad, *s. f. spirituality*
Espiritualizar, *v. a. to spiritualize*
Espiritualmente, *adv. spiritually*
Espirituoso, sa, *adj. V.* Espiritoso
Espita, *s. f. tap; cock* || *a span* [*dent*
Esplendente, *a.* 2. *splen-*
Espléndidamente, *adver. splendidly*
Esplendidez, *s. f. esplendor*
Espléndido, da, *adj. splendid*
Esplendor, *s. m. splendor*
Esplendorear, *v. neut. to shine* [*liancy*
Esplendoridad, *s. f. bril-*
Esplénico, ca, *adj. belonging to the spleen*
Espliego, *s. m. lavender*
Espodio, *s. m. spodium*
Espolada, *s. f. a stroke with a spur*
Espolazo, *s. masc. a great stroke with a spur*
Espoleadura, *s. f. a hurt with the spur*
Espolear, *v. a. to spur*
Espoleta, *s. the fusee of a bomb*
Espolin, *s. masc. a little shuttle* || *a thin flowered silk*
Espolinado, da, *adj. weaved with flowers*
Espolio, *s. m. spoils*
polista, *s. m. a renter of the spoils of dead prelates*
Espolon, *s. masc. a cock's spur* || *starling of a bridge* || *the beak of a ship* || *kibes*
Espondeo, *s. m. spondee*
Espondil, *s. m. the chine-bone*
Espondilio, *s. m. spondyle*
Esponja, *s. f. spunge* || *pumice-stone*
Esponjadura, *s. f. soaking, swelling of a spungious body*
Esponjar, *v. a. to swell by soaking* [*proud*
Esponjarse, *v. r. to grow*
Esponjoso, sa, *adj. spungious* [*bethroting*
Esponsales, *s. m. pl. a*
Espontaneamente, *adver. spontaneously*
Espontaneidad, *s. f. spontaneity* [*spontaneous*
Espontaneo, nea, *adject.*
Esponton, *s. m. half-pike*
Esportear, *v. a. to carry out in frails* [*frail*
Esportilla, *s. f. a little*
Esportillero, *s. m. a porter that plies with a frail*
Esportillo, *s. m. a frail*
Esporton, *s. m. a great frail*
Esportula, *s. f. a fee paid to the judges, etc.*
Esposa, *s. f. a spouse; a bride*
Esposas, *s. f. pl. manacles*
Esposo, *s. m. a spouse; a bridegroom*
Espotático, ca, *adj. free; voluntary* || *fictitious*
Espuela, *s. f. a spur*
Espuela de caballero, *comfrey*
Espuerta, *s. f. a frail*
Espulgadero, *s. masc. the place where t go to louse,*
Espulgador, *s. m louses, etc.*
Espulgar, *v. a. to pick fleas,*
Espulgo, *s. m. lo*
Espuma, *s. f. sc*
Espumadera, *s. mer*
Espumajo, *s. m*
Espumajoso, sa *of scum*
Espumar, *v. a. to froth*
Echar espuma la boca, *to f mouth with p*
Espumilla, *s. f.*
Espumillon, *s.*
Espumoso, sa, *a*
Espundia, *s. f. per in horses*
Espurio, ria, *adj*
Esputo, *s. m. sp*
Esquadra, *s. f. or rule* || *the t of a foot-com squadron of s*
Esquadrar, *v. a.*
Esquadría, *s. f. squaring*
Esquadron, *s. m dron of horse*
Esquadronar, *v. up soldiers drons*
Esquadroncillo, *little squadro*
Esquela, *s. f. a l*
Esqueleto, *s. m.*
Esquero, *s. mas leather-purse*
Esquiciar, *v. a.*
Esquicio, *s. m. a*
Esquifada, *s. f. t of a skiff*
Esquifar, *v. a. t boat*

fe, *s. m. a skiff*
la, *s. f. a little bell*
hearing
lador, *s. m. shearer*
lar, *v. a. to shear*
ep
leo, *s. m. shearing*
lla, *s. f. a squill*
lmar, *v. a. to gather*
fruit of a land
lmo, *s. m. the fruit*
produce of a land
ilo, *s. m. shearing*
ilon, *s. m. a small*
l
ina, *s. fem. outward*
gle; corner
inancia, *s. f. squi-*
ncy [*corners*
inar, *v. a. to make*
inazo, *s. m. an acute*
tward angle
inela, *s. f. armour*
the legs
inencia, *s. f. squi-*
ncy [*a ship*
ipar, *v. a. to equip*
ipazon, *s. m. equip-*
nt
ivar, *v. a. to eschew;*
avoid
ivarse, *ver. r. to dis-*
in; to scorn; to coy
ivez } *s f. disdain;*
iveza } *coyness*
ivo, va, *a. scornful*
ilidad, *s. f. stability*
le, *a. 2. stable*
lear, *v. a. to tame*
stable beasts
lecedor, *s. m. esta-*
lisher
lecer, *v. a. to esta-*
sh
lecimiento, *subs. m*
ablishment || *statute*
lemente, *ad. firmly*
lerizo } *s. m. land-*
lero } *lord* || *groom*
|| *one that looks to sta-*
bles [*stable*
Establillo, *sub. m. a little*
Establimiento, *s. m. Voy.*
Establecimiento
Establo, *s. m. stable*
Estaca, *s. f. stake* || *a slip*
of a tree || *a club* or
cudgel [*pins*
Estacas, *pl. tholes — iron*
Estacada, *s. f. palisade* ||
a list to fight in
Estacar, *v. a. to fix a sta-*
ke in the ground || *to*
tie a beast to a stake
Estacazo, *s. m. a blow*
with a stake
Estacha, *s. f. the rope that*
is let out after the wha-
le is struck
Estacion, *s. f. state; situa-*
tion || *season; time* ||
station
Estacionario, ria, *a. sta-*
tionary [*stake*
Estacon, *s. m. a great*
Estacte, *s. m. stacte*
Estada, *s. f. a stay in a*
place
Estadal, *s. m. a measure*
of a fathom
Estadio, *s. m furlong* ||
a race to run
Estadista, *subs. m. a sta-*
tesman
Estadizo, za, *a. stagnant*
Estado, *s. m. state* || *fa-*
thom [*stake*
Estadoño, *s. m. a sharp*
Estadouder, *s. m. stadtho-*
der [*spunging*
Estafa, *sub. f. sharping;*
Estafador, *s. m. a shar-*
per; a pilferer
Estafar, *v. a. to trick; to*
spunge
Estafermo, *s. m. a figure*
set up to ride at, and
strike it with lances
Estafero, *s. m. footman*
Estafeta, *s. f. a courier*
or *express* || *post-office*
Estafetero, *s. m. a post-*
man
Estala, *s. f. a stable*
Estalacion, *s. f. a degree*
of honour, or *preceden-*
cy [*to crack*
Estallar, *v. n. to burst;*
Estallido, llo, *subst. m.*
crack; report
Estambor, *s. m. stern-post*
Estambrar, *v. a. to twist*
yarn
Estambre, *sub. m. yarn;*
worsted
Estambres, *pl. stamina*
Estameña, *s. f. stamine*
Estampa, *s. f. print; cut*
|| *stamp* || *pattern*
Estampar, *v. a. to print*
|| *to stamp*
Estampero, *s. m. one who*
makes or *sells prints*
Estampido, *s. m. report of*
a gun, etc.
Estampilla, *sub. f. a little*
print || *a stamped seal*
Estancar, *v. a. to stop*
Estancarse el agua, *to stand*
as in a pool
Estancia, *sub. f. abode;*
stay || *a bed-room* ||
stanza
Estancias, *pl. quarters in*
a camp
Estanco, *s. m. a monopo-*
ly || *the place appoin-*
ted to sell in that way
|| *stay; staying* || *ar-*
chives, etc. || *pool*
Estandarte, *s. m. stan-*
dard [*gury*
Estangurria, *s. f. stran-*
Estanque, *sub. m. pool;*
pond
Estanquero, *s. m. mono-*
polist

Estanquillo, s. m. a little shop where they sell tobacco, etc.

Estanquito, s. m. a little pool

Estantal, s. m. buttress

Estante, s. m. a coffin for books

Estanterol, s. m. the mid-part of the galley

Estantigua, s. f. phantom; spectre

Estantio, tia, adj. stagnant || flow

Estañador, s. m. a pewterer [over

Estañar, ver. act. to tin

Estaño, s. m. tin || pool; pond

Estaquillar, v. a. to put wooden pegs in shoes

Estar, v. n. to be || to stand

Estarse, v. r. to be stayed or detained

Estarcir, v. a. to prick a design, and rub it over with coal-dust

Estatera, s. f. steel-yard || stater

Estática, s. f. staticks

Estatua, s. f. statue

Estatuaria, s. f. the statuary [tuary

Estatuario, s. m. a sta-

Estatuir, v. a. to establish

Estatura, s. f. stature

Estatulario, ria, adj. belonging to a statute

Estatuto, s. m. statute

Estay, s. m. stay

Este, s. m. the east-wind

Este, ta, to, pron. this, that, it

Estela, subs. f. steerage way; rake [tle

Estelario, s. f. ladies man-

Estelífera, ra, a. starry

Estelion, s. m. a newt

Estelion, s. m. toad-stone

Estelionato, s. m. stellionate

Estelon, s. m. V. Estelion

Estentórea (voz), a stentorean voice

Estepa, s. f. the holy rose

Estera, s. f. a mat

Esterar, v. a. to mat

Estercar, v. a. V. Estercolar [ging

Estercoladura, s. f. dun-

Estercolar, v. n. to dung

Estercolar, v. a. to dung the ground

Estercolero, s. m. a dunghill || one that carries dung

Estercuelo, s. m. stercoration [graphy

Estereografía, s. f. stereo-

Estereográfico, ca, a. belonging to stereography

Estereometría, sub. f. stereometry

Estereometrico, ca, adj. belonging to stereometry [maker

Esterero, sub. m. a mat-

Estéril, a. 2. steril

Esterilidad, s. f. sterility

Esterilizar, v. a. to make steril

Esterilla, s. f. a little mat || a small golden or silver-lace

Esterlin, s. m. stérling

Esternon, s. m. sternum

Estero, s. m. a salt marsh || the matting

Esterquero, s. m. V. Estercolero [hill

Esterquilinio, s. m. a dung

Esteva, s. f. the plough-handle

Estevado, da, adj. bow-legged || bunch-backed

Estiar, v. n. to stop; to stand

Estibia, s. f. V. Espibio

Estilo..., s. m. a

Estiercol, s. m.

Estilar, v. n. ...se; to use

Estilar, v. a. to

Estilicidio, s. m

Estilo, s. m. ...mon

Estilogloso, s. ...cle of the to

Estima, s. f. es

Estimabilidad, ...worth; exce

Estimable, a. 2

Estimacion, s. ...tion || estee ...ral instinct

Estimador, s. m

Estimar, v. a. t... to estimate

Estimativa, s. ...culty of ju... estimating || the beast

Estimular, v. ... || to stimula

Estimulo, s. m ...an incentive

Estinco, s. m. ...kind of newt

Estinia, s. f. co... of the nerve...ses, etc.

Estio, s. m. the

Estiomenado, ...ten; corrup

Estiomeno, s. ...tification in

Estipendiario, s...diary

Estipendio, s.

Estipite, s. m. ...or pillar

Estipticidad, s.

Estiptico, ca, ... || costive || n

Estipulacion, s...lation

Estipular, v.

.f. a currier's
[sively
nte, adv. extens
a, adj. grave;

.m. V. Estiron
a. to stretch;
out
. r. to be proud
r
v. a. V. Estirar
m. a sudden
tug; a jerk
a stock; a race
straw to stuff
ng with
. 2. estival
tr. act. to stow
a ship || to
cram a thing

, a. estival
.f. thrust; pass
, s. m. a spanish
ion for the stock-

f. a sort of quil-
stuff
, a. to quilt gar-
to stew meats
f. a stole
, s. f. stolidity
da, adj. foolish
. m. aum. de

, adj. 2. stoma-

r, v. a. to anger
rse, v. r. to sto-
[mach
, s. m. the sto-
de estómago, a
resolution
ero, s. m. a belly-

illo, s m. dim.
mago
al, a. 2. sto-
t

Estomático, ca, *adj. stomachick*

Estomaticon, na, *adj. V.* Estomatical

Estomaticon, *s. m. a plaster for the stomach*

Estónce, *y* Estónces, *adv. then*

Estopa, *s. f. tow || oakum || the coarsest cloth*

Estopada, *s. fem. a distaff full of tow || a fleece of tow*

Estopeño, ña, *adj. of tow*

Estoperoles, *s. m. pl. round headed nails*

Estopilla, *s. f. a sort of hempen cloth*

Estopon, *s. m. the coarsest hemp || sarp-cloth*

Estoposo, sa, *adj. belonging to,* or *like the tow*

Estoque, *s. m. rapier: tuck*

Estoqueador, *s. m. one who thrusts with the point*

Estoquear, *v. a. to thrust with the point of a sword*

Estoqueo, *s. m. the act of thrusting passes*

Estoraque, *s. m. storax*

Estorbador, *s. m. hinderer || hindrance*

Estorbar, *v. a. to hinder; to obstruct, etc.*

Estorbo, *s. m. hindrance; obstacle*

Estornija, *s. f. the trigger of a cart*

Estornino, *s. m. a starling*

Estornudar, *v. a. to sneeze*

Estornudo, *s. m. a sneeze*

Estotro, tra, *pron. that other*

Estoyco, ca, *adj. stoical*

Estoyco, *s. m. stoick*

Estracilla, *s. f. dim. de* Estraza [*ting-paper*

Papel de estracilla, *blot-*

Estrada, *s. fem. street || cause way*

Estrada encubierta, *the covered way in fortification*

Estradiote, *s. m. one that rides with the stirrups longs*

Estrado, *s. m. estrade || a court of justice*

Estrafalariamente, *adver. disorderly*

Estrafalario, *s. m. a sloven, ragged fellow*

Estragadamente, *adv. viciously; lewdly*

Estragamiento, *s. masc. lewdness*

Estragadar, *v. a. to spoil; to waste || to corrupt; to viciate*

Estrago, *s. mas. havock; waste || destruction || corruption of manners*

Estrambosidad, *s. f. strabism*

Estrambote, *s. m. an addition to the end of a verse, etc.*

Estrambótico, ca, *adject. strange; irregular*

Estrangol, *s. m. the strangles*

Estrangul, *s. m. the reed of a hautboy, etc.*

Estranguria, *s. f. strangury*

Estrapazar, *v. a. to laugh at; to scorn*

Estratagema, *s. f. stratagem*

Estratiote, *s. m. a sort of house-leek* [*ship*

Estrave, *s. m. stem* (*of a*

Estraza, *s. f. rags || outcast; trasch, etc.*

Papel de estraza, *blotting-paper* [to rear

Estrazar, *v. a.* to rend;

Estrechamente, *adv. straitly* || *exactly* || *severely* || *stingily*

Estrechar, *v. a. to straiten* || *to constrain* || *to stop*

Estrecharse, *v. r. to lessen one's spences* || *to knit a friendship*, etc.

Estrecharse de ánimo, *to despond*

Estreches, *s. f. straitness* || *union; connexion* || *a great danger* or *pain* || *misery*

Estrecho, *s. m. strait* or *streight*

Estrecho, cha, *adj. straight; narrow* || *barren* || *poor* || *stingy*

Estrechura, *s. f. straitness*

Estregadera, *s. f. a hard brush*

Estregadero, *s. m. a place the beasts rub themselves against*

Estregar, *v. a. to rub*

Estrella, *s. f. star.*

Estrellada, *s. f. star-wort*

Estrellado, da, *adj. starry*

Huevos estrallados, *poached eggs*

Estrellamar, *s. f. lily of the valley*

Estrellar, *a. 2. belonging to stars*

Estrellar, *v. a. to dash to pieces* || *to cast a thing in one's dish* || *to poach eggs*

Estrellarse con uno, *to withstand one's attempts*

Estrellera, *s. f. a beast that holds up its head*

Estrellita, *s. f. a little star*

Estrellizar, *v. a. to adorn with stars*

Estrellon, *s. m. a large star*

Estrelluela, *s. f. a small star*

Estremecer, *v. a. to shake*

Estremecerse, *v. rec. to quake; to tremble*

Estremecimiento, *s. mas. trembling*

Estremezo, *s. m. trembling*

Estremiche, *s. m. transom*

Estrena, *s. f. handsel* || *a new-year's gift*

Estrenar, *v. a. to handsel*

Estrenarse, *v. r. to begin to exercise one's self in.....*

Estreno, *s. m. begining*

Estrenque, *s. m. a cable made of rushes*

Estrenuo, nua, *adj. strenuous*

Estreñido, da, *adj. stingy*

Estreñir, *v. a. to bind*, or *wring hard*

Estreñirse, *v. r. to confine one's self*

Estrepito, *s. m. a noise*

Estriar, *v. act. to flute a column* [*flutings*

Estrias, *s. f. pl. striæ;*

Estribadero, *s. m. a prop*

Estribar, *v. n. to carry; to rest; to lie* or *lean*

Estribar, *v. a. to support; to prop*

Estribería, *s. f. a place where the stirrups are kept*

Estribillo, *s. m. a burden (of a song)*

Estribo, *s. m. stirrup* || *buttress* || *the step of a coach*

Estribord, *s. m. starboard*

Estricote (al), *adv. confusedly* or *scornfully*

Traer á uno al estricote, *to keep one at a bay*

Estrictamente, *ad. strictly*

Estriges, s. f. pl. screech-*owl*

Estrola, *s. f. a*

Estropajear, *v.* ... *with a dish*

Estropajo, *s.* ... *clout*

Lengua de es... *stammerer*

Estropajoso, sa... *ged; sloven,* ... *bleiome* or ... *stammering*

Estropear, *v. a* ... || *to mix* ... *lime*

Estropecillo, ... *de* Estropiezo

Estropiezo, *s.* ... *bling stone*,

Estrovito, *s.* ...

Estrovo

Estrovo, *s. m.* ... *cable so calle*... *ship*

Estructura, *s.* ...

Estruendo, *s.* ... *noise* || *tumu*... *sion* || *pom*... *dour* || *name*

Estruendosamen... *with great no*... *pously*

Estruendoso, sa, ... *tumultuous* ...

Estrupar, *v. a.* ... prar

Estruxadura, *s.* ...

Estruxamiento, ... *s. m.*

Estruxar, *v. a.* ... *to press*

Estruxar el dine... *with money* ... *reluctance*

Estruxarse, *v. r* ... *one's expence*

Estruxon, *s. m* ... *squeezing of*

Estuario, *s. m.* ...

Estuche, *s. m.* ...

che del Rey, the first rgeon of the King
co, s. m. stucco
diador, s. m. one who dies [scholar
diantazo, s. m. a great
diante, s. m. a scholar; a student
diantico, s. m. a young tty scholar
diantil, a. 2. belonging to the study
diantillo, s. m. a little paltry scholar
diantino, na, adj. belonging to students
dianton, s. m. an old, gged scholar
diar, v. a. to study
dio, s. m. study || a hool || a closet
diosamente, adv. studiously [diousness
diosidad, s. f. stu-
dioso, sa, adj. studious [house
fa, s. f. stove; hot-
far, v. a. to warm a om
filla, s. f. a little muff a foot-stove [ly
ltamente, adv. foolish-
lticia, s. f. folly
osa, sa, adjec. hot; rning
pendamente, adver. onderfully
pendo, da, adj. stupendous
pido, da, adj. stupid
por, s. m. stupor
prador, sub. m. one at stuprates
prar, v. a. to stuprate
pro, s. m. stupration
que, s. m. stucco
rar, v. a. to dry by forces of the fire
ion, s. m. sturgeon

Esula, s. f. the greatest kind of spurge
Etele, int. lo! behold!
Eter, s. m. ether
Etéreo, rea, adj. ethereal
Eternal, a. 2. eternal
Eternamente, } adv eternally
Eternalmente, }
Eternidad, s. f. eternity
Eternizar, v. a. to eternize
Eterno, na, adj. eternal
Etesios (vientos), s. m. pl. etesian winds
Etica, s. f. ethicks [gy
Etimología, s. f. etymolo-
Etimológico, ca, adj. etymological
Etiqueta, s. f. ceremonial
Etimologista, s. m. etymologist [stone
Etites, sub. f. the eagle-
Etna, s. m. a volcano. etc.
Etnico, ca, adj. ethnick
Eubolia, s. f. a speaking or advising well
Eucaristía, s. f. eucharist
Eucarístico, ca, adj. eucharistical
Euforbio, s. m. euphorbium
Eufrasia, s. f. euphrasy
Eunuco, s. m. eunuch
Eupatorio, s. m. hemp-agrimony
Euro, s. m. the east-wind
Euro austro, euro noto the south-east-wind
Europeo, pea, adj. European
Eutrapelia, s. f. pleasant jesting with innocence
Evacuacion, s. f. evacuation
Evacuar, v. a. to evacuate
Evadir, v. a. to evade
Evagacion, s. f. roving or rambling thoughts
Evanecer, v. n. to vanish

Evangélico, ca, adj. evangelical [pel
Evangelio, s. m. the gos-
Evangelista, s. m. evangelist [gelise
Evangelizar, v. a. to evan-
Evaporacion, s. f. evaporation [rate
Evaporar, v. n. to evapo-
Evaporar, v. a. to exhale
Evasion, s. f. evasion
Evehente, adj. m. ascending
Evento, s. m. an event
Eversion, s. f. eversion
Eviccion, s. f. eviction; dispossession
Evidencia, s. f. evidence
Evidenciar, v. a. to evidence
Evidente, a. 2. evident
Evidentemente, adv. evidently
Evitable, a. 2. evitable
Evitacion, s. f. a shunning [to avoid
Evitar, v. a. to shun;
Eviterno, na, adj. eternal
Evo, s. m. an age
Evocacion, s. f. evocation
Evocar, v. a. to conjure up; to invoke [tly
Exabrupto, adv. abrup-
Exâccion, s. f. receipt; gathering || impost; tax || exaction || exactness [perate
Exâcerbar, v. a. to exas-
Exáctamente, adv. exactly
Exâctitud, s. f. exactness
Exácto, ta, adj. exact
Exáctor, s. m. receiver; gatherer
Exâgeracion, s. f. exaggeration
Exâgerador, s. m. amplifier [rate
Exâgerar, v. a. to exagge-

Exâltacion, *s. f. exaltation*
Exâltar, *v. a. to exalt*
Exâmen, *s. m. examen*
Exâminacion, *s. f. examination*
Exâminador, *s. m examiner*
Exâminar, *v. a. to examine*
Exângue, *a. 2. exanguious*
Exânime, *a. 2. exanimated*
Exârar, *v. a. to engrave*
Exârcado, *s. m. exarchy*
Exârco, *s. m. exarch*
Exâsperar, *v. a. to exasperate*
Excavar, *v. a. to excavate*
Exceder, *v. n. to exceed*
Excelencia, *sub. f. excellence*
Excelente, *a. 2. excellent*
Excelentemente, *adv. excellently*
Excelentísimo, ma, *adj. must excellent*
Excelsamente, *adv. highly; lofty*
Excelso, sa, *adj. lofty; high*
Excêntricamente, *adver. excentrically*
Excentricidad, *s. f. excentricity*
Excéntrico, ca, *adj. excentrick*
Excepcion, *s. f. exception*
Excepcionar, *v. a. to start up an exception* or *objection*
Exceptacion, *s. f. exception*
Exceptar, *v. a. to except*
Excepto, *prep. except*
Exceptuar, *v. a. to except*
Excesivamente, *adv. excessively*
Excesivo, va, *adj. excessive*
Exceso, *sub. m. excess* || *rapture; extasy*
Excitar, *v. a. to excite*

Exclamacion, *s. f. exclamation*
Exclamar, *v. n. to exclaim*
Excluir, *v. a. to exclude*
Exclusion, *s. f. exclusion*
Exclusiva, *s. f. exclusion*
Excluso, sa, *p. p. excluded*
Excogitable, *a. 2. imaginable*
Excogitar, *v. a. to excogitate*
Excomulgador, *s. m. one who excommunicates*
Excomulgar, *v. a. to excommunicate*
Excomunion, *s. f. excommunication*
Excoriacion, *s. f. excoriation*
Excrecencia, *s. f. excrescence*
Excrementar, *v. n. to void excrements*
Excrementicio, cia, *adj. excrementitious*
Excremento, *s. m. excrement*
Excrementoso, sa, *adjec. excremental*
Excursion, *sub. f. excursion; inroad*
Excurso, *s. m. excursion; digression*
Excusa, *s. f. excuse*
Excusabaraja, *s. f. a basket of osiers, with a handle and a cover to it*
Excusable, *a. 2. excusable*
Excusadamente, *adver. needlessly* or *unseasonably*
Excusado, da, *adj. needless; superfluous*
Excusado, *s. m. a certain tribute wich the clergy pay to the King*
Excusador, *s. m. vicar*
Excusar, *v. a.* to excuse || to exempt || to avoid

Excusarse, ...
ne; to re...
Exe, *s. m.* ...
axis
Exêcrable, ...
Exêcracion ...
tion
Exêcrador, ...
Exêcrando ...
crable
Exêcrar, *v* ...
Execucion ...
Executable ...
be execu...
Executar, ...
Executar e...
distrain ...
an exec...
Executivan...
peditiou...
Executivo, ...
ditious ||...
sing
Executor, ...
Executoria ...
executio...
Executoria ...
tain a ...
Executoric...
executor...
Exêdra, *s.* ...
etc. wit...
for stud...
Exêgético ...
getical
Exemplar ...
plar || *e*...
Exemplar, ...
Exemplarr...
exempla...
Exemplific...
exempli...
Exemplo, ...
Exêncion, ...
Exêntar, ...
Exênto, ta ...
exempte...
Exênto, ...
Exêquial...

ias, sub. f. pl. exe-
's ; obsequies
ible, a. 2. that can
btained or executed
er, v. a. to excerci-
to practise
cio, s. m. excercise
itacion, s. f. exerci-
on [ser
itador, s. m. exerci-
itar, v. a. to exercise
ito, s. m. an army
acion, s. f. exhala-
s
iar, v. a. to exhale
arse, v. r. to evapo-
|| to overwork one's
[ted
isto, ta, adj. exhaus-
icion, s. f. exhibi-
i
ir, v. a. to exhibit
tacion, s. f. exhor-
on
tador, ra, adj. that
orts
tar, v. a. to exhort
tatorio, ria, adjec.
ortatory
to, s. m. a writ so
led in the courts of
ice
mar, v. a. to dig a
se out of the ground
, subs. m. a spot a
und without the
n, that is common
ncia, s. f. exigency
r, v. a. to exact
o, gua, adject. exi-
us
, s. m. exile
iamente, adv. nota-
; excellently
io, mia, adjec. exi-
ius
ir, v. a. to exempt
ncia, s. f. existence
nte, a. 2. existent

Existimacion, s. f. existimation [ve; to think
Existimar, v. a. to belie-
Existir, v. n. to exist
Exito, s. m. issue; end; success
E'xôdo, s. m. exodus
Exôneracion, s. f. exoneration [rate
Exônerar, v. a. to exone-
Exôrable, a. 2. exorable
Exôrbitancia, s f. exhorbitance [bitant
Exôrbitante, a. 2. exhor-
Exôrcismo, s. m. exorcism
Exôrcista, s. m. exorcist
Exôrcizar, v. a. to exorcise
Exórdio, s. m. exordium
Exôrnacion, s. f. exornation
Exórnar, v. a. to adorn
Exótico, ca, adj. exotick
Expanso, s. m. expensum
Espavecerse, v. r. to be frightened
Expectable, a. 2. notable
Expectacion, s. f. expectation
Hombre of expectacion, a man of consideration
Expectativa, s. f. expectation || a favour in expectance
Expectoracion, s. f. expectoration [torate
Expectorar, v. a. to expec-
Expedicion, s. f. expedition || dispatch
Expedicionero, s. m. Officer at the Pope's court for dispatches
Expedido, da, adj. dispatched || expeditious
Expediente, s. m. expedient || activity in business; facility, etc.
Expediente, a. 2. expedient

Expedir, v. a. to expedite; to dispatch
Expeditamente, adv. expeditiously
Expedito, ta, adj. expeditious
Expoler, v. a. to expel
Expendedor, s. m. an expensive man || one that tenders false money || a seller of stolen things
Expender, v. a. to expend
Expensas, s. f. pl. expenses [rience
Experiencia, s. f. expe-
Experimentado, da, adj. experienced
Experimentador, s. m. one who makes experiments
Experimental, a. 2. experimental [periment
Experimentar, v. a. to ex-
Experimento, s. m. experiment
Experto, ta, adj. expert
Expiacion, s. f. expiation
Expiar, v. a. to expiate
Explanacion, s. f. explanation [de
Explanada, s. f. esplana-
Explanar, v. a. to explain
Explayar, ver. a. to expand; to dilate
Explicacion, s. f. explication
Explicaderas, s. f. pl. the manner of explaining himself [cate
Explicar, v. a. to expli-
Explícitamente, adv. explicitly [cit
Explícito, ta, adj. expli-
Exploracion, s. f. exploration
Explorador, s. m. explorator || a spy or scout
Explorar, v. a. to explore
Exploratorio, sub. m. a probe

Expósito, ta, *adject. a foundling*
Expositor, *s. m. expositor*
Expremijo, *s. m. a wooden trough used by cheese-makers*
Expresamente, *adv. expressly*
Expresar, *v. a. to express* || *to spueeze out*
Expresion, *s. f. expression* || *squeezing out*
Expresivo, va, *adj. expressive*
Expreso, sa, *adj. express*
Expreso, *s. m. an express*
Exprimidera, *s. f. a little press to squeeze out the juice of herbs, etc.*
Exprimido, da, *adj. dry, lean, etc.*
Exprimir, *v. a. to squeeze out to express* || *to infer* or *conclude*
Exprobracion, *s. f. exprobation* [*openly*
Expuestamente, *adver.*
Expuesto, ta, *p. p. exposed; expounded*
Expugnacion, *s. f. expugnation*
Expugnador, *s. m. one who takes by assault, etc.* [*pugn*
Expugnar, *v. a. to ex-*
Expulsion, *s. f. expulsion*
Expulsivo, va, *adj. expulsive* [*sed*
Expulso, sa, *adj. expul-*

extasy
xtáti co, ca, *adj. extatick*
Extemporal, *a. 2. extemporary*
Extemporaneamente, *adv. extemporally*
Extender, *v. a. to extend*
Extendidamente, *adv. extensively* [*wide*
Extendido, da, *adj. large;*
Extendimiento, *s. m. extending; extension*
Extensamente, *adv. extensively*
Extension, *s. f. extension*
Extensivamente, *adv. extensively* [*sive*
Extensivo, va, *adj. exten-*
Extenso, sa, *adj. large; wide; spacious*
Extenuacion, *s. f. extenuation* [*nuate*
Extenuar, *v. a. to exte-*
Exterior, *a. 2. exterior; outward*
Exterior, *s. m. the out-side*
Exterioridad, *s. f. outward-shew*
Exteriormente, *adv. exteriorily* [*terminator*
Exterminador, *s. m. ex-*
Exterminar, *v. a. to exterminate* || *to banish*
Exterminio, *s. m. extermination* || *banishment*
Externo, na, *adj. extern*
Extinguible, *a. 2. extinguishable* [*guish*
Extinguir, *v. a. to extin-*

|| *to export*
Extrajudicial, *judicial*
Extrajudicialm *extrajudicia*
Extramuros, *the walls*
Extrangería, *te* or *manne reigner*
Extrangero, *foreigner;*
Extrañamente *strangely*
Extrañamient *putting awa ment*
Extrañar, *ver away; to* || *to banish der at* || *to c ke, etc.*
Extrañez, } *s.*
Extrañeza, } *m sion* || *novel larity* || *ama*
Extraño, ña, *neous* || *stra*
Extraordinaria *extraordina*
Extraordinario *extraordina*
Extravagancia *travagance*
Extravagante, *travagant* || *ry*
Extravagantes *decrees of*

rd to the canon-law
·enarse, *v. r. to ex-*
asate
·iar, *v. a. to put*
of the way || *to mis-*

·iarse, *v. r. to shift*
s quarters, etc.
·io, *s. m. straying*
ror; ill conduct
·adamente, *adver.*
ctly || *extremely*
·ado, da, *adj. per-*
|| *extreme* || *merry;*
rful [*tremely*
·amente, *adv. ex-*
·ar, *v. a. to put the*
hand to... to finish
·árse, *v. r. to do the*
ost endeavours || *to*
way || *to be stiff a*
ose
·auncion, *s. f. ex-*
eunction [*ty*
·idad, *s. f. extremi-*
·o, ma, *adj. last*
treme
en ó por extremo,
extremely
·o, *s. m. extremi-*
extreme; excess
·ecamente, *adver.*
nsically
·eco, ca, *adj. ex-*
ical
·ar, *v. a. to expel*
rce [*rance*
·ancia, *s. f. exube-*
·ante, *a. 2. exube-*
[*cerate*
·rar, *v. a. to exul-*
·ion, *s. f. exulta-*

·, *v. n. to exult*

F.

m. fa or f (musi-
te)

Fabear, *v. a. to ballot with beans* [*musick*
Fabordon, *s. m. church*
Fábrica, *s. f. fabrick* || *manufacture* || *fabrick-lands* [*tion*
Fabricacion, *s. f. fabrica-*
Fabricadamente, *ad. art-fully*
Fabricador, *s. m. manu-facturer* || *builder*
Fabricante, *s. m. builder; workman*
Fabricar, *v. a. to fabrick* || *to manufacture*
Fabril, *a. 2. belonging to all* || *manufacturer mechanick arts*
Fabriquero, *s. m. a buil-der* || *church-warden*
Fabuco, *s. m. beech-mast*
Fábula, *s. f. fable*
Fabulacion, *s. f. fiction; tale* [*tor*
Fabulador, *s. m. fabula-*
Fabular, *v. a. to invent fables* or *fictions*
Fabulilla, ita, *s. f. a lit-tle fable*
Fabulista, *s. m. fabulist*
Fabulizar, *v. a. V.* Fabu-lar [*bulously*
Fabulosamente, *adv. fa-*
Fabulosidad, *s. f. the fal-sity* or *vanity of fables*
Fabuloso, sa, *adj. fabu-lous*
Faccion, *s. f. exploit; atchievement* || *faction* || *form; shape*
Facciones, *pl. the features*
Faccionario, ria, *adject. partisan; favourer*
Faccioso, sa, *adj. factious*
Facecia, *s. f. facetious-ness*
Facecioso, sa, *adj. face-tious*
Fa·eta, *s. f. facet*

Faceto, ta, *adject. gay; merry*
Facha, *s. f. the face*
Fachada, *s. f. the front of a building* || *a large face*
Facial, *a. 2. intuitive*
Fácil, *a. 2. facile; easy*
Facilidad, *s. f. facility*
Facilitar, *v. a. to facili-tate*
Fácilmente, *adv. easily*
Facineroso, rosa, sa, *adj. facinorous* [*desk*
Facistol, *s. m. a reading-*
Faco, *s. m. a small horse*
Factible, *a. 2. that can be made* or *done*
Facticio, cia, *adj. facti-tious* [*factor*
Factor, *sub. m. maker* ||
Factoría, *s. f. factory*
Factura, *sub. f. fashion; making* || *invoice*
Fáculas, *s. f. pl. spots (in the sun)*
Facultad, *s. f. faculty* || *science* || *ability*
Facultativo, va, *adj. be-longing to any faculty*
Facundía, *s. f. eloquence*
Facundo, da, *adj. well-spoken; eloquent*
Fada, *s. f. a small sort of apple* [*man*
Fadrin, *s. m. a journey-*
Faena, *s. f. the working of a ship* [*fagot*
Fagina, *sub. f. fascine* || Meter fagina, *to tell sto-ries*
Falacia, *s. f. fallacy*
Falagüeño, ña, *adj. V.* Halagüeño [*duck*
Fálaris, *sub. f. a sort of*
Falaz, *a. 2. fallacious*
Falbala, *s. m. furbelow*
Falcado (carro) *s. m. an-cient chariot with scy-*

thes sticking out on both sides
Falcar, *v. a. to mow*
Falcas, *sub. f. pl. wash-boards* [*new moon*
Falcata (luna), *s. f. the*
Falce, *s. f. a scythe*
Falcinelo, *s. m. a martin*
Falconete, *s. m. falconet*
Falda, *s. f. petticoat* || *that part of any garment that hangs down* || *the lower part of a mountain*
Faldamento, *s. m. V.* Falda
Faldar, *s. m. tass* (*in armour*)
Faldellin, *s. m. under-petticoat*
Faldero, ra, *adj. belonging to petticoats*
Perrillo faldero, ó de falda, *s. m. a lap-dog*
Faldillas, *subs. f. pl. the skirst of a garment*
Faldistorio, *s. m. a sort of stool used by the bishops*
Faldon, *s. m. the lappet of a gown, etc.* || *a fillet* (*in architecture*)
Faldriquera, *s. f. V.* Faltriquera
Faldulario, *s. m. an old, ragged petticoat, etc.*
Falencia, *s. f. want of certitude, contingency*
Falibilidad, *s. f. fallibility*
Falíble, *a.* 2. *fallible*
Falimiento, *s. m. deceit; fraud*
Falir, *v. n. to fail*
Falla, *s. f. V.* Falta || *an ancient women's hood*
Fallar, *v. a. to ruff*, or *trump*
Falleba, *s. f. an iron bar for windows*

Fallecedero, ra, *adj. that can fail* [*die*
Fallecer, *v. n. to fail* || *to*
Fallecimiento, *s. m. death V.* Falta
Fallo, *s. m. sentence passed upon criminals* || *renouncing at cards*
Falordia, *s. f. fallacy; deceit*
Falsa, *s. f. dissonance*
Falsabraga, *s. f. false bray* (*in fortification*)
Falsada, *s. f. the flight of a hawk*
Falsamente, *adv. falsely*
Falsario, ria, *adj. forger*
Falseador, *s. m. falsifier*
Falcear, *v. a. to falsify* || *to bend a sword, etc.*
Falsear el cuerpo, *to cover one's body* — las guardas, *to bribe the guards*
Falsear, *v. n. to fall; to decay, etc.*
Falsedad, *s. f. falcity*
Falsete, *s. m. a faint treble* (*in musick*)
Falsificacion, *s. f. falsification*
Falsificador, *s. m. falsifier*
Falsito, *s. m. a little liar*
Falso, sa, *adj. false*
Falta, *s. f. want* || *fault; error*
Tiene quatro faltas, *she has gone three months with child*
Faltar, *v. n. to fail* || *to want* || *to break one's word, etc.* || *to die*
Faltar la escopeta, *to miss firing*
Faltitta, *s. f. a little fault*
Falto, ta, *adj. wanting; deficient* || *stingy* || *mad* [*tous*
Faltoso, sa, adj. *necessi-*
Faltriquera, *s. f. a pocket*

Falua, } s
Faluca, }
Fama, *s. f*
Fame, *s. f*
Famélico,
Familia,
men; ;
ligious
Familiar,
Familiar, *a*
a Prin
spirit
Familiar d
a titula
inquisi
Familiarc
who af
Familiari
liarity
Familiari
ke fam
|| *to fa*
Familiari
familia
Familiarn
miliarl
Familiatu
the fam
Oficio
Famosam
mously
Famoso,
Fámula,
maid
Famulici
ce of a
Fámulo,
Fanal, *s.*
thorn |
Fanático,
Fandango
so call
tertain
Fandang
who d
cing th
Faneca,
fish
Faneg

s. f. as much
a bushel of corn
[dantly
las, *adv. abun-*
, *v. n. V.* Fan-
r
s. f. boasting;
g
, *s. m. a boas-*
low; a bully
, na, *adj. she-*
of little value
ada, *s. f. brag-*

zar, *ver. n. to*
to brag
aría, *s. f. rodo-*
ing
a, *s. f. anger*
ises on trivial

, *v. n. to fancy*
s. f. fancy || *pri-*
sh of wit
, sa, *adj. Voy.*
ico
, *s. f. fantasm*
proud, haughty

n, *s. m. a proud,*
ful man
mente, *adver.*
ically
, ca, *adj. fan-*
l
, *s. m. V.* Fan-

.m. street-porter
, *ver. a. to beat*
| *to brandish the*

a, *s. f. entan-*
| *deceit; fraud*
e || *little-tattle*
a, *s. m. chatterer*
ero, *y* faramal-
. m. a tattling,
nt fellow
, *s. f. profes-*

sion of comedian, etc. || *cheat; falshood*
Farandulero, *s. m. comedian; player* || *a cheat; a sharper*
Farante, *s. m. a herald* || *an envoy* || *a player that speaks the prologue* [*stuffs up*
Farcinador, *s. m. he who*
Farda, *s. f. a tax paid for watering the lands*
Fardar, *v. a. to furnish with cloaths*
Fardel, *sub. m. fardel* || *knapsack* [Fardel
Fardelillo, *s. m. dim. de*
Fardillo, *sub. m. a little bundle*
Fardo, *s. m. a bundle* or *bale of goods*
Farellon, *subs. m. cape; promontory*
Fares, *s. m. pl. tenebres*
Farfalá, *s. f. furbelow*
Farfalloso, sa, *adj. stammerer*
Farfan, *s. m. a christian horse-soldier in the army of the Moors*
Farfante, } *subs. m. a*
Farfanton, } *bully*
Farfantonada, } *s. f. brag-*
Farfantonería, } *ging; rodomontado*
Fárfara, *s. f. colt's-foot*
Farfulla, } *s. m. stam-*
Farfullador, } *merer*
Farfullar, *v. n. to stammer* || *to talk* or *do hastily* [*of pap.*
Farinetas, *s. f. pl. a kind*
Faringe, *s. m. the upper end of the œsophagus*
Farisaismo, *s. m. pharisaism*
Farisaico, ca, *adj. pharisaical*
Fariseo, *s. m. pharisee*

Faro, *s. m. pharos; lighthouse*
Farol, *s. m. a lantern*
Farolero, *s. m. one who lights lanterns*
Farolillo, *sub. m. a little lantern*
Faron, *s. m. V.* Fanal
Farota, *s. f. a bold, impudent woman*
Faroton, *s. m. a bold, impudent man*
Farpado, da, *adj. cut in points*
Farpas, *s. f. pl. the points of a standard, etc.*
Farra, *s. f. a fish so called*
Farrago, *s. m. hodge-podge; farce*
Farro, *s. m. peeled barley*
Farsa, *s. f. a farce; a droll* || *a company of players*
Farsante, *s.* 2. *a player*
Farseto, *s. m. a doublet*
Farsista, *s. m. a player*
Fartes, *s. m. pl. a kind of fritters* [*and just*
Fas, *s. m. that is right*
Fascal, *s. masc. a heap of ten sheaves of corn*
Fasces, *s. f. pl. fasces*
Fascinacion, *s. f. fascination* [*nate*
Fascinar, *v. a. to fasci-*
Fasoles, *s. m. pl. french beans*
Fasquiar, *v. a to loath*
Fastidiar, *v. a. to loath* || *to disgust; to tire, etc.*
Fastidio, *s. m. loathing* || *disgust*
Fastidiosamente, *adv. fastidiously* [*dious*
Fastidioso, sa, *adj. fasti-*
Fastigio, *s. m. top* || *the height* or *pinnacle*
Fasto, *s. m. pomp; vain-shew* || *pride*

Fastos, *pl. calendar; records*

Fastoso, } *adj. ostentatious*
Fastuoso, }

Fatal, *a.* 2. *fatal*

Fatalidad, *s. f. fatality*

Fatalmente, *adv. fatally*

Fatídico, ca, *adj. fatidical*

Fatiga, *s. f. fatigue*

Fatigador, *s. m. one who wearies*

Fatigar, *v. a. to weary; to fatigue*

Fatigoso, sa, *adj. wearisome* [ria

Fator, fatoría. *V.* Factor, Factoría

Fatuidad, *s. f. foolishness; fatuity*

Fatuo, ua, *adj. fatuous*

Fatura, *s. f. V.* Factura

Fauce, *s. f. throat; gullet*

Faufau, *s. m. pride; solemnity*

Fauno, *s. m. a fabled god of the woods*

Fausto, *s. masc. pomp; wain-shew*

Fausto, ta, *adj. happy*

Faustoso, sa, *adj. ostentatious*

Fautor, *s. m. fautor*

Favila, *s. f. live coal*

Favo, *s. m. honey-comb*

Favonio, *s. m. the west-wind*

Favor, *s. m. favour*

Favorable, *a.* 2. *favourable*

Favorablemente, *adv. favourably* [favour

Favorcillo, *s. m. a little favour*

Favorecedor, *s. m. favourer*

Favorecer, *v. a. to favour*

Favorido, da, *adj. favoured*

Faxa, *s. f. a swaithing band* || *fascia* || *fesse*

Faxas de piernas or calzas, garters

Faxar, v. a. to swathe

Faxardo, *s. m. a kind of minced pie*

Faxero, *s. masc. a child's roller*

Faxo, *s. m. V.* Haz

Faxos, *plur. children's cloaths*

Fayado, *s. m. a garret*

Fayanca, *s. f. an unsteady posture of the body*

Faysa, *s. f. V.* Faxa

Faysan, *s. m. a pheasant*

Faz, *s. f. face* || *front* || *the right side of a stuff, etc.*

Faz á faz, *face to face* — á prima faz, *at the first sight* or *meeting*

Fazoleto, *s. m. a handkerchief*

Fe, *s. f. faith* || *fidelity* || *assurance* or *testimony*

Fealdad, *s. f. deformity; ugliness* || *turpitude*

Feamente, *adv. uglily* || *dishonestly*

Febeo, bea, *adj. belonging to god Apollo*

Feble, *a.* 2. *feeble; weak* || *short of weight*

Feble, *s. m. feeble, weak-side* [weakness

Febledad, *s. f. feebleness; weakness*

Feblemente, *adv. feebly; weakly*

Febo, *s. m. Apollo; sun*

Febrero, *s. m. february*

Febricitante, *a.* 2. *troubled with an ague*

Febrífugo, ga, *adj. febrifuge*

Febril, *a.* 2. *Febrile*

Fecal (materia), *s. f. human excrements*

Fecha, *s. fem. date (of a writing)* [teeth

Fechar, *v. a. to gnash the teeth*

Fecho, *s. m. V.* Hecho

Fechoría, *s. f. a base and ignoble action*

Fecial, *s. fem* ...
sort of pri...
rald of arm...

Feculento, ta ...
lent

Fecundamente ...
fully; abu...

Fecundar, *v.* ...
fecund

Fecundidad, ...
dity

Fecundizar, *v* ...

Fecundo, da, ...

Feeza, *s. f. ug*...

Felice, *a.* 2. ...

Felicidad, *s. f* ...

Felicitar, *v. a* ...
tulate

Feligrés, *s. m* ...

Feligresía, *s.* ...

Feliz, *a.* 2. *ha*...

Felizmente, *a*...

Felonía, *s. f.* ...

Felpa, *s. f. sh*...

Felpa rabona, ...
ling

Felpado, da, *a* ...

Felpilla, *s. fe*...
silken, sha...

Felpudo, da, *a* ...

Feluca, *s. f. fe*...

Femenil, *a.* 2 ...
womanish

Femenilmente ...
man-like

Femenino, na ...

Fementidamen...
unfaithfully

Fementido, da, ...
faithful

Feminal, *a.* 2. ...

Famineo, nea, ...
manish; fem...

Fendiente, *s. m* ...
blow [ni...

Fenecer, *v. a.* ...

Fenecimiento, ...

Fenicoptero, ...
mant (a b...

a, *adj. belon-*
ay
. anemony
. phenix
s. m. fenny-
[*menon*
s. m. pheno-
j. deformed;
honest; base
f. fruitfulness
ıtal; unlucky
2. fruitful;

n. a coffin
ia || holydays
ıarket || a fai-

), s. m. vaca-
in a court of
[*the feria*
belonging to
to buy or sell
s fairing
adj. ferine
s. an ancient
ıoney
s. m. a sort of
boiled in oil
n, *s. fem. fer-*
s
v. a. to leaven
. n. to ferment
o, va, *adject.*
ive
. m. leaven;

s. f. ferocity
ferocious
a. ferociously
: an iron club
V. Herrar
adj. of or be-
iron || fierce

V. Herreria
s. m. a cloak
n. the burnt
lying

Ferreteado, da, *adj. studded with iron*
Ferrion, *s. m.* } *passion;*
Ferriona, *s. f.* } *raving*
Ferro, *s. m. anchor*
Ferropea, *s. f. irons; fetters*
Fértil, *a.* 2. *fertile*
Fertilidad, *s. f. fertility*
Fertilizar, *v. a. to fertilize*
Férula, *s. f. ferula; palmer*
Ferviente, *a.* 2. *fervid*
Fervor, *s. m. heat-fervency*
Fervorcillo, *s. m. dim. de* Fervor
Fervorizar, *v. act. to stimulate*
Fervorosamente, *adver. with fervour*
Fervoroso, sa, *adj. fervid; fervent*
Festear, *v. a. V.* Festejar
Festejador, ra, *adj. courteous; obsequious, etc.*
Festejar, *v. a. to feast; to court*
Festejo, *s. mas. a feast || obsequiousness; attendance paid to one, etc.*
Festero, *s. m. an officer in a church who takes care of the feast, of the musick, etc.*
Festin, *s. m. a banquet, a feast* [*tion*
Festinacion, *s. f. festina-*
Festival, *a.* 2. *festival*
Festivamente, *a. merrily*
Festividad, *s. f. festivity || festival*
Festivo, va, *adj festival*
Dias festivos. *holy-days*
Feston, *s. m. festoon*
Fétido, da, *adj. fetid*
Feto, *s. m. fœtus*
Feudal, *a.* 2. *feodal*
Feudalidad, *s. f. the quality of fees*

Feudar, *v. a. to feoff*
Feudatario, ria, *a.* y *f. feudatory*
Feudista, *s. m. feudist*
Feudo, *s. m. fief*
Fiado (al), *adver. upon thrust*
Fiador, ra, *s. bail; security*
Fiador, *s m. the loop of a cloak || creance (in falconry) || astay (in a gun), etc.*
Fiambre, *adj. cold meat*
Fiambrera, *s. f. cold meat || a hamper to carry cold meat in || foppery; impertinence*
Fianza, *s. f bail; surety*
Fiar, *v. act. to bail one || to trust; to credit || to confide in*
Fiar, *v. n. to confide in; to rely upon*
Fiat, *s. m. consent; assent*
Fibra, *s. f. fibre*
Fibroso, sa, *adj. fibrous*
Fibula, *s. fem. buckle; clasp, etc.*
Fibulas, *pl. futures*
Ficcion, *s. f. fiction || grimace, etc.* [*fish*)
Fice, *s. m. whiting* (*a*
Ficédula, *s. f. beccafigo*
Ficticio, cia, *adj. fictitious*
Ficto, ta, *adj. feigned; fictious || vain; useless*
Fictura, *s. f. feint; disguise*
Fidedigno, gna, *adj. that deserves to be credited*
Fideicomisario, *s. mas. a feoffee of trust*
Fideicomiso, *s. m. a feoffment of trust*
Fidelidad, *s. f. fidelity*
Fideos, *s. m. pl. vermicelly*
Fido, da, *adj. faithful*

Fiducia, *s. f. confidence; faith*
Fiebre, *s. f. an ague*
Fiel, *a. 2. faithfull || believer*
Fiel, *s. m. overseer of the weights and measures || the judge of the field || the tongue of a balance*
Fieldad, *s. f. the office of the* fiel *|| surety*
Fielmente, *a. faithfully*
Fieltro, *s. masc. felt || a cloak against the rain*
Fiera, *s. f. a wild beast*
Fieramente, *adv. fiercely*
Fiereza, *s. f. fierceness || ugliness*
Fiero, ra, *adject. fierce || ugly || wild; savage || huge; excessive || horrible*
Fieros, *s. m. pl. threats; bravadoes*
Fierro, *s. m. V.* Hierro
Fierros, *pl. irons; fetters*
Fiesta, *s. f. feast; festival || holy day*
Fiestas, *pl. easter-days || vacation time || demonstrations of kindness*
Figmento, *s. m. earthenware*
Figo, *s. m. V.* Higo
Figon, *s. m. a cook's shop || V.* Figonero *|| a bardash*
[Figonero, ... *to a cook*]

notes (in musick) || court-cards
Hacer figuras, *to make faces*
Figurable, *a. 2. figurable*
Figurada, *s. f. an insignificant* or *impertinent action, etc.*
Figuradamente, *adv. figuratively*
Figurado, da, *adj. figurative*
Figural, *a. 2. belonging to a figure*
Figurar, *v. a. to figure*
Figurarse, *v. r. to imagine; to fancy*
Figurativo, va, *adj. figurative*
Figurería, *s. f. V.* Figurada
Figurero, *s. m. one that makes faces*
Figurilla, *s. f. a little figure*
Figuron, *s. masc. a great figure || a boasting, impertinent fellow*
Fil, *s. m. the tongue of a balance || equilibrium*
Fila, *s. fem. a file of soldiers, etc.*
Filaciga, *s. f. V.* Filástica
Filadez, *y* Filaiz, *s. f. ferret-silk*
Filamentos, *s. m. pl. filaments*
Filandrias, *s. f. pl. filanders*
Filantrópos, *s. m. bardock*
Filar, *a. 2. belonging to*

stuff made
Fileno, na, *a. effeminate*
Filete, *s. m. (architecture) edging || a*
Filetear, *v. a. edge* or *ed*
Fileton, *s. m.* Filete
Filiacion, *s.*
Filial, *a. 2.*
Filiar, *v. n. own desce*
Filicida, *s. m. his son*
Filigrana, *s. work*
Filili, *s. m. neness, et*
Filipéndula, *dula*
Filipichin, *s*
Filis, *s. m. ce; gente*
Filisteo, tea *gigantick*
Fillo, *s. m.*
Fillos, *pl. ters*
Filo, *s. m. librium; edge of a sharpenin*
Filología, *s. f. philo*
Filológico, *lological*

mente, *adv. phi-*
ically
, ca, *adj. philo-*
[pher
, *s. m. philoso-*
fa, *adj. philo-*
al
a, *s. f. filtration*
, *a. to filter*
. *m. a filter* || *a*
s. f. the hem of
ent
m. human ex-
st [purpose
masc. end || *aim ;*
at length. En fin,
: *to conclude*
(dia de los), *s. m.*
ule-day
. *2. final*
l, *adv. finally*
, *v. act.* y *n. to*
; *to end*
nte, *adv. finally*
te, *adv. finely*
ato, *s. m. death*
. *n. to die*
v. r. to long for...
. *f. a substancial*
ty ; a fund, etc.
reath, etc.
, *a. 2 stable ; las-*
s. f. fineness ||
ess || *gallantry* ||
ll gift [gnedly
nente, *adv. fei-*
, da, *adj. feigned*
r, *s. m. feigner*
ento, *s. m. feint ;*
ise
v. a. to feign || *to*
ck ; to ape || *to for-*
ries, etc.
, *a. 2. that may be*
d
o. s. m. the balance
ing of an account

Dar finiquito, *to lay all at stake*
Finítimo, ma, *adj. bordering on*
Finito, ta, *adj. finite*
Fino, na, *adject. fine* || *faithful*
Finta, *s. f. a tribute paid to the prince*
Fintas, *pl. feints (in fencing)*
Finura, *s. f. V.* Fineza
Firma, *s. f. hand ; signature*
Firmamento, *s. m. firmament* || *a prop ; a stay*
Firmar, *v. a. to sign or subscribe* || *to affirm*
Firmarse, *v. r. to attribute to one's self any name*
Firme, *a. 2. firm*
Firmemente, *adv. firmly*
Firmeza, *s. f. firmness*
Fiscal, *s. m. the king's sollicitor* || *a censurer*
Fiscal, *a. 2. fiscal*
Fiscalear, } *v. a. to accuse ; to charge*
Fiscalizar, }
Fisco, *s. m. the exchequer*
Fiseter, *s. masc. a sort of whale*
Fisga, *s. f. a harpoon* || *a jest ; a reflection*
Fisgar, *v. a. to play upon a man ; to jeer*
Fisgon, *s. m. a jesting, scoffing fellow*
Física, *s. f. physick*
Físicamente, *adv. physically*
Físico, ca, *adj. physical*
Físico, *s. m. a physician*
Fisil, *a. 2. easy to be cleaved*
Fisonomía, *s. f. physiognomy*
Fisonómista, *y* Fisonomo, *s. m. physiognomist*

Fistol, *s. m. a cunning artful man at play*
Fístola, *s. f. fistula*
Fistolado, da, *adj. fistulous*
Fístula, *s. f. a pipe*
Fistular, *a. 2. belonging to a pipe [lous*
Fistuloso, sa, *adj. fistu-*
Fitonisa, *s. f. pythoness*
Fixa, *s. f. hinge-hook*
Fixacion, *s. f. fixation*
Fixado, da, *adj.* (en el blason) *fitched*
Fixamente, *adv. fixedly*
Fixar, *v. a. to stick in* || *to fix*
Fixeza, *s. f. steadfastness* || *fixedness* || *fixity*
Fixo, xa, *adj. fixed ; steady*
Flacamente, *adv. weakly*
Flaco, ca, *adject. weak ; feeble [lation*
Flagelacion, *s. f. flagel-*
Flagelo, *s. m. a whip*
Flagicio, *s. m. an enormous crime*
Flagicioso, sa, *adj. flagitious*
Flagrar, *v. n. to sparkle*
Flama, *s. f. a flame*
Flamante, *a. 2. flaming*
Flambante, *a. 2. like so many flames*
Flamear, *v. a. to shiver*
Flamenco, *s. m. flammant (a bird)*
Flamenquilla, *s. f. a little plate for fruit*
Flameo, *s. m. a veil worn by the bride*
Flamígero, ra, *adj. flaming ; glittering*
Flámulas, *s. f. pl. pendents (in a ship)*
Flanco, *s. m. flank ; side*
Flanqueado, da, adj. defended by lateral fortifications

Flanquear, v. a. to flank
Flaon, s. m. custard
Flaquear, v. n. to totter || to be dispirited || to slacken
Flaqueza, s. f. leanness || weakness [flask
Flasco, s. m. a powder-
Flato, s. masc. a blast of wind || flatulency
Flatoso, sa, adj. V. Flatuoso
Flatulento, ta, adj. flatulent
Flatuoso, sa, adj. flatuous
Flauta, s. f. a flute
Flautas de órgano, organ-pipes
Flautada (voz), s. f. soft sweet voice
Flautero, tista, s. m. a flute-maker || a piper
Flautos pitos, amusements; pastimes
Flavo, va, adj. yellow
Flébil, a. 2. sad; mournful
Flebotomar, v. a. to phlebotomise
Flebotomía, s. f. phlebotomy [botomist
Flebotomiano, s. m. phle-
Flecha, s. f. arrow
Flechador, s. m. an archer
Flechar, v. act. to shoot arrows
Flechastes, s. m. pl. the ratlinges of the shrouds
Flechazo, s. m. a flight-shot
Flechería, s. f. a body of archers
Flechero, s. m. an archer
Flegma, etc. V. Flema, etc.
Flegmon, s. m. V. Flemon
Flema, s. m. phlegm
Flemático, ca, adj. phlegmatick
Fleme, s. m. fleam
Flemon, s. m. phlegmon
Flemoso, sa, adj. full of phlegm
Flemudo, da, adj. slow; lazy
Flequezuelo, s. m. small fringes
Fletamiento, s. m. freighting
Fletar, v. a. to freight
Flexibilidad, s. f. flexibility
Flexible, a. 2. flexible
Flexion, s. fem. flexion; flexure
Flibote, s. m. a fly boat
Flinflon, s. m. a plump; fresh-coloured man
Flocadura, s. f. fringing
Floña, s. f. trifle; impertinence [ged
Floqueado, da, adj. frin-
Floquecillo, s. m. a small fringe
Flor, s. f. flower; bloom; blossom || maidenhead; virginity || a cheat or cheating trick
Flor de cobre, verdigrease — de harina, flour — de vino, the mother on decayed wines — de cordovan, the smooth glossy side of the leather — de la canela, choice cinnamon — de especie, the spice called mace — de la oracion, flourish — de lis, the flower-de-luce
Flores de mano, artificial flowers
Flordelizar, v. a. to flourish with flowers-de-luce
Floreado (pan), s. masc. bread made with flour
Florear, v. act. to adorn with flowers
Florear el naype, to prepare cheating ca[...] la harina, to [...] searce
Florearse, v. r. to [...]
Florecer, v. n. to bl[...] || to flourish
Florecilla, ita, s. f. a[...] flower
Floreo, s. m. a flo[...] in fencing, etc.
Florero, s. m. a flow[...] || a flower-mak[...] picture full of fl[...] || a verbose, [...] talker
Floresta, s. f. a for[...] forest-work
Florestero, s. m. fo[...] keeper
Floreta, s. f. a bit of [...] leather added to a [...]
Floretada, s. f. a fill[...]
Florete, s. m. a pla[...] with swords
Floretear, v. a. to a[...] with flowers
Floridamente, a. elega[...]
Floridito, ta, adj. dim[...] Florido
Florido, da, adj. blo[...]med; blown || ex[...]lent; exquisite || cl[...] serene
Estilo florido, a fl[...] style || pascua flor[...] palm-sunday
Florifero, florigero, adj. floriferous
Florin, s. m. florin
Flortisado, da, adj. b[...]ded with a flower[...]luce
Floron, s. masc. flo[...]work; flourish
Floroncos, s. m pl. h[...]
Flos sanctorum, s. m[...] book containing th[...]ves of saints
Flota, s. f. a fleet

f. } rubbing; friction
to rub
a. *flothfully*
. V. Flaquear
f. *looseness-*
the wool that
ff from cloth
n on fruit, etc.
V. Floxedad
dj. flexible ||
ose || *slothful*
s. f. fluctua-
. to fluctuate
. fringe
ophtalmy
, s. m. a little
adj. fluid
to flow
. V. Frualera
. of the river
ial, fresh wa-
ush, at cards
f. flowing ||
. flux; flood
ibras, flow of
le risa, a fit
ng — de san-
ly-flux — de
ooseness
uxe del mar.
off lood and
. sea-calf
focus || *touch-*
rtise
ject. soft and
ongy
. heart-money
f. a fire with
nes
asc. heart ||

touch-hole || *a cook-room (in a ship)*

Fogonádura, *s. f. the partners of a mast*

Fogosidad, *s. f. heat; impetuosity*

Fogoso, sa, *adj. ignited; fieri* || *hot; unruly*

Fogote, *s. m. fire-brand*

Foja, *s. f. leaf of a book*

Folga, *s. f. mirth; recreation*

Foliar, *v. a. to mark the number of any book*

Folias, *s. f. pl. a sort of dance*

Folículo, *s. m. follicle*

Folio, *s. m. the leaf of a book* || *a folio* || *a sort of mercury*

Folio volante, *a loose sheet; a pamphlet*

Folla, *s. f. a confused, disorderly skirmish, etc.*

Follada (pasta), *s. f. a good puff-paste*

Follado, da, *adj. set in puffs; hollow*

Follage, *s. masc. leaves; leaved branches* || *foliage* || *tinsel*

Follar, *v. a. to blow with the bellows* || *to shape like leaves*

Follero, *s. m. who makes* or *sells bellows*

Folleta, *s. f. a measure of wine*

Folletero, *s. m. V.* Follero

Folleto, *s. m. a quire of paper* || *a news-paper*

Follon, na, *adj. slothful* || *nave*

Follonería, *s. fem. sloth; idleness*

Fomentacion, *s. f. fomentation*

Fomentador, *s. m. fomenter*

Fomentar, *v. a. to foment*

Fomento, *s. m. fomenting* || *fewel* || *incentive*

Fomes, } *s. m. incentive*
Fómite, }

Fondable, *a.* 2. *that may be sounded*

Fondear, *v. a. to sound — to visit the cargo on board of a ship*

Fondeo, *s. m. the visit of a ship's cargo*

Fondillon, *s. m. the lees of any cask*

Fondo, *s. masc. bottom; ground* || *the depth* || *a fund*

Dar fondo, *to cast anchor* — echar a fondo, *to sink a vessel, etc.*

Fondon, *s. m. V.* Fondillon

Fonil, *s. m. a tunnel to fill casks with*

Fonsadera, *s. f. a duty for keeping the ditches in repair*

Fontal, *a.* 2. *first; principal*

Fontana, *s. f. fountain*

Fontanar, *s. m. spring of water*

Fontanar, *a.* 2. *belonging to a fountain*

Fontanche, *s. mas. a top-knot*

Fontanería, *s. f. the art of making conduits* || *conduits; pipes*

Fontanero, *s. m. conduit-maker*

Fontano, na, *adj. V.* Fontanar

Fontanoso, sa, *adj. full* or *adorned with fountains*

Fontecica, *s. f. a little fountain*

Foque, *s. m. a triangular sail of the bowsprit*

Foragido, da, *adj. a mountaineer robber*

Foral, *a.* 2. forensick

Foraneo, nea, *adj. strange; foreign*

Forastero, ra, *adj. foreign; strange*

Forastero, *s. m. a stranger*

Forcejar, *v. n. to struggle; to strive*

Forcejon, *s. m. struggling; striving*

Forcejudo, da, *adj. strong; robust*

Forense, *a. 2. forensick*

Forero, ra, *adj. done according to the law*

Fórfolas, *s. f. pl. scabs on the head*

Forja, *s. f. a forge || mortar*

Forjador, *s. m. forger*

Forjadura, *s. f. forging*

Forjar, *v. a. to forge*

Forma, *s. fem. form || a mould || a shoe maker's last || a block || host*

Formable, *a. 2. that may be formed*

Formacion, *s. f. formation || form*

Formador, ra, *adj. former*

Formadura, *s. fem. form; figure*

Formal, *a. 2. formal*

Foamalidad, *s. f. formality*

Formalizar, *v. a. to form*

Formalizarse, *v. r. to formalize*

Formalmente, *adv. formally*

Formar, *v. a. to form; to frame; to make*

Formar queja, *to put up a complaint*

Formativo, va, *adj. formative*

Formejar, *v. act. to stow goods in a ship*

Formeros, *s. m. pl. lateral arches in a vault*

Formicante (pulso), *s. m. the pulse when it is low and weak*

Formidable, *a. 2. formidable*

Formidoloso, sa, *adject. fearful || formidable*

Formon, *s. masc. a great chisel*

Fórmula, *s. f. formule*

Formulario, *s. m. formulary*

Formulilla, *s. f. a little formule*

Fornicacion, *s. f. fornication*

Fornicador, *s. m. fornicator*

Fornicar, *v. a. to commit fornication*

Fornicario, ria, *adj. lewd; lecherous*

Fornido, da, *adj. strong; robust*

Fornimiento, *s. m. provision; store*

Fornir, *v. a. to furnish; to provide; to store*

Fornituras, *s. f. pl. sortment of printing letters*

Foro, *s. m. the bar; the court*

Forquina, *s. f. a fork*

Forrage, *s. m. forage || abundance or mixture of things of little value*

Forrageador, *s. m. forager*

Forragear, *v. a. to forage*

Forrar, *v. a. to line*

Forro, *s. m. lining || sheathing*

Fortachon, *s. mas. a very strong and well-built man*

Fortalecer, *v. a. to strengthen; to fortify*

Fortaleza, } *s fem. fortitude*
Fortalidad. } *|| strength || fortress*

Fortezuelo, *s. m. fortlet*

Fortificacion, *s. f. fortification*

Fortificar, *v. a. to fortify*

Fortin, *s. m. a fortlet*

Fortuitame
tuitousl

Fortuito,

Fortuna, *s*
storm

Fortuna de
omelet
moza de f
whore

Fortunar,

Fortunilla
Fortuna

Forzadame
|| necess

Forzado, *s*
slave

Forzado, d
Consonan
zados, *b*

Forzador,

Forzal, *s.*
of a com

Forzar, *v.*
take by

Forzosa,
draught
Hacer la f
to compe

Forzosamen
sarily ||

Forzoso, sa

Forzudo, d
robust

Fosa, *s. f.*
grave

Fosado, *s. m*

Fosal, *s. m.*

Fosca, *s. f.*

Fósforo, *s.*
ning sta

Fosico, *s. m*

Foso, *s. m*
trench

Fótula, *s. f*

Foxa, *s. f.*

Foya, *s. f.*
coals

Fracasar, *v*
to piec

m. a fall with
|| disaster; ill

f. fracture ||

f. fracture
a strawberry-
[grante
1. 2. V. Fra-
e, in the fact
f. V. Fraga
. a frigate
masc. a little

fragile; frail
s. f. fragility
, a. frailty;

s.m. fragment
s. f. craggi-
way || thick-
wood
, adj. craggy;
tony, etc.
s.f. fragrancy
a. 2. fragrant
a smith's forge
s. m. forger
a. to forge
V. Fragosidad
s f. rasberry
, s. m. rasber-

f. a sort of dart
s. m. a strap
ickle
e, adv. frankly
ly
, s. f. frangi-

, na, adj. be-
o the Francis-
r

masc. franck
money)
, adject. frank
eral
s. m. godwit

Frangente, s. m. an accidental misfortune
Frangible, a. 2. frangible
Frangir, v. a. to break
Frangollo, s. mas. boiled corn
Frangote, s. m. a pack
Franja, s f. fringe
Franjon, s. masc. a great fringe [fringe
Franjuela, s. fem. a little
Franquear, v. a. to franchise; to make free || to make a present
Franqueza, s. f. franchise || liberality
Franquicia, s. f. franchise || a privileged place
Franquísimamente, adv. very liberally
Frasca, s. f. dry leaves
Frasco, s. m. a decanter || a little powder flask
Frase, s. f. phrase
Frasquera, s. f. a case of bottles
Frasqueta, s. fem. frisket (in a printer's press)
Frasquito, s. m. dim. de Frasco [reprimand
Fraterna, s. fem. a severe
Fraternal, a. 2. fraternal
Fraternalmente, adv. fraternally
Fraternidad, s. f. fraternity
Fraterno, na, adj. fraternal (murderer)
Fratricida, s. m. fratricide
Fratricidio, s. m. fratricide (murder)
Fraudo, s. m. Fraudulencia, s. f. fraud; fraudulency
Fraudulentamente, adv. fraudulently
Fraudulento, ta, adject. fraudulent
Fraudulosamente, adver. fraudulently

Fraustina, s. f. a blockhead
Fray, title given to friars — fray juan, brother john
Fraylada, s. f. any action done by a friar
Frayle, s. masc. friar || monk-fish
Fraylecico, cillo, cito, s. m. a little friar || a child in a friar's habit || an ope (a bird)
Fraylego, ga, adj. monkish [kish
Frayleño, ña, adj. mon-
Fraylería, s. f. a company of friars
Fraylesco, ca, adj. monkish [friar
Fraylezuelo, s. m. a little
Fraylía, s. f. monachism; monkery
Frazada, s. f. a shagged blanket [Frazada
Frazadilla, s. f. dim. de
Fregacion, s. f. rubbing
Fregadero, s. m. scullery
Fregado, s. m. scouring
Fregador, s. m. scullery || a rubber
Fregadura, s. f. } rubbing; scouring
Fregamiento, s. m. } rubbing; scouring
Fregajo, s. m. a swab
Fregar, v. a. to rub — to scour
Fregatriz, } s. f. a chair woman
Fregona, } s. f. a chair woman
Fregoncilla, s. f. a young scouring wench
Freir, v. a. to fry in a pan
Frémito, s. m. a noise; a roar; a bellowing
Frenar, v. a. to bridle || to refrain
Frendiente, a. 2. furious
Frenero, s. m. a bit-maker
Frenesí, s. m. phrenesy

Frente, s. f. the fore-head || the blank space at the top of a writing || front: face [fore-head
Frentecilla, s. f. a little
Freqüencia, s. f. frequency
Freqüentacion, s. f. frequenting || frequency
Freqüentar, v. a. to frequent || to do a thing often
Freqüentativo, va, adject frequentative
Freqüente, a. 2. frequent
Freqüentemente, ad. frequently
Fresa, s. f. a straw-berry
Frescal, a. 2. a little cool or fresh [a cod
Frescal, s. m. a fish like
Frescamente, adv. freshly || quietly
Fresco, ca, adject. cool || fresh || new || sweet; not salted
Lugar fresco, a pleasant, cool place
Fresco, s. m. cool; cool-
military order || a lay-sister
Freylar, v. a. to receive one as a knight of a military order
Freyle, s. m. a knight of a military order
Freza, s. f. fry || dung || track || the noise silk-worms make when they awake
Frezar, v. n. to dung || to eat (said of silk-worms, when they awake)
Frialdad, s. f. coldness || frigidity [heavily
Friamente, adv. dully;
Friático, ca, adj. chilly || dull; heavy
Fricacion, s. f. friction
Fricar, v. a to rub
Fricasea, s. f. fricassee
Friccion, s. f. friction
Friega, s. f. friction with flannel, etc.
Friera, s. f. chilblain
Frígido, da, adj. cold
Fringilago, s. m. titmouse
Frison, s. m. ders horse
Frisuelos, s. of french
Fritada, s. f.
Fritillas, s. f.
Fritura, s. f.
Frivolamente lously
Frivolo, la,
Froga, s. f.
Frogar, v. a. bricks
Frondosidad, ves of a dance of
Frondoso, sa leaves || ce
Frontal, s. m pendium
Frontalera s. laces or antipendi
Fronte, s. f.
Frontera, s.
Fronterizo, lies upon || borderi

the ten-
hrown in
ubbing
rub
adj. fruc-
. to bear
tify
. Frito
ad. fruit-
[ful
adj. fruit-
gal
frugality
uition
njoy
. fruitive
m. a puc-
; a deceit
pucker;
to lie; to
[brass
. latten;
futility
j. futile;
adj. frus-
frustrate
. to be di-
a, adject.
s
pancakes,
ol. borders
d flowers
ure
it bearing
fruit-tree
to produce
[man
fruit-wo-
the fruite-
fruit-house
fruiterer ||
t || a nap-
INGLES.

kin to lay over fruit || *a picture of fruits*

Frutier, *s. m. the chief fruiterer*

Frutifero, ra, *adj. fruitful*

Frutificar, *v. a. V.* Fructificar

Frutilla, *s. f. a little fruit* || *a bead* || *a straw-berry* || *a by-dish*

Frutillar, *s. m. the place where straw-berries grow*

Fruto, *s. m. fruit; product; profit, etc.*

Frutuoso, sa, *adj. fructuous*

Fuca, *s. f. V.* Fico

Fúcar *s. m. a rich man*

Fuego, *s. m. fire*

Fuego de Sn. Anton, *St. Anthony's fire* — de artificio, *fire-work* — de ladrones, *the fire that burns backwards towards the chimney* — fatuo, *ignis fatuus*

Fuegos, *pl. beacons fired to alarm the country*

Fueguecillo, *s. m. dim. de* Fuego

Fuellar, *s. m. gilt paper they apply on a wax taper*

Fuelle, *s. m. bellows* || *a tale bearer*

Fuelles, *pl. rumples*

Fuen, *s. f. fountain*

Fuente, *s. fem. fountain; spring* || *an ewer to wash hands* || *a bason of water* || *issue; fountanel* [Fuente

Fuentecilla, *s. f. dim. de*

Fuera, *adv. out; without* || *besides; more over*

Fuera! *int. make way*

Fuercecilla, *s. f. a little force*

Fuero, *s. m. law; statute; ancient custom, etc.*

Fuero ecclesiastico, *ecclesiastical court*

Fueros, *pl. privileges; liberties*

Fuerte, *s. m. a fort*

Fuerte de campaña, *fortlet*

Fuerte, *a.* 2. *strong; able, powerfull*

Fuertecillo, *s. m. a little fort*

Fuertemente, *a. strongly*

Fuerza, *s. f. force; strength*

Fuerzas, *pl. forces; troops*

Fuga, *s. f. flight* || *a fugue* || *prop; buttress*

Fugacidad, *s. f. fugacity*

Fugaz, *a.* 2. *apt to run away* || *unsteady; unstable*

Fugitivo, va, *adj. fugitive*

Fuina, *s. f. foin*

Fulanito, ta, *s. f. such a little one*

Fulano, na, *s. such a one*

Fulga, *s. f. a moorhen*

Fulgente, *a.* 2. *shining; fulgent* [*shining*

Fúlgido, da, *adj. bright;*

Fulgor, *s. m. brightness*

Fulgurar, *v. a. to dart rays of light*

Fuliginoso, sa, *adj. fuliginous*

Fullerazo, *s. m. an arrant sharper*

Fullería, *s. f. sharping or cheating at play*

Fullerito, *s. m. dim. de* Fullero [*play*

Fullero, *s. m. a sharper at*

Fullena, *s. fem. a feigned quarrel* [*nation*

Fulminacion, *s. f. fulmi-*

Fulminado, da, *adj. thunder-struck* [derer

Fulminador, *s. m.* thun-

Fulminar, *v. a.* to strike

with a thunder-bolt || *to fulminate* || *to storm; to chafe*

Fulmíneo, nea, *adj. belonging to*, or *like the thunder* [*dering*

Fulminoso, sa, *adj. thun-*

Fumante, *a.* 2. *smoking*

Fumar, *v. a. to smoke*

Fumarada, *s. f. a puff of smoke* || *a pipe full of tobacco*

Fumaria, *s. f. fumitory*

Fumífero, ra, *adj. smoky; famous*

Fumorolas, *s. f. pl. cavities wich exhale a sulphureous smoke*

Fumosidad, *s. f. smoking*

Funámbulo, *s. m. a rope-dancer*

Funcion, *s. f. function* || *a feast; a publick act* || *a battle an engagement a compliment*

Funda, *s. f. case* || *scabbard* || *mould of button*

Funda de almohada, *a pillow-case*

Fundacion, *s. f. foundation* || *endowment*

Fundadamente *adv. upon a good ground*

Fundador, *s. m. a founder*

Fundago, *s. m. a publick magazine* [*mental*

Fundamental, *a.* 2. *funda-*

Fundamentar, *v. act. to found* || *to establish*

Fundamento, *s. m. foundation* || *fundamentals*

Fundar, *v. a. to found*

Fundar su opinion, *to ground one's opinion*

— mayorazgo, *to settle an estate of inheritance*

Fundería, *s. f. a foundery*

Fundible, *adj. fusible*

Fundíbulo, *s. m. a machine for throwing of stones*

Fundicion, *s. f. melting; casting* || *a cast* (*in printing*)

Fundidor, *s. m. a founder*

Fundir, *v. a. to melt* or *cast*

Fundo, *s. m. ground; land*

Fúnebre, *a.* 2. *funeral; mournful*

Funependulo, *s. m. a pendulum*

Funeral, *a.* 2. *funeral*

Funeral, *s. m. funeral; obsequies* [Fúnebre

Funereo, rea, *adj. Voy.*

Funestar, *v. act. to make fatal*

Funesto, ta, } *adj. fatal;*
Funestoso, sa, } *unlucky*

Furente, *a.* 2. *furious*

Furia, *s. f. fury*

Furibundo, da, *adj. furious*

Furiosamente, *adv. furiously*

Furioso, sa, *adj. furious*

Furion, *s. m. a chariot*

Furor, *s. m fury*

Furor poético, *a poetical rapture*

Furrier, *s. m. harbinger*

Furriera, *s. f. a woman that takes charge of all the keys in the King's palace*

Furrieta, *s. f. bravado* [*ly*

Furtivamente, *ad. furtive-*

Furtivo, va, *adj. furtive*

Fusado, y Fuselado, *adj. fusile* (*in heraldry*)

Fusca, *s. f. a with dusk*

Fusco, ca, *adj. dark brown*

Fusil, *s. m. fusil*

Fusilazo, *s. m. a musket-shot*

Fusilería, *s. f.* a company *of fusileers*

Fusilero, *s. m.* a fusileer

Fuso, *s. m. fusil* [...] *raldry*)

Fusta, *s. f. a foist* [...]

Fustan, *s. m. fust*[...]

Fuste, *s. m. the* [...] *saddle, etc.* || [...] *tion; basis*

Cosa de fuste, *a* [...] *much consequ*[...]

Fustete, *s. m. a* [...]

Fútil, *a.* 2. *futil*[...]

Futilidad *s. f. fu*[...]

Futura, *s. f. surv*[...]

Futurario, ria *ad*[...] *ging to future* [...]

Futuricion, *s. f. f*[...]

Futuro, ra, *adj.* [...]

Futuro, *s. m. fut*[...]

Futuros continge[...] *ture contingen*[...]

G.

GABACHO, *s. m.* [...] *despicable dirt*[...]

Gaban, *s. m. felt-*[...]

Gabardina, *s. f. ga*[...]

Gabarra, *s. f. a li*[...]

Gabarro, *s. m. a* [...] *in the hollow o*[...] *se's pastern* || [...] *bad quality of* [...] *a mistake in* [...] *accounts*

Gabata, *s. f. a* [...] *bowl*

Gabazo, *s. m. th*[...] *of the sugar-ca*[...]

Gabola, *s. f. gabe*[...]

Gabinete, to, *s.* [...] || *cabinet*

Gaboto, *s. m. a* [...] *shuttlecock wit*[...] *dores*

Gaburones, *s. m.* [...] *of the masts*

Gachas, *s. fam. p*[...] pudding *made* [...] wer, honey, [...]

. *adj. squat-*
. *adj. a spoi-*
a tenderling
ook
pectacles
to hook in
. *crookedness*
gers || *leprosy*
a. a hook; a
iect. crooked-
leprous
t. jet
pledge
es, pay; wa-
rofits
a branch cut
tree || *a bunch*
a cluster, etc.
adj. full of
etc.
rich splendid
gance; grace-
, *a court-day*
la de... *to boast*
[*thief*
m. a subtle
l. catch-poles,
, *etc.* || *street-*
[Goloso
ra, *adj. Voy.*
. *fine; neat;*
ldressed
. *a gallant*
e, *adv. gal-*
s. m. a little
gallant
f. a plant, or
lled
, *adject. fine;*
|| *witty; con-*
. *s. galant* ||
handsome
s.m. a gallant

Galantear, *v. a. to court; to gallantize*

Galantemente, *adv. gallantly* || *liberally*

Galantéo, *s. m. court ship*

Galantería, *s. f. gallantry* || *liberality* || *gracefulness* [ment

Galanura, *s. f. fine orna-*

Galápago, *s. m. a tortoise* || *a center (for an arch)* || *maltlong; maltworm* || *a cheating, cunning man*

Galapo, *s. m. a laying-top*

Galardon, *s. m. a reward*

Galardonador, *s. m. rewarder* [ward

Galardonar, *v. a. to re-*

Galarin, ó gallarin, *s. m. a progressive multiplication by two, by three, etc.*

Galavardon, *s. m. a long slouching fellow*

Galaxia, *s. f. the galaxy* or *milky way*

Galbana, *s. f. chichling* || *sloth* [ful

Galbanero, ra, *adj. sloth-*

Galbano, *s. m. galbanum*

Galdre, *s. m. a great loose coat* [Galdre

Galdrecillo, *s. m. dim. de*

Galdrope, *s. m. a particuliar rope in a ship*

Galdrufa, *s. f. whirligig*

Galeaza, *s. f. galeas*

Galeo, *s. m. a sword-fish*

Galeon, *s. m. galeon*

Galeoncillo, *s. m. a little galeon*

Galeota, *s. f. a galiot*

Galeote, *s. m. a galley-slave*

Galera, *s. f. galley* || *a long waggon* || *a house of correction* || *a printer's galley*

Galerero, *s. m. the master of a long waggon*

Galería, *s. f. gallery*

Galerista, *s. m. a marine* or *soldier aboard a galley* [lark

Galerita, *s. fem. copped*

Galerno, *s. m. the north-west-wind*

Galfarro, *s. m. a scoundrel*

Galfarros, *pl. catch-poles*

Galga, *s. f. a greyhound bitch* || *stone cast from a place defended* || *itch* or *scab*

Galgo, *s. m. a greyhound* || *a lank fellow*

Galgueño, ña, *adj. lank as a greyhound*

Gálgulo, *s. m. loriot*

Galibo, *s. m. a table* or *register of the building of ships*

Galicano, na, *adj. gallican*

Gálico (mal), *the french pox*

Galio, *s. m. cheese-rennet*

Galiopsis, *s. f. a sort of nettle*

Galladura, *s. f. the sperm of an egg*

Gallarda, *s. fem. galliard (a dance)*

Gallardamente. *adv. pleasantly; briskly*

Gallardear, *v. a. to do any thing with grace, etc.*

Gallardete, *s. m. a sort of flag* or *of streamer*

Gallardía, *s. fem. grace; pleasantness* || *boldness* || *generosity*

Gallardo, da, *a. graceful* || *liberal* || *valiant; bold*

Gallareta, *s f. a moor duck*

Gallarin, *s. m. V.* Galarin

Gallaruza, *s. f. a sort of coat with a cape to it*

Gallear, *v. n. to tread the*

Gallicinio, s. m. *the crowing of a cock*
Gallillo, s. m. *uvula*
Gallina, s. f. *a hen* || *a coward*
Gallina ciega, *a woodcock* || *hood-man blind* — de rio, *a moor hen*
Gallinaza, s. *hen's dung* || *carrion crow; turkey buzzard*
Gallinería, s. f. *poultry-market* || *a hen-roost* || *cowardice*
Gallinero, s. m. *a poulterer* || *a hen-roost*
Gallineta, s. f. *a young hen* || *a moorhen*
Gallineta ciega, *snipe*
Gallinoso, sa, *adj. coward*
Gallipavo, s. m. *a turkey cock*
Gallipuente, s. m. *a little open bridge*
Gallito, s. masc. *a young strutting amorous beau*
Gallo, s. m. *a cock* || *a fish*

Galope, s. m. *gallop*
Galopeado, da, *adj. done with precipitation*
Galopeado, s. m. *a boxing; a cudgelling, etc.*
Galopear, v. n. *to gallop*
Galopeo, s. m. *galloping*
Galopin, po, s. m. *a cabbin-boy* || *a scullion*
Gama, s. m. *the gamut*
Gama, s. f. *a doe*
Gamarra, s. f. *martingal*
Gamba, s. f. *a leg*
Gambalúa, s. m. *a tall, thin weak man*
Gámbaro, s. m. *a craw-fish*
Gambeta, s. fem. *a cross-caper* || *an affected gesture, etc.*
Hacer gambetas el caballo, *to curv.t*
Gambox, s. m. *a child's cap* [*trough*
Gamella, s. fem. *yoke* ||
Gametría, s. f. *a superstitious transposition of letters, in a word*

Ganadero,
Ganadillo,
tle flock
Ganado,
vermin
Ganado m
cattle —
Ganador,
winner
Ganancia,
Hijo de g
tard chi
Gananciose
ful; pro
Ganapan,
porter
Ganapierde
at cards
Ganar, v.
gain; to
Ganar el p
one's ca
vento, *t*
Ganchero,
guides r
Gancho, s.
hook || *a*

|| to bow ; to bend
ero, ra, a. wicked ;
nish
, s. f. a sort of wa-
-fowl || a thing of
value || an unex-
ted fortune
so, sa, adject. who
ks through the nose
ena, s. f. gangrene
enarse, v. r. to gan-
ne
enoso, sa, adj. of
nature of gangrene
ear, v. n. to speak
ugh the nose
il, s. m. a great fis-
g boat
o, sa, adj. desirous
ron, s. m. a young
se || a tall lean man
, s. m. a goose || a
wn
a, s. f. a picklock ||
he executioner
uar, v. a. to pick a
k
, s. masc. a hired
sgman or herdsman
nía, s. f. a company
herdsmen, etc.
lo, s. m. yelping
les, s. masc. pl. the
oat; the gullet
r, v. n. to yelp || to
hoarse
rata, s. m. a pen-knife
a, } s.m. wind-pipe ||
la, } a kind of fritter
ntada, s. f. the thro-
ng of a hook
ntear, v. n. to throw
ook || to scrawl ; to
ibble || to shuffle
ateo, s. m. V. Gara-
da [hook
atillo, s. m. a little
to, s. mas. hook ||
ments

Garabatos, pl. pot-hooks and hangers
Mozo de garabato, a thief
Garabatoso, sa, adj. enticing ; alluring
Garanbayna, s. f. a superfluous finery in dress
Garambaynas, pl. grimaces ; ridiculous gestures || pot-hooks and hangers
Garante, s. m. a guarantee
Garantía, s. f. guaranty
Garañon, s. m. a stallion ass, etc. || a lascivious man
Garapiña, s. f. a particle of congealed liquor || a sort of gold and silver laces
Bizcochos de garapiña, a kind of fine and delicate biscuit
Garapiñar, v. act. to congeal any liquid by ice
Garapiñera, s. f. a vessel used for congealing
Garapita, s. f. a thick net to catch the smallest fish
Garapito, s. masc. a little worm
Garapullo, subs. masc. a little dard used among school-boys
Garatusa, s. f. cajoling ; coaxing [a market
Garavito, s. m. a stall in
Garba, s. f. a sheaf
Garbanzal, s. m. a field where the chich-pease grow
Garbanzo, s. m. chich-pea
Garbanzuelo, s. m. a distemper in the feet of beasts
Garbar, } v. a. to bind up
Garbear, } into sheaves
Garbias, s. fem. a sort of fritters

Garbillador, s. m. a sifter
Garbillar, v. a. to sift
Garbillo, s. m. a sieve
Garbin, s. m. a cap made of a sort of network
Garbino, s m. the south-west wind
Garbo, s. m. gracefulness || liberality
Garboso, sa, adj. graceful; of a good air, etc.
Garbullo, s m. a confused huddle of people
Carcero, adj. m. who catches herons
Carces, s. m. a top (in a ship)
Garceta, s. f. young hern || a flock of hair upon the temples
Garcetas, pl. gaskets || the first antlers of a deer
Garduña, s. f. a weasel
Garduño, s. m. a subtle, cunning thief
Garfa, s. f. claw ; talon
Garfa, s. fem. a catching with claws or talons
Garfear, v. n. to lay hold of with a hook
Garfada, s. f. V. Garfa
Garfio, s. m. a hook ; a grapple
Gargagear, v. a. to spit out thick phlegm, etc.
Gargageo, s. m. a spitting
Gargajal, s. m. a placefull of spittles
Gargajazo, s. m. aum. de Gargajo
Gargajiento, ta, adj. that is full of phlegm
Gargajo, s. m. a clod of phlegm ; a glander || an ugly, ill disposed child
Gargajoso, sa, adj. Voy. Gargajiento
Garganta, s. f. the throat || the neck || instep ||

strait (*between hills*)
Hacer de garganta, *to sing sweed and fine*
Gargantada, *s. f. a gulp of water, etc. that is cast up*
Garganteador, *s. m. a quaverer*
Garganteaduras, *s. f. pl. the sutures by wich the sails are patched up*
Gargantear, *v. n. to quaver; to trill*
Garganléo, *s. m. quavering*
Gargantilla, *s. f. a necklace*
Garganton, na, *a. glutton*
Gárgara, *s. fem. the noise made in gargling*
Gargarismo, *s. m. gargarism*
Gargarizar *v. n. to gargle*
Gargol *adj. V.* Huero
Górgola *s. f. the spout of a gutter* || *lintseed*
Gárgoles, *s. masc. pl. the notches of a cask*
Cargüero *s. m. throat; gullet* || *weasand*
Gariofilata, *s. f. a plant so called*
Gariofilea, *s. f. wild carnation*
Gariofilo, *s. m. a clove-tree*
Garita *s. f. centry-box*
Garitero *s. m. one that keeps a gaming house* || *a gamester*
Garito, *s. m. a gaming house*
Garlador, *s. m. prattler*
Garlar, *v. a. to prattle*
Garlito, *s. m. a bow net* || *a snare*
Garlocha, *s. f. a sort of dart*
Garlopa, s. f. a large plane
Garnacha, s. f. gown (*of a counsellor, etc.*) || *office of a counsellor* || *counsellor; magistrate* || *a sort of hypocras*
Garo, *s. masc. a kind of lobster* || *pickle*
Garra, *s. f. a clutch; a claw; a talon* || *the man's hand*
Garrafa, *s. f. a flagon*
Garrafal, *a. 2. uncommonly big*
Garrafiñar, *v. a. to snatch with the claws*
Garrama, *s. f. a duty formerly paid by the moors* || *robbery; theft*
Garramar, *v. a. to rob; to steal*
Garrancha, *s. f. a sword*
Garrancho, *s. m. a broken bough, a splinter, etc.*
Garrapata, *s. f. tick* (*insect*) || *a very short man* || *a catch-pole*
Garrapatear, *v. act. to scribble* [*of moth*
Garrapato, *s. m. a kind*
Garrapatos, *pl. pot-hooks and hangers*
Garrar, *v. n. to drag the anchors*
Garridamente, *adv. gayly; finely; neatly*
Garrido, da, *adj. gay; airy; neat, etc.*
Garroba, *s. f. carob-bean*
Garrobilla *s. f. the wood of the carob-tree, when minced for dying*
Garrobo, *s. m. carob-tree*
Garrocha, *s. f. a sort of dart*
Garrochear, *v. a. to fret the bull with the garrocha*
Garrochon, *s. m. a spear used in the bull-feasts*
Garrofa, *s. f. carob-bean*
Garron, *s. masc. an old cock's spur* || *the heel*

Garrotaz
with
Garrote
a pac
ding
Dar ga
Garrotil
nancy
Garruch
Garruch
gles (
a sail
Gárrulo
talkat
Garulla
of poc
Garza, *s*
Garzo, *s*
Garzo, *z*
Garzon,
|| *a y*
Garzone
the yo
Garzoní
mann
man
Andar
act lik
Garzota,
of her
Gasa, *s.*
Gastador
thrift
Gastar,
waste
emplo
use of
Gastarse
(*speak*
ties) ||
Gasto, *s*
Gata, *s.*
grass
fore to
a mou
Gatada,
|| *a s*
a ho
Gataf

herbs and cream
aba, *s. f. an affec-*
ubmission, etc.
s. m. a great cat
tazos, *to deceive;*
eat; to steal
iento, *s. masc. a*
ching
v. n. to climb like
|| to creep on all
| to steal and run
, *s. f. cat's hole*
, *s. f. a parcel of*
| a feigned submis-
, etc.
, ca, *adj. of,* or
ging to a cat
a, *s. m. killer of*
a, na, *a. like a cat*
, *s. m. a kitten || a*
r for teeth || the
r of a gun || a
of flesh on the
of some mules ||
tle boy who picks
ets
. m. a cat || a purse
t's-skin || a subtle
er || a winch (en-
)
montes, *a cat-a-*
ntain—de algalia,
vet-cat—paul, *a*
key
, na, *adj. V.* Ga-
rio, *s. m. a confu-*
mixture of liquors
amus y Gaudete,
. mirth; joy; en-
tainment
to, *s. m. wild eglan-*
[whore
, *s. f. a common*
, *s. f. a draw in a*
net, etc.
s. f. a top (in a
ship) || a box (in a mad-house) || a ditch

Gavias, *pl. the main sail, and the bow-sprit sail*

Gaviero, *s. m. a top-man*

Gavieta, *s. f. the fore top*

Gaviete de las lanchas, *s. m. cat-head*

Gavilan, *s. m. a sparrow-hawk*

Gavilanes, *pl. the two cross-bars in the great Spanish sword-hilts*

Gavilancillo, *s. m. a little sparrow-hawk || prickle of an artichoke's leaf*

Gavilla, *s. f. faggot sheaf || a pack of knaves, etc.*

Gavillero, *s. m. the place where the faggots* or *sheaves are put*

Gavion, *s. m. a gabion || a broad hat*

Gaviota, *s. f. a sea-gull; a sea-cob*

Gaya, *s. f. a striped cloth*

Gayadura, *s. f. a trimming with laces of different colours*

Gayar, *v. a. to trim with laces of different colours*

Gayata, *s. f. a shepherd's [hook*

Gayo, *s. m. a jay*

Gayomba, *s. f. the broom of the gardens*

Gayta, *s. f. a bag-pipe || a sort of haut boy || a cymbal || a clyster || the neck* or *head*

Gayteria, *s. f. gaudiness in dress*

Gaytero, *s. masc. a bag-piper || one who dresses one's self with gaudiness, etc.*

Gaytero, ra, *adject. gay; lively; shining, etc.*

Gatafaton, *s. m. an idle or impertinent discourse*

Gazapa, *s. f. a lie*

Gazapaton, *s. m. V.* Gazafaton

Gazapela, *s. fem. quarrel; [strife*

Gazapera, *s. f. a coney-burrow*

Gazapillo, *s. m. dim. de* Gazapo

Gazapo, *s. masc. a young rabbit || a crafty knave*

Gazela, *s. f. an antelope; a gazel*

Gazeta, *s. f. gazette*

Gazetero, *s. m. gazetteer*

Gazetista, *s. m. a news-monger*

Gazies, *s. m. pl. the Turkish slaves who embrace the christian religion*

Gazmiar, *v. a. to rob and eat dainties*

Gazmiar, *v. neut. to complain,* or *resent*

Gazmoles, *s m. pl. the pip*

Gazmoñada, *y* Gazmoñería, *s. f. hypocrisy*

Gazmoñero, *y* Gazmoño, *s. m. an hypocrite*

Gaznatada, *s. f. a blow on the throat*

Gaznate, *s. m. the throat*

Gaznatico, *s. m. a small throat*

Gazofilacio, *s. m. a trea- [sury*

Gazpachero, *s. m. one who makes* or *carries the soop*

Gazuza, *s. f. a sharp ap- [petite*

Gefe, *s. m. V.* Xefe

Gelasidos (dientes), *s. m. pl. the fore teeth*

Gelatina, *s. f. a gelly*

Geliz, *s. m. an overseer of silk*

Gelosía, *s. f. V.* Celosía

Gemal, geme. *V.* Xemal. Xeme

Gemecer, v. n. to sight; to groan
Gemela, s. f. the flower of a jessamin staff grafted in the orange-tree
Gemelos, s. m. pl twins || fishes of the masts
Gemido, s. masc. groan; groaning [groans
Gemidor, s. m. one that
Geminacion, s. f. gemination
Geminar, v. a. to double; to repeat
Géminis, s. m. gemini || a sort of plaster
Gemino, na, adj. double; twofold
Gemir, v. n. to groan || to whistle, as the wind does || to roar
Genciana, s. f. gentian
Genealogío, s. f. genealogy
Genealógica, ca, adj. genealogical [logist
Genealogista, s. m. genea-
Generable, a. 2. generable
Generacion, s. f. generation || kind; sort
General, s. m. a general || a form (in a school)
General, a. 2. general
Generalato, s. m. generalship [lity
Generalidad, s. f. genera-
Generalif, life, s. masc a fine country-seat; a pleasure-garden
Generalísimo, s. m. a generalissimo
Generalmente, adv. generally [nerative
Generativo, va, adj. ge-
Genéricamente, adv. generically [rical
Genérico, ca, adj. gene-
Género, s. masc. genus || kind; sort || gender
Géneros, pl. commodities

Generosamente, adv. generously
Generosidad, s. f. generosity || nobleness of birth || boldness; resolution
Generoso, sa, adj. noble || generous || blod courageous
Génesis, s. m. genesis
Genetliaca, s. fem. genethliacks
Genetliáco, s. m. genethliatick
Genetliaco, ca, adj. genethliacal
Gengibre, s. m. ginger
Genial, a. 2. genial
Genio, s. m. genius
Genital, a. 2. genital
Genitivo, s. m. genitive
Genitivo, va, a. generative
Genitor, s. m. genitor
Genitura, s. f. generation; procreation || seed
Genizaro, s. m. mongrel || a janissary
Génoli, y Génuli, s. m. a bright red colour, used by painters
Gentalla, s. f. V. Gentualla
Gente, s. f. people || nation || army || a person
Gente bahuna, ó baxa, the mob — de la hampa, licencious, debauched people — del gordillo, the most vile populace — de modo y traza, gentlemen — de pelo, ú de peluza, the rich and opulent people — de trato, tradesmen — principal, the nobility or gentry
Gentecilla, s. fem. mob; rabble [then
Gentil, s. m. gentile; hea-
Gentil, a. 2. genteel || bold; lively || excellent

Gentileza, ness || l terity || dress || behavio
Gentilhom leman
Gentílico,
Gentilidad
Gentilism
Gentilizar the rites
Gentilmen teelly
Gentío, s. ber of p
Gentualla ble
Genuflexi flection
Genuino,
Geodesía,
Geodético, sical
Geografía,
Geográfico graphic
Geógrafo, pher
Geomancía
Geomántic mancer
Geómetra,
Geometral tral
Geometría
Geométric geometr
Geométric metrica
Geórgicas,
Geótico, c trial
Gerarca, s
Gerarquía
Gerárquico rarchic
Gerga, e
Gerifalt

| *a small sort of*
rin
m, *s. f. the cant among gipsies, gibberish* || *any difficult to apnd, etc.*
esco, ca, *adj. being to the cant age*
la, *s. f. V.* Geri-|| *concubinage*
o, na, *adj. ge-*
?
ico, *subs. m. an ypliphick*
te, *s. m. a drink with almonds mutton broth*
o, *s. m. a gerund*
rt, *s. m. a key ssick*
s. f. pl. gests
, *v. a. to gesticu-*

, ra, *adj. that gestes*
acion, *s. f. gestion*
ar, *a.* 2. *belonto a ridiculous re*
s. m. the face || *ld motion of the gesture* || *situa-*; *disposition* ||
; *appearance*
f. a great lip || *a room*
:on tanta gotà, *to mouths at one*
. *f. a bunch on ck*
, da, *adj. crooounchbacked, etc.*
v. a. to overload;
down || *to tire;*

, *adj. crooked;*

gibbous || *hilly; uneven* [Xiferada, etc.
Giferada, ria, ro. *Voyez*
Gigantazo, *s. m. a great giant*
Gigante, *s. m. a giant*
Gigante, *a.* 2. *uncommonly huge, etc.*
Gigantea, *s. f. sun flower*
Giganteo, tea, *adj. gigantick*
Giganticida, *s. m. a killer of giants*
Gigántico, ca, *adj. Voy.* Giganteo
Gigantilla, *s. f. a figure of pasteboard representing a short and bulky woman*
Gigantizar, *v. n. to grow giant like*
Giganton, *sub. m. a very great giant*
Gigote, *subs. m. minced meat; hash; capilotade, etc.* [*vigour*
Gijas, *s. f. pl. fatness* ||
Gilguero, *s. m. a goldfinch*
Gimelgas, *s. f. pl. fishes of the masts, etc.*
Gimnasio, *s. m. gymnasium*
Gimnosofista, *s. m. gymnosophist*
Ginebra, *s. f. a Moorish instrument made with several round sticks* || *any confusion* [*cake*
Ginebrada, *s. f. a kind of*
Ginesta, *s. f. broom*
Gineta, *s. f. a sort of savage cat* || *a short spanish lance*
Cabalgar á la gineta, *to ride with the stirrups very short* — tener los cascos á la gineta, *to be giddy brained*

Ginete, *s. m. a light horseman*
Ginglar, *v. n. to vibrate, as a pendulum does*
Ginjol, *s. m. jujube* || *jujube-tree*
Gira, *s. f. a bit of a cloth* || *a merry-making; a feast*
Hacer giras, *to tear*
Girafa, *s. f. cameleopard*
Giralda, *s. f. a vane shaped like a statue*
Giraldete, *s. m. a short upper garment*
Girándula, *s. f. girandol*
Girapliega, *s. f. a sort of electuary*
Girar, *v. n. to turn*
Girasol, *s. m. girasole; sun-flower*
Girel, *s. m. a sort of caparison*
Girifalte, *s. m. gerfalcon*
Giro, ra, *adjec. pretty; perfect; complete*
Giro, *s. m. a circular rapid motion* || *a transfer; a paying with bills* || *contour* || *bravado* [*ragoo*
Girofina, *s. f. a kind of*
Girofle, *s. m. a clove-tree*
Giron, *s. m. a gore in a garment* || *a rag* || *giron (in heraldry)*
Gironado, da, *adj. made with many gores* || *ragged* || *gironnee (in heraldry)* [*a vine*
Girpear, *v. a. to dig round*
Giste, *s. m. the froth of beer*
Gitanamente, *adv. cunningly; gipsy-like*
Gitanear, *v. a. to flatter;* to coax; to play the gipsy [cheating
Gitaneria, *s. f.* coaxing;

Gitano, na, *s. a gipsy*
Glacial, *a.* 2. *glacial*
Gladiator, *s. m. gladiator*
Gladíolo, *s. m. corn-flag*
Glandífero, ra, *adj. glandiferous*
Glándula, *s. f. glandule*
Glanduloso, sa, *adj. glandulous*
Glasé, *s. m. a glazed silk*
Glasto, *s. m. woad*
Glaucio, *s. m. an herb of a seagreen colour*
Gleba, *sub. f. a clod of earth*
Globo, *s. m. a globe*
Globoso, sa, *adj. globose*
Gloria, *s. f. glory* || *a sort of glazed stuff* || *a kind of custard*
Gloriarse, *v. r. to glory in*
Glorieta, *s. f. arbour; bower*
Glorificacion, *s. f. glorification*
Glorificador, *s. m. he who glorifies*
Glorificar, *v. a. to glorify*
Gloriosamente, *adv. gloriously*
Glorioso, sa, *adj. glorious*
Glosa, *s. f. gloss; comment*
Glosador, *s. m. glossator*
Glosar, *v. a. to gloss; to comment* || *to censure*
Gloton, *s. m. a glutton*
Glotonazo, *s. m. a great glutton*
Glotoncillo, *s. m. a little glutton; a gulchin*
Glotonear, *ver. n. to eat greedily*
Glotonería, } *s. f. gluttony*
Glotonía, }
Glutinoso, sa, *adj. glutinous*
Gnomon, *s. m. gnomon* || *a carpenter's rule*

Gnomónica, *s. f. gnomonicks*
Gnomónico, ca, *adj. belonging to the gnomonicks* [*ment*
Gobernacion, *s. f. govern-*
Gobernador, *s. m. a governor* [*helm*
Gobernalte, *s. m. rudder;*
Gobernar, *v. a. to govern*
Gobierno, *s. m. government*
Muger de gobierno, *a house-keeper*
Gobio, *s. m. a gudgeon*
Goce, *s. m. enjoying; of the wages, etc.*
Gocho, *s. m. a hog*
Godible, *a.* 2. *merry; joyful* [*bred, etc.*
Gofo, fa, *adj. uncivil; ill-*
Goja, *sub. f. a basket* or *pannier*
Gola, *s. f. gullet; weasand* || *neck-piece* || *gorget* || *a band (of a churchman)* || *the gorge of a bastion* || *an ogee*
Goldre, *s. m. a quiver*
Golfillo, *s. m. a little gulf*
Golfin, *s. m. a dolphin*
Golfo, *s. m. a gulf* || *the main ocean* || *a chaos; a confusion*
Golilla, *s. f. a little band starched, stift, and sticking out under the chin, like a ruff*
Golilla, *s. m. one who wears a* golilla
Golillero, ra, *s. one who makes* or *washes* golillas
Gollete, *s. m. the narrow neck of a bottle, etc.*
Gollería, *s. f. V.* Gullería
Golmagear, *v. a. Voyez* Golosmear
Golondrina, s. f. *a swallow*

Golondri
swallo
Golondro
desire
Golosame
Golosazo,
glutton
Golosear
Golosina,
dainty
appetit
Golosismo
ness; l
Golosmea
Golosinar
Golosinea
Goloso, s
|| *licke*
Golpazo,
stroke
Golpe, *s.*
Golpe de
numbe
agua,
water
Cerradu
spring-
Golpeade
ce that
much
Golpeado
cloth t
wove
Golpeado
Golpeadu
Golpear,
strike
Golpecillo
Golpeo, s
Golusmie
Goloso
Goma, s.
Goma ará
Gomecillo
der of
Gomia, s
pent ||
Gomos

...ice, s. m. a door-hinge
...dola, s. f. gondola
...rrea, s. f. gonorrhoea
...al, a. 2. fat; big || of a large size
...zo, za, adj. very fat, etc. [fat man
...flon, s. m. a pursy
...le, s. m. fat || greasy; ...ly || thick || big || coarse
...lobo, s. m. petty-...llen; wool-blade
...lon, na, adj. that is very fat
...or, s. m. fatness || bigness || thickness
...ra, s. f. fatness
...a, s. f. food for hawks
...ear, v. n. to quaver || to warble
...earse, v. r. to endeavour to talk, as little children do
...eo, s. m. quavering || warbling
...ería, s. f. the talking of a little child
...ojo, s. m. a weevil || a little weakly boy
...ojoso, s. m. eaten by weevils [silk-stuff
...oran, s. m. a thick
...orita, s. f. a bubble
...oritas, pl. quavering; trills
...oritear, v. n. to quaver; to trill
...otero, s. m. a pedlar
...uera, s. f. a sort of ruff [dart
...guz, s. m. a kind of
...igori, s. m. a splendid entertainment made for the ecclesiasticks
...rja, s. f. the throat || a knee bolted close to the stem [merry
...ir de gorja, to be

Gorjal, s. m. the collar of a doublet || neck-piece
Gormador, s. m. one who vomits
Gormar, v. a. to vomit by overcharging the stomach
Gorra, s. f. a cap; a bonnet || the coming of a spunger || a spunger; a parasite [tada
Gorrada, s. f. V. Gorre-
Gorrero, s. m. cap-maker || a parasite [ping
Gorretada, s. f. cap; cap-
Gorrete, s. m. a round cap [|| a calot
Gorrilla, s. f. a little cap
Gorrin, } Gorrino, } s. m. a porker
Gorrion, s. m. a sparrow
Gorrista, s. m. parasite; spunger
Gorro, s. m. around cap
Gorron, s. m. a great cap || a spunger; a mumper || pivot || a round smooth flint || a whoremonger
Gorrona, s. f. a common whore [Gorron
Gorronazo, s. m. aum. de
Gorullo, s. m. any little knob or lump
Gota, s. f. a drop || the gout
Gota artética, arthritis— coral, the falling-sickness — serena, gutta seren [with drops
Goteado, do, adj. spotted
Gotear, v. n. to fall drop by drop
Gotera, s. f. gutter || the fringes of a bed
Goteron, s. m. aum. de Gotera [de Gotera
Goterencillo, s. m. dim.
Gótico, ca, adj. gothick

Gotoso, sa, adj. gouty
Gozar, v. a. to enjoy; to possess
Gozarse, v. r. to rejoice; to be glad
Gozne, s. m. hinge
Gozo, s. m. joy; gladness
Gozoso, sa, adj. joyful
Gozque, s. m. a cur-dog
Gozquejo, s. m. dim. de Gozque
Grabador, s. m. engraver
Grabar, v. a. to grave, or engrave
Grabazon, s. m. engraving
Gracejante, a. 2. merry; facetious [jest
Gracejar, v. n. to joke; to
Gracejo, sub. m. mirth; facetiousness || lisping
Gracia, sub. f. grace || favour; kindness || a man's name || flash of wit || thanks; thankfulness
De gracia, gratis
Graciable, a. 2. gracious || grantable
Graciadei, s. f. an herb like hyssop
Graciosamente, adv. garcefully || gratis
Graciosico, ca, adj. dim. de Gracioso
Graciosidad, s. f. gracefulness
Gracioso, sa, adj. graceful || merry; facetious || gracious; benevolent || gratuitous
Gracioso, s m. a buffoon
Grada, s. f. step; stair || the grate of a monastery || foot stool
Gradas, pl. judgement-seat || seats raised over one another
Gradacion, s. f. gradation
Gradar, v. a. to harrow

Gradual, s. m. gradual
Gradual, a. 2. gradual
Gradualmente, adv. gradually
Graduando, s. m. he who is near to take his degrees

|| to give the degrees
Grafioles, s. m. pl. a kind of biscuit
Grafómetro, sub. m. an instrument to measure

Grajuné,

f. cow-grass
Gramalla, s. f. a sort of gown worn by magistrates [hanger
Gramallera, s. f. a pot-
Gramar, v. a. to knead

nadier
Granadilla, s. f. a kind of flower
Granadillo, s. m. a fine sort of speckled indian wood
Granado, s. m. a pomegranate-tree
Granado, da, adj. of the best sort
Granar, v. n. to seed || to grow to grain; to run to seed
Granate, s. m. granate
Granazon. s. f. seeding
Grancanon, s. m. fat canon (printing letter)
Grande, a. 2. great; big; large || grand
Grande, s. m. a grandee of spain [ty big
Grandecillo. lla, adj. pret-
Grandemente, ad. greatly
Grandeza, s. f. greatness || grandeur || the dignity of a grandee of spain

propt
Grangero, ...
|| a trad...
Granguardi...
guard
Granico, s. ...
grain, o...
Granilla, s...
seed || co...
Granillo, s...
grain || ...
ples, etc...
gain || a...
Granizar, ...
Granizo, s...
web in t...
Granja, s. ...
Grano, s. m...
|| berry ||...
|| a pimp...
pox || a g...
Granuja, s. ...
stone of ...
Granujado, ...
ned || ful...
Granulacio...
nulation
Granzas, s. ...

the gum of juniper-ree || ink of the China
...iento, ta, *adj. greasy*
...so, sa, *adject. fat* || *greasy; unctuous*
...o, s. m. *fat; a fat ...*
...mes, s. m. pl. *a mea... dish so called*
...samente, *adver. graciously*
...ficacion, s. f. *gratification*
...ficador, *sub. m. one who gratifies*
...tificar, v. a. *to gratify*
...til, s. m. *point or reef-...*
...tis, *adv. gratis*
...titud, s. f. *gratitude* || *agreeableness*
...to, ta, *adj. agreeable* || *thankful*
...tonada, s. f. *a sort of stewed meat*
...tuitamente, *adv. gratuitously*
...tuito, ta, *adj. gratuitous*
...tulacion, s. f. *gratulation*
Gratulatorio, ria, *adjec. gratulatory*
Gravamen, s. m. *charge; obligation; oppression, etc.*
Gravar, v. a. *to burden; to oppress*
Grave, a. 2. *heavy* || *grave* || *grievous* || *stately; proud* || *weighty; of consequence*
Gravear, v. a. *to weigh*
Gravedad, s. f. *heaviness* || *gravity* || *weight; importance* || *stateliness; pride*
Gravedoso, sa, *adject. proud; haughty*
Gravemente, *adv. grievously*

Graveza, s. f. *weight* || *grievousness*
Gravitar, v. a. *to load moderately*
Gravoso, sa, *adjec. onerous; burdensome*
Graznador, ra, *adj. croaking, etc.*
Graznar, v. n. *to croak; to cry*
Graznido, s. m. *the croaking of a raven, etc.*
Grecismo, s. m. *grecism*
Greda, s. f. *chalk*
Gredal, *sub. m. the place where chalk is found*
Gredoso, sa, *adj. chalky*
Grefier, *sub. m. the lord high-steward of the houshold*
Gregal, s. m. *the north-east-wind*
Gregal, a. 2. *gregarious*
Gregalizar, v. n. *to decline towards the north-east*
Gregario, *adj. m. gregarious*
Gregoriano, na, *adj. gregorian*
Gregorillo, s. m. *a neck-kercheif*
Greguería, s. f. *a confusion of voices*
Gregüescos, s. m. pl. *a sort of wide breeches*
Gregüesquillo, s. m. *old, ragged breeches*
Greguizar, v. a. *to speak in imitation of the greek dialect*
Gremial, s. m. *one of the pontifical garments*
Gremio, s. m. *the lap* || *body; company; guild*
Gremio de la iglesia, *the pale of the church*
Greña, *sub. f. entangled hair, etc.*
Andar á la greña, *to pull off the hairs in fighting*

Greñudo, da, *adj. whose hair stands up on end, etc.*
Gresca, s. f. *bustle; tumult* || *quarrel; fray*
Greuge, s. m. *grievance; complaint*
Grevas, s. f. *greaves*
Grey, s. m. *a flock; a herd*
Gribar, v. a. *to drive or fall to leeward*
Gridelin, a. s. m. *gridelin*
Grieta, s. f. *chap in the skin, etc.*
Grietas, *pl. scratches, or sellander (horse-disease)*
Grifa (letra) s. f. *the secretary hand*
Grifo, s. m. *griffin*
Grifos, *plur. entangled hairs*
Grillar, v. n. *to make a noise like a cricket* || *to shoot, to sprout out*
Grillera, *sub. f. the hole where a cricket lives*
Grillete, s. m. *fetters*
Grillo, s. m. *a cricket*
Grillos, *pl. fetters; irons*
Grillotalpa, *sub. f. mole-cricket*
Grima, s. f. *fright; horror*
Grimazos, s. m. pl. *odd figures of men in painting*
Grimpolas, *subst. f. the ship's pendents*
Griñon, *sub. m. a nun's stomacher* || *apricot peach*
Gris, s. m. *grey-colour* || *minever* || *raw weather*
Grita, s. f. *a crying out; a bawling*
Gritador, ra, *adj. bawling; bawler*

Gritar, *v. n. to cry out; to bawl*
Gritería, *s. f. a bawling*
Gritillo, *s. m. a little cry*
Grito, *subs. m. a cry; a shout, etc.*
Gropos, *s. m. pl. cotton that is put into ink*
Grosca, *s. f. a sort of venomous serpent*
Grosella, *s. f. gooseberry*
Groseramente, *adv. clownishly*
Grosería, *s. f. clownishness*
Grosero, ra, *adj. coarse || clownish; unmannerly*
Groseza, *s. f.* } *bigness; size*
Grosor, *s. m.* }
Grosura, *s. f. fat; fatness || the offal of a beast*
Groto, *s. m. a pelican*
Grua, *s. f. a crane*
Grueras, *s. f. pl. holes in the pullies that lift up the sails*
Gruero, (halcon) *a hawk trained for the crane*
Gruesa, *subst. f. a gross* (*twelve dozen*) *|| the chief revenue of a prebend, etc.*
Grueso, sa, *adject. big; great; huge || gross*
Grueso, *s. m. bigness || the gross; the principal, etc.* [*cranes do*
Gruir, *v. a. to cry, as*
Grulla, *s. f. a crane*
Grullada, *s. f. a company of people*
Grumete, *s. m. a ship-boy*
Grumo. *s. m. lump; clod; clot || heap*
Grumoso, sa, *adj. rugged; grumous*
Gruñido, s. m. grunting
Gruñidor, s. m. grunter

Gruñir, *v. a. to grunt || to creak, to screak*
Grupa, *s. f. croup*
Grupada, *s. f. the beating of the waves, etc.*
Grupera, *s. f. crouper*
Grupo, *s. m. group*
Gruta, *s. f. grot; grotto*
Grutesco, *s. m. grotesque*
Guacamayo, *s. m. a sort of parrot*
Guachapear, *v. a. to trouble* or *beat the water wich the feet*
Guachapear la herradura, *v. n. to be loose*
Guácharo, *s. m. weeper || an infirm* or *hydropick*
Guacharrada, *s. f. a sudden fall upon mud* or *water*
Guadafiones, *sub. m. pl. locks; fetters*
Guadamacil, *sub. m. gilt leather*
Guadamacilería, *sub. f. a gilt-leather-maker's shop* or *trade*
Guadamicilero, *s. m. a gilt-leather-maker*
Guadaña, *s. f. a scythe*
Guadañero, *s. m. a mower*
Guadapero, *s. m. a wild pear-tree*
Guadarnes, *subs. m. the place where the horse-trappings are kept || harness-keeper*
Guadixeno, *s. m. a poniar* or *dagger*
Guadramáña, *s. f. cheat; fraud* [*same*
Gualatina, *s. f. a sort of*
Gualda, *s. f. woad*
Gualderas, *s. f. pl. the sides* or *cheeks of the carriages of cannon*
Gualdo, da, *adj. yellow*

Gualdrapa, *horse-cl*
Gualdrapea or *intern natural*
Gualdraper *fellow*
Guanlada, *the open*
Guante, *s. the hand*
Guantería *shop*
Guantero,
Guañir, *v*
Guapament
Guapazo, *bold*
Guapear, *courage self in h*
Guapeton, *courage*
Guapeza, *:*
Guapo, pa *couragec ce || gall*
Guarda, s.
Guardas, *of a loc*
Guardabra:
Guardacab *low piec to save t being w*
Guardacad *contriva to keep t*
Guardacart *cartridg*
Guardadan *gentlma the ladi*
Guardador *|| a cov*
Guardafrer *wing-tr*
Guardafue *bars,*

da infante, s. m. far-
ingale [hair
ja, s. f. a look of
dajoyas, s. m. a cas-
t to keep jewels in ||
keeper of the jewels
dalado, s. m. rails
ng bridges, etc.
damancebos, s. m. a
pe on board a ship,
which the boys hold
t
damangier, s. m. a
try; a larder || the
g's pantry || the
ief officer of it
damen, s. m. the per-
s set to guard any
ce that people may
piss in it
damuger, s. f. one of
queen's-waiting-
men
dapies, s. m. V. Brial
dapolvo, s. m. any
th spread to keep off
dust
dapuerta, s. f. Voy.
tepuerta
dar, v. a. to keep ||
guard || to defend;
shield
dar la cama, to be
k in the bed || la ca-
, to cover the face
rdarse, v. r. to be upon
e's guard || to abs-
in from [beware
rda! int. take care;
rdario, s. m. King's
her (a bird)
rdaropa, sub. f. ward
be
rdaropa, subs. m. the
eper of the ward robe
rdasol, s. m. an um-
rella
rdatimones, s. m. guns
ced near the stern

Guardavela, s. m. clue-lines
Guardia, sub. f. guard || one that guards
Guardia de corps, a life-guard man || cuerpo de guardia, guard-house
Guardian, s. m. guardian || a sequestree
Guardian de navio, the boatswain
Guardiania, s. f. dignity of the guardian of the Franciscans
Guardilla, s. f. garret || dormer-window
Guardines, s. m. pl. small ropes a board ships
Guardoso, sa, adj. frugal; close; saving || niggard; covetous
Guarecer, v. n. to recover one's health
Guarecer, v. a. to protect; to defend || to keep or preserve
Guarida, s. f. a den || a lair || a place of refuge
Guarismo, s. m. arithmetick || a figure [metical
Guarismo, ma, adj. arith-
Guarnecer, v. a. to furnish; to provide || to lace a garment || to surround
Guarnicion, s. f. a garrison || lacing; embroidery, etc. || hilt || dress; ornament
Guarniciones, pl. armour || horse-trappings
Guarnicionero, sub. m. a horse's furniture-maker
Guay! int. alas! woe me!
Tener muchos guayes, to be much afflicted
Guaya, s. f. lamentation
Hacer la guaya; to la-ment

Guayaco, s. m. guaiacum
Guayapil, y guaypin, s. m. a kind of American cloke [lament
Guayar, v. n. to wail; to
Gubia, subs. f. a joiner's gouge
Guedeja, s. f. a lock of hair on the temples
Guedejar, v. a. to set off the head with locks of hair [Guedeja
Guedejilla, s. f. dim. de
Guedejudo, da, adj. that wears much hair on the temples
Gueltre, s. m. money
Güermeces, s. m. pl. a pimples in the throat of a hawk, etc.
Guerra, s. f. war
Guerra campal, open war
Guerreador, ra, s. a warrior [war
Guerrear, ver. a. to wage
Guerrero, ra, adj. warlike
Guerrilla, s. f. a little war
Guia, s. f. a guide || the chief stock a vineyard
Carta de guia, a pass; a safe conduct
Guias, pl. trains of gunpowder || the reins
Guiador, s. m. a guide
Guiamiento, s. m. guiding
Guiar, v. a. to guide; to lead; to conduct
Guija, s. f. a pebble
Guijarral, s. m. a pebbly place
Guijarrazo, s. m. a stroke of a pebble-stone
Guijarreño, ña, adj. like a pebble-stone
Guijarrillo, s. m. a little pebble-stone
Guijarro, s. m. a pebble-stone

cherry || hoist of a flag
Guindal, s. m. a cherry-tree
Guindalera, s. f. an orchard of cherry-trees
Guindaleta, s. f. a sort of rope
Guindaleza, s. f. top-rope
Guindar, v. a. to hoist up || to get or obtain || to hang [kles
Guindastes, s. m. pl. tac-
Guindo, s. m. a common cherry-tree
Guíndola, s. f. an engine on board ships, to take weighty things in them
Guinea, s. f. a guinea
Guineo, s. m. a dance of the negroes
Guiñada, } s. f. wink;
Guiñadura, } winking || a ship's lee-way
Guiñapo, s. m. a rag || a ragged person
Guiñar, v. act. to wink with the eyes || to sail

Guisar, v. a. to dress meat || to manage or dispose
Guiso, s. m. seasoning; sauce [ning
Guisote, s. m. ill seaso-
Guita, s. f. a small cord
Guitarra, s. f. a guitar || a mallet to pound the parget
Guitarrero, s. m. one that makes or sells guitars || a player upon the guitar [guitar
Guitarrilla, s. f. a little
Guitarrista, s. m. a player on the guitar
Guitarron, s. m. a great guitar
Guito (caballo), s. m. a head-strong horse
Guiton, s. m. a lazy beggar
Guitonear, ver. neut. to mump; to wander
Guitonería, s. f. wandering; beggary
Guizgar, v. a. to incite; to stimulate

Gurupa, per
Grupa, pe
Gusanera, s.
where the
Gusaniento,
of worms
Gusanillo, s.
worm—dr
purl
Gusano, s. m
Gusarapa, s.
rapo [
Gusarapillo,
Gusarapo, s.
insect so c
Gustadura,
Gustar, v.
to assay—
please
Gustillo, sub
pleasure
Gusto, s. m.
—liking;
fancy
A' gusto,
tion; to c
Libro de gu
sant book

H

ss. ah! eh!
f. a bean
ub. m. a field of
v. a. to have
v. imp. to hap-
o succeed
. m. substance;
; riches
s. f. the custom
r goods that are
ed
, pl. wages; pay,
lth; substance
s. m. ploughing
nents
, v. r. to behave
la, s. f. french-
. a. fit; able; ||
s; active || cle-
lful
d, s. f. ability ||
ness; dexterity
ion, s. f. habili-
[litate
, v. a. to habi-
, a. 2. habitable
n, s. f. habita-
[tant
r, s. m. inhabi-
v. a. to inhabit
, sub. m. a very
habit
subs. m. habit;
|| the badge of
nighthood || ha-
ustom
ion, s. f. habit;
[ted
lo, da, a. habitua-
, a. 2. habitual
mente, adv. ha-
ly
dad, sub. f. cus-
abit

Habituarse, *v. r. to accustom one's self*

Habitud, *s. f. habitude || relation; reference*

Habla, *s. f. tongue; language || speech; conference || words*

Hablador, *s. m. a talkative fellow*

Habladorcillo, *s. m. a little chatterer*

Habladorísimo, ma, *adj. very talkative*

Habladuria, *s. f. chat; chattering || an impertinent discourse*

Hablar, *v. a. to speak; to talk*

Hablatista, *s. m. a prating fellow*

Hablilla, *sub. f. idle talk* or *story*

Haca, *s. f. a little horse; a nag*

Hacanea, *s. f. a pad*

Hacecito, *s. m. a little faggot, etc.*

Hacedero, ra, *adj. that may be done*

Hacedor, *s. m. the creator || a maker || a factor || a nimble, quick person*

Hacendar, *v. act. to give estates*

Hacendarse, *v. r. to buy estates*

Hacendilla, *s. f. a little work* or *business*

Hacendosillo, lla, *a. dim.* de Hacendoso

Hacendoso, sa, *a. expeditive; diligent*

Hacenduela, *s. f. V.* Hacendilla

Hacer, *v. a. to make; to do || to form of materials || to commit; to put in act || to accustom*

Hacer limosnas, *to give alms* — gasto, *to spend* — humo, *to smoke* — la comida, *to dress the meat* — uno ausente, *to believe one absent* — gente, *to raise soldiers* — pedazos, *to pull to pieces* — chunga, chacota, chanza, *to ridicule* — agua, *to take water in, for a ship* — aguas, *to make water* — alarde, *to muster, or to boast of* — cara, frente, rostro, *to face, to resist* — costilla, *to suffer, to bear with patience* — de tripas corazon, *to pluck up a spirit* — fiesta, *to keep a holiday* — fiestas, *to endear, to fondle* — merced, ó mercedes, *to grant a favour* — sombra, *to protect* — ventaja, *to exceed, to surpass* — una bestia, *to fatten a beast*

Hacer noche, *to be night* — hace frio, *it is cold*

Hacerse, *v. r. to accustom on'es self*

Hacerse á la vela, *to fail* — atras, *to go back*

Hacha, *s. f. a torch; a flambeau || axe*

Hacha de armas, *a battle-axe*

Hachazo, *s. m. a stroke with an axe*, or *with a flambeau*

Hachear, *v. a. to cut with the axe*

Hachero, *s. m. a clandlestick to hold a torch || one that works with an axe*

Hacheta, *subs. f. a little torch* or *axe*

Hacho } s. m. a torch of
Hachon } rush and pitch

Guinda, s. f. a common cherry || hoist of a flag
Guindal, s. m. a cherry-tree
Guindalera, s. f. an orchard of cherry-trees
Guindaleta, s. f. a sort of rope
Guindaleza, s. f. top-rope
Guindar, v. a. to hoist up || to get or obtain || to hang [kles
Guindastes, s. m. pl. tac-
Guindo, s. m. a common cherry-tree
Guindola, s. f. an engine on board ships, to take weighty things in them
Guinea, s. f. a guinea
Guineo, s. m. a dance of the negroes
Guiñada, } s. f. wink;
Guiñadura, } winking || a ship's lee-way
Guiñapo, s. m. a rag || a ragged person
Guiñar, v. act. to wink

ses the victuals
Guisar, v. a. to dress meat || to manage or dispose
Guiso, s. m. seasoning; sauce [ning
Guisote, s. m. ill seaso-
Guita, s. f. a small cord
Guitarra, s. f. a guitar || a mallet to pound the parget
Guitarrero, s. m. one that makes or sells guitars || a player upon the guitar [guitar
Guitarrilla, s. f. a little
Guitarrista, s. m. a player on the guitar
Guitarron, s. m. a great guitar
Guito (caballo), s. m. a head-strong horse
Guiton, s. m. a lazy beggar
Guitonear, ver. neut. to mump; to wander
Guitonería, s. f. wandering; beggary
Guizgar, v. a. to incite;

people
Gurupa, p
Grupa,
Gusanera, where th
Gusaniento of worm
Gusanillo, worm— purl
Gusano, s.
Gusarapa, rapo
Gusarapillo
Gusarapo, insect so
Gustadura,
Gustar, v. to assay please
Gustillo, s pleasure
Gusto, s. m —liking fancy
A' gusto tion; to
Libro de g

H

st. *ah ! oh !*
f. a bean
ub. m. *a field of*
v. a. *to have*
v. imp. *to hap-*
o succeed
m. *substance ;*
; riches
s. f. *the custom*
or goods that are
ed
, pl. *wages ; pay,*
lth ; substance
, s. m. *ploughing*
nents
, v. r. *to behave*
ola, s. f. *french-*
. a. *fit ; able ;* ||
e ; active || *ole-*
ilful
d, s. f. *ability* ||
ness ; dexterity
tion, s. f. *habili-*
[*litate*
r, v. a. *to habi-*
e, a. 2. *habitable*
on, s. f. *habita-*
[*tant*
r, s. m. *inhabi-*
v. a. *to inhabit*
, sub. m. *a very*
habit
subs. m. *habit ;*
s || *the badge of*
nighthood || *ha-*
ustom
tion, s. f. *habit ;*
n [*ted*
lo, da, a. *habitua-*
l, a. 2. *habitual*
mente, adv. *ha-*
ly
idad, sub. f. *cus-*
habit

Habituarse, v. r. *to accustom one's self*
Habitud, s. f. *habitude* || *relation ; reference*
Habla, s. f. *tongue ; language* || *speech ; conference* || *words*
Hablador, s. m. *a talkative fellow*
Habladorcillo, s. m. *a little chatterer*
Habladorísimo, ma, adj. *very talkative*
Habladuria, s. f. *chat ; chat'ering* || *an impertinent discourse*
Hablar, v. a. *to speak ; to talk* [*fellow*
Hablatista, s. m. *a prating*
Hablilla, sub. f. *idle talk* or *story* [*a nag*
Haca, s. f. *a little horse ;*
Hacanea, s. f. *a pad*
Hacecito, s. m. *a little faggot, etc.*
Hacedero, ra, adj. *that may be done*
Hacedor, s. m. *the creator* || *a maker* || *a factor* || *a nimble, quick person*
Hacendar, v. act. *to give estates* [*tates*
Hacendarse, v. r. *to buy es-*
Hacendilla, s. f. *a little work* or *business*
Hacendosillo, lla, a. *dim.* de Hacendoso
Hacendoso, sa, a. *expeditive ; diligent*
Hacenduela, s. f. *V.* Hacendilla
Hacer, v. a. *to make ; to do* || *to form of materials* || *to commit ; to put in act* || *to accustom*
Hacer limosnas, *to give alms* — gasto, *to spend* — humo, *to smoke* — la comida, *to dress the meat* — uno ausente, *to believe one absent* — gente, *to raise soldiers* — pedazos, *to pull to pieces* — chunga, chacota, chanza, *to ridicule* — agua, *to take water in, for a ship* — aguas, *to make water* — alarde, *to muster*, or *to boast of* — cara, frente, rostro, *to face, to resist* — costilla, *to suffer, to bear with patience* — de tripas corazon, *to pluck up a spirit* — fiesta, *to keep a holiday* — fiestas, *to endear, to fondle* — merced, ó mercedes, *to grant a favour* — sombra, *to protect* — ventaja, *to exceed, to surpass* — una bestia, *to fatten a beast*
Hacer noche, *to be night* — hace frio, *it is cold*
Hacerse, v. r. *to accustom on'es self*
Hacerse á la vela, *to sail* — atras, *to go back*
Hacha, s. f. *a torch ; a flambeau* || *axe*
Hacha de armas, *a battle-axe*
Hachazo, s. m. *a stroke with an axe*, or *with a flambeau*
Hachear, v. a. *to cut with the axe*
Hachero, s. m. *a clandlestick to hold a torch* || *one that works with an axe*
Hacheta, subs. f. *a little torch* or *axe*
Hacho } s. m. a torch of
Hachon } rush and pitch

Hachuela, *s. f. small axe*
Hácia, *prép. to wards*
Hacienda, *s. f. an estate in the country* ‖ *wealth; riches* ‖ *work; business* [*giving*
Hacimiento, *s. m. thanks*
Hacimiento do rentas, *a publick auction*
Hacina, *subs. f. a heap of sheaves*
Hacinador, *s. m. one who heaps up sheaves*
Hacinar, *v. a. to heap up sheaves, etc.* ‖ *to grow wealthy*
Hacino, *s. m. a niggard; a scraping fellow*
Hadado, da, *adj. happy*
Hadador, *s. m. a fortune-teller* [*tunes*
Hadar, *v. a. to tell for-*
Hadas, Hadadas, *s. m. pl. fairies* ‖ *the fatal sisters; fates*
Hado *fate; destiny*
Hadrolla *ub. f. cheat in*

of any planet
Hala! *int. hold! peace! ho there!*
Halacuerdas, *s. m. a young unexperienced sailor*
Halagador, *s. m. fawner*
Halagar, *ver. a. to fawn upon; to caress, etc.*
Halago, *s. m. caresses; fawning on*
Halagüeñamente, *adv. kindly lovingly*
Halagüeño, ña, *a. kind loving fawning*
Halar, *v. a. to hall or haul*
Halcon, *subs. m. falcon; hawk*
Halconear, *v. n. to look up, with contempt, etc.*
Halconera, *s. f. the place where hawks are kept*
Halconero, *s. m. falconer*
Halda, *sub. f. a skirt of a garment, etc.* ‖ *a sack of sarp-cloth*
Haldada, *s. f. a skirt full of any thing*
Haldear, *v. n. to tuck up on'es gown in going along* [*lied*
Haldudo, da, *a. big-bel-*
Halieto, *s. m. balbuzard*
Hálito, *s. m. breathing*
Hallador, *s. m. finder*
Hallar, *v. a. to find*
Halarse, *v. r. to be* ‖ *to be present* ‖ *to meet; to be found*
Hallazgo, *s. m. finding* ‖ *a thing found by chance* ‖ *the reward given for finding a thing lost*
Hallulo, *s. m. bread baked under the ashes*
Halon, *s. m. halo*
Hamaca, *s. f. hammock*
Hamadríades, *s. f. pl. the nimphs of the woods*
Hambre, *s. f. hunger* ‖ *famine* ‖ *a greedy desire*
Hambrear, *v. n. to hunger*
Hambrear, *v. a. to starve; to famish* [*gry*
Hambriento, ta, *a. hun-*
Hambron, *s. m. hunger-starred*
Hamecces, *s. f. pl. a disease in hawks*
Hampa, *s. f. bragging; bravado*
Gento de la hampa, *rogues and whores*
Hampon, na, *a. proud; elate*
Hanega, *s. f. V.* Famega
Hao! *int. ho!*
Haragan, *sub. m. a lazy fellow* [*fully*
Haraganamente, *ad. sloth-*
Haraganear, *v. n. to* ... *a lazy life*
Haraganería, } *s. f.* ...
Haragania, } *lazi*...
Haraldo, *s. m. a her*...
Harapo, *s. m. a rag*...
Harbar, *v. a. to d*... *thing in haste an*...
Harija, *s. m. mill-d*...
Harina, *s. f. meal*
Harinero, *s. m. meal*... ‖ *the place wher*... *kept*
Harinero, ra, *a. me*...
Harmaga, *s. f. wild*...
Harnero *s. m.* ...
Haron, na, *a. slow;* ... *zy; idle*
Haron, *s. m. cukoo*...
Hartar, *v. a. to fil*... *satiate*
Hartazgo, *s. m. sati*...
Harto, ta, *a. satisf*... *sufficient or co*...
Harto *adv. enough*
Hartura *s. f. satiety*
Hasta *prép. till;* ... *to even to*
Hastial *s. m. the* ... *wall of a vault*
Hastiar *v. a. to loa*... *to disgust to tire*
Hastío *s. m. loathi*...

Hataca *s. f. a pot-*...
Hatajo, *subs. m. a* ... *flock or herd* ‖ *cro*... *throng*
Hatería, *s. f. the prov*... *given to the sheph*... *for the whole wee*...
Hatero, *s. m. the* ... *of the shepherds* ... *brings provision*
Hato ... *m. flock;* ... ‖ *company* ‖ *mil*... *de* ‖ *provision fo*... *shepherds* ‖ *cloth*... *goods*

n. a coat of
a beech-tree
s. a grove of
es
e right side of
bundle; fagot
urface
u
field covered
ves
ra., *a field to*
ed
V. Azada, etc.
exploit achie-
f. primming;
cruple, etc.
ra, *adj. who*
uples, etc.
nte, *adv. bol-*
ically
a, *a. that per-*
at exploits
f. V. Azcona
! eh! ho!
aquí, *see here,*
qui, *here it is*
, *s. f. a week*
rio, *sub. m. he*
eek it is to be
rio, ria, *adj.*
futile; use-
a-heben, *a kind*
grapes
f. a buckle
s. m. a set of
a. to buckle
a needle-full
, etc. || fibre ||
; string, etc.
l. hair || sun-
s. m. hebraism
a, } *a. hebrew*

Hebreo, *s. m. a hebrew*
Hecatombe, *s. m. hecatomb*
Hechicera, *s. f. a witch*
Hechicería, *s. f. witchcraft*
Hechicero, *s. m. a wizard*
Hechicero, ra, *adj. charming; inticing*
Hechizar, *v. a. to bewitch || to intice; to charm*
Hechizo, *s. m. witchcraft || charm; allurement || pastime*
Hechizo, za, *a. done purposedly*
Hecho, cha, *a. made; done || accustomed; inured*
Hecho, *s. m. action; deed*
El hecho de una causa, *the matter of fact*
Hechura, *s. f. the making || fashion || deed; effect || form || figure; statue || creature*
Heciento, ta, *a. dreggy*
Hedentina, *sub. f. stinck; fetidness*
Heder, *v. n. to stinck*
Hediente, *a. 2. stincking*
Hediondez, *s. f. stinck*
Hediondo, da, *adj. stincking; fetid || troublesome*
Hedor, *s. m. fetidness*
Hedrar, *v. a. to dig again*
Hegira, *s. f. hejira*
Helada, *s. f. hoar-frost*
Helar, *v. a. y n. to freeze*
Helarse, *v. r. to be extremely cold || to be dried with the frost*
Helecho, *s. m. fern*
Helena, *s. f. corpo santo; saint Helmo*
Helíaco, ca, *a. heliacal*
Helice, *s. f. the great bear (a constellation) || helix*
Helioscopio, *s. m. sea-lettuce || helioscope*

Heliotropio, *s. m. heliotrope*
Helxine, *s. f. pellitory of the wall*
Hematites, *s. f. a stone of a dark red colour*
Hematoso, sa, *a. turning chyle into blood*
Hembra, *s. f. a female || a woman's hair, when long and slender*
Hembra de corchete, *the eye of a claps*
Hembrilla, *s. f. a kind of corn*
Hembruno, na, *a. belonging to a female*
Hemina, *s. f. hemina*
Hemionite, *s. f. spleenwort*
Hemisferio, *s. m. hemisphere*
Hemistichio, *s. m. hemistich*
Hemorroo, } *s. m. a kind*
Hemorroyda, } *of snake*
Hemorroydas, *s. f. pl. hemorrhoids*
Henchimiento, *s. m. a filling*
Henchir, *v. a. to fill*
Hendedor, *s. m. one that cleaves*
Hendedura, *s. f. a cleaving; a crack*
Hender, *v. a. to cleave || to break, to get, or go through*
Hendrija, *s. f. a cranny; a little chink*
Henil, *s. m. hay-loft*
Heno, *s. m. hay*
Heñir, *v. act. to knead dough*
Hepática, *s. f. liver-wort*
Heptacordo, *s. m. heptacordus*
Heptágono, *s. m. heptagon*
Heráldico, ca, *a. belonging to an herald*
Heraldo, *s. m. an herald at arms.*

Herbolario, *s. m. herba-*

Herboso, sa, *a. herbous*

Hercúleo, lea, *a. hercu-lean*

Hérculos, *s. m. epilepsy*

Heredad, *subs. f. estate; farm, etc.* || *inheritance*

Heredamiento, *s. m. in-heritance*

Heredar, *v. a. to inherit* || *to give an estate, etc*

Heredero, *s. m. an heir* || *one who sells wine of his own growth*

Hereditario, ria, *a. here-ditary*

Herege, *s. m. an heretick*

Heregía, *s. f. heresy*

Herejote, ta, *a. an obsti-nate heretick*

Herencia, *sub. f. inheri-tance* [*siarch*

Heresiarca, *sub. m. here-*

Heretical, *a. 2. heretical*

Hereticar, *v. n. to be he-retick* [*cal*

Herético, ca, *adj. hereti-*

Hermanar, *v. act. to ac-knowledge as brother* || *to match; to pair*

Hermanar, *v. n. to live in a brotherly manner* || *to join in league, etc.*

Hermanazgo, *s. m. brother-hood* [*hood; fraternity*

Hermandad, *s. f. brother-*

La santa hermandad, *a brotherhood instituted to suppress robbers*

Hermanear, *v. act. to use one like a brother*

Hermanico, illo, ito, *s. m. a little brother*

Hermano, *s. m. a brother* || *a brother-in-law*

Hermano-carnal, *own bro-ther*—de leche, *a foster brother*

Hermanos del trabajo, *street-porters* — medio hermano, *half-brother*

Hermano, na, *a. fit; fit-ted; alike, etc.*

Hermosamente, *ad. beau*

Herrador, *s*

Herradura, *shoe*

Herrage, *s.*

Herramental *rier's pou*

Herramienta *iron-too bull's hor*

Herrar, *v. a. with iron a horse* || *ves* or *cat iron*

Herren, *s.*

Herreñal, *s. sowed wi*

Herrería, *s shop* or *noise*

Herrero, *su*

Herreruelo,

Herrete, *s.*

Herron, *s. m.*

Herronada, *stroke* [*c*

Herrumbre,

to hesitate
s. f. hetero-
[dox
a, a. hetero-
nea, a. he-

. m. pl. he-

phthisick;
n
dj. hectick;

V. Hética
m. a sixth
) [dron
m. hexae-
m. hexagon
sb. m. hexa-

f. a fathom
regs; lees;

l. hyades
V. Invierno
adj. fertile;
etc.
n. chimera
, adv. gent-

r. to play
an
. a gentle-

r, a gentle-
cient house
s. a proud,
tleman
iete, guillo,
y country-

nobleness;
obless; gen-
[whore
n. son of a
lra [lick
a. hydrau-
pitcher
m. hydro-

Hidrofilacio, s. m. *a subterraneous cavity full of water* [phoby
Hidrófobo, s. m. *hydro-*
Hidrografía, s. f. *hydrography* [graphick
Hidrográfico, ca, a. *hidro-*
Hidromancía, s f. *hydromancy* [dromantick
Hidromántico, ca, a. *hy-*
Hidrometría, s. f. *hydrometry*
Hidropesía, s. f. *dropsy*
Hidrópico, ca. a. *hydropick; dropsical*
Hidrostática, s. f. *hydrostaticks*
Hidrotecnia, s. f. *the science of water-engines*
Hiel, s. m. *the gall*
Hiel de tierra, *fumitory*
Hiena, s. f. *hyena*
Hienda, s. f. *dung*
Hierarquía, s. f. V. Gerarquía [flífico
Hieroglífico, s. m. V. Gero-
Hierro, sub. m. *iron* || *an iron-tool* || *a sword*
Hierro de fuego, *a marking-iron for cattle, etc.*
Hierros, pl. *irons; chains*
Higa, s. f. *an amulet to keep people from evil eyes*
Hacer la higa, *to laugh at one; to scoff or scorn him* [liver
Higadillo, lla, s. *a little*
Hígado, s. m. *the liver* || *courage; resolution*
Higo, s. m. *a fig*
Higrómetro, s. m. *hygrometer*
Higuera, s. f. *a fig-tree*
Higuera infernal, *spurge* — loca, *wild fig-tree*
Higueral, s. m. *orchard of fig-trees*
Hija, s. f. *a daughter*

Hijada, etc. V. Ijada, etc.
Hijastra, subs. f. *a step-daughter*
Hijastro, s. m. *a step-son*
Hijezno, s. m. *the young of any bird*
Hijico, ca, } s. *minion;*
Hijito, ta, } *dearling*
Hijo, s. m. *a son*
Hijos, pl. *young shoots; sprigs* [dalgo
Hijodalgo, s. m. V. Hi-
Hijuela, s. f. *a little daughter* || *a kind of mattress* || *a square past board laid upon the chalice* || *a trench*
Hijuelo, s. m. *a little son or boy*
Hila, s. f. *file; row* || *a slim gut* || *a tent (to put into wounds)* || *the spinning*
Hilas, pl. *lint (for wounds)*
Hilacha, s. f. *a ravelling thread*
Hilada, s. f. *a course or lay of stones, etc.*
Hiladillo, s. m. *ferret-silk*
Hilado, sub. m. *what has been spun*
Hilador, s. m. *spinner*
Hilandera, s. f. *a spinster*
Hilar, v. act. *to spin* || *to make a well compacted discourse, etc.*
Hilaracha, s. f. *a ravelling thread*
Hilaza, s. f. V. Hilado
Hilera, s. f. *file; row; rank* [tle thread
Hilico, illo, ito, s. m. *a lit-*
Hilo, s. m. *thread* || *wire* || *a stream of vinegar, etc.*
Hilo de gente, *a row of people* — de perlas, *a string of pearls*
Hilvan, s. m. *basting.*

Hilvanar, *v. a. to basle*
Himeneo, *s. m. hymen*
Himno, *s. m. hymn*
Hincapié, *s. m. the act of setting the foot fast against....*
Hacer hincapié, *to persist; to hold on*
Hincar, *v. a. to stick in*
Hincar la rodilla, ó hincarse de rodillas, *to kneel down*
Hincha, *s. f. hatred; enmity* [*dly*
Hinchadamente, *ad. prou-*
Hinchado, da, *a. proud; haughty*
Hinchamiento, *s. m. swelling*
Hinchar, *v. a. to sweell || to puff up*
Hincharse, *v. r. to sweell || to grow proud*
Hinchazon, *s. f. swelling || pride*
Hinchir, *v. a. to fill*
Hiniesta, *s. f. broom*
Hinojo, *s. m. knee || fennel*
Hipar, *v. n. to hiccough || to sob || to pant*
Hipecoo, *s. m. a plant so called* [*baton*
Hipérbaton, *s. m. hyper-*
Hipérbola, *s. f. hyperbole (in mathematicks)*
Hiperbole, *s. m. hyperbole (in rhetorick)*
Hiperbólico, ca, *adj. hyperbolical*
Hiperbolizar, *v. a. to hyperbolize*
Hiperdulía, *s. f. a worship paid to the holy virgin*
Hipérico, *s. m. St.-John's wort*
Hipermetría, *s. f. a figure when a verse-has one syllable above measure*
Hipo, *s. m. hiccough || ardent desire || anger; enmity* [*centaur*
Hipocentauro, *s. m. hippo-*
Hipocístide, *s. m. hypocist* [*choly*
Hipocondría, *s. f. melan-*
Hipocondríaco, ca, } *a. hypocondriacal*
Hipocóndrico, ca, } *a. hypocondriacal*
Hipocondrios, *s. m. pl. hypocondres*
Hipocras, *s. m. hyppocras*
Hipocresía, *s. f. hypocrisy*
Hipócrita, *s. y a. 2. hypocrite; hypocritical*
Hipocriton, *s. m. a great hypocrite*
Hipogrifo, *s. m. hippogriph*
Hipopótamo, *s. m. hippopotamus* [*sis*
Hipostásis, *s. f. hyposta-*
Hipostáticamente, *ad. hypostatically*
Hipostático, ca, *adj. hypostatical*
Hipoteca, *s. f. mortgage*
Hipotecar, *v. a. to mortgage* [*thecary*
Hipotecario, ria, *a. hypo-*
Hipotecario, *s. m. mortgagee* [*nuse*
Hipotenusa, *s. f. hypote-*
Hipótesis, *s. f. hypothesis*
Hipotético, ca, *a. hypothetical*]*posis*
Hipotiposis, *s. f. hypoty-*
Hirsuto, ta, *adj. hairy*
Hisca, *s. f. bird-lime*
Hiscal, *sub. m. a rope of three strands*
Hisopada, *s. f. quantity of water sprinkled with the hyssopo* [*kle*
Hisopear, *v. a. to besprin-*
Hisopo, *s. m. hyssop || a holy-water sprinkle*
Hispanismo, *s. m. a sp[...] nish idiotism*
Hispano, na, *a. Spa[...]*
Hispano, *s. m. a span[...]*
Historia, *s. f. history[...] a picture represe[...] any memorable ev[...]*
Historiador, rial, *sub.[...] historian*
Historial, *a. 2. histor[...]*
Historiar, *v. a. to w[...] histories || to paint[...] tory-pieces*
Histórico, *s. m. histo[...]*
Histórico, ca, *a. hi[...]cal* [*riogra[...]*
Historiógrafo, *s. m. h[...]*
Historiógrafo, fa, *adj.[...] longing to an histo[...]grapher*
Histrion, *s. m. a j[...] pudding; a buffo[...]*
Histriónico, ca, *a. h[...]trionical*
Histrionisa, *s. f. actr[...]*
Hita, *s. f. a nail-wit[...] a head*
Hito, ta, *adj. black*
Hito, *s. m. a mark || [...] white to shoot at || [...] pin to quoit at* [*qu[...]*
Jugar al hito, *to play [...]*
Hobacho, cha } *a. slow [...] heavy*
Hobachon, na } *a. slow [...] heavy*
Hocicar, *v. a. to turn u[...] with the snout*
Hocicar, *v. n. to fall upo[...] the face || to miscarr[...]*
Hocico, *s. m. the snout [...] a hog, etc. || great sti[...]king-out lips*
Hocicudo, da, *a. that [...] a sharp-pointed snou[...] etc.*
Hocino, *s. m. a hedging-bill || an orchard on [...] side of a strait*
Hocinos, pl. *straits be[...]ween hills*

s. m. a little
lv. this year
s. a hearth
f. a loaf
.f. a bon fire
blaze or flash
a leaf || a thin
s sword-blade
: of paper
a, tin
v. a. to make
'e
s. f. puff-paste
s. f. the leave
om the trees ||
ranches || use-
ds, etc. || the

a. to turn over,
s a book
, a. full of lea-

.f. a little leaf
d of wafer
hold! ho!
m. cambrick
s. f. holland
, sub. f. isin-
olland
ente, adv. spa-
|| quietly
da, a. large ;
s
estar holgado,
ell to pass
s. f. quiet; ease
ess || pleasure;
on
v. n. to rest, to
|| to rejoice or
ne's self
fiesta, to keep
y ; not to work
, s. m. an idle

ar, v. n. to be
loiter, etc.
ría, s. f. idleness

Holgin, na, *adj. belonging to a witch*

Holgon, *sub. m. a merry fellow*

Holgorio, *s. m. mirth ; merry-making*

Holgueta, } *s. f. a feast ;*
Holgura, } *a merry-making*

Hollar, *v. a. to tread ; to trample*

Hollejo, *sub. m. skin of grapes, etc.*

Hollin, *s. m. soot*

Holocausto, *s. m. holocaust*

Homarrache, *sub. m. one that is disguised in ridiculous habit*

Hombracho, *s. m. a great lusty man*

Hombre, *s. m. a man || husband*

Hombrear, *v. n. to push with the shoulders || to make one's self equal to another || to behave like a man (speaking of youth)*

Hombrecillo, zuelo, *s. m. a little dwarf*

Hombrecillos, *pl. hops*

Hombrillo, *s. m. a shoulderband in a shirt*

Hombro, *s. m. shoulder*

A' hombros, *adv. on the shoulders*

Hombron, *s. m. a great big man || a man of great note*

Hombruno, na, *a. mannish ; manly*

Olor hombruno, *a rank scent under the arm-pit*

Homenage, *s. m. homage*

Torre del homenage, *the chief* or *highest tower*

Homiciano } *s. m. homicide (manslayer)*
Homicida }

Homicidio, *s. m. homicide (manslaying)*

Homilia, *s. f. homily*

Homilista, *s. m. homilist*

Hominicaco, *s. m. a little mean coward*

Homogeneidad, *s. f. homogeneity*

Homogéneo, nea, *a. homogeneous*

Homólogo, ga, *adj. homologous*

Honda, *sub. f. a sling to cast-stones*

Hondamente, *adv. deeply*

Hondarras, *s. f. pl. dregs ; lees*

Hondazo, *s. m. a cast of a sling*

Hondear, *v. a. to sling*

Hondero, *s. m. slinger*

Hondillos, *s. m. pl. the seating of breeches*

Hondo, da, *a. deep*

Hondon, *s. m. the bottom || hole ; cavity*

Hondonada, *s. f. depth ; cavity*

Hondura, *s. f. depth*

Honestamente, *adv. honestly*

Honestar, *v. act. to honour || to excuse*

Honestidad, *s. f. honesty*

Honesto, ta, *a. honest*

Precio honesto, *a moderate or reasonable price*

Hongo, *s. m. mushroom || agarick ; tinder*

Hongoso, sa, *adj. fungous*

Honor, *s. m. honour*

Honorable, *a. 2. honourable*

Honorablamente, *adv. honourably*

Honorario, ria, *a. honorary*

Honorificamente, *ad. honourably*

Honorificencia, *s. f. honour ; worship*

Honorifico, ca, *a. honourifick*

Honra, *s. f. honour ; respect* || *esteem ; fame* || *chastily* || *any favour granted*

Honras, *pl. funeral ; obsequies*

Honradamente, *adv. honourably* || *honestly*

Honradez, *s. f. honesty ; probity*

Honrado, da, *a. honourable* || *honest*

Honrador, *s. m. honourer*

Honrar, *v. a. to honour* || *to favour ; to protect* || *to do credit to ; to be honour of* || *to raise, to greatness* || *to praise*

Honrilla, *s. f. impertinent niceties in point of honour*

Honrosamente, *adv. honourably*

Honroso, sa, *adj. honourable* || *honest* || *tenacious of honour*

Honrudo, da, *a. very tenacious of honour*

Hopa, *s. f. a tunick* or *close coat*

Hopalanda, *s. f. a tunick with a long tail to it*

Hopear, *v. n. to wag the tail* [*fox, etc*

Hopo, *sub. m. tail of a*

Hoque, *sub. m. a pair o gloves* (*a present*)

Hora, *s. f. an hour* || *a particular time*

Horas, *pl. a little prayer-book* [*rectly*

A' la hora, *adv. now ; di-*

Hora, *adv. now*

Horadar, *v. a. to pierce ; to bore*

Horado, *s. m. a hole* || *a grotto, etc.*

Horario, ria, *a. horary*

Horca, *s. f. a gallows* || *a fork* || *a rope of onions*

A' horcajadas, ó á horcajadillas, *adv. astraddle*

Horcajadura, *s. f. the joining of the tighs*

Horcajo, } *s. m. a forked*
Horcate, } *horse-collar*

Horchata, *s. f. sugar'd barley-water*

Horcon, *s. m. a great fork*

Hordiate, *s. m. barley-water* [*tal*

Horizontal, *a. 2. horizon-*

Horizontalmente, *adver. horizontally*

Horizonte, *s. m. horizon*

Horma, *s. f. a shoe-maker's last* || *a block for hats, etc.*

Hormero, *s. m. last-maker*

Hormiga, *s. f. an ant*

Hormigo, *s. m. a sort of mess to eat on fasting days* [*mortar*

Hormigon, *s. m. a sort of*

Hormiguear, *v. neu. to smart, like the stinging of ants* || *to stir* or *wag continually*

Hormiguero, *subs. m. an ant s nest* || *a strong* || *a swarm* [*ant*

Hormiguilla, *s. f. a small*

Hormiguillo, *s. m. a distemper in a horse's hoof* || *V.* Hormigo

Hormilla, *subs. f. a little last, etc.* [*work*

Hornabeque, *s. m. a horn-*

Hornacho, *s. m. excavation in a hill*

Hornachuela, *s. f. a hole in a wall* [*full*

Hornada, *s. f. an oven-*

Hornage, s. m. furnage

Hornaguear, *v. a.* to dig the ground in order to *take out fossile co*

Hornaguera, *s. f. fos coals*

Hornaza, *s. f. furnace*

Hornazo, *s. m. a sort rich cake*

Hornear, *v. a. to set br in the oven*

Hornecino, na, *a. bast*

Hornería, *s. f. the bak trade*

Hornero, *s. m. a bak*

Hornija, *s. f. a bavin, heat the oven*

Hornilla, *s. f. a kind chafing-dish*

Hornillo, *sub. m. a li oven* || *a small min*

Horno, *s. m. oven*

Horno de cal, *a lime-ki*
— de vidrio, *a gla house* [*sig*

Horóscopo, *s. m. hor*

Horquilla, *s. f. a li fork* || *the cleaving the ends of hair*

Horrendo, da, *a. horri* || *uncommon*

Hórreo, *s. m. a granary*

Horrero, *s. m. a granary keeper*

Horrible, *a. 2. horrible*

Horriblemente, *adv. horribly*

Hórrido, da, *a. horrid*

Horrísono, na, *adj. that has a dreadful sound*

Horro, *s. m. liberty*

Horro, ra, *a. free*

Horror, *s. m. horror*

Horroroso, sa, *a. horribl*

Horrura; *s. f. filth ; nast ness* || *the thick of a fo rest* || *horror*

Hortal, *s. m. a kitchen garden* [*her*

Hortaliza, *s. f. any pot*

Hortelano, *s. m. a gard ner* || *ortolan*

, s. f. a wooden
, s. f. nettle
a, a. brown; dark
red || dull; stern
ud
ble, a. 2. hospita-
[pitably
blemente, ad. hos-
dor, s. m. one who
es guests; host
go, s. m. the act
pitality || inn ||
r, v. a. to lodge
ntertain as a guest
ria, s. f. a sort of
al for monks || a
to entertain stran-
ro, sub. m. host;
ord [hospital
, s. m. a sort of
, a. 2. hospitable
, s. m. an hos-
lero, ra, s. a ma-
of an hospital
lidad, s. f. hospi-
[pitably
mente, adv. hos-
insalutato, adv.
ut taking leave
lo, lla, a. a little
etc.
s. m. an inn
o, s. m. landlord
, s. f. an inn
sub. f. victim ||
consecrated wafer
o, s. m. the wa-
r
r, v. a. to chastise
ire; to vex
, s. m. as much of
as the rain and
beats on || the
g of the rain on...
, 2. hostile

Hostililidad, s. f. hostility
Hostilizar, v. n. to commit hostilities
Hoy, adv. to day [ning
Hoy de mañana, this morning
Hoya, s. f. ditch || grave
Hoyada, s. f. a deep place
Hoyo, s. m. pit || pockhole, etc. || grave
Hoyoso, sa, adj. pitted; full of holes
Hoyuelo, s. m. cherry-pit
Jugar al hoyuelo, to play at chuck-farthing
Hoz, sub. f. a sickle || a strait between hills
Hozadura, s. f. the turning up with the snout
Hozar, v. act. to root or rout (as swines do)
Hucha, s. f. a hutch; a trough || a money-box || spare-money
Huchoho, s. m. the word used by falconers to call down the hawk
Huebra, s. f. an acre of land || a couple of mules
Huebrero, s. m. a servant who ploughs the land
Hueca, s. f. a spiral groove in the end of the spindle
Hueco, s. m. hollow; hole
Hueco, ca, adj. hollow || proud; haughty
Huélfago, s. m. difficulty and shortness of breath
Huelga, s. f. rest; resting || a merry-making, etc.
Huelga de la bala, the wind of a bullet
Huelgo, s. m. the breath
Huella, s. f. print; track
Huello, s. m. the place where the foot treads || step; gait
Huequecito, s. m. a little hole

Huérfano, na, adj. orphan
Huero, ra, adj. addle || sickly
Huerta, s. f. a kitchen-garden || an orchard
Huerto, s. m. a garden close with walls
Huesa, s. f. grave
Hueso, s. m. a bone || the stone of any fruit
Huesos, pl. the teeth || the rafters or timbers in a roof
Huesped, sub. m. host || landlord || guest
Huéspeda, s. f. landlady || a female guest
Huevar, v. a. to lay eggs
Huevecico, s. m. a small egg [sells eggs
Huevero, s. m. one who
Huevo, s. m. an egg
Huevo empollado, an egg with chicken — huero, an addle egg
Huevos rebueltos, buttered eggs — de pescado, the spawn of fish
Huida, s. f. flight
Huidero, s. m. the form of a hare, etc.
Huidizo, za, a. that runs away
Huir, v. n. to fly; to run away || to avoid; to shun [to fly
Huirse, v. r. to escape;
Hulano, s. m. V. Fulano
Hule, s. m. cere-cloth
Humanamente, adv. humanely || humanly
Humanar, v. a. to give the human nature || humanize
Humanarse, v. r. to take the human nature || to grow humane kind, etc.
Humanidad, s. f. huma-

nity || *nakedness* || *sex* || *corpulency* || *human frailty*

Humanidades, *pl. human learning* [*nist*

Humanista, *s. m. huma-*

Humano, na, *a. human* || *humane*

Humareda, *s. f. abundance of smoke* || *trouble; confusion*

Humazo, *s. m. a smoky paper held under the nose of one that sleeps*

Humear, *v. n. to smoke*

Humedad, *s. f. humidity*

Humedecer, *v. a. to humect) to moisten*

Húmedo, da, *adj. humid*

Humero, *s. m. the funnel of a chimney*

Humidad, *s. f. humidity*

Humido, da, *adj. humid*

Humildad, *s. f. humility* || *meanness of condition, etc.*

Humildad de garabato, *a false submission*

Humilde, *a. 2. humble* || *low; mean* [*bly*

Humildemente, *a. hum-*

Humillacion, *s. f. humiliation*

Humilladero, *s. m. a little chapel on the highways, etc.*

Humillador, *s. m. one who humbles*

Humillar, *v. a. to humble*

Humillo, *s. m. a little puff of pride*

Humo, *sub. m. smoke* || *a mourning crape*

Humos, *pl. houses* || *pride*

Humor, *s. m. humour*

Hombre de humor, *a merry man*

Humorada, *s. f. good or jovial humour*

Humorado, da, (bien, ó mal), *adj. that has humours well or ill disposed* [*to an humour*

Humoral, *a. 2. belonging*

Humorazo, *s. mas. a very jovial humour*

Humoso, sa, *adj. smoky*

Humúscula, *sub. f. a cormorant* [*king*

Hundimiento, *s. m. sin-*

Hundir, *v. a. to sink; to drown* || *to melt* || *to pull or bear down* || *to confound; to puzzle; to nonplus*

Hura, *s. f. a furuncle on the head*

Huracan, *s. m. hurricane*

Huraco, *s. m. a hole*

Hurañamente, *adv. with distrust or scorn*

Hurañeria, *s. f. distrust* || *scorn, disdain*

Huraño, ña, *adj. distrustful* || *disdainful*

Hurgar, *v. a. to stir*

Hurgon, *s. m. a fire-fork* || *a thrust; a pass*

Hurgonazo, *s. m. a great thrust or pass*

Hurgonear, *v. act. to stir with a fire-fork* || *to thrust with the point*

Hurgonero, *s. mas. Voy.* Hurgon [*ferreter*

Huron, *s. m. a ferret* || *a*

Huronear, *v. a. to catch with a ferret* || *to ferret; to search*

Huronera, *s. f. the hole of a ferret*

Hurtadillas (á) *adv. by stealth*

Hurtar, *v. a. to steal.*

Hurtar el cuerpo, *to slip aside*

Hurtarse, *v. r.* to fly, to escape

Hurto, *s. m. theft*

A'hurto, *ad. by stealth*

Husada, *sub. f. a spindle full*

Husillo, *s. mas. the* [illegible] *or spindle of a press etc.*

Husillos, *pl. trenches*

Husmeador, *sub. m.* [illegible] *who smells about*

Husmear, *v. a. to* [illegible] *about* || *to guess,* [illegible] *suspect*

Husmear, *v. n. to* [illegible]

Husmo, *s. m. ranknes*[illegible] *the meat, when tain*[illegible]

Huso, *s. m. a spindle*

I

Iberia, *s. f. one of the ancient names of Spain*

Ibèro, ibèrio, ibér[illegible] *adj. of, or belonging to iberia*

I'bis, *s. f. ibis*

Icáco, *s. m. a sort of* [illegible] *plum-tree* [illegible]

Icneumon, *s. m. ichne*[illegible]

Icnografía, *s. f. ichnography* [*graphi*[illegible]

Icnográfico, ca, *adj. ich*[illegible]

Iconoclasta, *s. m. iconoclast.*

Iconología, *s. f. iconol*[illegible]

Icor, *s. m. ichor*

Icosaedro, *s. m. icosaedron* [*jaundi*[illegible]

Ictericia, *s. f. the yello*[illegible]

Ictericiado, da, *adj. jaundiced*

Ictérico, ca, *adj. icteric*[illegible]

Ida, *s. f. a going*

Idas en casa de uno, *frequent visits*

Idea, *s. f. idea* || *plan project; scheme* || *plan so called*

Ideal, *a. 2. ideal*

Ignorado, da, *adj. unknown*
Ignorancia, *sub. f. ignorance*] || *silly*
Ignorante, *adj. ignorant*
Ignorantemente, *adv. ignorantly*
Ignorar, *v. a. not to know*
Ignoto, ta, *adj. unknown*
Igual, *a. 2. equal* || *even*
Iguala, *s. f. a contract; a bargain* || *a level*
A' la iguala, *a. likewise*
Igualacion, *s. f. equalling* || *equation*
Igualado (dexar á uno) *to beat one soundly*
Igualador, ra, *s. one who equals* or *evens*
Igualar, *v. a. to equal* || *to esteem equally* || *to even; to level*
Igualarse, *v. r. to compare one's self* || *to league*, or *joint with one*
Igualdad, *s. f. equality*
Igualdad de ánimo, *equanimity*
Igualmente, *adv. equally*
Iguana, *sub. mas. a great lizard of the west-indies* [*fillet of pork*
Ijada, *sub. f. the flank* ||
Tener su ijada, *to have a blind side*
Ijadear, *v. n. to pant*
Ijares, *s. m. pl. ilia*
Ilacion, *s. f. illation*
Ilapso, *s. m. illapse*
Ilecebra, *s. f. allurement*
Ilegal, *a. 2. illegal*
Ilegalidad, *s. f. illegality*
Ilegalmente, *a. illegally*
Ilegítimamente, *adv. unlawfully* [*timacy*
Ilegitimidad, *s. f. illegi-*
Ilegítimo, ma *adj. unlawful* || *illegitimate*
Ileso, sa, *adj. unhurt*

Iliaca (pasion), *s. f. the iliack passion*
Ilícitamente, *adv. unlawfully*
Ilícito, ta, *a. illicit*
Ilimitado, da, *a. illimited*
Ilion, *s. m. ileum; ileon*
Iluminacion *s. f. illuminacion colouring*
Iluminador *s. mas. one who illumines alluminor*
Iluminar, *v. a. to illumine; to illuminate* || *to colour prints, etc.; to alluminate.*
Iluminativo, va, *adj. illuminative*
Ilusion, *s. f. illusion*
Ilusivo, va *adj.*
Iluso, sa, *adj. deceived*
Ilusor, *s. mas. deceiver* || *mocker*
Ilusorio, ria, *adj. illusory*
Ilustracion, *s. fem. illustration* || *divine inspiration* || *ligth*
Ilustrador, *s. m. one who illustrates*
Ilustrar, *v. act. to illustrate* || *to ligth* || *to inspire*
Ilustre, *a. 2. illustrious*
Ilustremento, *adv. illustriously* [*ness*
Ilustreza, *s. f. illustrious-*
Ilustrísima, *s. fem. a title given in spain to the bishops, etc.*
Imágen, *s. f. an image*
Imágen celeste, *a constellation*
Imaginable, *a. 2. imaginable*
Imaginacion, *s. f. imagination*
Imaginar, *v. n.* to imagine || to adorn with images or statues

Imaginariamente, *adver. in imagination*
Imaginario, ria, *adj. imaginary* [*tuary*
Imaginario, *s. m. a statuary*
Imaginativa, *s. f. imagination; fancy*
Imaginativo, va, *adj. full of invention or device*
Imagineria, *s. f. imagery*
Iman, *s. m. load-stone*
Imbeato, ta, *adj. unhappy*
Imbecil, *a. 2. weak; frail*
Imbecilidad, *s. f. weakness*
Imbele, *a. 2. not fit for war; weak*, etc.
Imbierno, *s. mas. V.* Invierno
Imbornales, *sub. mas. pl. scupper-holes*
Imbuido, da, *adj. imbued*
Imbuir, *v. a. to imbue; to instruct*, etc.
Imitable, *a. 2. imitable*
Imitacion, *s. f. imitation*
Imitador, ra, *s. to imitator*
Imitar, *v. a. to imitate*
Imitativo, va, *adj. imitative*
Impaciencia, *s. f. impatience*
Impacientar, *v. a. to put out of patience*
Impaciente, *a. 2. impatient*
Impacientemente, *adver. impatiently*
Impacto, ta, *adj. thrust; put into; set upon*, etc.
Impalpable, *a. 2. impalpable* [*odd*
Impar, *a. 2. un equal* ||
Imparcial, *a. 2. impartial* || *retired from society* [*tible*
Impartible, *a. 2. impar-*
Impartir, *v. a. to impart*

Impasible, *a. 2. impassible* [*trepidly*
Impávidamente, *adv. intrepid*
Impávido, da, *adj. intrepid* [*peccability*
Impecabilidad, *s. f. im-*
Impecable, *a. 2. impeccable* [*potent*
Impedido, da, *adj. im-*
Impedimento, *s. m. hindrance; impediment*
Impedir, *v. a. to hinder*
Impeditivo, va, *adj. that hinders*
Impeler, *v. a. to impel*
Impenetrabilidad, *s. fem. impenetrability*
Impenetrable, *a. 2. impenetrable*
Impenitencia, *s. f. impenitence* [*tent*
Impenitente, *a. 2. impeni-*
Impensadamente, *adver. unexpectedly*
Impensado, da, *adject. unexpected*
Imperar, *v. act. y n. to reing; to command*
Imperativo, *s. m. imperative* [*perative*
Imperativo, va, *adj. im-*
Imperatoria, *s. f. master-wort* [*perial*
Imperatorio, ria, *adj. im-*
Imperceptible, *adj. imperceptible* || *incomprehensible*
Imperceptiblemente, *adv. imperceptibly*
Imperfeccion, *s. f. imperfection* [*perfect*
Imperfecto, ta, *adj. im-*
Imperfecto, *s. m. preter imperfect*
Imperial, *a. 2. imperial*
Imperial, *s. f. the roof a a coach*
Imperiales, s. m. pl. the imperialists

Impericia, *s. f. ignoran*
Imperio, *s. m. empire*
Imperiosamente, *adv. imperiously*
Imperioso, sa, *adj. imperious*
Imperito, ta, *adj. ignorant; unskilful*
Imperscrutable, *a. 2. in-scrutable*
Impersonal, *a. 2. impersonal* [*impersonal*
Impersonalmente, *adv*
Impersuasible, *a. 2. that cannot be persuaded*
Impertérrito, ta, *adj. fearless*
Impertinencia, *s. f. impertinence* || *importunity*
Impertinente, *a. 2. impertinent* || *importunate* [*impertinently*
Impertinentemente, *adv*
Imperturbable, *a. 2. unmoveable*
Impervio, via, *adj. impervious* [*ti*
Impetra, *s. fem. impetra*
Impetracion, *s. f. impetration*
I'mpetu, *s. mas. impetus* || *impetuosity*
Impetuosamente, *adv. impetuously*
Impetuosidad, *s. f. impetuosity*
Impetuoso, sa, *adj. impetuous* [*piously*
Impiamente, *adver. im*
Impiedad, *s. f. impiety*
Impio, pia, *adj. impious*
Impireo, rea, *adj. empyreal*
Implacable, *a. 2. implacable* [*implacabl*
Implacablemente, *adv*
Implaticable, *a. 2. intractable* || *impracticabl*

ion, implicancia, *plication*
, *v. a. to entan- perplex* || *to im-*
, *v. n. to imply*
mente, *adv. im-*
, ta, *adj. impli-*
[*ploring*
ion, *s. fem. im-*
, *v. a. to implore*
, *adj. 2. unsea-*
[*luted*
, ta, *adj. unpol-*
rable, *adj. 2. be- whatever ex-*
, *v. a. to impose*
y a crime to one
ach; to instruct
npose upon
le, *a. 2. insup- le* [*tance*
ncia, *s. f. impor-*
ute, *a. 2. impor-*
ntemente, *adver. ly; profitably*
, *v. n. to con- o matter; to be of ance* || *to amount*
nacion, *s. f. im- nacy*
nadamente, } *adv.*
namente, } *im- ately* || *out of*
nar, *v. a. to im-*
[*tunity*
nidad, *s. f. impor-*
no, na, *adj. im- nate* || *unseaso-*
lidad, *s. fem. im- ility*
litar, *v. act. to impossible* || *to*

Imposible, *a. 2. impossible* [*sition* || *tax*
Imposicion, *sub. f. impo-*
Imposta, *s. f. impost* (*in architecture*]
Impostor, *s. m. impostor*
Impostura, *s. f. imposture*
Impotencia, *sub. f. impotence*
Impotente, *a. 2. impotent* [*practicable*
Impracticable, *a. 2. im-*
Imprecacion, *s. f. imprecation*
Impregnacion, *s. f. impregnation*
Impregnarse, *v. r. to impregnate*
Imprenta, *s. f. printing* || *printing house*
Imprescindible, *a. 2. inseparable*
Imprescritible, *a. 2. that is without prescription*
Impresion, *s. f. impression* || *influence*
Impresionar, *v. a. to imprint in the mind*
Impreso, *s. m. any thing printed*
Impreso, sa, *adj. printed*
Impresor, *s. m. a printer*
Imprestable, *adj. 2. that cannot be lent*
Imprimacion, *subs. f. the priming of a canvass*
Imprimadera, *s. f. a tool used in priming canvass*
Imprimador, *s. mas. one who primes*
Imprimar, *v. a. to prime the cloth* [*to imprint*
Imprimir, *v. a. to print;*
Improbabilidad, *s. f. improbability* [*bable*
Improbable, *a. 2. impro-*
Improbablemente, *adver. improbably*

Improbar, *v. act. to improbate*
Improbo, ba, *adj. wicked* || *hard and fruitless*
Improperar, *v. a. to reproach; to upbraid*
Improperio, *s. m. an injurious reproach*
Impropiamente, *adv. improperly* [*priety*
Impropiedad, *s. f. impro-*
Impropio, pia, *adj. improper*
Improporcion, *s. f. disproportion*
Improporcionado, da, *adj. unproportionable*
Impróspero, ra, *adj. unprosperous*
Impróvidamente, *ad. improvidently*
Impróvido, da, *adj. improvident*
Improvisamente, *adver. unexpectedly* [*pected*
Improviso, sa, *adj. unex-*
De improviso, *adv. suddenly* [*dence*
Imprudencia, *s. f. impru-*
Imprudente, *adj. 2. imprudent*
Imprudentemente, *adv. imprudently*
Impúdicamente, *adver. lewdly* [*ness*
Impudicicia, *s. f. lewd-*
Impúdico, ca, *adj. immodest; lewd*
Impuesto, *s. m. impost; tax* [*posed*
Impuesto, ta, *p. p. im-*
Impugnacion, *s. f. opposition; contradiction*
Impugnador, *s. mas. impugner*
Impugnar, *v. a. to impugn*
Impugnativo, va, *adject. that impugns*
Impulsar, *v. a. to impel*

3457

f. impurity

Impuro, ra, *adj. impure*

Imputable, *a.* 2. *that can be imputed* [*tion*

Imputacion, *s. f. imputa-*

Imputador, *s. m. imputer*

Imputar, *v. a. to impute*

Inacabable, *a.* 2. *that cannot be finished*

Inaccesibilidad, *s. f. want of access.*

Inaccesible, *a.* 2. *inaccessible* || *incomprehensible*

Inaccesiblemente, *adv. inaccessibly* [*cessible*

Inacceso, sa, *adj. inac-*

Inaccion, *s. f. inaction*

Inadvertencia, *s. f. inadvertency*

Inadvertidamente, *adv. inadvertently*

Inadvertido, da, *adj. inconsiderate* || *unobserved* [*fected*

Inafectado, da, *adj. unaf-*

Inagenable, *a.* 2. *inalienable*

Inapetencia, *sub. f. inap-*

Inapetente, *a.* 2. *that has no appetite*

Inaplicacion, *s. f. inapplication*

Inaplicado, da, *adj. supine; careless* [*luable*

Inapreciable, *a.* 2. *inva-*

Inarticulado, da, *adject. inarticulate*

Inaudito, ta, *adject. unheard of*

Inauguracion, *s. f. inauguration* || *auguration*

Inaugurar, *v. act. to augurate*

Inaveriguable, *a.* 2. *that cannot be avered*

Incansable, *a.* 2. *indefatigable* [*defatigably*

Incansablemente, *adv. in-*

Incantable, *a.* 2. *that cannot be sung*

Incapacidad, *s. f. incapacity*

Incapaz, *a.* 2. *incapable*

Incardinacion, *s. f. profit obtained by the govern-*

Incensario, …

Incentivo, *s.* …

Incensurable … *cannot be* …

Inceptor, *s. m* …

Incertidumbre … *certitude*

Incesable, }
Incesante, }

Incesablemente …

Incesantemente … *santly*

Incesto, *s. m* …

Incestuosamente … *incestuous* …

Incestuoso, … *cestuous*

Incidencia, … *dence* || *i*… *an incide*…

Incidente, *a.* …

Incidente, *s.* … *dent*

Incidentemente … *cidentally*

Incidir, *v.* …

Incienso, *s.* …

o, sa, adj. unised
-ipto, ta, adj. inscribed
. f. incision || n a verse)
dientes) s. m. ors
n. a comma
ria, adj. that
s. m. inciter
o, } s. m. incitation
te, }
a. to incite
va, excitative
a, s. f. inclemencia, in
air
, a. 2. inclemency [tion
a, s. f. inclina-
v. a. to incline
ad, or bow || to
e || to be alike
, v. r. to incli-
bend to || to
wn to one
, adject. illus-
famous
a. to include
f. an hospital
dlings
s. f. inclusion
iente, adv. in-
y
adv. inclusi- [sive
va, a. inclu-
, adj. p. p. in-
la, adj. begun
finished
va, adject. be- [verable
, a. 2. irreco-
ta, adj. unk-

Incógnito, *adv. incognito*
Incognoscible, *a. 2. that cannot be known*
Incombustible, *a. 2. incombustible*
Incombusto, ta, *adj. unburnt*
Incomerciable, *a. 2. that is not negociable || insociable || impracticable*
Incómodamente, *adv. incommodiously*
Incomodar, *v. act. to incommode*
Incomodidad, *s. fem. incommodity*
Incómodo, da, *adj. incommodious*
Incomparable, *a. 2.* } *incomparable*
Incomparado, da, *adj.* }
Incomparablemente, *adv. incomparably*
Incompartible, *a. 2. indivisible* [ciless
Incompasivo, va, *adj. merciless*
Incompatibilidad, *s. fem. incompatibility*
Incompatible, *a. 2. incompatible*
Incompetencia, *s. f. incompetency*
Incompetente, *a. 2. incompetent*
Incompetentemente, *adv. incompetently*
Incomponible, *a. 2. that cannot be compounded || incompatible*
Incomportable, *a. 2. unsufferable*
Incomposibilidad, *s. fem. incompatibility*
Incomposible, *a. 2. incompatible*
Incomprehensibilidad, *s. f. incomprehensibility*

Incomprehensible, *a. 2. incomprehensible*
Incomunicable, *a. 2. incommunicable*
Inconcerniente, *a. 2. improper*
Inconcusamente, *adv. unquestionably*
Inconcuso, sa, *adj. unquestionable*
Inconexíon, *s. f. want of connexion*
Inconexô, xâ, *adj. unconnected || independent*
Inconfidencia, *s. f. mistrust || disloyalty*
Inconfidente, *a. 2. mistrustful || disloyal*
Incongruencia, *s. f. incongruity*
Incongruente, *a. 2. incongruous*
Incongruentemente, *adv. incongruously*
Incongruo, grua, *adj. incongruous*
Inconmensurable, *a. 2. incommensurable*
Inconmutable, *a. 2. incommutable*
Inconocido, da, *adj. unknown* [conquerable
Inconquistable, *a. 2. unconquerable*
Inconseqüencia, *s. f. inconsequence*
Inconseqüente, *a. 2. inconsequent*
Inconsideracion, *s. f. inconsiderateness*
Inconsideradamente, *adv. inconsiderately*
Inconsiderado, da, *adj. inconsiderate*
Inconsiguiente, *a. 2. inconsequent* [solable
Inconsolable, *a. 2. inconsolable*
Inconsolablemente, *adv. inconsolably*

Incontextable, *a.* 2. *incontestable*
Incontinencia, *s. f. incontinence* [*tinent*
Incontinente, *a.* 2. *incon-*
Incontinente, **ti**, *adv incontinently*
Incontrastable, *a.* 2. *invincible* [*disputable*
Incontrovertible, *a.* 2. *in-*
Inconvencible, *a.* 2. *that cannot be persuaded*
Inconveniencia, *s. f. inconvenience*
Inconveniente, *a.* 2. *inconvenient*
Inconveniente, *s. m. inconvenience*
Inconversable, *a.* 2. *insaciable*
Inconvertible, *a.* 2. *inconvertible*
Incordio, *s. m. a bubo in the groin* [*poration*
Incorporacion, *s. f. incor-*
Incorporal, *a.* 2. *incorporeal* [*corporate*

dulity
Incrédulo, **la**, *adj. incredulous* [*ble*
Increible, *a.* 2. *incredi-*
Incremento, *s. m. increment*
Increpacion, *s. f. increpation* [*pate*
Increpar, *v. a. to incre-*
Incruento, **ta**, *adj. unbloody* [*tation*
Incrustacion, *s. f. incrus-*
Incrustar, *v. a. to incrust*
I'ncubo, *s. m. incubus; nightmare*
Inculcar, *v. a. to inculcate* [*pable*
Inculpable, *a.* 2. *incul-*
Inculpablemente, *adver. inculpably*
Inculpado, **da**, *adj. unblameable*
Incultamente, *adv. without ornament, etc.*
Incultivable, *a.* 2. *uncultivable*
Inculto, **ta**, *adj. incult*

Indebido,
due || *in*
Indecencia
Indecente,
Indecenter
decentl
Indecible,
Indeciblen
inexpre
Indecision
minatio
Indeciso,
termine
Indeclinab
clinable
Indecoro,
Indecorosa
indecen
Indecoroso
decorou
Indefenso,
Indeficient
fectible
Indefinible
Indefinido
defined
Indeleble,

, s. f. indem-
demnification
on, s. f. in-
, v. a. to in-
cia, s. f. in-
cy
:e, } a. 2. inde-
te, } pendent
te- } adv. in-
:te- } depen-
dently
.ble, a. 2. inde-
le || irresolute
ıcion, s. f. in
ation
ıdamente, adv.
inately
ıdo, da, adj.
inate
. s. f. indevo-
[vout
a, adj. inde-
. dial-hand ||
collection of
things
ı, adj. indian
y [tion
s. f. indica-
. masc. sign;
a. to indicate
va, adj. indi-
s. m. the in-
mood
s. f. indiction
. mas. token;
nomon; hand
|| the fore fin-
[gives tokens
s. m. one who
. a. to give a
sign || to con-
. token; sing
. indigo
: Ingles.

I'ndico, ca, adj. indian
Indiestro, tra, adj. unhandy; unskillful
Indiferencia, s. f. indifference [rent
Indiferente, a. 2. indifferent
Indiferentemente, adv. indifferently
Indigencia, s. fem. indigence
Indigente, a. 2. indigent
Indigestible, a. 2. indigestible [gestion
Indigestion, sub. f. indigestion
Indigesto, ta, adj. indigested || troubled with an indigestion || harsh; untractable
Indignacion, s. f. indignation [worthily
Indignamente, adv. unworthily
Indignar, v. a. to irritate
Indignarse, v. r. to be filled with indignation
Indignarse la llaga, to rankle [|| indignation
Indignidad, s. f. indignity
Indigno, na, adj. unworthy || base
Indiligencia, s. f. negligence
Indio, dia, adj. indian
Indirecta, s. f. an indirect proposition, etc.
Indirectamente, adv. indirectly [rect
Indirecto, ta, adj. indirect
Indisciplinable, a. 2. indocile; froward
Indisciplinado, da, adj. undisciplined
Indiscrecion, s. f. indiscretion
Indiscretamente, adver. indiscreetly
Indiscreto, ta, adj. indiscret
Indisculpable, a. 2. inexcusable

Indisoluble, a. 2. indissoluble [dissolubly
Indisolublemente, ad. indissolubly
Indispensable, a. 2. indispensable
Indispensablemente, adv. indispensably
Indisponer, v. act. to indispose
Indisposicion, s. f. indisposition [disposed
Indispuesto, ta, p. p. indisposed
Indisputable, a. 2. indisputable
Indisputablemente, adv. indisputably
Indistintamente, adver. indistinctly
Indistinto, ta, adj. indistinct
Individuacion, s. f. specification || individuity
Individual, a. 2. individual [viduality
Individualidad, s. f. individuality
Individualmente, ad. individually
Individuamente, adver. without being divided; jointly
Individuar, v. a. to individuate || to specify
Individuo, s. m. an individual
Individuo, dua, adj. individual [sible
Indivisible, a. 2. indivisible
Indiviso, sa, adj. unparted; undivided
Por indiviso, jointly
Indócil, a. 2. indocile
Indocilidad, s. f. indocility
Indocto, ta, adj. ignorant
I'ndole, s. m. genius
Indolencia, s. f. indolence
Indolente, a. 2. indolent
Indomable, } a. 2. untameable
Indomeñable, } ungovernable

man that wants portion
Indubitable, *a.* 2. } *indu-*
Indubitado, da, *a.* } *bitable*
Indubitablemente, } *adv.*
Indubitadamente, } *indu-bitably*
Induccion, *s. f. induction*
Inducia, *s. f. a truce*
Inducidor, ra, *s. inducer*
Inducimiento, *s. m. in-ducement*
Inducir, *v. a. to induce*
Inductivo, va, *adj. in-ductive*
Indulgencia, *s. f. indul-gence* [*gent*
Indulgente, *a.* 2. *indul-*
Indultar, *v. a. to pardon* || *to exempt*
Indulto, *s. m. pardon* || *grant; privilege* || *in-dulto*
Indumento, *subs. m. gar-ment; vesture*
Indústria, *s. f. industry*
De indústria, *adv. de-signedly*

Inepcia, *s. f. foolery*
Ineptamente, *adv. unap-tly* || *foolishly* [*tude*
Ineptitud, *s. fem. inepti-*
Inepto, ta, *adj. unapt* || *foolish; impertinent*
Inercia, *s. f. inertness*
Inerme, *a.* 2. *unarmed*
Inerrante, *a.* 2. *fixed*
Inerte, *a.* 2. *inert; slow*
Inescrutable, *a.* 2. *ins-crutable* [*searchable*
Inescudriñable, *a.* 2. *un-*
Inesperadamente, *adver. unexpectedly*
Inesperado, da, *adject. unexpected*
Inestimabilidad, *s. f. qua-lity that makes inesti-mable*
Inestimable, *a.* 2. *ines-timable* [*ble*
Inevitable, *a.* 2. *inevita-*
Inevitablemente, *ad. ine-vitably*
Inexcusable, *a.* 2. *inex-cusable* || *indispensable*

Infaceto,
pid; w
Infacundo
eloquen
Infalibilid
libility
Infalible,
Infalibilem
fallibly
Infamacio
tion
Infamador
Infamar,
Infamative
famato
Infamatori
Infame, *a*
Infameme
mously
Infamia,
Infancia,
Infancino,
green o
Infando,
ked; v
Infanta,
Infantado

. m. a gent-
, da, adj. be-
o a gentleman
a. 2. indefa-
iente, adver.
ably
act. to infa-
[happily
ite, adv. un-
, adject. un-
. f. infection
a. to infect
adj. infected
d, s. f. infe-
[fecund
da, adj. in-
2. unhappy
s. f. infelicity
. unhappy
e, adv. un-
s. f. inference
, adj. inferior
l, sub. f. infe-
s. to infer
, s. m. merils,
penny morris
s play)
. 2. infernal
. a. to cast in
vex; to molest
, s. f. infesting
a. to infest ||
, adj. offen-
rtful
f. infection
v. a. to infect
, s. f. infidelity
. infidel; un-
2. unfaithful;
ous
, adver. un-

Infierno, s. m. hell || a place under ground
Infimo, ma, adj. lowest; meanest
Infinidad, s. f. infinity || a world [nitely
Infinitamente, adv. infi-
Infinitivo, s. mas. infinitive mood
Infinito, ta, adj. infinite
Infinito, adv. infinitely
Infirmar, v. a. to weaken; to enfeeble
Inflacion, s. f. swelling || puffing up
Inflamable, a. 2. inflameable
Inflamacion, s. f. inflammation
Inflamar, v. a. to inflame
Inflar, v. a. to swell || to puff up
Inflexibilidad, sub. f. inflexibility [ble
Inflexible, a. 2. inflexi
Inflexion, s. f. inflexion
Influencia, s. f. influence
Influir, v. a. to influence
Influxo, s. m. influence
Informacion, s. f. information
Informante, s. m. an inquisitor or inquirer
Informar, v. a. to inform
Informarse, v. r. to enquire about a thing
Informe, s. m. information || pleading; brief
Informe, a. 2. informous
Informidad, sub. f. deformity
Infortuna, s. f. unlucky influence of the stars
Infortunadamente, adv. unfortunately
Infortunado, da, adj. unfortunate [tune
Infortunio, s. m. misfor-
Infosura, s. f. repletion; surfeit (speaking of beasts
Infraccion, s. f. fracture || infraction
Infractor, s. m. infringer
Infrascripto, ta, adject. writen beneath
Infructífero, ra, adj. unfruitful
Infructuosamente, adv. unfruitfully
Infructuoso, sa, adj. unfruitful
I'nfulas, s. f. pl. the mitre of the bishops, etc.
Infundir, v. a. to infuse
Infusion, s. f. infusion
Infuso, sa, adj. infused
Ingenerable, adj. 2. that cannot be generated
Ingeniar, v. act. to contrive; to invent ingeniously [deavour
Ingeniarse, v. r. to en-
Ingeniatura, s. f. industry; ingeniousness
Ingeniera, s. f. a trap to catch birds [neer
Ingeniero, s. m. an engi-
Ingenio, s. m. wit; genius || engine
Ingenio de azúcar, ingenio; sugar house
Ingeniosamente, adv. ingeniously
Ingeniosidad, s. f. ingeniousness [nious
Ingenioso, sa, adj. inge-
Ingénito, ta, adj. unbegotten
Ingente, a. 2. vast; large; big [genuously
Ingénuamente, adv. in-
Ingenuidad, s. fem. ingenuity || natural liberty
Ingénuo, nua, adj. ingenuous || naturally free
Ingerir, v. a. to graft
Ingle, s. m. the groin

Inglete, *s. m. a diagonal line*
Inglosable, *adj.* 2. *that cannot be glossed on*
Ingobernable, *a.* 2. *ungovernable*
Ingratamente, *adv. ungratefully* [*titude*
Ingratitud, *s. fem. ingra-*
Ingrato, ta, *adj. ungrateful* [*dient*
Ingrediente, *s. m. ingre-*
Ingreso *s. mas. ingress* || *custom duty* || *receipt*
Inguinario ria, *adj. of, or belonging to, the groin* [*no taste*
Ingustable, *a.* 2. *that has*
Inhábil, *a.* 2 *unapt; uncapable* || *unhandy*
Inhabilidad, *s. f. inability*
Inhabilitacion, *s. f. disabling*
Inhabilitar, *v. a. to disable* [*bitable*
Inhabitable, *a.* 2. *unha-*
Inhabitado, da, *adj. uninhabited*
Inherencia, *s. f. inherency*
Inherente, *a.* 2. *inherent*
Inhibicion, *s. f. inhibition*
Inhibir *v. a. to inhibit*
Inhibitorio, ria, *adj. prohibitory*
Inhiesto, ta, *adj. standing upright*
Inhonestamente, *ad. dishonestly* [*honest*
Inhonesto, ta, *adj. dis-*
Inhospitable, } *a.* 2. *inhos-*
Inhospital, } *pitable*
Inhospitalidad, *s. f. inhospitality*
Inhumanamente, *ad. inhumanly* [*humanity*
Inhumanidad, *sub. f. in-*
Inhumano, na, *adj. inhuman*

Inicial, *a.* 2. *initial*
Iniciar, *v. a. to initiate*
Inimicicia, *s. f. enmity*
Inimicíssimo, ma, *adject. very contrary*
Inimitable, *adj. inimitable* [*telligible*
Inintelígible, *a.* 2. *unin-*
Iniquamente, *adv. wickedly*
Iniquidad, *s. f. iniquity*
Iniquo, qua, *adj. iniquitous*
Injuria, *s. fem. injury* || *abuse; name*
Injuriador, *sub. m. one that injures etc.*
Injuriar, *v. a. to injure* || *to call one names*
Injuriosamente, *adv. injuriously*
Injurioso, sa, *adj. injurious* [*justity*
Injustamente, *adv. un-*
Injusticia, *s. f. injustice*
Injusto, ta, *adj. unjust*
Inlegible, *a.* 2. *that cannot be read*
Inmaculado, da, *adj. immaculate*
Inmaduro, ra, *adj. unripe*
Inmanejable *a.* 2. *intructable*
Inmanente, *a.* 2. *immanent* [*marcessible*
Inmarcesible, *adj.* 2. *im-*
Inmaterial, *a.* 2. *immaterial*
Inmaturo, ra, *adj. unripe*
Inmédiacion, *s. f. contiguity*
Inmediatamente, } *adver.*
Inmediate, } *immediately*
Inmediato, ta, *adj. immediate* [*memorial*
Inmemorable, *a.* 2. *im-*
Inmemorablemente, *adv. beyond memory*

Inmemoria
morial
Inmemoria
morial p
Inmensame
mensely
Inmensidad
sity
Inmenso,
Inmensura
measura
Inmérito,
served
Inmersion,
Inminente
nent
Inmoble, *a*
ble
Inmoderaci
Inmoderad
immode
Inmoderad
moderat
Inmodestam
immode
Inmodestia
desty
Inmodesto,
Inmódico,
sive
Inmolacion
tion
Inmolador
Inmolar, *v*
late
Inmortal, *a*
Inmortalid
mortalit
Inmortaliza
immorta
Inmortalme
mortally
Inmortifica
being un
Inmortifica
unmorti
Inmoto, ta
Inmovible
Inmobil.

ovibilidad, *s. f. im-*
obility [*table*
adable, *a.* 2. *immu-*
undicia, *s. f. filth;*
rt [*clean; foul*
ndo, da, *adj. un-*
ine, *a.* 2. *exempt;*
te
midad, *s. f. immu-*
ty [*mutability*
utabilidad, *s. f. im-*
itable, *a.* 2. *immu-*
ble
acion, *s. f. immu-*
tion [or *alter*
utar, *v. a. to change*
cible, *adj. that can-*
t be born
to, ta, *adj. innate*
vegable, *a.* 2. *inna-*
gable [*testable*
gable, *a.* 2. *incon-*
ble, *a.* 2. *not noble*
minado, da, *adj. that*
not to be named
to, ta, *adj. unknown*
vacion, *s. fem. inno-*
tion
vador, *s. mas. inno-*
tor [*vate*
var, *v. act. to inno-*
merable, *a.* 2. *innu-*
erable
pta, *a. f. unmarried*
ediencia, *s. f. diso-*
dience
ediente, *a.* 2. *disobe-*
nce [*observance*
servancia, *s. f. non-*
servante, *adj.* 2. *not*
servant
encia, *s. f. innocence*
nte, *a.* 2. *innocent*
ntes, *s. m. pl. chil-*
rmas day
entemente, *adv. in-*
cently
ioso, sa, *adj. that is*
e out of the pres-
cribed time, or *against*
the laws
Inope, *a.* 2. *poor*
Inopia, *s. fem. poverty;*
scarcity
Inopinable, *a.* 2. *unex-*
pected || *incredible*
Inopinadamente, *adver*
unexpectedly
Inopinado, da, *adj. unex-*
pected [*dinate*
Inordenado, da, *a. inor-*
Inorme, *a.* 2. *V.* Enorme
Inpromptu, *adv. out of*
hand [*pore*
Inpromptu, *s. m. extem-*
Inpuribus, *adv. nakedly*
Inquietacion, *s. f. inquie-*
tude
Inquietador, *s. m. distur-*
ber [*quietly*
Inquietamente, *adv. un-*
Inquietar, *v. act. to dis-*
quiet
Inquieto, ta, *a. unquiet*
Inquietud, *s. f. inquie-*
tude
Inquilino, *s. m. lodger,*
inmate || *possessor in*
the name of another
Inquiridor, *s. m. inquirer*
Inquirir, *v. a. to inquire*
Inquisicion, *s. f. inqui-*
sition
Hacer inquisicion, *to*
burn useless papers, etc.
Inquisidor, *s. m. inqui-*
sitor
Inquisitivo, va, *adj. in-*
quisitive [*tiableness*
Insaciabilidad, *s. f. insa-*
Insaciable, *adj.* 2. *insa-*
tiable
Insaciablemente, *adv. in-*
satiably [*ble*
Insanable, *a.* 2. *incura-*
Insania, *s. f. madness*
Insano, na, *a. mad*
Inscribir, *v. a. to inscribe*
Inscripcion, *s. f. inscrip-*
tion
Inscripto, ta, *p. p. inscri-*
bed [*grave*
Insculpir, *v. act. to en-*
Insecable, *a.* 2. *that can-*
not be dried
Inseccion, *s. f. incision*
Insecto, *s. m. insect*
Insensato, ta, *adj. mad*
Insensibilidad, *s. fem. in-*
sensibility
Insensible, *adj.* 2. *insen-*
sible [*sensibly*
Insensiblemente, *adv. in-*
Inseparable, *adj.* 2. *inse-*
parable
Inseparablemente, *ad. in-*
separably [*ried*
Insepulto, ta, *a. unbu-*
Insercion, *s. f. insertion*
Inserir, } *v. a. to insert*
Insertar, }
Inserto, ta, *a. inserted* ||
grafted
Insidia, *sub. f. embush;*
snare
Insidiar, *v. act. to lay*
snares
Insidiosamente, *adv. in-*
sidiously
Insidioso, sa, *a. insidious*
Insigne, *a.* 2. *notable;*
famous, etc. [*bly*
Insignemente, *adv. nota-*
Insignia, *s. f. sign; to-*
ken; mark of honour,
etc. || *colours; ban-*
ner, etc.
Insimular, *v. a. to accuse*
Insinuacion, *s. f. insinua-*
tion || *a registering*
Insinuar, *v. act. to insi-*
nuate
Insipidez, *s. f. insipidity*
Insípido, da, *a. insipid*
Insipiencia, *s. fem. igno-*
rance
Insipiente, *a.* 2. *ignorant*

Insolencia, s. f. insolence
Insolente, a. 2. insolent || unusual
Insolentemente, adv. insolently [wholly
Insólidum, ad. insolido;
Insoluble, a. 2. indissoluble || that cannot be paid [vent
Insolvente, adj. 2. insol-
Insondable, adj. 2. that cannot be sounded || impenetrable
Insoportable, a. 2. insupportable [tion
Inspeccion, s. f. inspec-
Inspector, s. m. inspector
Inspiracion, s. f. inspiration [inspires
Inspirador, s. m. one who
Inspirar, v. a. to inspire
Inspirar, ver. n. to blow gently [lity
Instabilidad, s. f. instabi-
Instable, a. 2. unstable
Instalacion, s. f. installation
Instalar, v. a. to install

gator
Instigar, v. a. to instigate
Instilacion, s. f. instillation
Instilar, v. a. to instill
Instinto, s. m. instinct || instigation
Institor, subs. m. a merchant's factor || a shop's foreman, etc.
Institucion, s. f. institution [tor
Instituidor. s. m. institu-
Instituir, v. a. to institute [tutes
Instituta, s. f. the insti-
Instituto, s. m. institute (order or rule of life)
Instridente, adj. 2. pressing together
Instruccion, s. f. instruction [ted
Instructo, ta, a. instruc-
Instructor, } s. m. instructor
Instruidor, }
Instruir, v. a. to instruct
Instrumental, a. 2. instrumental

Insultar, v.
to attack
smartly
Insulto, s. n
Insuperable
perable ||
hable
Intacto, ta,
Integérrimo
upright
Integral, a.
I'ntegramen
rely; whe
Integridad,
|| entire
nity
I'ntegro, gr
whole ||
nest
Inteleccion,
Intelectivo,
Intelectivo,
lective
Intelectual,
Intectualida
wer or f
derstandi

ıncia, sub. f. *inance*
ie, s. f. *intem-*
re
ta (noche) s. f.
dark night
tivamente, adv.
onably
tivo, va, a. *un-*
able
ı, s. f. *intention*
ıadamente, adv.
edly
ıado, da (bien ó
. *well-affected* or
cted
ıal, a. 2. *inten-*

ıalmente, adver.
ionally
cia, s. f. *care;*
istration || *in-*
ıcy
te, s. m. *inten-*
steward
ıente, ad. *inten-*
[*ness*
ı, s. f. *intense-*
o, va, adj. *inten-*

sa, a. *intense*
, v. act. *to intend*
mpt
, s. mas. *intent;*
tion
ıa, s. f. *a great,*
arious purpose,
[*while*
adv. *in the mean*
lencia, s. f. *inter-*
on || *inconstancy*
ermission of the

lente, a. 2. *chan-*
le || *intermitting;*
ular
lacion, s. f. *inter-*
ion [*lary*
r, a. 2. *interca-*

Intercalar, v. a. *to intercalate* [*cede*
Interceder, v. n. *to inter-*
Interceptar, v. act. *to intercept* *cession*
Intercesion, sub. f. *inter-*
Intercesor, s. mas. *intercessor*
Intercesoriamente, adv. *by intercession*
Intercesorio, ria, a. *that intercedes*
Intercolunio, s. m. *intercolumniation* [*tal*
Intercostal, a. 2. *intercos-*
Intercutáneo, nea, a. *that is between the skin and flesh*
Interdecir, v. a. *to interdict; to forbid*
Interdiccion, s. f. *interdiction*
Interes, s. m. *interest* || *gain; profit* || *price; value*
Interesable, } a. 2. *pro-*
Interesal, } *fitable*
Interesado, da, adj. *self-interested*
Interesar, v. n. } *to gain*
Interesarse, v. r. } *a part* or *interest in a thing*
Interesar, v. a. *to interest*
Interese, s. m. *V.* Interes
Interin, adv. *in the mean while; by interim*
Interinamente, adv. *in the mean while*
Interinario, ria, } a. *that*
Interino, na, } *has a charge in commendam*
Interior, a. 2. *interior; inward*
Interioridad, s. f. *the inward* or *inner part*
Interiorísimo, ma, a. *very interior*
Interiormente, adv. *inwardly*

Interjeccion, s. f. *interjection*
Interlineal, adj. 2. *interlineary*
Interlocucion, s. f. *interlocution* [*locutor*
Interlocutor, s. m. *inter-*
Interlocutorio, ria, a. *interlocutory*
Interlunio, s. m. *the time when the moon is invisible*
Intermedio, s. m. *an interlude* || *interposition*
Intermedio, dia, adj. *intermediate*
Interminable, a. 2. *interminable* || *that cannot be decided, etc.*
Intermision, s. f. *intermission*
Intermitencia, s. f. *interruption; intermitent pulse* or *ague*
Intermitente, a. 2. *intermittent* [*mit*
Intermitir, v. a. *to inter-*
Internamente, adv. *inwardly*
Internar, v. a. *to penetrate inwardly*
Internarse, v. r. *to creep into one's favour, etc.*
Internecion, s. f. *slaughter; carnage*
Interno, na, adj. *internal*
Internodio, s. m. *the space between two joints*
Internuncio, s. m. *internuncio* [*mons*
Interpelacion, s. f. *sum-*
Interpelar, v. a. *to summon; to require*
Interpolacion, s. f. *interpolation*
Interpolar, v. a. *to interpolate*
Interponer, v. a. *to intermix* || *to interpose*

Interpretativo, va, adj.
Intérprete, s. m. *interpreter* [*terposed*
Interpuesto, ta, p. p. *in-*
Interregno, s. m. *interregnum*
Interrogacion, s. f. *interrogation* || *a note of interrogation*
Interrogante, a. 2. *who interrogates*
Punto interrogante, *a note of interrogation*
Interrogar, v. a. *to interrogate* [*terrogative*
Interrogativo, va, adj. *in-*
Interrogatorio, s. m. *interrogatory*
Interrogatorio, ria, adj. *belonging to an interrogatory* || *interrogative*
Interromper, } v. a. *to interrupt*
Interrompir, }
Interrupcion, s. f. *interruption* [*tion*
Interseccion, s. f. *intersec-*
Intersticio, s. m. *inters-*

mate || *inward*
Intitular, v. a. *to entitle*
Intitulata, s. f. *title of an act, etc.* [*rable*
Intolerable, a. 2. *intole-*
Intonso, sa, a. *unshaved* || *ignorant; foolish*
Intransitable, a. 2. *impassable*
Intransitivo, va, adj. *intransitive*
Intratable, a. 2. *intractable* || *inpracticable*
Intrépidamente, adv. *intrepidly* [*dity*
Intrepidez, s. f. *intrepi-*
Intrépido, da, adj. *intrepid* [*te; entangled*
Intrincable, a. 2. *intrica-*
Intrincadamente, ad. *intricately* [*gle*
Intrincar, v. a. *to entan-*
Intrínsecamente, ad. *intrinsically*
Intrínseco, ca, adj. *intrinsick* || *inward* || *silent; close; reserved*
Introduccion, s. f. *intro-*

ity; clou
Inurbano, *courteous*
Inusitadame *sally*
Inusitado, da
Inútil, a. 2 *needless*
Inutilidad, s
Inutilizar, v. *useless an ble*
Inútilmente, *lessly* || *in*
Invadeable, *cannot be*
Invadir, v. a
Invalidacion, *dating; in*
Inválidament *hout force*
Invalidar, v.
Inválido, da,
Inválido, s. n *lid* or *disa*
Invariable, a. *ble*
Invariablemen

iblemente, adv. in-
ibly
ion, sub. f. inven-
|| trick; device ||

ionero, s. m. in-
r || a wheedler ||
im man
ible, a. 2. that can-
e sold
r, v. a. to invent
riar, v. a. to in-
ory [tory
rio, s. m. inven-
iva, s. f. imagina-
; genius [tive
vo, va, adj. inven-
, s. m. invention
r, s. m. inventer
undo, da, adj. im-
nt
imil, a. 2. unlikely
imilitud, s. f. un-
ihood
ada, s. f. the win-
season
dero, s. m. a win-
g-place
r, v. n. to winter
izo, za, a. wintry
imil, a. 2. unli-

on, s. f. inversion
, sa, p. p. inverted
r, v. a. to invert
dura, s. f. investi-
[tigable
gable, a. 2. inves-
gacion, s. f. inves-
ion [tigate
gar, v. a. to inves-
r, v. a. to invest
adamente, adver.
terately
ado, da, adj. in-
ate
arse, v. r. to grow
erate, or old
v. a. to send

Invicto, ta, adj. unconquered [etc.
Invidia, etc. V. Envidia,
Invierno, s. m. winter
Invigilar, v. a. to watch diligently [ble
Invincible, a. 2. invinci-
Inviolable, a. 2. inviolable [violably
Inviolablemente, adv. in-
Inviolado, da, adj. unviolated
Invirtuoso, sa, adj. that wants virtue
Invisibilidad, s. f. invisibility
Invisible, a. 2. invisible
Invisiblemente, adv. invisibly [tory verse
Invitatorio, s. m. invita-
Invocacion, s. f. invocation
Invocar, v. a. to invoke
Invocatoria, s. f. invocation [invokes
Invocatorio, ria, a. that
Involuntariamente, adv. involuntary
Involuntariedad, s. f. a doing things contrary to the will
Involuntario, ria, adjec. involuntary
Invulnerable, a. 2. invulnerable [to graft
Inxerir, inxertar, v. act.
Inxerto, ta, p. p. grafted
Inxerto, s. m. a graft
Inyeccion, s. f. injection
Iónico, ca, adj. ionick
Ipso facto, ad. immediately; out of hand
Ipso jure, adv. with or by right
Ir, v. n. to go
Ir á la mano, to hinder; to with-hold. Irle á una persona alguna cosa, to concern

Irse, v. r. to go away or out || to leak || to be dying
Irse de boca, to be lavish of one's tongue — en la lumbre, to boil over
Ira, s f. anger; wrath
Iracundia, s. f. wrath; indignation
Iracundo, da, a. passionate [dia
Irascencia, s. f. V. Iracun-
Irascible, a. 2. irascible
Irenarca, s. m. a peculiar magistrate among the ancient Romans
Irino, na, a. made with the flower iris
Iris, s. m. iris (the rainbow) || any thing of various colours || pacificator; mediator || iris (flower)
Ironía, s. f. irony
Irónicamente, adv. ironically
Irónico, ca, adj. ironical
Irracional, } a. 2. irra-
Irracionable, } tional
Irracionablemente, adv. irrationally
Irradiacion, s. f. irradiation [te
Irradiar, v. a. to irradia-
Irreconciliable, a. 2. irreconciliable
Irrecuperable, a. 2. irrecuperable
Irrecusable, a. 2. inevitable
Irreducible, a. 2. irreducible || obstinate; stiff
Irrefragable, a. 2. irrefragable
Irrefragablemente, adv. irrefragably
Irregular, a. 2. irregular
Irregularidad, s. f. irregularity

Irregularmente, *adv. irregularly*
Irreligion, *s. f. irreligion*
Irreligiosamente, *adver. irreligiously* [*gious*
Irreligioso, **sa**, *a. irreli-*
Irremediable, *a. 2. irremediable*
Irremidiablemente, *adv. irrecoverably* [*sible*
Irremisible. *a. 2. irremis-*
Irremisiblemente, *adver. irremissibly* [*rable*
Irreparable, *a. 2. irrepa-*
Irreprehensible, *a. 2. irreprehensible*
Irreprehensiblemente, *ad. irreprehensibly*
Irresistible, *a. 2. irresistible* [*irresistibly*
Irresistiblemente, *adver.*
Irresoluble, *a. 2. that cannot be resolved* || *irresolute* [*lution*
Irresolucion, *s. f. irreso-*
Irresoluto, **ta**, *adj. irresolute* [*rence*
Irreverencia, *s. f. irreve-*
Irreverente, *a. 2. irreverent* [*vocability*
Irrevocabilidad, *s. f. irre-*
Irrevocable, *a. 2. irrevocable* [*revocably*
Irrevocablemente, *ad. ir-*
Irrision, *s. f. irrision*
Irrisorio, **ria**, *adj. ridiculous*
Irritable, *a. 2. irritable*
Irritacion, *s. f. irritation*
Irritador, *s. m. provoker*
Irritar, *v. a. to irritate* || *to provoke* || *to annul*
Irrito, **ta**, *adj. invalid, of no force*
Irrupcion, *s. f. irruption*
Isagoge, *s. f. introduction*
Ischion, *s. m. ischium; the hip-bone*
Isla, *s. f. an island*

Islan, *s. m. a sort of veil laced round*
Isleño, **ña**, *adj. y s. insular; islander*
Isléo, *s. m. a small island*
Isleta, **lilla**, *s. f. a little island*
Islilla, *s. f. flank*
Islote, *s. m. islet*
Isógono, **na**, *adj. equiangular*
Isoperímetro, **tra**, *adjec. isoperimetrical*
Isopleuro, *adj. m. equilateral*
Isósceles, *a. m. isosceles*
Ispida, *s. f. King's fisher*
Istmo, *s. m. isthmus*
Istriar, *v. a. to flute a column*
Item, *adv. item*
Iterable, *a. 2. that may be reiterated*
Iteracion, *s. f. reiteration*
Iterar, *v. a. to iterate*
Itinerario, *s. m. itinerary*
Iva, *s. f. ground-pine; herb-ivy*
Ixia, *s. f. a birdlime*
Izaga, *s. f. a place full of rushes* [*up*
Izar, *v. a. to hoist* or *pull*
Izquierda, *sub. f. the left hand* [*left*
A' la izquierda, *on the*
Izquierdear, *v. n. to go on the left* || *to mistake*
Izquierdo, **da**, *subs. left-handed*
Izquierdo, **da**, *adj. left* || *crooked* || *whose hams are too close*

J.

J**ABALI'**, *s. m. a wild boar*
Jabalina, *s. f. a wild sow* || *a javelin*

Jabalino, **na**,
Jabardear, *v.*
as bees do
Jabardillo, *s.*
ng of coun
Jabardo, *s. m.*
a pack of
Jabato, *s. m.*
boar
Jaca, *s. f. V.*
Jacerina, *s.*
mail
Jacinto, *s. m.*
Jaco, *s. m. a*
a nag
Jactancia, *s.*
Jactancioso,
glorious;
Jactarse, *v. r*
Jaculatoria,
latory pray
Jade, *s. m.*
of precious
Jadear, *v. n.*
Jadeo, *s. m.*
Jaecero, *s. m*
furnitures
Jaen, *adj. a*
Jaez, *s. m. a*
a horse ||
|| *likeness*
Jaez de cama
for a bed -
Jaez, *thin*
Jaharrar, *v.*
a wall
Jaharro, *s.*
Jalbegar, *v.*
wash wit
paint one
Jalbegue, *s*
washing ||
paint
Jaldado, **da**
bright yel
Jalde, *a. 2.*
Jaldo, **da**,
Jaldre, *s.*
colour

y
'ver
jamas, *for*
l. jambs
f. the place
throw the
eep
s. to throw
ordure of
gammon;
pieces of
ed together
people, in-
-wreck
dj. an ap-
ven to some
a garden ||
a ship
overed bal-
ship
gardening
n. gardener
e edging of
, etc.
like a wild
[*cher*
jar or *pit-*
rras, *to set*
a kimbo
to go often
r wine || *to*
to hough ||
the hough
a garter ||
f the garter
a little-pot
er-pot
pot
a great pot
[*stone*
the jasper-
to speckle;

Jaula, *s. f. a cage* || *a cell (in a mad-house)*

Jaulilla, *s. f. a kind of net-cap*

Jayan, *s. m. a great raw-boned fellow*

Jayanazo, *s. m. aum. de* Jayan

Jazmin, *s. m. jasmine*

Jesuchristo, *s. m. Jesus-Christ*

Jesuita, *s. m. a jesuit*

Jesuita, *adjec. belonging to Jesus*

Jesuítico, ca, *a. jesuitical*

Jesus, *s. m. Jesus*

Decir tos jesusos, *to pray for one that is dying*

Jesusear, *v. n. to repeat many times the name of Jesus*

Jo! *int. V.* Cho

Joa, Joba, *s. f. an addition made to certain timbers* [*sely*

Jocosamente, *adv. joco-*

Jocoserio (estilo), *s. m. a merry and serious style mixed together*

Jocoso, sa, *adj. jocose*

Jocundidad, *s. f. jocundity*

Jocundo, da, *adj jocund*

Jofayna, *s. f. V.* Aljofayna

Joliez, *subs. f. festivity; merriment*

Jolito, *s. m. rest; quiet* || *a dead calm*

Jónico, ca, *adj. ionick*

Jonjolí, *s. m. sesame*

Jordan, *s. m. any thing that makes young*

Jorfe, *s. m. a stone-wall without mortar*

Jorgina, *s. f. a witch*

Jornada, *s. f. a day's journey* or *work* || *an act of a play* || *a battle*

Jornal, *s. m. day-wages*

Jornalero, *s. m. a journeyman*

Joroba, *s. f. a bump* or *hump* || *a vexatious sollicitation*

Jorobado, da, *a. bunch-backed* [*molest*

Jorobar, *v. a. to vex; to*

Jostrado (virote), *s. m. a shaft that has a round head at the end*

Jóven, *a.* 2. *young*

Joveneto, *s. m. a youth*

Jovial, *a.* 2. *belonging to Jupiter* || *jovial*

Jovialidad, *s. f. jovialness*

Joya, *s. f. a jewel* || *a reward* or *present* || *the astragal of a column*

Joyas, *pl. a bride's clothes*

Joyante (seda), *sub. f. a very fine glossy silk*

Pólvora joyante, *the finest shining gunpowder* [*little value*

Joyel, *s. m. a jewel of*

Joyería. *s. f. a jeweller's shop*

Joyero, *s. m. a jeweller*

Joyo, *s. m. darnel; cockle*

Joynela, *s. f. a small jewel*

Juanete, *s. m. the knuckle-bone of the thumbs and great toes, when it sticks out more than ordinary* || *the trinket*

Juanetudo, da, *adj. that has sticking-out bones in the toes* [*cloth*

Juarda, *s. f. a stain in a*

Jubertar, *v. act. to hoist the boat into the ship*

Jubetería, *s. f. a broker's shop* or *street*

Jubetero, *s. m. a broker*

Jubilacion, s. f. jubilation

Jubilado, s. m. a veteran magistrate, etc.

or paltry doublet
Júdas, s. m. a traitor
Judayco, ca, a. judaick
Judaysmo, s. m. judaism
Judayzar, v. n. to judaise
Judería, s. f. jews quarter
Judía, s. f. kidney-bean
Judicacion, s. f. judging
Judicante, s. m. a supreme judge
Judicativo, va, adj. belonging to a judge
Judicatura, s. f. judicature
Judicial, a. 2. judicial
Judicialmente, adv. judicially
Judiciaria (Astrología), s. f. the judicial astrology
Judíciario, sub. m. astrologer
Judicioso, sa, a. judicious
Judiego, ga, adj. judaick
Judihuelo, s. m. son of a jew || kidney-bean
Judío, día, s. a jew, or jewess
Judío, día, adj. jewish

life
Jugador, s. m. a gamester
Jugador de manos, a juggler
Jugar, v. n. to play || to jest to be in jest
Jugareta, s. f. the playing without knowing the game [buffoon
Juglar, s. m. a jester; a
Juglaresa, s. f. a jesting merry woman
Juglería, s. f. buffonry
Juguete, s. m. jest; joke; humour || a play-thing; a toy [to jest
Juguetear, v. n. to play;
Jugueton, na, adj. wanton; sportful
Juicio, s. m. judgment || the sentence against a criminal [ciously
Juiciosamente, adv. judi-
Juicioso, sa, a. judicious
Julepe, s. m. julap
Julio, s. m. july
Julo, s. m. the fore-mule
Jumelas, s. f. pl. cheeks;

Junquillo, s.
Junta, s. f.
sembly ||
or putting
heap; co
Junta de méc
sultation
Juntadura,
tura
Juntamente,
Juntar, v. a
Juntarse, v.
gether ||
|| to copu
Junto, adv
near; ha
Junto, ta, p
Por junto,
lesale; by
Juntera, s.
plane
Juntura, s.
Júpiter, s. m
Jura, s. f.
giance
Juradería, s.
of a jurad
Jurado, s. m

ıente, *adv. juri-*
y [*cal*
, cā, *adj. juridi-*
ulto, *s. m. juris-*
t [*tion*
ion, *s. f. jurisdic-*
cia, *s. f. juris-*
nce
to, *s. m. juris-*
t
lencia, *s. f. juris-*
nce
s. m. jurist
s. m. perpetual
of property || *an*
ity settled upon
ing's revenue
s. m. bee-eater
d) [*broom*
, *s. f. butcher's*
s. m. a kind of
or mess
. f. just; tilt
, *s. m. close-coat*
, *s. m. tilter*
nte, *adver. justly*
t
v. n. to tilt or *just*
, *s. f. justice* || *the*
s of justice
, *v. a. to execute*
go, *s. m. the offi-*
a judge
ro, ra, *adj. that*
justice; severe
cion, *s. f. justifi-*
n || *justice*
damente, *adver.*
iably
dor, *s. m. justifier*
ır, *v. a. to justify*
tivo, va, *adjec.*
ying
, *s. m. a waistcoat*
ut sleeves
ta, *adj. just* || *fit*
ct || *close; strait*
m. a just
s y en verenjus-

tos, *with reason* or *without it*
Juvenil, *a.* 2. *juvenile*
Juventud, *sub. f. youth* || *young people*
Juzgado, *s. masc. court; judgment seat*
Juzgamundos, *s. masc. a backbiter*
Juzgar, *v. a.* y *n. to judge*

K

KALI, *s. m. alkali*
Kármes, Kérmes } *s. m. kermes*
Kirieleyson, *sub. m. lord have mercy upon us* (*a form of prayer*) || *burial; funeral*
Kiries, *s. m. pl. that part of the liturgy wich contains the* kirieleyson — *repetition* or *abundance; a legend*

L

LA, *art. the*
Lábaro, *s. m. constantine's imperial standard*
Labe, *s. f. spot* || *blemish*
Laberinto, *s. m. labyrinth*
Labia, *sub. f. a peruasive eloquence*
Labial, *a.* 2. *labial*
Labio, *s. m. a lip*
Labor, *subs. m. labour* || *work* || *order; simetry* || *a seamstress's work* || *tillage*
Labores, *pl. embroideries; chased works, etc.*
Laborante, *s. m. labourer*
Laboratorio, *s. mas. laboratory* [*or till*
Laborear, *v. a. to plough*,
Laborera, *s. fem. a skilful work-woman*

Laborió, *s. m. tillage*
Loborioso, sa, *adj. laborious*
Labrada, *s. f. a field tilled and ready for sowing* [*bandman*
Labrador, *sub. m. husbandman*
Labrador, ra, *s. a country-man* or *woman*
Labradoresco, ca, *a. rustick; clownish*
Labrandera, *s. f. a seamstress* [*of stone*
Labrante, *s. m. a hewer*
Labrantío, tía, *a. arable manurable*
Labranza, *sub. f. tillage; husbandry* || *ploughing* || *a tilled land*
Labrar, *v. a. to work* || *to till* || *to build* || *to sew; to embroider, etc.* || *to geld* || *to train; to manage, etc.*
Labrar á fuego, *to cauterize a horse*
Labriego, *s. m. a country-man; a peasant*
Labrusca, *sub. f. a wild vine*
Laca, *s. f. lac* [*footman*
Lacayo, *s. m. lackey;*
Lacaynelo, *s. m. a little* or *young lackey*
Lacear, *v. act. to adorn with knots*
Lacerado, da, *a. ragged; wretched* || *unhappy* || *miser; stingy*
Lacerar, *v. a. to rend; to tear in pieces* || *to break*
Lacerar, *ver. n. to live wretchedly* [*gardlines*
Lacéria, *s. f. poverty* || *nig-*
Lacería, *s. f. knots of ribbands, etc.*
Lacio, cia, *a.* lank; *fading*, etc. [*cisely*
Lacónicamente, *ad. con-*

Lactancia, s. f. the time that a child sucks; lactation
Lácteo, tea, a. milky
Via láctea, milky-way
Lacticinio, sub. m. milk-food
Lactúmen, sub. m. scabs that break out on children who suck too much
Ladano, s. m. labdanum
Ladear, v. act. to move from side to side
Ladearse, v. r. to swing one's body in walking || to incline, or bend to...
Ladear, v. n. to decline (speaking of the magnetical needle)
Ladera, s. f. the side of a hill
Ladilla, s. f. a crab-louse
Ladillo, s. m. a leathern boot in the ancient coaches
Ladino, na, adject. that speaks any tongue per-

Ladronera, s. f. a nest of thieves || a trench, or sluice for mills
Ladronicio, s. m. a theft
Lagaña, s. f. blear-eyedness [eyed
Lagañoso, sa, adj. blear-
Lagar, s. m. the wine-press
Lagarejo, s. m. } dim. de
Lagareta, s. f. } lagar
Lagartera, s. f. a lizard's hole || a very old and weak castle, etc.
Lagartera, (ave) a bird that catches the lizards
Lagartezna, } s. f. a little
Lagartija, } brown lizard
Lagartijera. V. Lagartera
Lagarto, s. m. a lizard || the cross of the order of santiago
Lago, s. m. a lake
Lagotear, v. n. to flatter; to coax
Lagotería, s. f. flattery; coaxing [a coaxer

... || broc...
of gold
Lambrija, s. ...
a lean, th...
person
Lamedad, s. ...
Lamedor, s. ...
licks || loc...
ry) || allur...
Lamentable, ...
mentable
Lamentacion, ...
tation
Lamentador, ...
Lamentar, v. ...
Lamentar, v. ...
Lamentarse, ...
Lamento, s. m...
Lamentoso, s...
mentable
Lamer, v. a. ...
Lamia, s. f. b...
sea-fish) ||
common w...
Lamido, da, ...
licked up ||
Lámina, s. f. ...
metal || a c...

la, s. f. a little
| a coarse wollen
ı, s. m. the case
h the glass-lamp
l
a, sub. mas. the
evil || farcy
, s. m. burdock
ab [the body
, pl. spots in
e lampazo, a fo-
rk in a suit of
ıgs
, na, a. mas. a
ess || hairless ||
[great lamp
, s. m. a kind of
, s. f. a lamprey
, v. a. to dress
lamprey
ıela, } s. f. a little
la, } lamprey;
n
, s. f. corn-sal-
[sea-fish
, sub. f. a sort of
wool || money
s. f. a maulking
nnons)
dj. 2. woolly;
n
m. a cast || the
of a net || chan-
ccident || end;
|| lucky time
de lance, to buy
penny-worth
l. missive wea-
incidents, in a
, s. f. plantain
sub. f. a rack to
ars on
s. m. a lancer
s. f. lancet
, s. f. } a prick
s. m. } with a

Lancha, s. f. a broad flat stone || pinnace; boat
Lanchada, sub. f. a boat's full lading
Lanchazo, s. m. a stroke with a great flat stone
Lancilla, s. f. a little lance
Lande, s. f. acorn
Landre, s. fem. a sort of gland or swelling || money tied in the corner of a handkerchiefs, etc.
Landrecilla, s. f. a glandule in the calf's thigh etc.
Lanería, s. fem. the shop where wool is sold
Lanero, sub. m. one that deals in wool || the house where the wool is kept
Langaruto, s. m. a long slim fellow
Langosta, sub. f. a grasshopper || a large lobster || a sharper
Langostin, s. mas. a little sea-lobster
Langostino, s. m. a little grass-hopper without wings
Langoston, s. m. a great grass-hopper; a locust
Languidez, } sub. f. lan-
Languideza, } guor; languishment
Lánguido, da, a. languid
Lanificio, s. m. working of wool
Lanilla, s. f. the nap of a cloth's right-side || a sort of stuff
Lanteja, s. f. a lentil
Lantejuela, s. f. a spangle
Lanterna, s. f. a lanthorn
Lanudo, da, a. woolly
Lanza, s. f. a lance || the pole of a coach || a lancer [in the rest
Lanza in ristre, the lance
Lanzada, s. f. a wound of a lance
Lanzada de moro zurdo, a great wound of a lance or spear
Lanzadera, sub. f. a weaver's shuttle
Lanzamiento, s. m. darting; casting
Lanzar, v. a. to dart; to cast || to turn out || to vomit
Lanzon, s. masc. a short thick lance [lance
Lanzuela, s. fem. a little
Laña, s. f. a cramping iron
Lañar, v. a. to bind stones with cramping irons || to open fishes to salt them
Lapa, s. f. a lepar or patella || burdock || a pellicle on the wine || the scum of any thing
Lapachar, s. m. a muddy place [case
Lapicero, s. m. a pencil-
Lápida, s. f. a flat square stone (for inscriptions, etc.)
Lapidaria, s. f. the art of a lapidary
Lapidario, s. m. lapidary
Lapídeo, dea, adj. lapideous
Lapidoso, sa, a. stony
Lapislázuli, s. mas. lapis lazuly [crayon
Lapiz, sub. mas. pencil;
Lapizar, v. a. to draw with crayons
Lapizar, s. mas. a stony-place
Lapso, sub. m. proces or tract of time

Laque, *s. m. a running footman*

Lardar, } *ver. act. to*
Lardear, } *baste meat in roasting* || *to vex*, *to chastise*

Lardero (martes) *s. masc. shrove-thuesday*

Lardo, *s. m. lard*

Lardon, *s. m. an addition in the margin*

Lardosillo, lla, *a. greasy*

Lares, *s. m. pl. the house hold gods* || *house; home*

Larga, *s. f. delay*

Largamento, *ad. largely*

Largar, *v. a. to let go; to loose*

Largar las velas, *to loosen any sail*

Largaria, *s. f. length*

Largo, ga, *a. long; large* || *liberal* || *copious* || *expeditious*

Largo, *adv. largely*

Largomira, *s. f. a prospective-glass*

Largon, na, *a. very long*

Largor, *s. m. length*

Largueado, da, *a. striped*

Largueros, *sub. masc. pl. upright stones, in the doors, etc.*

Largueza, *s. f. length* || *liberality*

Largura, *s. f. length*

Laringe, *s. m. larynx*

Laro, *s. m. a sea-mew*

Lasamiento, *s. m. weariness* [*fritter*

Lasaña, *subs. f. a kind of*

Lascivamente, *adv. lasciviously*

Lascivia, *subst. f. lasciviousness* || *excess*

Lascivo, ra, *a. lascivious — of a pleasant green colour*

Laserpicio, *s. m. a plant so called*

Lasitud, *s. f. weariness*

Laso, sa, *a. weary*

Lastar, *v. a. to pay* or *suffer for another*

Lástima, *subs. f. compassion; pity* || *grief; misfortune*

Lastimar, *v. a. to hurt* || *to move with pity*

Lastimarse, *v. r. to take pity on* || *to complain of...*

Lastimero, ra, *a. pitiful*

Lastimosamente, *adv. lamentably*

Lastimoso, sa, *a. lamentable*

Lasto, *sub. m. the charge one is at in recovering the money paid for another*

Lastrar, *v. a. to ballast*

Lastre, *s. m. ballast; last*

Lata, *s. f. thin*

Latas, *pl. poles* or *perches in the roofs* || *beams, in a ship*

Latamente, *adv. widely*

Lateral, *a. 2. lateral*

Latido, *s. m. the beating of the heart* || *pricking; pungency* || *barking*

Latigazo, *subs. m. a lash with a wip*

Látigo, *s. m. a whip; a scourge* || *a plume* or *feather* [*lasts*

Cordel de látigo, *whip-*

Latiguear, *v. n. to smack a whip*

Latin, *s. m. latin*

Latinajo, *s. m. low-latin*

Latinamente, *ad. in latin*

Latinear, *v. a.* to latinize

Latinidad, *s. f.* latinity

Latinismo, *sub. m. latinism*

Latinizar, *v. a. to* || *to speak latin sonably*

Latino, na, *a. lat*

Vela latina, *a sail*

Latinoso, sa, *adj ging to the latin*

Latir, *v. n. to bea heart does* || *t to ache violen bark*

Latitar, *v. n. to l*

Latitud, *subs. f. l latitude*

Lato, ta, *a. wide*

Laton, *s. m. latte*

Latonero, *s. mas. works latten*

Latría, *s. f. the due to god alc*

Latrina, *subs. f. office*

Latrocinio, *s. m.*

Laud, *s. m. a lut*

Laudable, *a. 2. l*

Láudano, *s. m. la*

Laudar, *v. a. to p*

Laudatoria, *s. f.*

Laudatorio, ria, *sing*

Laude, *s. f. a tor with an in: on it*

Laudes, *pl. the l*

Tocar á laudes, *one's self*

Laudemio, *s. m. alienation; la*

Launa, *s. f. lami*

Laurea, *s. fem. garland of lau*

Laureado, *s. m. takes a degre university* || *a reat*

Laurear, *v. a. with laurel degree in th*

laurel
: a crown of
ory (round
' a saint) ||
'el
adj. belon-
:rel
ias. laurel;
. pl. dish-
V. Lavatorio
baptism. ||
m. a wash-
. a washer
f. washing
er
masc. pl. a
. m. a laver
. m. a wild
f. laundress
. f. laundry
m. a wash-
f. lavender
wash
, to white-
plaster
. f. a clyster
m. washing
tive decoc-
[water
m. pl dish-
broad flat
sh || a shoal
to loosen ;
. a. laxative
f. quality ;
ay ; secular
knot of rib-
|| slip-knot
. lazaretto
m. a boy

who leads a blind man
Lázaro, *s. mas. a ragged beggar || a crafty, cunning fellow.* || *V.* Lazarillo
Lazo, *s. m. a slip-knot* || *a snare* || *knot; tie; band*
Lazos, *pl. flourishes in writing*
Leal, *a. 2. loyal*
Lealmente, *adv. loyally*
Lealtad, *s. f. loyalty*
Lebeche, *s. m. the south-west wind*
Lebrada, *s. f. hare-ragoo*
Lebraston, *s. m. an old hare* || *a cunning subtle man*
Lebratillo, *s. m. a leveret* [*hound*
Lebrel, *subs. m. a grey*
Lebrillo, *s. m. an earthen pan*
Lebron, *s. m. a great hare* || *a coward*
Lebruno, na, *a. leporine*
Leccion, *s. f. reading* || *lesson*
Lechada, *s. f. the wetting* or *moistening of lime*
Lechal, *a. 2. sucking*
Leche, *s. m. milk*
Leche de gallina, *star of Bethlehem* — de manteca, *butter-milk* — de pez, *milt*
Lechecillas, *s. f. pl. sweet-bread*
Lechera, *s. f. a milk-maid*
Lechero, *s. m. a milk-man*
Lechero, ra, *a. milky*
Lechetrezna, *sub. f. any milky plant*
Lechigada, *s. f. litter of pigs, etc.* || *a pack of rogues*
Lechino, *s. m. a match of lint*

Lecho, *sub. m. a bed* || *a layer*
Lechon, *s. m. hog ; pig*
Lechoncillo, *s. m. a sucking-pig*
Lechuga, *s. f. lettuce*
Lechuga crespa, *endive-leafed lettuce*—merciana, *the cabbage-lettuce* — parrada, *broad-leafed lettuce* — romana, *the roman lettuce*
Lechuguero, *sub. m. one who sells lettuces*
Lechuguilla, *s. f. a ruff-band* [*lettuce*
Lechuguino, *s. m. a young*
Lechuza, *s. f. an owl*
Lechuzo, za, *a. sucking*
Lechuzo, *s. m. a summoner* || *a gatherer of taxes*
Lector, *s. m. a reader* || *lector ; letturer*
Lector en teología, *a professor of divinity*
Lectoral, *adj. the canon whose office is to explain the holy scriptures*
Lectoría, *s. f. the office of a reader*
Lectura, *sub. f. lecture ; reading* || *pica (a printing letter)*
Ledamente, *adv. merrily*
Ledo, da, *adj. merry ; joyful*
Leer, *v. a. to read* || *to teach a science*
Legacía, *s. f. embassy* || *legation*
Legado, *s. m. ambassador* || *pope's legate* || *legacy* [*of papers*
Legajo, *s. m. a bundle*
Legal, *a. 2. legal* || *loyal ; faithful*
Legalidad, *s. f. legality*

Legar, *v. a. to send* || *to bequeath*
Legatario, *s. m. a legatee*
Legendario, *subs. m. the book of legends*
Legible, *a.* 2. *legible*
Legion, *s. f. legion*
Legionario, *s. m. legionary*
Legislador, *s. m. legislator* || *censurer*
Legislar, *v. n. to make* or *establish laws* || *to censure*
Legisperito, *s. m. jurisconsult* [*lawyer*
Legista, *s. m. civilian ;*
Legítima, *s. f. portion, share in the father's goods*
Legitímacion, *s. f. legitimation*
Legítimamente, *ad. lawfully* [*mate*
Legitimar, *v. a. to legiti-*
Legitimidad, *s. f. legitimacy* [*mate*
Legítimo, ma, *a. legiti-*
pleton
Lema, *s. m. argument ; subject* || *lemma*
Lencería, *s. f. linen-clothes* || *the linen-drapers street* [*per*
Lencero, *s. m. linen-dra-*
Lendrera, *s. f. a small-toothed comb to take out the nits*
Lendrero, *s. m. a place full of nits* [*nits*
Lendroso, sa, *adj. full of*
Lengua, *s. f. tongue* || *an interpreter* || *a bell's clapper*
Lengua del agua, *the edge of the water*—de buey, *bugloss* — de ciervo, *hartstongue*—de cordero, *lambs-tongue* — de caballo, *horse-tongue*— de perro, *hounds-tongue* — serpentina, *adder's-tongue*
Lenguado, *subs. m. sole* (*a sea-fish*)
Lenguage, *s. m. language*
Lentamente
Lente, *s. m.*
Lenteja, *s. f*
Lenteja de ag
Lenticular, *a*
lar
Lentisco, *s. m*
Lentitud, *s.*
Lento, ta, *ad*
Lentor, *s. m*
Lenzuelo, *s.*
chief
Leña, *s. f. f*
Cargar de le
one
Leñador, *s. m*
Leñera, *s. f.*
Leñero, *s. m*
wood || *wo*
pile
Leño, *s. m.*
tree ; a l
ship ; boa
Leñoso, sa,
Leon, *s. m.*
Leona, *s. f.*
Leonado, da
Leoncillo, *s.*

lj. slow; lazy;

em. damage;
ong
an awl
dject. hurt ||

east-wind
lethal
f. litany || *a*
ded story
lur. rogation

m. lethargy
joy; gladness
. *act. to make*

a letter || *the*
writing || *mot-*
(*in printing*)
nbio, *a bill of*

learning
e letras, *a lear-*
; *a great scho-*

, *s. f. assembly*
f litterature ||
r *folly spoken*
ivity
. *m. a learned*
lawyer
, *s. f. V.* Letra-

m. inscription
. *fem. dim. de*
a poetical com-
so called
. *fem. house of*
[*letter*
masc. a great
pl. papers in
tters set up at
s of churches
s. m. electuary
weighing an-
departing || *rai-*
diers || *depar-*

Pieza de leva, *a signal gun for sailing*

Levas, *pl. tricks; devices, etc.*

Levada, *s. fem. a bout* or *turn, at fencing*

Levadas, *plur. flourishes made with the lance*

Levadizo, za, *adject. to be lifted*

Puente levadiza, *a draw-bridge*

Levadura, *s. f. leven*

Levantador, *s. m. raiser of troubles, etc.*

Levantamiento, *s. m. raising* || *insurrection*

Levantar, *v. a. to raise; to lift* || *a build* || *to impute* || *to defend* or *protect*

Levantar la caza, *to rouse* or *start game* — falso testimonio, *to accuse falsely* — gente de guerra, *to raise soldiers* — la tabla, *to take away after dinner*

Levantarse, *v. r. to rise up* || *to recover* || *to grow more* or *greater in any respect*

Levantarse a las estrellas, *to grow very haughty* — con algo, *to take possession of any thing* — de la cama, *to raise out of bed* — á mayores, *to take upon one* — el pueblo, *to mutiny* — del juego, *to give over play*

Levante, *s. mas. levant; east* || *the east-wend*

Estar de levante, *to be unsettled*

Levantisco, ca, } *adj. le-*
Levantino, na, } *vantine*

Levar el áncora, *to weigh anchor*

Leve, *a.* 2. *light*

Levedad, *s. m. lightness*

Levemente, *adv. lightly*

Levia'an, *s. m. leviathan*

Levita, *s. m. levite*

Levítico, *s.* [illegible]*cus*

Lexia, *s. f.* [illegible] *ash in*

Ley, *s. f.* [illegible]*lty* || *legality* || *goo*[illegible]*llay*

Leyenda, *s. f. reading* || *what is read*

Lia, *s. f. a withe of osier-twigs to bind with*

Lias, *pl husks of grapes*

Liar, *v. a. to bind; to tie*

Liarlas, *to fly secretly*

Libar, *v. a. to suck* || *to taste*

Libelar, *v. a. to draw petitions, declarations, etc.*

Libelático, ca, *adj. that denies his religion for fear of tortures*

Libelo, *s. mas. petition; memorial, etc.* || *libel*

Libelo infamatorio, *defamatory libel*

Liberal, *a.* 2. *liberal* || *quick; active*

Liberalidad, *s. f. liberality*

Liberalmente, *adv. liberally* || *quickly*

Libertad, *s. f. liberty* || *exemption; freedom*

Libertado, da, *adj. impudent*

Libertador, *s. m. deliverer*

Libertar, *v. a. to set free; to enfranchise* || *to free; to clear*

Libertino, *s. m. the son of a bond-man made free* [*west-wind*

Libicoáfrico, *s. masc. the*

Libiconoto, *s. masc. the south-west-wind*

Libidinoso, sa, adj. libidinous

treasurer

Librancista, *s. m. one who has an order to receive money* || *he that gives such orders*

Libranza, *s. f. V.* Libramiento

Librar, *v. a. to deliver; to free* || *to give an order* or *warrant for money* || *to give a nun leave to talk at te grate*

Librazo, *s. m. a great book*

Libre, *a. 2. free; clear* || *bold*

Librea, *s. f. livery*

Librear, *v. a to weigh* or *sell by pounds*

Libremente, *adv. freely*

Librería, *s. f. book-trade* || *a book-seller's shop* || *a library*

Librero, *s. m. a book-seller*

Libreta, *s. f. a little pound* || *a loaf one pound weight*

Librilla, *s. f. a little pound*

Librillo, ito, *s. m. a little*

fully

Licito, ta, *adj. lawful*

Licor, *s. m. liquor*

Lictor, *s. m. lictor*

Lid, *s. f. strife; contention; combat*

Lidiador, *s. masc. combatant; contender*

Lidiar, *v. n. to strive; to contend; to combat*

Liebraston, *s. m a leveret*

Liebre, *s. m. a hare* || *a coward*

Liendre, *s. f. a nit*

Liento, ta, *adj. moist; damp*

Lienzo, *s. m. linen-cloth* || *a handkerchief* || *a picture*

Lienzo listado, *striped linen* — de muralla, *a side* or *curtain of a vall*

Liga, *s. f. garter* || *birdlime* || *league; alliance* || *allaying of metals*

Ligadura, *s. f. ligature* || *a band* || *union*

that are fir

Ligio, *a. m.*

Ligula, *s. f.*

Ligustrino,

or *belongin*

vet

Ligustro, *s.*

Lila, *s. fem.*

Flanders

Lilac, *s. f. lil*

Lilao, *s. m. a*

tation

Lilayla, *s. f. a*

len-stuff ||

Lililies, *s. m.*

lilies

Lima, *s. fem.*

smiths use |

a lemon-tr

Limadura, *s.*

Limar, *v. act.*

polish

Limaza, *s. f.*

Limazo, *s. ma*

without she

Limbo, *s. m.*

|| *limb* || *the*

Limera, *s. fem*

, *a. circums-*
canty
nitado, *a nar-*
ed man
nea, *adj. bor-*
a. *to limit*
n. limit
mud; dirt
s. lemon || *le-*
|| *a shaft of a*
. f. lemonade
da, *adject. of*
our
s. m. a little
f. alms
s. m. alms-
[*ritable*
ra, *adj. cha-*
adj. limous
f. cleaning;
s. f. a brush
es, *s. mas. a*
er
. m. cleanser
, *adv. clean-*
ly
a. to clean;
r. to clear
of any accu-
f. cleanliness
[*neat*
adj. clean;
m. cleaning
er
n. lineage ||
m. genealo-
m. one that
ch of his fa-
[*aloes*
sc. lignum
flax-plot

Linaria, *s. fem. linaria; toad-flax*
Linaza, *s. f. linseed*
Lince, *s. m. lynx*
Lincurio, *s. m. a precious stone so called*
Lindamente, *adv. finely; curiously*
Lindar, *v. a. to limit; to bound* [*dary*
Linde, *s. 2. limit; boun-*
Linde, *a. 2. contiguous; bordering on*
Lindero, *s. m. boundary*
Linderos, *pl. signs; tokens*
Lindeza, *s. f. fineness; curiousness*
Lindo, da, *adject. fine; curious; beautiful* || *good; perfect*
Lindo, *s. m. a beau; a fop*
Linea, *s. f. line* || *limit; boundary* || *kind; sort*
Lineal, *a. 2. lineal*
Lineamiento, *s. m. lineament* [*lines*
Linear, *v. act. to draw*
Linfa, *s. f. lymph*
Linfático, ca, *adj. lymphatick*
Linguete, *s. m. the pawl of a capstern*
Linimento, *s. m. liniment*
Lino, *s. m. flax* || *linen* || *sail*
Lintel, *s. m. lintel*
Linterna, *s. f. lantern*
Linternero, *s. m. lantern-maker*
Liños, *s. m. pl. the rows in wich vines are planted*
Lio, *s. m. bundle; pack; fardle*
Liquable, *a. 2. liquable*
Liquacion, *s. f. liquation*
Liquar, } *v. act. to liquefy*
Liquefacer, }

Liquidacion, *s. f. settling; clearing*
Liquidambar, *s. masc. an odoriferous medicinal liquor*
Liquidamente, *adv. like a liquid*
Liquidar, *v. a to liquefy* || *to liquidate; to clear*
Líquido, da, *adj. liquid*
Liquor, *s. m. liquor*
Lira, *s. f. a lyre* || *a sort of poetical composition*
Lírico, ca, *adj. lyrick*
Lirio, *s. m. a lily*
Lirio cardeno, *the flower-de-luce*
Liron, *s. m. a dormouse*
Lirondo, da, *adj. pure; unmixed*
Mondo y lirondo, *adver. without mixture*
Lis (flor de), *s. f. a flower-de-luce*
Lisamente, *adv. smoothly* || *plainly*
Lisera, *s. f. a berm*
Lisiado, da, *adj. desirous*
Lisiar, *v. a. to hurt; to maim* [*plain*
Liso, sa, *adject. smooth* ||
Lisonja, *s. f. flattery*
Lisonjeador, *s. m. a flatterer*
Lisonjear, *v. a. to flatter*
Lisonjero, *s. m. a flatterer*
Lisonjero, ra, *adj. flattering*
Lista, *s. fem. a band* || *a stripe in a stuff* || *a list*
Listado, da, *adj. striped*
Listo, ta, *adject. ready; quick*
Liston, *s. m. a broad band or stripe* || *a kind of ribband*
Listoncillo, *s. m. a little ribband*

Listonería, *s. f. a bundle* or *knot of ribbands*
Lisura, *s. f. smoothness* || *plainness ; ingenuity*
Litargirio, *s. m. litharge*
Lite, *s. f. a suit of law*
Litéra, *s. f. a litter*
Literal, *a. 2. litteral*
Literalista, *s. m. one who undestands the litteral sense*
Literalmente, *adv. litterally*
Literario, ria, *a. literary*
Literato, ta, *adj. literate*
Literatura, *s. f. literature*
Litigante, *s. m. litigant*
Litigar, *v. a. to litigate*
Litigio, *s. m. litigation*
Litigioso, sa, *adj. litigious*
Litispendiancia, *s. f. litispendance*
Litócola, *s. f. lithocolium*
Liturgía, *s. f. liturgy*
Livianamente, *adv. lightly*
Liviandad, *s. f. lightness* || *levity* || *lasciviousness*
Liviano, na, *adj. light* || *lascivious*
Livianos, *s. m. plur. the lights*
Lixa, *s. f. the sea-dog*
Liza, *s. f. mil'er's thumb* || *the lists* (*to fight*)
Llaga, *s. f. a wound ; a sore*
Llagar, *v. a. to wound*
Llama, *s. f. flame*
Llamada, *s f. a call* || *a marginal note* || *the chamade*
Llamador, *s. m. a caller* || *a knocker*
Llamamiento, *s. m. calling* || *convocation* || *the drawing the humour to a place* || *inspiration*
Llamar, *v. a. to call* || *to convoke* || *to summon* || *to draw the humour to a place*
Llamar á la puerta, *to knock to the door*
Llamarse, *v. rec. to bear such a name*
Llamarada, *s. f. a flash of fire*
Llamativo, va, *adj. that provokes to drink ; salt*
Llana, *s. f. a trowel*
Llanada, *s. f. a plain*
Llanamente, *adv. plainly*
Llaneza, *s. f. plainness* || *incivility*
Llano, na, *adject. flat ; smooth ; even* || *plain* || *kind* || *uncourteous* || *fácil*
Carnero llano, *a wether-mutton*—hombre llano, *plebeian*
Llanta, *s. f. colewort*
Llantas, *pl. bands of iron about the wheels*
Llanten, *s. m. plantain*
Llanto, *s. m. weeping ; mourning*
Llanura, *s. f. fla'ness ; evenness* || *plainness*
Llares, *s. masc. pl pot-hangers*
Llave, *s. f. a key* || *a lock of a gun*
Llavero, *s. m. keeper of the keys* || *a key-chain*
Lleco, ca, *adj. untilled*
Llegada, *s. fem. arrival ; coming*
Llegar, *v. n. to arrive ; to come to...* || *to reach* || *to touch*
Llenamente, *adv. copiously*
Llenar, *v. a. to fill*
Llenarse, *v. r. to glut one's self* || to grow angry ; *to fret*
Lleno, s. *masc.* plenty ; *abundance* || perfection
Lleno, na, *adj. ful*
Hombre lleno, *learned man*— d *entirely* — dar d *to hit a thing fa*
Lleudar, *v. a. to p in dough*
Llevada, *s. f. the c*
Llevadero, ra, *ad portable* [
Llevador, *s. m. a*
Llevar, *v. a. to ca gather taxes* || or *produce* || *to* || *to draw to on nion* || *to guide,* || *to manage* ||
Llevar á cuestas, *on the back*
Llevarse, *v. r. to passion*
Lloradera, *s. f. a*
Lloradero, ra, *adj. table*
Llorador, *s. m. a*
Lloraduelos, *s. m weeps and crie ry turn*
Llorar, *v. a. to cry ; to lamen*
Lloro, *s masc. crying*
Lloron, *s. m. a c cries much* || *crying lubber*
Lloroso, a, *adj. mournful*
Llovediza (agua) *rain-water*
Llover, *v. n. to*
Llovioso, sa, *adj*
Llovizna, *s. f. rain*
Lloviznar, *v. n.*
Llueca (gallina) *brood-hen*
Lluvia, s. f. rai
Lluvioso, sa,
Loa, s. f. pr

mendation || prologue
Laable, a. 2. laudable
Laablemente, adv. laudably
Loador, s. m. panegyrist || flatterer
Loar, v. a. to praise
Loba, s. f. a she-wolf || a wide cassock without sleeves || a ridge between two furrows
Cerradura de loba, a stock-lock
Lobado, s. m. a particular swelling in the horses
Lobagante, s. m. a sort of sea-lobster
Lobanillo, s. m. a wen
Lobezno, s. m. a wolf's cub
Lobo, s. m. a wolf
Lobo marino, a sea-wolf || cerval, ó cervario, an ounce
Lóbrego, ga, adj. dark; dismal
Lobreguecer, v. n. to grow toward night
Lobreguez, s. f. darkness
Lobuno, na, adj. wolfish
Local, a. 2. local
Localidad, s. f. locality
Locamente, adv. madly || excessively
Locarias, s. m. a fool
Loco, ca, adject. mad || fool; rash || fertile, abundant
A' tontas y á locas, at random
Loco, s. m. a madman
Casa de locos, a madhouse
Locucion, s. f. locution
Locura, s. f. madness || foolery
Locutorio, s. m. locutory
Lodazal, s. mas. slough; mire
Lodo, s. m. mud; mire; dirt
Lodoso, sa, adj. muddy; miry
Logarítmico, ca, adj. logarithmick
Lógaritmos, s. m. pl. logarithms
Lógica, s. f. logick
Lógico, ca, adj. logical
Lógico, s. m. logician
Lograr, v. act. to get; to gain; to pucharse || to get good of.... || to attain its end
Lograrse, v. r. to obtain one's desire
Logrear, v. a. to lend money to use
Logreria, s. f. usury
Logrero, s. m. usurer || monopolist
Logro, s. m gain; lucre || interest; use || usury || possession; enjoyment
Dar á logro, to lend upon usury
Loma, s. f. a rige or top of a hill
Lombarda, s. f. a sort of cannon || a kind of cabbage
Lombardada, s. f. a shot of a lombarda
Lombardear, v. a. to shoot off a lombarda
Lombriguera, s. f. southern wood
Lombriz, s. f. a worm
Lomillo, s. masc. dim. de Lomo
Lominhiesto, ta, adj. long backed and upright || proud; haughty
Lomo, s. m. the loins || back; ridge, etc. || the wrong side
Lona, s. f. sail-cloth
Longa, s. fem. a long (in musick)
Longanimidad, s. f. longanimity
Longamino, na, a. patient; steady in the adversity
Longaniza, s. f. a great sausage
Longimetria, s. f. longimetry
Longinqüo, qüa, a. far; remote
Longitud, s. f. length || longitude
Longitudinal, a. 2. longitudinal
Longitudinalmente, adv. according the length
Longura, s. f. length
Lonja, s. fem. burse; exchange || a grocer's shop || a church-porch || a strap || a slice or cut || leash (in falconry)
Lonjero, } s. m. a grocer
Lonjista, }
Looc, s. m. a lohock
Loor, s. m. praise
Loquacidad, s. f. loquacity
Loquaz, a. 2. loquacious
Loquear, v. n. to extravagate || to play; to toy
Loquero, s. m. keeper of the mad-people
Loquesca, s. f. the behaviour of madmen
Loriga, s. fem. cuirass || verril
Lorigado, da, adj. armed with a cuirass
Lorigon, s. m. a strong cuirass
Loro, s. masc. a kind of parrot
Loro, ra, adj. yellow, of of a gold colour || darkbrown
Losa, s. fem. a flat broad stone || a sort of snare
Losange, s. m. lozenge
Losar, v. a. to pave with broad stones
Losilla, s. f. dim. de Losa
Loteria, s. f. lottery
Loto, s. m. lote-tree

Loxôdromica, s. f. loxodromy
Loza, s. f. earthen ware
Lozanear, v. n. to sport; to brisk one's self up
Lazania, s. f. the green of the plants || joy; gayety || vigour briskness
Lozano, na, adj. green || gay; brisk
Lúbrico, ca, adj. slippery
Lucerna f. a lamp
Lucérula, s. f. a plant so called
Lucero, s. mas. the morning-star | splendor; brightness
Lucha, s. f. wrestling || struggle
Luchador, s. m. a wrestler
Luchar, v. a. to wrestle || to struggle
Lucidamente adv. splendidly
Lúcido, da, adj. lucid
Luciente, a. 2. bright; shining
Luciérnaga, s. f. a glow-worm
Lucifer, s. m. Lucifer
Lucifero, ra, adject. that brings light
Lucifugo, ga, adject. that flies from the light
Lucillo, s. m. a tomb
Lucimiento, s. m. brightness; splendor
Lucio, cia, adj. bright; shining
Cascos lucios, an empty skull
Lucio, s. m. pike (fish)
Lucir, v. a. to shine
Lucirse, v. rec. to dress one's self with elegance, etc. [tive
Lucrativo, va, adj. lucrative
Lucro, s. m. lucre; gain
Luctuosa, s. f. in the fees

paid to the church at a funeral
Luctuosa, sa, adj. mournful
Lucubracion, s. f. lucubration
Lucubrar, v. a. to lucubrate [stock
Ludibrio, s. m laughing-
Ludir, v. neut. to rub against...
Luego, adv. immediately; by and by || then || therefore

cause; reason; matter || opportunity; time
Lugar comun, the house of office — lugares comunes, common places; topicks — en lugar, instead
Lugarcillo, } s. m. a little
Lugarillo, } village
Lugaron, s. mas. a great village
Lugarteniente, s. masc. a lieutenant
Lugubre, a. 2. lugubrious
Luir, v. n. to rub two things together
spoil them
Lumbrada, } s. f. a great
Lumbrarada, } fire
Lumbre, s. f. fire || brightness
Lumbres, tinder-box
Lumbre, } s. f. the sharp
Lumbrera, } pointed plait of a horse-shoe
Lumbrera, s. f. a light || a dormer-window; a loover [ry
Luminar, s. m. a luminary
Luminária, s. f. a publick illumination || bon fire || window

Luminoso, sa, adj. luminous
Luna, s. f. the moon || silver (in chymistry)
Luna de espejo, a looking glass
Lunacion, s. f. lunation
Lunada, s. f. a gammon of bacon
Lunar, s. m. a mole on the skin
Lunar, a. 2. lunar
Lunario, s. m. lunary
Lunático, ca, adj. lunatick
Lunes, m. monday
Luneta, s. f. a vault with small round windows
Lunetas, pl. the spots in a peacock's tail
Lúnula, s. f. lunula
Lupanar, s. m. brothel
Lupia, s. f. a wen
Lupino, na, adj. of, or belonging to a wolf
Luquete, s. m. a zest
Lustracion, s. f. lustration
Lustral, a. 2. lustral
Lustrar, v. a. to expiate or purify by lustrations || to set a gloss upon
Lustre, lustre gloss
Lustro, s. m. a lustrum
Lustrosamente, adver. brightly
Lustroso, sa, adj. glossy
Luteranismo s. m. lutheranism
Luto, s. m. mourning
Luxó, s. m. luxury
Luxuria, s. f. luxury lust
Luxuriar v. n to be lewd
Luxuriosamente adver. luxuriously
Luxurioso, sa, adj. luxurious lewd
Luz, s. f. light
Luces, pl. the light of a house [twilight
Entre dos luces, in the

M

ᴀcᴀ, s. f. a bruise in fruit || spot || cheat; ud
na, s. fem. a kind of oden weapon
reno, s. m. a bragg ng boasting fellow
rron, s. m. macaroon
rrónea, s. f. a macaonick poem
rrónico, ca, adj. macaronick
rse, v. r. to be corrupted by a bruise
ar, v. a. to beat with mallet
racion, s. f. maceration [rate
rar, v. a. to macerina, s. f. a saucer
' a chocolate dish
ro, s. m. mace-bearer
ta, s. f. a flower-pot
he handle of any tool
tas, pl. mallets (in a p)
aca, s. m. a troublesome, heavy fellow
acar, v. a. to pound; bruise || to molest; plague
acon, s. m. V. Maca
ado, s. m. a hatchet
ar, v. a. V. Machacar
etazo, s. m. a blow or und with the mate [cutlass
ete, s. mas. a sort of
o, s. m. male || a he le || a he goat || a at hammer or sledge he log on which the il is fixed || hook; v
a. m. strong

Machon, s. mas. a kind of pillar [ewe, etc
Machorra, s. f. a barren
Machota, s. f. } a kind of
Machote, s. m. } mallet
Machucadura, s. f. bruise; bruising
Machucar, v. a. to bruise
Machucho, cha, adj. ripe; prudent [lank || faded
Macilento. ta, adj. lean;
Macis, s. f. mace
Macizamente, adv. firmly; solidly
Macizar, v. act. to make solid or massive
Macizo, za, adj. massive, solid [heraldry)
Macle, s. m. mascle (in
Macocas, s. f. pl. a sort of great figs
Macolla, s. f. a bundle of spikes of corn, etc.
Mácula, s. f. stain; spot || blemish
Macular, v. a. to stain || to blemish
Maculatura, s. f. maculature [stains, etc.
Maculoso, sa, adj. full of
Madama, s. f. madam
Madamisela, s. f. a woman affected in her dress, etc.
Madera, s. f. wood; timber || an unripe fruit
Madera del ayre, the horn of any beast
Maderada, s. fem. raft of timber
Maderage, } s. mas. the
Maderámen, } wood-work of a building
Maderamiento, s. m. timber-work; wainscot, etc.
Maderar, v. a. to plank; to wainscot, etc.
Maderería, s. f. a timber-merchant's wood-yard
Maderero, s. m. a wood-monger. V. Maderista
Maderillo, s. m. dim. de Madero
Maderista, s. m. one who guides rafts of timber
Madero, s. m. a piece of timber
Madexa, s. f. skein || fillet; hair-lace || a lazy, dull person [skein
Madexuela, s. f. a little
Madona, s. f. madam
Madrastra, s. f. stepmother
Madre, s. f. a mother || the channel of a river || matrix || common sewer || a founder's mould [a mother
Madrear, v. n. to act like
Madrecilla, sub. fem. the womb of birds
Madreperla, s. f. mother of pearl [suckle
Madreselva, s. f. honey-
Madrigado (toro), s. m. a bull that has leaped the cows
Madrigal, s. m. madrigal
Madriguera, s. f. a burrow || a nest of thieves, etc.
Madrina, s. f. god-mother || protectrice || prop
Madriz, sub. f. matrix || metropola || the place where a quail has his nest
Madrona, s. f. a too much indulgent mother
Madroñal, s. m. a grove of arbute-trees [tree
Madroñero, s. m. arbute-
Madroño, s. m. arbute-tree || arbute-berry || the red colour
Madrugada, s. f. the break of day || an early rising
De madrugada, adver.

Maduramente, *adv. ripe-*
Madurar, *v. a. y n. to ripen* [*rative*
Madurativo, va, *a. matu-*
Madurez, *s. f. maturity; ripeness* [*ture*
Maduro, ra, *a. ripe; ma-*
Maese, *s. m. master*
Maesecoral, *s. m. leger de main*
Maestra, *s. f. mistress*
Maestral, *a. 2. magisterial*
Maestral, *s. m. the north-west-wind*
Maestralizar, *v. n. to decline to the west (speaking of the needle of the compass)*
Maestramente, *adv. masterly*
Maestrante, *s. m. a breaker of horses*
Maestranza, *s. f. an Academy; a riding-house || all the several trades that belong to the building of ships*

gisterial gravity, etc.
Maestro, *s. m. master || main top-mast*
Maestro, tra, *adj. first; main*
Magacen, *s. m. a magazine*
Maganto, ta, *adj. lean; pale-faced; ill-looked, etc.*
Magaña, *s. f. a defect in the inside of a cannon*
Magarza, *s. f. camomile*
Magdaleon, *s. m. magdaleon*
Magenca, *s. f. digging*
Magencar, *v. a. to dig the vineyards*
Magestad, *s. f. majesty || superiority; authority*
Magestuosamente, *adver. majestically*
Magestuosidad, *s. f. majesty; grandeur*
Magestuoso, sa, *adj. majestick*
Magia, *s. f. magick*
Mágico, *s. m. magician*
Mágico, ca, *a. magical*

Magníficamen
gnificently
Magnificar, *s*
Magnificat, *s. cat*
Magnificencia
Magnifico, ca
ficent
Magnitud, *s. f*
|| grandeu
Magno, na,
Mago, *s. m. among the a magicia*
Magro, gra,
Magro, *s. m.*
Magrujo, ja
Magüer, *adv*
Maguey, *s. aloes*
Magujo, *s. m on shipbo*
Magulladura
Magullamien
sing || bru
Magullar, *v.*
Maherimient
pressing

. m. a pestle ||
er || a block-
coxcomb
pl. bones (for
e)
s, f. pounding;

s, s. m. a silly
ome fellow
m.
for
. a. to pound;
|| to vex; to

, s. f. fresh pork
. a braggado-

. a. to put straps
oes
. f. haw-thorn-
strap
s. m. a vineyard
anted || a young

evil; ill || hurt;
ake; pain ||
|| sore
s, the pox
. ill
bad; ill
. the postman's
manill
da, s. f. a coarse
oth
e, adv. wickedly
za, s. f. misfor-

er

fling; quarrelsome, etc.

Malaventurado, da, *a. unfortunate*

Malbaratador, *s. m. a waster; a spendthrift*

Malbaratar, *v. a. to waste; to spend away || to di- disorder* [*ried*

Malcasado, da, *a. ill-ma-*

Malcocinado, *s. m. tripes; offal, etc.*

Malcomido, da, *a. hungry*

play at cards

Malcriado, da, *a. ill-bred*

adver.

a. wicked

Maldecimiento, *s. m. evil-speaking*

Maldecir, *v. a. to curse*

Maldiciente, *a.* 2. *evil-speaker.*

Maldicion, *s. f. malediction || a curse*

Maldito, ta, *a. maledicted*

ne

pervert;

to deprave

Malecon, *subs. m. dike; cause-way*

Maledicencia, *s. f. slander; detraction*

Maleficiar, *v. a. to vitiate; to adulterate || to bewitch*

Maleficio, *s. m. malefice*

Maléfico, ca, *a. malefick*

Maleta, *s. f. cloak-bag; portmanteau*

Maleton, *subs. m. aum. de* Maleta

Malevolencia, *s. f. malevolence; ill-will*

la, *a. malevo-*

f. wickedness

|| a place full of briars

Malgastar, *v. a. to lavish; to mispend*

Malhadado, da, *adj. unhappy*

Malhecho, *s. m. misdeed*

Malhecho, cha, *a. ill-done*

Malhechor, *s. m. malefactor*

Malherido, da, *a. dangerously wounded*

Malhojo, *s. m. riff-raff; sorry stuff*

Malicia, *s. f. malice*

Maliciar, *v. a. to vitiate; to adulterate*

Malicia, *v. n. to suspect*

Maliciosamente, *adv. maliciously*

Maliciosa, sa, *a. malicious*

Malignamente, *adv. maligny*

Malignidad, *s. fem. malignity*

Maligno, na, *a. malicious*

Malilla, *sub. f. manill || a tale-bearer*

Malla, *s. f. armour of mail || the mesh of the net*

Mallar, *v. a. to arm with a coat of mail*

Mallero, *sub. m. one who makes coats of mail*

Mallo, *s. m. mallet || mall*

Malmeter, *v. a. to waste; to squander away*

Malmirado, da, *a. uncourteous*

Malo, la, *adj. bad; ill || wicked naught || sick*

Ser malo, *to be wicked.*

Estar malo, *to be sick*

Malo! *int. so much the worse*

Malograr, *ver. a. to disappoint; to break the measures, etc.*

Malograrse, *v. r. to be disappointed*

Malogro, *subs. m. disappointment*

Malparar, *v. a. to hurt; to blemish*

Malparir, *v. a. to miscarry*

Malparto, *sub. m. miscarriage*

Malquerencia, *s. f. ill will*

Malquerer, *ver. a. to bear an ill will*

Malquistar, *v. a. to set together by the ears*

Malquistarse, *r. to be troublesome* or *insupportable*

Malquisto, ta, *a. hated*

Malrotar, *v. a. to waste, to squanders*

Malsin, *s. m. a tale-bearer; an informer*

Malsi ar, *v. to carry tales; to play the informer*

Malsindad, } **Malsineria**, } *s. f. a mischievious accusation* or *tale*

Maltratamiento, *s. m. ill usage*

Maltratar, *v. a. to misuse || to spoil; to rumple, etc.*

Maltrato, *s. m. misusage; abuse*

Malva, *s. f. mallows*

Malvadamente, *adv. wickedly*

Malvado, da, *a. wicked*

Malvar, *subs. m. a place where mallows grow*

Malvasia, *s. f. malmsey*

Malvavisco, *s. m. marsh-mallows*

Malvis, *s. m. mavis*

Mama, *s. f. a dug* or *teat || mamma*

Mamada, *subs. f. the time which a child sucks*

Mamadera, *s. f. a sucking bottle*

Mamador, *s. m. sucker*

Mamalmo, *s.* *booby*

Mamauton, n

Mamar, *v. n.*

Mamario, ria, *adj. mammary*

Circulo mamario, *areola*

Mamelmos, *s. m. pl. a kind of soldiers formerly in Egypt*

Mamila, *s. f. the fleshy part of the breast*

Mamilar, *a. 2. mammillary*

Mamola, *s. f. a chuck under the chin*

Hacer la mamola, *to coax to cheat*

Mamon, *m. an over-*

M

M

much

Mamotreto *s. m. memorandum-book; depositary, etc*

Mamparar, *s. f. folding-screen*

Mamparar, *v. a. to defend; to fence off*

Mamparo, *s m. a parrying with the hand*

Mamparos, *pl. the divisions of the cabbins in a ship*

Mampesado, *s. m. the night-mare*

Mampirlan, *s. m. a wooden step* or *stair*

Mamporro, *s. m. a blow given*

Mampost

made

stones and mortar

Mampostero, *s. m. a mason*

Mampuesto, *s. m. unhewed stones and mortu*

Mamujar, } **Mamullar**, } *v. a.*

herb

ning water

Manar, *v. n. to flow || to abound || to come from*

Manato, *s. m. a kind of sea-fish*

Manca, *s. f. the left-hand*

Mancar, *v. a. to maim || to fail; to fall short || to disable*

Manceba, *s. f. a concubin.*

Mancebia, *s. f. a bawdy-house*

Mancebo, *s. m. a young man || a bachelor || journey-man*

Mancera, *s. f. the plough tail*

Mancerina, *s. f. a saucer for a chocolate-dish*

Mancha, *s. f. a spot; stain || a blemish*

Manchar, *v. a. to spot, stain || to blemish*

Manchega, *s. f. worst of various colours for garters, etc.*

Mancilla, *s. f. a wound a sore || spot; blemi. || pity*

Manciparse, *v. r. to yield to subm*

Manco, ca, *a. lame of a hand* or *arm || defecti*

Mancomun, (**De**) *ad. jointly*

Mancomunarse, *v. r.*

; to len..

subs

tato

ada, *s. f. offer ; promise* || *a legacy*
adadera, *s. f. V.* Demandera
adadero, *s. m. a messenger* || *a street-porter*
adado, *s. m. a command* || *a message*
adamiento, *s. m. commandement*
s dies mandamientos, *the ten commandments*
adar, *v. a. to command* || *to offer* or *promise* || *to bequeath* || *to send*
adarria, *s. f. calking-mallet*
adatario, *s. m. a proxy*
adato, *s. m. command; commandment* || *the washing of the feet on maundy-thursday* || *a letter of attorney*
adil, *s. m. an apron* || *horse-cloth*
ndilejo, *s. m. a coarse ragged apron*
ndilon, *s. m. a coward*
ndo, *s. m. power ; authority* || *government ; management*
ndoble, *s. m. a two-handed blow* || *a severe reprehension*
ndon, *s. m. one who commands imperiously*
ndra, *s. f. a sheep-fold* || *a cottage*
ndrágora, *s. f. mandrake*
ndria, *s. f. a coward*
ndron, *s. m. stroke of a stone* or *ball*
nducar, *v. a. to eat*
nea, *s. f. locks (for horse's legs)*
near, *v. a. to shackle horse*
ecilla, *s. f. a. little hand* || *clasp of a book*

Manecillas de cabrito, *kid's feet*
Manejable, *a. 2. tractable*
Manei..., *v. a. to handle* || *... manage*
Manejarse, *v. r. to move one's self*
Manejo, *s. m. handling* || *manage* || *management*
Maneota, *subst. f. locks ; shackles*
Manera, *s. f. manner* || *pocket* || *the cod-piece*
Manero, ra, *adj. portable in the hand*
Maneruelo, la, *adj. dim.* de Manero
Manezuela, *s. f. a little hand*
Manfla, *s. f. concubine*
Manga, *s. f. a sleeve* || *a sort of portmanteau* || *a long file ; of soldiers, etc.* || *a net little a purse* || *a straining bag* || *a water-spout*
Manga de cruz, *a case of silk that hangs under a crucifix* — de pica, *the spear of a pike* — de broquel, *the handle of a buckler*
Mangajurro, *s. m. sleeve that covers the hands*
Manganilla, *s. f. a juggling trick*
Mango, *subst. m. handle ; helve*
Mangonada, *s. f. a thrust with the arm*
Mangonear, *v. n. to stroll idly about*
Mangorrero, ra, *adj. common ; in every hand* || *wandering ; strolling*
Cuchillo mangorrero, *a knife that has a bad haft*

Mangote, *s. mas. a great haft* or *handle*
Mangual, *s. m. a mace of arms*
Mangueras, *sub. fem. pl. pump-hoses*
Manguero, *s. m. chief; commander*
Mangueta, *s. f. a bladder, etc. to give a clyster with* || *an upright beam* or *post*
Manguitero, *s. m. maker of muffs*
Manguito, *s. m. a muff*
Manía, *s. f. madness* || *odd fancy*
Manía lupina, *lycanthropy*
Maniaco, ca, *adj. dull ; stupid*
Maniatar, *ver. a. to bind the hands*
Maniático, ca, *a. maniack*
Manicordio, *sub. mas. V.* Manacordio.
Manida, *s. f. abode*
Manifacero, ra, *a. turbulent ; busy-body*
Manifactura, *s. f. manufacture*
Manifestacion, *s. f. manifestation*
Manifestador, *s. mas. one who manifests*
Manifestamiento, *s. mas. manifestation*
Manifestar, *v. a. to manifest*
Manifiestamente, *ad. manifestly*
Manifiesto, ta, *a. manifest*
Manifiesto, *s. m. a manifesto*
Manija, *s. f. haft ; handle* || *locks ; shackles* || *verril*
Manijero, *sub. m. head-journeyman*
Manilla, *s. f. a bracelet* || *manacles ; hand-cuffs*

prodigal

Manirotura, s. f. *prodigality*

Manivacío, cia, a. *idle; out of work*

Manjar, s. m. *any meat*

Manjar blanco, *a white dish made of almonds and jelly*

Manjares, *plur. the four suits at cards*

Manjolar, v. a. *to carry a hawk on the fist*

Manlieva, s. f. *a tax paid out of hand*

Mano, s. f. *a hand || elephant's trunk || handful || pestle || a quire of paper*

Manos, *pl. the fore feet of a beast*

Manos de carnero, *trotters*

Manobre, s. m. *a labourer*

Manojear, v. a. *to divide by handfuls*

Manojo, s. m. *handful*

Manopla, s. f. *a gauntlet || hand-leather || a very*

ness of hands

Manquera, s f. *lameness || default*

Mansamente, *ad. meekly*

Mansedumbre, s. f. *meekness* [*bed-chamber*

Mansion, s. f. *mansion ||*

Manso, sa, *adj. meek; mild; tame*

Manso, *sub. m. the bell-bearer that leads the flock* [*suete*

Mansueto, ta, *adj. man-*

Manta, s. *fem. a woollen blanket || a horse-cloth || a piece of hangings || a mantelet for the sieges*)

Mantas, *pl. the principal feathers in the hawk's wings*

A' manta, ó á manta de dios, *plentifully*

Manteador, s. *mas. tosser in a blanket*

Manteamiento, s. m. *tossing in a blanket*

Mantear, v. a. *to toss in a*

Mantener su

keep one's w

Manteniente, s

downright s both hands

Mantenimiento

maintenanc

Manteo, s. m.

man's clok man's unde

Mantequora, s.

Mantequero, s.

seller

Mantequilla, s

cake of butt

Mantera, sub.

makes wome

Mantilla, s. f.

horse-cloth

Mantillas, pl.

clothes || chil

Mantillon, s.

ragged fell

Manto, s. m.

veil || a man pretence, et

Manton, sub.

mantle or c

Manumisor, *sub. m. one who manumits*
Manumitiente, *s. m. V.* Manumisor
Manumiso, sa, *adj. manumited* [*numit*
Manumitir, *v. a. to ma-*
Manus Christi, *sub. m. a kind of electuary*
Manuscrito, *s. m. a manuscript*
Manuscrito, ta, *a. writ by hand*
Manutencion, *s. f. maintenance* || *preserving; upholding*
Manutener, *v. a. to maintain* || *to preserve*
Manutisa, *sub. f. a small sort of pink*
Manzana, *s. f. an apple* || *a sword's pommel*
Manzanal, *sub. m. an orchard of apple-trees*
Manzanar, *s. m. V.* Manzanal [*mille*
Manzanilla, *sub. f. camo-*
Manzanilla bastarda *mandlin*—loca, *maywed*
Manzanillas, *plur. knobs on chairs, etc.*
Manzano, *s. m. an apple-tree*
Manzer, *s. m. the child of a common whore*
Maña, *s. f. handiness; dexterity* || *an ill habit* || *cheat; cunning* || *a bundle of hemp*
Mañana, *s. fem. the morning* [*row*
Mañana, *adver. to mor-*
Mañanar, *v. n. to come to the next day*
Mañanear, *v. act. V.* Madrugar
Mañanica, *s. f. the break of day*
Mañear, *v. a. to manage a business with dexterity*
Mañeró, ra *adj. active; busy* || *handy; dexterous* || *mild; tractable* || *bail; security*
Mañosamente, *adv. handily* || *cunningly*
Mañoso, sa, *a. handy* || *crafty; cunning*
Mañuela, *sub. f. a crafty trick*
Mañuelas, *pl. a sly cunning fellow*
Mapa, *s. f. a map*
Mapalia, *s. f. a cottage* || *a sheep-pen*
Maquila, *subs. f. miller's fee; multure*
Maquilandero, *sub. m. a vessel* or *measure for the miller's fee*
Maquilar, *v. act. to measure and reserve the miller's fee*
Maquilero, } *sub. m. one*
Maquilon, } *who measures at the mill*
Máquina, *s. f. machine; engine* [*chination*
Maquinacion, *s. fem. ma-*
Maquinar, *v. act. to machinate*
Maquinaria, *s. f. machinery* || *mechanicks*
Maquinete, *s. m. a sort of hatchet*
Maquínica, *s. f. mechanicks* [*nist*
Maquinista, *s. m. machi-*
Mar, *s. 2. the sea*
Mar en leche, *a calm* or *smooth sea* — ir de mar á mar, *to go in a great state*
Maraguto, *s. m. V.* Foque
Maraña, *s. f. a heath* || *an entangled skein of silk, etc.* || *intricacy*
Marañado, da, *a. entangled* [*dis*
Maravedi, *s. m. marave-*
Maravilla, *s. f. wonder* || *great night shade* || *melilot*
Maravillar, *v. a. to cause admiration*
Maravillarse, *ver. r. to wonder*
Maravillosamente, *adv. wonderfully*
Maravilloso, sa, *a. wonderful*
Marbete, *s. m. a piece of paper to mark cloth with*
Marca, *s. f. a mark; a note marches; bounds; limits* || *the measure* or *size of some things*
Espada de marca, *a sword of due size.* Papel de marca mayor, *the largess sort of paper*
Marcador, *s. m. a marker*
Marcar, *v. a. to mark*
Marcear, *v. act. to shear sheep in the month of march*
Marcha, *s. fem. march; marching* || *the signal with the drum to march*
Marchamar, *v. a. to mark goods in the custom-house*
Marchamero, *s. m. marker in the custom-house*
Marchamo, *sub. mas. the mark put upon goods*
Marchante, *s. m. V.* Merchante
Marchar, *v. n. to march*
Marchazo, *s. m. a braggadochio*
Marchitable, *adj 2. that will fade* [*to wither*
Marchitar, *v. a. to fade*

Marchitura, *s. f. fading; withering*
Marcial, *s. m. an odoriferous powder for gloves*
Marcial, *a. 2. martial*
Marco, *s. m. a frame || a mark (weight) || standard (for measures) || a shoemaker's size*
Marea, *s. f. a breeze blowing from the sea || the tide*
Mareado, da, *a. sea-sick*
Mareamiento, *s. m. sea-sickness*
Marear, *v. a. to guide a ship || to vex; to plague || to sell publickly*
Marearse, *v. r. to be sea-sick || to be damaged by sea-water*
Mareo, *s. m. sea-sickness || grief* [*to the sea*
Marero, ra, *a. belonging*
Mareta, *sub. f. a violent strong tide || a wind that rises by degrees*
Marfaga, *sub. f. counterpane*
Marfil, *s. m. ivory*
Marga, *s. f. mourning || coarse hempen-cloth*
Margarita, *s. f. a pearl*
Márgen, *sub. f. margin || bank; border, etc.*
Margenar, *v. a. V.* Marginar
Marginal, *a. 2. marginal*
Marginar, *v. a. to note in the margin*
Mária, *s. f. mary*
Marial, *s. m. a book containing the praises of the virgin mary*
Marial, *a. 2.* } *belonging to the blessed virgin mary*
Mariano, na, *a.* }
Marica, *s. f. a magpie || an effeminate fellow || a long thin asparagus* [*nate fellow*
Maricon, *s. m. an effemi-*
Maridable, *a. conjugal*
Maridage, *s. m. marriage*
Maridar, *v. n. to marry*
Maridillo, *sub. m. a little pitiful husband || a foot-stove*
Marido, *s. m. husband*
Marimacho, *s. m. a manly woman; a virago*
Marimanta, *s. fem. bull-beggar*
Marimorena, *s. f. quarrel*
Marina, *s. f. a sea-coast || the marine || a sea-piece* (*in painting*
Mariñage, *s. m. navigation; sailing || the men of a ship*
Marinería, *s. f. the sailing* or *piloting || sea affairs*
Marinero, *s. m. mariner; seaman*
Marinesco, ca, *a. belonging to mariners*
Marino, na, *a. belonging to the sea*
Marion, *sub. mas. a pike (fish) || a coward*
Mariposa, *s. f. a butterfly*
Mariposilla, *s. f. a little butterfly*
Mariscal, *s. m. marshal || farrier*
Mariscal de logis, *a quarter-master*
Mariscalía, *sub. f. marshalship*
Mariscar, *v. a. to gather shell-fish*
Marisco, *s. m. shell-fish*
Marisma, *sub. m. a lake* made by the water of *the see*
Marital, *a. 2* marital
Marítimo, ma, *a.* *ritime* [*lo*
Marlota, *s. fem.*
Marlotar, *v. a. t* *to squander*
Marmita, *s. porri* *kettle*
Marmiton, *s. m.* *lion*
Mármol, *s. m.*
Marmolejo, *s. m* *marble pillar*
Marmoleño, ña *marble || marl*
Marmolería, *s. f.* *marble*
Marmóreo, rea,
Marmota, *s. f. m*
Maroma, *s. f. cab*
Marques, *s. m. m*
Marquesa, *s. f.* *ness || a large put over a lent*
Marquesado, *sub* *quisate*
Marquesita, *s. f*
Marra, *s. fem.* *great iron sle*
Marraga, *s. fem* *woven with goat's hair ||*
Marrajo, *sub. m.* *sea-fish*
Marrajo, ja, *a.* *ning*
Marrana, *sub. f*
Marrano, *s. m* *hog*
Marrano, na, *a* *dicted; excommunicated*
Marrar, *v. a. to*
Marras, *adv. for*
La noche de ma *night past*
Marregon, *s. m.*
Marro, *s. m. a g* quoits || want (a sport)

ɪ qu oit
m. Turky
[tai
V. Maltro-
hore bound
. f. craft;
, a. crafty;
ɪ sea-hog ;
rten
rten-skin
. m. many-
ly || a sly
ow
ɪ. Mars (a
n. love; a
anxious
uesday
f. a blow
mer
ub. m. one
ith a ham-
[mer
ct. to ham-
a hammer
r, sub. m.
f. a kind of
m. egret ||
irginal) ||
of a paper-
tinete, *to*
f. cuisses
l
f. a poll-
artinmass
a martyr
n. martyr-
. to martyr
m. mar-

Marzadga, *s. f. a tribute paid in march*

Marzal, *a.* 2. *of*, or *belonging to, the mouth of march*

Marzo, *sub. mas. march (month)*

Mas, *adv. more || but*
A' lo mas, *at most.* A' mas andar, *with all speed*

Masa, *s. f. dough-paste || mortar || a mass; a lump*

Masar, *v. a. to knead*

Mascabado, (azúcar), *sub. m. the coarsest sort of sugar*

Mascada, } *s. f. chewing*
Mascadura, }

Mascar, *v. a. to chew*

Máscara, *s. f. a mask || a masquerader || a masquerade* [*mask*

Mascarilla, *sub. f. a little*

Mascaron, *s. m. a great frightful mask || an ugly face* [*culineness*

Masculinidad, *s. f. mas-*

Mascnlino, na, *adj. masculine*

Masecoral, } *s. m. V.* Macsecoral
Masicoral, }

Masteleros, *sub. m. pl. the top masts*

Masticar, *v. a. to chew*

Mastiles, *s. m. pl. masts of a ship || feet of a bed, etc.*

Mastin, *s. m. a mastiff*

Mastina, *s. f. a mastiff-bitch*

Masto, *sub. m. the tree on wich another is grafted*

Mastranzo, *sub. m. wild mint*

Mastuerzo, *s. m. garden-cresses* [*der*

Mastuerzo salvage, dittan-

Mata, *s. fem. a bush; a shrub || a set* or *plant*

Matacan, *sub. m. an old shifting hare || a poison to kill dogs || a painful labour || a game at cards*

Matacandelas, *sub. m. an extinguisher*

Matacandil, *s. m. a sort of lobster*

Matachin, *s. masc. matachin*

Matachines, *plur. matachin-dance*

Matadero, *s. m. slaughter-house*

Matador, *s. m. a murderer || matadore*

Matadura, *s. f. a hurt on a horse's back || a wearisome fellow*

Matafuegos, *sub. m. a fire man || a pump*

Matalahuga, *s. f. anise || anise-seed*

Matalon, *adj. m. a sorry horse; a jade*

Matalotage, *sub. m. the victuals put on board of a ship*

Matalote, *a. V.* Matalon

Matanza, *sub. f. killing || slaughter || obstinacy*

Matar, *ver. a. to kill || to put out a candle || to hurt* or *wring a horse's back || to tire a man || to urge earnestly*

Matarife, *s. m. a butcher*

Matarrata, *s. f. a game at cards*

Matasanos, *s. m. a quack*

Matasiete, *sub. m. a bragadochio*

Mate, *s. m. mate (at chess)*

Matearse, *v. r.* to spring up in stalks [*maticks*

Matemática, *s. f. mathe-*

Materialidad, s. f. materiality
Materialmente, adv. materially || coarsely
Maternal, a. 2. maternal
Maternidad, s. f. maternity [ternal
Materno, na, adj. mater-
Matigüelo, sub. m. a doll stuffed with straw
Matiz, s. m. shadowing
Matizar, v. a. to shadow; to variegate
Maton, s. m. a ruffian; a cut-throat
Matorral, sub. m. a place full of bushes or briars
Matoso, sa, adj. full of bushes, etc.
Matraca, sub. f. a wooden rattle || a scoff || a headstrong man
Matraquear, v. a. to scoff; to jeer [rer
Matraquista, s. m. a jee-
Matrero, ra, adj. sly; crafty
Matricaria, s. f. mother-

to the morning
Matutino, na, a. V. Matutinal
Estrella matutina, morning star [a cat
Mau, sub. m. mewing of
Maula, s. f. a thing found by chance, etc. || a cunning trick || a bad paymaster [knave
Buena maula, a rake; a
Maulería, s. fem. a shop where remnants of silk, etc. are sold || tricking; cheating
Maulero, sub. m. a piece-broker || a cheating fellow [wing cat
Maullador, sub. m. a me-
Maullar, v. n. to mew
Maullido, } sub. m. mewing
Maullo, }
Mausoleo, s. m. mausoleum
Maxilla, sub. f. a cheek; or cheek-bone
Máxima, s. f. maxim || || thought: opinion

ancestor
Mayor, s. f
. a syllogi
Mayoral, s
herdsma
Mayorana,
Mayorazgo,
an estat
sons || th
Mayorazgui
writer u
Mayordome
minister
Mayordomi
wardshi
Mayordome
ward || s
Mayoría, s
principa
V. Mayo
Mayorista
in the h
the gran
Mayormen
Maytinant
who ass
Maytines,
Mayúscula

s. fem. bread
soup given
ey slaves
b. m. march-

. a brick
. fem. a dun-

a. to squeeze
ith the fingers
. a mallet || a

da, *a. repre-*
alls, etc. (*in*
)
s. f. masonry
f. a spindle-
ear of corn
dj. 2. block-
wkward
, me
ó decir la) *to*
make water
as much as is
once
. m. a pissing-

the sperm of
|| an ancient
coin
. 2. belonging
in meaja
. to piss
b. f. a kind of

sub. f. mecha-
a mean base

ente, *adv. me-*
lly || basely
ca, *a. mecha-*
mean; base
z, *s. f. mean-*
|| a swing
, s. m. a cradle
. m. a stirring-
[ring
, s. f. the stir-
m. mecenas

Mecer, *ver. act. to stir* or *mix together || to rock*
Mecha, *sub. f. a wick || a match || a lunt || a tent for a wound || a bit of bacon to lard with*
Mechar, *ver. act. to lard fowls, etc.*
Mechera, *s. f. a larding-pin* [*lamp*
Mechero, *sub. m. pipe of*
Mechinal, *s. m. a scaffolding-hole*
Mechon, *sub. m. a great wick || a tuft of hair, etc.* [*tuft*
Mechonoillo, *s. m. a little*
Mecoacan, *s. m. mechoacan*
Meda, *s. f. a heap of sheaves, etc.*
Medalla, *s. f. a medal*
Medallon, *s. m. medallion*
Medar, *v. a. to heap up sheaves, etc.*
Medero, *s. m. a fagot of wine-branches*
Media, *s. f. a stocking*
Mediacion, *s. f. distance between two objects || mediation*
Mediador, *s. m. mediator*
Mediana, *sub. f. the flesh that is near the neck of the animal*
Medianamente, *adv. indifferently; so so*
Medianería, *sub. f. contiguity of two houses*
Medianero, *s. m. mediator*
Medianero, ra, *a. middle*
Pared medianera, *partition-wall*
Medianía, } *s. f. measure; mediocrity*
Medianidad, }
Medianista, *s. m. the student in one of the middle classes*

Mediano, na, *adj. middling; moderate*
Mediante, *ad. by means of*
Mediar, *v. n. to mediate; to interpose || to be between...*
Mediastino, *s. m. mediastin* [*diately*
Mediatamente, *adv. me-*
Mediato, ta, *a. mediate*
Medicable, *a. 2. medicable* [*cament*
Medicamento, *s. m. medi-*
Medicar, *v. a. to medicine*
Medicastro, *s. m. quack doctor*
Mediceas (planetas) *s. f. pl. satellites of Jupiter*
Medicina, *s. f. physick*
Medicinal, *adj. 2. medicinal*
Medicinar, *v. a. to medicine* [*cian*
Médico, *sub. m. a physi-*
Médico, ca, *a. medical*
Medida, *s. f. measure*
Medidor, *s. m. measurer*
Mediero, *sub. m. seller of stockings*
Medio, *sub. m. middle; midst || mean; medium*
Medios, *pl. means; riches*
Medio, dia, *adj. half || twin*
Medio cañon, *a demi-cannon* — dia, *noonday*
Mediocre, *adj. 2. mean; middling; moderate*
Mediocridad, *s. f. mediocrity*
Medir, *v. a. to measure || to scan a verse*
Medirse, *v. r. to moderate one's self*
Meditacion, *s. f. meditation*
Meditar, *v. a. to meditate*

[illegible], adv. mathematically

[illegible], s. m. mathematician; the material [illegible]

[illegible], adj. [illegible]

[illegible], s. f. matter [illegible]

[illegible], a. material

[illegible], a dull [illegible] man [illegible]

[illegible], s. f. materiality

[illegible], adv. materially [illegible]

[illegible], a. maternal

[illegible], s. f. maternity

[illegible], adj. [illegible]

[illegible], sub. m. a doll stuffed with straw

[illegible] s. m. [illegible]

[illegible] to [illegible]

[illegible] s. m. a [illegible]; a cut-throat

[illegible] in a place [illegible]

[illegible], adj. full of [illegible]

[illegible] sub. f. a [illegible] a stiff [illegible] strong man

[illegible]

[illegible], s. f. [illegible]

[illegible] the husband [illegible]

[illegible] s. f. matin, the [illegible] first draught [illegible]

[illegible] s. f. [illegible]

[illegible], adv. [illegible]

[illegible] s. m. [illegible]

[illegible] pl. [illegible]

[illegible] belonging to the morning

[illegible] sub. m. morning of [illegible]

[illegible], s. f. a thing found [illegible]

[illegible] s. f. in a shop where [illegible] all [illegible] cheating

[illegible] sub. m. a [illegible]

[illegible] s. f. maxim [illegible] thought; opinion

[illegible]

[illegible] s. m. [illegible] ships

[illegible] s. m. [illegible]

[illegible]

morra, s. fem. bread
at || the soup given
the galley slaves
apan, sub. m. marck-
ane
ari, s. m. a brick
morra, s. fem. a dun-
eon
mar, v. a. to squeeze
bruise with the fingers
to, s. m. a mallet || a
andle
tonado, da, a. repre-
enting walls, etc. (in
eraldry)
zonezia, s. f. masonry
zorca, s. f. a spindle-
ull || an ear of corn
zorral, adj. 2. block-
head; awkward
, pron., me
a (pedir ó decir la) to
want to make water
ada, s. f. as much as is
pissed at once
eadero, s. m. a pissing-
place
eaja, s. f. the sperm of
an egg || an ancient
spanish coin
eajal, a. 2. belonging
to the coin meaja
lear, v. a. to piss
leauca, sub. f. a kind of
duck
lecánica, sub. f. mecha-
nicks || a mean base
action
lecánicamente, adv. me-
chanically || basely
lecánico, ca, a. mecha-
nical || mean; base
lecaniquez, s. f. mean-
ness || a swing
lecedoro, s. m. a cradle
lecedor, s. m. a stirring-
staff [ring
lecedura, s. f. the stir-
cenas, s. m. mecenas

Mecer, ver. act. to stir or
mix together || to rock
Mecha, sub. f. a wick || a
match || a lunt || a tent
for a wound || a bit of
bacon to lard with
Mechar, ver. act. to lard
fowls, etc.
Mechera, s. f. a larding-
pin [lamp
Mechero, sub. m. pipe of
Mechinal, s. m. a scaffol-
ding-hole
Mechon, sub. m. a great
wick || a tuft of hair,
etc. [tuft
Mechoncillo, s. m. a little
Mecoacan, s. m. mechoa-
can
Meda, s. f. a heap of shea-
ves, etc.
Medalla, s. f. a medal
Medallon, s. m. medallion
Medar, v. a. to heap up
sheaves, etc.
Medero, s. m. a fagot of
wine-branches
Media, s. f. a stocking
Mediacion, s. f. distance
between two objects ||
mediation
Mediador, s. m. mediator
Mediana, sub. f. the flesh
that is near the neck
of the animal
Medianamente, adv. in-
differently; so so
Medianería, sub. f. conti-
guity of two houses
Medianero, s. m. mediator
Medianero, ra, a. middle
Pared medianera, parti-
tion-wall
Mediania, } s. f. mea-
Medianidad, } sure; me-
diocrity
Medianista, s. m. the stu-
dent in one of the mid-
dle classes

Mediano, na, adj. mid-
dling; moderate
Mediante, ad. by means of
Mediar, v. n. to mediate;
to interpose || to be bet-
ween...
Mediastino, s. m. medias-
tin [diately
Mediatamente, adv. me-
Mediato, ta, a. mediate
Medicable, a. 2. medica-
ble [cament
Medicamento, s. m. medi-
Medicar, v. a. to medicine
Medicastro, s. m. quack
doctor
Mediceas (planetas) s. f.
pl. satellites of Jupiter
Medicina, s. f. physick
Medicinal, adj. 2. medi-
cinal
Medicinar, v. a. to medi-
cine [cian
Médico, sub. m. a physi-
Médico, ca, a. medical
Medida, s. f. measure
Medidor, s. m. measurer
Mediero, sub. m. seller of
stockings
Medio, sub. m. middle;
midst || mean; me-
dium
Medios, pl. means; riches
Medio, dia, adj. half ||
twin
Medio cañon, a demi-
cannon — dia, noon-
day
Mediocre, adj. 2. mean;
middling; moderate
Mediocridad, s. f. medio-
crity
Medir, v. a. to measure
|| to scan a verse
Medirse, v. r. to moderate
one's self
Meditacion, s. f. medita-
tion
Meditar, v. a. to meditate

Medroso, sa, *a. fearful || frightful*
Medula, *s. f. marrow*
Medular, *a. 2. medullar*
Meduloso, sa, *adj. full of marrow*
Megido, da, *adj. mixed with water and sugar*
Mego, ga, *adj. gentle; mild, etc.*
Mejor, *a. 2. better*
Mejor, *adv. better*
Mejora, *s. fem. improvement || jointure*
Mejoramiento, *s. m. bettering*
Mejorana, *s. f. marjoram*
Mejorar, *v. a. to better; to improve || to give by way of advantage*
Mejorar, *v. n. to recover || to grow better*
Mejorarse, *ver. r. to put one's self in a better station*
Mejoría, *sub. f. improvemente || growing better*

they put under the yoke
Melenudo, da, *a. that has much hair*
Melero, *s. m. honey-seller || the place where honey is kept*
Melgacho, *s. m. sea-dog*
Melífero, ra, *a. melliferous* [*fluously*
Melifluamente, *adv. melli-*
Melifluo, flua, *adj. mellifluous*
Meliloto, *sub. m. melilot || a fool*
Melindre, *s. f. a sort of fritter || coyness*
Melindrear, *v. n. to prim; to coy*
Melindrero, ra, *a. prim; coy; precise*
Melindrillo, *s. m. a kind of thin lace*
Melindrisar, *v. a. V.* Melindrear [lindrero
Melindroso, sa, *a. V.* Me-
Mella, *sub. f. a gap in a knife, etc.*

Membrana, *s.*
brane
Membranoso,
braneous
Membrete, *s.*
sheet || a b
Membrilla, *s*
quince
Membrillar,
chard of
Membrillero
Membrillo
ce-tree
Membrudamen
Membrudo, d
limbed; st
Mementos, *s.*
mento
Memo, ma, *a.*
dull, etc.
Memorable, *a*
Memorando, d
rable
Memorar, *v. a*
Memoratísimo
very memo
Memoria, *s. f.*

, s. m. one that silk
s. m. the furni- a house
v. a. to wind silk
, s. f. mention
r, v. a. to men-
ion, s. f. beggary
ite, a. beggar
tes, pl. the men- friars
ad, s. f. mendi-
, v. a. to men- ; to beg
, s. m. a beggar
z, s. f. beggary
iente, adv. faul-
sa, adj. faulty
, s. m. a piece en bread
illo, s. m. dim. drugo
v. a. to stir; to to manage or
, v. r. to do any a hurry
. m. motion;
, s. m. want; ffice; employ- [sary
ster, it is neces-
s, pl. natural ies || the tools rkman
so, sa, a. needy
s. f. spoon meat
, sub. m. handy an
s. m. a rag
subs. f. defect; overty || sha- onour
nte, ad. igno-

Menguado, da, a. cowardly || silly; stupid || mad || stingy
Menguante, s. f. the ebbing of the sea || the decrease of the moon || decay
Menguar, v. n. to decrease || to decay || to want
Menino, s. m. a minion, at court
Meniscos, s. m. pl. lunula
Menjuí, s. m. benjamin
Menjurge, s. m. a mixture of diverse liquors
Menologio, s. m. menology [called
Menonia, s. f. a bird so
Menor, a. 2. less || minor (under age)
Menor, s. f. the minor of a syllogism
Menorete (al, ó por lo), adv. at the least
Menoría, s. f. minority
Ménos, adv. less
Menoscabador, s. m. one that impairs
Menoscabar, v. a. to impair
Menoscabo, s. m. impairing [piser
Menospreciador, s. m. des-
Menospreciar, v. act. to despise [sing
Menosprecio, s. m. despi-
Mensage, s. m. message
Mensagero, sub. m. messenger
Menstruacion, sub. f. the monthly courses of a woman
Menstrual, adj. 2. menstrual
Menstruar, v. n. to have the monthly courses
Menstruo, sub. m. a woman's monthly courses || a menstruum

Menstruo, ua, a. menstrual
Menstruosa, adj. f. with the monthly courses
Mensual, a. 2. monthly
Mensualmente, ad. monthly
Mensura, s. f. measure
Mensurable, a. 2. mensurable [rer
Mensurador, s. m. measu-
Mensurar, v. a. to measure
Menta, s. f. mint
Mental, a. 2. mental
Mentalmente adv. mentally
Mente, s. f. the mind
Mentecatería, s. f. folly
Mentecato, ta, a. fool
Mentidero, s. m. a place where the news-mongers meet
Mentir, v. a. to lie || to differ from...
Mentira, s. f. a lie || a fault (in printing)
Mentirilla, s. f. a little lie
Mentirosamente, adv. falsely
Mentiroso, sa, a. lying; liar || false; deceitful || faulty
Menuceles, s. m. pl. trifles
Menudamente adv. particularmente || by little and little
Menudear, v. a. to repeat again and again
Menudencia, s. f. littleness
Menudencias, pl. small matters
Menudillos, s. m. pl. giblets
Menudito, ta, adj. very small
Menudo, da, adj. small; slender || slight
Hombre menudo, a man

that looks into every little thing
A' menudo, *often.*—Por menudo, *by little and little*
Menudos, *pl. the pluck of any beast* || *small brass money*
Meollada, *s. f. fried brains*
Meollo, *s. m. marrow* || *brain* || *the kernel of a nut, etc.*
Meon, *s. m. who pisses often* [*body*
Mequetrefe, *s. m. a busy-*
Meramente, *adv. purely*
Merar, *v. act. to mix liquors*
Mercachifle, *s. m. a pedlar*
Mercadante, *s. m. a merchant*
Mercadear, *v. n. to trade; to traffick*
Mercader, *s. m. a merchant*
Mercadería, *subs. f. merchandise* || *trade*
Mercado, *s. m. a market*
Mercaduría, *s. f. V.* Mercadería
Mercancía, *sub, f. trade; traffick*
Mercancías, *plur. goods; commodities*
Mercante, *sub. m. a merchant* [*tile*
Mercantil, *a. 2. mercan-*
Navío mercantil, *a merchant ship*
Mercar, *v. a. to buy*
Merced, *sub. f. salary* || *reward* || *courtesy; favour* || *a title given in spain to every polite person* || *a religious order so called*
. Estar á merced, *to be at one's mercy*
Mercenario, *s. m. mercenary* || *a friar of the order* de la merced
Mercería, *s. f. mercery*
Mercero, *s. m. mercer; haberdasher*
Merchan } *s. m. a merchant*
Merchante }
Merculino, na, *a. belonging to wednesday*
Mercurial, *s. m. mercury (a plant)*
Mercurial, *a. 2. mercurial*
Mercurio, *s. m. mercury*
Merdelon, na, *adj. filthy*
Merdoso, sa, *adj. turdy*
Mere, *adv. merely*
Merecedor, *s. m. deserver*
Merecer, *v. a. to deserve; to merit*
Merecidamente, *ad. deservedly*
Merecido, *s. m. a deserved punishment*
Merecimiento, *s. m. merit*
Merendar, *v. act. to eat one's bever* || *to dine*
Merendero, *s. m. a crow who devours the seed on ploughed land*
Merendona, *s. f. a splendid bever*
Meretricio, cia, *a. meretricious*
Meretriz, *s. f. a whore*
Mergansar, *s. m. a kind of wild goose*
Mergo, *s. m. a puffin*
Meridiano, *s. m. meridian*
Meridiano, na, *a. belonging to the noon*
Meridional, *adj. 2. meridional*
Merienda, *sub. f. bever; collation* || *dinner* || *lunch*
Merindad, s. f. the office or jurisdiction of the Merino
Merino, *s. m. a sort of magistrate* || *overseer of the cattle and pasture*
Méritamente, *adv. deservedly*
Meritar, *v. a. to merit*
Meritísimo, ma, *a. very deserving*
Mérito, *s. m. merit; desert*
Meritorio, ria, *adj. meritorious*
Merla, *s. f. black-bird*
Merlon, *s. m. merlon (fortification)*
Merluza, *s. f. stock-fish*
Merma, *s. f. diminution; decrement*
Mermar, *v. act. to diminish; to decrease*
Mermelada, *s. f. marmalade* [*nu*
Mero, ra, *adj. pure;*
Mero, *s. m. a fish not like a perch*
Merria, *s. f. a sledge*
Mes, *s. m. a month* || *woman's course*
Mesa, *sub. f. a table* || *landing-place (in a stair-case)* || *a pla...* *the income of an a...* *etc.* || *a party, at ... liards*
Mesa de cambiador, *a ... ker's shop* or *coun...*
Mesada, *sub. f. mon... wages, etc.*
Mesadura, *s. f. the ... ling off of the ha...*
Mesana, *s. f. fore-m...*
Mesar, *v. a. to pull ... hair off*
Meseguero, *s. m. k... of the harvest, etc.*
Mesentérico, ca, *adj. ... senterick*
Mesenterio, *s. m. m...*
Meseraycas (venas) ... pl. mesaraick v...
Mesero, *s. m. a...*

craftsman who is paid so much monthly
Mesias, s. m. messiah
Mesiazgo, s. m. the dignity of the messiah
Mesilla, s. f. a little table
Mesnada, subs. f. an ancient company of men of arms
Mesnadero, s. m. the captain of such a company
Meson, s. m. an inn
Mesonage, s. m. a place where there are many inns [keeper
Mesonero, s. m. an inn-
Mesonista, a. 2. a servant in an inn
Mesta, s. f. assembly of the herdsmen
Mestal, s. m. uncultivated ground
Mesteño, ña, adj. belonging to the mesta
Mestizo, za, a. mongrel
Mesto, s. m. a sort of oak
Mestura, s. f. meslin
Mesturar, v. a. to mix
Mesura, s. f. modesty || courtesy [destly
Mesuradamente, adv. mo-
Mesurado, da, a. modest; grave || courteous
Mesurar, v. act. to make one behave modestly || to be cautious in one's actions, etc.
Meta, s. f. bound; limit
Metacarpo, s. m. metacarpus [sicks
Metafísica, s. f. metaphy-
Metafísico, ca, adj. metaphysick
Metáfora, s. f. metaphor
Metafóricamente, adver. metaphorically
Metafórico, ca, a. metaphorical
Metal, s. m. metal || latten || the sound of human voice || the quality of any thing
Metalario, s. m. one who works in the metals
Metalepsis, sub. f. metalepsis [lick
Metálico, ca, adj. metal-
Metalla, s. f. a bit of a leaf of gold
Metamorfósis, s. f. metamorphosis
Metanea, s. f. a figure in rhetorick so called
Metatésis, s. f. metathesis
Metedor, s. m. he who introduces, etc. || a smuggler || children's cloth
Metedurìa, s. f. the smuggling
Metemuertos, s. m. a servant on the stage || a pimp
Metempsícosis, s. f. metempsychosis
Metéoro, s. m. meteor
Meteorológico, ca, a. meteorological
Meter, v. a. to put in; to introduce, etc. || to smuggle
Meter paz, to part a fray
—zizaña, to sow discord
Meterse, ver. r. to intermeddle || to knit friendship with one || to sink in the mud || to disembogue one self [ful
Meticuloso, sa, adj. fear-
Metido, s. m. a lye made with urine and dove's dung
Metimiento, s. m. putting in, etc.
Metódicamente, adv. methodically
Metódico, ca, adj. methodical
Método, s. m. method
Metonimia, s. f. metonimy
Metopa, s. f. metope
Metralla, s. f. case-shot
Metresa, s. f. a sweet-heart
Metreta, s. f. a measure containing about twelve gallons
Métricamente, adv. metrically
Métrico, ca, a. metrical
Metrificador, s. m. a versifier [sify
Metrificar, v. a. to ver-
Metrista, s. m. a versifier
Metro, s. m. metre; verse
Metropoli, s. f. metropolis
Metropolitano, s. m. metropolitan
Metropolitano, na, adj. metropolitan
Mexilla, s. f. the cheek
Mezcla, s. f. mixture || variegation [tly
Mezcladamente, adv. mix-
Mezclador, s. m. a mingler || a tell tale
Mezcladura, s. f. } mixture
Mezclamiento, s. m. } mixture
Mezclar, v. a. to mix; to mingle || to set a variance
Mezclarse, v. r. to marry bellow one's self
Mezereon, s. m. mezereon
Mezquinamente, adv. stingily
Mezquindad, s. f. poverty || stinginess
Mezquino, na, adj. poor || stingy
Mezquita, s. f. a mosque
Mi, pron. my
Mi, s. m. mi (in musick
Miaja, s. f. a little crum or bit
Micho, s. m. puss; kitten
Mico, s. m. an ape
Microcosmos, sub. m. microcosm

Micrómetro, *sub. m. micrometer* [*cope*

Microscopio, *s. m. micros-*

Miedo, *s. m. fear*

Miel, *s. m. honey*

Mielga, *s. f. fodder* || *the sea-cat* || *a rake*

Miembrecito, *s. m. dim. de* Miembro

Miembro, *s. m. a limb*, or *member*

Mienta, *s. f. mint*

Miente, *s. f. mind*

Parar miéntes, *to take notice of.... to reflect on....*

Miéntras, *adv. whilst*

Miera, *s. f. oil of juniper*

Miércoles, *s. m. wednesday* [*wednesday*

Miércoles corvillo, *ash-*

Mierda, *s. f. turd*

Mierla, *s. f. black-bird*

Mies, *s. f. harvest*

Miga, *sub. f. a crum* or *crumb* || *a little bit* || *the principal substance of....*

Migas, *pl. a dish so called*

Migaja, *s. f. a small crum* or *bit* [*scraps*

Migajas, *pl. remnants;*

Migajada, *s. f. a small bit*

Migajon, *s. m. a piece of crumb without crust* || *substance*

Migajuela, *sub. f. a very little bit*

Migar, *v. a. to crumble*

Migratorio, ria, *adj. migratory*

Mijo, *s. m. millet* || *maize*

Mijo del sol, *ground sel*

Mil, *s. m. thousand*

Mil en rama, *milfoil*

Milgrero, *s. m. one who easily believes miracles*

Milagro, *s. m. miracle* || *voiive*

Milagrosamente, *adv. miraculously* [*lous*

Milagroso, sa, *a. miracu-*

Milano, *s. m. a kite*

Milanos, *pl. cat's-tails; ragged catkins*

Milenta, *s. f. thousand*

Milésimo, ma, *adj. thousand*

Milicia, *s. f. warfare* || *soldiery* || *militia*

Miliciano, na, *a. belonging to the militia*

Soldado miliciano, *a militia man.*

Militante, *a. 2. militant*

Militar, *a. 2. military*

Militar, *s. m. a soldier*

Militar, *v. a. to serve as a soldier* || *to prove*

Militarmente, *adv. militarily*

Milite, *s. m. soldier*

Milla, *s. f. a mile*

Millar, *s. m. a thousand* || *between three and four pounds of cocoa*

Millarada, *s. f. the quantity of one thousand*

Echar milaradas, *to boast of one's riches.*

Millon, *s. m. a million*

Milocha, *s. f. a comet*

Mimar, *v. a. to coax; to wheedle*

Mimbral, *s. m. an ozier-plot*

Mimbre, *s. m. ozier*

Mimbrear, *v. n. to work with oziers* || *to vibrate, brandish*

Mimbrera, *s. f.* } *an ozier-*
Mimbreral, *s. m.* } *plot*

Mimbroso, sa, *adj. made with oziers*

Mimo, *s. m. a mimick* || *coaxing* || *primming*

Mimoso, sa, *a. prim; coy*

Mina, *s. f. a mine* || *an attick coin* || *spring of water*

Minador, *s. m. a miner*

Minar, *v. act. to undermine* [*tals*

Minera, *s. f. mine of me-*

Mineral, *s. m. mineral* || *spring*

Mineral, *a. 2. mineral*

Minero, *s. m. a miner* || *mineral* || *spring*

Miniatura, *s. f. miniature*

Minimo, ma, *a. the least*

Mínimos, *s. m. pl. the minimes*

Minio, *s. m. minium*

Ministerio, *s. m. office; employment* || *ministry*

Ministrar, *v. a. to exercise an office* || *to give; to afford*

Ministril, *s. m. a subaltern minister* || *a minstrel* [*pipes*

Ministriles, *pl. musical*

Ministro, *s. m. minister*

Minorar, *v. a. to lessen*

Minorativo, va, *adj. lessening*

Minoridad, *s. f. minority*

Minotoro, *s. m. minotaur*

Minucia, *s. f. small tithe of fruits* || *trifle*

Minúscula, (letra), *s. f. small letter*

Minuta, *s. f. minute* (*in writing*) || *memorandum; depositary*

Minutar, *v. a. to minute*

Minuto, *s. m. minute* (*in a degree, etc.*)

Miñosa, *s. f. a worm*

Mio, mia, *pron. mine*

Mio, *s. m. puss*

Mira, *subs. f. the aim*, or *sight of a gun* || *intention; design*

Mirabel, *s. m. a sort yellow honey-suckl*

, *s. m. miro-*
mente, *adv. mi-*
ly [culous
, sa, *a. mira-*
f. look; ogle;

s. m. a place to
at
, *a. prudent*
s. m. spectator
y; mirador
s. f. looking ||

, *s. m. the em-*
the moors
o, *s. m. looking*
g
a. to look || *to*
to purpose || *to*
to value
m. sun-flower
, *s. m. a toy; a*

black-bird
o, *s. m. gravi-*
iseness
v. r. to be for-
ave, precise
. affected gra-
ck-bird
n. looker on
myrrh
a, *a. made or*
h myrrh
s. m. a sort

. myrtle
the mass.
o, *s. m. a priest*
his first mass
s. missal
m. a boy that
mass.
, *s. f. miscel-*

v. 2. miserable
nte, *adv. mi-*

Miserere, *s. m. procession in which is sung the plasm* miserere || *the twisting of the guts*
Miséria, *s. fem. misery* || *trifle* [*pity*
Misericordia, *s. f. mercy;*
Misericordiosamente, *adv. mercifully* [*ciful*
Misericordioso, sa, *a. merciful*
Mísero, ra, *a. miserable*
Misérrimo, ma, *adj. very miserable*
Mision, *s. f. mission*
Misionarío, } *s. m. missionary*
Misionero, }
Misiva (carta), *s. f. a missive letter*
Mismo, ma, *a. the same*
Misterio, *s. m. mystery*
Misteriosamente, *adver. mysteriously*
Misterioso, sa, *a. mysterious*
Mística, *s. fem. mystical theology*
Místicamente, *adv. mystically* [*cal*
Místico, ca, *adj. mysti*
Misticon, *s.m. one who affects mysticalness, etc.*
Mitad, *s. f. half; moiety*
Mitan, *s. m. a slight sort of holland*
Mitigacion, *s. f. mitigation*
Mitigador, *s. m. one who mitigates*
Mitigar, *v. a. to mitigate*
Mitigativo, va, *adj. mitigating*
Mitología, *s. f. mythology*
Mitológico, ca, *a. mythological* [*gist*
Mitólogo, *s. m. mytholo-*
Mitote, *s. m. an indian dance*
Mitra, *s. f. a mitre*
Mitrado, *a. m. mitred*

Mitridático, ca, *a. belonging to mithridate*
Mitridato, *s. m. mithridate*
Mixtifori, *a. of the secular and ecclesiastical competence*
Mixtilineo, nea, *a. mixtilineal*
Mixtion, *s. f. mixture*
Mixto, ta, *a. mixt*
Mixto, *s. m. a mixt body*
Mixtura, *s. f. mixture*
Mixturar, *v. act. to mix*
Miz, *s. m. puss*
Miz, mizo, *s. m. a cat*
Moble, *a. 2. moveable*
Mocadero, } *s. m. a handkerchief*
Mocador, }
Mocarro, *s. m. snot*
Mocear, *v. a. to act like young people*
Mocedad, *s. fem youth* || *folly of youth*
Moceton, na, *a. a lusty young fellow* or *girl*
Mochada, *s. fem. a blow with the head*
Mochar, *v. a. V.* Desmochar
Mochazo, *s. mas. a blow with the but-end of a musket*
Mocheta, *s. f. the chapiter of a pillar*
Mochil, *s. m. a boy that serves the husbandmen*
Mochila, *s. f. a kind of caparison* || *a portmanteau*
Mochiler, } *s. m. a boy that follows the camp.*
Mochilero, }
Mochin, *s. m. the hangman*
Mocho, cha, *adj. bare; smooth* || *shaved*
Carnero mocho, a sheep that has the horns cut

candle) || *recrement of iron*
Mocoso, sa, *adj. snotty* || *contemptible*
Moda, *s. f. mode ; fashion*
Modal, *a.* 2. *modal*
Modal, *s. m. any particular quality* or *manner*
Modelo, *s. m. model*
Moderacion, *s. f. moderation* || *abatement*
Moderadamente, *adv. moderately* [*rate*
Moderado, da, *adj. mode-*
Moderador, *s. m. moderator*
Moderar, *v. a. to moderate* || *to abate*
Moderarse, *v. a. to countain one's self.*
Moderatorio, ria, *a. which can moderate* [*ly*
Modernamente, *adv. new-*
Moderno, na, *a. modern*
Modestamente, *adv. modestly*
Modestia, *s. f. modesty*
Modesto, ta, *a. modest*

fruits)
Modorrilla, *s. f. the third watch of the night* || *a disease among the sheep*
Modorro, ra, *a. drowsy* || *dully ; stupid*
Modrego, *s. m. a dunce ; a block-head*
Modulacion, *s. f. modulation*
Modular, *v. n. to modulate* [*melody*
Módulo, *s. m. module* ||
Modurria, *s. f. folly ; foppery*
Moeda, *s. f. an old grove of oaks*
Mofa, *s. f. scoff; jeer*
Mofador, *s. m. scoffer ; jeerer*
Mofadura, *s. f. jeering*
Mofante, *s. m. V.* Mofador
Mofar, *v. a. to scoff; to jeer* [*up cheeks*
Mofletes, *s. m. pl. puffed*
Moga, *s. f. money*
Mogate, *s. masc. glazing*

Mobarra, *s. f*
a pike, etc
Moharrache }
Moharracho }
Mohatra, *s. f*
Mohatrar, *v.*
ve price, a
Mohatrero, r
sells abov
buys unde
Mohecer, *v.*
Mohina, *s. f.*
gust
Mohino, na,
Macho mohi
born of a
she-ass.
Mohino, *sub.*
plays alone
ny others
Moho, *s. m.*
diness || *id*
Mohoso, sa,
Mojada, *sub.*
wetting ||
wound wi
weapon

the measure mojona || *a measure used in castile* || *setting of land-marks*
Mojonar, *v. a. to set land-marks*
Mojonera, *s. f. the place where the land-mark stands*
Mojonero, *s. m. a sort of excise-man*
Mola, *s. f. a moon-calf*
Molada, *s. f. the quantity of colour ground at one time*
Molar, *a.* 2. *belonging to a mill-stone*
Moldar, *v. a. to mould*
Molde, *s. m. a mould* || *a printer's form*
Libro de molde, *a printed book*
Moldear, *v. a. to mould*
Moldura, *s. f. a moulding*
Mole, *s. f. a mass; a lump*
Mole, *a.* 2. *soft; mellow* || *slow; sluggish*
Moledor, *s. m. a grinder* || *a troublesome person*
Moledura, *s. f. grinding*
Molendero, *s. m. grinder*
Moler, *v. a. to grind* || *to chew to tire, to vex*
Molestador, *s. m. molester*
Molestamente, *adv. troublesomely*
Molestar, *v. a. to molest*
Molestia, *s. f. pain; grief*
Molesto, ta, *adj. troublesome*
Moleta, *s. f. a little grind* || *a painter's mullar*
Molicie, *s. f. softeness* || *effeminacy*
Molienda, *s. f. grinding* || *grist* || *weariness*
Molificar, *v. a. to mollify*
Molimiento, *s. m. grinding* || *pounding* || *weariness*

Molinero *s. m. miller*
Molinero, ra, *a. belonging to the mill* || *to be grinded*
Molinete, *subs. m. a little mill* || *a turnstile*
Molinillo, *s. m. a coffee-mill* || *a chocolate-stick*
Molino, *s. m a mill*
Molino de viento, *a wind mill* — de sangre, *the mill moved by men* or *beasts*
Molla, *s. f. crumb of bread*
Mollar, *a.* 2. *soft; tender* || *credulous*
Mollear, *ver. n. to grow soft; to give over*
Molledo, *s. m. brawniness*
Molleja, *subs. f. calve's sweet-bread* || *gizzard*
Mollejon, *sub. m. aum.* de Molleja || *a fat lazy fellow*
Mollejuela, *s. f. dim de* Molleja
Mollentar, *v. a. to soften*
Mollera, *s f. the mould of the head*
Molleta, *s. f. snuffers* || *a loaf of flower*
Mollete, *s. m. manchet*
Molletes, *pl. fat cheeks*
Mollina / Mollizna, *s. f. a soft shower of rain*
Molliznar / Mollizncar, *v. n. to rain softly and small*
Mollondro / Mollondron, *s. m. a dull, heavy fellow*
Moloso, *sub. m. a foot in latin poetry*
Moltura, *s. f. miller's fee*
Momarracho, *subs. m. a ridiculous* or *hideous masker*
Momentaneamente, *adv. momentally*
Momentaneo, nea, *a. momentary*

Momento, *s. m. moment*
Momeria, *s. f. mommery*
Momio, mia, *adj. lean; scraggy*
Carne momia, *mummy*
Momo, *s. m. a ridiculous gesticulation, etc.*
Hacer se momo, *to hold all stakes*
Momperada, *adj. f. fine; shining well-calendered*
Mona, *s f. she monkey*
Monacal, *a.* 2. *monachal*
Monacato, *sub. m. monachism*
Monacillo, *s. m. a boy that serves at the altar, in a convent*
Monacordio, *s. m. claricord* || *monochord*
Monada, *subs. f. an apish trick*
Monago, *s. m. a monk*
Monaguillo, *s. m. V.* Monacillo
Monaquismo, *s. m. monachism*
Monarca, *s. m. a monarch*
Monarquía, *s. f. monarchy*
Monárquico, ca, *a. monarchical*
Monasterio, *s. m. a monastery*
Monástico, ca, *a. monastick*
Monda, *s. f. the pruning of trees* || *cleaning*
Mondadientes, *sub. m. a tooth-picker*
Mondadura, *s. f. picking; cleansing*
Mondaorejas, *s. m. an ear picker*
Mondar, *v. a. to pick; to cleanse* || *to shell nuts, etc.* || *to shave, etc.*
Mondejo, *s. m. a paunch of hog stuffed*
Mondo, da, *a. clean; pur*
Mondonga, *s. f. a serv of the queen's ladi*

Moneda, *s. f. money; coin*
Monedar } *v. a. to coin*
Monedear } *money*
Monedero, *s. m. coiner*
Monería, *subs. f. an apish trick*
Monesco, ca, *a. apish*
Monetario, *s. m. a chest. etc. to keep ancient coins in*
Monfies, *s. m. pl. robbers on the hills*
Monge, *s. m. a monk*
Mongia, *s. f. monachism || a monachal prebend, etc.*
Mongil, *s. m. a nun's habit || mourning weeds for a woman*
Mongío, *s. m. the state of a nun || a cloathing, in a nunnery*
Monicion, *s. f. monition || publication of matrimony*
Monigote, *s. m. a lay friar*
Monillo, *s. m. a woman's jumps without sleeves*

with one wheel in it
Monopetálo, la, *a. monopetalous* [*ly*
Monopolio, *s. m. monopo-*
Monosilabo, ba, *a. monosyllabical*
Monóstrofe, *s. m. a song containing but one stanza*
Monseñor, *s. m. mylord*
Monsiur, *s. m. sir*
Monstruo, *s. m. a monster*
Monstruosamente, *adver. monstrously*
Monstruosidad, *s. f. monstrousness*
Monstruoso, sa, *a. monstrous*
Monta, *s. f. amount; total || intrinsick value || the sounding to horse. || V.* Acaballadero
Montàdero, *s. m. V.* Montador
Montado, *s. m. a horseman || a harnassed horse*
Montador, *s. m. one who*

armed with
handed swor
Montaña, *s. f. a*
Montañes, sa,
taineer
Montañeta, *sub*
mountain
Montañoso, sa,
Montar, *v. n. t*
to amount ||
Montaraz, *a.*
taineer || wil
Montas, *adv. in*
thoug
Montazgar, *v.*
or *pay the* mo
Montazgo, *subs*
paid for the
the flocks
Monte, *subs. m*
mountain || a
great head of
stock at card
Monte de piedad
house; pawn
Montea, *s. f. th*
of stones || or
cal draught

, s. m. a huntsman
a. 2. living in the
tains
ontes, a wild cat
, sub. f. a certain
of knights
no, na, adj. V.
s
s. m. V. Monta
, s. m. a heap || a
nasty fellow
o, sa, adj. moun-
us
, s. f. a beast for
addle
ento, s. m. monu-

, s. m. monsoon
s. f. a doll repre-
ng the fashions ||
| drunkeness
. m. the knot that
up the women's
| crest; tuft
, da, adj. tufted;
d.
r, ver. n. to blow
nose [chief
o, s. m. handker-
e, subs. m. a blow
the fist upon the

ear, v. a. to blow
nose very often
earse, v. r. to cuff
nother
ró, ra, a. snotty
o, sub. m. dim. de
|| pip (in birds)
, s. f. snivel
ubs. f. mulberry ||

o, s. m. a maho-
n sectary
o, cha, adj. dark-
t
, s. f. a dwelling-

da, a. purple

Morador, s. m. dweller
Moral, sub. m. mulberry-tree
Moral, s. f. morality
Moral, a. 2. moral
Moraleja, subs. f. moral; morality
Moralidad, s. f. morality
Moralista, s. m. moralist
Moralizar, v. a. to moralise
Moralmente, adv. morally
Morar, v. n. to dwell
Moratoria, sub. f. respite; delay
Morbidez, s. f. softness of the flesh (in painting)
Mórbido, da, a. morbid
Morbífico, ca, adj. morbifick
Morbo, s. m. sickness; disease
Morbo caduco, the falling-sickness — galico, the french-disease
Morboso, sa, a. sick; ill || unwholesome
Morcella, sub. f. a spark from the candle
Morcilla, subs. f. a hog's pudding
Morcillero, s. m. one who makes or sells black puddings
Morcillo, s. m. muscle
Morcillo (caballo), s. m. a black horse
Morcon, subs. m. a great pudding || a fat unwieldy fellow
Mordacidad, s. f. mordacity
Mordante, s. m. a printer's visorium
Mordaz, a. 2. mordacious
Mordaza, s. f. a gag
Mordazmente, adv. railingly; sharply
Mordedor, s. m. biter
Mordedura, s. f. a bite

Morder, v. a. to bite || to prick
Mordicacion, sub. f. prickings
Mordicar, v. a. to prick
Mordido, s. m. a bit taken off with the teeth
Mordiente, s. m. a gilder's varnish
Mordihui, s. m. a weevil
Mordimiento, s. m. a bite
Mordiscar, v. a. to bite; to nibble
Mordisco, } s. m. a bite
Mordiscon, } || a bit
Morel de sal, s. m. a dark brown colour
Morena, s. f. a brown loaf
Morenillo, ito, adj. of a brown colour
Morenillo, s. m. a black powder used by the sheaters of sheep
Moreno, na, adj. dark-brown
Morera, s. f. white mulberry-tree
Morería, s. f. the Moors quarter
Morfex, s. m. a cormorant
Morga, s. f. dross of the oil
Moribundo, da, adj. in a dying condition
Moriego, ga, a. Moorish
Morigeracion, s. f. moderation in living
Morigerar, v. a. to tutor; to bring up
Morillo, sub. m. a little moor || an andiron
Morir, v. n. to die
Morirse, v. r. to grow stiff
Morisco, ca, a. Moorish
Moriscos, s. m. pl. men descended from Moors
Morisma, s. m. the Moorish religion || a multitude of Moors

Moro, *s. m. a Moor*
Moro, *a. m. that has no water in it (speaking of wine)*
Morocada, *sub. f. a blow given by a ram with the head*
Moron, *s. m. a little hillock*
Moroncho, cha, *adj. V.* Morondo
Morondanga, *s. f. an heap of rubbish, etc.*
Morondo, da, *adj. bald || bare* [nía
Moronía, *s. f. V.* Alboro-
Morosamente, *ad. slowly*
Morosidad, *s. f. slowness*
Moroso, sa, *a. slow; heavy*
Morquera, *s. f. a sort of thyme*
Morra, *sub. f. the upper part of the head || mora (a game)*
Morrada, *sub. f. a blow with the head*
Morral, *s. m. a sort of bag to feed a horse as*

Mortal, *a. 2. mortal*
Mortalidad, *s. f. mortality* [*tally*
Mortalmente, *adv. mor-*
Mortandad, *s. f. mortality (plague, etc.)*
Mortecino, na, *adj. that dies of itself*
Morterada, *s. f. a kind of sauce*
Morterete, *s. m. a very small sort of cannon* or *mortar*
Mortero, *s. m. a mortar*
Morteruelo, *s. m. a small sort of instrument like a mortar*
Morteruelos, *pl. a hog's liver dissolved with lard, salt, etc.*
Morticinio, *s. m. morkin*
Mortífero, ra, *adj. mortiferous* [*fication*
Mortificacion, *s. f. morti-*
Mortificar, *v. a. to mortify*
Mortuorio, *s. m. a funeral*
Morueco, *s. m. a ram*
Mórula, *s. f. a short delay*

Mosquear, *v.* ...
flies away
Mosqueo, *s.* ...
ving the flie...
Mosquero, *s.* ...
hanged for ...
settle on
Mosqueruela, *s* ...
of sweet-scen...
Mosqueta, *s. f.* ...
Mosquetazo, *s.* ...
shot
Mosquete, *s. m*...
Mosquetería, ...
of musketeer...
(in a play-...
Mosqueteril, *a* ...
ging to the ...
Mosquetero, *s.* ...
keteer || he ...
in the pit
Mosquil, *a. 2.* ...
Mosquino, na, ...
adj.
Mosquitero, *s.* ...
curtain
Mosquito, *s. m* ...
a perpetual

s. m. mustard-
thick must
v. n. to distil;
new wine || to
must into casks
. f. a bundle of
igs
, s. f. the place
he vine-twigs

sub. m. a cake
with must and
[wine
m. must; new
, a. 2. that may
n
, s. m. teacher
; gnomon || a
; a shew-glass,

v. a. to show
, ca a. strayed
ignorant
a mote; a lit-
in a cloth, etc.
s. m. the clerk
market
s. f. a wag-tail
m. a motto || a
ame
. a. to variega-
little tufts
, s. m. scoffer
v. a. to scoff; to

. m. anthem
ver. a. to cut
air
s. m. a lay-friar
. m. mutiny
v. a. to relate
otive || to give
on
s. m. motive
a, a. that moves
s. f. wag-tail
ta, } adj. easy
, } to be de-
ceived

Motonería, *s. f. assemblage of pullies*
Motones, *s. m. pl. the pullies in a ship*
Motor, *s. m. motor*
Motril, *s. m. V.* Mochil
Motriz, *adj. f. motive*
Motu proprio, *adv. of his own will*
Movedizo, za, *adj. moveable; unstable*
Movedor, *s. m. mover*
Mover, *v. a. to move || to stir || to miscarry*
Movible, *a. 2. moveable*
Móvil, *a. 2. moveable*
Móvil, *s. m. mobile*
Primer móvil, *primum mobile*
Movilidad, *s. f. mobility*
Movimiento, *s. masc. motion*
Moyana, *subs. f. a small sort of culverin || bran-bread*
Moyo, *s. m. a bushel*
Moyuelo, *s. m. a middle sort of bran*
Mozalbete, } *s. m. a young*
Mozalbillo, } *man*
Mozallon, *s. m. a robust young man*
Mozarabes, *subst. m. pl. Christians that lived among the Moors*
Mozcorra, *s. f. a common whore*
Moznado, da, *adj. that has neither teeth, tongue, nor claws (in blasonry)*
Mozo, za, *adj. young*
Mozo, *s. m. a servant || a street-porter || a bachelor || a cat || a beetle*
Mozuelo, *s. m. a robust young man*
Mozuelo, *s. m. a boy*
Mu, *s. f. sleep (a childish word) || lowing of a cow, etc.*
Muceta, *s. f. bishop's camail*
Muchacha, *s. f. a girl*
Muchachada, *sub. f. childishness*
Muchachear, *v. a. to act in a childish manner*
Muchachería, *s. f. childishness || a company of children*
Muchachez, *s. f. childhood*
Muchacho, *s. m. a boy*
Muchedumbre, *s. f. multitude*
Mucho, cha, *adj. abundant; numerous*
Mucho, *adv. much*
Mucilago, *s. m. mucilage*
Muda, *s. f. change || a sort of women's paint || moulting of birds || mew; coop*
Mudable, *a. 2. mutable*
Mudamente, *ad. dumbly*
Mudanza, *s. f. change*
Mudar, *v. a. to change || to moult* or *mew*
Mudarse, *v. r. to remove house*
Mudez, *s. f. dumbness*
Mudo, da, *adj. dumb*
Mue, *s. m. mohair*
Mueble, *a. 2. moveable*
Muebles, *s. m. pl. goods moveables*
Mueca, *subs. f. gesture; grimace*
Muela, *s. f. a grind-stone || a mill-stone || hillock*
Muelas, *p. the grinders*
Muelle, *s. m. spring (in any machine) || a mole (in the sea)*
Muelle, *a. 2. soft; tender*
Muellemente, *adv. softly*
Muer, *s. m. mohair*
Muérdago, *s. m. mistletoe*

Muermo, s. m. glanders (in a horse)
Muermoso, sa, adj. that has the glanders
Muerte, subs. f. death || murder || skeleton
Muerto, s. m. a dead man
Muerto, ta, p. p. dead
Muesca, s. f. notch
Muestra, s. f. show; sample || pattern; model || token || muster || a dial || a watch
Mufla, s. f. the cover of a refiner's furnace
Muga, s. f. bound; limit
Muger, sub. f. woman || wife
Mugercilla, s. f. a silly mean woman
Mugeriego, ga, adj. feminine || womanish
Mugeriego, s. m. the women of a place
Mugeril, a. 2. womanish
Mugerilmente, adv. womanly
Mugido, s. m. lowing
Mugil, s. m. mullet (a fish)
Mugir, v. n. to low
Mugre, s. f. greasiness; nastiness
Mugriento, ta, adj. greasy; nasty [vine
Mugron, s. m. layer of a
Muharra, s. f. the head of a pike, etc.
Muir, v. a. to milk
Mujol, s. m. mullet
Mula, s. f. a she-mule
Muladar, s. m. a dung-hill [to a mule
Mular, a. 2. belonging
Mulatero, s. m. muleteer
Mulato, ta, adj. mulatto
Mulero, sub. m. servant who takes care of the mules

Muleta, subs. f. a little young she-mule || a crutch
Muletada, s. f. a herd of mules [driver
Muletero, s. m. a mule-
Muleto, s. m. a little he-mule
Mulilla, s. f. a buskin
Mulla, s. f. a digging
Mullidor, s. m. one who makes soft || beadle
Mullir, v. a. to make soft || to dig or turn up the earth || to convoke
Mulo, s. m. a he-mule
Multa, s. f. a mulct; a fine [fine
Multar, v. a. to mulct, or
Multiforme, a. 2. multiform
Multilátero, ra, adj. that has many sides
Multiplicable, a. 2. multipliable [tiplication
Multiplicacion, s. f. mul-
Multiplicador, s. m. multiplicator || multiplier
Multiplicar, v. a. y n. to multiply
Multíplice, a. 2. manifold
Multiplicidad, s. f. multiplicity
Multíplico, s. m. multiplication
Multitud, s. f. multitude
Mundano, na, a. } worldly
Mundial, a. 2. }
Mundificar, v. a. to mundify
Mundificativo, va, adjec. mundificative
Mundillo, s. m. a warming-pan || a lace-maker's cushion
Mundinovi, } s. m. a raree-show
Mundinuevo, }
Mundo, s. m. the world
Municion, s. f. ammuni-

tion || the gun
De municion
Municionar, with ammu
Municipal, a pal
Municipe, s.
Municipio, s. or town municipiu
Munificencia ficence
Munífico, ca,
Muniteria, s. fortifying
Muñeca, s. f. || a rag ti knot
Muñeco, s. m
Muñequear, the wrist (
Muñequera,
Muñequería, died affecta
Muñidor, s. m
Muñir, v. a. assembly
Muñon, sub. muscle of
Muñones, p nions of a
Muradal, s. m
Mural, a. 2.
Muralla, s. f.
Murar, v. a. mure up
Murceguillo,
Murciégalo,
Murciélago,
Murecillo, s. || a little m
Murena, s. m
Murice, s. m shell-fish)
Murmugear,
Murmullo, s.
Murmuracio speakin

dor, *s. m. evil-*
r
r, *v. a. to mur-*
to mutter || *to*
evil; to rail
o, *s. m. murmur*
ng
m. a wall
s. f. heaviness in
d
ria, *adj. heavy;*
melancholy
f. myrtle
, *s m. pl. myr-*
ries
f. muse
r la musa, *to dis-*
he malice of one
, *sub. f. shrew-*

a, *sub. f. a bird*
es upon flies
m. moss || *musk*
a, *adj. oak-co-*

s. m. a muscle
o, sa, *adj. mus-*

, *s. f. muslin*
. m. museum
, *s. f. the nose-*
f a bridle
, *s. m. shrew-*
|| *a kind of spid.*

s. m. moss || *the*
g up of the ears
orse)
s. f. musick
a. 2. musical
s. m. a musician
a, *adj. musical*
sub. m. a little

m. thigh
pl. breeches
. *s. m. an ani-*
erated by a ram
he-goat

Musitar, *v. n. to mutter*
Mustela, *s. f. a sea-lamprey*
Mustiamente, *adv. sadly; languishingly*
Mustio, tia, *adj. melancholy; languishing*
Muta, *subst. f. pack of hounds*
Mutabilidad, *s. f. mutability*
Mutacion, *s. f. mutation; change*
Mutilacion, *s. f. mutilation*
Mutilar, *v. a. to mutilate*
Mutual, *a. 2. mutual*
Mutualmente, *adv. mutually*
Mutuo, tua, *adj. mutual*
Mutuo, *s. m. loan*
Muy, *part. very*
Muy, *adv. much*

N

Naba, *s. f. a radish*
Nabal, *s. m. a turnip-plot*
Nabal, *a. 2. belonging to a turnip*
Nabar, *s. m. a turnip-field*
Nabería, *s. f. a ragoo or soup of turnips*
Nabillo, *sub. m. a little turnip*
Nabina, *s. f. turnip-seed*
Nabiza, *s. f. a little sort of turnip*
Nabla, *s. f. a psaltery*
Nabo, *sub. m. a turnip* || *the spindle of a stair-case*
Nacar, *sub. m. mother of pearl*
Nacara, *s. f. a sea-conch*
Nacarado, da, *adj. of the colour of mother of pearl*
Nacela, *s. fem. a small boat* || *stria*
Nacer, *v. n. to be born* || *to spring up* || *to rise; to arise*
Nacido, da, *adj. born* || *sprung up* || *natural; innate* || *proper; fit*
Nacido, *s. m. swelling; abscess*
Nacimiento, *s. m. birth* || *nativity* || *rise; spring*
Nacion, *sub. f. nation* || *a stranger*
De nacion, *from the birth*
Nacional, *a. 2. national*
Nacionalidad, *s. fem. the properties of a nation*
Nacionalmente, *adv. nationally*
Nada, *s. f. nothingness* || *nothing*
Nada, *adv. not at all* || *little; very little*
Nadaderas, *s. f. plur. corks or bladders to learn to swim with*
Nadadero, *s. m. a swimming-place.*
Nadador, *s. m. swimmer*
Nadal, *s. m. birth; nativity*
Nadar, *v. n. to swim*
Nadería, *s. f. a trifle*
Nadie, *s. m. no body*
Nadir, *s. m. nadir*
Nado (á) *adv. swimming*
Nafa, *s. f. orange-flower-water*
Naguas, *s. f. pl. petticoat*
Nalga, *s. f. buttock*
Nalgada, *s. m. gammon; ham*
Nalgatorio, *sub. mas. the breech*
Nalgudo, da, *a. that has fat buttocks*
Nalguear, *ver. n. to wag the buttocks, in walking*
Nao, *s. m. a ship*
Napeas, s. f. pl. nymphs of the woods

Napelo, *s. m. wolf's-bane*
Naphta, *s. f. naphta*
Naquaracuna, *s. f. a sort of song or dance*
Naranja, *s. f. orange*
Naranjada, *s. f. conserve made with oranges*
Naranjado, da, *a. orange-coloured*
Naranjal, *sub. masc. an orange-garden*
Naranjazo, *sub. m. a blow with an orange*
Naranjera, *sub. f. orange woman*
Naranjero, *s. m. orange-tree* [*green orange*
Naranjilla, *sub. f. a little*
Naranjo, *s. m. an orange-tree*
Narciso, *s. m. daffodil* || *a sort of precious stone* [illegible] *a bean* [illegible] *tick*
Narcótico, ca, *a. narco-*
Nardino, na, *a. made of spikenard*
Nardo, *s. m. spikenard*
Narices, *s. f. pl. the nostrils*
Naricisimo, ma, *a. that has a very great nose*
Narigal, *s. m. the nose*
Narigante, *a. 2. that has a great nose* [*nose*
Narigon, *sub. m. a great*
Narigudo, da, *a. that has a great long nose*
Narigueta, guilla, *s. f. a little short nose*
Nariz, *s. f. the nose* || *the sharp point of the bridge's starlings, etc.*
Narizado, da, *a. that has a great long nose*
Narracion, *s. f. narration*
Narrador, *s. narrator*
Narrar, *v. a. to tell; to relate* [*rative*
Narrativa, *s. fem. a nar-*

Narrativo, va, } *a. narrative*
Narratorio, ria, }
Narria, *s. f. a sledge*
Narval, *s. m. a sea-unicorn* [*weel*
Nasa, *s. f. a bow-net or*
Naso, *s. m. the nose*
Nasqui, *s. m. name of* Nasa
Nasturcio, *s. m. nasturtium*
Nata, *s. f. cream*
Natas, *pl. custard*
Natal, *s. m. birth; nativity* || *the birth-day*
Natal, *a. 2. natal*
Natalicio, cia, *a. natalitione*
Natatil, *a. 2. that swims or floats on the water*
Nateron, *sub. m. cream-cheese*
Natillas, *s. f. pl. custard*
Natio, *s. m. birth*
Natio, tia, *adj. native; natural*
Natividad, *s. f. nativity*
Nativo, va, *a. native*
Natura, *s. f. nature*
Natural, *sub. m. nature; temper*
Natural, *a. 2. natural*
Naturaleza, *sub. f. nature* || *privy parts* || *ingenuousness*
Naturalidad, *s. f. naturalization* || *naturality* || *ingenuousness*
Naturalisimo, ma, *a. very natural*
Naturalista, *s. m. a naturalist* [*ralization*
Naturalizacion, *s. f. natu-*
Naturalizar, *v. a. to naturalize*
Naturalizarse, *v. r. to accustom one's self*
Naturalmente, *adv. naturally*
Nauclero, *s. m. a pilot*

Naufragar, *v. n. to suf[fer] shipwreck*
Naufragio, *sub. m. shi[p]wreck* [||
Náufrago, ga, *a. ser[...]*
Naumaquia, *sub. f. nau[ma]machy*
Nausea, *s. f. qualm; re[t]ching to vomit*
Nausear, *ver. n. to ne[...]*
Nauta, *s. m. a sailor*
Naútica, *s. f. navigati[on]*
Naútico, ca, *a. nautic[al]*
Nava, *s. f. a plain*
Navaja, *s. f. a razor* || *boar's tusk*
Navajada, *s. f. a cut w[ith a] razor* || *a wound w[ith] a boar's tusk*
Navajero, *s. m. the c[ase] for razors* || *a rag [to] clean the razor*
Navajilla, *s. fem. a li[ttle] razor*
Navajo, *s. m. a mea[...] rain-water*
Navajon, *s. m. a dag[ger] shaped like a razo[r]*
Naval, *a. 2. naval*
Navazo, *s. m. V.* Na[...]
Nave, *s. f. a ship* || [...] *of a church*
Navecilla, cita, *s. f. a little ship* [
Navegable, *a. 2. navi[gable]*
Navegacion, *s. f. navi[ga]tion*
Navegador, } *s. m. navi[]gator*
Navegante, }
Navegar, *ver. n. to [navi]gate*
Naveta, *s. f. an inc[ense] box* || *a draw in a [ca]binet*
Navichuelo, *s. m. a [little] ship*
Navidad, *s. f. chris[tmas]*
Navideño, ña, *a.* [...]

he time of
a ship
rra, *a man*
. *fem. pl. the*
the springs
m. a rough
. *a card to*
m. one who
of an ele-
,} *s. m. a na-*
,} *zareen*
em. cream-
calaminte
goshawk
a mist
em. juniper-
. *a. nebulous*
a. to play the
gross igno-
lly; foppery
nce
. *f. house of*
[*cessarily*
ite, *adv. ne-*
a, *a. neces-*
. *f. necessity*
rait
pl. necessa-
s
r. a. to ne-
n. to want
adv. igno-
mprudenty ||
. ignorant ||
|| *foolish;*
fool

Nèctar, *s. m. nectar*

Nefa, *s. f. orange-flower-water* [*nously*

Nefandamente, *adv. hei-*

Nefando, da, *adj. nefandous*

Pecado nefando, *sodomy*

Nefario, ria, *a. nefarious*

Nefas (por fas, ó por) *adv. justly* or *injustly*

Nefasto, *a. m. unlucky*

Nefrítico, ca, *a. nephritick*

Negacion, *s. f. negation*

Negado, da, *adj. inept; of no capacity*

Negador, *s. m. one who denies*

Negar, *v. a. to deny* || *to disown* || *to refuse* || *to prohibit* || *to conceal*

Negarse, *v. r. to excuse one's self*

Negativa, *s. f. negative* || *negation*

Negativamente, *adv. negatively*

Negativo, va, *a. negative*

Negligencia, *s. f. negligence*

Negligente, *a. 2. negligent* [*negligently*

Negligentemente, *adver.*

Negociacion, *s. f. negociation* || *trade; commerce* [gocio

Negociado, *s. m. V.* Ne-

Negociador, *s. m. negociator* || *merchant; dealer* [*chant*

Negociante, *sub. m. mer-*

Negociar, *v. n. to negociate* || *to trade* || *to suborn*

Negocio, *sub. m. affair; business* || *trade; commerce*

Negocioso, sa, *adj. diligent in doing business*

Negozuelo, *s. m. dim. de* Negocio [*black*

Negrear, *ver. n. to look*

Negrecer, *v. n. to grow black*

Negregnear, *v. n. to look blackish*

Negregura, *s. f. blackness*

Negreta, *s. f. a blackish sort of wild duck*

Negrilla, *s. f. a kind of black sea-fish*

Negrillo, *sub. m. a little negro* || *a black elm*

Negro, gra, *a. black*

Negra ventura, *bad luck*

Negro, *s. m. a negro*

Negrura, *s. f. blackness*

Negruzco, ca, *a. blackish*

Neguijon, *s. m. a distemper in the teeth, that turns them black*

Neguilla, *s. fem. gith* || *a constant denial*

Nema, *s. f. the seal upon a letter*

Nemine discrepante, *adv. unanimously*

Nemoroso, sa, *a. belonging to a word*

Nene, *s. m. a little infant*

Nenufar, *sub. m. water-lily*

Neófito, *s. m. neophyte*

Neomenia, *s. f. neomenia*

Nepote, *s. m. nephew*

Nequaquam, *ad. by no means*

Nereydas, *s. f. pl. sea-nymphs* [*with nerves*

Nerviar, *ver. act. to bind*

Nervino, na, *a. nervine*

Nervio, *sub. m. sinew; nerve*

Nerviosidad, etc. *V.* Nervosidad, etc.

Nervosamente, *ad. vigorously*

Nervosidad, *s. f. nervo-*

sity || *flexibility* or *ductility*
Nervoso, sa, *a. nervous*
Nervudo, da, *a. nervous; sinewy*
Nesciencia, *s. fem. ignorance*
Nesciente, *a. 2. ignorant*
Nesga, *s. f. a gore* (*in a garment*)
Néspera, *s. f. a medlar*
Netezuelo, *s. m. a little young grandson*
Neto, *sub. m. a pillar's pedestal* [*pure*
Neto, ta, *a. neat; clean;*
Neuma, *s. 2. expression rather by actions than words*
Neutral, *a. 2. neutral*
Neutralidad, *s. f. neutrality*
Neutro, tra, *a. neuter*
Nevada, *s. fem. a fall of snow*
Nevar, *v. n. to snow*
Nevasca, *s. fem. a fall of snow*
Nevatilla, *s. f. wag-tail*
Nevera, *s. fem. a snow-house; an ice house*
Nevería, *s. f. the place where the snow* or *ice is sold*
Nevero, *sub. m. seller of snow* or *ice* [*snow*
Nevisca, *s. fem. a fall of*
Nevoso, sa, *a. snowy*
Nexô, *s. m. knot, tie*
Ni, *conj. neither*
Niara, *s. f. a chaff-house*
Nicerobino, *a. mas. said of an ancient precious ointment*
Nicho, *s. m. a niche*
Nicociana, *s. f. nicotian*
Nidada, *s. fem. a whole nest of birds*
Nidal, *sub. mas. nest* || *the nest-egg* || *basis; ground*
Nidificar, *ver. n. to build one's nest*
Nidillo, *s. m. a little nest*
Nido, *s. m. nest*
Niebla, *s. f. mist; fog* || *mil dew*
Niego, *s. m. a nias-hawk*
Niel, *s. m. a chasing* or *engraving on the plate*
Nielar, *v. a. to chase* or *engrave* [*nerve*
Niervecico, *s. m. a little*
Niéspera, *s. f. a medlar*
Nieta, *s. f. a grandaughter* [*grandson*
Nietecito, *s. m. a young*
Nieto, *s. m. a grandson*
Nietro, *s. m. a measure of liquids*
Nieve, *s. f. snow*
Nigromancia, *s. f. necromancy*
Nigromante, } *s m. necromancer*
Nigromántico, }
Nigromántico, ca, *a. necromantick*
Nigua, *s. f. a small sort of worm* [*much*
Nimiamente, *adver. too*
Nimiedad, *s. f. excess*
Nimio, mia, *a. too much; excessive*
Ninfa, *s. f. a nymph*
Ninfea, *s. f. nenuphar*
Ninfo, *s. m. a bean; a fop*
Ningun, *a. m.* } *none*
Ninguno, na, *a.* }
Nininana, *s. f. any foolish unmeaning thing* || *hum; the humming of a tune*
Niña, *s. f. a little girl* || *the pupil of the eye*
Niñada, *s. f. childishness*
Niñato, *s. m. a calf taken out of the belly of cow* [*c*
Niñear, *v. n. to play*
Niñería, *sub. f. child ness* || *trifle*
Niñero, *sub. m. he th fond of children*
Niñeta, *s. f. a little or pupil*
Niñez, *s. f. childho infancy*
Niñita, *s. f. V.* Niñeta
Niño, *s. m. a little b*
Niño, ña, *a. infant; c*
Niño de la piedra, *a fo ling*
Nioto, *s. m. a sea-dog*
Niquiscocio, *s. m. a t*
Níspero, *s. m. medl medlar-tree*
Níspola, *s. f. medlar*
Nítido, da, *adj. cl neat; shining*
Nitral, *s. m. nitrous of earth*
Nitrería, *s. fem. salp house* [*p*
Nitro, *s. m. nitre,*
Nitroso, sa, *a. nitrou*
Nivel, *s. m. a level*
A' nivel, *ad. level;*
Nivelar, *v. a. to level*
No, *part. no, not*
Nobiliario, *s. m. boo peerage.* [*n*
Nobilísimo, ma, *adj.*
Noble, *a. 2. noble*
Noblemente, *adv. no*
Nobleza, *s. f. noblen nobility* [*dark*
Noche, *sub. fem. nig*
Noche buena, *christ night* — toledana *night when a man not sleep a wink*
Boca de noche, *ni* fall — prima noche close of the even media noche, *m*

ena, s. m. a cake on christmas

, la, a. of an ill-lack colour

, sub. m. a wild nut

s. f. notion

, a. 2. notional

va, a. hurtful

a, s. f. a glow-

o, ga, adj. tha rs in the night

il, a. 2. noctur-

ncia, s. fem. th st time of th [na

, na, a. noctur

, s. m. nocturn

, s. fem. node, ty

m. node; nodus

l. the nodes of a

s. f a nurse

s. fem. a sauce with walnuts, etc

, m. } a walnut-

, s. f. } tree

lo, da, adj. of a t colour

, sub. m. an or- of walnut-trees

, s. f. nolition

ngere, s. m. noligere

amente, ad. na- specially

ía, s. f. renown

o, da, adj. fa- renowned

niento, s. m. na- || nomination

, v. a. to name || tion || to nomi-

b. m. name || fame; renown || nick-name || the watch-word || noun

Nomenclatura, sub. f. nomenclature

Nomina, s. f. a catalogue of names [mination

Nominacion, s. fem. no-

Nominador, sub. m. one who nominates

Nominal, a. 2. nominal

Nominar, ver. a. to name or nominate

Nominativo, s. m. nominative

Nomino, s. m. a man capable of any honourable employment [ber

Non, s. m. an odd num-

Quedar de non, to remain alone — pares ó nones, even or odd

Nona, s. f none

Nonada, s. fem. a little; some what

Nonadilla, sub. f. dim. de Nonada

Nonagenario, ria, a. ninety years of age

Nonagésimo, ma, a. ninetieth

Nonagonal, a. 2. belonging to the number nine

Nonágono, s. m. nonagon

Nonnato, ta, a. the child cut out of the mother's womb

Nono, na, a. ninth

Non plus ultra, s. m. the utmost pitch

No obstante, adv. not with-standing

Noque, s. m. a tan-pit

Noquero, s. m. a tanner

Norabuena, s. f. congratulation

Noramala (dar la) to condole with one

Nord, sub. m. the north wind

Nordest, } s. m. north-

Nordeste, } east

Nordestear, v. n. to decline towards the north-east

Nordovest, } s. m. north-

Norueste, } west

Nordovestear, v. n. to decline towards the north-west

Noria, s. f. a sort of water-engine || a well

Norial, a. 2. belonging to the noria

Norma, s. f. a carpenter's rule || a rule; a direction] north-east

Nornordeste, s. m. north-

Norte, s. m. the north || the north-star

Nortear, v. a. to observe the north-star

Nos, pron. we; us

Nosomántica, s. f. the art of curing by enchantments

Nosotros, tras, pron. we

Nota, s. fem. a mark || a note || censure || style

Notable, a. 2. notable

Notable, s. m. a preliminary note

Notablemente, ad. notably [to censure

Notar, ver. a. to note ||

Notar cartas, to endite letters

Notaria, s. fem. notary's business or closet

Notario, s. m. a notary || one who writes the dictamen of another

Noticia, s. f. notion

Noticias, pl. learning; erudition [notice

Noticiar, ver. a. to give

Noticioso, sa, a. that has notice of || learned

Notificacion, *s. f. notification*
Notificar, *v. a. to notify*
Noto, *sub. m. the south-wind* [*bastard*
Noto, ta, *adj. known* ||
Notoriamente, *adv. notoriously*
Notoriedad, *s. f. notoriety*
Notorio, ria, *a. notorious*
Novacion, *s. f. novation*
Noval, *a. f. novale*
Novar, *v. a. to renew a contract, etc.*
Novato, ta, *adj. novice; new.*
Novator, *s. m. novator*
Novecientos, tas, *a. pl. nine hundred*
Novedad, *s. f. novelty*
Novel, *a.* 2. *new; novice*
Novela, *s. f. a novel*
Novelador, *s. m. one who writes novels*
Novelería, *s. f. a narration of novels* or *fables*
Novelero, ra, *adj. that likes to hear news* || *changing; inconstant*
Novena, *s. fem. a nine days-devotion*
Novenario, *s. m. a nine days-mourning*
Noveno, *s. m. the ninth part of the tithes*
Noveno, na, *a. ninth*
Noventa, *s. m. ninety*
Novia, *s. f. a bride*
Noviciado, *s. m. noviciate*
Novicio, cia, *a.* y *s. novice*
Noviciote, *s. m. a great lusty novice*
Noviembre, *sub. m. november*
Novillada, *sub. f. a drove of steers* [*steer*
Novillejo, *s. m. a young*
Novillero, *s. m. a steer-stall* || *a steer-keeper* || *a pasturage for the steers*
Novillo, *s. m. a steer* || *a cuckold* [*moon*
Novilunio, *s. m. the new-*
Novio, *sub. m. a bride-groom*
Novisimo, ma, *adj. very new* || *the last*
Novísimos, *s. m. pl. the four last things that happen to man*
Noxâ, *s. f. hurt; damage*
Nubada, *s. f. a shower*
Nubado, (cameloto) *watered camlet*
Nubarrada, *s. f. V.* Nubada [Nubado
Nubarrado, da, *adj. V.*
Nubarron, *s. m. a large cloud*
Nube, *s. fem. a cloud* || *a web in the eye*
Nubecilla, *s. fem. a little cloud*
Nubiloso, sa, *a. cloudy*
Nublado, *s. m. a cloud* || *an impending misfortune*
Nublado, da, *a. cloudy*
Nublar, *v. a. to cloud*
Nublarse, *ver. r. to fade away* || *to vanish*
Nublo, bla, *adj. cloudy, dark*
Nubloso, sa, *a. cloudy* || *contrary; adverse*
Nuca, *sub. f. nape of the neck*
Núcleo, *s. m. kernel of a nut, etc.*
Nudamente, *ad. nakedly*
Nudillo, *s. m. a knuckle*
Nudo, *s. m. a knot* || *node* || a gnar
Nudo, da, *a. naked*
Nudoso, sa, *a. knotty*
Nuegados, *sub. m. pl. a sweet pasty ma[de of] honey and nut[s]*
Nuera, *s. f. a d[aughter]-in-law*
Nueso, sa, *a. V.*
Nuestramo, *sub. master*
Nuestro, tra, *a.*
Nueva, *s. f. new*
Nuevamente, *ad* || *lately*
Nueve, *s. m. nin*
Nuevo, va, *a. n*
Nuez, *s. f. a nut*
Nueza, *s. f. brion*
Nugatorio, ria, *trifling*
Nulamente, *adv force* or *effica*
Nulidad, *s. f. n vice; defect*
Nulo, la, *a. nul*
Númen, *s. m. a poetical ge*
Numerable, *a. rable*
Numeracion, *s. ration*
Numerador, *s.*
Numeral, *a.* 2.
Numerar, *v. a. ber* || *to mark number*
Numerario, ria *merary*
Numerata pecun *money*
Numéricamente *merically*
Numérico, ca, *rical*
Número, *s. m. n figure* || *unit verse* [
Numerosamente
Numerosidad, *s. rosity*
Numeroso, sa
Numisma, *s.*

...no, s. m. money || an ancient coin
...mulario, s. m. a banker
...nca, adv. never
...nciatura, s. f. nunciature
...ncio, s. m. nuncio || an envoy || the bedlam of toledo
...ncupativo, va / ...ncupatorio, ria, a. nuncupatory
Nupcial, a. 2. nuptial
Nupcias, s. m. pl. nuptials; wedding
Nusco (con) adv. with us
Nutra, / Nutria, s. f. an otter
Nutricio, cia, adj. nutritious
Nutricion, s. f. nutrition
Nutrimental, a. 2. nutrimental
Nutrimento, s. m. nutriment
Nutrir, v. a. to nourish
Nutritivo, va, adj. nutritive
Nutriz, s. f. nurse
Ñagaza, s. f. bird-call
Ñaque, sub. m. a heap of rubbish
Ñiquiñaque, a word of contempt for any trifling thing
Ñoclos, s. m. pl. a sort of macaroons
Ñoño, ña, a. old; doting
Ñora, s. f. V. Noria

O

O! int. ho!
Obcecado, da, a. blinded
Obduracion, s. f. obduration
Obedecer, v. a. to obey
Obedecimiento, s. m. / Obediencia, s. f. obedience
A' la obediencia, your most obedient
Obediencial, a. 2. obedient
Obediente, a. 2. obedient
Obedientemente, ad. obediently
Obelisco, s. m. obelisk || a mark in a book in the form of a cross
Obelo, s. m. V. Obelisco
Obencadura, subs. f. the shrouds of a ship
Obenques, s. masc. plur. shrouds
Obesidad, s. f. obesity
Obeso, sa, adj. obese
O'bice, s. m. obstacle
Obispado, s. m. bishoprick || episcopacy
Obispal, a. 2. episcopal
Obispalía, sub. f. bishop's palace || bishoprick
Obispar, v. n. to be made a bishop || to die
Obispillo, s. m. a mock bishop among scholars || a great sausage || rump
Obispo, s. m. a bishop
Obispo de anillo, a titular bishop
Objeccion, s. f. objection
Objetar, v. a. to object
Objetivo, va, adj. objective
Objeto, s. m. object
Oblacion, s. f. oblation
Oblada, s. f. oblation in a funeral
Oblata, s. f. an offering of money made to a church || the wafer and wine before the consecration
Obléa, s. f. wafer
Oblier, s. m. a wafer-man
Obligacion, s. f. obligation
Obligado, s. m. a contractor for sea provisions, etc.
Obligante, a. 2. obliging; kind
Obligar, v. a. to oblige
Obligatorio, ria, a. obligatory
Obliquamente, adv. obliquely
Obliquidad, s. f. obliquity
Obliqüo, qüa, a. oblique
Oblongo, ga, adj. oblong
Obnoxio, xia, adj. obnoxious
O'bolo, s. m. obole
Obra, s. f. action; deed || work
Obra prima, curious work — la obra del escurial, a very long work — obra de dos leguas, about two leagues
Obras, pl. works: writings
Obras muertas, dead works or upper works of a ship — vivas, quick works
Obrada, subs. f. a day's work || an acre of land
Obrador, s. m. a workman || work-house
Obragero, s. m. an overseer of workmen
Obrar, v. a. to work || to operate || to go to the stool
Obrecica, cilla, cita, s. f. a little work
Obrepcion, s. f. obreption
Obrepticio, cia, a. obrepticious
Obreria, sub. f. workmanship || a revenue settled for the church-reparations
Obrero, s. m. workman; journeyman || a church-warden
Obrilla, s. f. a little work
Obrizo (oro), sub. m. the purest gold
Obscenamente, adv. obscenely

Obscurecimiento, *sub. m.*
Obscuridad, *s. f. obscurity ; darkness*
Obscuro, ra, *a. obscure ; dark* [*quious*
Obseqüente, *adj.* 2. *obse-*
Obsequiar, *v. a. to court ; to be obsequious*
Obsequias, *s. f. pl. obsequies*
Obsequio, *subs. m. obsequiousness*
Obsequiosamente, *ad. obsequiously*
Obsequioso, sa, *a. obsequious* [*tion*
Observacion, *s. f. observa-*
Observador, *s. m. observator*
Observancia, *s. f. observance || rite*
Observantes, *s. m. pl. the strictest order of the Franciscan friars*
Observar, *v. a. to observe*
Observatorio, *s. m. observatory*
Obsesion, *s. f. obsession*

Obtener, *v. a. to obtain*
Obtento, *s. m. prebend ; living, etc.*
Obtestacion, *s. f. obtestation*
Obtusángulo, *a. m. obtusangular* [*dull*
Obtuso, sa, *adj. obtuse ||*
Obvencion, *s. f. profits ; perquisites*
Obviar, *v. n. to obviate*
O'bvio, via, *adj. obvious*
Obyecto, *s. m. an objection or reply*
Oca, *subst. f. a gooze || a sweet american root*
Ocal, *a.* 2. *a kind of pear*
Ocasion, *s. f. occasion*
Ocasionado, da, *adj. quarrelsome*
Ocasional, *a.* 2. *occasional*
Ocasionalmente, *adv. occasionally*
Ocasionar, *v. a. to occasion || to bring into danger*
Ocaso, *s. m. the sun set || the west || the death*

from any w
in play, etc
Ocio, *s. m. le*
ness ; sloth
Ociosamente,
unfruitfull
Ociosidad, *s.*
Ocioso, sa, *a*
leisure || un
Ocozoal, *sub.*
snake
Ocosol, *s. m. a*
Ocre, *s. m. oc*
Ocroto, *s. m.*
Octaedro, *s. m*
Octágono, *s. n*
Octava, *s. f.*
stanza of e
diapason
Octavar, *v. n.*
taves (in m
Octavario, *s.*
that lasts ei
Octavo, va, *a*
Libro in oct
tavo
Octavo, *s. m.*
Octosilábico,

ulto, ta, *adj. occult*
ipacion, *s. f. seizing; invading* || *occupation*
upador, *s. m. occupier; occupant*
upar, *v. a. to seize; to invade* || *to occupy* || *to busy; to employ* || *to take up* [*rence*
urrencia, *sub. f. occur-*
urrir, *v. n. to occur*
a, *s. f. an ode*
iar, *v. a. to hate*
io, *s. m. hatred*
ioso, sa, *adj. odious*
oratísimo, ma, *a. very odoriferous*
orato, *sub. m. smell; smelling*
orífero, ra, *adj. odoriferous*
o, *s. m. leather bottle*
ecillo, *s. m. dim. de* dre
ería, *s. f. leather-bottle-maker's shop.*
ero, *sub. m. leather-bottle-maker or seller*
icnemo, *s. m. stone-curlew* [*pigeon*
as, *s. f. a sort of wild*
ate, *s. m. white-tail; horse-match*
noruestte, *s. m. west-north-west*
te, *s. m. west*
sudueste, *s. m. west-south-west*
ndedor, *s. m. offender*
nder, *v. a. to offend*
nderse, *v. r. to take offence*
nsa, *s. f. offence*
nsar, *v. a. to offend*
nsion, *s. f. offence; injury* [*sive*
nsivo, va, *adj. offen-*
sor, *s. m. an offender*
, *s. f. an offer*

Ofertorio, *s. m. offering* || *offertory*
Oficial, *s. m. workman; handycraftsman* || *a journey man* || *an officer*
Oficial eclesiástico, *official*
Oficialazo, *s. m. an able work-man*
Oficialejo, *s. m. a pitiful work-man, etc.*
Oficialía, *s. f. officialty*
Oficiar, *v. a. to officiate*
Oficina, *s. f. shop; work-house, etc.* || *the treasure's office, etc.*
Oficinas, *pl. offices* (*in a house*)
Oficio, *s. m. office*
Oficiosidad, *s. f. diligence and application to work* || *officiousness*
Oficioso, sa, *adj. laborious; diligent* || *officious* [*makes offers*
Ofrecedor, *s. m. he who*
Ofrecer, *v. a. to offer*
Ofrecerse, *v. r. to occur*
Ofrecimiento, *s. m. offer; offering* || *promise*
Ofrenda, *s. f. an offering*
Ofrenda, *v. a. to make an offering*
Oftalmia, *s. f. ophtalmy*
Oftálmico, ca, *adj. ophtalmik*
Ofuscacion, *s. f.* } *offuscation*
Ofuscamiento, *s. m.* } *offuscation*
Ofuscar, *v. a. to offuscate*
Oidas (de) *adv. as it is reported; by hearsay*
Oido, *s. m. the hearing* || *the ear*
Oidodecir, *s. m. hearsay*
Oidor, *s. m. hearer* || *a magistrate so called*
Oidoría, *s. f. the office of* oidor

Oir, *v. a. to hear* || *to give attention*
Ojal, *s. m. button hole*
Ojaladera, *s. f. she that makes button-holes*
Ojaladura, *s. f. the hole range of button-holes*
Ojalar, *v. a. to make button-holes*
Ojanco, *s. m. a cyclop*
Ojeada, *s. f. ogle; leer*
Ojear, *v. a. to eye; to look at*
Ojera, *s. f. a spot or wrinkle under the eye*
Ojeriza, *sub. f. ill-will; grudge*
Ojerudo, da, *adj. that has spots or wrinkles under his eyes*
Ojete, *s. m. eyelet-hole*
Ojetear, *v. a. to make eye-let-holes*
Ojialegre, *a. 2. gay-eyed*
Ojienxuto, ta, *adj. that weeps hardly and seldom*
Ojinegro, gra, *adj. black-eyed* [*eyed*
Ojizarco, ca, *adj. blue-*
Ojizayno, na, *adj. squint-eyed*
Ojo, *s. m. the eye* || *the sight*
Ojo de aguja, *the hole of a needle* — de buey, *ox-eye* — de chibo, *a sort of fish* — de puente, *the arch of a bridge* — de red, *the mesh of a net* [*care!*
Ojo! *int. beware! take*
Ojota, *s. f. American women's shoes*
Ojuelo, *s. m. a little eye*
Ojuelos, *pl. spectacles*
Ola, s. f. a wave
Ola! int. hold! hoe!
Oleada, s. f. a great wave

Oleaza, *s. f. the water remaining after the oil is pressed out*

Olecranon, *s. m. a prominent bone in the elbow*

Oledero, ra, *adj. giving scent*

Oledor, *s. m. smeller*

O'leo, *s. m. oil || the holy oil || oiling*

Oleomiel, *s. m. an oil oozing out of a tree in Syria*

Oleoso, sa, *adj. oily*

Oler, *v. n. to smell || to be like*

Oler, *v. a. to smell; to scent || to peep; to observe curiously*

Olfato, *s. m. smell; smelling*

Oligarquia, *s. f. oligarchy*

Oligarquico, ca, *adj. oligarchick*

Olimpiada, *s. f. olympiad*

Olímpico, ca, *adj. olympick*

Olimpo, *s. m. olympus ||*

hotch-potch

Ollas, *pl. whirl-pool in the sea*

Ollas, de fuego, *fire-pots*

Ollaza, *s. f. a great pot*

Ollazo, *sub. m. a blow given with a pot*

Ollejo, *s. m. V.* Hollejo

Olleria, *s. f. a potter's shop*

Ollero, *s. m. a potter*

Ollica, Ollilla, Olluela, } *s. f. a little pot*

Olmeda, *s. f. a grove of elm-trees*

Olmo, *s. m. elm-tree*

Olor, *s. m. odour; smell || sign; token || a good or bad name*

Olorcillo, *s. m. dim.* de Olor

Oloroso, sa, *adj. odoriferous*

Olvidadizo, za, *adj. forgetful*

Olvidado, da, *adj. forgot || forgetting*

Olvidar, *v. a. to forget*

Omitir, *v. a.*

Omnímodo, *neral*

Omnipotenci *potence*

Omnipotente *potent*

Omnipotente *with omn*

Omoplatas, *s. f. pl.*

Omoplatos, *s. m. pl.*

Onagra, *sub prim-rose*

Onagro, *s. n*

Once, *s.* 2. *e*

Oncear, *v. or give by*

Onceje.a, *s. catch sma*

Oncejo, *s. n*

Onceno, na,

Onda, *s. f.*

Ondear, *v.*

Oneroso, sa

Onfacino (A *oil of gre*

peya, s. f. ono-
mia
s, s. f. bugloss
sub. f. a sort of
s
f. an ounce
nte, adv. obscu·
l, s. f. opacity
ca, adj. opaque
; melancholy
s. m. opal
s. f. option
s. f. opera
n, s. f. operation
v. a. to operate
, s. m. a work-
o, va, adj. ope-
, sa, adj. opero-
borious
s. f. opiate
n, s. f. oppilation
v. a. to oppilate
ma, adj. rich;
, abundant
e, a. 2. opinable
e, a. 2. opiniative
v. n. to opine
, s. f. opinion
cita, s. f. a slight
on
s. m. opium
, ra, adj. splen-
copious
cion, s. f. help;
ur
amo, s. m. opo-
mum
, v. a. to oppose
se, v. r. to be con-
|| to stand over-
nst || to vie with
her for a living,
[nanax
aco, s. m. opopa-
amente, adv. op-
ely

Oportunidad, s. f. opportunity [tune
Oportuno, na, a. opportune
Oposicion, s. f. opposition
Opósito, s. m. hindrance; opposition
Al opósito, adv. over-against
Opositor, s. m. opposer || competitor
Opresion, s. f. oppression
Opresor, s. m. oppressor
Oprimir, v. a. to oppress
Oprobrio, sub. m. opprobrium
Optar, v. a. to choose
Optativo, s. m. optative
O'ptica, s. f. opticks
O'ptico, ca, adj. optical
Nervios ópticos, the optick nerves [well
O'ptimamente, adv. very well
O'ptimo, ma, adj. very good
Opuestamente, adv. with opposition
Opuesto, ta, adj. opposed; opposite || contrary [site
Opuesto, s. m. the opposite
Opugnacion, s. f. oppugning || attack-assault || objection
Opugnador, s. m. oppugner || attacker
Opugnar, v. a. to oppugn || to attack
Opulencia, s. f. opulence
Opulentamente, ad. opulently [rich
Opulento, ta, a. opulent; rich
Opusculillo, s. m. dim. de Opúsculo
Opúsculo, s. m. opuscule
Oquedal, s. m. a wood of lofty trees
Oqueruela, s. f. a knot in the thread, etc.
Oracion, s. f. oration; speech || orison; prayer
Oracional, s. m. a prayer-book
Oráculo, s. m. an oracle
Orada, s. f. gilt-head
Orador, s. m. orator
Orar, ver. neut. to make a speeck || to pray
Orate, sub. m. a fool; a madman
Oratoria, s. f. oratory
Oratoriamente, adv. in a rhetorical style
Oratorio, s. m. a house-chapel || oratorio
Oratorio, ria, adj. oratorical
Orbayar, v. n. to drizzle
Orbayo, s. m. drizzling rain
Orbe, s. m. a circle || a sphere || the world || orb || a sort of fish
Orbicular, a. 2. orbicular
O'rbita, s. f. orbit
Orca, s. f. ore (a great seafish)
Orco, s. m. ore || the hell
O'rden, s. 2. order
Ordenacion, s. f. ordering || order; ordinance
Ordenadamente, adv. orderly
Ordenador, s. m. orderer
Ordenamiento, s. m. ordinance; law, etc.
Ordenando, } Ordenante, } s. m. one that is to be ordained
Ordenanza, sub. f. order; disposition || ordinance; decree
Ordenar, v. a. to order || to appoint || to prescribe || to ordain
Ordenarse, v. r. to receive the holy orders
Ordeñador, ra, a. milker
Ordeñar, v. a. to milk

Ordinacion, *s. f. ordination*

Ordinal, *a.* 2. *ordinal*

Ordinariamente, *adv. ordinarily*

Ordinario, *s. m. the ordinary* || *the post; a courrier* || *daily expence* || *common way* || *women's monthly courses*

Ordinario, ria, *adj. ordinary*

Oreades, *s. f. pl. nymphs of the mountains*

Orear, *v. a. to blow; to cool* || *to air*

Orearse, *v. r. to take fresh air* [*gold*

Orecer, *v. a. to turn into*

Orégano, *s. m. wild marjoram*

Oreja, *s. f. an ear* || *the latchet* or *strap of a shoe*

Oreja de abad, *a sort of fritter* || *kidney wort*

Oreja de raton, *mouse-ear*

Orejeado, da, *adj. warned; informed* [*ears*

Orejear, *v. a. to wag the*

Orejeras, *s. f. pl. something to screen the ears from cold*

Orejon, *sub. m. a peach dried in slices* || *orillon*

Orejudo, da, *adjec. that has great ears*

Oreo, *sub. m. a pleasant temperate air*

Oreoselino, *sub. m. wild celery*

Orfandad, *sub. f. orphanism*

Orfebrería, *s. f. a goldsmith's ware* or *trade*

Organero, *s. m. organmaker*

Organico, ca, *adj. organical* || *harmonious*

Organillo, *s. m. a little organ*

Organista, *s.* 2. *organist*

Organizacion, *s. f. organization*

Organizar, *v. a. to organize* || *to tune the organ*

O'rgano, *s. m. an organ* || *the organs of the body*

Orgullo, *s. m pride* || *activity; eagerness*

Orgullosamente, *adver. proudly*

Orgulloso, sa, *a. proud* || *active; eager*

Oricalco, *s. m. orichalcum*

Oriental, *a.* 2. *oriental*

Oriente, *sub. m. orient; east* || *whiteness of the pearls*

Orifice, *s. m. gold-smith*

Orificia, *s. f. the goldsmith's trade*

Orificio, *s. m. an orifice*

Origen, *s. m. origin*

Original, *s. m. an original*

Original, *a.* 2. *original*

Originalmente, *adv. originally* [*to occasion*

Originar, *v. a. to cause;*

Originarse, *v. r. to take its origin from...*

Originario, ria, *adj. originally issued* || *originary* [*nal*

Origineo, nea, *adj. origi-*

Orilla, *s. f. brink; edge; border* || *list; selvage* || *shore; bank* || *bed's side* || *the wall (in the streets)* || *a cold bleak wind* || *end; limit*

Orillar, *v. n.* } *to come*
Orillarse, *v. r.* } *to the brinks* or *sides*

Orillo, *s. m. the list of the cloth*

Orin, *s. m. rust*

Orina, *s. f. urine*

Orinal, *sub. m. urinal chamber-pot*

Orinar, *v. a.* y *n. to*

Orinionto, ta, *adj.*

Orinque, *s. m. b*

Oriol, *s. m. a witwal*

Orion, *s. m. orion*

Oriundo, da, *adj. originally issued*

Orla, *s. f. skirt; border; edge* || *orle*

Orlador, *s. m. one that borders* or *edges*

Orladura, *s. f. border; edge* [*edge*

Orlar, *v. a. to border; to*

Orlo, *s. m. a wind-instrument like a cornet*

Ormesi, *sub. m. a sort of mohair*

Ornadamente, *adv. with ornament*

Ornamentar, *v. a. to adorn*

Ornamento, *s. m. ornament*

Ornar, *v. a. to adorn*

Ornatísimo, ma, *adj. very adorned*

Ornato, *s. m. ornament*

Oro, *s. m. gold*

Oros, *pl. the suit of diamonds in cards*

Orobias, *sub. m. a sort of incense* [*haughty*

Orondo, da, *adj. proud;*

Oropel, *s. m. tinsel*

Oropéndola, *s. f. a goldhammer* [*ment*

Oropimente, *s. m. orpi-*

Oroyéndola, *s. f. witwal*

Orozuz, *s. m. licorice*

Orquesta, *s. f. orchestre*

Ortega, *s. fem. a sort of bustard*

Ortiga, s. f. a nettle

Ortivo, va, adj. ortive

Orto, s. m. the rising of any planet

xô, xâ, *adj. ortho-* [*gular*
nio, *a. m. rectan-*
ıfia, *s.f. orthogra-*
ífico, ca, *adj. or-*
raphical
ıfo, *s. m. ortho-*
hist
, *s.f. rocket (herb)*
terpillar
s. m. the husk of
grapes
s.f. a sort of eart-
ware
ver. neut. to sail
nst the wind
, *s. m. a sty in the*
a snare to catch
with
on. you
f a she-bear
yor, *Charle's wain*
iente, *adv. boldly*
shly
(á), *adv. purpo-*
|| *boldly*
, *s. f. boldness* ||
eness
ıta, *s.f. skeleton*
v. n. to dare
, *sub. m. charnel-*
e [*tion*
ion, *s. f. oscilla-*
ıcia, *s.f. oscitancy*
, *s. m. a kiss*
s. f. a bear's den
s m. ossuary
, *s. m. a bear's cub*
a, *s.f. osprey*
, *sub. f. belveder*
nt)
m. a bear
ion, *s. f. shew*
ivo, va, *adjec. os-*
ive
ıcion, *s.f. shewing*
ntation
, *v. a. to shew*

Ostentar, *v. n. to make a parade* or *shew of...*
Ostento, *sub. m. a prodigious thing* [*tuous*
Ostentoso, sa, *adj. sump-*
Osteología, *s. f. osteology*
Ostiario, *sub. m. ostiary (of a church)*
Ostiatim, *adv. from door to door*
Ostra, *s. f. an oyster*
Ostracismo, *s. m. ostracism* [*bed*
Ostrera, *s. f. an oyster-*
Ostro, *s. m. oyster* || *the south wind*
Ostugo, *s. m. footstep*
Osudo, da, *adj. bony*
Otacusta, *sub. m. a tale-bearer; a make-bate*
Otañez, *subst. m. an old gentleman-usher of a lady* [*ver; a spy*
Oteador, *s. m. an obser-*
Otear, *v. act. to observe from a high place* || *to spy*
Otero, *s. m. hill; hillock*
Oto, *s. m. bustard*
Otona, *s. f. an African (flower)* [*time*
Otoñada, *s. f. autumn-*
Otonar, *v. n. to shoot up in the autumn* || *to work at the vintage*
Otoño, *s. m. autumn*
Otorgamiento, *sub. m. a grant* || *obligation; bond*
Otorgar, *v. a. to grant*
Otro, tra, *adjec. other; another* [*besides*
Otrosí, *adv. moreover;*
Ova, *s. f. sea-weed*
Ovacion, *s. f. ovation*
Oval, *a. 2. oval*
O'valo, *s. m. an oval*
Ovar, *v. n. to lay eggs*
Ovario, *s. m. an egg (in architecture)* || *ovary*
Ovecico, *s. m. a little egg*
Oveja, *s. f. a sheep; an ewe*
Ovejas, *pl. glamas*
Ovegero, *s. m. a shepherd*
Ovejuela, *sub. f. a little sheep*
Ovejuno, na, *adj. of*, or *belonging to, a sheep*
Overo, ra, *adj. flea-bitten-grey*
Overo, *s. m. a pigeon*
Ovest, *sub. m. the west-wind*
Ovillar, *v. n. to wind up into a bottom*
Ovillarse, *v. r. to squat; to crouch*
Ovillejo, *s. m. a little bottom* || *a sort of poetical composition*
Ovillo, *s. m. a bottom of thread, etc.* [*rous*
Ovíparo, ra, *adj. ovipa-*
Ovispillo, *sub. m. bird's rump* || *anus*
O'volo, *s. m. an egg (in architecture)*
Ovoso, sa, *adjec. full of sea-weeds*
Ox, *a word to drive away birds, etc.*
Oxalá, *ad. would to God*
Oxalme, *s. f. a sort of brine* or *pickle*
Oxear, *ver. a. to drive away birds; to beat bushes, etc.*
Oxeo, *subst. m. driving away birds, etc.*
Echar un oxeo, *to beat bushes in order to start the game* [*thorn*
Oxiacanta, *sub. f. haw*
Oxicrato, *s. m. oxycrat*
Oxigonio, *a. m. oxygon*
Oximaco, *s. m. a sort of bird of prey*

Oximel, *s. m. oxymel*
Oxte! *int. make way* || *ó' pho!*
Oyente, *s. m. by-stander*

P

PABELLON, *s. m. pavilion* || *a tent bed* || *flag* || *arbour; bower*
Pabilo, *s. m. the match of a candle*
Pablar, *v. a. to talk*
Pábulo, *s. m. aliment; food*
Paca, *sub. f. a beast in Brasil* || *a bundle; a ball*
Pacado, da, *adj. pacified*
Pacato, ta, *adj. peaceful*
Paccion, *s. f. paction; pact*
Paccionar, *v. a. to make a pact*
Pacedero (campo), *s. m. a field that affords pasture to cattle, etc.*
Pacedura, *s. f. pasture*
Pacer, *v. a. to feed; to graze*
Pachon, *sub. m. a heavy lumpish man* || *a hunting dog*
Pachorra, *s. f. slowness, heaviness*
Paciencia, *s. f. patience*
Paciente, *a. 2. patient*
Pacientemente, *adv. patiently*
Pacificacion, *s. f. pacification* || *peace, quiet*
Pacificador, *s. m. pacificator*
Pacíficamente, *adv. peaceably*
Pacificar, *v. a. to pacify* || *to appease*
Pacífico, ca, *adj. pacifick; peaceable*
Paco, *subst. m. a sort of American sheep*

Pactar, *v. act. to make a pact*
Pacto, *s. m. pact: paction*
Padecer, *v. a. to suffer*
Padecimiento, *s. m. a suffering*
Padilla, *s. fem. a little frying-pan* || *a sort of shovel*
Padrastro, *s. m. a step-father* || *obstacle; hindrance* || *a hill that overlooks a town, etc* || *a flaw in one's nails*
Padre, *s. m. father*
Padres, *pl. the father and mother* || *fore fathers; ancestors*
Padres nuestros, *paternoster*
Padrear, *v. n. to ressemble to one's father* || *to engender or beget*
Padrina, *s. f. god-mother*
Padrinazgo, *s. m. quality and function of godfather*
Padrino, *s. m. a god-father* || *a second in a challenge*
Padron, *sub. m. a roll of names* || *a publick monument* || *a note of infamy* || *a father that spoils his children*
Paflon, *s. m. the ceiling*
Paga, *s. f. pay, payment*
Pagadero, ra, *a. payable*
Pagadero, *s. m. the place of time of the payment*
Pagador, *s. m. pay-master* || *payer*
Pagaduría, *s. f. a paying-place*
Pagamento, *sub. m. payment*
Paganismo, *s. m. paganism*
Pagano, na, *s. pagan* || *peasant*
Pagano, na, *adj. pagan*

Pagar, *v. a. to pay*
Page, *s. m. a nobleman's page* || *a ship-boy*
Pages, *p. whip; jerk*
Pagecico, cillo, cito, *s. m. a little page*
Pagel, *s. m. a roach*
Página, *s. f. a page (of book)*
Pago, *s. m. payment* || *a farm, etc.*
Pago de viñas, *a territory that is all vineyards*
Carta de pago, *an acquittance*
Pago, ga, *paid*
Pagote, *s. m. a drudge* || *a servant to a pimp or whore*
Paguro, *sub. m. a sort of little crab*
Pairar, *v. n. to stand still with the sails spread*
Pais, *sub. m. a region; a country* || *a landscape*
Paisage, *s. m. landscape*
Paisana, *sub. f. a sort of dance*
Paisanage, *s. m. the inhabitants of a country*
Paisano, na, *adjec. from the same country*
Paja, *s. f. straw*
Paja larga, *a tall slim fellow*
Paja trigueña, *wheat straw*
Pajada, *s. f. chopt straw boiled in water with bran*
Pajado, da, *a. of a straw colour*
Pajar, *s. m. straw-loft*
Pajaza, *sub. f. the coarse straw that is left by the horse in eating*
Pajazo, *s. m. a blow with straw*
Pajera, *s. f. a little straw lo[ft]*
Pajero, *s. m. one who sells or carries straw*
Pajita, *s. f. a little s[traw]*

adj. covered
of straw ||
lour
a, a thatched

f. a match to
ndle-with
stubble; chaff
shovel || bas-
l || battle door
ade of an oar
tom of a bezel
per leather of

f. a word
sub. f. ill lan-
[tive
ra, adj. talka-
sub. f. a little
an ill word of
nt
ger, sub. m. a
o speaks like a

, s. a. talker ;
r
s. f. a word of
int || a bitting
[cious
ga, adj. pala-
s. m. a courtier
m. a palace
} s. f. a bit
} of pure gold
a mine
f. a shovel-full
m. palate
ver. a. to put
r sugar in the
f a new-born

, v. r. to taste
a thing
. m. tasting ;
g
m. paladin
ente , adver.
[manifest
, adj. open ;

Palafren, *s. m. palfry*
Palafrenero, *s. m. a groom*
Palamallo, *s. m. pall-mall*
Palamenta, *s. f. all the oars of a galley, etc.*
Palanca, *s. f. lever; bar pole || palank || a tackle*
Los de la palanca, *porters that carry burdens*
Palancada, *sub. f. a blow with a pole*
Palancana, } *s. f. a sort of*
Palangana, } *oblong bason*
Palanquera, *s. f. a rail, a fieldgate*
Palanquin, *s. m. a palanquin || a small tackle*
Palatina, *s. f. a tippet*
Palatinado, *s. m. palatinate*
Palatino, *s. m. Palatine*
Palatino, na, *adj. palacious*
Palazo, *s. m. a blow with a shovel* or *with a cudgel*
Palazon, *subs. m. all the masts and yards of a ship*
Palco, *s. m. a scaffold*
Paleador, *s. m. one who works with a shovel*
Palenque, *s. m. the lists to fight in*
Palero, *sub. m. one who makes* or *sells shovels*
Palestra, *s. f. wrestling-place || wrestling*
Paleta, *s. f. a little shovel || painter's pallet || shoulder-blade || trowel || spattle*
Paletilla, *sub. f. dim. de* Paleta || *brisket*
Paleto, *s. m. a buck*
Paleton, *s. m. the key-bit*
Paletoque, *s. m. a jerkin with short skirts*
Palia, *s. f. a silk veil*, or *square pastboard laid upon the chalice*
Paliacion, *s. f. palliation*
Paliadamente, *adv. in a palliate manner*
Paliar, *v. a. to palliate*
Paliativo, va, } *adj. pal-*
Paliatorio, ria, } *liative*
Palidez, *s. f. paleness*
Pálido, da, *adj. pale; wan*
Palillero, *sub. m. he that makes* or *sells tooth-picks || tooth-pick-case*
Palillo, *s. m. a little stick || tooth-pick*
Palillos, *pl. bones (for bone-lace) || drum-sticks*
Palinodia, *s. f. palinody*
Palio, *s. m. a canopy || a bishop's pall || the goal at running*
Correr el palio, *to run a race* [*cut, etc.*
Palitoque, *s. m. a stick ill-*
Paliza, *s. f. a cudgelling*
Palizada, *s. f. palisade || a water-stop made of piles, etc.*
Palma, *s. f. palm-tree || a branch of a palm-tree || victory || palm (hand's breadth || horse-hoof*
Palmachristi, *s. f. palmachristi*
Palmada, *sub. f. a stroke with the palm of the hand || clapping of hands*
Palmadica, *s. f. dim. de* Palmada
Palmadilla, *s. f. a sort of dance. || V.* Palmadica
Palmar, *s. m. a grove of palm-trees || fuller's thistle*
Palmar, *a. a. that is a palm long || belonging*

to the palm-tree || *evident; manifest*
Palmario, ria, *a. manifest*
Palmatoría, *s. f. palmer; ferula* || *flat wax-candlestick*
Palmear, *ver. n. to clap with the hands*
Palmejares, *subst. m. pl. breast-hooks (in a ship)*
Palmera, *s. f. palm-tree*
Palmero, *s. m. palmer; pilgrim*
Palmeta, *s. f. ferula*
Palmilla, *s. f. a sort of coarse cloth*
Palmito, *s. m. a kind of palm-tree*
Palmo, *s. m. palm (measure)*
Palmotear, *v. a. to strike with the palm of the hand* || *to clap with the hands*
Palmoteo, *s. m. clapping of hands*
Palo, *s. m. stick; staff; cudgel* || *a piece of timber*, or *of wood* || *a stroke with a cudgel* || *suit, at cards* || *the stalk of a fruit* || *a perch for a hawk* || *pale (in heraldry)*
Palos, *pl. mash*
Dar de palos, *to cudgel*
Paloma, *s. fem. a female dove*
Paloma zurrana, *a wild-pigeon* — torcaz, *a ring-dove* — tripolina, *a rough-footed pigeon*
Palomaduras, *s. fem. pl. seams of the sails*
Palomar, *s. m. pigeon-house*
Palomear, *v. n. to shoot pigeons*
Palomera, *sub. f. a place exposed to all winds*
Palomería, *s. f. the sport of shooting pigeons*
Palomero (virote), *s. m. a dart to kill wild pigeons with*
Palomilla, *sub. f. a little dove* || *fumitory* || *the arch of a saddle* || *a white horse* || *console; corbel*
Palomina, *s. f. pigeon's dung* || *fumitory* || *a black grape*
Palomino, *s. m. a young pigeon*
Palomo, *s. m. a male dove*
Palomo calzado, *a rough-footed pigeon*
Juan palomo, *a good for nothing fellow*
Palon, *s. m. a streamer (in blasonry)*
Palor, *s. m. paleness*
Palotada, *sub. f. a stroke with a stick etc.*
Palote, *s. m. drum-stick*,
Paloteado, *sub. m. a sort of dance with small sticks*
Palotear, *v. n. to make a noise with small sticks* || *to dispute; to wrangle*
Palpable, *a. 2. palpable*
Palpablemente, *adv. palpably*
Palpadura, *s. f.* } *feeling*
Palpamiento, *s. m.* }
Palpar, *v. a. to feel* || *to know evidently*
Palpebra, *s. f. the eye-lid*
Palpitacion, *s. f. palpitation*
Palpitar, *v. n. to palpitate*
Palta, *s. f. an American fruit like a pear*
Palto, *subs. m. a kind of pear-tree*
Palude, *s. f. marsh; morass*
Paludoso, sa, *a. ma*
Palumbario (halcon...) *m. the hawk that ...ches wild pigeons*
Palurdo, da, *adj. ...tick; clownish*
Palustre, *a 2. belo... to a marsh*
Palustre, *s. a trow...*
Pámpana, *s. f. a vin...*
Pampanada, *s. f. the ... of the young sho... vines*
Pampanage, *s. m. a... dance of vine-lea... superfluous orna...*
Pampanilla, *s. f. a ... used by the Ameri...*
Pámpano, *s. m. a ... branch*
Pampanoso, sa, *adj. ... of vine-branches*
Pampirolada, *s. f. a ... so called* || *folly; ...pery*
Pamplilla, *s. f. a ... pellitory of the w...*
Pamplina, *s. f. m... ear* || *trifle*
Pamposado, da, *a.* ...
Pampringada, *s. f. ... of bread with dri... of fat bacon, etc*
Pan, *s. m. bread* || ...
Pan de especias, *gi... bread* — de azucar ... *gar-loaf* — de ro... *cake of roses* — ... bon, *a great p... hard soup* — de ... *mass of solid g...* cuchillo, *wild ... lain* — porcino ... *bread* — y quesill... *wort*
Panes, *pl. the corn* ...
Panace, sub. f. a ... (plant)
Panacea, s. f. p...

: panado
v. a. to make
sell
ub. f. baker's
s. f. baking ||
se
. m. a baker
. m. whitlow
. honey-comb
. m. whitlow
m. a stupid
w
f. a kick
s. f. a garland
ts of flowers
f. armour for
n. the belly
ca, adjec. V.
co
. m. pancreas
, ca, a. pan-
n. to bow; to
sink
. fem. a mer-
dger
pl. pandects
m. a flexure
iddle of any
s. f. multitu-
urs || a stroke
tabour || fol-
ry
s. m. a blow
bour
s. m. a little
, v. n. to play
tabour
, s. m. playing
tabour
, s. m. player
tabour
s. m. a little
m. a tabour

|| an empty talker || a comet

Pandilla, s. f. a plot to cheat others

Pandillero, Pandillista, s. m. a caballer; a factious fellow

Pando, da, adj. inclined; crooked || heavy; bumpish

Pandorga, s. f. a noise of many instruments || a fat lazy woman || a comet [small loaf

Panecillo, cito, s. m. a

Panegírico, s. m. panegyrick

Panegirista, s. m. panegyrist

Panel, s. m. pane

Panera, s. f. corn-loft || a basket, etc. for the bread [satyrs

Panes, s. m. pl. fauns;

Panetela, s. f. panado

Panetería, s. f. antry

Panetero, s. m. pantler

Pánfilo, sub. m. a slow, dull fellow

Paniaguado, s. m. a servant, etc. allowed meat and drink || comrade; friend

Pánico, ca, adj. panick

Panículo, s. m. pannicle

Paniego, ga, adj. bread-eater [corn-land

Tierra paniega, good

Paniego, s. m. a sack for coal

Panificar, v. a. to grub up; to till

Panilla, s. fem. a certain measure of oil

Panizo, s. m. pannick; (a sort of millet)

Panoja, s. fem. a stalk of pannick

Pantalla, s. f. a screen

Pantano, s. m. slough || plunge

Pantanoso, sa, a. sloughy

Panteon, s. m. pantheon

Pantera, s. f. panther

Pantómetra, s. f. a sector

Pantómimo, s. m. pantomime

Pantorrilla, s. f. the calf of the leg

Pantorrillera, s. f. a stoking that makes the calf appear greater

Pantorrilludo, da, a. that has great calves

Pantuflazo, s. m. a blow with a slipper

Pantuflo, s. m. slipper

Panza, s. f. paunch; belly

Panzada, s. f. a blow on, or with the belly || a belly full of any food

Panzudo, da, a. paunch-bellied

Pañal, s. m. child-bed-linen || the lappet of a skirt

Pañales, plu. swaddling clothes || childishness

Pañalon, s. m. aum. de Pañal || one whose skirt hangs out at his breeches [draper

Pañero, s. m. woollen-

Pañetes, s. m. pl. a sort of drawers

Pañito, s. m. a bit of cloth

Pañizuelo, s. m. a little handkerchief

Paño, subst. m. cloth || breadth of a cloth || carpet || hangings || a natural spot or speck || a web in the eye || sails [clothes

Paños, pl. clothes; suit of

Pañol, subst. m. a ship's bread-room, etc.

Pañoso, sa, adj. ragged.

Papado, *s. m. papedom*

Papafigo, *s. m. beccafigo*

Papagaya, *s. f. a female parrot*

Papagayo, *s. m. a parrot || a kind of tulip || a fish like a tench*

Papahigo, *s. m. a sort of riding-hood for foul weather || a beccafigo the top-sail*

Papal, *a. 2. papal*

Papalina, *s. f. a cap with points on the ears*

Papalmonte, *adver. with the pope's authority*

Papanatas, *s. m. a dunce*

Papandujo, ja, *adj. soft; mellow*

Papar, *v. a. to eat pap, etc. || to neglect any thing*

Papar moscas, ó viento, *to stand gaping in the air*

Páparo, *s. m. a clown; a booby*

Paparrabias, *s. m. a pas-*

Papeleta, *s. f. a bill; a note, etc. || a cornet of paper*

Papelillo, *s. m. a little bit of paper*

Papelina, *sub. f. a cup || poplin*

Papelista, *s. m. a man that is always busy among papers*

Papelito, *s. m. a little paper*

Papelon, *s. m. a prolix writing || pasteboard*

Papera, *s. f. hernia gutturis*

Papero, *s. m. a pot to make pap*

Papialbillo, *s. m. a kind of ferret*

Papilla, *s. f. pap for children || coaxing; cheating*

Papillo, *sub. m. dim. de* Papo

Papion, *s. m. a kind of ape*

Papiro, *s. m. papyrus*

Papirolada, *s. f. a sauce so called*

Paquebot,

Paquete,

Par, *s. m.*

Pares, *pl.*

Par, *a. 2.*

Par, *adv.*

Para, *prep*

Parabien, *tulation*

Parabiener *who giv*

Parábola, *parabol*

Parabolan *who use*

Parabólico *bolick*

Paracronis

Paracleto,

Paraclito,

Parada, *s. pause; ping – bound || or stake*

Paradèra, *dam*

r game || a news-monger
ado, da, a. slow || idle
ador, sub. m. a docile orse || one who plays eep or high || a car-ier's inn
doxa, s. f. a paradox
adóxico, ca, a. para-oxical
fernales (bienes) pa-aphernalia
frasear, v. a. to pa-aphrase [phrase
frasi, s. fem. a para-
afraste, sub. m. para-hrast
afrásticamente, adv. araphrastically
afrástico, ca, adj. pa-aphrastical
afrenales. Voy. Para-rnales
age, s. m. a part of the ea; birth || a place || ituation
agoge, s. f. paragoge
agon, gonar. V. Pa-angon, etc.
ágrafo, sub. m. para-raph
aiso, s. m. paradise
aláctico, ca, adj. pa-allactick
alaxe, } s. f. paral-
alaxis, } lax
alelepípedo, s. m. pa-allelopiped
alelismo, s. m. paral-lism
alelo, la, a. parallel
alelo, s. m. a parallel
alelogramo, s. m. pa-allelogram
alio, sub. m. a sort of silk-thistle
alipómenon, s. m. pa-alipomena
lisis, s. f. a palsy

Paraliticado, da, a. pal-sical, palsied
Paralítico, ca, s. y a. 2. a paralitick
Paralogismo, sub. m. pa-ralogism [ralogize
Paralogizar, v. a. to pa-
Paramentar, ver. act. to adorn
Paramento, s. m. orna-ment || caparison, etc. the smooth surface of a stone || parament
Parámetro, sub. m. para-meter
Páramo, s. m. a desert || an open-empty place
Parancero, s. m. a bird-catcher
Parangon, s. m. paral-lel; comparison
Parangona, s. f. primer (a printing-letter)
Parangonar, } ver. a. to
Parangonizar, } compare
Paraninfo, sub. m. para-nymph
Paranza, s. fem. a hut to wait for passage of game
Parapeto, s. m. parapet; breast-work
Parar, sub. m. a game at hazard
Parar, v. a. to stop || to prepare || to use ill || to stake (at play)
Parar, v. n. to stop; to stay || to go; to meet at... || to end; to come to...
Pararse, v. r. to stop || to be irresolute
Parasceve, s. m. the holy friday [selene
Parasolene, s. fem. para-
Parasito, s. m. parasite
Parasol, sub. m. an um-brella

Parástades, sub. m. pl. pi-lasters
Parástata, s. f. prostare
Parasismo, sub. m. pa-roxism
Paratilla, s. f. a summary explication of the law-titles [gimlet
Parauso, s. m. a smith's
Parazonio, s. m. a sort of danger
Parca, s. f. a destiny
Parcamente, ad. scarcely
Parchazo, sub. m. a large plaster
Parche, s. m. a plaster || a drum
Parcial, a. 2. being the part of a whole || par-tial || intimate friend || sociable
Parcialidad, s. f. partia-lity || a party or faction || sociableness
Parcializar, v. a. to par-tialize [tially
Parcialmente, adv. par-
Parcidad, s. f. parsimony
Parcionero, s. m. a part-ner or partaker
Parcísimamente, adver. very scarcely
Parco, ca, adj. slingy || frugal; sober
Pardal, s. m. a sparrow || a tiger || a cameleo-pard || a plover (bird)
Pardal, a. 2. clownish || cunning crafty
Pardear, v. n. to appear dark or brown
Pardelas, s. m. a kind of sea-bird
Pardillo, s. m. a linnet
Pardillo, lla, adj. of a greyish colour
Pardo, s. m. a tiger
Pardo, da, a. grey
Pardusco, ca, a. greyish

Parear, v. a. to pair; to match

Parecer, s. m. opinion; judgment || mien; physiognomy

Parecer, v. n. to seem || to appear || to be like; to resemble

Parecer bien, ó mal, to look well or ill

Parecerse, v. r. to appear

Parecido, da, a. alike

Pared, s. f. a wall

Paredes, pl. house

Paredaño, ña, a. parted only by a wall

Paredilla, s. fem. a little wall

Paredon, s. m. an old wall of some ruined structure [couple

Pareja, s. fem. a pair or

Parejas, p. doublets (at dice) || gleek (at cards)

Parejo, ja, adj. equal; alike

Parejura, s. f. equality; likeness

Parélias, s. m. a parhelion

Parénesis, s. f. parenese

Parenético, ca, a. parenetick [exequies

Parentacion, s. f. solemn

Parental, a. 2. parental

Parentela, s. f. parentage

Parentesco, s. m. kindred

Paréntesis, sub. f. parentesis [or matching

Pareo, s. m. the pairing

Parergon, s. m. an additional ornament

Pargamino, s. m. parchment

Parhelio, s. m. parhelion

Párias, s. f. pl. a tribute one prince pays to another

Paricion, s. f. bringing forth a child

Parida, sub. f. a lying-in woman

Paridad, s. f. parity

Paridera, s. f. the place where cattle bring forth their young

Paridera, a. f. teeming, fecund [woman

Parienta, s. fem. a kinswoman

Pariente, s. m. a kinsman

Parientes, pl. parents; parentage

Parietales, s. m. pl. parietalia

Parietaria, s. f. pellitory of the wall

Parificar, v. act. to prove by an example

Pario (mármol), sub. m. parian marble

Parir, v. a. to bring forth a child, etc.

Parla, s. fem. prating; chattering

Parladillo, s. m. an affected phrase

Parlador, s. m. a talkative man

Parlamental, a. 2. belonging to a parliament

Parlamentar, ver. n. to parley

Parlamentario, sub. m. a member of a parliament

Parlamentario, ria, adj. parliamentary

Parlamento, sub. mas. a speech || a parliament

Parlar, v. a. to chat; to prate || to warble

Parla en baldo, an empty talker

Parlatorio, s. m. conversation || parlour (in a convent)

Parlería, s. f. prating; chatting || report; tale || warbling of birds

Parlerito, ...

Parlero, ra, ... that ear... warbling

Parlota, s. ... on trifles

Parlon, na, ...

Parlotear, ... long con...

Parmesano, ... san

Parnaso, s. m...

Paro, s. m. ...

Parola, s. f. ... loquacity on trifles

Paroli, s. m...

Parolina, s. ...

Paroniquia, ... telow-wo...

Paronomasia ... nomasia

Parótida, s. ...

Paroxismal, ... ting to pa...

Paroxismo, s...

Parpadear, ... kle with ...

Párpado, s. ...

Parpalla, Parpallota, Parpasola, } ...

Parpar, sub. ... the goose

Parque, s. m...

Parquedad, ... mony

Parra, s. f. a ... a wall || ... honey into

Párrafo, s. m... || alinea

Parral, sub. ...

Parrar, v. n. ... spread the

Parricida, s. ...

Parricidio, s. ... (murder ... ther, et...

fem. a sort of
pot
pl. gridiron
f. a wild vine
. a goose
m. a parson
s. f. parish ||
hurch
, adj. 2 paro-
dad, *s. f. the*
l right
o, na, *s. pa-*
r || *customer*
, *s. f. parsi-*
part || *side* ||
arty (in law-
l. parts ; en-
ts || *party; fac-*
ivy parts
. partly
a. to deliver
s. fem. a little
[*of a ship*
s. f. departure
f. a midwife
. f. mid-wifery
ub. m. a man
s. f. a partisan
. 2. partible
s. f. partition ;
o, ra, *a. par-*
n, *s. f. par-*
v. n. to par-
v. a. to impart
a. 2. partici-
ub. m. parti-
[*cle*
f. a parti-

Particular, *a. 2. a particular* [*ticular*
Particular, *s. m. a par-*
Particularidad, *s. f. particularity* || *privity ; intimacy*
Particularizar, *ver. a. to particularize*
Particularizarse, *v. r. to affect singularity*
Particularmente, *ad. particularly*
Partida, *s. f. departure* || *death* || *a party of soldiers* || *an article of an account* || *a set or party (at play)*
Partidas, *pl. parts ; natural endowments*
Partidamente, *adver. by parts*
Partidario, *s. m. a partisan*
Partido, *s. m. party ; faction, etc.* || *condition* || *contract ; agreement* || *territory*
Muger del partido, *a common strumpet*
Partido, da, *a. departed* || *divided* || *generous ; liberal*
Partidor, *s. m. a divider* || *wood-cleaver* || *a bodkin to part the hair with* || *he that cuts, at cards* || *divisor*
Partija, *s. f. partition*
Partimento, } *s. m. parting ; dividing*
Partimiento, }
Partir, *v. a. to part ; to divide* || *to cleave* || *to depart*
Partirse, *v. r. to depart ; to go away*
Parto, *s. m. a woman's delivery* || *a new-born child* || *production*

Estar de parto, *to be in labour* [|| *a wager*
Partura, *s. f. a contract*
Parturiente, (muger) *s. f. a woman that lays in*
Parúlis, *s. m. an abscess in the gums*
Parva, *s. f. a heap of corn upon the barn-floor*
Parvedad, } *s. f. smallness ; parvity*
Parvidad, }
Parvificencia, *s. f. parsimony* *little*
Parvo, va, *adj. small ;*
Parvulez, *s. f. littleness*
Parvulito, ta, *adj. very little*
Párvulo, la, *adj. little ; small* || *innocent ; simple* || *humble ; lowly*
Pasa, *s. f. raisins* || *passage of birds*
Pasacable, *s. m. a sort of chacoon*
Pasada, *s. f. going thró ; passage* || *a party (at play)* || *procedure ; dealing*
Pasadera, *s. f.* } *a thing that passes or goes through another*
Pasadero, *s. m.* }
Pasadero, ra, *a. passable*
Pasadía, *s. f. necessaries ; competency*
Pasadizo, *s. m. a passage ; a gallery, etc.*
Pasador, *s. m. he that carries over* || *a smuggler* || *an arrow ; a shaft* || *a kind of bolt* || *splicing fid*
Pasados, *s. m. pl. forcefathers, ancestors*
Pasage, *s. m. passage*
Pasagero, *sub. m. a passenger* [*tory*
Pasagero, ra, *a. transi-*
Lugar pasagero, *a the-*

rough fare aves pasageras, travelling birds

Pasagonzalo, *sub. m. a slight blow*

Pasamaneria, *s. f. a laceman's work* or *trade*

Pasamanero, *s. m. a laceman*

Pasamano, *sub. m. orris; lace* || *ballister, along the stairs*

Pasamiento, *s. m. passage*

Pasante, *s. m. a disciple of a physician, etc.* || *a tutor in an university*

Pasante de pluma, *a writing clerk*

Pasapasa, *s. f. juggling*

Pasaporte, *s. m. a passport*

Pasar, *ver. n. to pass; to come,* or *go through, by, over* || *to run* || *to be over; to cease* || *to die* || *to be reputed* || *to enter into one's thought*

Pasar, *ver. a. to pass; to carry over* || *to go beyond; to exceed* || *to allow* || *to skip; to omit* || *to dry figs* or *grapes* || *to strain* || *to bolt* or *sift meal*

Pasar de parte á parte, *to run through*

Pasarse, *ver. r. to go over to the enemy* || *to fade* || *to sink (said of ink on paper)*

Pasatiempo, *s. m. pastime*

Pasavolante, *s. m. a blunder* || *a sort of culverin*

Pasavoleo, *sub. m. a term used in playing at ball*

Pascasio, *s. m. a scholar that goes home upon all great holydays*

Pascua, *s. f. passover* || *easter*

Pascua de Espíritu santo, *Pentecost* — de Natividad, *christmas* — de flores, ó florida, *palm-sunday*

Pascual, *a. 2. paschal*

Paso, *sub. m. the permission signed to a paper, that it may have its effect* || *passport*

Pascadero, *s. m. walking-place*

Pascador, *s. m. a walker* || *pacer* || *walking-place*

Pasear, *v. a. y n. to walk* || *to pace*

Pasearse, *v. r. to walk*

Paseo, *s. m. walk; walking* || *walking-place* || *going; pace*

Pasibilidad, *s. f. passibility*

Pasible, *a. 2. passible*

Pasillo, *s. m. a little pace* or *passage*

Pasion, *s. f. passion*

Pasionaria, *s. f. a kind of flower*

Pasionario, *s. m. a book used to sing the passion*

Pasionero, Pasionista, } *s. m. he who sings the passion, in the holy week*

Pasito, *s. m. a little pace*

Pasito, *ad. softly; gently*

Pasivamente, *adv. passively*

Pasivo, va, *a. passive*

Pasmado, da, *a. swooned away*

Pasmar, *v. a. to cause a spasm* || *to stupify* || *to chill* or *benum*

Pasmarse, *v. r. to swoon away*

Pasmar, *v. n.* to be astonished, stupified

Pasmarota, *s. f. a feigned swoon*

Pasmo, *s. m.* [illegible] *astonishment; stupefaction* || *a wonder*

Pasmosamente, *adv.* [illegible] *astonishment, stu*[illegible]

Pasmoso, sa, *adj. wonderful* [illegible]

Paso, *s. m. step;* [illegible]

Paso, sa, *a. past*

Paso, *ad. softly;* [illegible]

Paso, *int. softly*

Paspié, *s. m. a passe-pied*

Pasquin, *s. m.* Pasquinada, *s. f.* } *pasquin*[illegible]

Pasquinar, *v. a. to* [illegible] *pasquinades*

Pasta, *s. f. paste* || [illegible] || *constitution; temper*

Pastar, *v. n. to feed* || *to graze*

Pastar, *v. a. to pasture*

Pasteca, *s. f. a pulley* or *block in a ship*

Pastel, *sub. m. a pie; a pasty* || *a blot* || *a parte (in fortification)* || *woad* || *pastel* || *a monk (in printing)*

Pasteleria, *s. fem. pastry-work* || *pastry-cook's shop*

Pastelerito, *s. m. dim. de* Pastelero

Pastelero, *s. m. pastry-cook*

Pastelillo, *sub. m. a little pie or pasty*

Pastelon, *s. m. a great pie*

Pastilla, *s. f. pastil*

Pastinaca, *s. f. parsnep* || *a kind of thornback*

Pasto, *sub. m. pasture* || *food*

A' pasto, *ad. plentifully*

Pastor, *s. m. a shepherd* || *a pastor* || *a blot*

Pastora, *s. f. a shepherdess*

Pastoral, *a. 2. pastoral* [ru[illegible]

ente, *adv. she-*
like
, cito, cillo, *s.*
tle shepherd
v. a. to pas-
keep sheep
s. f. a pastoral
s. m. the state
pherd
s. f. the office of
erd || company
erds
, cia, *a.* } *pas-*
a. 2. } *toral*
ente, *adver. V.*
mente
a, *a. fat; full;*

s. f. pasture
, *sub. m. pastu-*

a paw; a foot
ale goose
f. a sort of coin
s. m. patache
m a clown
. m. a patacoon

ib. f. a kick || a
oot step
sub. m. one that
ge feet
lo, *s. m. min-*
r
ver. n. to move
eet very nimbly
amp with one's

. m. clattering
e feet
s. f. a ridicu-
deavour
, *s. f. a sort of*

m. a clown; a

. s. f. clownish-
implicity; ig-

Patarata, *s. f. a tale; an idle story*
Pataratero, *s. m. a teller of idle stories*
Patarraez, *sub. m. back-stay, in a ship*
Patata, *s. f. patatoe*
Paté, *s. f. cross patée (in herald)*
Pateadura, *sub. f. clattering with the feet*
Patear, *ver. act. to stamp with one's feet || to kick || to trot or run*
Patena, *s. f. patine*
Patente, *a. 2. open; manifest; plain*
Patente, *s. f. a patent*
Pagar la patente, *to pay one's entrance* or *initiation* [*festly*
Patentemente, *ad. mani-*
Patera, *s. f. a patine*
Paternal, *a. 2. paternal*
Paternidad, *s. f. paternity*
Paterno, na, *a. paternal*
Paternoster, *s. m. pater noster*
Patesca, *sub. f. a sort of pulley in a ship*
Pateta, *s. m. a lame*
Patético, ca, *a. pathetick*
Patiabierto, ta, *a. that has the legs opened*
Patialbillo, *s. m. a kind of ferret*
Patíbulo, *s. m. the gallows* [*or foot*
Patica, *s. f. a little paw,*
Patico, *s. m. a gosling*
Paticoxo, xa, *a. lame*
Patiestebado, da, *a. bow-legged* [*ven-footed*
Patihendido, da, *a. clo-*
Patilla, *s. f. a little paw or foot || the trigger of a gun*
Patillas, *pl. the devil*

Patin, *s. m. a little court-yard || the great sea-swallow; a scray*
Patines, *pl. skates*
Patinejo, } *s. m. a little*
Patinillo, } *court-yard*
Patino, *s. m. a gosling*
Patio, *s. m. a court-yard || pit of a play-house*
Patitieso, sa, *a. benummed || amazed*
Patituerto, ta, *a. splay-footed*
Patizambo, ba, *a. crook-legged*
Pato, *s. m. a goose*
Pato, ta, *a. equal*
Patochada, *s. f. foppery; blunder*
Patojo, ja, *a. splay-footed*
Patología, *s. f. pathology*
Paton, *s. m. he that has large feet*
Patraña, *s. f. an idle story*
Patria, *s. f. native country*
Patriarca, *s. m. patriarch*
Patriarcado, *sub. m. patriarchate* [*chal*
Patriarcal, *a. 2. patriar-*
Patriciado, *sub. m. patriciate*
Patricio, *s. m. a patrician* [*cian*
Patricio, cia, *adj. patri-*
Patriedad, *s. f. V.* Patrimonialidad
Patrimonial, *a. 2. patrimonial*
Patrimonialidad, *s. f. the state* or *condition of the natives of a country*
Patrimonio, *s. m. patrimony*
Patrio, tria, *a. of one's country || of one's father*
Patriota, *s. m. compatriot*

the house || *the first galley*

Patronado, *s. m. V.* Patronato,

Patronado, da, *a. of patronage*

Patronalo, } *s. m. patro-*
Patronazgo. } *nage; advowson* || *foundation of a benefice*

Patronímico, *s. m. patronymick name*

Patrono, *s. m. V.* Patron

Patrulla, *s. f patrole*

Patrullar, *v. n. to patrole*

Patudo, da, *adj. that has great paws* or *feet*

Patullar, *v. n. to paddle* || *to be very busy*

Paulina, *s. f. decree of excommunication* || *ill language* [*poor*

Paupérrimo, ma, *a. very*

Pausa, *s. fem. a pause* || *rest; repose* || *slowness*

Pausadamente, *adv. leisurely; slowly*

Pausado, da, *adj. staid;*

Paviota, *s. f. a gull (sea-bird)*

Pavo, *s. m. a turkey-cock*

Pavo real, *a pea-cock*

Pavon, *s. m. a pea-cock*

Pavonada, *s. fem. a short walking, etc.* || *pageantry*

Pavonar, *ver. a. to paint dark brown*

Pavonazo, *sub. m. a red brown colour*

Pavonear, *v. n.* } *to struct*
Pavonearse, *v. r.* }

Pavor, *s. m. fear*

Pavorde, *sub. m. the provost of a chapter*

Pavordía, *sub. f. provostship*

Pavorido, da, *a. frighted*

Pavorosamente, *ad. fearfully* [*full*

Pavoroso, sa, *adj. fright-*

Pavura, *s. f. fear*

Páxara, *s. fem. a female bird*

Paxarear, *v. n. to fowl* || *to ramble about*

sparrow

Paxarota,

Paxarotada

Paxarraco,

Paxaruco,

Payla, *s. f.*
sort or *p*

Paylon, *sub*
Payla

Payo, ya, *a*

Paz, *s. f.*
eveness,
counts,

Paz, *int. pe*

Pazguato, t
stupid

Peage, *s. m*

Peagero, *s.*
rer

Peal, *s. m*
the stocki
the foot

Peana, }
Peaña, }
a stool

Pebete, *s. m*
fume || *p*

Pebetero, *s*

dor, ra, *adj. y sub. a* ...*ner*
...dora, *s. f. a whore*
...dorazo, *s. m. a great* ...*ner*
...minoso, *a. sinful*
...ato, *a.* 2. *peccant*
..., *v. n. to sin* || *to go* ...*ainst a rule, etc.*
..., *s. m. a fisch* || *clay*... ...*d*
...zillo, *sub. m. a little* ...*ch* [*colour*
...lo, ña, *a. of a pitch*
...mela, *s. fem. a little* ...*ce*
...uelo, *sub. m. a little* ...*t* || *a small fish*
...a, *s. f. tribute; tax*
...ar, *v. a. to pay a tax*
...mo, *sub. m. a great* ...*east, etc.*
..., *s. m. V.* Pechina
...era, *s. f. plastron.* ...*a breast-leather* || *a* ...*man's breast*
...eria, *s. f. the act* or ...*ligation of paying a* ...
...ero, ra, *a. taxable*
...ero *s. m. a bib*
...ecolorado, *sub. m a* ...*net* [*at cards*
...igonga, *s. f. a game*
...ina, *s. fem. a cockle-* ...*ell worn by the pil-* ...*ims*
...o, *s. m. the breast* || ...*woman's breast* || ...*urage* || *tribute; tax*
...uga, *s. f. the breast* ...*a fowl, etc.*
...ugon, *s. m. a blow on* ...*e breast*
...uguera, *s. fem. hoo-* ...*ng-cough, etc.*
...gar, *v. a. to pinch*
...o, *s. m. a pinch*
..., *s. f. a fish-pond*

Pecinal, *s. m. meer; pool*
Pécora, *s. f cattle* || *a sly cunning man*
Pecorea, *s. f. plundering of soldiers*
Pecoso, sa, *a. freckly*
Pectoral, *s. m. a breast-cross* || *a breast-plate*
Pectoral, *a.* 2. *pectoral*
Peculado, *s. m. peculation*
Peculiar, *a.* 2. *peculiar*
Peculiarmente, *ad. peculiarly*
Peculio, *s. m. peculium; substance*
Pecunia, *s. f. money*
Pecuniario, ria, *adj. pecuniary* [*nious*
Pecunioso, sa, *adj. pecu-*
Pedacico, cito, *sub. m. a little bit*
Pedage, *s. m. toll-money*
Pedagogía, *s. f. pedagogy*
Pedagogo, *sub. m. pedagogue* [*neous*
Pedáneo, *adj. m. peda-*
Pedante, *s. m. pedant*
Pedantería, *s. f. pedantry*
Pedantesco, ca, *adj. pedantick*
Pedantismo, *sub. m. padantry* || *the herd of pedants*
Pedazo, *s. m. bit; piece; fragment* [*bit*
Pedazuelo, *s. m. a little*
Pedernal, *s. m. a flint*
Pedestal, *s. m. pedestal*
Pedestre, *adj.* 2. *pedestrious* [*upon one foot*
Pedicox, *sub. m. a jump*
Pedicular, *a.* 2. *pedicular*
Pedículo, *s. m. pedicle*
Pedido, *s. m. tribute; tax* || *petition*
Pedidor, *s. m. asker*
Pedidura, *s. f. demand; asking*

Pedigon, *s. m. importunate asker*
Pedigüeño, ña, *adj. that is always asking, etc.*
Pedimento, *s. m. petition*
Pedir, *v. a. to demand; to ask* || *to beg*
Pedo, *s. m. a fart*
Pedorrera, *s. f. frequency of farts*
Pedorreras, *plur. close trunk-breeches*
Pedorrero, ra, *adj. y s. farter*
Pedorreta, *sub. f. a fart with the mouth*
Pedorro, ra, *a. y s. farter*
Pedrada, *s. f. a casting* or *stroke of a stone* || *cockade* || *a wipe; a taunt*
Pedrea, *sub. f. the act of flinging many stones at*
Pedrecita, *sub. f. a little stone* (*place*
Pedregal, *s. m. a stony*
Pedregoso, sa, *a. stony* || *troubled with the gravel* [*musket*
Pedreñal, *s. m. a sort of*
Pedrera, *s. f. a quarry*
Pedrero, *sub. m. a stone-cutter* || *a pederero* || *a slinger* || *a lapidary* || *a foundling*
Pedrezuela, *s. f. a little stone*
Pedrisco, *s. m. large hail*
Peer, *v. n. to fart*
Pega, *sub. f. conglutination* || *glue* || *pitch* || *a varnish upon the earthen ware* || *magpie*
Pegadillo, *s. m. a small plaster*
Pegadizo, za, *a. viscid; clammy* || contagious
Pegado, s. m. a plaster
Pegadura, s. f. glug ...

pitching || *conglutination*
Pegajoso, sa, *a. viscid* || *contagious* || *sweet; mild* || *alluring*
Pegamiento, *s. m. gluing*
Pegar, *ver. a. to glue* || *to pitch* || *to stick* || *to cudgel* || *to infect*
Pegar fuego, *to set on fire*
Pegar, *v. n. to take root* || *to attack* || *to quarrel* || *to be contiguous* || *to fall asleep* || *to taunt*
Pegarse, *v. r. to cling*
Pegaso, *s. m. Pegasus*
Pegata, *sub. fem. a trick played to one*
Pegote, *s m. any sticking clammy thing*
Peguera, *s. fem. heap of pine-branches, etc. to draw pitch out*
Peguero, *s. m. one who draws* or *sells pitch*
Pegujal, *s. m. a stock of goods, cattle, etc.* || *a man's own property*
Pegujalero, *sub. m. the owner of a small flock, etc.* *wool, etc.*
Pegujon, *s. m. a pellet of*
Pel, *s. f. skin*
Pela, *s. m. a boy richly dressed*
Pelada, *s. f. a sheep's skin without wool*
Peladera, *s. f. falling of the hair*
Peladillas, *s. f. pl. large, smooth comfits* || *pebble-stones* [*bare*
Pelado, da, *adj. bald* ||
Pelador, *s. m. one who makes bald, etc.*
Peladura, *s f. the making bald*
Pelafustan, *s. m. vagrant*
Pelage, *s. m. hair's quality*
Pelambre, *s. m. hair* || *pulling off hair* || *baldness*
Pelambrera, *s. f. a tan-pit to take the hair off the skins* || *abundance of hairs. V.* Peladera
Pelamen, *s. m. V.* Pelambre
Pelamesa, *s. f. tearing off hair* [*tunny*
Pelamide, *s. fem. young*
Pelandusca, *s. f. a common whore*
Pelar, *v. a. to make bald* || *to pick a fowl* || *to peel* || *to pare*
Pelayre, *s. m. one who teazes cloth with a teazel*
Pelayria, *s. f. the act of teazing cloth*
Pelaza, } *s. fem. scuffle;*
Pelazaga, } *fray*
Peldefebre, *s. m. a sort of camlet* [|| *fray*
Pelea, *s. f. fight; battle*
Peleador, *s. m. a fighter*
Pelear, *v. a. to fight*
Pelearse, *v. r. to box*
Pelechar, *v. n. to breed new hair, etc.* || *to grow rich, etc.*
Peleona, *s. fem. scuffle; fray* [*basset, etc.*)
Pelete, *s. m. a punter* (*at*
Peleteria, *s. f. furrier's trade* or *shop*
Peletero, *s. m. furrier; skinner*
Peliagudo, da, *a. sharp-haired* || *entangled* || *witty; subtle*
Peliblando, da, adj. that has very soft hairs
Pelicabra, *s. f. a satyr*
Pelicano, *s. m. a pelican*
Pelicano, na, *adj. grey*-[illegible] *haired* [*hair*[illegible]
Pelicorto, ta, *adj. shor*[illegible]
Pelicula, *s. f. pellicle*
Peliforra, *s. f.* [illegible] *strumpet* [*dan*[illegible]
Peligrar, *ver. n. to*[illegible]
Peligro, *s. m. danger*
Peligrosamente, *ad. dan*-*gerously* [illegible]
Peligroso, sa, *a. dange*[illegible]
Pelilargo, ga, *adj. long-haired*
Pelillo, *s. m. short hair*
Pelinegro, gra, *a. black-haired*
Pelirubio, bia, *adj. fair-haired* [*hair*[illegible]
Pelitieso, sa, *adj. rough*[illegible]
Pelito, *s. m. a little hair*
Pelitre, *s. m. wild pellitory* [[illegible]
Pelitrique, *s. m. bawbles*
Pella, *s. fem. a pellet; a bal* || *a mass of metal* || *a lump of butter, etc.* || *a sort of heron*
Pellada, *s. fem. a blow with a snow-ball, etc.* || *a trowel ful of mortar*
Palleja, *s. fem. a skin or hide* || *a strumpet*
Pellejoria, *s. fem. a skinners shop* || *skinners street*
Pellejero, *s. m. skinner*
Pellejina, *s. f. a thin skin*
Pellejo, *s. m. skin; hide* || *leather-bottle*
Pellica, *s. fem. a blanket made of fine furs*
Pellico, *sub. m. the skin wore by shepherds* || *a wipe; a taunt*
Pellizcar, *v. a. to pinch* || *to steal*
Pellizco, *s. m. a pinch; a bite* || *remorse*

le monja, *a sort* *aroons*
s. m. an ancient garment
ra
, s. m. a tuft of *etc.*
m. V. Pelmazo
ia, s. f. slowness
s. m. a flat mass *eavy mess*
za, adj. slow; *h*
m. hair || down || a flaw (in dia-, etc.)
fre, red hair
ba, against the
a, adj. bald || covetous
. fem. falling of *r*
, s. fem. poverty *tousness*
s. f. V. Pelona
, a. hairy
. fem. a ball || a || a tennis-court *ld wench*
sub. m. a blow ball
m. goat-hair to *iairs, etc.*
v. n. to toss (at || to dispute
ver. a. to debate *ount*
, v. r. to quar- *fight*
sub. f. women's [*balls*
, s. f. a heap of
s. m. seller or *of balls || he that* *balls, at ten-* *t || fray; scuffle*
. fem. a little

Peloton, *sub. m. a large ball || a tuft of entangled hair || a knot of people || platoon*
Pelta, *s. f. a kind of shield*
Peltre, *s. f. pewter*
Peltrechar, *v. a. V.* Pertrechar
Peltrero, *s. m. a pewterer*
Peluca, *s. f. a periwig*
Pelucon, *s. m. a large wig*
Peludo, da, *a. hairy*
Peludo, *s. m. a rush-mat*
Peluquería, *s. f. periwig-maker's shop*
Peluquero, *sub. m. periwig-maker*
Peluquin, *s. m. a bag-wig*
Pelusa, *s. fem. down (on peaches, etc.) || wealth*
Pena, *s. f. pain; trouble || punishment || fine*
Pena, *ó* sopena de, *upon pain of*
Penachera, *s. f.* } *tuft ||*
Penacho, *s. m.* } *crest of a helmet || pride*
Penadamente, *adv. painfully*
Penadillo, lla, *adj. that affords drink with difficulty*
Penado, da, *a. painful || V.* Penadillo
Penal, *a. 2. penal*
Penalidad, *s. fem. pain || penalty*
Penar, *v. n. to suffer || to long for*
Penar, *v. a. to punish*
Penarse, *v. r. to be grieved* (*hold-gods*
Penates, *s. m. pl. house-*
Penca, *s. f. prickly leaf of a thistle, etc.; cardes || the hangman's whip*
Pencar, *v. a. to whip at the cart's tail*

Pencazo, *s. m. a stroke with a whip*
Pencudo, da, *adj. sharp-leaved*
Pendanga, *s. f. a strumpet*
Pendejo, *sub. m. the hair about the privy parto || a coward*
Pendencia, *s. f. quarrel; fray* [*rel*
Pendenciar, *v. n. to quar-*
Pendenciero, ra, *a. quarrelsome*
Pender, *v. n. to hang || to depend || to boggle; to waver*
Pendiente, *s. m. declivity || ear-pendant*
Pendiente, *a. 2. hanging*
Pendil, *s. m. mantle*
Tomar el pendil, *to run away secretly*
Péndola, *s. f. a pen || a pendulum || balance of a watch*
Pendolero, ra, *a. hanging*
Pendolista, *s. m. a quick writer || a cheating, crafty fellow*
Pendon, *s. m. standard; pennon, etc. || banner || streamer || a titter or stander*
Péndulo, la, *a. pendulous*
Penetrabilidad, *s. f. penetrability*
Penetrable, *a. 2. penetrable* [*tration*
Penetracion, *s. f. pene-*
Penetrador, *s. m. penetrant* [*of....*
Penetral, *s. m. the inside*
Penetrante, *a. 2. deep*
Penetrar, *ver. a. to penetrate*
Penetrativo, va, *a. penetrative*
Peninsula, *s. fem. peninsula*

Penitencia, s. fem. penitence || penance
Penitencial, a. 2. penitential
Penitenciar, v. a. to impose a penance
Penitenciaria, s. fem. the penitentiary's court or dignity
Penitenciario, s. m. penitentiary
Penitenciario, ria, a. relating to the penitentiary
Penitente, a. y s. 2. penitent
Penosamente, adv. painfully
Penoso, sa, a. painful
Penoso, s. m. a beau
Pensado, da, a. thought on || premeditated
De pensado, adv. purposedly
Pensamiento, s. m. the understanding || a thought || quickness
Pensar, v. a. to think || to give beasts their allowance
Pensativo, va, a. thoughtful
Pensier, s. m. pansy (a flower)
Pensil, s. m. garden in the air || any beautiful garden
Pension, s. f. pension || trouble; incumbrance
Pensionar, v. a. to impose a pension
Pensionario, s. m. boarder || pensionary
Pensionista, s. m. pensioner
Pentadáctilo, } Pentafilon, } s. m. cinquefoil
Pentágono, s. m. a pentagon
Pentámetro, s. m. pentameter

Pentatemo, s. m. the pentateuch
Pentecostes, s. m. Pentecost
Penúltimo, ma, a. last but one
Penumbra, s. f. penumbra
Penuria, s. f. penury
Peña, s. f. } Penado, s. m. } a rock
Peñascal, sub. m. a rocky place
Peñasco, s. m. a rock || a sort of silk stuff
Peñascoso, sa, a. rocky
Peñedo, s. m. a rock
Peñiscola, s. f. peninsula
Peñol, s. m. a great rock || the end of the ship's yard
Peñon, sub. m. a great lofty rock
Peon, s. m. a walker || a foot-soldier || a day-labourer || a pawn, at chess || a gig
A peon, adv. upon one's legs
Peonada, s. f. a day's work
Peonage, s. m. a company of men on foot
Peonería, sub. f. as much ground as may be tilled in one day
Peonia, s. f. piony
Peonza, s. f. a boy's top || a very short man
Peor, a. 2. worse
Peor, adv. worse
Peoría, s. f. growing worse
Pepian, s. m. kid of lamb cut in small pieces and stewed
Pepinar, s. m. the cucumber-ground
Pepinazo, s. m. a blow of a cucumber
Pepino, s. m. cucumber
Pepion, s. m. an ancient gold coin

Pepita, s. f. kernel o… ples, etc. || grape-… || pip
Pepitoria, s. f. the gi… of a goose, etc. || a … gle-mangle
Peplide, s. f. wild pu…
Peplo, s. m. milk-thi…
Pepon, s. m. a water… lon [|| inf…
Pequeñez, s. f. small…
Pequeñito, ta, adj. little
Pequeño, na, adj. lit…
Pequeñuelo, la, adj. little
Pera, s. f. a pear
Perada, s. f. conserv… pears
Peral, s. m. a pear-t…
Peraleda, s. f. an orc… of pear-trees
Peranten, sub. m. … honeysuckle || a … indian fan
Perayle, s. m. V. Pe…
Peraza, s. f. a great p…
Percances, s. m. pl. … quisites; vails; p…
Percatar, v. n. to th… to consider
Percebimiento, s. m. … parative
Percebir, v. a. V. Per…
Percepcion, s. f. pe… tion
Perceptible, a. 2. pe…
Perceptivo, va, adj. … may perceive
Percha, subs. f. a po… perch || a peg || a … to catch partridg… prop of a vine
Perchas, pl. floor tim… (in a ship)
Perchon, s. m. the p… pal shoot of a vin…
Perchonar, ver. n. … snares

s. to receive
to perceive
} *s. m. a kind of vulture*
a. 2. striking
s. to dull ; to
f. percussion
n. striker
. to lose || *to*
orrupt
f. perdition
loss || *dama-*
, *adv. des-*
[*gnedly*
, *a. lost desi-*
a. lost || *who*
m. a wicked
[*loses*
a, *adj. that*
f. V. Perdi-
a. to broil on
| *to prepare ;*
m. a young
pl. small shot
} *s. m. dim. de* Perdigon
perro) *s. m.*
log
) *s. m. perdi-*
partridge
s. pardon
, *with your*
[*nable*
a. 2. pardon-
s. m. forgiver
a. to pardon;
|| *to exempt ;*
e with
, *s. m. a bul-*
r

Perdulario, ria, *a. negligent* [*ting*
Perdurable, *a.* 2. *everlas-*
Perdurablemente, *adver. perpetually*
Perecear, *v. a. to delay* or *putt off by idleness.*
Perecedero, ra, *a. perishable* [*poverty*
Perecedero, *s. m. misery;*
Perecer, *v. n. to perish*
Perecimiento, *s. m. perishing*
Peregrinacion, *s. f. peregrination* || *pilgrimage*
Peregrinamente, *adver. strangely*
Peregrinar, *v. a. to peregrinate* || *to go a pilgrimage* [*geness*
Peregrinidad, *s. f. stran-*
Peregrino, na, *adj. rare ; strange* || *travelling*
Peregrino, na, *s. a traveller* || *a pilgrim* || *a stranger*
Perendeca, *s. f. a common whore*
Perendengue, *sub. m. ear pendant*
Perennal, *a.* 2. *perennial*
Perennalmente, *adv. continually*
Perenne, *a.* 2. *perennial*
Loco perenne, *a madman without intervals*
Perennemente, *adv. continually*
Pèrennidad, *s. f. perennity* [*remptory*
Perentorio, ria, *adj. pe-*
Perexil, *s. m. parsly*
Pereza, *s. f. sloth ; laziness* [*fully*
Perezosamente, *adv. sloth-*
Perezoso, sa, *adj. slothful*
Perfeccion, *s. f. perfection*
Perfeccionar, *v. a.* to *perfectionate*

Perfectamente, *adv. perfectly* [*fective*
Perfectivo, va, *adj. per-*
Perfecto, ta, *a. perfect*
Perficionar, *v. a. to perfect ; to finish*
Perfidia, *s. f. perfidiousness*
Pérfido, da, *a. perfidious*
Perfil, *s. m. profile* || *the out side of a picture, etc.*
Perfilado, *s. m. a grave formal person*
Perfiladura, *s. f. the drawing the first lines of a picture*
Perfilar, *v. a. to draw the first lines of a picture*
Perfilarse, *ver. r. to shew one's self in profile*
Perfoliata, *sub. f. a sort of plant* [*enjoys*
Perfruidor, *s. m. he that*
Pèrfumador, *s. m. a perfumer*
Perfumar, *v. a. to perfume*
Perfume, *s. m. a perfume*
Perfumería, *s. f. a perfumer's shop*
Perfumero, *s. m. perfumer* [*functory*
Perfunctorio, ria, *a. per-*
Pergamino, *s. m. parchment*
Pergeñar, *v. a. to dispose* or *execute with skilfulness* [*terity*
Pergeño, *s. m. skill ; dex-*
Pericardio, *s. m. pericardium* [*pium*
Pericarpo, *s. m. pericar-*
Pericia, *s. f. skill*
Perico, *sub. m. false hair for women* || *a parroquet*
Pericon, *s. m. a large fan*
Pericraneo, *s. m. pericranium*
Periecos, *s. m. pl.* periœci

Perigeo, *s. m. perigee*
Perihelio, *s. m. perihelium*
Perilla, *s. f. a little pear*
De perilla, *adver. to the purpose*
Perillan, *s. m. a knave; a sly crafty fellow*
Perillos, *s. m. pl. a kind of sweet paste*
Perilustre, *a.* 2. *very illustrious*
Perímetro, *s. m. perimeter*
Perínclito, ta, *a. great; heroical*
Perinola, *s. f. a totum*
Periodico, ca, *a. periodical*
Periodo, *s. m. a period*
Periostio, *s. m. periosteum*
Peripatético, ca, *a. peripatetick*
Periquillos, *s. m. p. a kind of sweet meat*
Perisoios, *s. m. pl. perisciens*
Peristáltico, ca, *a. peris-* [*taltick*
Perito, ta, *a. skilful*
Peritóneo, *sub. m. perito-*

Permanencia, *s. f. permanency*
Permanente, *a.* 2. *perma-* [*nent*
Permision, *s. f. permission*
Permisivo, va, *adj. that contains a permission*
Permiso, *s. m. permission*
Permiso, sa, *p. p. permitted*
Permisor, } *s. m. one who*
Permitidor, } *permits*
Permitir, *v. a. to permit || to allow*
Permixtion, *s. f. mixture*
Permuta. } *s. f. per-*
Permutacion, } *mutation*
Permutar, *ver. a. to per mute*
Pernada, *s. f. a fling with the leg || a gambol*
Pernaza, *s. m. a great leg*
Perneador, *s. m. a good walker*
Pernear, *v. n. to stir* or *shake the legs*
Perniabierto, ta, *a. open-legged*
Perniborra, *s. m. one that*

Pe:ol, *s. m.*
Perone, *s. n*
Peroracion, *s.*
Perorar, *v.*
de an ora
with imp
Perpendicula
pendicula
Perpendicula
perpendic
Perpendículo
pendicle ||
Perpetracion
tration
Perpetrador,
Perpetrar, *s*
trate
Perpetua, *s*
flower
Perpetuacion
petuating
Perpetuamen
petually
Perpetuan,
Perpetuar, *s*
petuate
Perpetuidad,
Perpetuo, tu

. *f. a bitch* ||
ess
f. a pack of
se caresses
, *adver. in a manner*
m. a great dog
s. m. one that
sily angry || *a*

f. a dog-ken-
nd pay-master

.f. many dogs
| *a pack of ro-*

rías á one, *to names*
n. a dog-keeper
, *a. fit for dogs*
ra, *a poor jade*

s. m. a little dog

m. the cock of [*dog*
oosero, *terrier*
m. a little dog
ero, *a lap-dog*
. *a dog*
guas, *a water-*
ra, *a setting-* [*hound*
o, *a blood-*
a large hound
, *to cheat; to*

, *s. m. pl. top*
masts
f. bran-bread
, *a. doggish*
, *s. f. perse-* [*secutor*
, *sub. m. per-*
nto, *s. m. per-*

a. to pursue || *to prosecute* || *to persecute*

Persevante, *s. m. a pursuivant at arms*
Perseverancia, *s. f. perseverance*
Perseverar, *v. n. to persevere*
Persiana, *s. f. a kind of silk stuff* || *a sort of lattice-window*
Persicaria, *s. f. arse-smart*
Persignarse, *v. r. to cross one's self*
Persignumcrucis, *s. m. a gash; a flash*
Pérsigo, *sub. m. a sort of peach*
Persistencia, *sub. f. persistance*
Persistir, *v. n. to persist*
Persona, *s. f. a person*
Personado, *s. m. personate* (*sort of benefice*)
Personage, *s. m. personage*
Personal, *a. 2. personal*
Personalidad, *s. f. personality*
Personalmente, *adv. personally*
Personeria, *s. f. office of attorney, etc.*
Personero, *s. m. an attorney; an agent*
Personilla, *s. f. a paltry person*
Perspectiva, *sub. f. perspective*
Perspicacia, *s. f. perspicacity*
Perspicaz, *a. 2. perspicacious*
Perspicacidad, *s. f. perspicuity*
Perspicuo, cua, *a. perspicous*
Persuadir, *ver. a. to persuade*
Persuasible, *a. 2. suasible*
Persuasion, *s. f. persuasion*
Persuasivo, va, *adj. persuasive*
Pertenecer, *v. n. to belong; to appertain* || *to pertain*

Pertenencia, *s. f.* } *what belongs or pertains to*
Pertenecido, *s. m.* }
Pértica, *s. f. a perch* (*measure*)
Pértiga, *s. f. a perch; a pole*
Pértigo, *s. m. coach-pole*
Pertiguería, *s. f. the office of a verger*
Pertiguero, *s. m. a verger of a church*
Pertinacia, *s. f. pertinacity*
Pertinaz, *a. 2. pertinacious*
Pertinazmente, *adv. pertinaciously*
Pertinente, *a. 2. pertinent*
Pertinentemente, *adver. pertinently*
Pertrechar, *v. a. to furnisch; to provide; to store*
Pertrechos, *s. m. pl. furniture; stores*
Perturbacion, *s. f. perturbation*
Perturbadamente, *adv. disorderly*
Perturbador, *sub. m. perturbator*
Perturbar, *v. a. to trouble; to disturb.*
Peruetano, *sub. m. a wild pear* or *pear-tree*
Perulero, ra, *a. native of Perú* || *rich; wealthy*
Perversamente, *adv. perversely*
Perversidad, *s. f. perversity*
Perversion, *s. f. perversion*
Perverso, sa, *a. perverse*
Pervertidor, *s. m. perverter*
Pervertir, *v. a. to pervert*
Pesa, *s. f. a weight*
Pesas, pl. plummets of a clock, etc.

Pesadamente, *adv. heavily* || *grudgingly*

Pesadez, *s. f. heaviness; weight* || *dullness* || *fatness in person* || *pain; grief* [*mare*

Pesadilla, *s. f. the night*

Pesado, da, *adjec. heavy, weighty* || *dull* || *troublesome* || *very fat*

Pesador, *s. m. a weigher*

Pesadumbre, *s. f. heaviness* || *grief; sorrow*

Pésame (dar el), *to condole with*

Pesar, *s. m. grief; sorrow; grudging*

A' pesar, *adv. grudgingly*

Pesar, *v. n. to weigh; to be heavy* || *to have a value for* || *to be sorry for*

Pesar, *v. a. to weigh*

Pesaroso, sa, *a. sorrowful*

Pesca, *s. f. fishing* || *all sorts of fish*

Pescada, *s. f. stock-fish*

Pescadería, *s. f. fish-market* [*ger*

Pescadero, *s. m. fish-monger*

Pescadillo, *s. m. a little fish* [*fish*

Pescado, *s. m. fish* || *stock-*

Pescador, *s. m. a fisherman*

Pescante, *s. m. a sort of crab or crane* || *a coach-box*

Pescar, *ver. a. to fish* || *to catch*

Pescozon, *s. m. a blow on the neck*

Pescozudo, da, *a. that has a great brawny neck*

Pescuezo, *s. m. the neck* || *the nape of the neck* || *the breast*

Pesebre, *s. m. a manger*

Pesebrera, *s. f. the manger-range*

Pesebron, *s. m. the bottom of a coach*

Peseta, *s. f. a sort of silver coin*

Pesete, *s. m. curse; cursing*

Pesga, *s. f. weight*

Pesiatal! *inter. odds my life!*

Pesillo, *s. m. gold-weights*

Pésimamente, *adver. in a very bad manner*

Pésimo, ma, *a. very bad*

Peso, *weight* || *a pair of scales* || *a kind of silver coin* [*beans*

Pésoles, *s. m. pl. french*

Pespuntar, *v. a. to stitch, as they do fine caps, etc.*

Pespunte, *s. m. fine stitching*

Pesquera, *s. f. fishery*

Pesquería, *s. f. fishing* || *fishery*

Pesquisa, *sub. f. search; inquiry*

Pesquisar, *v. a. to search; to inquire*

Pesquisidor, *s. m. inquirer; examiner*

Pestaña, *s. f. eye-lashes* || *an edging or welt*

Pestañear, *v. n. to move the eye-lids*

Peste, *s. f. plague; pestilence* || *an excessive abundance*

Pestiferamente, *adv. in a contagious manner*

Pestífero, ro, *adj. pestiferous*

Pestilencia, *s. f. pestilence*

Pestilencial, *a. 2. pestilential*

Pestilencialmente, *adver. V.* Pestiferamente

Pestilente, *a. 2.* pestilential [*a door*

Pestillo, *s. m.* the bold of

Pestorejo, *s. m. the* ... *of the neck*

Pestorejon, *s. m. a* ... *on the neck*

Pesuña, *s. f. a foot or* ... *of a beast* || *the* ... (*in a horse*)

Petaca, *s. f. a sort of* ... *made or covered* ... *leather*

Pétalo, *s. m. a petal*

Petaquilla, *s. f. dim.* ... Petaca

Petardear, *v. a. to* ... *up with a petard* || ... *shark; to sponge*

Petardero, *s. m. a pe*... *deer* || *a sharking fe*...

Petardo, *s. m. a petard* ... *sharking; sponging*

Petate, *s. m. a shar*... *fellow*

Peticano, **Peticanon**, *s. m.* ... *non* [*a pr*... *ting letter*

Peticion, *s. f. petition*

Petillo, *s. m. a little c*... *rass* || *a stomacher*

Petimetre, *s. m. a beau* ... *fop* [*a little*

Petis, *s. m. a name give*...

Petitorio, ria, *a. petito*...

Petitorio, *s. m. a ridi*... *lous, troublesome* ... *mand*

Peto, *s. m. a cuirass* ... *stomacher*

Petral, *s. m. V.* Pretal

Petraria, *s. f. a petra*...

Petrera, *s. f. a fight* ... *stones* [*co*

Petrificacion, *s. f. pe*...

Petrificar, *v. a. to pe*...

Petril, *s. m. V.* Preti...

Petrina, *s. f. V.* Preti...

Petrisca, *subs. f. a f*... with stones

Petróleo, subs. m. pe... rock-oil

Pe...

, s. f. petulance
, a. 2. petulant
. m. a fish || a
ing fellow
r, sub. m. mer-

s. f. combing
s. m. the curling
ssing of hair ||
nish man
, s. m. one that
carder || com-
oth
, s. f. combing
combed off
a. to comb one's
cut steep down
ckle hemp || to
ne's style
sub. m. a large
a cross piece of

b. m. a comb ||
card wool || an
o dress hemp ||
p
texedor, a slaie
sub. m. a comb-
shop
sub. m. a comb-

a fish [nium
f. pitch || meco-
, hard rosin
m. the stalk of a
a nipple || pro-
y
s. f. a linch-pin
f. } a wag-
s. m. } tail
, s. f. phalanx
, sub. m. a sort
der || a kind of

utico, ca, adjec.
ceutick
, s. f. pharmacy
s. m. a medi-

Pharmacopea, s. f. pharmacopeia
Pharmacópola, s. f. pharmacopolist
Phase, s. m. passover
Phases, s. f. pl. phases
Philaucia, s. f. self-love
Pia, s. f. a pied nag
Piada, s. f. pieping
Piador, sub. m. a pieping chick, etc.
Piadosamente, adv. piously || pitifully
Piadoso, sa, a. pitiful
Piamente, adv. piously
Pian piano, adv. softly; without hurry
Piar, v. n. to piep; to pip || to long for
Piara, s. f. a herd of swines, etc.
Pica, s. f. a pike
Picacho, s. m. the sharp point of any thing
Picacureba, s. f. a turtle-dove of brasil
Picada, s. f. a prick
Picadero, s. m. a riding-house
Picadillo, sub. m. minced meat
Picado, subs. m. a design pricked
Picador, s. m. a jockey || a riding-master || a block to mince meat upon
Picadura, s. f. pricking || a prick || a slash in a garment
Picafigo, s. m. beccafigo
Picamaderos, subs. m. a wood-picker
Picante, s. m. sharpness; poignancy
Picaño, ña, adj. ragged; knavish
Picaño, s. m. a patch on a shoe

Picapedrero, s. m. a stone-cutter
Picaporte, s. m. a latch
Picar, v. a. to prick || to peck || to bite || to sting || to itch || to mince meat
Picar la amarra, to slip the cable — un caballo, to spur or to manage a horse
Picarse, v. r. to be offended at.... || to pretend to...; to set up for... || to taint; to be spoiled || to rut
Pícaramente, adver. roguishly
Picarazo, s. m. aum. de Pícaro
Picardear, ver. a. to play wanton tricks || to drink hard, etc.
Picardía, s. f. knavery || malice; craftiness || a lewd action || a gang of knaves [rabble
Picaresca, s. f. rascality;
Picaresco, ca, a. } roguish; knavish || bantering
Picaril, a. 2. }
Picarillo, s. m. dim. de Pícaro
Pícaro, s. m. a rogue; a knave || a malicious, cunning man
Pícaro de cocina, a scullion
Pícaro, ra, a. mischievous; hurtful || merry; gay.
Picaron, } s. m. aum. de Pícaro
Picaronazo, }
Picarote, }
Picatoste, s. m. a toast
Picaza, s. f. a magpie
Picazo, s. m. a blow with a pike, etc.
Picazon, s. m. itching || anger

peak || *a wood-picker* || *a fraction*

Picolete, *s. m. a cramp-iron in a lock*

Picon, *s. m. a sharp biting jest* || *small coal*

Picor, *s. m. smart; smarting*

Picoso, sa, *a. pitted with the small pox*

Picota, *subs. f. a gallows built with stones* || *a pillory* || *the top of a mountain, etc.*

Picotada, *s. f.*
Picotazo, *s. m.* } *a wound made by a bird's bill*

Picote, *subs. m. a kind of cloth* [*to prate*

Picotear, *v. a. to peck* ||

Picotearse, *v. r. to quarrel; to squabble*

Picotero, ra, *a. talkative*

Pictima, *s. f. epithem*

Pictórico, ca, *a. relating to picture*

Picudo, da, *adj. pointed ;*

Piedad, *s. f. piety* || *pity*

Piedra, *s. f. a stone* || *large hail*

Piedra aguzadera, *a grindstone* — azufre, *brimstone* — pomez, *pummice-stone* — de toque, *touch stone* — iman *load stone* — infernal, *infernal stone* — filosofal, *philosopher's stone*

Piedras, *pl. counters* (*at play*)

Piedrecica,
Piedrecilla,
Piedrezuela, } *s. f. a little stone*

Piel, *s. f. skin* || *leather; hide*

Piélago, *sub. m. the main sea; the deep*

Piélago de odre. *V.* Piezgo

Pienso, *s. m. the common allowance given to a beast*

Pierna, *s. f. a leg* || *a quarter of a walnut* || *a breadth of a sheet*

Piernas, *pl. the strokes of*

harrow

Pigmeo, m

Pigre, *a.*

Pigricia,
ness

Pigro, gr

Pihua, *s. f.*

Pihuela, *s*
hawks

Pihuelas,

Piisimo, m

Pijota, *s.*

Pijote, *s.*

Pila, *s. f*
fountain
|| *a sto*
font in
ly-wate
a pile

Pilada, *s.*
of mort
bout

Pilar, *s. m*
fountain

Pilarejo, *s*
pillar

Pilastra, *s.*

Pilastrilla

age, s. mas. plundering; pillage
ar, v. a. to plunder || to catch
on, s. m. a large vase of a fountain || a sugar-loaf || the weight of a steel-yard
enero, ra, a. vulgar; known to every body
ongo, ga, a. lean; dry
astaña pilonga, a dry chesnut
otage, s. m. pilotage
loto, s. m. a pilot || a great drinker
ltraca,} s. f. poor wretched meat
ltrafa,}
mental, s. mas. a place full of guinea pepper
mentero, s. m. a pepper-box || a pepper plant
menton, s. m. guinea-pepper
mienta, s. f. pepper
imiento, s. m. a pepper-plant || guinea-pepper
impido, sub. m. a sort of sea-fish
impin, s. m. a sort of play among children
impinela, s. f. pimpernel
impollar, sub. m. a little coppice-wood
mpollo, s. m. a sprout of a tree or plant || the bud of a rose, etc. || a spark; a coxcomb
na, s. f. a conick stone, etc.
nas, plur. battlemens || jaunts of a wheel
nabete, s. m. a sort of fine pine-tree
náculo, s. m. pinnacle
nal,} s. m. a grove of pine-trees
nar,}
nariego, ga, a. belonging to the pine
aza, s. f. a pinnace

Pincel, s. m. a pencil
Pincelada, s. f. a stroke of a pencil
Pincerna, s. 2. a cup-bearer
Pinchadura, s. f. a prick
Pinchar, v. a. to prick
Pinco, s. m. a flyboat
Pineda, s. f. a sort of garters
Pingajo, s. m. a hanging rag
Pinganello, s. m. icicle
Pingorotudo, da, a. high
Pingue, s. m. pink (a ship)
Pingüe, a. 2. fat
Pingüedinoso, sa, a. fat; greasy
Pingüedo, s. f. fatness
Pinillo, s. m. spicknel; mald-mony
Pinillo oloroso, wild dill
Pinjantes, sub. m. pl. jewels hanging to a woman's head-dress
Pinjar, v. a. to hang
Pino, s. m. a pine-tree || a ship; a boat
Pinole, s. m. a sweet powder mixed with the chocolate
Pinoso, sa, a. full of pine-trees
Pinta, s. f. seam; cicatrice || a spot || a mark in a card, etc. || a drop || a pint
Pintas, pl the spotted fever || a game like the basset
Pintacilgo,} s. m. goldfinch
Pintadillo,}
Pintado, da, a. speckled; spotted
Pintar, v. a. to paint || to describe || to imagine
Pintaroxo, s. m. a linnet
Pintarrajo, s. m. dawbing; plaistering
Pintilla, s. f. dim. de Pinta
Pintiparado, da, a. exactly alike

Pintiparar, v. a. to compare
Pintojo, ja, a. speckled; spotted
Pintor, s. m. a painter
Pintoresco, ca, a. belonging to the picture
Pintorrear, v. a. to party-colour
Pintura, sub. f. painting; painture || a picture
Pinulas, s. f. pl. pinnules
Pinzas, s. f. pl. pincers; nippers
Pinzon, s. m. chaffinch
Pinzote, s. m. the tiller of the helm
Piña, s. f. a pine-apple || ananas
Piñata, s. f. an earthen-pot
Piñon, s. m. the kernel of a pine-apple || pinion
Piñonata, s. f. preserved pine-apple-kernels
Piñonate, sub. m. a paste made of kernels of pine-apples and sugar
Piñoncillo, s. m. dim. de Piñon
Piñuela, s. f. a kind of silk stuff
Pio, ia, a. pious || merciful
Pia madre ó mater, the pia mater
Pio, s. m. a word used to call the chickens
Piojento, ta, a. lousy
Piojenta,} s. f. penny-grass
Piojera,}
Piojería, s. f. lousiness
Piojicida, s. 2. killer of lice
Piojo, s. m. a louse
Piojoso, sa, adj. lousy || avaricious
Piojuelo, subs. m. a little louse
Piola, s. f. a small cable
Piorno, s. m. broom
Pipa, s. f. a pipe || a tobacco-pipe || the fuses of a bomb.

Picar, *v. a. to smoke tobacco*
Pipi, *s. m. a sort of bird in Africa*
Pipian, *s. m. an American ragoo*
Pipiar, *v. n. to pip ; to chirp*
Pipiripao, *s. m. a splendid banquet*
Pipo, *s. m. lesser spotted wood-pecker*
Pipote, *s. m. a small pipe* or *cask*
Pipotillo, *s. m. dim. de* Pipote
Pique, *s. m. grudge ; bickering* || *peek, at picket* || *the bottom*
Estar á pique, *to be upon the point* — echar á pique, *to sink a ship*
Piques, *pl. the crotches, in a ship*
Piquera, *s. f. the passage for bees in a bee-hive*
Piquería, *s. f. a body of pike-men*
Piquero, *s. m. a pike-man*
Piqueta, *sub. f. a kind of pick-ax*
Piquete, *sub. m a slight prick* || *a little hole* || *a stake ; a pole* || *a picket of soldiers*
Piquillo, *s. m. a little bill* or *beak*
Pira, *s. f. a funeral pile ; a pyre*
Piragua, *s. f. pirogue*
Piramidal, *a.* 2. *pyramidical*
Piramidalmente, *adv. pyramidically*
Pirámide, *s. f pyramid*
Pirata, *s. m. a pirate*
Piratear, *v. n. to pirate*
Piratería, *s. f. piracy*
Pirático, ca, *a. piratical*
Piromancia, *sub. f. pyromancy*
Piromántico, *sub. m. one that professes the pyromancy*
Pironio, *s. m. pyrrhonian*
Pironismo, *s. m. pyrrhonism*
Piropo, *s. m. a carbuncle*
Pirotecnia, *s. f. pyrotechny*
Pisa, *s. f. the act of treading* [*a kick*
Pisada, *s. f. a foot-step* ||
Pisador, *s. m. treader*
Pisar, *v. n. to tread*
Pisaverde, *s. m. a bean ; a nice fop*
Piscator, *s. m. almanack of Milan*
Piscatorio, ria, *a. piscatory*
Piscina, *s. f. a fish-pond*
Piscis, *s. m. pisces*
Pison, *s. m. a rammer*
Pisotear, *ver. a. to tread repeatedly*
Pista, *s. f. a trace*
Pistar, *v. a. to pound in a mortar*
Pisto, *s. m. jelly-broth*
Pistola, *s. f. a pistol*
Pistoletazo, *s. m. the shot of a pistol*
Pistolete, *s. m. a little pistol*
Pistrage, } *s. m. bad* or
Pistraque, } *insipid broth*
Pita, *s. f. a sort of aloes* || *a cry used to call the hens* [*the* pita
Pitaco, *s. m. the stalk of*
Pitagórico, *s. m. pythagorician*
Pitancería, *s. f. the place where pittance* or *alms is given out*
Pitancero, *sub. m. distributer of allowances* or *alms ; pittancer*
Pitanza, *sub. f. pittance ; allowance* || *alms* || *salary* [*ness*
Pitaña, *s. f. blear-eyed-*
Pitañoso, sa, *a. blear-eyed*
Pitar, *v. a. to wi... pay* || *to distr... pittance, etc.*
Pitarra, roso. *V... noso*
Pitillo, *subs. m.*
Pitipie, *s. m. sc... map, etc.*)
Pito, *s. m. a s... wood-pecker ... dian bug*
Piton, *s. m. a l...* || *tubercle* || *b...*
Pitones, *pl. sto... dren play-wit...*
Pitorra, *s. f. wo...*
Pituita, *s. f. ph...*
Pituitoso, sa, *a.*
Pixa, *s. f. a ma... member*
Pixide, *s. f. a li...*
Pizarra, *s. f. sla...*
Pizarral, *s m. sla...*
Pizarrero, *s. m.*
Pizca, *s. f. a sma...*
Pizcar, *v. a. to p...*
Pizco, *s. m. a pi...*
Pizpereta (muge... *active, indust... man*
Pizpirigaña *sub. ... among childr...*
Placa, *s. f. an an...*
Placabilidad, *s. ... bility*
Placable, *a.* 2. *p...*
Placacion, *s. f. a...*
Placarte, *s. m. p...*
Placear, *v. a. to ... to proclaim*
Pláceme, *s. m. c... lation*
Placenta, *s. f. p...*
Placenteramente *joyfully*
Placentero, ra, *... merry*
Placer, *v. im...*
Placer, *s. m.*

ramente, *adver. pu-*
-kly
ro, ra, *a. common;*
blick || *relating to a*
rket-place
ta, *s. f. a little mar-*
-place
ble, *a. 2. gentle;*
d
do, da, *a. placid*
ente, *a. 2. pleasant;*
asing [|| *region*
, *s. f. wound; sore*
s, *pl. the four cardi-*
l points || *the points*
the compass.
r, *v. a. to plague*
so, sa, *a. plaguy;*
rtful
, *sub. m. a plan* || *the*
d of a ship || *list; roll*
, *s. f. a trowel* || *a*
ge of a book, etc. ||
plain
mayor, ó primera
na, *the staff-officers*
a regiment
da, *s. f. a plain*
ha, *s. f. a plate of*
tal || *a smoothing-*
n || *a taylor's goose*
hear, *v. a. to plate*
o iron linen
hon, *sub. f. a great*
te of metal
huela, *sub. f. a little*
te
o, *sub. m. the great*
by (a sea-bird)
s, *s. m. pl. flat floor*
bers
ta, *s. f. a planet*
tario, ria, *a. plane-*
y
a, *s. f. V.* Planco
cie, *s. f. a plain*
forio, s. m. planis-
e [*plane*
s. m. a plan || *a*

Plano, na, *a. plain; even*
Planometria, *s. f. plani-metry*
Planta, *s. f. a plant* || *the sole of the foot* || *nurse-ry; seed-plot* || *planting* || *a plan (in architec-ture)*
Plantas, *pl. braggings*
Plantacion, *s. f. planta-tion*
Plantador, *s. m. a plan-ter* || *planting-stick*
Plantage, *s. m. plantain*
Plantar, *v. a. to plant* || *to set* || *to execute a plan*
Plantarse, *ver. r. to stand on one's feet*
Plantario, *s. m. a nursery*
Plantear, *v. a. to make a draught of*
Plantecica, *s. fem. a little plant*
Plantel, *s. m. a nursery* || *an orchard*
Plantificacion, *s. f. plan-tation* || *a plan*
Plantificar, *ver. a. to exe-cute a plan* || *to cuff; to kick, etc.*
Plantilla, *s. fem. a little plant or plan* || *the first sole of a shoe, etc.*
Plantillar, *v. a. to new-sole shoes* || *to new-foot stockings*
Plantío, *s. m. planting* || *a nursery of young trees*
Plantista, *s. m. a bully; an hector*
Planto, *s. m. lamentation, mourning* [*set*
Planton, *s. m. a plant; a*
Plañideras, *s. f. pl. the mourners*
Plañido, *s. m. mourning; lamentation*
Plañir, *v. a. to lament; to bewail*

Plasma, *s. f. a plasm*
Plasmar, *v. a. to shape; to form*
Plasta, *s. f. any sort of soft paste*
Plata, *s. f. silver*
En plata, *adv. briefly; plainly*
Plataforma, *s. f. plat-form*
Platanal, Platanar, Plátano, *s. m. the plane-tree*
Platazo, *s. m. a great dish*
Plateado, da, *adj. of the silver-colour*
Platear, *v. a. to silver.*
Platel, *s. m. a little dish*
Plateria, *sub f. the silver smiths street*
Platero, *subs. m. a silver smith* (*smith*
Platero de oro, *a gold*
Plática, *s. f. discourse; speech* || *practice*
Platicable, *a. 2. practica-ble* [*tionner*
Platicante, *s. m. practi-*
Platicar, *v. a. to discourse; to converse* || *to practise*
Plático, ca, *a. experienced*
Platificar, *v. a. to change to silver*
Platija, *s. f. a plaice*
Platilla, *s. f. a sort of fine linen*
Platillo, *s. m. a little dish* || *slander*
Plato, *s. m. a dish*
Hacer plato, *to boast*
Platónicamente, *adv. in a platonick manner*
Platónico, ca, *a. platonick*
Platucha, *s. f. a plaice*
Plausibilidad, *s. f. plausi-bility*
Plausible, *a. 2. plausible*
Plausiblemente, *adv. plau-sibly*

Plauso, *s. m. applause*
Plaustro, *s. m. a cart*
Playa, *s. f. flat sea-shore*
Playazo, *subs. m. a great shore*
Playero, *s. m. a fisherman that brings fish from the sea-coast*
Playon, *subs. m. a great shore*
Plaza, *s. f. a market* || *a fortified place* || *a place or square* || *office ; employment*
Sentar plaza, *to enlist for a soldier* — pasar plaza, *to have a name*—plaza, plaza, *make way*
Plazo, *s. m. term ; time ; adjournment* || *lists*
Plazuela, *s. f. a little place*
Plebe, *s. f. the common people*
Plebeyo, ya, *a. plebeian*
Plebezuela, *s. f. the rabble*
Plebiscito, *s. m. plebiscitum*
Pleca, *s. f. a reglet*
Plectrillo, *s. m. dim. de* Plectro
Plectro, *sub. m. a bow to play on a violin, etc.*
Plegable, *a. 2. pliable*
Plegadamente, *adv. intricately ; confusedly*
Plegadera, *s. f. a folding-stick*
Plegador, *s. m. a folder* || *a weaver's beam* or *roller*
Plegadura, *s. f. folding up*
Plegar, *v. a. to fold up*
Plegaria, *s. f. a prayer*
Plenamente, Plenariamente, } *adver. fully*
Plenario, ria, *adj. full ; plenary*
Plenilunio, *s. m. the full* [*moon*
Plenipotencia, *s. f. plenipotency*
Plenipotenciario, *s. m. plenipotentiary*
Plenitud, *s. f. plenitude ; fulness*
Pleno, na, *adj. full*
Pleonasmo, *s. m. pleonasm*
Pleura, *s. f. pleura*
Pleuresía, *s. f. pleurisy*
Pleurítico, ca, *adj. pleuritick*
Pleyades, *s. f. pleiades*
Pleyta, *s. f. a mat of rushes*
Pleyteador, *s. m. one who is at law* || *wrangler ; chicaner*
Pleytear, *v. a. to be at law*
Pleytesía, *s. f. an agreement ; a covenant*
Pleytista, *a. 2. belonging to a cause* || *litigious*
Pleyto, *s. m. a law-suit* || *the papers belonging to a law suit* || *a dispute*
Pliego, *sub. m. a fold* || *a sheet of paper* || *a packet of letters*
Pliegue, *s. m. a plait ; a fold*
Plinto, *s. m. plinth*
Plomada, *s. f. a black lead pencil* || *a perpendicular line* || *a plummet*
Plomar, *v. a. to put a leaden seal to*
Plomazon, *s. f. a gilder's* [*cushion*
Plomizo, za, *a. like lead*
Plomo, *s. m. lead-plummet*
Plomoso, sa, *a. like lead*
Pluma, *s. f. a feather* || *a quill* || *a pen* || *wealth* || *fart*
Plumado, da, *a. feathered*
Plumage, *s. m. plumage* || *a plume*
Plumagear, *v. a. to move ; to stir ; to wag*
Plumagería, *s. f. feather-work* || *quantity of feathers* || *a feather-shop*
Plumagero, *s. m. a feather-man*
Plumario, *s. m. a scrivener ; a lawyer*
Plumaye, *s. m. plumage*
Plumbeo, bea, *a. leaden* || *like lead*
Plumeo, mea, *a. feathered*
Plumería, *s. f. V.* Plumageria
Plumero, *s. m. a feather-besom* || *a pen-case*
Plumífero, ra, *a. having feathers*
Plumilla, *s. f. a little fea-* [*ther*
Plumion, *s. m. V.* Plumon
Plumista, *s. m. a scrivener ; a lawyer, etc.*
Plumon, *s. m. the down of birds* || *a feather-bed*
Plumoso, sa, *a. feathered*
Plural, *a. 2. plural*
Plural, *s. m. plural number*
Pluralidad, *s. f. plurality*
Pluvia, *s. f. rain*
Pluvial, *a. 2. pluvial*
Pluvial, *sub. m. a plover* || *a cope*
Pluvioso, sa, *a. pluvious*
Pneumático, ca, *a. pneumatick*
Poas, *s. f. pl. cringles of the bowline*
Pobeda, *sub. f. a grove of poplars*
Poblacho, *s. m. the mob* [*the rabble*
Poblacion, *s. f. the peopling* || *a town* || *populousness*
Poblado, *s. m. a town ; a village, etc.*
Poblador, *s. m. a founder of a colony, etc.*
Poblar, *v. a. to people*
Poblazo, *s. m. a populous town, etc.*
Pobo, *s. m. white pop*[lar]
Pobre, *a. 2. poor*

f. a poor man ‖
ar
o, lla } adj. poo-
, ta } rish
ia, s. f. V. Po-
ite, adv. poorly
s. f. a gang of
people
s. m. almoner
s. f. a strumpet
s. m. a poor or
fellow
n, s. f. a gang of
s ‖ stinginess
o, lla, adj. dim.
rete
, s. m. a beggar
s. f. poverty
o, ma, adj. very
, s. m. the aggre-
beggars
m. a well digger
s. f. a hog-sty
s. f. a medicinal
[draught
ubs. f. potion ;
a. little ; few
es, seldom — po-
o, by degrees
s. m. drink
f. pruning
, s. f. a pruning-
s. m. a pruner
s. f. the gout in
t
a. to prune
, s. m. one em-
d by another
s. m. the season
ning
s. m. a setting-
[tinado
e podenco, a bas-
lo, s m. dim. de
s. power

Poder, v. a. to be able ‖ may ; can
Poderhabiente, s. m. V. Podatario
Poderío, s. m. power ; authority ‖ wealth
Poderosamente ad. powerfully
Poderoso, sa. adj. powerful ‖ wealthy
Podon, s. m. a pruning knife
Podre, s. m. pus ; matter
Podrecerse, v. r. to rot ; to putrify [trefaction
Podrecimiento. s. m. pu-
Podedumbre, s. f. rotteness
Podricion, podrir, etc. V. Pudricion, etc.
Poema, s. m. a poem
Poesia, s. f. poesy ; poetry
Poeta, s. m a poet
Poética, s. f. art of poetry
Poéticamente, adv. poetically
Poético, ca, a. poetical
Poetisa, s. f. poetress
Poetizar, v. a. to poetize
Poeton, s. m. a great poet (ironically)
Poinos, s m. pl. gauntree or gauntry ; horse
Polaca, s. f. the upper part of a shoe [polacre
Polacre, s. m. poluque ;
Polar, adj. 2. polar
Polayna, sub. f. spatterdash [block
Polea, s. f. a pulley ‖ a
Poleada, s. f. pap for children
Polémica, s. f. the art of offinding and defending a fortified place ‖ dogmatical theology
Polémico, ca, a. polemical
Polenta, s. f. a pudding made of the meal of maize
Poleo, s. m. pennyroyal ‖ ostentation
Polevi, sub. m. a kind of very high heels in the shoes
Poliantea, s. f. polyanthea
Poliarquía, s. f. polygarchy
Poliárquico, ca, a. relating to polygarchy
Pólice, s. m. the thumb
Policia, s. f. police ; polity ‖ politeness ‖ neatness
Policitacion, s. f. an offer or promise
Policresta (sal), s. f. polychrest
Poligamia, s. f. polygamy
Poligamo, ma, a. polygamist
Poligiota, s. f. polyglot
Polígono. s. m. a polygon
Polígono, na, a polygonal
Poligrafía, s. f. polygraphy [dron
Polihedro, sub. m. polye-
Polilla, s. f. a moth
Polinche, s. m. a receiver of stolen goods
Polipétalo, la, a. polipetalous
Pólipo, s. m. polypus
Polipodio, s. m. polypody
Polir, v. a. to polish
Polisílabo, ba, adj. poly syllabical
Polispastos, s. f. a machine with many pullies
Política, s. f. politicks ; policy ‖ politeness
Políticamente, adv. politically
Político, ca, a. political
Político, s. m. politician
Póliza, s. f. an order given to pay any sum

Póliza de seguro, *a policy of insurance*
Polizon, *s. m. an idle slovenly boy*
Polla, *s. f. a young hen || a girl || a pool (at cards)* [*chicken*
Pollastro, *sub. m. a great*
Pollastron, *s. m. a lofty strong-limbed lad*
Pollazon, *s. m. a hatch; a covey*
Pollera, *sub. f. a coop || a sort of petticoat*
Pollería, *sub. f. poultry-market*
Pollero, *s. m. a poulterer || a hen-roost*
Pollico, *subs. m. a young chick* [*ass-colt*
Pollinejo, *s. m. a young*
Pollino, *s. m. an ass-colt || an ass*
Pollito, *s. m. a little chick*
Pollo, *s. m. a chick*
Polluelo, *s. m. a young chick*
Polo, *s. m. pole*
Poltron, na, *adj. lazy; slothful* [*chair*
Silla poltrona, *an elbow-*
Poltronería, *s. f. laziness*
Poltronizarse, *ver. r. to grow idle; lazy*
Polucion, *s. f. pollution*
Poluto, ta, *a. polluted*
Polvareda, *s. f. a cloud of dust* [*verise*
Polvificar, *v. a. to pul-*
Polvillo, *s. m. small dust*
Polvillos, *plur. a sweet powder for the hair*
Polvo, *s. m. dust || a pinch of snuff*
Pólvora, *s. f. gun powder*
Polvoreamiento, *s. m. dusting; powdering*
Polvorear, *v. a. to dust; to powder*

Polvoriento, ta, *a. dusty*
Polvorin, *s. m. priming powder || a priming-powder-case*
Polvorista, *sub. m. gun powder-maker*
Polvorizar, *v. act. to pulverise*
Polvoroso, sa. *a. dusty*
Poma, *s. f. an apple || perfuming-pan* or *box || a pomander*
Pomada, *s. f. pomatum*
Pomar, *sub. m. an apple-orchard* [*stone*
Pómez, *s. f. the pumice-*
Pomífero, ra, *a. bearing apples*
Pomo, *s. m. an apple || any sort of fruit || a pomander || pommel || a nosegay* [*pump*
Pompa, *subs. f. pomp || a*
Pompear, *v. n. to strut; to look big*
Pomposamente, *adv. pompously* [*pous*
Pomposo, sa, *adj. pom-*
Poncela, *s. f. a maid; a virgin* [*quor*)
Ponche, *s. m. punch* (*li-*
Poncho, cha, *adj. lazy; idle*
Ponchon, na, *a. aum. de* Poncho
Poncil, *sub. m. a sort of great lemon*
Ponderable, *a. 2. ponderable || important*
Ponderacion, *s. f. ponderation || exaggeration*
Ponderado, da, *adj. presomptuous; arrogant*
Ponderador, *s. m. ponderer || he that extols* or *magnifies*
Ponderar, *v. a. to weigh || to ponder || to extol; to magnify*

Ponderativo, va, *a. exaggerating*
Ponderosamente, *ad. considerately*
Ponderosidad, *s. f. ponderosity*
Ponderoso, sa, *a. ponderous || cautious; circumspect* [*egg*
Ponedero, *s. m. nest*
Ponedero, ra, *a. that lays eggs || that may be put* or *set*
Ponedor, *s. m. one who puts* or *sets || out bidder*
Ponentisco, ca, *adj. occidental*
Poner, *v. act. to put; to set; to lay*
Poner fin, *to make an end*
— la lengua en alguno, *to talk ill of one* — en depósito, *to deposite* — árboles, *to plant trees*
— campo, *to pitch the camp*
Ponerse, *v. r. to go about something || to betake one's self to... || to oppose; to resist*
Ponerse el sol, *to set* — en ostentacion, *to take state upon one* — en cobro, *to put one's self in safety*
Poniente, *s. m. the west || west wind*
Ponleví, *s. m. V.* Polevi
Pontage, } *s. m. pontage,*
Pontazgo, } *bridge-toll.*
Pontificado, *s. m. pontificate*
Pontifical, *s. m. pontifical || pontificalia*
Pontifical, *a. 2. pontifical*
Pontificalmente, *ad. pontifically*
Pontificar, *v. a. to govern the church as the*

ves || *to celebrate mass*
pontificalibus
tifice, *s. m. Pontiff*;
ontifice [*tifical*
tificio, cia, *adj. pon-*
ton, *s. m. ponton*
zoña, *s. f. poison*
zoñar, *v. a. to poison*
zoñoso, sa, *a. poiso-*
ous
a, *s. f. poop; stern*
ar, *v. a. to dally with;*
make slight of...
eses, *s. m. the fore-*
ays [*straw*
ote, *sub. m. a sort of*
ulacho, *s. m. the low*
abble
ular, *a.* 2. *popular*
ra popular, *the popu-*
r favour
ularmente, *adv. po-*
ularly [pulacho
ulazo, *s. m. Voy.* Po-
loso, sa, *a. populous*
uedad, *s. f. smallness;*
itleness || *meanness of*
irit
aillo, lla, *a. very little*
simo, ma, *adj. the*
ast that may be
aito, ta, *a. very little*
, *prep. for* || *by*
tal, *so that* — por acá
por allá, *here or there*
por ventura, *per ad-*
nture
cel, *s. m. a small pig*
elana, *s. f. china-wa-*
|| *a great earthen* ||
owl || *white colour mi-*
d with azure
ino, *s. m. a young*
g || *bruise; blow*
ino, na, *adj. belon-*
ng to a pig
ion, s. f. portion
oncica, *s f. a small*
tion

Porcionista, *s. m. he who has a right to one of the shares*
Porcipelo, *s. m. bristle*
Porcuno, na, *a. of* or *belonging to swine*
Pordiosear, *v. a. to beg*
Pordiosería, *s. f. beggary*
Pordiosero, *s. m. a beggar*
Porfía, *s. f. contention; strife* || *obstinacy* || *importunity*
A' porfía, *in emulation of one another*
Porfiadamente, *adv. obstinately*
Porfiado, da, *a. obstinate*
Porfiador, *s. m. a wrangler* || *an obstinate man*
Porfiar, *v. a. to contend positively* || *to stand obstinately in a thing*
Pórfido, *s. m. porphyry*
Poro, *s. m. a pore*
Porosidad, *s. f. porosity*
Poroso, sa, *a. porous*
Porque, *conj. because* || *why*
Porque, *s. m. cause; motive* [*wild board*
Porquera, *s. f. soil of a*
Porquería, *s. f. nastiness; filtiness* || *dirt; filth* || *incivility*
Porqueriza, *s. f. a hog-sty*
Porquerizo, } *s. masc. a*
Porquero, } *swineherd*
Porqueron, *s. m. a catch-pole* [*swine*
Porquezuelo, *s. m. a little*
Porra, *s. f. a club* || *pride; vanity* || *a dunce; a fool* [*way*
Hacer porra, *to stop in the*
Porrada, *s. f. a blow with a club* || *folly; impertinence*
Porrazo, *s. m. a blow with a club, etc.*

Porrería, *sub. f. footery; foppery*
Porreta, *sub. f. the green leaf of a leek, etc.*
En porreta, *adv nakedly*
Porrilla, *s. f. a farrier's hammer*
Porrina, *s. f. the corn, wheen green*
Porro, ra, *adj. dunce; stupid*
Porron, *s. m. a water-pot*
Porrudo, *s. m. a crook*
Porta, *s. f. the port* (*the grand seignor's court*)
Portas, *pl. ports* (*in a ship*)
Portacartas, *s. m. the courier's mail*
Portada, *s. f. front; frontispiece* || *the little page*
Portadas, *plur. a weaver's warp*
Portaderas, *s. f. pl. Voy.* Aportaderas
Portador, *s. m. a bearer*
Portal, *s. m. porch; entry; hall* || *pórtico* || *a gate* [Portal
Portalazo, *s. m. aum. de*
Portalejo, *s. m. dim. de* Portal
Portaleña, *s. f. embrasure* || *a board sawed for doors*
Portalero, *s. m. an officer at the avenues of a town; to receive the duties, etc.* [lejo
Portalico, *s. m. V.* Porta-
Portalo, *s. m. a little door in a ship's side*
Portamanteo, *s. m. a portmanteau*
Portanario, *s. m. the pylorus*
Portanto, *s. m.* ambling
Andar de portanto, to amble

Portantillo, *sub. m. dim. de* Portante

Portanveces, *s. m. vicar; vice-gerent* [*holes*

Portañolas, *s. f. pl. port-*

Portapaz, *s. 2. pax*

Portar, *v. a. to carry*

Portarse, *v. r. to behave; to demean*

Portátil, *a. 2. portable*

Portazgo, *subs. m. toll; turnpike*

Portazguero, *s. m. a gatherer of a toll*

rtazo, *s. m. a blow given by the door*

Porte, *s. m. carriage || postage || the burden of a ship || gait || countenance* [*hire*

Portear, *v. a. to carry for*

Portearse, *v. r. to travel* (*speaking of birds*)

Portento, *s. m. portent*

Portentoso, sa, *adj. portentous*

Porterejo, *s. m. a paltry porter*

Portería, *s. f. the main door of a convent, etc. || the porters lodge or office* [terejo

Porterillo, *s. m. V.* Por-

Portero, ra, *s. a porter; a door-keeper*

Portezuela, *s. f. a little door; a vicket*

Pórtico, *s. m. a portico*

Portillo, *s. m. a breach in a vall, etc. || a notch or gap || way; expedient*

Portillos, *pl. back-doors*

Porton, *s. m. interior gate*

Pos (en), *adv. behind*

Posa, *s. f. a stop; a rest*

Posas, *pl. knel || the buttocks*

Posada, *subs. f. lodging; dwelling || inn*

Posaderas, *sub. f. pl. the buttocks*

Posadero, *s. m. inn-keeper || a rest for a musket, etc.*

Posar, *v. n. to lodge || to rest || to lay down one's burden || to sit down to dinner*

Posavergas, *s. f. pl. a sort of yards used anciently*

Posdata, *s. f. postcript*

Poseedor, *s. m. possessor*

Poseer, *v. a. to possess*

Poseso, sa, *p. p. possessed*

Pagar el poseso, *to pay one's entrance*

Posesion, *s. f. possession*

Posesional, *a. 2. relating to*, or *including, possession*

Posesivo, va, *a. possessive*

Posesor, *s. m. possessor*

Posesorio, ria, *a. possessory* [*ty*

Posibilidad, *s. f. possibili-*

Posibilitar, *v. a. to make possible*

Posible, *a. 2. possible*

Posible, *s. m. wealth*

Posicion, *s. f. position*

Positivamente, *adv. positively*

Positivo, va, *a. positive*

De positivo, *adv. positively* [*nary*

Pósito, *s. m. a publick gra-*

Positura, *s. f. positure || posture*

Poso, *s. m. rest || dregs; grounds*

Poson, *s. m. V.* Posadero

Pospelo (á), *adv. against the hair* or *grain || unseasonably*

Pospierna, s. f. the thigh

Posponer, v. act. to postpone

Posta, s. *f.* post || post-*house || post-horses || post-stage || hail-shot || a lay* or *stake* (*at pla*

Postar, *v. a. to bet; to*

Poste, *s. m. a post; a pillar; a prop*

Postear, *v. a. to post; to ride post* [*som kno*

Posteleros, *s. m. pl tra*

Postema, *s. f. apostume*

Postemoro, *s. m. a knife to open apostumes*

Postergar, *v. a. to leave behind*

Posteridad, *s. f. posterity*

Posterior, *a. 2. posterior*

Posterioridad, *s. f. posteriority*

Posteriormente, *ad. after*

Postigo, *sub. m. a back-door || a wicket || one fold of a double door*

Postiguillo, *s. m. dim de* Postigo

Postila, *sub. f. marginal note; postil*

Postilacion, *s. f. the act of writing marginal notes*

Postilar, *v. act. to write marginal notes*

Postilla, *s. f. a scab*

Postillon, *s. m. postilion || a jade*

Postilloso, sa, *a. scabby*

Postizo, za, *adj. sham; false || done after*

Posmeridiano, na, *adjec. post-meridian*

Postor, *s. m. out bidder*

Postracion, *s. f. prostration*

Postrador, *s. m. he who prostrates another*

Postrar, *v. a. to prostrate*

Postrarse, *v. r. to prostrate*

Postre, adj. 2. last

Postres, s. m. pl. desert fruit

rer, a. 2. last
reramente, ad. lastly
rero, ra, a. last
rimeramente, adver.
stly [Novísimos
rimerías, s. f. pl. V.
rimero, ra, a. last
ulacion, s. f. postu-
tion
tulados, s. m. pl. pos-
ulates (in mathema-
cks [postulates
tulador, s. m. one who
tular, v. a. to postulate
tumo, ma, a. posthu-
mous
tura, sub. f. posture ||
osition || planting ||
he set rate of commodi-
ies || agreement; trea-
' || wager || women's
aint || a bird's egg
turas, pl. young trees
ransplanted
able, a. 2. potable
age, sub. m. pottage ||
reens; roots
agería, s. f. greens or
oots for a soup
e, sub. m. an earthen-
ot || a flower-pot
encia, s. f. potency;
ower || possibility
encial, a. 2. potential
encialmente, adv. po-
entially
entado, s. m. potentate
ente, a. 2. powerful;
otent || strong; lusty
entemente, ad. power-
ully [night
estad, sub. f. power;
ísimo, ma, a. chief;
rincipal
ra, s. f. a rupture
ranca, sub. f. a young
are
ero, s. m. a surgeon
at cures ruptures

Potrico, s. m. a little colt
Potrilla, s. f. an old man
that plays the pretty
fellow
Potro, s. m. a colt || an
engine to rack malefac-
tors || a frame of farriers
|| an earthen chamber-
pot || a bubo
Potroso, sa, a. bursten
Poya, s. f. furnage
Horno de poya, a com-
mon oven [on a bench
Poyal, s. m. a cloth to lay
Poyata, s. f. a cup board
in a wall
Poyo, s. m. a stone bench
|| the judge's fee
Poza, sub. f. a puddle of
water
Pozal, s. m. a pail || the
brim of a well
Pozo, s. m. a well
Pozuela, subs. f. a small
puddle
Práctica, s. f. practice
Practicable, a. 2. practi-
cable [tically
Prácticamente, adv. prac-
Practicante, s. m. a young
physician or surgeon
Practicar, v. a. to practise
Práctico, ca, a. practical
Practicon, s. m. one capa-
ble more by practice
than study
Pradal, s. m. a meadow
Pradecillo, s. m. a little
meadow
Pradera, } s. f. a mea-
Pradería, } dow
Praderoso, sa, a. relating
to a meadow
Pradico, dillo, s. m. a lit-
tle meadow
Prado, sub. m. a meadow
|| a publick walking-
place [tick
Pragmática, s. f. pragma-

Pragmático, ca, a. prag-
matick
Prasio, s. m. a coarse sort
of emerald
Pravedad, s. f. pravity
Pravo, va, adj. wicked;
perverse
Praxis, s. f. practice
Pre, s. m. a soldier's daily
pay [the hands
Premanibus, adver. into
Preámbulo, s. m. preamble
Prebenda, s. f. a prebend
Prebendado, s. m. a pre-
bend or prebendary
Prebestad, s. f. } pro-
Prebestadgo, s. m. } vost-
ship
Preboste, s. m. a provost
Precacion, s. f. supplica-
tion [rique
Precario, ria, a. preca-
Precaucion, s. f. precau-
tion [cautious
Precautelar, v. act. to be
Precaver, v. a. to prevent
any danger
Precedencia, s. f. prece-
dence
Preceder, v. a. to precede
Precelente, a. 2 excellent
Preceptista, s. 2. one who
gives precepts
Preceptivo, va, a. precep-
tive
Precepto, s. m. a precept
Preceptor, s. m. preceptor
Preces, s. f. pl. prayers
Precesion, s. f. reticence
Preciado, da, a. precious
Preciador, s. m. prizer
Preciar, v. a. to prize; to
value [brag of
Preciarse, v. r. to boast, or
Precio, s. m. price; va-
lue; worth
Preciosamente, adv. pre-
ciously [ness
Preciosidad, s. f. precious-

Precioso, sa, *a. precious*
|| gay; merry
Precipicio, *s. m. a preci-*
pice [*pitation*
Precipitacion, *s. f. preci-*
Precipitadamente, *ad. pre-*
cipitately
Precipitar, *v. a. to preci-*
pitate [*fall*
Precipite, *a. 2. ready to*
Precipitosamente, *ad. has-*
tily
Precipitoso, sa, *a. steep ||*
inconsiderate
Precipuo, pua, *a. chief;*
principal
Precisamente, *adv. preci-*
sely || necessarily
Precisar, *v. a. to oblige;*
to force
Precision, *sub. f. precise-*
ness || necessity
Preciso, sa, *a. precise ||*
necessary
Precito, ta, *adj. reproba-*
te; damned
Preclaro, ra, *a. famous;*
illustrious
Precocidad, *s. f. precocity*
Preconizacion, *s. f. preco-*
nising [*conize*
Preconizar, *v. a. to pre-*
Preconocedor, *s. m. one*
who foresees; provident
Preconocer, *v. a. to foresee*
Precoz, *a. 2. precocious*
Precursor, ra, *a. precur-*
sor [*sor*
Predecesor, *s. m. predeces-*
Predecir, *v. a. to foretell*
Predefinicion, *s. f. pre-*
determination
Predefinir, *v. a. to prede-*
termine [*destination*
Predestinacion, *s. f. pre-*
Predestinar, *v. a. to pre-*
destinate
Predeterminacion, *sub. f.*
predetermination

Predeterminar, *v. act. to*
predetermine
Predial, *a. 2. predial*
Prédica, *s. f. a sermon*
Predicable, *a. 2. that may*
be preached upon ||
praise-worthy || predi-
cable (in logick)
Predicacion, *sub. f. prea-*
ching || a sermon
Predicadera, *s. f. a pulpit*
Predicaderas, *pl. eloquen-*
ce
Predicado, *s. m. the attri-*
bute, in a proposition
Predicador, *s. m. a prea-*
cher
Predicamental, *a. 2. rela-*
thing to a predicament
Predicamento, *s. m. pre-*
dicament || reputation
Predicante, *s. m. a pre-*
dicant
Predicar, *v. a. to preach*
|| to preach up [*pit*
Predicatorio, *s. m. a pul-*
Prediccion, *s. f. prediction*
Predileccion, *s. f. predi-*
lection [*red*
Predilecto, ta, *a. prefer-*
Predio, *s. m. a farm; a*
demesne [*dominate*
Predominar, *v. a. to pre-*
Predominio, *s. m. predo-*
minance [*minence*
Preeminencia, *s. f. pree-*
Preeminente, *a. 2. pree-*
minent [*sublime*
Preexcelso, sa, *a. great;*
Preexistencia, *sub. f. pre-*
existence
Preexistir, *v. n. to pre-exist*
Prefacio, *s. m. the preface*
(in the mass)
Prefacion, *s. f. a preface*
(in a book)
Prefacioncilla, *s. f. a lit-*
tle preface
Prefecto, *s. m. a prefect*

Prefectura, *s. f. prefec-*
ture [*rence*
Preferencia, *sub. f. prefe-*
Preferible, *a. 2. preferable*
Preferir, *v. a. to prefer*
Preferirse, *v. r. to offer*
or present one's self for...
Prefigurar, *v. a. to pref-*
gurate
Prefinir, *v. act. to fix a*
term or delay
Prefixar, *v. a. to prefix*
Prefixo, xa, *a. prefixed*
Prefulgente, *adj. 2. res-*
plendant; glistering
Pregon, *s. m. proclama-*
tion || a crier
Pregonar, *ver. a. to pro-*
claim by a crier
Pregonero, *s. m. a crier*
Pregunta, *s. f. a question*
Preguntador, *sub. m. one*
that asks many ques-
tions
Preguntar, *v. a. to ask*
questions
Preguntón, *sub. m. a tea-*
sing asker of questions
Prejudicial, *a. 2. to be pre-*
judged
Prelacía, *s. f. prelacy*
Prelacion, *s. f. prelation*
Prelada, *sub. f. the supe-*
rior of a monastery
Prelado, *s. m. a prelate ||*
a superior of a convent
Preliminar, *a. 2. preli-*
minary
Preliminares, *sub. m. pl.*
preliminario
Prelucir, *ver. a. to shine*
before hand
Preludio, *s. m.* } *a prelu-*
Prelusion, *s. f.* } *de*
Premática, *s. f. a prag-*
matick [*mature*
Prematuro, ra, *adj. pre-*
Premeditacion, *s. f. pre-*
meditation

ditar, v. a. to pre-
litate [der
ador, s. m. a rewar-
ar, v. a. to reward
o, s. m. a reward ||
rize || any thing gi-
to boot in an ex-
nge
oso, sa, a. crowded
rouble some; tea-
y [ses
sas, s. f. pl. premi-
cion, s. f. predeter-
ation
nstratenses, sub. m.
remonstratenses or
bertins
ra, s. f. V. Aprieto
a, s. f. a pledge; a
n || household goods
bre de buenas pren-
, a man of good
's
ar, v. a. to give or
a pawn
ar, v. n. to win a
with good words,
leness, etc.
edero, s. m. a hoock;
aps, etc.
edor, s. m. one who
's, etc.
er, v. a. to take; to
ch || to seize; to ar-
|| to set off || to leap
er, v. n. to take root
catch fire
eria, s. f. a broker's
p
ero, s. m. a broker
ld cloaths, etc.
ido, sub. m. dress;
b; attire || a pattern
laces
imiento, s. m. ta-
g; seizing
cion, s. f. prenotion
, s. f. a press
lo, s. m. the gloss of a cloth when calen-
dered
Prensadura, s. f. pressing
Prensar, v. a. to press
Prensista, s. m. a pressman
Prenunciar, v. a. to foretell; to presage
Prenuncio, sub. m. a pro-
gnostick or presage
Preñada, a. f. with child
|| big with young
Pared preñada, a wall
that bellies out
Preñado, s. m. } pregnan-
Preñez, s. f. } cy
Preocupacion, s. f. preoc-
cupancy || preposses-
sion
Preocupar, v. a. to preoc-
cupate || to prepossess
Preordinacion, sub. f. pre-
dination [ordain
Preordinar, v. a. to pre-
Preparacion, s. f. } prepa-
Preparamiento, s. m. } ration
Preparar, v. a. to prepare
Preparativo, s. m. a pre-
parative
Preparativo, va, adj. pre-
paratory
Preponderar, v. n. to pre-
ponderate
Preponer, v. a. to prefer
Preposicion, s. f. prepo-
sition
Prepósito, sub. mas. the
provost of a collegiate
church || the superior of
a religious order
Prepositura, s. f. provost-
ship || dignity or office
of a superior
Preposteracion, s. f. pre-
posterousness
Prepóstero, ra, adj. pre-
posterous [werful
Prepotente, a. 2. very po-
Prepucio, s. m. prepuce
Prerogativa, s. f. prero-
gative
Presa, s. f. taking; cat-
ching || a prize || prey
|| gain; profit || the
hawks talon || handle ||
flood-gate; mill-dam,
etc. [broth
Presa de caldo. jellily-
Presada, s. f. the green
colour of a leek
Presagiar, v. a. to presage
Presagio, s. m. a presage
Presagioso, sa, adj. in-
cluding a presage
Presago, ga, adj. that
presages [thood
Presbiterado, s. m. priest-
Presbiteral, a. 2. priestly
Presbiterato, s. m. priest-
hood [chancel
Presbiterio, sub. mas. the
Presbítero, s. m. presbyter;
priest [cience
Presciencia, sub. f. pres-
Prescindir, v. a. to abs-
tract [cito
Prescito, ta, adj. V. Pre-
Prescribir, v. a to pres-
cribe [cription
Prescripcion, s. f. pres-
Prescriptible, a. 2. that
may be prescribed
Prescripto, ta, p. p. pres-
cribed
Presea, s. f. a jewel; a
rich ornament, or gift
Presencia, s. f. presence
Presencial, a. 2. relating
to presence
Presencialmente, adv. in
one's town person
Presentacion, s. f. presen-
tation
Presentador, s. m. patron
of a benefice
Presentalla, s. f. a votive
Presentaneamente, adv.
presently

Presontillo, *s. m. a small*
Presentimiento, *s. m. presentiment*
Presentir, *v. a. to foresee*
Preservacion, *s. f. preservation* [*ver*
Preservador, *s. m. preser-*
Preservar, *v. a. to preserve* [*servative*
Preservativo, *s. m. a pre-*
Preservativo, va, *adj. preservative* [*dentship*
Presidencia, *sub. f. presi-*
Presidente, *s. m. a president* [*son*
Presidiar, *v. a. to garri-*
Presidiario, *s. m. one banished to any strong place in Africa*
Presidio, *s. m. a garrison-town* || *help; protection*
Presidir, *v. a. to preside*
Presilla, *s f. a loop* || *a sort of linen*
Presion, *sub. f. pression; pressure*
Preso, *s. m. a prisoner*

Preste, *s. m. a priest that celebrates mass*
Preste Juan, *Prester John; the Emperor of Ethiopia*
Prester, *s. m. a hurricane*
Presteza, *s. f. quickness*
Prestigiador, *s. m. a juggler*
Prestigio, *s. m. a prestige; a juggler's trick, etc.*
Prestigioso, sa, *adj. prestigious* [*mony*
Prestimonio, *s. m. presti-*
Prestiños, *s. m. pl. a kind of fritters* [*ready*
Presto, ta, *adj. quick;*
Presto, *adv. quickly; readily*
Presumidamente, *adver. presumptuously*
Presumido, da, *adject. proud; presumptuous*
Presumir, *v. act. to presume*
Presumir, *ver. n. to presume too much upon*

oppressi
danger
haste ;
Presurosan
ligently
Presuroso,
Pretal, *s. m*
ther
Pretenden
Pretender,
tend || *to*
or *aspir*
Pretendien
tender
Pretension
Pretenso,
Pretensor,
der
Pretericion
omitting
name of
— prete
Preterir, *v*
mention
son in a
Pretérito,
rit; pas

, s. m. a pretexte;
ence
ar, v. a V. Pre-

sb. m. a rail to
e breast on
s. f. a girdle
', s. m. a blow
girdle
, sub. f. a little

. m. a pretor
s. f. pretorship
, a 2. of, or be-
g to a pretor
.o, na, adj. pre-

s. m. pretorium
ria, adj. V. Pre-

s. f. pretorship
r, v. n. to prevail
cion, s. f. preva-
n
dor, s. m. a pre-
tor
r, v. a. to pre-
'e
to, s. m. preva-
n of an attor-
:c.
n, s. f. prepa-
|| provision;
foresight || ad-
caution || pre-
z
mente, adv. be-
nd
), da, adj. pro-
abundant; full
ident; wary
, v. a. to pre-
o foresee; to be
|| to prevent || to
r inform
e, v. r. to pro-
o be cautious
. a. to foresee
v. a. to pervert

Previlegiar, gio. V. Privilegiar, etc,
Previo, via, adj. previous
Prevision, s. f. prevision
Previsto, ta, adject. foreseen [glory
Prez, s. m. honour; fame;
Priapismo, sub. m. priapism
Priesa, s. f. haste; speed || fight || throug
Prietamente, adver. closely; pressingly
Prieto, ta, adj. blackish || stingy
Prima, s. f. prima (a canonical hour) || she cousin || the smallest string of an instrument || the female hawk
Primacía, s. f. primacy
Primacial, a. 2. belonging to a primate
Primado, s. m. a primate || primariness
Primado, da, adj. primary
Primal, s. m. a silk-twist, etc.
Primal (cordero), s. m. a lamb the firstyeaned in the year
Primamente, adv. prettily; curiously
Primariamonte, adv. primarily [primary
Primario, ria, adj. first;
Primavera, sub. fem. the spring || a silk cloth full of flowers
Primazgo, sub. m. cousinship [cousin
Primearse, v. r. to call
Primer, a. m. the first
Primera, s. fem. primero (a game)
Primeramente, adv. first
Primería, s. f. primariness
Primeriza, s. f. a woman delivered of his first child [primary
Primerizo, za, adj. first;
Primero, ra, adj. the first || the former
Primero, adver. first || before
Primicerio, ria, adj. first; primogenial
Primicerio, s. m. the dean of some churches
Primichon, s. m. a little skain of silk
Primicias, s. f. pl. first fruits || essay
Priicmlerio, s. m. V. Primiciero
Primigenio, nia, adjec. first-born
Primilla, s. f. the pardon of a first fault
Primísimo, ma, adj. very curious, etc.
Primitivo, va, adj. primitive
Primo, ma, adj. first || skilful || delicate; curious [a negro
Primo, s. m. a cousin ||
Primo hermano, a cousin german
Primogénito, ta, adject. first-born
Primogenitura, s. f. primogeniture
Primoprimus, s. m. an undeliberated motion
Primor, s. m. skilfulness || delicacy; curiousness [dial
Primordial, a. 2. primor-
Primorear, v. n. to excel in any art
Primorosamente, adv. curiously
Primoroso, sa, adj. curious; delicate; excellent || skilful
Princesa, s. f. a princess

Principela, *s. f. a sort of camlet*

Principiador, *sub. m. one that begins* [*ner*

Principiante, *s. m. begin-*

Principio, *sub. m. beginning* || *principle*

Principios, *pl. first course of meat*

Pringada, *s. f. a slice of bread pressed upon fat bacon boiled soft*

Pringar, *v. a. to grease* || *to baste a capon, etc.* || *to wound* || *to blot a man's reputation*

Pringarse, *v. r. to misbehave in an employment*

Pringon, *s. m. greasing* || *a spot of grease*

Pringon, na, *adj. greasy*

Pringue, *s. 2. the dripping of fat bacon, etc.*

Prior, *s. m. a prior*

Prior, *a. 2. prior; anterior*

Priora, *s. f. prioress*

put to a ferret

Privacion, *s. f. privation*

Privada, *s. f. privy; necessary house*

Privadamente, *adv. intimately*

Privado, *s. m. a favourite*

Privado, da, *adj. private* || *privy; familiar*

Privanza, *s. f. intimacy; favour*

Privar, *v. a. to deprive*

Privar, *v. n. to be in favour; to be very intimate*

Privarse de juicio, *to turn mad* — de razon, *to be drunk* [*vatively*

Privativamente, *adv. pri-*

Privativo, va, *adj. privative* || *private; particular* [*lege*

Privilegiar, *v. a to privi-*

Privilegiativo, va, *adj. including a privilege*

Privilegio, *s. m. a privilege* [*tage*

tion; es

Probanza,

-proof

Probar, *v.*

try; to t

Probática,

Probatorio

batory

Problema,

Problemát

problem

Problemát

problem

Procacidad

Procaz, *a.*

Proceder,

ding; p

Proceder,

Procedido

Procedimi

ceeding

Proceloso,

Prócer, *s.*

a great

Prócer, *a*

Procero, r

Proceridad

...so, s. m. progress || ...cess
...nto, s. m. prepara... ; making ready
...ama, ...amacion } s. f. pro... clama... || acclamation
...lamar, v. a. to pro...im
...live, a. 2. proclivous
...o, s. m. lover ; sweet...rt [sul
...onsul, s. m. procon...
...onsulado, s. m. pro...nsulship
...onsular, a. 2. procon...lar [tion
...reacion, s. f. procrea...
...eador, s. m. procrea...
...ear, v. a. to procreate
...ura, s. f. a letter of ...orney
...uracion, s. f. admi...tration || a letter of ...orney || an attor...'s office || procura...n-money
...urador, s. m. an at...ney ; a proctor || a ...curator
...uraduría, s. f. proc...ship || an attorney's ...dy
...urar, v. a. to procure ...to sollicit
...urrente, s. m. a cape ...nning into the sea
...icion, s. f. prodition; ...achery
...igalidad, s. f. prodi...lity [digally
...igamente, adv. pro...
...igio, s. m. a prodigy
...igiosamente, adver. ...odigiously
...igioso, sa, adj. pro...ious
...o, ga, adj. prodigal

Proditorio, ria, adj. proditory [tion
Produccion, s. f. production
Producibilidad, s. f. producibleness
Producible, a. 2. producible [cer
Producidor, s. m. produ...
Producir, v. a. to produce
Productivo, va, adj. productive [duced
Producto, ta, p. p. pro...
Producto, s. m. produce ; product
Proejar, ver. act. to row against the wind or stream
Proel, s. m. a sailor who works in the prow
Proemial, a. 2. introductory [preface
Proémio, s. mas. proem ;
Proeza, s. f. prowess
Profanacion, s. f. profanation
Profanador, s. m. profaner
Profanamente, adv. profanely [fanation
Profanamiento, s. m. pro...
Profanar, v. a. to profane
Profanidad, s. fem. profaneness || an excessive luxury
Profano, na, adjec. profane || worldly-minded
Profecía, s. f. prophecy
Proferir, v. a. to utter ; to speak [rirse
Proferirse, v. r. V. Prefe...
Profesar, v. a. to profess
Profesion, s. f. profession
Profeso, sa, adj. y f. professed monk or nun
Profesor, s. m. professor
Profeta, s. m. prophet
Profetal, a. 2. written by the prophets
Profetar, v. a. to prophesy

Profèticamente, adv. prophetically
Profético, ca, adj. prophetical
Profetisa, s. f. prophetess
Profetizar, v. a. to prophesy [cient
Proficiente, adj. profi...
Proficuo, cua. adj. profitable
Profligar, v. a. to overthrow ; to root
Prófugo, ga, adj. fugitive ; wandering
Profundamente, ad. deep; deeply
Profundar, v. a. to dig || to dive into ; to go to the bottom of....
Profundidad, s. fem. profoundness ; depth
Profundizar, v. a. V. Profundar
Profundo, da, adj. deep ; profound
Profusamente, adv. profusely
Profusion, s. f. profusion
Profuso, sa, adj. profuse || copious
Progénie, s. f. progeny ; off-spring
Progenitor, s. mas. progenitor
Progenitura, s. f. progeny
Progimnasma, s. m. beginning ; essay
Progresion, s. f. progression
Progresivo, va, adj. progressive
Progreso, s. m. progress
Prohibicion, s. f. prohibition
Prohíbir, v. a. to prohibit
Prohibitivo, va, } adject.
Prohibitorio, ria, } prohibitory
Prohijador, s. m. adopter

Prohijamiento, *s. m. adoption*

Prohijar, *v. a. to adopt for a son*

Prolacion, *s. fem. pronunciation*

Prole, *s. fem. issue ; offspring ; a child*

Prolegómeno, *s. m. prolegomena*

Proletario (Autor) *s. m. a paltry writer*

Prolífico, ca, *adj. prolifick*

Prolixamente, *adv. prolixly*

Prolixidad, *s. f. prolixity* || *tediousness*

Prolixo, xa, *adj. prolix* || *who stands upon trifles* || *tedious*

Prólogo, *s. m. prologue*

Prolongacion, *s. fem. prolongation*

Prolongadamente, *adver. with prolongation*

Prolongado, da, *adject. oblong*

Prolongamiento, *s. mas. prolonging*

Prolongar, *v. a. to prolong*

Proloquio, *s. m. a short and witty sentence*

Prolusion, *s. f. a prelude*

Promediar, *v. a. to divide by halves* || *to entermeddle*

Promedio, *s. m. middle*

Promesa, *s. f. a promise*

Prometedor, *s. m. promiser*

Prometer, *v. a. to promise*

Prometerse, *v. r. to hope ; to flatter one's self*

Prometido, *sub. m. a promise* || *an out-bidding*

Prometimiento, *sub. m. a promise*

Promiscuamente, *adver. promiscuously*

Promiscuo, cua, *adj. promiscuous* || *equivocal*

Promision, *s. f. promise ; promising* || *promission*

Promisorio, ria, *adj. promissory*

Promocion, *s. f. promotion*

Promontorio, *s. m. promontory* || *mountain ; hill, etc.*

Promotor, *s. m. promoter* || *proctor*

Promovedor, *s. m. promoter ; instigator*

Promover, *v. a. to promote*

Promulgacion, *sub. f. promulgation*

Promulgador, *s. m. promulger*

Promulgar, *v. a. to promulgate ; to promulge*

Proncidad, *s. f. proneness*

Prono, na, *adjec. prone ; inclined*

Pronombre, *s. m. a pronoun*

Pronosticacion, *s. f. prognostication*

Pronosticador, ra, *adjec. prognosticator*

Pronosticar, *v. a. to prognosticate*

Pronostico, *sub. m. a prognostick*

Prontamente, *ad. promptly ; readily*

Pronteza, } *s. f. promptness ; quickness*
Prontitud, }

Pronto, ta, *adj. prompt ; ready*

Prontuario, *s. m. a tablebook ; a depositary, etc.*

Pronuba, *s. f. the woman that presides at a wedding*

Pronunciacion, s. f. pronunciation

Pronunciar, *v. ... nounce*

Propagacion, s ...

Propagador, *s. ... gator*

Propagar, *v. a ...*

Propagativo, v ... *propagates*

Propalar, *v. a. to divulge*

Propasar, *ver. ... beyond ; to*

Propensamente ... *propensity*

Propension, *s. ... sity*

Propenso, sa, *a... se ; inclined*

Propiamente, ... *perly*

Propiciacion, ... *tiation*

Propiciador, *s. ... tiator*

Propiciar, *v. a ...*

Propiciatorio, ... *pitiatory*

Propicio, cia, ... *tious*

Propiedad, *s. ...* || *propriety*

Propietariamen... *right of prop...*

Propietario, ri... *proprietor ;*

Propina, *sub. ... pay ; salary*

Propinar, *v. a ... to drink*

Propinquidad, ... *pinquity*

Propinquo, qua...

Propio, pia, *a...* || *fit*

Propio, *sub. ... disposition*

Propisimament... properly

Proponedor,

ı. to propose

. f. propor-

ın de, pro-
'to

e, a. 2. pro-
!

adv. pro-
portiona-
bly

), da, adjec.
able

. a. 2. propor-
[portion

dad, s. f. pro-

nente, adv.
ally

, v. a. to pro-

s. f. proposi-

n. discourse;
'k || purpose;

, purposedly
, to the pur-

. f. proposi-
ress; repre-

ı, p. p. pro-
rposed

o, s. m. a for-
ınce; a bul-

s. f. the act
of pushing
nemy
row

le, proportio-

. a. to share
ıably to....
m. a sharing
ıably to....

s. f. proro-
gation

Prorogar, v. a. to prorogue

Prorumpir, v. n. to issue or spring out with violence || to burst out

Prosa, s. fem. prose || a tedious discourse

Prosador, s. m. a prose-writer || a satirical, censorious man

Prosapia, s. f. race; generation

Prosayco, adj. prosaick

Proscribir, v. a. to proscribe

Proscripcion, s. f. proscription

Proscripto, ta, a. y sub. proscribed; proscript

Prosecucion, s. f. prosecution

Proseguible, a. 2. that may be prosecuted

Proseguimiento, s. m. prosecuting [secute

Proseguir, v. a. to pro-

Prosélito, s. m. proselyte

Prosevante, s. m. a pursuivant

Prosista, s. m. a prose-writer || a talkative man

Prosit! int. lat much good may it do you!

Prosodia, s. f. prosody || babbling; pratling || poesy

Prosopopeya, s. f. prosopopeia || ostentation

Prósperamente, adv. prosperously

Prosperar, v. a to give good success

Prosperar, v. n. to prosper [rity

Prosperidad. s. f. prospe-

Próspero, ra, adj. prosperous [tution

Prostitucion, s. f. prosti-

Prostituir, v. a. to prostitute [tute

Prostituto, ta, adj. prosti-

Proteccion, s. f. protection

Protector, s. m. a protector

Protectora, } s. f. protec-
Protectriz, } tress; protectrice

Proteger, v. a. to protect

Protervamente, ad. arrogantly; impudently

Protervia, } s. f. proter-
Protervidad, } vity

Protervo, va, a. arrogant; impudent

Protesta, } s. f. protes-
Protestacion, } tation

Protestante, a. y s. protestant

Protestar, v. a. to protest

Protesto, s. m. protest || protestation

Proto, the first in his line

Protocolo, s. m. protocol

Protomartir, s. m. protomartyr

Protomédico, subs. m. the first physician

Protonotario, s. m. protonotary

Prototipo, s. m. prototype

Provecho, s. m. profit; advantage; gain

Provechosamente, ad. profitably [table

Provechoso, sa, a. profi-

Provecto, ta, a. stricken in years

Proveedor, s. m. provider; purveyor.

Proveeduría, sub. f. purveyance || store-house

Proveer, v. a. to provide || to bestow a place upon one || to decree

Proveerse, ver. r. to ease one's body

Proveido, s. m. a decree

Provoido, da, *a. that has got a place*
Provcimiento, *s. m. providing*
Provena, *s. f. layer of a vine*
Provenir, *v. n. to proceed from*
Proverbiador, *s. m. a collection of proverbs*
Proverbial, *a. 2. proverbial*
Proverbialmente, *ad. proverbially*
Proverbio, *s. m. proverb* || *presage*
Providamente, *ad. providently*
Providencia, *s. f. providence*
Providencial, *a. 2. providential*
Providente, *a. 2.* } *provident*
Próvido, da, *a.* } *provident*
Provincia, *s. f. a province* || *an important matter*
Provincial, *a. 2. s. m. provincial*
Provincialato, *s. m. provincialship*
Provision, *s. f. provision* || *a providing one with a benefice* || *grant; patent.*
Proviso (Al), *adv. out of hand*
Provisor, *s. m. provider; provisor* || *a bishop's vicar-general*
Provisoría, *s f. the office of a provisor, etc.* || *the pantry in a monastery*
Provisto, ta, *p p. provided*
Provocacion, *s. f. provocation*
Provocador, *s. m. a provoker*
Provocar, *v. a. to provoke*
Provocativo, va, *a. provocative*
Próximamente, *ad. nearly* || *lately*
Proximidad, *s. f. proximity*
Próximo, ma, *a. near; next*
Próximo, *s. m. a neighbour*
Proyectar, *v. a. to project*
Proyecto, *s. m. a project* || *a draught*
Proyecto, ta, *a. extended; dilated*
Prudencia, *s. f. prudence*
Prudencial, *a 2. prudential*
Prudencialmente, *ad. prudencially*
Prudente, *a. 2. prudent*
Prudentemente, *ad. prudently*
Prueba, *sub. f. a proof* || *trial; essay* || *a shew* or *sample*
A' prueba, ó de prueba, *proof*
Pruina, *s. f. the hoary-frost*
Pruna, *s. f. a plum*
Pu, *s. f. the excrements of a child*
Pu! *int. fy!*
Pua, *subs. f. a point* || *a graft* or *graff* || *a sly cunning fellow*
Pubertad, *s. f. puberty*
Pubes, *sub. m. the bone about the privy parts*
Pública, *s. f. thesis on the publick law*
Publicacion, *s. f. publication*
Publicador, *s. m. publisher*
Publicamente, *adver. publickly*
Publicano, *s. m. a publican*
Publicar, *v. a. to publish*
Publicidad, *s. f publicity* || *a publick place*
Publico, ca, a. publick
Casa pública, a. bawdy-house
Público, s. m. the publick
Pucelana, *s. f. pozzolana*
Puchada, *s. f. a poultice made with meal and water*
Puches, *s. m. pl. hasty pudding made of flower, honey, etc.*
Puchecilla, *s. f. a sort of pap*
Puchera, *s. f. V.* Olla
Pucherico, *s. m. dim. of* Puchero
Puchero, *s. m. an earthen pot, a pipking* || *the meat boiled in the pot*
Pudendo, da, *a. shameful*
Partes pudendas, *the privy parts; the pudenda*
Pudicicia, *s. f. pudicity*
Pudor, *sub. m. modesty; shamefacedness*
Pudricion, *s. f. rottenness*
Pudridero, *s. m. a rotting place; a dung-hole, etc.*
Pudrigorio, *s. m. a sickly man*
Pudrimiento, *s. m. putrefaction, rottenness*
Pudrir, *v. act. to rot* || *to vex; to teaze*
Pudrir, *ver. n. to rot; to putrify*
Pueblo, *s. m. a town or village* || *the people* || *the vulgar the mob*
Puente, *s. 2. a bridge* || *the deck of a ship*
Puente levadiza, *a draw-bridge*
Puentecilla, *s. f. a little bridge* || *the bridge of a fiddle, etc.*
Puerca, *sub. f. a sow* || *a wood-louse* || *the nut of a screw*
Puercas, pl. *scrofulous swellings*
Puercamente, ad. *nastily*

co, s. m. hog; swine
wild boar
co, ca, adj. nasty;
rty || clownish; unci
l [years
ricia, subs. f. boyish
ril, adj. 2. puerile;
yish [lity
rilidad, s. f. pueri-
rilmente, ad. boyishly
rro, s. m. a leek
rta, s. f. a door; a
ate || custom; duty
rta principal, fore door
rasera, ó falsa, back
or
tecica, cilla, s. f. a
tle door
to, s. m. port; har-
ur || a streight (bet-
een hills)
to seco, a frontier-
vn where goods pay
luty
, ad. then || since ||
w, why
que, since that
ta, s. f. a slice; a
t; a piece || a lay or
ke (at play)
to, ta, p. p. put;
aced
pues del sol puesto,
ter sun set
to, ad. since
to que, although
to, s. m. a place ||
childbed || post; em-
oyment
int. fy!
l, s. m. a boxer
a, sub. f. a battle; a
ht
acidad, s. f. ardour,
gerness in fighting
ar, v. n. to fight; to
ve
, a. 2. warlike
f. out-bidding

Pujador, s. m. out-bidder
Pujamiento, sub. m. out-bidding
Pujamiento de sangre, blotches; breaking out
Pujante, adj. 2. strong; powerful
Pujanza, s. f. strenght; might; power
Pujar, v. n. to grow up; to over-top || to strive
Pujar, v. a. to out-bid || to hesitate; to stammer
Pujavante, sub. m. a farrier's buttress
Pujo, s. m. tenesmus || desire, longing
Pulcritud, s. f. beauty
Pulcro, cra, adj. handsome || sparkish; womanish
Pulga, s. f. a flea
Pulgas, pl. little tops (to play with)
Pulgada, s. f. an inch
Pulgar, s. m. the thumb
Pulgarada, s. f. a blow or pression with the thumb || a pinch of snuff, etc.
Pulgon, s. m. a vine-fretter
Pulguera, sub. f. a place full of fleas || flea-wort
Pulgueras, pl. V. Empulgueras
Pulguilla, s f. a little flea
Pulican, s. m. Pelican (a tooth-drawer's instrument)
Pulicia, s. f. V. Policia
Pulidamente, adver. curiously; delicately
Pulidero, s. m. V. Pulidor
Pulidez, s. f. finery; attire; dress
Pulido, da, a. fine; curious; nice
Pulidor, s. m. polisher || polishing-iron, etc.

Pulimento, s. m. polish; gloss
Pulir, v. a. to polish || to set off a discourse
Pulirse, v. r. to dres one's self finely
Pulla, s. f. joke; jest; banter || a sort of eagle
Pulmon, s. m. the lungs
Pulmonaria, s. f. pulmonary; lungwort
Pulmonía, s. f. consumption
Pulpa, s. f. pulp
Pulpejo, s. m. the brawny flesh of fingers, etc.
Pulpería, subs. f. a shop where they sell wine, brandy, etc.
Pulpero, s. m. one that keeps a pulpería
Púlpito, s. m. a pulpit
Pulpo, s. m. a polypus or many-feet
Pulposo, sa, a. pulpous; pulpy
Pulque, s. m. the juice of a tree called maguey
Pulsacion, } s. f. pulsation
Pulsada, }
Pulsar, v. a. to touch || to feel one's pulse
Pulsar, v. n. to beat as the pulse
Pulsativo, va, a. beating
Pulsera, s. f. a band put on the pulse
Pulseras, pl. bracelets
Pulsista, s. 2. one that knows well the pulse
Pulso, s. m. the pulse || strenght in the wrist || care; attention
Pulular, v. n. to spring up; to multiply
Pundonor, s. m. the point of honour
Pundonoroso, sa, a. nice in points of honour

Pungimiento, *sub. m. a pricking*

Pungir, *v. a. to prick* || *to nettle*

Pungitivo, va, *a. prickly*

Punicion, *s. f. punition*

Punir, *v. a to punish*

Punta, *s. f. a point* || *a sharp top* || *a printer's bodkin* || *quickness; quick taste* || *sharpness; acrimony*

Punta de agrio, *a touch of sharpness*

Puntas, *pl. purls of laces* || *the bull's horns*

Puntacion, *s. f. punctuation*

Puntada, *s. f. a stich*

Puntal, *s. m. a prop*

Puntapie, *s. m. a kick; a spurn*

Puntar, *v. a. to point in writing*

Puntear, *ver. a. to play upon a guitar by pricking the strings* || *to point* || *to stipple*

Puntera, *s. f. house leek*

Punteria, *s. f. a pointing* or *levelling at; aim.*

Puntero, ra, *a. pointer; aimer*

Puntero, *s. m. a fescue* || *a farrier's bodkin* || *a stone-cutter chisel*

Puntiagudo, da, *a. sharp pointed*

Puntilla, *subs. f. a little point* or *purl*

Andar de puntillas, *to walk on tiptoe*

Puntillazo, } *s. m. a kick;*
Puntillon, } *a spurn*

Punto, *s. m. a point* || *a moment* || *a stitch* || *the size of a shoe* || *the ace at cards* or *dice* || *a note in musick* || *a dot* || *a stop* || *hole in a stirrup-leather* || *the sight of a gun*

Hombre de punto, *a man of honour* — Punto en boca, *silence* — dar punto, *to give over*, or *to give a hint*—al punto, *immediately*

Puntoso, sa, *a. having many points* || *punctilious*

Puntuacion, *s. f. punctuation*

Puntual, *a. 2. punctual* || *certain* || *fit; proper*

Puntualidad, *s. f. punctuality* || *certainty* || *fitness*

Puntualizar, *v. a. to imprint in one's mind* || *to put the last hand to...*

Puntualmente, *ad. punctually*

Puntuar, *v. a. to point in writing*

Puntura, *s. f. a prick*

Punzada, *s. f. a prick* || *a grief; a trouble*

Punzadura, *s. f. a prick*

Punzante, *a. 2. prickly*

Punzar, *v. a. to punch; to prick* || *to trouble*

Punzon, *s. m. a bodkin*

Punzoncico, *s. m. a little bodkin*

Puñada, *s. f. a fisty-cuff*

Puñado, *s. m. a handful*

Puñal, *s. m. a dagger; a poniard*

Puñalada, *s. f. a stab with a dagger*

Puñete, *s. m. a fisty-cuff*

Puñetes, *pl. ruffles* || *bracelets*

Puño, *subs. m. a fist* || *a handful* || *wrist-band* || *a ruffle* || *the handle of a sword* || *the clue of a sail*

Pupa, *s. f. the pus[...]* *a pimple* [...]

Pupila, *s. f. the pu[...]*

Pupilage, *s. m. p[...] vity* || *a boarding[...]*

Pupilar, *a. 2. pu[...]*

Pupilero, *s. m. [...] keeps a boarding[...]*

Pupilo, *s. m. a pu[...] one that is at a bo[...]ding-school*

Puposo, sa, *a. pimpl[...] scabby*

Puramente, *ad. pure[...]*

Pureza, *s. f. purity*

Purga, *s. f. a purge*

Purgacion, *s. f. purga[...]* || *justification*

Purgaciones, *pl. wo[...] courses*

Purgante, *a. 2. purg[...]*

Purgar, *v. a. to purg[...]*

Purgarse, *v. r. to ju[...] one's self*

Purgativo, va, *a. pu[...]tive*

Purgatorio, *s. m. pur[...]*

Puridad, *s. f. purity* || [...] *crecy.*

En puridad, *clear[...]*

Purificacion, *s. f. puri[...]cation* || *cleansing*

Purificadero, ra, *a. p[...]fying*

Purificador, *s. m. puri[...]* || *purificatory*

Purificar, *v. a. to pur[...] to cleanse.*

Purificatorio, ria, *a. [...]rificatory*

Puro, ra, *a. pure*

Púrpura, *s. f. purple*

Purpurado, *s. m. a [...]dinal*

Purpurar, *ver. a. to purple* || *to dress purple*

Purpurear, *v. n. [...] a purple colo[...]*

...o, rea, *a. purple*
..., *sub. f. a lowest of wine*
...to, ta, *a. purulent*
...*m. pus*
...ime, *a. 2. pusillous*
...midad, *s. f. pusility*
..., *s. f. pustule*
... *f. a whore*
...no, *subs. m. the ... or race of whores*
...r, *v. n. to whore*
...o, *a. y subs. m. a ...-monger*
...o, va, *a. putative*
...io, *s. m. V.* Puno
... *s. m. a pitcher*
... *v. n. V.* Putañear
..., *s. f. wheredom ... awdy-house*
..., ca, *a. whorish*
... *m. a bardash*
..., *s. m. a puet*
...ccion, *s. f. putre...n*
..., da, *a. putrid*
... *s. m.* Pozzolana

Q

...DERNA, *s. f. a ...rter*
...nas, *pl. two fours ...ce*
...nal, *s. m. a sort of ...e on a shipboard*
...nario, ria, *a. made ...ur parts*
...nillo, *s. m. dim. de* ...lerno
...no, *s. m. a stit... book || a loose sheet ... book || a pocket-... || a book of ac...s, etc. || a suit of*

Quadra, *s. f. a room or hall || a stable || the square plot the house stands on || the quarter of a ship || the chest of a horse*
Caballo ancho de quadra, *a full-chested horse*
Quadrado, *s. m a square || quadrature || quadrate (in printing) the gusset, in a skirt*
Quadragenario, ria, *adj quadragenarious*
Quadragésima, *s. f. quadragesima*
Quadragesimal, *a. 2. quadragesimal*
Quadragésimo, ma, *adj. fortieth*
Quadrangular, *a. 2. quadrangular*
Quadrángulo, *s. m. quadrangle*
Quadrante, *s. m. quadrant || a sun-dial || the smallest piece of money*
Quadrar, *v. a. to square || to quadrate; to agree*
Quadratura, *s. f. quadrature* [*square*
Quadrete, *s. m. a little*
Quadrienal, *adj. 2. quadrennial*
Quadrienio, *s. m. the space of four years*
Quadriga, *s. f. a coach, etc. with four horses*
Quadril, *s. m. the hip*
Quadrilátero, ra, *a. quadrilater* [*quadril*
Quadrilla, *s. f. a troop; a*
Quadrillero, *s. m. the chief of a quadril || an officer* or *trooper of the* santa-hermandad
Quadrillo, *s. m. a little square || a sort of square dart* or *arrow*

Quadrilongo, *s. m. a parallelogram*
Quadrimestre, *s. m. the space of four months*
Quadriple, *a. 2. quadruple*
Quadrisilabo, ba, *a. quadrisyllable*
Quadrivio, *s. m. a place having four ways meeting in a point*
Quadivista, *subs. m. one who uses four measures in an affair*
Quadro, *s. m. a square || a rectangle parallelogram || a picture || a square bed in a garden || any frame*
Quadrupedal, *a. 2.* } *quadruped*
Quadrupédante, *a. 2.* }
Quadrúpede, *a. 2.* }
Quadrúpedo, da, *a.* }
Quadrupede, *s. m. a. quadruped*
Quadruplicacion, *s. f. quadruplication*
Quadruplar, *v. a. to quadruplicate*
Quádruplo, pla, *a. quadruple*
Qual, *pron. what || which || any*
Qual, *ad. as; like*
Qualidad, *s. f. V.* Calidad
Qualquier, *a. whoever*
Qualquiera, *a. whoever || any*
Quan, *ad. how*
Tan hermosa quan ingrata, *as handsome as ungrateful*
Quando, *ad. when || although*
Cada y quando, ó quando quiera, *whensoever*
Quantía, *s. f. quantity || quality; noble birth, etc.*
Quantidad, *s. f. quantity*
Quantioso, sa, *a. in great*

quantity || *rich; wealthy*
Quanto, ta, *a. how much*
Quantos, *how many*
Quanto mas, *how much more*
Quanto media legua, *about half a league*
Quantoquiera, *whensoever*
Quarango, *s. m. a tree that produces the jesuit's bark*
Quarenta, *s. m. forty*
Quarentena, *s. f. quarantine* || *the lent*
Quaresma, *s. f. lent*
Quaresmal, *a. 2. belonging to the time of lent*
Quarta, *s. f. a quarter of a yard, etc.* || *a fourth (in musick)* || *a quart or fourth (at piquet)* || *a quarter wind*
Quartago, *s. m. a nag*
Quartal, *s. m. a quarter of a measure*
Quartana, *s. f. the quartan ague*
Quartanario, ria, *a. that has a quartan ague*
Quartar, *v. a. to plough the land for the fourth time*
Quartazo, *s. m. a great room etc.*
Quartear, *v. a. to divide into quarters*
Quartel, *s. m. a quarter* || *stanza of four verses* || *quarter of a town* || *quarters in a camp* || *house; lodging* || *powder-room*
Quartelado *a. m. quartered (in heraldry)*
Quarteron, *s. m. a quarter of a pound, etc.* || *the son of a mongrel and a spanish woman*
Quarterones, *pl. panes; pannels*
Quarteta, *s. f. stanza of four verses*
Quartete, } *s. m. V.* Quarteta
Quarteto, }
Quartilla, *s. f. a quartern* || *the quarter of a sheet of paper* || *the horse's pastern*
Quartillo, *s. m. the fourth part of the* azumbre, *etc.*
Quarto, *s. m. a quarter of a hour, etc.* || *house; lodging apartment* || *room; chamber* || *a small brass coin* || *a quarter of mutton*
Quartos, *pl. money* || *members*
Quarto, ta, *a. fourth*
Quarton, *s. m. a large piece of timber*
Quasi, *adv. V.* Casi
Quaternario, ria, *a. quaternary*
Quaternidad, *s. f. quaternity*
Quaternion, *s. m. quaternion*
Quaterceno, na, *a. fourteenth*
Quatralbo (caballo) *s. m. a horse that has four white feet*
Quatralbo, *s. m. a commodore of four galleys*
Quatrero, *s. m. a horse-stealer*
Quatridial, *a. 2.* } *of four days standing*
Quatridiano, na, *a.* }
Quatriduano, na, *a.* }
Quatrin, *sub. m. a small coin like a farthing* || *money*
Quatrinca, s. f. four persons or things together; *quaternion*
Quatro, *s. m. four*
Quatrocientos, tas, *a.* ... *hundred*
Quatropea, *s. f. a* ... *horses sold at* ...
Quatropeado, *s. m.* ... *ticular step in dan*...
Quantrotanto, *s. m.* ... *times as much*
Que, *pron. that* || *wh*...
Quebrada, *s. f. an* ... *ven ground*
Quebradero, *s. m. br*...
Quebradero de cab... *vexation of spirit*
Quebradillo, *s. m.* ... *den heel of a sho*...
Quebradizo, za, *a. f*... *brittle*
Voz quebradiza, *a* ... *ble voice*
Quebrado, *s. m. a* ... *tion (in arithmet*...
Quebrador, *s. m. br*...
Quebradura, *s. f.* ... *king* || *rupture* ... *tenness*
Quebramiento, *sub.* ... *breaking* || *a ban*... *tey*
Quebrantable, *a. 2.* ... *gible*
Quebrantador, *sub.* ... *breaker* || *a stone-*...
Quebrantadura, *s. f.* ... *ture; fracture*
Quebrantahuesos, *s.* ... *sort of eagle* || *a* ... *blesome man*
Quebrantamiento, ... *breaking* || *fract*... *rupture* || *wearin*... *infringement* || *re*... *annulling*
Quebrantar, *v. a. to* ... || *to bruise* || *to we*... || *to tire* || *to rep*... *annul*
Quebranto, *s. m.* ...

|| weariness || pity ||
...ess; damage
...ebrar, v. a. to break
...ebrar, v. n. to break;
to turn bankrupt
...ebrarse, v. r. to get a rupture
...eda, s. f. the nine ó clock bell, when all shall be at home
...edada, s. f. a staying
...edar, v. n. to stay; to remain
...edar, v. a. to leave
...edarse, v. r. to be at a stand
...edito, ad. softly; gently [still
...edo, da, adj. quiet;
...edo, ad. low || softly; gently
...eja, s. f. a complaint || resentment
...ejarse, v. r. to complain
...ejicoso, sa, a. whinning; whimpering
...ejido, s. m. complaint; lament
...ejoso, sa, a. one who complains of another
...ejumbroso, sa, a. V. Quejicoso
...ema, s. f. burning || conflagration
...emadero, subs. m. the place where malefactors are burnt
...emador, s. m. burner
...emar, v. a. to burn || to blast || to waste an estate
...emazon, s. f. a burning || an excessive heat || itching || a nipping jest
...erella, s. f. a complaint
...erellante, a. 2. plaintiff [plain
...erellarse, v. r. to com-
...relloso, sa, a. plain-
tive || whinning; whimpering
Querencia, s. f. the place any beast generally resorts to; form, kennel, etc. [to love
Querer, v. a. to will ||
Querer, s. m. will || love
Queridillo, s. m. a little favourite
Querido, da, a. beloved
Mi querido, my dear
Querubin, s. m. cherub
Quesadilla, s. f. a cheese-cake
Quesera, s. f. a cheese-monger's shop || a dairy where cheese is made
Quesería, s. f. the season of making cheeses
Quesero, s. m. a cheese-monger
Quesillo, sub. m. a small cheese
Queso, s. m. cheese
Questa, s. f. a begging; a gathering
Qüestion, s. f. question || debate; quarrel
Qüestion de tormento, rack; torture
Qüestionable, a. 2. questionable
Qüestionar, v. a. to debate a matter
Qüestionario, s. m a collection of questions
Qüestor, s. m. questor || a friar that begs for his order
Qüestuario, ria, } adj. lucrative;
Qüestuoso, sa, } quæstuary
Qüestura, s. f. questorship
Quetzale, s. m. a bird of America
Quexigal, s. m. a grove of holms
Quexigo, s. m. a holm
Quibey, s. m. a venemous plant of America
Quicial, s. m. the door-post, where the hinges are made fast
Quicio, s. m. a hinge
Quidam, s. m. a certain man [essence
Quididad, s. f. quiddity;
Quiditativo, va, adj. belonging to the essence
Quid pro quo, s. m. quid pro quo
Quiebra, subs. f. chap; chink; gap || breach || loss; damage || bankruptcy
Quiebro, s. m. trilling; quavering || inflexion of the body
Quien, pron. who || what
Quienquiera, adj. whosoever
Quietacion, s. f. quiet
Quietamente, a. quietly
Quietar, v. a. to quiet
Quiete, s. f. quiet
Quieto, ta, a. quiet; still
Quietud, s. f. quietude; quietness
Quijera, s. f. iron-pieces in the cross-bow
Quilatador, s. m. assayer (in the mint)
Quilatar, v. a. to assay or try silver, etc.
Quilate, s. m. carat
Quilla, s. f. the keel of a ship [other
Quillotro, tra, adj. this
Quillotro, s. m. disturbance; trouble
Quilo, s. m. the chile
Quimera, s. f. quarrel
Quimerista, a. 2. quarrelsome
Quina, } s. f. the jesuit's
Quinaquina, } bark; quinquina

Quinas, *pl. two fives* || *the arms of Portugal*
Quinario, *s. m. the number of five*
Quince, *s. m. fifteen*
Quinceno, *a. fifteenth*
Quincurion, *sub. m. the leader of five soldiers*
Quindenio, *s. m. the space of fifteen years*
Quinientos, tas, *a. five hundred*
Quinolas, *s. f. pl. a game at cards*
Quinquagenario, *fifty years old*
Quinquagésima, *quinquagesima*
Quinquagésimo, ma, *adj. fiftieth* [*quefoil*
Quinquefolio, *s. m. cin-*
Quinquenio, *sub. m. the space of five years*
Quinquillería, *s. f. hardware*
Quinquillero, *s. m. hardware-man*
Quinta, *s. f. a country-house* || *a quint* (*at piquet*) || *a fifth* (*in musick*)
Quinta esencia, *quintessence* [*tal*
Quintal, *s. m. a quin-*
Quintaleño, ña, *a. that weighs a quintal*
Quintañon, na, *a. very old* [*fifth*
Quintar, *v. a. to take the*
Quintería, *s. f. a farm*
Quinterno, *sub m. five sheets of paper*
Quintero, *s. m. a farmer*
Quintil, *s. m. july*
Quintilla, *s. f. stanza of five verses*
Quintillo, *s. m. fifth story*
Quinto, *s. m. the fifth*
Quinto, ta, *a. fifth*

Quintuplo, pla, *a. quintuple* [*in a gain*
Quiñon, *subs. m. a share*
Quiñonero, *s. m. sharer; partner*
Quirite, *s. m. a roman gentleman of old*
Quirúrgico, ca, *a. chirurgical*
Quisicosa, *s. f. a riddle*
Quistion, *s. f. V.* Question
Quisto (Bien, ó mal) *a. well or ill beloved*
Quita, *s. f. an acquittance*
Quita! *int. away! avaunt*
Quitacion, *s. f. wages; salary*
Quitador, *s. m. who takes away* [*quittance*
Quitamiento, *s. m. an ac-*
Quitapelillos, *sub. m. a flatterer; a pickthank*
Quitapesares, *s. 2. a consolation*
Quitar, *v. a. to take away* || *to fetch out of pawn* || *to pull*
Quitarse, *v. r. to abstain from; to rid one's self of* [*brella*
Quitasol, *sub. m. an um-*
Quite, *subs. m. a taking away* || *obstacle; hindrance*
Quito, ta, *a. quit; clear; free; rid*
Quixada, *s. f. a jaw*
Quixal, *s. m. grinder-tooth*
Quixar, *s. m. grinder-tooth* || *jaw*
Quixero, *s. the side of an artificial canal*
Quixo, *s. m. the ore of any mine*
Quixones, s. m. pl. bastard parsley
Quixotada, s. f. a ridicu-*lous action or undertaking*
Quixote, *s. m. thigh-armour* || *a foolish* ...*rious person* [*xota*
Quixotería, *s. f. V.* Qu...
Quiza, **Quizas**, *adv. perhaps*
Quociente, *s. m. quotient*
Quodlibetal, *a. 2.* **Quodlibético** ca, *a.* par... do... ca...
Quodlibeto, *s. m. a paradox* [*Ameri...*
Quoque, *s. m. a tree*
Quotidianamente, *adv. daily*
Quotidiano, na, *adj. daily; quotidian*
Quotidie, *adv. daily*
Quotidie, *s. m. a thing that happens every day* || *a husband*

R

Rabadan, *s. m. a chief among the shepherds*
Rabadilla, *s. f. the rump*
Rabadoquin, *s. m. a sort of long gun*
Rabanal, *s. m. a ground where radishes grow*
Rabanero, *adj.* ... (*said of garments*)
Rabanil *s. m. a little radish* || *a touch of sharpness in the* ... || *desire; longing*
Rabaniza, *s. f. the seed of radishes*
Rábano, *s. m. a radish*
Rabear, *v. a. to wag the tail*
Rabel, *s. m. a rebeck* || child's breech
Rabelillo, s. m. a little rebeck [*side*
Rabera, sub. f. th...

s. m. a rabbi
, s. f. rage
r, v. a. to rage
an, } a. m. rubi-
ano, } can
orto, ta, adj. short-
led || that wears
rt cloaths
ta, s. f. fretting
orcado, s. m. frega-
bird [tailed
argo, ga, adj. long-
ico, ca, adj. rabbi-
al
ismo, s. m. the doc-
e of the rabbies
ista, s. 2. rabbinist
o, s. m. a rabbi
samente, adver. fu-
usly [mad
ose, sa, a. furious;
alsera (Muger), s. f.
aucy, impudent wo-
n
a, s. f. the tip of a
ing-rod
, s. m. a tail
de junco, the tro-
k bird
n, na, a. short-tai-
l; cropped
seada, } s. f. bes-
seadura, } pattering
sear, v. a. to bespat-
; to splash
so, sa, adj. that has
ragged or daggled
il
do, da, a. long-tailed
menta, s. f. } par-
mento, s. m. } rel
mado, da. adj. hea-
d up like grapes
mar, v. a. to glean
mo, s. m. a bunch;
cluster [cination
cinacion, s. f. ratio-
inar, v. a. to ratio-
te; to reason

Raciocinio, s. m. a reasoning
Racion, s. f. a daily allowance || a prebend
Racionabilidad, s. f. rationality
Racional, s. m. rationalness; reason
Racional, a. 2. rational
Racionalidad, s. f. rationality [tionally
Racionalmente, adv. ra-
Racionero, s. m. a canon of a church
Racionista, s. 2. one that has a daily allowance
Rada, s. f. a road for ships
Radiado, da, a. starlike
Radiante, a. 2. radiant
Radicacion, s. f. radication
Radical, a. 2. radical
Radicalmente, adv. radically
Radicar, v. n. } to take
Radicarse, v. r. } root
Radio, s. m. radius
Radioso, sa, adj. radiant
Raedera, s. f. a scraper; a scraping tool
Raedizo, za, a. that may be easily scraped
Raedura, s. f. scraping; scrapingness
Raer, v. a. to scrape
Raer con rastro, to rake
Rafa, s. f. a buttress, a pillar, etc. set at distances in mud walls
Ráfaga, s. f. squalls
Rafe, s. f. eaves
Raicilla, s. f. a small root
Raido, da, adj. saucy; impudent [a root
Raigal, a. 2. relating to
Raigon, s. m. a large old root
Raiz, s. f. a root || the origine; the first cause
|| the lower part of...
Bienes raices, immoveable goods
Raja, s. f. a chip || a shiver or splinter || a gap; a cleft || portion; share || a kind of cloth
Rajadillo, s. m. a sort of sweet-meat
Rajar, v. a. to cleave; to split || to tell many boasting lies
Rajeta, s. fem. a kind of cloth
Rajuela, s. f. a little chip
Ralea, s. f. race; stock; kind [thin
Ralear, v. neut. to grow
Raleza, s. fem. thinness; rarity
Ralladura, s. f. rasping; grating || raspings
Rallar, v. a. to rasp; to grate
Rallo, s. m. a rasp
Rallon, s. m. a sort of dart
Ralo, la, adj. rare; thin
Rama, s. f. bough; twig
Ramadan, sub. m. a fast kept by the Mahometans
Ramal, s. m. the end of a cord untwisted || a halter
Ramalazo, s. m. a blow with the ramal
Rambla, s. f. a gravelly or sandy place
Ramera, s. f. a common whore
Rameria, s. f. a bawdy-house || whoredom
Ramerita, s. f. dim. de Ramera
Ramero (halcon), s. m. a brancher
Rameruela, s. fem. a poor distressed whore

Ramificacion, s. f. *ramification* [*mify*
Ramificarse, v. r. *to ra-*
Ramillete, s. m. *a nosegay* || *a pyramid of fruits, etc.*
Ramilletero, ra, s. *nosegay-man* or *woman*
Ramilletero, s. m. *an artificial flower-pot*
Ramito, sub. m. dim. de Ramo
Ramo, s. m. *a bough; a branch*
Ramo de taberna, *a tavern-bush* — Domingo de ramos, *palm-sunday*
Ramon, s. m. *boughs cut off to feed the cattle with*
Ramonear, ver. n. *to gather or cut small boughs for cattle*
Ramoso, sa, adj. *full of boughs; branchy*
Rampa, s. f. *the cramp*
Rampante, a. m. *rampant* (*in heraldry*)
Ramplon (hierro), s. m. *a cramping-iron*
Herrar de ramplon, *to shoe a horse with frost-nails* [*stalk*
Rampojo, s. m. *grape's*
Rana, s. f. *a frog*
Ranazarzal, *a land frog*
Ranacuajo, s. m. *bull-head*
Ranchería, s. f. *a cottage, etc. where many people live together*
Ranchero, s. m. *the chief of a rancho*
Rancho, s. m. *the company that lies in one chamber, etc.*
Rancho de santa Bárbara, *gun-room*.—hagan rancho, *make way!*

Rancio, cia, adj. *rancid; rusty*
Rancio, s. m. *rancidness*
Rancioso, sa, adj. *rancid*
Rancor, s. m. *rancour*
Randa, s. f. *net-work lace, etc.*
Randal, s. m. *net-work*
Rangifero, s. m. *a rein-deer*
Rangua, s. f. *a piece of iron wherein a pivot plays*
Ranilla, s. f. *a little frog* || *the frush of a horse's foot*
Ranillas, pl. *the scratches in a horse's heels*
Raninas, s. f. pl. *ranular veins*
Ranquear, v. n. *to go lame in the hips*
Ránula, s. f. *ranula*
Ranúnculo, s. m. *ranunculus*
Rapacejo, s. *shagged end of a cloth, etc.* || *a little boy*
Rapacería, s. f. *a boyish trick* || *a gang of boys*
Rapacidad, s. fem. *rapaciousness*
Rapacilla, s. f. *a pretty young girl* [*ving*
Rapadura, s. f. *the sha-*
Rapagon, s. m. *a lad without beard*
Rapar, v. a. *to shave* || *to take away by force*
Rapaz, a. s. *rapacious*
Rapaz, za, s. *a boy or girl*
Rapazada, s. f. *boyishness*
Rápidamente, ad. *rapidly*
Rapidez, s. f. *rapidity*
Rápido, da, adj. *rapid*
Rapiña, s. f. *rapine*
Ave de rapiña, *a bird of prey*

Rapiñar, v. a. *to pillage; to rob*
Rapista, s. m. *a barber*
Raposa, s. f. *a fox*
Raposera, s. fem. *a fox's kennel*
Raposería, s. f. *craftiness*
Raposo, s. m. *a he-fox*
Raposuno adj. *of or belonging to a fox*
Rapto, s. m. *a rape*
Rapto, ta, adj. *taken or snatched away*
Raptor, s. m. *a ravisher*
Raqueta, s. f. *a racket*
Raquítico, ca, a. *ricketty*
Raquitis, s. f. *the rickets*
Raramente, adv. *rarely; seldom* [*tion*
Rarefaccion, s. f. *rarefac-*
Rarefacerse, v. r. *to rarefy* [*fied*
Rarefacto, ta, p. p. *rare-*
Rareza, Raridad, } s. f. *rarity*
Raro, ra, adj. *rare*
Ras, s. m. *an even superficies*
Ras con ras, adver. *level; touching one another*
Rasadura, s. f. *the act of smoothing the corn-measure*
Rasamente, ad. *clearly; openly*
Rasar, v. a. *to strike the corn to level it with the bushel* [*rake*
Rascador, s. m. *scraper;*
Rascadura, s. f. *scraping; scratching* || *a scratch*
Rascar, v. a. *to scrape; to scratch*
Rascon, s. m. *a rayle*
Rascuñar, rascuño. V. Rasguñar, etc.
Rasero, s. m. *a strickle*
Rasgados (ojos), s. m. *large or full eyes*

adura, *s. fem. a rending; a tearing*
ar, *v. a. to tear; to* ...ad || *to make an arpeggio*
o, *s. m. a flourish* (...*s writing*) || *a witty* ...*oke* || *a piece of prudence, etc.*
on, *s. m. a rent in* *garment*
uear, *v. a. to flourish* (*in writing*) || *to* ...*ke an arpeggio*
uñar, *ver. act. to* ...*atch* || *to sketch*
uño, *s. m. a scratch* ...*s sketch* [*serge*
la, *s. fem. a sort of*
m, *s. f. shaving* || ...*ping*
, *s. m. sattin*
, sa, *adjec. plain;* ...*ooth* [*ther*
mpo raso, *fair weather*
a, *s. f. the chaff*, or ...*n of corn* || *the* ...*rd of an ear of corn* *fish-bone* || *grape's* ...*lk* or *bunch*
adillo, *s. m. a cheat* ...*cards*
adura, *s. f. the scraping* || *scrapings*
ar, *v. a. to scrape* || ...*rob*
uetas, *s. f. pl. a scraper* (*for ships*)
illar, *v. a. to comb* ...*card flax, etc.*
illo, *s. m. V.* Rasillo
ra, *s. f. a sledge* || ...*awing* || *track*
rallar, *v. a. to ma*... *a snapping with a* ...*hip*
ar, *v. a. to draw;* ...*rag*

Rastrear, *v. a. to trace; to track*
Rastrero, *s. m. overseer of the slaughter-houses*
Rastrero, ra, *adj. trailing; dragging* || *vile; mean*
Rastrillador, *sub. m. one that hackles hemp*
Rastrillar, *v. a. to hackle hemp* || *to rake*
Rastrillo, *s. m. an hackle* or *brake to dress hemp* || *flax-comb* || *portcullis* || *a cover for the pan of a gun* || *a rake*
Rastro, *s. m. track; trace* || *a sledge* || *slaughter-house* || *sign; token*
Rastrojera, *s. f. fallow-ground* [*corn*
Rastrojo, *s. m. stubble of*
Rasura, *s. f. shaving* || *scraping*
Rasuras, *pl. lees of wine*
Rasurar, *v. a. to shave*
Rata, *s. f. a. she-rat* || *a great rat* || *quota*
Rata por cantidad, *in proportion to the quantity*
Ratafía, *s. f. ratafia*
Ratear, *v. a. to diminish* or *share proportionably* || *to rob; to pilfer* || *to crawl* or *creep*
Rateo, *s. m. proportional distribution*
Ratería, *s. f. pilfery*
Ratero, ra, *adj. creeping* || *mean; vile; base*
Ladron ratero, *a pick-pocket* [*cation*
Ratificacion, *s. f. ratification*
Ratificar, *v. a. to ratify*
Ratihabicion, *s. f. ratification*
Ratina, *s. f. rateen*
Rato, *sub. m. a. rat* || *a while*

A' ratos, *ad. sometimes; by fits*
Raton, *subs. m. a rat; a mouse*
Ratonar, *v. a. to gnaw; as mouses do*
Ratonera, *s. f. mouse-trap*
Raudal, *s. m. a torrent*
Raudo, da, *adj. rapid; impetuous*
Rauta, *s. f. road*
Raya, *s. fem. a line; a streak* || *border; limit* || *the fish thorn-back*
Tres en raya, *five-penny morris* [*ring on*
Rayano, na, *adj. bordering on*
Rayar, *v. a. to streak* || *to underline*
Rayar, *v. n. to excel; to get the better*
Rayar el alba, *to peep* or *dawn*
Rayo, *s. m. beam; ray* || *radius* || *a spoke of a wheel* || *a thunderbolt*
Raynela, *s. f. a little line* or *streak*
Raza, *s. f. race; breed* || *quality; nature*
Razago, *sub. m. a coarse sort of linen*
Razon, *s. f. reason* || *account* [*ble*
Razonable, *a. 2. reasonable*
Razonablejo, ja, *a. dim. de* Razonable
Razonablemente, *adver. reasonably*
Razonamiento, *s. m. reason; reasoning*
Razonar, *v. n. to reason* || *to discourse* || *to talk*
Re, *s. m. d, musical note*
Reaccion, *s. f. reaction*
Reacio, cia, *adj. restiff; stubborn*
Real, *sub. m. a camp* || *real; a Spanish coin*

Asentar el real, *to encamp*
Real, *a. s. real* || *royal* || *sincere; plain*
Galera real, *the commander's galley*
Realce, *sub. m. relievo; embossed work* || *addition of value, beauty, etc.* [*organ*
Realejo, *s. m. a portable*
Realengo, ga, *adj. royal*
Reálete, *sub. m. a sort of coin*
Realeza, *s. f. royal magnificence, etc.*
Realidad, *s. f. reality, sincerity*
Realillo, *s. m. a sort of coin*
Realmente, *adv. really*
Realzado, da, *a. embossed*
Realzar, *v. a. to raise* || *to heighten; to set off*
Reasumir, *v. a. to reassume* [*ming*
Reasuncion, *s. f. reassu-*
Reata, *sub. f. a cord that ties many mules one by ones* || *the fore mule that draws in a cart*
Votar de reata, *to vote blindly as others*
Reatadura, *s. fem. tying again*
Reatar, *v. a. to bind* or *tie again* || *to vote as others*
Reato, *s. m. guilt*
Reaventar, *v. a. to winnow again*
Rebalsa, *s. f. a puddle*
Rebalsar, *v. a. to settle in a puddle*
Rebanada, *s. f. a slice*
Rebanadilla, *s. f. a little slice*
Rebanar, *v. a. to slice; to cut in slices*

Rebañadera, *s. f. a hook; a tenter*
Rebañar, *v. a. to rake; to scrape* || *to gather into a flock*
Rebañego, ga, *adj. of*, or *belonging to a flock*
Rebaño, *s. m. a flock of sheep* || *a heap*
Rebate, *s. m. strife; debate; quarrel*
Rebatiña, *s. f. scramble; scrambling*
Andar á la rebatiña, *to scramble*
Rebatir, *ver. a. to beat back; to repulse* || *to abate, in accounts*
Rebato, *s. m. an alarm* || *a sudden surprise*
Coger de rebato, *to surprise.* Tocar á rebato, *to beat the alarm*
Rebaxa, *s. f. abatement*
Rebaxar, *v. a. to lower* || *to abate of the price*
Rebaxo, *s. m. a groove*
Rebelarse, *v. r. to rebel* || *to fall out with one*
Rebelde, *a.* y *s. rebel* || *contumacious*
Rebeldía, *s. f. rebellion* || *contumacy*
Rebelion, *s. f. rebellion*
Rebellin, *s. m. a ravelin*
Rebelon, *a. m. restiff*
Rebencazo, *s. m. a stroke with a bull's pizzle*
Rebenque, *s. m. a bull's pizzle, etc. to chastise the galley-slaves with*
Rebien, *adv. very well*
Rebisabuelo, *s. m. a great great grand father*
Rebisnieto, } *s. m. a great*
Rebiznieto, } *grand-son*
Rebociño, *s. m. a cloak worn by women*
Rebollidura, *s. fem. a de-*

fect in the insi-
cannon
Rebosar, *ver. n.*
(*speaking of*
when over-flow
Rebosadura, *s. f.*
flowing
Rebosar, *v. n. t*
Rebotar, *v. a. t*
back a ball || *to*
nail [*rebo*
Rebote, *s. m. rel*
Rebotica, *s. f. a*
thecary's back-
Rebotiga, *s. f. ba*
Rebotin, *sub. m.*
leaves of a mu
tree || *raw silk*
Rebozar, *v. a. V.*
bozar
Rebozo, *s. m. V.*
Rebramar, *v. n.*
or *roar again o*
quently
Rebudiar, *v. n. to*
as the wild boa
Rebueno, na, *ad*
good [*the*
Rebujar, *v. a. to*
Rebujo, *s. m. the*
putting the ma
Rebullir, *v. n. to*
move [*to w*
Reburujar, *v. a. t*
Reburujon, *subs.*
bundle
Rebusca, *s. f. se*
gleaning || *re*
shreds, etc.
Rebuscar, *v. a. t*
|| *to search*
Rebuznador, *subs*
braying ass
Rebuznar, *ver. n.*
like an ass
Rebuzno, *s. m. a l*
Recabar, *v. a. to*
Recadero, *sub. m*
senger

ᵼdo, s. m. a message a compliment or gift at one sends || the ne- ssaries ingredients materials || daily ovisions || abundan- ; copiousness || a iting, in a law-suit
er, ver. neut. to fall ain; to relapse
ida, s. f. a relapse
lar, v. a. to strain ugh
lcadamente, adver. ly as if crammed or d down || repeatedly
lcar, v. a. to stuff; ram; to tread down
lcarse, ver. r. to re- st; to tell over and r again
lcarse el pie, to ain one's foot
lcitrar, v. n. to kick; spurn
lzar, v. a. to prick a ign and rub it over th coal-dust
mar, ver. a to em- oider
mara, s. fem. a with wing-room || a war- be || a gentleman's ipage
mbiar, v. act. to re- nge || to shine
mbio, s. m. chan- g again || re-ex- nge (in trade)
mo, s. m. embroide- -work; embossed- rk
acanilla, s. f. a feig- l limping || tergiver- ion
ntacion, s. f. recan- ion
ton, s. m. a stone

Recapacitar, v. a. to re- volve in one's mind
Recapitulacion, s. f. re- capitulation
Recapitular, v. a. to re- capitulate
Recargar, v. a. to load or charge again; rechar- ge || to lodge a new writ against one
Recargar la calentura, to redouble or increase
Recargo, sub. m. impea- ching again || a new writ against one || the increase of a fever
Recata, s. f. tasting again
Recatadamente, ad. pru- dently
Recatado, da, a. wary || modest
Recatar, ver. a. to taste again || to conceal ca- refully
Recatarse, v. r. to be cau- tious [pen
Recatear, v. a. to chea-
Recato, s. m. cautious- ness; wariness || secre- cy || modesty
Recaton, s. m. the but- end of a spear, etc.; ferrel
Recatonazo, s. m. a blow with the end of a spear
Recaudacion, s. f. reco- very; gathering
Recaudador, s. m. a re- ceiver of rents, etc.
Recaudamiento, s. m. V. Recaudacion
Recaudar, v. a. to reco- ver; to receive
Recaudo, s. m. recovery || a message
Recavar, v. a. to dig again
Recazo, s. m. hilt || the back-side of a knife
Recentadura, s. fem. the portion of leaven left fort the next-time
Recental (cordero), s. m. a sucking lamb
Recentar, v. a. to put the leaven in the dough
Recepcion, s. f. reception
Receptáculo, s. m. recep- tacle
Receptador, s. m. recei- ver of stolen goods
Receptar, v. a. to receive stolen goods || to abet a criminal
Receptarse, v. r. to run to a place of refuge
Recepto, s. m. a place of refuge
Receptor, s. m. a receiver
Receptoría, s. f. the cash or office of a receiver
Receta, s. f. a recipe || a receipt
Recetar, v. a. to prescri- be, or order
Recetario, s. m. a book wherein the write the physician's prescrip- tions
Recetor, s. m. a receiver
Rechazar, v. a. to repul- se; to push or drive back
Rechazo, s. m. repulsing
Rechinar, v. n. to screak; to creek || to look gruff
Rechino, s. m. screaking; creeking
Reciamente, ad. strongly
Recibidero, ra, adj. re- ceivable
Recibidor, s. m. a receiver
Recibimiento, s. m. recei- ving; reception || an- tichamber [|| to admit
Recibir, v. a. to receive
Recibo, s. m. reception || a receipt; or acqui- tance

Recien, *adv. recently*
Reciente, *a. 2. recent*
Recientemente, *adv. recently*
Recinto, *s. m. inclosure; circumference*
Recio, cia, *adj. strong || great; bulky || hard-hearted* [*hardly*
Recio, *adv. strongly* ||
Hablar recio, *to speak big*
Récipe, *s. m. a recipe*
Recipiente, *s. m. a recipient* [*ving*
Recipiente, *a. 2. recei-*
Reciprocamente, *ad. reciprocally*
Reciprocar, *v. a. to make reciprocal*
Reciprocarse, *v. r. to correspond reciprocally*
Reciproco, ca, *adj. reciprocal*
Recision, *s. f. rescission*
Recisimo, ma, *adj. very strong* [*tion*
Recitacion, *s. f. recita-*
Recitado, *s. m. a recitativo*
Recitar, *v. a. to recite*
Recitativo, va, *adj. recitative* [*rigor*
Reciura, *s. f. strength* ||
Reclamacion, *s. f. reclamation*
Reclamar, *v. a. to reclaim || to oppose; to protest against*
Reclamo, *s. m. a bird-call || reclamation || reclaiming || a catch-word || inticement*
Reclo, *subst. m. absence from the choir by leave*
Reclinar, *v. a. to recline; to lean*
Reclinatorio, *subs. m. a prop to lean on*

Recluir, *v. a. to shut up*
Reclusion, *s. f. shutting up || a prison*
Recluso, sa, *adj. recluse*
Reclusorio, *s. m. a prison, etc.*
Recluta, *s. f. recruit*
Reclutar, *v. a. to recruit*
Recobrar, *v. a. to recover*
Recobrarse, *v. r. to recover one's health, etc.*
Recobro, *s. m. recovery*
Recocer, *ver. a. to boil over again*
Recocho, cha, *adj. too much boiled*
Recocido, da, *adj. versed; experienced*
Recodo, *s. m. an angle or corner*
Recogedero, *sub. m. the place wherein things collected are put*
Recogedor, *s. m. he that collects*
Recoger, *v. a. to retake || to collect; to gather || to squeeze; to wring || to shut up*
Recogerse, *v. r. to retire || to go home || to go to bed*
Recogida, *s. f. a recluse*
Recogimiento, *s. m. a gathering || retirement || refuge || retired living || a house for women to live in retirement || recollection* [*tion*
Recoleccion, *s. f. recollec-*
Recoleto, ta, *a. y s. a kind of Franciscan friars* or *nuns || one that lives in retirement*
Recomendable, a. 2. recommendable
Recomendacion, s. f. recommendation

Recomenda
commen
Recompens
Recompens
pensatio
Recompens
compens
Reconcent
concentr
Reconcilia
concilia
Reconcilia
conciler
Reconcilia:
Reconcome
scratch
Reconcomi
tion ma
scratch
picion ||
Recóndito,
te; hidd
Reconfesar
fess agai
Reconoced
viser
Reconocer,
to revis
ledge || *t*
or *behol*
Reconocido
teful
Reconocim
now led,
tude || *re*
Recontar,
again ||
Reconvalec
cover he
Reconvenc
ting; re
Reconveni
tort; to
Recopilaci
tulation
Recopilar,
tulate ||
Recoqui
fut fe

s. f. remem-
[mind
a. to call to
ver. r. to re-

n. to awake
r. a. to run
rvey || to run
k || to mend;

memoria, *to*
ad—los caña-
beg
. m. out-pa-

a. to shorten
|| to cut pa-
[again
r. a. to sew
a. to incline
ver. r. to lay
down
: the buying
illages what
's to sell again
of hounds
m. a turning
r
m. one who
and there in
ll again
s f. recrea-

a. to recreate
a. to increase
to, *s. m. in-*
[ment
s. m. recre-
recreation
adv. upright-
[gular
la ; *a. rectan*
s. m. a rec-
[cation
, *s. f. rectifi-*
. a. to rectify
ca, *a. recti-*

rectitude
Ingles.

Recto, ta, *a. right*

Rector, *s. m. a rector*

Rectorado, *sub. m. rectorship*

Rectoral, *a. 2. rectoral*

Rectorar, *v. n. to be elected a rector*

Rectoria, *s. f. rectory || rectorship*

Recua, *sub. f. a drove of mules, etc.*

Recudimiento, *s. m. an order to receive rents || the profit a thing yelds*

Recudir, *ver. a. to yeld profit* or *benefit*

Recuento, *s. m. an inventory* [*brance*

Recuerdo, *s. m. remem-*

Recuero, *s. m. mule-driver* [*ground*

Recuesto, *s. m. a rising*

Recular, *v. n. to fall* or *go back*

Reculo, la, *a. without a tail (applied to poultry)*

Recuperable, *a. 2. recoverable*

Recuperacion, *s. f. recuperation*

Recuperador, *s. m. one who recovers*

Recuperar, *v. a. to recuperate ; to recover*

Recuperarse, *v. r. to make up one's losses*

Recura, *s. f. a comb-maker's saw*

Recurar, *v. a. to cleave or make the teeth of a comb*

Recurrir, *ver. a. to have recourse to*

Recurso, *s. m. recourse || recursion*

Recusacion, *s. f. exception in law || refusal*

Recusar, *ver. a. to except against || to refuse*

Red, *s. f. a net || net-work || a grate* or *lattice || the speaking room of a monastery || a place where they deliver out any thing through a grate*

Red barredera, *a drag-net*

— de araña, *cobweb*

Redada, *s. f. a cast of a net*

Redaño, *s. m. omentum*

Redar, *v. a. to cast the net*

Redarguecion, *s. f. retorting*

Redarguir, *v. a. to retort*

Redecilla, *sub. f. a small net || a bag-net*

Rededor, *s. m. compass ; circumference*

Al rededor, *adv. round about*

Redemir, *v. a. to redeem*

Redencion, *s. f. redeeming || redemption || help*

Redentor, *s. m. redeemer*

Redero, *s. m. a net-maker*

Redicion, *s. f. repetition*

Rediezmo, *s. m. the taking a tithe over again*

Redil, *s. m. hurdles to fold sheep in*

Redimir, *v. a. to redeem*

Redistribucion, *s. f. new distribution*

Rédito, *s. m. revenue*

Reditnable, } *a. 2. that*
Reditual, } *yields a revenue*

Redituar, *v. a. to yield a revenue*

Redoblado, da, *adj. thick and short*

Redoblar, *v. a. to redouble, (in musick), to repeat the same note; to strike the same string || to rivet a nail*

Redoble, *s. m. a second stroke on the same string*

Redomilla, *sub. f. a little vial* [*roundly*

Redondamente, *adver.*

Redondear, *v. a. to round, to make round* || *to clear from debts, etc.*

Redondel, *s. m. a round mat*

Redondez, *s. f. roundness*

Redondilla, *s. f. a sort of poetical composition; a roundelay*

Redondo, *s. m. a piece of money*

Redondo, da } *a. round* || *got clear from debts; free, etc.* || *irreprehensible* || *unarmed*

A' la redonda, *adver. round about*

Redondon, *s. m. a great circle* or *round*

Redopelo (al), *adj. against the hair* or *grain*

Redopelo, *sub. m. strife; quarrel*

Redor, *s. m. a round mat*

plication

Reduplicar, *v. a. to reduplicate*

Reduplicativo, va, *a. reduplicative*

Reedificacion, *s. f. re-edifying* [*fy; to rebuild*

Reedificar, *v. a. to re-edi-*

Reembolsar, *v. a. to reimburse*

Reembolso, *sub. m. reimbursement*

Reemplazar, *v. a. to replace; to make amends*

Reemplazo, *s. m. replacing; compensation*

Reoncuentro, *s. m. a rencounter*

Reengendrador, *s. m. one that regenerates*

Reengendrar, *v. a. to regenerate*

Reengendrarse, *ver. r. to arise; to spring*

Refaccion, *s. f. refection* || *restitution*

Refalsado, da, *a. receitful*

cacao
Refirma
Refitolo
has t
tory
Refiteri
Reflecti
to be
Reflexa
cunn
Reflexi
Reflexi
flect,
Reflexiv
reflec
Reflexiv
Reflexo
of the
Reflexo
Reflore
flour
Refluxo
Refocil
cing
Refocil
|| *to*
Refocil

ne, s. m. reform
ada, s. f. } a sort of
ado, s. m. } ribbon
ar, v. a. to streng-
; to reinforce
arse, v. r. to reco-
one's strength
to, s. m. a deeper
ch cut along the
dle of a dry ditch
cion, sub. f. refrac-
[fractory
tario, ria, adj. re-
to, ta, a. refracted
, s. m. a proverb
cillo, s. m. a little
erb
amiento, subs. m.
ing; friction
ar, v. a. to rub
on, s. m. a rub-
or friction
amiento, s. m. re-
ning
ar, v. a. to bridle
refrain [ter-sign
dar, v. a. to coun-
dario, s. m. an of-
that counter-signs
data, s. f. counter-
[her
cador, s. m. refres-
cadura, s. fem. re-
hing
car, v. a. to refresh
o begin again || to
w or revive a grief
car la memoria, to
ind
car, v. n. to cool
carse, ver. r. to re-
h nature
co, s. m. refresh-
t; repast
fresco, adv. again
ga, s. f. a fray; a
rrel
rante, s. m. the
|| a refrigeratory

Refrigerante, a. 2. cooling; refrigerative
Refrigerar, v. a. to refrigerate
Refrigerativo, va, adjec. refrigerative
Refrigeratorio, s. m. the cooler
Refrigerio, s. m. refreshment || consolation
Refringir, v. a. to refract a ray
Refuerzo, s. m. reinforcement || succour; relief [one
Refugiar, v. a. to shelter
Refugiarse, v. r. to refuge to...
Refugio, s. m. refuge
Refulgencia, s. f. refulgence
Refulgente, a. 2. refulgent
Refundicion, s. f. melting again
Refundir, v. a. to melt again; to new-cast
Refunfuñadura, s. f. } muttering; grumbling
Refunfuño, s. m. }
Refunfuñar, v. neut. to grumble; to mutter
Refutacion, s. f. refutation
Refutar, v. a. to refute
Regadera, s. f. watering-pot
Regadío, s. m. watering || a watered place
Regadizo, za, adjec. that may be watered
Regádor, s. m. a waterer || a comb-maker's tool
Regadura, s. f. watering
Regajal, s. m. a watery, slabby, dirty place
Regajo, s. m. a puddle
Regaladamente, adver. daintily

Regalado, da, adj. dainty || nice; delicate
Regalador, s. m. a liberal, generous, magnificent man || a polishing-tool
Regalamiento, s. m. making much of...
Regalar, v. act. to make much of... || to treat daintily || to entertain
Regalarse, v. r. to regale one's self || to dissolve; to melt
Regalía, s. f. the prerogative of a king; regalia
Regalicia, } s. f. licorice
Regaliz, }
Regaliza, }
Regalillo, sub. m. a little present || a muff
Regalo, s. m. a present || treat; entertainment
Regalon, na, adj. dainty-mouthed || spoiled child [ring
Regamiento, s. m. watering
Regañado, da, adj. given or done with reluctance
Regañar, v. n. to snarl; to growl || to grumble, or mutter
Regañar los dientes, to gnash the teeth
Regaño, subs. m. grumbling; growling
Regañon, na, s. a snarling, growling dog || a grumbling fellow || the north-wind
Regar, v. a. to water
Regata, s. fem. trench; gutter
Regate, s. m. quick and irregular motion || subterfuge
Regatear, ver. n. to use subterfuges

Regatear, v. a. *to cheapen; to haggle* || *to elude*

Regatería, s. f. V. Regatonería [*ter*

Regatero, s. m. *a huckster*

Regaton, s. m. *a huckster* || *a cheapener* || *the but-end of a spear*

Regatonear, v. n. *to play the huckster*

Regatonería, s. f. *a huckster's shop* or *trade*

Regazar, v. a. *to tuck up*

Regazo, s. m. *the lap of a woman, etc.*

Regencia, s. fem. *governing; ruling* || *regency* || *professorship*

Regeneracion, s. f. *regeneration* [*nerate*

Regenerar, v. a. *to rege-*

Regentar, v. a. *to govern as a regent*

Regente, s. m. *a regent* || *a president of a council* || *a professor*

Regiamente, ad. *royally*

Regibado, da, a. *crookbacked*

Regidor, s. m. *a ruler; a governor* || *an alderman*, or *sheriff*

Regidor, ra, adj. *ruling; governing*

Régimen, sub. m. *rule; government*

Regimiento, sub. m. *government* || *regimen* || *a course of diet* || *a council of regency* || *the magistrates of a town* || *sheriffalty* || *a regiment*

Regio, gia, adj. *royal*

Aqua regia, *aqua regalis*

Region, s. f. *region*

Regir, v. a. *to govern; to rule*

Registrador, s. m. *an examiner* || *a register* || *a keeper of rolls*

Registrar, v. a. *to examine; to look into* || *to registrer* || *to search goods at the custom-house*

Registro, s. m. *search; searching* || *a tassel* || *a register* || *the custom-house* || *the entry-book of a custom-house*

Registros, pl. *the stops in the organ*

Regitar, v. act. *to vomit (speaking of hawks)*

Regitivo, va, adjec. *that rules* or *governs*

Regla, s. f. *a rule* || *woman's courses*

Regladamente, ad. *orderly; regularly*

Reglado, da, adj. *orderly; regular*

Reglamento, s. m. *regulation; rule*

Reglar, a. 2. *regular*

Reglar, v. a. *to rule* || *to regulate*

Reglarse, v. r. *to regulate one's expenses, etc.*

Regnícola, a. y s. *a native of a kingdom* || *a denison*

Regocijadamente, adver. *merrily*

Regocijar, v. a. *to rejoice*

Regocijarse, v. r. *to rejoice at*

Regocijo, s. m. *joy; mirth*

Regodearse, ver. r. *to delight in* || *to sport; to wanton*

Regodeo, sub. m. *merry-making; sporting* || *delighting in*

Regojo, sub. m. a bit of broken bread || a little small fellow

Regojuelo, s. m. dim. Regojo

Regoldar, v. n. *to* [...] || *to boast*

Regolfar, ver. n. *to* [...] *round like a whirl*[...]

Regolfo, s. m. *a* [...] *pool* || *a gulf*

Regona, s. fem. *a* [...] *road* || *a deep* [...]

Regordete, a. m. [...] *and fat*

Regordido, da, adj. [...] *fed up with fat*

Regostarse, v. r. *to* [...] *light in* [*deli*[...]

Regosto, s. m. [...]

Regresar, v. n. *to* [...] *into a benefice* [...]

Regresar, v. a. *to* [...] *a benefice* || *to* [...] *one's self to...*

Regresion, s. fem. [...] *back; return*

Regreso, s. m. *regres*[...]

Regüeldo, s. m. *a* [...] || *a boast; a brag*

Reguera, s. fem. *trench*, *gutter*

Reguero, s. m. *rivulet*

Regulacion, s. f. *regula-tion* || *computation* || *comparison*

Regulado, da, a. *regu*[...]

Regular, v. a. *to regul*[...]

Regular, a. 2. *regular*

Regularidad, s. f. *regularity* [*gula*[...]

Regularmente, adv. [...]

Régulo, s. m. *any pe*[...] *sovereign* || *a basil*[...] || *regulus*

Regurgitar, v. n. *to* [...] *over; to overflow*

Rehabilitacion, s. f. *rehabilitation* [*inst*[...]

Rehabilitar, v. a. *to* [...]

Rehacer, v. a. *to* [...] *make again* || *to* [...]

acerse, *v. r. to recover one's strength || to rally after disorder*
acimiento, *sub. m. a rising again || recovery || rallying of broken troops*
acio, cia, *a. V.* Reacio
echo, cha, *adj. done again || rallied || strong-limbed*
en, *s. m. an hostage*
nchir, *v. a. to fill* or *stuff again*
ndija, *s. f. a cranny*
rir, *v. act. to mark again the measures, [again*
rvir, *ver. n. to boil*
lar, *v. a. to writhe* or *twist again || to strain the cable*
lar, *v. n. to shake; stagger*
lete, *s. m. a shuttlecock.*
lo, *s. m. staggering*
nchimiento, *s. m. the filling* or *stuffing again*
llar, *v. a. to trample again*
yar, *v. a. to dig again*
yo, *s. m. a deep ditch*
ida, *s. f. a precipitate flight || the doubling of a stag*
ir, *v. a.* y *n. to fly to double, as stags || to reject*
ndir, *v. a. to sink* or *drown again || to melt again || to waste an estate*
rtado (ciervo), *s. m. stag that doubles*
sar, *v. a. to refuse*
, *a. 2. risible*
gracion, *s. f. restoration of one to his own*

Reintegrar, *v. a. to restore one to his own*
Reintegrarse, *v. r. to recover one's estate*
Reintegro, *s. m. V.* Reintegracion
Reir, *v. n. to laugh || to be pleasant*
Reir el alba, *to dawn*
Reirse, *v. r. to laugh at*
Reiteracion, *s. f. reiteration [rate*
Reiterar, *v. a. to reiterate*
Reivindicacion, *subst. f. claim; claiming*
Reivindicar, *v. a. to claim*
Reja, *s. f. a plough-share || iron-grate of a window [window, etc.*
Rejado, *sub. m. a grated*
Rejalgar, *s. m. realgar*
Rejazo, *subs. m. a blow with a plough-share*
Rejo, *sub. m. any iron-point || the sting of a bee, etc. || strength*
Rejon, *subst. m. an iron bar ending in a sharp point || a spear used in the bull-feasts || a sort of poniard*
Rejonazo, *s. m. a blow with a* rejon
Rejoneador, *sub. m. one who wounds the bull with a* rejon
Rejonear, *v. a. to wound the bulls with the* rejon
Rejoneo, *s. m. the act of wounding bulls with the* rejon
Rejuela, *s. f. a little grate || a fire-pan*
Rejuvenecer, *v. neut. to grow young again*
Relacion, *s. f. relation*
Relacionar, *v. a. to relate or report*
Relacionero, *sub. m. one who sells songs, etc. in the streets*

Relamerse, *v. r. to lick one's lips savourily*
Relámpago, *subst. m. a lightning || a web in the horse's eye*
Relampaguear, } *to lighten || to glitter*
Relampaguzar, }
Relance, *s. f. a new cast of net || chance; accident [ce*
De relance, *ad. by chance*
Relapso, sa, *a. relapsed*
Relatar, *v. a. to relate*
Relativo, va, *a. relative*
Relator, *sub. m. relater; reporter*
Relatoria, *s. f. the function of reporting the cause [again*
Relavar, *ver. a. to wash*
Relaxacion, *s. f.* } *relaxation || release*
Relaxamiento, *s. m.* }
Relaxar, *v. a. to relax || to release*
Relaxarse, *v. r. to slacken || to take to a loose life || to be loose in the body*
Relente, *s. m. the softness caused by the dew*
Relentecer, *v. n.* } *to grow soft, supple, etc.*
Relentecerse, *v. r.* }
Relevacion, *s. f. a raising || diminution of taxes, etc. || pardon*
Relevante, *a. 2. raised; noble*
Relevar, *v. a. to raise; to extol || to emboss || to unload; to discharge || to relieve*
Relex, *s. m. retreat (in architecture) || rut of a wheel || the landing*

Relieve, s. m. *relievo* || *offals; scraps, etc.*

Religar, ver. a. *to bind again*

Religion, s. f. *religion*

Religionario, s. m. } *a cal-*
Religionista, s. 2. } *vinist*

Religiosamente, adv. *religiously*

Religiosidad, s. fem. *religiousness* [*gious*

Religioso, sa, adj. *reli-*

Religioso, sa, s. *a monk* or *nun*

Relinchar, v. n. *to neigh*

Relinchido, } s. m. *a neig*
Relincho, } *hing*

Relindo, da, adjec. *very pretty, fine, etc.*

Reliquia, s. f. *remains* || *relick*

Rellanar, v. a. *to plain* or *smooth again*

Rellanarse, ver. r. *to sit stretched out in a chair* || *to sink with too much weight, etc.*

Rellenar, ver. a. *to fill* or

in one's eyes

Remachadas (narices), s. f. pl. *a broad flat nose*

Remachar, v. a. *to rivet* or *clinch a nail* || *to make fast*

Remador, s. m. *a rower*

Remanecer, v. n. *to remain* || *to appear suddenly* [*mainder*

Remanente, s. m. *the re-*

Remangar, v. a. *to tuck up the sleeves, etc.*

Remanso, sub. m. *a standing water in a river*

Remar, v. n. *to row*

Rematadamente, adv. *absolutely* || *desperately*

Rematado, da, adj. *quite lost; desperate*

Rematar, v. a. *to end; to finish* || *to close an account* || *to strike up a bargain*

Rematar, v. n. *to end* || *to adjuge in an auction*

Rematarse, v. r. *to perish; to be ruined, etc.*

Remesar,

Remeson, *that is t* || *a sho*

Remeter, *again*

Remiendo *a botch spot* or

Remilgars *pretty f to brick*

Remilgo,

Reminisce *miniscen*

Remirado

Remirar, *again* | *roughly*

Remisame *missly*

Remisible

Remision *back* || *missnes*

Remiso,

Remisorio *may re*

mojar, v. a. to soak; to steep; to water

mojo, s. m. soaking; steeping

molacha, s. f. beet-root

molcar, v. a. to tow a ship

molinarse, v. r. to turn about || to troop; to flock

molino, s. m. a whirlwind || a whirl-pool || the turn of the hair on the top of the head || a spiral line || a troop; a flock || trouble; disturbance

molon, s. m. the wild boar's upper tusk

molon, na, adj. slothful

molonearse, ver. r. to slacken; to be slow, etc.

molque, s. m. towing

mondar, v. a. to clean or prune again

monta, s. f. new horses (in war)

montar, v. a. to frighten the game || to give new horses to soldiers || to stuff again a saddle, etc.

montarse, v. r. to fly very high || to use lofty expressions, etc.

moquete, s. m. a fisty-cuff || a sharp sword || the courting a lady

mora, s. f. remora

mordedor, ra, a. that causes remorses

morder, v. a. to bite again || to cause remorses

mordimiento, s. m. a remorse

mostar, ver. a. to put must into old wine

Remostarse, Remostecerse, v. r. to grow sweet again like new wine

Remosto, s. m. the putting must into old wine

Remoto, ta, adj. remote; distant

Remover, v. a. to remove; to stir

Removimiento, s. m. removing

Remozar, v. a. to make young

Remozarse, v. r. to grow young

Rempujar, v. a. to push; to thrust

Rempujo, s. m. a push; a thrust || the flying out of a roof

Rempujon, s. m. a push, or thrust

Remudar, v. a. to change again

Remugar, v. a to ruminate

Remuneracion, s. f. remuneration

Remunerador, s. m. a rewarder

Remunerar, v. a. to remunerate

Remuneratorio, ria, adj. remunerating

Remusgar, v. n. to suspect

Ren, s. m. the rein, or kidney

Renacer, v. a. to be born again || to revive || to spring up again

Renacimiento, s. m. new birth || regeneration || revival

Renacuajo, sub. m. bull-head

Rencilla, s. f. quarrel

Rencilloso, sa, adj. quarrel some

Renco, ca, adj. loose or lame in the hips

Rencor, s. m. rancour

Rencorioso, sa, Rencoroso, sa, a. rancorous

Rendajo, s. m. V. Arrendajo

Rendicion, s. f. reddition

Rendidamente, adv. submissively

Rendija, s. f. a cranny; a little chink

Rendimiento, s. m. yielding up || surrendering || submission || weariness || a rent, or revenue

Rendir, v. a. to yield up || to surrender || to yield; to bring forth || to vomit

Rendirse, v. r. to be even spent || to surrender or submit

Rendon, s. m. V. Rondon

Renegado, da, adj. renegade || wicked; perverse

Renegador, s. m. a renegade || a swearer

Renegar, ver. a. to deny obstinately || to curse and swear

Renegar, v. n. to abjure one's religion || to abhor

Renglon, s. m. a line (in writing)

Renglones, pl. writings

Renglonadura, s. f. a line

Rengo, ga, adj. that has got a hurt in the loins

Reniego, s. m. a renouncing the God, etc.

Renitencia, s. fem. reluctance

Renitente, a. s. reluctant

Renombre, s. m. a surname

Renovacion, s. f. renovation; renewal

Renovador, s. m. renewer

Renovar, v. a. to renew

Renovero, s. m. a broker || an usurer.

Renquear, *v. n. to go lame in the hips*
Renta, *s. f. rent; revenue*
Rentar, *v. a. to yield rent* or *revenue*
Renteria, *s. f. a farm*
Rentero, *s. m. a farmer*
Rentilla, *sub. f. a small rent || a game at cards*
Rentoy, *s. m. a game at cards*
Renuencia, *s. f. reluctance; repugnance.*
Renuevo, *s. m. a young shoot of a tree || a nursery renewing.*
Renuncia, *s. f. renunciation || cession; giving up* [*be renounced*
Renunciable, *a. that may*
Renunciacion, *s. f. renunciation*
Renunciar, *v. a. to renounce || to give up || to refuse* or *reject || to contemn || to renounce* or *revoke* (*at cards*)
Renuncio, *s. m. renounce* (*at cards*)
Reñido, da, *a. fallen out with one* [*war*
Guerra reñida, *bloody*
Reñir, *v. n. to quarrel; to contest || to chide; to rebuke* [*question*
Reñir, *v. a. to debate a*
Reñon, *s. m. V.* Riñon
Reo, *s. m. a criminal; a guilty person || defendant || series; sequel || a sort of fish*
Repajo, *s. m. a place for cattle to graze || a thicket of young trees*
Repantigarse, *v. r. to sit stretched out at one's full ease*
Repapilarse, *v. r. to glut one's self*

Reparable, *a. 2. repairable || remarkable*
Reparacion, *s. f. reparation* [*|| censurer*
Reparador, *s. m. repairer*
Reparamiento, *s. m. repair; repairing*
Reparar, *v. a. to repair || || to observe; to examine || to mend || to make a stand || to parry in fencing || to be cautious*
Repararse, *v. r. to contain one's self*
Reparo, *subst. mas. repair; reparation || regard; notice; observation || doubt; difficulty; obstacle || defence; intrenchment, etc.*
Reparticion, *s. f. repartition || assessment*
Repartidor, *s. m. distributer || assessor*
Repartimiento, *s. m. distribution || assessment*
Repartir, *v. a. to distribute || to assess*
Repasadera, *s. f. a kind of carpenter's plane*
Repasar, *v. a. to repass || to look* or *read over again || to repeat*
Repasion, *s. f. reaction*
Repaso, *s. m. the looking* or *reading over again || review; revision || a reprimand* [*again*
Repastar, *ver. a. to feed*
Repasto, *s. m. new food* or *pasture*
Repatriar, *v. n. to return to one's country*
Repecho, *sub. m. the side of a hill*
Repelar, *v. a.* to pull off *the hair* || to take by little parties

Repeler, *v. a. to to beat back*
Repelo, *s. m. pul the hair || a fla the nails || the way* or *sense || quarrel*
Repelon, *s. m. a the hair || a litt pulled out*
Repeloso, sa, *a.*
Madera repelosa, *that has an ill*
Repensar, *v. a. t over again*
Repente, *s. m. a motion*, or *eve*
De repente, *ad denly*
Repentinamente,
Repentino, na, *a.*
Repenton, *s. m. a event*, or *moti*
Repercudida, } *s.*
Repercusion, } *c*
Repercusivo, va *percussive*
Repercutir, *v. a. cute*
Repercutir, *ver.*
Repertorio, *s. m tory*
Repesar, *v. a. t*
Repeso, *sub. ma ghing again || ghing place*
Repetencia, } *s.*
Repeticion, } *ti*
Repetidamente, *peatedly*
Repetidor, *s. m.*
Repetir, *v. a. to*
Repicado, *s. m. a nice beau*
Repicapunto, (d nicely; curio
Repicar, a. a. t mince || to repeek

que, s. m. chimes ||
repeat (a picket)
quete, s. m. chime on
bells || occasion;
counter || a clatte-
g of tongues
a, s. f. modillon
car, v. a. to pinch
co, s. m. a pinch
cion, s. f. repletion
to, ta, a. replete
ca, s. f. a reply
car, v. n. to reply
con, na, adj. that
ll always reply
llo, s. m. cabbage-
ad
lludo (hombre) s. m.
short squat man
ner, v. a. to put or
again || to replace
to reinstate || to subs-
ute [tion
rtacion, s. f. modera-
rtado, da, a. mode-
te; sober
rtar, ver. a. to re-
ss; to refrain
rtarse, v. r. to curb
e's passion
rtorio, s. m. a reper-
ry || a calendar [ly
adamente, ad. quiet-
sar, v. n. to repose
to rest; to sleep || to
still
sarse, v. r. to settle
aid of any liquor)
sicion, s. f. reposi-
on || reinstating
so, s. m. repose; rest
steria, s. f. an office;
buttery
stero, s. m. butler;
ficer || a kind of car-
t
egunta, s. f. a new
stion
untar, ver. a. to

question over and over
again
Reprehender, v. a to re-
prehend [prehensible
Reprehensible, a. 2. re-
Reprehension, s. f. repre
hension
Reprehensor, s. m. repre-
hender
Represa, s. f. a mill-dam;
a flood-gate || resent-
ment
Represalia, } s. f. repri-
Represaria, } sal
Represar, v. a to stop the
water, etc.
Representable, a. 2. that
may be represented
Representacion, s. f. re-
presentation
Representador, s. m. One
that represents
Representante, sub. m. a
player [present
Representar, v. a to re-
Representativo, va, adj.
representative
Reprimenda, s. f. a re-
primand
Reprimir, ver. a. to re-
press; to refrain
Reprobacion, s. f. repro-
ving || reprobation
Reprobar, v. a. to reprove
|| to reprobate
Réproba, s. m. a repro-
bate [proach
Reprochar, ver. a. to re-
Reproche, sub. m. a re-
proach [duction
Reproduccion, s. f. repro-
Reproducir, v. a. to re-
produce
Reptil, a. 2. reptile
República, s. f. republick
Republicano, na, a. re-
publican [publican
Republicano, s. m. a re-
Repúblico, s. m. a man

full of zeal for the pu-
blick good, or fit for
the publick employ-
ments
Repudiacion, s. f. repu-
diation [diate
Repudiar, v. a. to repu-
Repudio, s. m. repudia-
tion
Repuesto, sub. m. provi-
sions made before hand
De repuesto, adv. before
hand
Repuesto, ta, p. p. of re-
poner
Repugnancia, s. fem. re-
pugnance
Repugnante, adj. 2. re-
pugnant
Repugnar, v. a. to repugn
Repulgar, v. a. to hem
Repulgo, s. m. a hem in
a garment || the edge
of a pie
Repullo, s. m. a violent
shake or jump
Repulsa, s. f. a repulse
Repulsar, v. a. to repulse
or repel
Repunta, s. f. a point of
land || a sign of anger,
etc. || a quarrel
Repuntar, ver. n. to flow
(speaking of the tide)
Repuntarse, v. r. to turn
(said of a wine) || to
quarrel [purge
Repurga, s. fem. a new
Repurgar, v. a. to purge
or clean over again
Reputacion, s. f. reputa-
tion
Reputar, v. a. to repute
Requebrador, sub. m. one
that courts
Requebrar, v. a. to court;
to make love
Requemado, da, a. adust;
burnt || very brown

Requemar, v. a. to burn again
Requemarse, v. r. to consume away with grief, etc.
Requerimiento, s. m. requiring; intimation
Requerir, v. a. to intimate; to notify || to require || to verify || to take care of...
Requerir de amores, to court; to make love
Requeson, s. m. curds
Requësta, s. f. a request
Requëstar, ver. a. to request || to court a lady
Requiebro, s. m. an amorous, flattering expression
Requisito, sub. m. the requisite
Requisito, ta, a. requisite
Res, s. f. a head of cattle
Resaber, ver. n. to affect a tedious learning
Resabiar, ver. n. to practise an ill habit || to have an ill taste or savour
Resabiarse, ver. r. to fly into a passion
Resabio, s. m. an ill habit or custom || a jadish trick in a horse || an ill taste or savour
Resaca, s. f. surf
Resalir, v. n. to jut out; to project
Resaltar, v. n. to reflect; to rebound || to jut out
Resalte, s. m. a jutting or leaning out
Resalto, s. m. reflecting; rebounding. || V. Resalte
Resaludar, v. a. to resalute
Resalutacion, s. f. resalutation
Resarcir, v. a. to make amends for; to repair
Resbaladero, s. m. a slide; any slippery place
Resbaladino, na, a. slippery
Resbaladura, s. fem. the print of a slipping
Resbalar, v. n. to slide; to slip
Resbalon, sub m. a slipping
Rescaldar, v. a. to heat or warm again
Rescatar, ver. a. to buy again || to redeem; to ransom || to exchange
Rescate, s. m. redeeming
Rescoldo, s. m. hot ashes || fear; suspicion
Rescontrar, v. a. to compensate (in accounts)
Rescribir, v. a. to write again || to answer to a letter
Rescripto, s. m. a rescript
Rescuentro, s. m. a compensation
Resellar, v. a. to coin or seal again
Resello, s. m. coining, sealing again
Resembrar, v. a. to sow again
Resentido, da, a. resentful
Resentimiento, sub. m. resentment || a slit; a chink
Resentirse, ver. r. to resent || to chink; to gape
Reseña, s. f. a muster or review
Reserva, s. f. reserve
Reservacion, s. f. reserving
Reservado, da, a. reserved; cautious; shy
Reservar, v. a. to reserve
Reservarse, v. r. to keep one's self
Resfriado, p. m. a cold
Resfriado, da, a. that has got a cold
Resfriamiento, s. m. cooling
Resfriar, v. a. to cool
Resfriarse, ver. r. to get a cold || to cool; to relent
Resfriecer, v. n. to grow cold
Resfrio, s. m. the growing cold || a cold
Resguardar, v. a. to preserve or defend
Resguardarse, v. r. to be cautious
Resguardo, s. m. care, caution || defence; shelter || security
Residencia, s. fem. residence || residentship the trial of a governor, etc. when he resigns his employment
Pedir residencia, to call to an account tomar residencia, take to an account
Residenciar, v. a. to make the trial of a governor, etc.
Residente, s. m. a resident
Residir, v. n. to reside
Residuo, s. m. residue
Resigna, } s. f. resignation
Resignacion, }
Resignante, sub. m. a resigner
Resignar, v. a. to resign
Resina, s. f. a resin
Resinoso, sa, a. resinous
Resistencia, s. fem. resistance
Resistero, } s. m. reflection or violent heat of the sun
Resistidero, }
Resistir, v. n. to resist
Resma, sub. f. a ream paper

...sol, s. m. *the reverberation of the sun*
...solano, s. m. *a warm sunny place*
...sollar, v. n. *to breathe thick*
...solucion, s. f. *resolution*
...solutamente, ad. *resolutely*
...solutivo, va, a. *resolutive*
Resoluto, ta, a. *resolute; resolved*
Resolver, v. a. *to resolve*
Resonacion, s. f. *reflection of the sound*
Resonancia, s. f. *resounding || consonance*
Resonante, a. 2. *resounding*
Resonar, v. n. *to resound*
Resoplar, ver. neut. *to breathe hard and frequently*
Resoplido, } subs. mas.
Resoplo, } *hard and frequent breath*
Respaldar, s. m. V. Espaldar
Respaldar, v. a. *to write on the back of a bill, etc.*
Respaldarse, v. r. *to lean on the back of a chair || to put one's shoulder out of joint*
Respaldo, s. m. *the back of a chair, etc. || writing on the back*
Respectivamente, ad. *respectively*
Respectivo, va, a. *respective* [*relation*
Respecto, s. m. *respect;*
Respecto, ad. *with respect to* [*table*
Respetable, a. 2. *respec-*
Respetar, v. a. *to respect*
Respeto, s. m. *respect*
Estar de respeto, *to be in ceremony*
Respetosamente, ad. *respectfully*
Respetoso, sa, a. *respectful* [*pectfully*
Respetuosamente, ad. *res-*
Respetuoso, sa, adj. *respectful*
Réspice, s. m. *an offering made in the mass*
Respigadera, s. f. *a gleaner woman* [*ner*
Respigador, s. m. *a glea-*
Respigar, v. a. *to glean*
Respigon, sub. m. *a flaw in one's nails*
Respingar, v. n. *to kick*
Respingo, s. m. *a kick || a pert peevish answer*
Respiracion, s. f. *respiration; breath*
Respiradero, sub. m. *the pipe of the lungs || a hole to let in the air*
Respirar, ver. n. *to respire; to breathe*
Resplandecencia, s. fem. *resplendence*
Resplandecer, ver. n. *to shine; to glitter*
Resplandeciente, adj. 2. *resplendent*
Resplandor, s. m. *splendor; brightness*
Responder, v. n. *to answer*
Respondidamente, adver. *with correspondence; symetry, etc.*
Respondon, na, a. *grumbling; that has always an answer* [*ponsible*
Responsable, adj. 2. *res-*
Responso, } s. m. *a es-*
Responsorio, } *ponse*
Respuesta, s. f. *an answer || the report of a gun*
Resquebradura, } s. f. *a*
Resquebrajadura, } *crack; a chop; a slit; a cleft*
Resquebrajar, ver. a. V. Resquebrar
Resquebrajo, sub. m. V. Resquebrajadura
Resquebrar, ver. act. *to crak; to slit; to cleave*
Resquicio, s. m. *chink; cleft; cranny || way; means; opportunity*
Resta, s. fem. *the rest, or remainder*
Restablecer, v. a. *to re-establish*
Restablecerse, v. r. *to recover one's health, etc.*
Restablecimiento, s. mas. *re-establishment*
Restallar, v. n. *to snap*
Restañar, v. a. *to stop the blood, etc.*
Restaño, s. m. *a silver or gold stuff || a pool*
Restante, sub. m. *what remains*
Restar, v. a. *to substract || to remain*
Restauracion, s. f. *restoration* [*res*
Restaurador, s. m. *restorer*
Restaurar, v. a. *to restore*
Restaurativo, va, a. *restorative* [*torative*
Restaurativo, s. m. *a res-*
Restitucion, s. f. *restitution*
Restituir, v. a. *to return; to refund || to restore*
Restituirse, ver. r. *to return; to go back*
Restitutorio, ria, a. *relating to the restitution*
Resto, sub. m. *rest; remainder || a stake (at play) || substraction*
Restriccion, s. f. *restriction*

Restricto, ta, a. *restrained*

Restringir, v. a. *to restrain* || *to restringe*

Restriñir, v. a. *to stop* || *to restringe*

Resucitador, sub. m *one that revives*

Resucitar, ver. a. y n. *to resuscitate; to revive*

Resudacion, s. f. *perspiration*

Resudar, ver. a. y n. *to perspire; to sweat*

Resuello, s. m. *a thick and short breath*

Resueltamente, adv. *resolutely*

Resuelto, ta, a. *resolute* || *quick; expeditive*

Resulta,
Resultancia, } *s. f. a rebound* || *a result*

Resultar, ver. n. *to rebound* || *to result*

Resúmen, s. m. *summary*

Resumidamente, ad. *summarily*

Resumir, v. a. *to resume* || *to reduce*

Resuncion, s. f. *resuming*

Resurreccion, s. f. *resurrection*

Resurtir, ver. n. *to spurt up; to rebound*

Retablo, s. m. *altar-piece* || *a picture* || *a puppet shew*

Retacar, v. a. *to strike a ball twice (at billiards)*

Retaco, s. m. *a small gun* || *a large, sort of billiard-stick* || *a thick and short man*

Retador, s. m. *a challenger. V.* Retar

Retaguarda,
Retaguardia, } *s. fem. the rear of an army, etc.*

Retahila, s. fem. *a file of soldiers, etc.*

Retajar, v. a. *to cut; to pare; to clip* || *to make a pen again* || *to circumcise*

Retal, s. m. *shreds; parings, etc.*

Retallar, ver. n. *to sprout again*

Retallo, sub. m. *a new sprout*

Retama, s. f. *broom*

Retamal, s. m. *a place full of brooms*

Retamera, s. f. *the place where they heap up the broom*

Retamero, ra, a. *relating to the broom*

Retar, v. a. *to challenge* || *to charge a man with treason and to offer to make it good in combat*

Retardacion, s. f. *retardation; delay*

Retardar, v. a. *to retard; to delay*

Retazo, s. m. *bid; piece* || *shreds*

Retejar, v. a. *to new tile* || *to mend cloaths*

Retejo, s. m. *new tiling*

Retemblar, v. n. *to tremble repeatedly*

Reten, sub. m. *a spare thing; provision, etc.*

Retencion, s. f. *retaining* || *reservation* || *retention of urine*

Retenedor, s. m. *he who stops or retains*

Retener, v. a. *to retain* || *to reserve* || *to detain; to stop*

Retentar, v. a. to try or attempt again

Retentiva, s. f. prudence; reservedness

Reteñir, v. a. to die again

Reteñir, v. n. *to tinkle; to jingle*

Retesmiento, s. m. *coagulation; curdling*

Retesar, v. a. *to harden* || *to stretch*

Reticencia, s. f. *reticence*

Retina, s. f. *the retina*

Retinte, sub. mas. *dying over again* || *a tinkling noise*

Retiñir, v. n. *to tinkle; to jingle*

Retiracion, s. f. *retiration*

Retirada, sub. f. *retreat; retirement*

Retirado, da, a. *retired; solitary*

Retirar, v. a. *to draw or get out* || *to withdraw*

Retirarse, v. r. *to retire* || *to go home* || *to go out or away* || *to fall out with one*

Retiro, s. m. *retreat; retirement* || *falling out with one*

Reto, s. m. *a challenge. V.* Retar

Retocar, ver. a. *to touch again* || *to revise; to correct*

Retoñar,
Retoñecer, } *v. n. to sprout out again*

Retoño, sub. mas. *a new sprout*

Retoque, s. m. *finishing; correcting*

Retorcedura, s. f. *twisting again*

Retorcer, v. a. *to twist again* || *to retort*

Retorcido, s. m. *a kind of sweet meat*

Retorcimiento, subs. m. *twisting again*

Retórica, s. f. *rhetorick*

Retóricas, pl. talkativeness; rhetorications

Retórico, ca, a. rhet-cal

etórico, s. m. a rhetorician
etornar, v. n. to return
etornar, v. a. to turn, or turn up || to render like for like
etornelo, s. m. a flourish; a voluntary (in musick)
etorno, s. m. return || an exchange
etorta, s. f. a retort
etortero (al), ad. round about [to wreath
etortijar, v. a. to twist;
etortijon, s. m. twisting
etozador, s. m. wanton; dallier
etozar, v. n. to play the wanton; to dally
etozar con el verde, to sport; to frolick — la risa, to burst with laughing [dalliance
etozo, s. m. wantoness;
etozon, na, a. wanton; lascivious
etrabar, v. a. to set people by the ears
etraccion, s. f. retraction [tation
etractacion, s. f. retrac-
etracto, s. m. redemption; redeeming
etraer, ver. a. to draw back; to withdraw || to dissuade || to reproach again || to resemble || to redeem
etraerse, v. r. to retire; to fly to...
etraido, s. m. a man retired in a privileged place
etraimiento, s. m. refuge; shelter
etranca, s. f. a crupper for a beast of burden
etratador, s. m. a painter that draws by the life
Retratar, v. a. to draw by the life || to imitate || to retract or recant
Retratarse, v. r. to recant
Retrato, s. m. a picture drawn by the life || redemption; redeeming
Retreta, s. f. the tattoo
Retrete, s. m. a closet
Retribucion, s. f. retribution [bute
Retribuir, v. a. to retri-
Retroceder, ver. n. to go back; to retrograde
Retrocesion, s. f. } retrogradation
Retroceso, s. m. }
Retrogradacion, s. f. retrogradation
Retrogradar, v. n. to retrograde
Retrógrado, da, a. retrograde [again
Retronar, v. a. to thunder
Retrovender, v. a. to sell again
Retrovendicion, s. f. selling again
Retrucar, v. n. to strike one ball against the other at billiards || to revy (at play)
Retruécano, s. m. a quibble, a pun
Retruque, s. m. a renvy or paroly (at play)
Retuerto, ta, adj. very crooked
Retular, v. a. to write an inscription or title
Rétulo, s. m. an inscription; a title
Retumbante, adj. 2. resounding [sound
Retumbar, v. a. to re-
Retumbo, s. m. a resounding; a great sound
Reuma, s. f. a rheum
Reúmatico, ca, a. belonging to, or troubled with, a rheum
Reumatismo, s. m. rheumatism
Reunion, s. f. reunion
Reunir, v. a. to reunite
Revalidacion, s. f. ratification
Revalidar, v. a. to ratify
Revelacion, s. f. revelation; revealing
Revelador, s. m. revealer
Revelar, v. a. to reveal
Revendedor, sub. mas. a huckster
Revender, ver. a to sell things by retails
Revenirse, v. r. to decay; to grow stale; to take damp, etc. || to be out of conceit with a thing
Reventa, s. f. retailing
Reventadero, s. m. any bad place in a road || a painful work
Reventar, ver. n. to burst || to work hard || to spring out
Reventar, v. a. to plague; to molest
Reventon, s. m. bursting a great difficulty || a hard work
Rever, v. a. to review; to revise [beration
Reverberacion, s. f. rever-
Reverberar, v. a to reverberate
Reverdecer, v. n. to grow green again
Reverencia, s. fem. reverence [verencear
Reverenciador, s. m. re-
Reverencial, adj. 2. reverential [vere
Reverenciar, v. a. to

Reverendisimo, ma, *adj. most reverend*
Reverendo, da, *a. reverend*
Reverendas, *f. pl. dimissory letters from one bishop to another*
Reverente, *a. 2. reverent*
Reversible, *a. 2. revertible*
Reversion, *s. f. reversion*
Reverso, *s. m. reverse of a coin, etc.*
Reverter, *v. n. to revert*
Reves, *s. m. the wrong-side || a back stroke || a misfortune* [*way*
Al reves, *ad. the wrong*
Revesado, da, *adj. stubborn; peevish || hard; difficult*
Revesar, *v. a. to vomit*
Revesino, *s. m. a game at cards*
Revestir, *v. a. to put one garment over another || to overcast a bastion with stone*
Revestirse, *v. r. to be prepossessed || to grow proud*
Revezar, *n. n.* } *to take*
Revezarse, *v. r.* } *one's turn with another*
Revezo, *sub. m. taking turns*
Revision, *s. f. revision*
Revista, *s. f. a review; a revising* [*cause*
Revistar, *v. a. to revise a*
Revisto, ta, *p. p. of rever*
Revivir, *v. n. to revive*
Revocable, *a. 2. revocable* [*tion*
Revocacion, *s. f. revoca-*
Revocar, *v. a. to revoke || to paint the out-side of a wall || to go back*
Revoco, *s. m. the polish, etc. given to a wall*

Revolar, *v. n. to fly again*
Revolcadero, *s. m. wallowing-place*
Revolcarse, *v. r. to wallow; to roll, or tumble || to be prepossessed with..*
Revolear, *ver. n. to fly swiftly and round, as swallow does*
Revoleteo, *sub. masc. a quick motion of birds in flying*
Revolotear, *v. n. V.* Revolear.
Revoltillo, *s. m. a bundle of several things || disorder; confusion*
Revolton, *sub. m. a sort of worm feeding upon leaves*
Revoltoso, sa, *adj. turbulent; seditious*
Revolucion, *s. f. revolution*
Revolvedor, *s. m. a seditious man; a disturber*
Revolver, *v. a. to turn; to turn up || to wrap; to roll up || to stir about || to set at variance; to disturbe*
Revolver los humores, *to revulse humours*
Revolver, *v. n.* } *to turn;*
Revolverse, *v. r.* } *to turn round* [*voco*
Revoque, *s. m. V.* Re-
Revuelo, *s. m. the new flying of a bird || flying back || confusion*
De revuelo, *ad. swiftly; quickly* [*volver*
Revuelto, ta, *p. p. of re-*
Revulsion, *s. f. revulsion*
Revulsivo, va, } *a. that*
Revulsorio, ria, } *causes a revulsion*

Rey, *s. m. a King*
Reyerta, *s. f. a [...] quarrel*
Reyezuelo, *s. m. [...] king || a wren (bird)*
Reyna, *s. f. a que[...]*
Reynado, *s. m. R[...]*
Reynar, *v. a. to r[...]*
Reyno, *s. m. kin[...] realm*
Rezado, *s. m. offi[...]vine service*
Rezaga, *s. f. the [...] an army* [
Rezagar, *v. a. to [...]*
Rezagarse, *ver. r. [...] behind; to lag*
Rezago, *s. m. res[...]due; remainde[...]*
Rezar, *v. a. to p[...] recite || to fore[...] grumble; to mu[...]*
Rezelador, *s. m. t[...] that serves to m[...] mares hot, befo[...] receive stallion*
Rezelar, *v. a. to [...] suspect || to m[...] mares hot befo[...] receive the stal[...]*
Rezelarse, *v. r. to*
Rezelo, *s. m. fea[...]picion; mistru[...]*
Rezeloso, sa, *a. f[...] suspicious*
Rezno, *s. m. a tick*
Rezo, *sub. m. a p[...] divine service*
Rezongador, *sub. [...] grumbling fello[...]*
Rezongar, *v. a. to [...]ble; to mutter*
Rezonglon, } *s. m. [...]*
Rezongon, } *[...]bling[...]tering fellow*
Rezumarse, *v. r. [...] out; to leak || [...]pire*

s. f. strength ||
the mouth of a
o, } s. m. a little river; a brook
s. m. the ridge of
. f. shore; bank
, ña, a. belonging to a shore or bank
o, ga, a. that in near a river
s. m. edge; edge border; hem, increase
, v. a. to edge; to
bría, s. fem. the y of a ricohombre
te, ad. richly
ub. m. a wealthy an
erra), s. fem. a hat produces a time after the g down of corn
, a. rich || noble ious
bre, } sub. m. a e, } grandee; n of the realm
mente, adv. riusly
s, s. fem. ridicuss
, la, } a. ridiouso, sa, } lous
. m. watering
m. a gold or silgot [bridle
s. f. the rein of a
la suelta, a round — á media rienhalf speed — á toda, a full speed
. m. risk; danger
strife; quarrel
r

Rifar, v. n. to strive; to quarrel [cast lots
Rifar, v. a. to draw or
Rifirafe, sub. m. a slight quarrel
Rigidez, s. f. rigidness; sternness [stern
Rígido, da, adj. rigid;
Rigor, s. m. rigor; harshness
En rigor, rigorously
Riguridad, s. f. rigor
Riguroso, sa, a. rigorous
Rija, s. fem. a lacrymal fistula [heap
Rima, s. fem, rhyme || a
Rimar, v. a. to rhyme || to search; to ferret about
Rimbombar, v. n. to resound; to echo
Rimbombe, } s. m. resound;
Rimbombo, } echoing
Rimero, s. m. a heap; a pile
Rincon, s. m. a corner
Rinconada, s. f. the corner formed by two houses, etc. [corner
Rinconcillo, s. m. a little
Ringla, } s. f. a row of
Ringlera, } houses, etc.
Ringlero, sub. m. a line drawn with a pencil
Ringorango, s. m, a flourish (in writing)
Rinoceronte, s. m. a rhinoceros
Riña, s. f. a quarrel
Riñon, s. m. a kidney
Riñonada, s. fem. the fat about the kidneys || a ragoo of kidneys
Rio, s. m. a river
Riostra, s. f. king-posts (in architecture)
Ripia, s. f. a shingle
Ripiar, v. a. to fill with rubbish || to cover with shingles

Ripio, sub. mas. rubbish (small bits of stone) || a botch (in poetry)
Riponce, s. m. rampious
Riqueza, s. fem. wealth; riches || richness
Riquísimante, adv. most richly [rich
Riquísimo, ma, a. most
Risa, s. f. laughter
Risada, s. f. a fit of laughter [crag
Risco, sub. m. a rock; a
Risibilidad, s. f. risibility
Risible, a. 2. risible || comical pleasant || ridiculous
Ristra, s. fem. a rope of onions, etc. [a lance
Ristre, s. m. the rest for
Risueño, ña, adj pleasing; smiling
Rito, s. m. rite || custom; manner
Ritual, s. m. ritual
Rival, s. m. a rival
Rivera, s, f. a rivulet
Rixa, s. f. a fray; a quarrel
Rixador, ra, a. quarrelsome
Rixo, s. m. inclination to sensuality
Rixoso, sa, adj. quarrelsome || inclined to sensuality
Riza, s. f. the root of the green barley given to horses || havock; destruction
Rizar, ver. a. to curl the hairs || to plait linen nicely
Rizo. s. m. curl || plait || a shorn velvet
Rizo, za, a. curled
Roa, s. f. V. Roda
Roano, a. m. roan
Rob, s. m. rob (of fruits)
Robador, s. m. a robber

gall-bearing oak-trees
Roblizo, za, *adj. strong; stout*
Robo, *s. m. theft; robbery*
Roborante, *adj. 2. corroborant*
Roborar, *v. a. to strenghten* ||
Roborativo, va, *a. corroborative*
Robra, *s. f. a bill of sale*
Robrar, *ver. a. to draw a bill of sale* || *to clench a nail*
Robre, *s. m. V.* Roble
Robustamente, *adv. robustly*
Robustez, **Robusticidad**, **Robustocidad**, *s. fem. robustness*
Robusto, ta, *a. robust*
Roca, *s. f. a rock*
Rocadero, *s. m. a painted cap like a mitre* || *a cornet of paper* || *the end of the distaff about wich they fasten the flax*

Rodado (caballo), *s. m. a dappled horse*
Rodador, *s. m. any thing that rolls*
Rodadura, *s. f. tumbling; rolling*
Rodaja, *s. f. a little wheel* || *a rowel*
Rodapelo. *V.* Redopelo
Rodapie, *s. m. the base* or *fringe of a bed*
Rodar, *ver. a. to roll* || *to roll* or *tumble down*
Rodar mundo *to ramble*
Rodear, *v. a. to encompass* || *to turn*, or *wind round*
Rodear, *v. neut. to turn round about* || *to periphrase*
Rodela, *s. fem. a round target*
Rodelero, *s. m. the soldier that wears a rodela*
Rodeo, *sub. m. compass* || *a way about* || *delay; excuse; pretence*

Rodomiel, ...
şatum
Rodrigar, ...
Rodrigon ...
for a vi...
Roedor, *s.* ...
Roedura, ...
Roel, *sub.* ...
heraldry
Roer, *v.* ...
talk ill ...
Roete, *s.* ...
the pom...
into wi...
Rogacion, ...
entreaty
Rogacione...
Rogador, ...
prays
Rogar, *v.* ...
entreat; ...
Rogativa, ...
entreaty
Rogativas ...
prayers
Rol, *s. m.* ...
Roldanas, ...
(in a sh...

strong woman
lo, da, *a. that*
a cold
·se, *v. r. to get*

, *s. m. a cold;*
tion; a pose
s. f. steel-yard
s. m. the spa-
ngue || spanish

, pl. shifts; eva-
[ly
romance; *plain-*
r, *v. a. to trans-*
o spanish
o, ra, *adj. that*
es or sings spa-
allads || that
terfuges
o, *s. m. a book*
ish ballads
ta, *sub. m. one*
ites in spanish

, *v. a. to weigh*
steel-yard
, *v. n. to pre-*
ate
na, *a. roman ||*
nd white (said
t)
, *ver. a. to turn*
nish
, *s. m. a long,*
spanish ballad
s. fem. the sour

. m. rhomb
s, *s. m. rhom-*
[pilgrim
sub. f. a woman
s. m. a plot of
planted with
y
s. f. pilgrimage
s. m. a pilgrim
ary || a little
h

Romo, ma, *a. flat-nosed || blunt; blunted; dull || the mule got by a horse on a she-ass*

Rompedor, *s. m. one who wears out many clothes, etc. || breaker*

Romper, *v. a. to break || to wear out clothes, etc. || to pierce,* or *open || to wound || to grub up an untilled ground || to fall to open enmity*

Romperse, *v. r. to learn with; to grow sharp, etc.*

Rompeesquinas, *s. m. a fierce bully; a noisy fellow*

Rompimiento, *s. m. rupture; breaking || a falling out || a cleft; a crack || a glory (in painting)*

Ronca, *s. f. a bravado*

Roncador, *s. m. a snorer*

Roncamente, *adv. hoarsely || clownishly*

Roncar, *v. n. to snore || to hector; to swagger*

Roncear, *v. n. to be idle* or *lazy || to flatter; to coax*

Roncería, *s. f. laziness; slothfulness || flattery; coaxing*

Roncero, ra, *adj. lazy; slothful || flatterer*

Roncha, *s. f. a blister; a wheal || sharping; spunging*

Ronchar, *v. a. V.* Ronzar

Ronchon, *s. m. aum. de* Roncha

Ronco, *s. m. snoring*

Ronco, ca, *adj. hoarse || harsh*

Roncon, *s. m. the drone of a bag-pipe*

Ronda, *s. fem. a round || the rounds*

Rondador, *s. m. one that goes the rounds*

Rondar, *v. a. to go the rounds || to haunt a place much*

Rondis, } *s. m. the lower*
Rondiz, } *part in a precious stone*

Rondon (de), *ad. abruptly,* or *intrepidly*

Ronfea, *s. f. a two-handled sword*

Ronquear, *ver. n. to be hoarse*

Ronquedad, }
Ronquera, } *s. f. hoarseness*
Ronquez, }

Ronquido, *s. m. a snoring*

Ronzal, *s. m. a halter*

Ronzar, *v. a. to chew,* or *crack hard things*

Roña, *s. fem. the scab in sheep || dirt; nastiness || craftiness; cheat*

Roñería, *s. f. cunning; cheat; deceit || covetousness*

Roñoso, sa, *a. scabby || dirty; nasty || crafty; cunning || stingy; covetous*

Ropa, *s f. all the furniture of a house in linen, silk, etc. || clothes || robe; gown*

Ropa de levantar, *a morning gown* — de mesa, *table-linen* — blanca, *linen*

Ropage, *s. m. clothes; clothing || a stately suit*

Ropavejería, *s. f. a broker's shop*

Ropavejero, *s. m. a broker*

Ropería, *s. f. a broke*

gall-bearing oak-trees

Robliso, za, *adj. strong; stout*

Robo, *s. m. theft; robbery*

Roborante, *adj.* 2. *corroborant*

Roborar, *v. a. to strenghten* || *to corroborate*

Roborativo, va, *a. corroborative*

Robra, *s. f. a bill of sale*

Robrar, *ver. a. to draw a bill of sale* || *to clench a nail*

Robre, *s. m. V.* Roble

Robustamente, *adv. robustly*

Robustez, } *s. fem. robustness*
Robusticidad,
Robustocidad,

Robusto, ta, *a. robust*

Roca, *s. f. a rock*

Rocadero, *s. m. a painted cap like a mitre* || *a cornet of paper* || *the end of the distaff about wich they fasten the flax*

Rodado (caballo), *s. m. a dappled horse*

Rodador, *s. m. any thing that rolls*

Rodadura, *s. f. tumbling; rolling*

Rodaja, *s. f. a little wheel* || *a rowel*

Rodapelo. *V.* Redopelo

Rodapie, *s. m. the base* or *fringe of a bed*

Rodar, *ver. a. to roll* || *to roll* or *tumble down*

Rodar mundo, *to ramble*

Rodear, *v. a. to encompass* || *to turn*, or *wind round*

Rodear, *v. neut. to turn round about* || *to periphrase*

Rodela, *s. fem. a round target*

Rodelero, *s. m. the soldier that wears a* rodela

Rodeo, *sub. m. compass* || *a way about* || *delay; excuse; pretence*

Rodomiel, *…*
…atum

Rodrigar, …

Rodrigon, …
for a vin…

Roodor, *s.* …

Roedura, *s* …

Roel, *sub.* …
heraldry

Roer, *v. a* …
talk ill o…

Roeto, *s. m* …
the pome…
into win…

Rogacion, …
entreaty

Rogaciones…

Rogador, *s* …
prays

Rogar, *v.* …
entreat; …

Rogativa, …
entreaty

Rogativas, …
prayers

Rol, *s. m.* …

Roldana, …
(in a sh…

...ous, *strong woman*
...lizado, da, *a. that got a cold*
...lizarse, *v. r. to get cold*
...lizo, *s. m. a cold; fluxion; a pose*
...na, *s. f. steel-yard*
...nce, *s. m. the spanish tongue || spanish lad*
...nces, *pl. shifts; evasions* [*ly*
...uen romance, *plain-*
...ncear, *v. a. to translate into spanish*
...ncero, ra, *adj. that composes or sings spanish ballads || that uses subterfuges*
...ncero, *s. m. a book of spanish ballads*
...ncista, *sub. m. one who writes in spanish tongue*
...near, *v. a. to weigh with a steel-yard*
...near, *v. n. to preponderate*
...ano, na, *a. roman || black and white* (*said of a cat*)
...anzar, *ver. a. to turn into spanish*
...anzon, *s. m. a long, tedious spanish ballad*
...aza, *s. fem. the sour dock*
...bo, *s. m. rhomb*
...boydes, *s. m. rhomboid* [*pilgrim*
...era, *sub. f. a woman*
...eral, *s. m. a plot of ground planted with rosemary*
...eria, *s. f. pilgrimage*
...ero, *s. m. a pilgrim, rosemary || a little ... of fish*

Romo, ma, *a. flat-nosed || blunt; blunted; dull || the mule got by a horse on a she-ass*
Rompedor, *s. m. one who wears out many clothes, etc. || breaker*
Romper, *v. a. to break || to wear out clothes, etc. || to pierce, or open || to wound || to grub up an untilled ground || to fall to open enmity*
Romperse, *v. r. to learn with; to grow sharp, etc.*
Rompeesquinas, *s. m. a fierce bully; a noisy fellow*
Rompimiento, *s. m. rupture; breaking || a falling out || a cleft; a crack || a glory* (*in painting*)
Ronca, *s. f. a bravado*
Roncador, *s. m. a snorer*
Roncamente, *adv. hoarsely || clownishly*
Roncar, *v. n. to snore || to hector; to swagger*
Roncear, *v. n. to be idle* or *lazy || to flatter; to coax*
Ronceria, *s. f. laziness; slothfulness || flattery; coaxing*
Roncero, ra, *adj. lazy; slothful || flatterer*
Roncha, *s. f. a blister; a wheal || sharping; spunging*
Ronchar, *v. a. V.* Ronzar
Ronchon, *s. m. aum. de* Roncha
Ronco, *s. m. snoring*
Ronco, ca, *adj. hoarse || harsh*

Roncon, *s. m. the drone of a bag-pipe*
Ronda, *s. fem. a round || the rounds*
Rondador, *s. m. one that goes the rounds*
Rondar, *v. a. to go the rounds || to haunt a place much*
Rondis, } Rondiz, } *s. m. the lower part in a precious stone*
Rondon (de), *ad. abruptly,* or *intrepidly*
Ronfea, *s. f. a two-handled sword*
Ronquear, *ver. n. to be hoarse*
Ronquedad, } Ronquera, } Ronquez, } *s. f. hoarseness*
Ronquido, *s. m. a snoring*
Ronzal, *s. m. a halter*
Ronzar, *v. a. to chew,* or *crack hard things*
Roña, *s. fem. the scab in sheep || dirt; nastiness || craftiness; cheat*
Roñeria, *s. f. cunning; cheat; deceit || covetousness*
Roñoso, sa, *a. scabby || dirty; nasty || crafty; cunning || stingy; covetous*
Ropa, *s f. all the furniture of a house in linen, silk, etc. || clothes || robe; gown*
Ropa de levantar, *a morning gown* — de mesa, *table-linen* — blanca, *linen*
Ropage, *s. m. clothes; clothing || a stately suit*
Ropavejeria, *s. f. a broker's shop*
Ropavejero, *s. m. a broker*
Roperia, *s. f. a broker's*

trade, or *shop* || *vestiary of friars*
Ropero, *s. m. a broker* || *that sells new clothes* *a friar that takes care of the vestiary* || *cheesemonger*
Ropeta, *s. f. a little coat or garment*
Ropilla, *s. f. clothes of little value* || *a waist coat with hanging sleeves*
Ropita, *s. f. V.* Ropeta
Ropon, *s. m. a gown of ceremony*
Roque, *s. m. a rook* (*at chess*)
Ni rey ni roque, *no body*
Roquero, ra, *a. rocky* || *seated on a rock*
Roquete, *sub. m. a short surplice*
Rorro *s. m. an infant*
Rosa *s. f. a rose*
Rosado da *a. of a rose-colour*; *made of roses*
Rosal, *s. m. a rose-bush*
Rosario, *s. m. a rosary* || *chain pump* || *the back-bone*
Rosca *s. f. a screw* || *a sweet cake with a hole in the middle*
Roscon, *s. m. aum. de* Rosca
Rosco, sca, *a. rosy*
Roseta, *s. fem. a little* or *artificial rose*
Roseton *s. m. a great rose*
Rosicler, *s. m. a bright rose-colour*
Rosmaro, *s. m. a sort of sea-calf*
Roso, sa, *a. ruddy*
Rosoli, *s. m. rosasolis*
Rosquilla, *s. fem. a little sweet round cake*
Rostrado, da, *a. shaped like a beak*
Rostrillo, } *sub. m. seed-*
Rostrino, } *pearl* || *a sort of head-dress*
Rostrituerto, ta, *a. wry-looked*
Rostro, *sub. m. a beak* || *the face*
Hacer rostro, *to face an enemy*, *etc.*
Rota, *s. f. rout*; *defeat* || *rumb* || *the rota*
Rotacion, *s. rotation*
Rotamente, *adv. lewdly*
Roto, ta, *adj. broken* || *ragged* || *lewd*
Rótula, *s. fem. the knee-ball* || *trochisk*
Rotular, *v. a. to put on a title*, *etc.*
Rótulo, *s. m. a title*; *an inscription* || *a bill posted up*
Rotunda, *s. f. a rotundo*
Rotundidad, *s. f. rotundity*
Rotundo, da, *a. rotund*; *round*
Rotura, *s. f. a rent in a garment*, *etc.*
Roxear, *ver. n. to redden* || *to blush*
Roxo, xa, *a. red*
Roya, *s. f. the dampness of corn*
Roza, *s. fem. weeding* || *rubbing* || *a weeded field*
Rozagante, *a.* 2. *sumptuous*; *showing*; *dragging* (*said of gown*) || *gay*; *brillant*
Rozar, *v. a. to weed* || *to browse* || *to rub*
Rozarse, *v. r. to cut*, or *interfere* || *to stammer* || *to resemble*
Roznar, *v. n. to bray like an ass* || *to chew*
Roznido, *s. m. braying* || *chewing*
Rozno, *s. m.* as
Rozo, *s. m. chip*
Rua, *s. f. a stre*
way
Ruan, *s. f. a sor*
Ruano, na, *a. r*
Caballo ruano,
Ruar, *v. n. to ro*
or ride about t
Rubeta, *s. fem.*
frog
Rubí, *s. m. a ru*
Rubia, *s. f. mac*
Rubial, *sub. m.*
where madde
Rubican (caball
a rubican hor
Rubicundo da,
rubicund
Rubificar, *v. a.*
Rubin, *s. m. rus*
Rubio, bia, *a.*
fair-haired
Rubion (trigo),
red wheat
Rubo, *s. m. a bu*
Rubor, *sub. m.*
modesty || *sha*
Rúbrica, *s. f. r*
flourish added
signature; *ch*
Rubricar, *v. a.*
cate || *to sign*
flourish
Rubriquista, *sub*
that knows
bricks
Rubro, bra, *ad*
ruddy
Ruc, *s. f. a bir*
immense size
Rucio, cia, *a. gr*
Rucio rodado, *dap*
Ruda, *s. f. rue*
Rudamente, *adv.*
coarsely
Rudera, *s. f. rubb*
Rudeza, *s. fem.*
|| *dullness*

ub. m. pl.
ij. coarse ;
igh ; harsh
ill
listaff
wheel || a
ound fish ,
t of veal ||
arquebuse
la , cita , s.
heel
rolling || a
bout a gar-
|| a round
[treaty
rayer ; en-
no, s. m. a
wheel
roller used
tre
ria, a. slo-
gged
, s. f. sport;
a ruffian ;
. to pimp
f. pimping
a , a. of, or
o , a pimp
d-haired ||
izled
wrinkle
o wrinkle
. roaring
to roar like
ake a noise;
c.
cosa , to be
bout
f. rugosity;
. rugose
n. rhubarb
oise || fray;
. adv. with

Ruidoso, sa, *a. noisy*
Ruin, *a. 2. vile ; base || mean ; paltry ; despicable || wicked ; perverse || covetous ; stingy*
Ruina, *s. f. ruin*
Ruinar, *v. a. to ruin*
Ruinoso, sa, *a. ruinous*
Ruindad, *s. f. a base action || covetousness*
Ruinmente, *adv. vilely ; wickedly*
Ruiponce, *s. m. rampion*
Ruipóntico, *sub. m. centaury*
Ruiseñor, *s. m. nightingale*
Rular, *v. a. to roll*
Rumba, *s. f. V.* Arrumbadas
Rumbo, *s. m. rumb (at sea) || course ; way ; method || ostentation ; pomp*
Echar de rumbo, *to boast*
Rumbosamente, *ad. pompously*
Rumboso, sa, *adj. pompous ; magnificent*
Rumia, *s. f. rumination*
Rumiador, ra, *ruminant*
Rumiar, *ver. a. to ruminate ; to chew the cud || to muse on*
Rumo, *sub. m. the first hoop in the head of a cask*
Rumor, *s. m. rumour*
Rumorcillo, *s. m. a little rumour*
Runfla, *s. f. a great number* or *quantity*
Runrun, *s. m. rumour ; noise*
Ru[illegible], *v. a. to make notches in the casks*
Rupicapra, *s. f. shamoy ; wild-goat*
Ruptura, *s. f. rupture*

Ruqueta, *s. fem. rocket (herb)*
Rural, *a. 2. rural*
Rusco, *sub. m. butcher's broom*
Rústicamente, *adv. rustically*
Rusticidad, *s. fem. rusticity*
Rústico, ca, *a. rustick*
Rústico, *s. m. a clown*
Rustiquez, } *s. f. rusticalness*
Rustiqueza, }
Ruta, *s. f. road ; way || itinerary*
Rutilante, *a. 2. shining ; glittering*
Rutilo, la, *a. of the gold-colour*
Ruxada, *s. fem. a sudden shower*
Ruxar, *v. a. to water*

S.

SA'BADO, *s. m. saturday || sabbath*
Sábalo, *s. m. shad (fish)*
Sábana, *s. f. a sheet (for a bed) || altar-cloth*
Sabandija, *s. f. any worm or such small creature || a short ugly person*
Sabanilla, *s. f. a small sheet || handkerchief ; towel, etc. || altar cloth*
Sabañon, *s. m. chilblain*
Sabatarios, *s. m. pl. the jews*
Sabático, ca, *a. sabbatical*
Sabatina, *s. f. the office of saturday in the church*
Sabatino, na, *adj. sabbatical*
Sabatismo, *s. m. sabbatism*
Saber, *sub. m. learning science*
Saber, *v. a.* to know || to be learned
Saber, *v. n.* to taste || to please

Sabiamente, *adv. wisely*
Sabido, **da**, *a. learned*
Sabidor, *sub. m. one that knows* or *understands*
Sabiduría, *s. f. wisdom* || *knowledge* || *learning; science*
Sabina, *s. f. savin* (*herb*)
Sabio, **bia**, *a. wise*
Sabio, *s. m. a wise man*
Sabiondez, *s. fem. much knowledge joined to much cunning*
Sabiondo, **da**, *a. that has knowledge joined to malice*
Sable, *s. m. sabre*
Saboca, } *s. f. a little sort*
Saboga, } *of shad*
Sabor, *sub. m. savour; relish*
Saborear, *v. a. to give a savour; to season*
Saborearse, *v. r. to savour*
Saboyana, *s. f. a kind of woman's petticoat* || *a sort of pie*
Sabrosamente, *ad. savourily*
Sabroso, sa, *a. savoury*
Sabueso, *s. m. a blood-hound*
Sábulo, *s. m. hard sand; gravel*
Sabuloso, sa, *a. san .,*
Saca, *s. f. exportation* || *a great sack*
Sacabala, *s. f. an instrument to take out the balls of a wound*
Sacabalas, *an instrument to extract a shot out of a cannon, etc.*
Sacabocado, } *s. m. a nip-*
Sacabocados, } *ping tool*
Sacabuche, *s. m. a sackbut.* || *V.* Sacatrapos
Sacadinero, *sub. masc. a wheedle to get one's money* || *shining gewgaws*
Sacadura, *s. f. a cut made in cloaths to make them sit easy*
Sacaliña, *s. fem. a sort of dart* || *a wheedle, etc. to obtain one's end*
Sacamanchas, *s. m. one that takes out spots* || *one that publishes other men's faults*
Tierra sacamanchas, *fullers earth*
Sacamiento, *s. m. a taking* or *drawing out*
Sacamuelas, *s. m. a tooth-drawer* || *any instrument to draw out teeth*
Sacanabo, *s. m an instrument to extract the bomb, out of a mortar*
Sacapelotas, *s. m. V.* Sacatrapos
Sacar, *v. a. to take out; to draw out*
Sacar á luz, *to produce* — en limpio, *to clear* — por el rastro, *to discover by the track*
Sacatrapos, *s. m. a rag-gatherer* || *a worm* (*to unload a gun*) || *a cunning sharper*
Sacerdocio, *s. mas. priesthood*
Sacerdotal, *a.* 2. *sacerdotal*
Sacerdote, *s. m. a priest*
Sacerdotisa, *s. f. a priestess*
Sachadura, *s. f. weeding*
Sachar, *v. a. to weed*
Sacho, *s. m. a weeding-hook*
Saciable, *a.* 2. *that may* be satiated
Saciar, *v. a.* to satiate
Saciedad, *s. f.* satiety
Saco, *sub. m. a sack; a bag* || *sack-cl... king; pillagi...*
Sacomano, *s. m. pillage*
Sacramental, *a. ...mental*
Sacramentalmen... *sacramentall...*
Sacramentar, *v. ... the sacramen...*
Sacramentarse, *... transubstanti... self*
Sacramentario, ... *sacramentari...*
Sacramente, *ad...*
Sacramento, *s. ... ment* || *myste...*
Sacratísimo, ma... *sacred*
Sacro, *s m. sak...* || *saker-gun... ning thief*
Sacrificadero, *s... place where ... fices were ma...*
Sacrificador, *s. ... ficator*
Sacrificar, *v. a. ... fice*
Sacrificio, *sub. ...*
Sacrilegamente, *... crilegiously*
Sacrilegio, *s. m ... lege*
Sacrílego, ga, *a...*
Sacrismoche, } *s. ...*
Sacrismocho, } *s... in black, b... tatters*
Sacristan, *s. m. a sexton*
Sacristana, *s. f. ...*
Sacristanía, *s. f. ... of a sexton*
Sacristía, *s. f. ... vestry.* V. Sac... the stomach
Sacro, cra, ...

…, ta, *adj. must*

s. f. a shake || …ish *word*

…da, *adj. hard*; …*tern*

…, *s. m. shaker* || …*ng-pole, etc.*

…a, *sub. f. a sha-*

…nto, *s. m. sha-* …*c.* || *snapping at* …*v. a. to shake* || …; *to chastise* || …*s back; to repel* …*ap at*

…*f. arrow*

…*s f.* } *a wound* …*s. m.* } or *the shot* …*arrow*

…*ver. a. to shoot* …*rrows*

…*s. f. a loop-hole*

…*s. m. an archer*

…*f. a sort of tur-* …*tch* || *a loop-hole*

…*s. fem. a little*

…*s. m. a channel* …*water-mill* || *a* …*peg*

…*s. m. a great ar-* …*dart*

…*f. a witch*

…d, *s. f. sharpness* …*ll in a dog* || *sa-*

…no, ma, *a. most* …*ious*

…, *s. m. a liquor* …*distils from a cer-* …*plant*

…*2. sagacious*

…nte, *adv. saga-* …*ly*

…*a. 2. belonging* …*arrow* || *sagittal*

…*s. m. an archer* …*tarius*

Sagma, *s. f. a measure in architecture*

Sago, *s. m. a loose upper coat*

Sagradamente, *adv. sacredly*

Sagrado, da, *a. sacred*

Sagrado, *sub. m. a sanctuary; an asyle*

Sagrar, *v. a. to consecrate*

Sagrario, *s. m. a sanctuary; a holy-place* || *tabernacle*

Ságula, *s. f. dim. de* Sago

Sahornarse, *v. r. to tear off one's skin*

Sahorno, *s. m. excoriation*

Sahumador, *s. m. a perfumer* || *a perfuming pan*

Sahumadura, *s. f. a perfuming* || *a perfume*

Sahumar, *ver. a. to perfume*

Sahumerio, } *s. m. a per-*
Sahumo, } *fuming with the smoke of sweets burnt, etc.* [*dripping*

Sain, *s. m. suet; grease;*

Sainar, *v. a. to fatten*

Saja, } *s. f. scarifi-*
Sajadura, } *cation*

Sajar, *v. a. to scarify*

Sal, *s. f. salt*

Sala, *s. f. a hall; a large room* || *tribunal* || *feasting; ball, etc.*

Saladar, *s. m. a ground made barren by sea-water*

Saladero, *s. m. a salting tub or place*

Salado, da, *adj. merry; witty, etc.*

Salado, *s. m. the sea. V.* Saladar || *salt-meat*

Salador, ra, *s. one who salts meat, etc.*

Salador, *sub. m. V.* Saladero

Saladura, *s. fem. salting; saltness*

Salamandra, *s. fem. salamander*

Salamanquesa, *s. f. a newt*

Salar, *v. a. to salt*

Salariar, *ver. act. to pay salary*

Salario, *s. m. salary*

Salce, *s. m. willow; sallow-tree*

Salceda, *s. f. willow-plot*

Salcicha, *s. f. a sausage*

Salcichon, *s. m. a thick and short sausage* || *a kind of fascine*

Saledizo, za, *a. jutting out*

Salero, *s. m. a salt-seller* || *a salt-box*

Saleta, *s. f. a little hall*

Salgada, } *s. f. sea-purs-*
Salgadera, } *lain*

Salida, *s. f. a going out* || *a way out* || *a sally* || *a walking place near a town* || *issue; end; success* || *way; means* || *getting off*

Salidizo, za, *a. jutting out*

Salina, *s. f. a salt-pit*

Salinero, *s. m. salt-maker* || *salt-man*

Salino, na, *a. saline*

Salir, *v. a. to go out* || *to peep or dawn* || *to spring; to come forth* || *to arise* || *to succeed* || *to excel* or *out-do* || *to cost; to amount*

Salir de madre, *to overflow the banks* — de seso, *to run mad*

Salirse, *v. r. to break off* a treaty, etc. || to run out

Salirse de religion, to quit a religious order

[illegible], sa, *a. of, or be-longing to, the salt petre*

Saliva, *s. f. spittle; saliva*

Salivacion, *s. f. salivation*

Salival, *a. 2. salival*

Salivar, *v. a. to salivate*

Salivoso, sa, *adj. full of spittle*

Sallar, *v. a. to weed the corn*

Salma, *s. f. a great large sack.* || *V.* Tonelada

Salmear, *ver. a. to sing psalms*

Salmista, *s. m. psalmist*

Salmo, *s. m. a psalm*

Salmodia, *s. f. psalmody* || *psalter*

Salmodiar, *v. a. to sing* or *rente psalms*

Salmon, *s. m. a salmon*

Salmonada (Trucha), *s. f. a salmon-trout*

Salmonete, *s. m. mullet* (*a sea-fish*)

Salmorejo, *s. m. a same*

Salpicar, *v. a. to splash* || *to tarnish; to spoil*

Salpicon, *s. m. cold beef cut in slices and eaten with oil, vinegar, etc.*

Salpimentar, *v. a. to season with salt and pepper* [*can serpent*

Salpinga, *s. f. an Affri-*

Salpresar, *v. a. to salt* or *powder meat*

Salpuga, *s. f. a kind of venemous ant*

Salsa, *s. f. a sauce*

Salsafras, *s. m. sassafras*

Salsaparrilla, *s. f. sarsaparella*

Salsera, *s. f. a saucer*

Salsereta, } *s. f. a little*
Salserilla, } *saucer*

Salserilla de color, *a small dish with red paint*

Salsero, *s. m. thyme*

Salsifrax, } *s. f. sassa-*
Salsifragia, } *fras*

Salsilla, *s. f. a paltry sauce*

Saltabancos, *s. m. a quack*

jump |
skip a
vious
|| *to fl*
Saltaregl
cular
mather
Saltaren,
the gu
grass h
Saltarin,
Saltaterar
sort of
Saltatriz,
dancer
Salteador
way m
Salteamie
robbery
sault
Saltear, *v.*
highwa
surprise
Salteo, *su*
enravis
Salterio,
|| *a psa*

ub. m. a kind of hopper
a. 2. salubrious
ad, s. f. salubrity
. f. health || sa-
pl. salutes
, adj. 2. whole-
mente, adver. somely
r, s. m. saluter
ack pretending tural gift of cu- istempers, etc.
v. a. to salut || end to cure with , etc.
s. m. a salute,
, s. f. a sort of ness on the salt
n, s. f. a saluta-
[wholesomely
mente, adver.
, ra, a. whole-
a tasting meat nk before the etc. || a volley harge
, s. f. salvation
, s. f. a sand-
[meal
ub. m. bran of
s. m. saviour
adj. 2. savage; coarse; clow-
, s. f. coarse- lownishness
, s. f. wild beast
vagina, a meat a wild taste
lia, s. f. safe-
, s. m. saving a refuge, a

Salvante, adv. save; saving
Salvar, v. a. to save
Salvarse, v. r. to escape a danger, etc.
Salvatiquez, s. fem. rudeness; clownishness
Salve, int. hail! god save you!
Salve, s. f. salve regina
Salvia, s. f. sage
Salvilla, s. f. a salver
Salvo, va, a. safe
Salvo, adv. save; under || saving; without prejudice to [conduct
Salvoconduto, s. m. safe-
Sambenito, sub. m. a sort of garment put by the inquisitors
Samblage, s. m. a joining [instrument
Sambuca, s. f. a musical
Sampsuchino, sub. m. an onguent made with marjoram, etc.
Sampsuco, s. m. marjoram
Samuga, s. f. V. Xamuga
San, adj. saint
Sanable, a. 2. sanable
Sanalotodo, s. m. a plaster put upon any sore
Sanamente, adv. plainly; simply; honestly
Sanar, ver. a. to heal; to cure
Sanar, v. n. to be healed
Sancion, s. f. sanction
Sancochar, ver. a. to boil any meat without seasoning it
Sanctasanctorum, s. m. sanctuary; the holy of holies
Sandalia, s. f. a sandal
Sandalino, na, adj. made of, or like the, sandalwood

Sándalo, sub. m. sandalwood || wild-mint; penny-wort
Sandaraca, s. f. sandarack
Sandez, s. f. folly
Sandía, s. fem. a water-melon
Sandio, dia, a. fool; mad
Sandix, sub. m. a sort of lead-calx
Saneamiento, s. m. answering for
Sanear, v. a. to answer for; to make good || to repair; to retrieve
Sangradera, s. f. a lancet || a draining out the water
Sangrador, s. m. a bleeder || a trench to convey water
Sangradura, s. f. the part of the arm where the vein is opened
Sangrar, v. a. to let blood || to drain the water out || to get money out of one
Sangrar, v. n. to bleed
Sangraza, s. fem. watery blood
Sangre, s. f. blood || race
Sangría, s. f. blood-letting || a draining out the water || a getting out the money. V. Sangradura
Sangriento, ta, a. bloody
Sangual, s. m. a kind of eagle
Sanguaza, s. fem. watery blood
Sanguífero, ra, adj. sanguiferous
Sanguijuela, s. f. a leech
Sanguinaria, s. f. blood-wort || bloot-stone
Sanguinario, ria, a. sanguinary

Sanguineo, nea, *a. sanguineous*
Sanguino, na, *adj. sanguine*
Sanguinolento, ta, *adj. sanguinolent*
Sanguinoso, sa, *a. bloody* || *sanguinary*
Sangüis, *s. m. the blood of J. C. in the eucharist*
Sanguisorva, *s. f. a kind of burnet*
Sanguja, *s. f. a leech*
Sanícula, *s. fem. sanicle; self-heal*
Sanidad, *s. fem. health* || *candour*
Sano, na, *adj. sound; healthy* || *safe* || *sound; whole* || *honest; sincere, etc.*
Santa, *s. fem. a female saint*
Santamente, *ad. holily* || *sincerely* || *plainly*
Santasantorum, *s. m. V.* Sanctasanctorum
Santelmo, *sub. m. Saint-Elme's fire*
Santero, ra, *s. one that goes about questing for a saint, etc.*
Santiago, *s. m. an order of knights in Spain*
Santiago y cierra España, *the war-cry used by the spaniards*
Santiamen, *sub. m. a moment*
En un santiamen, *adv. in the twinkling of an eye*
Santico, ca, *sub. a little saint*
Santidad, *s. f. holiness; sanctity*
Santificacion, *s. f. sanctification*
Santificador, *s. m. sanctifier*
Santificar, *v. a. to sanctify*
Santiguada, *s. f. the sing of the cross*
Santiguadera, *s. fem. the act of blessing*
Santiguador, ra, *sub. one pretends to cure by blessing*
Santiguar, *v. a. to bless, to make signs of the cross upon sick people* || *to chastise*
Santiguarse, *v. r. to bless* or *cross one's self*
Santiguo, *s. m. the sign of the cross*
Santimonia, *s. f. holiness*
Santiscario, *s. m. a whim; a foolish fancy*
Santísimo, ma, *a. most-holy*
El santísimo, *the holy sacrament*
Santo, ta, *a. holy*
Santo, *s. m. a saint*
Santon, *s. m. a Mahometan monk* || *an hypocrite*
Santoral, *s. m. collection of legends* or *sermons*
Santuario, *sub. m. sanctuary* || *a temple* or *church*
Santurron, na, *s. an hypocrite*
Saña, *s. f. wrath; fury*
Sañoso, sa, *adj. angry; furious*
Sañudamente, *adv. angrily*
Sañudo, da, *adj. angry; wrathful; furious*
Sapiencia, *s. f. wisdom*
Sapiente, *a. 2. wise*
Sapillo, *s. m. a little toad* || *ranula*
Sapo, *s. m. a toad*
Saponaria, *s. f. soap-wort*
Saporífero, ra, *adj. savoury*
Saquear, *v. a. to sack; to pillage*
Saqueo, *s. m. sacking; pillage*
Saquera, *s. f. a needle used to sew*
Saquilada, *s. f.* … *wheat that i*… *full*
Saquillo, *s. m. a*…
Saraguete, *s. m*… *ball*
Sarampion, *s. m*…
Sarao, *sub. m.* … *meetting for*
Sarcia, *s. f. a l*…
Sarcillo, *s. m.* … *hook*
Sarcócola, *s. f.* … *gummy juice*
Sarcófagos, *s.* … *among the* … *sarcophagou*…
Sarcótico, ca, … *cotick*
Sarda, *s. f. a k*…
Sardesco, *s. m*… *of the sardin*…
Sardina, *s. f. a*…
Sardinero, ra, … *sells pilchar*…
Sardineta, *s. fe*… *pilchard*
Sardio, } *s. m.*
Sardo, } *stor*…
Sardonia, *s. f.* … *called*
Risa sardonia… nica, *a sar*… *sardonick la*…
Sardonix, *s. f.*…
Sarga, *s. f. ser*…
Sargenta, *s. f.* … *of order of s*…
Sargentear, *v.* … *duty of a ser*…
Sargentería, *s.*…
Sargento, *s. m.*…
Sargenton, *s. m*… *big-boned* … *virago*
Sargo, *s. m.*…
Sarguela, *s*… *light se*…

'. a. to scarify
.f. scarification
ador, sub. masc.
ho gathers up the
hes of vines
ar, v. a. to ga-
p the branches of
ines, after pru-

era, s. f. a place
up the prunings
ies
to, s. m. a twig
nch of a vine cut
ind
f. the itch or man-
:hing [mangy
sa, adj. itchy;
lo, sub. m. blot-
breaking out ||
'ings, etc.
', v. n. to bite,
u do
, s. f. a battle
.f. a net made of
)
s. m. a rattling
throat
ub. m. a kind of
oat
m. the fur that
's on a man's ton-
a hot fever ||
r about a cham-
t, etc.
f. } a string of
. m. } beads, etc.
. f. a frying-pan
le sarten, pan-
, fritters, etc.
a, s. f. a frying-
ill
), s. m. a blow
frying-pan
.f. a woman tay-
antua-maker
m. a taylor
, s. m. a paltry

Satanas, s. m. satan
Satélite, s. m. armed attendant; guard
Satélites, p. satellites
Sátira, s. f. satire (poem)
Satírico, ca, adj. satirical
Satirio, s. m. a water-rat
Satirion, s. m. satyrion
Satirizar, v. a. to satirise
Sátiro, s. m. a satire
Satisfaccion, s. f. satisfaction
Satisfacer, v. a. to satisfy
Satisfactorio, ria, adj. satisfactory
Satisfecho, cha, p. p. satisfied
Sativo, va, adjec. that is cultivated
Sato, s. m. a sowed field
Sátrapa, s. m. satrap
Saturacion, sub. f. saturation
Saturar, v. a. to saturate
Saturnal, a. 2. belonging to saturn
Fiestas saturnales, saturnals
Saturnino, na, adj. saturnine
Satuino, s. m. saturn
Sauce, sub. m. willow or sallow-tree
Saucedal, s. m. a willow-plot
Sauco, s. m. elder-tree
Sauco de agua, whitten-tree
Saudade, s. f. desire; longing for
Sauquillo, s. m. a dwarf-elder
Sauz, s. m. V. Sauce
Sauz gatillot, s. m. agnus castus
Saxâfrax. V. Saxifraga
Saxâtil. a. 2. living among rocks
Saxífraga, } sub. f. saxi-
Saxífragia, } frage
Saya, s. f. a woman's upper petticoat or gown
Sayal, s. m. coarse sackcloth

Sayalero, s. m. a weaver of sackcloth
Sayalesco, ca, adjec. made of the cloth called sayal
Sayaza, s. f. aum. de Saya
Sayazo, s. m. aum. de Sayo
Sayete, s. m. dim. de Sayo
Saynete, s. m. any daintiness || any thing pleasing || a sauce; a seasoning || intermesses || interlude (in a play)
Saynetillo, s. m. dim. de Saynete
Sayno, s. m. a sort of hog in the west-indies
Sayo, s. m. a loose upper coat
Sayo dominguero, a sunday garment
Sayon, s. m. hangman; executioner || catchpole
Sayonazo, sub. m. aum. de Sayon
Saynelo, sub. m. a little upper coat or jerkin
Saz, s. m. a willow-tree
Sazon, s. f. season || savour || humour; temper
En sazon, adv. seasonably
Sazonar, v. a to season || to ripen
Sazonarse, v. r. to grow ripe
Se, pron. one's self; himself; herself; themselves; itself
Se dice, it is said
Sebesten, s. m. jujube-tree
Sebillo, s. m. a sort of paste for the hands
Sebo, s. m. tallow
Seboso, sa, adjec. tallowish
Seca, s. f. dryness || the mint || wen; tumor.

Secar, *v. a. to dry*
Secarse, *v. r. to wither; to pine away* || *to be extremely thirsty* || *to look* or *talk bluntly*
Secas (**á**), *adv. dryly*
Pan á secas, *dry bread*
Secaral, *sub. m. a dry sandy place*
Seccion, *s. f. a section*
Seceno, na, *adj. belonging to the number six*
Secesion, *s. f. secession*
Secluso, sa, *adj. secluded*
Seco, ca, *adj. dry* || *lean* || *austere; rough; sharp*
Secrecion, *s. f. secretion; separation*
Secrestacion, *s. f. sequestration* [*trator*
Secrestador, *s. m. seques-*
Secrestar, *v. a. to sequester* [*tion*
Secresto, *s. m. sequestra-*
Secretas, *s. f. pl. secret prayers* (*in the mass*) || *a necessary house*

Secular, *a. 2. secular*
Secularidad, *s. f. secularity* [*larize*
Secularizar, *v. a. to secu-*
Secundario, ria, *adj. secondary*
Secundariamente, *adver. secondly* || *in the second degree, etc.*
Secundina, *s. f. secondine*
Secura, *sub. f. drought; dryness*
Sed, *s. f. thirst*
Seda, *s. f. silk* || *silk-stuff* || *a hog's bristle*
Sedadera, *s. f. an instrument for dressing the hemp*
Sedal, *s. m. a fishing-line* || *seton; rowel*
Sede, *s. f. a see*
Santa sede, *the holy see*
Sedentario, ria, *adj. sedentary*
Sedeña, *s. f. the hurds of the silk*
Sedeño, ña, *adj. silky* || *bristly*

mow
Segazon, *s.*
reaping ||
Seglar, *a.*
lay; a la
Segmento,
ment
Segregacion
Segregar, *v*
gate
Segri, *s. m.*
Seguida, *s.*
|| *train;*
De seguida
ther | *o*
ther
Mugeres de
mon who
Seguidilla,
couplets ||
Seguidillas,
ness
Seguido, *d*
rent; con
Seguidor, *s.*
|| *black l*
ting on
Seguimiento

dario, ria, *adj. se-dary* [*second*
do, da, *adjec. the*
don, *s. m. the youn-son*
, *s. f. an axe*
amente, *adv. secu-*
ar, *v. a. to secure*
eja, *sub. f. a small ; a hatchet*
idad, *s. f. security*
o, ra, *adj. secure ;* || *sure*
o, *s. m. a safe-con-t; a passport* || *in-ance*
s. m. *six*
, *pl. the sices on the*
ento, tas, *adjec. six*
idred
ion, *s. f. selecting ;*
ice [*chosen*
o, ta, *adj. elected ;*
o, *s m. the select*
tes, *s f. selenites*
ide, *s. f. a kind of*
or, *s. m. a sealer*
ura, *s. f. a sealing*
, *v. a. to seal*
s. m. a seal
: el sello, *to con-le*
e Salomon, *tadpole*
s. f. a wood
co, ca, *adj. of the ds ; wild, etc.*
quez, *s. f. wildness*
, sa, [illegible] Selvático
a, *s. f. a week*
ería, *s. f. a weekly* [*rian*
ero, *s. m. septima-*
nte, *s. m. counte-e ; aspect* || *face ; out-side ; sem-*

Sembradío, día, *adj. that may be sowed*
Sembrado, *s. m. a sowed field*
Sembrador, *s. m. a sower*
Sembradura, *s. f. sowing*
Sembrar, *v. a. to sow*
Sembrar moneda, *to scatter money* — nuevas, *to spread news* — zizaña, *to sow discord*
Semeja, *sub. f. likeness* || *sign ; token*
Semejable, *a. 2. like* || *comparable*
Semejante, *a. 2. like*
Semejantemente, *adver. likely* [*blance*
Semejanza, *sub. f. resem-*
Semejar, *v. n. to resemble*
Semen, *s. m. seed*
Semencera, *s. f. V.* Sementera
Semental, *a. 2. belonging to the seed* or *sowing*
Sementar, *v. a. to sow*
Sementera, *s. f. sowing* || *sowing-time* || *a sowed field* || *seed of discord*, etc. [*bag*
Sementero, *s. m. a seed-*
Sementino, na, *adj. relating to the sowing-time* [*months*
Semestre, *adjec. 2. of six*
Semestre, *s. m. six months, semestra*
Semi, *half*
Semibreve, *sub. f. semibrief* [*mioircle*
Semicírculo, *s. m. a se-*
Semideo, *s. m. a demi-god*
Semidiámetro, *s. m. semidiameter*
Semidifunto, ta, *a. half-dead* [*god*
Semidios, *s. m. a demi-*

Semidormido, da, *a. half-asleep*
Semigola, *s. f. half-gorge (in fortification)*
Semilla, *s. f. seed*
Semilunio, *sub. m. half-lunation*
Seminal, *a. 2. seminal*
Seminario, *sub. m. seminary* || *nursery*
Seminarista, *s. m. a seminarist*
Semioctava, *s. f. stanza of four verses*
Semiracional, *a. 2. dull ; stupid*
Semirecto (angulo), *sub. m. an angle of* 45 *degrees*
Semis, *s. m. six ounces*
Semitono, *s. m. a semitone* [*alive*
Semivivo, va, *adj. half*
Semivocal, *sub. f. semivowel*
Semivulpa, *s. f. a quadruped living in America*
Sémola, *sub. f. the wheat when peeled*
Sempiterna, *s. f. a sort of serge* [*piternal*
Sempiterno, na, *adj. sem-*
Sen, } *s. f. sena*
Sena, }
Senado, *s. m. senate* || *senate-house*
Senador, *s. m. senator*
Senario, *s. m. the number of six* || *a verse of six feet most ordinarily iambick*
Senas, *s. f. pl. two sices, at dice*
Senatorio, ria, *adj. senatorial*
Senciente, p. a. of sentir
Sencillamente, *adv.* ingenuously
Sencillez, *s. f.* thinness ||

ingenuity ‖ simplicity ; silliness

Sencillo, lla, a. genuine ; natural ‖ thin ‖ ingenuous ; sincere ‖ simple ; silly

Senda, s. f. a path

Senderar, } v. a. to open a path ‖ to guide through paths
Senderear, }

Sendero, s. m. a path

Sendos, das, adj. pl. each of them

Sene, s. m. an oldman

Senectud, s. f. oldage

Senescal, s. m. seneschal

Senescalia, s. f. the office or dignity of a seneschal

Senil, a. 2. senile

Senites, s. f. selenites

Seno, s. m. breast ‖ the woman's breasts ‖ bosom ‖ lap ‖ refuge ‖ a fold in a garment ‖ gulf ; bay ; sinus ‖ a sine ‖ sinus (in a wound)

Senogil, s. m. Voy. Cenogil,

Sensacion, s. f. sensation

Sensibilidad, s. f. sensibility

Sensibilisimo, ma, adjec. most sensible

Sensible, a. 2. sensible

Sensible, s. m. sensibility

Sensiblemente, adv. sensibly

Sensitiva, s. f. sensitive [plant

Sensitivo, va, adj. sensitive

Sensual, a. 2. sensual

Sensualidad, s f. sensuality

Sensualmente, adv. sen[sually

Sentada, s. f. a sitting

De una sentada, all at once

Sentadillas, (cabalgar á) to ride sitting

Sentado, da, adj. sedate ; sober ; staid

Pulso sentado, a sedate pulse

Sentamiento, s. m. seat ; setting ; site

Sentar, v. a. to set ; to place ‖ to beat down the seams

Sentar partidas, to enter accounts — plaza de soldado, to list one's self a soldier — con esos, to go into place

Sentarse, v. r. to sit down

Sentarse en cuclillas, to sit on one's legs — en la conclusion, to be obstinately resolved

Sentencia, s. f. sentence

Sentenciar, v. a. to sentence

Sentenciario, s. m. collection of sentences

Sentencion, s. m. a rigorous sentence

Sentencioso, sa, adj. sententious

Sentible, a. 2. sensible

Senticar, sub. m. a place full of thorns, of briars, etc.

Sentidisimo, ma, adject. very touchy, etc.

Sentido, da, adj. touchy ; exceptious

Sentido, s. m. sense

Sentimiento, s. m. sense ; feeling ‖ grief ; trouble ‖ sentiment ; opinion ‖ a crack in a wall ‖ resentment

Sentina, sub. f. sink of a ship

Sentir, v. a. to feel ‖ to hear ‖ to judge ; to be of opinion

Sentirse, v. r. to ... to crack (a wall)

Sentir, s. m. sense ; feeling ‖ sentiment ...

Seña, s. f. sign ; the watch-word

Señal, s. m. sign ; token ‖ bound ; scar, etc. left by wound

Señaladamente, ad... cially

Señalamiento, s. m...

Señalar, v. a. to ... to mark out ‖ with a flourish ... the day, etc. ... mon ‖ to mak... in fencing ‖ to ... goals

Señalarse, v. r. to ma... one's self eminent...

Señaleja, sub. f. a li... mark

Señar, v. n. to make sig[ns]

Señero, sub. m. one th[at] makes signs

Señor, s. m. a lord ‖ master

El gran señor, the gran[d] seignior

Señora, sub. f. a lady ‖ mistress [re...

Señoreage, s. m. seign[iorage]

Señorear, v. a. to rule ... govern ; to lord it ‖ subject ‖ to call a m... señor

Señorearse, v. r. to pl[ay] the lord

Señoria, s. f. lordship ; seigniory [Se...

Señorico, ca, s. dim.

Señoril, a. 2. belonging ... the lord of a manor

Señorio, s. m. lord... domination

Señorito, ta, *sub. dim. de* Señor
Señuelo, *s. m. a lure to call hawks*
Seor, *s. m. V.* Señor
Separable, *a. 2. separable*
Separacion, *s. f. separation*
Separadamente, *adv. separately*
Separador, *s. m. a separator* || *an anatomist*
Separar, *v. a. to separate* || *to dissect* or *anatomize*
Sepedon, *s. m. a sort of serpent*
Sepelir, *v. a. to bury*
Sepia, *sub. f. cuttle-fish; sound*
Septenario, *sub. m. septenary number* || *the space of seven days*
Septenio, *s. m. the space of seven years*
Septentrion, *sub. m. septentrio*
Septentrional, *a. 2. septentrional*
Septiembre, *sub. m. september*
Séptima, *s. f. a septieme* or *seventh (a piquet)*
Séptimo, ma, *adj. seventh*
Septuagenario, ria, *adjec. septuagenary*
Septuagésina, *s. f. septuagesima*
Septuagésimo, ma, *adjec. seventieth*
Septuplo, pla, *adj. septuple*
Sepulcral, *adj. 2. sepulchral*
Sepulcro, *s. m. a sepulchre*
Sepultar, *v. a. to bury*
Sepultura, *s. f. sepulture; burial* || *a burying place*
Sepulturero, *s. m. grave-digger*

Seqüaz, *a. 2. follower; sectator; sequacious*
Sequedad, *s. f. dryness* || *roughness*
Sequedal, *s. m. a dry land*
Sequela, *s. f. sequel; consequence*
Sequencia, *s. f. a kind of hymn*
Sequeral, *s. m. a dry land*
Sequero, *s. m. a dry season*
Sequeroso, sa, *adj. dry*
Seqüestracion, *sub. f. sequestration*
Seqüestrar, *v. act. to sequester*
Seqüestro, *s. m. sequestration* || *sequestrator*
Sequete, *s. m. a dry piece of bread, etc.* || *roughness* || *a short stroke (at billiards*
Sequía, *s. f. dryness*
Sequillo, *s. m. a kind of rush*
Sequío, *s. m. a dry season*
Sequísimo, ma, *adj. very dry*
Séquito, *s. m. train; retinue*
Ser, *v. n. to be*
Ser de alguno, *to be a friend to one*
Ser, *s. m. the being, essence* or *existence of.....*
Sera, *sub. f. a basket*, or *frail*
Serado, *s. m. V.* Serage
Seráfico, ca, *adjec. seraphical*
Serafin, *s. m. seraphim*
Seraphina, *s. f. a sort of woollen cloth*
Serage, *s. m. many frails full of coal*
Serapino, *s. m. V.* Sagapeno
Serasquier, *s. m. seraskier*
Serba, *s. f.* sorb; service

Serbal, *sub. m. sorb; service-tree*
Serenar, *ver. a. to make serene* || *to calm; to pacify* || *to put out all night in the dew*
Serenar, *v. n. to grow serene; to clear up, etc.*
Serenata, *s. f. a serenade*
Serenero, *s. m. the cover of the head to defend from the dew*
Serenidad, *s. f. serenity*
Serenísimo, ma, *adject. most serene*
Sereno, *s. m. the evening dew*
Sereno, na, *adj. serene*
Seriamente, *adver. seriously*
Sérico, ca, *adj. silken*
Serie, *s. f. series*
Seriedad, *s. f. seriousness* || *sincerity*
Serijo, } Serillo, } *sub. m. a little frail* or *basket*
Serio, ria, *adj. serious* || *sincere*
Sermon, *s. m. a sermon* || *a tongue*
Sermonario, ria, *adject. belonging to a sermon*
Sermonario, *s. m. a book of sermons*
Sermonear, *v. a. to preach*
Sermonizacion *s. fem. a speaking in publick* || *talk; discourse*
Serojas, *s. f. p. the whithered leaves that fall from trees*
Seron, *s. m. a great frail*
Serosidad, *s. f. serosity*
Seroso, sa, *adj. serous*
Serpa, *s. f. layer of a vine*
Serpear, *v. a. to go winding like a serpent*
Serpentaria, *s. f.* dragonwort

pent ; serpentine
Serpenton, s. m. a great serpent || serpent (a musical instrument)
Serpiente, s. m. serpent ; snake
Serpigo, sub. m. a sort of tumour
Sérpol, s. m. wild thime
Serradizo, za, adjec. that may be sawed
Serrador, s. m. a sawyer
Serraduras, s. f. pl. saw-dust
Serrallo, s. m. seraglio
Serranía, s. f. a mountainous country
Serrano, na, adjec. y s. mountaineer
Serrar, v. a. to saw
Serrezuela, sub. f. a little saw
Serrin, sub. m. saw-dust
Serron, sub. m. a great saw used between two men
Servador, s. m. preserver
Servible, a. 2. servicea-
Servidumbre, sub. f. servitude || a necessary house
Servil, a. 2. servile
Servilla, s. fem. a sort of light shoe
Servilleta, sub. f. a table-napkin [lely
Servilmente, adv. servi-
Serviola, sub. f. cat-head (in a ship)
Servir, v. a. to serve || to wait || to help || to grant a supply to the king
Servirse, v. r. to allow ; to approve of || to make use of
Servitud, s. f. servitud
Sesada, s. f. fried brains
Sesear, v. n. to lisp
Seseli, s. m. sesely ; hart-wort
Sesen, sub. m. a certain piece of money
Sesenta, s. m. sixty
Sesenton, sub. m. a man sixty years old
Sesera, s. f. the part of
Seso', s. m.
sense ; jud
iron, etc.
on over the
Hablar en s
seriously
Sesquiáltero,
Sesquimodio,
hel and a
Sesquitercio,
and a thir
Sesteadero, }
Sesteador, }
ter dinner
Sestear, ver.
nap after a
Sesudamente
dently ; wi
Sesudo, da, a
wise
Seta, s. f. bris
room || a th
ger (in a
great lip ||
Setecientos,
ven hundr
Setena, s. f.
of seven ||

ı. *f. severity*
v. r. to take
look angrily
adj. severe ||
rious
cruelty
, ria, *adject.*
ry
, *s. f. sexage-*
[*tieth*
, ma, *adj. six-*
m. a space of

V. Sextula
sex
sexte || *a si-*
picquet)
m. an old ro-
sure
. *m. sesterce*
sextile
f. a sextain
dj. sixth
fem. a sort of

imself, her-
nselves
sí out of his
De por sí, *by*

n. a subterra-
oom to keep
ol in summer
a sibyl
. 2. *whistling;*

, *a. sibylline*
a shekel
ub. m. syco-
[*tree*
m. sycamore.
f. a kind of
l plant
, adj. sideral
ider
mowing; or
ne

Siembra, *s. f. sowing* || *sowing-time*

Siempre, *adv. always*

Siempreviva, *s. f. house-leek* || *amaranth*

Sien, *s. f. the temple of the head*

Sierpe, *s. fem. serpent; snake* || *an ugly woman* || *a passionate person* || *any thing that moves by undulation*

Sierpecilla, *sub. f. a little serpent*

Sierra, *s. f. a saw* || *a long ridge of mountains*

Siervo, va, *adj. y s. slave* || *servant*

Siesta, *sub. f. the heat of the day from noon forwards* || *afternoon's nap; zest*

Siete, *s. m. seven*

Sietemesino, na, *adject. born the seventh month*

Sieteñal, *a.* 2. *seven years old*

Sigilacion, *s. f. sealing*

Sigilar, *v. a. to keep a secret*

Sigilo, *s. m. a seal* || *secrecy due to confession, etc.*

Sigilosamente, *adver. se-* [*crety*

Sigiloso, sa, *adj. secret; close*

Siglo, *sub. m. a century; an age*

Signáculo, *s. m. the impression of a seal*

Signar, *v. a. to sign*

Signarse, *ver. r. to cross one's self*

Signatura, *s. fem. sign; token* || *signature*

Signífero, ra, *adj.* that *bears a sign* [*fication*

Significacion, *s. f.* signi-

Significado, *s. m. a thing signified*

Significador, ra, *a. that signifies*

Significar, *v. a. to signify*

Significativo, va, *adj. significative*

Signo, *s. m. a sign* || *a seal* [*wing*

Siguiente, *adj.* 2. *follo-*

Sílaba, *s. f. a syllable*

Silabario, *s. m. syllabar*

Silbar, *ver. act. y n. to whistle* or *hiss* || *to hiss at; to mock*

Silbato, *s. m. a whistle*

Silbido, } *s. m. whistling*
Silbo, }

Silenciario, ria, *adj. silent; still*

Silenciario, *s. m. one who commands silence*

Silenciero, ra, *adj. that commands silence*

Silencio, *s. m. silence*

Silenciosamente, *adv. silently*

Silencioso, sa, *adj. silent*

Silépsis, *s. f. syllipsis*

Silquerillo, *s. m. dim de* Silguero

Silguero, *sub. m. a gold finch*

Silería, *s. fem. the place where the* silos *are*

Silero, *s. m. V.* Silo

Silibo, *sub. m. a kind of thistle*

Silicio, *s. m. V.* Cilicio

Siligo, *sub. m. a black grain growing among the corn*

Siliqua, *s. f. cod; husk; shell*

Silla, *s. f. a chair* || *a bishop's seat* or *see* || *a saddle*

Silla real, a throne — de mano, a sedan or chair

—volante, *flying-chair*
—doblegable, *folding-chair* [*face*
De silla á silla, *faceto*
Sillar, *sub. m. a stone cut out square for building*
Sillera, *s. f. a place where a sedan is kept*
Sillería, *s. fem. a row of chairs* || *seats* or *stalls in a cathedral, etc.* || *a chair-maker's shop* || *a building with square stone*
Sillero, *s. m. he that makes* or *sells chairs* || *a saddler*
Silleta, *s. f. a litle chair* || *a close-stool-pan*
Silletero, *s. m. a chairman* || *one that makes sells* or *mends chairs*
Sillita, *s. f. V.* Silleta
Sillon, *s. m. a great chair* || *a side-saddle*
Silo, *s. m. a granary under ground, to lay up corn in*
Silogismo, *sub. m. a syllogism* [*gistical*
Silogístico, ca, *adj syllo*
Silogizar, *v. n. to syllogize*
Siluro, *s. m. a sturgeon*
Silva, *s. f. V.* Selva
Silvanos, *s. m. pl. sylvans*
Silvestre, *a. 2. wild*
Sima, *s. f. a deep pit; a dungeon*
Sima de vicios, *an abyss of vice*
Simado, da, *adj. deep*
Simbólico, ca, *adj. symbolical* || *analogous*
Simbolizacion, *s. f. symbolizing; analogy; sympathy, etc.*
Simbolizar, *v. n. to symbolize*
Símbolo, *s. m. symbol*

Simetría, *s. f. symmetry*
Simétrico, ca, *adj. symmetrical* [*ape*
Simia, *s. f. a monkey; an*
Simiente, *s. f. seed*
Simienza, *s. f. V.* Sementera
Símil, *a. 2. like*
Símil, *s. m. likeness* || *a simile*
Similitud, *s. f. similitud*
Simio, *s. m. an ape*
Simonía, *s. f. simony*
Simoníaco, ca, *adj. simoniacal* [*niack*
Simoníaco, *s. m. a simo-*
Simpar, *adj. 2. without equal*
Simpatía, *s. f. sympathy*
Simpatícamente, *a. sympathetically*
Simpático, ca, *adj. sympathetical*
Simplazo, *sub. m. a very silly fellow*
Simple, *adj. 2. simple* || *single; only; bare* || *plain; without ornament* || *simple; downright* || *insipid* || *silly; simpleton*
Simple, *s. m. a medicinal plant*
Simplecillo, *s. m. a silly fellow* [*ply*
Simplemente, *adv. sim-*
Simpleza, *sub. f. simpleness* || *roughness*
Simplicidad, *s. f. simplicity*
Simplicísimo, ma, *adject. very simple*
Simplicista, *s. m. a simpler*
Simplísimo, ma, *a. very silly; simpleton*
Simplista, *s. f. a simpler*
Simplon, } *s. m. a most*
Simplonazo, } *silly fellow*

Simulacion, *s.*
tion
Simulacro, *s.*
Simuladament
gnedly
Simular, *v. a.*
dissemble
Simultad,
Simultaneidad
concourse
neous thing
Simultáneo,
multaneous
Sin, *prep. wit*
Sinagoga, *s. f.*
Sinalefa, *s. f.*
Sincel, Sincel
cel, etc.
Sinceramente
cerely
Sincerar, *v.*
Sinceridad, *s.*
Sincero, ra,
Síncopa, *s. f.*
Sincopal (Cal
an ague w
Sincopal, *s. f.*
Sincopar, *v.*
pate
Síncope, *s. n*
Sincopizar, *v.*
syncopes
Sincopizarse,
swoon
Sindéresis, *s.*
Sindicado, *s.*
|| *sentence*
Sindicar, *v.*
or *impeach*
Síndico, *s. m.*
of the fines
cations || *a*
Sinédoque, *s.*
che
Sinfonía, *s. f.*
|| *a cymbal*
Sinsito, *s. m.*
Singladura,
way

glones, *sub. m. p. the crotches in a ship*
gular, *a.* 2. *singular*
gularidad, *s. f. singularity*
gularísimamente, *adv. most singularly*
gularizar, *v. a. to singularize*
gularmente, *adv. singularly || separately*
gulto, *s. m. sob; sigh; groan* [*hand*
iestra, *s. fem. the left*
iestramente, *adv. sinistrously || wickedly*
iestro, tra, *adj. left || sinister; sinistrous || wicked; perverse*
iestro, *s. m. a vice*
igual, *adj.* 2. *without equal* [*injustice*
justicia, *s. f. wrong;*
número, *s. m. an innumerable quantity*
no, *adv. if not; unless*
noca, *s. f. a fever that lasts a day*
nocal, *a.* 2. *that lasts a day (said of a fever)*
nodal, *a.* 2. *synodical*
nódico, ca, *a. synodick || synodical*
nodo, *s. m. synod || conjunction of two planets*
onimia, *s. f. the use of synonimous words*
ónimo, ma, } *a. synoni-*
ónomo, ma, } *mous*
ónimo, *s. f. m. a synonima*
ople, *s. m. sinople*
razon, *s. fem. wrong; injustice*
nsabor, *s. m, distaste; disgust*
sonte, *s. m. the mocking bird*
axis, *s. f. syntax*

Sintesis, *s. f. synthesis*
Sintético, ca, *a. synthetick*
Síntoma, *s. m. symptom*
Sintomático, ca, *a. symptomatick*
Sinuosidad, *s. f. sinuosity*
Sinuoso, sa, *a. sinuous*
Sio, } *s. m water-smal-*
Sion, } *lage*
Sipedon, } *s. m. a kind of*
Sipidon, } *serpent*
Siquiera, *adv. at least*
Sire, *s. m. sir*
Sirena, *s. f. a siren*
Sirga, *s. f. towing || a rope to tow a ship a long*
Sirgar, *v. a. to tow a ship*
Sirgo, *s. m. a silk twist*
Sirguero, *s. m. a gold finch*
Sirio, *s. m. syrius; dog-star* [*east wind*
Siroco, *s. m. the south-*
Sirtes, *s. f. pl. syrtis*
Sirviento, *s. m. a servant*
Sisa, *s. f. the lessening of any thing by substracting some small part, etc. || the sloping* or *shaping of a garment || size for gilding || borax for soldering*
Sisas, *sub. f. taxes upon meat* or *drink; excise, etc.*
Sisador, *s. m. one that makes the market penny, etc. || excise-man*
Sisar, *v. a. to make the market penny || to take away; to lessen, etc. || to slope in cutting*
Siselis, *s. m. sesely*
Sisimbrio, *s. m. a kind of cresses*
Sison, *s. m. a tailor that cuts cabbage* too o*ften || a sort of bird*
Sistema, *s. f. system*

Sistemático, ca, *a. systematical*
Sístole, *s. f. systole*
Sistro, *s. m. sistrum*
Sitiador, *s. m. besieger*
Sitial, *s. m. a stool withhout a back*
Sitiar, *v. a. to besiege*
Sitibundo, da, *a. thirsty*
Sitio, *s. m. place; site; seat || a siege || a fine country-seat*
Bienes sitios, *immoveables goods*
Situacion, *s. f. situation*
Situado, *s. m. an assignment upon a branch of revenue*
Situar, *v. a. to situate || to assign upon....*
Situarse, *ver. r. to get a place, an employment*
Sizigia, *s. f. syzigia*
So, *prep. under*
So! *int. used stop horses*
Soasar, *v. a. to half roast*
Soba, *sub. f. kneading || beating*
Sobaco, *s. m. the arm-pit*
Sobado, *s. m.* } *handling;*
Sobadura, *s. f.* } *rumpling*
Sobajar, *v. a. to handle roughly; to rumple, etc.*
Sobaquera, *s. f. a cut in the sleeves*
Sobaquina, *sub. f. the ill scent of arm-pits*
Sobar, *v. a. to knead || to beat; to chastise || to rumple*
Sobeba, *s. f. the noseband of a bridle*
Sobarbada, *sub. f. a jerk whith a bridle || check; reprimand*
Sobarcar, *v. a. to carry* or *tuck up under the arm*
Soberanamente, adv. soveteignly

noble || *fiery mettle some* (*said of a horse*)
Soberbiosamente, *adver. proudly*
Soberbioso, sa, *adj. proud*
Sobina, *s.f. a wood-peg*
Sobon, } *s. m. a lazy; idle fellow*
Sobonazo, }
Sobornador, *s. m. a suborner*
Sobornal, *subst. m. the overplus in measure or charge*
Sobornar, *v. a. to suborn*
Soborno, *s. m. subornation; bribe*
Sobra, *s. f. overplus*
Sobras, *pl. the remnants of a dinner, etc.*
De sobra, *adv. superabundantly*
Sobradillo, *s. m. a little garret* || *a shed over a shop, etc.*
Sobrado, *s. m. a garret*
Sobrado, da, *adj, superfluous* || *impudent* || *wealthy* [*lazy*

Sobreasar, *v. a. to over-*
Sobrebeber, *v. a. to drink one glass after another*
Sobrecama, *s. f. counterpane*
Sobrecaña, *s. f. a splent* (*a disease in a horse's leg*) [*ge; over-charge*
Sobrecarga, *s. f. surchar-*
Sobrecargar, *v. a. to surcharge; to over load* || *to beat down the seams*
Sobrecargo, *s. m. supercargo*
Sobrecarta, *s. f. the cover of a letter* || *a second letter or order*
Sobrecartar, *v. a. to reiterate an order, etc.*
Sobrecebadera, *s. f. bowsprit-top-sail*
Sobreceja, *s. f. the part of the forehead near the eye brows*
Sobrecejo, *s. m. a frowning* [*cingle*
Sobrecincho, *s. m. a sur-*
Sobrecoger, *v. a. to sur-*

Sobrel
per-
Sobrel
cip
Sobrel
mu
win
Sobrel
to
wit
Sobre
sive
Sobre
pet
De so
ter
Sobre
ve-
Sobre
Sobre
nat
Sobre
sup
Sobre
nan
Sobre
put
Sobre

(So)brequilla, *s. f. stemson*
(So)breronda, *s. f. counter-rond*
(So)breropa, *s. f. an upper garment*
(So)bresaliente, *a. 2. standing above* or *beyond another* || *supernumerary* [*a picket*
Soldados sobresalientes,
Sobresalir, *v. a. 2. to jut out* || *to over-top* || *to excel*
Sobresaltar, *v. a. to rush violently upon; to assail* || *to surprise*
Sobresalto, *s. m. a surprise; a sudden assault, etc.* [*wares*
De sobresalto, *adv. una-*
Sobresanar, *v. a. to heal superficially* || *to palliate*
Sobresano, *adv. superficially* || *feignedly*
Sobreseer, *v. n. to supersede* [*securely*
Sobreseguro, *adv. safety;*
Sobreseimiento, *s. m. superseding*
Sobresello, *s. m. one seal put upon another*
Sobresembrar, *v. act. to sow over again*
Sobresolar, *v. a. to new-sole shoes* || *to put one floor upon another*
Sobrestante, *sub. m. overseer; supervisor*
Sobrestante, *a. 2. next*
Sobresueldo, *s. m. a gratification*
Sobresuelo, *sub. m. one floor put upon another*
Sobretarde, *s. f. the evening* [*coat*
Sobretodo, *s. m. upper-*
Sobretodo, *adver. above all; especially*

Sobrevenir, *v. n. to survene; to supervene*
Sobreverterse, *ver. r. to over flow*
Sobrevesta, *s. f. an upper-coat without sleeves*
Sobrevestir, *v. a. to put one garment over another* [*wind*
Sobreviento, *s. m. a large*
Ponerse a sobreviento, *to gain the weather gage of a ship* — ir á sobreviento, *to sail with a scant wind*
Sobrevista, *s. f. viser*
Sobreviviente, *s. longest liver*
Sobrevivir, *v. n. supervive; survive*
Sóbriamente, *adv. soberly*
Sobriedad, *s. f. sobriety*
Sobrina, *s. f. a niece*
Sobrino, *s. m. a nephew*
Sóbrio, bria, *a. sober*
Socapa, *s. f. a pretence*
A' socapa, *adv. privately; secretely*
Socarra, *s. f. singing* || *craftiness*
Socarrar, *v. a. to singe*
Socarren, *s. m. the eaves of a house*
Socarron, na, *adj. sly; cunning; crafty*
Socarronamente, *adver. craftily*
Socarronería, *s. f. craftiness; waggery*
Socarronísimo, ma, *adj. most crafty* [*under*
Socava, *sub. f. a digging*
Socavar, *v. a. to dig under; to undermine*
Socavon, *s. m a cave dug under a hill*
Sochantre, *sub. m. subchanter* [*ness*
Sociabilidad, *s. f. sociable-*

Sociable, *a. 2. sociable*
Sociedad, *s. f. society*
Socio, *s. m. a companion*
Socolor, *s. m. a pretence*
Socolor, *adv. under colour*
Socorredor, ra, *adj. that helps* or *succours*
Socorrer, *v. a. to succour; to relieve*
Socorro, *s. m. succour; relief; aid*
Socrocio, *s. m. a plaster of the saffron colour* || *pleasure*
Socrocio mithridátrico, *mithridate*
Soda, *s. f. glass-wort*
Sodomía, *s. f. sodomy*
Sodomita, *s. masc. a sodomite*
Sofaldar, *v. a. to tuck up the coats*
Sofaldo, *s. m. tucking up*
Sofisma, *s. m. sophism*
Sofista, *s. m. a sophister*
Sofistería, *s. f. sophistry*
Sofísticamente, *adv. sophistically*
Sofisticar, *v. a. to cavil*
Sofístico, ca, *a. sophistical*
Soflama, *s. f. a. little flame* || *reverberation of the fire* || *blush* || *captious and deceiving words*
Soflamar, *v. a. to shame one* || *to deceive with fair words*
Soflamero, *s. m. one who deceives with fair words*
Sofocar, *v. a. to suffocate*
Sofreír, *v. a. to fry lightly*
Sofrito, ta, *p. p. of sofreír*
Sofrenada, *sub. f. a jerk with a bridle* || *check; reprimand*
Sofrenar, *v. a. to give*

jerk with the bridle || *to check*

Soga, *s. f. a rope made of* esparto || *a measure for the lands, etc.*

Soga! *int. fy! fy upon!*

Soguear, *v. a. to measure with a rope*

Soguero, *sub. m. a rope-maker*

Soguilla, } *s. f. a little*
Soguita, } *rope* || *fillet; hair-lace*

Soguillo, *s. m. hair-lace*

Sohez, *a. 2. mean; base; vil*

Sojuzgador, *s. m. subduer*

Sojuzgar, *v. a. to subdue*

Sol, *s. m. the sun* || *sol* or *g, (musical note)*

Solacear, *v. a. to solace*

Solado, *s. m. a boarded* or *paved floor*

Solador, *sub. m. one that paves with square tiles, etc.* [*lely*

Solamente, *adv. only; so-*

Solana, *s. f. a sunny place* || *the rent paid for a house*

Solanazo, *s. m. aum. de* Solano

Solano, *sub. m. the east-wind*

Solapa, *sub. f. a lapping over in a garment* || *a false pretence, etc.*

Solapadamente, *adv. dissemblingly; deceitfully*

Solapado, da, *a. crafty, deceitful*

Solapar, *v. a. to lap over; like a garment* || *to conceal; to colour, etc.*

Solape, } *s. m. V.* Solapa
Solapo, }

A'solapo, *adv. by stealth*

Solar, *s. m. the ground a house stands on* || *the ancient mansion-house of a family*

Solar, *a. 2. solar*

Solar, *v. a. to lay a floor; to pave* || *to new-sole shoes*

Solariego, ga, *a. belonging to the stock* or *mansion-house*

Solaz, *sub. m. comfort; pleasure*

Solazar, *v. a. to solace; to comfort*

Solazarse, *v. r. to recreate one's self*

Solazo, *s. m. a burning sun* [*rejoicing*

Solazoso, sa, *a. pleasing;*

Soldada, *s. f. salary; wages* [*med soldier*

Soldadado, *s. m. a refor-*

Soldadesca, *s. f. soldiery*

Soldadesco, ca, *adj. soldierly*

Soldadico, } *s. masc. a*
Soldadillo, } *little paltry soldier*

Soldado, *s. m. a soldier*

Soldador, *s. m. soderer* || *sodering-iron*

Soldadura, *s. f. sodering* || *soder*

Soldan, *s. m. soldan*

Soldar, *v. a. to soder;* or *solder* || *to mend*

Soldemente, *adv. only*

Solecismo, *s. m. solecism*

Solecito, *s. m. a burning sun* [*litariness*

Soledad, *s. f. solitude; so-*

Solejar, *s. m. an open; sunny place*

Solemne, *a. 2. solemn* || *gay; merry*

Solemnemente, *adv. solemnly*

Solemnidad, *s. f. solemnity*

Solemnísimo, ma, *a. most solemn*

Solemnizador, ra, *s.* [...] *who solemnizes*

Solemnizar, *v. a.* [...] *lemnize* [...]

Soleó, *s. m. a* [...]

Soler, *v. n. to be* [...] *to use*

Solera, *sub. f. the* [...] *part of a wall* || [...] *lees* [...]

Solercia, *s. f. indu*[...]

Soleta, *s. f. a new* [...] *to a stocking*

Soletar, } *v. a. to* [...]
Soletear, } *le stockin*[...]

Soletero, ra, *s. one* [...] *soles old stockings*

Solevacion, *s. f.* }
Solevamiento, *s. m.* } [...] *a sedition*

Solevantar, *v. a. to* [...] || *to persuade* [...] *to change places*

Solevar, *v. a. to ris*[...]

Solfa, *sub. f. musi*[...] *harmony* || *singin*[...] *cudgelling*

Solfeador, *s. m. an* [...] *cian* || *he that* [...] *lime*

Solfear, *v. a. to sin*[...] *notes* || *to beat ti*[...] *to chastise; to las*[...]

Solfeo, *s. m. singi*[...] *lash; cudgelling*

Solfista, *s. 2. a great* [...] *sician*

Solicitacion, *s. f. sol*[...]

Solicitador, ra, *s. sol*[...]

Solícitamente, *adv.* [...] *citously*

Solicitar, *v. a. to so*[...]

Solícito, ta, *a. solici*[...] *careful*

Solicitud, *s. f. solici*[...]

Sólidamente, *adv. so*[...]

Solideo, *s. m. a cal*[...] leather cap

Solidez, *s. f. soli*[...]

la, *adj. solid*
m. a solid
ır, *v. n. to speak*
ne's self
), *s. m. soliloquy*
sub. m. mercury
ate
n. a throne
nente, *adv. so-*
ria. *adj solitary*
, *a. wont; usual*
. *a. all alone*
ra, *s. f. lifting*
ving
v. a. to ease to
derneath || *to re-*
to steal
. *m. lifting un-*
th [*fish*)
f. sole (*a sea-*
, *v. a. to singe*
s. m. a scullion
fty knave
, *s. f. scullery-*
[*crafty knave*
, *s. m. a most*
m. a pickerel
n. a pike (*fish*)
v. n. to sob
s. m. a sob
a. alone; only
, ó á sus solas,
ly
. *a solo*
. only; solely;
[Solomo
, *s. m. dim. de*
. *m. a chine of*
, *a. 2. solstitial*
s. m. solstice
, za, *adj. loose-*
ntied
s. m. one who
etc.
a. to loosen;
to let go; to

Soltar qüestiones, *to solve* or *explain obscure questions*
Soltarse, *v. r. to exercise one's self to...* || *to give one's self over to lewdness, etc.*
Soltería, *s. f. a single life*
Soltero, ra, *sub. a single man* or *woman*
Soltura, *s. f. loosening; untying* || *release; enlargement* || *agility; dexterity* || *impudence; lewdness*
Soluble, *a. 2. soluble*
Solucion, *s. f. untying* || *solution*
Solutivo, va, *adj. dissolving*
Solvente, *a. 2. solvent*
Solver, *v. a. to untie* || *to solve* or *resolve*
Solviente, *a. 2. solvent*
Soma, *s. f. bran*
Sombra, *sub. f. shadow; shade* [*arbour*
Sombrage, *s. m. a green*
Sombrajo, *s. m. a shady place* [brar
Sombrar, *v. a. V.* Asom-
Sombrear, *v. a. to shadow a picture*
Sombrerazo, *s. m. a very large hat* || *a blow with a hat*
Sombrerera, *s. f. a hat-case* || *butterbur*
Sombrerería, *s. f. hatter's shop*
Sombrerero, *s. m. a hatter*
Sombrerillo, ito, *s. m. a little hat*
Sombrero, *s. m. a hat* || *the roof of a pulpit* || *the quality of a Spanish Grandee*
Sombrio, bria, | Sombroso, sa, } *a. shady*

Someramente, *adv. superficially* [*ficial*
Somero, ra, *adj. super-*
Someter, *v. a. to subdue*
Someterse, *v. r. to submit*
Sometico, ca, *a. sodomite*
Somnolencia, *sub. f. sleepiness*
Somo, *sub. m. top of a hill, etc.*
Somonte, *s. m. what is rough, uncouth, etc.*
Somorgujador, *s. m. a diver*
Somorgujar, *v. a. to dive under water* [*geon*
Somorgujo, *s. m. a plun-*
A' lo somorgujo, *adv. under water* || *secretely; by stealth* [morgujar
Somormujar, *v. a. V.* So-
Somormujo, Somormujon, *V.* Somorgujo
Sompesar, *v. a. to weigh by hand* [*noise*
Son, *s. m. a sound* || *a*
Sonable, *a. 2. sonorous* || *noisy* || *famous; renowned*
Sonada, *s. f. sonata*
Sonadera, *s. f. the blowing of one's nose*
Sonadero, *s. m. a handkerchief. V.* Sonadera
Sonado, da, *a. famous; renowned* || *a thing much spoken of*
Sonador, *s. m. one who blows his nose with noise* || *handkerchief*
Sonajas, *s. f. pl. a kind of tabour*
Sonajera, *s. f. a woman that plays on the sonajas*
Sonajero, *s. m. a rattle; a small bell, etc.*
Sonante, *a. 2. sonorous*
Sonar, *v. n. to sound*

Sonar, *v. a. to play upon an instrument* || *to relate to....*

Sonarse, *ver. r. to blow one's nose* || *to be reported abroad*

Sonata, *s. f. sonata*

Sonco, *s. m. endive*

Sonda, *sub. f. plummet; sounding-lead*

Sondalesa, *s. f. a sounding-plummet*

Sondar, } *v. a. to sound*
Sondear, } *the depth of waters, etc.*

Sonecillo, *sub. m. a light sound*

Sonetazo, *sub. m. a very good sonnet*

Sonetico, *s. m. a little pretty sonnet* || *a light sound*

Soneto, *s. m. a sonnet*

Sonido, *s. m. a sound*

Sonlocado, **da**, *adj. hare-brained* [*rously*

Sonoramente, *adv. sono-*

Sonoridad, *s. f. sonorousness*

Sonoro, **ra**, } *a. sonorous*
Sonoroso, **sa**, } || *upright*

Sonreirse, *v. r. to smile*

Sonrisa, *s. f.* } *a smile*
Sonriso, *s. m.* }

Sonrodarse, *v. r. to stick in the mire (said of the wheels)*

Sonrosar, } *v. a. to die*
Sonresear, } *in a rose-colour*

Sonrosearse, *v. r. to blush*

Sonroseo, *s. m. blushing*

Sonrozar, *v. a. to ashame*

Sonroxo, *sub. m. shame; blush*

Sonsaca, *s. f. seducing; cheating; pumping*

Sonsacador, **ra**, *s. wheedler*

Sonsacar, *v. a. to wheedle; to pump a thing out of one*

Sonseque, *s. m. V.* Sonsaca

Sonsonete, *s. m. a little sound caused by hitting softly on any thing*

Soñador, *s. m. a dreamer*

Soñar, *v. a. to dream*

Soñarrera, *s. f. the dreaming much* || *a heavy sleep*

Soñoliento, **ta**, *adj. sleepy* || *sluggard*

Sopa, *s. f. a sop or soup*

Sopaborracha, *wine-sop*

Sopalanda, *s. f. a dress worn by vagabonds, etc.*

Sopapo, *s. m. a blow under the chin* || *sucker of a pump*

Sopar, *v. a. to sop*

Sopaypa, *s. f. a kind of fritter* [*use or treat ill*

Sopear, *v. a. to sop* || *to*

Sopena, *adv. upon pain of*

Sopesar, *v. a. V.* Sompesar

Sopetear, *v. a. to sop* || *to use ill*

Sopeton, *s. m. a large sop* || *a sudden box on the ear* [*denly*

De sopeton, *adv. sud-*

Sopilla, *s. f. dim. de* Sopa

Sopista, *s. m. V.* Sopon

Soplado, **da**, *adj. over curiously dressed*

Soplador, **ra**, *s. a blower* || *a make-bate*

Soplamocos, *s. m. a blow given on the nose*

Soplar, *v. a. y n. to blow* || *to whisper; to prompt* || *to blow a man (at draughts)* || *to blow one up* || *to drink hard* || *to accuse; to inform against*

Soplarse, *v. r. to trim up one's self*

Soplillo, *sub. m. a* [...] *puff of wind*, [...] *a very thin silk*, [...]

Soplo, *sub. m. br*[...] *puff; blowing* || [...] *per; information* [...] *tale carried*

Soplon, **na**, *s. f.* [...] *former* || *a tale* [...]

Sopon, *s. m. a fellow* [...] *goes to convents* [...] *a soup*

Soponcio, *s. m.* [...]

Sopor, *s. m. heav*[...] *sleepiness*

Soporifero, **ra**, } *a.* [...]
Soporoso, **sa**, } *ri*[...]

Soportable, *a. 2.* [...] *table*

Soportal, *sub. m.* [...] *king-place unde*[...] *tico*

Soportar, *v. a. to su*[...] *to bear with*

Sor, *s. f. sister (a nun)*

Sor, *ó seor*, *s. m.*

Sorba, *s. f. a sor*[...]

Sorbedor, *s. m.* [...] *sups up*

Sorber, *v. a. to su*[...] *to swallow up*, [...] *sume*

Sorbete, *s. m. she*[...]

Sorbeton, *s. m.* [...] Sorbo

Sorbible, *a. 2. sor*[...]

Sorbicion, *s. f. so*[...] *potion*

Sorbito, *sub. m.* [...] *draught; a sip*

Sorbo, *s. m. a dr*[...] *a gulp* || *a sorb tree*

Sorce, *s. m. a m*[...]

Sordamente, *ad*[...]

Sordera, } *s. f*[...]
Sordez, }

Sordidez, *s.* [...]

do, da, *a. sordid*
na, *s. f. a little pipe*
a mute
a sordina, *privately*
, da, *adj. deaf* ||
ent || *that does not*
and [*slowness*
a, *s. f. heaviness*;
awiron, *s. m. a back-*
oke [*prise*
rehender, *v. a. to sur-*
resa, *s. f. a surprise*
a, *s. f. ballast* || *a tun-*
's side
ro, ra, *a. sluggish*;
cause ill ballasted
ador, *sub. m. he that*
sts the lots || *he that*
tacks the bull at the
ll feasts
ar, *v. a. to cast lots*
to attack the bull
o, *s. m. the act of*
sting lots
ro, *s. m. a diviner*
ja, *s. f. a ring*
rer sortija, *to ride at*
ring
jon, *s. m. a great ring*
legio, *s. m. witche-*
ft; *witchery*
lego, *s. m. one who*
sts lots [*per coat*
l, *s. m. a great up-*
, *sub. f. glass wort*;
ll wort
gadamente, *ad. quiet-*
; *calmly*
gado, da, *adj. quiet*;
lm
gar, *v. a. to quiet*;
still; *to calm*
gar, *v. n. to get rest*
to repose; *to sleep* ||
grow quiet
ego, *s. m. quietness*;
llness; *calmness*
o (Al, ó de) *adver.*
pe; *athwart*

Soso, sa, *adj. unsavoury*; *insipid*
Sospecha, *s. f. suspicion*
Sospechar, *v. a. to suspect*
Sospechosamente, *adver. suspiciously* [*cious*
Sospechoso, sa, *a. suspi-*
Sosquin, *s. m. a blow given cunningly or treacherously*
Sosten, *s. m. a support*; *a prop, etc.* [*ter*
Sostenedor, *s. m. suppor-*
Sostener, *v. a. to sustain*; *to support* [*taining*
Sostenimiento, *s. m. sus-*
Sostituir, *v. a. to substitute* [*tute*
Sostituto, *s. m. a substi-*
Sota, *s. f. the knave* (*at cards*)
Sotacaballerizo, *s. m. an officer under the master of the horse*
Sotacochero, *s. m. an under-coachman*
Sotacola, *s. f. a crupper*
Sotacomitre, *s. m. an under-boatswain* (*in a galley* [*der-minister*
Sotaministro, *s. m. an un-*
Sotamontero, *s. m. an under-huntsman*
Sotana, *s. f. a cassock*
Sotanl, *sub. m. a kind of under-petty-coat*
Sotanilla, *s. f. a little cassock* [*neous cellar*
Sótano, *s. m. a subterra-*
Sotaventar, *v. a. to drive to leeward*
Sotavento, *s. m. the lee side*
Sotechado, *s. m. a cart-house, etc.*
Soterraneo, nea, } *a. subterraneous*
Soterraño, ña, }
Soterraneo, *s. m. a vault under ground*
Soterrar, *v. a. to burry* || *to put under ground*

Sotil, sotileza. *V.* Sutil, sutileza [*or thicket*
Sotillo, *s. m. a little wood*
Soto, *sub. m. a wood*; *a thicket*
Soto, *prep. under*
Sotoministro, *s. m. an under-minister*
Sotrozo, *s. m. linch-pin*
Sotuer, *s. m. saltier*
Su, *pron. his*; *her*
Su padre de v. m. *your father*
Suadir, *v. a. to persuade*
Suasible, *a. 2. that may be persuaded*
Suasion, *s. f. persuasion*
Suasivo, va, *a. persuasive*
Suave, *a. 2. sweet*; *pleasant*; *soft*
Suavemente, *adv. sweetly*; *softy* [*sweetness*
Suavidad, *s. f. suavity*;
Suavizar, *v. a. to make sweet or soft*
Subalternar, *v. a. to subject* [*tern*
Subalterno, na, *a. subal-*
Subalterno, *sub. m. a subaltern*
Subcinericio, cia, *a. baked under hot ashes*
Subdelegacion, *s. f. subdelegation* [*delegate*
Subdelegado, *s. m. a sub-*
Subdelegar, *v. a. to subdelegate*
Subdiaconado, } *s. m. subdeaconship* [*deacon*
Subdiaconato, }
Subdiácono, *s. m. a sub-*
Súbdito, ta, *a. subject*
Súbdito, *s. m. a subject*
Subdividir, *v. a. to subdivide* [*vision*
Subdivision, *s. f. subdi-*
Subduplo, pla, *adj. subduple*

Subida, s. f. *going up* || *a rising; an ascent* || *increase*
Subidero, ra, a. *rising*
Subidero, s. m. *a step; a stair, etc.*
Subido, da, a. *lofty; high* || ***proud***; *haughty*
Subido de quilates, *very fine*, or *pure*—de color, *high coloured*
Subidor, s. m. *one that* ***raises, etc.***
Subir, v. a. ***to raise; to*** *lift up* || ***to come up*** *stairs* [***rise***
Subir, v. n. *to go up; to*
Subirse de punto, *to take* *state upon one* — de talones, *to grow proud*
Súbitamente, adv. *suddenly* [*taneous*
Subitáneo, nea, a. *subi-*
Súbito, ta, a. *sudden*
Súbito, De súbito, } ***abver. suddenly***
Subjugar, v. a. *to subdue*
Subjuntivo, s. m. *subjunctive*
Sublevacion, s. f. } Sublevamiento, s. m. } *a rising; a sedition*
Sublevar, v. a. ***to move a*** *sedition*
Sublimacion, s. f. ***lifting up*** || ***sublimation***
Sublimado, sub. m. *sublimate*
Sublimar, v. a. *to lift up* || *to sublimate*
Sublimatorio, ria, a. *sublimatory*
Sublime, a. 2 ***sublime***
Sublimemente, adv. *sublimely* [*mity*
Sublimidad, sub. f. *subli-*
Sublunar, adj. 2. *sublunary*

Subministracion, s. f. *affording supplying*
Subministrador, sub. m *one who supplies or affords*
Subministrar, v. a. *to supply; to afford*
Subordinacion, s. f. *subordination*
Subordinar, v. a. *to subordinate*
Subpolar, a. 2. *lying under the pole* [*tion*
Subrepcion, s. f. *subrep-*
Subrepticio, cia, a. *surreptitious*
Subrigadier, s. m. *an officer of horse under the brigadier* [*gation*
Subrogacion, s. f. *surro-*
Subrogar, v. a. *to surrogate*
Subsanar, v. a. *to exculpate* || *to make amends for....* [*cription*
Subscripcion, s. f. *subs-*
Subscribir, v. a. *to subscribe* [*cribed*
Subscrito, ta, p. p. *subs-*
Subseguirse, v. r. *to follow* [*quent*
Subseqüente, a. 2. *subse-*
Subsidiario, ria, a. *subsidiary*
Subsidio, s. m. *subsidy*
Subsiguiente, a. 2. *sub-* *sequent* [*tence*
Subsistencia, s. f. *subsis-*
Subsistir, v. a. *to subsist*
Subsolano, s. m. *the east* *wind*
Substancia, s. f. *substance* || ***wealth*** || *value*
Substancial, adj. 2. *subs-***tantial**
Substanciar, v. a. to make an abridgment or summary || to enquire about...; to verify || to draw a brevial of the case

Substancioso, sa, a. *substantial; juicy*
Substantivar, v. a. *to make like a substantive*
Substantivo, a. m. s. *substantive* [*titution*
Substitucion, s. f. *subs-*
Substituidor, sub. m. *one who substitutes*
Substituir, v. a. *to substitute* [*tute*
Substituto, s. m. *a substi-*
Substraccion, s. f. *subtraction* [*tract*
Substraer, v. a. *to subs-*
Substraerse, ver. r. *to fly from....* [*tend*
Subtender, v. a. *to sub-*
Subtensa, s. f. *subtense*
Subterráneo, nea, a. *subterraneous*
Suburbano, Suburbio, } s. m. *a suburb*
Suburbano, na, a. *suburban* [*sion*
Subversion, s. f. *subver-*
Subvertir, v. a. *to subvert*
Succino, s. m. *yellow amber*
Succion, s. f. *suction*
Suceder, v. n. *to succeed* || *to inherit* || *to happen*
Sucesion, s. f. *succession*
Sucesivamente, adv. *successively* [*sive*
Sucesivo, va, a. *succes-*
Suceso, s. m. *success*
Sucesor, s. m. *successor*
Suciamente, adv. *nastily*
Suciedad, s. f. *nastiness; filth* [*cintly*
Sucintamente, adv. *suc-*
Sucintarse, v. r. *to lessen* one's *expenses*
Sucinto, ta, adj. succint || tucked up
Sucio, cia, adj. nasty; filty; dirty

, sub. m. moisture ||
ce || gravy
o, sa, adj. full of
isture ; juicy
oo, s. m. succubus
s. m. the south || the
ith-wend
lero, s. m. handker-
ef || a stove ; a hot-
use || a gutter
r, v. a. to sweat
rio, s. m. handker-
ief [east wind
st, s. m. the south-
r, s. m. sweat
rifero, ra, } adj. su-
rifico, ca, } dorifick
rifico, s. m. a sudo-
ick [west-wind
uest, sub. m. south-
adest, s. m. south-
ith-east
adonest, s. m. south-
ith-west
este, s. m. south-west
recita, s. f. dim. de
egra
ra, s. f. a mother-
law
ro, s. m. father-in-
v
, s. f. the sole of the
e || sole (fish) || the
oved wood of a par-
ion
s, pl. sandals
lo, s. m. pay ; wad-
|| a penny
, s. m. the ground
floor || a story || bot-
n || dregs ; lees
a, s. f. untying
as, plur. fetters for
rses feet
amente, adv. loose-
lewdly || nimbly
, ta, adj. untied ||
bly ; quick || free ;
|| talkative

Suelto de lingua, evil-speaker [dream
Sueño, sub. m. sleep || a
Suero, s. m. whey || serosity
Suerte, s. f. fate ; destiny || chance; hazard || a lot || a sort ; a kind ; a manner || race
Suficencia, s. f. sufficiency
A' suficiencia, adv. sufficiently
Suficiente, a. 2. sufficient
Suficientemente, adv. sufficiently [cation
Sufocacion, sub. f. suffo-
Sufocador, s. m. he that suffocates
Sufocar, v. a. to suffocate || to put out the fire || to stop [fragant
Sufragáneo, a. y s. m. suf-
Sufragar, v. a. to help ; to favour
Sufragio, sub. m favour ; assistance || vote ; suffrage
Sufrible, adj. 2. } tolera-
Sufridero, ra, a. } ble
Sufridísimo, ma, a. most patient
Sufrido, da, adj. patient ; that will suffer much
Sufridor, sub. m. one who suffers with patience and resignation
Sufrimiento, s. m. patience ; resignation
Sufrir, v. a. to suffer ; to endure [fumigation
Sufumigacion, s. f. suf-
Sufusion, s. f. suffusion
Sugerir, v. a. to suggest
Sugestion, s. f. suggestion
Sugesto, s. m. a pupilt
Sugeto, s. m. a person || a subject || occasion ; motive ; matter
Sugo, s. m. juice ; moisture

Sugecion, s. f. subjection
Sujetar, v. a. to subject || to make a thing fast
Sujeto, ta, adj. subject ; liable, etc.
Sulcar, Sulco. V. Surcar, Surco
Sulfonete, s. m. a match to light the fire with
Sulfúreo, rea, a. sulphurous
Sultan, s. m. sultan
Sultana, s. f. sultana
Suma, sub. f. a sum || a summary
En suma, adv. in short
Sumamente, adv. highly ; extremely
Sumar, v. a. to sum
Sumar, v. n. to amount to
Sumariamente, adv. summarily [cess
Sumaria, s. f. verbal pro-
Sumario, sub. m. a summary [mary
Sumario, ria, adj. sum-
Sumergir, v. act. to submerge ; to drown
Sumersion, s. f. submersion
Sumidad, s. f. the summit ; the top
Sumidero, s. m. a sink
Sumiller de cortina, s. m. a chaplain of honor to the king — de corps, the king's esquire of the body [tery
Sumillería, s. f. the but-
Sumir, v. a. to swallow
Sumirse, v. r. to sink into the ground
Sumision, s. f. submission
Sumiso, sa, adj. submissive
Sumista, s. m. one who makes summaries, etc.
Sumo, ma, a. the highest || the most excellent

El sumo pontífice, *the pope* [monte

Sumonte, *s. m. Voy.* So-

Súmula, *s. f. a sum; an abridgment*

Sumulista, *s. m. V.* Sumista

Suncho, *sub. m. an iron that fastens the pump, on board a ship*

Suntuario, ria, *adj. sumptuary* [tuously

Suntuosamente, *ad. sump-*

Suntuosidad, *s. f. sumptuousness*

Suntuoso, sa, *a. sumptuous*

Supeditacion, *s. f. trampling on; subduing*

Supeditar, *v. a. to trample on; to subdue, etc.*

Superable, *a. 2. superable*

Superabundancia, *s. f. superabundance*

Superabundante, *a. 2. superabundant*

Superabundantemente, *ad. superabundantly*

Superabundar, *ver. n. to superabound*

Superádito, ta, *adj. superadded*

Superano, *s. m. the treble (in musick)*

Superar, *v. a. to overcome* [mainder

Superavit, *s. m. the re-*

Superbo, ba, *adj. V.* Soberbio

Supercheria, *s. f. fraud; trick* || *incivility*

Superchero, ra, *a. deceitful* [rerogation

Supererogacion, *s. f. supe-*

Superfetacion, *s. f. superfetation* [cial

Superficial, *a. 2. superfi-*

Superficialmente, *adver. superficially*

Superficie, *s. f. superficies*

Superfluamente, *adv. superfluously*

Superfluidad, *s. f. superfluity* || *superfluousness*

Superfluo, flua, *a. superfluous* [ephod

Superhumeral, *sub. m. an*

Superintendencia, *s. f. superintendence*

Superintendente, *sub. m. superintendent*

Superior, *a. 2. superior; upper*

Superior, *s. m. a superior*

Superiorato, *subs. m. the being superior; superiority* [riority

Superioridad, *s. f. supe-*

Superiormente, *adv. better; excellently*

Superlativo, va, *adj superlative* [perlative

Superlativo, *s. m. the su-*

Superno, na, *adj. supreme; the highest*

Supernumerario, ria, *adj. supernumerary*

Supersticion, *s. f. superstition*

Supersticiosamente, *adv. superstitiously*

Supersticioso, sa, *a. superstitious*

Supervencion, *sub. f. supervention* [vene

Supervenir, *v. n. to super-*

Supino, na, *a. supine*

Ignorancia supina, *gross ignorance*

Supino, *s. m. the supine*

Súpitamente, *adj. V.* Súbitamente [fication

Suplantacion, *s. f. falsi-*

Suplantar, *v. a. to falsify a writing* [ment

Suplemento, s. m. supple-

Súplica, s. f. petition; request [cation

Suplicacion, s. f. suppli-

Suplicaciones, *pl. small wafers rolled up*

Suplicacionero, *s. m. one that makes or sells small wafers* [plicant

Suplicante, *s. m. a sup-*

Suplicar, *v. a. to supplicate; to intreat*

Suplicio, *sub. m. punishment; pain* [makes up

Suplidor, *s. m. one that*

Suplir, *v. a. to make up; to supply* || *to tolerate; to bear with*

Suponedor, *s. m. supposer*

Suponer, *v. a. to suppose*

Suposicion, *s. f. a supposition* || *a forgery*

Supositorio, *s. m. a suppository*

Suprema, *s. f. the supreme council of the inquisition*

Supremamente, *ad. to the last end* [[illegible]

Supremo, ma, *a. supreme*

Supresion, *s. f. suppression*

Supreso, sa, *p. p. suppressed* [press

Suprimir, *v. a. to sup-*

Supuesto, *s. m. an individual*

Supuesto, ta, *p. p. of* Suponer [se it

Supuesto que, *adv. suppo-*

Supuracion, *s. f. suppuration*

Supurar, *v. a. to bring to suppuration* [rate

Supurar, *v. n. to suppu-*

Supurativo, va, } *adj. sup-*
Supuratorio, ria, } *purative*

Suputacion, *s. f. supputation*

Suputar, *v. a. to supputate*

Sur, *s. m. the south-wind*

Sura, *s. f. one of the bones in the leg*

, v. a. to furrow
, v. a. V. Zurcir
s. m. a furrow
ero, s. m. harbour;
en, etc.
, v. a. to come to
|| to spring out
a, s. f. postern-gate
back-door || a sally
o, s. m. a prepara-

or, sub. m. a pur-
or || a water-spout
niento, sub. m. sup-
ing; furnishing ||
parative
, v. a. to supply;
furnish
efecto, to take effect
, v. n. to spring out
, ta, p. p. of Surgir
, s. m. surtout; up-
coat
pron. their
nt. up! come!
ar, v. a. to suscitate
adv. above
cto, ta, a. suspect;
picable
ndedor, sub. m. one
t suspends
nder, v. a. to suspend
amase
nderse el caballo, to
nce
nsion, s. f. suspen-
|| suspense || ama-
ent
nsivo, va, a. what
the faculty of sus-
ding
nso, sa, p. p. of Sus-
der [pensory
nsorio, ria, a. sus-
rar, v. a. to sigh || to
for
, s. m. a sigh || a
of sweet meat ||

Susten, Sustener. V. Sosten, etc.
Sustentacion, s. f. sustainaing
Sustentáculo, s. m. a support; a poop, etc.
Sustentador, sub. m. one that sustains, etc.
Sustentamiento, s. m. sustenance; maintenance
Sustentante, s. m. sustainer; respondent
Sustentar, v. a. to sustain; to support || to maintain || to defend conclusions, etc.
Sustentar mucha casa, to keep a great family
Sustento, s. m. sustenance; food
Sustillo, sub. m. dim. de Susto
Sustitucion, Sustituir. V. Substitucion, etc.
Susto, s. m. fear; fright; trouble
Susurrador, s. m. whisperer; mumbler, etc.
Susurrar, v. n. to murmur || to mumble || to whisper [tered about...
Surrarse, v. r. to be mut-
Susurro, s. m. murmur; murmuring || whispering; muttering
Sutil, a. 2. subtil || subtle
Sutileza, s. f. subtility; thinness || subtlety
Sutilidad, s. f. subtility
Sutilizar, v. a. to subtilize || to talk finely
Sutilmente, adv. subtly
Sutorio, ria, a. relating to the shoe-maker's trade
Sutura, s. f. suture
Suya, s. f. intent; mind
Suyo, ya, pron. his; her; its
Suyos, s. m. pl. his relations; his people

T

TA! int. softly; take care
Taba, s. f. small bone ||
Tabaco, s. m. tobacco
Tabalada, s. f. a box on the ear || a blow given with the breech
Tabalario, s. m. the breech
Tabalear, ver. a. to stir; to wag
Tabalear, v. n. to make a noise with the fingers upon a table
Tabananzo, s. m. a cuff on the ear [shop)
Tabanco, s. m. stall (mean
Tábano, s. m. a gad-fly
Tabaola, s. f. a confused noise; a fray, etc.
Tabaque, sub. m. a little basket [tacks
Tabaques, pl. small nails;
Tabaquera, s. f. a snuff-box || the bowl of a tobacco-pipe
Tabaquería, s. f. the shop where snuff is sold
Tabaquero, s. m. a seller of snuff
Tabaquillo, s. m. a little basket
Tabaquista, s. 2. a connoisseur in snuff || a great taker of snuff
Tabardete, } sub. m. the
Tabardillo, } spotted fever
Tabardo, sub. m. a coat worn by country people
Tabellion, s. m. tabellion; notary
Taberna, s. f. a tavern
Tabernáculo, s. m. tabernacle
Tabernero, s. m. a publican; a tavern-keeper
Tabi, s. m. tabby
Tabicar, v. a. to make

partition || to shut; to close

Tábido, da, a. tabid

Tabique, s. m. a partition of lath and plaster

Tabla, s. f. a board; a plank || a table || a picture || a banker's counter

Tabla de rio, that part where the river runs smoothest

Juego de tablas, the game of tables [buckler

Tablachina, s. f. a wood-

Tablacho, s. m. sluice; flood-gate

Tabladillo, sub. m. dim. de Tablado

Tablado, s. m. a scaffold || the floor of a stage

Tablado, da, a. covered with boards

Tablage, s. m. the boards sawed off from a tree, etc. || a gaming house

Tablagería, s. f. the vice of haunting gaming-houses || the gaming-house-keeper's wages

Tablagero, s. m. one who makes scaffolds || receiver of taxes, etc. || a gaming-house's keeper || a butcher

Tablar, s. m. garden-bed

Tablazo, s. m. a blow with a board or table

Tablazon, s. m. heap of boards, etc.

Tablear, v. a. to divide a garden into beds

Tablero, s. m. tables to play on || a chess or draught-board || a shop-board || a banker's counter || a sort of nail || a gaming-house || the publick || a square stone for an inscription

Tableta, s. fem. a little board or table || a tablet to write on || a sweet lozenge

Tableteado, s. m. a noise made with, or upon boards

Tabletear, v. n. to make a noise with boards

Tabletilla, s. f. a sweet lozenge

Tablica, s. fem. a little board or table

Tablilla, s. fem. tablet || a kind of wafer || a sweet lozenge

Tablilla de meson, a sign hung out

Tablillas, pl. the cushions of a billiard-table

Tablon, sub. m. a large board or plank

Tabloza, sub. f. painter's pallet

Tabuco, s. m. a closet

Tabuquito, s. m. a little closet

Taburete, sub. m. stool; cricket [stool

Taburetillo, s. m. a little

Taca, s. f. stain; spot

Tacamaca, s. f. a kind of gum or rosin

Tacañear, v. n. to play the knave

Tacañería, s. f. knavery || stinginess

Tacaño, s. m. a knave

Tacaño, ña, adj. sly; crafty; deceitful || stingy [spot

Tacar, v. a. to stain; to

Taceta, s. f. a vessel used in the oil-presses

Tacha, s. f. a blemish; a defect || a small nail

Tachar, v. a. to blemish to blot out || to blame

Tachon, s. m. a rasure || galloon; lace || a stud

Tachonar, v. a. to lace || to stud

Tachonería, s. f. adornment with laces or studs

Tachoso, sa, a. blemished

Tachuela, s f. a tack; a sprig

Tácitamente, ad. tacitly

Tácito, ta, a. tacit

Taciturnidad, s. f. taciturnity

Taciturno, na, a. silent; not talkative || dull; melancholy

Taco, s. m. a wood-peg || the wad or rammer of a gun || a kue, at billiards || one draught of wine upon another || oath || a sort of lance

Tacon, sub. m. the heel-piece of a shoe

Taconear, v. n. to make a noise with the heels in walking

Táctica, s. f. tacticks

Tacto, s. m. the feeling

Tafallo, s. m. a patched garment

Tafanario, s. m. the breech

Tafetan, s. m. taffety

Tafetanes, pl. colours; standards, etc.

Tafilete, s. m. a kind of thin leather

Tafiletear, v. a. to adorn with thin leather

Tafurea, s. f. a flat bottom boat

Tagarino, s. m. an ancient Moor or Moriaco

Tagarnina, s. fem. a sweet thistle good to eat

Tagarote, s. m. the [illegible]

rt of falcon || a writ-
ng clerk || a poor
ntleman
arotear, v. n. to write
ry quickly
alí, s. m. a shoulder-
lt
aral, sub. m. a place
ll of tamarisks
eño, a. m. that has a
ad beard
ona, s. f. a horse-mill
onero, s. m. a miller
ulla, s. f. a particu-
r measure or portion
f land
ur, s. m. gamester
urería, s. fem. a ga-
ing-house || a chea-
ng-trick
a, s. f. a score; a tally
ada, s. fem. a cut; a
ash; a slice || hoarse-
ess
adera, s. fem. a chap-
ing-knife || a sluice
dam
adero, s. m. a chop-
ing-block [Tajada
adilla, s. fem. dim. de
ador, s. m. a cutter ||
chopping-board
adura, s. f. a cut; an
ncision
amar, s. m. cut-water
| the starling of a
ridge
ar, ver. a. to cut; to
lash; to slice || to
ake a pen
o, s. m. cut; cutting
| a slash; a gash || a
hopping-block
ion, sub. m. a great
hopping-block
juela, s. f. } a four-leg-
uelo, s. m. } ged stool
, a. 2. such
ual, such as it is

Con tal, provided that
Tala, s. fem. the cutting down of trees || pruning; lopping || havock; ravage
Talabarte, s. m. a belt
Talador, s. m. ravager
Taladrar, v. a. to bore; to pierce
Taladro, s. m. a wimble; a piercer || a hole
Talamera, s. f. a tree prepared to catch wild pigeons
Talamo, s. m. a nuptial bed || the room where the married couple receives the compliments, etc.
Talanquera, s. f. a rail, etc. about the place prepared for a bull-feast, etc. || a place of refuge
Talante, sub. m. talent; parts || will; pleasure
Talantoso, sa, a. peaceable; gentle
Talar, ver. a. to cut down || to prune; to lop || to ravage; to waste
Talar, adj. 2. trailing; dragging
Talares, s. m. pl. winged shoes of Mercury
Talasomeli, s. m. a kind of purgative composition
Talavera, s. fem. earthen [ware
Talco, sub. m. talk (a transparent stone)
Talega, s. fem. a bag || a purse
Talegazo, s. m. a blow with a bag [sack
Talego, sub. m. a bag or
Talegon, s. m. a great bag
Taleguilla, s fem. a little bag; a pouch

Talento, s. m. talent
Talidad, s. f. what makes a thing such as it is
Taliestro, s. m. thalictrum; meadow-rue
Talion, s. m. requital; retaliation
Talionar, ver. a. to retaliate
Talisman, s. m. talisman
Talla, s. fem. carving; graving || carved work; cut || land-tax || ransom
Media talla, half relief
A' media talla, in haste; carelessly, etc.
Talladura, s. f. carving
Tallar, sub. m. a ground where the plants begin to sprout out
Tallar, v. a. to carve || to cut out
Tallarin, sub. m. a paste cut in small bits
Tallazo, sub. m. aum. de Talle || a man of an enormous size
Talle, s. m. size; pitch; stature || shape; waist || fashion; manner
Tallecer, v. n. to sprout out; to grow to a stalk
Tallecillo, s. m. dim. de Talle
Taller, s. m. any workshop || college; academy, etc.
Talleres, pl. an ancient coin in Spain
Tallista, s. m. a carver
Tallo, s. m. stalk; stem
Talludo, da, a. that has a great stalk || old; obsolete, etc.
Talmud, s. f. talmud
Talmudista, s. m. talmudist
Talon, s. m. the heel

Taloncar, *v. n. to go with great speed*
Taloneeco, ca, *a. belonging to the heels*
Talparia, *s. f. a tumour or abcess in the pericranium*
Talque, *sub. m. clay to make crucibles*
Talvina, *s. f. milk (white juice of some seeds)*
Tamandoa, *s. m. a quadruped in Brasil*
Tamañamente, *adver. as great or big as another*
Tamañito, ta, *a. so little || fearful*
Tamaño, *sub. m. magnitude; bigness; bulk*
Hombre de tamaño, *a man of consideration*
Tamaño, ña, *a. so great or big little; small*
Tamaras, *s. f. pl. cluster of dates || faggot of brush wood || chips*
Tamarindo, *s. m. tamarind*
Tamarisco, } *s. m. tamarisk*
Tamariz, }
Tamarizquito, ta, } *adj. so little*
Tamarusquito, ta, }
Tambalear, *v. n.* } *to move to and fro*
Tambalearse, *v. r.* }
Tambaleo, *sub. m. movement to and fro*
Tambanillo, *s. m. a jutting out (in a building)*
Tambarillo, *sub. mas. a small trunk with the top round*
Tambesco, *s. m. a swing (sport)*
Tambien, *conj. as well; also*
Tambo, *s. m. an inn*
Tambor, *s. m. a drum || a drummer*

Tamborete, *s. m. cap of the mast head*
Tamboril, *s. m. a timbrel || the breech*
Tamborilada, *s. f.* } *a blow on the breech, etc.*
Tamborilaso, *s. m.* }
Tamborilear, *v. n. to play on a timbrel || to praise; to cry up*
Tamborilero, *s. m. one that plays on a timbrel*
Tamborillo, *s. m. a little drum for children*
Tamborin, } *sub. m. V.* Tamboril
Tamborino, }
Tamboritear, etc. *V.* Tamborilear, etc.
Tamiz, *s. m. a sieve*
Tamo, *s. m. the hurds of hemp beaten, etc. || straw worn to dust, etc.*
Tamorlan, *s. m. the great kan of the Tartars || a proud, haugty man*
Tampoco, *adv. as little; neither*
Tamujo, *s. m. a sort of furze-bush*
Tan, *conj. as; so*
Tan, *s. m. the sound of a drum, etc.*
Tanaceto, *s. m. tansy*
Tanda, *s. f. an alternative turn || a task*
Tanganillas (en), *adver. staggeringly*
Tanganillo, *s. m. dim. de* Tángano
Tángano, *s. m. a but (to play at quoits) || the game of quoits*
Tangente, *s. f. a tangent*
Tangible, *a. 2. tangible*
Tangidera, *sub. f. a great cable*
Tantaranton, sub. masc. the noise made with a drum

Tanteador, … *calculat…*
Tantear, *v*… *late; to try, etc. to delib… deem ||* … *rate or t…*
Tanteo, *su*… *tion; m… reflectio… tion || re… ting; ta…*
Tantico, *s.*…
Tanto, *s.* … *copy || a*…
Tantos, *p*… *play or with*
Tanto, ta …
Tanto, *ad*… *many; many ||*
Tanto mej… *better — much th*…
Tañedor, … *upon m… ments*
Tañer, *v.* … *some m… ment*
Tañer, *v.* … *to conce*…
Tañido, *s.* … *of a bell… sical ins*…
Tao, *s. m* … *the lette*…
Tapa, *s. f.* … *of a box… piece of*
Tapaboca, … *on the m… hand*
Tápacas, *s*…
Tapadera, …
Tapadero …
Tapadil…

ring one's self
rantle
s. m. eaves
s. m. one that
' || a cover
, s. f. a pistol-
s. m. pl. capers
s m. V. Brial
a. to stop up
ver
} s. m. V.
in, } Tantaran-
tan
se, v. r. to co-
's face with a
s. m. a cover
le ill done, etc.
da, a. brown;
apetados, mour-
nes
m. a carpet
f. a mud wall
s. m. one that
mud walls
ub. m. a sort of
to make mud
a rammer to
th
. a. to make a
all || to wall
nce
s. f. tapestry;
gs
s. m. tapestry-
upholsterer
la, adj. close-
s. fem. a buil-
etc. with mud
[perujarse
se, v. r. V. Ta-
s. m. V. Tape-
. m. tapestry;
s || a turky-
vet

Tapizar, *v. a. to hang a room, etc.*
Tapon, *s. m. a cork*
Tapsia, *s. fem. a sort of plant*
Tapujarse, *v. r. to cover one's face with a cloak, etc.*
Tapujo, *s. m. the act of covering one's face*
Taque, *s. m. a sound like knocking at a door*
Tara, *s. f. tare and tret || a tally* [work
Taracea, *s. fem. inlaid*
Taracear, *v. a. to inlay*
Taragallo, *sub. m. a stick tied across a dog's neck*
Taragontía, *s. f. dragon-wort*
Tarando, *s. m. a tarend*
Tarángana, *s. f. a kind of pudding*
Tarantela, *s. fem. a brisk tune played to a person bitten by the tarantula*
Tarántula, *s. f. tarantula*
Tarantulado, da, *a. bitten by the tarantula*
Tarara, *s. f. the sound of a trumpet*
Tararira, *s. fem. a merry feast*
Tarasca, *s. f. a pasteboard-serpent carried about towns, etc. || an ugly, roguish woman*
Tarascada, *s. f. a bite || ill language*
Tarascar, *v. a. to bite, as dogs do* [rasca
Tarascon, *s. m. V.* Ta-
Taravilla, *s. f. mill-clapper || a great talker || talkativeness*
Taray, *s. m. tamarisk*
Tarazana, *s. f.* } *dock;*
Tarazanal, *s. m.* } *arsenal*

Tarazar, *v. a. to bite || to tear || to grieve*
Tarazon, *s. m. a piece; a slice* [slice
Tarazoncillo, *s. m. a little*
Tarbea, *s. f. a large square hall*
Tardador, *s. m. one that stays or delays*
Tardano, na, *adj. tardy; slow*
Tardanza, *s. f. delay*
Tardar, *v. n. to stay long; to delay*
Tarde, *s. f. the evening*
Tarde, *adv. late*
Tardecita, *s. f. evening; night* || slowly
Tardiamente, *adv. late-*
Tardío, día, *adj. tardy; slow || backward*
Tardo, da, *adj. tardy; slow || dull*
Tardon, na, *adj. very slow* or *dull*
Tarea, *s. f. a task*
Targum, *s. m. targum*
Tarifa, *s. f. tariff*
Tarima, *s. f. estrade*
Tarimilla, *s. fem. a little estrade* [estrade
Tarimon, *sub. m. a great*
Tarja, *s. f. a spanish coin || a tally,* or *score || a target*
Tarjas, *pl. strokes*
Tarjar, *v. a. to score*
Tarjeta, *s. fem. a little target*
Tarquin, *s. m. the mud that is taken out in cleasing a pond*
Tarquinada, *s. f. a rape*
Tarreñas, *s. f. pl. child's snappers*
Tarro, *s. m. a large wide earthen vessel*
Tarta, *s. f. a tart*
Tártago, *s. m. spurge ||*

Tartamudo, da, *a. stam-*
Tartana, *s. f. a tartane*
Tartáreo, rea, *adj. tartarean* [*rize*
Tartarizar, *v. a. to tarta-*
Tártaro, *s. m. the hell* || *tartar*
Tartera, *s. f. V.* Tortera
Taruga, *s. f. a wild beast in the west-indies*
Tarugo, *s. m. a wooden-pin*
Tas, *s. m. a little anvil*
Tasa, *s. f. assize; rate* || *diet* [*rate*
Tasacion, *s. f. setting a*
Tasadamente, *adv. barely; scantily*
Tasador, *s. m. one who sets a rate*
Tasajo, *sub. m. a slice or cut of hung beef, etc.*
Tasar, *v. a. to rate; to set a price upon...* || *to prescribe a diet, etc.*
Tascar, *v. a. to beat hemp* || *to browse*
Tascar el freno, *to champ*

Tataranieto, *sub. mas. a grand-son's grand-son*
Tate! *int. take care! no more of that!*
Tato, *s. m. a sort of scaly lizard* || *a young brother*
Tato, ta, *a. stammerer* || *the youngest child*
Tau, *s. m. V.* Tao
Taumaturgo, *sub. m. one who makes miracles*
Taurete, *sub. m. stool; cricket*
Tauro, *s. m. taurus*
Tautología, *s. fem. tautology*
Tauxía, *s. fem. damask-work*
Tavellado, da, *a. marked with the mark of the manufacturer*
Taxâtivo, va, *adj. that limits; that fixes the bounds*
Taxea, *s. f. V.* Atarxea
Taybique, *s. m. V.* Tabique

Teatral, ·
Teatro, *s*
stage
Techado,
Techar, ·
house
Techo, *s*
house |
Techumb
of the roof
Tecla, *s.*
of orga
Teclado,
of an o
Teclear,
upon t
totry s
Te Deum
Tediar, ·
to hate
Tédio, ·
aversi
Tedioso,
Tegual, ·
tax or
Teja, *s.*
Tejadillo

sub. m. shard of a || the game of quoits
small bar of gold
ew-tree [tile
eta, s. f. shard of a
ela, s. f. a little tile
hard of a tile
lo, sub. m. dim. de
jo
, s. f. web; linen;
th; any thing that is
wen || a gold or sil-
r tissue || toils to take
ld beasts || the lists
tilting, etc. || any
m — a caul
mones, s. m. pl. hu-
n figures suppor-
g any part of a buil-
g [loom
, sub. m. a weaver's
raña, s. f. a cobweb
io, s. m. telephium
a, s. f. a large nail
the plough
copio, s. m. a teles-
pe [paper
a, s. fem blotting
on, s. m. a sort of
ong silk cloth
la, s. f. a little web
.
as, s. f. p. a kind of
soles (sea-fishes)
o, s. m. an onguent
ade with honey, etc.
z, s. m. a caparison
za, s. f. a counter-
ne
nio, s. m. the office
here the king's offi-
rs sit to receive the
ties
a, s. m. wilfulness;
stinacy; theme
ático, ca, a. obsti-
te; positive
ladera, s. f. a sort
drinking-cup || a

cramp-fish. Voy. Tembleque
Temblador, ra. s. y adj. one that trembles
Temblante, adj. 2. trembling [bleque
Temblante, s. m. V. Tem-
Temblar, v. n. to tremble; to quake
Tembleque, s. m. an ornament worn by women on the head
Temblequear, } ver. n. to
Tembletear, } quake
Temblon, na, adj. trembling || fearful
Temblor, s. m. a trembling; a quaking
Temblor de tierra, an earthquake
Tembloso, sa, a. that is often trembling
Temedero, ra, a. to be feared
Temedor, ra, s. one that fears [dable
Temedor, ra, a. formi-
Temer, v, a. to fear
Temerariamente, adver. rashly
Temerario, ria, a. rash; temerarious
Temeridad, s. f. rashness
Temeron, s. m. a bully; a hector [fully
Temerosamente, ad. fear-
Temeroso, sa, a. timorous; fearful || formidable
Temible, adj. 2. formidable; terrible
Temor, s. m. fear; dread
Temoso, sa, a. positive; obstinate [drum
Témpano, s. m. a kettle-
Temperamento, ad. constitution; temper || temperature || medium; mean

Temperancia, } s. f. tempe-
Temperanza, } rance
Temperar, v. a. to temper, to moderate
Temperatura, s. f. temperature
Temperie, s. f. temper
Tempero, sub. m. time; season; disposition of a ground to receive the seeds
Tempestad, s. f. time; season || tempest; storm
Tempestividad, s. f. seasonableness
Tempestivo, va, a. seasonable
Tempestuoso, sa, a. tempestuous
Templa, s. f. a kind of paste or size used by painters [perately
Templadamente, ad. tem-
Templadico, ca, adj. a little tempered
Templado, da, a. temperate
Templador, s. m. moderator || a tuner; a pitch-pipe [ring
Templadura, s. f. tempe-
Templanza, s. f. temperance || moderation || temperature || harmony (in a picture) || temper of steel
Templar, v. a. to temper || to tune an instrument
Templario, sub. mas. a knight-templar
Temple, s. m. temperature || temper || agreement in tune || the order of the knights-templars
Pintura al temple, the painting in water colours

[illegible]

Temporalizar, *ver. a. to make temporal and perishable*

Temporalmente, *ad. temporally*

Temporaneo, nea, *adj. temporal; perishable*

Temporario, ria, *a. temporary* [*poral*

Temporero, ra, *a. tem-*

Temporizar, *v. n. to temporize* [*forward*

Tempranal, *a. 2. hasty; forward*

Tempranamente, *adver. early; betimes*

Tempranero, ra, *a. V.* Tempranal

Temprano, *adv. early*

Temprano, na, *a. hasty; forward*

Temulento, ta, *a. drunk*

Tenacear, *v. a. V.* Atenacear

Tenacear, *v. n. to be tenacious in one's opinion*

[illegible]

Tenca, *s. f. a tench*

Tencion, *s. f. a holding*

Ten con ten, *adv. with proportion and equality || by degrees*

Ten con ten, *s. m. moderation*

Tendal, *s. m. a tilt. V.* Tendalero

Tendales, *pl. the shafts of a cart* [dedero

Tendalero, *s. m. V.* Ten-

Tendalete, *subst. m. the awning of a ship*

Tendedero, *s. m. a place to hang or lay clothes out to dry*

Tendedor, *s. m. one who spreads, etc. V.* Tender

Tendejon, *s. m. a large tent* [*line*

Tendel, *s. m. a mason's*

Tendencia, *s. f. tendency*

Tendente, *a. 2. tending; driving*

Tender, *v. a. to spread abroad; to stretch out*

|| the
ce || th
a fort
nancy
Tener,
have;
keep ||
dersta
ber
Tener ex
value
oblige
bien,
appro.
Tener,
Tenerse
stand
Tenería
Tenésmo
Teniente
etc. ||
vetous
Teniente
Tenor,
conte
music.
Tension
Tentacio

ıamente, *adv. sligh- ; weakly*
ıdo (ser), *to be obli- ł to...*
ıe, *a. 2. tenuous ; in || weak || slight ; little value, etc.*
ıidad, *s. f. tenuity*
ıo, ua, *a. V.* Tenue
ıta, *s. f. a provisio- l possession*
r, *v. a. to die ; to ıge*
racia, *s. f. theocracy*
rático, ca, *adj. theo ıtical*
onía, *s. f. theogony*
ɔgal, *a. 2. theologi- l*
ɔgal, *s. m. doctor of ʋinity; theologist || a ɛbend bestowed upon ne but doctors of di- ıity* [*divinity*
ɔgía, *s. f. theology;*
ógicamente, *adver. ɛologically*
ógico, ca, *adj. theo- ıical*
ɔgizar, *v. n. to speak on theological mat- s* [*gical*
ogo, ga, *adj. theolo-*
ogo, *s. m. a theolo- ın ; a divine*
ema, *s. f. theorem*
ía, } *s. f. theory*
ica, }
ico, ca, *adj. theore- k*
o, sa, *adjec. full of ın and apt to burn*
ofía, *s. f. theology ; ʋinity*
, *s. m. turf*
péutica, *s. f. thera- ıtick*
r, *adj. third*
a, *sub. f. a devout woman of the third or- der of St. Francis || a third (in musick) || a tierce (at piquet) || a mediatrix* [*ly*

Terceramente, *ad. third-*
Tercería, *s. f. mediation || depositing goods in a third hand || pimping; bawding*
Tercerilla, *s. f. a stanza of three verses*
Tercero, *sub. m. a third person || a devout man of the third order of St. Francis || a media- tor || a tither || a pimp*
Tercero, ra, *adj. third*
Tercerol, *s. m. the after- most of the slaves that row in a galley*
Tercerola, *sub. f. a short carbine*
Tercelo, *s. m. a tiercet*
Tercia, *s. fem. the third part of a yard — tierce*
Terciado, *subst. m. short broad sword* [*ague*
Terciana, *s. f. a tertian*
Tercianario, *s. m. a man troubled with a tertian ague* [*taffety*
Tercianela, *s. f. a kind of*
Terciar, *v. a to cross ; to lay cross*
Terciar la capa, *to throw the ends of the cloak over the shoulders*
Terciar, *v. n. to comple- te the number of three || to tertiate || to plough a third time || to me- diate,* or *interpose || to pimp* or *bawd*
Tercio, cia, *adj. third*
Tercio, *s. m. a third part || a regiment || media- tion ; interposition*
Tener buenos tercios, *to be strong* or *well-limbed*

Terciopelado, *subs. mas. wrought velvet*
Terciopelero, *s. m. a vel- vet-maker*
Terciopelo, *s. m. velvet*
Terco, ca, *adj. obstina- te ; positive ; hard*
Terebintina, *s. f. turpen- tine* [*ne-tree*
Terebinto, *s. m. turpenti-*
Tereniabin, *s. m. a li- quid manna*
Terete, *a. 2. fat ; plump*
Tergiversacion, *s. f. ter- giversation*
Tergiversar, *ver. act. to shuffle ; to use fetches*
Teriaca, *s. f. treacle*
Teriacal, *a. 2. theriacal*
Tericia, *s. f. the jaundice*
Terliz, *s. m. ticken for beds || trellis*
Terma, *s. f. hot baths*
Terminacion, *s. f. end ; conclusion || termina- tion*
Terminajo, *s. m. a barba- rous word*
Terminal, *a. 2. that ter- minates*
Terminar, *v. a. to termi- nate ; to bound*
Terminar, *v. a. y n. to end*
Terminillo, *s. m. an af- fected word*
Término, *sub. m. term || bound || time || man- ner ; behaviour || dis- trict ; territory*
Terminole, *s. m. an af- fected* or *obsolete word*
Termómetro, *s. m. ther- mometer*
Terna, *s. f. three per- sons for an employ- ment* [*dice*
Ternas, *pl. two trois (at*
Ternario, ria, *a. ternary*

Ternario, *s. m. a ternary; a ternion*
Ternecico, ca, *adj. very tender*
Ternejon, *s. m. V.* Ternerón
Ternera, *s. f. a cow-calf*
Ternero, *s. m. a bull-calf*
Terneron, *s. m. a man easily moved*
Ternezuela, *s. f. dim. de* Ternera
Terneza, *s. f. tenderness*
Ternezuelo, la, *adj. very tender*
Ternilla, *s. f. gristle*
Ternilloso, sa, *a. gristly*
Ternísimamente, *adver. most tenderly*
Ternísimo, ma, *adject. most tender*
Terno, *s. m. a ternary or ternion* || *apparel; dress*
Echar ternos, *to swear; to curse*
Ternura, *s. f. tenderness*
Terquedad, } **Terquería**, } **Terqueza**, } *sub. f. obstinacy; positiveness*
Terrado, *s. m. a flat roof; a terrace*
Terrage, *s. m. V.* Terrazgo
Terraja, *s. f. an iron-tool to make screws*
Terral, *sub. m. a land-breeze*
Terraplen, *s. m. platform*
Terraplenar, *v. a. to fill with earth* || *to make a platform of earth*
Terrapleno, *s. m. Voy.* Terraplen
Terráqueo, quea, *adject. terraqueous*
Terraza, *s. f. an earthen vessel with two handles*
Terrazgo, *s. m. any piece of ground* || *the rent paid for a field*
Terrear, *v. n. to show itself (said of the earth in a sown field)*
Terregoso, sa, *a. cloddy*
Terremoto, *subst. m. an earthquake*
Terrenal, *a. 2. terrestrial*
Terrenidad, *s. f. ground; soil*
Terreno, na, *adj. terrestrial* || *earthly*
Terreno, *s. m. ground; soil* || *a space of ground*
Terreo, rea, *adj. earthy; earthen*
Terrera, *s. f. a piece of ground among rocks* || *a kind of lark*
Terrero, *s. m. a terrace* || *a place of rendezvous* || *a place of exercise* || *a but to shoot at*
Hacer terrero, *to court a lady*
Terrero, ra, *adj. terrestrial* || *humble; base, etc.*
Terrestre, *a. 2. terrestrial*
Terrestridad, *s. f. quality of the soil*
Terretremo, *s. m. earthquake*
Terrezuela, *s. f. a little land, etc.*
Terribilidad, *s. f. terribleness*
Terrible, *a. 2. terrible*
Terriblemente, *adv. terribly*
Terribleza, *s. f. terribleness*
Terrícola, *s. m. an inhabitant of the earth*
Terrífico, ca, *adj. terrifick; dreadful*
Terrígeno, na, *adj. generated in the earth*
Terrin, *s. m. a countryman*
Terrino, na, *a. earthy; earthen*
Territorio, *s. m. territory*
Terromontero, *s. m. an earthy hill*
Terron, *s. m. a clod of earth* || *a clot; a lump*
Destripa terrones, *a clown*
Terroncillo, *s. m. a little clod, etc.*
Terrontera, *s. f. a steep land, etc.*
Terror, *s. m. terror*
Terrosidad, *s. f. quality of the soil*
Terroso, sa, *adj. earthy; terreous*
Terruño, *s. m. ground; soil*
Tersar, *v. a. to cleanse; to polish*
Terso, sa, *adject. clean; clear; polished*
Tersura, *s. f. neatness; niceness*
Tertil, *s. m. a duty paid upon silk*
Tertulea, } **Tertulia**, } *sub. f. a club or meeting of persons*
Tertuliano, na, *adj. one belonging to a club*
Tesaurizar, *v. a. to treasure up*
Tesauro, *s. m. a vocabulary*
Tesera, *s. f. a square bone, etc. used by the Romans for watchword, etc.*
Tesis, *s. f. thesis*
Teso, sa, *adj. V.* Tieso
Teso, *s. m. the top of a hill, etc.*
Teson, *s. f. wilfulness; positiveness*
Tesorar, *v. a. to treasure up*
Tesorería, *s. f. treasureship* || *treasury*
Tesorero, *s. m. a treasurer*
Tesoro, *s. m. treasure; treasury*
Testa, *s. f. the fore-head* || *head; noddle* || *the front of an army*

taceo, cea, *adj. testaceous*
tador, *s. m. a testator*
tadura, *s. f. razure; scratch in writing*
tamentaria, *s. f. the execution of a will*
tamentario, *s. m. the executor of a will*
tamentario, ria, *adj. testamentary*
tamento, *s. m. testament; will*
tar, *ver. a. to make one's will* || *to raze; to scratch; to blot out*
tarudo, da, *adj. headstrong; obstinate*
tera, *s. f. front; facing* || *a stay-band* || *armour for the horse's head*
terada, *sub. f. a blow with the head* || *obstinacy* [*a place, etc.*
tero, *s. m. the front of*
tículo, *s. m. testicle*
tificacion, *s. f. testification*
tificar, *v. a. to testify*
tificativo, va, *adject. testifying* [*evidence*
tigo, *s. m. witness;*
timonial, *a. 2. testimonial* [*monial*
timonial, *s. m. a testi-*
timoniar, *v. a. to depose; to give evidence*
timoniero, *sub. m. a false witness*
timonio, *s. m. testimony; witness; evidence*
vantar un testimonio, *to accuse one falsely*
imoñero, ra, *adj. a false witness* || *impostor hypocrite*
, *s. m. a testoon*

Testudo, *s. f. a tortoise (among the ancient Romans)*
Testuz, } *s. m. the nape*
Testuzo, } *of the head*
Tesú, *s. m. a tissue*
Tesura, *s. f. hardness; solidness* || *an affected gravity*
Teta, *s. f. a teat; a pap; a breast*
Tetar, *v. a. to suckle*
Tetera, *s. f. a tea-pot*
Tetilla, *s. f. a little teat*
Teto, *s. m. V.* Teta
Tetona, *a. fem. that has great breasts*
Tetracordio, *s. m. tetrachord* [*dron*
Tetraedro, *s. m. tetrae-*
Tetrágono, *s. m. a tetragonal figure*
Tetragrámaton, *s. m. the name of God composed of four letters*
Tetrarca, *s. m. a tetrarch*
Tetrarquía, *s. f. tetrarchy*
Tétrico, ca, *adj. tetrical; tetricous*
Tetro, tra, *adj. dark*
Tetuda, *a. f. V.* Tetona
Teucrio, *s. m. the bitter sage*
Texedor, ra, *s. a weaver*
Texedura, *s. f. weaving*
Texer, *v. a. to weave*
Texido, *subs. m. tissue; cloth; linen, etc.*
Texo, *s. m. a yew-tree*
Texon, *s. m. a badger; a brock* || *a yew-tree*
Texto, *s. m. text*
Textorio, ria, *adjec. belonging to weaver's trade*
Rayo textorio, *a shuttle*
Textual, *a. 2. textuary*
Textualista, *s. m. textuarist*

Textura, *s. f. texture*
Tez, *s. f. the colour of one's face; complexion*
Tezado, da, *adj. black*
Ti, *pron. thee*
Tia, *s. f. aunt*
Tiara, *sub. f. tiara* || *the pope's triple crown*
Tibia, *s. f. a flute*
Tibiamente, *adv. lukewarmly* [*ness*
Tibieza, *s. f lukewarm-*
Tibio, bia, *a. lukewarm*
Tibor, *s. m. a china-jar*
Tiburon, *s. m. a shark (sea-fish)* [*time*
Tiempecillo, *s. m. a short*
Tiempo, *sub. m. time* || *age; years* || *weather* || *tense*
Tienda, *s. f. a tent* || *a shop* || *a tilt or awning*
Tienta, *s. f. a surgeon's probe*
Tiento, *s. m. the feeling or groping* || *the stick of a blind man* || *caution; care; prudence* || *a rope-dancer's pole* || *a painter's maulstick* || *a flourish in musick before playing* || *a stroke*
Andar á tientas, *to walk groping* [*derly*
Tiernamente, *adv. ten-*
Tierno, na, *adj. tender*
Tierra, *s. fem. earth* || *a man's country* || *land* || *field*
Tiesamente, *adv. stiffly* || *strongly*
Tieso, sa, *adj. hard; solid* || *strong; robust* || *stiff* || *bold* || *headstrong*
Tieso, *s. m. hardness; solidness*
Tiesto, *s. m. a pot*

|| *a pot to set flowers*

Tifon, *subs. m. a whirl-wind*

Tigre, *s. m. a tiger*

Tildar, *v. a. to make a title* or *dash; to accent* || *to blemish; to brand* || *to rase; to blot out*

Tilde, *s. m. a title; a dash; an accent*

Tildon, *s. m. aum. de* Tilde

Tilla, *s. f. a ship's deck*

Tilo, *s. m. a linden-tree*

Timbal, *s. m. a kettle-drum* [*drummer*

Timbalero, *s. m. kettle-*

Timbre, *sub. m. helmet* (*in blasonry*)

Timiama, *s. f. a kind of perfume* || *red storax*

Timidamente, *adv. fearfully*

Timidez, *s. f. timidity*

Timido, da, *adj. timid; fearful* [*pole*

Timon, *s. f. helm* || *coach-*

Timonear, *v. n. to steer at sea*

Timonel, *s. m. steersman*

Timonera, *s. f. the helm-port*

Timonero, *s. m. steersman*

Timorato, ta, *adj. timorous; scrupulous*

Timpanillo, *s. m. dim. de* Timpano

Timpano, *s. m. a kettle-drum* || *the tympanum of the ear* || *tympan* || *axis* [*V.* Tinaja

Tina, *s. f. a dier's copper.*

Tinada, *s. fem. a heap of fire wood*

Tinado, } *s. m. a hut to*
Tinador, } *shut sheep in*

Tinaja, *s. f. an earthen jar*

Tinajeria, *s. f. the place where the earthen jars are kept*

Tinajero, *s. m. one who makes earthen jars. V.* Tinajeria

Tinajilla, *s. fem. a little earthen jar*

Tinajon, *sub. m. a great earthen jar* [jilla

Tinajuela, *s. f. V.* Tina-

Tinea, *s. f. moth*

Tinelo, *s. m. a dining-room* [*con*

Tinge, *s. m. a sort of fal-*

Tinieblas, *s. f. p. darkness* || *tenebres* (*a service in the Romish Church*)

Tino, *s. m. judgement; sense* || *facility, etc. got by the habit*

Tinta, *s. f. die; tincture* || *ink* [*tinge*

Tintar, *ver. a. to die; to*

Tinte, *s. m. dying* || *die; hue; colour* || *a dier's shop*

Tintero, *s. m. an inkhorn*

Tintillo, *sub. m. reddish wine* || *a fool*

Tinto, ta, *adj. died*
Vino tinto, *red wine*

Tintor, *s. m. a dier*

Tintoreria, *s. f. die-house*

Tintorero, ra, *s. a dier*

Tintura, *s. f. tincture; dying* || *die; hue; colour* || *women's paint*

Tinturar, *v. a. to die; to tinge* [*stinginess*

Tiña, *s. f. scurf; scall* ||

Tiñoso, sa, *adj. scurfy* || *stingy* [*oldman*

Tio, s. m. *an uncle* || *an*

Tiorba, s. f. *a theorbo*

Tiple, sub. m. *the treble* (*in musick*)

Tipo, s. m. *a type*

Tipografia, *s. f. typogra-phy* [*phi*

Tipógrafo, *s. m. typogra-*

Tipmna, *s. f. V.* Ti...

Tiquismiquis, *s. m. affec-ted words or expres-sions*

Tira, *s. fem. a band; a swelt of cloth, etc.*

Tirabraguero, *subs. m. a truss* (*for a rupture*)

Tirabuzon, *sub. m. cork-screw*

Tiracol, } *s. m. a shoul-*
Tiracuello, } *der-belt*

Tirada, *s. fem. throwing* || *a distance from one place to another* || *a long while*

Tiradera, *s. f. an arrow* || *the string of a bow*

Tirado (oro), *s. m. gold wire or thread*

Tirador, *s. m. one that throws; shooter* || *press-man* (*among printers*)

Tirador de oro, *a gold wire-drawer*

Tiramira, *s. f. a long ridge of mountains* || *a long and narrow way etc.* [*and let go*

Tiramollar, *v. a. to pu...*

Tiranamente, *ad. tyrannically*

Tirania, *s. f. tyranny*

Tiránicamente, *adv. tyrannically* [*nical*

Tiránico, ca, *adj. tyran-*

Tiranillo, *s. m. a petty tyrant* [*nise*

Tiranizar, *v. a. to tyran-*

Tirano, *s. m. a tyrant*

Tirano, na, *adj. tyrannical* [*ched, etc.*

Tirante, a. 2. *stiff; stre...*

Tirante, sub. m. *a beam, in a roo...*

Tirantes, *pl. traces (for draught-horses)*
Tirantez, *s. f. the length*
Tirapie, *s. m. shoe-maker's stirrup*
Tirar, *ver. n. to throw; to cast; to shoot* ‖ *to draw; to pull; to pluck* ‖ *to get* ‖ *to stretch* ‖ *to incline to* ‖ *to lug* or *tug*
Tirela, *s. fem. a kind of striped stuff*
Tireta, *s. fem. a tagged point*
Tiricia, *s. f. the jaundice*
Tirilla, *s. f. a little band* or *welt* ‖ *a woman's tucker*
Tirillo, *s. m. a little piece of cannon*
Tiritaña, *s. fem. linsey-woolsey*
Tiritar, *ver. n. to shiver with cold*
Tiritona, *s. f. a feigned shivering*
Tiro, *s. m. a throw; a cast; a shot* ‖ *a gun* or *cannon* ‖ *a charge (for a gun, etc.)* ‖ *a theft* ‖ *wrong; hurt* ‖ *a cheat* or *trick* ‖ *a trace (for draught-horses)*
Tiros, *pl. the hangers of a belt*
Tirocinio, *s. m. apprenticeship* ‖ *probation-time*
Tiron, *s m. tyro. V.* Estiron
Tirria, *sub. f. aversion; antipathy*
Tirteafuera! *int. stand away! draw off! be gone!*
Tirso, *s. m. Bacchus's javelin*
Tisana, *s. f. ptisan*
Tisica, *s. f. phthisick*
Tisico, ca, *a. phthisical*
Tisis, *s. f. phthisick*
Tisú, *s. m. a tissue*
Titere, *s. m. puppet-show*

Titerero, } *s. f. a puppet-player*
Titerista, }
Titi, *s. m. a very little monkey*
Titilacion, *s. f. titillation*
Titimalo, *sub. m. milk-thistle*
Titiritayna, *s. fem. any merry feast*
Titiritero, *s. m. a puppet-player*
Tito, *s. m. a sort of kidney-beans* ‖ *a chamber-pot*
Titubear, *v. n. to stagger; to waver*
Titular, *a. 2. titular*
Titular, *v. a. to entitle; to affix a title*
Titular, *v. n. to obtain a title from the king*
Titulillo, *s. m. a little title*
Andar en titulillos, *to stand upon trifles*
Titulizado, da, *adj. one who has a title*
Titulo, *s. m. title* ‖ *voucher*
Tixera, *sub. fem. a pair of scissars* ‖ *a sawing trestle* ‖ *a shearer* ‖ *the first feather in a hawk's wing* ‖ *a trench*
Tixerada, } *s. fem. a cut with the scissars*
Tixeretada, }
Tixeretas, *s. f. pl. little scissars* ‖ *stings of a vine*
Tixeretear, *v. n. to give repeated cuts with scissars*
Tizna, *s. f. a black matter to smutt with*
Tiznar, *v. a. to smutt; to besmut* ‖ *to blemish*
Tizne, *s. 2. soot*
Tiznon, *s. m. black spot*
Tizo, *s. m. a coal that is not well kindled*
Tizon, *s. m. a fire-brand* ‖ *blasted corn* ‖ *a blemish*

Tizona, *s. f. a sword*
Tizonazo, *s. m. a stroke with a fire-brand*
Tizoncillo, *s. m. a little fire-brand* ‖ *blasted corn*
Tizonera, *s. f. coal-pit*
To! *a word used to call a dog*
Toaja, } *s. f. a towel* ‖ *a pillow-case*
Toalla, }
Toalleta, *s. f. a little towel* ‖ *a napkin*
Toba, *s. fem. soft sandy stone; ragstone* ‖ *scurf on the teeth*
Tobaja, Toballa. *V.* Toaja, etc.
Toballeta, } *sub. f. Voy.* Toalleta
Tobelleta, }
Tobera, *s. f. a hole for the bellows in a goldsmith's furnace*
Tobillo, *s. m. the ancle-bone*
Toca, *s. fem. a woman's coif*
Tocado, *s. m. a head-dress*
Tocador, *s. m. one who touches, etc.* ‖ *a night-cap* ‖ *a lady's dressing room*
Tocamiento, *s. m. a touch* ‖ *contact*
Tocante, *adv. touching; relating to*
Tocar, *v. a. to touch* ‖ *to reach* ‖ *to play on any instrument* ‖ *to sound a trumpet* ‖ *to wind a horn* ‖ *to beat a drum* ‖ *to move* or *affect* ‖ *to dress the head* ‖ *to beat* or *chastise* ‖ *to cheat*
Tocar, *v. n. to touch; to concern; to belong to* ‖ *to fall to one's lot or share*
Tocarse, *v. r. to put on hat*

Tocayo, ya, *a. namesake*
Tochedad, *sub. f. roughness* || *ignorance* || *folly; silliness*
Tochear, *v. a. to bar the door with a round pole*
Tocho, *s. m. a round-pole; a bar*
Tocho, cha, *adj. rough; clownish* || *ignorant* || *fool; silly*
Tochura, *s. f. buffoonry*
Tocinero, ra, *s. one who sells bacon*
Tocino, *s. m. bacon*
Tocon, *s. m. the stump of a tree, or of a limb*
Todavia, *adv. nevertheless* || *also*
Todo, da, *a. all; whole*
Todo, *s. m. the whole*
Toesa, *s. fem. six feet; a fathom*
Toga, *s. f. toga* || *a magistrate's gown*
Togado, da, *adjec. that wears a gown*
Tolanos, *s. m. pl. lampass (horse's disease)*
Toldadura, *s. f. a cloth spread to keep off the sun*
Toldar, *ver. a. to cover with a tilt, etc.*
Toldero, *s. m. a huckster*
Toldillo, *s. m. a sedan*
Toldo, *sub. m. a tilt; an awning; a pavilion, etc.* || *an huckster's shop* || *pride; ostentation*
Tolerable, *a. 2. tolerable*
Tolerablemente, *adv. tolerably*
Tolerancia, *s. f. patience* || *sufferance* || *toleration*
Tolerar, *v. a. to suffer* || *to tolerate*
Toletes, *s. m. pl. tholes*
Tolle, tolle, *int. take away*
Tollo, *s. m. a sea-cat* || *slough; mud*
Tolondro, } *s. m. swelling; bruise; blow* || *a blunderer*
Tolondron, }
Tolones, *s. m. p. lampass*
Tolva, *s. f. the hopper of a mill*
Tolvanera, *s. f. a wirlwind of dust*
Toma, } *s. f. a taking* || *a pinch of snuff; a dish of coffee, etc.* || *an aperture made to take water out of a river*
Tomada, }
Tomadero, *s. m. hold* || *the aperture made to take water out of a river*
Tomado, *s. m. a sort of furbelow*
Tomador, *s. m. taker*
Tomadores, *pl. gaskets*
Tomadura, *s. f. a taking* || *a pinch of snuff, etc.*
Tomajon, na, *adj. one that takes every thing*
Tomar, *v. a. to take; to lay hold of* || *to leap the mare, etc.* || *to take away; to steal*
Tomar por tal parte, *to strike up such a way* — prestado, *to borrow* — la sangre, *to stanch bleeding* — de coro, *to learn by heart*
Tomarse, *ver. r. to grow rusty* || *drunk*
Tomarse de vino, *to grow drunk*
Tomate, *s. m. a red fruit so called*
Tomento, } *cow's hair, hards, etc.*
Tomiento, }
Tomillar, *s. m. a ground where thyme grows*
Tomillo, *s. m. thyme*
Tomin, *s. m. a weight of twelve grains*
Tominejo, *s. m. a very small bird in the west-indies*
Tomiza, *s. fem. a small cord of esparto*
Tomo, *s. m. a tome, or volume* || *bulk; substance* || *importance; value*
Tomon, na, *a. V.* Tomajon
Ton, *s. m. a tone* || *motive; occasion*
Tona, *s. f. the surface of any liquor*
Tonada, *s. f. a song*
Tonadica, } *s. f. a little song*
Tonadilla, }
Tonante, *a. m. thundering*
Tonar, *v. a. to thunder*
Tondino, *s. m. a moulding so called*
Tonel, *s. m. a cask*
Tonelada, *s. f. a tun*
Tonelería, *s. f. cooperage*
Tonelero, *s. m. a cooper*
Tonelete, *s. m. the lower part of a Roman garment*
Tono, *s. m. tone* || *tune*
Tonsura, *s. f. tonsure* || *shearing*
Tonsurar, *v. a. to shave one's crown* || *to shear*
Tontada, *s. f. folly; foppery; impertinence*
Tontazo, *sub. m. a great silly fellow*
Tontear, *v. n. to play the fool*
Tontedad, } *sub. f. folly; silliness*
Tontería, }
Tontillo, *sub. m. hoop; fardingale*
Tonto, ta, *a. fool; silly*
Tontonazo, za, *adj. aum. de Tonto*
Toñina, *s. f. a tunny*

Topa, *s. f. a pulley*
Topacio, *s. m. a topaz*
Topada, *s. f. V.* Topetada
Topadizo (hacerso), *to go to meet one*
Topador, *s. m. one who strikes or meets || a ram that butts*
Topar, *v. a. to strike* or *beat against || to meet || to butt || to consist* or *lie in || to agree*
Toparca, *s. m. toparch*
Toparquía, *s. f. toparchy*
Tope, *s. m. the striking* or *running against... || point; matter || obstacle; hindrance || fray; quarrel || the top of a mast, etc.*
Topetada, *s. f. a butting*
Topetar, *v. a. to butt, as rams do || to strike* or *beat against... || to stumble*
Topeton, *s. m. a striking* or *running against...*
Topetudo, da, *adj. that butts*
Tópico, ca, *adj. topical*
Topinaria, *s. f. a mole-hill* [*stumbler*
Topo, *s. m. a mole || a*
Topografía, *s. f. topography* [*graphical*
Topográfico, ca, *a. topo-*
Topógrafo, *s. m. topographer*
Toque, *s. m. a touch || contact || the touching gold on a touchstone || point; matter || a stroke or blow || a ring of bells || the beat of drum*
Toquero, *s. m. a weaver of a fine sort of head-dress* [*coif, etc.*
Toquilla, *s. fem. a little*

Tora, *s. f. a jew-family || the tribute that a jew family paid*
Torada, *s. f. a number of bulls*
Toral, *adjec. 2. that has most strength*
Torbellino, *s. m. a whirlwind*
Torce, *s. f. the link of a chain, etc. || a necklace*
Torcecuello, *s. m. a wryneck*
Torcedero, *s. m. an instrument to twist with*
Torcedor, *s. m. a twister || a twisting-spindle*
Torcedura, *s. f. twisting || tart sort of wine*
Torcer, *v. a. to twist; to wrest || to bend || to retort* [*one's way*
Torcer, *v. n. to go out of*
Torcerse, *v. r. to retract an opinion || to be put out of joint || to turn; to be spoiled*
Torcida, *s f. match; wick*
Torcidamente, *ad. crookedly; aslope* [*silk*
Torcidillo, *s. m. twisted*
Torcido, *s. m. a kind of sweet meat* [*gripes*
Torcijon, *s. m. colick;*
Torcimiento, *s. m. twisting || bending || going out of the way || periphrasis*
Torculado, *s. m. the worm of a screw*
Tórculo, *m. a little press*
Tordillo (caballo), *s. m. a flea bitten horse*
Tordo, *s. m. a thrush*
Tordo, da, *a. V.* Tordillo
Toreador, *s. m.* one that rides at bulls
Torear, *ver. n.* to ride at bulls in the bull-feasts

|| to drive a cow to the bull
Toreo, *s. m. a bull-feast*
Torero, *s. m. a footman that fight bulls*
Tores, *sub. m. torus (in architecture)*
Torete, *sub. m. a lively young bull*
Torga, *s. f. a stick tied across a hog's neck*
Toril, *sub. m. the place where they shut up the bulls for the bull-feasts*
Torillo, *s. m. a young or little bull || perineum*
Torionda, *s. f. a cow that is in lust*
Torloroto, *s. m. a sort of flute among shepherds*
Tormenta, *s. f. a storm; a tempest* [mentar
Tormentar, etc. *V.* Ator-
Tormentar, *ver. n. to be beaten by a tempest*
Tormentario, ria, *adjec. belonging to cannons*
Tormentila, *s. f. tormentil* [*sprit-top-mast*
Tormentin, *sub. m. bow-*
Tormento, *s. m. torment || the rack || a cannon*
Tormentoso, sa, *adject. stormy*
Tormo, *s. m. a rock separate from all others*
Torna, *s. f. restitution || return*
Tornaboda, *s. f. the second day's feast at a wedding*
Tornada, *s. f. a return || a trip*
Tornadizo, za, *a. deserter; renegade*
Tornadura, *s. f.* restitution || return || a measure of about ten feet
Tornar, *v. n.* to retur

Tornar, *v. a. to turn; to return*

Tornasol, *s. m. turnsol || any changeable colour*

Tornasolado, da, *adj. of a changeable colour*

Tornátil, *adjec. 2. made with a turner's wheel*

Tornaviage, *s. m. return from a journey*

Tornaviron, *s. m. Voy.* Torniscon

Torneador, *s. m. a turner || a fighter in a tournament*

Tornear, *v. a. to turn, as turners do || to turn about || to fight in a tournament*

Torneo, *s. m. a tournament*

Tornera, *s. f. a nun who looks to the turning-box*

Tornero, *s. m. a turner*

Tornillero, *s. m. a deserter*

Tornillo, *s. m. a screw* or *vice || desertion*

Torniscon, *s. m. a blow with the back of the hand*

Torno, *s. m. a turn || a turner's lath || a spinning-wheel || a turning-box || axis || regress*

Toro, *s. m. a bull || torus (in architecture)*

Torondon, *s. m. V.* Tolondro

Toronja, *s. f. a kind of citron*

Toronjil, *subs. m. balm-gentle*

Toronjo, *s. m. a citron-tree*

Toroso, sa, *adj. strong; robust*

Torozon, *s. m. griping of the guts*

Torpe, *adj. 2. torpid || dull; slow || base; vile || obscene; filthy*

Torpedad, *s. f. V.* Torpeza

Torpedo, *s. m. cramp-fish*

Torpemente, *adv. dully; slowly || basely*

Torpeza, *s. f. dullness; slowness || turpitude, obscenity || baseness; vileness*

Torrar, *v. a. to toast || to torrefy*

Torre, *s. f. a tower || a steeple || a country-seat*

Torres de viento, *castles in the air*

Torrear, *v. a. to fortify with towers*

Torrefaccion, *s. f. torrefaction*

Torrejon, *s. m. a small tower; a turret*

Torrente, *s. m. a torrent*

Torreon, *s. m. a large tower*

Torreznada, *s. f. an omelet with slices of bacon in it*

Torreznero, *s. m. a lazy fellow that sits always over the fire*

Torrezno, *s. m. a rasher of bacon || a large volume*

Tórrido, da, *adj. torrid*

Torrijas, *s. f. pl. slices of bread soaked in eggs, then fried in oil, etc.*

Torrontera, *s. f.* } *a hill*
Torrontero, *s. m.* }

Torrontes, *s. f. a kind of white grape*

Torta, *s. f. a pie* or *pasty*

Tortada, *s. f. a great pie of pigeons*

Tortera, *s. f. a pasty-pan || a notch in the end of the spindle*

Torticeramente, *adver. wrongly*

Tortijon, *s. m. griping of the guts*

Tortilla, } *s. f. a little*
Tortita, } *pasty || an omelet*

Tórtola, *s. f. turtle-dove*

Tortolico, *s. mas. young turtle-dove*

Tortolilla, } *s. m. a little*
Tortolillo, } *turtle-dove*

Tórtolo, *s. m. the male of the turtle-dove*

Tortozon, *s. m. a kind of grape*

Tortuga, *s. f. a tortoise*

Tortuosamente, *ad. crookedly*

Tortuoso, sa, *a. tortuous*

Tortura, *sub. f. crookedness || torture; rack*

Torvisco, *s. m. spurge*

Torvo, va, *adj. torvous; fierce*

Torzal, *s. m. any thread twisted*

Torzon, *s. m. griping of the guts*

Torzonado, da, *a. griped*

Tos, *s. f. cough*

Toscamente, *av. coarsely*

Tosco, ca, *adj. coarse; rough || rude; clownish*

Tosecilla, *s. f. an affected cough*

Toser, *v. n. to cough*

Tosidura, *s. f. coughing*

Tosigar, *v. a. to poison*

Tósigo, *s. m. the venemous juice of the yew tree || any poison || pain; grief*

Tosigoso, sa, *a. poisoned*

Tosquedad, *s. f. coarseness; roughness*

Tostada, *s. f. a toast*

Tostador, *s. m. toaster, a toasting iron, etc.*

Tostar, *v. a. to toast; parch*

Toston, *s. m. chi*

...se, *when toasted* ‖ *a silver coin, in Portugal*
Total, *a. 2. total; entire*
Total, *s. m. total*
Totalidad, *s. f. totality*
Totalmente, *adv. totally*
Totilimundi, *s. m. a rareeshow*
Totovía, *sub. f. a tufted lark*
Toucan, *s. m. toucan (a bird in Brasil)*
Toxicado, da, *a. poisoned*
Tóxico, *s. m. poison*
Toxo, *sub. m. a kind of broom*
Toyson, *s. m. fleece*
Toza, *s. m. slump*
Tozal, *s. mas. hill; eminence*
Tozolada, *s. f.* } *a blow*
Tozolon, *s. m.* } *on the nape of the neck*
Tozudo, da, *a. headstrong*
Tozuelo, *s. m. the nape of the neck*
Traba, *s. f. a linking; a knitting, etc.* ‖ *tie; knot; chain* ‖ *obstacle; hindrance*
Trabas, *pl. fetters (for the horse's legs)*
Trabacuenta, *s. f. a mistake in any account* ‖ *quarrel; dispute*
Trabadero, *s. m. the thinner part of a beast's foot*
Trabado, da, *a. strong; robust*
Trabadura, *s. f. joining together*
Trabajadamente, *adver. laboriously*
Trabajado, da, *adj. troubled; grieved, etc.*
Trabajador, *sub. m. a labourer*
Trabajar, *v. n. to work* ‖ *to labour* ‖ *to warp (as boards do)*
Trabajar, *v. a. to trouble; to disorder* ‖ *to work* ‖ *to manage a horse*
Trabajillo, *s. m. dim. de* Trabajo
Trabajo, *s. m. work; labour* ‖ *pain; trouble; grief*
Trabajosamente, *ad. laboriously*
Trabajoso, sa, *a. laborious; troublesome* ‖ *imperfect*
Trabal (clavo), *s. m. a nail that serves to join beams together*
Trabar, *v. a. to link; to knit; to join together* ‖ *to contend for; to dispute* ‖ *to fight* ‖ *to lay hold on* ‖ *to censure* ‖ *to shackle*
Trabar la vista, *to squint*
Trabarse de palabras, *to quarrel with one*
Trabazon, *s. m. knitting; joining together* ‖ *connexion*
Trabe, *s. f. a beam*
Trábea, *sub. fem. gown (among the ancients)*
Trabilla, *s. fem. dim. de* Traba
Trabon, *sub. m. an iron ring put to the feet of a horse*
Trabuca, *s. f. serpent (a kind of fire-work)*
Trabucacion, *s. f. confusion, disorder*
Trabucante, *adj. 2. that weighs; of full weight*
Trabucar, *v. a. to overturn; to turn topsy-turvy* ‖ *to trouble; to confound*
Trabucar, *v. n. to stumble* ‖ *to bear down the weight*
Trabucarse, *v. r. to mistake, to equivocate*
Trabucazo, *s. m. a blunderbuss's shot* ‖ *a sudden misfortune*
Trabuco, *s. m. a blunderbuss* ‖ *a battering-ram, etc.*
Tracamundana, *s. f. a ridiculous exchange*
Tracias, *s. mas. north-north-west wind*
Tracista, *s. m. one that draws the model of a work, etc.* ‖ *a cheat; a sharper*
Tracto, *s. m. a space of time*
Tradicion, *s. fem. tradition*
Traduccion, *s. f. translation*
Traducir, *v. a. to translate* ‖ *to change*
Traductor, *s. m. translator*
Traedor, *sub. m. he that brings or carries*
Traer, *v. a. to bring; to carry; to fetch* ‖ *to wear* ‖ *to draw* ‖ *to persuade or engage*
Traer en lenguas, *to speak ill of...* — las piérnas, *to rub the legs*
Traerse bien, *to be nicely dressed*
Trafagar, *v. n. to traffick* ‖ *to travel; to wander*
Trafago, *s. m. traffick* ‖ *care; trouble*
Trafagon, *s. m. a trading man* ‖ *a busy-body*
Trafalmejo, ja, *a. bold*
Traficacion, *s. f. traffick*
Traficar, *v. n. to traffick*
Traficante, *s. m. a trading man*

Tráfico, *s. m. traffick*
Tragacanta, *s. fem. tragacanth*
Tragacete, *s. m. a moorish dart*
Tragadero, *sub. mas. the weasand pipe || abyss; gulph*
Tragador, *sub. m. a devourer; a glutton*
Tragafees, *s. m. a traitor*
Tragaldabas, *s. m. a glutton* [*runner*
Tragaleguas, *s. m. a great*
Tragaluz, *s. f. a dormer-window; an oval*
Tragamallas, *sub. mas. a cheat; a sharper*
Tragantada, *s. f. a very large draught*
Traganton, na, *sub. a glutton*
Tragar, *v. a. to swallow; to devour* [*draught*
Tragazo, *sub. m. a large*
Tragazon, *s. f. gluttony*
Trage, *s. m. apparel; garb; dress || colour; pretence*
Tragear, *v. a. to dress a person*
Tragedia, *s. f. tragedy*
Tragedioso, sa, *adj. tragical* [*of stag*
Tragélafo, *s. m. a kind*
Trágico, ca, *a. tragical*
Trágicamente, *adv. tragically* [*comedy*
Tragicomedia, *s. f. tragi-*
Tragin, *s. m. carriage*
Traginante, *s. m. a carrier* [*goods*
Traginar, *v. a. to carry*
Traginero, *s m. a carrier*
Tragino, *s. m. carriage*
Tragio, *sub. m. a plant so called*
Trago, *s. m. a draught of any liquor*

A' tragos, *by degrees*
Tragon, na, *a. glutton*
Tragonia, *s. f. gluttony*
Tragopana, } *s. f. a sea-*
Tragopánade, } *war (a large bird)*
Traguillo, } *s. m. a little*
Traguito, } *draught; a sip*
Traicion, *s. f. treason*
Traicionero, ra, *a. treasonable*
Traida, *s. f. bringing; fetching*
Traidor, *s. m. a traitor*
Traidor, ra, *adj. traiterous* [*terously*
Traidoramente, *ad. trai-*
Traidorcico, ca, *s. a little traitor*
Trailla, *sub. f. a leash || a sort of cart*
Traiña, *s. f. V.* Boliche
Traite, *s. m. dressing of cloth*
Trama, *s. f. woof || plot*
Tramador, *s. m. weaver || plotter* [|| *to plot*
Tramar, *ver. a. to weave*
Trámite, *s. m. a path*
Tramo, *s. m. a piece of land, etc. || a flight (of a stair-case)*
Tramojo, *s. m. the lowest and hardest part of the reed of any grain || the tie that binds the sheaves*
Tramontana, *s. fem. the north-wind* or *side || pride*
Tramontano, na, *a. ultramontane*
Tramontar, *v. n. to set beyond the mountains* (said of the sun)
Tramontarse, v. r. to run *away*
Tramoya, s. fem. *wing;* decoration ; machine

(of a stage) || cheat; fraud
Tramoyista, *s. m. decorator; machinist || a cheat; a deceiver*
Trampa, *s. f. a trap; a pitfall; a snare || a cheating trick*
Trampal, *s. m. a slough; a miry place* [*fig*
Trampantojo, *s. m. pre*
Trampear, *v. n. to shark; to sharp || to cheat, t trick*
Trampilla, *s. fem. a littl cheat* or *fraud*
Trampista, *s. m. a sharpe*
Tramposo, sa, *adj. sha king; cheating*
Tranca, *s. f. a door-bar*
Trancada, *s. fem. a larg stride || a blow wit a bar*
Trancahilo, *s. m. a kno in the thread* [*a shi*
Trancanil, *s. m. knee, i*
Trancar, *v. a. to bar*
Trancazo, *sub. m. a blow with a bar*
Trance, *s. m. a ticklis* or *dangerous point || the last gasp*
Trance de armas, *a battl*
Trancelin, *sub. m. littl tresses*
Tranchete, *s. m. shoema ker's cutting-knife*
Tranco, *sub. m. a larg stride || threshold*
Tranquera, *s. f. a palisade* [*post || linte*
Tranquero, *sub. m. door*
Tranquilamente, *adver quietly*
Tranquilar, *v. a. to quiet,* to tranquilize
Tranquilidad, s. f. tranquillity [tranqui
Tranquilizar, ver. a

s. *f. a little*

a, *adj. tran-*
n; quiet
. beyond
. s. fem. tran-

na, *a. tran-*

cia, *s. fem.*
ency
tal, *adj. 2.*
ent
, *ver. n. to*

ver. act. to

sub. m. pro-
se
adj. 2. pas-
sient [*fer*
. a. to trans-
le, *a. 2. that*
ansfigured
ion, *s. fem.*
ation
se, *v. r. to be*
ed
, *s. f. trans-*

tâ, *a. trans-*

v. a. to copy
transparent

, *ver. act. to*

ion, *s. fem.*
ation
lor, *sub. m.*
er
niento, *s. m.*
ing
, *ver. a. to*

tivo, va, *adj.*
he power of
ing
v. a. to rub

one thing against ano-ther

Transfretar, *v. a. to go over the sea*

Transfuga, **Transfugo**, *s. m. a run-away; a de-serter*

Transfundir, *ver. a. to transfuse*

Transfusion, *s. f. trans-fusion* [*transgress*

Transgredir, *ver. act. to*

Transgresion, *s. f. trans-gression*

Transgresor, *s. m. trans-gressor* [*tion*

Transicion, *s. f. transi-*

Transido, da, *a. starved with hunger, etc.* || *stingy* [*sact*

Transigir, *v. a. to tran-*

Transitar, *v. n. to pass*

Transitivo, va, *a. tran-sitive*

Transito, *s. m. passage*

Transitoriamente, *adver. transitorily*

Transitorio, ria, *a. tran-*

, *adv. metaphorically*

Translaticio, cia, **Translato, ta**, *a. me-taphorical*

Transmarino, na, *adj. transmarine*

Transmigracion, *s. fem. transmigration*

Transmigrar, *ver. n. to transmigrate*

Transmisible, *a. 2. trans-missive*

Transmision, *s. f. trans-mission* [*mit*

Transmitir, *v. a. to trans-*

Transmutable, *a. 2. trans-mutable*

Transmutacion, *s. fem. transmutation*

Transmutar, *ver. a. to transmute*

Transmutativo, va, **Transmutatorio, ria**, *a. ha-ving the po-wer of transmuting*

Transparencia, *s. fem. transparency*

Transparentarse, *v. r. to be or grow transparent*

Transparente, *a. 2. trans-parent*

Transpiracion, *s. f. trans-piration*

Transpirar, *v. n.* **Transpirarse**, *v. rec. to transpire*

Transportacion, *s. fem. transportation*

Transportamiento, *sub. m. transportation* || *a transport; a violent motion*

Transportar, *ver. a. to transport* || *to trans-pose*

Transportarse, *ver. r. to fall into a passion*

Transporte, *s. m. trans-port*

Transportin, *sub. m. an upper mattress upon a bed*

Transposicion, *s. f. trans-position*

Transubstanciacion, *s. f. transubstantiation*

Transubstanciar, *v. a. to transubstantiate*

Transversal, *a. 2. trans-versal* || *collateral*

Transadera, *s. fem. twisted knot; tresses*

Tranzar, *v. n. to twist into tresses*

Trapa, *s. f. V. Tripula*

Trapacear, *v. a. to cheat in selling, etc.*

Trapaceria, *s. f. a cheat; a fraud*

Trapacero, ra, *adj. V.* Trapacista

Trapacete, *s. m. a broker's or a banker's book*

Trapacista, *s. m. a cheater in selling, etc.*

Trapajo, *s. m. a rag; a tatter* [*tattered*

Trapajoso, sa, *a. ragged;*

Trápala, *s. f. a confused noise of clattering with the feet, etc.*

Trapaza, *s. f. a cheat; a fraud* [cear

Trapazar, *v. a. V.* Trapa-

Trapazo, *sub. m. an old rag, etc. ‖ a knavish trick*

Trapería, *s. f. a draper's shop ‖ a place full of rags ‖ a ragman's shop*

Trapero, *s. m. a ragman*

Trapezio, *s. m. trapesium*

Trapiche, *s. m. a sugar-mill* [Trapo

Trapillo, *s. m. dim. de*

Trapisonda, *s. f. bustle; tumult*

Trapo, *s. m. rag; tatter; clout ‖ ragged people ‖ cloth ‖ a suit of sails*

Traque, *s. f. the noise of a squib when bursting*

Traquea, *s. f. weasand; wind pipe*

Traquear, *v. n. to crack; to creek; to burst ‖ to cry like a story ‖ to clatter like a drum etc. ‖ to move; to stir*

Traqueo, *s. m. crackling; creeking ‖ moving; stirring*

Traquiarteria, *s. f. weasand; wind-pipe*

Traquido, *s. m. the report of a gun*

Tras, *prep. after; behind*

Trast as, *s. m. a noise*

Trasalpino, na, *adj. trasalpine*

Trasañejo, ja, *a. three years old*

Trasca, *s. f. a thick strap*

Trascabo, *s. m. the tripping up one's heels*

Trascanton, *subs. m. a stone-stud in the corner of a street*

Trascender, *ver. n. to transcend*

Trascender, *v. a. to discover; to perceive*

Trascolar, *v. a. to strain a liquor*

Trasconejarse, *ver. r. to stop behind*

Trascordado, *sub. m. a forgetful man*

Trascordarse, *ver. r. to forget*

Trascoro, *s. m. the back-side of a choir*

Trascorral, *s. m. a back-yard ‖ the breech*

Trasdobladura, *s. f. trebling* [*ble*

Trasdoblar, *v. a. to tre-*

Trasdoblo, *s. m. treble, triple*

Trasegador, *sub. m. one who decants*

Trasegar, *v. a. to decant; to pour from one vessel into another ‖ to turn up* [*ge the mark*

Traseñalar, *v. a. to chan-*

Trasera, *s. f. back-side*

Trasero, ra, *a. that comes behind*

Trasero, s. m. the breech

Traseros, pl. ancestors

Trasfogar, ver. a. to turn over a book

Trasfundicion, *s. f. tran[s]fusion* [...]

Trasgo, *s. m. an hobg[oblin]*

Trasguear, *v. n. to pla[y] the hobgoblin*

Trasguero, *s. m. one wh[o] plays the hobgoblin*

Trashoguero, *sub. m. an iron back to a chim[ney] ‖ a great log to lay [be]hind the fire*

Trashojar, *v. a. to tur[n] over a book*

Trashumar, *v. a. to dri[ve] the flocks from the pa[s]tures to the mountain[s] etc.*

Trasiego, *s. m. the pa[s]sing from one place [to] another ‖ decanting*

Trasijado, da, *a. thin lean*

Traslacion, } *s. f. trans-*
Trasladacion, } *lation*

Trasladador, *s. m. a trans[lator]*

Trasladar, *v. a. to trans[port] ‖ to translate*

Traslado, *s. m. a copy [of] a writing* [pa

Traslapar, *v. a. V.* Sola

Traslativo, va, *a. meta[phorical]*

Trasloar, *v. a. to prai[se] with excess*

Traslucido, da, adj. } *transpa-*
Trasluciente, a. 2. } *rent*

Traslucirse, *v. r. to shin[e] or appear through ‖ [to] be transparent*

Traslumbramiento, *s. m. dazzling*

Traslumbrarse, *v. r. to b[e] dazzled ‖ to disappe[ar]*

Trasluz, s. m. a light th[at] shines trough...

Trasmallo, s. m. tra[...]

hollow mallet
at mall)
, adv. behind-
ıa, s. f. the day
morrow
, v. a. to un-
se, v. r. to pe-
through...
r, ver. n. V.
tar
, s. f. tart sort
[transmute
, ver. act. to
, etc. V. Trans-
da, s. f. the last
the watching
t
, ver. neut. to
ll night
ar, ver. a. to
he names
acion, s. fem.
ny
er. a. to hear
tc.
v. a. to rave;
rio, ria, a. ex-
ary
ver. a. to turn
c. with a sho-
n, s. f. con-
; making over
ento, sub. m.
ssion
v. n. to pass
to go over
v. a. to trans-
pass over || to
ain || to run
|| to exceed ||
ress || to pierce
d, etc.
sub. m. con-
making over

|| pain; grief || transgression

Traspeynar, v. a. to comb again [wrestling

Traspie, s. m. a trip in

Dar traspies, to reel; to stagger

Traspillarse, v. r. to grow lean [transplant

Trasplantar, ver. act. to

Trasponedor, s. m. one that transfers, etc.

Trasponer, v. a. to transfer; to remove || to transpose || to get out of sight || to transplant

Trasponerse, ver. r. to slumber || to set (said of the sun, etc.)

Trasportar, etc. V. Transportar

Traspuesta, s. f. transfering || a sudden disappearing || an angle, etc. in a mountain || a part of building behind another

Traspuesto, ta, p. p. of trasponer (room

Trasquarto, s. m. a back-

Trasquero, s. m. one who makes or sells straps

Trasquilador, sub. m. a shearer

Trasquiladura, s. f. shearing [|| to clip

Trasquilar, v. a. to shear

Trasquilimocho, cha, a. shorn close

Trasquilones, sub. m. pl. notches in hair that is ill cut

Traste, s. m. a fret (in a musical instrument. V. Trasto

Dar al traste, to sink down

Trasteado, s. m. the frets of an instrument

Trasteador, s. m. one that turns the lumber over

Trastear, ver. a. to turn over the lumber of a house || to play finely on an instrument

Trastejador, s. m. a tiler

Trastejadura, s. f. tiling

Trastejar, v. a. to mend the tiles of a house || to patch

Trastejo, s. m. tiling

Trastera, s. f. wardrobe

Trastería, s. f. old household-goods

Trastesado, da, a. hard

Trastienda, s. f. a back-shop

Trasto, s. m. a piece of lumber [goods

Trastos, pl. household-

Trastornable, a. 2. moveable || changeable

Trastornado, s. m. a madman || a drunk-man

Trastornador, s. m. overthrower || a pragmatical fellow

Trastornadura, s. f. overthrowing

Trastornar, v. a. to overthrow; to turn topsy-turvy || to make a man change his mind

Trastornarse, v. r. to fall asleep || to be mad or drunk [wing

Trastorno, s. m. overthro-

Trastocamiento, sub. m. changing || exchange.

Trastrocar, v. a. to change the order, etc. || to exchange

Trastrueco, } s. m. chan-
Trastrueque, } ging

Trastumbar, ver. a. to make fall

Trasudadamente, adver. laboriously

Trasudar, v. a. to sweat

with fear, etc. to transsuede

Trasudor, *s. m. a sweat*

Trasuntar, *ver. a. to copy; to transcribe* ‖ *to abridge*

Trasuntivamente, *ad. by transcription* ‖ *summarily*

Trasunto, *s. m. a copy*

Trasvenarse, *v. r. to extravasate* [*flow*

Trasverter, *v. n. to over-*

Trasvinarse, *v. r. to run out of a cask (said of wine)*

Tratable, *a. 2. tractable*

Tratadillo, *s. m. a little treatise* [‖ *a treaty*

Tratado *s. m. a treatise*

Tratador, *s. m. a negotiator; an intermedler*

Tratamiento, *s. m. treatment; usage*

Tratante, *s. m. a dealer*

Tratar, *v. a. to touch; to handle* ‖ *to treat* ‖ *to use* ‖ *to deal; to trade*

Tratillo, *s. m. a little trade*

Trato, *s. m. trade; traffick* ‖ *treatment; usage* ‖ *dealing* ‖ *management* ‖ *manner; behaviour* ‖ *plot* ‖ *a title given to one*

Traversas, *s. f. pl. backstays (in a ship)*

Traves, *s. m. bent; slope; obliquity* ‖ *misfortune a flank (in fortification)*

De traves, ó al traves, *athwart; a slope.*

Travesaño, *s. m. a transom* [vesar

Travesar, *v. a. V.* Atra-

Travesear, *v. n. to be unquiet; turbulent* ‖ *to speak in a lively manner* ‖ *to live lewdly*

Travesero, na, *a. placed across*

Flauta travesera, *a german flute* [*ter*

Travesero, *s. m. a bolster*

Travesia, *sub. f. a crossway* ‖ *passage* ‖ *traverse (in fortification)* ‖ *large or quartering wind* [*guised*

Travestido, da, *adj. dis-*

Travesura, *s. f. a child's petulance, etc.* ‖ *quickness of wit* ‖ *obscenity*

Traviesa, *s. f. V.* Travesia [*wart*

A' traviesas, *adv. ath-*

Travieso, sa, *a sloping; cross* ‖ *quick; unquiet* ‖ *lewd*

Traza, *s. f. a plan* ‖ *a scheme*

Trazador, *s. m. the drawer of a plan* ‖ *a schemer*

Trazar, *ver. a. to draw a plan* ‖ *to scheme*

Trazo, *s. m. the delineation of a plan*

Trazos, *pl. the folds of a drapery*

Trasumarse, *v. r. to transpire* [*vet*

Trébedes, *s. f. pl. a tre-*

Trebejar, *v. n. to toy; to play* [*toy*

Trebejo, *s. m. a child's*

Trebejos, *pl. pieces (at chess)* ‖ *tools*

Trebol, *s. m. trefoil*

Trece, *s. m. thirteen*

Estarse en su trece, *to be* obstinate [teen

Treceno, na, adj. thir-

Trecemesino, na, adj. *thirteen months old*

Trecésimo, ma, *a. the thirtieth*

Trechel, *s. m. a coarse sort of wheat*

Trecho, *sub. m. space; distance*

Trecientos, tas, *a. three hundred*

Trefe, *a. 2. light; weak; that easily bends, etc.* ‖ *troubled with the phthisick*

Trefedad, *s. f. the phthisick* [*rest*

Tregua, *s. fem. truce* ‖

Treinta, *a. thirty*

Treintanario, *s. m. thirty*

Treinteno, na, *adj. thirtieth*

Treintena, *s. fem. the thirtieth part*

Troja, *s. fem. a brickoll (at billiards)*

Tremebundo, da, *adject. dreadful*

Tremedal, *sub. m. a quaking bog* [*ful*

Tremendo, da, *a. dread-*

Trementina, *s. f. turpentine*

Tremer, *v. n. to tremble*

Tremes, *a. 2.*, Tremesino, na, *adj.* } *three months old*

Tremielga, *s. f. crampfish*

Tremolante, *a. 2. flying; wavering in the air*

Tremolar, *v. a. to set up a standard; to hoist a flag*

Tremolar, *v. n. to fly; to waver or play in the air*

Tremolina, *s. f. a commotion in, or of the air* ‖ *bustle; tumult*

Tremor, *s. m. trembling, quaking*

Tremulo

...mulamente, *adv. in a remulous manner*
...mulante, *a.* 2. } *tremu-*
...mulento, ta, *a.* } *lous*
...mulo, la, *a.* }
...n, *s. m. train*
...na, *s. f. a scarf*
...nado, da, *a. reticu-ated*
...ncas, *s. f. pl. bits of eeds put in bee-hives*
...ncellin, *s. m.* } *little*
...ncilla, *s f.* } *tresses*
...ncillo, *s. m.* }
...neo, *s. m. a sledge*
...nos, *s. m. pl. the la-entations of jere-iials*
...nque, *s. m. a dike*
...ntenario, *s. m. thirty*
...nza, *s. fem. a twist; esses; plait*
...nzadera, *s. f. a frame weave tresses || a ibbon of thread*
...nzado, *s. m. the hair visted into tresses*
...nzar, *ver. a. to wist ito tresses*
...o, *s. m. square sail; ig sail*
...pa, *s. f. a climbing || he border of a gar-nent || a beating*
...padera, *s. fem. bind-eed*
...pador, *s. m. a rope-ancer || a climber*
...panar, *v. a. to trepan*
...pano, *s. m. a trepan*
...pante, *a.* 2. *sly; cun-ing*
...par, *v. n. to climb*
...pidacion, *s. f. trepi-ation* [*lous*
...pido, da, *adj. tremu-*
..., *s. y a. three*
...ñejo, ja, *a. three rs old*

Tresdoblar, *v. a. to triple*
Tresdoble, *s. m. the triple*
Tresquilar, etc. *V.* Trasquilar
Treta, *s. fem. a pass* or *thrust* (*in fencing*) *a trick; a stratagem*
Triaca, *s. f. treacle*
Triangular, *a.* 2. *triangular*
Triángulo, *s. m. a triangle* [*gular*
Triángulo, la, *a. trian-*
Triaquero, *s. m. treacle seller* [*rians*
Triarios, *s. m. pl. tria-*
Tribu, *s.* 2. *a tribe*
Tribuir, *v. a. to give || to attribute* [*lation*
Tribulacion, *s. f. tribu-*
Tribular, *v. a. to afflict*
Tribuna, *s. fem. pulpit* (*among the ancients*) *|| church-gallery*
Tribunado, *s. m. tribune's office*
Tribunal, *s. m. tribunal*
Tribúnico, ca, } *a. tribu-*
Tribunicio, cia, } *nitial*
Tribuno, *s. m. a tribune*
Tribntacion, *s. fem. a tribute* [*tribute*
Tributar, *v. a. to pay a*
Tributario, ria, *adj. tributary*
Tributo, *s. m. a tribute*
Tricésimo, ma, *a. thirtieth*
Triclinio, *s. m. a dining-room*
Tricorne, *a.* 2. *having three horns*
Tridente, *adj.* 2. *having three teeth*
Tridente, *s. m. a trident*
Trienal, *a.* 2. *triennial*
Trienio, *s. m. the space of three years*
Trifauce, *adj. m. having three mouths* (*said of cerberus*)

Trífido, da, *adj. divided in three*
Trifolio, *s. m. trefoil*
Triforme, *adj.* 2. *having three forms*
Trigaza, *s. f.* } *the wheat-*
Trigazo, *s. m.* } *straw, when short and chopped* (*tieth*
Trigésimo, ma, *a. thir-*
Trigla, *s. fem. mullet* (*a sea-fish*)
Triglifo, *s. m. triglyph*
Trigo, *s. m. corn; wheat*
Trigono, *s. m. trigon*
Trigonometría, *s. f. trigonometry*
Trigonométrico, ca, *adj. trigonometrical*
Trigueño, ña, *adj. of the wheat colour*
Triguero, ra, *adj. that grows in wheat-lands*
Triguero, *s. m. a sieve || a corn-merchant*
Trilingüe, *adj.* 2. *having or speaking three tongues*
Trilla, *s. f. mullet* (*a sea-fish*) *|| thrashing*
Trilladera, *s. f. V.* Trillo
Trillado (camino), *s. m. a beaten road*
Trillador, *s. m. a thrasher*
Trillar, *v. a. to thrash; to tread out corn || to frequent a road || to beat*
Trillo, *sub. m. an instrument to trash corn with*
Trimestre, *s. m. the space of tree months*
Trinado, *s. m. trilling; quavering* [*quaver*
Trinar, *v. n. to trill; to*

Trinca, *s. f. three things of the same kind, class, etc.* [*here*

Trincas del baupres, *las-*

Trincapiñones, *sub. m. a young hare-brained fellow*

Trincar, *v. a. to break into pieces* || *to jump*

Trincar la nao, *to sail close the wind*

Trinchante, *s. m. a gentleman-carver* || *a carving-knife* [*meat*

Trinchar, *ver. a. to carve*

Trinchea, *s. f. a trench*

Trinchear, *v. a. to make trenches* [chero

Trincheo, *s. m.* V. Trin-

Trinchera, *s. f. trench* || *intrenchment*

Trincherar, *v. a. to make trenches* || *to intrench*

Trinchero, *s. m. a trencher*

Trincheron, *s. m. a large intrenchment*

Trinchete, *sub. m. shoemaker's cutting knife*

Trineo, *s. m. a sledge*

Trinidad, *s. f. trinity*

Trinitarios, *s. m. pl trinitarians*

Trinitaria, *s. fem. pansy (flower)*

Trino, na, *a. containing three things* || *trine*

Trinomio, *s. m. an algebraical quantity of three terms*

Trinquetada, *s. f. a sailing with only the fore-sail*

Trinquete, *s. m. the fore-mast* || *the fore-sail* || *a tennis-court* [*bear*

Triones, *s. m. the great*

Tripa, *s. f. gut; tripe* || *paunch; belly*

Tripas, *pl. the inside of a fruit*

Tripartir, *v. a. to divide into three parts* [*tite*

Tripartito, ta, *a. tripar-*

Tripastos, *sub. m. the assemblage of tree pullies*

Tripe, *s. m. mock-velvet*

Tripería, *s. f. tripery* || *tripe-house*

Tripero, ra, *s. a tripe-man, or woman*

Tripero, *s. m. a woollen-cloth put upon the belly*

Tripicallero, ra, *s. a tripe-man, or woman*

Tripilla, *s. f. a little gut*

Tripitrape, *s. m. a mass of ridiculous things heaped together*

Tripitropà, *s. f. a violent revolution in the guts*

Tríplica, *s. f. an answer to a reply*

Triplicar, *ver. a. to treble* or *triple* || *to answer to a reply*

Tríplice, *adj. 2. triple; treble* [*city*

Triplicidad, *s. f. tripli-*

Triplo, pla, *a. triple*

Triplo, *s. m. the triple,* or *treble*

Trípoda, } *sub. f. vessel,*
Trípode, } *stool, etc. upon three legs; a tripod*

Tripon, na, *a. paunch-bellied*

Triptongo, *sub. m. triphthong*

Tripudiar, *v. n. to dance*

Tripudio, *s. m. a merry dancing*

Tripudo, da, *a. paunch-bellied*

Tripulacion, s. fem. the *manning of ships*

Tripular, *v. a. to man a*

-ship || *to mix; termix*

Triquete (á cada *at every step*

Triquitraque, *su clattering nois*

Trireme, *s. m. tr*

Tris, *sub. m. th of a glass wh break it* || *an i*

Venir en un tris, *in a trice*

Tris tras, *a cl*

Trisa, *s. f. a sha*

Trisagio, *s. m. th repeated song seraphins* || *a f lasts three day*

Trisca, *s. f. the treading on nu etc.*

Triscador, *s. m. a ring, turbulen*

Triscar, *v. n. to noise by tread shels, etc.* || *to others by noise*

Trisecar, *v. a. to three equal pa*

Triseccion, *s. f. t*

Trisílabo, ba, *a. bical*

Trisílabo, *s. m.*

Triste, *a. 2. sad, ful*

Tristemente, *ad*

Tristeza, *s. f. sorrow*

Tristísimo, ma,

Trisulco, ca, *adj three points*

Triton, *s. m. T sea god)*

Trituracion, *s. ration*

Triturar, *v. a.*

Triumvirato, *s. virate*

Triumviro, *s*

nfador, s. m. triumpher
ınfal, a. 2. triumphal
ınfante, a. 2. triumphant
ınfar, v. n. to triumph to play trumps
nfo, s. m. a triumph a trump at cards
ial, adj. 2. trodden ile; trivial
ialidad, s. f. trivialness [vially
ialmente, adver. tri-
io, sub. m. a place here three ways meet
a, s. f. a little bit; a agment
as, p. haliards; gears
cable, a. 2. that may trucked
a trocada, la trocadil-, } ad. on the contrary
cader, ra, s. one who ucks
car, v. a. to truck; to exchange || to vomit
carse, v. r. to change ne's manners, etc.
catente, s. m. a ridiculous exchange
cha, s. f. a footpath; cross-way
chemoche, adver. at andom; rashly
cisco, s. m. trochisk
co, s. m a kind of fish
feista, sub. m. a conueror
feo, s. m. a trophy
glodita, s. m. a trolodyte
mpa, s. f. a hunter's orn || a trumpet || an lephant's trunk || a ort of top, for boys || a w's harp
pada, s. f. a blow given by sudden meeting face to face
Trompar, v. a. to deceive
Trompazo, s. m. a great blow
Trompero, s. m. one that makes tops or gigs || a deceiver
Trompeta, s. f. a trumpet [peter
Trompeta, s. m. a trum-
Trompetear, ver. n. to sound a trumpet
Trompetero, s. m. a trumpeter
Trompetilla, s. f. a little trumpet || a horn to help the hearing || the trunk of a bee, etc.
Trompicar, v. n. to stumble often or violently
Trompicar, v. a. to supplant
Trompico, s. m. a child's top or gig
Trompicon, s. m. a violent stumble
Trompillar, v. n. to stumble
Trompo, s. m. a child's top or gig
Trompon, sub. m. a great top or gig
A' trompon, De trompon, } adv. disorderly
Tron, s. m. the noise of a cannon shot
Tronada, s. f. a tempest with thunders
Tronador, ra, adj. thundering
Tronar, v. n. to thunder
Troncal, a. 2. belonging to a trunk
Troncar, v. a. to cut off short || to mutilate || to lame a book, etc.
Tronchar, v. a. to cut the stalks of cabbages, etc. || to snap off boughs of a tree, etc.
Tronchazo, sub. m. aum. de Troncho
Troncho, s. m. the stalk of a cabbage, etc.
Tronchudo da, adj. having a great stalk, etc.
Tronco, sub. m. trunk; stock [ded
Tronco, ca, a. mutila-
Troncon, sub. m. a great trunk
Tronera, s. fem. a loophole || a dormer window; an oval, etc. || a hare-brained fellow
Troneras, plur. billiard-hazards
Tronido, s. m. the noise of thunder, etc.
Tronitoso, sa, adj. thundering
Trono, s. m. a trone
Tronzar, ver. a. to break into pieces || to gather or plait a coat
Tronzonar, v. a. to cut in pieces
Tropa, s. f. a troop
Tropel, sub. m. a noise made with the feet || croud; multitude || the noise of many people || precipitation || confusion, disorder
Tropela, s. fem. precipitation with confusion and disorder || wrong; injury
Tropellar, v. a. to trample on
Trompezadero, sub. m. a stumbling-place
Tropezar, v. n. to stumble
Tropezarse, ver. r. to cut or interfere (said of a horse)
Tropezon, s. m. a stumble

Tropezon, na, } adj. that
Tropezoso, sa, } stumbles often; stumbling-horse, etc.
Trópico, s. m. a tropick
Trópico, ca, a. tropical
Tropiezo, s. m. a stumbling || a stumbling-block
Tropilla, s. fem. a little troop
Tropo, s. m. trope
Tropologia, s. f. tropology
Tropológico, ca, a. tropological
Troque, s. m. truck; exchange
Troqueo, s. m. a trochee
Trotar, v. n. to trot || to run
Trote, s. m. a horse's trot
Troton, na, a. trotting
Trotoneria, s. fem. continual trotting or running
Trova, s. fem. a metrical composition
Trovador, ra, s. a finder
Trovador, s. m. a poet; a bard || a verse-maker
Trovar, v. a. to find or meet by chance || to make verses || to imitate a metrical composition || to invert the sense of words
Trovista, s. m. a poet; a bard || a verse-maker
Trox, s. fem. a granary to keep corn in || the church
Troxa, } s. f. a soldier's
Troxada, } knapsack
Troxado, da, a. shut up in a knapsack
Troxe, s. f. V. Trox
Troza, s. f. mizen parrel-truss
Trozeo, sub. m. a parrel-truss
Trozo, s. masc. a stump-piece || a regiment of horse
Trucha, s. f. a trout
Trucha salmonera, a salmon-trout
Truchuela, s. f. the smallest sort of the fish called poor jack || a little trout
Trucidar, v. a. to kill
Trucos, s. m. pl. the play of billiards; trucks
Truculento, ta, a. cruel; bloody; truculent
Trué, sub. m. a kind of linen-cloth
Trueco, sub. m. truck; exchange
A' trueco, provided that
Trueno, s. m. the noise of the thunder; of the cannon, etc.
Trueque, sub. m. truck, exchange
Trufa, s. f. a fib; a sham; a fun
Trufaldin, na, s. a player or dancer on stage
Truhan, s. m. a buffoon
Truhanear, v. n. to play the buffoon
Truhanería, s. fem. buffoonry
Truhanillo, s. m. dim. de Truhan
Trujal, s. m. an oil-mill || a soap-maker's caldron
Trujaman, s. m. an interpreter; a truchman || a broker
Trujamanear, v. n. to interpret || to play the broker
Trujamanía, s. f. brokerage
Trulla, s. f. bustle; tumult; rout
Trullo, s. m. a teal
Truncamiento, sub. m. a cutting off, etc.
Truncar, v. a. V. Troncar
Trunco, na, a. V. Tunto
Truque, sub. m. a game at cards
Truquero, s. m. a keeper of billiards
Tú, pron. thou
Tu, pron. thy; thine
Tubo, s. m. a tube
Tudel, sub. m. the brass pipe of a bassoon, etc.
Tudesco, s. m. a sort of great coat
Tuera, s. f. the fruit of coloquintida
Tuerca, s. f. the nut or worm of a screw
Tuero, s. m. a fire-brand
Tuertas (á), adv. wrongfully
Tuerto, ta, a. crooked; awry || one-eyed || squint-eyed
Tuerto, sub. m. wrong; injury
Tuertos, pl. twisting of the guts; gripes
Tuétano, s. m. marrow
Tufarada, s. f. a strong scent
Tufo, sub. m. a steam or exhalation from the earth || the strong scent of burning charcoal, etc.
Tufos, pl. side-locks of hair along the temples || pride
Tugurio, s. m. a hut; a cottage
Tuicion, s. f. tuition; defense
Tuitivo, va, a. that defens or protects
Tulipa, s. f. a small tulip
Tulipan, s. m. a tulip
Tullido, da, adj. lame of the limbs cripple, etc.
Tullidura, s. f. the dun of a hawk
Tullimiento, s. m.

raction or *weakness of he nerves*
llir, *v. n. to dung; to mute (said of a hawk)*
llir, *ver. a. to maim; cripple*
lirse, *ver. r. to grow cripple*
nba, *s. f. a tomb || the roof of a coach || a fall*
nbado, da, *a. rounded in the top; vaulty*
nbaga, *s. f. pinchbeck a ring of pinchbeck*
nbagon, *s. m. a large ring*, or *bracelet of pinchbeck*
nbar, *v. a. to tumble; make fall || to teaze with mockery || to run; to make drunk, c.*
nbar, *v. n. to tumble; fall upside down*
nbarse, *ver. r. to lay down to sleep*
nbo, *s. m. a tumble*
nbo de olla, *grounds*
nbon, *s. m. a coach, c. with a vaulty roof*
nido, da, *adj. tumid; swelled*
nor, *s. m. tumour; swelling || pride*
nulo, *s. m. a tomb; monument || a funeral decoration*
nulto, *s. m.* } *tumult*
nultuacion, *s. f.* }
nultuar, *v. n.* } *to make tumult; to tumultate*
nultuarse, *v. r.* }
nultuariamente, *adv. tumultuarily*
nultuario, ria, *a. tumultuary*
ltuosamente, *adv. tumultuously*

Tumultuoso, sa, *adj. tumultuous*
Tuna, *s. fem. an American fig, and fig-tree || the idle life that rogues and beggars live*
Tunante, *s. m. a beggar; a vagabond*
Tunar, *v. n. to mump; to beg*
Tunda, *s. f. the shearing of cloth || a beating*
Tundente, *a. 2. that makes a bruise* or *contusion*
Tundicion, *s. fem. the shearing of cloth*
Tundidor, *s. m. a shearer of cloth*
Tundidura, *s. f. shearing*
Tundir, *ver. a. to shear cloth*
Tundizno, *s. m. the hair of the cloth, when sheared*
Túnica, *s. f. a tunick || [a tunicle*
Tunicela, *s. fem. a little tunick || the little film that is over a nut, etc.*
Tupa, *s. f. heaping up, etc. || the eating to satiety*
Tupé, *s. m. a toupee*
Tupir, *v. a. to heap up; to pull close*
Tupirse, *v. r. to fill the belly*
Turar, *v. n. to last*
Turba, *s. fem. a rout; a crowd || turf; peat*
Turbacion, *s. f. trouble; disorder [sorderly*
Turbadamente, *adv. di-*
Turbado, da, *a. disordered || astonished; out of countenance*
Turbador, *s. m.* disturber
Turbamulta, *s. f.* a crowd *of people*

Turbante, *s. m. a turban*
Turbar, *v. a. to trouble; to disturb*
Turbarse, *v. r. to confound one's self, to be out of countenance*
Turbativo, va, *adj. that disturbs*
Túrbido, da, *a. turbid*
Turbino, *s. m. turbith*
Turbio, bia, *adj. thick; muddy || unlucky || dark; obscure*
Turbion, *s. m. a sudden short storm || a strong gust of wind*
Turbit, *s. m. turbith*
Turbon, *s. m. V.* Turbion
Turbulencia, *s. fem. turbidness || turbulence*
Turbulentamente, *adver. turbulently*
Turbulento, ta, *a. turbid || turbulent*
Turco, ca, *s. Turk*
Turco, ca, *a. Turkish*
Turgida, *s. f. a certain part of an ox's hide*
Turgencia, *s. f. turgency*
Turgente, *a. 2. turgid; swelling*
Turíbulo, *s. m. a censer*
Turiferario, *s. m. thuriferary*
Turma, *s. f. a testicle*
Turmas de tierra, *truffles*
Turnar, *v. n. to altern*
Turnio, nia, *a. goggle-eyed || stern*
Turno, *s. m. a turn*
Turon, *sub. m. a field-mouse*
Turquesa, *s. fem. a turquoise || a mould to cast bullets in*
Turquesado, da, *a.* of a turquoise colour
Turqui, *a.* deep blue

Turrar, *v. a. to toast* || *to scorch*

Turron, *sub. m. a sweet meat made of almonds, honey, etc.*

Turronero, *s. m. one who makes or sells the turron*

Turumbon, *sub. m. swelling; bruise*

Tusilago, *s. m. colt's foot*

Tuson, *s. m. a fleece*

Tusona, *s. f. a strumpet*

Tútano, *s. m. marrow*

Tutear, *v. a. to thou and thee*

Tutela, *s. fem. tutelage; guardianship*

Tutelar, *a. 2. tutelar*

Tutía, *s. f. tutty*

Tutor, *s. m. tutor; guardian*

Tutoría, *s. fem. guardianship*

Tutriz, *s. f. tutoress*

Tuyo, ya, *pron. thine; thy own*

Tuyos, *pl. thine; those of thy party; thy kindred*

El mio y el tuyo, *meum et tuum*

U

UBE'RRIMO, ma, *adj. most fruitful*

Ubi, *s. m. place; room; space*

Ubicacion, *s. f. existence in a determined place*

Ubicarse, *v. r. to exist in a determined place*

Ubiquidad, *s. f. ubiquity*

Ubiquitario, ria, *a. ubiquitarian*

Ubre, *s. f. udder*

Ubrera, *sub. f. a sore in a child's mouth*

Ucé, *your worship (the same as vuestra merced)*

Ucencia, *s. fem. your excellence*

Ufanamente, *ad. proudly; arrogantly*

Ufanarse, *v. r. to boast; to grow proud*

Ufaneza, } Ufanía, } *s. fem. pride; arrogance* || *briskness*

Ufano, na, *adj. proud; arrogant* || *brisk; merry*

Ugier, *s. m. V.* Uxier

Ulcera, *s. f. ulcer*

Ulceracion, *s. f. ulceration*

Ulcerar, *v. a. to ulcerate*

Ulceroso, sa, *a. ulcerous*

Ulmaria, *s. f. mead-sweet*

Ulterior, *a. 2. further*

Ultimadamente, } U'ltimamente, } *adver. lastly*

Ultimar, *v. a. to finish; to put an end to*

Ultimidad, *s. f. the being the last*

U'ltimo, ma, *adj. last; ultimate*

U'ltimas, *s. f. pl. the final syllables*

Ultra, *adv. besides; moreover*

Ultrajamiento, *s. m. outraging; outrage*

Ultrajar, *v. a. to outrage*

Ultraje, *s. m. an outrage*

Ultramar, *a. 2. ultramarine*

Ultramar, *s. m. ultramarine country* || *ultramarine (paint)*

Ultramarino, na, *adj. ultramarine*

Ultramarino, } Ultramaro, } *sub m. ultramarine (paint)*

Ultramontano, na, *adj. ultramontane*

Ultriz, *a. fem. revenger; avenger*

Ultróneo, nea, *a. ultroneous*

U'lula, *s. f.* ...

Ululato, *s. m* ...

Umbilical, ... *lical*

Umbral, *s.* ... || *lintel*

Umbralar, *s* ...

Umbrático, ... *ting to sh*...

Umbría, *s.* ... *place*

Umbrío, bri...

Umbroso, ...

Un, *a. m.* ...

Unánime, *a.* ... *mous*

Unanimemen...

Unanimidad ... *nimity*

Uncia, *s. fem* ... *coin* || *an* ...

Uncion, *s.* ... *the extrem*...

Unciones, *p*... *frictions*

Uncionario, ... *with mer*... *tions*

Uncir, *v. a.* ...

Undecágono ... *cagon*

Undécimo, ...

Undisono, n... *a noise lik*... *ling*

Undoso, sa, ...

Ungarina, *s* ... *coat made* ... *rian fashi*...

Ungido, *s.* ... *anointed*

Ungimiento, ... *ting, un*...

Ungir, *v. a.* ...

Unguentario ... *lating to* ... *perfumer*

Unguenta... *maker*

ients || a perfumer || a place where the ointments are kept
güente, } sub. m. ointment · unguento, } ment · unguent || perfume
icamente, adv. only; singularly
caule, a. 2. that has but one stalk
cidad, s. f. the being only and singular
ico, ca, a. only; sole; singular
cornio, s. m. unicorn
idad, s. f. unity
idamente, ad. jointly
ificar, v. a. to make one of many
iformar, v. a. to make uniform
iforme, a. 2. uniform
iforme, s. m. uniform; regimental clothes
iformemente, a. uniformly [mity
iformidad, s. f. uniformity
igénito, a. m. the only begotten
ion, s. f. union
ir, v. a. to unite
ison, s. m. unison
isonancia, s. f. unison || monotony
isono, s. m. unison
isono, na, a. unison
itivo, va, } a. unitive
itoso, sa, }
ituoso, sa, }
iversal, a. 2. universal
iversalidad, s. f. universality [versally
iversalmente, ad. universally
iversidad, s f. university [verse
iverso, s. m. the universe
iverso, sa, a. universal
ivocacion, subs. f. the being univocal

Univocarse, v. r. to be univocal
Unívoco, ca, a. univocal || like || united || unanimous
Uno, s. m. one
Uno, na, a. one; a; an
Uno á uno, ó por uno, one by one [ter
Untador, s. m. an anointer
Untadura, s. f. } an anointing or daubing
Untamiento, s. m. }
Untar, v. a. to anoint || to daub
Untar las manos, to grease one in the fist; to tip one
Úntaza, sub. f. a coarse ointment || grease
Unto, s. m. any ointment || fat; grease
Unto de las ruedas, gome
Untoso, sa, } adj. unctuous
Untuoso, sa, }
Untuosidad, s. f. unctuosity
Untura, s. f. anointing; daubing || any unctuous matter
Uña, s. f. nail || hoof || talon; claw; clutch || a scab growing upon beasts where they are galled
Uña de caballo, colt's-foot — de asno, foal's-foot — de vaca, cow-heal
Uñas de ancla, the flukes of an anchor
Uñada, s. f. a mark made with the nail
Unarada, s. f. a scratch with a nail
Uñate, s m. a pinching with the nail
Uñero, s. m. a whitlow || a flaw in one's nails || a nail that enters into the flesh
Uñeta, s. f. a play among children
Uñidura, s. f. a yoking
Uñir, v. a. to yoke
Upar, v. n. to struggle in order to rise high
Uracho, s. m. the aperture at wich the urine issues
Uraño, ña, a. V. Huraño
Urbanamente, adv. courteously
Urbanidad, s. f. urbanity
Urbanísimo, ma, a. most courteous
Urbano, na, a. courteous; civil || dwelling in the town
Urca, s. f. a howker || an ore [semary
Urce, s. m. a kind of rosemary
Urdidera, s. f. a woman that wharps || a weaver's beam
Urdidor, ra, s. one that wharps
Urdidor, s. m. a weaver's beam
Urdidura, s. f. warping
Urdiembre, } subs. m. the warp
Urdimbre, }
Urdir, v. a. to warp || to contrive
Urétera, s. f. urethra
Uréteres, s. m. pl. ureters
Urgencia, s. f. urgency
Urgente, a. 2. urgent
Urgir, v. n. to urge
Urina, s. f. urine
Urinario, ria, a. urinary
Urna, s. f. an urn
Urnica, s. f. a little urn
Urnicion, s. f. a futtoc-timber
Uro, s. m. ure-ox
Urraca, s. f. a magpie
Ursa, s. f. a she bear

Usacion, s. f. the wearing out [marily
Usadamente, adv. custo-
Usado, da, a. worn out || experienced
Al usado, ad. at usance
Usage, s. m. usage; use; habit
Usagre, s. m. a letter
Usanza, s. f. usage; use
Usar, v. a. to use || to exercise || to accustom
Usarse, v. r. to be in fashion
Usencia, s. f. your reverence
Useñoria, Usia, Usiria, } s. f. your lordship (the same as vuestra señoria)
Usier, s. m. V. Uxier
Usitado, da, adj. used; customary
Uso, s. m. usage; use || || usance || wearing out or off
Ustaga, s. f. a kind of pulley (on board a ship)
Usted (an abbrevation of vuestra merced) you, sir; you madam.
Ustion, s. f. ustion; burning
Usual, adj. 2. usual || social
Usuario, ria, a. usufructuary [tion
Usucapion, s. f. usucap-
Usufructo, s. m. usufruct
Usufructuar, v. a. to have the temporary use of any thing
Usufructuario, ria, adj. usufructuary
Usura s. f. usury || gain; profit
Usurar, Usurear, } v. a. to usure to get a profit, etc.
Usurario, ria, adj. usurious
Usurero, s. m. an usurer
Usurero, ra, a. usurious
Usurpacion, s. f. usurpation [per
Usurpador, s. m. an usur-
Usurpar, v. a. to usurp
Ut, s. m. ut (a musical note)
Utensilio, s. m. utensil
Utensilios, pl. soldier's free quarters
Uteral, a. 2. Uterino, na, a. } uterine
Uterinos, pl. brothers or sisters by the mother's side
U'tero, s. m. the womb
U'til, a. 2. useful; profitable
Util, s. m. profit || utility
Utilidad, s. f. utility
Utilisimo, ma, a. most useful
U'tilmente, ad. usefully
Utilizar, v. a. to be profitable
Utilizarse, v. r. to get some benefit from....
Utrera, subs. f. a young heifer
Utrero, s. m. a steer
Uva, subs. f. a grape || a bunch of grapes || the berry of a grape || a drunk-man
Uva de gato, house-leek — de perro, the wild bay tree — crespa ó espina, a goose-berry—lupina, wolf-bane — taminia, stavesacre — pasa, a raisin
Uvada, sub. f. plenty of grapes
Uvagdemaestre, s. m. the master of the wagons
Uvate, s. m. thick confection of grapes
Uvea, s. f. uvea, (tunic of the eye) [pe
Uvero, s. m. seller of gra
Uvilla, s. f. a small sort of grapes
Uxier, sub. m. usher; door-keeper

V

Vaca, s. f. a cow || bee || the stock that two ga mesters have in common
Vacacion, s. f. vacation; holidays || vacancy
Vacada, sub. f. a herd of cows
Vacancia, s. f. Vacante, s. m. } vacancy
Vacante, a. 2. vacant void
Vacar, v. n. to be vacan || to attend; to min
Vacatura, s. f. vacancy
Vacia, s. f. V. Bacia
Vaciadero, s. m. a sink
Vaciadizo, za, a. hollow low; empty; cast in mould, etc.
Vaciador, s. m. emptie || an emptying instru ment
Vaciamiento, s. m. emptying
Vaciar, v. a. to empty || to cast in a mould
Vaciar el vientre, to eas one's self
Vaciarse, v. r. to speak inconsiderately
Vaciedad, s. f. emptines
Decir vaciedades, to tal nonsense
Vacilacion, s. f. vacilation; tottering
Vacilar, v. n. to totte to stagger

Vacin, Vacinica. *V.* Bacin, Bacinica
Vacío, cía, *adj. empty* || *void; vacant* || *vain; presumptuous* || *foolish*
Vacío, *s. m. void space; vacuum*
De vacío, *ad. emptily*
Vaco, ca, *a. void; vacant*
Vacuidad, *s. f. vacuity*
Vacuno, na, *a. belonging to cows*
Vacuo, *s. m. vacuum*
Vade, *sub. m. a scholar's port-folio*
Vadeable, *a. 2. fordable*
Vadear, *v. a. to ford* || *to overcome a difficulty* || *to sound a business*
Vademecum, *s. m. V.* Vade
Vadera, *s. f.* } *a ford*
Vado, *s. m.* } *a ford*
Vadoso, sa, *a. that has many fords*
Vafe, *s. m. a bold stroke*
Vagabundo, da, *a. vagabond*
Vagamente, *adv. indefinitely*
Vagamundear, *v. n. to play the vagabond; to stroll about*
Vagamundo, da, *a. vagabond*
Vagar, *v. n. to ramble; to wander* || *to stray*
No me vaga, *I am not at leisure*
Vagar, *sub. m. leisure* || *sloth-fulness*
Estar, ó andar de vagar, *to be idle*
Vagaroso, sa, *a. wandering; vagrant*
Vagazo, *s. m. the husks of grapes* or *olives, when pressed*
Vagido, *s. m. the squall of children*
Vago, ga, *a. wandering* || *light; fickle* || *vague*
Vagueacion, *s. f. inconstancy* or *wavering of the mind*
Vaguear, *v. n. to wander; to ramble about*
Vaguedad, *s. f. inconstancy; wavering*
Vaguemaestre, *s. m. Cartaker*
Vagnido, *s. m. giddiness* || *danger of ruin, etc.*
Vaguido, da, *a. troubled with a giddiness*
Vahanero, ra, *a. slothful; vagrant*
Vahar, *v. n. V.* Vahear
Vaharada, *s. f. breath*
Vaharera, *s. f. a pustule in the mouth of sucking children*
Vaharina, *s. f. vapour; steam* || *mist*
Vahear, *v. n. to steam*
Vaho, *s. m. steam; vapour*
Vahuno, na, *a. V.* Bahuno
Vaida, *s. f. a half-round vault*
Vaido, *s. m. V.* Vagido
Val, *s. m. vale; valley* || *a sink; a common sewer*
Valar, *a. 2. belonging to an inclosing wall*
Valar, *v. n. to bleat*
Vale, *s. m. a farewell* || *a promissory note*
Valedero, ra, *a. valid; lawful*
Valedor, *s. m. favourer; supporter*
Valentacho, *s. m. a bully*
Valentía, *sub f. valour; courage* || *a courageous action* || *boasting language* || *quickness of the wit*
Hambre y valentía, *a proud beggar*
Valentísimamente, *adv. most valiantly*
Valentísimo, ma, *a. most valiant* || *most versed, experienced*
Valenton, *s. m. a bully; a hector*
Valentonada, *s. f. a bragging*
Valentonazo, *subs. m. a braggadochio*
Valer, *v. n. to be worth* || *to be useful* || *to be in favour* || *to have the power* or *virtue*
Valer, *v. a. to favour; to protect*
Valerse, *ver. r. to make use of*
Valerse de uno, *to enjoy the favour of one*
Valeriana, *s. f. valerian*
Valerosamente, *adv. valiantly*
Valeroso, sa, *a. valorous* || *powerful; efficacious*
Valetudinario, ria, *a. valetudinarian*
Valía, *s. f. value; worth* || *favour* || *faction; party*
A' las valías, *at the stated price*
Validacion, *s. f. validation*
Válidamente, *ad. with validity*
Validar, *v. a. to validate*
Valido, da, *a. that makes use of* || *that is in favour*
Valido, *s. m. a favourer* || *V.* Balido
Válido, da, *a. valid*
Mendigos válidos, *sturdy beggars*
Valiente, *a. 2. strong* || *valiant* || *powerful; efficacious* || *excellent* || *great; excessive*
Valiente, *s. m. a bully*
Valientemente, *ad.* str

gly || valiantly || excessively

Valimiento, s. m. value; worth; utility || favour || protection

Valioso, sa, a. wealthy

Valiza, s. f. the beacon, or buoy of a shoal

Valla, s. f. intrenchment; palisade || a rail fixed round

Valladar, sub. m. an intrenchment

Valladear, v. a. to surround with intrenchments, etc.

Vallado, s. m. intrenchment; palisado

Vallar, v. a. to fortify; to intrench

Valle, s. m. a valley

Vallecico, Valiecillo, Vallejo, } s. masc. a little valley

Valona, s. f. a large sort of band

Valones, s. m. pl. great walloon breeches

Valor, s. m. value; worth || valour || validity || power; efficacy

Valorar, Va orear, } v. a. to value

Váloría, subs. f. value; price; estimation

Valua, s. f. value

Valuacion, s. f. valuation

Valuar, v. a. to value

Válvula, s. f. valve || sucker of a pump

Vanagloría, subs. f. vainglory

Vanagloriarse, v. r. to boast; to be proud of...

Vanagloriosamente, adv. proudly

Vanaglorioso, sa, a. vainglorious

Vanamente, ad. vainly || superstitiously || inconsiderately || proudly

Vanear, v. n. to talk idly

Vanguardia, s. f. the van of an army

Vanidad, s. f. vanity

Vanidoso, sa, a. vainglorious

Vanisimamente, ad. most proudly

Vano, na, adj. vain || empty || proud

Vapor, s. mas. vapour; steam || breath

Vaporable, a. 2. that may vapour away

Vaporacion, s. f. evaporation

Vaporar, Vaporear, Vaporizar, } v. n. to vapour away; to evaporate

Vaporoso, sa, a. vaporous

Vapulacion, s. f. Vapulamiento, s. m. } whipping

Vapular, v. a. to whip

Vaquear, v. a. to leap the cows [of cows

Vaquería, subs. f. a herd

Vaquerillo, s. m. dim. de Vaquero

Vaquerizo, za, a. belonging to the cows

Vaquero, s. m. a cowkeeper

Vaquero, ra, a. belonging to cow-keepers

Vaqueta, s. f. a calf's leather. V. Baqueta

Vaquilla, Vaquita, } s. f. a. heifer

Vara, s. f. a rod; a twig; a wand || a yard (measure) || a hawk's pearch

Vara real, a scepter

Varas, pl. the shafts of a coach, etc. [rays

Varas de luz, beams;

Varaderos, s. m. pl. certain timbers so called on board ships

Varal, s. m. any long pole || a tall fellow

Varapalo, s. m. a long pole || a blow with pole || grief; affliction

Varar, v. a. to launch ship

Varar, v. neut. to run aground || to miscarry

Varascato, s. m. arbour work [with a ro

Varazo, sub. m. a strok

Varchilla, s. f. a certain measure of corn

Vardasca, s. f. a thin ro

Vardascazo, s. m. a blow with a thin rod

Vareador, s. m. he th beats down with a po

Varaage, s. m. the measuring by yards

Varear, v. a. to beat dow with a pole || to strik a bull, etc. with a spe || to measure or sell b yards

Varearse, v. r. to gro lean, etc.

Varejon, s. m. a great po

Varenga, s. f. floor-tim ber (on board a ship

Vareta, sub. f. a sma wand || a lime-twig || nipping jest || an inc rect proposition, etc

Varetas, pl. stripes, any staff

Varetear, v. a. to strip

Variable, a. 2. variabl

Variacion, s. f. variati

Variamente, ad variou

Variar, v. a. y n. to va

Várice, s. f. a varix

Varicoso, sa, a. varic

Variedad, s. f. variety variation

Varilla, subs f. a

wand, or *rod* || *a curtain-rod* || *a thin sharp point*
Varilla de cuello, *the throat*
Varillas, *pl. the bones of the jaws*
Vario, ria, *a. various* || *variable* || *vague* || *party-coloured; speckled, etc.*
Varios, *pl. some*
Varon, *s. m. a male (said of men)* || *a full grown man* || *a man of consideration* || *a baron*
Hijo varon, *a son*
Varonía, *sub. f. the male line* || *a barony*
Varonil, *a. 2. manly*
Varonilmente, *adv. manlily*
Varraquear, *v. n. to grumble*
Vasallage, *s. m. vassalage* || *subjection; dependence*
Vasallo, *s. m. a vassal*
Mal vasallo, *a good for nothing fellow*
Vasar, *s. m. a cupboard; a shelf, etc.*
Vascongado, da, *adj. of biscay*
Vascuence, *s.m. a biscayan tongue*
Vasera, *s. f. a cupboard* || *the case in wich an urinal is kept* || *glass-basket*
Vasija, *sub. f. a vessel* || *casks*
Vasijilla, *s. f. dim. de Vasija*
Vasillo, } *s. m. a small*
Vasito, } *vessel*
Vaso, *s. m. a vessel; a cup, etc.* || *a ship; a boat* || *the body of the hive, etc.* || *capacity* || *a horse's hoof* || *a chamber-pot, etc.*
Vástago, *s. m. sucker; sprig*
Vastedad, *s. f vastness*
Vasto, ta, *adj. vast.* || *V.* Basto
Vate, *s. m. a poetical prophet* || *a diviner* || *a bard; a poet*
Vaticinador, *s. m. a vaticinator*
Vaticinar, *v. a. to vaticinate*
Vaticinio, *s. m. vaticination*
Vaxilla, *s. f. table-utensils*
Vaya, *s. f. scoff; jest; sham*
Vayna, *s. f. a sheath; a case; a scabbard* || *cod; husk; shell*
Vaynazas, *s. m. a lazy sluggish fellow*
Vaynica, } *sub. f. a thin*
Vaynilla, } *husk, etc.* || *fringe* || *vanilla*
Vayven, *sub. m. a wavering; a staggering* || *fluctuation; uncertainty* || *danger; peril*
Vecero, *s. m he that comes to perform anything in his turn*
Vecinamente, *ad. nearly*
Vecindad, *sub. f. neighbourhood; vicinity* || *the inhabitants of a town, etc.* || *abode; dwelling place* || *likeness*
Vecindario, *s. m. the number of inhabitants in a town* || *a list of them*
Vecino, na, *a. neighbour* || *near* || *inhabitant* || *settled in a place* || *like*
Vecino, *ad. near; not far*
Veda, *s. f.* prohibition by *law*
Vedado, *s. m. a forbidden place*
Vedamiento, *s. m. prohibition*
Vedar, *v. a. to forbid*
Vedegambre, *s. m. white ellebore*
Vedija, *s. f a lock of hair* or *wool*
Vedijas, *pl. the scrotum*
Vedijilla, *s. f. dim. de* Vedija
Vedijoso, sa, } *a. full of*
Vedijudo, da, } *locks of hair* or *tufts of wool*
Vedriado, da, *a. glazed*
Veduño, *s. m. the ground a vine yard stands on*
Veedor, *s. m. overseer; inspector, etc.*
Veeduría, *s. f. the office of an inspector*
Vega, *s. f. a plain pasture ground by a river's side*
Vegada, *sub. f. a. turn; taking of one's turn*
A' las vegadas, *by turns*
Vegetable, } *a. 2. vegetable*
Vegetal, }
Vegetácion, *s. f. vegetation*
Vegetarse, *v. r. to vegetate*
Vegetativo, va, *a. vegetative*
Vehemencia, *s. f. vehemence*
Vehemente, *a. 2. vehement*
Vehementemente, *adv. vehemently*
Vehículo, *s. m. vehicle*
Veinte, *s. m. twenty*
Veintena, *s. f. the twentieth part* || *score; twenty*
Veintenar, *subs. m. the twentieth part*
Veinteno, na, *adj.* twentieth
Veintésimo, ma, *a.* tw[illegible]

Veintidoseno, na, *a. relating to the number of two and twenty*
Veintiquatreno, na, *a. relating to the number of four and twenty*
Vejancon, na, *adj. very old; decrepit*
Vejestorio, *s. m. old clother; old lumber, etc.*
Vejete, *s. m. a ridiculous old man*
Vejez, *s. f. old age*
Vejezuela, *s. f. a little old woman* [*old man*
Vejezuelo, *s. m. a little*
Vejote, *s. m. a very old man*
Vela, *s. f. watching* || *a watch* || *lucubration; labour; study* || *sentinel; sentry* || *pilgrimage* || *candle* || *sail* || *a horse's ear*
Velacho, *s. m. the fore sail*
Velacion, *s. f. a watching* || *a wedding*
Velada, *s. f. a watching*
Velado, *s. m. a new-married man*
Velador, *sub. m. one that watches much* || *a watch-man;* || *a sentinel* || *a large lamp, etc. to work by at night*
Velage, *s. m. a complete suit of sails* [*ding*
Velambres, *s. f. pl. a wed-*
Velamen, *s. m. a complete suit of sails*
Velar, *v. n. to watch;* || *to espouse; to wed*
Velarte, *s. m. a sort of fine cloth*
Veleidad, *s. f. velleity*
Velejar, *v. n. to sail*
Veleria, *s. f. a tallow-chandler's shop*

Velero, *s. m. a chandler*
Velero, ra, *adj. good sailer*
Veleso, *s. f. tooth-wort*
Veleta, *s. f. a weathercock*
Velete, *s. m. a thin vail*
Velicacion, *s. f. vellication* [*cate*
Velicar, *ver. a. to velli-*
Velilla, *s. f. a little candle* || *a small sail*
Velillo, *s. m. a little veil* || *a sort of web like gauze*
Vellecillo, *s. m. soft down*
Vellera, *sub. f. a woman that pulls off the down from the other women face*
Vellido, da, *a. downy*
Vello, *s. m. down; soft hair* || *the nap on a cloth*
Vellocino, *s. m. a fleece*
Vellon, *s. m. a fleece* || *brass money*
Vellorí, } *s. m. a sort of*
Vellorin. } *cloth*
Vellorita, *s. f. primrose; cowslip*
Vellosilla, *s. f. mouse-ear*
Velloso, sa, *a. downy* || *hairy*
Velludo, da, *a. hairy*
Velludo, *sub. m. velvet; shag, etc.*
Vellutero, *s. m. a weaver of velvet, etc.*
Velo, *s. m. a vail or excuse; pretence*
Velocidad, *s. f. velocity; swiftness* [*swiftly*
Velocisimamente, *ad. most*
Velocisimo, ma, *a. most swift*
Velon, s. m. an oil-lamp
Velonera, s. f. the stand on wich the oil-lamp is usually placed

Velonero, *s. m. he t*
makes or sells oil-la
Veloz, *a. 2. swift*
Velozmente, *ad. swif*
Veludo, *sub. m. vel*
shag, etc.
Vena, *sub. f. a vein* ||
grain of wood
Venablo, *sub. m. a h*
man's spear
Venadero, *sub. m. a*
boar's hold, etc.
Venado, *s. m. a kin*
stag
Venaje, *s. m. the str*
or current of the w
Venal, *a. 2. belongin*
the veins || *venal*
Venalidad, *s. f. venal*
Venate, *s. m. whit*
(a bird)
Venático, ca, *adj.*
has a little of the m
man
Venatorio, ria, *a. be*
ging to ***hunting;***
natick [
Vencedor, ra, *a. con*
Vencedor, *s. m. con*
ror; vainquisher
Vencejo, *sub. m. a ti*
bind the sheave
martlet (a bird)
Vencer, *ver. a. to va*
quish; to conquer
overcome || *to bend*
Vencible, *a. 2. conq*
rable
Vencida, *s. fem. over*
ming; conquest
Vencido, da, *a. due*
be paid
Vencimiento, *sub. m*
Vencida || *bending*
Venda, *s. f. a fillet*
the head, etc. || a
dem
Vendaje, s. m. th
of a broker; br

Vendar, *ver. a. to bind with fillets*
Vendaval, *s. m. a south-west-wind*
Vendedera, *s. fem. a woman seller*
Vendedor, *s. m. a seller*
Vendeja, *s. f. a publick sale*
Vender, *v. a. to sell*
Vendible, *a. 2. vendible; saleable*
Vendicion, *sub. f. vendition; sale*
Vendimia, *s. f. vintage*
Vendimiador, *s. m. a vintager*
Vendimiar, *ver. a. to gather the grapes*
Veneficiar, *ver. a. to bewitch. V.* Beneficiar
Veneficio, *sub. m. witchcraft. V.* Beneficio
Venéfico, ca, *adj. venemous*
Venenar, *v. a. to poison*
Venenario, *s. m. an apothecary*
Veneno, *sub. m. poison || any pharmaceutick composition || drug || paint*
Venenosidad, *s. f. poisoning quality.* [*mous*
Venenoso, sa, *adj. vene-*
Venera, *s. f. a scollop-shell || a vein in mines*
Venerable, *a. 2. venerable* [*nerably*
Venerablemente, *ad. ve-*
Veneracion, *s. f. veneration*
Venerador, *s. m. he that venerates* [*rable*
Venerado, da, *adj. vene-*
Venerar, *ver. a. to venerate* [*real*
Venereo, rea, *adj. vene-*
Venero, *s. m. a vein in mines || a vein of water || the horary line in a sun-dial*
Veneruela, *s. f. a little scollop-shell*
Vengador, ra, *s. revenger; avenger*
Vengala, *s. f. a thin sort of silk-stuff || a cane* or *staff denoting command* [*revenge*
Vengancilla, *s. f. a light*
Venganza, *s. f. a revenge*
Vengar, *v. a. to revenge* or *avenge*
Vengativo, va, *adj. revengeful*
Venia, *s. fem. pardon || leave; licence*
Venial, *a. 2. venial*
Venialidad, *s. f. venialness* [*nially*
Venialmente, *adver. ve-*
Venida, *s. fem. coming; arrival || return || overflowing*
Venidero, ra, *a. future*
Venideros, *s. m. pl. descendants; posterity*
Venilla, *s. fem. a small vein* [*cle*
Venino, *s. m. a furun-*
Venir, *ver. n. to come || to fit, as apparel || to amount*
Venir á menos, *to decline, to fall to a worse state*
Venoso, sa, *a. veiny*
Venta, *s. f. a sale || an inn* [*hound*
Ventador (Perro), *a blood-*
Ventaja, *s. f. advantage*
Ventajosamente, *adver. advantageously*
Ventajoso, sa, *ad. advantageous*
Ventalla, *s. f.* the sucker *of a pump*
Ventalle, *s. m. a fan*
Ventana, *s. f. a window || nostril*
Ventanage, *s. m. all the windows of a house*
Ventanazo, *s. m. a noise made in shutting a window with force*
Ventanera, *s. fem. a woman that is always gazing at the window*
Ventanero, *s. m. he who makes frames for windows*
Ventanica, *s. f. a little window*
Ventanico, *s. m. a little window-shutter*
Ventanilla, *s. f. V.* Ventanica [tanico
Ventanillo, *s. m. V.* Ven-
Ventar, } *ver. n. to blow*
Ventear, } *(said of the wind) || to smell || to enquire || to expose to the wind*
Ventearse, *v. r. to swell || to fart* [*keeper*
Ventero, ra, *s. an inn-*
Ventilacion, *s. f. ventilation || discussion*
Ventilar, *v. a. to ventilate || to winnow || to discuss, to debate*
Ventilar, *v. n.* } *to cir-*
Ventilarse, *v. r.* } *culate (said of the wind, etc.*
Ventisca, *s. f. a strong gust of wind*
Ventiscar, *v. n. to blow hard (said of the wind when it raises the snow)*
Ventisquero, *s. m. the place where the wind has blown the snow in heaps*
Ventolera, *s. f.* a gust of wind || pride; haughtiness

Ventor, *sub. m. a blood-hound; a ranger*
Ventorrillo, } *s. m. a little*
Ventorro, } *despicable inn*
Ventosa, *s. f. cupping-glass || air-hole*
Ventosear, *v. n.* } *to fart*
Ventosearse, *v. r.* }
Ventosidad, *s. f. ventosity || a fart*
Ventoso, sa, *a. windy*
Ventrada, *s. f. a litter*
Ventral, *a. 2. belonging to the venter or belly*
Ventregada, *s. f. a litter || the coming of many things together*
Ventrera, *s. f. belly-band*
Ventriculo, *sub. m. ventricle* [*bellied*
Ventrudo, da, *a. large-*
Ventura, *s. f. good luck || venture*
Venturero, ra, *a. accidental; fortuitous*
Venturero, ra, *s. adventurer*
Venturilla, *s. fem. some good luck*
Venturina, *s. f. a kind of precious stone of a yellowish colour*
Venturo, ra, *a. future*
Venturon, *s. m. a great unexpected luck*
Venturosamente, *adver. luckily*
Venturoso, sa, *a. lucky*
Venus, *s. f. Venus*
Venustidad, *s. f. beauty; gracefulness*
Venusto, ta, *a. beautiful; graceful*
Ver, *v. a. to see || to consider || to understand || to find || to foresee*
Ver, *s. m. shew; appearance; outside*
A mi ver, *in my opinion*
Vera, *s. f. the sea-shore*
Veras, *pl. truth; verity || eagerness* [*earnest*
De veras, *adv. in good*
Veracidad, *s. f. veracity*
Veranada, *s. f. the summer for the beasts*
Veranar, } *v. n. to pass*
Veranear, } *the summer*
Veraneo, } *sub. m. the*
Veranero, } *place where beasts pass the summer*
Veranico, } *s. m. a short*
Veranillo, } *summer*
Veraniego, ga, *a. of, or belonging to, the summer || sick during the hot summer || imperfect; defective*
Verano, *s. m. summer*
Veraz, *a. 2. veracious*
Verbal, *a. 2. verbal*
Verbalmente, *adv. verbally* [*blade*
Verbasco, *sub. m wool-*
Verbena, *s. f. vervine*
Verberacion, *s. f. verberation*
Verberar, *v. a. to verberate* [*example*
Verbigracia, *adver. for*
Verbo, *s. m. a word; a term; a verb*
Echar verbos, *to swear, to curse*
Verbosidad, *s. f. verbosity*
Verboso, sa, *a. verbose*
Verdacho, *s. m. a light green colour || a kind of mineral green earth*
Verdad, *s. f. truth*
Verdaderamente, *adver. truly*
Verdadero, ra, *a. true; real; sincere*
Verdal, *a. 2. greennish*
Verdasca, *s. a thin rod*
Verde, *sub. m. the green colour || verdigrease || tartness of wine || grass*
Verde, *a. 2. green || tart || brisk; lusty; fresh*
Verdea, *s. f. verde; verdea*
Verdear, *ver. n. to grow green* [*green*
Verdecelledon, *s. m. sea-*
Verdecer, *v. neu. to grow green*
Verdecillo, *s. m. a green-finch* [*green*
Verdegay, *s. m. a light*
Verdeguear, *ver. n. to look or grow green*
Verdemar, *s. m. a stone of a sea-green colour used by painters*
Verdemontaña, *s. m. a mineral of a green colour*
Verderol, *sub. m. a kind of shell-fish* [*finch*
Verderon, *s. m. green-*
Verdete, *sub. m. verdigrease*
Verdin, *s. m.* } *harshness; tart-*
Verdina, *s. f.* } *ness of wine, etc.*
Verdinegro, gra, *a. deep green*
Verdino, na, *adj. of a fine green colour*
Verdiseco, ca, *adj. half dry*
Verdolaga, *s. f. purslain*
Verdor, *s. m. greenness || green years; youth || briskness; lustiness*
Verdoso, sa, *a. greenish*
Verdoyo, *sub. m. a green moss that grows upon stones, etc.*
Verdugado, *s. m. a fardingale*
Verdugo, *sub. m. executioner; hangman || scion; sprig || a w*

raised, or *a mark left with a lash*

Verdugon, *s. m. a great scion* or *wheal*, *etc. V.* Verdugo

Verduguillo, *s. m. a little scion* || *a tubercle on a leaf* || *a narrow razor*

Verdulero, ra, *sub. an herb-man* or *woman*

Verdura, *s. f. greenness*, *etc. V.* Verdor || *any pot-herb*

Verduras, *pl. a forest-work suit of hangings*

Vereda, *s. f. a path*

Veredario, ria, *adj. an epithet applied to postilions*, *post-horses*, *etc.*

Veredero, *s. m. a messenger that carries to small districts*

Veredilla, *s. fem. a little path*

Verga, *s. f. rod; wand; pole* || *a yard* || *a man's privy member*

Vergajo, *s. m. a bull's pizzle*

Vergel, *sub. m. orchard* || *flower-garden*

Vergeta, *s. fem. a small rod*, *etc.*

Vergonzante, *s. m. a poor person ashamed to beg*

Vergonzante, *a.* 2. *ashamed* || *shameful*

Vergonzosamente, *adver. bashfully* || *shamefully*

Vergonzoso, sa, *a. bashful* || *shameful*

Verguear, *v. a. to beat with a rod*

Vergüenza, *s. f. shame* || *a shameful action* || *the point of honour* || *the pillary* [*parts*

Vergüenzas, *pl. the privy*

Verguer, } *s. m. a verger*
Verguero, }

Vergueta, *s fem. a small rood; a twig* [*pole*

Vergueta, *s. f. a catch-*

Vericueto, *s. m. a rough*, *uneven place*, *etc.*

Vericuetos, *pl. circumlocutions*, *etc.*

Verídico, ca, *a. veridical*

Verificacion, *s. f. verification*

Verificar, *v. a. to verify*

Verificativo, va, *a. verifying*

Verisímil, *a.* 2. *likely*

Verisimilitud, *s. f. likeliness* [*grate*

Verja, *s. f. lattice-work;*

Vermicular, *a.* 2. } *vermi-*
Verminoso, sa, *a.* } *nous*

Vernal, *a.* 2. *vernal*

Vero, ra, *a. true*

Verónica, *s. f. fluelling*, *speedwell*

Veros, *sub. m. pl. vaire* (*in heraldry*)

Verosímil, *a.* 2. *likely*

Verosimilitud, *s. f. likeliness*

Verraco, *s. m. a hog*

Verraquear, *v. neut. to grumble*, (*as a hog does*)

Verriondez, *s. f. the lust of hogs*

Verriondo, da, *a. in lust* || *withered* || *ill boiled*

Verrocal, *s. m. V.* Berrocal [*wort*

Verrucaria, *s. fem. wart-*

Verruga, *s. f. a wart*

Verrugoso, sa, } *adj.*
Verruguiento, ta, } *warty*

Verruguilla, *s. f. a little wart* [*round*

Versar, *ver. n.* to turn

Versarse, *v. r.* to make *one's self skilful*, etc.

Versatil, *a.* 2. *that will turn; versatile*

Versicula, *s. f. the place where the choir-books are laid up*

Versiculario, *s. m. a keeper of the choir-books* || *he that sings the verses* [*of a chapter*)

Versículo, *s. m. a verse*

Versificar, *v. a. to versify*

Versillo, *sub. m. a little verse*

Version, *s. f. version*

Versista, *sub. m. a verse maker*

Verso, *sub. m. a verse* || *a small piece of cannon*

Vertebra, *s. f. the chine-bone*

Vertedero, *s. m. a sink*

Vertedor, *s. m. gutter*, *etc.* || *a scoop*

Vertellos, *s. m. pl. parrels*

Verter, *v. a. to spill; to shed* || *to translate*

Vertibilidad, *sub f. aptness to move* or *turn; verticity*

Vertible, *a.* 2. *moveable* || *versatile*

Vertical, *a.* 2. *vertical*

Vertice, *sub. m. vertex* || *top; summit*

Verticidad, *s. f. verticity*

Vertiente, *s m. the running down of waters* || *the steep of a hill*, *etc.*

Vertiginoso, sa, *a. vertiginous* [*giddiness*

Vértigo, *s. m. vertigo;*

Véspero, *s. m. the evening star*

Vespertillo, *s. m. a bat*

Vespertino, na, *a. of the evening*

Vestala, *s. f. a vestal*

Veste, *s. f. a garment*

Vestidillo, *s. m. a petty ragged garment, etc.*

Vestido, *s. m. a garment* || *a suit of clothes*

Vestidura, *s. f. a garment* || *sacerdotal clothes*

Vestigio, *s. m. footstep* || *remain*

Vestiglo, *s. m. an horrible monster; a phantom*

Vestimenta, *s. f.* }
Vestimento, *s. m* } *raiment; garment*

Vestir, *v. a. to clothe* || *to adorn* || *to overcast a bastion with stone, etc.* || *to dress one's self*

Vestuario, *s. m. an attiring-room*

Veta, *s. f. a vein of metal, etc.* || *stripe (in a stuff)* || *a ribbon*

Vetado, da, *adj. full of veins*

Veterano, *s. m. veteran*

Vetilla, *s. f. a little vein*

Vexacion, *s. f. vexation*

Vexámen, *s. m. a nipping jest; a scoff* || *a critical examination*

Vexar, *v. a. to vex* || *to criticise*

Vexiga, *s. f. bladder* || *blister* || *vesicle*

Vexigas, *pl. pimples of the small pox*

Vexigatorio, ria, *blistering*

Vexigatorio, *s. m. a vesicatory*

Vexigazo, *sub. m. a blow with a bladder full of wind*

Dar un vexigazo, to play a trick

Vexigüela, }
Vexiguilla, } *s. f. a little bladder, etc.; a vesicle*

Vexiguero, *s. m. a rook (among gamesters)*

Vexilo, *s. m. standard; colours, etc.*

Vez, *s. f. a time* || *a turn* || *a glass* or *draught of wine, etc.*

Una vez, *once* — dos veces, *twice* — tres veces, *thrice* — cien veces, *a hundred times, etc.*

A' veces, *sometimes* || *by turns*—tal vez, *perhaps* — tal vez, ó tal qual vez, *sometimes*

Veces, *pl. place; room; stead*

Vezar, *v. a to accustom*

Vezo, *s. m. custom; use* || *V.* Bezo

Via, *s. f. a way*

Via lactea, *the milky way*

Viadera, *sub. f. a piece of wood in a weaver's loom*

Viador, *s. m. a traveller*

Viage, *s. m. a voyage, a journey*

Viagero, }
Viajador, } *a s. m. a traveller*

Viajar, *v. n. to travel*

Vial, *a. 2. belonging to the roads* or *to travelling*

Vianda, *s. f. meat; victuals*

Viandante, *s. m. a traveller* || *a passenger*

Viaraza, *sub. f. looseness (in a horse)* || *a blunder*

Viático, *s. m. viaticum*

Vibora, *s. f. a viper*

Viborrillo, la, *s.* }
Viborrezno, *s. m.* } *a little young viper*

Vibracion, *s. f. vibration*

Vibrar, *v. a. to brandish;*

nan which
ith the af-
seeing
. the ear-
when gla-
o glaze ear-
the glass-
a house ||
rtition
idriera, *a*
e person
fem. glass-
lass-seller's
. m. glass-
ss seller
glass
. glassy
V. Vidrio
elonging to
m. *V*. Ve-
i old wo-
very old-
[*man*
. an oldish-
n oldman
cks of hair
oles
old
V. Bieldo
. m. a soft
wind || *air*
. the belly ;
s. m. ven-
m. friday ||
e day
beam
the beam ,
a press

Vigésimo, ma, *a. twentieth*

Vigilancia, *s. f. vigilance*

Vigilante, *a.* 2. *vigilant*

Vigilar, *v. n. to watch ; to take care of...*

Vigilia, *s. f. watching* || *labour ; study* || *ever ; vigil*

Vigor, *s. m. vigour*

Vigorar, *ver. a. to give vigour* [*gorously*

Vigorosamente, *adv. vi-*

Vigoroso, sa, *a. vigorous*

Vigotas, *s. f. pl. ribs of a parrel*

Viguería, *s fem. timber-work ; the beans of a building, etc.*

Vigueta, *s. f. a little bean*

Vihuela, *s. f. a sort of lute*

Vihuelista, *s. m. one who plays upon the* Vihuela

Vil, *a.* 2. *vile*

Vilano, *s. m. the down of a thistle's flower*

Vileza, *s. f. vileness*

Vilicacion, *s. f. management*

Vilipendiar, *v. a. to despise ; to abuse*

Vilipendio, *sub. m. contempt ; abuse* [*vile*

Vilísimo, ma, *adj. most*

Villa, *s. f. a town*

Village, *s. m. a village*

Villanage, *sub. m. the country people* || *villanage ; soccage*

Villanchon, *s. m. a clown*

Villancico, *s. m. a sort of pastoral poem* or *song*

Andar en villancicos, *to repeat frivolous excuses, etc.*

Villanciquero, *s. m. one who composes* villancicos

Villanería, *s. f. V.* Villanage, *and* villanía

Villanesco, ca, *a. belonging to the country ; clownish*

Villanía, *s. f. lowness of birth, etc.* || *a base action ; a villainy* || *an unmannerly expression, etc.*

Villano, na, *a. meanly extracted* || *clownish ; rustical* || *coarse ; unmannerly* || *base ; shameful*

Villano, *sub. m. a clown* || *a rustical dance*

Villanote, *s. m. aum. de* Villano.

Villar, *s. m. a great village* || *a particular game at billiards*

Villazgo, *sub. m. a tax upon the towns*

Villeta, *s. fem. a little town ; a borough*

Villete, *s. m. a billet. V.* Billete

Villivina, *s. f. a kind of linen* [*seat*

Villoría, *s. f. a country*

Villorin, *s. m. a coarse sort of cloth*

Villorrio, *s. m. a small paltry village*

Vilmente, *adv. vilely*

Vilo (en), *ad. in the air*

Vilordo, da, *a. heavy ; lazy ; dull*

Vilorta, *s. f. a ring made of osier, etc.*

Vimbre, *s. m. osier*

Vinagera, *sub. f. a mass cruet*

Vinagre, *s. m. vinegar*

Vinagrera, *s. f. vinegar bottle or cruet*

Vinagrero, *sub. m. vinegar-man*

Vinagrillo, s. m. a sort of paint made with vinegar || a rosy vinegar used in snuff
Vinagroso, sa, a. rough; austere [dresser
Vinatiego, s. m. a vine-
Vinatero, sub. m. a merchant of wine
Vincapervinca, s. f. periwinkle
Vinculable, adj. 2. that may be entailed
Vincular, v. a. to entail an estate || to make fast
Vinculo, s. m. tie; bond; knot || an entail || a thraldom
Vindicacion, s. f. vindication || revenge
Vindicar, v. a. to vindicate || to revenge || to claim or demand
Vindicativo, va, a. vindicative; revengeful || apologetick
Vindicta, s. f. revenge
Viniebla, s f. dog's tongue (an herb)
Vino, s. m. wine
Vinolencia, sub. f. drunkenness
Vinolento, ta, adj. given to wine or drunk
Vinosidad, s. f. vinosity
Vinoso, sa, a. vinous || given to wine
Viña, s. f. a vineyard
Viñadero, s. m. keeper of vineyards [dresser
Viñador, sub. m. a vine-
Viñedo, s. m. a district that is all vineyard
Viñero, s. m. the landlord of many vineyards
Viola, s. f. a viol || a violet || a gilly-flower
Violaceo, cea, adj. of a violet-colour

Violacion, s. f. violation
Violado, da, a. of a violet colour || chiefly made of violets
Violador, s. m. violator
Violar, v. a. to violate || to force a woman || to profane || to spoil
Violencia, s. f. violence || a rape
Violentamente, adv. violently
Violentar, v. a. to force; to use violence
Violento, ta, a violent
Violeta, s. f. a violet
Violin, s. m. a violin; a fiddle || a fiddler
Violinista, s. m. a skilful fiddler
Violon, s. m. a bass-viol || one who plays upon the bass-viol
Violoncillo, s. m. pocket-violin || a paltry fiddler
Viperino, na, a. viperine
Vira, s. f. a quarrel of a cross-bow || a welt of a shoe
Viraton, sub. m. a large dart
Vireo, s. m. green finch
Virey, s. m. viceroy
Vireyna, sub. f. viceroy's wife
Vireynato, } sub. m. viceroyatly
Vireyno, }
Virgen, s. f. a virgin
Virgen, a. 2. virgin
Virginal, a. 2. virginal
Virginea, s. f. tobacco of Virginia
Virgineo, nea, a. virginal
Virginidad, s fem. virginity
Virgo, s. m. virgo
Virgula, s. fem a little rod, etc. || a comma
Virgulilla, s. f. a comma

Virgulto, s.
bush
Viril, s. m
to set b
ate.
Viril, a. 2
Virilidad,
manhoo
Virilla, s.,
Virilmente
manly
Virio, s. m
Viripotent
riageab
girl).
Virolento,
the smal
with it
Virotazo,
wound
- V. Vir
Virote, s.
a cross
ring pu
of slav
bully
Virtual, a
Virtualida
lity
Virtualme
Virtud, s
Virtuosam
tuously
Virtuoso,
|| pou
cious
Viruelas,
small p
Virulenci
Virulente
lent
Viruta, s
Visage, s
grimac
Visagra,
Visceras
bowe
Viscor
Visc

the sight of
ɔiser
s. f. visibi-

visible
, ad. visibly
·m. vision ;
parition ||
[visionary
ia , *adj. y s.*
isier
n. a visit ,
| visitation
searching ||
|| a visitant
:el , *a gaol-*

f. visitation
. a visiter ||

to visit || to
ɔnquire into
that can see
ɔ. a. to have
ɔse of
f. a glimp-
ɔerfect sight
re ; suspi-

limmering;
the gloss of

o. *V.* Biso-

a. visual
ɔ. a viceroy
eve
vespers
ht || aspect;
: || vision ;
|| notice ;

na , *one who*
goods and

before — á
ing ; near ;
ectly ; wit-
ion

Vistas , *pl. the windows and doors of any edifice*
Vistillas , *s. f. pl. an high place to discorver the country from*
Vistosamente , *ad. beautifully*
Vistoso , sa , *a. gay ; beautiful*
Visual , *a. 2. visual*
Vital , *a. 2. vital*
Vitalicio , cia , *a. during the life of one*
Vitalidad , *s. f. vitality*
Vitando , da , *avoidable*
Vitela , *s. f. a young heifer || vellum*
Vitelina , *a. f. of a dark colour (speaking of the bile)*
Vitor , Vitorear , Vitoria , etc. *V.* Victor , etc.
Vitreo , trea , *a. vitreous ; glassy*
Vitrificacion , *s. f. vitrification*
Vitrificar , *v. a. to vitrify*
Vitriolo , *s. m. vitriol*
Vitualla , *s. f. victuals*
Vituallado , da , *adj. victualled*
Vituperable , *a. 2. vituperable*
Vituperacion , *s. f. vituperation ; blame*
Vituperador , *s. m. a blamer*
Vituperar , *v. a. to vituperate ; to blame*
Vituperio , *s. m. blame ; censure || a shameful action*
Vituperiosamente , *adver. shamefully*
Vituperioso , sa , *a. shameful ; ignominious*
Viuda , *s. f. a widow*
Viudedad , *s. f.* } *widowhood*
Viudez , *s. f.* }
Viudita , *s. f. an young widow*

Viudo , *s. m. a widower*
Viva ! *int. let him live !*
Vivac , *s. m. an extraordinary night guard*
Vivacidad , *s. f. vivacity ; liveliness || vitality*
Vivacisimo , ma , *a. most lively*
Vivamente , *adv. lively ; sprightly*
Vivandero , *s. m. a sutler*
Vivaque , *s. m. a small quarter for soldiers*
Vivar , *s. m. a warren || a park*
Vivaracho , cha , *a. brisk ; gay ; lively*
Vivaz , *a. 2. long-vived || strong || gay ; active ; lively*
Vivera , *s. f.* } *a park || a warren || a pond*
Vivero , *s. m.* }
Víveres , *s. m. pl. provisions ; victuals*
Viveza , *s. f. liveliness ; sprightliness*
Vividero , ra , *a. habitable*
Vividor , *sub. m. a long-vived man || one that knows how to live well*
Vividor , ra , *a. lasting ; durable*
Vivienda , *s. f. a dwelling*
Viviente , *a. 2. living*
Vivificacion , *s. f. vivification*
Vivificador , *sub. m. one that vivifies*
Vivificar , *v. a. to vivify*
Vivificativo , va , *a. vivifical*
Vivífico , ca , *a. vivifick*
Vivíparo , ra , *a. viviparous*
Vivir , *v. n. to live*
Viva v. m. mil años , ó muchos años , i thank you .
Vivo , va , adj. alive ...

the strongest part of... *any jutting out in a building* || *mange*

Vizcacha, *s. f. a kind of hare in America*

Vizcondado, *sub. m. viscounty*

Vizconde, *sub. m. a viscount* [*countess*

Vizcondesa, *sub. f. a vis-*

Voace, } *your worship;*
Voarce, } *you, sir* (*used for* usted *or* vuestra merced)

Vocablo, *s. m. a word*

Vocabulario, *s. m. vocabulary*

Vocacion, *s. f. vocation* || *the name given to a church*

Vocal, *a.* 2. *vocal*

Vocal, *s. f. a vowel*

Vocal, *s. m. one that votes in an election*

Vocalmente, *ad. orally*

Vocativo, *s. m. vocative*

Voceador, *s. m. a bowler*

ladle of a water-mill

Voladero, ra, *a. that does or can fly* || *transitory*

Voladero, *s. m. a precipice*

Volador, ra, *a. flying*

Volador, *s. m. a bean* || *a flying fish*

Volandas (en), *a. flying through the air*

Volandero, ra, *a. flying; hanging in the air* || *casual* || *instable*

Volante, *a.* 2. *flying*

Ciervo volante, *bull-fly*

Volante, *s. m. a sort of thin veil* || *a shuttle cock* || *a running footman*

Volanton, *s. m. the bird that is ready to fly*

Volar, *ver. n. to fly* || *to flutter* || *to fly about* || *to disappear*

Volar, *v. a. to blow up with gun-powder* || *to fly at* (*said of a hawk*)

Volatería, *s. f. the haw-*

volca
Voltari
tanc
Voltari
Volteac
vaul
Voltear
abou
tumb
Voltear
overt
Voltege
to pu
Voltere
Volteta
Volubil
bility
Voluble
|| *ch*
Volúme
Volumi
mino
Volunt
mina
Volunt
volun

'nge one
ther
to sing
, to de-
!o turn;
hat may
m. tur-
'he twis-
'the guts
ec. that
[nut
omiting
'dj. that
) vomit
'omitive
a vomi-
mit
a vomit
ng one's
. mitory
ıdj. vo-
racity
ulf; an
a. gulfy
cious
ortese
adject.
'ou
talk to
ye and
'on. ye;
plural
voter ||
te in an
to vow
'. Botar
'otive
|| a vo-

tive || *a vote* || *an oath* || *a curse*

Voz, *s. f. a voice* || *a singer* || *a vote* || *the sound of an instrument* || *a report* [*fame*

Pública voz, *a common*

Voznar, *v. n. to cry like; a swan* [*excellence*

Vuecelencia, *s. fem. your*

Vuelco, *s. m. a turn; a turning about*

Vuelo, *s. m. flight of a brid, etc.* || *elevation of the mind*

Vuelos, *pl. ruffles*

Vuelta, *s. f. a turning about* || *an overturning* || *a change* || *a return* || *the back side* || *a ruffle* || *a ploughing*

Venir de vuelta, *to come back* — otra vuelta, *another time* — andar á vueltas, *to quarrel* — tener vueltas, *to be inconstant*

Vuelto, ta, *p. p. of* volver, *turned*

Vuesamerced, *s. f. your worship* [*lordship*

Vuesaseñoría, *s. f. your*

Vueso, sa, } *pron.*
Vuestro, tra, } *yours*

Vulgacho, *s. m. the mob*

Vulgar, *adj. 2. vulgar; common* [*rity*

Vulgaridad, *s. f. vulga-*

Vulgarizar, *v. a to divulge* || *to translate into vulgar tongue*

Vulgarizarse, *v. r. to become common*, or *vulgar* [*garly*

Vulgarmente, *adv. vul-*

Vulgata, *s. fem. vulgar translation of the bible*

Vulgo, *s. m. the vulgar; the mob; the multitude*

Vulnerable, *a. 2. vulnerable* [*ding*

Vulneracion, *s. f. woun-*

Vulnerar, *ver. a. to infringe; to break* || *to wound*, or *blemish*

Vulnerario, ria, *adject. vulnerary*

Vulpeja, *s f. a fox*

Vulto, *s. m. face; visage* || *V.* Bulto

Vulva, *s. f. the womb*

Vusted, *s. m. your worship* (*used for* vuestra merced)

X

XABALON, *s. m. one of the small beams in forming á roof*

Xabalonar, *v. a. to place the small beams in forming a roof*

Xabalcon, *s. m. V.* Xabalon [balonar

Xabalconar, *v. a. V.* Xa-

Xabardillo, *s. m. V.* Jabardillo

Xabeba, *s. fem. a sort of Moorish flute*

Xabeca, *s. f. a large net*

Xabega, *s. f. V.* Xabeba || *V.* Xabeca

Xabeguero, ra, *adj. belonging to the net called* Xabega

Xabeguero, *s. m. he that fishes with the* Xabega

Xabeque, *s. m. a xebeck*

Xable, *s. m. a croe or notch of a cask*

Xabon, *s. m. soap*

Xabonado, *s. m soaping* || *the linen, when souped* [ping

Xabonadura, sub. *f.* soa-

Xabonaduras, plur. soaping-water

Xabonar, *v. a. to soap; to wash with soap* || *to scold*
Xaboncillo, *s. m.* V. Xabonete
Xabonera, *s. f. soap-wort*
Xaboneria, *s. f. a soap-house* [*boiler*
Xabonero, *s. m. a soap-*
Xabonete, **Xabonete de olor**, } *subst. m. a wash-ball*
Xácara, *sub. f. a song so called* || *a sort of dance* || *a gang of young people singing at night through the streets* || *vexation* || *lie; story*
Xacarear, *ver. n. to sing* Xacaras || *to vex; to teaze*
Xacarero, *s. m. one who likes to sing* Xácaras || *a jovial fellow*
Xácaro, *s. m. a bully; a boaster* á lo xácaro, *ostentatiously*
Xacena, *s. f. a cross-beam*
Xaco, *s. m. a garment wore anciently by soldiers*
Xada, *s. f. hoe*
Xadiar, *v. a. to hoe*
Xaga, *s. f. a wound*
Xalapa, *s. f. jalap*
Xalear, *v. a. to call the dogs in hunting*
Xallulo, *s. m. a sort of cake baked on charcoal*
Xalma, *s. f.* V. Enxalma
Xaloque, *s. m. the south-west wind*
Xalxacolt, *s. m. a sort of pear-tree in America*
Xamacuco, *s. m.* V. Zamacuco
Xamar, *v. a. to call*
Xambrar, *ver. a.* V. Enxambrar

Xamete, *s. m. an ancient sort of cloth*
Xamuga, *s. f. a sort of saddle for women*
Xamuscar, *v. a.* V. Chamuscar
Xanable, *s. m. senvy*
Xandalo, la, *adj. affected in speaking or walking*
Xano, na, *adj.* V. Llano
Xantio, *s. m. burdock*
Xantoline, *s. f. worm-seed*
Xapoypa, *s. f. a sort of pancake*
Xaque, *s. m. a check at chess*
Xaque y mate, *checkmate*
Xaque de aqui, *go out*
Xaquear, *v. a. to check the king (at chess)*
Xaqueca, *s. f. megrim*
Xaqueta, *s. fem. a sort of loose upper garment*
Xaquetilla, *s. f. dim. de* Xaqueta
Xaqueton, *s. m. aum. de* Xaqueta || *a hector*
Xáquima, *s. f. a halter*
Xaquimazo, *s. m. a blow with a halter* || *misfortune*
Xara, *s. f. a sort of cistus* || *a kind of dart* or *arrow*
Xarabe, *s. m. sirup*
Xarabearse, *v. r. to make use of sirups*
Xaral, *s. m. a place full of shrubs* or *bushes*
Xaramago, *sub. m. wild rape* [*press*
Xarayz, *sub. m. a wine-*
Xarcia, *s. f. a bundle* or *heap of several things*
Xarcias, pl. *the riggings of a ship* || *fishing-tackling*
Xareta, *sub. f. a netting*

used on board a shi
|| *V.* Jareta
Xarife, *s. m. cheriff*
Xarifo, fa, *adj. curio*
beautiful; lovely
Xaropar, *v. a. to ad*
julaps, etc.
Xaroparse, *v. r. to ma*
use of julaps, etc.
Xarope, *sub. m. julap*
any bitter drench
Xaropear, *v. a.* V. Xaropar [*hounds*
Xauria, *s. f. a pack of*
Xauto, ta, *adj. insipid*
Xazilla, *sub. f. footstep;*
track
Xea, *s. fem. an ancient duty paid upon goods*
Xeera, *sub. f. a drained marsh*
Xefe, *s. m. a chief; commander*
Xemal, *adjec. s. long of half a foot*
Xeme, *s. m. half a foo*
|| *the female face*
Xenape, *s. m. senvy*
Xepe, *s. m. allum*
Xeque, *s. m. lord; com*
mander; governor
Xera, *s. f. as much lan*
as a pair of oxen ca
plough in a day
Xerapellina, *s. f. old rag*
ged clothes
Xerga, *s. f. any coars*
cloth or *stuff* || *can*
straw-bed
Xergon, *s. m. a straw-be*
|| *the paunch*
Xerguilla, *s. f. a sort*
cloth half silk, ha
wool
Xerife, *s. m. cheriff*
Xeringa, *s. f. a syringe* ||
troublesome insta
ces, etc.
Xeringar, *v. a. to*

ge || *to molest ; to plague* [*ging*
Xeringazo, *s. m. syringe*
Xervilla, *s. f. V.* Servilla
Xeta, *s. f. V.* Geta
Xia, *s. f. V.* Chia
Xibia, *s. f. cuttle-fish* || *V.* Xibion
Xibion, *s. m. cuttle-bone*
Xicara, *s. f. a dish used to drink chocolate out of*
Xifa, *s. f. the bad part of the meat that they throw away when they kill beast*
Xiferada, *s. f. a wound with a butcher's knife*
Xiferia, *s. fem. the butcher's business*
Xifero, *s. m. a butcher* || *a butcher's knife*
Xifero, ra, *adj. belonging to a butcher* || *dirty ; filthy*
Xilguero, *s. m. goldfinch*
Xilobálsamo, *sub. m. the balm-tree*
Xímia, *s. f. a she-ape*
Xímio, *s. m. a he-ape*
Xiride, *s. fem. stinging corn flag* [*reed*
Xisca, *s. f. a kind of wild*
Xitar, *v. a. to drive out* or *away*
Xixallar, *s. m. a place full of* xixallos
Xixallo, *sub. m. a sort of cytisus* [*horses*
Xo, *a word used to stop*
Xuagarzo, *s. m. a thorny bush that grows in mountainous places*
Xubete, *s. m. an ancient armour*
Xucla, *s. fem. one of the seven signs that the Arabs place on their consonants to denote some vowel*
Xugo, *s. m. juice ; gravy ; moisture*
Xugosidad, *s. f. juiceness*
Xugoso, sa, *adj. juicy*
Xugue, *s. m. filthiness ; grease, etc.*
Xulo, *s. m. the leader of the flock*
Xurel, *sub. m. a sort of sea-roach*
Xutà, *s. f. a kind of goose in America*

Y

Y *part. conj. and.*
Ya, *adv. already* || *now* || *another time* || *at last* || *sometimes*
Yacer, *v. n. to lye in a place*
Yacija, *s. f. a bed, etc. where one lies* || *grave; tomb*
Yactura, *s. f. a loss*
Yambo, *s. m. an iamb*
Yámbico, ca, *a. iambick*
Yantar, *s. m. food ; meat* || *an ancient tax*
Yaro, *s. m. calves-foot (herb)*
Yedra, *s. f. ivy*
Yegua, *s. f. a mare*
Yeguacería, *s. f. a stud of mares*
Yeguada, *s. f. a herd of mares*
Yegüerizo, } *s. m. a keeper of mares*
Yegüero, }
Yelmo, *s. m. a helmet*
Yelo, *s. m. frost* || *ice*
Yema, *s. fem. bud ; eye ; button* || *the yolk of an egg*
Yema del dedo, *the end* or *top of the finger*
Yentes y vinientes, *comers and goers*
Yerba, *s. f. herb* || *any venemous plant* || *herbage ; grass*
Yerbas, *pl. pot-herbs*
Yermar, *v. a. to dispeople*
Yermo, *s. m. a desert ; a solitude*
Yermo, ma, *adj. desert*
Yernalmente, *adv. like a son-in-law*
Yernar, *v. a. to force one to be a son-in-law*
Yernecillo, *s. m. a paltry son-in-law*
Yerno, *s. m. a son-in-law*
Yerro, *s. m. error ; mistake*
Yerto, ta, *adject. stiff ; stretched out, etc.*
Yervo, *s. m. fitch ; vetch*
Yesal, } *s. m. plaster-quarry*
Yesar, }
Yesca, *s. fem. tinder* || *a thing quite dry* || *incentive of any passion*
Yesera, *s. fem. plaster-quarry*
Yesería, *s. f. the building with plaster*
Yesero, *s. m. a plasterer*
Yeso, *subst. m. plaster ; parget*
Yeson, *s. m. rubbish*
Yezgo, *s. m. a dwarf elder*
Yo, *pron. I*
Yogar, } *v. n. to stay ; to abide*
Yoguir, }
Yuca, *s. f. yucca-root*
Yugada, *s. f. an acre of ground*
Yugo, *s. m. a yoke*
Yuguero, *s. m. a ploughman*
Yugular, *a. 2. jugular*
Yunque, *s. m. an anvil*
Yunta, *s. f. a yoke of oxen*
Yuntería, *s. f. the place where they keep the oxen, etc.* [*uni*
Yunto, ta, *adj. joi*

f. an horizon-
in oil-mills
f. command
ion, s. f. juxta-

.f. jujube

Z

word used to
dogs
s. f. a kind of
loes
.f. } the run-
ento, } ning of
} a ship
d [aground
ver. n. to run
s. m. the run-
round
a sort of ship
a. to stir; to
or mix || to
to throw down,

} s. f. plun-
a, } ging; sin-
ddenly into wa

. a. to plunge;
uddenly under

, v. r. to plun-
sink || to hide
lf
} s. f. a noisy
} quarrel
ub. m. a little
or market
a. to frighten
[bowl
a dutch ware-
f. flight; run-
ay || clearing
ip
. to adorn; to
|| to clear a
[run away
r. to fly; to

Zafareche, *s. m. a pond*

Zafari (granada), *s. f. a pomegranate that has square kernels*

Zafariche, *s. m. a board to put earthen pots on*

Zaferia, *s. f. a hamlet || a farm*

Zafiedad, *s. f. rusticity; clownishness*

Zafio, fia, *adj. rude; unpolished; gross*

Zafir, } *s. m. saphire*
Zafiro, }

Zafirino, na, *adjec. of a shaphire colour*

Zafo, fa, *adj free; without hindrance, etc. || safe; free from danger or hurt*

Zafon, *s. m. V.* Zahon

Zaga, *s. f. back; backside || the load put in the back part of a cart*

Zaga, *s. m. he who is the last player*

Zagal, *s. m. a stout youth || a young shepherd || an under petticoat*

Zagala, *subst. f. a young maid, or shepherdess*

Zagalejo, ja, *sub. a very young shepherd or shepherdess* [*petticoat*

Zagalejo, *s. m. a sort of*

Zagalito, *s. m. dim. de* Zagal

Zaguan, *s. m. a porch*

Zaguanete, *s. m. a little porch*

Zaguero, ra, *adject. the last; the hindmost*

Zahareño, ña, *adj. haggard || wild; fierce, disdainful*

Zaheo (dobla), *s. f. an ancient gold coin*

Zaheridor, *s. m. he that reproaches*

Zaherimiento, s
reproach
Zaherir, *v. a. to*
Zahinas, *s. f. p*
of pap
Zahon, *s. m. g*
wide breeches
Zahonado, da, *a*
Zahondar, *v. a.*
to sink in the
Zahori, *sub. m.*
pretends to se
bowels of th
etc.
Zahorra, *s. f. ba*
Zahumar, Zahu
Sahumar, etc.
Zahurda, *s. f. a*
|| any filthy
Zalá, *sub. f. the*
prayers or wo
Hacer la zalá,
one
Zalagarda, *s. f.*
buscade || a s
tack || a snare
quarrel, etc.
Zalama, } *a*
Zalamería, } *ter*
Zalamero, ra, *s*
terer
Zalea, *s. f. a she*
dried but not
Zalear, *v. a. to*
to drag || to
by crying za,
Zalema, *s. f. a*
bow
Zaleo, *s. m. the*
sheep pulled
by the wolf ||
shaking [
Zalona, *s. f. a l*
Zamacuco, *s. m.*
a silly fellow
kenness
Zamanza, *s. f.*
ling; a wh
Zamarra, *s.*

of sheep skins with the wool on
marrear, *v. a. to drag and tear || to cudgel || to press close in a dispute* [Zamarro
marrico, *s. m. dim. de*
marrilla, *s. f. a small sheep's skin || a sort of penny-royal*
marro, *s. m. a garment made* or *lined with sheep skins || a sheep's skin || a dunce*
Barbas de zamarro, *a thick dirty beard*
marron, *s. m. aum. de* Zamarro
mbarco, *s. m. a large strap tied round the mules drawing a coach*
mbo, *s. m. a wild beast in America*
mbo, ba, *a. splay foot*
mboa, *s. fem. a sort of quince || a kind of citron*
mbomba, *s. f. a pastoral drum* or *timbrel*
mbombo, *subs. mas. a clown; a rude witless fellow*
mborondon, na, } *adj.*
mborotudo, da, } *gross; rude; clownish*
mbra, *s. f. a Moorish feast* or *dance || a merry-making*
mbucarse, *v. r. to hide one's self suddenly || to put one's cards under the stock*
mbuco, *s. m. hidding one's self suddenly, etc*
mbullida, *s. f. sinking into the water suddenly || a particular trick in fencing*
bullirse, *ver. r. to plunge; to sink suddenly into water*
Zampalimosnas, *s. m. a beggar* [*toh*
Zampapalo, *s. m. a glut-*
Zampar, *v. a. to put one thing in another suddenly || to eat voraciously*
Zamparse, *v. r. to rush suddenly into a place*
Zampatortas, bodigos, etc. *s. m. a glutton*
Zampoña, *s. f. a pastoral instrument consisting of several pipes || a poor of the hospital || an unwitty saying*
Zampuzar, *v. a. to put* or *sink into water || to hide*
Zampuzo, *s. m. sinking under water || hiding*
Zanahoria, *s. f. parsnep || a vain and false compliment*
Zanca, *s. f. a bird's leg || a spindle shank*
Zancas de araña, *shifts; subterfuges*
Zancada, *s. fem. a large step; a stride*
Zancadilla, *s. f. a trip || a snare; a fraud*
Zancado, da, *a. insipid*
Zancajear, *v. a. to tread aukwardly kicking up the heel* [*a coach*
Zancajera, *s. f. the step of*
Zancajiento, ta, *adj. V.* Zancajoso
Zancajo, *sub. m. heel || a dull fellow*
Zancajoso, sa, *adj. splay foot || dirty; bedaggled || dull; blundering*
Zancarron, *subst. m. the heel's bone || any bone dry and without flesh || an old, lean, ugly person || an ignorant professor*
Zanco, *s. m. stilts || one who dances with stilts*
Zancudo, da, *adj. long-legged*
Zandalia, Zándalo, *Voy.* **Sandalia, Sándalo**
Zandía, *s. fem. a water-melon*
Zanefa, *s. f. V.* Cenefa
Zanga, *s. fem. a play at cards in four*
Zangala, *s. f. buckram*
Zangamanga, *s. f. deceit; fraud*
Zangandongo, } *s. m. an*
Zangandullo, } *idle or silly fellow*
Zángano, *s. m. a drone*
Zanganear, *v. n. to ramble about; to be very idle, etc.*
Zangarilla, *s. f. a kind of temporary mill*
Zangarilleja, *sub. fem. a young dirty girl*
Zangarrear, *ver. act. to scratch the guittar*
Zangarriana, *s. f. a distemper in the head among sheep || melancholy* [*idle lad*
Zangarúllon, *s. m. a tall*
Zangolotear, *v. a. y n. to move indecently*
Zangoloteo, *s. m. indecent motion of one's body* [*tear*
Zangotear. *V.* Zangolo-
Zangoteo. *V.* Zangoloteo
Zanguanga, *s. f. a feigned infirmity to avoid work* [*idle fellow*
Zanguayo, *sub. m. a tall*
Zanja, *s. f. a ditch || the foundation of a house etc.*

Zanjar, *v. a. to dig; to lay the foundations*

Zanjon, *s. m. a great or deep ditch*

Zanjoncillo, *s. m. dim. de* Zanja

Zanqueador, **ra**, *sub. one who spreads or opens his legs || a great walker*

Zanqueamiento, *s. m. the act of spreading the legs*

Zanquear, *v. n. to spread or open one's legs in walking || to trot; to ramble*

Zanquilargo, **ga**, *a. long-legged*

Zanquilla, **Zanquita**, *s. f. a short-thin-legged person*

Zanquituerto, **ta**, *adject. bow-legged*

Zanquivano, **na**, *a. that has spindle shanks*

Zapa, *s. fem. a pioneer's spade || shagreen*

Caminar á la zapa, *to undermine*

Zapador, *s. m. a sapper*

Zapar, *v. a. to sap*

Zaparrada, *s. f. V.* Zaparrazo

Zaparrastrar, *v. a. to drag one's garment along the ground*

Zaparrastroso, **sa**, *adjec. that drags his garment loose along the ground || clumsy; ill done*

Zaparrazo, *s. m. a blow given by falling || sudden misfortune, etc.*

Zapata, *sub. f. a piece of leather put under a hinge, etc. || console; corbel || a half boat*

Zapatazo, *sub. m. a blow with a shoe || a noisy fall*

Zapateado, *s. m. a sort of [dance*

Zapateador, *s. m. one who makes a noise with the shoes*

Zapatear, *v. a. to strike or to make a noise with the shoes || to cut or interfere*

Zapatearse, *v. r. to stand against*

Zapatera, *s. f. a shoe maker's wife*

Zapateria, *s. f. shoe maker's shop or business*

Zapateria de viejo, *a cobbler's shop*

Zapaterillo, *s. m. a paltry shoe maker*

Zapatero, *s. m. shoemaker*

Zapatero de viejo, *a cobbler*

Zapateta, *s. f. a blow on the shoe*

Zapatico, *s. m. a small shoe*

Zapatilla, *s. f. a little piece of leather || hoof*

Zapatillas, *pl. pumps*

Zapatillero, *subst. mas. shoe maker that makes pumps*

Zapatillo, *s. m. a small shoe*

Zapato, *s. m. a shoe*

Zapaton, *sub. m. a great clownish shoe || wooden shoe*

Zapatudo, **da**, *adj. that wears clownish shoes*

Zape, *a word used to drive away a cat*

Zapear, *ver. a. to drive away a cat by crying* zape

Zapito, *s. m. a wooden vessel to milk cows into*

Zapote, *s. m. an American fruit and tree*

Zapuzar, *v. a. V.* Zampuzar

Zaque, *s. m. a leather-bottle*

Zaquear, *v. n. to p[...] wine from a leath[...] into another*

Zaquizami, *s. m. a g[...]*

Zar, *s. m. Czar*

Zara, *s. f. maize*

Zarabanda, *s. f. sarab[...]*

Zarabutero, **ra**, *ad[...] lying; deceitful*

Zaradion, **Zaradique**, *s. m. a [...] dicine [...] to cure [...]*

Zaragotana, *s. f. flea-[...]*

Zaragoci, *ad[...] plum* [...ured

Zaraguelles, *s. m. pl. [...]*

Zaramago, *sub. m. [...] rape*

Zaramagullon, *s. m[...] ver (a sea-fowl)*

Zarambeque, *s. m. a [...] ce very gay of the [...] groes*

Zaramullo, *s. m. a [...]*

Zaranda, *s. f. a siev[...]*

Zarandador, *s. m. si[...]*

Zarandajas, *s. f. pl. s[...] trifles of little val[...] scraps of a dinner*

Zarandar, **Zarandear**, *v. a. to [...]*

Zarandero, *s. m. sif[...]*

Zarandillo, *s. m. a [...] sieve || a little brisk fellow*

Zarapallon, *s. m. a [...] ragged fellow*

Zarapatel, *s. m. a s[...] ragoo*

Zarapeto, *sub. m. a [...]*

Zarapito, *s. m. a ki[...] sea-gull*

Zaratan, *s. m. a canc[...] the breasts of won[...]*

Zaraza, *s. f. printed [...]na-cotton*

Zarazas, *pl. a mer[...] to kill rats, e[...]*

Zarcear, *ver. n[...]*

he water-pipes with
rambles
ceta, s. f. a moor-hen
cillo, s. m. an ear-ring
cillos, pl. strings of a
ine
co, ca, adj. light blue
evitz, s. m. the eldest
on of the Czar
gatona, s. f. flea-worth
iano, na, a. czarian;
zarish
itza, s. f. czarina
. an engine to
wind up silk
pa, s. f. the dirt that
ticks to dragging garments || paw [anchor
par, ver. a. to weigh
pastroso, sa, adject.
dirty; ragged
pazo, s. m. the noise
made by some thing
falling down
rposo, sa, adj. dirty
rracatería, s. f. false
caresses
rracatin, s. m. huckster; broker; retailer
rrapastra, s. f. Voyez
Zarpa
rrapastron, sub. m. a
dirty; ragged fellow
rrapastroso, sa, adjec.
dirty; ragged
ria, s. f. dirt
rriento, ta, adj. dirty
rza, s. f. briar; bramble [north-wind
rgagan, s. m. a cold
rzaganete, s. m. dim.
de Zarzagan
rzagavillo, subst. m. a
stormy north wind
rzahan, sub. m. a thin
striped silk
zaidea, s. f. raspberry
al, s. m. a place full
brambles

Zarzamora, s. f. a blackberry [parilla
Zarzaparrilla, s. f. sarsa-
Zarzaparrillar, s. m. the place where the sarsaparilla grows
Zarzaperruna, sub. f. dog-briar
Zarzarosa, s. f. wild rose
Zarzo, sub. m. hurdle of reeds, etc.
Zarzoso, sa, adj. full of brambles
Zarzuela, s. f. a comedy or farce in two acts
Zas, the noise made by a blow — a blow
Zascandil, s. m. an unexpected accident || a sly cunning fellow
Zata, } s. fem. raft of
Zatara, } timber
Zatico, } s. m. a small
Zatillo, } bit of bread
Zatiquero, s. m. a pantler
Zato, s. m. a bit of bread
Zayda, s. f. a sort of hern
Zayno (caballo), s. m. a horse all of one dark colour || a head-strong horse
Mirar de zayno, to look upon one with an ill eye
Zazoso, sa, adj. lisping
Zea, s. f. spelt
Zebra, s. f. a zebra
Zoda, s. f. the name and pronunciation of the letter Z [(root)
Zedoaria, s. fem. zedoary
Zelador, s. m. zealot
Zelar, v. a. to be zealous or jealous
Zelo, sub. m. zeal || rut; lust (in beasts)
Zelos, pl. jealousy
Zeloso, sa, adj. jealous
Zelotipia, s. f. jealousy
Zenit, s. m. zenith

Zenzalino, na, a. belonging to gnats
Zenzalo, s. m. a gnat
Zequí, sub. m. a golden coin, among Moors
Zequía, s. f. a canal
Zeta, s. f. V. Zeda
Zeugma, s. f. zeugma
Zilórgano, s. m. a kind of organ
Zipizape, sub. m. a noisy quarrel with blows
Zirigaña, s. f. flattery; adulation
Zitara, s. f. V. Acitara
Zizaña, s. f. darnel || dissention
Zizañero, ra, adj. who raises dissention
Zócalo, s. m. zocle. foot; stand [ripeness
Zocato, ta, a. pale with
Zoclo, subs. m. buskin || wooden shoe
Zoco, s. m. wooden shoe || buskin || socle
Zocoba, s. f. a particular plant and tree in America
Zodíaco, s. m. zodiac
Zofra, s. fem. a Moorish carpet
Zollipar, v. n. to sob
Zollipo, s. m. a sob
Zolocho, cha, adj. silly; foolish
Zoma, s. f. V. Soma
Zomas, pl. uneven ridges in the fields
Zompo, pa, a. V. Zopo
Zona, s. f. zone
Zoncería, s. f. insipidy || silliness [unsavoury
Zonzo, za, adj. insipid;
Ave zonza, a silly witless person
Zonzorrion, s. m. a dull silly fellow
Zopas ó zopitas, lisping

Zopisa, s. f. pitch
Zopo, pa, adj. maimed; lance
Zopo, s. m. an unhandy, aukward fellow
Zoquete, sub. m. a short and thick piece of wood || a large piece of bread || a short and fat person || a dunce; a blockhead
Zoquetero, ra, a. beggarly
Zoquetudo, da, a. gross; rude; ill-made
Zorita (paloma), s. f. a wild pigeon [whore
Zorra, subst. f. a fox || a Estar una zorra, to be drunk — cazar una zorra, to make one's self drunk dormir, ó desollar la zorra, to sleep one's self sober
Zorrastron, s. m. a very sly, cunning fellow; a volpone
Zorrazgo, s. m. a great fox || V. Zorrastron
Zorrera, s. f. a fox's hole || a smoky house, etc. || heaviness; drowsiness
Zorrería, s. f. the trick of a fox || any sly trick [lump...
Zorrero, ra, adj. heavy; Perro zorrero, a fox-dog
Zorrilla, s. f. a little fox || a sort of onguent
Zorrillo, s. m. a little fox
Zorro, s. m. a he fox || an idle fellow
Zorros. pl. the fox's tail or skin
Zorrococlo, s. m. a kind of cylindrical wafers || a fellow that looks dull, but who knows well his advantage || kindness; fair words, etc.
Zorronglon, na, a. dull, slow; who does any thing unwillingly, etc.
Zorrullo, s. m. V. Zurrullo
Zorruno, na, a. relating to a fox
Zorzal, s. m. a feldfare
Zorzaleña (Aceytuna), s. f. a small round sort of olives
Zoster, s. m. a distemper so called [fellow
Zote, s. m. a heavy dull
Zoylo, s. m. zoilus
Zozobra, sub. f. a foul or strong wind || trouble; grief
Zozobrar, v. n. to be in danger of foundering at sea || to be in great trouble, etc.
Zua, } s. f. V. Azuda
Zuda; }
Zubia, s. f. a place where many waters meet
Zuciedad, Zucio. V. Suciedad, Sucio
Zueco, s. m. a wooden-shoe || a galosh [style
Zueco (Estilo) a plain
[illegible], sub. m. brimstone. V. Azufre
Zufrir, v. a. to suffer. V. Sufrir
Zuiza, s. f. a sort of sport, like a muster of soldiers || a quarrel
Zuizon, s. m. a dart. V. Chuzo
Zulaque, s. m. a kind of cement or mastick
Zulla, s. f. spanish sainfoin || turd
Zullarse, v. r. to squirt it out
Zullenco, ca, a. who lets fly all under him
Zullon, s. m. a wind expelled without noise
Zumacal, } s. m. a place
Zumacar, } full of sumach
Zumacar, ver. a. to tan skins with sumach
Zumacaya, s. f. V. Sumaya
Zumaque, s. m. sumach || wine
Zumaya, s. f. screech-owl
Zumba, s. f. a bell hanging on the neck of cattle || a nipping jest
Zumbar, v. n. to hum; to buz || to tingle, or tinkle (said of the ears) to scoff; to play upon one
Zumbarse, v. r. to jest
Zumbel, sub. m. frown; angry aspect
Zumbido, } s. m. a hum-
Zumbo, } ming or buzzing noise
Zumbon, na, a. jesting; jovial [pigeon
Zumbon, s. m. a kind of
Zumiento, ta, a. juic
Zumillo, s. m. a sort of dragon-wort
Zumo, s. m. juice; moisture
Zumoso, sa, a. juicy
Zuño, s. m. frown; frowning
Zupia, s. f. a bad wine || any bad liquor || dregs; ground
Zura, } s. f. a wild pi-
Zurana, } geon
Zurcidera, s. f. a woman that darns
Zurcidor, ra, s. a darner
Zurcidor, s. m. a pimp
Zurcidura, s. f. [illegible]
Zurcir, v. a. [illegible] || seam [illegible] tily || [illegible] ries

Lightning Source UK Ltd.
Milton Keynes UK
UKHW031415280119
336340UK00010B/806/P